ISBN 978-0-266-95329-6
PIBN 10914837

DOCUMENTS AND PROCEEDINGS

OF THE

HALIFAX COMMISSION, 1877,

UNDER THE

TREATY OF WASHINGTON OF MAY 8, 1871.

IN THREE VOLUMES.

VOLUME III.

WASHINGTON:
GOVERNMENT PRINTING OFFICE.
1878.

H

APPENDIX L.

No. 32.

MICHAEL MACAULAY, of Gloucester, Mass., fisherman and master mariner, called on behalf of the Government of the United States, sworn and examined.

By Mr. Foster:

Question. You are skipper of a schooner out of Gloucester?—Answer. Yes.

Q. What is the name?—A. The Noonday.

Q. Where were you born?—A. In Prince Edward Island.

Q. How many years have you been fishing?—A. About twelve years.

Q. The first part of the time for mackerel and at present for cod?—A. Yes.

Q. How do you happen in here?—A. I came in here with a sick man from the Grand Banks.

Q. And you have been in command of this vessel two years?—A. Yes; about that.

Q. Before that you were fishing as a sharesman?—A. Yes.

Q. How many years were you cod-fishing?—A. Seven years, I guess.

Q. Where?—A. On the Grand Bank.

Q. Now, when you began to go cod-fishing to the Grand Bank, how did you supply yourselves with bait?—A. We took it from home. We used to get some on the Banks in the summer time.

Q. What did you take with you?—A. Salt bait, pogy slivers.

Q. Slivers are pogies and menhaden cut off the bones?—A. Fish cut off the bone each side.

Q. What else?—A. We used to put that on, and what we used to pick up on the Bank; small halibut and other small fish.

Q. How long is it since you began to go to Newfoundland for bait?—A. Well, it is about four years since I have first been there for herring. I guess we were there as soon as any of them.

Q. When you go to Newfoundland for herring, how do you get it?—A. We take it out of the seines.

Q. How do you pay for it?—A. We pay so much.

Q. How much, usually?—A. Well, there are certain times they charge pretty high. At other times they don't charge so high. We paid as high as $25 this summer, and took as much as we wanted.

Q. How many times have you been in this summer for bait?—A. I have been in for herring twice.

Q. What else have you been for ?—A. Squid, twice.

Q. How did you get squid ?—A. Well, they caught them; jigged and took them alongside the first time, and we bought them salted the second time.

Q. Who jigged them the first time ?—A. The natives.

Q. How much did you pay for them ?—A. Two dollars a barrel.

Q. The salt squid did you get last time ?—A. Yes.

Q. Does this answer for bait ?—A. It is not so good ; but we could not get anything else.

Q. How many times have you been to Newfoundland for bait ?—A. Since I have been skipper ?

Q. Yes.—A. Well, I have been about six times in two years.

Q. And how many times did you go before that, while you were sharesman ?—A. I have been back and forward for the last four years. I have been there as much as, I suppose, ten or twelve times before I went skipper.

Q. Now, won't you tell the Commissioners what is the longest and what is the shortest time that it has ever taken to go from the Bank into Newfoundland to get bait and return to the fishing ground ?—A. The shortest time I have been would be about nine days.

Q. What is the longest ?—A. I have been four weeks.

Q. How did that happen ?—A. I could not get it. I was hunting it up, trying to get it.

Q. Now, you have fished with salt bait taken from home, not going near Newfoundland, and you have gone in as a skipper half a dozen times, and as sharesman ten or twelve times to buy bait ?—A. Yes.

Q. I want you to state whether in your opinion the advantages of going to Newfoundland to procure bait are worth anything.—A. Well, when we used to carry bait from home, we used to catch some fish, but since we went to run fresh bait we didn't catch half the quantity we used to catch, I don't think, when we used to take bait from home, because we lose half our time and more looking for fresh bait.

Q. You lose half your time ?—A. Yes.

Q. You don't consider it an advantage ?—A. No; I don't consider it an advantage at all.

Q. Have you ever got caplin there for bait ?—A. No; I never took any caplin. I have never been in a vessel that had any.

Q. Now, before you were cod-fishing you made some mackerel voyages, I think ?—A. Yes; I have been four or five years for mackerel before I went for cod.

Q. What vessels were you in ? Begin with the earliest mackerel schooner you were in.—A. I have been in the Moonlight. That was the first vessel, John Spriggan, captain.

Q. What year ?—A. About 1865, I guess.

Q. How many barrels of mackerel did you take that year ?—A. Well, I took off and on about 150 barrels, I guess.

Q. Where did you take them ?—A. Most of them around the Magdalens.

Q. What was the next schooner you were in ?—A. The Easterwood, Captain Galasky.

Q. How many barrels of mackerel did you take in her ?—A. Well, between 180 and 190. I could not be certain; off and on, about that.

Q. Where were they taken ?—A. We caught them between the North Cape and around the Magdalens; up between the Magdalens and North

Cape. We used to fish in different places, but the most part was taken around the Magdalens. ,

Q. What was the third schooner you were in ?—A. The Charles P. Thompson. No, I was mistaken. The second schooner I was in was the James Bliss.

Q. Who was the captain ?—A. James Walsh.

Q. How many barrels did you take in her ?—A. Two hundred and forty.

Q. Where were they taken ?—A. Part of them to the northward of North Cape, what we call Bradley Bank, and abroad off North Cape.

Q. Were any of those taken within three miles ?—A. No, we didn't catch any. I don't know but we tried and got a few there, but not anything over a dozen or so.

Q. Where was that ?—A. It was to the westward of North Cape—what they call Tignish.

Q. You think you caught a dozen barrels inshore ?—A. No, not a dozen; we might have caught a dozen or twenty mackerel to a man.

Q. What was the fourth vessel you were in mackereling ?—A. The Charles P. Thompson was the fourth.

Q. What year was that, do you remember ?—A. Well, it was about 1869, I guess.

Q. Who was her captain ?—A. Edward Cash.

Q. How many barrels of mackerel did you take in her ?—A. About 95 barrels; between that and 100. We caught them up northward.

Q. Was she a new vessel ?—A. No. ' The James Bliss was a new vessel.

Q. Now I would ask you, so far as your observation goes, what is the principal fishing-ground for mackerel-schooners in the Gulf of St. Lawrence ?—A. Where I have principally fished in my time was around the Magdalens. That was the principal ground in my going to fish.

Q. Did you ever fish much off the Bight of Prince Edward Island ?—A. No, I never did.

Q. Have you been there ?—A. Yes; I have been there working up and down shore, but I never fished any there. I might have tried abroad off East Point, or abroad off the North Cape; but I have never been in a vessel that fished in the bend of the island, because it is a place where they don't want to fish very often.

Q. Why not?—A. Because they don't like the ground. They don't like to fish. They don't call it a very safe place to fish.

Q. Is it a place that is avoided by—— A. Fishermen ? Yes.

Q. Why ?—A. Because it is a place where, if they are caught with the wind easterly or northeasterly, we can't get out.

Q. You lived at Prince Edward Island 20 years ?—A. Yes; I was born there and lived there until I came to Gloucester.

Q. Do you ever fish there from the shore ?—A. Well, I have gone fishing there from the shore. What part of the island did you live at ?—A. At St. Peter's, right in the bend.

Q. Did you ever see boats fishing on the island ?—A. Yes.

Q. I would like to know how far from the shore these fishing boats around Prince Edward Island go out for mackerel, or used to when you were there ?—A. I would judge in my way that they would go from three to five miles.

Q. One question more; as you have been sailing out of Gloucester now for some years, what is the principal fishing business of Gloucester ?—A. I should think codfish and halibut the principal.

By Mr. Davies:

Q. You lived at St. Peter's ?—A. Yes.

Q. How long since you lived on the island ?—A. Twelve years.

Q. That would be 1865 ?—A. Yes.

Q. That was when you first went in the Moonlight ?—A. Yes.

Q. You have never been on the island since you left there ?—A. No.

Q. How old are you now ?—A. About 33.

Q. You left the island when you were about 21 ?—A. Yes.

Q. Are your people engaged much in St. Peter's in the fisheries ?—A. They do go fishing a good deal. They catch fish enough for themselves any way.

Q. That is just what I want to know. I never understood that you engaged in the fisheries largely ?—A. Well, they catch always enough for themselves. I don't know that they catch any more. That is all, I guess.

Q. There are no fishing-stages there ?—A. No, they can't keep fishing-stages there.

Q. It is a very exposed place ?—A. To my recollection that is so.

Q. Then you never were at any of the fishing-stages fishing on the island ?—A. No.

Q. You never were to Rustico, New London, Cascumpec, or Tignish ? —A. No.

Q. You never saw them fishing there ?—A. I have seen the boats fishing there.

Q. Will you venture the assertion that those boats fishing off those places fish farther than three miles ?—A. I should think off Rustico they fish as much as ten miles.

Q. As a general rule, you think that ?—Yes, because it is a place with shoal water, and they have to go quite a piece off.

Q. Do you give that as your actual opinion or mere supposition ?—A. My opinion is that I have seen them ages outside of ten miles.

Q. Where ?—A. Where I have been fishing up and down in those vessels.

Q. But you have said you never fished around Prince Edward Island ? —A. Well, I said I have made passages up and down the island.

Q. What year was that you made passages ?—A. Well, probably I have been—I don't know-=but I have been every year I have been in the bay. Probably we might work up from the northward up as far as East Point.

Q. Now, every man who was brought here from Rustico, and every man at Rustico who has made an affidavit, has stated that three-fourths to nine-tenths of the fish caught in that harbor are caught within three miles of land.

Mr. FOSTER objects to this question, for which, after a short argument, the following question was substituted.

By Mr. Davies:

Q. Here is a deponent, Alexander McNeil, who says:

I would think the number of fishing-boats at Rustico harbors would number about one hundred and fifty.

My twenty years' experience has proved to me that the best mackerel-fishing around our coast is about a mile from the shore, in from 7 to 10 fathoms of water.

All the fish caught by the boats are taken within a mile of the coast, many of them within half a mile, during the months of July and August, but during the months of September and October the boats take their catch farther out, say two miles or two and a half. It is a very rare occasion that they go out three miles or beyond it.

Of the total catch in the boats, over nine-tenths is caught well within the three-mile limit.

Have you sufficient experience off Rustico Harbor to give evidence in contradiction of that I have read?—A. Well, I state what I have said. I have seen boats over ten miles fishing for mackerel off Rustico.

Q. Have you had sufficient experience of fishing off Rustico to give any evidence?—A. I have never fished off Rustico.

Q. Will you say it is true or not?—A. I can't tell.

Q. How far have you been fishing off Rustico Harbor?—A. I never fished.

Q. How often have you passed within three miles there?—A. I don't know—very seldom.

Q. Did you ever?—A. I don't know that I did.

Q. Then you can't possibly tell whether the boats fish there or not?—A. I say I have seen them fishing off ten miles.

Q. Were they large or small boats?—A. Large.

Q. How often have you seen them fish off ten miles?—A. Five or six times.

Q. Is that as often as you have been there?—A. Probably that is as often.

Q. Have you seen them fishing in other parts of the island?—A. Yes.

Q. What other parts?—A. Up and down the shore. I have seen boats off shore fishing.

Q. Now, here is Daniel Ross, of Rustico, fish merchant. He says:

I myself am a practical fisherman and engage personally in the catching and curing as well as in the sale of the fish.

That the best mackerel-fishing is about one mile or one mile and a half from the coast-line of the shore, and very frequently the best catches are made much closer to the shore than that.

That the mackerel-fishing prosecuted in boats from the shore is chiefly within the limit of two miles; at times the schools of mackerel go farther out, extending as far as three miles and beyond that, but I have no hesitation in positively swearing that at least nine-tenths (9-10ths) of the mackerel caught by the boat-fishermen are caught within the three-mile limit.

Would you like, from your experience, to contradict that?—A. I could not tell you where they were caught, but I have said what I have said, that I have seen them fishing outside of three miles.

Q. How many boats did you see there?—A. I didn't count them.

Q. I want to know if you yourself ever fished up and down the coast of the island?—A. I might have tried, but never anything inside of three miles. I have never been in within three miles.

Q. When you were living on the island did you never see the American fleet sailing up and down?—A. Often.

Q. Many of them?—A. There used to be a good many.

Q. What number used you consider there were?—A. I could not tell; I don't know that I ever counted.

Q. How many was the fleet of American vessels supposed to be?—A. How many vessels?

Q. Yes. How many American vessels were there in the fleet sailing up and down?—A. Sometimes as high as three or four; sometimes ten or fifteen.

Q. Did you ever see as many as 100 at one time going past?—A. No.

Q. What would take them into that dangerous place?—A. Many of them passed up and down, probably——

Q. Have you any idea that they were fishing?—A. They may have been some of them fishing half way across.

Q. You could not see that?—A. Well, you could see them half way across.

Q. What? Twenty-eight miles from shore?—A. It is only twenty-eight miles across from East Point to Magdalen Islands.

Q. You were not at East Point. You were at St. Peter's.—A. You can't tell. I have been up and down.

Q. Well, you say, then, you have been at East Point?—A. I have been there often.

Q. Have you ever seen the fleet around East Point?—A. I have seen vessels in there.

Q. That is not what I asked you. Have you ever seen the fleet there? —A. Yes; I have seen the fleet.

Q. How many would you see?—A. Probably fifteen or twenty.

Q. You have never seen them within three miles there?—A. Not fishing—I never did.

Q. Have you seen them at all within three miles?—A. I have seen them sailing within three miles.

Q. Fifteen or twenty?—A. Yes.

Q. Were they not fishing?—A. I could not say they were fishing.

Q. Could you say they were not fishing?—A. Yes.

Q. How could you say that?—A. They were sailing. They don't fish when they are sailing.

Q. Have you never seen them within three miles unless they are sailing?—A. I have seen them at anchor within three miles.

Q. What were they doing there then?—A. They were making lee; it was blowing too hard.

Q. You don't know whether they were fishing then or not?—A. I never saw them.

Q. They go there for shelter, to that dangerous place?—A. There is no danger there. They have a way to get out of that part of the bay; but in the bend they haven't.

Q. Did you ever catch fish in Bay Chaleurs?—A. I did.

Q. In what vessel?—A. Well, what do you call Bay Chaleurs?

Q. Don't you know? As a master-mariner, don't you know where Bay Chaleurs is?—A. Well, I have fished across from the Magdalens.

Q. But don't you know what Bay Chaleurs is?—A. Yes.

Q. Well, why do you ask me?—A. Well, I call it right across from Magdalens to Bay Chaleurs. Wherever we fish down there we call it Bay Chaleurs.

Q. You call it Bay Chaleurs?—A. Yes; I call it Bay Chaleurs fishing.

Q. It has a good reputation for fishing, has it, the Bay Chaleurs; has it, among American fishermen?—A. Well, that is what I always hear them call it.

Q. Have you ever been in the Bay Chaleurs proper fishing?—A. Yes, I have.

Q. In what vessel?—A. I have been in the Charles P. Thomson.

Q. Any other?—A. I might be in the James Bliss too.

Q. Might you in any other vessel?—A. No.

Q. Will you swear you were not in Bay Chaleurs in the Moonlight or Easterwood?—A. I might be there working up and down. I don't know if ever I fished in there.

Q. You have no recollection of ever fishing in the Bay Chaleurs?—A. I don't know if ever I fished there.

Q. In the other two vessels you did; where did you fish?—A. We tried once at North Cape; that is, in the bay and well to the westward of it.

Q. Point out on the map where North Cape is.—A. Well, I know where it is.

Q. I want you to show it on the map.—A. (Witness points to North

Cape, Prince Edward Island.) That (pointing to waters between North Cape and Miramichi Bay) is what I call Bay Chaleurs fishing.

Q. Do you know Miscon Point ?—A. Yes.

Q. Did you go around Point Miscou ?—A. I have been to anchor there, not fishing.

Q. Then you have been inside of Point Miscou at anchor ?—A. Yes.

Q. Were there other vessels there too ?—A. There might be.

Q. Have you seen other vessels there ?—A. Yes.

Q. Have you ever tried to fish in that bay ?—A. No.

Q. Have you heard of other vessels fishing there ?—A. I have heard of other vessels fishing there.

Q. You never tried to fish yourself ?—A. No, I have never fished in a vessel that fished up in the bay, but I have been in vessels that fished off Miscou light.

Q. Did they make good catches ?—A. No, nothing extra.

Q. How many did you catch off there ?—A. Well, we might catch a dozen barrels or so.

Q. Did you ever fish on the Cape Breton shore ?—A. I have been down to Margaree once.

Q. In the fall ?—A. Yes.

Q. Is that known to be a good fishing-ground among the Americans ?—A. I have heard talk that it used to be.

Q. Did you fish there ?—A. I have been there once.

Q. Did you catch any fish ?—A. Nothing worth speaking of.

Q. There were other vessels there; what year was that ?—A. About 1868.

Q. What time of the year ?—A. In the fall.

Q. That was after the mackerel-fishing in the bay was done ?—A. No, it was about the first of the month, the first of October.

Q. Is that the season when they generally go to Margaree ?—A. Yes, I have never been there but once.

Q. The time you went did they go ?—A. There was a dozen sail when I called there.

Q. How long did you stay to see whether there were fish there or not ?—A. One day.

Q. You can't tell whether the others caught them or not ?—A. No.

Q. Have you ever been to Seven Islands ?—A. No.

Q. Nor up the shores of the river St. Lawrence ?—A. No.

Q. Nor around Bonaventure ?—A. No, I have never been around Bonaventure, but I have been once at anchor at Port Daniel.

Q. Have you heard of this being a good fishing-ground ?—A. No; I have heard it mentioned that fish were caught there, but never that it was a good fishing-ground.

Q. You don't know what quantities were caught, of course ?—A. No.

Q. Did you ever ask whether it was good or not ?—A. No.

Q. You never were a master of a vessel during those years you were in ?—A. No; I was a mere hand.

Q. You caught 95 barrels one year, 150 another, 180 a third, and 240 another year. Were these very small catches ?—A. Yes.

Q. And you never caught any within three miles ?—A. I don't know but we might catch a few; never anything worth speaking of.

Q. And you didn't try ?—A. We did try once or twice.

Q. Had you a license to fish when you were there ?—A. I could not exactly tell you.

Q. But you ran in to try ?—A. We were in making lee.

Q. You never tried to keep outside ?—A. I could not tell you; I have seen some vessels keep outside. I have seen them making lee and getting under way and running out.

By Mr. Whiteway:

Q. You have been seven years cod-fishing?—A. Yes, about seven years.

Q. Part of these at Grand Bank?—A. Yes, all.

Q. You commenced in '71, I think?—A. Yes, about that.

Q. Can you tell me what vessel you were in that year?—A. I have been in the Midnight.

Q. How many trips?—A. Three trips; that is, on the Grand Banks.

Q. Do you recollect the quantity of fish you took each trip?—A. Well, I could not exactly say.

Q. Did you use salt or fresh bait?—A. Salt.

Q. What bait did you first take?—A. Slivers the first trip. We got squid on the bank the second trip, and then used salt bait the last trip.

Q. Did you take any salt bait for the second trip?—A. Yes, sir.

Q. You didn't use it?—A. No.

Q. What quantity did you take each trip?—A. Ten or fifteen barrels each trip.

Q. What vessel were you in the second trip?—A. I have been in the Midnight two years.

Q. How many trips did you make that year?—A. Two.

Q. What quantity did you take; do you remember?—A. I could not recollect.

Q. Did you use salt bait or fresh?—A. We used salt bait.

Q. Altogether, for the two trips?—A. No; we got some fresh bait on the Bank—some squid one trip; we caught them on the Bank.

Q. On the first trip you used altogether salt bait?—A. Yes.

Q. The third year, what vessel were you in?—A. I was in the Noonday.

Q. Do you remember how many trips you made?—A. I was mistaken; in the third year I was in the Enola C.

Q. Do you remember how many trips?—A. I was only in her one trip; I was fresh fishing in the spring, and then went for salt fish.

Q. Fresh fishing on the American coast?—A. No; on the Grand Banks. We made three trips. We went in March; about the first of March.

Q. Do I understand that you went about the first of March and made three trips for fresh fish?—A. Yes.

Q. Then you made one trip for salt fish; do you recollect the quantity of fish you took?—A. I could not say; something over 140,000 pounds.

Q. That is salt fish?—A. Yes.

Q. You don't recollect the quantity of fresh fish you took?—A. No.

Q. Did you use salt bait that season?—A. Yes; we did catch some fresh bait on the Bank part of the trip.

Q. That is, on the salt-fishing trip you used partly salt bait and partly fresh?—A. Yes.

Q. The fourth year, what vessel were you in?—A. The Noonday.

Q. How many trips did you make that year?—A. Two trips.

Q. Do you remember the quantity you took?—A. We took 170,000 pounds the first trip.

Q. That would be in '74?—A. Yes.

Q. How much did you take the second trip?—A. We had 165,000.

Q. What bait did you use?—A. Fresh bait caught on the Banks.

Q. Now the fifth year, what vessel were you in ?—A. The Noonday.

Q. How many trips did you make ?—A. I made one salt trip.

Q. How much fish did you catch ?—A. We caught 110,000.

Q. How many trips did you make for fresh fish ?—A. We made three trips for fresh fish.

Q. Where did you get your bait that year ?—A. In Newfoundland.

Q. That is the first year you went to Newfoundland, is it ?—A. No ; we were in the year before that.

Q. You stated before that you got bait on the Banks, now you say you got it in Newfoundland. Which is correct ?—A. We got our bait in Newfoundland the fifth year.

Q. That is 1875 ?—A. Yes.

Q. Is that the first year you got it in there ?—A. Yes.

Q. Just now you said you had been into Newfoundland for bait in 1874 ? Then you have only been in three years ?—A. And this year.

Q. That is '75, '76, and '77—only three years ?—A. Didn't I tell you I was in the first trip in the Noonday.

Q. Did you go into Newfoundland for fresh bait in 1874 for the first time, or was it in 1875 ?—A. I told you——

Q. Just answer simply ?—A. 1874.

Q. Then you were incorrect just now when you said you caught it that year on the Banks ?—A. Well, I caught part of it. The first trip we went into Newfoundland, and the second trip got it on the Banks.

Q. You went into Newfoundland in the spring for your first bait ?—A. Yes.

Q. Where did you go ?—A. To Fortune Bay.

Q. Did you take a seine and catch the bait yourself ?—A. No.

Q. Did you employ people there to catch it for you ?—A. Yes.

Q. How many barrels of bait did you get ?—A. Somewhere about 40 barrels.

Q. And you gave them $25 or thereabouts ?—A. Not that year ; it was $50 that year.

Q. Well, now, in 1875 you say you got 110,000 pounds of fish. What vessel were you in in 1876 ?—A. The Noonday.

Q. How many trips ?—A. One trip.

Q. How many fish did you take ?—A. 80,000—78,000.

Q. Had you made any trips for fresh fish in the spring ?—A. Yes.

Q. How many ?—A. Three or four—four.

Q. Where did you get bait for the fresh fish ?—A. We got it down the shore here ; some in Prospect.

Q. You caught the fresh bait yourselves ?—A. No ; we bought it there.

Q. Did you employ people to catch it for you ?—A. They came alongside with it, and we bought it from them.

Q. What was it ?—A. Herring.

Q. The trip you made for salt fish, where did you get bait ?—A. Some on the Cape Breton shore. We got the first bait on the Cape Breton shore, and the next in St. John's.

Q. For the first three or four trips you went for fresh fish, and then you went for a trip for salted fish ?—A. Yes.

Q. For the first bait for the salt fish you went to Cape Breton ?—A. Yes.

Q. And the second bait to St. John's ?—A. Yes.

Q. What time did you go into St. John's ?—A. We went there about the last of October.

Q. What bait did you get then ?—A. Squid.

Q. Was that fresh squid ?—A. Yes.

Q. Then you went to the Banks and completed your trip ?—A.. Well, part of a trip; we didn't get much of a trip at that.

Q. You completed your 78,000 pounds ?—A. Yes.

Q. And returned home ?—A. Yes.

Q. What time did you get home ?—A. I could not exactly say.

Q. Now, this year, what vessel were you in ?—A. The Noonday again.

Q. What were you doing this year ?—A. Salt-fishing.

Q. All the year ?—A. Yes.

Q. How many trips have you made ?—A. I am on the second now.

Q. Returning home ?—A. No.

Q. Are you going out now ?—A. I am going to the Banks. I have made one trip.

Q. How much did you take ?—A. Off and on about 100,000.

Q. Where did you get bait for that trip ?—A. At Fortune Bay.

Q. What time of the year?—A. About the 10th of May, the first bait.

Q. You live at Gloucester.—A. Yes.

Q. What time did you leave Gloucester ?—A. We left on the 2d day of March.

Q. Where did you go in the interim between that and the 10th of May ?—A. Fishing on the Banks, on Grand Bank.

Q. What bait did you use ?—A. We took a little bait from home— enough to start with. I was fishing halibut, salt halibut.

Q. With what bait were you fishing ?—A. We caught bait on the ground.

Q. You went from home without any bait at all ?—A. We took enough to start with.

Q. What did you take ?—A. About two or three thousand herring— three thousand.

Q. They were frozen herring ?—A. Yes.

Q. Wl e ·e did you get them ?—A. They came from down East.

Q. Did you go directly from that into Fortune Bay for fresh bait ?— A. I fished on the Banks near two months.

Q. Did you go from that, after the 10th of May, to Fortune Bay for fresh bait ?—A. Yes.

Q. Did you catch any bait in Fortune Bay ?—A. No.

Q. Had you a herring seine on board ?—A. No.

Q. Did you see many of your countrymen in there looking for bait ?— A. Yes.

Q. A great many of them ?—A. A good many.

Q. Did they catch bait themselves, some of them ?—A. No, they never catch bait. They have it seined there.

Q. Were you on board their vessels ?—A. Yes, I was.

Q. Are you not aware that many of them take down large herring seines and get bait themselves ?—A. I never heard it.

Q. You never heard of their having barred any of the coves there ?— A. No.

Q. During the last spring, in Fortune Bay, have they not barred herrings in the coves ?—A. O, yes; they have them barred as long as six weeks waiting for the Americans to come for them; that is the natives I am speaking of.

Q. Have not the American cod-fishers, some of them, taken large herring-seines with them and used them for taking herring and barring the coves ?—A. No; I haven't heard of it.

Q. You are now going out on your second trip ?—A. Yes.

Q. Now, you have given us an account of your voyages, in 1874, 1875, 1876, and 1877; those are the years you used fresh bait?—A. Yes.

Q. You don't recollect your voyages for 1871, 1872, and 1873; those were the years you used salt bait?—A. Those years we used salt bait.

Q. You alleged just now that during the years you used salt bait your voyages were superior to those made when you used fresh bait?—A. Yes.

Q. Well, you don't remember your catches when you used salt bait?—A. I don't remember the quantity of fish we took home, because I was a hand. Probably I might have known if I had inquired into it.

Q. How is it you pledge your oath that during the years you used salt bait you took more fish than when you used fresh bait, when you don't remember what quantity of fish you took with the salt bait?—A. Well, I might have known nearly, but I could not tell exactly what fish we took to a pound or so.

Q. You have told me distinctly that you did not remember the quantities you took in 1871, 1872, and 1873?—A. No, I could not say exactly.

Q. You can't remember?—A. No. I know I got a good deal more money.

Q. If you can't remember the quantity of fish you took how can you say you took more than in the four succeeding years?—A. Well, I can tell, because the last two years I have been skipper myself, and the other two I have been with a man that had been in this vessel before I took her. I knew the number of fish because he and I worked together, and I found out what number. These other years I never asked the skippers probably the number of fish we landed.

Q. Well, you still affirm upon oath that you took larger quantities of fish with salt bait than with fresh?—A. Well, not with salt bait, but that and what we caught on the Banks.

Q. You stated now that you took a larger quantity with salt bait than with fresh?—A. Well, I didn't state that, but we catch bait on the Banks as well as using salt bait. I told you we were catching part on the Banks.

Q. Then you say you caught a larger quantity when you didn't go into the coast of Newfoundland?—A. Yes.

Q. You are sure as to that now?—A. Yes.

Q. You can't tell the Commission what quantity you took during those years? You can't remember?—A. Well, I could not tell you the certain number.

Q. Then how can you tell that the number was larger or smaller?—A. Because I made more money.

Q. Do you remember the amount of money you made in 1871?—A. Well, I could tell you, I suppose.

Q. Will you tell us?—A. I might figure it up.

Q. Will you tell us what money you made in 1871? Can you recollect?—A. I could not exactly tell you.

Q. In 1872? If you can't, answer yes or no.—A. What do you mean? Salt fish?

Q. What money did you make in 1872?—A. I made about $500 I think.

Q. That is fresh and salt?—A. Yes.

Q. For the season?—A. Yes.

Q. All the other hands made the same?—A. Yes.

Q. Do you remember what you made in 1873?—A. No; I could not exactly tell you.

147 F

Q. Do you remember what you made in 1874?—A. No.

Q. In 1875?—A. I can't exactly tell you what I made.

Q. In 1876?—A. I didn't keep any run of it like that.

Q. You can't tell about 1876?—A. No; I didn't keep any run of it.

Q. I suppose you can't say as to this year because it is not ended yet?—A. Probably if I figured it up I could tell you what I made.

Q. Now, you say you have been four years into Newfoundland for bait. During the last two years you have been master and during the first two years you were a hand on board?—A. Yes.

Q. That is all?—A. Yes; that is all into St. John's.

Q. Were you into any other port—Long Harbor?—A. No; I was in Cape Breton.

Q. You were in St. John's once, that is, on the Newfoundland coast, in 1876?—A. Yes.

Q. This year you have been in four times. Where have you been?—A. I have been to Long Harbor, and I have been to Fortune Bay twice, and I have been to Bay Bulls once, and St. John's once. Well, I have been in several places up and down the shore looking for bait, but did not get any.

By Sir Alexander Galt:

Q. Where did you usually fish on the Grand Banks?—A. Well, I could not tell you the certain spot, because we fished all over it pretty much.

By Mr. Whiteway:

Q. Can't you tell the latitude and longitude of the place you fished? —A. We did not fish in any one certain spot.

By Sir Alexander Galt:

Q. Is it not a long way to go from the Bank to Fortune Bay? Are there not places along here (pointing to the coast from Cape Francis to Cape Race) where you can get bait?—A. We might not find any bait there. We go all over looking for it.

By Mr. Whiteway:

Q. You go to Fortune Bay in the spring before you go to the Bank at all?—A. No.

Q. Do you mean to say you go into Fortune Bay from the Banks and then go out again?—A. Yes.

Q. Now, when you go into Fortune Bay is it on the Grand Banks you are fishing or to the southward?—A. It is on the Grand Bank.

Q. Are you on the Grand Banks or on St. Peter's and Green Banks when you go to Fortune Bay for bait?—A. We are on the Grand Bank.

Q. Always?—A. Yes.

Q. Now, you say you can't tell upon what part of the Grand Banks you fished?—A. No; you probably set trawls in the evening, and if you find no fish you are under sail next morning. You are under sail nearly every day. We were under sail nearly every day last trip. We fish in 44 latitude one day, and next time we set trawls it will be in 44½, next time in 45.

Q. You fish at different places?—A. Yes.

Q. Do you keep a log-book?—A. Yes.

Q. On board ship?—A. Yes.

Q. Have you that here now?—A. No.

Q. Could you tell the date you left fishing at the Grand Banks to go into Saint John's for bait this year?—A. I could not exactly say.

Q. Can't you remember ?—A. I don't know if I could exactly tell you now.

Q. Do you remember the date you got back after being in there ?—A. We got back the 24th of last month.

Q. Well, now, you left Saint John's the 24th September ?—A. We got back the 24th.

Q. Well, now, do you remember what time you left Saint John's ?—A. I left on the 22d September.

Q. How long were you in Saint John's ?—A. Well, I have been——

Q. On that occasion I mean. How long had you been there ?—A. I had been there two days.

Q. Well, how long had you been coming from the Banks into Saint John's ?—A. About 36 hours.

Q. That altogether makes five and a half days. Then it takes you five and a half days?—A. Yes; and then I have been three weeks looking for bait.

Q. But I am speaking of this occasion ?—A. Yes.

Q. You were about five and a half days ?—A. Yes.

Q. You are clear upon that point ?—A. Yes.

Q. Now, how came you to swear just now that the shortest time you were in there was seven days?—A. Well, I didn't say. I said I have been over three weeks.

Q. You said you were thirty-six hours coming in from the Banks ?—A. I said I was thirty-six hours coming in from the Banks. I didn't go directly to Saint John's then. But then when I got my bait, when I left I got it at Saint John's; it was salt bait. I was looking for fresh bait and could not get it. We gave up hopes of getting fresh bait, and then went to Saint John's and got salt bait.

Q. Then you were not correct when you said you were thirty-six hours ?—A. Well, you didn't ask me. You asked me in a different way. You asked me how long I was coming in from the Banks, and I told you. But I was longer than that looking for bait, because I didn't go directly to Saint John's when I came looking for bait. When I gave up every other place, I came to Saint John's.

Q. You were thirty-six hours going to St. John's, and you were two days in St. John's ?—A. I was not at that time.

Q. I was only speaking of one voyage and kept you to one particular trip. You told me you were clear it took five and a half days for the trip.—A. I didn't say such a word, that it took me five and a half on this trip.

Q. Do I understand you now that you were not correct in making the statement that it took thirty-six hours to go into St. John's and that you remained in St. John's two days and took two days to go out again ?—A. I left the bank and run for St. John's and I have been in there and got through my business before I left St. John's, and went all round the coast looking for fresh bait.

Q. What business had you in St. John's ?—A. We wanted to find out where we could get bait.

Q. Had you any other business ?—A. Not anything large.

Q. How long did you remain in St. John's to find out where you could get bait ?—A. We came in on Saturday evening about dark and lay there until Monday morning.

Q. Then where did you go to ?—A. To a place called Portugal Cove.

Q. When do you go there ?—A. We were there a night or so. We got there some time about four o'clock and were there until next morning.

Q. You didn't get bait there ?—A. No.

Q. Where then did you go ?—A. Up the shore.

Q. To what place ?—A. Broad Cove.

Q. Did you get bait there ?—A. No.

Q. How long did you remain ?—A. We went there in the morning and were away next evening.

Q. Where then ?—A. To the northward, to Bonavista.

Q. Did you get bait there ?—A. No.

Q. How long did you remain there ?—A. Two days.

Q. Where did you go from there ?—A. To Heart's Content.

Q. Did you get bait there?—A. No; we staid there three days.

Q. Where did you go then ?—A. We worked back to St. John's. We worked on shore down along, trying different places. We tried the coves inside and along shore.

Q. When did you get back to St. John's ?—A. The day of the week ? I could not exactly tell you.

Q. How long did you remain there then ?—A. Two days.

Q. Did you get fresh bait there ?—A. No; we took salt bait.

Q. What detained you that long getting salt bait ?—A. Well, the first evening we were in there they caught a few squid, a very few, and we remained there until next morning to see whether they would catch, thinking probably they might strike in and we could get some. Next morning they didn't get any, so we took salt squid, and the wind was kind of ahead, so we didn't go out until next day.

Q. How long did it take you around all this coasting voyage ?—A. It was about three weeks from the time we left until we got back.

Q. Can you tell me when you left the Banks ?—A. No.

Q. Now, don't you know a great number of harbors and places where you could get bait between St. John's and Portugal Cove?—A. There have been vessels in every harbor from St. Peter's to St. John's and didn't get any.

Q. American vessels have been in every harbor from St. Peter's to St. John's and haven't got any bait?—A. Not any fresh bait. They were looking for fresh bait. I don't know but some of them might have got it.

Q. What time during this year did those vessels go into all those harbors between St. Peter's and St. John's and get no bait ?—A. From the middle of last month.

Q. From the middle of September to the first of this month—during fifteen days ?—A. Well, some there might be from the first of the month; there might be some there.

Q. That is American vessels in all the ports between St. Peter's and St. John's and got no bait ? Were you in any of those ports yourself?—A. No; I have been there and to the northward of St. John's.

Q. How do you know they were there ?—A. I have seen vessels going along there.

Q. How many have you seen ?—A. Five or six.

Q. Can you name one ?—A. There was one captain said he had been up and down all along the shore, from St. Peter's up and down, and didn't get any fresh bait.

Q. Where did you fall in with him ?—A. In St. John's.

Q. Was that the first time or the last ?—A. The last time.

Q. Did he take fresh bait or salt ?—A. I was not in his company all the time. I could not correctly tell you whether he got salt or fresh bait.

Q. Now, you have detailed your expedition in for bait this year; you were in also last year ?—A. Yes.

Q. Can you tell me the time you left the fishing ground last year to go in for bait ?—A. No; I can tell you the time I was gone.

Q. Can you tell me the port to which you went ?—A. St. John's.

Q. Direct from the Banks ?—A. Yes.

Q. You can't tell the time you left the Banks ?—A. No.

Q. How long did it take you to go in ?—A. About 38 hours, I suppose.

Q. Did you get bait in St. John's ?—A. Yes.

Q. Fresh ?—A. Yes.

Q. Did you return immediately to the fishing ground ?—A. Yes.

Q. How long were you in St. John's ?—A. I was there five days.

Q. You remained in St. John's five days on that occasion last year ?—A. Yes.

Q. Were you detained by no other cause than the procuring of bait ?—A. That is all.

Q. Was there no bait there to be had ?—A. There was, but they could not catch enough at once, and we had to wait for the morning and evening catch, and buy what they would bring aboard.

Q. Did you go in the harbor or remain in Freshwater Bay ?—A. The vessel remained in Freshwater Bay.

Q. Why did she remain there ?—A. That is where they catch the bait.

Q. You did not go into St. John's; was it not to avoid paying the light-dues ?—A. No; it was not.

Q. State whether it was that or not.—A. No; I don't know if it was that; it was not that.

Q. Did you pay light-dues ?—A. No.

Q. How long did it take you to get out to the fishing grounds at the Banks ?—A. I could not say.

Q. Cannot you remember how long—38 hours ?—A. It took nine days from the day we left to when we got back.

Q. Did you make any other trip to Newfoundland for bait last year ?—A. Not from the Banks. We took bait from Cape Breton when going there.

Q. The only two voyages you made in for bait since you have been master are the one just referred to, when you went round to Bonavista and got salt bait, and one in 1876, when you anchored in Freshwater Bay, outside of St. John's, and got bait and came out again ?—A. Yes.

Q. Those were the only two trips you went in for fresh bait, excepting in Fortune Bay ?—A. That is all.

Q. Fresh bait, I believe, is very superior to salt bait for taking fish ?—A. If it was on the Bank, it is; but when you have to spend half your time looking for it, it is not.

Q. Then, if you had plenty of fresh bait you would consider it far superior to salt bait for catching fish ?—A. Yes.

Q. Did you ever get any ice in St. John's ?—A. No.

Q. Where did you get your ice ?—A. Which time ?

Q. At any time.—A. We got ice in St. John's the last trip.

Q. You got ice in St. John's last year ?—A. Yes.

Q. Had you no other business in St. John's besides that of getting bait ?—A. No other business.

Q. Did not your men jig bait themselves ?—A. No.

Q. Have you ever jigged bait there either when captain or hand?—A. I never jigged any bait in St. John's.

Q. Did any of your crew?—A. No; nor any of my crew.

Q. Have any of your crew jigged squid in any other port than St. John's?—A. No; not that I know of. While they were with me I never saw them jig for squid.

Q. You always employed others to get bait?—A. They come alongside, and we buy bait from them.

Q. You employ them to catch bait for you?—A. They come alongside and they catch it.

Q. Do they come alongside with squid to sell, or do they come and ask what quantity of bait you want, and you tell them and they go and catch it?—A. They come alongside with bait. They never come near except with bait.

Q. They never come to ask whether you want bait or not?—A. No.

Q. How often has that occurred that they have come alongside with bait?—A. That is with squid.

Q. How often has it occurred that they have come alongside with squid?—A. All the times I have ever been there for bait, they have come alongside, and have had the bait—squid—in their boats.

Q. You got salt bait that year?—A. Salt squid.

Q. Last year you got fresh squid?—A. Fresh bait.

Q. And you were five days in St. John's before you got it?—A. Yes; waiting till they caught it.

Q. Do you mean to say that they did not come on board to know what quantity of bait you wanted?—A. They came on board the first morning I was there and had bait in their boats.

Q. And then you told them what quantity of fish you wanted, and they went and caught it?—A. They had bait to sell and I bought what they had.

Q. Then you told them what quantity you wanted, and they went and caught it?—A. Yes. At last they had more than I wanted.

Q. Bait was very abundant?—A. I did not want all the bait they had caught, the last morning I was there.

Q. That is the only time you got fresh squid from the people there?—A. Yes; the last time last year.

Q. You got it the year before?—A. No.

Q. That was the only time you got fresh squid?—A. I got no fresh squid that trip, but on the first trip.

Q. I thought you were in for bait only once that year?—A. I told you I was in St. John's four times this year.

Q. You told me you were in Fortune Bay.—A. Twice in Fortune Bay and twice on the coast.

Q. You have been more than once in St. John's this year?—A. Once in what I call St. John's.

Q. Have you been at any other time on the coast besides at Fortune Bay?—A. Yes.

Q. Where did you go?—A. In Bay of Bulls.

Q. When were you in Bay of Bulls?—A. I went in there the last day of July.

Q. When did you leave the Banks to go there?—A. I was right from home.

Q. You went from home to the Bay of Bulls?—A. Yes.

Q. And got bait there, in how long a time?—A. They caught it the same day we went in there.

Q. And you proceeded at once to the Banks?—A. Yes.

Q. How long was it before you got on the fishing grounds?—A. About two days.

Q. You got the bait the first day you went in?—A. Yes.

Q. Then you were only three days altogether in getting bait and proceeding to the Banks?—A. Yes; I had come from home then.

Q. How do you reconcile that with the statement you made that the shortest time in which you got bait was nine days?—A. There is a difference. I was asked the time it took from leaving the Banks to get back. I did not go there from the Banks.

Q. You draw a distinction between leaving home and going to Newfoundland to get bait and going from the Banks there for bait?—A. I was asked what time was taken between leaving the Banks to get bait and getting back again. I don't know but that I was three weeks from the time I left home till I got there.

Q. In 1875 you were a hand. Do you recollect what time you left the Banks to go into the coast for bait?—A. No; I do not.

Q. Do you remember how often you went in?—A. Once, I think.

Q. Do you recollect to what place you went?—A. To Fortune Bay.

Q. That was the only part of the coast to which you went for bait in 1875, and you went there but once?—A. That is all.

Q. In 1874, how often were you on the coast of Newfoundland for bait?—A. Once, I think.

Q. Those were the two years you were a hand?—A. Yes.

Q. How was it you said you were 10 or 12 times into that coast for bait before you were master, and six times since you were master?—A. I did not mean in Newfoundland getting bait. I was asked how often I took fresh bait.

Q. It is, then, not correct as you have stated, that you were into Newfoundland for bait ten or twelve times before you were master. Did you state that or not?—A. I don't think I did—that I went into Newfoundland that number of times for bait.

Q. As a matter of fact, you were there once in 1874, once in 1875, once this year; once in 1876.

Q. Then you were there once in 1874, once in 1875, once in 1876, and twice this year?—A. Yes.

Q. That makes five times you went on the coast of Newfoundland for bait?—A. Five times altogether. I have been four times this year, twice for squid and twice for herring.

Q. You were there once in 1874, once in 1875, once in 1876, and four times in 1877. Is that a fact?—A. That is the fact.

Q. Any other statement you may have made in regard to the times you have been in for bait is incorrect?—A. I was asked how often I had been in for fresh bait.

Q. You were asked how often you had been into Newfoundland for fresh bait?—A. I did not understand that it was only Newfoundland.

Q. You were there once in 1874, once in 1875, once in 1876, and four times in 1877. That is a correct statement?—A. Yes; that is a correct statement.

Q. Any other statement you made as to the number of times you went into Newfoundland for bait is incorrect?—A. Yes.

No. 31.

STEPHEN J. MARTIN recalled on behalf of the Government of the United States.

By Mr. Dana:

Question. I have learned since you were on the stand, what I did not know before, that you have been engaged in halibut fishing?—Answer. Yes.

Q. During the time you were in the Bloomer, were you halibut fishing?—A. Yes.

Q. Where did you fish?—A. Part of the time at the George's, but the biggest part of the time, seven years out of the ten or eleven years, we fished in different parts of the Bay of Fundy, from Yarmouth to Seal Island.

Q. That includes all the region about, I suppose. You have heard something about Cape Sable Island?—A. Yes.

Q. During time you were fishing in that region, were you fishing deep sea or inshore?—A. In deep water; never within fifteen miles of the shore. Sometimes we sighted Yarmouth light or Seal Island light.

Q. Did you ever see any other persons fishing as close inshore as three miles?—A. We were not near enough to see.

Q. Did you go in at all?—A. Twice; once into Bryer Island after herring, and once into Yarmouth after alewives.

Q. When you were at Bryer Island, did you find any other fishermen there?—A. Nobody but ourselves.

Q. Did you speak with any, either going or coming?—A. No.

Q. Did you get your bait at home?—A. We went to Bryer Island to try and get some bait, but did not get any. We got 400 or 500 herrings and came right away.

Q. Did you take bait from home?—A. Always.

Q. Is it the practice among the American fishermen to procure the bait from home?—A. Yes; when going only that short distance, they always take their bait from home.

Q. As far as your information extends, you know nothing of any halibut which is not taken outside in deep water?—A. No.

By Mr. Weatherbe:

Q. What was the last year you fished?—A. 1861.

Q. Where did you fish?—A. We caught one trip about 15 miles west of Yarmouth light. We could see the light on a clear night.

Q. From Yarmouth and to the west?—A. Yes; and towards Seal Island.

Q. Yarmouth was farthest you went west on that coast?—A. Yes; unless we went up to Bryer Island.

Q. You fished altogether west of Yarmouth?—A. Yes.

Q. You only fished at Yarmouth and west of Yarmouth?—A. Sometimes we would go as far off as Seal Island and Brown's Bank. We have been eastward on that coast.

Q. You never tried inshore fishing?—A. No.

Q. Did you ever land at Sable Island?—A. Never in my life.

Q. You never fished there in sixteen years?—A. No.

Q. You never fished for halibut lately?—A. Not since 1861.

Q. You stated, when you were here before, that halibut was a deep-sea fish?—A. We sometimes fished in 75 or 80 fathoms.

Q. You did not make anything out of halibut fishing?—A. No.

Q. Lately there has been a good deal of money made out of halibut fishing in the Gulf of St. Lawrence?—A. Not in the Gulf of St. Lawrence.

Q. Do you know anything about halibut fishing in the gulf?—A. No.

Q. You never heard of it?—A. No.

Q. Not off Anticosti?—A. Not to my knowledge. I have heard tell of it.

Q. You never heard of any halibut fishing except as deep-sea fishing?—A. I have heard of a few halibut being caught down at Miquelon and St. Pierre.

Q. Sixteen years ago?—A. Yes.

Q. Since that you have heard nothing about it?—A. No; I never paid much attention to it. I might have heard about it, but never gave it any attention.

Q. Do you know that it had lately been discovered that it was a shore-fishery?—A. No.

Q. You never fished any since 1860?—A. No.

No. 33.

EZRA TURNER, of Isle of Haut, Deer Isle, State of Maine, fisherman, called on behalf of the Government of the United States, sworn and examined.

By Mr. Foster:

Question. You live on the south part of Deer Isle, on Penobscot Bay, and in the State of Maine?—Answer. Yes.

Q. And the name of your place of residence is Isle of Haut?—A. Yes.

Q. How far is that from Mount Desert?—A. Twenty miles.

Q. How old are you?—A. I was 64, 12th of last March.

Q. When were you first in the Gulf of Saint Lawrence?—A. About 1829.

Q. What for?—A. I was for codfish that trip.

Q. When were you first in the Gulf of Saint Lawrence after mackerel?—A. In 1831.

Q. How many years have you been fishing in the Gulf of Saint Lawrence for mackerel?—A. I have been from that time till 1865.

Q. Thirty-five years?—A. Yes.

Q. When were you first skipper?—A. In 1831.

Q. Of what schooner?—A. The Porpoise.

Q. You were pretty young when you were first skipper?—A. There were younger skippers than I was.

Q. How old were you?—A. About nineteen.

Q. How many years were you in the Porpoise?—A. I was in her 17 years.

Q. In succession?—A. Yes.

Q. Where was she from?—A. She belonged to the town of Deer Isle, when Isle of Haute and Deer Isle were one.

Q. She belonged to the place where you live?—A. Yes.

Q. Where did she pack out?—A. The first three years I fitted and packed at Isle of Haute, and the next fourteen years I fitted and packed in Gloucester.

Q. State to the Commission what was your principal fishing-ground for mackerel in the Gulf of St. Lawrence.—A. I have been all over it, but the principal ground is Banks Bradley and Orphan and the Magdalen Islands. Late in the fall down at Margaree there is considerable hovering about there among the fleet.

Q. Have you caught mackerel within three miles of the shore any-where, and, if so, name all the places, and tell the Commission all you know about the extent of the fishing at those places?—A. I got 90 barrels one day. I did not judge myself anything more than three miles out, and I don't think I was. I think I was within three miles of the land; when we hove to after we had done fishing, we were six or seven miles off. The wind was right off land.

Q. Where was that?—A. At Margaree. Aside of that, I don't recollect getting a dozen barrels of mackerel at any place inshore round the whole bay.

Q. In one day, do you mean, or altogether?—A. In any one time. I might have picked up fifty barrels, aside of these wash-barrels, inside of the line all round the bay.

Q. So far as you have observed fishing within three miles of the shore, where is the most of it done in the gulf?—A. At Margaree Island, the most I have seen done. It is the only place there is any fish inshore that I know of.

Q. Why is that? Explain.—A. When the fish come down out of the bay in the fall we calculate that those which go through the Gut of Canso strike Margaree, unless the wind blows from the south and then they go round Cape North. They strike down to Margaree. Sometimes we can get them half way across to East Point, and afterwards two-thirds of the way from there towards Margaree, and if there is a heavy north wind it drives them near the shore. I never saw them caught inside of one mile or two miles, for the land there is very high, and one mile does not look much distance where the land is so high.

Q. When you speak of fishing off Margaree do you know if there is any fishing between the island and mainland there?—A. I never saw a mackerel caught there, but I don't know that it has not been done.

Q. When you measure distances do you measure them from the mainland or the island?—A. From the island.

Q. Then you mean inshore of the island?—A. Yes. I consider the island land.

Q. Have you ever fished off Prince Edward Island?—A. Yes. I have fished all round the east side wherever anybody fished.

Q. Did you fish within three miles of the shore there?—A. No. It is a rare thing that ever you get mackerel within the three miles. When they come within three miles they rise in schools, and we never calculate to do much out of them, but from four to six or seven miles off is the common fishing ground there.

Q. Did you ever go to Seven Islands in the gulf?—A. Yes, I have been there three times. I never got 20 barrels of mackerel.

Q. How near inshore did you try there?—A. I tried close in there and I did not find any. They used to catch them broad off and then the story was that some vessels caught them close in. Some of the English boats told me they had done well close in to St. Anne.

Q. St. Anne is on the other side of the river?—A. It is on the south side, right across.

Q. Did you ever try seining for mackerel in Bay St. Lawrence?—A. Yes. I took a seine once and went up to Seven Islands, and from there down through the Straits to Anticosti, down by Mingan, up through the inside of Mecatina, to St. Augustine and Dog Island, and from there to Old Fort. I was ordered to go and stop there.

Q. Where is Old Fort?—A. It is on the Labrador coast.

Q. What success had you in seining?—A. I never got a scale. I went from there to Five Islands, Newfoundland, Bonne Bay, and over to the

Magdalen Islands, and got there the first of September, and landed my seines and boats without one scale.

Q. What year was that?—A. I cannot tell that. It was when I was in the Blondel.

Q. Was it 10, 15, or 20 years ago?—A. It was 15 years ago.

Q. That season after first September did you try catching mackerel in the usual way, with hook and line?—A. Yes; all I got.

Q. How many did you get?—A. 270 barrels.

Q. Where?—A. At the Magdalen Islands and broad off New London and about 30 or 40 barrels southeast of East Point.

Q. What was the last year you fished in the Gulf of St. Lawrence?—A. I think it was 1865.

Q. You came from home here on a request by letter or telegram. Did you bring any books or memoranda with you?—A. No.

Q. You have not any means of fixing dates?—A. No. I did not know for what I was wanted, or what you were going to do with me.

Q. Do you recollect being in the Gulf of St. Lawrence once when there was a cutter there, and the limits within which you were to fish were pointed out?—A. I do, well.

Q. Tell me what the cutter was?—A. I cannot tell her name, because there was none on her, but I heard the name of her. The captain was Captain Daly.

Q. Where did she come from?—A. From Halifax. He sent for me to come on board.

Q. I should like to fix the time as nearly as possible. You hardly remember the year?—A. I cannot; I was in Highland Lass that year, I am pretty sure.

Q. Do you remember whether it was before the Reciprocity Treaty?—A. It must have been.

Q. The Reciprocity Treaty began in 1854; then it must have been twenty-odd years ago?—A. Yes.

Q. Describe what sort of a cutter it was, where it came from, where you saw it, and tell the whole story.—A. He gave a general invitation to all American skippers to come on board and see where their limits to fish were. There were 30 or 40 sail of vessels round there, but they all cleared out, except one or two, as soon as he came in.

By Sir Alexander Galt:

Q. Where did that occur?—A. In Port Hood.

WITNESS (to Mr. Foster). I staid there. The captain sent his boat down alongside a vessel which was there (I forget the name) and told the skipper he wanted him to come on board. He went to another one, and then came round to me and said, "The captain wants you to go on board." I went on board. The captain told me what his orders were from Halifax, and he showed me his marks on the chart. I well recollect three marks. One was from Margaree to Cape St. George, and then a straight line from East Point to Cape St. George, and then another straight line from East Point to North Cape. The captain said, "If you come within three miles of these lines, fishing or attempting to fish, I will consider you a prize."

Q. That is to say, you were excluded from three miles drawn from point to point across the Bend of Prince Edward Island?—A. Yes. He made those lines from the shore marks.

Q. I want to ask you generally whether you regard the Magdalen Islands as a safe fishing-ground?—A. Yes; as safe as any place in the bay.

Q. It is rather boisterous there when there is a wind?—A. Where is it not?

Q. How could you protect yourself?—A. There is no wind, but you can make a lee under the Islands, because you can go all round them.

Q. How about the north shore of Prince Edward Island?—A. We consider it a very bad place.

Q. Why?—A. You are embayed, and the tide sets in there so from the easterly that it is almost impossible to beat out. When the wind has blown two hours the sea is so sharp a vessel can do nothing.

Q. Do you regard that portion of the mackerel fishery which lies within three miles of the shore in the Gulf of St. Lawrence as important and valuable to American fishermen?—A. There is a very small part of the mackerel caught within three miles of the land there or anywhere or at the Magdalen Islands, that I know of, and I have always fished with all the fleet and vessels there, although at times I have seen good fishing at Margaree. Sometimes at Margaree the vessels fish within three miles of the land. That is all the important inshore fishing I know of in the whole bay.

Q. In regard to the herring fishery at Grand Manan, have you been in that neighborhood after herring?—A. Yes, I suppose I was the man who introduced that business.

Q. How many years ago was that?—A. That is 25 years ago, I guess.

Q. Did you go there to catch herring or to buy them?—A. That is the way all our vessels do; they go and buy them from the inhabitants there who fish the herring and freeze them.

Q. Do you know of any herring being caught by American fishing-vessels in British waters about Grand Manan?—A. No; I never knew any American vessel go there to fish for them. I have known the inhabitants there to charter American vessels and the skipper, and to give the vessel such a part and the skipper such a part—say they would give them two shares. The vessel would lie in the harbor and they would fish the herring, freeze them, and sell them. If there were four parties they would reckon one share for the vessel, one share for the captain, which with the others would make six shares. They several times wanted to charter me to come down in the winter.

Q. Have you ever seen American vessels there with herring nets?—A. I never did. Our nets and our fishermen cannot compete with Nova Scotia fishermen for herring.

Q. Why not?—A. Their nets are finer and they understand the hanging of them better. I have sold nets there and the people have taken them and seamed them over, and the nets would do as well again as they did when I had them. There is no American I ever knew or heard of who went there to catch herring.

Q. When were you there last?—A. I was down there last year, last winter. I only stopped a little while.

Q. You have now been speaking of the frozen herring?—A. Yes; they are frozen herring.

Q. Have you ever known any American vessels to fish for herring to salt or smoke in that vicinity?—A. No; not there.

Q. Eastport and Campobello are close to each other?—A. Yes.

Q. And the line between the two countries, Campobello being British and Eastport American, is the center of the channel, is it not?—A. Yes.

Q. Which has the most inhabitants, Eastport or Campobello?—A. If you take the whole of Campobello there is not much difference, but Eastport is the more thickly peopled. There are three villages in Campobello. The people told me they had no trouble over the fishing, and

I talked with them particularly about it. They say when the pollock are on our side their boats are here, and when on their side our boats are there, so they never have any trouble about the fishing-grounds.

Q. Do you know of any fishing done in boats there except pollock-fishing?—A. No.

Q. What kind of fish for mercantile purpose is pollock; is it a valuable or a cheap fish?—A. It is a cheap fish. Not so valuable as cod.

Q. What do they sell for per pound?—A. They go from $1.25 to $3 per quintal.

Q. Within the last few years?—A. Yes. They make a good deal of oil; they are well livered.

Q. And that pollock fishery, as you understood, is common to the boats of the two places?—A. That is what they told me when I saw the boats there together.

Q. They make a reciprocity treaty for themselves?—A. That is as I understood it. At Eastport the people told me that if herring were at Grand Manan they would go over, and if they were on their side the people of Grand Manan would come over and fish in West Bay. They never had any trouble.

Q. Is your information about the State of Maine sufficiently extensive to enable you to state whether the fisheries of Maine, cod and mackerel particularly, have been increasing or decreasing, say for the last ten years?—A. I should say they have been decreasing.

Q. Explain.—A. The town I live in once had twenty sail of vessels over 50 tons; now it has not got one.

Q. What did these vessels do?—A. Fished for codfish and mackerel.

Q. Did the same vessels do one business one part of the year and the other business the other part?—A. Yes.

Q. Do you include the whole of Deer Isle in that or merely your town?—A. I can tell you for the whole of Deer Isle. There used to be fishing firms there that owned and fitted out vessels. There were three firms at Burnt Cove, Deer Isle. There were two firms at Green's Landing, Charles Eden and S. Green. The Warrens had twenty sail of vessels. Now there is not one solitary fishing-stand in the whole town of Deer Isle, and no one fishes for pollock or mackerel, unless it be the two Webbs. The Webbs have three vessels left. The Warrens have one or two vessels left. Charles Eaton has not a vessel. There is a not a fleet or a barrel in Burnt Cove.

Q. Take other towns on the coast which you know of in the vicinity of Booth Bay?—A. I am not so well posted in regard to Booth Bay of late years. A new firm from Cape Cod has gone there, and they say is starting business there. I know the fishing business went down there greatly. McClentick, one of the principal fish-dealers, told me that it was about played out with them.

Q. What is the Cape Cod firm fishing for?—A. They are fishing for everything, I believe. They fit out vessels, and buy fish, herring and mackerel.

Q. Give me the name of the firm.—A. I cannot remember it.

Q. Are there any other towns you recollect about?—A. Yes; there is the town of Vinalhaven. There used to be 50 sail of vessels there, and it was one of the greatest places for codfish-making in the State. Now there is not one vessel goes out of the harbor where there used to be a fleet. There are four or five vessels belong to the island and scattered all round I believe George Hopkins is the only one in that town who has made codfish this year.

Q. Do you know anything about Portland?—A. I have not been at

Portland for seven or eight years. But I know about Bucksport and Castine; they have broken up in regard to fishing.

Q. They have stopped the business?—A. All except a few barrels.

Q. What did Castine used to do?—A. Castine used to be the mainstay of all fishing. Everybody went there to fit out, and it used to own a good many Bankers itself, and it used to supply vessels with salt and everything else. Now the salt-stores are all gone and the vessels are all gone. I don't know of one vessel that has gone out of Castine to the Banks this year, and there used to be 70, 80, or 90 sail of Bankers fit out there yearly. There are more Bankers going out of Bucksport than Castine, because there are none from Castine, but nothing to what they used to be.

Q. You remember the old bounty system?—A. I think I do.

Q. What was it, and what was the effect of its withdrawal?—A. It used to cost about nine shillings to the dollar to get it.

Q. How do you mean?—A. They would get an old vessel, and hire a crew to go in her, and the wages and expenses would eat up all the bounty and considerably more.

Q. What do you mean by getting an old vessel?—A. When the bounty was on, anybody who had an old vessel would let a man take her for nothing. If you had an old vessel you would say to me, "I will give you her to use this season if you will give me the bounty." The earning of the bounty would be no expense to you, and if I could make the vessel earn anything I would get it. That is the way bounty catching was carried on where I live.

Q. Would not that increase the number of vessels by keeping old vessels afloat?—A. Yes; vessels which ought to have been dead. That is the way the bounty system was carried on in our locality; but there were vessels which earned the bounty and the bounty helped them.

Q. The bounty was given exclusively on cod-fishing vessels?—A. Yes.

Q. Did those old vessels which went cod-fishing, partly induced to do so by the bounty, go after mackerel any part of the year?—A. They used to go after everything.

Q. But not during the four months they were earning their bounty?—A. No.

Q. The rest of the year they went fishing for everything?—A. Yes; they did not go a great distance off.

Q. Was the effect of withdrawing the bounty to diminish the number of vessels and to place old and poor vessels out of employment?—A. Yes; old vessels that were not good for anything.

By Sir Alexander Galt:

Q. A question was asked you whether fishing on the coast of Maine had increased or diminished, and you said it had decreased; and you spoke of the number of vessels. Where did those vessels usually fish at the time to which you referred?—A. Our vessels used to go to Labrador, Brown's Banks, and Western Banks, and all round.

Q. Along the whole coast?—A. Yes.

Q. And to the Grand Banks?—A. Some, but very few; I went to the Grand Banks in one vessel.

By Mr. Foster:

Q. Did your vessels come to the gulf for mackerel?—A. No; not the old bounty catchers.

By Mr. Weatherbe:

Q. You have named all the places where the vessels fished ?—A. The bounty catchers? Yes.

Q. You say the effect of the bounty was, as far as your personal acquaintance with it goes, that people had to pay about nine shillings on the dollar to get it ?—A. Yes.

Q. The vessels you spoke of as fishing from the several towns on your coast—where did they fish? Did you think Sir Alexander Galt's question referred to the bounty vessels ?—A. I thought the bounty catchers were meant. The other vessels fished all over the shores.

By Hon. Mr. Kellogg: ·

Q. Fishing for cod or mackerel ?—A. Both. I mean the firms which have carried on the fishing.

By Sir Alexander Galt:

Q. I had no reference whatever to the bounty system. I want to know where those vessels you spoke of as sailing out of all the ports on your coast usually fished—whether they fished in the gulf or on your own coast ?—A. All over the whole coast.

Q. Everywhere ?—A. Yes; everywhere in the gulf, about home, and everywhere else. The same as they fish now.

By Mr. Weatherbe :

Q. How far south of your place do they fish ?—A. For spring mackereling they go as far as Cape May.

Q. Those vessels you speak of went and fished in the same places as the Gloucester fishermen fished ?—A. Exactly.

Q. And they failed of late years ?—A. Yes.

Q. And your coast fishery has failed of late years ?—A. Yes.

Q. Generally ?—A. Yes.

Q. Do you know the reason the fishery on your coast has failed; is it overfishing ?—A. I always thought it cost all the fish were worth to get them, anyhow.

Q. Has your fishery diminished of late years ?—A. It was nothing but unlimited credit that ever kept the fishermen up, I contend.

Q. Then their credit failed ?—A. Yes.

Q. Is that the only reason ?—A. I don't know what other reason there is. That is reason enough, is it not ? They are not able to carry it on. They cannot make it profitable.

Q. Is that the only reason you have to give ?—A. Yes.

Q. That want of credit has stopped them ?—A. The credit has stopped and the business has stopped. There is no profit in the business, they say. That is what has made it stop.

Q. There used to be a profit in the business for years and years ?—A. I don't know about that.

Q. Was there never any capital in the business ?—A. There was some.

Q. For years and years there was capital in the business? For twenty years ?—A. Yes.

Q. There was capital in the business twenty years, was there ?—A. I don't think I understand you.

Q. Was there capital invested to carry on the fishing business on the coast of Maine ?—A. I suppose there was, or else I don't know how it could be carried on.

Q. For a large number of years ?—A. Yes.

Q. For 20 years ?—A. Yes.

Q. For the last five or six years there has been no capital in it?—A. Yes; for about the last 10 years.

Q. The fishing has been given up?—A. Because they did not find it profitable; there is no profit in it.

Q. How is it they have failed?—A. I cannot tell you more than there is no profit in the business.

Q. For twenty years they found a profit in it?—A. I don't know about that.

Q. Don't you know it?—A. They did not show it; if they made money they would be likely to show it in some way or other.

Q. When there was a large number of fishermen or firms carrying on the fishery business during those 20 years, and had capital invested in it, do you know whether they made money out of it?—A. No; I cannot swear as to what other people made.

Q. For the last 10 years it has not been profitable?—A. I know the business has all gone down.

Q. Are the fish to be caught there now, and were they of late years?—A. They fish on the same ground now as they did then.

Q. Do you know that the fisheries have failed?—A. I don't know. I don't suppose they have.

Q. Do you know anything about it?—A. I know as much as anybody.

Q. How do you know as much as anybody?—A. I am in the way of knowing what vessels bring in at Gloucester, Booth Bay, and Mount Desert.

Q. For twenty years there was capital invested in the fishing business?—A. Yes.

Q. For the last 10 years the capital has been withdrawn?—A. Withdrawn or lost.

Q. Do you know why?—A. No.

Q. Can you tell me, in regard to those 10 years, when the capital was invested, anything about the statistics of the catches and vessels?—A. No.

Q. For the last ten years can you tell anything about the statistics of the catches or vessels?—A. I don't keep books, and I cannot tell you how much a man lost or gained.

Q. Have you been engaged in the fishing business yourself?—A. I have not been engaged in cod fishing, and not much mackereling.

No. 33.

WEDNESDAY, *October* 3, 1877.

The Conference met.

The cross-examination of EZRA TURNER, of Isle of Haut, Deer Isle, State of Maine, called on behalf of the Government of the United States, was resumed.

By Mr. Weatherbe:

Question. You are acquainted with a place called Lubec?—Answer. I am.

Q. I will give you the names of some places and ask you if you are acquainted with them: Lubec, Perry, Pembroke, Eastport, Cutler, Machias, Campobello, West Isles, Point Lepreau.—A. I am acquainted with Point Lepreau, Cutler, Eastport, and Lubec. Machias I was never in but once.

Q. How often have you been in the other places?—A. I cannot tell you; a great many.

Q Recently, how often ?—A. I have not been there these three years.

Q. In any of them ?—A. Yes; I was in Cutler two years ago.

Q. Since the Washington Treaty came into operation have you been there ?—A. When did that come into operation ? I was in Cutler two years ago; I have not been in Eastport these three years.

Q. Can you give the Commission any statistics in regard to the fisheries at those places ?—A. I cannot.

Q. Have you taken any pains to obtain and make up statistics ?—A. No; that is as to the quantity caught, you mean.

Q. Anything at all with regard to the fisheries. Have you made up statistics ?—A. No.

Q. None whatever ?—A. No.

Q. You have spoken of Grand Manan ?—A. Yes.

Q. When were you there last ?—A. Two years ago, I think.

Q. How long were you there ?—A. I was there a fortnight.

Q. How many years were you there previously ?—A. Grand Manan is a place I often go to.

Q. How often have you been there since the Washington Treaty came into force ?—A. I cannot say.

Q. Give the number of times as near as you can ?—A. I was at Grand Manan two years ago, and staid a fortnight. I have been there off and on these fifty years.

Q. Take the last four years, how long have you been there altogether; one month ?—A. No; I never staid a month there.

Q. Altogether, during the last four years, have you been there three weeks ?—A. Yes.

Q. During the last ten years how long have you spent there ?—A. I cannot tell.

Q. Can you give any idea ?—A. I cannot remember.

Q. We have gone to a great deal of trouble in regard to getting statistics of Grand Manan fishery and the fishery on that coast; I want to know what you know about it ?—A. I have been going off and on to Grand Manan, sometimes staying one day and one night, and sometimes three or four days, and once two weeks. That was the longest time I ever stopped on one occasion at Grand Manan.

Q. Generally you only staid one day, and went away the next day ?—A. Yes.

Q. Did you take any opportunity while there to gather any statistics with regard to the fisheries ?—A. I knew how they were doing in fishing.

Q. Do you know how many boats they use ?—A. They use boats and vessels clear round there.

.Q. Did you, during the period you were there, make inquiries; and, if so, to what extent, and from whom ?—A. As to how many boats were there?

Q. As to statistics about the fisheries ?—A. No.

Q. Anything at all ?—A. No; I could see for myself.

Q. Did you make any inquiries whatever ?—A. Yes; about the fishing, from Mr. Caskill, the largest merchant there.

Q. And with regard to the number of boats engaged ?—A. I did not ask the number of boats engaged.

Q. You did make inquiries, from whom ?—A. Mr. Caskill, of Grand Manan.

Q. He resides there now ?—A. He is there now.

Q. On what subject did you make inquiries ?—A. I asked him how the fishing was this year, and he said very bad as yet.

148 F

Q. What year was that?—A. Four years ago; it was in July I was there.

Q. Give any other inquiries you made and tell me from whom you made them.—A. I did not make any inquiries about the fishing from anybody else.

Q. You asked no other question but what you have said?—A. Not from him.

Q. From any person else?—A. From John Beales, who left Moose-a-beck and went down there, bought a place, and staid there and fished.

Q. What did you ask him?—A. How he had done in fishing, and he said a good deal better than when he was up at Moose-a-beck. It was fishing in a small boat.

Q. That was all you asked him?—A. Yes.

Q. Did you make any other inquiries?—A. I don't recollect that I did.

Q. Do you know Walter B. McLaughlin, fishery overseer, Grand Manan?—A. I do not.

Q. You have heard of him?—A. I don't think I ever heard that name. How long has he been overseer?

Q. A great many years. He is county councilor, captain of the militia, justice of the peace, and light-house keeper; he was born in Nova Scotia, and resided all his life at Grand Manan, and is 48 years old. You know where the light-house is?—A. Yes, and been to it.

Q. I will read you some extracts from Mr. McLaughlin's testimony. After showing that he had taken up a good deal of time in preparing statistics, he says as follows with regard to American boats:

Q. Well, those boats—those American boats—do they equal or outnumber ours?—A. I think they outnumber ours. I would not say positively. I am convinced in my own mind that they outnumber ours.

Q. Those boats supply the coast of Maine with fish?—A. Yes.

Q. Our people do not compete with them in those markets?—A. Our fish go to Boston, Portland, or New York. Those boats supply their own coast.

Q. How often do they go home with their fish?—A. They fish a week or so and then go home. They have a nice little cabin in the boat and the men sleep in that. As soon as they get a load they go home.

Q. How do they keep their fish?—A. They salt them.

Q. How is it about the fresh fish?—A. Well, when they come for fresh fish in the winter time, of course they have larger boats or vessels.

Q. And the fish that are taken by the Americans in the summer they salt?—A. Certainly, unless they sell them fresh in the American market. It that case the vessels come supplied with ice. There are a few that run to Machias and other places with fresh fish, the same as they do to Eastport or Lubec; but any that make a business of selling the fish fresh must have an ice-house.

Q. Those American boats that you spoke of all fish within three miles?—A. Yes; I consider that they all fish within three miles—a marine league. Boat-fishing means that.

Q. Now, about how many American vessels fish on the coast during the season?—A. It would be hard to tell that. It has never been my duty to count them.

Q. They come in large numbers and they generally outnumber ours?—A. Yes; our people at Grand Manan fish but little in vessels.

Q. Do these vessels come in fishing within three miles?—A. At a certain time of the year. In winter it is entirely within. The fall and winter fishing is entirely within.

Q. What besides herring are caught in summer?—A. Cod, pollack, and hake.

Q. They catch in boats and vessels both?—A. Yes.

Q. Now, in the spring, are you not visited by the Grand Manan fleet from Gloucester?—A. Yes; they used formerly to come to Grand Manan direct. Generally now they go to Eastport and get the Eastport people to catch bait for them.

Q. When you say "formerly," do you mean after the Treaty of Washington?—A. Yes. They did not come before that much. It is since 1871 that have come principally. They will come down every spring.

*   *   *   *   *

Q. And now they come chiefly to Eastport to employ Eastport fishermen, who catch the fish and bring them to them?—A. The big vessels are not fitted out for herring-fishing. They take an Eastport vessel in company with them, and come over and anchor in our waters. They bring their own fishermen with them, and anchor in our waters, and get their bait there. They sometimes come in the fall for bait.

Q. Where have they gone this year?—A. I think to Campobello, Deer Island, and those places.

Q. Still in British waters?—A. Yes; we have the herring fishery.

Q. How many came down in the spring?—A. To the Grand Manan grounds, I should say forty sail. I would not say positively.

Q. As a practical fisherman, you say about forty sail of them?—A. Yes.

Q. Do you see them come in the fall?—A. Yes; at all times of the year.

Q. Then you believe the amount you have given is an underestimate?—A. I know it must be over half a million dollars; that is, our old $500,000.

Q. That is within the mark for your own island?—A. Yes.

Q. Of the British catch?—A. Yes; our own Grand Manan people, because sometimes they come over from Campobello and other places, but I have nothing to do with that.

Q. Well, now, is the American catch larger or smaller?—A. I think it is larger.

Q. Have you any doubt?—A. No; because their appliances are so much better than ours, and I think their men outnumber ours.

Q. I suppose they are just as assiduous in using their appliances?—A. Just as much so. One of their vessels will take more haddock in a short time than ours will in a whole year. One of theirs took 150,000 pounds in a week, while all of ours took only 50,000 pounds in the whole year. That was sold fresh.

Do you know anything about that, whether it is true or not true?— A. Some of it is exactly true, and some of it I don't know about. About the Eastport boats outnumbering the Grand Manan boats, I don't know whether that is true or not.

Q. Mr. McLaughlin further said :

Q. On the mainland you say our catch must be half a million, and the American catch is equal to that?—A. Yes; I think so, because they come down in the winter and follow these fine harbors up.

Q. You make for the mainland and islands a million and a half to be the catch of the Americans, and the same for our own people?—A. I think that would be fair.

Q. That is within our waters, within three marine miles?—A. Yes.

Are you able to say anything about that, whether it is correct or not?—A. I have been at Grand Manan all my days. I know but just one place round there where you can get bottom within three miles, I was going to say. That is right between Swallow's Tail and Long Island, where it is not more than three miles from land to land. There is good hooking there, and that is where all the Grand Manan fishermen go for hake, cod, and pollack. I cannot say about the Eastport people, for they are so much connected with the Grand Manan people. The East-port vessels go there to fish, and the Grand Manan people come and fish in Passamaquoddy Bay. I never heard of any trouble. They told me at Eastport there was no trouble about the fishing in the river. In regard to herring catches, it was Campobello men who chartered Eastport ves-sels, and they always tried to charter me. They get the vessels to go in and live in, and give the skipper a certain share and the vessel a certain share, and carry their own nets, and catch the fish. I never knew an American carry a net there in my life. I have been there when the men have caught herrings from St. John's to Campobello, along the whole shore. I have been there six years running buying herring, and I never saw an American vessel fishing there in my life, except those chartered in that way. They got a Lubec pinkey there once. Four men at Campobello chartered her. They had no skipper on her then, and they gave a certain share for the use of the vessel. I don't know what the catch was.

Q. I will also read some extracts from the testimony of Mr. James McLean, merchant, Letite Passage, N. B. Do you know Letite Pas-sage?—A. Yes.

Q. Do you know Mr. James McLean, merchant, there?—A. I don't know the name. I cannot recollect the name of one man there, though I know a good many by sight.

Q. Mr. McLean said:

Q. You live close to the shore of the bay?—A. Close to the shore.

Q. There are a number of harbors at that part of the coast; in which harbor do you carry on business?—A. We have a store at Letite and another at Black Bay.

Do you recognize him. They are both places in the Bay of Fundy?—A. They are 50 miles apart.

Q. He keeps a store at each place. Are you acquainted with him?—A. I am not acquainted with him.

Q. Mr. McLean said:

Q. You are acquainted with the fishery from Lepreau to Letite?—A. Yes; very well.

Q. That is along the mainland?—A. Yes.

Q. Among the islands lying along the coast are Campobello, Deer Island, and some minor islands?—A Yes.

Q. Besides Grand Manan?—A. Yes.

＊　　　　＊　　　　＊　　　　＊　　　・　　＊　　　　＊

Q. On the mainland, take from Lepreau to Letite, how many vessels and boats are employed by British subjects?—A. From Lepreau to Letite I should think there are between 50 and 60 vessels.

That is what he says with regard to British fishing-vessels. Mr. McLean further says:

Q. Before the treaty of Washington, in 1871, how did you deal with the fish? Did the Americans come in as much after the abrogation of the Reciprocity Treaty and before they commenced under the Washington Treaty?—A. Not catching herrings.

Q. Did they do so after 1871?—A. Yes.

Q. Tell the Commission how you dealt with the herring before 1871?—A. We dealt with them as we do now. The Americans came down and bought them; if not, we loaded a vessel ourselves and shipped them frozen to New York.

Q. Since the Washington Treaty, the Americans have come down and fished a great deal?—A. Yes.

Q. Are the fishing-grounds in your locality entirely in British waters?—A. Our herring fishery is altogether in British waters—all that I know of; I don't know of any in American waters.

Q. Is that correct?—A. Yes.

Q. Mr. McLean said also:

Q. How many fish in the winter time?—A. In the herring-fishing on our coast in winter there are from 100 to 125 American vessels fishing, small and large.

Is that true?—A. I should think it was, if they call it fishing when Gloucester vessels come down.

Q. Are there that number of American vessels fishing in those waters?—A. I want you to tell me what you call "fishing," whether by money, hook and line, or nets. That many vessels go there to buy herring. If you refer to 125 sail of American vessels, I will grant that number of American vessels go there.

Q. How do you know that?—A. I never counted them, but seeing so large a number, and knowing so many, and that gentleman stating the number to be 125, I don't doubt it.

Q. He does not refer to Gloucester vessels. Is it true or not?—A. I cannot swear to it. He says it is so, and I think it is.

Q. He does not refer to Gloucester vessels?—A. He does not refer to any places.

Q. He says:

Q. That is from Lepreau to Latite?—A. Yes, off Beaver Harbor, Black's Harbor, Black Bay, and Lepreau.

Q. What size are the vessels?—A. They range from 10 up to probably 40 or 50 tons.

Is that correct?—A. No.

Q. Are you able to contradict it ?—A. Yes; as regards the vessels I have seen.

Q. Have you any means of knowing ?—A. No; except what I saw during the six years I was there.

Q. You have been to those places ?—A. Yes.

Q. How often ?—A. Six winters running.

Q. Within the last four years, how often ?—A. I have not been there the last four years.

Q. Have you been there the last ten years ?—A. Yes.

Q. Have you been there the last six years ?—A. Yes, I think so.

Q. Not since ?—A. I don't think so.

Q. Are you able to speak with regard to the fisheries there during the last six years ?—A. No; but I never heard there had been any great change.

Q. Have you endeavored to get any statistics in regard to the fishing on your own coast or any of those coasts ?—A. No; I never knew they were wanted.

Q. You never made any inquiries ?—A. No.

Q. Then you don't undertake to contradict any of this evidence ?—A. I say there never were 125 sail of American vessels of that description buying herring there during the six years I was there or one-fourth of that number.

Q. I am asking in regard to recently ?—A. I cannot say what were there last winter.

Q. Mr. McLean said further :

Q. All the rest of the fleet of 150 vessels fish for herring ?—A. Yes, of the 100 or 125 vessels.

Q. Will you state to the Commission the process of fishing, what the Americans do when they come down there ?—A. They come down in their vessels. They frequent our harbors in blustering weather, and in fine weather they go out in the morning and set their nets.

Is that correct ?—A. They never used to do so when I was there.

Q. You are not able to say anything about the fishing there since always the Washington Treaty ?—A. That is new fishing to me. They used to stay in the harbors while I was there, and set their nets.

Q.

They have anchors to their nets and large warps, and set a gang of nets, two or four nets to a boat. The nets are allowed to remain out all night and are taken up in the morning, if it is not windy. If it is too windy the vessels remain in harbor, and the nets have to remain in the water until there is a chance to get them taken in. The vessels do not take up the nets ; the boats are sent after them, and in blustery weather it is not a very nice job. The herring is taken on board the vessels. Sometimes if there is a large catch the men take the herring to the beach and freeze them ; if there is only a small catch they freeze them on deck, but they cannot freeze the fish so well on deck as on shore.

Q. These vessels which receive the herring as soon as frozen are different vessels ?—A. Yes. They are outside of the 125 I mentioned.

Q. These are the American vessels which are in the harbors with buyers on board ?—A. Chiefly American vessels.

* * * * * *

Q. It is much more convenient to land ?—A. Yes; with large quantities it is much more convenient to land.

Q. Is it not a very great convenience and privilege to the Americans to be allowed to do so ?—A. I should think so ; I look upon it as such.

Q. The Americans themselves consider it a privilege to land ?—A. I suppose so.

Q. Obviously it is a very great privilege ?—A. It looks that way. I know that all our fishermen have to land to freeze the fish, and the Americans follow the same methods. There is no difference between them at all ; at least I do not see any difference. They fish in the harbor just in common with our own men.

Has that changed any since you were there ?—A. Yes; I never saw an American heave a net while I was there and never heard of one. I never saw a Gloucester vessel have a net.

Q. You are acquainted with the Bay of Passamaquoddy?—A. Yes.

Q. Mr. McLean says:

Q. Was that not at one time a great herring-ground?—A. It was once a splendid fishing-ground.

Is that correct?—A. Yes.

Q. Since the negotiation of the Washington Treaty, and since the Americans have fished there, what has become of it?

Q. Are you able to answer that?—A. The fishing-ground is there yet.

Q. I will read you Mr. McLean's answer:

A. It has been destroyed within the last two years. It is now no good whatever.

You are not able to say anything about that?—A. I did not know there had been any eruption there that had made any alteration in the bay.

Q.

Q. This has been done by American fisherman?—A. Not altogether. The American fishermen helped to do it; a great many Americans were concerned in it, but our fishermen were in it too.

Q. Were your fishermen driven to it, in order to compete with the Americans?—A. They have to do it; they must do it.

Were you aware of the nature of the fishing that went on there?—A. Yes.

Q. Was there any trawling there in your day?—A. No. That is a herring-ground.

Q. Mr. McLean says:

Q. Another mode of fishing—trawling—is practiced with larger fish, such as pollack, haddock, &c. Explain the effect of it?—A. Trawling has been pursued, as I understand it, during the last six or seven years.

A. There was no trawling in Passamaquoddy Bay while I was there; so the people told me. I talked with them about fishing.

Q. When you gave direct evidence I understood you to be giving evidence down to the present time with regard to the value of the British fisheries; you were not doing so? You cannot speak of the fisheries within the last six years?—A. No.

Q. You did not intend to speak of the last six years?—A. No.

Q.

Q. Along the coast of Maine, say from Eastport westward, there lives a large population who fish entirely in our waters?—A. Yes. They come from Lubec, Perry, Pembroke, and Eastport, and along by Cutler, and westward of Lubec, and still farther away than that.

Q. And from Machias?—A. I think so.

Q. They all come and fish in our waters?—A. Yes.

That is since the Washington Treaty?—A. I think a good deal of that is correct. Those boats come over and try in British waters, over at Grand Manan.

Q.

Q. Within three miles of their coast there is no fishing of which you are aware?—A. Yes.

Q. And this is a population that lives by fishing alone?—A. From Eastport and along there they follow fishing for a livelihood, beyond question.

Is that correct?—A. Yes.

Q.

Q. So that a large body of American fishermen gain their whole livelihood in our waters?—A. Yes; those that fish there do.

Q. What would you say is the quantity of herring alone that comes to Eastport in the course of the season—how many millions go to that small town during this period?

Are you able to answer that?—A. I could not.

Q. The witness answered it in this way :

A. I should think, at the least calculation, from seven to ten millions.

A. He means herrings by the count I suppose.

Q. Are there from seven to ten millions ?—A. I cannot say.

Q.

Q And of all the herring caught by you, more than three-quarters goes to Americans, either for food or bait ?—A. Of frozen herring ? Yes.

Q. And of the $50,000 or $60,000 worth that you take, what proportion goes to the Americans ?—A. About one-third.

Q. Where do you sell the rest ?—A. In the Dominion and New Brunswick ; some are shipped to the West Indies.

I suppose you were not acquainted with those matters at all. Have you any knowledge of them ?—A. Yes ; I have. I think that statement is correct.

Q. Are you acquainted with Mr. James Lord, of Deer Island ?—A. I am not acquainted in Deer Island. There are two Deer Islands. I belong to what is called Deer Isle.

Q. How many vessels have Campobello fishermen now ?—A. I cannot tell. A good many of their skippers go out of Gloucester. I don't know how many vessels are owned at Campobello ; I could not give you an idea.

Q. Mr. James Lord is fishing overseer at Deer Island ?—A. Yes.

Q. He said :

Q. Now, is it part of your official duty to ascertain the number of boats and vessels engaged in the fishery there ?—A. It is.

Q. Can you tell me what is the number of schooners or vessels ?—A. There are 28 vessels engaged in the fishery in my district.

Q. Of what tonnage ?—A. The aggregate tonnage is about 700 tons.

Q. How many men are employed there ?—A. I have a memorandum. (Reads.) There were 171 men engaged in the vessels fishing.

Q. How many boats are there ?—A. 234.

*   *   *   *   *   *   *

Q. Do the Americans fish much on the coast ?—A. Yes ; they fish in common with our fishermen, on the same fishing grounds.

Is that correct ?—A. They do. Eastport fishermen and those people are all one.

Q.

Q. How many vessels have they ?—A. I should think they had full as many as our folks.

A. Should think it is likely that Eastport has.

Q.

Q. Campobello employs about how many vessels and how many boats ?—A. I could not give you exactly the number. I should say it was about equal to West Isles. I should not think there would be much difference.

Are you aware of that ?—A. Eastport, Lubec, and Campobello are all one, and the people live in sight of one another, and get on agreeably about fishing. I talked with them about it when I was at Eastport seeing them.

Q.

Q. Then off Campobello there is about $180,000 worth taken by our people ?—A. I should say so.

Q. And $180,000 worth at West Isles ?—A. Yes.

Q. And the Americans take an equal catch in both places ?—A. Yes.

Is that correct ?—A. I should think so.

Q.

Q. All within three miles?—A. Yes: with the exception of one or two vessels from Deer Is and that go outside. The chief catches are inshore.

Is that correct?—A. Yes.

Q.

Q. Well, when I asked you for an estimate of the catch, and you gave me $180,000, you did not include in that amount the fish that was caught outside?—A. No.

You do no include that either, I presume?—A. No.

Q.

Q. That is about a million?—A. Yes.

Q. Have you any doubt you are underestimating rather than overestimating it?—A. No doubt that is under, if anything.

Q. That is taken by British subjects?—A. Yes.

Q. Then the American fishermen, do they take on these coasts as much every year as the British subjects, or more?—A. I think they do fully as much. I have no doubt. If I were going to say either more or less, I would say more.

A. I don't think that is correct.

Q. Do you know anything about it?—A. Nothing more than that I was there fishing. I have not been there for six years, but I know about it.

Q. What was the quantity when you were there—$900,000?—A. I can give no kind of estimate.

Q. Would it be $500,000?—A. I could not give any kind of an estimate.

Q. Would you undertake to say it was not $500,000?—A. No; I could not say any amount.

Q.

Q. Is there any fish on the American shore at all? Are you aware of any fish within the three-mile limit?—A. There are none worth talking about. None of our fishermen ever visit that coast for the sake of fish.

What do you say?—A. I say that is not true. Before I left home there was a Grand Manan vessel in at Deer Island, the skipper of which wanted me to pilot him down to Isle of Haut not to catch mackerel. I would have done it if I had not had a boat of my own.

Q. You are able to qualify the statement by that instance; are you able to give any other instance?—A. I have known of British vessels being in our waters.

Q. Tell me what vessels they were.—A. I don't know. Grand Manan vessels have no names painted on their sterns.

Q. Then never mind their names. How many were there; did you count them?—A. There have been three which I have been acquainted with.

Q. How long ago was that?—A. Thirty years ago the first one; and she belonged to Brier Island; the last ones were on Sunday last or Sunday previous.

Q. Those are the only ones you can mention at present?—A. Yes.

By Mr. Foster:

Q. Was it this summer you saw the two vessels?—A. Sunday before last.

Q. The quantity of ten millions of herrings was spoken of. Can you give the Commission an idea of what herring are worth each?—A. They vary in size.

Q. If you take the value of 1,000 or 100 herring?—A. If they averaged one cent they would do very well, I think.

Q. Do they average one cent? How many are there in a barrel, and what is the price of a barrel?—A. I cannot say. I had very hard luck.

I lost $600 the first cruise. and on the other three or four cruises I hardly got out square. I was very unlucky. If you don't hit the market at Gloucester you get shoved overboard.

Q. That is when they want bait ?—A. Yes.

Q. Did you intend to assent to the statement that all the herring-fishing you know of is in British waters ?—A. Not by any means. In winter it is the only place where they catch them. I don't know but that there is as good fishing on our shore, but we never catch them in winter, and never tried; but we do in spring and summer, and now they are doing as well in Portland herring-fishing as was ever done anywhere.

Q. There is herring-fishing all along the United States coast ?—A. I rather think there is.

Q. You say you did not mean to say in cross-examination that all the herring-fishing is in British waters. Will you enumerate the places on the United States coast where herring are caught in considerable quantities, and the season of the year when they are caught ?—A. I don't know of any place on the whole coast but which, at certain times of the year, has large quantities of herring. At Isle of Haut, for instance, we were getting from 5 to 15 barrels a night in one net when I left there. They were small-sized herring; the nets were one-inch mesh. They sunk the nets and lost some of them. The people had no means of smoking the herring, so they salted them for lobster bait. There are 100 sail vessels which make it a practice to go in the fall to catch herring. They make Portland their headquarters. They strike for Wood Island, and go eastward to Cape Porpoise, and clear along into Boston Bay, and down by the Graves, and they catch more herring than is caught anywhere I know of in British North America.

Q. Did you mean to assent to the statement that American vessels fish for herring in British waters as a fact you know of ?—A. Not with nets. They buy herring there. I never knew an American to have a net there, and I never heard of one.

Q. Did you mean to assent to the statement that there were several fishing towns in Maine which gained their whole livelihood by fishing in British waters ?—A. I do not know of any such business.

Q. Will you state whether you understand that there are any fishing towns in Maine the inhabitants of which get their living by fishing in British waters ?—A. I don't know of one.

Q. Did you mean to say, in answer to Mr. Weatherbe's question, that there were any towns on the coast of Maine the inhabitants of which get their living by fishing in British waters ?—A. No; but I do think the people of Eastport and Grand Manan are like one, and fish back and forth.

Q. That is what you stated yesterday ?—A. Yes.

Q. You say that the frozen herring business, as far as you know, is carried on in British waters entirely ?—A. Yes.

Q. In answer to questions put to you yesterday with regard to the failure of the fisheries of Maine, did you refer to the failure of the fishing business or to the failure of the catch of fish ?—A. I meant the fishing business.

Q. How is it as to the catch of fish off the coast of Maine ?—A. I cannot say that the catch has materially altered there, although fish are not so plentiful as they used to be. But I don't think that the change in the catch makes so much difference as the price and expense of getting them, for Maine is about bankrupt from end to end in the fishing business.

Q. When the fishing-vessels of your own town and its vicinity, and the other places you spoke of yesterday, were engaged in fishing, where did they catch their fish? Was it off the shores of the United States or off the coast of the British provinces, or both?—A. From the Grand Banks to Cape Cod, in every place where they now carry it on. They had equally as good vessels as anybody, and went all over the shores.

Q. After what kind of fish?—A. All kinds. They did not go so much for halibut our way as for codfish and mackerel. But it is estimated by the best judges of the fisheries that our State has depreciated 60 per cent., and in a good many places I know it has 100 per cent.

Q. What has depreciated?—A. The fishing business.

By Mr. Weatherbe:

Q. The reason they do not try to fish on the coast of Maine is because the fishing is better up in the Bay of Fundy?—A. They cannot live by fishing, go where they will.

Q. I thought you told Mr. Foster that you did not know but that the fish were there, but you did not try to fish them there?—A. I did not say we tried to fish for them. I say I did not know but what the fishing is very nearly the same as usual.

Q. Your fishermen do not now try to catch fish on the coast of Maine?—A. They try somewhere; it is their business.

Q. I understood you to say they do not try to catch fish on the coast of Maine?—A. I did not say so.

Q. Do they try?—A. Yes; we have plenty of vessels and boats all the time trying to fish on the coast of Maine.

Q. But the whole business, you say, is bankrupt?—A. Pretty much so; pretty much abandoned. There used to be 125 sail of vessels which fitted out from Castine; I don't know of one this year.

No. 34.

SAMUEL T. ROWE, of Gloucester, Mass., fisherman, called on behalf of the Government of the United States, sworn and examined.

By Mr. Foster:

Question. Your business has been that of a fisherman and skipper of fishing vessels all your life?—Answer. Yes.

Q. How old are you?—A. 55 years.

Q. What was the first year you were in the Gulf of Saint Lawrence fishing for mackerel?—A. I was there in 1845.

Q. You had been in the gulf a good many times before you were captain, had you not?—A. No; only one year; one trip.

Q. When were you first captain?—A. In 1846.

Q. What was the vessel?—A. Champion.

Q. When were you in the gulf next?—A. In 1851.

Q. In what schooner?—A. O'Connell.

Q. Were you in the gulf afterward?—A. Yes.

Q. In what years?—A. 1851, 1852, 1853, and 1855.

Q. You were not there in 1854?—A. No.

Q. As skipper every time?—A. Yes.

Q. Were you there in any other vessels?—A. I was there in the Oconowoc.

Q. What years were you in the gulf in that vessel?—A. 1856, 1857, and 1858; three years.

Q. Then what schooner did go in?—A. I was in the Alferetta in 1859.

Q. How many years did you remain in that vessel?—A. From 1859 until last year.

Q. Were you in the gulf all those years?—A. No.

Q. Do you remember how many years you were in command of that vessel in the gulf?—A. I was in the gulf all but two years, I think, 1870 and 1871. I have not been in the gulf since 1874.—I was skipper of the vessel.

Q. I will take your experience of fishing in the gulf in the Alferetta, beginning in 1859. How large a schooner was she?—A. 55 tons.

Q. New measurement?—A. Yes.

Q. In 1859 what was your catch?—A. 220 barrels.

Q. In 1860 what was it?—A. We got about the same.

Q. In 1861?—A. We got 310 barrels, I think.

Q. 1862?—A. We got 420 or 425 barrels; I could not say to four or five barrels.

Q. 1863?—A. We made two trips, and got 330 barrels each trip.

Q. Take that year when you had 330 barrels each of two trips, and tell the Commission where they were caught.—A. They were mostly caught at the Magdalen Islands. The first trip was all caught at the Magdalen Islands.

Q. And the second trip?—A. The largest part was caught at the Magdalen Islands and between that and Margaree, about half way across, I think.

Q Were any of the second trip in 1863 caught inshore?—A. No.

Q. In 1864 what was your catch?—A. I think 320 barrels each trip. We made two trips.

Q. For what quantity was your vessel fitted?—A. 330 or 340 barrels.

Q. Those years you got nearly full fares each time?—A. Nearly.

Q. Where were those two trips in 1864 taken?—A. Mostly at the Magdalen Islands; about 50 or 60 barrels were taken at Margaree broad off on the fall trip.

Q. Those taken at Margaree, were they taken inshore or off shore?—A. I should judge five or six miles out, out of the range of the island, between that and Cape Mabou.

Q. In 1865 what did you catch?—A. We made two trips, and caught 240 and 225 barrels.

Q. Where were those taken?—A. Mostly at Magdalen Islands; some few might have been caught somewhere else. We caught some few some years on the fall trip between Cape George and Port Hood, round the Fisherman's Bank, and between the island and Cape George.

Q. In 1866 what did you catch?—A. 300 barrels the first trip and 115 the second.

Q. Where did you take the first trip?—A. At Magdalen Islands.

Q. All of them?—A. Yes.

Q. Where did you take the second trip?—A. We got part of them at Magdalen Islands. We caught the trip round in different places; but most of them we got at Magdalen Islands, 70 or 80 barrels.

Q. Were you licensed in 1866?—A. Yes.

Q. In 1867 you were in the gulf again?—A. Yes.

Q. Were you then licensed?—A. Yes; I think so.

Q. How many barrels did you get in 1867?—A. 300 barrels.

Q. Where were they taken?—A. At Magdalen Islands.

Q. Did you fish anywhere else?—A. No; I don't think we did on that trip.

Q. In 1868 were you in the gulf again?—A. Yes.

Q. Were you licensed that year?—A. I don't think we were.

Q. How many barrels did you get?—A. Somewhere about 230 barrels, I think.

Q. Where were those taken ?—A. Most of them at Magdalen Islands. That is mostly our fishing-ground, except late in the fall, when we get a few round at other places.

Q. In 1869 were you in the gulf?—A. Yes.

Q. How many did you get then ?—A. About 260 barrels, I think.

Q. Where were they taken ?—A. We got most of them at Magdalen Islands. Some, I think, we caught between Cape George and Margaree. We got some in some years off Cape Breton, between Cape George and Port Hood, and off Fisherman's Bank. Late in the fall we would go round there, and sometimes pick up a few barrels, thirty or forty, and some vessels less.

Q. In those years were you in the habit of fishing in the Bend of Prince Edward Island ?—A. I have been there, but I have fished there very little.

Q. Did you then fish within three miles of the shore ?—A. No. The very few times I was there to try, I generally tried from seven to ten miles out. I have not been there for a number of years.

Q. In 1870 were you on the American coast or in the gulf ?—A. On the United States coast.

Q. Fishing for mackerel ?—A. I think we were cod-fishing in 1870.

Q. You were not in the gulf in 1870 and 1871 ?—A. No.

Q. Were you in the gulf in 1872 ?—A. Yes.

Q. How many barrels did you get ?—A. 315, or about that number.

Q. Where were those taken ?—A. We got most of them at Magdalen Islands. We caught a few at Margaree, between that and Chetacamp.

Q. Inshore or out ?—A. I think we were out four miles.

Q. In 1873 what did you get in the gulf?—A. I think 290 barrels.

Q. How long were you in getting them ?—A. We went into the gulf in July and came out somewhere about October 20.

Q. In 1874 were you there again ?—A. Yes.

Q. What did you get then ?—A. I think we had about 315 barrels that year.

Q. Will you describe that voyage ?—A. In 1874 we were there all the season. We went into Canso and landed fifty barrels of mackerel. We afterwards took them on board and carried them home.

Q. How many barrels did you get that year ?—A. 315 barrels.

Q. Were those packed barrels ?—A. No ; sea barrels.

Q. The collector at Port Mulgrave says you made two trips, and got 230 barrels the first trip and 170 the second. That is not so ?—A. No ; it is not so.

Q. Did you ever give anybody the statement that it was so ?—A. No ; I never did. I only made one trip in 1874.

Q. Where were your fish taken that year ?—A. At the Magdalen Islands.

Q. All of them ?—A. Yes.

Q. If I have added up this statement correctly, you have caught in the Gulf of St. Lawrence nearly 5,000 barrels—4,930. You have been up here during 14 seasons, and you got 19 trips; the average of your trips is $259\frac{9}{19}$ barrels, and the average of your seasons, $352\frac{1}{4}$ barrels. Now, I want you to take your last trip in the gulf in 1874, when you obtained 315 sea barrels, as you say, and let me see how profitable that was to you. In the first place, with whom did you fit out ?—A. With Rowe & Jordan.

Q. Mr. Rowe, of that firm, is your brother ?—A. Yes.

Q. As captain that year in the Alferetta, you had in the first place your own catch as sharesman, I suppose ?—A. Yes.

Q. Who caught the most mackerel on board that year?—A. I did.

Q. You were high-liner, as it is called?—A. Yes.

Q. Has the captain choice of positions?—A. Yes. He has one of the best berths; there are two about alike, and the captain has one of them. He has his choice anyway.

Q. What did your share come to?—A. Somewhere about $125 or $130, I think.

Q. Did that include your percentage as captain?—A. No.

Q. What percentage did you have as captain?—A. 3½ per cent.

Q. What was your net stock that year?—A. It was in the neighborhood of $2,300, I suppose.

Q. And on that you had a percentage of 3½ per cent.?—A. Yes.

Q. Did you make anything else out of the voyage than what you have mentioned?—A. No. I owned one-half of the vessel.

Q. Did the vessel make or lose money that year?—A. She lost $150 for the whole fishing season. We began fishing in April and we knocked off in the latter part of October.

Q. Then you did something else besides fishing for mackerel?—A. Yes. We went cod-fishing in the spring.

Q. How did you do at cod-fishing that year?—A. We did very well.

Q. Did you make or lose on the cod-fishing trip?—A. I do not think that we lost much. In fact, I do not think that we lost anything.

Q. Was the cod-fishing less or more profitable than the mackerel-fishing?—A. I could not tell exactly. I suppose the vessel was about square when she came to the bay.

Q. You were about square on the year's cod-fishing?—A. Yes.

Q. And how was it at the end of the year?—A. One hundred and fifty dollars were sunk.

Q. What was your share of the loss?—A. One-half.

Q. Was that making any allowance for interest or depreciation?—A. No.

Q. Was the vessel insured?—A. Yes; but she could not pay her bills within $150.

Q. You seem to have made quite as good catches of mackerel as the average for any one who has been here so many years?—A. We used to do about as well as the average, I guess.

Q. Have you got rich on it?—A. O, no; I have not got much of anything. I own a house, and that is about all. The vessel has been run about out.

Q. What do you mean by that?—A. She has run until she has sunk what she is worth.

Q. Is the vessel lost?—A. Some years she sunk considerable, and other years she made something.

Q. You are 55 years of age, and you have been fishing ever since you were a boy?—A. I began when I was ten years old, and have been at it steadily since I was 15.

Q. How much are you worth?—A. I have a house worth about $3,000, I suppose, and that is about all I have. I have no vessel now; that is how well I have done; and there are a good many as badly off as I am.

Q. If you were going to the Gulf of St. Lawrence to fish, should you regard the privilege of fishing within three miles of the shore as important to the success of your voyage?—A. No, I should not, because I have never fished there much. They drive you off there a great deal.

Q. You seem to have had licenses during two years; why did you take them out?—A. Well, they did not cost much, and I thought they might trouble me and drive me around. They drove us out of a harbor once.

Q. What do you mean by this ?—A. They stopped us from going into the harbor. This was a good while ago, and I thought I would take out a license. It did not amount to much, and if I found anything inshore; I then had a right to catch fish there.

Q. The first year you paid 50 cents a ton on 55 tons for your license; what did you pay the second year ?—A. I forget; but I think it was $1 a ton. I won't, however, be certain about it.

Q. Have you ever fished for mackerel on Georges Bank ?—A. O, yes.

Q. You have gone there on purpose to fish for mackerel ?—A. O, yes; and for a number of years.

Q. Without going into the details of the voyages, will you state whether it is a good fishing ground ?—A. It is a good fishing ground. I have got a good many mackerel there.

Q. You have been cod-fishing a good deal, I notice ?—A. Yes.

Q. How have you supplied yourself with bait ?—A. We always got our bait home. During the first part of the season we would go to Cape Cod and the sound for it. Generally, after the first one or two trips, when the frozen herring were gone, we went over across to Cape Cod, to what is called the Shoals, and procured bait until it came our way, and we then baited during the rest of the year at home.

Q. Have you ever got bait where you were fishing on the Banks ?—A. Yes.

Q. What kind of bait ?—A. Herring.

Q. Have you ever been to Newfoundland for bait ?—A. Yes; but not for fresh bait. I went there after frozen herring.

Q. Did you buy or catch the herring ?—A. I bought them.

Q. For bait for your own vessel ?—A. No; but a cargo. I took them home.

Q. How often did you purchase them ?—A. I did so for a few years.

Q. Where did you go for them ?—A. To Fortune Bay.

Q. Did you go there prepared to fish for them ?—A. No; and I never saw any one who did so, when I went there. It is now a number of years since I was there.

Q. In how many Prince Edward Island harbors have you been ?—A. I have been in Georgetown, and Malpeque, and in Cascumpeque once, in 1851. I went there for barrels. The man who fitted us out then had barrels there and he wanted us to go and take them.

Q. Why did you go to Malpeque ?—A. To make a harbor. I was never there a great deal.

Q. How many times have you been fishing there ?—A. I was about there mostly all one year, I think, and I might have been in there four or five times.

Q. How many times were you in Georgetown ?—A. I do not think I was there over two or three times. I was in Georgetown Harbor for the first time, I think, in 1874, save once. I was there in 1856 or 1857, and I do not think that I was there again until 1874.

Q. Are those harbors of such a kind that fishing-vessels in bad weather can easily enter them ?—A. No; those which are on the north side of the island are not so.

Q. Why not ?—A. Well, it is kind of shoal water about them, and it is generally pretty rough there when the wind is blowing on shore. When the wind is to the westward and off shore, they do well enough, but when the wind is blowing on shore, they are considerably rough.

Q. When the wind is off shore, there is no particular danger to be experienced when entering them ?—A. No.

Q. Have you been in the habit of going to Port Hood ?—A. Yes ; I have been there a number of times.

Q. At what season of the year ?—A. Late in the fall, to make a harbor ; when we are going to the Magdalen Islands, we are sometimes there for ten days or a week ; and in the fall, when we are down around that way, we generally spend the night in there.

Q. When, in the autumn, do you generally get into the vicinity of Port Hood ?—A. We never get over there until along about the 10th or the middle of October. Some are there earlier.

Q. Where, on the whole, has been your fishing ground ?—A. It has been at the Magdalen Islands. We went to Bank Orphan on our first trip some years.

Q. Have you usually fished in company with the greater part of the Gloucester vessels ?—A. Well, yes. A good many vessels fished around the Magdalen Islands. Some days you will only see a few there when a large fleet is there, and some days you will see a good many there.

Q. Why ?—A. Because they are all around the islands. The mackerel are found all about them, and the vessels fish all around them.

Q. Have you ever fished in the Bay of Chaleurs ?—A. No ; I was never there but once, and that was in 1874.

Q. Did you go in to try for mackerel ?—A. Yes.

Q. What was your luck ?—A. We never caught a mackerel.

Q. Did you ever fish off Seven Islands ?—A. Yes ; once.

Q. When ?—A. In 1852, I think.

Q. That was a good many years ago ?—A. Yes.

Q. Did you catch any fish there ?—A. No ; we got nothing there, and we did not stop long.

By Mr. Davies :

Q. What kind of a harbor is Port Hood ?—A. Well, it is a middling good harbor, though it is nothing extra.

Q. It is a pretty fair harbor ?—A. Yes.

Q. When you were there in the fall, were many of the fleet there ?—A. Yes.

Q. How many ?—A. I do not know, as I could not exactly say ; sometimes 150 vessels and sometimes 60 would be there ; but I do not think that I ever saw over 200 vessels there at one time.

. Q. There were always from 60 to 200 in that harbor when you were in it ?—A. Not always ; but this would be the case a good many times late in the fall. I was never there save late in the fall.

Q. When you were then there you would always find in it a fleet more or less large ?—A. Yes.

Q. And you think the numbers varied from 60 to 150 and 200 ?—A. Two hundred were the most I think I ever saw there at once ; and a good many of them were English vessels, from Lunenburg and La Have.

Q. These vessels were all engaged in fishing, I suppose ?—A. Yes.

Q. And I believe you were there every fall ?—A. I was there almost every fall.

Q. It is one of the fishing-grounds well known to fishermen in the fall ?—A. Yes ; for those who fish that way ; some fish the other way, down to the Magdalen Islands and half-way across between them and Cheticamp ; and if the wind is to the eastward, they make Port Hood their harbor, as there is no other harbor in which one can run about there.

Q. The shores of Cape Breton Island, from Port Hood to Cheticamp and Margaree, &c., are well known to all fishermen as good fishing-grounds in the fall ?—A. Yes; spells of mackerel are found there.

Q. And as a rule, the fleet go there some little time at any rate ?—A. Yes; some of the vessels go that way.

Q. You were accustomed to go there every fall, for a greater or less time ?—A. We never fished at Margaree a great deal.

Q. But you were at Port Hood or Cheticamp ?—A. Almost every fall. We would be there a week, I suppose.

Q. And off Sydney ?—A. No; I was never around Cape North.

Q. But you were around the Cape Breton shore every fall ?—A. Yes; our vessels were there late in the fall.

Q. And sometimes you were there for a week, and sometimes for 10 days ?—A. Yes.

Q. Were good catches made there at these times ?—A. I never saw but one good catch made there and that was taken between Margaree and Cape Mabou.

Q. Is that on Cape Breton ?—A. Yes.

Q. Between Margaree Island and the mainland a good catch was made ?—A. Yes.

Q. Were many vessels then there ?—A. No; there were 25 or 30 sail.

Q. What do you call a good catch as taken there ?—A. 60 or 70 barrels.

Q. Apiece ?—A. Yes; but all vessels do not catch alike.

Q. Your judgment would be that each of these 25 or 30 vessels caught 60 or 70 barrels ?—A. I do not think that all did so. I understood you to ask what I thought a good catch was. Some of them did not get more than 30 barrels.

Q. Do you know what the vessels took at the time ?—A. O, yes.

Q. What did they take ?—A. One vessel caught 70 barrels, and we got 50.

Q. Would that be the general average ?—A. I could not tell. We saw them all catching fish around us, but vessels do not always fish alike. There is a good deal of difference between them. One might catch 100 barrels, and another not one-half that. I have seen this happen often.

Q. You understood that they made good catches ?—A. I know that another vessel, my brother's, took 70 barrels.

Q. Have you any doubt as to this being the average for the fleet ?—A. I do not think that it was; but I think they all got a large share.

Q. Within what time did you take them ?—A. We got them all during one day.

Q. What have you caught there every fall ?—A. I have obtained very few there, that fall excepted.

Q. You went there nevertheless ?—A. Yes; but we got most of our stock at the Magdalen Islands.

Q. Did the fleet also go there ?—A. They went somewhere, but I do not know where.

Q. I understand you to state that you do not know where the fleet went ?—A. I could not tell. I know that they left the Magdalen Islands, but I could not say whether they went to Margaree or Prince Edward Island.

Q. But they either went to Margaree or Prince Edward Island ?—A. Of course; when fishing, vessels go from one place to another, and it is hard to tell where they go.

Q. I heard a witness state—I think it was yesterday—that the mackerel strike in on the Cape Breton shore when going down ?—A. They generally do so.'

Q. And the vessels follow them ?—A. But it is not often that they stop more than a day or two.

Q. Did you take the 50 barrels close inshore ?—A. No; we were five or six miles outside of the range of Margaree Island, I should think, from the look of it. We were to the southwest of Margaree Island.

Q. You were between Margaree Island and Mabou ?—A. Yes.

Q. When was this ?—A. In 1864.

Q. Would you undertake to swear at this length of time what distance you were then from the shore ?—A. Well, I think it was what I have told you.

Q. You then had a right to fish inshore ?—A. Yes; I think we were about five miles off shore.

Q. Would you swear to this ?—A. I could not; we never measured it.

Q. Can you positively state the distance ?—A. No; no farther than I have done to the best of my judgment. Generally, a man can tell two miles from five or six.

Q. I have heard witnesses say that they could not tell three miles from five.—A. I do not know about that; but I should think they could.

Q. You think that there is no difficulty in telling the distance from shore ?—A. O, yes. One could not tell it exactly, but I think a man ought to tell whether he was three or five miles off.

Q. You think there is no difficulty about it ?—A. I should not think so.

Q. Is your memory very accurate ?—A. Well, sometimes it is, and sometimes I cannot remember some things.

Q. What did you say you caught in 1874 ?—A. 315 barrels.

Q. And that only ?—A. Yes; and we made one trip that year.

Q. When did you go to the bay ?—A. In July.

Q. Is your memory sufficiently clear on that point to state whether it was in June or July ?—A. Yes; it was in July, after the 4th; it might have been on the 8th of that month.

Q. You are reported in the return to which Mr. Foster called attention, to have been in the Gut on June 25th ?—A. No; that is a mistake or a misstatement.

Q. Where were you September 1st, 1874 ?—A. I do not know exactly; but I think that about that time we went to Canso.

Q. Can you tell me how many barrels you had on board then ?—A. Yes. We , I think that we had somewhere about 270—260 or 270 barrels. ll

Q. You cannot remember the number exactly ?—A. No; not within 10 or 15 barrels.

Q. You landed a portion of them ?—A. Yes; 50 barrels.

Q. Do you know David Murray, collector of customs at the port there ?—A. No.

Q. How often have you been in Canso ?—A. I was there every year I was in the bay.

Q. And you do not know Mr. Murray ?—A. I suppose I may have seen him, but I could not tell him now if I saw him. I suppose I have been in his office.

Q. Do you know the man ?—A. I know there is such a man.

Q. Have you ever spoken to him ?—A. I could not say that I have, but I have spoken either to him or to his clerk. I have been at his office.

Q. Do you know him ?—A. I do not say that I do, but I have seen him or his clerk. I have been at his office.

Q. What did you go there for ?—A. To get a permit to land mackerel.

Q. Were you accustomed to tell him what your catch was?—A. Yes, sometimes; when he asked me I used to tell him.

Q. Was he accustomed to ask you about it ?—A. I do not know that he was.

Q. You gave voluntary information on the subject ?—A. No; I did not tell without being asked.

Q. If he did not ask you and if you did not give him voluntary information, how is it you say you were accustomed to state what your catch was?—A. I told him it when he asked me about it, but I could not swear that he asked me about it.

Q. Do you mean at any special time ? Don't quibble about it.—A. No; I could not swear that Murray ever asked me what my catch was, and I do not swear whether I know the man.

Q. Do you or do you not know the collector of Port Mulgrave, David Murray ? Have you ever seen him ?—A. I do not know, but I have been at his office.

Q. Have you there seen a man you believed to be him ?—A. I do not know as I took notice. I went there for a permit; it was given me and I went off.

Q. Did you ever state at his office what your catch was ?—A. I do not remember that I ever did so.

Q. Did you state to me a few moments ago that you had done so ?—A. I do not know as I did.

Q. Do you recollect stating that you told him or his clerk what your catch was ?—A. I told you I did so if he asked me about it.

Q. Did they ask you about it ?—A. I could not say; they may and they may not. I cannot recollect.

Q. Do I understand you to say that your recollection is an absolute blank on that point; you do not remember stating your catch or whether they asked you about it ?—A. No; I do not.

Q. Were you there on October 20, 1874 ?—A. No.

Q. You were not there at Port Mulgrave ?—A. No.

Q. Were you there September 1st, 1874 ?—A. Well, I was only there that once. I do not know when it was, but I think it was somewhere in the first part of September. That is the only time we were there save when we came from home. We stopped at Pirate's Cove, two or three miles below Port Mulgrave.

Q. Is that where Murray's office is ?—A. No.

Q. And you do not know whether you saw him or not ?—A. No.

Q. But you may have seen him ?—A. I do not know the man. I could not tell him if I saw him.

Q. In this report to which your attention has been called, it is mentioned that the Alferetta, a Gloucester vessel, landed fish there the 1st of September, and was there October 20th, 1874, on the second trip with 170 barrels.—A. That is not correct.

Q. What was your total catch that year ?—A. 315 barrels or thereabouts.

Q. Mr. Murray reports it 400 barrels ?—A. That is the way report get carried round, repeated many times; and they thus make one have more fish than be caught. I think this is the case sometimes.

Q. Were you more than once in the Gut of Canso that year ?—A. We were there three times on our way up, and on our way home, and once to land some fish.

Q. Did you stop there when you were going home?—A. Yes; to take the 50 barrels on board.

Q. In whose charge were they left?—A. In Mr. Hartley's.

Q. Did you inform him what your catch was?—A. I do not recollect; but most likely I did. He most always seemed to ask what it was.

Q. And if you did so inform him, of course you told him the truth?—A. Yes. I would tell him what we had.

Q. You never fished in the Bay of Chaleurs?—A. No; save once, when we tried and failed.

Q. Did you try near the shore there?—A. We tried all over the bay.

Q. Did you try there near the shore within the three-mile limit?—A. Yes; I think we did.

Q. When was this?—A. It was a number of years ago.

Q. During the Reciprocity Treaty?—A. Yes, I think so.

Q. Was a portion of the fleet accustomed to resort to the Bay of Chaleurs to fish?—A. Only a very few vessels were in it when we were there.

Q. Were the fleet accustomed to repair there for the purpose of fishing?—A. I could not tell, I am sure.

Q. Did you never hear that this was their custom?—A. I have heard that some vessels went there.

Q. That a portion of the fleet did so?—A. Some vessels—yes.

Q. Did you hear that a portion of the fleet was accustomed to fish there?—A. I do not know that I ever heard of more than 10 or 12 sail of our vessels being there at one time.

Q. And if they were there, you do not know whether this was the case or not?—A. Of course; I only know what I have heard.

Q. Did you never fish around Bonaventure?—A. Yes, off and on.

Q. But anywhere along the shore?—A. No.

Q. Have you fished about Seven Islands?—A. Yes, once; but I did not catch anything.

Q. You never fished there again?—A. Yes.

Q. Do you know whether any portion of the fleet was accustomed to fish there at times?—A. There were not a great many vessels there then; perhaps there were 8 or 10.

Q. But during the year?—A. I do not think so.

Q. You know that some vessels go there?—A. Well, some few do.

Q. Did you ever fish around the shores of Prince Edward Island?—A. Yes, but very little. I have tried there off and on, at different times, and over across to East Point, Magdalen Islands, and then come right back to Malpeque.

Q. Have you fished around East Point?—A. I have tried there.

Q. Close in shore?—A. I do not think that I was ever within the three-mile limit.

Q. Are you positive about this?—A. No.

Q. You may have fished there within the three-mile limit?—A. Yes; but I could not say.

Q. You were on the Alferetta in 1863?—A. Yes.

Q. And you caught about 330 barrels each trip?—A. Yes.

Q. Did you catch any portion of the first trip in 1863 within three miles of Prince Edward Island?—A. We never caught a fish in sight of Prince Edward Island.

Q. That year?—A. No; we came out of Souris and went straight to the Magdalen Islands; and we never left there until we started for home, in the latter part of August, I think.

Q. Do you know John F. Campion?—A. Yes; he was with us that trip.

Q. Do you know that he has been examined here?—A. Yes.

Q. Have you had his statement read to you?—A. Yes, I have seen it

Q. And you heard what he said about that first trip in the Alferetta?—A. Yes.

Q. He was asked—

Q. What was your catch in the Alferetta that year?—A. During the one trip that I was in her we caught 300 barrels.

Q. Were they caught outside the three-mile limit or close inshore?—A. Some were caught between East Point, Margaree, and the balance around the island and the Magdalen Islands.

Q. What distance were you from the shore?—A. One-third of that trip was caught between East Point and the Magdalen Islands, and the balance close to the shore of both islands.

A. That is not correct; we never hove to in sight of the island.

Q. Your memory differs from his on that point?—A. Well, I cannot help that. We went right straight to the Magdalen Islands, and we left there the latter part of August.

Q. And you are equally sure that you did not catch any fish that year within the three-mile limit, as you are that you did not do so any other year?—A. I am certain as to that year, because we were full of mackerel when we went home.

Q. Do you mean to speak from your recollection as to that year, respecting the distance you fished from the shore, as distinct from and better than for other years?—A. No; but I can tell when we catch fish at the Magdalen Islands—when we get whole fares there.

Q. You are just as sure respecting other years as this year?—A. I do not know about other years when we get fish at different places; but when I catch a whole trip at a certain place, I recollect that pretty well.

Q. You did not catch that whole trip at the Magdalen Islands?—A. Yes, we did.

Q. Where did you catch the second trip that year?—A. Mostly at the Magdalen Islands, and between them and Margaree.

Q. Did you take any portion of it at Margaree?—A. No; but the last day we fished after we left Magdalen Islands, we were just in sight of Margaree.

Q. You do not appear to have fished, except on one occasion, within three miles of the shore?—A. I never caught any fish inshore to amount to anything.

Q. In 1866 you took out a license?—A. Yes.

Q. You had fished in the bay for 14 years previously, and though you had never caught any fish inshore, you deemed it necessary to take out a license then?—A. I thought the license was cheap, and I had heard a good deal about vessels being driven round, and so I thought I would take one.

Q. But you did not catch any fish that year within the three-mile limit?—A. I do not know that we did, save at the Magdalen Islands.

Q. The price of the licenses doubled the next year, and still you took out another. What explanation have you to make as to your motives for doing so?—A. If we found mackerel anywhere inshore, we could have fished there.

Q. And still during sixteen years you had never taken any fish within three miles of the shore?—A. Yes; but I might not have got fish at the Magdalen Islands that year, and then I could have gone somewhere else.

Q. Had you an impression that the fishery would fail that year at the Magdalen Islands ?—A. No; the license did not cost a great deal. I only paid half of it, and I thought it best to be sure, and be on the safe side.

Q. Then the possible failure of the fishing at the Magdalen Islands had nothing to do with your motives in doing so ? You must have had some other motives ?—A. We then had a right to go anywhere we had a mind to.

Q. When you had the license ?—A. Of course.

Q. But why did you do so, when for 16 years you had never caught any fish there ?—A. We did not know what we would do.

Q. Had you heard from others that the fleet were accustomed to take the fish inshore ?—A. Well, no; I do not know as I ever heard of anybody catching a great many fish within the three-mile limit ; but I know the fish were caught 5, 6, 7, and 8 miles off shore, and the like of that.

Q. Or 4 miles off ?—A. Yes; I suppose so; but I cannot say what others have done.

Q. You have heard of the fish being taken within 4 miles of the coast ?—A. I suppose that some few have been caught there.

Q. Have you so heard ?—A. I could not say. When talking about these matters, fishermen do not state any regular distance. A man does not say he caught his fish 4 or 3 miles off shore, but that he fished off East Point or Malpeque, or wherever he may have been. They generally do not state the distance.

Q. You have heard that the fleet fished off East Point, and Malpeque, and Margaree, without reference to distance ?—A. Well, I suppose that off Margaree mackerel have been taken inshore ; more are so caught there than elsewhere.

Q. Did you hear from the captains in the fleet that they were accustomed to take fish off the places I have named ?—A. Yes. I knew that they do take them there.

Q. Did you hear that this was their custom ?—A. I do not know that any special man came and told me he did so, but if I asked a man where he caught his mackerel, he would say at such a place, wherever it might be.

Q. Did you ever hear from the captains in the fleet that they took their mackerel at East Point, Malpeque, or Margaree ?—A. Well, I have heard of mackerel being caught at all those 3 places, but never heard of them having been taken at any regular distance off shore that I know of.

Q. But what you heard from these captains had nothing to do with your taking out licenses ?—A. Well, I do not know as it did. When a man comes to the bay for a trip of mackerel if he does not find them at one place he generally goes to another; and if you have a license you can go all round.

Q. You have stated that you did not do that ?—A. I did not because I found mackerel somewhere else.

Q. Therefore you did not want licenses ?—A. We did not know what we were going to do when we took them out.

Q. But you had had an experience of sixteen years there ?—A. Yes; but I did not know what would happen sixteen years to come. There is a good deal of difference between the two.

Q. Have you heard that of late years the mackerel have changed their habits somewhat, and are found nearer the shore than used to be the case ?—A. Yes; I have heard of them being caught by boats off Prince Edward Island, but never so nigh the shore as is now represented.

I have been up and down the island, and I have seen boats fishing four miles off and three miles off and outside, I think.

Q. When was this?—A. I do not know that it was in any particular year, but it was when I was up the island around Malpeque and came down by East Point.

Q. Do you know the distance from the shore at which mackerel are now taken off Prince Edward Island?—A. No. I have not been in the bay since 1874.

Q. Did your experience, then, inform you, or had you heard it from others, that the habits of the mackerel had somewhat changed, and that they were now found and taken closer inshore than they used to be?—A. No; I do not know as this was the case.

Q. You never heard of it?—A. I do not think that I did.

Q. But you stated just now that you had heard something about it?—A. I do not recollect saying so.

Q. You said that the boats were now taking fish inshore?—A. I have heard of that since I came down here.

Q. But never previously?—A. No; I do not know as I ever did.

Q. You said you have lost a good deal of money on some of these trips?—A. No, not a great deal; but I have not made much.

Q. But you have made money?—A. I have a house, and that is all.

Q. Were you a member of a firm?—A. No.

Q. You were merely a fisherman?—A. Yes.

Q. For what firm did you go out?—A. I have fished for a number of firms; the last one was that of Rowe & Jordan.

Q. Are you aware whether these firms made money or not?—A. Well, I could not say; I suppose that some do, and that some do not—on the fish after they are landed. I do not think that the vessels make much money, but I do not know. We used to get an average stock.

Q. What would be a fair charter a month for a vessel of 75 tons?—A. I could not tell you.

Q. Did you never charter one?—A. No; I never heard of a vessel having been chartered at any place for ten or twelve years; but this used to be done.

Q. Do you not know what a fair ordinary charter for a vessel of that size is?—A. It would be about $200 I suppose for a large vessel.

Q. But for a vessel of 75 tons?—A. A vessel of small size for the fishing season of perhaps nine months, would cost, I suppose, about $100 a month; but I do not know for certain what would be the charge. I have not known any vessels to be chartered for a good many years.

Q. Did you go to McGuire's or Hartley's when you went to Cape Breton in 1874?—A. I went to Hartley's.

Q. You are quite sure about that?—A. We always fitted out there; we never fitted out at any other place.

Q. Had you during the seasons you were fishing, or say in 1874, any British fishermen with you—Cape Breton men, Nova Scotians, or Prince Edward Islanders, besides Americans?—A. I do not know that we had any in 1874.

Q. Do you remember whether you had or not?—A. No; I do not remember all the names of the crew.

Q. In 1863, when Campion was with you, had you any other colonial fishermen with you?—A. We had one man who belonged to the island.

Q. Who was he?—A. He lived at Gloucester then, and his name was Frank Chivari, think.

Q. It was not Simon Chivari?—A. He went by the name of Frank.

Q. Do you remember any other colonial fishermen who were with you during any of the years when you were fishing ?—A. No ; I do not know as I do. We had one or two one year, but I do not know as I could recollect their names.

Q. I would like you to do it if you can.—A. We had one man named Jim Rose, I think.

Q. Where was he from ?—A. Prince Edward Island. I think that was his name.

Q. What year was this ?—A. I could not tell you exactly. It was eight or nine years ago, I think.

By Mr. Whiteway:

Q. You said you had been to Fortune Bay, Newfoundland, for frozen herring ?—A. Yes; that was 12 or 13 years ago.

Q. You have not been there since ?—A. No.

Q. Are you aware whether the herring are now shipped from there in bulk or in barrels ?—A. We took them in bulk.

Q. And frozen herring are invariably shipped in bulk?—Yes. I never knew them to be shipped in any other way.

By Mr. Foster:

Q. You told Mr. Davies you once saw as many as 200 vessels in Port Hood ?—A. Yes; a good many English vessels were in the fleet at the time.

Q. What year was this ?—A. I do not know as I could tell the year exactly. I suppose it was somewhere about nine or ten years ago; it was at the time of a heavy breeze, I remember.

Q. Can you tell how many of these vessels were British ?—A. O, well, I suppose that nearly one-half of them were so; I should think that these vessels numbered 80 or 90 sail sure.

Q. They were not all fishing vessels, were they ?—A. Yes; some were cod-fishers and a good many mackerel-fishers.

Q. When you were at Port Hood in 1874, how many American vessels were there there then ?—A. The fleet was not very large that year.

Q. How many did it number ?—A. I could not exactly tell; sometimes a greater and sometimes a lesser number was there; perhaps there were 40 sail.

Q. Were you at Port Mulgrave June 25, 1874 ?—A. No; we were then at home.

Q. When did you leave home ?—A. After the 4th of July. We always left home after this date, one year excepted, and that was in 1856, to the best of my knowledge. We then went after poor mackerel.

Q. Could the Alferetta have been there on the 25th of June, 1854 ?—A. No; I do not think so.

Q. Do you only think not ?—A. No. I owned half of her, and we were on George's Bank at that date. We always go there up to the 4th of July.

By Mr. Weatherbe:

Q. Did you call at Hartley's on the way through ?—A. I think that we did.

By Mr. Foster:

Q. You did not leave Gloucester that year until after the 4th of July?—A. No.

Q. How do you know that you were not there on the 20th of October? Where were you then ?—A. In the bay. We might have been going out at that date. We generally leave the bay about the 20th or the 25th of October.

Q. Did you stop at Pirate's Cove?—A. Yes, we always do stop there.

Q. Were you in Pirate's Cove on the 20th of October, 1874?—A. We might have been. We generally go out the 20th or the 25th of that month, though some vessels stay a little later.

Q. You were in the bay somewhere on that 20th of October?—A. Yes.

By Mr. Weatherbe:

Q. You are mistaken about Port Mulgrave; all the part you mention is Mulgrave?—A. I do not know but that it is.

By Mr. Foster:

Q. Where is the place at which Murray's office was?—A. It was at the place we call Mulgrave.

Q. The first date, 25th of June, cannot be right?—A. No.

Q. But on the 20th of October you may have been at Pirate's Cove?— A. I could not say that, but we might have then been going out of the bay.

Q. What did you stop there for that year?—A. We had some mackerel to take in; some 50 barrels.

Q. And what else had you to do there?—A. We put a few empties ashore to make room for the others, and took in a little wood, water, &c.

Q. How many empty barrels did you remove?—A. As many as we had landed.

Q. Can there be any mistake at all about the number of mackerel?— A. No, I do not think it. There cannot be any mistake. We did not make but one trip that year, and we did not have a full trip. I am sure of that.

Q. As to John F. Campion, I notice on the 33d page of the evidence, British side, that he was examined and answered as follows:

Q. This was in the year 1865?—A. I was then in the Alferetta still; her captain was named Cash.

Who was then captain of the Alferetta?—A. I was her skipper every year since she was built.

Q. Were you part owner of her in 1865?—A. Yes, and ever since she was four months old up to last fall.

Q. Was Campion with you in 1865?—A. No. He was never with us save on one trip.

Q. Is there a Gloucester captain named Cash?—A. Yes, but I could not say whether he was fishing that year. I only know one captain of that name.

Q. In 1863 Campion was with you on one trip?—A. Yes, it was on the first trip.

Q. Was it the first trip of the year?—A. It was the first mackerel voyage.

Q. Was he with you cod-fishing?—A. He went on the first trip. We shipped him at the Island after we went down there.

Q. He says you shipped him at Gloucester?—A. We did not do so; he shipped at the island.

Q. His evidence is as follows on this point:

Q. And the next year, 1863?—A. I was also then in the fishing business.
Q. In what vessel?—A. The schooner Alferetta, Captain Rowe.
Q. Did you begin early that year?—A. Yes; we started in July.
Q. Where did you go?—A. We came to the Bay of the St. Lawrence.
Q. Was she a Gloucester schooner?—A. Yes.

Q. Did you go that season to the Southern fishing grounds along the American coast ?—A. No. I was in Gloucester when the vessel went out there, but I did not go.

Q. Why ?—A. Simply because I did not think there was any money in the transaction. I remained idle, as did many others at the time that year. I had never any faith in the Southern fisheries, because I saw that a great many people who went there did not make much.

Q. A good many others were idle as well as yourself ?—A. Yes.

Q. You waited until fishing commenced in the Bay of St. Lawrence ?—A. Yes.

His evidence continues:

Q. One-third were caught altogether outside the limits ?—A. Yes. We went home with the trip. I think it was in August we returned to Gloucester. We caught about 300 barrels.

Q. He means packed, I suppose; that was about the number we packed. He shipped with us on that trip at Souris.

Q. Are you positive about that ?—A. We went to the bay one hand short; men were not very plenty at Gloucester. Vessels often have to go that way. The cook's wife wanted to go down, and we accommodated her; and then when we went in this man wanted to go and we shipped him.

By Hon. Mr. Kellogg:

Q. Did I understand you to say you had licenses for 3 years ?—A. No; but for 2 ——, 1866 and 1867.

Q. In 1866, 50 cents a ton was charged ?—A. I think so.

Q. And the next year $1 ?—A. Yes; and I think the price was raised the third year to $2, but we did not take out any that year, and that is the reason why vessels did not then purchase them, I think.

Q. I should like you to state more fully what considerations you had in addition to those you have mentioned, if there were any, for taking out licenses.—A. Well, I do not think there were any others. When we had a license we could go any where without being bothered, and this might have been the case 4, 5, and 6 miles off shore.

Q. The sense of being secure whenever you went in the bay was your motive, or part of it ?—A. Yes; I suppose so. I have heard of vessels having been sometimes so bothered, but this was never the case with me save once.

By Mr. Davies:

Q. During the 23 years you fished in the bay were you ever interfered by the cutters ?—A. Yes; once.

Q. Where were you then ?—A. Going to Gaspe; this was in 1852 or 1853; I would not be certain about the year.

Q. You were then within the limits ?—A. We were not fishing; we were going to a harbor in company with some 25 vessels.

Q. Did they board you ?—A. Yes; every vessel was boarded.

Q. From 1852 to 1866 you were never interfered with by the cutters ? —A. No.

By Mr. Foster:

Q. Explain what happened at the time you were boarded off Gaspé.— A. It looked stormy and quite a fresh breeze was blowing when we were working up there. Most of the fleet were there, and the men on a steamer had boarded them and forbidden them to go in; and when we got there they boarded us and did the same thing. This occurred about 10 o'clock in the forenoon, and we staid round till late in the afternoon; it may have been 4 o'clock when they told us that we could go in, and we did so.

By Mr. Weatherbe:

Q. Give the name of the captain of that cutter.—A. I could not tell either his name or the steamer's name. I forget them now; it is so long ago, and I do not know that I knew them at the time.

<h2 style="text-align:center">No. 35.</h2>

Moses Tarr, of Gloucester, Massachusetts, fish-merchant and fisherman, called on behalf of the Government of the United States, sworn and examined.

By Mr. Trescot:

Question. You are a native of Gloucester?—Answer. Yes.

Q. State to the Commissioners what your business and occupation have been in Gloucester; what positions you have held, and the character of the experience you have had.—A. I commenced to go a fishing when a boy. I worked on a farm, and afterwards, early in life, I fished some. I have made mercantile voyages, and have, subsequent to that time, been in a commercial and fishing business, owning and fitting a large number of vessels, and I have held under two or three administrations office under the General Government. I have been president of a Gloucester Mutual Fire Insurance Company for several years, and was, during our rebellion, four or five years doing business at Charlotte-town, Prince Edward Island. I have done most of the different classes of business for New England men.

Q. So that in various capacities, partially in the custom-house, partially as president of an insurance company, partly as fisherman, and partly as fish-merchant you have had a large and full experience of the Gloucester fisheries?—A. Yes, I have.

Q. Now, with regard to the mackerel-fishing of Gloucester, has it increased or declined in the course of your experience?—A. It has, in the course of my experience, done both. In my first knowledge of it our vessels were small and the catch quite small, and it grew to be an important business subsequent to 1833, 1834, and 1835. About our earliest fishing in the Gulf of St. Lawrence, I should say, for mackerel was from 1832 to 1834. I don't remember the date of the first catching of mackerel in the bay. I was in 1832 there myself as a youngster, for codfish. I don't remember knowing anything about any mackerel in the bay or mackerel-fishing at that time, or previous to that time.

Q. Then it grew up from that time?—A. The mackerel fishery in the Gulf of St. Lawrence grew up from about that time. That was the first. We commenced by a vessel or two at a time. Perhaps the two first years they didn't catch but a few hundred barrels, or a few thousand perhaps, and it grew from that time up to eighteen hundred and some of the earliest years of forty, forty-one, and forty-two. It afterward declined and nearly failed out. I had a vessel that came in, after being there for the whole season, with as low as 30 or 60 barrels. I have known the mackerel to be very plenty on our coast for a series of years and then to run down, and almost no fish; only 100 barrels would be an ordinary fair catch for the season.

Q. Now, what, according to your recollection and knowledge of the Gloucester business, was the fleet employed in the mackerel fishery in the gulf when it was at its highest?—A. I should think it was at its highest during the rebellion.

Q. What was the number of the fleet employed then?—A. I should think we had over two hundred vessels.

Q. What is it now in the gulf from Gloucester?—A. We had when I came away vessels that were considered to have gone there 68.

Q. When you say that the number of vessels employed in the gulf was larger during the rebellion, and that the fishing of mackerel was at its height, must there not have been some exceptional demand for mackerel? Was there not an exceptional demand arising from the demand for the Army?—A. Yes; everything ran high. But I think we had had a larger number of vessels there before, say in '49, '52, or '53, but not so much tonnage.

Q. Then, if I understand you, within the last series of years the mackerel fishery of Gloucester has declined rather than increased?—A. It has declined; yes.

Q. Now, has the mackerel fishery of Gloucester declined as compared with its cod-fishery; so far as the industry of Gloucester as a fishing-port is concerned, what is the relation of the mackerel to the cod fishery?—A. Well, I should think the relative importance of the two classes of business, if I understand you aright, would be seventy-five per cent. codfish to twenty-five per cent. mackerel.

Sir ALEXANDER GALT. Are you asking him generally?

Mr. TRESCOT. I am asking him as to the relations that the two industries bear to each other in Gloucester. He says 75 per cent. codfish and 25 mackerel.

Sir ALEXANDER GALT. That is both on the American coast and in the gulf?

Mr. TRESCOT. Yes.

Q. Do you know what is the relation of the cod fishery to the mackerel fishery this year?—A. Well, I should think it was 90 per cent.

Q. Do you know what the relative values of the cod fishery and the mackerel fishery were last year in Gloucester?—A. I don't know.

Q. Now, from your experience in the various capacities in which you have done business in Gloucester, as fisherman, as fish merchant, as president of an insurance company, as being in the custom-house, what would you suppose would be the profit of fishing in Gloucester; is it large or small?—A. Small.

Q. What is it derived from, the fishing or the handling of the fish?—A. The handling of the fish. The earnings of the fishermen are very small for a family to live on in Gloucester, as everywhere else. They labor ten months in the year in Gloucester, and I think that the average earnings of fishermen would be considered good when they averaged $300 apiece.

Q. Then, I understand that the profit of the fisheries in Gloucester, as you understand the industry of the town, is a mercantile profit and not a fishing profit?—A. It is a mercantile profit. The fish are brought in. When the vessel arrives at the wharf they are purchased with a fair competition, there being 40 or 50 purchasers, and the crews are paid off as soon as the fish are weighed out, and the fish then become a mercantile rather than a fishing interest.

Q. Now, with your experience of fishing and what you have seen and known, have you ever been able to form an opinion as to the gulf fisheries; that is, as to what per cent. of those caught there are caught in deep water and what per cent. within three miles?—A. I have had some acquaintance with it by my business, and being in the bay fishing for mackerel myself two years, and knowing those who have been.

Q. What would you say was the percentage?—A. Well, very small. If I had to set it down, I should say there was 15 per cent. caught within the three-mile limit.

Q. You referred to the fact, as I understood, that you had been living at Prince Edward Island four years?—A. I did. Well, I went home, perhaps, twice a year.

Q. When you lived at Charlottetown, what were you doing?—A. My main business was the purchasing of produce. The purchasing of oats was the main business, and as incidental to the business I have shipped 10,000 to 20,000 bushels of potatoes, and what fish I dealt in, that is, mackerel, not codfish. I competed with two or three others for them.

Q. Can you give me the extent of your purchase of fish in any year?— A. My purchases of mackerel were small. There was a Mr. Hall and one or two other parties there who owned and were running boats themselves, and their fish came to them. What fish I bought were such as the farmers and fishermen living on the north side of the island caught and brought into market without regard to those places that had stations. I could not say that I bought more than 200, or 300, or 400 barrels while I was living at Charlottetown.

Q. Are you familiar with the habits and ways of the boat-fishermen on the island?—A. Yes; I have been invited out there to give an opinion in relation to the manner of their curing their fish. They were premature in the business, and didn't understand the business as we did. I used to go out to Rustico, to Malpeque, to Souris, and across the island to Bouche, I believe it is, and those places. I used to see there, and I understand the manner of their fishing.

Q. Now, with regard to that boat-fishing, with your knowledge of it in your four years' residence there and purchasing of fish from those people, can you form any idea from what they have told you, or what you saw, as to the distance at which they caught fish? How did they carry on that fishery, when did they go out, how far did they go, and when did they come in?—A. The boats there are manned, except the fishermen's and farmers' boats, by three, and perhaps some smaller ones by two, and up to four men. They go about daylight in the morning; between that and sunrise. The distance from the shore depends entirely upon where they find mackerel or codfish such as they are fishing for, and they are not likely to catch them within two miles—seldom within that. Two miles is a very short distance from the land. Sometimes they are inside of that, undoubtedly, and from that they go to three, four, five, six, and seven miles, and exceptionally beyond that.

By Sir Alexander Galt:

Q. When did you say you were living in Prince Edward Island?—A. From the fall of 1861 to the fall of 1866.

By Mr. Trescot:

Q. And about the character of this fish—you have dealt more or less in them all during that time; how did you find them?—A. Well, the mackerel-fishing commences its course about the 10th or 20th of June. That would be my judgment. The earliest fish are seldom caught before the 20th of June. Then the mackerel are poor and are like all other poor mackerel, even if taken care of they are No. 3. They increase from that and become No. 2, and when you get along to the middle or the 10th of August the mackerel generally, in seasons of good fishing, are then very handsome fair mackerel. But no one can testify what the mackerel will be next year through the season by what it is this year.

Q. What was the preparation of the fish by these people from whom you bought? How did it compare with the preparation by thorough mackerel fishers?—A. Well, we should not sell any of them that time for a fancy article. They were put ashore in the little barns and places where they kept them and many of them were careless with them, and would be a week, perhaps, filling a barrel. While they were waiting some of them would be injured. But some that were acquainted with the business cured them comfortably well.

Q. Can you give me any idea of the amount of fish caught around the shores of Prince Edward Island?—A. Well, I think the year I was there they would range from 4,000 to 7,000 barrels—not exceeding 7,000 barrels, maybe.

Q. The shore fisheries?—A. Yes; the island fisheries.

Q. These fish were bought up by the merchants who dealt in fish and were exported?—A. Yes.

Q. Who bought most largely?—A. Mr. Hall and Mr. Carvell—Mr. Hall, I think, most largely.

Q. What proportion of them did Mr. Hall get?—A. I suppose he got nearly half. The rest were distributed among such as came into competition for them.

By Mr. Weatherbe:

Q. When did you leave the island; ten years ago?—A. I left the island—well, I left my business there in the spring of 1866.

Q. You have resided in the States since that?—A. I have always resided in the States; my residence in the island was only a temporary home for the season.

Q. How many years were you doing business there?—A. From 1861—the fall of 1861—until 1865.

Q. Have you read over the evidence with regard to the boat fishery that has been given before the Commission?—A. No, I haven't read any testimony.

Q. I presume you know most of the men residing in Rustico?—I am somewhat familiar with them.

Q. Do you know Alexander McNeil?—A. Yes.

Q. Churchill?—A. Yes.

Q. And Marshall?—A. Yes.

Q. These are all respectable men?—A. Yes.

Q. Men of truth?—A. Yes; I don't know anything to the contrary, as far as I know.

By Sir Alexander Galt:

Q. You spoke of the commencement of the mackerel fishery in the bay as being about 1830?—A. I think I said 1832 or 1833.

Q. I understood you to say it declined about 1841?—A. Yes, it fell off, I think, about 1841.

Q. Then it increased again until the time of the war?—A. No, not entirely until the time of the war. It fell off again after that, but we were doing as well in 1852, '3, '4 again; that would be my remembrance. But I think we got as many mackerel in the gulf in the few years of the war as any other time.

Q. Now again it has fallen off, I understand you to say?—A. Entirely; it has almost entirely fallen off as far as any profitable business is concerned.

Q. You said there were only 68 vessels this year?—A. Yes.

Q. Has it declined periodically on the American coast also?—A. Yes.

Q. I wanted to ask you just this, whether the fishing is good at the same time in your observation on the American coast and in the Gulf of St. Lawrence, or whether it fluctuates and is good on your coast and bad in the gulf in the same year and *vice versa*?—A. I don't think there could be a distinct line drawn there, but I think it is sometimes the case that it resolves itself into that in a measure.

Q. It is occasionally good on the American coast and occasionally in the gulf, but not usually good on both coasts at the same time?—A. I have known it to be good on both coasts, but when we can find it good at home we should rather fish there.

Q. It has not been very good this year?—A. No, it is not.

By Mr. Trescot:

Q. How does the fishing on the coast compare with the fishing in the gulf?—A. With the same kind of fishing, do you mean?

Q. No; but with the kind of fishing that is practiced, which is seine fishing altogether. How does the seine-fishing on the coast compare with hand-line fishing in the gulf? Is it or is it not cheaper?—A. With the same quantity of fish taken, we can do it a good deal cheaper at home.

By Mr. Weatherbe:

Q. Generally speaking, it is cheaper fishing?—A. Yes; it is cheaper at home, because at home we can catch 100 barrels to-day and pack them to-morrow.

Q. You are only speaking now of the years when it is prosperous on your coast?—A. Yes.

Q. You are not speaking of an average of, say, 10 or 15 years? Take the most prosperous fishing on your coast and the most prosperous years in the gulf, there is more to be made in the gulf-fishing?—A. No, sir; not with the same class of fishing.

Q. I suppose you didn't make up any estimate?—A. No; but I have it in my mind and in my books.

Q. Had you been in the business of mackerel-fishing on your own coast before you came into the gulf?—A. Yes.

Q. Do you carry it on yet?—A. No; I gave it up altogether.

By Mr. Davies:

Q. When you speak of 15 per cent. of the mackerel being caught in-shore, do you embrace in that the mackerel caught by the boats?—A. No; that has nothing to do with the provincial fishermen. I speak of our catch.

By Mr. Weatherbe:

Q. You commenced in 1861 down there in Charlottetown?—A. Yes; the first business I did there was in the fall of 1861.

Q. You had an establishment at Cascumpec?—A. No.

No. 36.

BENJAMIN ASHBY, of Noank, Connecticut, fisherman, called on behalf of the Government of the United States, sworn and examined.

By Mr. Dana:

Question. Noank is situated to the eastward of New London?—Answer. Yes, about seven miles from New London.

Q. It is between New London and Stonington?—A. Yes, about mid-way.

Q. Are you now attached to the United States schooner Speedwell?—A. No, I am not,

Q. How many years had you been fishing?—A. Forty-four this last April.

Q. How old were you when you began?—A. Nine years old.

Q. You are Benjamin Ashby, junior. Your father is living, and a fisherman?—A. He is living, but he is too big to be a fisherman; he has been.

Q. Now, when did you first go in charge of a vessel ?—A. I had charge of a vessel thirty-three years.

Q. You took charge of a vessel 32 years ago ?—A. Yes.

Q. That was in 1845, was it ?—A. Before that. I had a vessel built in 1843, and I had had charge of a vessel then two or three years.

Q. Did you sail out of Stonington ?—A. I sailed out of Noank, Connecticut, every time. I never failed to go out of the port, and always from the same custom-house too.

Q. Now, in what kind of fishing have you been engaged during this long period ?—A. Halibut-fishing.

Q. Substantially that has been exclusively your occupation ?—A. That has been all my business up till the last two or three years, until I gave up the business, and gave it into somebody else's hands.

Q. Where have you caught your halibut ?—A. The majority of them on Nantucket shoals.

Q. What other places ?—A. Upon the Georges, in May and June and part of July; and for seven years, two trips a year, I have been over on to Brown's Bank. I have been in sight of Seal Island twice, and Cape Sable two or three times.

Q. With those exceptions, it has been on the Georges and Nantucket shoals ?—A. What we call the Southwest Georges.

Q. Those are nearer ?—A. Yes.

Q. What is the course of the halibut business—when do you leave port, for instance ?—A. We leave about the middle of March.

Q. Then you go first to the Southwest George's ?— A. Southeast from Nantucket shoals.

Q. How long do you usually fish there ?—A. Till the 1st of May.

Q. Then after the 1st of May you go to the George's ?—A. Yes, sir; we stay until July. The last of July we are on the northeast part of the George's.

Q. Then where ?—A. For the last seven years I have gone across to LaHave and to Brown's.

Q. Before the last seven years where did you go in the autumn ?—A. We used to quit. I didn't know anything about coming over to this shore at all for halibut.

Q. How is the halibut business carried on now from the places in that region ?—A. It is not carried on at all from Noank, because there is only one vessel fishes at all, and she has only been one trip this season. This same vessel was to Mobile all winter.

Q. These halibut you carry fresh to market ?—A. Yes, all fresh to New York.

Q. Your vessels are smacks, are they ?—A. Yes, with wells in them.

Q. About how often do you run into New York ?—A. About once a month. One trip a month is about the biggest we can do.

Q. What kind of bait do you use ?—A. I don't know how to answer you—whether to say menhaden, hardheads, pogies, or what.

Q. You mean the same thing, do you ?—A. Yes; it is pogies or menhaden. I suppose you all understand it. It is one kind of fish altogether, but has a good many names.

Q. I want you to state to the Commission how long you keep that bait in ice. You have a special way of icing it, haven't you ? Now, how long are you able to keep it in the way you prepare it for use ?—A. Well, do you want me to plan out an ice-house ?

Q. No; how long can you use it iced in the way you ice it ?—A. Well, the way I have put it up to preserve it I have fished with it when it has stood in ice 33 days, and have caught fish with it just as well as when we first commenced to fish with it.

Q. Then you are able, with iced bait, to go out on those shoals of Nantucket and the George's catching until you go back to New York ordinarily. You required no fresh supply?—A. We never pretend to make any fresh supply.

Q. You never did all these 40 years?—A. No.

Q. Now, tell these gentlemen how you prepare that bait to keep it so well.—A. I have an ice-house. The ice is cut 22 inches square in our State the way we take it in. We stow two cakes in breadth and three in length in the house, whether it is 12 inches thick or 20 inches thick. We leave a whole tier in the bottom. Then we take these pogies and put them four inches thick; then about the same thickness of fine ice, as fine as we can pound it—snow would be better. We put the same thickness of ice that we have of fish. Then we put another tier of fish, and then some ice again, till we stow from 7,000 to 10,000 of these fish right in one house. Then we fill all round the sides and all over the top with the fine ice, and then cover it with canvass to keep it. I have fished with it when it has been 33 days, and it has been good bait to fish with.

Q. Now you have a floor of cakes of ice?—A. Yes, we call them in our vessels bed-rooms.

Q. What is the depth of pogies you put on?—A. About four inches.

Q. Then four inches of fine ice?—A. Yes.

Q. Ground up?—A. We pound it as fine as we can with the axe: we have no mills.

Q. Then four inches of ice, then pogies, then ice again?—A. Yes, we fill it full.

Q. What is the advantage of that mode of preparing the ice?—A. It is all frozen solid and good. The top of the ice, when it gets frozen, bears its own weight, and it is not on the fish. It forms a kind of a crust upon the fish, and there is no air gets through it, I suppose, and it does not make any weight on the fish underneath.

Q. In case there is any melting, what is the effect on the bait?—A. When it begins to melt and the crust breaks away the fish begin to decay.

Q. You avert that or prolong the period by your mode?—A. Yes.

Q. If the water forms there does it draw up?—A. No, it goes down. the sides. We have it stowed so that the water that forms goes each side of this house.

Q. It runs off?—A. Yes.

Q. Is your method of preserving this fish practiced in any other place than your region of New London and Noank?—A. I am not acquainted. I have seen Cape Ann fishermen stowing bait, but I never went in for the science of their stowing it. There is too much wood around the vicinity of the bait. I have seen them stowing herring. I never saw them stowing pogies.

Q. Now, you say you have been to Brown Bank one trip?—A. I have been about two trips a year for seven years.

Q. Did you use the same bait, prepared in the same way?—A. Yes.

Q. You had no occasion to go in for bait?—A. No.

Q. You never had?—A. No.

Q. Where is Brown's bank?—A. It is south of Cape Sable, about forty miles from land.

Q. You have been about two trips a year for seven years?—A. Yes.

Q. Have you been to LaHave Bank?—A. I have been about the same number of trips.

Q. How far is that from the land, Nova Scotia?—A. About 60 or 65 miles from Cape Sable, about south by east.

Q. With the same results?—A. Yes.

Q. You used your original pogies and menhaden that you brought from home?—A. Yes.

Q. Now you know Cape Sable, and Cape Sable Island?—A. I don't know Sable Island. I have never been down there—Cape Sable I mean.

Q. How near have you ever been to the shore there fishing?—A. I have fished two trips in my life within sight of Cape Sable light.

Q. Did you always see it?—A. No; once in a while; it was a red light; they have changed it now.

Q. How often have you been there?—A. About three times in my life-time, in 42 years; that is the furthest eastward I have ever fished.

Q. And you never fished nearer the land of Cape Sable than about 15 miles?—A. No; I think it was full 15 miles, if it was not more. I don't know how far you could see; it was very hard to see. It was a red light.

Q. How long can you keep this halibut in the wells on board your smacks?—A. Just as long as we might stay down here in cold water; we keep them in the well alive; we have had them in the well four weeks, just as bright as when they were taken from the water. When we go into Connecticut in the warm water they won't live.

Q. They will live off Nantucket Shoals and off the George's?—A. Through March, April, May, and the fore part of June.

Q. Now when it becomes warm, if there is any danger of their dying, what do you do?—A. We take them out and kill them and stow them in ice.

Q. Do you take more ice than enough to preserve your bait?—A. We have two or two and a half tons generally to preserve our bait. We generally take 25 or 30 tons of ice on the trip.

Q. For the purpose of stowing the halibut?—A. Yes.

Q. Do you give them any food in the wells?—A. No; I have had them there when we have thrown in a lot of menhaden. We have scooped them up and thrown them into the wells with the halibut, and I have taken forty-four out of a halibut after they have been in. But we don't pretend to feed them, because we hardly ever put any food in the wells.

Q. Do you find the halibut after such a long fast just as good as ever?—A. Do I think he is? Yes, sir; I think he is the best fish in the world with the exception of the salmon.

Q. After staying in the well he is just as good as when he is caught?—A. Yes; because he gets rid of all the filth, and he is all fish, what is left of him. He is a splendid fish and I like to catch him. I would quit my meals any time to catch a good halibut.

Q. Do the New London people catch fish the same way with smacks?—A. Yes; the same way.

Q. And they fish in deep waters?—A. Yes.

Q. Do you know anything about catching halibut inshore?—A. No; not unless on the Nantucket Shoals, in shoal water on the George's.

Q. Well, I don't call that inshore. I mean near the mainland?—A. No.

Q. Did you ever make port up here?—A. Yes; I have three times—in to northward of Cape Sable.

Q. What port?—A. Stoddart Island.

Q. That is somewhere about Cape Sable?—A. Northward of Cape Sable.

150 F

Q. What did you go for?—A. To ride out two hurricanes, two three of the hardest winds ever I saw blow. That was in—I don't r(ollect exactly the year. It was in September.

Q. Perhaps the Commission may all know, but from what size to wh size do you catch these halibut? I don't mean you to take an extra(dinary case, but how do they run?—A. They run about 60 poun(dressed; that is, the head and tail off, and the "innards" taken out.

Q. Do you take a good deal of pains to clean them?—A. Yes; ve much pains. We get all the blood out of the backbone, and eve thing.

Q. How do you do that?—A. We scrape it out with knives, and wa them with scrub-brooms. We scrub the blood out of the back bo very particularly to keep them.

Q. If you are going to keep halibut in ice for a long time your s(cess depends very much upon the pains you take in fully cleansi them?—A. Yes.

Q. So with the success in keeping bait a long time?—A. Just t same. We clean every bony fish. We take every fish when we wa to keep them a long time, and scrub the blood right out of the bac bone after the head is off, and wash them very clean. That leav nothing but the fish and the bone.

Q. How long do you think you could keep your ice; for instance, (the Grand Bank, if you wanted fresh bait for codfish, how long cou you keep the bait fresh?—A. I can't tell; because I never went ou salt-fishing cruise in my life. I have never been aboard a salt-fishi vessel. I can't tell anything about that.

Q. How do you catch halibut? Do you use trawls?—A. We u trawls and hand-lines. I call my two hands a trawl. I calculate u trawl would be equal to any other in the vessel.

Q. Which do you think the most of for success generally, the han lines or the trawls?—A. Hand-lines wherever we have fished. I ha got the marks to show about my trawls right on my hands.

Q. How is the number now and the quantity compared with what was any 20 or 40 years ago?—A. There is plenty this year by wha have heard and seen of our smacks. I haven't been halibut fishing.

Q. How does this year for halibut fishing on the coast of the Unit States—I mean the small banks, the Nantucket Shoals, and all arou that region—compare with other years?—A. They are plentier th they have been for 35 years.

Q. When your vessels from your town of Noank have got through t halibut fishing, what do they do?—A. Some of them haul up and so go south. I have always hauled up when I have got through the h but season.

Q. About pound-fishing off the coast of Nantucket and along Rho Island and Massachusetts, can you tell us about that?—A. I may you the best way I know. I have been in the pound business the last t years on the east end of Long Island. Last year at Elizabeth Isla All we had to contend with was Mr. Forbes, a big man from Boston.

Q. Well, he owns the island?—A. Yes.

Q. You didn't have a hard time after all?—A. We had a tip-top ti after he found out we didn't want to steal his deer or sheep.

Q. He accommodated you, didn't he, a good deal?—A. His sons ca aboard, and they were very polite. We furnished them with bait everything they wanted. They were very accommodating.. All we 1 to do was to send up to the farm-house and get our milk generally. furnished them with all the fish they wanted to eat for the summer.

Q. Take the pound-fishing along the coast; perhaps you could describe how the pounds are constructed ?—A. Yes; of course we can. We had fifty-seven stakes driven to set them on, some in thirty-five feet of water, some as deep as thirty-eight feet of water. We ran them in from that on the leader until they came into four feet of water.

Q. You drove the stakes in ?—A. Yes.

Q. How long are they? How high?—A. They are from thirty-five to forty-eight feet.

Q. They are laid out in a straight line at right angles with the shore?— A. First you drive these stakes down. Then there is a line rove through the bottom of the stake five feet from the end of the stake, through a hole bored in the stake. Then the net is bent on to these lines, and this net is hauled right down to the bottom.

Q. By a sort of cable or chain? Which is it?—A. We have out-haulers.

Q. What keeps them down ?—A. These ropes haul them down, and we belay them to the top of the stake.

Q. Do you have a block?—A. There is no block; nothing but the hole through the bottom of the stake.

Q. How far does this line run out to sea?—A. It doesn't run out at all.

Q. But how long is the line of stakes ?—A. Nine fathoms.

Q. Then at the end you have little openings for the fish to go into?— A. There is the mouth of the pound.

Q. Are there not two circular or semi-circular places ?—A. No; only one, on the inner part of the pound ; there is what we call the heart.

Q. That has two openings ?—A. Yes ; one on each side of the line.

Q. So that whichever way the fish are going they will have to turn in ?—A. Yes.

Q. It is owing to the peculiarity of the fish that they will not turn a sharp corner ?—A. I suppose so.

Q. Then in the heart there is a square box where they finally come up?—A. It is fifty to sixty feet square. We slack all these lines up. They are all cast off. We have out-haulers to haul the net right up to the top of the water. The fish are all pursed up into one corner.

Q. Now, is that a large business along that coast of Nantucket, Rhode Island, Massachusetts, and Elizabeth Island?—A. Yes; the biggest fishing in the world.

Q. Has it very much increased ?—A. Yes.

Q. How many men does it require to attend one of these pounds ?— A. It took three to attend ours—generally three. We had only one pound.

Q. How are the catches, great or small?—A. They are great. They catch anything that comes.

Q. What fish do you principally catch ?—A. When we first put on the string we catch halibut and herring or alewives, next mackerel; the next after the mackerel is the dog fish ; then we catch shark, about 25 pounds average; then shad and the chiguit.

Q. Do you catch menhaden ?—A. Then scup after that.

Q. What do you say of the scup as a fresh fish for market ?—A. It is the biggest fish in the Fulton market.

Q. What do you mean by the biggest fish. It bears the biggest price ?—A.

Q. Is there any other name for the scup ?—A. The paugey.

Q. That brings a high price ?—A. Yes.

Q. Is there a great deal of it?—A. Yes; very plenty. But this year

they have been very small, and we have taken them out. We hav
turned out as much as 2,500 barrels of small paugies. They were no
salable in the market, and we let them go to grow big.

Q. Does the halibut bring a high or low price?—A. It has run thi
season from five to ten cents a pound.

Q. But generally the halibut is abundant in the market and the pric
is low?—A. Yes.

By Sir Alexander Galt:

Q. Is the price you mentioned that which you would get for thei
when you brought them in?—A. No.

By Mr. Dana

Q. Now, can you tell me how many vessels are engaged in cod-fishin;
for the New York market from your town?—A. There are 32 or 33.

Q. Solely in that business?—A. Yes; altogether.

Q. When do they go to the Banks?—A. The fore part of April.

Q. Where?—A. To Nantucket Shoals altogether.

Q. Now, I want you to describe to the Court whether there is an abun
dance or otherwise of cod on the Nantucket Shoals; how it is as a cod
fishing region.—A. Well, it is very big field for fishing cod. Last yea
they found them plentier than for twenty-five or twenty-eight years
They have been very plenty all the season.

Q. This season?—A. Yes; they have plentier than for a good man;
years back. Right through the summer they have caught them ver,
plenty anywhere from eighteen to twenty-five fathoms of water.

Q. How often do they go in to New York?—A. Once a fortnight
about ten trips, from the first of April to the last of September. The
they quit that ice fishing, and along October and November they carr;
them alive in wells. They generally carry ice.

Q. You say they run into New York how often?—A. Once a fort
night. They have ten trips of ice-fishing and four trips in the wells.

Q. Now, how many vessels from New London engage in supplyin
New York with fresh codfish?—A. Well, I have looked over the lis
Somewhere between twenty-five and twenty-eight. There should b
more.

Q. Is Greenport engaged in the same business?—A. Yes. There ar
not near so many vessels.

Q. Well, these vessels, you say, are all smacks?—A. Yes.

Q. What tonnage?—A. Anywhere from 20 to 45 tons.

Q. When they have a fare, about how many fish on the average ar
they able to take in?—A. About 2,500 to a vessel. Some get more an
some less. Some have been in with 4,300 or 4,400 of fresh fish.

Q. How much did they sell for by the pound?—A. From three and
half to eight cents. They averaged about five cents a pound.

Q. What would be the average catch to a man?—A. Well, there a
about five men to a smack.

Q. How do you fit them out, on shares?—A. Yes. They averag
about three men to a vessel on shares, and a few men by the month
$20 and $25.

Q. Has this fishing for New York market with fresh fish been four
profitable?—A. No; they make a living. They just about make enou
to live through the winter and start even next spring.

Q. I suppose generally those engaged as merchants in it. doing a m
cantile business, make more money?—A. The men in Fulton mark
make more money. There is where we leave our money.

Q. I think you stated the number and quantity were as large as they ever had been ?—A. Yes.

Q. Did you say whether this scup you thought so highly of is abundant ?—A. Yes; it is plentier this year than for the past five or six years.

Q. What period of time are they to be found ?—A. May and June. They are very small this year. We turn them out to let them go another year.

Q. But when they are full grown how big are they ?—A. A pound and a quarter.

Q. How are the mackerel off Block Island and Rhode Island generally, and off Elizabeth Island ?—A. They have been very large and plenty this season. We have caught them in our pounds, and one vessel from our place did a pretty good business to the eastward of Block Island, and between Block Island and Gay Head, which is the western side of Martha's Vineyard.

Q. Then the blue fish ?—A. They have been very plenty.

Q. What seasons. How long are they there ?—A. Well, they are there in the fore part of June till the last of October.

Q. They are caught in Vineyard Sound ?—A. Yes.

Q. They send them mostly to New York ?—A. Yes; they are all prepared for the New York market.

By Mr. Davies:

Q. I have only a question or two to ask for information. Do you mean to say that these halibut in the tanks live for four weeks without food at all ?—A. Yes.

Q. And that they will keep up there ?—A. Just as bright as when put in.

Q. In fatness and weight ?—A. Yes.

Q. How do you account for it ? Do they get food in the water ?—A. I don't know anything about it, but they are just as bright after they have been four, five, or six weeks, and just as lively as when they were taken.

Q. Do you change the water ?—A. We have about six hundred holes in the bottom of the vessel. It is right throught the bottom, and the sea washes in through it.

Q. Do you say you didn't know anything about halibut on the Nova Scotia and Dominion shores until the last few years ?—A. For the last seven years.

Q. Have you gone up among them at all ?—A. No; I never was there catching halibut.

Q. There is the Island of Cape Sable ?—A. I never went round it. I made Cape Sable light three times.

Q. That pound-fishery; what coast is it on ?—A. The States of Connecticut and Massachusetts.

Q. Do you embrace Massachusetts in your statement about the pound-fishery ?—A. Yes; that is where we fished last season.

Q. How far off from the shores do you have these pounds ?—A. Maybe six hundred feet on the shore. We run a leader from the shore right off into thirty-six or thirty-eight feet of water.

Q. Do you catch mackerel in them ?—A. Yes. We got a lot of mackerel, some 280 odd barrels, and sent them to New York.

Q. They come pretty close in there ?—A. Yes; right along.

Q. What takes them in ?—A. I can't tell.

Q. Is it bait ?—A. There is no bait you can see that time of year.

Q. Are there many of those pounds ?—A. Yes.

Q. The whole ground is covered ?—A. Yes; wherever they can the stakes.

Q. I want to ask you whether these pounds injure the fishing the shores or not ?—A. No; the fish are just as plenty now.

Q. I don't speak of this year, for this is an exceedingly good year for five or six years along, have you noticed any diminution of the ing along there ?—A. No.

Q. Are most of the mackerel caught by the pound along that coast A. Yes; about all. There is only one of our vessels out of the St Connecticut for mackerel.

Q. How deep are they ?—A. About 40 feet; you have a stake of 52 feet.

By Mr. Dana:

Q. When you speak of Massachusetts you don't speak of Mass setts Bay, inside of Cape Ann and Cape Cod ?—A. No.

Q. You mean the south shore ?—A. Yes.

By Mr. Davies:

Q. I simply meant to ask you whether you embraced Massachu in the statement that the pound-fishing has not diminished the fi A. I speak of Buzzard Bay. It is south of Cape Cod.

No. 37.

THURSDAY, *October* 4, 18

The Conference met.

JOSEPH F. BROWN, of Gloucester, Massachusetts, master marine fisherman, called on behalf of the Government of the United S sworn and examined.

By Mr. Foster:

Question. You live in Gloucester ?—Answer. Yes.

Q. You are 34 years old ?—A. About that.

Q. Where have you been fishing this summer ?—A. On the nort of Prince Edward Island, at Tracadie.

Q. What is the name of the schooner you have been fishing in The Riverdale.

Q. What time did you go to the island ?—A. I arrived there the day of July.

Q. What has become of the schooner now ?—A. She was cast on Tracadie Beach the 22d day of September.

Q. How have you been fishing this summer ?—A. In boats.

Q. Not from a vessel ?—A. No.

Q. Did you go up to fish in boats ?—A. Yes; we fitted for that v expressly to fish in boats.

Q. How many boats did you take ?—A. Two seine-boats an dories.

Q. How many men ?—A. Twelve men to fish.

Q. You fished from what time to what time ?—A. From the 26t of July until about the 20th September.

Q. Until your vessel was cast away ?—A. Yes.

Q. How many barrels of mackerel did your boats catch ?—A hundred barrels.

Q. How far off from the shore have you been fishing in the boa summer ?—A. About three miles, in that vicinity. We have been far as five miles, and sometimes inhore.

Q. How many boats are there fishing out of Tracadie?—A. Nineteen, including ours.

Q. What size boats; how many men?—A. They averaged about four men, I should think.

Q. How did you happen to get your vessel stranded?—A. A gale of wind came up on the 21st. We parted both chains and went ashore.

Q. You hope to get your vessel off?—A. Yes; I think we shall.

Q. Now have you seen the mackerel vessels there this summer?—A. Yes; occasionally we have seen them pass up and down.

Q. What is the greatest number you have seen any one day?—A. I have seen as high as 30 sail.

Q. Do you know at all what luck they have fishing?—A. Well, I think the general average has been pretty poor.

Q. Tell all you know about that.—A. Well, the highest trip I have known or heard of is 350 barrels, and very few at that.

Q. What vessel got that?—A. I can't tell you that; but I can tell you of the George B. Loring that got 250 barrels. I can't tell the name of one that got 350 barrels.

Q. Do you know about the result of the fishing of any other vessels?—A. I was aboard the Wildfire six weeks ago. She had got 100 barrels and had been in the bay about a month; she had 21 men.

Q. Any others?—A. That is all I know.

Q. If you have any information about any other vessels, either succeeding or failing, you may state what you know.—A. Well, I heard that the mackerel-fishing in the bay had been a failure, as near as I can hear.

Q. Were you in the bay last year?—A. Yes.

Q. At the same place?—A. Just about the same voyage; we were not fitted quite as well as we were this year.

Q. What did you do last year, buy or catch?—A. We came mostly to buy; we caught 20 barrels.

Q. With boats?—A. We had one dory and the vessel's boats.

Q. Has your experiment this year been successful?—A. No; it has been poor.

Q. Would it have been successful if you hadn't lost your vessel?—A. No; we would have lost money if we hadn't lost our vessel.

Q. What have been the average prices of mackerel this summer at Tracadie—I mean after it is cured. Give us the highest and the lowest prices you have known.—A. The highest sold for $10.50, that is for 200 pounds of fish after they were cured.

Q. What is the lowest?—A. $3.50.

Q. What is the average?—A. About $7.00, I should judge.

Q. Now, you have been fishing for mackerel in the Gulf of St. Lawrence in former years a good many times I believe? What was the first year you were in the gulf?—A. The first year I was in a schooner called the Saline.

Q. What year?—A. '57, I think, as near as I can tell.

Q. You must have been a boy of 14?—A. Yes; that was when I first commenced.

Q. When were you first a skipper yourself?—A. I think in '64.

Q. How many trips have you made to the bay as skipper?—A. Two; last year and this year is all I have ever been master.

Q. When you were here before you have been as sharesman?—A. Yes.

Q. But you have been a skipper in mackerel vessels elsewhere?—A. Yes; I have been on our shore.

Q. What year did you say you were first a skipper ?—A. '64 I think it was.

Q. I will just run rapidly through your fishing experience since time. What was the first schooner of which you were in command A. The Eclipse.

Q. What did you do the first year ?—A. We followed the Geor fishing until along in July. Some time in the first of July. Then fi for mackerel on the shore between Mount Desert and Cape Cod.

Q. How many barrels of mackerel did you take off the shores of United States that year ?—A. Somewhere about 260 barrels I think

Q. Take the next year, 1865 ?—A. We were in about the same l ness—the same voyage. We landed about the same number of bar Somewhere in that vicinity.

Q. When fishing off the United States coast did you make one or a number of trips ?—A. We made a number of trips.

Q. What were you doing in 1866 ?—A. In 1866. I was in Bay (leurs or the Gulf of St. Lawrence.

Q. You use two terms. Do you mean one and the same thing A. One is called the Gulf of St. Lawrence and the other the Bay C curs. The fishermen call it Bay Chaleurs sometimes.

Q. It is the same thing you mean. The whole gulf goes by the n of Bay Chaleurs sometimes ?—A. Yes.

Q. What is the Bay Chaleurs proper ?—A. It is a small bay to northward. The fishermen call the whole gulf Bay Chaleurs.

Q. What was the size of the vessel you were in in 1866 ?—A. Al 140 tons.

Q. What was her name ?—A.

Q. How many barrels of mackerel did she take ?—A. 500 barrel: landed.

Q. Did you go home with that one trip ?—A. Yes; we were her the season.

Q. She was a large vessel. How many hands did she have ?—A men.

Q. Now, where were these mackerel caught ?—A. They were ca at different places in the bay, at Bradley, Orphan, and Magdalen, around Margaree and Port Hood, around there in the fall. Late in fall we got up as far as that.

Q. Have you been in the gulf fishing for mackerel since that year A. Not until last year.

Q. How many years had you been there before 1864 ?—A. I had l here four seasons.

Q. Taking your entire fishing experience, I wish you would tell Commission what was the principal ground on which you caught m erel. What was the principal fishing ground ?—A. Banks Bradley Orphan, and the Magdalen Islands were our principal fishing gro

Q. Now, to what extent have you fished within three miles of shore ?—A. Well, but very little. I don't recollect ever catching very few fish inside of three miles until this year.

Q. When you have been in boats ?—A. Yes.

Q. I wish you would explain to the Commission how the vessel-ing is carried on, and how the boat fishing is carried on, and what i difference between them, as you understand ?—A. Well, the vessel-ing is more in deep water and offshore. They go searching after In the boat-fishing, we lie and wait for the fish to come to us.

Q. Can the vessels get fish in the places where the boats us fish ?—A. Not to any extent.

Q. When the boats are fishing near shore?—A. No; never, when the boats are fishing near shore.

Q. When the boats are fishing near shore how do they take mackerel? Is it in large schools?—A. No; I think the mackerel all through the north shore, so far as I have seen, seem to be scattered and feed on bottom, and all the way we can get them is to anchor. When the vessels come in among us they never get anything at all. They have tried it this year two or three times right in among the boats, but never could do anything.

Q. Well, can the vessels catch mackerel enough to make a profitable voyage if they fish in the manner in which the boats do?—A. No, they cannot.

Q. What is the largest number of mackerel vessels you ever saw fishing together, that you recollect?—A. In one place?

Q. Yes.—A. I think I have seen 500 sail of vessels in Boston Bay in one fleet.

Q. What is the largest number you ever saw together in the Gulf of St. Lawrence?—A. Well, I think 250 sail is the largest.

Q. Where was that?—A. Around Port Hood and Margaree in the fall of the year, when they all collected there in October.

Q. What year was it?—A. I could not tell exactly, but I think that was 1866.

Q. Have you ever fished or been for fish to the Bay Chaleur, proper? —A. Into the bay? I have been there but I never caught any fish in the Bay Chaleur at all. I have been there once or twice.

Q. Have you fished in the bend of the island; that is, Prince Edward Island, in vessels?—A. I have tried. I have been in vessels that tried up the island, but never caught any mackerel to speak of in the bend.

Q. Is it safe or dangerous?—A. It is the most dangerous place I know of in the gulf.

Q. Why?—A. Such a deep bend and shoal water. It is impossible for a vessel to get out. After a wind has been three hours blowing it would be almost impossible for a vessel to get out.

Q. How is it with respect to taking refuge in the harbors?—A. The harbors are very dangerous to enter, except they get in before the breeze comes on or in the day time. They are not fit to enter in the night time in bad weather.

Q. Why?—A. They are barred harbors and shoal water.

Q. What do you mean by barred harbors?—A. A bar of land stretching across the mouth.

Q. Have you ever fished in the vicinity of Margaree?—A. I have.

Q. What time of the year?—A. October, I think.

Q. At what distance from the shore of the island have you fished in that vicinity?—A. I have fished all the way from three or four miles, but in sight of the land ten or fifteen miles off.

Q. Have you ever fished close inside of there?—A. No.

Q. Have you ever fished inside of three miles of the island?—A. I might have been in within three miles. I don't think I have caught any fish there.

Q. Have the mackerel been found this summer in schools?—A. No. I haven't seen a school of mackerel since I have been in the bay. No large body of mackerel I haven't seen.

Q. Can the vessels make a profitable catch of fish unless there is a large school?—A. No; I don't think they can.

Q. How do you manage in boats? How have you got your 100 barrels?—A. I have been out every morning when there was a chance at anchor, and remained until eight or nine o'clock. The highest number of fish we have caught to a man has been 260.

Q. Two hundred and sixty mackerel would make how much more or less than a barrel?—A. The last we caught, 260 would make a barrel. The first we caught it would take nearly 300 to a barrel.

Q. How does the quality of the mackerel you have been taking this summer in boats range?—A. They range about one-third 3's, about one-third 2's, and one-third 1's.

Q. Pretty good mackerel?—A. No. I call them pretty poor.

Q. Is that a poor average? How does it compare with the mackerel you used to take at the Magdalen Islands formerly when vessel-fishing?—A. It was a good deal better than they have been this year.

Q. Have you sold these hundred barrels?—A. No; I only judge about the value; I don't know.

Q. How have the boats that fished about you been doing in comparison with you?—A. They seem to think they have done very well. They seem to be satisfied.

Q. Have they caught any more than you have?—A. No; I think we have caught more than the average.

Q. Explain how it is that they can be doing well while you regard yourselves as losing money?—A. They are under no expenses. They are farmers, part of them, and they go out fishing when it suits, so that it is nearly all gain to them. I am under a good deal of expense.

Q. Have you ever seen the boats fishing with the vessels in former years?—A. No, sir; very seldom.

Q. Have you chartered any schooners, Gloucester schooners, within one or two years?—A. No; I chartered my own last year to D. C. & H. Babson.

Q. What did you get for her charter?—A. One hundred and fifty dollars a month for four months, to go to Tracadie and buy and catch mackerel—about the same voyage as this year, only last year we went mostly to buy.

Q. How were you employed last year?—A. I was hired.

Q. On wages?—A. Yes.

Q. I suppose you have no objections to state them?—A. No; they paid me $75 a month.

Q. To take charge of the vessel and twelve men?—A. Yes.

Q. Did you get anything but that?—A. Anything except that! No, sir; only $150 a month for the vessel and $75 a month for myself.

Q. How were the men paid?—A. Two were on shares, interested in the voyage, and others were hired from $35 to $15 a month.

Q. Are you speaking now of this year?—A. Last year.

Q. You only got ten barrels of mackerel last year. The result must have been unprofitable to the people who took the charter?—A. Twenty barrels we got, as near as I know; I don't know exactly. I was told then they had sunk between $1,500 and $1,600.

Q. When a vessel is fitted out for a mackerel-trip, with a dozen men on board or thereabouts, what is the average cost of provisions per day for the men?—A. About 45 cents.

Q. Do you mean for this year or last year?—A. I mean these last two or three years.

Q. How does that compare with what it was 7, or 8 or 10 years ago?—A. I should think it took 70 or 75 cents eight or nine years ago when things were high.

Q. Under the war prices?—A. Yes.

Q. In what depth of water do you catch mackerel?—A. From five to ten fathoms.

Q. Taking your experience of mackerel fishing in the Gulf of St. Lawrence, how much value do you attach to the right to catch fish within three miles of the shore?—A. Mine is not any. I will never pursue the business again in a vessel.

Q. You never would pursue it again?—A. No; this is my first year's experience, and I don't want any more.

Q. Then, you are not employed this year?—A. No; I am on my own account.

By Mr. Weatherbe:

Q. Where did you keep your vessel?—A. This season?

Q. Yes.—A. In Tracadie Harbor.

Q. Where was she—on the beach?—A. No; about southwest from the mouth of the harbor.

Q. Tracadie is a dangerous place, is it not?—A. Well, the harbor, I think, is very good. If you go out, it is a dangerous place outside.

Q. It is a dangerous place inside, is it not? Was it not inside you were lost?—A. We were not lost.

Q. Then it is not a dangerous place inside?—A. Well, it is not dangerous, because the vessel is there, and there is no danger. None of us were lost at all.

Q. Is it a usual thing for a vessel to go ashore inside of a harbor?—A. Well, it is very seldom among our vessels there. There were ten boats on the beach besides myself.

Q. But do you know whether it is usual for vessels to go ashore inside? Has it ever been known before?—A. Yes; in 1853 a large fleet went ashore—American vessels.

Q. Inside of a harbor?—A. Yes.

Q. Not since that?—A. Not that I know of.

Q. Have you heard of any on that dangerous coast of the island since that large gale?—A. Yes; I heard of two the fifth day of last July; two Nova Scotia vessels were cast away at St. Peter's.

Q. In 1876?—A. Yes.

Q. Any others have you heard of?—A. No.

Q. Since the great gale?—A. No; I haven't heard of others.

Q. How many have been cast away on the Magdalens?—A. Of late years? That I could not tell.

Q. Is it a dangerous place?—A. I don't consider it as dangerous as the island, the north side.

Q. But you don't know anything about how many vessels have been cast away?—A. Well, I know from the experience I had there. I have had experience there, and I judge by that.

Q. I am instructed that vessels leave there in consequence of the dangers of the coast, that they leave there and come to the other shores, the mackerel-fishing vessels—is that correct?—A. I don't think it is. They leave there in the fall to follow the mackerel.

Q. I got it from a very truthful man, and I want to ask you whether it is so or not, that it is such a dangerous place that they leave it early, and come to other coasts, to the Cape Breton coast, Sydney, St. Ann's, and Margaree?—A. I think they go to Margaree and Port Hood. Port Hood is the best harbor on the whole coast. That is the reason, I think, they go there.

Q. That is the reason they go there?—A. Well, the mackerel generally leave the Magdalens, and they follow the mackerel.

Q. At the time the stormy weather comes on they leave there?—A Yes.

Q. Then you are not under the necessity of encountering the danger if you are only there in the summer months. You would not say, as a master mariner, that there was any danger on the island in the summer months?—A. Oh, there is some danger. You may have a gale.

Q. Well, that is true of this harbor here. I think there have been some vessels wrecked in this harbor, but as a master mariner, do you say that in the summer months it is a dangerous thing to fish in the bend of Prince Edward Island?—A. Yes; I think it is a dangerous place for a vessel fishing in the summer, or any season.

Q. Yet there has not been a vessel lost except the two? Where were they lost?—A. At St. Peter's.

Q. That is not the bend of the island?—A. St. Peter's is not! It is as nearly in the bend as you can go, as far as I am informed.

Q. Then I am mistaken. Malpeque is the bend?—A. I would not be positive, but Tracadie is about 45 miles from East Point, and St. Peter's I think, is 11 or 12 miles to the eastward of that.

Q. That is, it is nearer the point?—A. Yes.

Q. Now, that cannot be anything like as dangerous as the center?—A. Well, that is nearly the center.

Q. Well, what time were these vessels lost that you speak of?—A The 5th day of July.

Q. Well, the master must have been at fault?—A. Well, I may be at fault now.

Q. I didn't wish to say so at all?—A. Well, you judge from that.

Q. Were you there when those other vessels were lost?—A. I was in Tracadie the 5th day of July, when they went ashore.

Q. Was that in the harbor?—A. No; they were outside. I was in the harbor.

Q. It was in the night?—A. I could not tell whether it was in the night or day.

Q. You don't know how they came to be lost; you had no conversation with them?—A. No; I know they were cast away, that is all.

Q. You don't know anything about what was the motive for casting them away?—A. Well, the wind was the occasion of it.

Q. You considered it a dangerous gale, then, in July? A. It was a heavy breeze.

Q. Had you made harbor to save yourselves?—A. Yes; we made harbor that morning early.

Q. Well, that is what those others should have done. A little fore thought would have saved them?—A. Perhaps they could not get there in season. I have been caught myself in gales of wind right near harbor, and had to go off.

Q. I cannot understand. Perhaps you will explain how you came to select Tracadie as a place for fishing. One would consider it was not the best place?—A. Well, I was there last year, and I thought by appearances there was a prospect of a very good year's work, and that I might do well. My vessel is not calculated for the fishing business, that is, for the mackerel business to go off shore, and that is the reason I went in boats instead of going in a vessel.

Q. Why didn't you go to the Magdalens or some better place?—A Well, I don't know that that is better.

Q. I thought, according to your view, that it was?—A. It is at some seasons.

Q. Why didn't you go to Port Hood?—A. We don't generally fish at Port Hood until late in the fall.

Q. The boats fish there all summer, don't they?—A. I don't know. I never fished in boats till last year and this year.

Q. When you were about engaging in the enterprise of boat-fishing, did you inquire as to the boat-fishing in any other places?—A. No; I never made any inquiries at all.

Q. You made no inquiries as to the best places, but just simply took a fancy to select Tracadie?—A. Yes; I was there last year, that is the reason.

Q. Then in your view you were induced to believe it would be a success?—A. I thought last year it looked favorable.

Q. Don't you think you are taking rather too gloomy a view of the future?—A. The whole mackerel I have got, allowing my vessel was afloat, would not pay the bills.

Q. Even with that, that is only one year; what did you do when you were here before?—A. I had made one or two prosperous voyages, and I have made pretty poor ones, very poor.

Q. How many voyages have you made altogether, in round numbers?—A. Six or seven full seasons.

Q. You mean more than one trip a season?—A. No; never but one trip.

Q. Well, how many of these trips have been successful, do you consider?—A. Two were very successful.

Q. Were those two early in the period over which you fished?—A. One, we came early and staid late. The other one, we came in July and went home decently early, probably in September. I could not say exactly when, as it was some time ago.

Q. But I asked whether they were early in the period over which you fished; were they at the beginning of your fishing?—A. One was the third year. The other was the fourth time.

Q. Now, if I understand you correctly, you never fished within three miles much?—A. No.

Q. Once or twice you mentioned when you tried inshore?—A. Yes; but we never caught anything to speak of.

Q. You never tried more than once or twice?—A. I would not say once or twice, or three or four times.

Q. But very few times indeed?—A. Yes.

Q. Had you a license, do you recollect?—A. No; I could not tell that. Last year and this year I was master. The other years I was not master.

Q. Then you don't know; do you know whether there were cutters?—A. I have never been boarded by cutters in the bay in my life.

Q. During any of the years that you fished, was it forbidden?—A. Never that I knew of.

Q. You understood that you had a right to go in for fish?—A. I didn't know.

Q. A good many American fishermen, we have understood, have fished at Bradley and Orphan and the Magdalens. A certain number have always gone there. Some of them have done pretty well and others haven't, and yet they never tried inshore fishing?—A. Well, this year I have known vessels try inshore, and they haven't done anything to my knowledge amongst the boats.

Q. But you were making losing voyages before?—A. This year?

Q. No; before. You made seven voyages and lost money on five of them. But you never tried inshore?—A. Well, we tried and we spoke to the boats and found there was nothing doing. When they did try they didn't do anything.

Q. But you didn't give it a successful trial, I should say. I may be wrong. Your general fishing was outside? Your idea of fishing was outside?—A. Yes; that is what we fitted for.

Q. Well, you failed year after year for five years and didn't try inshore?—A. O, we tried it.

Q. I asked you how often, and you mentioned once or twice, or three or four times. Now I am speaking of a successful testing of it for a season. What I would like to hear would be some person who has tested it for a season. For instance, we have had vessel after vessel, and witness after witness; we have had a hundred vessels that ran in as close as they could get to the shore, and then drifted off until they got beyond three miles, and then came in again, and repeated the operation, continuing that course of fishing for a whole season. We have had hundreds of them.—A. I don't think I was ever near enough.

Q. For instance, at St. Anns, we had the evidence of the collector of customs, of vessels at St. Anns running in there and drifting off in the way I have described. You never tried that?—A. No; I never tried to follow it up.

Q Perhaps you might try that next year. It might be a hint?—A. No; I don't think I shall. I have had two successive trips.

Q. You will make money out of these mackerel this year. What will you sell them for? You bought some at $3.50?—A. No, I didn't.

Q. You didn't buy any this year?—A. No, we didn't buy any mackerel.

Q. It was last year?—A. We went there purposely to buy, but didn't buy anything.

Q. You were giving the price they were selling for?—A. Yes.

Q. They were selling for $10.50 and $3.50?—A. Yes.

Q. You would have made money if you had bought them?—A. I don't think so. I would sell mine now for $10.50.

Q. There. But what will you sell them for at home?—A. I think $7.50, $11, and $16, is the last quotation.

Q. Did you have any colonial fishermen, province fishermen, on board your vessel any time?—A. No. Do you mean, did we have any employed? No.

Q. That is unusual for an American vessel not to have a majority of provincial men on board?—A. Yes; I should judge about two-thirds.

Q. Well, does it not occur to you that that may be the reason you didn't succeed. You wanted a little of the provincial element on board?—A. No; I don't think we needed that at all.

Q. Well, we have had many instances where they have done well and made large catches. They understood where to catch fish. Have you ever heard of the practice of lee-bowing boats?—A. No. I have heard of lee-bowing vessels.

Q. You have tried to lee-bow vessels?—A. Yes; I have tried that.

Q. You consider that all right enough?—A. Yes. I should consider it fair.

Q. Well, it is just as fair to lee-bow a boat as a vessel?—A. I don't know how to lee-bow a boat.

Q. Would it not be just as fair? I don't ask you whether you did it or not?—A. I don't know whether it is as fair or not, because I don't know how.

Q. That would not have the slightest effect on its fairness, whether you know or not?—A. I don't know anything about that.

Q. Suppose I tell you how?—A. Well, then it would be fair enough.

Q. Would you consider it fair, then ?—A. Yes, I would.

Q. You never tried it, and never saw it done, but you would consider it perfectly fair ?—A. Yes; perfectly fair.

Q. You have lee-bowed vessels, and would do it again ?—A. I have done that.

Q. That has been in the case of vessels out in deep water, where you don't succeed ?—A. O, we do succeed sometimes.

Q. In five trips out of seven you have been unsuccessful. But in the instances we have had of lee-bowing boats, and going wherever they could get them, they have been successful, and made money ?—A. Well, I haven't done that.

Q. Well, I only want to suggest that it may be done, and money made out of it. You say you never tried it, and never saw it done ?—A. I never lee-bowed boats, and never knew how it could be done. That is all the trouble there.

Q. There are no fishing stages at Tracadie ?—A. Yes.

Q. When were they put up there ?—A. There are two stages with buildings on them, and two besides with no buildings.

Q. When were they put there ?—A. Three of them were there last year, and one was put since.

Q. But not before that ?—A. I don't know.

Q. It is rather a new place ?—A. No; I don't think it is. I do not know. I could not tell you.

Q. Are they men who carry on fishing to a large extent themselves ?—A. No; not very large.

Q. Well, there has never been any large dealer or fish-merchant that had stages there like they have at other places ?—A. McDonald, of Georgetown, is interested in that one. I do not know how large it is. He has three boats.

Q. How many fishing stages are there at Rustico ?—A. I could not tell. I never was in.

Q. You never made inquiries ?—A. I have made some inquiries about Mr. Hall's boats. I know how many boats I have heard he has. He has a stage. I don't know how large it is.

Q. Then, at Tracadie, these boats from the island have done well ?—A. They think they have.

Q. You think so, too ?—A. Well, they think so.

Q. Well, the only reason you think you haven't is that you are under expenses ?—A. I am under great expenses.

Q. What is the expense ?—A. About $600 a month, I should judge.

Q. You didn't buy any fish ?—A. No.

Q. Last year you bought very few ?—A. I didn't buy any.

Q. You went there to buy—why didn't you ?—A. We could not buy to save much, to make anything.

Q. But you went there to buy ?—A. I was hired. I had charge of the vessel, and my employers managed the buying.

Q. What did you do during the season ?—A. Fished a little in boats.

Q. How long were you there ?—A. From the 5th of July to the 6th of August, one month and one day.

Q. You weren't in there very long ?—A. No.

Q. Did the boats do very well there ?—A. Not in that month.

Q. They did after that, I am told ?—A. Well, I am told they didn't do anything extra after that.

Q. In the fall they did well; they told us so themselves.—A. Well, I could not say for certain.

Q. Well, now, you must take a very gloomy view of affairs, because we are informed this is the best year they have ever had except one.—A. Well, if that is the case, why I need hardly go again. I had better give it up.

Q. We don't deny that, and I may disclose to you that that is our theory. Now is it a good year or not ?—A. It has been a poor year for me, very poor.

Q. Had you made no inquiries about others ?—A. I know about other boats.

Q. All along the coast they have a number of boats. Have you ever asked how many ?—A. No; I never asked that question. I suppose it would be impossible almost to find out.

Q. No, you would find out very easily. You could find out by reading this evidence. You have never asked how they got on at other places ? —A. I have asked boats four or five miles below my place, and I have asked them from Rustico, and they have done about the same as we have.

By Mr. Foster:

Q. What good would fishing stages at Tracadie do you ?—A. No good.

Q. There are two or three of them where you are ?—A. Four.

Q. You have never been to Rustico Harbor ?—A. No; but I have been up as far as to meet the boats. We have been up along the coast right off amongst the boats, and we have met the Savage Harbor boats.

Q. Have you ever inquired of the Rustico boats ?—A. Yes.

Q. What were you told about the quantity of the mackerel they were catching ?—A. They were doing about the same as we did.

Q. Now, what were you told last year as to the success of the boats through the whole season ?—A. Last year, as far as I can tell, it was a poor season.

Q. Who told you so ?—A. Most every one. They will tell you so now. The people there will tell you so, the fishermen.

Q. What is lee-bowing a vessel, and why do you say you don't know what lee-bowing a boat is ? Explain.—A. Well, a vessel we lee-bow under sail for mackerel, and drift with the wind; in lee-bowing we come under the vessel's lee and stop as near as we can under her lee-bow. Then we throw bait, and that bait gets underneath the other vessel and tolls off the mackerel; that is, sometimes it does and sometimes it does not; then we drift away from the other vessel with the mackerel. But the boats are at anchor, and spring up. There is no sail on the boats at all. I have never hove to at all.

Q. Why cannot a vessel lee-bow a boat at anchor ?—A. Because the boat is at anchor, and the vessel is under sail.

Q. Explain why. I do not understand why you cannot lee-bow her. —A. Well, I might shoot up alongside, but I would drift away from her.

Q. How long would you be within a short distance of a boat at anchor ?—A. I could not tell exactly, but we would drift away very fast. We drift two knots an hour in the vessel I am in.

Q. I don't understand why you could not draw the fish that the boats are fishing away.—A. I have seen that tried, and they could not do anything at all.

Q. Why not ?—A. That I cannot say—why not. They didn't get the mackerel away.

Q. Were the boats fishing in a school of mackerel, or fishing for mackerel from the bottom ?—A. From the bottom. They were scattered from a mile to a mile and a half apart.

By Mr. Davies:

Q. Were you there as late as the 22d of September ?—A. Yes.

Q. That was the day of the storm ?—A. Yes.

Q. Now I want to ask you, for a few days previously, a week or a ortnight previously, did you see any mackerel vessels along the coast? —A. Yes, the day before the breeze I saw six go up the bight toward Jascumpeque and Malpeque, and that way.

Q. Well, taking the week or fortnight previously, how many would rou say you have seen ?—A. I did not see a great many the last week or ten days we were there at all. The last day before the breeze I might have seen some passing and repassing, nothing to speak of. I suppose it was a month ago when I saw a large fleet.

Q. You did not go up along the coast to East Point the week previous to the 22d ? Did you go along toward East Point ?—A. No further than I went in a boat, sometimes five or six miles.

Q. I wanted to see whether you had seen the fleet that was at East Point at all ?—A. No; I didn't see the East Point fleet at all.

No. 38.

PETER H. MILLS, of Deer Isle, in the State of Maine, farmer and fisberman, called on behalf of the Government of the United States, sworn and examined.

By Mr. Trescot:

Question. Where is your place of residence ?—Answer. Deer Island.

Q. How long, have you been living there ?—A. About 26 years.

Q. Where is Deer Island ?—A. In Penobscot Bay; about 70 miles southward of Bangor.

Q. What has been your occupation ?—A. Fishing, farming, and some mechanical business.

Q. What has been, during 20 years, the chief occupation of the people of Deer Island? Fishing ?—A. Yes, sir; mackerel-fishing mostly.

Q. Well, in the 20 years of your experience has there been very much change in the character of the business ?—A. There has.

Q. How ?—A. It has depreciated.

Q. What was the average fleet of Deer Island when you knew it ?— A. I haven't any records, but from my judgment I should say perhaps 150 sail of vessel.

Q. About what tonnage ?—A. They would average 50 tons.

Q. What is the fleet now ?—A. There may be 25 sail of vessel, and there may not be so many.

Q. Where has the fleet fished; in the gulf ?—A. Years past they have fished in the gulf.

Q. Where are they fishing now mostly ?—A. On the coast of the United States.

Q. Well, then, to what do you attribute the depreciation; to the failure of the mackerel or of the profit in the business ?—A. There does not seem to be a profit in the business.

Q. In your 20 years' experience of Deer Island, has anybody realized a fortune ?—A. No; not that I know of.

Q. You know the neighborhood of Deer Island well? How far are you from Castine ?—A. 20 miles.

Q. Was there any time when that was a large fishing place ?—A. Yes.

Q. How is it now ?—A. It is dull, extremely dull.

151 F

ciated.

Q. With your experience of the fishery for twenty years, what is profit? Is it in the fishing, or in the handling of it afterwards?—A well, it is in the handling of the fish, the principal profit.

Q. Do you know anything of the fishing about Prince Edward Is —the shore fishing?—A. Well, I have been there a few years.

Q. You say you were a farmer and shore fisher yourself, at hom A. Yes.

Q. Were you familiar with the habits of the fishermen about Pi Edward Island?—A. Yes, I was.

Q. How far out did their boats catch fish when you knew them? V was the average run of their voyages?—A. Well, I never fished m in small boats from Prince Edward Island, but I had intercouse fishermen there. They told me they fished off twelve or fifteen mil

By Mr. Davies:

Q. Were you fishing at all in the bay?—A. Yes.

Q. Many years?—A. Not a great many years.

Q. Were you in an island vessel, or an American vessel?—A. Our island vessels—Deer Island.

Q. What years did you go to the gulf?—A. Well, sir, I only hav records of two years. I think I was there in 1853, and the year 1 but the dates of my other years in the gulf have slipped my memor

Q. When you speak of the island fishermen, and as to the distan which they were accustomed to fish from the shore, you have refer to these years, twenty years ago?—A. No, sir, inside of that. I fix the date of the time I had intercourse with them.

Q. I should like you to try, because there is a little variance bet what you say and the evidence we have. What was the last year were there?—A. I haven't the date of the last year I was there.

Q. But you can tell us about what it was, surely? You remember and 1856?—A. I have the records for them; that is all. I don't my memory.

Q. Does your memory entirely fail you apart from the records? No, sir, not entirely.

Q. Well, if it does not fail you entirely, perhaps you will tell m A. Well, I can't tell you that. I only have the dates of those two y It would be impossible for me to tell you the last time.

Q. Well, the time before the last?—A. Well, I can't tell you that only have the dates of these two years.

Q. How many years were you there altogether?—A. That I know.

Q. What fishermen did you converse with?—A. The boat fisher from the north side of Prince Edward Island.

Q. What part?—A. French Village, North Cape.

Q. That would be near Tignish?—A. Near about.

Q. Apart from what the fishermen told you would you tell this mission as the result of what you saw that the boats were accust to fish about 10 or 12 miles? Would you venture to assert that a best information you had from what you saw apart from what you said the fishermen told you?—A. No; I would not assert that fro own experience, because I never took pains to consider the distanc

Q. I want you to tell the size of the boats they fished in about Tig they were manned by two men, were they not ?—A. From two to three I think they averaged.

Q. What kind of boats are they ?—A. Large open boats manned by two or three men.

Q. Do you know the honorable Stanislaus Francois Poirier ? He has been a leading man in that section and must have been when you were there ?—A. No.

Q. I will just call your attention to his statement and ask you if it coincides with what you saw yourself when you were there. By the way, I want to draw a distinction between fishing for codfish or halibut and for mackerel. Do you mean that these boats fished off 10 miles fishing for mackerel, or that you were so informed ?—A. Not all; principally.

Q. Perhaps there is no difference of opinion between you at all. I will read his statement from the evidence:

Q. As a general rule are these fishing-grounds good for mackerel ?—A. They are very good.

Q. At what distance from the shore are the mackerel taken ?—A. From the 20th June up through July and August until the 20th September the mackerel are all caught within two miles of the shore around the portion of the island to which we refer. I have been fishing for these 40 years in my own locality and I may safely say that I have never caught mackerel outside of two miles from the shore around there.

Q. They were all taken within two miles of the coast ?—A. Yes.

Q. And your recollection extends over a period of 40 years ?—A. Yes. I was born i 1823, and I began fishing when I was 12 or 14 years of age. I think I can safely say can speak from recollection for forty years back.

What do you say to that ?—A. What is he speaking about—small boats ?

Q. He is speaking of the boats that fish around Tignish. Would you venture, from what experience you gained when there, to contradict his statement in that respect ?—A. No, sir ; I would not venture to contradict his statement.

Q. When you speak of the fishing being very much depreciated during the past year, did you refer to the fisheries along the coast of Maine ?—A. Yes.

Q. They are almost abandoned, are they not ?—A. Well, very nearly so.

Q. Your island, I think, is very near the line between New Brunswick and the State of Maine ?—A. No.

Q. How far from it ?—A. Perhaps 240 miles.

Q. And you think it has been abandoned because you found there was no profit in the business ?—A. Yes.

Q. The years you were in the gulf yourself, what vessel were you in ?—A. The D. R. Proctor, of Deer Island, and the Jane Otis.

Q. Were you pretty successful ?—A. Not very ; we brought out small trips.

Q. Where did you fish ?—A. Between Cape St. George and East Point, Prince Edward Island; between Port Hood and East Point; between East Point and the Magdalen Islands, up to the northward of the island, on those Banks, Bradley and Orphan.

Q. Did you try Bay Chaleurs at all ?—A. No.

Q. Your fishing was at the Magdalens and along the north shore of Prince Edward Island, from East Point to the Cape Breton shore ?—A. We didn't go around the Cape Breton shore, not down toward Margaree.

Q. To Port Hood ?—A. Yes.

Q. And your catches were not very large ?—A. No.

Q. Your experience was not very extensive?—A. Not very extensive in the gulf.

By Mr. Trescot:

Q. I think you misunderstood a question of Mr. Davies. He asked you about the time you had been at Prince Edward Island. You told him you could not recollect the date, but you can say whether it was within six, eight, or ten years?—A. I haven't been there for fifteen years; I will venture that.

Q. Now, with regard to another question. You stated, as I understand, and as the question I put would lead me to understand, that the mackerel fishery of Deer Island has very much diminished. You understood Mr. Davies to apply to the mackerel fishery in the gulf. I would like to know whether, in reply to his question, you meant to say that the fisheries all along the coast of Maine have diminished very much?—A. They have; yes, sir.

By Mr. Davies:

Q. As regards the gulf, you have not been there for 15 or 16 years?—A. No; but our vessels are coming and going there.

(The witness, being recalled, said he desired to make an explanation with regard to a part of his evidence, and proceeded to say that in speaking of the diminution of the fishing on the coast of Maine he did not know anything about the depreciation of the fish in the water on the coast, but that he meant to state simply that the business had not been so profitable in catching them as formerly.)

By Mr. Davies:

Q. The vessels that have engaged in the business have diminished in number?—A. Yes.

Q. And the catches of the vessels that are engaged in the business, have they been as large as in former years?—A. No, sir; they have not.

No. 39.

WILLIAM H. McDONALD, of Gloucester, Mass., called on behalf of the Government of the United States, sworn and examined.

By Mr. Trescot:

Question. You were born in St. John's, Newfoundland?—Answer. Yes.

Q. You live in Gloucester?—A. Yes.

Q. What business are you engaged in?—A. Cod-fishing a little, and herring-fishing in the winter.

Q. How long have you been cod-fishing as skipper?—A. Six years.

Q. You have been fishing on the Grand Bank all that time?—A. Yes.

Q. Do you take bait with you or purchase it?—A. I am two years taking bait from Newfoundland. In previous years I took it from home.

Q. How do the two systems compare together?—A. I know I have done nothing at all since I have gone in. I always got fish before.

Q. Then you have come to the conclusion you won't go in any longer?—A. No; I won't.

Q. What is the trouble?—A. We lose money by going in.

Q. Do you recollect what catch you made in the first four years when you used salt bait?—A. Yes. The first year we got about 3,700 quintals; the second year about 3,500; the third year 3,000; last year about 1,800, and this year about 1,400.

Q. Do you own your own vessels ?—A. Yes; part of them.

Q. How do you account for the falling off in your catches? What was he matter ?—A. We lost so much time going in.

Q. How many times did you go in for bait this year ?—A. Six times.

Q. How much time did it take ?—A. We lost about three months this ummer.

Q. How were you delayed so much ?—A. The bait was scarce.

Q. How long was the longest time ?—A. About five weeks.

Q. And the shortest ?—A. A week.

Q. Were you there these five weeks because you could not get bait, r were you detained from other causes ?—A. We could not get bait. We rere going around looking for it.

Q. Besides the expense of getting bait when you went into Newfound-and ports, did you pay light-dues ?—A. Yes; here are the bills. (Hands u bills paid in 1877, viz: Light-dues, $23.52; harbor-dues, $2.00; water-ates, $4.90; pilotage, $22.50. Total, $52.92.)

By Mr. Whiteway :

. Where do you reside ?—A. At Gloucester.

Q. How long have you resided there ?—A. Eight years.

Q. Previous to that you resided at St. John's, Newfoundland ?—A. Yes.

Q. Six years you have been on the Grand Banks fishing ?—A. Yes.

Q. What were you doing the other two years ?—A. Mackereling in he bay.

Q. Up the gulf ?—A. Yes, and down at Prince Edward Island.

Q. In what vessels ?—A. William Carson and Harvey C. Mackey.

Q. You were fishing on the coast of Prince Edward Island ?—A. Yes, ind round by Sydney and Cape Breton.

Q. Who was the master of the vessel ?—A. John MacMullin.

Q. Did you do pretty well there ?—A. We did decently well. We got 90 barrels.

Q. The first year ?—A. In one trip.

Q. Did you make a second trip that year ?—A. No.

Q. The second year, what did you get ?—A. Two hundred and fifty arrels, more or less.

Q. You made only one trip ?—A. Only one trip.

Q. You caught mackerel along the coast of Prince Edward Island and he coast of Cape Breton ?—A. Yes; not within the limits. We caught one within three miles of the land.

Q. What limits ?—A. We caught none within three miles of the land.

Q. Did you see any other vessels fishing there ?—A. Yes, hundreds.

Q. Were they on the north or south side of the island ?—A. On the orth side.

Q. Off what harbors were they fishing ?—A. We fished off Sidney and ot most there, and off East Point and Souris. We fished all round here and at Georgetown Bank.

Q. You would run in and out again as occasion required ?—A. Yes.

Q. As long as you found the mackerel, you would run in to land and ut again ?—A. We never ran in to land for mackerel.

Q. You went up and down the coast ?—A. Yes. We never caught any lackerel inshore.

Q. What harbors did you enter for shelter ?—A. Charlottetown, George-own, and Souris.

Q. Did you remain long in harbor at any time ?—A. Sometimes four r five days.

Q. They are pretty good harbors?—A. Yes, good harbors. George-town and Charlottetown are good harbors.

Q. Is there any difficulty in entering them in case of a gale of wind?—A. No.

Q. Then for four years you became master, of what vessel?—A. Henry A. Johnson.

Q. Was that the first year you went to the Banks?—A. Yes.

Q. Who was the owner of the vessel?—A. W. Parsons.

Q. You took your bait from where?—A. From home.

Q. From Gloucester?—A. Yes.

Q. What bait was it?—A. Salt pogies.

Q. How many voyages did you make that year?—A. Three.

Q. All for salted fish?—A. Yes.

Q. Did you use no fresh bait at all?—A. We caught squid on the Banks. There were plenty of squid on the Banks that year.

Q. Did you use any other fresh bait besides that squid?—A. We always used small halibut for bait.

Q. You made three voyages; did you keep a memorandum of the catch?—A. I never did.

Q. Are you quite sure of the sum total of your catch that year?—A. Yes.

Q. That you took 3,700 quintals in three voyages?—A. Yes.

Q. What was the size of the vessel?—A. 59 tons.

Q. The second year were you in the same vessel?—A. No; in the Carrie S. Dagle.

Q. How many voyages did you make?—A. Two.

Q. Did you use any salt bait?—A. We used all salt bait.

Q. Did you catch no fresh bait on the Banks?—A. We caught a trifling amount of squid.

Q. And the third year you were in the same vessel?—A. Yes.

Q. Did you make any memorandum of the voyages those two years?—A. No; I did not.

Q. Are you clear that the second year you got 3,500 quintals, and the third year 3,000 quintals?—A. Yes. I got somewhere near 3,000 quintals the third trip.

Q. How many trips?—A. Two.

Q. And the fourth year what quantity did you catch?—A. Somewhere about 2,000 quintals.

Q. How many trips did you make that year?—A. Two.

Q. You used salt bait during those four years?—A. Yes.

Q. Your catch decreased during the four years you were using salt bait from 3,700 quintals to 2,000?—A. Yes.

Q. And what was the first year you went to the Banks using fresh bait?—A. 1876.

Q. Did you take any salt bait with you?—A. Yes; a year ago this spring I took ten barrels of salt bait, I think.

Q. Did you make up your first trip with salt bait?—A. No.

Q. How many trips did you make last year?—A. Two.

Q. Did you get any squid on the first trip on the Banks?—A. No.

Q. Did you get any small halibut or other bait?—A. We had small halibut; we always get them.

Q. Having small halibut last year on the first trip, how was it that you did not complete the trip there?—A. There was so much fresh bait coming on the Banks that the fish would not take salt bait.

Q. There was so large a quantity of fresh bait coming on the Banks, you found salt bait no good?—A. No good.

Q. There was a large number of vessels coming from the coast of Newfoundland with fresh bait?—A. Last year they mostly got bait there.

Q. All the vessels got fresh bait there last year?—A. I would not say all.

Q. How large was the fleet with which you were fishing on the Banks?—A. I could not tell you the number of the vessels; it is impossible to tell that.

Q. Do you remember the number of bankers that went from Gloucester?—A. I do not.

Q. You then went in to Newfoundland for bait?—A. Yes.

Q. And last year was the first time?—A. Yes.

Q. Where did you go?—A. To Fortune Bay.

Q. In what season of the year?—A. In June, about first of June.

Q. Did you ever try to get bait at ports nearer than Fortune Bay; at ports between Cape Race and Conception Bay?—A. It was no use, for you could not get it at any other place at that time of the year.

Q. Did you try at any other?—A. No.

Q. You went to Fortune Bay and got herring?—A. Yes.

Q. There was a great number of American vessels in Fortune Bay last spring, catching herring, I believe?—A. There were not many; I don't know that there was anybody but ourselves when we were there.

Q. You had no difficulty in getting herring?—A. No.

Q. How long did it take you to go in for bait, get herring at Fortune Bay and return to the Banks?—A. You cannot do it in less than twelve days.

Q. How long did it take you on that occasion?—A. About twelve days. I never did it in less than one week.

Q. I am now speaking of the time you went to Fortune Bay, the first time you went in, which was last year. How long did it take you to go from the Banks to Fortune Bay, get bait, and return to the Banks?—A. About twelve days.

Q. Are you clear about it?—A. I am not exactly positive. I did not keep a log. I never did it in less than one week, and I know I did not do it in that time then.

Q. Do I understand that the shortest time occupied in going from the Banks to Fortune Bay and back to the Banks would be one week?—A. Yes.

Q. Were you in last year any other time except this once?—A. Yes; I was in other parts of Newfoundland.

Q. What?—A. Cape Royal.

Q. For squid?—A. Yes.

Q. How long did it take you on that occasion to go in, get bait, and return to the Banks?—A. Two weeks that time.

Q. You were all that time at Cape Royal?—A. No; I was not there all the time. I was at a place called Torbay. We had to leave there and go back to Cape Royal.

Q. You went in Cape Royal first?—A. Yes.

Q. How long did you remain there?—A. I went in the morning and left in the evening.

Q. Then you went to Torbay?—A. To St. John's, to get money.

Q. Did you enter the port of St. John's?—A. Yes.

Q. Last year?—A. Yes.

Q. Did you pay light-dues there?—A. Yes.

Q. You went to Torbay?—A. Yes.

Q. And round to Cape Royal?—A. Yes.

Q. After getting your bait at Cape Royal, when you returned there, how long did it take you to get out of the Banks?—A. One day and night.

Q. One night going out?—A. Yes. I may not have got just to where I fished, but I got on the Banks.

Q. On the fishing-ground?—A. Not on the fishing-ground.

Q. The Banks are all fishing-grounds?—A. No. There are parts where you cannot get a fish.

Q. Are those the only two occasions you were into Newfoundland for fresh bait last year?—A. I was in three times.

Q. Where did you go the third time?—A. To Portugal Cove, Conception Bay.

Q. How long did it take you to get there?—A. I went there direct from home—from the States.

Q. That was your second trip?—A. Yes.

Q. Did you go in for bait—squid?—A. Yes.

Q. What time of the year?—A. About 12th September.

Q. You employed the people there to get squid for you immediately on your arrival?—A. Yes.

Q. And how long was it before they succeeded in supplying your wants?—A. It took me about two weeks then. I got on the Banks on the 16th September.

Q. With a full supply of bait?—A. Yes.

Q. You then got your trip completed—by what time?—A. We did not get anything at all to speak of. We got about 200 quintals.

Q. And you returned at what time?—A. We returned home about 7th November.

Q. And you were on the Banks from 16th September to 7th November?—A. Not exactly all that time. I was in at Newfoundland when coming home.

Q. At what time did you leave the Banks?—A. Eleventh October.

Q. You staid in Newfoundland from 11th October till when?—A. On 22d October, I think, I started for home.

Q. You completed your fishing for that season?—A. Yes.

Q. This year did you go direct from Gloucester to the Banks, or did you go to Newfoundland first for bait?—A. We went to Newfoundland, Fortune Bay, first for bait.

Q. At what time of the year?—A. We left home about 23d April, and got to Newfoundland about 1st May.

Q. What part of Fortune Bay did you go to for bait?—A. Long Island.

Q. Were there many vessels there at that time getting bait?—A. Three or four.

Q. Did you take a seine with you?—A. No.

Q. Were any other American vessels there with seines?—A. No American vessel ever had a seine there.

Q. I am informed that a large number of American vessels went there this spring and caught bait themselves.—A. They would not be allowed to put a seine in the water there; they would be chopped down.

Q. Were you ever chopped down?—A. I never had a seine there, and never knew an American vessel with a seine there.

Q. You have not seen them there?—A. No; and I have traded there all the time in the winter time.

Q. You have been there for herring in winter?—A. Yes; during 4 winters.

Q. That is, in the months of February and March?—A. Yes.

Q. That is, for frozen bait?—A. For frozen herring.

Q. Is frozen herring shipped in bulk or in barrels?—A. In bulk.

Q. You never heard of any being shipped in barrels?—A. No.

Q. Then if any one said that there were barrels used it would be incorrect?—A. Of course; it is not so in winter.

Q. Not in Fortune Bay?—A. No.

Q. You never heard of such a thing as a·duty being charged on her-ring-barrels used for putting frozen herring in?—A. No; I never did.

Q. We had a witness here the other day who stated that on empty bar-rels used for putting herring in a duty was charged.—A. They do pay a duty on the barrels into which they put herring, but not frozen herring.

Q. You never heard of frozen herrings being put in barrels?—A. I have seen them put in barrels at Grand Manan, not at Newfoundland.

Q. Did you get your bait at Newfoundland soon after you went down?—A. No; there was quite a delay this spring before we got bait.

Q. You got it at Long Harbor?—A. Yes; it was very scarce. It was four or five days before we got bait.

Q. Before you could get the people to catch the bait for you?—A. Yes; there was very little there to catch; it was very scarce.

Q. Then you proceeded to the Banks; did you catch a good trip with that quantity of bait?—A. No.

Q. How much bait did you take with you?—A. About 45 barrels.

Q. How much did you pay for it?—A. $62.

Q. You fish altogether with trawls, I suppose?—A. Yes.

Q. A great number of vessels were fishing round you in the same way with trawls?—A. Yes.

Q. The large quantity of fresh bait scattered on the fishing-grounds, I suppose, has a tendency to keep the fish well on the ground?—A. The Bank fish never go off the grounds and never leave the Banks. There is plenty of proof of that. The shore fish of Newfoundland would not be liked in the States.

Q. What is the difference between the shore and Bank fish?—A. In the shore fish the nape is black, and that would not do for our market.

Q. What is its color in the Bank fish?—A. White.

Q. Are they otherwise exactly alike?—A. No; they are not alike at all. What you get inshore are small fish.

Q. Have you ever fished at the western part of Newfoundland, round Fortune Bay and that portion of the coast?—A. No.

Q. Then you have not seen the large fish they take there?—A. Yes; I have.

Q. Have you ever fished off Cape St. Mary's?—A. Yes.

Q. Are not the fish caught there large fish?—A. They are large, but are not the same as the Bank fish. A cargo was caught there by one of the American schooners six years ago, but it was never sold. It was caught by one of Mr. Lowe's schooners.

Q. There has lately been some of the American vessels fishing at St. Mary's?—A. I have not seen any.

Q. The fish caught off Cape St. Mary's are not like the Bank fish?—A. No.

Q. Are the fish caught at parts of the coast further west like Bank fish?—A. I never fished further westward than Cape St. Mary's.

Q. You say there is a difference in Bank and shore fish in other re-spects than that one has a black nape and the other a white nape?—A. There is a difference in every way.

Q. In what other respect?—A. The shore fish is not nearly so thick, not nearly so fat, and has a black nape.

Q. Anything else?—A. No.

Q. They have each the same number of fins ?—A. I suppose so. I never counted.

Q. But you are a great authority on codfish ?—A. Yes; I know about codfish.

Q. You noticed the size and thickness of the fish and the color of the nape, and yet you cannot say how many fins they have ?—A. No.

Q. Will you undertake to say that the Bank fish have not got a fin over and above the shore fish ?—A. No.

Q. Upon getting out on the first trip to the Banks you said you did not complete your codfish voyage ?—A. No.

Q. You came into Newfoundland again ?—A. I came to Fortune Bay again.

Q. About what time was that ?—A. About the 1st June.

Q. You got your herring, in how long ?—A. It was just exactly two weeks till I got on the Banks again.

Q. Did you then complete your voyage ?—A. No.

Q. Did you go in again ?—A. Yes.

Q. Where did you go ?—A. To Cape Royal.

Q. To any other place ?—A. No.

Q. How long were you at Cape Royal ?—A. Just one week going in and coming out again.

Q. Did you go in again ?—A. Yes.

Q. When ?—A. In July some time.

Q. Where did you go then ?—A. To Cape Royal again.

Q. Did you go to any other places, or did you get bait there and go out again ?—A. We went to the Bay of Bulls next time.

Q. Did you go to any other place besides the Bay of Bulls ?—A. No.

Q. How long were you in there ?—A. Something over one week.

Q. Were you in after that ?—A. Yes.

Q. When ?—A. In August.

Q. Where did you go ?—A. To Saint John's first.

Q. And out again from there ?—A. To Portugal Cove.

Q. How long were you there ?—A. Over two weeks.

Q. Did you go in again ?—A. I was in about the last of August.

Q. Where did you go then ?—A. I could not tell you all the places. I went to Saint John's and other places.

Q. How long were you then ?—A. Something over five weeks.

Q. Did you get bait ?—A. We got some salt squid, no fresh squid.

Q. You returned to the Banks ?—A. Yes.

Q. And did you complete your voyage at the Banks ?—A. I am right from the Banks going home.

Q. What quantity have you got ?—A. 1,500 quintals.

Q. Just now you said it was 1,400 quintals ?—A. It is between 1,400 and 1,500 quintals. I cannot say exactly.

Q. Then you made one trip this year ?—A. Yes.

Q. That is between 23d April, when you left Gloucester, and the present time ?—A. Yes, one trip.

Q. Were you not talking a little at random when you said you had spent half your time in getting fresh bait ?—A. I think I did spend half my time.

Q. I believe all American vessels leaving Gloucester in the spring go down to Fortune Bay, in the first place, to get bait ?—A. Not all of them.

Q. The great majority ?—A. A good many of them.

Q. On the way to the Banks ?—A. Yes, I suppose so.

Q. And those which do not go into Newfoundland get their bait some.

where on the Nova Scotia coast?—A. I don't know exactly where. I suppose they get it somewhere round the shores on their own coast, or some other place.

Q. And you say that the greater number, in fact nearly all American vessels, went into the Newfoundland coast this year for bait?—A. Yes.

By Mr. Trescot:

Q. You say you are on your way home from the Banks?—A. Yes.

Q. When did you get into Halifax?—A. Last night.

Q. What brought you here; did you come for a harbor?—A. Yes.

Q. Have you been in the habit of going to Grand Manan for herring?—A. I never was there.

By Mr. Whiteway:

Q. Do not a great number of American vessels anchor in Freshwater Bay instead of going into the Port of St. John's?—A. I don't know. I saw a couple anchored there this summer. I anchored in the Narrows myself, and was charged for anchoring.

By Mr. Trescot:

Q. What were you charged?—A. Six dollars. I was fined.

By Mr. Foster:

Q. What were you fined for?—A. I was fined for anchoring in the Narrows. There was no wind, and we could not get in.

By Mr. Whiteway:

Q. Were you not obstructing navigation, and was it not the harbor-master's boat which went out to you?—A. Yes.

Q. You were liable to be fined for obstructing navigation?—A. There were three vessels lying there. There was plenty of room for any other vessels to go in.

Q. And you were ordered out?—A. We went out.

By Hon. Mr. Kellogg:

Q. You spoke about going into Georgetown and Charlottetown Harbors?—A. Yes.

Q. They are at the southern side of Prince Edward Island?—A. Yes.

Q. Have you ever been in the harbors on the north side?—A. No; I have been in no harbors except on the south side.

Q. Are those quiet harbors?—A. Yes.

By Mr. Whiteway:

Q. Were you in Fortune Bay in January when you went for frozen herring?—A. I think on the 2d of January.

No. 40.

WILLIAM A. DICKEY, of Belfast, Maine, fisherman, called on behalf of the Government of the United States, examined.

By Mr. Dana:

Question. When did you begin to go fishing?—Answer. I commenced in 1858; I went as a hand, as sharesman.

Q. At that time were there many vessels from Belfast engaged in the fishing business?—A. Ten or twelve sail.

Q. Fishing for cod and mackerel?—A. Yes.

Q. What has become of the mackerel trade and fishermen of Belfast?

—A. There are but two of us who fish for mackerel with vessels of any size; that is, excepting small vessels.

Q. Are your mackerel-men now mainly engaged in fishing on th American coast?—A. They have been for the last six years.

Q. You went into the bay-fishing in 1858. Do you know for how man barrels the vessel fitted?—A. The vessel fitted for 400 or 500 barrels.

Q. And you caught how many?—A. About 270 barrels, I think.

Q. Did you catch any fish inshore then?—A. I was a boy, a youn fellow, and I don't remember particularly. We caught part of then inside the lines. We fished inshore and off, but the whole quantity w caught inshore I don't remember.

Q. In 1859 did you go fishing again?—A. Yes.

Q. Were you in the bay?—A. Yes, one trip, late.

Q. Do you recollect how many you caught?—A. From one hundre and forty to one hundred and fifty barrels.

Q. Were any of those caught inshore?—A. That year we fished alto gether at Bank Orphan, or pretty much so. We may have caught few inshore. I cannot say the quantity.

Q. From 1860 to 1865 where were you fishing?—A. For those fiv years I was skipper of the same vessel, fishing on our shores. I fishe for cod one trip in the spring and afterwards on our shores.

Q. You made one trip in the early spring for cod?—A. Yes.

Q. Where did you go?—A. To Western Banks and Banquero.

Q. What kind of bait did you have?—A. Salt clams.

Q. No fresh bait?—A. No.

Q. How long were you generally on the Banks?—A. We generall left home 25th or 27th April and got back generally before 4th July.

Q. And then you went mackerel fishing on your own coast?—A. O our own shores.

Q. What part of the American shore did you fish on?—A. We fishe from Mount Desert Rock to Cape Cod.

Q. With menhaden bait?—A. Yes; with salt bait.

Q. Do you come into port often?—A. We harbor occasionally whe there is a wind.

Q. I mean do you land your fish?—A. Yes; we land them wheneve we get a voyage; sometimes two or three times and sometimes not more than twice.

Q. You could go in often enough to get fresh pogies and menhaden i you wished?—A. We never use fresh bait for mackerel, but salt bai altogether.

Q. After 1865 did you go in the bay again?—A. I could not say whether the next time was in 1865 or 1866. I know it was the last yea the treaty was on.

Q. You had a right then to go where you liked?—A. Yes.

Q. Did you catch any mackerel inshore?—A. We caught a few at Margaree and at Magdalen Islands that year. We fished some at Margaree.

Q. Did you make any attempt to fish inside the line?—A. At the Magdalen Islands there were no fish inside. We were out some distance.

Q. Did you know that fact by trying yourself or by reports, or by both?—A. We tried in and off shore.

Q. That year there was no fish inshore?—A. We did not get any in shore at Magdalen Islands. At Margaree we probably fished inshore within two, three, or four miles.

Q. When did you next go to the bay?—A. I skipped one or two years. I am not certain but that I staid at home and went cod-fishing a trip and mackereling. The first year after the treaty was up I was at home. I am certain of that.

Q. You mean you went cod-fishing?—A. Yes.

Q. What else did you catch?—A. I was catching menhaden for oil, I, think, that year.

Q. Are there plenty of menhaden to be found on your coast?—A. Yes. Steamers get each from 25,000 to 26,000 barrels almost every year. I think there are 31 steamers this year.

Q. Where do they take the pogies. Is there a place to manufacture the oil near Portland?—A. There are several of them there, and at Round Point and Booth Bay.

Q. When did you next go into the bay?—A. 1867 or 1868, I don't know which; 1867, I think, but I could not be certain.

Q. What did you catch?—A. Mackerel.

Q. How many trips did you make?—A. Two trips; we landed one small trip and sent it home.

Q. What did you catch the first trip?—A. I think 190 or 200 barrels.

Q. What did you get the second trip?—A. About 70 barrels I think we carried home.

Q. Out of those 260 barrels, how much did you catch inshore?—A. We, perhaps, might have caught 40 barrels. We fished some inshore and some off shore. We had a license that year.

Q. Having a license, you tried inshore, did you?—A. Yes, we tried inshore; but the fishing was not as good inshore, and there was better fishing off shore; and we got the greater part of them off shore.

Q. Do you mean there were more fish off shore, or was it in regard to their fatness?—A. There were more off shore.

Q. You did not catch enough inshore to pay the license?—A. I don't remember whether we did or not.

Q. Were you master then?—A. Yes.

Q. You tried the inshore fishing?—A. Yes; we tried it when we were inshore.

Q. Take the next four years, where were you fishing?—A. I don't remember whether I was in the bay next year or not. In 1869 or 1870 I think I was in the bay.

Q. Did you have a license?—A. No, we had no license then.

Q. You had a license only one year?—A. Yes.

Q. Were you cod-fishing during the next four years at all?—A. No.

Q. Only catching mackerel?—A. Yes.

Q. Generally, where did you catch your fish when you were in the bay?—A. We caught some at Magdalen Islands, and from Point Miscou to North Cape and Bank Bradley.

Q. During that period of time where did you find your largest and best fish?—A. We fished on what we call the West shore, between Point Escuminac and northward of North Cape, ten or twelve miles out. We did the best there, I think.

Q. During the whole of the four years, where did you find any fish inshore? Did you try inshore?—A. I was only two of those four years in the bay, and the other two I was on our shores; I think in 1869 and 1870 or 1868 and 1869 I was in the bay.

Q. During those two years, where did you find your best fishing—without regard to particular localities—inshore or out?—A. We found the best fishing off shore. We did not find any vessels inshore at all. We were in a new vessel, the cutters were there, and we did not try inshore at all. We fished at Magdalen Islands.

Q. Did you find satisfactory fishing?—We got a fair trip, though we

did not fill all our barrels. We got 215 barrels, I think, one trip, ε
190 barrels the second trip.

Q. That is pretty good fishing ?—A. Yes, good fishing.

Q. Since 1871 where have you been fishing ?—A. I have been sein
on our shores.

Q. At what parts of the American coast ?—A. From Mount Des
Rock to Cape May, Delaware. We commence there in the spring ε
work eastward.

Q. Were you fishing inshore or out or both along the Americ
coast ?—A. Off shore and inshore.

Q. How many have you taken there ?—A. We took all the way fr
350 to 1,000 barrels. Last year we had about 1,000 barrels.

Q. You had good luck on the American coast ?—A. Yes, we have 1
good fishing there for five or six years.

Q. How has it been this year ?—A. There was good fishing early t
year, in May, south. Since then there has been very little done.

Q. At what time did you come into the bay this year ?—A. 10th Δ
gust.

Q. Are you in Halifax with your vessel ?—A. Yes.

Q. For a harbor ?—A. We came into harbor last night.

Q. You did not come to Halifax as a witness ?—A. No.

Q. Were you homeward bound when you made Halifax ?—A. Yes.

Q. How many barrels have you got ?—A. From 118 to 120 barrels.

Q. During all the time you have been cod-fishing, you say you hε
gone to the Banks in spring and to your own coast in summer ; hε
you been in for fresh bait ?--A. We did not used to go in for bait th
I have not been cod-fishing the last nine years or longer.

Q. While you were fishing you used salt bait altogether ?—A. Yes

Q. Do you know anything about weir and pound fishing on the co
of Maine ?—A. I never was engaged in weir or pound fishing.

Q. You have seen it ?—A. I have seen a number of pounds.

Q. And heard about it ?—A. I have heard there is a considera
quantity taken.

Q. You cannot give any account of it ?—A. No.

By Mr. Doutre :

Q. How many times have you been in the bay ?--A. About six
seven times.

Q. Six or seven different seasons or trips ?—A. Different seasons.

Q. And sometimes you went two trips in one season ?—A. We hε
landed and sent home a trip, but I have never been home and bε
on a second trip.

Q. Where did you land any trip ?—A. We landed a trip the first yε
I was in the bay at Cascumpeque. That is about 19 years ago.

Q. How did those fish reach home ?—A. They were shipped home
a vessel.

Q. Have you ever fished on the coast of Gaspé ?—A. I never fish
on the coast of Gaspé. I have been there twice.

Q. You never tried to fish there ?—A. No.

Q. Why did you go there if you did not intend to fish ?—A. We wε
into Gaspé from Bonaventure for water. We fished broad off on Bo.
venture Bank, about southeast, 40 or 50 miles.

Q. Was the Gaspé coast nearest ?—A. There was not much differeι
between that and North Cape, I think.

Q. Do you ever fish in Bay Chaleurs?—A. I never fished there, l
I have laid inside of the point about Shippegan. We caught a f
mackerel there one year.

Q. How far from the shore ?—A. From two to five or six miles.

Q. Do you remember the number of barrels you caught there ?—A. We caught one day off Shippegan, I think, 25 barrels.

Q. Did you ever fish in the Bend of Prince Edward Island ?—A. Very little. I heaved to twice off Cascumpeque. I never liked the place to fish.

Q. Did you not find fish there ?—A. Not many.

Q. How far from the coast were you when you tried ?—A. We tried inside of two miles and from that to seven or eight miles off.

Q. Did you fish on the coast of Cape Breton ?—A. Very little; a very little at Margaree.

Q. How far from Margaree were you when you fished ?—A. Probably from one mile to four or five miles off.

Q. Is that a good place for mackerel ?—A. It is a good place sometimes in the fall. It used to be some years ago.

Q. In what portion of the year did you fish there, fall or summer ?—A. I fished there a little while in summer the year I was there.

Q. How many barrels did you catch there ?—A. I might have caught 20 or 25 barrels there. I was probably there three or four or two or three days.

Q. You have fished at the Magdalen Islands ?—A. Yes; round the Magdalen Islands parts of two years.

Q. How far from the coast did you find the mackerel ?—A. The years we were there we got them ten or twelve from the islands—the main body of the fish.

Q. None nearer ?—A. Some we got within two or five miles, all the way from three to fifteen miles, but we fished principally ten or twelve miles off. That was in 1865.

Q. Where did you go to fish for cod ?—A. We went on Western Banks and Banquero.

Q. Did you take your bait with you ?—A. Yes.

Q. You did not buy any ?—A. No; we carried salt clams when I went.

Q. How long ago is that ?—A. I have not been for nine or ten years.

Q. Do you mean to say you never fished for mackerel otherwise than with salt bait ?—A. No; we never use fresh bait as heave bait. We use mackerel to put on our jigs, but for trawl bait we use salt bait altogether.

Q. When you fish on your own coasts, do you fish with salt bait ?—A. Yes; for mackerel we do.

Q. Is not fresh bait better ?—A. No, I don't know that it is. I never used it very often; not for mackerel.

Q. At North Cape what quantity did you take within two or three miles of the shore ?—A. We fished about 12 miles to the northward of North Cape.

Q. Was that the nearest point to North Cape you fished ?—A. We have fished nearer than that. We have tried all the way from inshore to out, but the principal part of the fish we caught out to the north, except this year, when we fished pretty handy in.

Q. You have come in from the bay ?—A. We have been in the bay this year.

Q. Where did you catch your fish ?—A. This year we caught the principal part of our fish from Escuminac to Port Hood. We fished some from West Cape to North Cape; we caught a few fish at East Point, and a very few at Port Hood.

Q. How far from the shore ?—A. We caught half, nearly half, I should say, inside of two or three miles; some within one mile, and from that out to eight miles.

Q. You caught half of them within those distances from the shore ?— A. I should say that this year we got one-half our fish inside of two or three miles of the shore.

Q. How long did it take you to catch those 120 barrels ?—A. We went through Canso on 10th of August, and have been fishing ever since.

Q. Did you ever try fishing round Canso?—A. We tried as we went. We tried off Port Hood a couple of days. At East Point we tried, and went from there to North Cape and tried there, and got a few mackerel, and we went from there to Escuminac and back again.

Q. Try to remember where you caught your fish this year, and tell the Commission exactly what proportion you took within three miles of the shore ?—A. I think about one-half.

Q. Not more than one-half ?—A. I think not more than one-half. Our best fishing was off Escuminac. We struck the fish when we were within sight of the top of the light, eight or ten miles out. We got fifty or sixty barrels off there the first week ; we caught nearly all of these outside of three miles. We worked in, and the last few days we were in the bay we were inside of three miles. I think we took 30 or 40 barrels out of those 50 or 60 outside.

Q. How many men composed your crew ?—A. Twelve.

Q. Was any British subject on board ?—A. Yes; we had one.

Q. Did you leave him at home, or have you got him still with you ?— A. We took him from home, and we have him now.

Q. What is his name ?—A. Lawrence Landerkin.

Q. Is he from Canso ?—A. No; he belongs to Newfoundland.

Q. Where did you take him ?—A. I shipped him in Portland.

Q. Did you see other American fishing-vessels while you were there ? .—A. Yes; there have been quite a number.

Q. How many did you see there together ?—A. We saw all the way from three to fifty-odd sail; American vessels and several English vessels.

Q. And they fished like you, inside, when they could find fish, and also outside ?—A. They all fished together, inside and out.   •

Q. And they took about the same proportion, one-half of their catches inshore ?—A. Yes; about the same.

Q. Do you think you did not take three-quarters of your catch inshore ?—A. Not this year, or any other year.

Q. Other years what was the proportion ?—A. I think we caught about three-quarters outside, and this year we caught fully one-half inside, or near about that. I kept no particular account of them, because it did not matter to me one way or the other.

Q. You say you saw about 50 sail fishing there ?—A. There were about 50 sail one day, and the rest of the time 3, 5, or 8, along there.

Q. They have all taken tolerably good catches ?—A. No; they have all done very slimly, or the greater part of them.

Q. You admit that you have not been very lucky ?—A. We have done about an average of the fleet, I should say.

Q. And the other vessels have done about the same as you ?—A. Some have got more and others have not got one-half or one-fourth. Some have got double what we did.

Q. And some, I suppose, three times what you did ?—A. Some vessels which went in early have got double what I have ; but some which went in when I did have not got more than half.

Q. Did you hear of any vessels having 300 or 400 barrels ?—A. No; I have not heard of vessels having 400 barrels. I heard of a vessel having 290 barrels. She is a large vessel and had a crew of 17 men, and had been in the bay all summer.

Q. Do you know the schooner Lettie ?—A. I know the schooner Lettie belonging to Charlottetown.

Q. Do you know Captain Macdonald ?—A. No.

Q. Do you know how many barrels the Lettie caught ?—A. No. I do not.

Q. Did you see her fishing with you ?—A. I don't remember seeing her this year.

Q. Have you not heard from fishermen that she caught 500 barrels ?—A. I have not heard anything about it.

Q. Have you seen any British vessels on the American coast fishing this year ?—A. Yes.

Q. How many have you seen ?—A. I did not see but one.

Q. Do you remember her name ?—A. No. I recollect seeing one.

Q. Do you know the name of her captain ?—A. No.

By Mr. Dana:

Q. This year, 1877, you think you have given a fair trial to inshore fishing ?—A. Yes; we had a good trial of it, I think.

Q. You did your best with it ?—A. Yes; we tried inshore.

Q. You caught from 118 to 120 barrels fishing inshore and outside ?—A. Yes.

Q. And how many packed barrels will they make ?—A. They will probably pack one hundred and seven or one hundred and eight.

Q. How much did the vessel fit for ?—A. We only fitted for 200 barrels this fall trip.

Q. As a commercial and money matter, is that bad or good ?—A. It is a poor trip.

Q. A losing one ?—A. It is losing money.

Q. Will it be a pretty considerable loss ?—A. For the time we were catching them, not much loss, but no money.

Q. It will not pay ?—A. It will not pay. Fishing will not pay anywhere this year, I guess.

Q. Were there any places where there was reported to be good inshore fishing which you did not try ?—A. The boats have done very well inshore, anchored, but we could not fish among them. The boats have done very well at Miminegash, Prince Edward Island, this year. They have done as well as they have done for some time. The boats at Cascumpeque have done very slimly this year, I have been told. The boats fish inshore to an anchor.

Q. Was there any place where vessels went inshore which was reported to you to have good fishing that you did not try ?—A. I did not see or hear of any.

Q. Is there any place where vessels went where they have done well inshore ?—A. I have not heard of it. The principal part of the fish this year has been caught inshore, as nigh as I can judge.

Q. Do you know by direct report or otherwise of any vessels fishing inshore or off shore that have done well this year ?—A. Some vessels that went early got good, fair trips; 5 or 6 vessels did that went in the bay in July; but those are the only ones I have heard of. Nothing was done since we went in; the vessels did not do anything in August.

Q. You said, in answer to one of the counsel, that you did not like the bend of the island. Why is this the case ?—A. I have not made a

practice of fishing there, any longer than with a good wind we could
from one end of it to the other, going or coming.

Q. What is the reason?—A. It is because it is a bad place, and I d
not like to stop there. It is well enough, however, close to North Ca
and East Point, where you can watch your chance to get round wh
there comes a northeaster.

By Mr. Doutre:

Q. I understand that your catch this year was an average one?—
I think we got an average with the American fleet, as far as I have hear
Mr. Murray, of the custom-house at Canso, said that we had an averag
or more than an average, with the American fleet.

Q. Do you not think that you came rather late fishing to, and ha\
come rather early from the bay?—A. I did not see any prospect
catching anything when I left, and so I thought I would come hom
Something may yet be done though.

Q. Is it not to your knowledge that the mackerel generally come in
abundance later than this date?—A. No; not of late years. I have no
during the last 5 or 6 years, heard of much being done late in the se
son in the bay.

Q. What is the quality of the mackerel which you have taken th
year?—A. Well, they run rather poor; they are mostly 2s, and th
mackerel. They have not had much food; they are not fat.

Q. What proportion is number ones?—A. I do not think one-quarte
if that. They, however, may be so this year, since mackerel are scarc

Q. What do you expect to get for number ones?—A. About $16
$18. I hear that they are worth that, but I do not know.

Q. Have you not heard that No. 1 mess mackerel are bringing $22?-
A. We have no mess mackerel; we did not mess any; and we ha\
very few fit for mess.

By Sir Alexander Galt:

Q. Did you fish with seines or hand-lines?—A. We fished with han
lines.

Q. Were many American vessels fishing with seines this year in th
gulf?—A. I did not see any use them, though a number had seines.
have not seen a school in the bay.

Q. When you spoke of menhaden-fishing, you spoke of a number
steamers being employed in it?—A. Yes.

Q. How far from the coast do these steamers take menhaden?—
They go sometimes 8 or 10 miles off, and sometimes inside of the islan
and among the islands.

Q. Do they take menhaden with purse-seines?—A. Yes.

By Hon. Mr. Kellogg:

Q. Do you generally seine for mackerel when they school?—A. Ye
Q. Do you do so at any other time?—A. No.

No. 41.

ELVARADO GRAY, seaman and fisherman, of Brooksville, Me., w
called on behalf of the Government of the United States, sworn, a
examined.

By Mr. Foster:

Question. You are a skipper of a Gloucester vessel?—Answer. Yes.
Q. What is the name of your vessel?—A. Plymouth Rock.
Q. How old are you?—A. Twenty-eight.

Q. How many years have you been skipper ?—A. Eight years, or 9 seasons. I have been skipper since I was 19.

Q. Since you have been skipper you have been engaged in the Bank cod fishery ?—A. Yes.

Q. Did you ever make mackerel trips in the bay ?—A. Yes.

Q. How many?—A. Four.

Q. During what years ?—A. In 1866 I was there for two trips.

Q. You were then very young ?—A. Yes. I was not master at the time.

Q. What was the name of the schooner you were in that year ?—A. The Reunion.

Q. What was her captain's name ?—A. Harvey Conroy.

Q. Did you take the first trip home to Gloucester that year ?—A. Yes.

Q. How many barrels of mackerel did you get in the bay that year ?—A. About 600 barrels.

Q. You have no means of telling the number accurately ?—A. No; I could not say for a certainty.

Q. Being a boy you did not have an interest in this matter like a skipper ?—A. That is very near the number—600 barrels. It is not it to a pound, but it is near enough.

Q. Where were they caught ?—A. The biggest part was taken on Banks Bradley and Orphan.

Q. Were any of them caught within the 3-mile limit ?—A. I do not remember of heaving to within three miles of land that year.

Q. When were you next in the gulf ?—A. I would not say for certain but I think it was in the fall of 1870.

Q. What was the name of your schooner that year ?—A. Henry L. Phillips.

Q. Were you skipper ?—A. Yes.

Q. How long were you in the gulf ?—A. We got in there sometime about the middle of September, I think, and were there till sometime in October.

Q. What did you catch ?—A. Something like 60 barrels.

Q. What had you been doing during the previous part of the year ?—A. Banking, on the Grand Banks.

Q. Where did you get these 60 barrels ?—A. Scattered all over the bay. There were no fish in the bay that year.

Q. When were you again in the bay ?—A. In 1872 I think on a fall trip.

Q. What was your schooner's name ?—A. George Clark. I was captain.

Q. How many barrels did you take ?—A. 70, I think.

Q. Where did you take them ?—A. The bigger part we got at the Magdalen Islands and the rest scattered through the bay.

Q. When were you next there ?—A. In 1873, in the George Clark, on a fall trip.

Q. What did you catch ?—A. 90 barrels, I think. We caught the bigger part of them at the Magdalen Islands, and the rest scattered through the bay. While I was in the bay I will say that we never got a barrel of mackerel within three miles of land.

Q. The first year, when you made two trips, you were there for the season ?—A. Yes.

Q. And the last three years you made fall trips ?—A. Yes.

Q. After you had been cod-fishing elsewhere ?—A. Yes.

Q. What have you done since 1873?—A. In 1874 and 1875 I was our coast.

Q. And what have you been doing in 1876 and 1877?—A. Banki:

Q. Where?—A. At the Grand and Western Banks.

Q. What is the name of the vessel of which you are skipper now' A. The Plymouth Rock.

Q. You were in the same vessel last year?—A. No, I was then in 1 schooner Knight Templar.

Q. How have you provided yourself with bait for Bank fishing 1. year and this year?—A. I took fresh bait from Gloucester this seasor the spring. My first trip was made to Western Bank; I also used fr bait last year.

Q. What did you take for bait?—A. Frozen herring, from Gloucest

Q. Did you obtain any other bait?—A. Yes, we went to St. Andre Bay, on the American side, and baited the second time.

Q. Where is that?—A. About Eastport.

Q. What bait did you get there?—A. Fresh herring.

Q. What did you do after you made your trip to the Western Bank ' A. We went to Newfoundland direct from Gloucester then.

Q. You did not provide yourself with bait at home?—A. No, we w to Fortune Bay and bought herring, putting them in ice.

Q. How often have you been to Newfoundland to buy bait this year' A. Four times.

Q. Have you ever caught any herring there?—A. No.

Q. Or caplin?—A. No.

Q. Have you ever obtained either save by purchase?—A. No.

Q. Did you ever get squid there?—A. Yes.

Q. How?—A. We bought them.

Q. Has there been any squid taken on your vessel?—A. Yes, wt Banking.

Q. Under what circumstances?—A. It is like this: when we go to N foundland and bait is plentiful it pays us better to buy it, and then on our trip, than to try and catch it ourselves, thus losing time, and wt squid are scarce, we catch a few, and help to make up what we want as to save time; that is our only object in catching them ourselves.

Q. Are your men at leisure to fish for squid?—A. No.

Q. What do they do at this time?—A. They have water to fill and ice to get; and as soon as the bait comes alongside, we have to 1 the men to hoist it on board.

Q. When do your men ever catch bait?—A. At nights.

Q. How many squid in all do you suppose your vessels ever jigged took?—A. At the outside, 20 barrels in 2 seasons—last year and t year.

Q. How long does it take you to go in from the Banks to Newfou land, obtain bait and return to your fishing grounds?—A. A fair av age time would be about a week.

Q. What is the longest time?—A. Nine days, to my knowledge.

Q. And the shortest?—A. Five days, I think.

Q. What did your bait cost in Newfoundland this year?—A. T whole thing, port charges and all cost me about $400 on the last trip

Q. Did you have these bills, I now hand you, to pay?—A. Yes;.

Q. What are they for?—A. This one, $4.80, was for water rates. cannot tell you what it is for, I am sure. We have to pay them whetl we fill in with water or not. It is a government bill. It rates 5 cei a ton.

Q. What is the next for?—A. Light dues; it amounts to $23.04.

Q. How much is that a ton ?—A. 24 cents, on 96 tons.

Q. Pass right on to the next.—A. Well, the next is a harbor master's bill—for fees.

Q. What is it for ?—A. I do not know unless it is for the trouble of anchoring in the harbor. It is a bill we have to pay in St. John's every time we anchor, and go out and in ; it amounts to $2.

Q. Pass right along to the next.—A. The next bill is for anchoring and clearing and so on.

Q. How much is it ?—A. I do not see any amount here. I do not know what it is. I do not know but what it is included in the water rate. It is a government concern.

Q. It is not carried out ?—A. No.

Q. I do not see any pilotage charge; how does that happen ?—A. Well, the trouble there is, when they speak us, and they are sure to do that, because they lie right in the mouth of the harbor, and you cannot go in by them without they speak you—for they are right in the door-yard—you are obliged to pay full pilotage whether you take them or not ; and so we took one, of course.

Q. Is there a pilotage bill there ?—A. No.

Q. How does that happen ?—A. We had a pilot, but he took us in and ran us on Cod Rock, and so I did not pay him anything. I told him if he would pay me the damage done my vessel I would pay pilotage fees, and so as he did not pay for the damage done the vessel, I did not pay pilotage—hence I have not got any bill.

Q. Otherwise you would have paid pilotage fees ?—A. Exactly so.

Q. The whole bills of the trip amounted to $400?—A. Yes; port charges and all.

Q. What do you think as to the difference between fresh and salt bait ?—A. Well, I think we would be just as well off if we had nothing to do with fresh bait; but in order to get a share of the fish now, I think that we have got to have fresh bait. But if all used salt bait, we could do just as well. We always used to get good trips with salt bait and shack before fresh bait was introduced.

Q. What was then used for salt bait ?—A. Clams, and porgies, and herring and squid sometimes.

Q. Did you use to obtain squid on the Banks ?—A. Yes.

Q. Do you do so now ?—A. They are scattered and not so plentiful there as they used to be.

Q. Is the squid a fish whose presence can be regularly depended on, or is its presence uncertain and migratory ?—A. Well, there are places where you are sure to get them on the Newfoundland coast.

Q. What about squid on the American coast ?—A. I know they are found there.

Q. Whereabouts ?—A. I have seen them around the coast of Maine.

Q. Are they found south of Cape Cod ?—A. Yes. They come there sometimes in May, and are caught in weirs, &c.

Q. In great abundance ?—A. I think not, but I do not know much about this.

Q. What proportion of the business of Gloucester is engaged in the cod fishery and what proportion in the mackerel fishery, as far as you are able to judge ?—A. I should say that two-thirds are engaged in the Bank fishery and one-third in the mackerel and herring fisheries.

Q. What proportion does the herring bear, compared with the mackerel fishery ?—A. One-half, I should think.

Q. Do they catch or buy herring ?—A. So far as my knowledge goes,

they have always bought herring. I have never been on a herring t
but I understand that this is the case.

Q. When you speak of one-sixth of the business of Gloucester be
engaged in the mackerel fishery, do you refer to the Gulf of St. L
rence mackerel fishery?—A. I should say that is for the whole thin

Q. Do you know about the mackerel fishery on the coast of the Uni
States?—A. I did not think about it; for the last two or three ye
most of the mackerel have been caught on our own coast. You
know that as well as I do.

Q. You said that your average time spent in getting bait was 7 days
A. About a week.

By Mr. Weatherbe:

Q. You fished in the Reunion in 1866?—A. Yes.

Q. That is the first time you went fishing?—A. O, no; but tha
the first time I was in the bay. I have fished since 1861, when I
11 years old.

Q. Where did you then fish?—A. On the Grand Banks.

Q. You did very well in the bay in 1866?—A. Yes.

Q. Why did you not stick to the Reunion?—A. When it comes
we make a change. Our mackerel season is up in the fall. I went t
trips to the bay in her.

By Mr. Foster:

Q. Do you know anything about the herring business at Grand]
nan?—A. Yes; but very little.

Q. Have you been there?—A. Yes.

Q. When?—A. Last spring and this year; but I did not take a
bait there. I took bait, however, last season at Bliss Island.

Q. Do you know of any catch of herrings being made by Americ
in that vicinity?—A. No; there has never been one to my knowled

By Mr. Weatherbe:

Q. Do you know where the Reunion went in 1867?—A. No; she l
then changed masters.

Q. Who was she owned by?—A. William Henry Steele, then, I thi

Q. Of Gloucester?—A. Yes.

Q. Is it the custom of Gloucester fishermen to remain in the emp
of the same owners?—A. No; they change about.

Q. Constantly?—A. Yes.

Q. The rule is to change about?—A. I do not know about that, l
they do so.

Q. What is the usual practice?—A. To make changes.

Q. Do they remain with the same owners year after year?—A. No

Q. Do you know what the Reunion caught in 1867?—A. No.

Q. Did you then make any inquiries about her?—A. No.

Q. Do you not hear what catches vessels make?—A. We do pre
well when we attend to our own business.

Q. You are not able to state the catches of other vessels?—A. No.

Q. Or to give any information in this respect save for your own v
sel?—A. No.

Q. Most of the fishermen would be likely to know only what th
own vessels did?—A. They will do pretty well if they know that.

Q. Some fishermen frequent certain places in the bay and oth
other places?—A. Yes.

Q. And some always go to the Magdalen Islands?—A. Yes; tl
is so.

Q. And others to the bend of the island ?—A. Yes.

Q. Then you would not be able to tell what others did ?—A. No.

Q. Have you ever met Charles W. Dunn, a fisherman, who has frequently fished in American vessels ?—A. I have met a man named Peter Dunn, but I do not know any Charles Dunn.

Q. He deposes:

That in 1870, I was about two months and a half fishing in the gulf, in the Reunion, during which time we got four hundred and thirty barrels of mackerel. She was seventy-four tons and carried fifteen hands.

A. Yes; but I thought she was sold out in California before that time.

Q. You do not remember her fishing that year ?—A. No; I know nothing about it at all.

Q. He continues:

That in 1871, I was in the Rambler for eight weeks, fishing in the gulf. We took out two hundred and eighty barrels of mackerel. We came into the gulf late that season. She was sixty-three tons, and that time carried thirteen hands.

That fully three-quarters of the fish taken in these schooners were taken close to the shore, or within three miles along this island, Miscou, Bay Chaleur, the Magdalens, and other places on the British coasts. Taking the season through, the inshore fishing is the best. I believe that it would not be at all worth while to fit out for this gulf if the vessels were not allowed to fish inshore.

Q. Had you a license when in the bay ?—A. No.

Q. You know nothing about the cutters?—A. Yes; when I was there, in 1872, there were cutters in the bay. There were plenty of cutters, but no fish.

Q. When there were plenty of cutters in the bay there were no fish for Americans ?—A. Yes; that is probable; but——

Q. Do you want to explain that any further ?——A. Just so; but the Nova Scotian vessels had the same trouble, too.

Q. Were they kept out?—A. The Nova Scotian vessels did not do any better than our own vessels. That is between you and me.

Q. We want to know about it.—A. That is the idea, and the true thing.

Q. That is just what we want to come at and ascertain.—A. Yes; go on.

Q. If you have any information to give about it. Were they kept out of the 3-mile limit ?—A. No.

Q. Were you ?—A. Yes; we were.

Q. Constantly ?—A. But there were no fish inshore or offshore.

Q. Were you kept constantly outside of the 3-mile limit ?—A. Well, no; I could not say that we were constantly, because the cutters would not be in sight all the time, of course.

Q. What vessel were you in then ?—A. The George Clark; year 1872.

Q. When the cutters were out of sight, would you steal inside of the 3-mile limit ?—A. No; we would not.

Q. You did not try to go in ?—A. No.

Q. You never fished inside of the 3-mile limit ?—A. No.

Q. You never hove to inside of the three-mile limit?—A. No; I do not think that I ever did so in my life. Of course if there had been any fish inshore or any inducement for us to go in we would have done so.

Q. And you never tried inshore in your life ?—A. I never did; no.

Q. You never heard of three-quarters of the fish being taken within the three-mile limit, as mentioned in C. W. Dunn's deposition ?—A. Yes; I have heard tell of vessels fishing inshore.

Q. And making large catches ?—A. No; I never heard that.

Q. If you had you would have gone in and tried ?—A. I think it is likely 1 would if I knew that there were plenty of fish inshore.

Q. If you had ever heard evidence like that I mentioned, you would have gone in and given the inshore fishery a trial ?—A. Well, I know a little more about that matter than the man who made that statement.

Q. Would you have done so or not ?—A. Well, of course if there were fish inshore and we knew it and had a chance to catch them we probably would do so.

Q. If you heard a hundred men swear what I have mentioned, would you do so ?—A. If I heard men swear to a lie and I knew it, that would be no temptation to me.

Q. But you would certainly be open to conviction ?—A. O, yes.

Q. If a hundred men so swore, would you be induced to give it a trial?—A. That would depend on circumstances.

Q. If you had a license, how much persuasion would have induced you to give the inshore fishery one trial ?—A. If I was going to fish inshore, I would have gone the right way about it and obtained a license.

Q. Do you not think you are a little prejudiced about this matter ?—A. No.

Q. What prejudice have you against those shores of ours ?—A. None.

Q. And you never once tried inshore ?—A. No, not in the bay.

Q. So of course you cannot speak about this fishery from your own knowledge; you must have some sort of prejudice in this regard ?—A. What is the use of our going to try for fish where we know there are no fish.

Q. Precisely, but you did not know; how did you find out ?—A. Were not the boats fishing right along as we went along the shore, and we could see whether they were getting fish or not. The boats were strung all around the shore.

Q. Now you are telling us something.—A. Yes; I am glad of it.

Q. How many thousand boats fished inside the three-mile limit around Prince Edward Island ?—A. I do not know, but I know that a great many boats fished around the coast.

Q. How much did these boats catch, on the average ?—A. I do not know.

Q. Did you ever try to ascertain ?—A. No.

Q. Did you ever make inquiries respecting this matter ?—A. No.

Q. Have you any idea respecting it ?—A. No.

Q. Do you know from personal observation what they caught ?—A. No.

Q. And yet you never tried inshore ?—A. Not within the three mile limit.

Q. The cutters never gave you any trouble ?—A. No; their men only boarded us and told us that we were not allowed to fish within three miles of the shore.

Q. And you obeyed the order ?—A. Yes.

Q. How far did you ever go inshore to fish ?—A. Well, probably within five or six miles of land.

Q. Have you any preference as to fishing six miles off, over four miles off ?—A. Well, of course there is no way for us to tell the exact distance.

Q. Have you any such preference ?—A. Of course not.

Q. Is five miles off any better than four and a half miles for fishing purposes ?—A. That does not amount to anything with me. We fish were we find fish. We catch them five miles offshore and ten miles off when the fish are there.

Q. If the fish were three and a half miles off shore, you would have no objection to catch them there ?—A. Not in the least.

Q. Have you any choice as to distance ?—A. No.

Q. You think that five miles off is better than three and a half miles for fishing ?—A. It does not make any odds.

Q. You think there is no difference between them ?—A. It does not make any odds where we find the fish.

Q. Do you think 5 miles off is a better distance to fish at than three and a half miles, as a usual thing ?—A. I could not say.

Q. Or better than 6, 7, or 8 miles off ?—A. I could not say.

Q. Or 10 miles off ?—A. I do not know any limit to it; there is none, as far as I can see.

Q. You don't know of there being any difference between three and a half miles and 15 miles off for fishing ?—A. No, we catch the fish out of sight of land sometimes, on Banks Orphan and Bradley.

Q. And sometimes you make bad voyages there ?—A. The best voyage I ever made was out of sight of land.

Q. We have had a good many bad years and failures through fishing out of sight of land ; we have heard of men failing year after year there, and yet they never tried to fish inshore, although they heard that there was good fishing inshore ?—A. Well, I do not think it.

Q. Do you not think that you are mistaken in——A. O, no.

Q. What about ?—A. The fishing.

Q. What about the fishing ?—A. Well, what you were speaking about —the limit.

Q. You said you had no choice about the limit, and that three and a half miles offshore was as good for fishing as 15 miles off.—A. Yes; I don't see any difference.

Q. But this is what I was going to observe : you might be mistaken about it; I am quite sure that there is a mistake ; you said you had done better outside the three-mile limit than—what ?—A. Yes. When I was in the bay in 1866, and that was the only year I did anything at all in the bay.

Q. You did better outside than what ?—A. In 1866 we caught all the mackerel I ever saw taken in the bay to amount to anything, and they were got offshore.

Q. You were in the bay in 1870, 1872, and 1873 ?—A. We were there in 1872 and 1873.

Q. In 1870 you were in the Henry L. Phillips as skipper ?—A. Then I was there in 1870 and 1872.

Q. And 1873 also, for you were four years in the bay ?—Well, all right.

Q. Besides 1866. Is that not correct ?—A. Yes. Then I was five trips in the bay instead of four.

Q. And in 1870 you only caught 60 barrels ?—A. I think so.

Q. And only 70 barrels in 1872 ?—A. I think so.

Q. And only 90 barrels in 1873 ?—A. Yes.

Q. It was an utter failure ?—A. Pretty much so. That was in the fall, after we got home from the Banks.

Q. That was a failure ?—A. Yes.

Q. Can you give us any earthly reason why you did not try inshore after 1870 ?—A. It was because there were no fish inshore.

Q. I thought you had done well enough and better outside ?—A. You misunderstood me this time.

Q. Then you do not say that the fishing was better outside ?—A.

There was no fishing in the bay in those years that amounted to thing inside or outside.

Q. But you told us you did not know anything about anybo catches except your own?—A. Yes.

Q. And you did not ask the men in the boats or make the sligl inquiry about what was caught inshore?—A. How do you know?

Q. You told us you made no inquiries of what the boats did.—A. cuse me, I do not think I told you any such thing. You asked me I knew, and I told you I could see the boats fishing around the shor

Q. I asked you if from personal observation you could tell what t caught, and you said you had enough to mind your own busir Have you made any mistake? Explain.—A. All I came here for to give a fair account of what I know about the fisheries—and if understood it as I do you would understand what I mean—and thꞓ what I am doing. I have no prejudice in this matter. When we v in the bay for mackerel it was easy enough for us to find out whel there were any mackerel inshore or offshore. Plenty of vessels boats were trying, and if there were no mackerel along the coast 1 not likely that without any inducement we would make ourselves li for seizure. It is easy enough to discover whether the fish are insl or not by running along it and looking at the boats. We can whether a man is catching fish or not by looking at him without ask a question; and by running along the coast and looking at the boats can see for ourselves.

Q. Did you ever make any inquiries as to the catch of the bo during the season?—A. No.

Q. Did you make any inquiries whatever of the boatmen witl spect to the boat-fisheries?—A. Well, I have talked the matter o while in the harbor I have seen men whom I have asked if any of boats were doing anything, or had done anything round the shore, the like of that, you know.

Q. In which harbor did you do this?—A. Well, in Port Hood.

Q. Whom did you ask?—A. Now, you have got me. I don't kɩ one boat-fisherman from another.

Q. How often did you so inquire in Port Hood, or anywhere else A. Perhaps I might have inquired once or twice, or it might have Ꮟ half a dozen times, I could not say which.

Q. Did you inquire in Port Hood as to what the average catch of boats was, or how they had done during the season?—A. No; I nᴇ asked, save as to whether they had done anything along the shore.

Q. During the season?—A. No; but at that time—that day or t week. I would ask if they had been doing anything inshore.

Q. That was after their fishing was over. You were not there till fall?—A. Yes.

Q. Then I suppose you found out that their fishery was over for season?—A. Do they not get mackerel on shore in the fall as well a the summer?

Q. What did you find out from them?—A. Well, the answer I from them was that the boats were doing nothing.

Q. They were not then fishing at all?—A. Well, they were tryinɡ seems.

Q. What is the fishing season for the boats?—A. Well, I do think that it belongs to me to answer that question.

Q. How often did you find out that the boats were doing nothing, ᵼ during what months?—A. Well, it was, say, in October that I m such inquiry.

Q. Were you on your way home in October?—A. No.

Q. Had you then just come into the bay?—A. I came in some time in September.

Q. How long did you wait there?—A. We generally left the bay about the middle of October. We used to do so.

Q. At what time in October did you make such inquiries?—A. Perhaps the first or perhaps the last of September.

Q. And you found out that the boats were doing nothing?—A. They said they were not.

Q. Then you did not try there?—A. No, not in there.

Q. Was that the reason why you did not try in there?—A. Partly; that might have been partly the reason.

Q. Did you ask what the boats had done, or usually did?—A. No.

Q. You then only made inquiry as to what the boat-fishers were doing that day or that week, as the case might be?—A. Yes.

Q. How did you learn that the shore fisheries were useless and worthless?—A. From what we could hear.

Q. What did you hear?—A. What you are talking about don't amount to anything as I can see. If we were in Port Hood Harbor and wanted to know whether there was any fishing round about there or not, we would see other skippers, &c., and find out in a very short time whether they had done anything off shore or on, and if there were no fish there we would go to what we considered the most likely place at which we could get them.

Q. I understood you to say you did not make inquiries of any other vessels, and that to mind your own business was as much as you could do. Then you did inquire what other vessels had caught?—A. Yes; naturally so.

Q. And did you find out what they caught?—A. No; I do not think it.

By Mr. Whiteway:

Q. Are you part owner of the vessel of which you are now captain?—A. No.

Q. Were you part owner of the Knight Templar?—A. No.

Q. You fished on the Grand Banks from 1861 to 1866?—A. Yes.

Q. You were a hand then?—A. Yes.

Q. You have been on the Grand Banks during the last two years?—A. Yes.

Q. And this is the extent of your experience in that fishing?—A. Yes.

Q. How many men are on board of your present vessel?—A. Fourteen, all told.

Q. In the spring, when the vessel is fitted out, do each of these men get a supply of articles to leave with their families—an advance?—A. I think so. I think that the firms supply them with outfits.

Q. The owners of the vessel supply them with a sufficiency for their families during their absence?—A. I think so, but I am not sure about it. I know that as a general thing the families draw on the men.

Q. During their absence, their wives or families get what they require?—A. Anything in reason, of course. I understand so.

Q. Is the ordinary cash price or a large profit charged for these articles?—A. I have never been a member of such a firm; but I think they get enough out of the business to run it of course—a fair profit.

Q. The firms do not charge the ordinary cash price in this relation?—A. Well, they ought not to; they are not going to get cash; I think they make enough to get a living out of the business.

Q. You know that they do charge a long profit?—A. No; I do not think that they do; but I think that they charge profit enough to make themselves whole, taking one year with another.

Q. Is their percentage 30 or 40 per cent. above the cash price?—A. It is 20 or 25 per cent., I think, over and above it.

Q. Is not a greater price than the ordinary cash price charged for the articles required for the fitting out of a vessel?—A. No, I do not think so.

Q. Do you know whether this is so or not?—A. I have been part owner of 3 vessels, and for outfits from spring to the fall we expected to pay probably 15 per cent. over and above the cash price in consideration for the delay.

Q. Then the supplier charges 15 per cent. over and above the cash price for articles supplied?—A. Yes; something like that; he has go to have it for the use of his money; such difference is 15 or 20 per cent. or somewhere along there; I could not say exactly what it is.

Q. What would it cost to pack and cure a barrel of mackerel for market?—A. I am not prepared to answer that question.

Q. Would $1 pay all such expenses?—A. I think not; the barrel it self is worth somewhere about a dollar; I think they charge $2 for packing a barrel of mackerel—for barrel and all.

Q. That leaves a handsome profit to the packer; something like 50 or 60 cents?—A. Yes, about that.

Q. What does it cost to cure a quintal of Bank codfish?—A. I could not state such cost correctly; we bring our fish in cured in quintals, and weigh them from the hatch and sell them.

Q. To the owners of the vessels?—A. Sometimes, and sometimes to others.

Q. But, as a general thing, the owner of the vessel takes the voyage as soon as the vessel arrives?—A. Yes.

Q. The fish is weighed out, and you are credited with a certain price for them?—A. Yes.

Q. What does it cost to cure for market dried codfish?—A. I think that at Beverly they charge 25 cents a quintal for making the fish after it comes from the hatch.

By Mr. Foster:

Q. Salt included?—A. They do not use any salt there; but in Gloucester they do.

By Mr. Whiteway:

Q. Is there any other expense?—A. Yes, if the fish are boxed up for market.

Q. Is there not an arrangement made among the vessel-owners and suppliers for the Bank fishery as to the price which they will credit the fishermen for their fish?—A. I think so.

Q. So that immediately after a vessel comes in with a cargo the price to be credited is known from such previous arrangement among the merchants?—A. Yes.

Q. What is the difference between the prices allowed by the merchants and the market-price for dried codfish?—A. I cannot say.

Q. Does not the owner of the vessel make a profit of something like $1 a quintal upon the fish when cured and ready for market?—A. I think they calculate to make seventy-five cents or a dollar; but they do not always obtain it.

Q. To what place did you go from Gloucester last year in the Knight Templar?—A. To the Western Bank first.

Q. Had you fresh bait?—A. Yes.

Q. Did you take it from Gloucester?—A. No.

Q. Where did you get it?—A. At Bliss Island, N. B.

Q. Did you go into any Dominion or Newfoundland ports for bait last year?—A. Yes.

Q. Where did you go?—A. Into Hermitage Bay, Newfoundland.

Q. When were you there?—A. The first of May.

Q. Was that after you had used up the bait you had taken from Bliss Island?—A. Yes; I took that bait to Western Bank, and afterwards went to Hermitage Bay and obtained herring.

Q. And you then proceeded to the Grand Bank?—A. Yes.

Q. Did you buy your bait there?—A. Yes.

Q. Did you go at any other time last year to Newfoundland ports for bait?—A. Yes.

Q. When?—A. I was at St. John's about the 1st of August, on my second trip.

Q. You had been in the mean time to Gloucester?—A. We went to Gloucester on the 19th of June with our first trip.

Q. What did you take on your first voyage?—A. 169,000 pounds.

Q. And you proceeded direct from Gloucester to St. John's?—A. We went to Canso; we could not get bait there, and then we went to St. Pierre Island. I bought salt bait there and went on the Bank with it, reaching the Bank on the 21st of July.

Q. You afterward went for bait to the Newfoundland coast?—A. Yes.

Q. When did you leave the Bank to do so?—A. I was on the Bank 10 days, leaving it about the 2d of August. I arrived in Newfoundland somewhere about the 3d or 4th of August.

Q. Is your memory distinct regarding the days?—A. Very nearly.

Q. You got bait in St. John's and then returned to the Bank?—A. No. I went in there to get ice and money.

Q. Money—for what purpose?—A. To buy bait and ice.

Q. Did you require to get water there?—A. No. We might at one time get ice in St. John's, and not bait, going to some other port for squid.

Q. Did you not then go to some other port for water and other articles?—A. When we used to go on long trips we took water enough for them, but now that we calculate to go in for fresh bait we do not take as much water with us, but fill up when we go in.

Q. You say your port charges and all at St. John's amounted to $400?—A. Yes, about that, for my last trip.

Q. Have you any account of it?—A. Not here, but I could produce it.

Q. You have given us items amounting to $29.84?—A. That is for port charges alone. I bought bait and ice besides.

Q. Were not several sums advanced to the crew in St. John's?—A. No.

Q. Do you never so advance money in port?—A. Sometimes we let them have a little money.

Q. Does not a great portion of this $400 consist of advances made to the crew?—A. No; it consists of what was paid for port-charges, bait, and ice. Our other expenses are not included in it. We do other trading around the coast.

Q. What other trading?—A. Suppose we want to buy anything for the vessel, such as a barrel of flour, we do so; but such expenses are not included in the $400.

Q. What articles did you buy there on this occasion?—A. I could not mention them all. I let the crew this year have a little money, and I bought some things myself, clothing, &c.

Q. Can you give us the particulars as to what you bought for the vessel?—A. I bought some rigging, some baskets for the handling of bait, and so on. I suppose you do not expect me to mention every article in detail. We never go in without spending some money.

Q. What did you pay for bait on this occasion out of this $400?—A. I could not tell you exactly, because we have to pay different prices for it. We may get bait for $12 at one time, and at another time it may cost us $100.

Q. Have you ever paid $100 for bait on one trip?—A. I think I have for bait and ice, and I do not know but more.

Q. What is the highest amount which you ever paid for bait alone on one trip?—A. Sixty-eight dollars, I think, for squid.

Q. And what is the lowest amount?—A. Twelve dollars and fifty cents for caplin.

Q. What do you pay for ice?—A. Different prices; they asked us $12 a ton this year.

Q. How many tons of ice do you take on one trip?—A. Six.

Q. How much do you pay for ice on a trip?—A. Twelve dollars a ton, in an ice country too.

Q. When did you pay this?—A. This year, to a Dutchman there. I don't know his name. It was Vamburgh, or what's his name, that keeps a confectionery shop?

Q. Lunburgh?—A. Yes.

Q. Do you mean to swear that you paid $12 a ton for ice?—A. Yes.

Q. How many tons did you get on this trip this year?—A. Five tons, I think.

Q. Are you clear about this?—A. Yes; I took ice there last year.

Q. That is for one baiting?—A. Yes.

Q. That makes $60 for ice, and, with $68 for bait, this makes $128; and adding to this sum $29.84, we have $157 for ice, bait, and port-charges. How is the difference between this amount and $400 made up?—A. We baited four times.

By Hon. Mr. Kellogg:

Q. Does this $400 cover more than one trip?—A. It covers the four baitings. This was for my last voyage.

By Mr. Whiteway:

Q. Between what dates did you bait?—A. Between the 1st of June and the last of August.

Q. You went in four times to St. John's?—A. No.

Q. But in to the coast?—A. Yes.

Q. If you had not got that bait at Newfoundland, you must have obtained it somewhere?—A. We might have taken salt bait.

Q. It would have cost more than fresh bait, would it not?—A. I could not say as to that.

Q. What do you pay per barrel for salt bait?—A. At Gloucester it costs, I guess, $4 a barrel.

Q. And herrings in Newfoundland cost $1 a barrel?—A. Yes.

Q. Would you require to buy ice, &c., in Gloucester?—A. Yes.

Q. And you would have to go a considerably greater distance from the Banks to Gloucester for these articles than to Newfoundland?—A. Yes.

Q. Then the cost of getting bait in Newfoundland is considerably less than it would be in Gloucester?—A. I think not.

Q. How is that?—A. If we are going to take bait from Gloucester, we would take probably 10 or 12 or 15 barrels, and the rest we would pick up on the Banks. If we were going to have salt bait, we would catch birds and porpoises, and get shack and mix it with them, and that would do us for the season.

Q. Does your getting fresh bait prevent you getting shack on the Banks?—A. Well, we consider fresh bait to be better than salt bait and shack. We have ice-houses and all that kind of thing, and we do not spend any time in looking after shack or in picking it up.

Q. It must take you some time to get it on the Banks?—A. Yes, of course; but when we have fresh bait we do not occupy any time in getting that at all. We do not then bother with it.

Q. What have you on your vessel in the harbor now?—A. About 10,000 pounds of codfish, caught within a fortnight.

Q. Where?—A. Just east of what is called Green Island, near Portland.

Q. You have not been in Newfoundland for bait for this trip?—A. No.

Q. Did you go there while on your former voyage this year?—A. Yes; four times.

Q. How many times did you go to Newfoundland for bait last year?—A. Three times.

Q. What was the longest time between the time you left the Banks till you returned to them, that you have ever consumed in obtaining bait there?—A. Nine days.

Q. And five days is the shortest time you ever so occupied?—A. Yes.

Q. Have you ever observed the lantz on the Banks?—A. Yes.

Q. During what months?—A. It is found there during all the months. I think it comes there in the last of June, and it is to be seen there in July and August—different schools are met with; the spring school is large and the August school small.

Q. Have you ever observed it there afterward?—A. I think it is there in September, and it is found there in October; I have seen them there in the last of the fall.

Q. Are the caplin found there?—A. Yes, about the Virgin Rocks and the southern part of the Grand Banks; I have seen them there about the first of July and the last of June.

Q. Have you noticed how long they continue on the Banks?—A. I think they stop there about a fortnight.

Q. In what depth of water have you there seen caplin?—A. In four or five fathoms.

Q. Is that the deepest water in which you have seen them there?—A. I have seen them in 40 fathoms; the codfish drive them right on to the surface of the water.

Q. You have always fished with trawls?—A. I have also fished with hand-lines; I have fished with trawls during the last two years. We used hand-lines altogether on my first voyage.

Q. Are you in the habit of taking up much seaweed on your trawls?—A. No; I do not know anything about that.

Q. You have not seen this happen?—A. No.

Q. Do you know as a matter of fact that seaweed is often brought up on the Banks?—A. I never knew of it.

Q. Have you taken the trouble at any time to examine the stomachs of codfish?—A. Yes.

Q. And have you found any small shell-fish in their stomachs?—Yes, plenty of them.

Q. Does that occur at all times during the fishing season?—A. Yes, more or less.

Q. What is the food which you have principally found in their stomachs on the Banks?—A. Caplin and lantz, and what we call Bank clams and crabs.

Q. Have you fished for cod on Western Banks, Grand Banks, and George's Bank?—A. Yes.

Q. Have you observed any difference between the cod on these several Banks?—A. Yes.

Q. Can you describe it?—A. Yes. The Western Bank cod are not nearly so large as the Grand Bank cod; there is more of a black nape on the former than on the latter, and the former are not so well fed, and they are very watery and slim. The Grand Bank cod are the largest fish, and they resemble each other more as to quality. They are large, white naped, and well fed—better fed than the Western Bank cod. The latter are small and black, and they are thinner than the others.

By Mr. Foster:

Q. What do you mean by black naped?—A. The nape is the belly part—it is a little thin skin over the belly of the fish.

Q. Your family does not have to get advances in your business?—A. No, and I am not posted much in that line.

No. 42.

FRIDAY, *October* 5, 1877.

The Conference met.

ROBERT H. HULBERT, fisherman, of Gloucester, was called, on behalf of the Government of the United States, sworn and examined.

By Mr. Foster:

Question. How old are you?—Answer. Thirty-five.

Q. Where were you born?—A. In Yarmouth, Nova Scotia.

Q. You have been a fisherman and captain of fishing and trading vessels for some years?—A. Yes.

Q. When did you first fish for mackerel in the Gulf of Saint Lawrence?—A. In 1861, I think.

Q. In what vessel were you then?—A. The Roger Williams.

Q. What was the name of her captain?—A. Lane.

Q. How many fish did you take?—A. Two hundred and sixty barrels, I believe, but I would not be certain.

Q. Have you any means of refreshing your memory as to dates and catches?—A. No.

Q. You are now pilot on the Speedwell?—A. Yes.

Q. Where did you catch your fish the first year you were in the gulf?—A. Principally at the Magdalen Islands. The last we caught were taken near Fisherman's Bank, between Cape George and Prince Edward Island.

Q. Were any portion taken within 3 miles of the shore?—A. I could not say; but probably not more than one-eighth were so caught, as I have found this to be the case on different trips made since.

Q. What were you doing from 1862 to 1865?—A. I was engaged in different kinds of fishing, but mostly in cod-fishing. I sometimes fished for mackerel on our own coast.

Q. When did you make your second mackerel trip to the gulf?—A. I cannot be certain as to the year, because it was some time afterwards.

Q. What was the name of your vessel?—A. The Pocumtuc, I think.

Q. Who was her captain?—A. George H. Hurlbert, my brother.

Q. You cannot fix that year accurately?—A. No.

Q. What was your catch?—A. About 180 barrels.

Q. Where were they taken ?—A. At the Magdalen Islands principally. Some were caught near Margaree Island, Cape Breton.

Q. How many were caught there ?—A. We only fished there one day, to the best of my recollection, and we got something in the neighborhood of 30 or 35 barrels.

Q. Were any taken that year by you within three miles of the shore ?—A. A certain number of vessels fish around Prince Edward Island and the coast of Cape Breton at different places. Some fish near the Port Hood Islands, on the west coast of Cape Breton.

Q. But where were these 180 barrels taken ?—A. At the Magdalen Islands principally. We staid there as long as we could, with regard to the weather. We left them somewhere near the middle of October; but I cannot remember the exact time.

Q. Where did you then go ?—A. To Port Hood, for a harbor.

Q. Were the mackerel you took near Margaree Island caught either within three miles of the island or the mainland ?—A. They were probably taken within three miles of Margaree Island.

Q. But not within three miles of the mainland ?—A. No.

Q. Were they taken outside of that island ?—A. Yes.

Q. When did you make your third trip to the Gulf of St. Lawrence ?—A. I cannot remember the year exactly; but the next vessel in which I went there was the Aphrodite, Captain Calderwood.

Q. How many barrels of mackerel did you take ?—A. Two hundred and seventy.

Q. Where were they taken ?—A. Principally between North Cape, Prince Edward Island, and Miscou Island, up the west shore.

Q. Was any portion of them taken within three miles of the shore?—A. We did not fish much in any other part of the bay. There did not seem to be any fish at the Magdalen Islands that summer of any consequence. The fish were scarce there that year, and we took the most part of our fish up in that part of the bay. We took none of any consequence anywhere else.

Q. To what part of the bay do you particularly allude ?—A. To that between North Cape and Point Miscou.

Q. Were they taken within three miles of the shore ?—A. I should not say that they were.

Q. Can you give any reason why they were not ?—A. It is because you cannot raise a body of mackerel in such shoal water as is generally found three miles from the shore on that part of the coast.

Q. What is the shoalest water in which you usually raise a school of mackerel ?—A. We cannot raise a school, to make it profitable to lay to and heave over bait, in short of 20 or 25 fathoms of water.

Q. Is the water as deep as that along the shore between North Cape and Point Miscou within three miles of the shore ?—A. I think not.

Q. Have you fished along the north shore of Prince Edward Island ?—A. Yes.

Q. You were only in the gulf for mackerel during three years ?—A. No; I was there two years since that.

Q. Did you fish along the bend of the island during the early years when you were in the bay ?—A. Yes; but very little; nothing of any consequence.

Q. How near the shore do you anchor when seeking a lee off the bend of the island ?—A. From 2 to 2½ miles of the shore.

Q. And then when you weigh anchor and try to fish again, do you begin to fish from the anchorage ground, or do you run out farther ?—A.

We then run off usually from 1 mile to 1½ miles, and perhaps 2½ miles before we try.

Q. What is the nearest point to the land at which you have known fishing to be done off Prince Edward Island?—A. From 3 to 5 and probably from 5 to 15 miles off.

Q. Why is it that a vessel, in order to fish advantageously, must raise a considerable school of mackerel?—A. You have to have a considerable body of fish alongside to make it profitable to heave bait over; bait costs considerable.

Q. How much bait would you throw over usually during a day's fishing?—A. From 2 to 2½ barrels.

Q. What does it cost per barrel?—A. It varies in price at different seasons; sometimes the price is as high as $8, and sometimes as low as $6.

Q. Can you fish even at the distance from the land you have mentioned off the north coast of Prince Edward Island and the bend of the island when the wind is on shore?—A. No.

Q. Why not?—A. Because the water is shoal, and the sea raises there very quickly and becomes rough, and of course as the wind increases the sea will naturally increase, and we have then to get out of there and go somewhere else.

Q. Is it a safe place to be in?—A. No, not when the wind is on shore.

Q. Is there any particular point from which the wind there chiefly blows?—A. Not that I know of; the wind varies there about the same as at any other part of the coast.

Q. How long does it ordinarily take to run the whole length of the island?—A. 11 hours, with a good breeze.

Q. Were you fishing up in these waters at any time when the cutters were here?—A. Yes, one year.

Q. That was the year you did not fix, and your third one, I suppose?—A. No, it was since then.

Q. Do you remember either during your first or third year's fishing here, going into Malpeque Habor and getting aground?—A. Yes.

Q. When was that?—A. The year I was in the Aphrodite. We went ashore going into Malpeque Harbor in the night.

Q. How did it happen?—A. The night was dark and stormy.

Q. What did you get ashore on?—A. On the bar while going in.

Q. Have you been in any of the other harbors in the bend of the island?—A. I was in Cascumpeque once.

Q. Were you in any others?—A. No; not on that side of the island.

Q. Is it easy to enter either Cascumpeque or Malpeque Harbors with a light wind?—A. No.

Q. Can fishing-vessels depend on getting into them and out of the way from the storm?—A. No.

Q. What, then, is the way of escape from a storm for fishing-vessels off the bend of the island?—A. When you see a storm commence, you must either go one way or the other to get out of the bend of the island—either around North Cape or down around East Point. The wind is generally so that you can fetch one way or the other.

Q. How quickly does a high wind get up there?—A. It varies considerably; sometimes a squall rises, and it blows very heavily in a very short time—in a few minutes, in fact; and sometimes the wind rises gradually.

Q. What do you say about the Magdalen Islands as a place for safe fishing?—A. This is a very good place for fishing, because we can make a lee with any wind.

Q. For some years after your first three years you were not in the Gulf of St. Lawrence ?—A. No.

Q. When were you there again ?—A. In 1872.

Q. In what vessel ?—A. The Hattie B. West; I was the skipper.

Q. How many barrels of mackerel did you take ?—A. Three hundred and seven.

Q. How long were you taking them ?—A. We went into the bay some time between the 1st and the 10th of August, and we left it on the 25th of October.

Q. Where were these fish taken ?—A. All at the Magdalen Islands.

Q. When did you leave the Magdalen Islands ?—A. About the 20th or the 21st of October.

Q. Where did you then go ?—A. To Georgetown, Prince Edward Island.

Q. For what ?—A. We started to go to Port Hood, but when we got across to East Point, Prince Edward Island, the wind came from the southward with such force that we could not fetch Port Hood, and as the wind blew fresh, we went into Georgetown and there made preparations to go home.

Q. Did you afterward go to Port Hood ?—A. Yes.

Q. Did you fish that year anywhere save at the Magdalen Islands ?—A. We tried one day from East Point up the island probably twelve miles on the north side, with some fifty sail of vessels.

Q. How far out were you ?—A. We tried all the way probably three to twelve miles off shore.

Q. With what success ?—A. We could not find anything; none of us got anything.

Q. This was in 1872 ?—A. Yes.

Q. What were you doing in 1873 ?—A. I was then again in the bay.

Q. In what vessel ?—A. The Joe Hooker.

Q. Were you skipper ?—A. Yes.

Q. When did you go into the bay ?—A. Somewhere about the 10th of July; but I would not be certain.

Q. How many barrels of mackerel did you take that season ?—A. We sent home by a freighter from Canso, 210½ barrels; we then returned, and got back the day before the storm of 1873.

Q. Did you send your fish home in a sailing-vessel or in a steamer ?—A. We shipped them in a sailing-vessel.

Q. What did it cost to send them home ?—A. Seventy-five cents a barrel.

Q. From what port did you send them ?—A. Port Hawkesbury.

Q. When ?—A. The gale took place on the 13th, I think, and—but I can hardly remember the date, though I have it all down in some of my books, which I haven't with me; it was somewhere about the 1st of August.

Q. What did you do after that ?—A. We took 270 barrels.

Q. Where did you catch your two fares of mackerel in 1873 ?—A. We caught our first trip on Bank Bradley and at the Magdalen Islands in the summer; and we took our second trip principally at the Magdalen Islands; we got some few at Prince Edward Island.

Q. How many did you take at Prince Edward Island ?—A. Probably one-eighth of the last fare, but no more.

Q. How near the shore was that portion taken ?—A. They were caught, I should say, from 5 to 15 miles off the land.

Q. Were you in Port Mulgrave that season ?—A. No.

Q. Your whole catch that year, in your two trips, was 480½ bar which went home to Gloucester ?—A. Yes.

Q. Have you the means of telling how much you made that year J self or how your vessel did ?—A. I could not give the exact stock it was somewhere in the neighborhood of $7,000.

Q. What was the quality of the mackerel ?—A. They were ones twos.

Q. With what firm did you fit out ?—A. Shute & Merchant, of (cester, who owned the vessel.

Q. And they packed out the mackerel ?—A. Yes.

Q. What have you been doing since ?—A. Principally seining ar on the coast of the United States.

Q. What did you do in 1874, seining ?—A. I did not go out until J and I believe we landed 800 barrels.

Q. How many trips did you make ?—A. Four, after the 1st of Jr

Q. What were you doing in 1875 ?—A. Seining, after the 1st of J

Q. Did you go cod-fishing in the spring ?—A. Yes.

Q. Where ?—A. To Sable Island Bank.

Q. How early did you begin your seining for mackerel ?—A. B 1st of June.

Q. And you took 500 barrels ?—A. Yes.

Q. In 1876, where were you ?—A. In the same business as in 187 was cod-fishing in the spring.

Q. When did you begin seining ?—A. About the same time, the 1 June.

Q. How did you succeed last year ?—A. We did very well.

Q. How many barrels did you get ?—A. I was in two different sels; and last spring 1 did not go cod-fishing at all.

Q. What did you do in your vessel ?—A. We went south for macl in her. We went away down the coast seining.

Q. How many barrels did you take on the first trip ?—A. We ca 100 barrels into New York fresh and we carried home 270 barrels.

Q. You got 370 barrels ?—A. Yes; 100 we sold in New York an we packed.

Q. How long were you making that trip ?—A. About 6 weel think.

. Q. What did you do afterwards ?—A. I went seining in another sel.

Q. How many barrels did you take ?—A. About 500, I think—d the best of the season.

Q. How many then did you get on the whole ?—A. About 870 ba during the whole summer.

Q. What were you doing last spring ?—A. I did not do anything I went seining.

Q. How many mackerel did you take this spring ?—A. I canno exactly, because we sold the most of them fresh in New York ; we them and carried them in fresh.

Q. You did not sell them by the barrel ?—A. No.

By Hon. Mr. Kellogg:

Q. Where did you go fishing ?—A. To the southward of New Y

By Mr. Foster:

Q. How many barrels did you pack besides the fresh ones ?—A. / we were done with the fresh ones we brought in 330 barrels salted

Q. What was the vessel's stock ?—A. She stocked on the first $5,112.

Q. How long did it take you to do that?—A. About 7 weeks, or prob·ably rather 8 weeks.

Q. Whereabouts were these fish taken?—A. All the way from 20 miles north of Hatteras to as far north as Nantucket.

Q. Where did you go on your next trip this season?—A. Down on the coast of Maine; we were a short time gone; we could not find any fish, and so we came home again.

Q. What did you do?—A. I believe we stocked about $500 on the second trip.

Q. Did you make a third trip this year?—A. Yes.

Q. Where?—A. At Block Island.

Q. What was your luck there?—A. It was very good, considering.

Q. How many barrels did you take?—A. 130.

Q. What did they sell for?—A. $22.50 and $23.50 a barrel. We sold them at Gloucester; they were Block Island mackerel.

Q. What was your stock?—A. I could not tell exactly, but we shared $79 each, and there were 14 men.

Q. What was the total amount all your trips this summer stocked, seined on the United States coast?—A. I heard it talked of at the time, and I think that it was somewhere in the neighborhood of $8,000.

Q. That was the result of the stocking out?—A. Yes; that was the total stock.

Q. When did you cease fishing this summer?—A. About the 1st of August.

Q. And soon afterwards you came up in the Speedwell as pilot?—A. Yes.

Q. You have been several times in the Gulf of St. Lawrence, and you have fished over our own coast from Hatteras up, and I should like to ask you a few questions respecting the food of the mackerel—where do you find it?—A. We find it usually from 20 to 50 miles off the land, during the early part of the season; generally we do not then find any food at the surface of the water; so their food at this time consists of shrimps and sand fleas, which we find inside of the fish.

Q. What do you find later?—A. We then find what we call red seed —I do not know its proper name, but it is something that looks round and red—with shrimps and little small fish of different kinds.

Q. How far out at sea have you found this food, this red stuff?—A. I have seen it, I may safely say, 40 miles southeast of George's.

Q. In what quantities?—A. I could not exactly say, because when we are out that way of course, if we see any fish, we have not much time to look after anything else.

Q. Have you found it in abundance or in small quantities? A. Some years it is very abundant, and more years when the mackerel do not play out that way, there probably won't be so much of it.

Q. Where and when do the mackerel first appear on the United States coast in spring?—A. We first find them somewhere abreast of Hatteras or a little to the northward of it—20 miles north of Hatteras.

Q. At what date?—A. From the 20th to the 25th of April.

Q. When are they at Cape Delaware?—A. That depends upon the weather; if you have northerly and easterly winds they won't come up very fast; they will then come very slowly along the coast, but if you have moderate southerly and westerly winds they will naturally work along a little faster than if it was a cold and backward spring. They vary considerably in the time of their appearance.

Q. Give us the average approximate dates when they make their ap·pearance off Cape Delaware.—A. It is something like fifteen days per-

haps at the average, but if it is not a moderate season it would prob
be from fifteen to eighteen days.

Q. I want to learn the average date of their appearance off
Delaware; which is the earliest and which the latest date ?—A. It w
be somewhere about the 10th of May, and perhaps sometimes a
earlier than that.

Q. At what date do they reach Sandy Hook ?—A. Probably a
the 15th of May they arrive there, and afterward they reach Mo
Point, at the east end of Long Island. They stop longer off New
than off any other part of the coast. We cannot tell exactly when
come to Montak, because after they leave the grounds off New Yor
think they go to the bottom and spawn; the schools are then broken
great deal at certain points; after they go along the coast of Long Is
or get down that way, they do not appear to be in as great a boc
they are off New York; they do not school so often in these quarte

Q. And you think that the schools begin to break up at that poin
A. Yes; as a general thing.

By Sir Alexander Galt:

Q. Is that at Sandy Hook ?—A. It occurs east of it on the coa
Long Island.

By Mr. Foster:

Q. When do the mackerel reach the vicinity of Cape Cod and
tucket ?—A. The schools vary considerably in this respect. The
that pass through by the Vineyard get through early, but the fish
go outside do not get along quite so early. Sometimes part of t
will get down through by the Vineyard by the 1st of June, or per
the 10th of June; but the fish that go outside will be a little later.

Q. Where are the spawning places for mackerel off the United St
coast ?—A. We think that a great quantity of them spawn on the so
west part of George's Bank and about Nantucket Shoals, off San
Head, and on the fishing-ground off there; a large fishing-grour
situated southeast or east of Nantucket.

Q. Coming north of Nantucket Shoals, where are the spaw
grounds found ?—A. Sankaty Head is where there is a light-hous
the eastern part of Nantucket Island, I believe.

Q. Southwest from George's Bank ?—A. Yes.

Q. Where do you find their spawning grounds, to the northwar
this ?—A. On the different Banks around Massachusetts Bay, I
pose, though I never caught any spawning there, but I have can
mackerel there at different times out of which spawn would run.

By Sir Alexander Galt:

Q. At what date was this the case ?—A. Probably from the 1s
the 15th of June; those fish do not all spawn at the same time. '
depends on the time when they arrive on the coast. Those that
through the Vineyard do not generally spawn until after they
through.

By Mr. Foster:

Q. Give the earliest and the latest dates for the spawning seaso
the different points on our coast ?—A. This would extend probably f
the 15th of June to the 1st of July.

Q. Then you think that their spawning is concluded on our coast
the 1st of July ?—A. Yes.

Q. How long do the different spawning times for the schools of m erel last?—A. Probably not more than 10 days, and perhaps not so long. When the mackerel are spawning, in our opinion, there is generally a dull spell, during which they do not school or go into deep water, as they have gone down, we think, to spawn. We do not then catch many of them, and before this dull spell commences, the spawn is running out of a great many of them quite freely. When we find that they have come up again in bodies—which is probably ten days or a fortnight after the opening of the dull spell—we find that the spawn is out of them.

Q. How soon do they begin to be in good condition after their spawning is over?—A. You can perceive that they have increased some in flesh in a fortnight's time afterwards.

Q. Name the points on the American coast at which the mackerel are taken in large quantities, beginning to the southward, and running northward, and the particular seasons when these fish are abundant at these points?—A. We find quite a body of fish after their spawning is through, out near the south shoal lightship at Nantucket, and off to the eastward of Nantucket Island; southeast of that we find quite a body of mackerel after their spawning is done, some years; and some years there will not be so many there; but generally a number of fish are taken there.

By Sir Alexander Galt:

Q. When does this take place?—A. From the 25th of June to the 10th of July, sometimes; the dates vary some.

By Mr. Foster:

Q. Mention the most southerly point where the mackerel are found in abundance?—A. We never find any extra fishing until we get somewhere near half-way between Cape Cod and Sandy Hook; along the coast there we find the fish considerably plentiful. We find them there north of the light-ship—say 20 miles north of it, off Delaware.

Q. How many mackerel did you ever know to be taken in one day there, by one vessel?—A. I have known 100 barrels to be taken there by vessels in one day.

Q. When you were with them?—A. Yes; I saw them at the time.

Q. When was this?—A. Somewhere along about the 1st of May.

Q. That was before they had spawned?—A. Yes; the date when they are so caught there varies sometimes; it is sometimes later and sometimes earlier. We sometimes take large quantities off Barnegat, from 15 to 45 miles off the land.

Q. Where is Barnegat?—A. It is situated probably five-eighths of the way from Cape Cod to Sandy Hook.

Q. How large a quantity have you known to be taken off Barnegat by the vessel?—A. Sometimes we get in one haul there 150 barrels and perhaps more. I have been there when 140 barrels were taken in a day at one haul of the seine.

Q. When was that?—A. Probably from the 1st to the 5th of May.

Q. What is the next point farther north?—A. Off New York, and Sandy Hook.

Q. When are they caught there?—A. Perhaps from the 5th to the 10th of May, and may be a little later. The fish remain some time off New York; their stay depends on the weather.

Q. How large a catch have you known to be taken in one day there?—A. This last spring we took as high as 180 barrels at one haul there.

Q. Which is the next point?—A. After the mackerel get by there, we do not find anything that is extra good fishing until we get down towards the South Shoal light-ship, near Nantucket; perhaps 1 may be some at Montauk, but there are not so many there as (about the light-ship. There is no extra good fishing near Montauk ing the first part of the season.

Q. How large a catch have you known to be made there?—A. schools at this point are generally broken up a great deal.

Q. You think that the schools break up?—A. Yes.

Q. How many barrels have you ever known to be taken there in day?—A. Perhaps from 20 to 40 barrels.

Q. What is the next place?—A. The next place, where we find 1 schools, is down about the South Shoal light-ship.

Q. You have omitted to mention Block Island?—A. Well, we d(find mackerel there to any amount early in the summer.

Q. How early do you find them there?—A. We find them the small schools about the same time as off Montauk.

Q. What is the season for fishing at Block Island?—A. Alon midsummer.

Q. After they have spawned?—A. Yes; fish have been caught summer near Montauk Point. Those are fish that do not come n any farther, but stay at Block Island all summer.

Q. Give an account of Block Island mackerel-fishing, and state quality caught, the times when taken, and the quantities of the cat made there.—A. They have been taken this year there in very s schools, and as low as 5 barrels in a school, though there have bee high as 200 barrels taken in a school this summer after the 1st of J there was nothing done before that there of any account.

Q. How was the fishing last year at Block Island?—A. We did have any vessels there last summer. One or two vessels went t and staid a short time, and two out of that number got trips.

Q. What is the quality of Block Island mackerel?—A. These fish commonly large enough and long enough for extra ones.

Q. By that you mean mess mackerel?—A. Yes.

Q. What are they sold for?—A. I do not know what price they I brought this summer. We did not mess our mackerel; but prob; they will bring from $26 to $27 a barrel.

Q. Is their price a good deal higher than that of any other mack which comes to the market?—A. Yes.

Q. Where is the next place at which the mackerel are found in a dance?—A. East of Block Island.

By Sir Alexander Galt:

Q. When are the fine mackerel which you have just mentioned tak —A. From the last of July and all through August.

By Mr. Foster:

Q. You say that this school of mackerel does not go farther nortl A. Yes.

Q. Explain why you think so.—A. I say so because we do not c any schools of that sized mackerel any distance to the nor'ard of point, or more than 20 miles to the north of Block Island. We ge odd mackerel, overgrown, in a school, once in a while, but we do meet with schools of such mackerel any distance north of Block Isl;

Q. You are satisfied that this school goes no father north?—A.

Q. Is that the commonly received opinion?—A. We have never ta notice of this fact until of late years, although those fish were there viously. Those who have fished there during different seasons tell that these fish have been there every season for a number of years.

Q. Where is the next place at which mackerel are taken?—A. We do not take many after we leave this point until we reach Nantucket.

Q. When are they found there?—A. After they have spawned.

Q. Give the dates as near as you can in this regard.—A. They are found here from the 20th or the 25th of June until the 10th of July perhaps; this would be about the period during which the largest body of fish is met with at this point.

Q. Is there a school which stays about Nantucket all summer?—A. No.

Q. Why do they go there?—A. I do not know. I suppose that part of them go there to spawn. This is where we miss them after they first come there; we lose the fish that first come on the coast there for a short time.

Q. What is the greatest catch which you have known to be made in a day by one vessel off Nantucket?—A. I have known vessels take a school, which they could not handle, there in a day; they would have to let a large quantity of the fish go out before they could handle the seine.

Q. What is the largest number of barrels which you have known to be brought on deck?—A. We took 200 barrels there this summer, and, after taking this quantity out, we gave the seine over to another vessel which took out an additional 150 barrels, and then a shark went through the seine, tearing it to pieces, so they lost the rest, and consequently we do not know how many barrels were in the seine.

Q. Why did you give away 150 barrels?—A. Because we could not dress any more than we had taken out. We had all we could take care of in good weather.

Q. And you know that 350 barrels were taken out of the seine before the shark destroyed it?—A. Yes.

Q. When was this?—A. I cannot give the exact date, but it happened some time between the 5th of June and the 10th of July.

Q. Had the fish then spawned?—A. Yes.

Q. It was after the mackerel were in good condition?—A. We got a very small quantity of twos out of this catch, and twos were the best we could get out of them at that time of the year.

Q. What is the case north of Nantucket Shoals?—A. We will find that same body of fish after they leave that place on George's Bank.

Q. Have you seined there?—A. Yes.

Q. What is the largest quantity which you have known one vessel to seine there in one day?—A. I can only speak in this relation concerning vessels in which I have myself been. We have taken 100 and 110 barrels at a haul there.

Q. At what time during the summer?—A. Probably about the 20th of July.

Q. Were those mackerel in good condition?—A. There were some ones among them then.

Q. They had fattened up some?—A. Yes.

Q. Where is the next point at which mackerel are found?—A. The next point of any consequence is situated on the coast of Maine, near Monhegan and Mount Desert Islands. Monhegan Island lies off the mouth of the Penobscot.

Q. How far is this from Mount Desert?—A. I do not know exactly, but it is somewhere about 40 miles from it.

Q. Is that in the Bay of Penobscot?—A. This island lies off shore— off the western part of Penobscot Bay, outside.

Q. How large an island is it?—A. I cannot tell exactly.

Q. Has it any inhabitants?—A. Yes; quite a number of fisherm
live on it. I suppose it has 100 inhabitants, and perhaps more.
belongs to the State of Maine.

Q. How large a catch have you known to be made there in a day
one vessel?—A. We do not generally catch there more than from 100
125 barrels in a haul. Sometimes, however, vessels get more there; b
I have known that to be done in a day.

Q. When?—A. From the last of July along through August.

Q. What is the quality of the fish caught in this locality?—A. A
that are large and long enough are fit for number ones.

Q. What does this indicate with respect to fatness?—A. There a
no particularly long ones; but at that time of the year, they are f
enough for ones, if they are long enough.

Q. What is the next place?—A. Well, we remain there the bigg
part of the season until the mackerel begin to move westward again.

Q. Do you not go nearer to Mount Desert than that?—A. We fi
the best fishing between Monhegan Island and Mount Desert; this
the ground we fish on from the last of July all through August.

Q. Over how large a space?—A. Along a coast of 40 miles perha;
and perhaps a little more; we fish all the way from 10 to 50 miles off t
shore there out to Jeffrey's Bank, and even farther than that.

At this point the examination of this witness was interrupted by
sent of the Commission, to allow of the hearing of other testimony.

No. 43.

CASTANUS M. SMALLEY, fisherman, of Belfast, Me., was called on
half of the Government of the United States, sworn and examined.

By Mr. Dana:

Question. Did you sail out of Rockland or Belfast?—Answer. M
vessel sails from Rockland.

Q. When did you begin to go fishing?—A. In 1858.

Q. Did you fish during 1858, 1859, and 1860?—A. Yes.

Q. In the bay?—A. Yes.

Q. How many trips did you make in 1858?—A. One.

Q. How many fish did you then catch?—A. 200 barrels.

Q. Did you catch any of these within three miles of the shore?—
No; they were all taken on Banks Orphan and Bradley.

Q. How many barrels did you catch in 1859?—A. About 175.

Q. And in 1860?—A. About 200 barrels.

Q. Did you pack out that number?—A. These were what we call se
barrels.

Q. Did you try to fish inshore?—A. Yes.

Q. In what way?—A. With hooks and lines and bait.

Q. Did you go in and drift out?—A. Yes; we hardly ever anch
when we are fishing for mackerel.

Q. What portion of your fish, at the outside, do you think you caug
inshore within three miles of the coast in 1860?—A. Possibly one-thir

Q. That is the outside figure?—A. Yes.

Q. Where did you find the most and the best mackerel during the;
three years—inshore or off shore?—A. Off shore.

Q. There is no question about that?—A. No.

Q. After 1860 you were not fishing for some years?—A. Yes.

Q. How many?—A. I think that I started fishing again in 1866, tl
year after the war.

Q. In what vessel were you in 1858?—A. The Georgiana, of Cohasset.

Q. And in 1859?—A. I was then in the same vessel.

Q. And in 1860?—A. I was then in the Star of Hope, of Cohasset.

Q. Were you in the service of the United States in the Army?—A. Yes.

Q. When did you join the Army?—A. In July, 1862.

Q. And until when did you stay in it?—A. Until the 7th of June, 1865.

Q. When did you next go fishing?—A. I next went to the bay, I think, in 1867.

Q. Did you fish in 1866?—A. Yes.

Q. Where?—A. Partly on our shore.

. In a fishing-vessel?—A. Yes.

Q. For what?—A. Mackerel.

Q. At what part of the American shore did you fish?—A. We fished all the way from Mount Desert Rock to Cashes Ledge and Cape Cod.

Q. In 1867 you came to the bay?—A. Yes.

Q. How many barrels of mackerel did you then catch?—A. About 200.

Q. What was the name of your vessel that year?—A. The Florence Reed.

Q. Where did you fish?—A. At the Magdalen Islands.

Q. Did you catch all your fish there?—A. Yes.

Q. Did you have a license in 1867?—A. Yes.

Q. And still you caught all your fish off the Magdalen Islands?—A. Yes.

Q. And made no use of your license?—A. No.

Q. Where did you fish in 1868?—A. On our shore.

Q. For mackerel?—A. For codfish and mackerel.

Q. Between Mount Desert and Cape Cod?—A. For mackerel; yes.

Q. Where did you fish for cod?—A. On the Western Bank for the spring trip.

Q. Were you in the bay in 1869?—A. Yes.

Q. And also in 1870?—A. Yes.

Q. What did you catch in 1870?—A. We carried out of the bay that year 200 barrels.

Q. That was the last time that you were then in the bay?—A. Yes.

Q. What did you fit for?—A. That was all the vessel would carry; we were full. I am in the same vessel now.

Q. What is her name?—A. The Esperanza.

Q. What portion of your fish was caught broad off shore and more than three miles from the coast?—A. From one-third to one-half were taken off shore and the rest, eel-grass mackerel, were caught inshore.

Q. Where?—A. Principally around Prince Edward Island.

Q. Of what quality were these mackerel?—A. They were poor.

Q. How came you to fish there for poor mackerel; were there none to be caught outside?—A. I presume that some were to be caught outside at the time, but if a man gets a catch of fish inshore, he is liable to stop there and see if he can get another one.

Q. Where were you fishing in 1871 and 1872?—A. On the American coast.

Q. Were you fishing for cod and mackerel?—A. We were cod-fishing on the spring trips, and we fished for mackerel during the rest of the season. In the spring we were on the Western Bank and not on the Grand Bank.

Q. How did you do?—A. Very well, indeed.

Q. Were you in 1873 in the bay again?—A. Yes.

Q. In what vessel were you in 1868?—A. The Esperanza.

Q. Were you in the same vessel in 1869?—A. Yes.

Q. Have you been in her ever since?—A. No.

Q. In 1869 you were in her?—A. Yes.

Q. In 1870?—A. Yes.

Q. In 1871?—A. Yes.

Q. In 1872?—A. I was in her.

Q. Iu 1873 you were in the bay again?—A. Yes.

Q. How many trips?—A. I made one in the vessel myself and c down, and the second trip I stopped ashore.

Q. Was that the Esperanza?—A. No, it was the Ernest F. Norw

Q. How many did you catch?—A. 230. I am pretty positive it that.

Q. Did you hear anything about the second trip?—A. I heard it 260.

Q. You learned that from whom?—A. From the master, Cap Adams.

Q. Is it true that the vessel got 400 barrels the second trip?—A. I do not think it is.

Q. Why not?—A. In the first place, I do not think the master w lie about it, and in the second place the vessel could not carry then

Q. That was in 1873, you are sure?—A. Yes.

Q. Those 230 caught when you were on board her, where were taken?—A. They were principally taken from Bank Orphan to] Port.

Q. Offshore?—A. Well, I should say so. I mean the principal of them was taken off shore.

Q. How many of the 230 do you think were taken near inshore? Well, it is a pretty hard matter for a man to stand on deck and whether it is within three or six miles, but a man's judgment would him. I should say that perhaps one-third of the whole trip was ta within between three and five miles.

Q. Do you think you took any within less?—A. Yes, there migh some.

Q. What proportion of the whole was taken within less than t miles?—A. There might be 30 or 40.

Q. You tried inside and outside?—A. Yes, we always did that.

Q. And you found a small catch inside, while they were largest most numerous outside?—A. Yes.

Q. In 1874, you were ashore?—A. Yes.

Q. In 1875, you were at home. In 1876 where were you?—A. I fishing.

Q. Where?—A. In the bay.

Q. Were you cod-fishing early in the spring?—A. Yes.

Q. How many months did you fish for cod?—A. We generally ca lated to get ready about the 20th of March and return somewhere ab June.

Q. Then you would go off in July to the bay for mackerel?—A. I believe I went through Canseau last year, the 26th day of July.] pretty positive it was the 26th.

Q. When did you return?—A. I came out of the bay somewhere tween the 2d and 5th of September; at any rate, I was home the of our State election.

Q. What day is the State election?—A. It is, I think, the second] day in September.

Q. You made two trips when in the bay. How was it that year?—A. Very dull.

Q. Did you try inshore and outshore both?—A. Yes.

Q. Now in 1877, this year, when did you go into the bay?—A. I went to the bay in August. I went through Canseau.

Q. Are you in here for harbor?—A. Yes.

Q. When did you come in?—A. Day before yesterday.

Q. Are you homeward bound?—A. Yes.

Q. When did you leave the fishing-grounds, or come through the Gut?—A. We came through Canseau a week ago; we came last Saturday.

Q. How much did you get all this time?—A. 110 barrels.

Q. And you tried inshore and outshore both?—A. Yes.

Q. What parts of the bay have you been?—A. We have been from what we call the West Shore to Port Hood.

Q. You fished all around?—A. Yes.

Q. And that is the best you could do?—A. Yes.

Q. How much can your vessel carry?—A. I fitted for 200. We had a small vessel.

Q. This won't pay?—A. No, I don't think it will.

Q. Did you heave to in the Bend?—A. Yes, I tried coming down. We hove to two or three times.

Q. Did you find anything?—A. Perhaps we might catch half a dozen mackerel.

Q. Not half a dozen barrels?—A. No.

Q. Those were not very large were they?—A. Well, they were what we term No. 2, small fry.

Q. You have been codfishing how many seasons, do you think, in all?—A. I have been codfishing five seasons in the same vessel. That is what we term spring fishing, not the season right through.

Q. Have you used salt bait or fresh?—A. Salt bait always, with the exception of one trip that we caught mackerel and had them spoil on our hands.

Q. Did you find the salt bait successful?—A. Yes.

Q. Hand-lining?—A. Yes.

Q. Have you a trawl also?—A. No, sir.

Q. You haven't found it necessary to go in for fresh bait?—A. No, sir.

By Mr. Weatherbe:

Q. I don't know whether you mentioned the number of barrels you caught in 1876?—A. I don't think I was asked it.

Q. About how many?—A. 120 barrels.

Q. What vessel had you in 1876?—A. The Esperanza.

Q. The same as now?—A. Yes.

Q. What is her tonnage?—A. 43 tons, American tonnage.

Q. She got pretty well for that tonnage?—A. Well, we didn't call it so, with 12 men.

Q. Are 12 men a fair average number in a vessel that size?—A. Yes, sir.

Q. You caught one-third inshore? Is that the average?—A. Yes, sir, generally.

Q. It is, in your best judgment?—A. In my best judgment we generally caught one-third or somewhere about that.

Q. That would be a fair average, I suppose?—A. Yes, sir.

Q. Sometimes more and sometimes less, but from one-third to one-half?

Mr. DANA. He didn't say that.

Mr. DAVIES. He said from one-third to one-half were taken insho

Q. You said you took two-thirds or one-half offshore ?—A. No, si

Q. Do you think that would be an average, one-third inshore; would be a fair average of the fishing of the mackerel-vessels insl generally ?—A. Generally speaking, of some vessels. There are s vessels that hang around inshore that are not fit to go out.

Q. They would catch more inshore ?—A. Yes, and poorer fish.

Q. One third, you think, would be a fair average for large vessels A. I am not going to speak of others besides my own.

Q. One-third would be a fair average ?—A. What I took out of bay, one-third was caught by the three-mile limit; but we might h been a little further off or a little nearer in. It is a hard matte judge.

Q. Do you think there is any considerable number of those po vessels that can't fish further out but hang inshore ?—A. There is q a number of them that never come by East Point. They daren't gc in the bend.

Q. They are American vessels ?—A. Some are, and some are not.

Q. About what proportion would you consider to be a fair prop tion of American vessels that hug the shore that way ?—A. I should there was four-fifths of them American vessels, because there is n great many English vessels that fish.

Q. What proportion of the fleet, I mean, that come into the gulf, l the shore that way and catch fish more inshore ?—A. There might one in twenty-five sail.

Q. Do you think there would be that many ?—A. Yes; there mi be one in twenty-five.

Q. You have seen them, I suppose, in the different years you h; been in the gulf ?—A. Yes; there are always two or three hang round in harbors that dare not try it outside. There are plenty of th poor vessels.

Q. You used a term, eel-grass mackerel ?—A. Yes.

Q. Well, is that a term that is used on your shores at all ?—A. T is a term that all those fishermen use when they catch mackerel insho They are an inferior quality, with black bellies. I have some of th on board now.

Q. Is it a term in use on your own shores ?—A. Yes.

Q. Then you consider that your mackerel caught inshore are infer to those caught outside ?—A. Yes; we think that is so anywhere.

Q. Couldn't you catch the best mackerel on your shore in close ?— Well, there are times when the mackerel will run in there to chase bait in.

Q. Is it not the fact that the best mackerel are caught inside at Bl Island ?—A. I never fished there. I don't think they catch any in Blo Island, within five or six miles of it.

Q. Are you acquainted with Rustico ?—A. I have been up and do' there.

Q. Are not they the very best quality of mackerel caught ?—A. would not call them so.

Q. That would be a matter of opinion ?—A. Well, I could not c them so. I prefer fishing in a little deeper water. To make good, ni white fish I prefer them caught in deeper water.

Q. What depth would you say ?—A. I want them over eight fathor You can't get a very big depth in the Bay of St. Lawrence anywh until you sail to the northward.

Q. Now, don't you think the same fish go out and in. Is it yc idea that certain schools keep in one place and certain schools another? Is it not your idea that the same mackerel go out and in?—A. Yes, it is my opinion that the mackerel go out and in, and we know they do. But it is my positive idea that the best fish that go into the Bay Chaleurs go through the strait and by Sydney.

Q. Do you mean the Strait of Canso?—A. No, the Strait of Belleisle and come down to Sydney.

Q. What time?—A. Well, they are passing up and down there after the month of August until they all go out.

Q. You think these are not the same as you catch off the north of the island?—A. No, I don't.

Q. Do you think your opinion is general?—A. Yes, sir.

Q. That they are a different class of fish altogether?—A. Yes.

Q. Might it not be just that you catch them later in the year when they are fatter?—A. Well, after September comes in they don't fat up much.

Q. Don't you think it is because you get later and fatter mackerel?—A. No, I don't think that is the reason. I don't think fish fatten any after the middle of September.

Q. At any rate take the coast of the island itself. If you fish out in deep water you think you catch better fish?—A. Yes.

Q. Then you must be under the impression that they divide and the best remain outside while the poor ones come inside?—A. I don't know but what one fish is as good as another, but it takes food to make the fish.

Q. Is it not a fact that they feed in close to the shore?—A. There is food, but not such healthy food as outside.

Q. That is your theory?—A. Yes.

Q. Then it is altogether a question of food. You think they get better food inside?—A. Yes.

Q. And if it turned out that they got better food inshore you would change your opinion? You would say, then, that you would catch more mackerel inshore than off? If you found that the mackerel got their food inshore, you would perhaps change your opinion with regard to the matter?—A. Well, if there was better fish inshore than off, I should know there was better food inshore.

Q. Well, if the mackerel feed in eight fathoms, wherever that is, to-day, are they not to be found inshore to-morrow? Don't the same mackerel move about?—A. They move just which way the food moves.

Q. Then they move about everywhere?—A. Well, I could not say for that. I have caught mackerel for four or five days in one place and not seen any again for three weeks.

Q. Was that the same school, do you think, or were they moving about?—A. I think the fish was moving about.

Q. The first you encountered would be away, and others would fill their places?—A. Yes.

Q. Off the bend of the island will you not find eight fathoms within a mile of the island in many places?—A. Yes, there are many places there that you will find eight fathoms within a mile, I presume.

Q. Within half a mile?—A. Well, I never looked personally on the chart. I never calculated to stop around there a great deal, anyhow.

Q. What you mean is, that if you find them in eight fathoms you would get the best mackerel there?—A. No, I don't mean that.

Q. Well, suppose you would catch them in eight fathoms, would you call them eel-grass mackerel?—A. No, if they were nice fish I should not. If they were poor fish, with black bellies, I would call them eel-grass mackerel. It doesn't make any odds if they were caught in two fathoms.

No. 44.

EDWARD A. GOOGINS, of Portland, Maine, called on behalf of Government of the United States, sworn and examined.

By Mr. Dana:

Question. You are in what vessel now ?—Answer. The Esperanza

Q. You are in here accidentally ?—A. Yes.

Q. You came in here for a harbor ?—A. Yes.

Q. You are bound home ?—A. Yes.

Q. You have got through your fishing ?—A. Yes.

Q. Now, when did you begin to go fishing ?—A. When I was 14 y old.

Q. You were born in the year ——— ?—A. 1834.

Q. That would make it 1848 when you went fishing ?—A. Yes.

Q. Where were you living then ?—A. At Trenton, Maine.

Q. That is the custom-house district of Ellsworth ?—A. Yes.

Q. At that time when you first went fishing where did you go ?—I went to Grand Manan.

Q. How many years were you fishing off Grand Manan ?—A. Se years.

Q. Until you were 21 ?—A. Yes.

Q. Were you a skipper any of that time ?—A. No; I was alwa hand.

Q. Seven years you were a Trenton fisherman off Grand Manan ?—Yes; Grand Manan and Nova Scotia.

Q. Now, where did you first go when the season began ?—A. In spring ?

Q. Yes.—A. Around Nova Scotia.

Q. To what part ?—A. Digby, Petit Passage, and Brier Island.

Q. For what ?—A. Codfish.

Q. That was spring fishing ?—A. Yes.

Q. During these seven seasons in the spring, when you caught co that part of Nova Scotia, where did you catch them ? How far 1 land ?—A. The principal part 12 miles from land ; we judged 12, 1 15.

Q. Did you ever know of the distance being measured any time ?—Only once ; around the island.

Q. What was the nearest to land that you ever fished ?—A. I miles.

Now, how do you know it was four miles ?—A. Well, there was : tle dispute there. The natives of the island made a complaint to a n of-war that the American fishermen fished within three miles of land ; and the place they called within three miles was "Gravelly tom," on the southeast part of Grand Manan, right off from Gi Manan, at the southeast end. They measured, and found it was miles from the nearest land to where the American fishermen fis Inside of that is deep water. On that it is shoal.

Q. So you were fishing on a shoal ?—A. Yes ; shoal water.

Q. It turned out to be four miles ?—A. Yes.

Q. That is the nearest you ever went ?—A. Yes ; the nearest I fished in an American vessel.

Q. And your codfish you caught twelve or fifteen miles off ?—A. 1 is the nearest we could judge.

Q. While you were fishing for cod there what bait did you use ?—Herring.

Q. Did you go in for it?—A. We went in for it.

Q. To what place?—A. A number of places.

Q. Whatever place was nearest?—A. Yes.

Q. When did you generally go, on what day?—A. Generally on Saturday. We used to calculate to go in on Saturday, because we didn't fish on Sundays.

Q. None of your vessels fished on Sundays?—A. None I know of.

Q. Do you know any American vessels that fished inside of three miles?—A. No; I never heard of any.

Q. Well, you would meet them going in for bait?—A. Yes.

Q. Was it the custom to talk very freely with one another?—A. Yes.

Q. Do you think you got free and honest reports of where they fished?—A. Well, very near, for the very reason that we lived right close by one another. We could find out after a while.

Q. Do you know of any, during those seven seasons, that fished nearer than three miles?—A. No.

Q. Was that cod fishery pretty successful?—A. Sometimes it was, and sometimes not.

Q. Taken as a whole?—A. Yes, it was, taken as a whole.

Q. Did you move to Grand Manan to live?—A. Yes.

Q. When did you move to Grand Manan? The next year after you were twenty-one?—A. The next year after.

Q. You had a house there and were married?—A. No; I was married; my wife belonged to the island.

Q. You went to Grand Manan to live?—A. Yes.

Q. You engaged in fishing?—A. Yes.

Q. Boat-fishing?—A. Yes.

Q. You changed from vessel-fishing to boat-fishing?—A. Yes.

Q. Describe this boat-fishing. How big were the boats?—A. Twenty feet keel.

Q. She had no forecastle?—A. No; only a small temporary cuddy we rigged up ourselves.

Q. I will go back to the time you were fishing in vessels. Why was it you didn't fish nearer than four miles?—A. One reason was that they would not allow us, and another reason was that we could not do as well.

Q. If you had been allowed, if you had been left to your own preferences, which would you do?—A. We would prefer to fish outside, for the reason that the boats were in there and they could get more bait than we got. Their own vessels that were there could not do so well inside as outside at the time I was there.

Q. What did you learn from the inhabitants, as well as from the vessels, as to the American vessels? Did they ever tell you that the American vessels were within three miles?—A. No, I never heard only the one complaint. That was before I went there to live, and while I was there to live I never heard any complaints of the American vessels fishing inside.

Q. How long were you there?—A. I was there nine years.

Q. During these nine years you had a boat or boats about 20 feet in length?—A. Yes.

Q. Intended for a single day?—A. Yes.

Q. To come in nights?—A. Yes. We took our dinners with us.

Q. Tell me, if you please, what fishing you did the different seasons of the year in boats?—A. Well, in the spring we used to commence in May generally, sometimes a little earlier.

154 F

Q. What did you catch then?—A. We would catch a very few fish, mostly hake.

Q. Well, the hake is a rather inferior fish?—A. Yes.

Q. Were they plenty or few?—A. They were scattering along i spring. We didn't calculate to do a great deal anyway.

Q. Now you have fished seven years outside for cod and nine in boats, I suppose mostly inside?—A. Yes, mostly inside.

Q. You can therefore compare them. Now which furnished the | est number and the best fish?—A. Outside.

Q. There is no question about it?—A. No question about that.

Q. The hake is an inferior fish for eating. What does it furni: A. It furnishes most oil of anything.

Q. What is next? After a few scattered cod and hake princi what is next?—A. The next is the hake in July and August to tember. We catch these by night.

Q. Night fishing. What is next?—A. Generally herring fishi the fall.

Q. From October to when?—A. To Christmas or New Year.

Q. That finishes the boat fishing for the season?—A. No. after the herring strikes in one place, it comes in another, and w enough for bait. In winter we get small codfish. They are smal they will do for pickling.

Q. And you set nets in the winter?—A. Yes.

Q. You set them from the Grand Manan?—A. Yes.

Q. Is it in the nets you catch small cod?—A. No; with line.

Q. Now, when the codfish are very abundant and better offshore did you take them inshore with boats?—A. Because I could be every night to see my family. I had a house on the island, and a little place. I could take care of that and be at home. I could d work and fish too. That is why I preferred boat fishing to vesse ing. I would not have to be gone all the time.

Q. Now, that year, 1865, you spoke of nine seasons when you boat fishing—what did you then do?—A. I moved across into Ma

Q. Near Eastport?—A. Yes.

Q. What is the name of the town?—A. Trescot, Washington Co

Q. How many years did you live at Trescot?—A. I lived there 1865 to the 28th of this last July.

Q. All that time working on shore?—A. Yes; I had nothing with fishing. This year I started fishing again.

Q. This vessel, the Esperanza, belongs to Rockland?—A. Yes.

Q. You were to the gulf?—A. Yes.

Q. How many were you fitted out for?—A. I understood, when we fitted for 240 barrels.

Q. How much have you got in all?—A. 110 barrels.

Q. That is in sea-barrels?—A. Yes.

Q. That is a very unfavorable result?—A. Well, I should think am not used to mackerel-fishing.

Q. You said the 28th July you went; did you go through Can A. Yes.

Q. Do you recollect the date?—A. No.

Q. How many days had you been out when you went through We were some time getting ready from the time I went aboard. were ten days, I think, going down.

Q. You can't recollect the date of your going through?—A. No

Q. You got in here night before last for harbor?—A. Yes.

Q. Have you been pretty well around the gulf?—A. Well, I

was there before. I could not tell you whether I have been pretty near around, or half, or a quarter of the way.

Q. Did you fish inshore as well as outside?—A. Well, it is useless to ask me any questions about that. As the land is low there I would not pass my judgment anything about this trip at all.

Q. About the distance?—A. No.

Q. This is your first experience of the bay mackerel-fishing?—A. Yes.

Q. It will probably be the last?—A. I think very likely it will. I don't think I made enough to entice me to go again.

By Mr. Foster:

Q. Your last knowledge of Grand Manan was the year 1865?—A. Yes.

By Mr. Davies:

Q. Off what shores did you fish this year in the Esperanza? Did you know the shores?—A. I didn't know the shores; I was a stranger there.

Q. You heard from those on board, though, what place?—A. They said they were fishing off the west shore, and there was one place they called North Cape, Prince Edward Island.

Q. East Point, Prince Edward Island. did you hear that?—A. Yes; I was there. We came down and up by it.

Q. Up and down the shore of the island?—A. We did not stop anywhere.

Q. You stopped at both ends?—A. Yes; we fished there.

Q. The fleet was fishing, I understand, chiefly about East Point and North Cape?—A. Yes.

Q. Many of them?—A. I should judge around North Cape there were fifteen or sixteen sail, perhaps twenty. I did not count them. At East Point I should think something like fifty sail when we were there.

Q. I suppose you didn't make any inquiries what they caught?—A. No.

Q. Did you go down the Cape Breton shore?—A. Only to Port Hood.

Q. Did you catch any there?—A. I think fifteen barrels, off shore.

Q. What other place?—A. I have mentioned all, except Georgetown.

Q. Well, that is part of Prince Edward Island. Whatever fish you did catch were caught in one or other of those places? You could not tell how far off?—A. No; you need not ask me any questions about that.

Q. You could see the land?—A. Yes.

Q. You saw the cows walking on it?—A. I don't think—I don't know that I ever saw one walking there; I don't know that they keep any cattle.

Q. Did you go ashore?—A. Once, in Georgetown. I saw a horse there once; that is the only kind of cattle I saw.

Q. It is a pretty good country for horses?—A. I don't know, I only saw one.

Q. Speaking seriously, do you mean to say you can't give an opinion as to the distance you were from the shore off East Point?—A. I could not.

Q. The captain of the Esperanza said they were fitted out for 200 barrels, not 240.—A. Well, I might have made a mistake; I might have misunderstood.

Q. What was the size of the vessel?—A. 43 or 44 tons.

Q. She would not like to carry more than 200 barrels. How many of a crew have you got?—A. Ten men.

Q. Just one question or two now about Grand Manan. You went in 1848, and fished for seven years on board American vessels?—A. Yes.

Q. You didn't fish there in American vessels after the Reciproc[i] Treaty came in ? It was before that that the complaint was made ?— I think it was. I was nothing but a boy at the time.

Q. You paid very little attention to where you were fishing ?—A know we were not fishing inside of that line, because there was nothi there to catch.

Q. There are plenty of fish to be caught within ?—A. No.

Q. The boat-fishing when you left there was chiefly inside ? Am I [r] correct in saying that the boats catch most of their fish inside ?—A. Y Sometimes they go out, but very seldom.

Q. I want to just understand correctly. Nearly all the fish cau[g] by the boats are caught inside ?—A. Yes.

Q. Then the fish are there to be caught ?—A. Yes.

Q. Very well; and did you as a boy, fishing, pay particular attenti to whether you were in or out ?—A. We knew we were out, becaus know all the grounds we were on. We fished on them year after ye

Q. You were asked why you didn't go in and said you were prohibite you said because the people didn't allow you.—A. I said because a m[a] of-war didn't allow us.

Mr. DANA. He gave two reasons.

Mr. DAVIES. I should say one would be quite sufficient.

Mr. DANA. He could dodge a man-of-war if it was worth while.

By Mr. Davies:

Q. Would you dodge a man-of-war to get inside ?—A. I don't kn what I might do. I never had the chance to try.

Q. The temptation was not thrown in your way. Now, I want to [a] you, do you know anything about the fishing carried on there in win' by American vessels ?—A. I do not.

Q. Then, for aught you know, they may fish inside altogether in w ter ?—A. They do not.

Q. Did I understand you correctly that you understood nothing ab[o] it ? You said you knew nothing about the fishing in there in winter A. No, nor summer either.

Q. I asked if you had ever fished aboard an American vessel winter about Grand Manan.—A. No; never.

Q. At any time of your life ?—A. No.

Q. Did you ever see any fishing there in winter ?—A. No.

Q. So you absolutely know nothing of it at all ?—A. No; I absolut know——

Q. Did I understand that you absolutely knew nothing of it at all A. I don't understand your question. I wish you would put it plain[e]

Q. I understand that you never fished on board a vessel in the win about Grand Manan ?—A. I have said.

Q. And also that you never saw an American vessel fishing in win anywhere about the island ?—A. Well, I could not go over the island at once. I never heard about it.

Q. Then am I correct in saying you know nothing about it ?—A know nothing about it further than that.

Q. I mean within or outside of three miles ?—A. I never saw [a] American vessel around there in the winter that I can recollect.

Q. Then I am correct in saying you know nothing about whether t[h] do or not ?—A. I never saw them. How can I tell ?

Q. Do you know Walter B. McLaughlin ?—A. I have seen him.

Q. How many years is it since you left Grand Manan altogether ? Twelve years, I think, or thirteen. I left in 1865.

Q. Then, since you have left Grand Manan you know nothing, I suppose, of the number of vessels ?—A. No; I have never seen the island, that I recollect, since, any more than at a distance.

Q. As to the period during the last twelve years, you don't profess to say anything about it at all ?—A. No.

Q. When you were there, after the end of the seven years, you fished in boats yourself ?—A. Yes.

Q. What kind of a man is McLaughlin; a respectable man ?—A. He is considered so.

Q. Is it possible that the fishing may have changed since you were there ? I will read Mr. McLaughlin's statement with reference to the Grand Manan fishery. He was asked: " Now, about how many American vessels fish on the coast during the season ? " He answers: " It would be hard to tell that. It has never been my duty to count them." He was asked: " They come in large numbers and they greatly outnumber ours ? " He answers: " Yes ; our people at Grand Manan fish but little in vessels." He is asked again: " Do these vessels come in fishing within three miles ? " And he answers: "At a certain time of the year. In winter it is entirely within. The fall and winter fishing is entirely within." Now that may be the case for the last twelve years ; you don't profess to know ?—A. I don't profess to know anything about that.

By Mr. Dana :

Q. While you were there you saw no American vessels fishing there ?—A. No.

No. 45.

ISAAC BURGESS, of Belfast, Me., fisherman, called on behalf of the Government of the United States, sworn and examined.

By Mr. Foster :

Question. You are one of the sharesmen on board the Eliza Poor, Captain Dickie, and are twenty-four years old ?—Answer. Yes.

Q. When did you begin fishing for mackerel in the Gulf of St. Lawrence ?—A. In 1868.

Q. You must have been a little fellow then ?—A. Yes; fifteen years old.

Q. Do you remember the name of the schooner ?—A. The Oak Grove, Captain Burgess.

Q. How many barrels did you take ?—A. 210 barrels.

Q. Where was she from ?—A. Belfast.

Q. How long was she taking them ?—A. She was somewhere in the neighborhood of seven or eight weeks. They were taken off shore on Bradley.

Q. Any within three miles ?—A. No.

Q. Take the next time.—A. 1869. I was in the James Jewett, Captain Henry Coombes.

Q. Where from ?—A. Belfast.

Q. How many barrels of mackerel did she take ?—A. 273.

Q. Now where were these taken ?—A. On the West Shore, Escuminac, North Cape, East Point, and some at Magdalens.

Q. Well, if any of those were taken within three miles of the shore, state at what place and how many ?—A. I don't think we caught any within three miles of the shore.

Q. What was the next year ?—A. 1872.

Q. What vessel?—A. The Mary Louise, Oscar Fitch, captain, Gloucester.

Q. What was her size?—A. 70 tons, I think.

Q. Did you make more than one trip?—A. Two trips.

Q. When did you go into the gulf?—A. We came in the first tr think, in June.

Q. What did you do with that first trip?—A. We took them bac Gloucester.

Q. How long were you gone the first trip?—A. About a month.

Q. How many barrels did you get?—A. 273 barrels the first trip

Q. Where did you take them?—A. We took them around the isl North Cape, and Magdalen Islands.

Q. How many at the Magdalens?—A. We got half our trip ther

Q. How many off the island?—A. Probably 40 or 50 barrels.

Q. When fishing off the island, how near shore did you fish?— don't think we fished less than four miles, four or five.

Q. Where else did you catch any part of your trip?—A. Some bet' Port Hood and East Point.

Q. Were those, any of them, within three miles?—A. No.

Q. Did you get any within three miles that trip?—A. A few at a ¡ called Rustico one day within three miles. That is all during that

Q. Well, how did you happen to be at Rustico?—A. We saw ¡ small boats in fishing, springing up, and we went in there and them. It came on to blow that night and we had to go out. It w; the Bend, and we had to get off shore.

Q. How many barrels did you get?—A. 80 barrels that day, Rustico.

Q. Take the next year?—A. That was 1874. I was in the A Salem, Captain Elbridge Love, of Booth Bay.

Q. How many barrels of mackerel did you take?—A. 173 barre

Q. How long were you getting them?—A. Somewhere in the n borhood of nine weeks.

Q. When did you begin?—A. We came away from home abou 1st of August. We were a week, I believe, getting down.

Q. Where were those taken?—A. They were taken at the Magda some around East Point, and some around Port Hood. The most o' trip at the Magdalen Islands.

Q. Now the Alice, Salem, is put down that year as having come i the 9th August one trip, and having gone home the 15th of Oct Are those dates about right? Did you begin about August and about the 15th October?—A. I think we did.

Q. But she is said to have taken 275 barrels?—A. 173 barrels w; we got aboard when I was aboard.

Q. Who was the fish merchant to whom she packed out?—A. Ch A. Dyer.

Q. May you be mistaken 100 barrels?—A. No; I am not.

Q. Most of those you say were taken at Magdalen Islands?—A.

Q. If any of them were taken within three miles, state where? They were not.

Q. Well, this year you are in the Eliza Poor. As we have heard her through others, I will not delay about that.

By Mr. Weatherbe:

Q. I didn't take down the year you made two trips and got 273 rels. What year was it?—A. That was in 1872.

Q. Where were you in 1870 and 1871?—A. In 1871 I was to wo Booth Bay in a factory.

Q. In 1874 you were in the Alice?—A. Yes.

Q. You are sure that was the year?—A. Yes.

Q. You left her. How many trips did you make?—A. Only one trip. I left her at Portland when she came home that trip.

Q. Who was the master?—A. Elbridge Love.

Q. Had you any Nova Scotia fishermen in her?—A. I don't know that we did. I cannot say. We had all kinds, Spaniards, Portuguese, French.

Q. Any from the provinces?—A. No; I don't think we did.

Q. None at all?—A. No.

Q. In some of these other years, did you have fishermen belonging to the provinces?—A. No; mostly from the State of Maine—from Belfast.

Q. But this year, 1874, you had foreigners?—A. Yes; we had mostly.

Q. Not much accustomed to fishing?—A. Poor fishermen generally.

Q. How many tons was she?—A. I think from 71 to 76 tons; 71, I am pretty sure.

Q. The previous vessel, what was her name?—A. The Oak Grove; that was 1868.

Q. In 1869?—A. I was in the James Jewett.

Q. The next one, what was the name?—A. That was in 1872—the Mary Louise.

Q. Had you Spaniards and Portuguese that trip?—A. No; mostly Americans.

Q. What was her tonnage?—A. I could not say exactly what the tonnage was. I think somewhere in the neighborhood of 70 or 75 tons.

Q. You caught your mackerel four miles off?—A. Yes.

Q. What proportion?—A. Half of them. I could not tell.

Q. I suppose that would be the distance you would select as being good fishing?—A. Yes, sir.

Q. That would be the best fishing you have?—A. Yes, sir.

Q. I suppose most of the fishermen fished that distance?—A. Yes; they generally fished off there, near four or five miles.

Q. It is considered about the best fishing, four or five miles?—A. Yes; it is.

Q. I suppose in some places the fish would go in three and a half miles?—A. Yes, some fish do.

Q. You would not mind coming in three and a half miles if you were four miles out. I suppose sometimes they would manage to get in three miles?—A. No vessels I have ever been in.

Q. I am not speaking of the vessels, but the fish—is there anything to stop them at four miles?—A. No.

Q. There is no obstruction of any kind. Just as good water?—A. Yes; only a little shallower.

Q. Just as good feed?—A. Yes.

Q. Perhaps better feed?—A. Well, most generally the gales drive them off, but they come back again.

Q. I suppose when the wind is a little off shore the best feed would be inside, closer in?—A. Yes.

Q. Closer inside than four miles?—A. I should say so.

Q. They would then go in pretty close?—A. Yes.

Q. You would then go in there and drift off?—A. Yes.

Q. And the fleet would do that. We have evidence of that. The fleet would run in as close as they could get and then drift off?—A. Yes; that was the way they fished.

Q. As close as they could get in?—A. Not within four miles.

Q. I was referring to a little closer. I wanted to come in a little closer if I could. I was throwing a little bait?—A. Well, probal there might have been some fellows go in handier.

Q. Some would go in nearer?—A. Yes; some of the captains went

Q. Let us make a compromise and say three miles and a half. Y don't object to that, do you? (No answer.)

No. 46.

CHARLES H. BRIER, of Belfast, Me., called on behalf of the Gove ment of the United States, sworn and examined.

By Mr. Trescot:

Question. You are a Belfast man?—Answer. Yes.

Q. When did you get here?—A. Night before last.

Q. You came in the Eliza Poor?—A. Yes.

Q. What brought her in?—A. The storm.

Q. How old are you?—A. Twenty-five.

Q. How long have you been fishing?—A. Fifteen years.

Q. When did you start?—A. When I was ten years old.

Q. What sort of fishing have you been doing?—A. Mackerel-fishii

Q. Where?—A. Four years in the bay and the rest on our coast.

Q. What four years in the bay?—A. '67, '68, '70, and '77.

Q. Well, the first year you went in what vessel?—A. The Atlan

Q. Where from?—A. Belfast.

Q. Where did you go to fish?—A. To the bay.

Q. Whereabouts in the bay?—A. From East Point to North Cape

Q. Did you make one or two trips?—A. One.

Q. How long was it?—A. Two or three months.

Q. Well, don't you recollect more particularly? Do you mean two three?—A. About three.

Q. What did you catch?—A. We caught mackerel.

Q. What was the result of your fishing?—A. 200 barrels.

Q. Now, what proportion of these did you take within three miles' A. Of the 200 barrels we took 100 within three miles.

Q. Then in 1868, what vessel were you in?—A. The Rippling Wa

Q. Where were you that year?—A. From North Cape to East Po and Escuminac.

Q. How many trips?—A. One.

Q. What tonnage was she?—A. Over 100 tons.

Q. How long did your trip last?—A. Three months.

Q. What did you take?—A. 250 barrels.

Q. Now, with regard to those 250 barrels, what proportion of th were taken within three miles?—A. They were taken off shore mos

Q. Where were you in 1870?—A. In the Eliza Poor.

Q. Where were you that year?—A. We went around the island Escuminac, the West Shore.

Q. Was that one or two trips?—A. One trip.

Q. What did you take that year?—A. About 200 barrels. We w there about three months.

Q. Now what proportion of that catch was taken within three mil —A. About one half.

Q. Then in 1877 what vessel were you in?—A. The Eliza Poor.

Q. What did you do that year?—A. We got 110 barrels.

Q. That is the same voyage you are coming in now?—A. Yes.

Q. When did you go?—A. The 9th August.

Q. When did you come out?—A. About a week ago; we came last Sunday.

Q. You got 110 barrels. What proportion of those were taken within three miles?—A. About one-half.

Q. Then only four years you have been in the bay?—A. Yes.

Q. The rest you have been on the coast; now, how does your fishing on the coast compare in point of success with the fishing in the gulf?—A. It is better on our coast the last ten years.

Q. I am talking of the time you have been there?—A. Yes.

Q. Is the fishing on the coast as expensive as in the gulf?—A. I don't think.

Q. In the fishing on the coast that you made, did you make long or short trips?—A. Short trips.

Q. Do you recollect your last trip?—A. Yes; we got between 900 and 1,000.

Q. In what time?—A. Five months, I should think.

Q. Well, you have been fishing fifteen years. As between fishing in the gulf and fishing in the bay, as a fishing industry, which is best?—A. I should rather fish on the coast, a great deal.

Q. Do you know anything about Prince Edward Island boat-fishing?—A. I have seen a good deal of it this year; we met the boats off the North Cape and East Point.

Q. How far did they come off?—A. A mile and a half to two and three miles.

By Mr. Doutre:

Q. Since fishing on the American coast is so much better than in the bay, why do you go in the bay?—A. Well, it failed this year; we had to go in the bay.

Q. When it is better at home you remain there, and when it is better in the gulf you go there?—A. Yes.

Q. That is quite sensible. You say it is not so expensive fishing on the coast. Please explain why.—A. Well, it does not cost so much. I don't know exactly. It is a good deal more expensive coming down to the bay than home.

Q. Well, why? Is it because you have more hands, or that more provisions are eaten—that they have a better appetite in the bay than on the coast? What is it?—A. I don't know.

Q. You don't fit on the American coast for three months because you may be only a week out?—A. We fit for three or four weeks.

Q. Very well, but you are not starting on such a long expedition as when you go to the bay. That is the reason you don't fit out so completely. Is it so?—A. We mostly always have to fit out once or twice in the bay.

Q. Suppose you had to fit out for the same length of time on the American coast that you have in the gulf, would it cost much less?—A. No, about the same thing.

Q. When you were in the Atlantic in 1867 where did she fish?—A. In the bend of the island, from East Point to North Cape.

Q. How far from the shore have you been fishing?—A. Fishing from ten to fifteen miles off most of the time.

Q. Did you go near shore?—A. Right off Malpeque we ran in.

Q. When you were going in the harbors didn't you fish in the neighborhood around the island?—A. We fished inshore part of the time. The great part of the time off shore, ten or fifteen miles, I should say.

Q. Can you state now where you were longer fishing, whether it was out ten miles, as you say, or near the shore?—A. Most of the time off shore.

Q. What have you to remind you of that?—A. I think becau would take quite a while to run inshore when we wanted to.

Q. What do you call inshore?—A. Two or three miles off.

Q. Can you find out easily whether you are three miles or four n or five miles off?—A. I don't know how we can.

Q. Suppose you were about five or four miles, would you call off shore or inshore?—A. I would call it inshore.

Q. Then, what leads you to say you caught about half your inshore and half out?—A. Because we did, I suppose. We had a lic to fish inshore, and we fished there.

Q. You were not afraid of going in there; so long as you found you fished there?—A. Yes.

Q. Well, you had no reason whatever, had you, to take a note of quantity taken inshore or outshore—what reminds you now of the fac A. I don't know anything to remind me, only that we fished about the time off shore, and caught about as many fishing off shore as in

Q. In your second trip did you follow about the same spots as in first trip?—A. We went to North Cape, Escuminac, and West Sho

Q. How far from shore?—A. Sometimes we would be in sight of and sometimes off shore.

Q. Well, if you were called upon to state what proportion you ca inshore and what proportion off shore?—A. We caught them m off shore.

Q. Well, that is not very definite?—A. We might have got 50 o 250 barrels inshore.

Q. Not more than that? In the Eliza Poor you got more inshore that?—A. Yes.

Q. Both years?—A. Yes.

Q. The mackerel that you caught on the Amercan coast—did you it, or was it sold fresh?—A. It was salted.

Q. How many trips did you make during the five months?—A. carried about 250 barrels a trip—from 50 to 250. The largest trips 250.

Q. Since 1870 you have not fished on the American coast. Wha did you make of the time during these years?—A. I worked on s part of the time, and part of the time I fished.

Q. From 1870 to 1877 you did not fish at all?—A. 1877?

Q. The last time you came in the bay was 1870?—A. Well, I fi on our coast.

Q. During that interval?—A. Yes.

Q. Did you fish last year?—A. Yes.

Q. What was your catch?—A. 900 or 1,000 barrels.

Q. What distance from the coast generally is the mackerel take the American shore?—A. Mostly off shore.

Q. For the last year or two?—A. The most of our fish are abroa

No. 47.

DEXTER F. WALSH, of Belfast, Me., fisherman, called on beha the Government of the United States, sworn and examined.

By Mr. Foster:

Question. You live at Portland?—Answer. No, at Belfast.

Q. You were in the Eliza Poor?—A. Yes.

Q. What was the first year you were ever mackereling in the Gt St. Lawrence?—A. 1867.

Q. How many barrels did you take ?—A. 300.

Q. Where ?—A. At Magdalens.

Q. Anywhere else ?—A. We caught about all there, I think.

Q. Take 1869, what vessel were you in ?—A. In the Morning Star,. Captain Moore.

Q. How many barrels of mackerel did you take ?—A. I think we took, in 1869, 240 barrels in two trips.

Q. How long were you here ?—A. About four months in the bay.

Q. Where were these taken ?—A. At the Magdalens mostly.

Q. Where else ?—A. I don't remember fishing anywhere else—West Shore and Prince Edward Island.

Q. In 1876 you were in the gulf again ?—A. No.

Q. Were you not in the gulf last year ?—A. Yes.

Q. In what schooner ?—A. The Alice M. Gould.

Q. How long were you here ?—A. Four months, two trips—one for cod and one for mackerel.

Q. How long were you in the gulf mackereling ?—A. Two months.

Q. How many men have you had ?—A. 14 mackereling.

Q. How many barrels have you got ?—A. 40.

Q. In two months ?—A. Yes.

Q. Where were these taken ?—A. At Port Hood, Cape George, and East Point.

Q. I need not ask you whether you made any money last year ?—A. I was cook and made $50 a month.

Q. But from catches was any money made ?—A. No. The crew came home in debt.

Q. Not only the vessel but the crew ?—A. The vessel and the crew both.

Q. This year you have been in the Eliza Poor ?—A. Since the 4th of August.

Q. We have had an account of the trip; I think I won't go over that again.

By Mr. Davies:

Q. Were you master of these vessels ?—A. No.

Q. You were in the Morning Star in 1869. Who was her captain then ?—A. George Moore.

Q. When you were there this year how many barrels did you take ?—A. 120.

Q. Where were you fishing ?—A. Around the west shore of Prince Edward Island, and Escuminac, some around East Point.

Q. Every year there are more or less got there ?—A. Yes.

Q. The first year, '67, you were not there at all ?—A. No; at the Magdalens.

Q. And since that you have been generally fishing those grounds ?—A. Yes. The second year we fished mostly at the Magdalens.

Q. The last year you have been fishing over this ground ?—A. Yes. I haven't been at the Magdalens this year at all.

Q. When; '76 ?—A. No; I was not there last year.

Q. Why didn't you go there last year and this year ?—A. I don't know why.

Q. The fleet was fishing around East Point and Port Hood ?—A. We had news from the Magdalens that they were not doing anything there, I suppose. We generally know what is going on all round the bay.

Q. You got a very small catch last year ?—A. Yes.

Q. That was not the average ?—A. Yes, I think it was.

Q. What time did you go in?—A. We went in, I think, some time about the 15th of August.

Q. You missed the best catches of the year?—A. We were cod-fishing when the best mackereling was going on. All the vessels did poorly anyway. Only a few vessels got a trip.

Q. In '69 you were off the island too?—A. Yes.

Q. Did you catch many off the island shore?—A. No. We got most of our trip off the Magdalens.

Q. How far off the island did the boats fish?—A. Four or five miles.

Q. The last witness said half a mile to a mile and a half or two miles?—A. They fished all distances.

Q. Why did you say four miles, then? Have you seen them over a mile or two or three miles?—A. Yes.

Q. Is not that generally the distance they fish?—A. I could not say.

Q. Why; haven't you been sufficiently long?—A. I have seen them fishing inside and outside of three miles.

Q. Haven't you been there sufficiently long this season and last season to see?—A. I should say the boats we saw this year were fishing three miles off.

Q. But you got your fish inside?—A. Some of them.

Q. The boats were outside of you?—A. Sometimes they were.

Q. How far would you be off when the boats would be outside of you?—A. Perhaps a mile.

Q. Then they might be outside of you and still be well within three miles?—A. Yes.

Q. You give it as your evidence that most of the time the boats were four miles from land; and when you say that you caught none within three miles, you mean that you caught them at the same distance as the boats?—A. Some of them fished four miles off and some further.

Q. The bulk I mean; do you mean that?—A. Yes; they fished four or five miles off.

Q. Do you know Charles H. Brien, who was examined here?—A. Yes.

Q. He stated that the boats fished from half a mile to a mile or two. Did he tell the truth or not?—A. I have seen them as near as that.

Q. You don't agree with him?—A. Yes, I do.

No. 48.

LAWRENCE LONDRIGAN, of St. Mary's Bay, Newfoundland, fisherman, called on behalf of the Government of the United States, sworn and examined.

By Mr. Foster:

Question. You were born in Newfoundland?—Answer. Yes.

Q. How long have you been away from there?—A. Three years this coming fall.

Q. How old are you?—A. Twenty-eight or twenty-nine years last fall.

Q. What did you do the first year you left Newfoundland?—A. The first year I was in America. I trawled on the coast of Maine.

Q. What schooner?—A. Liberator.

Q. From what port did she sail?—A. Westport, Me.

Q. You went trawling for what?—A. Codfish and hake principally.

Q. Whereabouts did you trawl?—A. Off the coast of Maine and along Seal Island Bay.

Q. You made short trips?—A. Yes.

Q. Were you getting fish to salt?—A. To sell green.

Q. To be salted ?—A. We salted them ourselves.

Q. What bait did you use ?—A. The first summer we used clams and afterwards pogies and menhaden.

Q. Salted ?—A. The clams were salted, but the pogies were kept in ice.

Q. Not sliver ?—A. We iced them ourselves.

Q. What were you doing last year ?—A. I was mackereling last summer.

Q. In what vessel ?—A. Lizzie Poore.

Q. On the United States coast ?—Yes.

Q. What were you doing last winter ?—A. I left to go in a vessel for frozen herring last December.

Q. What is the name of the vessel ?—A. J. W. Roberts.

Q. Where did she hail from ?—A. Rockport, Me.

Q. Who was her captain ?—A. P. Conley.

Q. When did she start from Rockport ?—A. 26th December.

Q. How long were you gone ?—A. We were at Beaver Harbor and round Grand Manan about two weeks.

Q. Were other vessels there ?—A. Yes.

Q. How many ?—A. Electric Flash, Madawaska Maid, Mary Turner, Episcatawa.

Q. How many frozen herring did you get ?—A. 300,000.

Q. Where did you obtain them ?—A. Some were bought frozen and some we bought green and took ashore, and some we froze on the deck of the vessel.

Q. What did you pay for them ?—A. For most of them fifty cents a hundred; for about 25,000, forty five cents a hundred.

Q. Did you catch any yourselves ?—A. No, we had no means of catching any.

Q. You purchased them for money ?—A. Yes, for money.

Q. This summer you have been in the Lizzie Poore ?—A. Yes.

Q. Have you any idea what your share is going to be ?—A. No, I have not the slightest.

By Mr. Davies:

Q. The fish you bought down at Grand Manan were frozen partly on deck and partly on shore ?—A. Yes, and some were bought frozen.

Q. Those you bought in a green state you landed ?—A. Some of them.

Q. And froze them there yourselves, and then transferred them to the vessel ?—A. Yes.

No. 49.

RICHARD HOPKINS, of Belfast, Me., fisherman, called on behalf of the Government of the United States, sworn and examined.

By Mr. Trescot:

Question. How old are you ?—Answer. Sixty-three years.

Q. Where do you live ?—A. At Belfast.

Q. Were you born there ?—A. No, at Vinehaven.

Q. How far is that from Belfast ?—A. Thirty-five miles.

Q. How many years have you been fishing ?—A. Forty years.

Q. What vessel are you now in ?—A. Esperanza.

Q. When did she come here ?—A. On Wednesday, I think.

Q. Who is captain of the vessel ?—A. Captain Smalley.

Q. She came from the gulf. How long have you been there ?—A. About five weeks.

Q. Of the twenty-five years you have fished there, what proporti
your fish did you catch outside, and what proportion within three mi
the shore?—A. I never saw a large deck of fish, during the time I
there, caught very near the shore. They were mostly small decks.
best fishing I have seen was on what we call Bank Bradley.

Q. That has been during the whole of the time you have been
ing?—A. Yes. I should say that nearly three-fourths of the fish I
taken in the bay have been taken off shore, 8, 15, 25, and 30 miles (

Q. During those forty years have you done much fishing on the U1
States coast?—A. Yes; I have fished a good deal in the States du
that time.

Q. Do you mean the coast of Maine, or clear down where the m
erel go?—A. The coast of Maine.

Q. You have not done much fishing on the shore from Cape Co
Hatteras?—A. No.

Q. Or off on the Georges?—A. No.

Q. You could not really compare the coast-fishing with the bay-fish
from what you have seen of it?—A. No.

Q. You don't know much of the United States coast-fishing?—A.

Q. When you did fish off that coast, was it with seine or hand l
—A. Hand line.

Q. Then you don't know anything about seine fishing, which has (
in of late years?—A. I have not been seining.

Q. With regard to your fishing in the bay. What did you find t
the best fishing-ground in the bay, during the forty years you have 1
there?—A. I think I have caught most fish at Magdalen Islands.

Q. Are the Magdalen Islands a tolerably safe place?—A. I cons
them about as safe as any part of the bay where you get mackerel.

Q. As safe as the Bend of Prince Edward Island?—A. Yes; sai

Q. Why?—A. The Bend of Prince Edward Island is not a very

place to fish unless you are well acquainted with the harbors, which are hard to get into in a storm.

Q. Do you know anything about the shore boat-fishing at Prince Edward Island?—A. No; I don't know more about it than that I have seen them off fishing a great many times in going up and down the shore.

Q. How far off did you meet the small boats?—A. One, two, three, or four miles off.

By Mr. Davies:

Q. You have been fishing a good many years, and you seem to have preferred the gulf fishing to that on the American coast?—A. I have been in the gulf eighteen seasons mackereling.

Q. I thought you said twenty-five seasons?—A. I was eighteen seasons mackereling, and the balance fishing for codfish.

Q. Have you fished in Bay Chaleurs proper?—A. Yes; I have been in Chaleurs Bay.

Q. Some of the witnesses have spoken of Chaleurs Bay as a pretty good fishing-ground; would you state it to be a pretty fair fishing-ground?—A. Well, I don't think it is a very good place to fish in. I never fished as much there as below; not half as much.

Q. What is the matter with it?—A. We never could find mackerel the same as in other places.

Q. Did you try it of late years or further back?—A. I have not fished there much within ten years.

Q. Previous to that you fished there?—A. Yes, more.

Q. Every year more or less?—A. Yes.

Q. When you were in Chaleurs Bay and found poor fishing, did you go far up?—A. Not a great way up; not more than 10 or 15 miles up the bay.

Q. What are the boundaries of Chaleurs Bay—from Miscou Point to Port Daniel?—A. Yes.

Q. When you have been fishing there, did you ever go along the shores?—A. Yes, we followed along the shores on both sides.

Q. The fleet used to fish there?—A. Yes, on both sides; but not very handy in to those shores, for we never could find fish very handy in to those shores.

Q. The center of the bay is as good fishing ground as the sides?—A. The center of the bay is fully better.

Q. Your fish were caught mostly in the center of the bay, I suppose?—A. Yes, mostly down at the mouth of the bay.

Q. You have not followed up the bay at all?—A. No.

Q. Perhaps you never went up at all?—A. Yes, I have gone up as far as Paspebiac.

Q. How many times?—A. Eight or ten times.

Q. Was the fleet accustomed to fish down at the mouth of the bay or to go up?—A. During the latter part of the season they fish below.

Q. What do you mean?—A. I never was there fishing in the fore part of the season.

Q. Then you don't know?—A. Not for the first part of the season. The latter part of the season they fish below.

Q. Do you know whether any bait which the fish follow is to be found round the shores—brit, for instance?—A. Yes, I have seen them in the water frequently.

Q. Where do you find them?—A. You see them on the fishing ground.

Q. I mean in the bay. Do you find them in round that shores?—A. I never took notice whether they were about in that bay much. Probably I have seen them. I don't recollect about it now.

Q. Leaving Bay Chaleurs, have you fished along the west co
New Brunswick ?—A. Not much.

Q. We have had evidence that some of the fleet fished there.
your vessel among them ?—A. A good many vessels go where I
see them during the time they are in the bay.

Q. Did you go further north than Bay Chaleurs—to Bonaventu
up round the River St. Lawrence ?—A. I have been at Bonav
several times.

Q. Have you been up at Seven Islands ?—A. No.

Q. You never fished at Seven Islands ?—A. No; I have neve
there.

Q. Have you been master of a vessel ?—A. I have been pilo
master of a vessel in the bay six times only.

Q. Have you been along the shore of River St. Lawrence ?—A
much.

Q. That part of the fisheries you don't know about?—A. I do I

Q. Whether the fish are taken inshore or out you cannot sa
having been there?—A. I have been round Anticosti fishing; we
did much there.

Q. Fishing for mackerel round Anticosti ?—A. Mackereli
never did much there.

Q. Coming down to Cape Breton; you have been at Marga
course ?—A. Yes.

Q. At what time of year did you generally go to fish there
In the fall.

Q. Is there any particular time when fishermen run to Margar
A. At the last of August and September.

Q. Is Sydney one of the places you went to?—A. I never fished

Q. Have you fished off Port Hood ?—A. I have.

Q. And from Cheticamp down to Margaree ?—A. Yes.

Q. You have also fished at Prince Edward Island ?—A. Yes.

Q. What parts of the island do you prefer ?—A. At East Point
between that and the Chapels.

Q. Between the two Chapels is good fishing ground ?—A. Yes.
found some there this season.

Q. The fleet generally go there more or less ?—A. I have seen
fleets there, never a large fleet.

Q. Have you been in any of the harbors along Prince Edward Is
—A. Yes.

Q. Have you fished off Rustico and Malpeque ?—A. Not muc
Rustico, some off Malpeque.

Q. And off Cascumpeque ?—A. Very little.

Q. Off North Cape ?—A. Yes.

Q. Off Miminegash ?—A. Yes.

Q. You took fish more or less at the different places where
went ?—A. Yes.

Q. Is Margaree considered by fishermen to be very good fi
ground ?—A. It has not been very good of late years.

Q. Was it formerly so considered ?—A. I have seen good fi
there.

Q. I believe the fishing grounds are changing. For instance
year you have not been to Bank Bradley ?—A. No.

Q. Why did you not go there ?—A. We had heard from there.

Q. That nothing was to be had there ?—A. I have not heard of
thing being taken there.

Q. The same with Bank Orphan. You have not been there this year?—A. No.

Q. Have you been at the Magdalen Islands?—A. In sight of them.

Q. You did not catch anything there?—A. No.

Q. So the fish are not now so much at the old places where you used to find them 20 years ago?—A. No.

Q. In what direction is the change tending? Are the fish nearer the shore than they used to be years ago?—A. I don't think any nearer than they used to be—not the body of the fish.

Q. This year about one-half of your catch was taken near the shore?—A. We did not get but very few of ours inshore this season.

Q. Did the fleet use purse-seines in deep water?—A. I did not see a seine hove in the bay.

Q. Why don't they use purse-seines in deep water if the fish are there?—A. I don't know. They don't very often heave them till they see the mackerel when schooling.

Q. Did you see any mackerel schooling there in deep water?—A. I did not.

Q. And therefore you did not throw your purse-seine?—A. We did not have a seine to throw. We had hand lines.

Q. What character are the fish you have got? What qualities—No. 1, No. 2, or No. 3?—A. I should say they would go by the cull here about one-half 2's and one-half 1's.

Q. Is that what you call a fair average for the catch?—A. Yes.

Q. Is it better than the average catch as regards quality?—A. The quality is not so good. I have been here a great many falls when three-quarters would be 1's.

Q. Would I be correct in assuming that of the fish caught by your vessels in the bay three-quarters are 1's?—A. Not this season.

Q. Generally?—A. Yes, as a general thing they used to be so in the fall, say from 1st August up to to 20th October.

Q. About three-quarters 1's and the others 2's?—A. Yes, that used to be about the average.

Q. I suppose you left the bay on account of the storm of the 22d?—A. There have been no fish caught since then.

Q. Did the storm cause you to leave?—A. We left because there was no mackerel.

Q. Before the storm came on the mackerel were there?—A. The mackerel were going—pretty well thinning out, I suppose, by the appearance of things.

Q. After the storm of the 22d they disappeared?—A. I saw none after the storm.

Q. Is it not customary for mackerel to disappear after a storm?—A. Not in all cases. It was getting late for them.

Q. I have heard it stated that when a storm comes on the mackerel generally disappear, and you don't see them for some days?—A. That is a common thing.

Q. You saw mackerel before the storm of the 22d?—A. Yes.

Q. They were not seen afterwards?—A. The day before the storm I saw mackerel and caught some.

Q. Did you see any afterwards?—A. No.

Q. So that it always, or very nearly always, happens that after a heavy storm you do not see mackerel for some days, do you?—A. No; but after a week's time you should see them if they are there.

Q. They return after a week's time?—A. Yes.

Q. Is there any difficulty in ascertaining the distance from the land?

155 F

For instance, if you were out 2, 3, or 4 miles would there be any diffi culty in telling the distance from the shore?—A. Well, no, not much difficulty about telling it.

Q. You think there would be no difficulty in telling whether you were two, three, or four miles off?—A. You can tell when you are out ten miles from land. When you are off ten miles Prince Edward Island, it looks low.

Q. Is there any difficulty when you are two, three, or four miles off, in ascertaining where you are exactly?—A. When you get the opinion of four or five men you can judge within a mile or half a mile.

Q. You think it would require the opinions of four or five men?—A. To see how they agree on it. Some might say they were four or five miles out, when they were not more than two miles from shore.

Q. They might think they were four or five miles out when they were only two?—A. Yes.

Q. One witness told us that a great many fish were taken four miles from land, and that there was good fishing-ground four miles out; is that a fact?—A. Who was it said so?

Q. A witness who was examined here to-day. What do you think of the statement that there is a very good fishing-ground just four miles out?—A. There might be, but I don't know where it is.

Q. You have been many years on the American coast?—A. Yes.

Q. Fishing mackerel?—A. Yes.

Q. How many miles from the coast did you as a general rule take your mackerel?—A. I have been out 60 miles.

Q. Is that the general distance?—A. No.

Q. What is the general distance?—A. Probably from 15 to 20 miles off.

Q. Are there many traps and pounds along the coast for catching mackerel?—A. No.

Q. You don't know about those, for you have not fished along the shores?—A. I never fished along the shore much.

Q. You have never been employed in connection with traps and pounds?—A. No.

Q. Do you know if much mackerel is caught in the traps and pounds? —A. No.

Q. What years were you fishing on the American coast?—A. I was there a year ago this fall.

Q. What other years?—A. I was fishing there three years ago this fall.

Q. Five years ago, were you there then?—A. Yes.

Q. Was the fishing you had then pretty good?—A. Yes, very good.

Q. Has it been increasing or diminishing?—A. It has increased.

Q. Within what time?—A. Up to one year ago. This season it has been nothing scarcely.

Q. Nothing at all?—A. There has been some fishing.

Q. Were 1875 and 1876 very good years?—A. Yes.

Q. How were 1870 and 1871?—A. The fishing was fair.

Q. What do you call fair?—A. It was just about an average of the last fifteen years.

Q. Have you noticed any decrease in fishing on that coast within the last ten years?—A. Some seasons the fishing was not as good, but mackerel have been there during that time.

Q. The mackerel have not been taken, but may have been in the water?—A. Yes.

Q. When you were in Bay St. Lawrence were you in the same vessel all the time ?—A. No, different vessels.

Q. What vessels were you in ?—A. It would take me some time to remember all the names. There were Castlemaine, S. S. Lewis, City Bilee, Bloomer, Clara, Lapwing, Forest Queen, Oak Grove.

Q. What year were you in the Forest Queen ?—A. I think it was 1854.

Q. You were not in her in 1864, were you ?—A. No.

Q. What year were you in the Oak Grove ?—A. The first year of the war, I think.

Q. That would be 1861 ?—A. Yes.

Q. Who was the captain ?—A. Captain Burgess.

Q. Any other vessel ?—A. Circassian.

Q. What catch did you take in the Oak Grove ?—A. About 160 barrels, I think. I know it was a small trip.

Q. Were you in the bay in 1867 and 1868 ?—A. I was there in 1868.

Q. Had your vessel a license ?—A. No.

Q. What was her name ?—A. I think her name was the same as the vessel I am now in—Esperanza.

Q. Then you had no license when in the gulf any of those years ?—A. No.

Q. How do you know that the vessels had no license ?—A. The crew had always to pay part of the license fee, and I do not pay any.

Q. Do you attach much importance to the bay fishing ? Do you value it much as a privilege ?—A. It has not been much of a privilege to me for the two or three last trips I have made there.

Q. Speaking generally as a fisherman of the United States, do you think the right to go down to the bay to fish is of much value ?—A. It does not seem to be much of late years.

Q. I don't mean to limit you to this year or last year, but I mean the right of fishing generally ?—A. For the last four years there have been but very few American vessels fishing in the bay.

Q. Do you look upon it as a valuable fishing-ground; you seem to have devoted most of your life to it in preference to anything else apparently ?—A. People have a great many minds about that. They might think it valuable when they started to go there, and afterwards think it is not.

Q. What is the general opinion among fishermen—that it is valuable or not ?—A. They think it has not been very valuable lately. I used to think it was valuable once.

Q. The catches were very large at one time ?—A. Pretty good some seasons.

Q. The years the catches were large you considered it valuable, and the years the catches were small you did not consider it valuable ?—A. Yes. When there was good fishing, and the fish fetched fair prices, it was a valuable fishery.

Q. Do you think the privilege of going to the bay is one of any value ? —A. It has not been so for the last three or four years, but before that I think a man would do as well there as going anywhere fishing.

By Mr. Trescot:

Q. Mr. Davies has been very anxious to know what you think of the value of the privilege of fishing in the bay. Do you think it would be worth while for the government and people of the United States to pay one million dollars a year for the privilege of fishing in it ?—A. No, I do not.

Q. Mr. Davies asked you if you had this year seen any of the f
schooling out off shore, and you told him no. Have you seen any ma
erel schooling inshore?—A. I did not see a school of mackerel while
was there.

Q. Either inshore or out?—A. No.

Q. Have you seen any of the horse mackerel this year in the bay'
A. No.

Q. Mr. Davies asked you also about fishing along the coast of Prir
Edward Island, and you spoke of fishing about East Point back a
forth. How far off did you fish, as a rule, when you fished at the islan
—A. This season?

Q. Yes.—A. All the way from six to eight and ten miles.

Q. Mr. Davies asked you why you had not been to Banks Brad
and Orphan this year, and you said there were no fish there. Did y
mean to say that the fishing at Banks Bradley and Orphan has fal
off, as a general rule, or only this year?—A. I was not there, but I
derstood there was not anything there. I learned that by other vesse

Q. This year?—A. At that time.

Q. You told Mr. Davies you thought in old times that about thr
fourths of the mackerel caught in the bay used to be No. 1's—how
back do you mean? Do you refer to this year, last year, or year befo
or a good while back?—A. A good while back.

Q. How many years back?—A. Twenty or thirty.

Q. You were also asked whether you left the bay on account of
storm, and you said no?—A. We did not leave on account of t
storm.

Q. Then you were asked whether, as a rule, mackerel did not disappe
when a storm came up, for a week, and were not to be found; had y
found any mackerel just before the storm?—A. Yes; I caught some t
day before.

Q. Anything like a large catch?—A. No; a very small one.

Q. Now, with regard to the difficulty of measuring distances. Wl
do you think would be the value of a man's opinion who stood on sho
and said a vessel was three miles or three miles and a half off?—A.
would not have so good a chance to be right as if he was standing or
vessel and looking at the shore.

Q. It is in all cases a very uncertain sort of calculation?—A. Ye
when the land is high it is more deceiving.

Q. Have you not found yourself deceived very often in the measu
ment of distances?—A. Yes.

Q. What do you think would be the value of a man's judgment
stating that he stood on shore and saw a fleet of 200, 300, 400, or 5
vessels fishing within three miles of land?—A. It would not amount
much.

By Mr. Davies:

Q. Did you understand what Mr. Trescot said to you?—A.
asked me what I thought the judgment of a man would be worth abo
the distance of a fleet of vessels off from the shore; it would be unc
tain whether they would be within three miles or two miles.

Q. What was the first year you came to the bay?—A. I think 18
I did not go after mackerel, but codfish.

Q. What was the first year you were in the bay for mackerel?—A.
1835, I think.

Q. Were the mackerel better then than in 1845 or 1855?—A. No.

Q. Not so good?—A. I don't think they were.

Q. They were better about 1860?—A. Yes; somewhere about then.

Q. And from that down to 1865 or 1870?—A. Yes; and since that time not as good.

Q. Those are the years they were better?—A. Yes.

By Mr. Trescot:

Q. Suppose a fleet of 200 or 250 vessels were fishing off shore, what space would be covered?—A. Sometimes when they are snugly together, they don't cover a very large body of water; and you can scatter them over a large surface. It depends on how snugly they are together.

By Hon. Mr. Kellogg:

Q. The first year you went into the bay cod-fishing, had you heard of mackerel-fishing there?—A. No. There was hardly a vessel from the States in the bay then.

Q. Had you heard of mackerel fishing there; had it begun then?—A. No; there was not much caught at that time.

By Mr. Foster:

Q. What year were you first in the bay for mackerel?—A. In 1835. In 1827 there was nothing doing in mackerel-fishing.

No. 50.

GEORGE O. CLARK, of Belfast, Me., fisherman, called on behalf of the Government of the United States, sworn and examined.

By Mr. Foster:

Question. You are one of the sharesmen of the Lizzie Poore?—Answer. Yes.

Q. How many years before that had you been in the gulf fishing?—A. Seven or eight years.

Q. What was the last year before this summer you were there?—A. 1870.

Q. In what schooner?—A. Banner, of Belfast, Captain McFarlane.

Q. How many barrels of mackerel did you catch?—A. About 160 or 165.

Q. And where were they taken?—A. Mostly round North Cape and the Bend of Prince Edward Island.

Q. What portion, if any, was taken within three miles of the shore?—A. 15 or 20 barrels.

Q. Where were those taken?—A. They were not taken a great way inside of three miles; about three miles off Kildare, this side of North Cape.

Q. Were you in the bay in 1869?—A. No.

Q. In 1868?—A. Yes.

Q. In what schooner?—A. Charles E. Moody, Frankford, Capt. Thos. Clark.

Q. How many barrels did she take?—A. About 200 barrels.

Q. Where were they taken?—A. Off Bonaventure, broad off.

Q. Were any of them taken within three miles of the shore?—A. No.

Q. Were you in the bay in 1867?—A. Yes.

Q. In what schooner?—A. Mary Lowe, of Gloucester, Captain Adams.

Q. How many barrels did you take?—A. About 250, I think.

Q. Where were those taken?—A. At Magdalen Islands, East Point, Margaree, and Cape North.

Q. If you took any of them inshore, state where you took them and how many ?—A. We got about 50 barrels at East Point, from 3 miles out; about the same number at the Magdalen Islands. From Point to Port Hood we got a few going across, and from there dow Cape North we got the rest of the catch, about 150 barrels.

Q. Do you say you were at Margaree ?—A. Yes.

Q. How near the shore did you take mackerel there ?—A. About t miles off.

Q. Three miles from the mainland or the island ?—A. From island.

Q. Were you in the bay in 1866 ?—A. Yes.

Q. In what schooner ?—Atlantic, of Bedford, Captain Coombs.

Q. How many barrels did you catch ?—A. About 60 barrels.

Q. Where did you get them ?—A. At the Magdalen Islands.

Q. How long were you in the bay ?—A. About six weeks.

Q. What was your earliest trip to the bay ?—A. In 1858.

Q. How many times between 1858 and 1866 were you in the bay ? Three times.

Q. When were you next there before 1866 ?—A. In 1860.

Q. In what schooner ?—A. Abegail, Captain Dunbar. We were ing for both cod and mackerel.

Q. On the same trip ?—A. Yes.

Q. How long were you in the gulf that year ?—A. About months.

Q. Do you remember what you took ?—A. 20 quintals of cod ε or 5 barrels of mackerel. We were not really catching mackerel. fitted out for codfish.

Q. What bait had you ?—A. We caught mackerel for bait.

Q. Where did you fish for cod ?—A. Away up Madeleine River.

Q. Were you in the bay in 1859 ?—A. Yes; In President, of Be Capt. Conway.

Q. Were you fishing for mackerel ?—A. For codfish and macker

Q. How much mackerel and how much codfish did you take ?— guess about 150 quintals of codfish and about 150 barrels of macke

Q. Where did you take the mackerel ?—A. Off Bonaventure.

Q. Within what distance of the shore ?—A. Just in, right off the

Q. In 1858 what schooner were you in ?—A. Columbia, of Be Capt. McFarlane.

Q. Fishing for mackerel ?—A. Yes.

Q. What did you get ?—A. I believe we got about 200 barrels.

Q. How old were you then ?—A. 12 years.

Q. Do you remember what was your fishing ground ?—A. Off N Cape and the Bend of Prince Edward Island.

Q. How near the shore at the bend of the island ?—A. I should t about 3 or 4 miles out.

By Mr. Davies:

Q. Did you ever fish in Bay Chaleurs ?—A. We have been into S pegan for a harbor.

Q. You never fished up in the bay ?—A. Not up in there.

Q. Then you know nothing about the fishing there ?—A. No.

Q. Have you ever heard of the fleet going there to fish ?—A. I be they have been there.

Q. Have you ever fished at Seven Islands ?—A. No, I don't l where they are.

Q. Nor up St. Lawrence River ?—A. I have been away up there ing.

Q. Fishing for mackerel?—A. For cod and mackerel.

Q. How far from the shore did you catch the mackerel there?—A. We caught them inshore. We caught them for bait.

Q. How far out?—A. One mile.

Q. When you were down at Cape Breton and Margaree, how far were you off from the island?—A. From 4 to 10 miles.

Q. You told Mr. Foster from three to ten?—A. He did not ask me anything about Cape Breton. He asked me the distance from Margaree Island.

Q. Then you were four miles from Cape Breton, and three miles from Margaree?—A. Yes.

Q. Could you tell the distance exactly or accurately?—A. No, I could not tell exactly.

Q. You had no reason for giving any special attention to it?—A. No.

Q. You may have been two miles or four miles out?—A. I might have been two miles and I might have been five.

Q. I suppose special attention is not given to the exact distance you are off shore. You don't pretend to measure?—A. No.

Q. When you spoke of off shore and inshore generally, it may have been two or four miles, you cannot tell?—A. Yes.

Q. You have been round Prince Edward Island?—A. Yes.

Q. And fished in the same way there, from two to five miles out, off and on?—A. Yes, from three to five miles and eight miles, according to how the weather was.

Q. If the fish had been plentiful would you have gone in?—A. I suppose we would if fish had been plentiful.

Q. At what distance out do the boats fish—two or three miles?—A. From one mile to three or four miles.

Q. I suppose you would be often fishing in among the boats?—A. No, we hardly ever went in among the boats.

Q. You never fished much about Rustico?—A. No, we never fished round at Rustico.

Q. At what parts of the island did you fish?—A. Off East Point, Georgetown, up at the Two Chapels, off New London, Malpeque, Cascumpeque, Kildare, North Cape, and from there to West Cape.

Q. All round the shores of the island?—A. Yes.

Q. Where were you the year you got 60 barrels in the Atlantic?—A. Mostly over at the Magdalen Islands.

Q. Had you a license that year to fish?—A. No.

Q. You did not try anywhere else?—A. We fished a little off Cape George.

Q. That trip appears to have been a great failure?—A. Yes.

No. 42.

MONDAY, *October* 8, 1877.

The Conference met.

Examination of ROBERT H. HULBERT, called on behalf of the Government of the United States, resumed.

By Mr Foster:

Question. When your examination ended on Friday, I was inquiring of you as to the fishery on the coast of Maine in the neighborhood of Mount Desert. Over how large a territory on the coast of Maine does the mackerel fishery extend, and how long does it last there?—Answer. Somewhere in the neighborhood of 90 miles, and perhaps more than that. I could not say for certain, for I never remember distances or courses.

Q. Ninety miles from what?—A. Ninety miles along the coast.

Q. Along about where?—A. Portland principally, and from thei Mount Desert.

Q. How many months does it last?—A. The principal part of fishing is from July 1 to August 25.

Q. How far out to sea does it extend?—A. Somewhere in the ne borhood of sixty miles.

Q. Could you give a general idea of what portion of all the mack that go into the markets of Maine and Massachusetts, and are inspec are caught between Mount Desert and Block Island, including Banks, offshore?—A. Probably, seven-eighths of all the mackere: spected.

Q. Do you include in that the mackerel which come from Bay Lawrence?—A. No; only those that are caught on the United St coast.

Q. Then, on our coast, the fishing for mackerel does not go n farther north than Mount Desert?—A. Nothing of any conseque Probably there are some mackerel go north of that, but very few of vessels go after it.

Q. About what season of the year, along from Mount Desert to] sachusetts coast, is the fishing at its height?—A. In July and Aug'

Q. When do the vessels that fish on the United States coast begi go south again?—A. The last of September, the 25th September erally; it depends a great deal on the weather.

Q. And how far south do they go?—A. We don't follow those m erel that go on the coast of Maine farther than the mouth of Vine: Sound; that is near Chatham.

Q. On the north side of Cape Cod?—A. Yes.

Q. And how late do you fish for them off in the vicinity of Chath —A. We fish there only a few days, because after the mackerel c mence to go down from there they go very fast; unless the weathe very fine we cannot fish at all for them.

Q. What is the latest season of the year when mackerel are fishe(the United States coast?—A. Nothing of any account is done ε the 15th November.

Q. Where are the mackerel fished so late as that?—A. Sometime Block Island, and sometimes in the vicinity of Massachusetts Bay.

Q. Do not your fishermen go farther south than Block Islan(autumn, to any extent?—A. No.

Q. What is the quality of the mackerel taken in autumn?—A. 1 are generally fat, but they begin to decrease after the last of Octob

Q. Within what period are the best mackerel taken off Maine,] sachusetts, and Block Island?—A. In September, and till 15th Octo perhaps they are the best.

Q. What is the quality of the mackerel taken in the spring be they spawn, everywhere?—A. All No. 3's.

Q. Wherever they are caught?—A. Yes.

Q. You have spoken in your examination of having seen food mackerel as far out as George's Banks. Will you describe the diffei kinds of mackerel food you have yourself observed?—A. The lar; quantity of food we find in mackerel is lantz. The largest we find about four inches in length.

Q. Lantz is a kind of sand-eel?—A. Something similar. Then we what we call all-eyes, a very small fish about half an inch in length. is a young fish of some kind, I don't know what.

Q. Have you any opinion in regard to what it is?—A. We someti think they are young mackerel. We don't know what they are because they are very young.

Q. Where have you found those all-eyes?—A. In great abundance at Block Island, and often twenty-five miles off the coast of that island.

Q. In what quantities have you found them?—A. They will sometimes cover miles of water. They will be on the surface of the water so that you can pick them up in your hand, and can take five or six in the palm of your hand.

Q. What extent of surface have you found covered with these little fish?—A. We find them from alongside of the vessel till we reach three or four miles off in a boat; we find them the whole distance. I don't know how far they may extend beyond, but quite a distance.

Q. Is there any other food for mackerel?—A. There is what we call cayenne; it is a seed of some kind or spawn.

Q. Is there any other food?—A. Hay-seed or red-seed; it has various names among different classes of people.

Q. What is that?—A. I don't know.

Q. It is animal?—A. It is something that has life, I suppose.

Q. How far out to sea do you find that?—A. On the George's Banks, and even to the north, west, and east of the George's.

Q. Is that found very extensively, or only in small quantities?—A. At some seasons very extensively, and at other seasons there will not be so much. We cannot tell exactly how extensive it may be.

Q. Is there any other mackerel food?—A. Sometimes the mackerel, when down near the bottom, feed on different kinds of fish near the bottom, such as shrimp. You find shrimp in mackerel at different times.

Q. And jelly fish?—A. I don't know that I ever found any jelly fish in them. I have seen mackerel tear them to pieces, but whether they eat them or not I don't know. I have seen mackerel jump at them, but probably it was for some other fish that were round the jelly fish.

Q. You carried fresh mackerel into the New York market?—A. Yes.

Q. That goes packed in ice, I suppose?—A. Yes.

Q. How many vessels are engaged in the business of carrying fresh mackerel into the New York market?—A. About fifty sail.

Q. And how many are engaged in the same trade for the Boston market?—A. Nearly the same number, to the best of my knowledge.

Q. Are those vessels of the same size as other vessels engaged in the fishing business elsewhere?—A. Smaller vessels run with fresh mackerel to Boston than to New York.

Q. What would you estimate as the average tonnage of vessels engaged in the fresh mackerel trade for New York, and also the average tonnage of vessels engaged in the same trade with Boston?—A. Probably somewhere in the neighborhood of 50 or 55 tons for Boston, and perhaps 10 or 12 tons more for New York, on an average.

Q. Not quite so large as the average of the Cape Ann fleet?—A. No.

Q. Can you give any idea of the quantity of fresh mackerel that goes into the New York market every season?—A. I should say about a fair average would be 40,000 mackerel to a vessel.

Q. Do you mean for the season or trip?—A. For the season.

Q. How many mackerel, such as go into the market, would there be on an average to a barrel?—A. Of such mackerel as were taken there las spring it would take in the neighborhood of 150 on an average to a barrel.

Q. How many fresh mackerel do you think go to the Boston market?—

A. I have not much idea what the quantity is. I don't know t:
could come near it.

Q. Do those fresh mackerel vessels make a few long trips or 1
short trips ?—A. They cannot keep out very long for the fish woul(
keep. They have to run in with the fish while they are good or
will lose them.

Q. About how long are the vessels out ?—A. Sometimes a week
perhaps ten days; not longer than ten days after they get fish on b

Q. Now, take your experience in fishing for mackerel in the G(
St. Lawrence. What value would you attach to the right to fish w
three miles of the shore in British dominions ?—A. What fish (
take inside of three miles ?

Q. You can take it in that way or in regard to its value.—A. I (
not tell exactly the value because the fish vary in price a great de

Q. How important do you regard it?—A. At the outside, I have 1
in my experience taken more than one-eighth of a fare inside of 1
miles.

Q. Do you think that seining mackerel perceptibly diminishe:
quantity of mackerel found in the sea ?—A. I cannot tell exactly, be(
sometimes I think we kill some very young fish. But seining has
going on a number of years, and even three years ago mackerel
just as plentiful as I ever saw them, and they were quite abundan1
year, while this year they are scarce. We cannot account for it.

Q. Have you ever known seining to be carried on successfully i
Gulf of St. Lawrence ?—A. No.

Q. Do you know any reason therefor?—A. I hardly know wha
reason may be; perhaps it may be the tide, or it may be that the n
erel do not school the same as they do with us. There are variou:
sons. We don't find many mackerel school on that fishing ground

Q. So far as it has been tried there, seining has not been successf1
A. No.

Q. Have you ever fished in the vicinity of Seal Island, near
Sable ?—A. I have fished on that fishing ground for codfish somet

Q. Have you ever fished for halibut there ?—A. No.

Q. Within what distance of Seal Island have you ever fished for
fish, and how have you happened to be there ?—A. Sometimes we
fish scarce on George's Bank or other Banks where we fish in sun
and we run over there and try; but we hardly ever get inside of fro
to 25 miles of Seal Island.

Q. What is the shallowest water you ever knew the halibut fishe
be prosecuted in ?—A. I could not tell that, because I am not muc
quainted with the halibut fishing, though I have been some few voy:

Q. You don't expect to catch halibut in much shallower water
codfish ?—A. No; generally deeper.

Q. And your codfish have not been taken within how far from lan
A. From 15 to 25 miles of Seal Island, and in that vicinity.

Q. You have made cod-fishing voyages; where to and how man
general terms?—A. I could not tell you exactly how many; qu
number.

Q. Where have you been ?—A. To the Grand Banks, Sable I:
Banks, and others.

Q. Have you tried both trawling and hand-line fishing ?—A. Ye

Q. What has been your bait ?—A. For general use, herring.

Q. And what else ?—A. Sometimes we used clams.

Q. Salt clams ?—A. Yes; and sometimes squid and menhaden.

Q. Menhaden slivers ?—A. Yes.

Q. Have you ever been in to Newfoundland to buy bait for codfish?—A. I have been there.

Q. To what port?—A. St. Mary's Bay.

Q. What did you buy?—A. We bought a lot of caplin; that was all we could get.

Q. Was that good bait?—A. No.

Q. Why not?—A. It would not keep any time in ice, and it was too small.

Q. What is the bait used on the George's Banks by codfishermen?—A. For the first three trips in the winter time they take frozen herring, and after that they use alewives and menhaden, which they get in Vineyard Sound.

Q. In regard to the mackerel fishing, what is the bait used for throw bait by mackerel vessels?—A. Menhaden slivers.

Q. How far north is the extreme point where menhaden is caught?—A. I don't hardly remember, but probably nothing north of Grand Manan Island, and I don't think they go that far.

Q. Can you give us the price of fresh mackerel in New York and Boston markets?—A. I don't know that I can correctly. The prices vary a great deal.

By Mr. Davies:

Q. You are now pilot on board the Speedwell and do not go mackerel fishing now?—A. Yes.

Q. Have you had much experience in the fisheries of the Gulf of St. Lawrence? How many seasons have you been there?—A. I think I have been there five seasons.

Q. And those seasons cover the whole of your experience there?—A. Yes.

Q. In regard to fishing off the American coast your experience has been more extended?—A. Yes.

Q. How many seasons were you there?—A. Five whole seasons, and parts of perhaps five other seasons.

Q. How far from shore were your mackerel taken on the American coast?—A. All the way from 5 to 50 miles from the land and also off the off-shore Banks. George's Banks are 133 miles from Cape Ann, and we find mackerel there and off the northeast edge of the Banks.

Q. Last year and the year before were very good fishing years?—A. Very favorable; we could not complain.

Q. I understand they were exceptionally good?—A. Yes.

Q. What was the condition of the mackerel fishery along the United States coast for the previous eight or ten years; had it been declining?—A. It does not appear to have been.

Q. When you say "it does not appear to have been," do you speak from actual experience?—A. From what I have seen myself.

Q. Did you examine the returns to see the quantity caught?—A. I don't know that I have properly, but as I am amongst the vessels, I have a pretty good chance of knowing how the others have been doing. At the close of every season when the vessels stop seining, I can see the reports of all the vessels and the quantity of fish landed. I have not those in my memory, because I never thought they would be of any assistance to me.

Q. Are you able to state whether there was a decline in the mackerel fishery off the coast of the United States during the seven or eight years previous to 1875?—A. Not to my knowledge; I could not say there was.

Q. Could you say there was not ?—A. No.

Q. In reply to Mr. Foster, where did you say seven-eighth inspected fish were caught ?—A. I said seven-eighths of the i fish in Maine and Massachusetts were caught between Block Is Mount Desert. Block Island is in the State of Rhode Island, an Desert is in Maine.

Q. Do you mean that to include all fish caught by American v A. I mean fish caught on the coast of the United States. I speaking of the fish caught in British waters.

Q. It does not refer to the fish caught by American vessels ir waters ?—A. No.

Q. You speak from your practical knowledge, having beer ground and seen the fish taken ?—A. Yes.

Q. You say that seven-eighths of the mackerel caught by A vessels in American waters are caught between those two poi Yes.

Q. And the other one-eighth is taken where ?—A. It is take southward of that, between Hatteras and Block Island.

Q. Have you examined the inspection returns ?—A. We generally every season when the fishing is done.

Q. You have not got any returns with you ?—A. No.

Q. When you make your return after a fishing voyage, d return embrace a statement of the places where the fish were i A. No.

Q. Does it embrace the fact that the fish were taken in Ame British waters ?—A. It does not.

Q. Then if an American vessel took a cargo of fish into one ports, it would not appear from the official returns whether the been caught in British or American waters ?—A. We see that is reported with so many barrels of fish from such a place.

Q. That is in the newspapers ?—A. Yes.

Q. Is there any official record kept ?—A. There is a record vessel kept by the owner.

Q. I understood you to say, speaking with regard to the Unite coast, that there is a special school of mackerel in the neighbc Block Island, which is known as Block Island mackerel ?—A.

Q. And that they remain there the whole season and do i north ?—A. They do not come north; we don't find them north

Q. I understood you to say that mackerel fishing on the A coast begins in May and does not end till November ?—A. It t early as 25th April. When it closes depends a great deal weather. If there is a blustery, cold autumn, the mackerel will so long; but if there is moderate weather, they will stay till vember.

. The fish remain on the coast, more or less, during that ti Ye.

Q. And are taken in large and small quantities the whole time ?—A. Not in large quantities in the latter part of the sea body of the fish have gone off the coast.

Q. All the fish taken before the spawning season you clas 3 ?—A. Yes; all that are long enough. They are threes ar threes.

Q. When you speak of American vessels fishing in the sp mackerel off the United States coast, they are fishing for the class of mackerel ?—A. Yes.

Q. You described the different places where mackerel spawn,

said the time of spawning varied at different places along the American coast ?—A. Yes.

Q. How do you know that mackerel spawn on George's Shoal ?—A. Because there is a certain quantity of them taken there before spawning, and others taken there after spawning.

Q. How do you know they spawn there? Have you seen young mackerel there ?—A. I have seen all-eyes, which we suppose are young mackerel, on the George's.

Q. Describe them.—A. It is a very small fish, probably not more than half an inch in length, and its eyes are more conspicuous than any other part of the body. You notice the eyes of the fish when swimming in the water before you observe the body.

Q. You call them all eyes for that reason ?—A. Yes.

Q. That is what makes you believe that mackerel spawn on George's Banks ?—A. Yes.

Q. Do I understand you to say that there are two schools of mackerel that come along the United States coast and that a distinct school comes along the Maine coast ?—A. The fish do not all come in to the coast at one time.

Q. At different times ?—A. Yes.

Q. And a little later as you come further north ?—A. Yes. The fish do not all strike the coast at one point. Sometimes the mackerel will strike a little to the north of Hatteras, and you will fall in with another school of fish 50 miles north, that will come near the coast, within 50 miles, and perhaps less.

Q. You said you found a body of fish frequenting Nantucket shoals, and you found that body afterwards on George's Banks ?—A. We find them sometimes at George's afterward; sometimes they don't get so far eastward as that. We usually find part of them on the George's, at the southwest part.

Q. The mackerel that are found off the coast of Maine remain there until they begin to return to their haunts for the winter, wherever those haunts may be ?—A. Yes; the mackerel on the coast of Maine and Massachusetts.

Q. Do you know whether fishermen ever take mackerel in the winter season in muddy places ?—A. I have heard of mackerel being taken out of the mud with a spear in the winter time.

Q. Whereabouts ?—A. In Cape Cod Bay, Bridgehampton Bay, and in the vicinity of Cape Cod.

Q. Did you ever examine the eye of the mackerel in early spring ?—A. Yes.

Q. Can you tell the Commission whether the eye is then in the condition in which you find it afterwards, during the mackerel season, or what difference is there ?—A. When we first find the mackerel in early spring, there is always a sort of scale over probably two-thirds of the eye. As the mackerel work north, the scale comes off, and the last mackerel we find, those in the middle of November, have the scale again, covering a quarter of the eye.

Q. It would then seem that in the spring the eye has a film over it, and as the season advances, this works off ?—A. Yes.

Q. And as the colder season comes on, the film covers the eye again ?—A. It appears that something grows over the eye as the weather grows colder.

Q. Have you heard of mackerel being taken in winter under the ice ?—A. I have heard of their being taken when the ice was on the flats, but not when the harbor was frozen.

Q. They were taken from the mud below the ice ?—A. Yes; deepest part of the island.

Q. When thus taken, would the film be over the eye ?—A. know. I only saw one caught in that way, and I did not take no that point.

Q. Do you know whether the mackerel winter in the mud ? could not say, but we have reason to think they do. That is the g opinion of fishermen—that the mackerel winter in the mud.

Q. Do the mackerel remain on George's Shoal all the season, mackerel do at Block Island ?—A. Some seasons they do, and seasons they remain there only a short time. They have been there some years during all the season.

Q. You were five seasons fishing in the gulf, I believe ?—A, Y

Q. At what special places did you fish while there ?—A. The pri part of my fishing in Gulf St. Lawrence was at the Magdalen Isla

Q. You never fished much in other parts ?—A. Not greatly; fished in other parts of the bay.

Q. Have you ever fished in Bay Chaleurs ?—A. Yes, one su We spent one week there one summer.

Q. What year was it ?—A. I cannot remember the year.

Q. Can you remember the vessel you were in ?—A. I think it the Pocumtuc.

Q. That would be some time in 1865 ?—A. About that time.

Q. Had you any license at that time ?—A. I cannot recollect w we had or not; but I don't remember hearing anything about a l

Q. Was there much of a fleet in Bay Chaleurs when you were th A. No; there were three vessels there.

Q. Where did you go ?—A. We went up as far as Port Daniel, north side of the bay.

Q. Did you fish close to the shores at all ?—A. We tried round bay, but we did not find anything.

Q. You did not go on the south side ?—A. No.

Q. Did you fish off the Gaspé coast, and up at Bonaventure ?- never fished there.

Q. Or at Seven Islands ?—A. No.

Q. You don't know anything about those fishing-grounds ?—A

Q. Have you tried along the west coast of New Brunswick Miscou Point to Miramichi ?—A. I fished part of one summer there.

Q. Did you fish close inshore there ?—A. We did not fish cl shore, for the water is too shallow to raise a body of mackerel fished from North Cape, Prince Edward Island, to Miscou Island

Q. Did you fish within three miles of the shore on the west New Brunswick ?—A. To my certain knowledge, I did not.

Q. Then you don't know anything of that fishing-ground ?—A.

Q. Have you fished within three miles of the shore at Prince E Island ?—A. Undoubtedly I have at different times.

Q. And you caught nothing to speak of ?—A. Yes; I anchored many times under the lee of the land at different parts of the isla

Q. You did not catch many mackerel ?—A. We never took bu few mackerel inside of what we supposed was three miles off sho cording to the soundings laid down on our chart, and the soundin found with our lead.

Q. What chart did you use ?—A. Eldridge's, mostly.

Q. An American chart ?—A. Yes.

Q. You did not use Bayfield's chart ?—A. Not much.

Q. From the chart you judged you were within three miles of the shore?—A. That is the way we judged, by our soundings.

Q. You tried the Cape Breton coast?—A. Yes.

Q. How did you find the fishing there?—A. I remember catching some mackerel one season near Margaree Island.

Q. Any quantity to speak of?—A. Somewhere in the neighborhood of 30 or 35 barrels.

Q. Those were all?—A. They were got in one day's fishing at the latter part of the season.

Q. You have already stated that you caught one-eighth of your mackerel inshore; where did you get them?—A. Inside of three miles at the Magdalen Islands.

Q. You never caught any mackerel at all, except 35 barrels, within three miles of the shore, except at the Magdalen Islands?—A. Yes; I have caught a few mackerel at different times, within three miles of the land, probably at Prince Edward Island. I have taken mackerel there inshore, in very small quantities, perhaps one barrel or two.

Q. Apart from the barrel or two caught at Prince Edward Island, you never caught any fish within three miles of the shore, but 35 barrels around Cape Breton?—A. That is the largest catch I took, knowing I was within three miles of the land.

Q. Did you catch many within four miles of the land?—A. No.

Q. Did you catch many within five miles?—A. No. You cannot raise a sufficient body of mackerel in less than 20 fathoms of water to lay to and heave bait. I am speaking as I found it.

Q. Do I understand you to say that you cannot raise a large body of mackerel within three or four miles of the shore?—A. I venture to say that I cannot do it, for there is not deep enough water.

Q. Then is it not curious that you can find them around the Magdalen Islands?—A. It is deeper water there than around any part of the coast.

Q. Does not this map (a chart of the coast of North America from the Strait of Belle Isle to Boston, including the banks and islands of Newfoundland) show that the soundings around Prince Edward Island and Cape Breton are deeper than those off Magdalen Islands?—A. I don't know but this map shows that.

Q. Would you say, looking at this map, that within three miles of Magdalen Islands you can find water 20 or 25 fathoms deep?—A. In some parts we do.

Q. Within three miles of the shore?—A. We do. I don't know that I can find it marked 20 fathoms deep.

Q. You have shown why mackerel cannot be caught at Prince Edward Island?—A. I don't say they cannot be caught there. I have caught them there myself in small quantities.

Q. Apart from the two or three barrels, you said mackerel were not to be had there, and you gave as a reason that the water was not deep enough?—A. Sometimes we took them inside of three miles at the Magdalen Islands; sometimes not within fifteen miles of land. It is giving a large proportion to say that one-eighth of my catches were taken within three miles of land.

Q. You did not say that it was giving a large or small proportion?—A. I did not want to put it down too small. I have seen many trips taken when no fish were taken anywhere except at Magdalen Islands, and there pretty well offshore.

Q. You gave evidence that one-eighth of the catch was taken inshore; none appear to have been taken inshore except 35 barrels off Cape Bre-

ton, and two or three barrels off Prince Edward Island ?—A. Di
that two or three barrels were taken off Prince Edward Island,
or three barrels each time we tried ?

Q. Would it surprise you to hear that three-fourths or seven-e
of the fish caught by boat-fishermen are taken within three mil
almost within two miles, of the shore ?—A. I would be very muc

Q. Your theory would fall to the ground ?—A. I should think a

Q. Your experience in the gulf is confined to five seasons ?—A
is all ; and part of that I remember very little of.

Q. You don't know what the other vessels have taken, or whei
catches were taken ?—A. No.

Q. You wish to confine your experience to that obtained in yo
sel ?—A. Yes.

Q. You wish the reason why mackerel could not be taken insl
be received that it is because the water is too shallow, and tha
must be 20 or 25 fathoms ?—A. That is the way I caught mackei
self.

Q. Do you mean that that is with hand-lines or seines ?—A. 1
with hand-lines. I have never been seining.

Q. Do you know why seines are not successful in the gulf?
don't know. I have heard various reasons given.

Q. Have you ever heard that it was because the mackerel we
close to the shore to enable the seiners to catch them ?—A. I have
that reason.

Q. Have you heard it from fishermen ?—A. I don't know but
have.

Q. Have you any doubt about it ?—A. I cannot say I have or
have not. I may have heard so.

Q. That they cannot seine mackerel because they are in too s
water ?—A. They have been seined there this summer.

Q. To any large extent ?—A. I don't know to how large an ex

Q. Do you know whether any seiners have adapted their seines
waters of the gulf ?—A. I cannot say as to that ; I have not beer

Q. So, practically, you know very little about the fishing in the g
A. I admit I know very little about it, and I will do less than I d

Q. You find your present position more profitable than that of a
erel fisherman ?—A. Probably my present position may not co
long.

By Mr. Whiteway :

Q. Have you been many seasons to the Grand Banks fishing?—
Q. How many times ?—A. Perhaps once or twice.
Q. When were those occasions ?—A. I cannot give you the da
Q. Nor the years ?—A. No.
Q. Did you fish with salt or fresh bait ?—A. I have been the
fished with salt bait altogether some seasons. When I sailed
Provincetown I fished with salt bait altogether.

Q. Have you ever used fresh bait on the Grand Banks ?—A.
part of a voyage, part of the season.

Q. Where did you get it ?—A. We bought it at Prospect,
Halifax.

Q. What year was it that you went into St. Mary's Bay for ca
A. That was the year I was in the Pocumtuc; in the spring we w
there. We did not go in exactly for bait, but in coming out we
some caplin. I cannot tell you the year.

Q. How many barrels did you buy ?—A. About 15 barrels.

Q. That is the only time you used caplin?—A. That is the only time I have used any.

Q. Are you sure the caplin you purchased at that time were perfectly fresh when you put them in ice?—A. I could not say. We got them from one or two boats which came up to us; but whether they had been caught 24 hours before or that morning I could not say.

Q. Suppose other parties who have had experience in the use of caplin for bait packed in ice pronounced it to be a fish which would keep longer than any other, would you be disposed to contradict the statement?—A. No; because I have only tried it once, and I speak as I found it.

Q. You fish with trawls and hand-lines?—A. We were fishing with trawls then.

Q. Fresh bait, I believe, is far superior to salt bait in fishing with trawls?—A. I did not find it so that season. We had salt clams, a very costly bait, and we got our trip on it.

Q. How much did you pay per barrel for that bait?—A. I think $10 that spring.

Q. Do you remember what you gave for the caplin?—A. From $1 to $1.50 per barrel. It was not over $2.

Q. The season you were fishing, were many American vessels fishing near you?—A. Yes.

Q. Were they using fresh or salt bait?—A. Some with fresh and some with salt bait. Those using fresh bait did not fish where we did. We could not catch fish where they were. We could not catch as many as we could by ourselves.

By Sir Alexander Galt:

Q. You spoke of the mackerel coming at different parts of the year to the coast and spawning?—A. Yes.

Q. They must be different schools of fish, I suppose?—A. Yes.

Q. They come from the deep waters and go inshore and spawn?—A. Yes.

Q. The fish spawning off Mount Desert would not belong to the same school as those which spawn off Sandy Hook?—A. Certainly not.

Q. Do you take the mackerel on St. George's Bank and the Banks in the gulf where the bottom is rocky and broken, or where it is sandy, or do you take them under both these circumstances?—A. Under both. But I do not know that I ever took much notice of that, because our seines do not go to the bottom, and we have not much idea of what the bottom is.

Q. What is the case with the places which you have described as those where you go?—A. Some are rocky, and more parts are sandy.

Q. Where is this so? Give an instance of it.—A. It is very rocky off Block Island.

Q. And you take them there, as I understand it, rather later in the season than at other places?—A. Yes. There is a place twenty-one miles southeast of Block Island where there is a small bank. A great many cod-fishermen lay there, and it is the best place for the large mackerel to play and show themselves.

By Hon. Mr. Kellogg:

Q. Do you consider that the mackerel go actually into the mud?—A. I do not know as they do so.

Q. Do you believe that this is the case?—A. Yes.

Q. But they are not of the nature of a mud fish at all?—A. I do not know that they are.

156 F

Q. What do you think as to the theory of mackerel migrati
you believe that they go south altogether, or that they merely
shore into deep water?—A. I do not think that they go very f
but rather that they go out to the northern edge of the Gulf S

Q. Do you think that they go altogether there?—A. Probab
not go; perhaps there are other places where they go; but I tl
they go away until they find warm water.

Q. Is that the character of any other fish, to migrate in
water?—A. We have schools of other kinds of fish that come
southward; there is the cod, which comes on the Banks.

Q. Is their migration as well established as that of the mac
A. I do not know but that it is.

Q. Have you observed where they strike?—A. I do not kno
have.

Q. What signs have you seen of codfish migrating?—A. Wel
caught them in different parts, of course.

Q. Are there signs of their migrating? Do they migrate in
water?—A. I do not think that they do; of course, we find
them on the Banks, but we do not know where they go to or co
I cannot tell.

Q. No more than you can with respect to the mackerel?—A.
know but this is the case.

Q. You do not know whether the mackerel go into deep wa
the Gulf Stream?—A. I do not know whether they go into th
all; that is only what I think is the case.

Q. Have you seen evidence enough in all your experience t
you clearly that the mackerel go into the Gulf Stream or spe
winter elsewhere?—A. I do not know as I could say.

No. 51.

JAMES CURRIE, master mariner and fisherman, of Pictou, w
on behalf of the Government of the United States, sworn and e

By Mr. Foster:

Question. How old are you?—Answer. Fifty-four.

Q. Have you ever fished for mackerel?—A. Yes.

Q. Where?—A. In the bays of Pictou; in what is called th
umberland Strait, from Cape George to Pictou Island, and fr
George to Murray Harbor, and also from Pictou Island again t
called the Gulf Wharf at Arisaig, and clear to the West Cape
Edward Island.

Q. In vessels or in boats?—A. In boats.

Q. How large were they?—A. Some of them were 20 feet
others 22 feet and 25 feet.

Q. How far out from the shore did the boats go when you
them?—A. From Pictou Harbor to the East Point of Pictou I
distance of 9 miles, and from the latter point to Arisaig Wharf
thing like 12 to 15 miles.

Q. From land to land?—A. Yes.

Q. How far out is most of the boat fishing with which
acquainted, done?—A. All I can tell you is that I have fis
along the shore, and that there we could not get anything wor
ing of.

Q. Estimate the distance out at which you fished.—A. Wh
shore fishing is done from half a mile to 1½ miles out, and no

of fish is to be got there, but you can go off shore 3 miles and outside of that, and get fish.

Q. Were you ever a pilot for a government vessel ?—A. Yes; this was before confederation—in 1854.

Q. What were the names of the vessel and her captain ?—A. Responsible was the vessel's name, and Philip Dodd the name of the captain.

Q. What was this vessel doing while you were pilot ?—A. We were looking after the American fishermen.

Q. For what purpose ?—A. To see that they did not intrude on the shore fisheries. We cruised on the north side of Prince Edward Island, around on the south side of Cape Breton, and occasionally on the north side of Cape Breton.

Q. How long were you on that vessel ?—A. Five or six months, I should say.

Q. Did you find the American vessels fishing within 3 miles of the shore ?—A. We did not find any fishing within three miles of the shore; they were all outside of that limit.

Q. Were any seizures made ?—A. None were made by the Responsible.

Q. Did you see any made by other vessels ?—A. No; but I heard of this being done.

Q. Who owned the Responsible ?—A. My father.

Q. And how did the government happen to have her under charge ?—A. They chartered her from my father.

Q. Have you seen the boats go off-shore and fish in company with United States vessels ?—A. Yes; I saw this occur between Port Hood and Margaree Island, where we used to cruise considerably. I saw Scotch boats, as I call them, pull off and make fast to American schooners, and get a good quantity of fish, loading their boats and going ashore; and that was outside of the three-mile limit.

Q. You saw them made fast to the American schooners ?—A. Yes.

Q. According to your observation, does fishing by the American vessels injure the boat fishery ?—A. No.

Q. Why not ?—A. Because, on the grounds where they fish, as far as I have seen, the Americans feed the fish by heaving over quantities of bait.

Q. Are any fishing-vessels fitted out from Halifax; and, if so, how many ?—A. I do not exactly know, but there are not many fitted out from Halifax.

Q. Are there any ?—A. I do not know of any.

Q. Do the fishermen up here in the provinces, as far as you have observed, get rich ?—A. No; they are generally poor.

Q. Do they lay up money ?—A. No.

Q. By whom is the money made on fish ?—A. By the merchants in Halifax.

By Mr. Thomson:

Q. Are you a practical fisherman yourself ?—A. Yes.

Q. How long have you been engaged in fishing ?—A. I caught my first fish when I was 14 years old.

Q. And how old are you ?—A. Fifty-four.

Q. And have you been engaged in fishing ever since you were 14 ?—A. No; not all the time. I have been a pilot as well as a fisherman.

Q. Do you call yourself a practical fisherman ?—A. I do.

Q. Have you gone on fishing-voyages ?—A. I am a practical boat-fisherman.

Q. You have not fished in any schooner ?—A. Yes; but not as erman. I have made trading trips, having gone to buy fish, but fish myself.

Q. You have not been in a vessel engaged in fishing ?—A. never been engaged in vessels as a fisherman.

Q. Then you are not a practical fisherman except as concerns —A. I should say that a man who understands boat-fishing coul fish on board of a schooner.

Q. You have never fished on a schooner ?—A. Not as a fishern

Q. Did you ever fish at all in the Bay of St. Lawrence ?—A.

Q. In boats ?—A. Yes.

Q. Where ?—A. Off St. Peter's.

Q. Did you go to reside there ?—A. No.

Q. You happened to fish there ?—A. I ran over there in a bo cause we could not then get any fish at home.

Q. You went there from Pictou ?—A. Yes.

Q. To which St. Peter's did you go ?—A. To St. Peter's on the side of Prince Edward Island.

Q. Did you go over there in an open boat ?—A. Yes.

Q. What is the distance across ?—A. I do not know as I cou you now exactly.

Q. What is about the distance ?—A. It is something like 125 n guess, around down to East Point; and then it is between 40 miles up the island to St. Peter's.

Q. That would make the distance 170 miles ?—A. I will not sv that.

Q. You went there in an open boat ?—A. Yes.

Q. How often did you try that experiment ?—A. Twice in n time. I was there this summer in a boat which I built myself was there twelve years ago.

Q. That would be in 1865 ?—A. I do not know about that; know that it is all of twelve years ago. We loaded with codfish

Q. You were not then mackerel-fishing ?—A. No; that was spring.

Q. You never fished for mackerel in the Bay of St. Lawrence at A. Yes; I have.

Q. When ?—A. Fifteen years ago.

Q. What were you in ?—A. A schooner.

Q. I thought you told me you never fished in a schooner ?— were trading, and sometimes when we could not buy any fish we to and caught them; but this was not making a summer's worl You asked me if I was a hired fisherman, and I told you that I w

Q. I asked you if you were in the habit of fishing in schoone I have done so; but not as a hired fisherman.

Q. What, then, was your business ?—A. I was hired under t trader of that schooner.

Q. What were you doing ?—A. Trading.

Q. Where ?—A. We were at North Cape, Cape Breton, and pre at Ingonish, Cape Breton, and then we went into the Bay of S rence and afterward to the south side of North Cape, Cape Bret

Q. Did you trade at Prince Edward Island ?—A. No; but pened to sail that way, and we heaved out the lines one evenin if we could catch any mackerel. We were going to Pictou w were caught by a head-wind and taken as far as Cascumpeque; t then headed off again and we came around East Point and wen

Q. You did not trade then ?—A. No.

Q. You did not go out to fish at all?—A. We had fishing-gear on board, and we went for the purpose of catching fish that day.

Q. But was your schooner fitted out for fishing?—A. No, but for trading; she had, however, fishing-gear on board.

Q. What do you call fishing-gear?—A. She had somewhere about six nets on board, and mackerel jigs and lines enough for six men, and such and such bait as we could buy as we went along the shore.

Q. Where did you get it?—A. At Little Canso, before we went round Scatarie.

Q. Had you barrels in which to put your fish?—A. Yes.

Q. Then you were on a kind of mixed trip—trading and fishing?—A. Of course. When we could not buy, we caught them if we could.

Q. How many fish did you catch during the whole trip?—A. We caught 150 barrels.

Q. Where?—A. Between Ingonish, Cape Breton, and St. Peter's, Prince Edward Island. We were not exactly close inshore.

Q. What do you call close inshore?—A. From one-half a mile to 1½ miles, and perhaps 1¾ or 3 miles off shore.

Q. But were you very nearly close inshore?—A. We were not inside of three miles from it anyway; none of them were taken within this limit.

Q. Not one of them?—A. No.

Q. I suppose that you would not have caught any within three miles of the shore if you could have done so?—A. Yes; we would, if we could have got any there.

Q. Did you try in there?—A. Yes.

Q. I suppose you knew that you had no right to fish there?—A. We were in a British schooner, and we had a right to fish anywhere where we could get fish.

Q. Did you attempt to fish within three miles of the shore?—A. I tell you plainly that we tried in there, but we could not get the fish there to any amount.

Q. What did you catch there?—A. I remember that one day we took 25 mackerel there.

Q. And that is the only day you do remember of having caught fish there?—A. No.

Q. What other days did you do so?—A. There are plenty more days when this was the case.

Q. I suppose you remember that day because so few were then caught?—A. Yes; it did not pay us much for that day's work.

Q. Other days you did much better work?—A. Yes.

Q. Do I understand you to state to the Commission that the inshore fisheries along Prince Edward Island are good for nothing?—A. I do not think that they are good for anything, between you and me.

Q. During how many years have you been acquainted with them?—A. I was fourteen when I caught my first fish.

Q. Was this on the shore of Prince Edward Island?—A. No; but off Sheet Harbor, down here. In 1857, my father moved to the town of Pictou, and the next spring we fitted out and went away around the shore fishing. My father is now in Nebraska.

Q. I understand you to state that, in your opinion, the inshore fisheries on the north side of Prince Edward Island—that is, within three miles of the coast, are good for nothing?—A. They are good for nothing; that is the way it lays now.

Q. And the way it has always lain so far as you are aware?—A. Yes.

Q. While you have been acquainted with them?—A. Yes.

Q. And that is your opinion under oath ?—A. I am on my oath.
my oath which I am looking after.

Q. And these fisheries are really good for nothing ?—A. The
really good for nothing.

Q. How often have you fished along the shore on the north s
Prince Edward Island, to justify you in giving that opinion ?—A
next year after I was in the Responsible I was fishing in the bay
was in 1854.

Q. How often did you fish there ?—A. I may say that since I
been in Pictou—that is since 1857, with the exception of some
when I have gone piloting, and more times when I went navigati
the West Indies, and when I was in one of your steamboats pilot
Boston, I have been engaged in fishing in the spring, summer, an
almost every year except four or five years.

Q. Have you been fishing for mackerel ?—A. Yes; and for co
hake.

Q. Within 3 miles of Prince Edward Island ?—A. Yes; and o
of 3 miles.

Q. I am speaking of inside of 3 miles from the shore ?—A. Ins
that distance I tell you plainly that mackerel cannot be caught t
amount.

Q. If you have no experience as to fishing within the 3-mile limi
can you say that this fishery is worth nothing ?—A. I say that fro
experience there are no fish to be got within 3 miles of the shor
they can be got outside of that.

Q. What experience have you of the fishing within 3 miles
northern side of Prince Edward Island ?—A. I think I have s
plainly enough. I tell you that you can catch no fish inshore; th
all caught outside.

Q. How often have you fished where I have mentioned ?—A.
twenty times at different times.

Q. How long were you there on each of these occasions ?—A.
pose sometimes two months, and sometimes three months, and so

Q. Were you in fishing vessels ?—A. I told you that I was n
hired fisherman on a fishing vessel. I was in fishing boats from
22 and 25 feet keel.

Q. Where did they belong to ?—A. Two of them I built myself

Q. When you were living at Pictou ?—A. Yes.

Q. Did you not tell me that you so fished only on two occasions
I said I did so on two occasions, and into two boats which I
mysel .

Q. You said you went there once this year and once twelve year
—A. Yes.

Q. How does it now happen that you say you have fished
twenty times ?—A. I say that I have fished there all of twenty ti

Q. In open boats ?—A. Yes; and I have been there from two to
months each time.

Q. In open boats ?—A. Yes.

Q. On each of these twenty occasions was your place of resi
Pictou ?—A. Yes.

Q. Did you not tell me that you had gone over there twice ?—A

Q. Did you ever go over there in any other boats but your own
Yes; but not from Pictou.

Q. Where did you go from ?—A. Murray Harbor. I went th
earn a living.

Q. Murray Harbor is on the south side of Prince Edward Island?—A. Yes.

Q. What did you go there for?—A. I was seeking for employment.

Q. And you were employed in boats there?—A. Yes.

Q. You went in boats from there to fish for mackerel?—A. Yes.

Q. What were you fitted out for generally?—A. For cod-fishing; but we could not get them on that shore, and so we went round to the north side of the island to see what we could do mackerel fishing.

Q. And you could not catch any mackerel?—A. Not inshore.

Q. Will you give us the names of the owners of these boats in which you were?—A. One of them was named Jackson; and I think that the other three are lost; they are dead now. I forget their names. Jackson is now living.

Q. And you remained fishing for three months?—A. For two or three months.

Q. And during this time you caught nothing?—A. Nothing to make it worth while.

Q. What did you get?—A. Something like 15 barrels of mackerel and 20 quintals of codfish.

Q. And that was all?—A. Yes.

Q. Is that a specimen of your catches all through these twenty times? —A. It is—about.

Q. Did you always go fishing there during those twenty times from Murray Harbor?—A. No.

Q. Where else did you go from?—A. We went once from Whitehead, down on this side of Canso.

Q. Where did you go then?—A. To the north side of the island. I was with Tom Munroe, who is living now.

Q. Did you fish inshore?—A. Yes.

Q. And you caught nothing?—A. Nothing to speak of; but we got some, of course.

Q. What induced you to go fishing there after the experience you had?—A. I was hard up, and did not want to remain idle. There were fish to be got there if you went off the shore far enough; but we had not the means, and we could not get them.

Q. But there were fish there?—A. Yes; off on the grounds; but we wanted capital in order to catch them.

Q. How was the fishing where you were?—A. I did not see any fish; if I had, I would have got some of them.

Q. You say that the inshore fisheries are worth nothing?—A. Yes.

Q. Why, then, did you continue to fish there?—A. You must understand that I was not master of the boat. I was only a hired man, and I had to do as my master told me; and that is the reason why we did not catch the fish.

. Did you not tell them that they could get no fish inshore?—A. Yes.

Q. And though you told them that it was of no use, they did fish inshore?—A. Yes; certainly.

Q. Do you not think that they had had some experience in fishing in that locality themselves?—A. Perhaps this was the case.

Q. Had they such experience or not?—A. I thought this was the case; but they did not keep to their arrangement with me; they were too frightened to go off shore, but some men are not frightened to do so in an open boat.

Q. And you are one of them?—A. Yes.

Q. Where did you put up at night?—A. In the cuddy, forward.

Q. You did not go inshore?—A. No.

Q. You did not then run into a harbor?—A. If it was dark and sto looking we certainly would go in for the night.

Q. Then on these different occasions you never made harbo night?—A. Yes; but not as a general thing.

Q. And on these different occasions you kept inshore?—A. The I was hired with did so.

Q. This was the case on the twenty occasions you speak of?—A. save on two of these occasions, when I went fishing in boats belon{ to myself.

Q. And on eighteen occasions you kept inshore?—A. Yes.

Q. And caught nothing there?—A. Yes; nothing worth speakin

Q. And these people would not go out beyond 3 miles to fish?—A.

Q. How far from the land did you keep?—A. From half a mil 1¾ and 2 miles.

Q. In other words, you actually fished eighteen times, for two or t months at a time, and you never caught more than 15 or 16 barrel fish?—A. No.

Q. You so fished during eighteen different seasons for three mo at a time?—A. Yes.

Q. How did you get provisions?—A. We took them with us.

Q. Did you take provisions for three months in an open boat?- Yes; they were stowed away in the cuddy.

Q. Was this an open boat?—A. Yes; with a cuddy forward. T were from four to five or six hands on board. A barrel of flour, other things, will do this number for six month's time.

Q. What was the size of the boat?—A. 20, 22, or 25 feet keel. can get boats down here with 18 feet keel that will carry 500 quin of codfish.

Q. And provisions for six months?—A. A barrel of flour, with o necessities, stores, will do it.

Q. Where do you stow them?—A. Forward.

Q. Not in the cuddy?—A. Yes.

Q. And you had barrels of fish on board, and salt, and all that?- Certainly.

Q. How many barrels had you on board?—A. A 300-quintal I could take about 150 barrels.

Q. How many had you on board?—A. About 100, I suppose, inc ing whole barrels and half barrels, to make stowage for the boat.

Q. How many barrels of salt had you?—A. We buy this by the h head, but to make ballast we put it into barrels, unheading them a use it. A hogshead holds 7 bushels.

Q. How many hogsheads had you?—A. About 15.

Q. You had besides 100 barrels to put fish in aboard?—A. Yes; we could stow fish away in bulk.

Q. And besides all these you had in an open boat provisions fo men for three months?—A. Yes.

Q. And all this in a boat of 25 feet keel?—A. Yes; that is don the country.

Q. And you never went into a harbor at all?—A. We used to do { it looked dark and stormy and the like of that.

Q. And you never went outside of the three-mile limit while on t voyages?—A. No; not in the boats in which I was a hired man. ·

Q. You did not do so these eighteen times?—A. No.

Q. Never at all?—A. No; not in the boats in which I was.

Q. And they would not go more than 1½ miles out?—A. No; but I saw boats outside of that.

Q. But they would not go there?—A. Yes.

Q. And this was done for eighteen different seasons; the same thing was done over and over again?—A. Yes.

Q. So that from this experience you swear positively that, in your opinion, the inshore fisheries on the north side of the Prince Edward Island are good for nothing?—A. They are good for nothing; and this is also the case with the shore fishery of Northumberland Strait.

Q. And if people came here and swore that plenty of fish are to be caught, and are caught, on the north side of Prince Edward Island, you would not believe one word of it?—A. No more than as to what I have stated; you may get there from 10 to 15 quintals of codfish, and perhaps from 15 to 20 barrels of mackerel; but this is not going to pay a crew.

Q. You do not believe it if people say that the best fishing is inshore?—A. No; not one word of it.

Q. In fact, the inshore fisheries are worth nothing?—A. Yes; but outside the limits you will get fish.

Q. But with that splendidly fitted out boat you never thought of going out there to try?—A. No.

Q. How far along the shores of Prince Edward Island did you fish on these occasions?—A. As far as Cascumpeque, I think.

Q. Did you fish off Rustico?—A. I cannot say that we hove a line off there.

Q. Did you sail up as far as that?—A. Yes; we went as far as Cascumpeque.

Q. Why did you not try there?—A. A fair wind was blowing, and we did not think it worth while.

Q. Is not Rustico considered the best fishing-ground around the island?—A. No.

Q. Where is the best fishing-ground around the island?—A. Off New London.

Q. That is the next harbor to Rustico?—A. Yes.

Q. Did you try there?—A. No.

Q. Why not?—A. Well, when I was there I was a hired man; I was not master of the boat, and I could not tell my master to go to work and fish there.

Q. Did he fish at Rustico?—A. We fished inshore, but we got nothing; what I call getting nothing is when a man makes a voyage, and when he comes back cannot pay his debts; that is nothing, and worse than nothing.

Q. You say you were in the schooner Responsible in 1853?—A. Yes.

Q. And you took no American vessels fishing in the bay within the three-mile limit?—A. No; one morning we found one inside at Magdalen Island, but when we came to examine, she was getting wood and water.

Q. You never saw any other American vessel inside of the limit?—A. No.

Q. Did you not see others, which got out of the way, and beyond the three-mile limit before you could take them?—A. No; we sailed along one foggy morning, and tried to catch them, but we could not.

Q. You wished to see if any were inside?—A. Yes.

Q. Why, then, did you try to catch them?—A. It was on account of the noise made about their imposing on the provinces; and the thing was to get them if we could.

Q. You knew that there were none within the three-mile limit ?
We sailed along the shore in a fog and tried to catch them. We s?
from cape to cape, in the vicinity of the three-mile line, but none of
American vessels attempted to come inside.

Q. Did you not say you tried to catch them inside ?—A. No
sailed from cape to cape, in the fog, but never found one of them in

Q. You never saw one of them ?—A. Not inside; but there
plenty outside in the fog; and I saw the Scotch boats make fast to t
and catch mackerel.

Q. Was this on foggy days ?—A. Yes; and other days, too.

Q. There were other government vessels in there at that time ?
Yes.

Q. And they happened to seize vessels ?—A. I think they ha
give some of them up afterward. Some seizures were made; but
not know whether they were legal or not. We did not see a chan?
make any legally.

Q. How many vessels were seized that year ?—A. I do not remem
just now.

Q. Of how many seizures did you hear ?—A. I could not tell you
now, it is so long ago, and I have not bothered my memory abo
since. I think that Leybold took one or two, as near as I can recol
and the brig Halifax was out at the same time. Sir Colin Campbel
a man-of-war brig, had something to do with some of them, an?
made more mischief with Nova Scotia fishermen for telling yarns a
these matters than with the Americans, and he did not let the for
out of Port Hood for a month.

Q. You seem to have a prejudice in this regard ?—A. No; I
none.

Q. I asked you what vessels were seized ?—A. I cannot give
either the names or the number of them.

Q. What did you hear about them ?—A. I do not remember just :

Q. How are you now employed ?—A. I have no employment at]
ent.

Q. Where do you reside ?—A. At Pictou.

Q. If I understand you aright, when the Americans came in to
within three miles of the shore the boat-fishermen made fast to
American fishermen ?—A. Yes; but this was not within but outsi?
the three-mile limit, and many of the boats thus got good catches.

Q. Do the American vessels come within the three-mile limit ?
Yes; to approach the harbors.

Q. But do they do so to fish ?—A. I cannot answer that more ?
to say that I have never seen them catch any fish inside of the t?
mile limit, though I have heard people say that they come to fish wi
three miles of the shore.

Q. Did you ever see them do so ?—A. No. I mean by seeing t
fishing seeing them haul the fish up.

Q. Did you ever so see them in the act of fishing ?—A. I never
them more than sailing along the bays, and so on.

Q. I understand you to say that you have been for forty years
gaged in fishing, and that during this time you never saw an Amer
vessel fishing within three miles of the coast ?—A. No.

Q. You never did ?—A. I never did.

Q. Either on the coast of Nova Scotia, of Prince Edward Islan?
of Cape Breton ?—A. No.

Q. You have seen them fishing very near the three-mile li

but never inside of it?—A. I have seen them inside of it, but I never saw them fishing inside of it.

Q. They were then merely sailing?—A. Yes.

Q. Then all these British boat-fishermen who made fast to the American vessels went outside of the three-mile limit to take advantage of the American bait?—A. Yes.

Q. And the Americans never came within the three-   limit at all?—A. Not that I have seen.

Q. Do you think it possible for them to have come inside of it without your having seen them?—A. Yes; I only stick to what I have seen myself.

Q. Do you not think it odd that this should be the case during these forty years?—A. I have heard people say that they came inside the limit to fish, but I have never seen them do so; I do not know as I ever did.

Q. Do you believe that the American fishermen have ever fished within the three-mile limit on the coast of Nova Scotia, of Prince Edward Island, or of Cape Breton?—A. Well, as to the believing part, I have heard men who tell the truth say that they have done so; but at the same time I have never seen it.

Q. Do you believe the persons who said so or not?—A. I have heard people say so.

Q. Do you believe them?—A. I believed one or two men occasionally; but I do not say whether this is the case or not. I did not see it.

Q. As far as your experience goes, you believe that the Americans never have fished within three miles of the land during the last forty years?—A. I do not know about that; that is getting it rather tight on a man. I might have an opinion that they did do it, and would not like to say that they did not do it; but I have not seen them do it.

Q. What is your opinion in this regard?—A. My opinion is, that I do not think that the intruding of the Americans on our shore is worth talking about. I believe this much, that if the people of Nova Scotia would give the American fishermen a little more freedom, the boat fishermen would have a better chance.

Q. You are strongly in favor of the Americans coming inside of the 3-mile limit to fish?—A. Yes; because then I would not have to row so far off on a calm morning.

Q. Why?—A. When there is no wind, we have to pull the boat off.

Q. What has that to do with this question?—A. We want to get alongside of the vessels, where the bait is thrown, and get some of the fish that the vessels raise.

Q. You mean that you cannot get any fish within three miles of the. shore at Pictou?—A. No.

Q. And you cannot get anything there unless the American schooners come there and throw bait out?—A. Yes—nothing worth speaking of.

. Q. Do the American schooners come off Pictou and throw out bait, as a rule?—A. I have seen them between East Point, Pictou Island, and Arisaig Wharf, or Gulf Wharf.

Q. And wherever they throw out bait, you go to fish?—A. I have seen them come quite close to the Three-Mile light, at Pictou Island, and raise mackerel half way between that point and the Gulf Wharf.

Q. And then you got some fish?—A. Yes.

Q. Then I understand that you wish the Commission to understand that unless the Americans come there and throw out bait, even the inshore fishery is good for nothing?—A. Yes; and you must not think

that I have any prejudice about it, for this is not the case; I h:
none.

Q. In point of fact, you say that unless the American fishermen :
allowed to fish off our coasts, our own fishermen cannot catch a
thing?—A. No.

By Mr. Foster:

Q. Does anybody get any considerable quantity of mackerel with
throwing out bait?—A. No; it takes a quantity of it to raise the ma
erel.

Q. Do the small-sized boats usually have a considerable quantity
bait to throw over?—A. No.

Q. Will you tell me how many men there were on board of the ves
or large boat on which you were?—A. There were six of us.

Q. Will you describe what kind of boat it was, and state its len;
and tonnage?—A. An open boat has no tonnage. The boat was of
feet keel, 11 feet 6 inches beam, and 5 feet 6 inches in depth of ho
she had something like 6 or 7 feet laid off for a forecastle, called
cuddy; the two sides of the boat were furnished with bunks for
men to sleep in; and then there was what was called standing room
the captain; and between this and the mainmast was another pl
where we stowed away nets, fishing-lines, and fishing-gear of all kind
a barrel of flour and a barrel of beef and a barrel of pork, if we wantec

Q. Do you know the boat's tonnage?—A. I could not tell you; n
of the boats are measured, because they are open. By keeping th
open, we get clear of custom-house taxes, while if we decked them i
and aft, we would have to pay taxes at every port which we entered

Q. Are they like the boats called in Newfoundland western bo
which stay out at sea?—A. Yes; pretty much.

Q. Which stay out for three and four weeks, and scarcely ever
beyond three miles from the shore?—A. They are not built on the sa
principle; we Nova Scotians call the western boats of Newfoundl:
jacks.

Q. How do these boats of yours compare in size with the Newfou
land jacks?—A. Ours are not quite so large.

Q. How much smaller are they?—A. If the jacks are of 25 tons t
den, our boats are something like 15 tons.

Q. I notice that Mr. Killigrew in his testimony speaks of western bc
manned by six men for six months, and states that their tonnage va:
from 22 to 28 tons, and that they follow the fish to different parts of
coast. Sir Alexander Galt asked him if they staid out at sea, and
replied:

Yes; perhaps for three or four weeks. They are something like our Bankers,
they only fish about a couple of miles from the shore. They scarcely ever go far
than that from the coast.

Q. You know what kind of boat this is?—A. Yes.

Q. And you say that if this is of 25 tons, yours are of 15 tons?—
Yes.

By Mr. Davies:

Q. What is the length of the keel?—A. Twenty-two feet.

Q. What is the beam?—A. Eleven feet six inches.

Q. Do you say that a boat of 22 feet keel has 11 feet beam?—
Eleven feet six inches we generally call it; the hold is some 5 fee
inches.

Q. And six feet is taken in the low for the cuddy?—A. Six or se
feet, I should say.

Q. It has two masts?—A. Yes.
Q. And is schooner-rigged?—A. Yes.

No. 52.

WILLIAM PERRY, fisherman and seaman, of Sheet Harbor, Nova Scotia, was called on behalf of the Government of the United States, sworn, and examined.

By Mr. Dana:

Question. How far is Sheet Harbor east of Halifax?—Answer. About 45 miles.

Q. During how many years have you lived there?—A. About twenty-five or thirty years.

Q. Do you recollect the year when you first went fishing?—A. No; I first went fishing with my father in the bay.

Q. For mackerel or cod?—A. For cod.

Q. Where did you go?—A. I used to go boat-fishing with him at home, and then my brothers and myself got a vessel and went on what we call the Banks, 15 or 20 miles off the coast of Nova Scotia, in deep water.

Q. You did not then go into the bay?—A. No; that would be early in the season.

Q. Are these Banks 15, or 20, or 30 miles out from the shore?—A. Yes; in from 60 to 75 fathoms of water.

Q. And there you caught codfish?—A. Yes.

Q. Did you go into the bay afterward?—A. Yes; in August and the latter part of July; and I have been here September.

Q. You were fishing on the Banks off Nova Scotia in May and June?—A. Yes.

Q. And afterward you went up the Gulf of Saint Lawrence?—A. Yes.

Q. Where did you go then?—A. Up about Prince Edward Island, and I have been up as far as Anticosti Island, over to Labrador, and around the Magdalen Islands.

Q. Were you cod-fishing still?—A. Yes; we fished out in the bay off the island.

Q. What was the tonnage of your vessel?—A. We had two vessels; one was very small and the other was of 25 or 30 tons or along there.

Q. What was the tonnage of the small vessel?—A. About 15.

Q. When you used to go into the bay to fish at the different places you have mentioned, how far off shore did you catch your fish?—A. From 8 to 12 and 15 miles.

Q. Have you tried the inshore fisheries?—A. Yes. We never do try for cod, however, inside of 8 or 10 or 12 miles from the shore; we consider it useless to do so in vessel fishing; of course the boats fish closer in.

Q. You have not been engaged in boat fishing in the bay?—A. No.

Q. Have you seen American vessels fishing in the bay?—A. Yes; very often.

Q. At about what distance off shore have you so seen them?—A. At all distances; some were 8 or 10 miles off, and others 3, 4, 5, and 6 miles off. I have seen them fishing very often on the ridge between Cape George and Prince Edward Island.

Q. There are shoaler and well-known places of fishing-grounds along there?—A. Yes.

Q. Did you devote yourself industriously to the fishing busin(
A. Yes ; as far as my means allowed me to do so I did.

Q. I suppose that you had not enough capital for large vesse
great outfits ?—A. No.

Q. Why do your people not do as the Americans do, and build
fine vessels, and go off and fish outside, and catch good large c;
and get large fish ?—A. I cannot tell you, unless they are afraid (
money.

Q. Or they have not got it ?—A. Yes.

Q. In your case, I suppose that you did not have it ?—A. No.

Q. In all this time, from 1863 to 1872, that you were fishing
were you part owner of all the vessels in which you were ?—A. Y

. Were you sole owner ?—A. No ; there were three of us—bro

. What are your brothers' names ?—A. John and Patrick.

. Where do they live ?—A. At Sheet Harbor.

. And you three owned the vessels ?—A. Yes.

. Did you all go fishing ?—A. Yes, and together.

Q. Under the Dominion flag ?—A. Yes.

Q. You had a right to go inside and fish as much as you liked
Yes.

Q. While you were cod-fishing did you occasionally take a ca;
mackerel ?—A. We used to take them for bait.

Q. Where ?—A. Sometimes where we were fishing, and some
closer in shore.

Q. You caught them where you were fishing for cod ?—A. Yes.

Q. Did you catch the greater or better part of these fish there or
in ?—A. We never could make a great catch of mackerel. We d
have the means to do so. We were not fitted up with bait mills
our catch of mackerel was very small, sometimes it consisted of a b
a half a barrel, or somewhere along there.

Q. What have you been doing since 1872 ?—A. Coasting and trading.

Q. You have not been fishing since then ?—A. No, save last year when I fished with seines for herring.

Q. Where ?—A. At the Magdalen and Anticosti Islands.

Q. Was your fishing a success or a failure ?—A. The fish were plentiful where we were.

Q. From what you learned from other vessels, what was the result of the mackerel fishing last year ?—A. These fish were then very scarce as I could understand.

Q. You know Halifax pretty well ?—A. Yes.

Q. Are there any fishing vessels fitted out in Halifax ?—A. I could not say, but I do not think that many are fitted out here. There may be some for all I know.

Q. Do you know of one ?—A. No, not down our way.

Q. But in the port of Halifax ?—A. I could not say that for certain I know of one so fitted out.

By Mr. Doutre :

Q. Who requested you to come here as a witness ?—A. Mr. Mackasey introduced me to these gentlemen, and they asked me a few questions concerning the matter and I gave them my opinion as far as my little experience goes.

Q. What were you asked ?—A. I was asked concerning the fisheries in and off shore.

Q. You were asked your opinion about them ?—A. Yes.

Q. Were you asked what you yourself had seen ?—A. Yes ; and what experience I had had in fishing.

Q. How often have you fished in the Gulf of St. Lawrence ?—A. I have fished there some three or four summers, three to the best of my knowledge, that is for part of the season.

Q. This includes the years when you were fishing with your brothers ?—A. Yes.

Q. Were you exclusively fishing for cod ?—A. Yes, we went for the purpose of catching cod.

Q. Where have you been fishing ?—A. In the bay, to Labrador, over about Anticosti, and down around Sydney and Cape North, and all around this shore.

Q. You were always looking for cod ?—A. Yes.

Q. How far did you fish from Anticosti ?—A. About 9 miles—between it and Labrador on the banks there. We generally made a harbor at Mingan, on the Labrador coast, and got our bait there.

Q. What are you doing now ?—A. Nothing. I sold my vessel this summer, and I am building a vessel, which is not yet finished.

Q. Where were you when the conversation took place which led to your coming here as a witness ?—A. I came up to Halifax on business, and being well acquainted with Mr. Mackasey my meeting him led to my coming here.

Q. You say you only fished for mackerel for bait ?—A. Yes.

Q. Where did you look for that bait ?—A. We often tried for it when laying at anchor on the ground where we fished for cod, and we would catch some mackerel there sometimes ; at other times we would go inshore and we would find some there.

Q. How far off shore ?—A. From 2 to 3 or 4 or 5 miles.

Q. What do you call inshore ?—A. Coming close to the land.

Q. What distance from it ?—A. I could not exactly say, but it would be 3 or 4 or 5 miles from it sometimes.

Q. You call 5 miles inshore ?—A. Yes—from where we would b
ing, and we would go in, may be half the distance between us and
shore, and try.

Q. Have you ever fished on American vessels ?—A. No.

Q. You say you have seen American vessels fishing ?—A. Yes.

Q. How near the shore ?—A. I should say within the 3-mile
sometimes, and sometimes farther off—8 or 9 miles off.

Q. Where did you see the larger number of them fishing ?—A. I
seen a very large fleet fishing on the ridges between Cape George, i
fall of the year when I would be going to the islands.

Q. How far from the coast ?—A. 8 or 9 miles as near as I can ju
and I have seen them fishing closer to and along the shore.

Q. Did you ever see a school of mackerel ?—A. Yes; and ma
one.

Q. Where ?—A. In all parts of the bay.

Q. Near the shore or away from the shore ?—A. Yes.

Q. What are your brothers doing now ?—A. One of them is fisl

Q. On his own account ?—A. Yes,

Q. Which one is this ?—A. John.

Q. Do you know whether he is fishing for cod or mackerel ?—A
is cod-fishing.

Q. Is that his usual occupation ?—A. Yes; he also goes he
fishing.

Q. With nets ?—A. Yes.

Q. Where did you take the barrel or half a barrel of mackerel v
you mention as having taken for bait ?—A. Wherever we coul
them. Sometimes it was where we were fishing, and sometimes
where.

Q. Where are herring generally taken ?—A. Great quantities of
are taken at the Magdalen Islands and at Anticosti, in the spring

Q. How far from the shore ?—A. Along the shore, in the harbor:

Q. A few acres from the shore ?—A. Yes.

Q. Have you been paid to come here ?—A. No.

By Mr. Dana:

Q. Did you come from home for the purpose of appearing here
giving evidence ?—A. No.

Q. Had you any idea when you left home of coming here as :
ness ?—A. No, not in the least.

Q. Did you then know, by the way, that the Commission was in
sion ?—A. No, I did not know the first thing about it until Mr. Mac
asked me my opinion on the matter; and that was before he spo
the Commission.

Q. He asked you your opinion ?—A. Yes; and what I thought :
it from my experience.

Q. Mr. Mackasey lives here ?—A. Yes.

Q. And what did you tell him ?—A. I told him what I thought c
matter, as far as my experience went.

Q. And then you came here ?—A. Yes.

Q. Has anything been said to you by any one requesting you t
tify to certain things, whether you believe them to be true or not'
No, not in the least.

Q. Nothing of the sort has occurred ?—A. No.

Q. And if any such thing has been said, you would have left the
that said it at once ?—A. Yes; it would have been useless to hav
anything of the sort to me.

No. 53.

THOMAS WARREN, of Deer Isle, Me., called on behalf of the Government of the United States, sworn and examined.

By Mr. Dana:

Question. Be so kind as to state your age.—Answer. Fifty-eight.

Q. When did you first ; go fishing no matter as to the exact date ?—A. About 1853.

Q. In the gulf ?—A. Yes.

Q. For what did you go; for mackerel, or cod, or both ?—A. Mackerel.

Q. The mackerel was rather a new thing then in the gulf ?—A. Comparatively ; yes.

Q. How long were you engaged in fishing ?—A. That season ?

Q. No; I didn't mean that season, but how many seasons did you go ?—A. I went five years in succession.

Q. Into the gulf ?—A. Yes.

Q. Your last trip was in '37 or '38 as a fisherman ?—A. '37.

Q. Where did you catch fish then ? I don't mean the place, but whether inshore or off shore ?—A. Do you refer to the first year ?

Q. To the first five years. You spoke of having been there from '33 to '37 ?—A. I was there five years.

Q. Without going into details, did you catch the fish you caught inshore or off shore, and in what proportion ?—A. It is a long time ago. I only speak from memory. In 1833 I was in a schooner named the Eagle.

Q. That is so long ago that we don't care much about the names, but only whether you can tell from memory whether those five years you caught off shore or inshore ?—A. In 1833 I was there for mackerel.

Q. Can you tell how it was these five years, or, if you prefer, take each year ?—A. Well, three of the five years I was there for codfish.

Q. Those were caught in deep water ?—A. Always.

Q. Two years you were for mackerel ?—A. Yes.

Q. These two years, where did you catch ?—A. In 1833 we got them all off shore. In 1837, the last year I was there, we got 23 barrels out of our trip very near St. Peter's, within three miles of the shore.

Q. You have no doubt they were within three miles of the shore ?—A. I am clearly of the opinion that they were within three miles.

Q. What was your whole trip ?—A. I don't recollect, perhaps 200 barrels. The vessel was small.

Q. Of those about 23 barrels were taken within three miles. After 1837 what did you do ?—A. I never went a fishing voyage after '37. I retired from fishing and went into the fitting business.

Q. That is, fitting fishermen ?—A. Yes.

Q. How long were you engaged in that business ?—A. About twenty-eight years, if I recollect aright.

Q. You continued in that business until you were appointed inspector or afterwards ?—A. My being appointed inspector did not interrupt my fishing business.

Q. When did you give up your business as an outfitter ?—A. In 1874.

Q. Then from the time you gave up fishing, 1837 to 1874, you were engaged as outfitter of vessels ?—A. Very slightly for the first four or five years.

Q. After that more largely. Am I right ?—A. Yes.

Q. How many years were you inspector in the State of Maine ?—A. I was appointed in 1862 and held office until '69.

157 F

Q. Seven or eight years ?—A. Seven years.

Q. Did your duties as inspector of fish generally carry yo
fishing ports of the State, and to what extent ?—A. Yes; I wa
fishing town once a year, and when complaints came, I was a
they came.

Q. What is the largest number of vessels you fitted for yo
one year ?—A. In 1862, if I recollect aright, I fitted out twent
of mackerel for the Bay Chaleurs, or St. Lawrence rather.
it the Bay Chaleur.)

Q. How many mackerel-men were fitted out from your place,
in former years—say from '60 to '62 ?—A. In 1862 we had t
number in the bay.

Q. How many had you then ?—A. 45 to 48.

Q. How many are there now ?—A. Well, I don't know tha
swer that question. From our town we have had about five i

Q. Is the number of vessels in other fisheries about the a
No; it has depreciated. There is not a quarter part of them

Q. When you had forty-five vessels, or from that to fort
1862, what proportion of them went into the bay ?—A. Nearl

Q. This year you have five in the bay ?—A. Yes.

Q. The year before, or the year before that, how was it ?
year, for instance.

Q. How many were in the bay ?—A. As near as I can rec
one.

Q. Five tried this year ? With what success, as they have t
from ?—A. Well, they have all lost money.

Q. Are you well acquainted with Castine ?—A. I am.

Q. Is that far from you ?—A. It is about fifteen miles to th

Q. Has Castine engaged much in mackerel or cod ?—A. It
engaged in cod, but of late years they have not done much ir
of fish.

Q. How many fishermen do you suppose are fitted fro
now ?—A. Not a mackereler.

Q. Take Camden; how many did they use to have and l
have they now ?—A. Camden has always been a small fisl
About eight vessels, if I recollect.

Q. Are there any now ?—A. Yes, there are, but I guess ther
three now.

Q. Are they in the bay ?—A. No, none in the bay.

Q. Take North Haven ?—A. Well, I guess they have had
there.

Q. Any there now ?—A. None.

Q. Eastport; how many did they use to have ?—A. When l
there in 1862 they had eight mackerelers.

Q. Are there any now in the bay ?—A. None—nowhere.

Q. Now those various places in which the number of ve
have gone in the bay have diminished to nothing, what are
sels doing now, where they still own them ?—A. Fishing on t
can shore. They are divided between seining on the shor
fishing.

Q. That leads me to ask you as to the condition of the mack
ing on the shores of Maine. How is it, and how how has it b
last eight or ten years ?—A. I don't know that I understand.

Q. The catch of mackerel on the shores of Maine; has it ir
diminished ?—A. It has decreased this year.

Q. I don't mean this year particularly, but take the gene

ten years past. How is the mackerel business of the coast compared with what it used to be?—A. My impression is there was as many mackerel put up on the coast of Maine last year, 1876, perhaps as there ever was. I only speak from recollection. I know they were very plenty.

Q. How is it as to summer-fishing grounds? Where are the summer-fishing grounds?—A. For mackerel? I should think three-fourths of all the mackerel there is taken in the United States is taken on the coast of Maine.

Q. Now include in that the mackerel which are taken by your vessels in the bay.—A. What do you say?

Q. Including the mackerel taken by your vessels in the bay, what proportion of all the mackerel taken, whether in the bay or on the coast, is taken on the American coast?—A. What part of them?

Q. Yes; what proportion of the whole?—A. I don't know.

Q. Have you any means of forming a judgment?—A. No; but I think the amount taken in the gulf is very small indeed compared with the mackerel packed in the States.

Q. You should know. You have had a long experience as inspector and otherwise.—A. Do you speak of that period for which I was inspector?

Q. I mean to include the whole period while you were inspector or an observer of the matter as a merchant.—A. I should think from '62 to '69—during that period of time I should think there was more than 50 per cent. of all the mackerel taken was taken in the Gulf of Saint Lawrence. I should think so.

Q. Since that time how has it been?—A. It is all run down to a point almost. Everything has been taken this way.

Q. You mean in Maine?—A. Maine and Massachusetts.

Q. Then what do you say of the bay-fishing now, its present condition? I don't mean just to-day, but historically, taking the last ten years, five years, three years, two years, and so on. What condition is it in?—A. Well, I should say it was worthless. You mean the St. Lawrence, do you? Well, I should say it was worthless.

Q. And practically the people have so treated it?—A. They have.

Q. They have either gone out of the fishing or gone to other places?—A. They have gone seining on our shores.

Q. When you seine on the American shores, how far do you go? What is the limit of your seining?—A. Well, our folks rarely go outside of the Georges. In fact, they don't go beyond that at all. Perhaps twenty miles from the shore would be the most common ground. All the way from Portland down to Mount Desert Rock.

Q. Then you would say between Georges and Mount Desert Rock was about the limit of your seining?—A. Yes.

Q. Is that business an increasing business?—A. It has depreciated a good deal this year.

Q. But within the last ten years it has been increasing?—A. Yes, I guess it has been. I guess these last ten years it has been.

Q. Now from 1854 to 1866 you recollect was the Reciprocity Treaty?—A. Yes.

Q. During that time you had free scope fishing the gulf. You fished without respect to the three-mile line. Now, during that time when you had free access to the coast, was there any difference in the general result of the fisheries? Was it any more favorable to the people of the United States then?—A. Well, the fishing was very good in the St. Lawrence until about the year 1868.

Q. Well, was it any more favorable? Was there any difference that

you observed between the fishing at the time you had liberty to
without respect to the three-mile limit and the time when there wa
obstruction?—A. Yes, sir. Since I was quite young and went t
myself in 1837 I have always thought it an advantage to us, the fis
within three miles.

Q. How did that compare in your opinion with the advantage of
ing duties laid upon British fish coming into your markets?—
should say, taking the duties into consideration, reciprocity was al
against us.

Q. Now you know the opinion of the fishing people in Maine. I
been your duty to examine and go to every town once a year. V
was the general opinion you found among the fishermen and fishers as to the benefit they got from the Reciprocity Treaty as fisher
balancing the privilege of fishing inshore against the removal of
duties?—A. Well, sir, I have spent a good deal of time, especially v
I was inspector for the State, in trying to get at public opinion in t
fishing towns. I have consulted a great many captains and owne
vessels. From 1860 to '63, '64, '65, and '66 there was not a great
said about it, because the mackerel were plenty in the Gulf of St.
rence; but so far as I know for several years before the treaty wa
pealed they were very glad to see the time coming that we shoul
placed back where we were under the Treaty of 1818. The feeling
strongly against reciprocity.

Q. That is with reference to the fishery clauses of the treaty?—A.
in reference to fish. I didn't refer to anything else.

Q. Do you say that from your observations and the experience
have had that there was a strong opinion among the people of M
engaged in the fisheries?—A. Yes.

Q. They preferred to go back to the arrangement by which they
excluded from the inshore grounds and had power to impose dutie
British fish?—A. Yes.

Q. Well, from your whole experience down to within the last
years, is there much value in your judgment in the inshore fishe
that is, within three miles?—A. I think there is a value.

Q. I asked if there was much?—A. No; I don't think it is great;
I think there is a value in the inshore fisheries.

Q. It is more for the boats than for vessels, is it not? How is tha
A. I don't know anything about boats. We only go there in ve
from 50 to 100 tons. There is a value and a fear. We were very
our way when we had the privilege of buying licenses of the En
folks.

Q. You are probably looking to a different point from that to w
I directed you, but you may go on with reference to the apprehens
you used to have when it was not permitted to you to go within. What
they?—A. Well, there were a great many captains that had no int
in the vessels, and they would seem to take risks that they ough
of fishing inshore. Somehow they seemed to have an impression
it was no harm to catch fish inshore if they were not caught.

Q. Now, what other reasons influenced you besides the fear tha
captains would actually go inshore?—A. Well, it was a great poi
determine when a vessel was within three miles. There was nothin
indicate it, and it was a matter of judgment between the American
sels and the cruisers. The vessels seemed to be apprehensive that
would be taken off three, four, five, or six miles.

Q. Now, from your experience, is it, or is it not, difficult to deter
from a vessel, especially when the shore is high, what distance yo

off?—A. I think it is a very difficult thing indeed to determine just the distance from shore.

Q. Now from which class of vessels—there were some naval vessels and those fitted out by the provinces—which class of vessels did you have trouble from?—A. They were all called cutters in '37, if my memory serves me right.

Q. Do you know from what you learned whether there was any difference in the treatment of the men and the liberties given to them, the degree of severity practiced, as between officers of the regular navy and those of the cutters fitted out by the provinces?—A. Well, I was not in the bay. When I was in the bay there were three sailing cutters. Of late years those captains seemed very exacting, but when the naval officers came they seemed to be more liberal and easy. They would go aboard and tell them what the regulations were, and leave documents with them, and advise them not to catch inside.

Q. How was it with the captain of the Canadian cutters?—A. They were very arbitrary.

Q. Were there frequent complaints?—A. Yes; I think so. I can't say. I saw two vessels taken down at Margaree one morning—Gloucester vessels, I think. They made a great deal of trouble that day, but really at that time I could not see that the cutters were to blame. I saw the vessels taken. They were within three miles.

Q. So far as position is concerned, the cutters were not in fault, but did you know anything about the conduct of the officers when they boarded them?—A. No; we were under sail, trying to get out of the way of the cutters.

Q. What was done, and what the people complained of, you were not witness of?—A. No.

Q. Now I want to ask you, going back to the year 1837, was there any other difficulty with reference to the right to draw the lines from headland to headland? I don't ask you whether you had this experience yourself?—A. Well, I heard that matter freely discussed among the American fishermen, but I knew nothing of it.

Q. You had no experience of it?—A. No.

Q. But you heard it discussed?—A. Yes.

Q. As a question between them and the cutters?—A. No, not to my knowledge. I have only been aboard vessels when they were telling about this, that, and the other thing being wrong, about the drawing of these lines from the headlands, and about the cutters exacting things that they ought not.

Q. For what reason was it, when the licenses were at a low fee, that your people took them?—A. For fear they would be seized. They knew, of course, that the three-mile limit, as it was understood, was an indefinite thing; it created a fear on the part of the captains that they might be innocently taken. Then again, as I have said, there were times when they were satisfied that the inside fisheries were valuable.

Q. So it was partly the value of the privilege of being able to fish where they liked, and partly the fear of being taken when they ought not to be?—A. Yes.

Q. Have you made any inquiries specifically as to the captures of those vessels and the rules laid down?—A. I have heard a great deal about it.

Q. You have no statistics?—A. No.

By Mr. Weatherbe:

Q. You were speaking of the lines drawn from headland to headland; what years did you refer to?—A. I referred particularly to the year

1837, and so in the year 1833, the two years I was mackerel-f
in the gulf.

Q. Well, you were not referring to any other years except those
No, I never was there.

Q. And you were only speaking of those years?—A. Yes, that
regard to the headland question.

Q. But you spoke of the cutters being very exacting?—A. W
course, I only spoke of what I heard aboard those vessels. I
nothing about it.

Q. You were just merely speaking of something you heard in
A. Yes.

Q. How often did you hear it that year?—A. Well, I was down
quite late in the fall, and it was a subject of constant conversat
board our American vessels.

Q. Don't you think you are mistaken?—A. About what?

Q. How many cutters were there?—A. Three I think.

Q. Did you ever see any cutter there that year?—A. I saw
take those two Cape Ann vessels. I think it was 1837. I may t
taken as to the year.

Q. You only saw one. Yes.

Q. How many did you say you saw?—A. I saw three of them, l
it was, cruising in the bay that fall I was there last time.

Q. Were they exacting to you?—A. No.

Q. They didn't annoy you?—A. No.

Q. You didn't fish inshore at all?—A. Yes, we did. I caught
is, the vessel I was in—23 barrels.

Q. But you caught those in one day?—A. Yes, one morning
breakfast.

Q. All the rest you caught outside?—A. Yes.

Q. You never caught any except the 23 barrels of macke
shore?—A. That is all ever when I was engaged in the bay.

Q. You caught these in the morning before breakfast?—A. Y

Q. You never tried to fish inshore any other time. You fish
shore every other time except that?—A. I think so.

Q. Was there a cutter in sight when you caught these?—A.]
If there had been we would not have been likely to catch them.

Q. You said you had an idea it was right?—A. I was only sp
of the opinions of the captain's.

Q. That was the only time you ran any risk?—A. Yes. We w
St. Peter's early in the morning and got becalmed.

Q. That is the only time you run any risk?—A. Yes.

Q. Where was that?—A. Right off St. Peter's.

Q. That was pretty good fishing. You had a pretty good time
Yes; that is the best fishing I ever saw in my life aboard a vesse

Q. One would wonder why you didn't try it again?—A. We dic
it then. We were coming out of harbor and got becalmed, and t
came up all around us solid, apparently, and just as soon a
breezed up the fish all left us; but during this time we had 23 t

Q. Well, you never tried it again?—A. I don't recollect that v
tried it again.

Q. The cutter never troubled or boarded you any time whateve
No.

Q. From what experience you have had, your own personal expe
the best fishing is inside?—A. Within three miles?

Q. Certainly.—A. Well, no.

Q. You never saw anything better than that catch of 23 barı

the time, and that is the only time you tried?—A. We were surrounded by hundreds of vessels.

Q. But, looking to your own personal experience, the best fishing there that you knew was within three miles?—A. Yes; well, I never saw 23 barrels caught, that I recollect, so quickly as we caught them that morning.

Q. And you never tried it any other time? (No answer.)

Mr. TRESCOT. Did he understand your question?

Mr. WEATHERBE. Did you understand?—A. Yes; I believe I understand.

Q. Then, with regard to the value of the inshore fisheries in the Gulf of St. Lawrence, you have no personal knowledge later than 1837?—A. No practical knowledge.

Q. But since that I understood you to say you had acquired knowledge by procuring information?—A. I commenced when I was done fishing to fit out vessels.

Q. Have you ever acquired any knowledge from others with regard to the value of the inshore fisheries since 1837?—A. I have invariably consulted all my captains.

Q. You recollect when the agitation was going on in regard to the Reciprocity Treaty in 1852 in your State?—A. Yes; in 1854. We were, down to that, against it.

Q. I suppose you are acquainted with Senator Hamlin?—A. Yes; and with Mr. Pyke, too. He voted against it. I circulated a petition.

Q. I am asking you with reference to Senator Hamlin. He took an interest in this question of the fisheries, did he not?—A. Yes; but I have really forgotten about it.

Q. You yourself, in 1852, did not consider the fisheries of the gulf of any value, I think?—A. In 1852? I always considered them of some value.

Q. How much value? In 1852-'54, for instance.—A. Well, I don't know any distinction, since I went fishing, in the value of the inshore fisheries.

Q. Now, you are here as officer of the government in the State of Maine, having collected statistics, and you have brought a book full of statistics, I suppose?—A. You said I came on purpose for this examination. I had a dispatch, and a very few moments after I got the dispatch I came unprepared.

Q. What I said was that you had collected statistics. It was known you had collected statistics. It was known you were a man likely to be well acquainted with the subject. Now, I want to ask you whether it was considered in the State of Maine in 1852, 1853, 1854, or any of those years, that the inshore fisheries were of a great deal of value?—A. Well, so far as I know, although I had not at that time traveled over the State of Maine, I probably got hold of the opinion of our fishing communities and towns, from Portsmouth to Eastport, and they were opposed to the opening of our markets to foreign fish, or, in other words to the Reciprocity Treaty.

Q. What I want to get at is this, whether the general feeling in that State was opposed to it, or whether the people were generally of the opinion that the inshore fisheries of the Gulf of St. Lawrence were of very little use to you. Tell us that?—A. So far as I know ever since I can recollect having anything to do in Bay Chaleurs they always were frightened at this three-mile restriction.

Q. You certainly understand my question. Were your fisherman of

the opinion that the three-mile inshore fisheries of the gulf were of
to them or not ?—A. I think they considered them of considerable va
    Q. You think they did ?—A. Yes.
    Q. Did that opinion continue, or, if not, when did the opinion char
—A. I don't know that that opinion has ever changed.
    Q. Let me read you just a few lines from the remarks of Senator H
lin. I suppose you are a supporter of his, that you have been, and
at this time ?—A. Yes.
    Q. He is a very able man ?—A. He is said to be.
    Q. After describing the magnitude and importance of the Amer
fisheries " as the great fountains of commercial prosperity and n:
power," he declared that " if American fisherman were kept out of t!
inshore waters, the immense amount of property thus invested w
become useless, and leave them in want and beggary, or in priso
foreign jails."—A. That was in 1852. That was from headland to h
land.
    Q. Now my impression was that they were discussing the ques
irrespective of the headland question. They were discussing the q
tion whether the fish were not caught within three miles of the sho'
    Mr. DANA. It may save you the trouble of examining if I state
known fact which cannot affect the witness' mind, that that speech
made while Great Britain claimed the whole Bay of Fundy and all tl
bays.
    Mr. WEATHERBE. He was arguing in favor of reciprocity. (To
witness.) Are you acquainted with Mr. Scudder, of Massachusett:
A. No.
    Q. Mr. Scudder, of Massachusetts, said, referring to the mackere

    These fish are taken in the waters nearer to the coast than the codfish are. A
siderable portion—from one-third to one-half—are taken on the coasts and in the
and gulfs of the British provinces. The inhabitants of the provinces take many of ·
in boats and with seines. The boat and seine fishery is the more successful and
fitable, and would be pursued by our fishermen were it not for the stipulations o
Convention of 1818, between the United States and Great Britain, by which it is
tended that all the fisheries within three miles of the coast, with few unimportan
ceptions, are secured to the provinces alone. Mr. Tuck, of New Hampshire, said:
inshore fishery, which we have renounced, is of great value, and extremely impor
to American fishermen. From the first of September to the close of the season
mackerel run near the shore, and it is next to impossible for our vessels to obtain
without taking fish within the prohibited limits. The truth is, our fishermen
absolutely and must have the thousands of miles of shore fishery which they hav
nounced, or they must always do an uncertain business. If our mackerel men are
hibited from going within three miles of the shore, and are forcibly kept away
nothing but force will do it), then they may as well give up their business first as
It will be always uncertain.

That was correct at that time ?—A. No; Mr. Tuck never went fisl
there.
    Q. I don't suppose Senator Hamlin did either?—A. No.
    Q. Were these opinions correct or not ?—A. I guess not.
    Q. They didn't represent the popular view ?—A. I guess they v
discussing the agitated question of the line from headland to headl:
    Q. I will have to read it again. "The truth is, our fishermen r
absolutely and must have the thousands of miles of inshore fishery wl
they have renounced, or they must always do an uncertain business
A. I understand perfectly. The idea of Mr. Tuck is that, because
sels are excluded from three miles, it must make the business uncert
    Q. Do you think it was a profitable business outside in the gul:
that time, if they were excluded from within three miles ?—A. It w:
profitable business. It was so in 1852, and it continued so until 1.
    Q. If the American fishermen had been excluded by force, rigi

from within three miles of the shore, it would have been a profitable business from 1854 to 1868 ?—A. Yes; the mackerel have been dropping off since as early as 1866. Since the period I have mentioned it has not been profitable anywhere.

Q. Was that true at that time—that which I have read ?—A. I guess it wants to be qualified some.

Q. Nobody seems to have controverted it in Congress ?—A. If that refers strictly to within three miles of the shore, they attach more consequence to that three-mile restriction than the fishermen generally do.

Q. You said Senator Hamlin was a popular man. Didn't he represent the fishermen's views at that time ?—A. I suppose he thought he was.

Q. Are you able to state that he did not ?—A. What do you say ?

Q. What great authority can you give us now that took a different view of the case at that time ?—A. I say he attaches a greater consequence to it than the fishermen generally.

Q. Give me the name of any man of eminence.—A. I should very much rather have an opinion on that question from practical mackerelmen than from the honorable Hannibal Hamlin.

Q. Can you give me the opinion of practical mackerel-men obtained at that time?—A. I have seen them since I came to Halifax. I have conversed with a great many that know more about the fisheries than ever he did.

Q. Your own experience that morning exactly coincides with Senator Hamlin's views ?—A. Yes.

Q. Well, now I ask you if you can give me the name of any practical mackerel-man who understood the question in 1852, and who would differ from Senator Hamlin ?—A. I recollect that there was that controversy, since you have brought it up, but it has left my mind, and perhaps I never should have thought of it unless you had brought it up.

Q. What was the feeling of your best fishermen ?—A. I am unable to say.

Q. But what their feelings are now, that we claim money, you are able to say ?—A. Are you claiming money; is that so ?

Q. You know that, don't you ?—A. Well, I have heard something about money compensation, but I didn't know you were sincere in it, really.

Q. You think this is a farce ?—A. I believe every word you say.

Q. I ask you whether you were not aware that the proceedings under which you were produced here were in consequence of a claim on the part of Great Britain for money ?—A. Well, I recollect it has been talked of that you claimed money.

Q. Did you know you were brought as a witness to give evidence to resist it ?—A. I know I came here to testify what I knew of the fishing in the bay.

Q. Did you know that the parties who brought you here were resisting a claim for money ?—A. No; I did not.

Q. Do you know the provisions of the Washington Treaty with regard to the fisheries ?—A. Well, the main part of the Washington Treaty I suppose I do know. I know we have a right of fishing inshore. Is not that correct ?

Q. Certainly.—A. And I thought that the Englishmen thought the free fishing on our coast was insufficient to compensate you for our privilege of fishing inshore, and you wanted so much money on top of that. I never knew there was any sum or anything of that kind.

Q. You did understand the question ?—A. I understood at the tim passed, but how many years is it since it passed ?

Q. Well, never mind. What did you suppose this Commission for ?—A. I haven't thought of it for years.

Q. You didn't know we were trying that very question now ?—A did.

Q. You gave your evidence with that knowledge ?—A. Yes.

Q. You think now that the value of the inshore fishery has changed A. No; I have the same opinion that I have always had. I have s all through that they were valuable to us.

Q. Now with regard to the right of carrying our fish free into United States, I suppose you think that is of no advantage to your fisl men, that provision of the treaty ?—A. I have no idea it is any advant to our side of the house.

Q. It is a disadvantage, isn't it ?—A. Yes; it is against us.

Q. Be kind enough to explain how ?—A. Well, all these things se to me to be regulated by supply and demand. If there is 100,000 t rels of mackerel hove into our market on top of what we produce tendency is to depreciate prices.

Q. If this provision of the treaty increases the supply of mackere: the United States market it will bring down the price of fish ?—A. St that again.

(Question repeated.)—A. I think it would have that tendency.

Q. That is the reason you think it is no advantage to your fisl men to have the privilege of fishing inside ?—A. No; putting both visions of the treaty together, it is no advantage, because the suppl: increased and the prices are depreciated.

Q. You will admit this, that it is an advantage to the consumers bringing down the price ? You will admit that ?—A. Yes.

Q. Then in point of fact it gives you cheap fish ?—A. The tendenc to cheapen them.

Q. For the people of the United States ?—A. Yes.

No. 54.

WILFORD J. FISHER, of Eastport, Me., called on behalf of the G ernment of the United States, sworn and examined.

By Mr. Trescot:

Question. Of what place are you a native ?—Answer. Grand Mar

Q. How old are you ?—A. Fifty-six.

Q. Where do you live now ?—A. At Eastport, Me.

Q. How old were you when you moved to Eastport ?—A. I could tell you without thinking.

Q. You are fifty-six years old now. How long have you lived Eastport ?—A. Since 1845.

Q. What is your present occupation at Eastport?—A. I am agen an express company, and am doing a general commission business.

Q. How long have you been doing that ?—A. For the last six ye

Q. Do you recollect how old you were when you left Grand Ma and went to Eastport?—A. I left Grand Manan when I was twenty-years of age.

Q. While you lived on Grand Manan what was your occupation ?—My father kept an extensive fishing establishment and was fitting fishing vessels. I worked with him until I was twenty-one or twe two years of age.

Q. Describe to the Commission what sort of business you were engaged in while assisting your father in this business?—A. Our business was fitting out fishermen, curing fish, drying fish, and marketing them after I got old enough.

Q. You were engaged in that until you were twenty-two?—A. Yes.

Q. About what time did you go into your father's business? Early?—A. I used to go to school in the day-time and work in the fish-yard night and morning before and after school. As I got older I took more charge of the business.

Q. As I understand you the time you left school and went into the establishment entirely you were twenty-one years old and were in charge of the whole department of fitting vessels, dealing with the fish, taking them to market included?—A. Yes.

Q. Well, after that what did you do?—A. After that I went to sea for two years.

Q. What do you mean when you say you went to sea; did you go as a fisherman?—A. No; I went in a merchant vessel.

Q. Your father's vessel?—A. No; in an American vessel.

Q. After that?—A. After that I brought up in Eastport and went into business.

Q. What sort of business at Eastport?—A. Fitting out fishermen and general business, curing fish, and trading in West India produce, and all kinds of business done by our general stores.

Q. How long did that continue?—A. 15 years.

Q. What did you do after that?—A. I went to Grand Manan again and weir-fished for 8 or 10 years. About that time I commenced to make herring oil. I had weirs at Grand Manan, and went over and engaged in the manufacture of herring oil and smoking herring.

Q. How long did you remain at Grand Manan?—A. 8 or 9 years, I think; I made no calculation and should not like to state exactly. Somewhere about that time.

Q. Well, after you went to Grand Manan did you return to Eastport?—A. Yes.

Q. You have been ever since at Eastport?—A. Yes.

Q. What business have you been in since?—A. Express and general commission business. I have been buying hake-sounds for parties in Boston.

Q. As I understood, when you went back to Grand Manan you were doing a weir business?—A. Yes, sir.

Q. What have you done with them?—A. I have them still.

Q. Do you work them yourself?—A. No; I rent them.

Q. You have been renting them ever since?—A. I have been renting them the last six years. Sometimes I rent them for an annual payment for the privilege, and some of the weirs I rent on a fifth, building the weirs myself. In other cases I make a trade with them to build the weirs for so much, and give me so much net proceeds. I make the best trade I can.

Q. How many weirs are you interested in?—A. Three large weirs. One we didn't build this year. Only two were built this year, on account of the smoked herring being very low.

Q. Are you still employed in smoking herring and curing them?—A. Yes; in the way I have stated.

Q. I want you to explain to the Commission the character of the business done at the weirs. What force have you employed there?—A. Well, the weirs are built in the eddies, places where the herring frequent. They are caught in the weirs. The weirs are built so that the

tide never leaves them. We are obliged to do that so as not to destr
the herring, to have none die in the weirs. They have a large ga
which takes boats 12 feet wide and we take them in masts and all. V
can open it twelve feet wide the whole height of the weir so that t
boat comes in without stepping the masts. We seine the herring th
are in the weir and put them in the boats, then take them ashore ai
wash them out, scale them and string them on sticks and put them
the smoke-house, smoke them and box them. After being boxed \
sell them wherever we can get most money for them.

Q. What force have you employed in those weirs?—A. When I fish
there myself I had five to twelve men according to the season. Sor
months we are obliged to employ more men than others.

Q. On each weir?—A. No; that would be what we call a gang.

By Sir Alexander Galt:

Q. How many men are required to manage one weir?—A. Twel
men to manage one weir.

Q. It would take twelve men?—A. Yes; that would be for two
three months; that is all.

By Mr. Trescot:

Q. What months?—A. October has usually been the best month i
the last two years. Six or eight years ago we used to catch them ev
earlier in the season. Sometimes we got a heavy haul of herring
April. Last year we got a very heavy catch in April.

Q. Then it comes in the fall again?—A. Yes; they come towards f
again. They vary with the seasons on account of the weather or sor
other cause we can't control. They are about sure to come withir
month or six weeks.

Q. Can you tell the Commissioners what is the proportion, as far
catching herring is concerned, in Grand Manan of the weir fishery
the sea fishery? Could you form any idea at all?—A. I don't kno
that I understand the question. You mean the proportion of herri
caught in weir to the proportion caught in nets?

Q. Yes; at sea in nets and boats.

Mr. THOMSON. What do you mean by at sea?

Mr. TRESCOT. I mean the proportion caught in weirs as compar
with those not so caught. I don't care whether inshore or out.—A. The
is none of the class we catch in weirs but very few that are caught
boats. The herring we smoke are smaller than these caught in nets ai
boats.

Q. Then the smoked herring are essentially from weirfi-shing?—
Yes; exclusively so, except as to a few large herring smoked late in t
year, or partly smoked, that they call bloaters.

Q. The herring fishery at Grand Manan consists of different class
of fish. There is the smoked herring, that is one class?—A. Yes.

Q. What others?—A. The other business is to catch them in nets i
bait to catch line fish with, and another business is to catch them in no
to freeze them and sell them fresh for food. There is a very few peo]
who follow the catching of herring to pack in barrels of salt because t
market has been so dull. It is not followed much and has not been i
a number of years to any extent. It is followed some, but not to t
extent it used to be.

Q. Now what are pickled herring?—A. They are herring caught
nets, put in barrels, and sold as pickled herring.

Q. They are the same kind that are caught and frozen, but not t
same kind that are smoked?—A. Just so.

Q. Then you have the smoked herring, the fresh herring caught for bait; the herring that is caught and frozen for bait and food, and the pickled herring, which you say is a very small proportion of the business; so I understand you?—A. You understand pretty nearly. But the freezing of the herring for food can only be done in cold weather, so that if the weather is not cold enough some of that is pickled, but not much is pickled otherwise, as the salt and barrels are an expense.

TUESDAY, *October* 1, 1877.

The Commission met.

Examination of WILFORD J. FISHER continued.

By Mr. Trescot:

Question. When you closed yesterday, you had described the way of fishing to the Commissioners, and stated that the smoked-herring fishery at Grand Manan was almost essentially a weir-fishery; can you give the Commission any idea of what the amount of smoked-herring business is at Grand Manan?—Answer. I estimate the amount of smoked herring cured at Grand Manan at 400,000 boxes.

Q. Annually?—A. Yes; annually.

Q. Where is the market for these smoked herring?—A. In the United States almost altogether.

Q. These herring are shipped directly from the Island of Grand Manan?—A. They are now, under the present arrangements, under the treaty.

Q. In what are they shipped? In American vessels or by parties in the island?—A. There are four English vessels that have been running in, one from New York and three to Boston. These vessels are owned by people at Grand Manan. Then there are occasionally other vessels chartered to load herring for Boston.

Q. Do I understand by that that they are chartered by Grand Manan people?—A. Yes.

Q. What vessels are these generally?—A. Just such vessels as they can pick up. It does not make any difference as to the character of the vessels running from Grand Manan to New York or Boston. Either English or American vessels can go.

Q. You say there are four vessels owned by people in Grand Manan in which they ship smoked herring to Boston and New York?—A. Yes; a large part of them; and a large part of them are sold at Eastport.

Q. Mostly caught in weirs?—A. Altogether in weirs.

Q. Then there would be no portion that would be caught by Americans?—A. No; unless they went there and leased part of the weir.

Q. It is all a Grand Manan fishery essentially; the cargo is shipped in Grand Manan vessels and shipped by the people of Grand Manan?—A. Yes; in addition to the smoked herring business at Grand Manan, the island of Campobello smokes, I should think, 250,000 boxes; Indian Island, Deer Island, and the rest of the small islands around the immediate vicinity about 50,000 more. I should say there were 700,000 boxes of smoked herring cured in our immediate vicinity on these British islands.

Q. These fisheries at Campobello, Deer Island, and the neighboring islands are all fisheries of the natives of those islands?—A. Yes.

Q. Now with regard to the frozen and pickled herring, what sort of a business is done at Grand Manan and the islands adjacent, to the best of your knowledge, in that article?—A. The frozen herring and pickled herring are the same herring, caught in the same way and by the same

men. The frozen herring business can only be carried on in the w
when the weather is cold. If a man sets his net for bait and gets
herring than he wants to use, he salts them in barrels; that is the
way he can utilize them at this time. In the winter season they fi
exclusively for this frozen herring business, but there are times in
winter season when thaws come on and soft weather; then, if a mar
his nets out and catches fish, he can't freeze them, and he then pi
them in barrels. But there is no way they can make so much m
out of herring as freezing them and selling them in a frozen stat
requires no barrels and no salt, and the outlay is labor altogether.

Q. Well, by whom is the catching of herring for the purpose of
ing conducted generally?—A. Mostly altogether in our vicinity by
minion fishermen. There is a small number of fishermen at Eas
that, when there is no herring there, would go down to Letite and
Bay, and amongst the islands; but the number of Dominion fishe:
is very small.

Q. What is the proportion of the foreign fishing compared with
of the natives at Grand Manan?—A. I think Eastport does not se
boats or vessels in the frozen-herring business on the shores of the
minion of Canada. Perhaps in relation to that I had better state
cumstance: there are a good many people living at Eastport wh
British subjects; they have British vessels; they fish in British ve
On the other hand, there is a number of American vessels that have
owned and are owned at Deer Island and other places on the Dom
side, that are owned and sailed by Dominion men, but still are t
American register; they have never been transferred. But the nu
of Americans who leave our place to go fishing for frozen herri
comparatively small in proportion to the whole number engaged i
business.

Q. What is done with these frozen herring, are they shipped?
Yes, sir. There is a good many of these bought at Eastport b
people there who engage in that business, and are shipped on the ste
to Boston. But a large quantity is sold to American vessels tha
there and buy them.

Q. For the purpose of bait?—A. No; mostly for food. I should
pose those that come for bait only take small quantities. Those
come from Gloucester carry away full loads.

Q. Well, besides these two herring fisheries, what are the fish
around Grand Manan?—A. The fishing around Grand Manan is co
pollock, haddock, and hake.

Q. Are these fisheries within three miles of the shore or off sho
A. Some are within three miles.

Q. Which? Tell the Commissioners where the fisheries are,
rule.—A. There is a time early in the spring and late in the fall
the fish come in close to the shores at Grand Manan, codfish and had
principally. The haddock around Grand Manan is caught in
mostly altogether—mostly within the three-mile limit. The pollock
codfish are mostly caught outside of the three-mile limit. Gra
ground is a great place for pollock, and that, in my judgment, is wi
the limit. The hake fishing, since trawling has commenced, they
gone off shore. It was always supposed that you had to get a m
bottom to catch hake. This trawling business has brought
new idea, and the fishermen have found their best hake last yea
this year on hard bottom between Campobello and Grand Man:
deep water—larger fish and more of them—and the fleet of vessels
have followed hake fishing this year have most all exclusively con

themselves to that fishing-ground which I consider without the three miles.

Q. Of these four fisheries, hake, haddock, pollock, and cod, what is the respective value? I mean as fisheries.—A. The quantity of hake, and their value, I could give you very near, but the others would be, of course, more liable not to be correct. I am largely engaged in the sound business. The quintal of hake makes one and a quarter pounds of sounds, and it is not only my business to know what sounds I buy myself, but how much are brought in the neighborhood, and whose hands they go into. This year the hake business has been larger than any year since my remembrance.

Q. This year, I understand, it has been offshore?—A. Yes, a very large catch. I estimate the quantity of sounds this year in our district, including in that Grand Manan and everything from Point Lepreau, 33,000 pounds. Perhaps it may be more, 1,000 pounds over. It will not, I think, go under. By taking a quarter from that you have the quantity of hake caught. Now, last year we didn't get quite ten tons of sounds altogether in the whole district.

Q. What I want to get at is this: What is the relative proportion that the hake fishing bears to the haddock, cod, or pollock? Which is the most valuable, I mean generally?—A. The inshore or offshore?

Q. Take it altogether, and then I will ask you separately. Is the haddock offshore or inshore?—A. It is offshore and inshore.

Q. How about the pollock?—A. The pollock is caught more offshore than in.

Q. Then the codfish?—A. The codfish are almost exclusively caught offshore, except, as I tell you, in the early spring or late in the fall there is a school of small codfish that strikes within the limits, and the people there catch them more or less.

Q. Then, as I understand, generally the codfish is an offshore fishery —the valuable codfish?—A. Yes.

Q. The hake i s offshore also?—A. Yes.

Q. The pollock is also offshore?—A. Yes.

Q. And the haddock is inshore and offshore?—A. Yes, but understand me, I don't say there is not a few hake, pollock, and cod inshore.

Q. I mean generally. Now of these four which is the most valuable? —A. At Grand Manan this year the hake fishery is the most valuable by far. At Campobello the hake offshore is most valuable.

Q. Now, by whom are these fisheries mainly conducted at Grand Manan?—A. They are conducted by the inhabitants of Grand Manan.

Q. Is there a large proportion of American fishermen engaged in these fisheries within your knowledge?—A. I know of Americans who go there and hire by the month to the weir fishermen.

Q. No, I am talking about the American boats and vessels?—A. The quantity of American boats and vessels that go there to fish inside is very small, very small indeed.

Q. Could you form any estimate what would be the annual value of the fishery at Grand Manan, taking the opposite coast, and taking the neighborhood generally, from your experience as a man of business with some practical acquaintance with the operations yourself as a merchant; what would be the annual value, including Grand Manan and the coast from Letite to St. Andrews and Lepreau?—A. I should set the value of the fish caught at Grand Manan at not over $400,000. They might go $500,000, but I think if I had $500,000 I would have some left.

Q. That is for Grand Manan. Now for the coast on the other side.—

A. From Point Lepreau to St. Andrews and all the islands conne
including Campobello, I should put less than a million. It is a p
hard thing to estimate, but I should say considerably less than a
ion, with everything included—herring, oil, the fish-tummies, sm
herring, hake sounds, and the fish themselves.

Q. That excludes Grand Manan ?—A. Yes; I put down Grand M
at $400,000, and all the other places around our vicinity at not o
million.

Q. Now, I will read some questions put to and answers made
gentleman supposed to be familiar with that portion of the fisheries
without asking you to contradict him, I want to ask you how far
judgment agrees with his. I refer to the evidence of James Mac
merchant, Letite, parish of St. George, Charlotte County, New B
wick; do you know him ?—A. Very well; I am very intimate with

Q. These are the questions and answers, if you will attend to th

Q. Judging from your practical knowledge of the fishery, being an owner of v
and dealing with the men who fish as you do, what do you say, at a low figure,
be the value of the fisheries and the actual worth of the fish caught by British su
between the points you mention from Lepreau to Letite; what would be a fair
age value from 1871 ?—A. I should estimate the quantity for Charlotte County an
adjoining islands. We all fish, and it would be difficult to separate the two.
Q. You are acquainted with the value of the islands as well ?—A. Yes; I visit
Manan occasionally, and the adjoining islands often.
Q. What is the catch of the whole ?—A. A low estimate for our fishing wou
$1,000,000 for each year.
Q. For British subjects ?—A. Yes.
Q. That is a low estimate ?—A. I think I am under the mark; in fact, I ha
doubt of it at all.
Q. And it may be a good deal more ?—A. Yes.
Q. You have not a shadow of a doubt that it is at least a million ?—A. No.
Q. And our American friends take a considerable amount more ?—A. They t;
many.
Q. They have more men and more vessels ?—A. Yes.
Q. And they take at least as much ?—A. Yes, fully as much as we do, if not m
Q. Have you any doubt that they take more ?—A. I believe that they take mo
Q. You have no doubt of it ?—A. No.

Q. With your knowledge, would you say that was an accurate a
ment of the fishing between Letite and Lepreau ?—A. I shall not
my estimate by hearing that.

Q. Do you know of any American vessels engaged in these wa
in those fisheries, taking anything like an approximate amount of a
ion ?—A. No; it is impossible. It is erroneous. The imports o
country would not show it, and cannot show it; it is impossible.

Q. Now, here is from another witness whom you may know
Walter B. McLaughlan, light-house keeper and fishery-overseer at G
Manan, in the county of Charlotte, New Brunswick ?—A. I have kⁱ
him from a boy.

Q. (Reads:)

Q. You are well acquainted with the fisheries of Charlotte County; take the
land fishing from Letite as far as Lepreau, is that a good fishing ground ?—A. It
sidered a good fishing ground; I am not personally acquainted with it, and ca
say from what I have heard. My duties have never carried me there.
Q. But your practical knowledge extends there ?—A. Yes.
Q. What would be the value of the mainland fishery, the British fishery alon
ing it from Letite to Lepreau ?—A. My own fishery is, say, $500,000; Campobell
West Isles must equal mine, and the mainland will certainly be more than b
that, if not equal to it.
Q. Well, then, you put Campobello and West Isles as about equal to Grand Man
A. Yes; speaking as I do. Not knowing exactly, I should say so.
• Q. That would be a half a million for these two islands, and a half a milli
Grand Manan, that makes a million, and you think the mainland is half as mt
either of those; that would be a fair estimate for the mainland ?—A. Yes; Cha

County is a very important fishing county. In 1861 I was a census enumerator, and I think the result of the fishing in that county nearly equalled that of all the other fisheries of the province, with the exception of St. John County.

Q. You put half a million as the catch of the British fishermen on the mainland for the year, and, in your judgment, the American catch is the same?—A. All I can judge is by what I hear; they come down in their vessels; I think they have their own way on the North Shore, very much more than on Grand Manan. I have a great deal of trouble with them there. But on the North Shore I think they have things pretty much as they want. I would say that they probably surpass our own catch.

Now does your judgment conform with that statement?—A. If I heard that correctly, he estimates Grand Manan at $500,000, and Campobello and the adjacent islands $500,000, and half a million for the mainland.

Q. If he means that the mainland is half of Campobello and West Isles, it would be only $250,000?—A. He is under my estimate, but I should not alter my estimate.

Q. You put half a million for the mainland for a year? You don't agree with him?—A. No; I think he should have added $250,000 more.

Q. Now he is asked if, in his judgment, the American catch is the same as the British, and answers, "All I can judge by is what I hear. They come down in their vessels. I think they have their own way on the North shore very much more than at Grand Manan." Have you any idea that that is correct?—A. No. As I have said before, of that amount caught there there is not one-fifth that is caught by Americans. I would be safe in saying less.

Q. At page 256 he is asked by Mr. Foster what he includes in the mainland. Mr. Thomson answers, "From Point Lepreau to Letite;" and the witness says, "From Point Lepreau to St. Andrew's." Then, the question is asked, "You make one million and a half taken by Americans and the same by British fishermen," and the answer is yes; and then he answers in the affirmative to the question whether that is a low estimate.—A. That is where we differ. I say that of one and a half million taken, not more that one-fifth of that quantity may be taken by American fishermen. That includes off shore and inshore.

Q. You have been living in Eastport of late years?—A. Yes.

Q. And you know the neighborhood of Eastport, Lubec, and Cutler?—A. Yes, very well, indeed.

Q. Now, we have been told, although I can't find the evidence—what are the occupations of those places?—A. Eastport is what you would call a fitting village or town, or whatever you may call it—about 4,000 population. The merchants there fit out fishermen, but those fishermen that they fit out are the same men that come up from those islands—they come up to Eastport and fit out there to prosecute this fishery on the North shore, at Grand Manan, and other places in the Bay of Fundy. The amount of American vessels fitted from Eastport in the fishery business is very small, and it is decreasing every year, because it has not been a paying business. Then Eastport sends a number of vessels to the Magdalen Islands in the spring for herring. That has been heretofore quite a business with us, and is still followed up. Not so much this last year as formerly, because last year before last they lost a great deal of money by the Magdalen herring, on account of the price of smoked Magdalen herring declining very much in the market. A good many people kept Magdalen herring lying in the smoke-house until this year. They didn't sell them until this year. Then there is a certain number of small boats and vessels which don't exceed 25 at the outside, in my estimation, that fit out for this fishery; that is, hake fishing and frozen herring off shore. That is about the extent at Eastport. Then

158 F

Lubec, which is in the same district as Eastport, I think fits six ve
with which they fish exclusively on the Bank. They don't fish o
inshore ground. I could name these vessels, but I didn't bring an
Then Lemoine, in Maine, has had at Grand Manan this year, fi
three vessels. They fish without the limits. What we call]
Narrows has had one. Cutler has had two. At Pembroke, Perr;
all these places the people are not fishermen. They don't go fi:
They may take a boat when the pollack is in, in the summer, a'
down one or two days, and catch a few fish to take home for the wi
use, but they don't make a practice of fishing and they have not.

Q. This question was asked Mr. Maclelan: "Along that coast.
Eastport and Lubec toward Mount Desert, are there not great nu
of fishing villages that depend upon fishing for a living?" An
answer was: "They are about the same as our own; they live on
ing, fishing, farming, lumbering, and so on, just exactly as ours (
know no difference between them." Then the question was a
"Without our fisheries could they live by fishing?" And the a
was: "No; because if they could they would not come to our fisl
They would not come so far away. They do not have fisheries of
own." Now, of course, without the fisheries they could not live b
ing; but do you know of any community from Eastport to Mount]
that depends upon fishing, and that would be compelled to go o'
Grand Manan waters to fish?—A. No; not for the last twenty
As I tell you, Lemoine had this year three vessels; last year it ha
They used to have eight or ten thirty years ago. And these men
gone into the Bank fishing to Grand Bank. This year there ar
three that have favored the Bay of Fundy fishing, and they fish (
Grand Manan Bank, at a place which is outside the limits.

Q. In your experience in the smoked-herring business could the
ness sustain a duty of a dollar a barrel?—A. Well, it has alway:
by the box. I think the old duty was five cents a bag.

Q. If that duty were reimposed what would be the effect?—A
people would have to stop smoking them now.

Q. How is it about the accuracy of this statement, accordi
your judgment: "Q. Now, taking Grand Manan, judging by tl
turns that the fishermen give you, can you tell us what each
makes by fishing? Do you know that from statements of their o
from personal observation?—A. I think $1,000 a year would t
utmost each would make. I don't mean clear; they certainly woo
clear that"?—A. I should think that was large. Still, as I don'
Grand Manan, and I don't know how the people live there now, I ;
rather not answer as to that.

Q. What would you estimate to be the money-value of the fisl
the average fisherman would catch there in a year?—A. They
have to be divided into a good many classes—the weir-fisherme
hake-fishermen, and the people of Grand Manan farm a good d
connection with their fishing. They all raise their own potatoe
have cows, and are well to do. It would be a pretty hard thing
to state.

By Mr. Foster:

Q. Did you ever know a fisherman who prosecuted that busin(
a living and got rich?—A. Some I know of since we had recip
both at Grand Manan and Deer Island, who went into the s;
herring and herring-oil business that are very well off.

Q. Well, that is business?—A. Yes, sir; but I never knew

who hauled the fish out of the water with his hands line-fishing that ever got rich.

Q. You have never known one that laid up money?—A. No; not in that business alone.

Q. Have you an opinion as to the effect of throwing gurry over on the fishing grounds?—A. That has been talked over among the fishermen for the last 40 years. I have somewhat changed my mind in regard to it. We used to think once it was a great injury, but I have about made up my mind that this gurry is devoured by sea-fleas, star-fish, and other insects that inhabit the water, and that it is not so great an injury as we have heretofore thought it. I have no doubt that the gurry thrown overboard will attract dog-fish, cat-fish, skates, and that kind of fish in large numbers while it lasts, but I don't think it injures the fishing grounds to the extent supposed.

Q. Do you think the effect would last from one season to another?—A. No.

Q. What do you say about the effect of trawling?—A. I think trawling is an injury to the fish, inasmuch as trawls set in the mouth of the bay will catch the mother fish as they come in to spawn. And I think they are an injury so far as they catch these mother fish. I don't think the trawls frighten the fish or drive them out, but I think they catch the mother fish as they come in to spawn, and thereby decrease the quantity.

Q. You speak of the mouths of the bays. Would it be the case off the coast on the Banks?—A. It would not do so much injury there. I don't know that it would do any injury there at all. It would only be an injury on spawning grounds or in the road—set in the road where the fish come in to spawn.

Q. On the spawning grounds or at the mouth of a bay of moderate size?—A. On the spawning grounds or in the road that the fish take to the spawning grounds, it would be an injury.

By Mr. Thomson:

Q. You live now at Eastport?—A. Yes.

Q. I understood you to say you came from Grand Manan?—A. I was born there and lived there until I was 22.

Q. I understood that you owned American vessels?—A. No.

Q. That you yourself owned American vessels or shares in them after you went to Eastport?—A. I owned shares in American vessels, freighting vessels, and I also owned a share in the brig I went to the coast of Labrador in. .

Q. Was that an American or English vessel?—American registry. I also owned a share in an English vessel that I went to Newfoundland herring fishing in.

Q. Well, in order to hold an American registry you must have been an American citizen?—A. Yes, sir.

Q. After leaving Grand Manan you were naturalized?—A. Yes.

Q. How long ago were you naturalized?—A. I was naturalized, I think, about 1851 or 1852; I am not certain. I had to live in the United States five years before I got naturalized.

Q. At present you are an American citizen and have been since 1851 or 1852?—A. Yes.

Q. Your sympathies are naturally with the American side of this question?—A. My sympathies are for the right, and have been ever since I was a boy in this fishery. Whatever is right.

Q. Well, that is a very wide term. It depends on our stand-point.

Your sympathies are with the American view of this question
Not unless they are right.

Q. Well, then, I will put it in another way. You think the Am
view is right ?—A. I don't know about that. I have my own view
I think they are right.

Q. Do your views differ from the American views; do you diffe
your neighbors in Eastport ?—A. I differ from some of them, and
with a good many Dominion people I have talked with. I hav
differed from some of them.

Q. Do you consider that the Americans ought not to pay an
under this Commission ?—A. No; I don't think they should. I
the markets they get are a full equivalent.

Q. Well, that is all I want to know. Your sympathies, then, ar
the American views ?—A. I don't take it on the line of sympat
take it on the line of right, of justice between man and man.

Q. At all events, your view is that the Americans should not
dollar ?—A. Not if they keep the markets open.

Q. Well, as the matter now stands ?—A. I think that is a full e
lent.

Q. That is your idea ?—A. For the inshore fisheries. I think th
ing of the American markets is an equivalent for the Dominion fi
inside of three miles.

Q. Well, when you say that, from what stand-point are you spe
the fisherman's or the merchant's ? Or do you take a broad, pi
view of the matter ?—A. I am speaking from my own judgment
business I have followed through life and am still following.

Q. Well, when you say that the free market is an entire equ
for our fisheries, who do you say the free market is given by ; at
expense ? Is it at the expense of the American fishermen or th
of the United States people ?—A. The free market and taking
duty is in favor of the fishermen.

Q. The American fishermen ?—A. No, the Dominion fishermen

Q. And against whom is it ?—A. If the duty was put on it wo
against the Dominion fishermen.

Q. Well, against whom is the taking off of the duty ?—A. It is a
the United States, of course.

Q. But what class in the United States ?—A. I don't know ho
intend to class them. I suppose the United States is a country,
the country takes it off, I suppose the country must make
amount.

Q. How did you class the British fishermen ? You thought it
advantage to them to have the duty off ?—A. Simply because i
him a better market for the fish he produces.

Q Tell me why you cannot class the Americans. Tell me wha
it has on the American fishermen, taking off the duty. Have
thought of it at all ?—A. I don't know that I ever heard a fish
speaking in regard to it.

Q. And you are serious, then, you never heard an American
man complain of this duty being taken off ?—A. I don't know
have.

Q. Have you ever thought of this, as a practical man, whe
affects the American fisherman at all or not ?—A. I have given it
deal of thought.

Q. Whom does it affect, the merchant or the fisherman ?—A
this, that to put on a duty of five cents a box on smoked herring

American Government would amount almost to a prohibition of the smoked-herring business.

Q. Well, how as to $2 a barrel on mackerel?—A. Mackerel is a fish I don't know much about. I never fished it. I have packed a good many while I was fish inspector at Eastport, twenty-five years.

Q. Are there any being smoked on the American shores as at Campobello?—A. Yes.

Q. Would they increase in price in consequence of a duty?—A. I cannot answer that question.

Q. Are you serious about that?—A. I am. If you put on a duty and call me after it has been in operation a few years, I will answer that question. I can't anticipate anything that might happen.

Q. You are serious in saying that five cents a box on herring would be a prohibition to British fisheries, but you can't say whether, if they were prohibited, it would have the effect of raising the price of American fish?—A. No, I could not say.

Q. Then, according to you, the influx of British fish has no effect upon the price of American fish at all?—A. I didn't say so.

Q. Well, do you say so? I think it follows from what you have said?—A. I don't say anything about it.

Q. Do you decline to give any opinion in regard to it?—A. I won't at the present time.

Q. Have you any doubt that the fish sent in from the British provinces has a sensible effect in making the price of fish smaller in the United States market?—A. They may have that tendency to keep the price down.

Q. Tell me if you believe they have that tendency or not?—A. I think they may have that tendency.

Q. Do you say that they have that tendency?—A. The more fish put on the market, of course the tendency is that way, but there is a point beyond which that tendency is inoperative. The moment you reach the point of the consumer, when he can't afford to pay, he has to buy some other article of food. Since my time the quantity of smoked herring sold in the United States markets has increased tremendously. The prices they are selling for now are 20 cents in New York, 21 cents in Boston, and 15 cents in Eastport. With the boxes of the present size that will pay the fishermen, but at the sizes they made boxes fifteen or twenty years ago, no fisherman could follow it. When you come to increase the price of herring over 25 cents per box the consumers won't buy them.

Q. There is a certain amount of fish of that description carried into the United States and certain prices are paid. I presume you got the same price for American fish as you got for English cured fish. Is it not so? I mean smoked fish in boxes.—A. Yes.

Q. I want you to tell me, if you will, whether the importation of that kind of fish from the provinces has any effect on the price of American fish?—A. I presume it may have some effect; but, as I told you before, I cannot answer that question, because last year smoked herring was 9 cents a box.

Q. Do you say it makes a difference or not—the importation of that fish from the provinces—on the price of American fish?—A. Last year we had the same supplies, and smoked herring were 9 cents a box; and this year, with still the same supplies, they are 15 cents a box at Eastport. I cannot tell what occasions the difference in price. I suppose the consumption rules it more than anything else.

Q. Does the importation of American fish affect the price, injuriously or otherwise, of American cured fish of the same description ?-could not tell you.

Q. You have no opinion on the subject at all ?—A. No.

Q. I now ask you if the fish that come in from the British pro have not the effect of making the fish cheaper to the consumer, ever effect it may have on the fishermen ?—A. I don't know but v may.

Q. Have you any doubt about it ?—A. I cannot form any correc mate, because the price is not two years alike. But there is one t can assure you, that the price of fish can never rise above a certain because it then gets beyond the reach of the consumer, and when i beyond the consumer's means he will not buy it.` Consequently th regulate itself.

Q. Does not the larger supply of fish that comes in from the pro' under the treaty, than what did before the treaty, have the eff diminishing the price of fish, and therefore diminishing the price consumer ?—A. I cannot answer the question; I don't know.

Q. Though you have dealt in fish forty years ?—A. Yes ; fully years.

Q. How often have you gone of late years to Grand Manan to how the fisheries are carried on ?—A. I have not been at Grand M much for the last six years.

Q. You have not been there for the last six years ?—A. I have there, but not much.

Q. How many visits in the last six years ?—A. Three or four vi

Q. And how long would the visit be on each occasion ?—A. No long.

Q. About how long ?—A. Sometimes one day, sometimes only hours.

Q. Then each visit would not average half a day ?—A. Perhaps

Q. And how many visits have you made in six years ?—A. I have perhaps four, maybe five.

Q. What season of the year would you visit Grand Manan ?—summer time.

Q. The summer time is not the brisk fishing-season there ?—A.

Q. I thought it was spring and fall ?—A. It depends on what k fish you have reference to.

Q. Take herring.—A. The frozen herring are only taken in the v The smoked-herring trade is in the summer at the center of the i Wood's Cove, and round there, and late in the fall at White Head, Islands, Two Islands, and other parts of the island. They don't mence their smoked-herring fishing there till later in the season.

Q. For six years you have only been there five times, on an av half a day at a time, and of course you have had no opportur knowing from personal observation what American vessels fished the island nor what American boats fished round the island. T obvious, is it not?—A. I think I have.

Q. Although you have not been there ?—A. Although I have no there.

Q. I said from personal observation.—A. I have not seen an can boat fishing at Grand Manan; not in the act of fishing.

Q. From personal observation you could not possibly say ?—A. not seen any fishing there. I deal with all those men.

Q. Then the information you have been pleased to give the Co sion in regard to the business done at Grand Manan has not been

personal knowledge, but from information received from other persons?
—A. I do not say so.

Q. Do you not state that now?—A. I lived in Grand Manan until I was 22 years of age.

Q. I confine you to the last six years. During the whole of that time you did not visit the island scarcely once a year, five times during six years. From personal observation you have admitted you cannot speak of the island during those years.—A. I told you I had not seen any fish caught there.

Q. All the information you have been pleased to give the Commission in regard to the fishing round Grand Manan, and the quantity taken by American and British subjects, has been based on hearsay?—A. It has been based on my own actual knowledge, and from conversation with Grand Manan people and others, and men engaged in the business.

Q. Is not that hearsay?—A. You may call it what you have a mind to; I don't purpose to call it hearsay.

Q. I understand you to swear that information you got from other persons, depending on others entirely for the truth of those statements, you decline to call hearsay?—A. I say you can call it hearsay. I come here and swear to the best of my judgment in regard to this matter, from my personal knowledge of Grand Manan, having been a long time resident there, having fished there, and having been through the whole thing; from conversation with men there engaged in the business, and having had business transactions with them, and from receiving accounts and getting my pay from weirs I own there, which is pretty good authority, in my opinion.

Q. I wish to get from you exactly what the authority is; that is hearsay, is it not? Do you say you own weirs there?—A. I own shares in weirs there.

Q. Who are the other owners with you, Grand Manan people or Eastport people?—A. With the exception of my sister, they are Grand Manan people. My sister owns a share with me; she lives in Eastport.

Q. She has not been naturalized?—A. No; I did not know it was required of women.

Q. Do you include the herring you take in your weirs in the American catch?—A. No; I pay the government a tax for the weirs, and I suppose they must claim the fishing.

Q. Do you include that portion of the fish out of the weirs which comes to your share as being part of the American catch?—A. I include it as being part of the Dominion catch, it being caught at Grand Manan.

Q. Though it is taken by an American citizen simply doing business in our waters, and you call that British catch?—A. I do; it was caught in British waters, and I pay $10 a year to the Dominion Government on each weir.

Q. Therefore it is British catch?—A. I presume so; it is caught in British waters and cured on British soil.

Q. Then if Americans come in and catch fish very nearly the same place in their vessels, which would be taken out of British waters, you would call that British catch?—A. British vessels cannot smoke herring on board their vessels.

Q. Do I understand that if American vessels come in and catch herring or any other fish within three miles of the shore, in British waters, that you call it British catch?—A. No; if an American vessel catches fish in British waters within three miles of the shore, I call it American catch, but caught in British waters.

Q. You have been pleased to put the value of all the catch round

Grand Manan at $400,000 a year?—A. Yes; I said that I call it, in judgment, not over $400,000; not to exceed $500,000.

Q. Do you mean British or American catch or both?—A. I mean that is caught within three miles by both parties or all men. A g many Nova Scotia people come down and camp. I mean that is catch of the island.

Q. This you give as your opinion from having been on the island season a year for six years, and that for half a day?—A. I gave opinion as being to the best of my knowledge, and I obtained it 1 reliable sources.

Q. Do you know Mr. W. B. McLaughlin?—A. I have known him a long time.

Q. Is he a respectable man?—A. Yes.

Q. Is he a credible man?—A. I should think so. I don't know thing to the contrary.

Q. He is not a man who would make a misstatement under oath fully?—A. I would not suppose he would.

Q. Are you aware that it was his business to find out what the ac catch of the British subjects was, and to make a return to the gov ment?—A. I was aware he was fishery warden. I pay my weir-ta him.

Q. You are not aware that it was his business to find what actual catch of the island was, and to make a return to the gov ment?—A. I don't know.

Q. Mr. McLaughlin has stated that such was his business, and f the returns made by the people themselves, which, he stated, were tirely under the mark, he found that their catch amounted to half a ion dollars. Are you prepared to contradict that statement?—A. 1 prepared to let my statement stand as based on my judgment.

Q. Either state that Mr. McLaughlin's statement is untrue or th is not.—A. I will not make any such statement. I will say that McLaughlin, I think, has erred in judgment.

Q. At page 254 of Mr. McLaughlin's testimony there is the follow

Q. Will you tell me what is the value of the fish taken by our own people each on the island?—A. Well, I could tell from my fishing returns of last year. I have brought them all.

Q. Do you make up your return for the whole year?—A. Yes; from the 1st Jan to the 31st December.

Q. You do not make it up for the fiscal year?—A. No; I am ordered to make to the 31st December. The return states itself that it is so made up. The amou my estimate, as I made it up from inquiry last year, is $383,891, but that is far r the real catch.

Q. You say that it is far under the actual value of the catch. How do you acc for its being under the amount?—A. Well, the fishermen are reluctant to give a count of what they make on account of the taxation. We have a free-school law and are taxed very heavily for it.

Q. It happens that you are an assessor of taxes?—A. I am at times, and I county councilor, and have been a census enumerator.

Q. And they do not like to give this information to you? You are the last per whom they want to give it?—A. Well, I tell them that the Marine Department lets such information go out of its possession. They tell me there is no need doing so; that I have it all in my hands. They say it is too thin.

Q. Then you believe the amount you have given is an underestimate?—A. I it must be over half a million dollars; that is our old $500,000.

He is a gentleman who swears that from the lips of the men t selves he got a statement that the catch each year amounted to $383 in round numbers $400,000, as being the British catch alone. He that is underestimated, and it is at least $100,000 more.—A. I ca help it; I have given you my opinion.

Q. With your means of obtaining information, do you still presume to put your opinion against his?—A. I do; I don't depart from it one particle.

Q. Although it was Mr. McLaughlin's business to obtain a return of the catch?—A. I have given a great deal of thought and care to it for years.

Q. Then I understand you to say that the catch amounts to $400,000 in round numbers, including the American catch and every catch all round the island?—A. Yes.

Q. Then Mr. McLaughlin has told an untruth deliberately, or those people lied to him when they said they caught $383,891 in value, and in round numbers $400,000; do you think the people have deliberately de ceived Mr. McLaughlin?—A. I don't say so; Mr. McLaughlin may have deceived himself; I don't say whether he has been deceived or the people have been deceived.

Q. He got those figures from statements of the people themselves.—A. I gave mine from my own judgment, and I know of no reason to alter them.

Q. Is it probable, in your judgment, that the people of the island deceived Mr. McLaughlin as to their catch?—A. I don't know.

Q. Is it probable?—A. I don't know what the people and Mr. McLaughlin may do together.

Q. Do you think it is probable?—A. Mr. McLaughlin, until a few years ago, had lived on Gannet Rock, which is a long way from the mainland, and was not connected with the fisheries.

Q. Mr. McLaughlin has stated that he went from house to house and asked each man as to his catch?—A. That may be.

Q. You know Grand Manan; do you believe the people would deliberately deceive Mr. McLaughlin, and make believe that they caught more fish than they actually did?—A. I don't know; I cannot answer that question; I don't know what the people of Grand Manan told Mr. McLaughlin.

Q. You cannot form any opinion as to whether the people would deceive him or not?—A. I don't wish to form any opinion, because I do not think it is necessary. I don't wish to form one without due consideration, and unless I know with whom he talked. I don't propose to have anything to do with Mr. McLaughlin's talk with the inhabitants.

Q. Do you admit that, if Mr. McLaughlin tells the truth, when he says that he went from house to house and made inquiries of each fisherman, he has better means of information than you?—A. I won't admit that. I know Mr. McLaughlin well, and I won't admit it.

Q. Do you intend the Commission to understand that Mr. McLaughlin is a man not to be relied on?—A. I don't wish to state anything of that kind. I have made my statement, Mr. McLaughlin has made his, and the Commission may choose between the two.

Q. You have sworn that you believe him to be a credible man?—A. Yes; as we speak of men, I have nothing to say against Mr. McLaughlin. He has lived in Grand Manan; I know him; and he has lived on Gannet Rock for a long time.

Q. Would his living on Gannet Rock alter his moral character?—A. Not a particle, but it deprives him of seeing the extent of the fishing at Grand Manan.

Q. That may be. Does it deprive him of the opportunity of going round and asking the different people what they caught?—A. No; he can go round.

Q. Do you believe the inhabitants would misinform him by telling him that they caught more than they did, for the purpose of increasing their taxes?—A. I could not answer the question; the inhabitants can answer it; I refuse to answer it.

Q. You say that, although Mr. McLaughlin had those means of information, you still put your judgment against his?—A. I do.

Q. Is there not as much fish taken around the island of Campobell and Deer Island, with its surrounding islands, the parish of West Isles as is taken round Grand Manan?—A. I should think that Grand Manan exceeds them both in smoked herring, and exceeds them largely in hake this year; but Deer Island exceeds Campobello in codfish and froze herring. It would be quite a calculation to figure it up.

Q. Is there as much fish taken round the two islands Campobello and Deer Island, and the parish of West Isles, as there is round Grand Manan?—A. Yes, and more.

Q. How often are you in the habit of visiting the mainland from Letite to Lepreau and to St. Andrew's?—A. I go to St. Andrew's once in while. There is very little fishing there. There is more law than fishing.

Q. It is the county town?—A. Yes.

Q. Are you in the habit of visiting Letite often?—A. No, I am not.

Q. Or St. George or Penfield?—A. No.

Q. Nor the parish of Lepreau?—A. No.

Q. Nor Back Bay?—A. No.

Q. Nor Mace's Bay?—A. No, and there are very few fish caught there

Q. How long is it since you have been to any of those places?—A. Some I never was at.

Q. Take St. George, which is a considerable town, how long is it since you were there?—A. I could not tell you the number of years; it is long time since. There is no fishing there.

Q. How long is it since you have been there?—A. A good many years.

Q. How long is it since you have been in any part of the parish of Penfield?—A. A good many years.

Q. And the parish of Lepreau?—A. I don't know that I was ever there but once or twice in my life.

Q. Do you know Mr. James McLean?—A. Yes; I see him very often and his brother, who lives at Eastport, who is junior partner in the firm of A. & J. McLean.

Q. Is Mr. James McLean a respectable and reliable man?—A. As far as I know him.

Q. He is not a man who would willfully make a misstatement under oath?—A. I could not tell you about that. Mr. McLean speaks for himself and I speak for myself.

Q. As far as you know, is he a man who you believe would not willfully make a misstatement under oath?—A. I could not answer the question.

Q. Have you no belief?—A. I assail no man's character; I did not come here to do that. I came here to give a fair, candid opinion in regard to this business, and I don't propose to be brought in conflict with any other man or injure any other man. If that is the purpose for which I was brought here I don't wish to say more.

Q. You were not brought here to ventilate and air your views, but for the purpose of answering such questions as might be put to you by the American and British counsel.—A. I was not brought here to tell whether Mr. James McLean was a reliable or unreliable man, I presume

Q. You were asked this question: Is Mr. James McLean a respectable man, in your judgment?—A. I told you I thought he was, as far as I know.

Q. You refuse to answer whether you believe he would tell a lie under oath?—A. I refuse to answer the question.

Q. Do you believe he would not tell a lie under oath?—A. That question I do not answer.

Q. Did you ever hear of his having been charged with telling a lie under oath?—A. I do not answer that question.

Q. Do you refuse to answer the question, whether you ever heard that he had been charged with telling a lie under oath?—A. Not unless the Commission enforces an answer. I don't wish to go into Mr. McLean's character.

Q. I insist on an answer to the question, whether you ever heard of Mr. McLean being charged with telling a falsehood under oath.—A. I don't know he was ever under oath.

Q. Did you ever hear any person say that he had made a misstatement under oath?—A. I don't know that I ever did.

Q. You don't remember having ever heard it said that Mr. McLean had made a misstatement under oath?—A. Fishermen say that he is a confounded story-teller; but you cannot always believe what they say. They say he lies to them. I don't know.

Q. Do you mean that he lied under oath?—A. I did not see him under oath. I don't know or wish to say anything in regard to that.

Q. You have said that the fishermen who take the fish out of the water do not make much money?—A. I made that statement; that of the men who caught fish with hook and line I never knew one to get rich.

Q. They have to deal with the fish merchants doing the same kind of business you are doing. I suppose the fish merchants get the profits?—A. I don't know. I know a great many fish merchants who do not get rich.

Q. Did you ever know any who did?—A. I know that I carried it on a long time and did not get rich.

Q. Did you ever know any who did?—A. In our vicinity? Yes, in connection with other business. We have a number of firms who are rich.

Q. You never have visited the main land, except an incidental trip to St. Andrews, because you say you were never in Pennfield, never at Letite, and never in Lepreau?—A. I never was in Lepreau more than once or twice in my life.

Q. Have you been there within the last ten years?—A. I have not.

Q. And yet, although you have never been on the main land, excepting an incidental visit to St. Andrews, you undertake to put your opinion of the catch on the main land against the opinion of a man like Mr. McLaughlin, whose special business it is to attend to the fishing off that coast?—A. I do.

Q. Do you know Mr. James Lord, of Deer Island?—A. Very well, indeed. I had a long conversation with him before he came down here. Mr. James Lord has been buying hake sounds for me for six years.

Q. He is a respectable man?—A. I think so.

Q. You do not think he would make a willful misstatement under oath?—A. I don't think he would. All men are liable to mistakes and to errors in judgment.

Q. You admit you are liable to mistakes?—A. It may be so. You may find men who won't agree with me.

Q. You won't admit you make mistakes?—A. I have given you ¦ opinion to the best of my judgment, and you have got it.

Q. Although you swear that all men are liable to make mistakes, y swear you are not?—A. I don't understand it in that way.

Q. You have stated there were Dominion men who own shares American vessels running to Eastport and elsewhere. Will you tell who they are?—A. I did not say so.

Q. You said American vessels owned by Dominion men?—A. I d and can give you their names.

Q. Give them?—A. There is the Sea Spray, which is chartered t year by a man named Powers, of Deer Isle, Maine, I think, and he is s¢ ing mackerel on the coast of Maine. Then there is the schooner Lo¢ out.

Q. They are American vessels?—A. Yes.

Q. What do you mean by chartered? There is a difference betw¢ owning and chartering?—A. A great deal of difference.

Q. I asked you who the Dominion owners were?—A. The Domin owners are the Holmeses.

Q. Where do they live?—A. In Deer Island some of them, and so at Beaver Harbor. There is the Charlotte Augusta, the captain which is William Holmes. She is owned by the family of Holmes v live at Fairhaven; and the Lookout is owned by the same family.

Q. Are they British subjects?—A. Yes.

Q. Living at Deer Island?—A. Yes.

Q. And not naturalized in the United States?—A. No, they are naturalized.

Q. They are owned by them, and American registered?—A. No, I not say that.

Q. The vessels are run in another name; in whose name do these ¥ sels run?—A. I could not tell you.

Q. How then do you know the vessels have Dominion owners A. I know it by hearing the parties themselves say so, and by talk with some of the principal owners of the vessels.

Q. Did you never inquire in whose name they were running?—A never went to the custom-house to see in whose name they were re¡ tered.

Q. You never asked?—A. No.

Q. Are they American registered?—A. They are American ves¡ running under American registry.

Q. Of course, you are aware that no British subject can own an Am¢ can vessel, or any share in an American vessel?—A. Yes.

Q. Round Deer Island and Campobello I think the fish are cau by boat fishermen?—A. Not altogether.

Q. There is a great quantity caught by them?—A. Deer Island is ¿ ting a great many small vessels.

Q. Fishing round their own island?—A. They don't fish there. Th is very little fishing round Deer Island.

Q. I am speaking of the fishing round Deer Island or West Isles?— The fishing at Deer Island and West Isles for frozen herring is follov in boats inshore, but the fishing is mostly done in vessels. There ai few boats there; some 22 feet boats.

Q. Round Deer Island, West Isles, and Campobello the fishing in British waters, and within three miles of the land?—A. Yes, and Grand Manan. Hake is caught out toward the Wolves outside of th miles.

Q. You know Quoddy River?—A. Yes.

Q. Where does it run ? It is a river running into the bay ?—A. Some call it Quoddy River; others call it Passamaquoddy Bay; there are different names for it.

Q. Passamaquoddy Bay is above.—A. Some people call it St. Andrew's Bay; it is always called St. Andrew's by the people with us. In fact, there is no river by the name of Quoddy River. I know of no river by the name of Quoddy River.

Q. You have lived at Eastport all the time you have stated, and you never heard of a salt-water current in the neighborhood of Deer Island and Campobello bearing the name of Quoddy River ?—A. I did not say so. A salt-water current and a river are two different things. A river is supposed to be fresh water, though salt water may flow into it.

Q. Is there not a salt-water current there commonly known as Quoddy River ?—A. Not by our people.

Q. Do you know the stream called Quoddy River ?—A. I know of no stream called Quoddy River. I know where Quoddy is, and the entrance to Quoddy Harbor.

Q. I understand you that, though living so long at Eastport, in close proximity to West Isles and Campobello, you never heard of the sea-current called Quoddy River ?—A. I don't know it by that name.

Q. What name do you know it by ?—A. On the way to Eastport, between Cherry Island and Campobello, and, in fact, all around Eastport on both sides of it, the currents are very swift. There is a shallow place we call the Ledges, which lies below Cherry Island, rather toward Eastport, where the tides of St. Andrew's Bay and Cobscook Bay, of which Eastport forms the end, meet. If you ask fishermen where they are going, they always say that they are going off to the Ledges. They will not tell you they are going to fish in Quoddy River. It is all Quoddy, and it is all this bay; but this particular point you are trying to come at, this shoal piece of ground that lies right on the point as the two swift currents come down by Moose Island, on which Eastport is built, we call the Ledges altogether.

Q. Will you tell me how you know those particular portions you have described are what I mean by Quoddy River ?—A. I don't know anything else you can mean.

Q. For you never heard of Quoddy River ?—A. I give you the boundaries of what I call Quoddy.

Q. You said you never heard of Quoddy River ?—A. I may have heard of it, but our fishermen do not call it so.

Q. Did you not tell me you never heard of Quoddy River ?—A. You asked me if I knew of a swift salt-water current called Quoddy River, and I told you I did not.

Q. I asked you if you had heard of Quoddy River, and you told me you never had.—A. I don't remember what answer I made to that.

Q. I ask you now, have you ever heard in your lifetime of what is called Quoddy River ?—A. I may by some people, but as a general thing we don't call it that.

Q. Have you ever heard of it ?—A. I think it is likely I have.

Q. Are you sure you have ?—A. I think it is likely I have.

Q. Are you sure you have ?—A. I could not name any man who said it.

Q. Have you heard of it ?—A. Let it go that I have.

By Mr. Trescot:

Q. You have been asked whether you undertake to contradict certain testimony given by Mr. McLaughlin; I want to call your attention to some questions and answers to show whether you mean to contradict

him, or whether it is not the fact that you are in agreement with hi
Mr. McLaughlin says:

Q. Do you make your return for the whole year?—A. Yes; from the 1st January
the 31st December.

Q. You do not make it up for the fiscal year?—A. No; I am ordered to make it
to the 31st December; the return states itself that it is so made up. The amount
my estimate, as I made it up from inquiry last year, is $383,691, but that is far und
the real catch.

Q. You say that is far under the actual value of the catch; how do you account
its being under the amount?—A. Well, the fishermen are reluctant to give an accou
of what they make, on account of the taxation. We have a free-school law now, a
are taxed very heavily for it.

Q. It happens that you are an assessor of taxes?—A. I am at times, and I am a cou
councilor, and have been a census enumerator.

Q. And they do not like to give this information to you; you are the last person
whom they want to give it?—A. Well, I tell them that the marine department ne
lets such information go out of its possession. They tell me there is no need of do
so; that I have it all in my hands. They say it is too thin.

Q. Then you believe the amount you have given is an underestimate?—A. I kn
it must be over half a million dollars; that is, our old $500,000.

Q. That is within the mark for your own island?—A. Yes.

Q. Of the British catch?—A. Yes; our own Grand Manan people; because someti
they come over from Campobello and other places, but I have nothing to do with th

Q. Well, now, is the American catch larger or smaller?—A. I think it is larger.

Q. Have you any doubt?—A. No; because their appliances are so much better th
ours, and I think their men outnumber ours.

In regard to the last portion of the answer, what is your judgme
as to the proportion of the American catch to the British catch?—
The American catch at Grand Manan is very small. I don't thinl
was called upon to make an estimate of the amount. The Americ
catch is very small indeed.

Q. What is the relation of the British to the American catch at Gra
Manan?—A. I have denied emphatically that there was any Americ
catch to amount to anything taken within three miles of the shore. T
American catch at Grand Manan is taken almost entirely outside of t
three miles.

By Mr. Thomson:

Q. I understood you to swear that within three miles round Gra
Manan there was no American catch whatever?—A. I did not say
I said very trifling.

Q. What do you call very trifling?—A. I think the catch inside of t
three-mile limit at Grand Manan by American boats is very trifling.

Q. Or schooners?—A. There is not any American schooner fishi
within three miles. You cannot mention and you cannot prove one.
do not believe but that $2,000 would buy all that is caught by Americ
boats inside of the three-mile limit.

Q. Then Mr. McLaughlin's statement that the Americans caug
$500,000 worth of fish there is and must be willfully false?—A. Insi
of three miles—yes, or he was mistaken.

By Mr. Trescot:

Q. Mr. McLaughlin's conversations as to the British catch could gi
him no information as to what was the American catch?—A. Not t
slightest. Mr. McLaughlin must have reckoned the value of all t
cargoes of frozen herring taken off the island and caught by Domini
subjects, or he must have reckoned the fish caught by American vess
at Grand Manan 15 miles out, or at the Ripplings 8 or 10 miles out
sea. He has made a gross mistake some way, but how I don't kn
He may be able to account for it; I cannot.

No. 55.

JOSEPH LAKEMAN, fisherman, of Grand Manan Island, was called on behalf of the Government of the United States, sworn and examined.

By Mr. Trescot:

Question. Where were you born ?—Answer. In Lubec, State of Maine.

Q. Where are you now living ?—A. On Grand Manan Island.

Q. Are you now a British subject ?—A. No.

Q. When did you move from Maine to Grand Manan ?—A. In 1845.

Q. Have you lived at Grand Manan since ?—A. Yes.

Q. What has been your occupation at Grand Manan ?—A. I began there in the green fish trade as a merchant, and I added to that weir and vessel fishing.

Q. And are you now weir and vessel fishing ?—A. I am not now vessel fishing, but I am weir fishing. I make that a specialty.

Q. What fish are caught at and in the neighborhood of Grand Manan ?—A. Herring principally, and also cod, pollock, and hake.

Q. What are you especially engaged in ?—A. The herring fishery.

Q. Smoked or frozen ?—A. Smoked mostly. We freeze some few, but not many.

Q. Have you any idea as to the number of boxes of herring put up on the average annually at Grand Manan in connection with the smoked herring fishery ?—A. From 300,000 to 500,000 boxes are put up. The number depends upon the run of the fishing about the island.

Q. Is the smoked-herring fishery of Grand Manan almost entirely a weir fishery ?—A. Yes; about all of it is so. Very few net herring are smoked.

Q. Who prosecutes the herring fishery, as a rule ? Is it a native fishery, or is it participated in by people outside—by Americans ?—A. I cannot now call to mind any person, American born, who is engaged in the business at the present time, except Mr. Small, who is engaged in it to a very limited extent—he is a native-born American, and has been naturalized—and myself.

Q. As far as the herring fishery goes, it is entirely a Grand Manan fishery, carried on by the native population ?—A. Yes, generally speaking this is the case.

. Where are the smoked herring sent ?—A. Mostly to the American market.

Q. In American or Grand Manan vessels ?—A. Within the last few years, since the new treaty came into operation, and Canadian fish were allowed to enter the American market free of duty, they have bought coasting-vessels.

Q. Who have done so ?—A. Our people.

Q. The Grand Manan people ?—A. Yes; they are owned at our island, and have been bought on the American side. American vessels have been converted into English vessels, and they are run to New York and Boston, taking there the fish of the island and smoked herring principally.

Q. Do you know anything about the frozen-herring business ?—A. Yes.

Q. How is it conducted, and what sort of a business is it ?—A. The herring which are frozen are caught principally by our people on the island, and sold to the American vessels, which come there for them.

Q. Do you know any appreciable proportion of American vessels which come there, catch herring, and freeze them ?—A. I do not.

Q. What other fisheries besides the herring fishery are carried on at and around Manan Island ?—A. The cod, pollock, and hake fisheries.

Q. Are they inshore or off-shore fisheries ?—A. The hake, until w a few years back, has been considered altogether an inshore fishery since the introduction of trawling it has extended into deep water off shore. They go out now earlier in the season than they used to fish for hake.

Q. It has become an off-shore fishery ?—A. Yes; it is carried o yond the 3-mile limit.

Q. How about the haddock fishery ?—A. We do not fish espec for haddock; those we take are caught promiscuously while we catching other fish.

Q. Can you state, from your experience since 1845, what propo of all the fisheries there, within 3 miles of the shore, is carried o American vessels or boats ?—A. When I went to Grand Manan Is in 1845, and for say 10 years subsequently, more was done by Ame vessels there than now, or than has been the case for the last 10 y There used to be quite a fleet of small vessels which came there Hancock County, in Maine, but within the past 10 or 12 years this has about all dropped off, with the exception of one or two vessels gone into another kind of fishing—Grand Bank fishing. They built larger vessels, and consequently they have dropped our i fisheries.

Q. What is your estimate as to the annual value of the whole G Manan fishery, taking it all in all ?—A. I should say that it woul exceed $50,000 on the average, with regard to the fisheries carri within the 3-mile limit. Taking into consideration the whole fis including the frozen-herring business. I could not with propriety p value at over $60,000 at the most. I could not go beyond that, should say that $50,000 is nearer the mark; and I am putting the f at the outside limit for the best years and the highest prices.

Q. You include everything caught about Grand Manan Island Yes; with the oil, sounds, and everything that is realized out o fishery.

Q. What number of boxes of smoked herring do you imagine is from Grand Manan to the American market ?—A. I should judge at least three-quarters of our catch is so sent, and this product am to from 300,000 to 500,000 boxes a year.

Q. What are they worth a box ?—A. This year they rule low they have ruled as high as 45 cents a box, and from that down to 15 cents. I have sold the catch of the season at Eastport for 45 a box.

Q. How many would be three-quarters of this catch ?—A. Cal average catch about 400,000 boxes, and then on the average 30 would be sent annually to the American market.

Q. What do you think they are worth ?—A. I should think that average, one year with another, would be 20 cents a box, or betwe and 15 cents.

Q. What would 300,000 boxes then be worth at 20 cents a box $60,000.

Q. What do you think is the value of the frozen-herring fis including bait and food and everything else ?—A. I should suppose the average quantity sent to the American market would be from 12 cargoes a year.

Q. What are they worth a cargo ?—A. About $1,000, on the av

Q. That would make $12,000 for frozen-herring ?—A. Yes; $10,000 to $12,000.

Q. What are the cod, hake, and pollock fisheries at Grand M

worth?—A. I should say that 10,000 quintals would be a fair average annual catch for the hake fishery.

Q. What is a quintal worth?—A. I should say that the average price is about $1.25 a quintal.

Q. That would make $12,500 as the annual value of this fishery?—A. Yes.

Q. What is the haddock fishery worth?—A. As a general thing haddock and hake go together.

Q. What is the cod-fishery worth?—A. I should say that on the average 12,000 and probably 13,000 quintals would be a fair average annual catch for this fishery at Grand Manan.

Q. What is a quintal of cod worth?—A. From $3.50 to $3.75 on the average, for large and small.

Q. What would 13,000 quintals then be worth?—A. $48,750.

By Sir Alexander Galt:

Q. Do you make this up at the rate of $3.75 or $3.50?—A. I have placed the rate at $3.75.

By Mr. Trescot:

Q. How much do these several totals make?—A. $133,450.

Q. Think a little and tell us what you meant by telling us a few minutes ago that in your opinion the value of the annual catch of the fisheries of Grand Manan Island only amounted to $50,000, or at the most to $60,000?—A. $500,000 I meant. Did I say $50,000? If I did, that was a slip of the tongue—and if I said $60,000 I meant $600,000.

Q. This is the annual proceeds of the Grand Manan fisheries?—A. No; the value of the hake sounds is yet to be considered.

Q. But as far as you have gone that is the case?—A. I want to add the value of 100,000 boxes of herring, which at 20 cents a box are worth $20,000, and the total figure is then $153,450, if I have made no mistake. This is the value of the average annual catch of smoked herring, frozen herring, hake, and cod at Grand Manan.

Q. You think that the catch of fish at Grand Manan, in which you agree with Mr. McLaughlin, is worth about $500,000?—A. I do not think that it is $500,000 a year actually; but I think that I can safely put it down at $500,000.

Q. What portion of the fishery there carried on within the 3-mile limit is conducted by Americans in American vessels. What part of this $500,000 is represented by American capital?—A. My estimate is for fish taken by people residing on Grand Manan Island, and who are considered to be citizens.

Q. Do any other people come there and fish?—A. Yes; some, but not many.

Q. How many American boats and vessels come within the 3-mile limit, off Grand Manan Island, to fish, and what is the value of their catch?—A. I do not know of an American vessel that fishes there within the 3 mile limit, that is, with lines. It may be, however, that some vessels that came there line-fishing last season set nets in there for the purpose of getting bait. I think it is quite likely that some of them have done so; I know that our weir fishermen supply most of the vessels with bait. We sell them bait out of our weirs; we open an account with them when they come there.

Q. Your experience, in this regard, dates back to 1845, and you have been weir-fishing all this time?—A Yes, principally.

Q. And you know something about the Grand Manan fisheries?—A. Yes.

159 F

☛ Q. Then state. what portion of the fishery within the 3-
ι there is carried on by Americans; give the value of the who
aud say what proportion of the $500,000 is taken by American
part of that estimate, $500,000, is caught by Americans. Tl
to what has been taken by our people on Grand Manan; it c
whole ground.

Q. And you say that the Americans do not carry on any fis
within 3 miles of the shore?—A. Yes; but some American v
off on the Banks. The value of the fish of all kinds taken
within the limits off Grand Manan is $500,000; but no fish
there, to my knowledge, by American fishermen, in boats or ι

Q. What is the population of Grand Manan?—A. Mr. Lorii
history of Grand Manan, issued last year, gives it at abou
2,500.

Q. Do you know much of the opposite side of the coast—
Lepreau, St. Andrew's and Deer Island, &c.?—A. No, not a ς
to my personal knowledge.

Q. Are you not obliged to know something about the fishe
coast, in connection with the management of your own busi
We learn what they are doing over there, and we secure repo
regard. For instance, if herring are caught there we natur
inquiries concerning their quality and quantity and such ma
as to how many are being put up, because we are intereste
branch of the business; but if I hear about the line fishing
there, I am not so immediately interested in that department
not care so much about it.

Q. How does the herring fishery on that coast compare wit
ring fishery of Grand Manan Island?—A. Their line-fishing is
tensive than ours, but their smoked-herring business is not so
as ours; they do not smoke as many herring as we do—at lea
stand not, but I do not know that this is the case from my ow
knowledge. They, however, make line and net fishing ι
specialty than do our island people, and they probably in
more herring for what is called the frozen-herring business.

Q. Is the fishery carried on there of greater or less valu
Grand Manan fishery?—A. I do not think that there is a gre
difference between the two. At least, I should not think
extent of our smoked-herring business would very nearly o
they do more than our vessels in other branches, and I woul
pose there would be any very great material difference betv
two fisheries.

Q. From your experience what do you suppose is the vι
whole fisheries carried on from Grand Manau Island up to
the whole of Charlotte County?—A. I would not like to esti
more than $2,000,000.

Q. That is for the whole fishery as mentioned?—A. Yes, I
it was overestimated at $2,000,000. I should think that one
quarter millions of dollars would be the full extent of its valι

Q. On that shore or up around Grand Manan do you belie
ble from anything you have seen that there is an Americ
carried on there, and an American catch taken there, in
altogether of the people of Grand Manan, and of the inhabitε
opposite from Letite of equal value with the British catch?—

Q. Or that if the value of the British catch there is a millioι
of the American catch there is also a million, and perhaps mι

am confident that nothing of the kind is the case. I give this as my honest opinion.

Q. You say you have been dealing in the smoked-herring business for a long time. Would that business stand an additional tax of 5 cents in gold per box, which is the amount of the old duty ?—A. No, it could not, this year in particular.

Q. Why ?—A. We are only getting this year, in the American market, 15 cents a box for our best quality of herring, after they are shipped.

Q. Would not the customer have to pay the duty ?—A. I think not.

Q. Why not ?—A. My experience is to the contrary. I cannot so understand it.

Q. Explain why you think so ?—A. I will tell you how the matter has worked in my experience. I have shipped direct in my own vessel from Grand Manan to Boston smoked herring with other kinds of fish when there was an average duty of 5 cents in gold a box on smoked herring, and I have sold those herring alongside of a man from Lubec who was also selling herring. Mine were equally as good, or if not better than his, and the reputation of Grand Manan herring stands higher than that of Quoddy herring, as is known by everybody who knows anything about it, because we have a better quality of fish. I have sold my herring in the Boston market alongside of Lubec herring, and for the same price which the latter obtained, while I also paid 5 cents a box in gold duty at the Boston custom-house. I once took a cargo of about 7,000 boxes there in the schooner Belle, and I left $350 in gold at the Boston custom-house, and if the consumer paid the duty I paid it also ; and so I came home minus $350 in gold, which, if no duty had been imposed on Canadian fish, I would have had in my pocket.

Q. If the captain from Lubec had gone there with the same cargo, obtaining the same price, he would have come away with these $350 in his pocket ?—A. Certainly he would; that is clear.

Q. You thus lost $350 ?—A. I did really lose it.

Q. In other words, without reference to duty you had in the American market to take the price which the American fisherman got there ?—A. I had to sell my fish at the same price which he got; the dealer could pay me no more than he paid him, for my herring were no better than his, and he could not afford to pay me any more for them, as he could get what he wanted from American fishermen ; so I was obliged to sell at the same price.

. Q. You do not believe that the herring fishery could stand the addition mentioned ?—A. It could not. It really could not. We were previously driven out of the business of shipping fish to the Boston market—this is the truth of it—until the renewal of reciprocity.

By Mr. Thomson :

Q. Did you ever reflect as to whether the imposition of a 5 cents duty on your fish did not raise by so much the price of the fish, so that you got to that extent a higher price for your fish ?—A. I think this is not the case. It could not do so. The $350 were taken out of my pocket in this way : they had a sufficient quantity of fish in the American market, which was kept supplied with all that was required at a certain price.

Q. What price did you get in that particular instance ?—A. I do not remember.

Q. Suppose that fish had been in such demand in the market that you got 20 cents more for them than you actually did receive, and that the Lubec man also obtained 20 cents more; do you think that you would have been paying the duty ?—A. Certainly I would.

Q. The American fishermen want the duty back on fish, I suppose?—
A. I do not know about that, I am sure; but they naturally would wish to have it back again, I suppose, in order to exclude our fish from their market.

Q. I suppose that the consumer got his fish cheaper, owing to the removal of the duty and the admission of your fish into the American market?—A. The consumer would then get his fish cheaper—the more fish that are put on the market the cheaper the consumer gets them.

Q. Do you think that the effect of the duty would be to keep you out altogether?—A. It would exclude us.

Q. In that particular case did you lose money?—A. O, I certainly did; that is, I lost money in this way: if my fish were as good—and they were so, of course—as those of my neighbor at Lubec, and if he sold his fish at 30 cents a box, and paid no duty, while I sold mine at 30 cents a box and paid 5 cents gold duty per box, I look upon it in this light, that I lost 5 cents in gold per box, which I would not have lost if I had operated on the American side. Besides there was quite a premium on gold at the time, and it cost me more to get my fish to the American market than it did the American to whom I refer.

Q. We will grant, for the sake of argument, that you did lose.—A. I understand that I did lose money, certainly.

Q. Do you mean that you really lost money?—A. I lost it in the sense I have mentioned.

Q. And otherwise, did you make money?—A. I certainly have made money in the smoked-herring business.

Q. But did you lose money on that particular transaction?—A. O, I really did make money on that transaction; that is clear; that is to say I made over and above a living, and I call that making money; but I would have made more money if it had not been for the duty.

Q. Would you have made any more with the duty off, if the price of herring then fell 5 cents per box all round in the American market?—A. Certainly I would not; that is clear.

Q. The duty had rather the effect of putting money into the pocket of the Lubec fishermen than of taking it out of yours?—A. I think not; I do not see it in that light.

Q. On that particular transaction, at any rate, you made money?—A. I got over and above a living.

Q. Why, then, did you say that you would be driven out of the American market?—A. I say this would be the case if a prohibitory duty were put on.

Q. Of course; but do you say that the imposition of a five cents duty would do so?—A. At the present time, with present prices of fish, that would do it; we could not then operate in the American market, and we could not make a living.

Q. Do you not think that the imposition of a five cents duty would raise the price five cents more in the American market?—A. No.

Q. Why not?—A. I do not see any reason why that should be the case, because our fish are not wanted in the American market. Our fish go into that market as a surplus.

Q. Then the result of this treaty is that the Americans get their fish a great deal cheaper than was the case before?—A. There are times when smoked herring are very plentiful on the American side, and then herring run low in price.

Q. Is not the result of the treaty, which admits your fish into the American market on equal terms with the American fish, to make the price of fish lower in that market?—A. It has that tendency evidently.

Q. Therefore the consumer gets his fish for less money?—A. Evidently he does. When herring are abundant the price is lower.

Q. It further follows that although a certain class of fishermen may lose something by this free admission of British fish into the American market, the American public gain by it?—A. By getting their fish at a low price? Of course it makes the price of fish lower in that market. That is clear.

Q. Then the consumer gets the fish cheaper?—A. He evidently does; the larger the quantity that is put on the market the less the price will be.

Q. You state that the annual value of the Grand Manan fisheries is from $500,000 to $600,000, but according to the figures which you gave Mr. Trescot such annual value amounted in all to only $153,000; will you explain how you account for the difference?—A. That is for the body of the fish, apart from the value of the oil and sounds.

Q. What is the value of the sounds?—A. It would take some time to figure that up.

Q. Would it amount to $50,000?—A. No.

Q. Would anything else be worth $50,000? You see that all these figures do not make $200,000; now where do you get your $500,000 or $600,000?—A. I said I did not believe that it would exceed that, and I do not think that it will come up to that amount.

Q. Is not $500,000 and $600,000 a mere random guess on your part?—A. I have no figures by which I know that it is correct.

Q. The figures you have mentioned only bring such value up to $153,000, leaving a difference of about $450,000 between that and $600,000; the fact is that you have not made any accurate calculation about this at all?—A. I have not; no.

Q. Do you know Walter McLaughlin, of Grand Manan Island?—A. Yes.

Q. He is a respectable man, is he not?—A. Yes; he has the reputation of it.

Q. And he is a truthful man?—A. Yes.

Q. You know that his business as fishery warden is to find out actually what the catch is, and I suppose that you will not put your judgment, in this respect, against his?—A. Well, that would depend on circumstances.

Q. Would you put your judgment as to the catch of Grand Manan against his, when it is his business to find out what it really is?—A. No; I do not think that I would.

Q. Do you know Mr. Lord, of Deer Island?—A. I do not, save from reputation.

Q. He has the reputation of being a straightforward man, has he not?—A. I never heard anything to the contrary.

Q. Do you know James McLean, of Black Bay?—A. Yes; I am well acquainted with him.

Q. He is a very respectable man?—A. He is.

Q. And a truthful man, as far as you are aware?—A. He is; yes.

Q. As to the main-shore fisheries, of course you would not put your opinion against that of Mr. McLean?—A. No; not with respect to some things.

Q. Surely you would not put your opinion as to the mainland fisheries against that of a man engaged in them, and who lives there?—A. When I speak from personal knowledge of anything, and if in this Mr. McLean's opinion differed from mine, I would give Mr. McLean credit for being truthful, and for not desiring to misrepresent the matter; but,

at the same time, I would not submit to his judgment in such
as being better than and superior to my own.

Q. No doubt; but with respect to matters about which you l
personal knowledge you would not put your judgment, founded o
hearsay, against that of Mr. McLean ?—A. Certainly not.

No. 56.

SYLVANUS SMITH, outfitter and vessel-owner, Gloucester, Mas
called on behalf of the Government of the United States, sworn,
amined.

By Mr. Foster:

Question. You have always lived in Gloucester, I believe ?—A
I formerly resided in Lockport, the adjoining town.

Q. How old are you ?—A. I am 48.

Q. You began life as a fisherman ?—A. Yes; I was very youn
I first went fishing.

Q. When did you first come to the Gulf of St. Lawrence ?-
1848.

Q. Did you then come as sharesman ?—A. Yes.

Q. In what vessel ?—A. The schooner Juniatta.

Q. How long was your trip and how many barrels did you t
A. We were 3 months on the voyage, and we took 300 barrels,
best of my recollection.   I have no record of that trip.

Q. When did you next go to the gulf fishing ?—A. In 1851.

Q. In what schooner ?—A. The Wave.

Q. As sharesman ?—A. Yes.

Q. How long were you on the trip ?—A. Two and a half mont

Q. How many barrels did you take ?—A. 280 barrels.

Q. Did you go fishing to the gulf in 1852, and, if so, in w
pacity ?—A. I did ; I went as master.

Q. In what vessel ?—A. The R. C. Parsons.

Q. What was her tonnage ?—A. About 80 tons, carpenters' m
ment.

Q. How many men were on board of her ?—A. About 12, I tl

Q. During how many years were you fishing successively in
C. Parsons ?—A. Four.

Q. In what vessel did you next go ?—A. The E. C. Smith.

Q. What was her tonnage ?—A. About 105 or 110, I think.

Q. How many men were on board of her ?—A. 17.

Q. During how many years were you in her ?—A. 5, I think.

Q. In what schooner did you next go ?—A. The Kit Carson.

Q. What was the number of men on board ?—A. 19.

Q. What was her tonnage ?—A. 145, or thereabouts.

Q. How many years were you on her ?—A. 4, I think.

Q. Which was the last year when you were in the Gulf of S
rence as a fisherman ?—A. 1864.

Q. In preparing yourself to give testimony here, have you lo
your books to ascertain the catches that were made on the
vessels in which you were ?—A. Yes ; I have carefully exami
books and found these different catches.

Q. Have you the catches of all these years ?— A. Yes, one ex
and I have the stock of that year, but not the number of barre
were then taken.

Q. You were 13 years in succession as skipper in the Gulf of S rence fishing for mackerel, and the last year you were there for that purpose was in 1864?—A. Yes.

Q. Have you prepared a statement giving the results of your fishing those years?—A. I have.

Q. Is this a copy of it?—A. It is.

Q. And that is correct?—A. It is.

Q. What was your share as sharesman on the Juniatta, in 1848?—A. It was $64; it might have been some few cents over.

Q. Where were your fish chiefly taken that year?—A. We then fished on Banks Orphan and Bradley, and what we call the Pigeon Hill ground, which lies off the west shore of New Brunswick, between North Cape and Point Miscou.

By Sir Alexander Galt:

Q. How long were you on that trip?—A. Three months.

By Mr. Foster:

Q. How long were you on the trip which you made into the gulf in the Wave in 1851?—A. Two and a half months.

Q. What was your catch?—A. 280 barrels.

Q. What was your share?—A. $88.69.

Q. Where did you fish that year?—A. On Banks Orphan and Bradley and some at the Magdalen Islands. We, however, caught the most of them on Bank Bradley.

Q. Give the catches for the various years when you were skipper, with the names of the schooners?—A. In 1852 I came into the bay in the R. C. Parsons; was 2 months on the voyage, and caught 100 barrels. In 1853 I was 3½ months on the voyage, and took 120 barrels. In 1854 I made two trips, and took 180 barrels on the one and 120 barrels on the other; was about 2 months on each voyage. In 1855 I made 2 trips, and was gone about 4½ months, but I have no account of the number of barrels which we caught that year; we stocked, however, $2,967.56 as the result.

Q. The year previously, when you took 300 barrels, what did your stock amount to?—A. The two stocks, as taken from my books, amounted to $2,937.56.

Q. What was the average price of mackerel that year?—A. $9.90.

Q. For the following year, for which you could not find the number of barrels caught though you have given the stock for that year accurately, as you do not know the number of barrels, you do not know what was the average price that year?—A. No.

Q. Will you tell the Commission what was your fishing ground during the years when you were in the R. C. Parsons?—A. Well, I fished on the Pigeon Hill ground and on Banks Orphan and Bradley most of the years that I was on that vessel, and I fished some in October on the Cape Breton shore.

Q. How far from the land did you fish off the Pigeon Hills?—A. Some 18 or 20 miles, I think, and along there.

Q. You have fished off the Cape Breton shore while you were in the R. C. Parsous?—A. Yes.

Q. I want you particularly to describe where you fished off that shore, and how near the land you did so, making your statement in as much detail as possible.—A. Well, the first year in which the R. C. Parsons came down there, we left home along about the middle of September, and we fished for a portion of the year at the Magdalen Islands, and towards the last of the trip in October we fished some around Margaree Island and Mabou.

▇ Q. How near to the shore did you fish off Cape Breton?—A.
we fished sometimes within a mile or 1½ miles of the shore, ▇
other times we fished 4 or 5 miles from the shore. There were
banks off there, and we sometimes fished on them, 7 or 8 miles
the shore.

Q. Off where?—A. Off from the shore of Margaree Island.

Q. Have you names for these little banks?—A. No; but we ▇
the soundings there and we often resorted to that place to fish.

Q. If you are able to estimate at all the quantity of mackerel ▇
you caught within 3 miles of the shore off Margaree Island, or
where about the Cape Breton coast, I would like to have you te
all you can about it. We are confining ourselves to the trips m▇d
the R. C. Parsons?—A. I think that the first season we got 100 ba▇
and I think that one-half of that trifle was caught within the 3
limit, around Margaree, in what we call Broad Cove.

Q. Now take your second year.—A. In 1853 we only made on▇
and we fished up around the Banks. I think we went home e▇
than usual that year. We caught some mackerel on that side, but
not recollect what quantity. We did not, however, get many that
on that shore.

Q. What portion of these 120 barrels, in your judgment, was ▇
within 3 miles of the shore that year?—A. We might have caug
dozen barrels, or about that quantity, but I could not state it pre▇
now.

Q. The following year, in the R. C. Parsons, you made two trip▇
got 300 hundred barrels; where did you catch them?—A. Most ▇
Orphan Bank and the Pigeon Hill ground, I believe.

Q. How late were you in the bay that year?—A. I think th▇
went out of it in the latter part of October; but I have not the ▇
date.

Q. Did you fish at all in 1854 within 3 miles of the shore any▇
that you remember?—A. Well, we might have tried for some fish i
lower part of the bay on the last trip when we were going home.

Q. What do you mean by the lower part of the bay?—A. The▇
down towards Port Hood. We sometimes fished off East Point. ▇
half way across was a bank on which we fished sometimes. We
fished from that over to the Cape Breton shore. Vessels resorted ▇
to fish.

Q. You have no record of the number of barrels you took th▇
year you were in the R. C. Parsons, though you have the amount o▇
year's stock; can you tell where you fished that year?—A. W▇
fished mostly over the same ground as previously; during a part o▇
year I fished at the Magdalen Islands.

Q. Give us the length of the trip and the number of barrels pe▇
which you caught while you were on the E. C. Smith?—A. We▇
5½ months out in 1856, that first year I was in her; we went in ▇
and we made two trips, which are put down as one in the state▇
We caught 600 barrels on the two trips—about 300 barrels each t▇

Q. I see that you have not carried out the stock for that year?—
could not find it.

Q. Do you remember where you finished that year?—A. I fish▇
Bank Orphan and caught some mackerel, about 50 barrels, in th▇
of Chaleurs, on that trip, I think.

Q. How far were you up the Bay of Chaleurs?—A. This was ▇
Port Daniel, off Paspebiac. We caught some fish up there durin▇
or two days.

Q. Within what distance from the shore?—A. We were off in the middle of the bay. I could not give the exact distance.

Q. Do you remember at all the width of the Bay of Chaleurs at that point?—A. No; but I should think that it was some 7 or 8 miles.

Q. Were you ever in the Bay of Chaleurs during any other year?—A. I have been in there for a harbor frequently.

Q. Where?—A. At Shippegan and Port Daniel.

Q. Have you ever fished there, that year excepted?—A. No; that was the only year when I caught any fish there.

Q. Did you at any other time try to fish there?—A. No; I do not know but that we might have done so when in a harbor, but I do not recollect of having tried there; that is the only year when I ever caught any fish in the Bay of Chaleurs to amount to anything.

Q. What was the result of your fishing the second year you were in the E. C. Smith?—A. We then caught 625 barrels; that was in 1857.

Q. How long were you out?—A. 5½ months. We went out in the very first of the season, and we staid the season through. I went away about the 1st of June or the last of May, and came out of the bay in the last part of the season.

Q. In November?—A. Yes.

Q. What was the result of your fishing in 1858?—A. We then caught 550 barrels.

Q. What length of time were you out?—A. During those years when I was exclusively fishing for mackerel we went into the bay in the very first part of the season.

Q. You have the stock for 1858; what was the average price per barrel that year?—A. $9.44. The stock amounted to $5,200.

Q. Did you send any fish home that year?—A. I did not.

Q. Did you do so in 1858?—A. Well, I did not ship any home; I did not land any to ship.

Q. You brought the whole of the 550 barrels back with you?—A. One year I shipped some with two of my brothers—100 barrels with one, and 180 barrels, I think, with both. I took them out in the bay, and I do not know but 1858 was that year.

Q. You transshipped them from one schooner to another in the bay?—A. They took them on board there and I took their supplies; that was the first of my shipping mackerel home.

Q. You think that may be the year, but you do not know?—A. I am not certain about it, but I think that is the year.

Q. What did you do in 1859?—A. I caught then 250 barrels.

Q. In what length of time?—A. We were 5 months on that trip.

Q. What did you do in 1860?—A. I was out 4 months and caught 220 barrels.

Q. What did they stock at?—A. $1,805.08; the average stock was $8.40.

Q. The next schooner you were in was the Kit Carson; what did you do in her?—A. In 1861, in the Kit Carson, I made a 4½ months' trip. I caught 520 barrels, and the average price was $4.43; stock, $2,303.02.

Q. How long were you in the Gulf of St. Lawrence in 1862?—A. Five months.

Q. What did you catch?—A. Six hundred and four barrels.

Q. Have you a memorandum concerning this trip?—A. I have no memorandum of the precise trip, but I have the number of barrels we then caught, as taken from my pass-book, kept on the wharf; it is what we call the tally-book. I have no memorandum concerning the precise stock for that year.

Q. What did you do in 1863?—A. I then went two trips; was out
months; caught 1,003 barrels; average price, $9.07; stock, $9,101.87

Q. And 1864?—A. I then made one trip; was out for 5½ mont
caught 1,126 barrels; average price, $10.75; stock, $12,104.82.

Q. Were all the prices which you have given for 1862, 1863, and 1
American currency prices?—A. Yes.

Q. 1864 was your last year in the Gulf of St. Lawrence?—A. Yes
skipper of a vessel.

Q. And during the two last years you were there you shipped ho
mackerel?—A. Yes.

Q. How?—A. By packet from the Strait of Canso.

Q. What did you pay?—A. $1 a barrel freight to Gloucester; t
was in currency.

Q. In what way did you ship mackerel home in 1864, and what
this cost you?—A. By packet; and I think it cost the same for freig
but I am not sure of that.

Q. During the 13 years you acted as skipper, I believe you cau
6,018 barrels of mackerel, and your average catch per year was 469 l
rels?—A. I have not figured that up.

Q. Did anybody ever sail out of Gloucester who was more succes
than yourself in catching mackerel?—A. Well, they all said that I
a pretty large share.

Q. Without showing any modesty about it, did anybody catch
many as yourself?—A. I think not.

Q. Was Andrew Leighton as near you as any one?—A. I think t
for the number of times I was fishing I got more than he did; but t
some years he was longer in the bay than I was, and got as many a
did, if not a few more.

Q. You stocked over 1,100 barrels in 1864?—A. Yes.

Q. What did you do afterwards?—A. I went into the fishing b
ness, and fitted out vessels.

Q. What was the style of the firm in which you first were?—
Rowe and Smith.

Q. How long were you in it?—A. Three years.

Q. This was in 1865, 1866, and 1867?—A. Yes.

Q. What is the name of your present firm?—A. Smith & Gott
went into this firm in 1868.

Q. What has been you business in this firm?—A. I was in the s
business as previously—the cod and mackerel business. We are
buyers and we ship fish to the West.

Q. I have a statement respecting your mackerel business in the
of Smith & Gott, both on the United States shore and in the Gulf of
Lawrence, but you have not given me a statement of your business du
the years when you were in the first firm; why did you not do so?—
When I came away I had only 2 or 3 days to look over my old bo
and I did not have access to the old books of the other firm for the
pose.

Q. You have a statement made up from the books of your pre

firm from 1868 to the present time; is this a copy of that statement?—
A. Yes; it is as follows:

Bay-trips from 1868 to 1876, inclusive.				Shore-trips from 1868 to 1876, inclusive.			
Year.	No. of vessels.	No. of barrels of mackerel.	Average price.	Year.	No. of vessels.	No. of barrels of mackerel.	Average price.
1868	5	625	$16 00	1868	5	1,961	$11 87
1869	7	1,097	16 00	1869	2	1,140	8 75
1870	7	1,038	13 00	1870	5	1,852	8 61
1871	5	1,413	8 00	1871	2	1,174	9 70
1872	3	789	14 00	1872	3	1,494	9 22
1873	6	2,291	9 25	1873	4	1,889	13 93
1874	7	2,800	6 00	1874	5	3,704	8 20
1875	3	623	11 33	1875	6	2,531	9 81
1876	3	319	10 30	1876	4	3,642	5 80
Total	46	10,995		Total	36	19,387	

Number of barrels of shore mackerel packed from 1868 to 1876 19,387
Number of barrels of bay mackerel packed from 1868 to 1876 10,995
Value of shore mackerel $176,998 00
Value of bay mackerel 111,699 00

The following table contains a statement of the trips I made in the
bay from 1848 to 1864, inclusive:

Year.	Name of vessel.	Length of trip.	No. of barrels.	
1848	Juniatta	3 months..	300	Shareman's share, $64.
1851	Wave	2½ months..	280	Shareman's share, $88 69.
1852	R. C. Parsons (12 men)	2 months..	100	
1853	......do	3½ months..	120	
1854	......do	2 months..	180	} Stocked, $2,937.56. Average price, $9 90.
1854	......do	...do	120	
1855	......do	4½ months..	....	Two trips; stock, $2,967.56.
1856	E. C. Smith (17 men)	5½ months..	600	
1857	......do	...do	625	
1858	......do	...do	550	Stock, $5,200. Average price, $9.44.
1859	......do	5 months..	250	
1860	......do	4 months..	220	Stock, $1.850. Average price, $8.40
1861	Kit Carson (19 men)	4½ months	520	Stock, $2,303.02. Average price, $4 43.
1862	......do	6 months..	604	
1863	......do	5½ months..	1,003	Stock, $9,101.87. Average price, $9 07.
1864	......do	...do	1,126	Stock, $12,104 82.

Sharesman from 1848 to 1851, captain from 1852 to 1864.
Thirteen years captain; 6,018 barrels. Average per year, 469.

WEDNESDAY, *October* 10, 1877.
The Conference met.
The examination of SYLVANUS SMITH was resumed.

By Mr. Foster.

Question. Will you state where you caught your mackerel from year
to year while you were in the E. C. Smith?—Answer. In 1856 we made two
trips; the first was caught on Bank Orphan, with the exception of about
50 barrels, as near as I can judge, which were taken in the Bay of
Chaleurs, and the second trip was caught at the Magdalen Islands.

Q. Whereabouts did you catch the fish in the Bay of Chaleurs?—A.
Up off Paspebiac, I think, or along there. We were up in that section
of the bay.

Q. How near the shore were you?—A. We were in the middle of the
Bay of Chaleurs; it would be hard to judge the distance, but we were
some 4 or 5 miles off shore.

Q. How wide is the bay there ?—A. I do not recollect exactly, bu think it is some 10 miles; that is, if my recollection is correct. It is so time since I was there.

Q. Where did you catch your mackerel in 1857?—A. On Banks Orph and Bradley and at the Magdalen Islands; and along in the fall, abc the time we went home, we fished towards the Cape Breton shore.

Q. Did you fish off the Cape Breton shore?—A. I do not recollect catching many mackerel there in 1857, but we then took a few off Mabc I think; we might have caught 50 barrels or so off that shore that ye but as to this I have to depend on my memory.

Q. When did you go towards the Cape Breton shore?—A. could r tell you now just the time, but we usually got there by the 10th or 1 15th of October.

Q. What harbor did you make there?—A. Port Hood usually.

Q. Where did you catch your mackerel in 1858?—A. We fished dur the early part of the season on what we call the Pigeon Hill grou and on Bank Orphan; and after September we went to the Magdal Islands.

Q. Did you fish off the Cape Breton shore in 1858 on your way home' A. We are almost always in the last part of the season—because t weather then becomes blowy—down about that way for a spell; I thi we caught some there that year, though I cannot recollect exactly, t I would not set the quantity at over 50 barrels.

Q. How long did you stay in the vicinity of Port Hood whither it 1 your habit in the autumn, while on your way home from the fish grounds, to go?—A. We generally made Port Hood our harbor wl there in bad weather; we would sometimes go in there when it v stormy, and then afterwards go out to grounds some distance off to fi: we generally made that our harbor for about two weeks in the last p of the season.

Q. You have described generally your fishing grounds for the res the season; and now explain at what different points in the vicinity Port Hood you used to fish?—A. We sometimes tried along the M garee shore; and if we did not find anything there, we would then off to the Magdalen Islands, or fish half way across between the C Breton shore and the Magdalen Islands, where there are good fish grounds. We used to try there, as it used to be a very good fish ground.

Q. This was half way across between Margaree Island and the M dalen Islands?—A. Yes.

Q. What fishing ground is situated there?—A. I do not know of: particular bank there, but we find that it is on the route by which mackerel come down the bay from the north; they are often met v there, and when they do not strike the shore, good fishing is to be ' in that quarter.

Q. Did you fish closer to the shore off Margaree Islands than e where?—A. We did; sometimes we fished there within two miles of shore and sometimes four or five miles off.

Q. In 1859, you caught 250 barrels in five months; where were t taken?—A. We had a very hard year that year, and we picked our up so slowly, that I can hardly call to mind where we got them. I ing five months we filled up the small number of barrels mentioned, we fished mostly at the Magdalen Islands, though we may have cau some few elsewhere; but still I cannot call to mind any particul: definite amount in this regard.

Q. Did you get any large catches at any place that season ?—A. No; we were a long time in the bay, and we only got a few mackerel.

Q. What do you call a large day's catch ?—A. 30, 40, or 50 barrels ; most always a catch of that kind will remain in my mind pretty well ; but I am not so likely to remember small catches.

Q. What is the biggest catch which you ever made in a day ?—A. 120 barrels, I think.

Q. When was this ?—A. In 1864.

Q. Where abouts were they taken ?—A. Broad off the Magdalen Islands.

Q. In 1860 you caught 220 barrels in four months ; where were they taken ?—A. We fished at the Magdalen Islands the most of that year.

Q. Did you try that autumn off the Cape Breton shore ?—A. We most always tried there ; but I do not recollect catching any fish that year off the Cape Breton shore. It was a very poor year down there.

Q. What is the largest number of barrels you remember taking in a day near Margaree Island ?—A. I caught 100 barrels during one day on that shore the last time I fished there.

Q. Was this within the three-mile limit ?—A. I think a portion of them was caught there ; during the fore part of the day we were within three miles of the shore.

Q. Of the island or mainland ?—A. We were within three miles of Mabou ; the barrels in question were wash-barrels, not sea-barrels, and 100 wash-barrels would pack out about 75 sea-barrels, probably.

Q. Is there a difference of one-quarter between wash-barrels and what they pack out ?—A. I should judge that 100 wash-barrels would be about 75 sea-barrels.

Q. And what is the difference between sea-barrels and what they pack out at home ?—A. It is usually one-tenth, and sometimes a little more.

Q. In 1861 you were in the Kit Carson, and in 4½ months took 520 barrels ; where did you catch them ?—A. We fished that year around the Magdalen Islands during the whole season.

Q. Did you fish at all that year around Prince Edward Island ?—A. I never fished there to get any mackerel. I have tried, but I never got fish there.

Q. Did you try there that year ?—A. I might have tried some as I passed along, but I never fished there much any way.

Q. Did you fish the first year you were in the Kit Carson near Port Hood, off the Cape Breton shore ?—A. We fished some off that shore, between Port Hood and Cape George during the last part of the season.

Q. Where is Cape George ?—A. Between Port Hood and Prince Edward Island, about half way across.

Q. You now mention another fishing ground ; what is it called ?—A. Fisherman's Bank ; it lies half way between Souris and Cape George.

By Hon. Mr. Kellogg :

Q. Do you refer, when speaking of Mabou, to Mabou River or to Cape Mabou ?—A. I mean Cape Mabou, a high bluff at the entrance of Broad Cove, east of Port Hood and of Mabou River.

By Mr. Foster :

Q. Did you fish at the mouth of Mabou River ?—A. I never saw any one fish there.

Q. The second year you were in the Kit Carson you caught 604 barrels; where were they taken ?—A. All the years I was in her I fished invari-

ably at the Magdalen Islands, except for a short time at the last pa
of the season, when we fished down about the Cape Breton shore.

Q. Then, shall we understand that during all the years you were i
the Kit Carson your exclusive fishing ground was in the vicinity of tl
Magdalen Islands except late in the autumn ?—A. While on that ve
sel I never fished anywhere else, that is, to catch any fish of any accoun
except late in the autumn, when almost every year I caught some mac
erel about the Cape Breton shore; not always inshore, but sometim
close inshore, and at other times, perhaps, some distance off; and the
we would make Port Hood our harbor in bad weather.

Q. You speak of never having caught any fish off Prince Edwar
Island when in your last two vessels, part of which you owned, I thin
the E. C. Smith and the Kit Carson ?—A. Yes.

Q. Those were large vessels?—A. Yes.

Q. Did you ever fish in those vessels within three miles of the sho
and catch any fish off Prince Edward Island ?—A. I never did. I mig
have hove to and caught a few scattered fish there, but I never caug
enough to detain us there.

Q. Were you in the habit of resorting to harbors on the north side
Prince Edward Island ?—A. I was never in those harbors with tho
vessels, save two or three times at Malpeque while in the first one.

Q. During the years of your fishing experience, what is the large
number of United States fishing-vessels that you have seen together
one time, so far as you can judge ?—A. Well, I do not know exactl
but I should think I have seen 200 together at one time.

Q. Where ?—A. At the Magdalen Islands.

Q. What is the largest number of United States fishing-vessels, a
cording to your best information, that was ever in the Gulf of St. La
rence in any one year fishing—speaking from what you have personal
observed, and what you have learned from others ?—A. I never to
the matter much into consideration, but there may have been at tim
perhaps, 400 such vessels in the bay. I have, however, no defini
knowledge on the subject.

Q. What is the greatest number of vessels of all descriptions that y
ever knew to be there ?—A. There was quite a large fleet of provinc
vessels there at one time, besides; I should think that their numb
was 100 or 150.

Q. When was this ?—A. I do not recollect the exact year, but I c
refer back to the vessel in which I was then to help my memory a litt
1 should think that this was somewhere in 1855 or 1856, or along the

Q. When you fished, did you usually fish with the greater part of t
Gloucester fishing fleet ? How many was the largest number of Glo
cester fishing-vessels that was ever there in one year, in your juc
ment ?—A. I can answer that merely by guess-work, having no stat
tics to guide me ; and I could not tell the number.

Q. Were you usually fishing with the Gloucester fleet ?—A. Duri
the last 5 or 6 years that I fished in the bay, I fished in company
the greater part of the Gloucester fleet.

Q. What, then, was the chief fishing ground of the Gloucester fl
during the last few years that you were fishing ?—A. The Magdal
Islands.

Q. Have you any means of knowing how many of the Gloucester fl
were fishing at the Magdalen Islands at the time of the gale in Augu
1873, when a good many went ashore there ?—A. I do not know t
number, but the largest part of the fleet was then there, I think ; i
own vessels in particular were all there.

Q. How many vessels did you then have there ?—A. Five or six, I think.

Q. It has been stated that 28 Gloucester vessels then went aground at the Magdalen Islands; how many of your vessels then went aground ?—A. One.

Q. One out of five or six ?—A. Yes; and the captain got her afloat in a couple of days,

Q. Can you tell how many Gloucester fishing-vessels are in the Gulf of St. Lawrence this year ?—A. I cannot.

Q. Nor last year ?—A. I could do so only as regards my own.

Q. How many had you there last year ?—A. Three; and I have two there this year.

Q. And how many the year before last ?—A. Three.

Q. During the last 10 years that you fished in the Gulf of St. Lawrence, you had the right, under the Reciprocity Treaty, to fish anywhere in the bay; how, then, did it happen that you did not fish much during this period within three miles of the shore in British waters ?—A. Well, we fished where we could find the most fish, and I suppose that the most fish were on the grounds on which we fished.

Q. Have you the result of your trips made to the Gulf of St. Lawrence and on the American shore since your fishing firm was organized in 1868 ?—A. I have them made up.

Q. How many vessels did you have in the gulf in 1868 ?—A. Five; we landed 625 barrels; average price, $16.

Q. The whole five vessels only caught 625 barrels ?—A. Yes.

Q. How many vessels did you have that year on our shore ?—A. Five.

Q. How many barrels did they land ?—A. One thousand nine hundred and sixty-one; average price, $11.87.

Q. How many vessels did you have in the gulf in 1869 ?—A. Seven; they landed 1,097 barrels; average price, $16.

Q. How many did you have on the American shore ?—A. Two; they landed 1,140 barrels; average price, $8.75.

Q. How many vessels did you have in the gulf in 1870 ?—A. Seven; they landed 1,038 barrels; average price, $13.

Q. And how many on our shore ?—A. Five; they landed 1,852 barrels; average price, $8.61.

Q. And in 1871 ?—A. We then had five vessels in the bay; they landed 1,413 barrels; average price, $8.

Q. How many had you on our shore?—A. Two; they landed 1,174 barrels; average price, $9.70.

Q. And in 1872 ?—A. We then had three vessels in the bay and three on our shore; the former landed 789 barrels, average price, $14; and the latter 1,494 barrels, average price, $9.22.

Q. And in 1873 ?—A. We then had six vessels in the bay and four on our shore; the former landed 2,291 barrels, average price, $9.25; and the latter 1,889 barrels, average price, $13.93.

Q. And in 1874 ?—A. We then had seven vessels in the bay and five off our shore; the former landed 2,800 barrels, average price, $6; and the latter 704 barrels, average price, $8.20.

Q. And in 1875 ?—A. We then had three vessels in the bay and six on our shore; the former landed 623 barrels, average price, $11.33; and the latter 2,531 barrels, average price, $9.81.

Q. And in 1876 ?—A. We then had three vessels in the bay and four on our shore; the former landed 319 barrels, average price, $10.20; and the latter 3,642 barrels, average price, $5.80.

Q. How does the result of those years sum up ?—A. The average catch in the bay per vessel during these ten years was 239 barrels, such average on our shore was 538½ barrels; the result of the stoc: the vessels which fished on our shore exceeded that of those w: fished in the bay by $65,299.

Q. I notice that since your fishing firm was organized the mack which have been taken on the United States shore have not brougt much by the barrel as the bay mackerel; will you explain the re: for this?—A. In the early part of the year the catch of our vessels quite large and prices then run low, while the mackerel caught then small and of poor quality, so that though the average number of bai taken on our shore is larger, the price realized has been smaller on average.

Q. Compare the prices of the shore and bay mackerel for the mo extending from the time when fishing usually begins in the bay—i June out to the end of the season.—A. Our bay fishing comme; about the 1st of July, and I have only the figures for the whole ca

Q. I only want to know whether the shore or the bay mackerel w sell at the higher price during those months?—A. Our shore fetch the most money.

Q. Suppose that you can catch mackerel on the United States s at the same time that you do so in the bay, and then compare prices of these mackerel caught from that date onward; would shore mackerel be more or less in price than the bay mackerel?. Well, I do not know that I could answer that question; I have n figured it up, and I have no statistics to guide me to a conclusioi specting it.

Q. How many vessels have you in the Gulf of St. Lawrence year?—A. Two.

Q. What are their names?—A. The Etta Gott and the Margie St

Q. What has been the result of their voyages?—A. The Etta has landed and shipped home 220 barrels, caught at the Magd Islands and Bird Rocks.

Q. How do you know where they were caught?—A. From what captain has written me, and what my brother, who was in the v and who came home, has told me.

Q. Did the Etta Gott go seining?—A. No, she went with hooks lines.

Q. How was it with the other vessel?—A. She went out on the day and carried a seine. I heard from her a day or two before I away, and she then had 60 barrels.

Q. Do you know where she had been fishing?—A. Yes; ar Prince Edward Island.

Q. How do you know that?—A. From letters which were frequ sent me.

Q. During how many years have you been in the habit of usi seine on the United States shore?—A. Some 10 years.

Q. And has a large part of the mackerel which has been caug that shore during the time that your present firm has existed taken with seines?—A. The largest part has been so taken.

Q. Have you prior to this year tried seining in the Gulf of St. rence?—A. No.

Q. Have you known seining to be successful there?—A. I never any one to make a voyage by seining there.

Q. Do you know any reasons why seining has not succeeded i Gulf of St. Lawrence?—A. One cause is due to the shallowness c water in it; and then the mackerel do not seem to school or play c surface of the water there as they do on our coast; these are the two chief reasons for it. Besides, the bottom in the gulf is of such a character that it does not well admit of seining; the seines are torn in it, and it has been found very difficult on that account. I never saw mackerel rise to the surface there anywhere else than around Prince Edward Island, where I have so seen some close in around the shore in the surf; but I have never seen mackerel rise to the surface around the Magdalen Islands.

Q. And you cannot seine them unless they do rise to the surface?— A. You have got to have them school on the surface of the water before you can so inclose them.

Q. When you are fishing generally and throwing bait over, do you not see them in the same way?—A. They then rise and come up alongside of the vessel, but they do not usually seine them in that way, but when they see the fish coming along in schools, they go out in boats and cast their seines around these schools.

Q. Why can you not seine them when you throw out bait and thus raise schools?—A. They usually do not seine them that way.

Q. You do not know whether it could be done or not?—A. O, yes; it has been tried and sometimes a few are caught that way; but not enough to make a business of it.

Q. Where were the best mackerel found in the gulf during the years when you were a fisherman?—A. I always found the best at the Magdalen Islands.

Q. What did you regard as the safest fishing-ground in the bay?—A. The Magdalen Islands.

Q. Why?—A. Because you can make a lee there with the wind in any direction.

Q. Since you gave up fishing yourself, you have, of course, no personal knowledge as to the particular places where your vessels and other Gloucester vessels have gone to; but have you any means of knowing their usual fishing-grounds?—A. Yes; by talking with the captains when they come home.

Q. Have you been in the habit of making inquiries on this subject?— A. I mostly talk the matter over with them, and ask where they have taken their voyage. This is mostly our first inquiry.

Q. Where have your vessels chiefly fished?—A. At the Magdalen Islands, in the bay, though in one case in particular some sixty barrels were once taken toward the last of the trip between Souris and Cape George; but that is the only instance which I recollect.

Q. Do you regard the fishing-grounds within three miles of the shore in the Gulf of St. Lawrence as of much or of little value?—A. I never considered them to be of any great value.

Q. How is it that the boats can do well fishing inshore when the vessels cannot do so?—A. Well, one man might go out and catch a few fish along shore; but if a vessel did so, when they came to divide the proceeds among the crew it would not pay them to stop there; one or two men might take a barrel of surf-mackerel in a day, and it would be a good day's work for them, though that would not pay 17 men.

Q. How much bait have you ever thrown over in a day in the Kit Carson, the largest vessel in which you fished?—A. I have thrown 6 barrels over in one day.

Q. How much did it cost a barrel?—A. It would average $5 or $6; however, on some days we would throw over but little bait.

Q. How deep do you think the water must be to enable a school of mackerel to be raised and to afford a good day's fishing?—A. Well, I

160 F

could not say that there is any rule for that. The fish often are on t
Banks when, perhaps, they may not be found in very shoal places in a
quantity, but still some mackerel might be there.

Q. I notice that you had some vessels in the gulf in 1866 and 18
when licenses were taken out. You have not examined the record
your business for those years, I believe?—A. No. I had only access
my own books, and the books containing that information were in t
possession of another concern.

Q. How many vessels did you have in the gulf in 1866?—A. Six
seven, I think, but I could not give the number exactly.

Q. If the figures that are given me are correct, you must have b
more than that; I will name them over. Was the Winged Arrow c
of the vessels you had in the gulf that year?—A. Yes.

Q. And the Eureka another?—A. She was owned by the master, t
was fitted out by us.

Q. Was the Ada L. Harris another?—A. Yes.

Q. And the Arequipa another?—A. Yes.

Q. Had you the A. J. Franklin also there?—A. Yes.

Q. And the Bridget Ann?—A. She was owned by the master, l
fitted out by us.

Q. And the Northerner?—A. Yes.

Q. And the Alferetta?—A. Yes; the captain, however, owned p
of her.

Q. And the Colonel Ellsworth?—A. Yes.

Q. Several of these were owned by you and the rest you fitted out'
A. Yes.

Q. These vessels are put down as having taken out licenses in 186
who paid for these licenses, and how were these payments charged'
A. My impression is that they were charged to the stock of the vesse

Q. So that one-half of their cost was paid by the men?—A. That
my impression.

Q. Explain why you took out licenses in 1866, when it was the ha
of your vessels to fish at the places you have mentioned.—A. Well,
thought it was better for the vessels to take out licenses to avoid a
liability of seizure which they might incur and to save them from p
sible annoyance.

Q. When you were in the bay before the Reciprocity Treaty, did
observe any cutters there?—A. O, yes; frequently. I saw them a
was boarded by them.

Q. But your vessel was never seized?—A. No; but I was threater
with seizure.

Q. Why?—A. I was once up in the Bay of Chaleurs; we were
a harbor during a storm, and on coming out the officer of a cut
boarded our vessel and other vessels, for quite a fleet had run do
there, and he used pretty violent language. He said that he wo
seize my vessel if he caught her in there again, and he indorsed a pa
stating that the vessel had been boarded.

Q. In what harbor had you been?—A. Shippegan.

Q. Had you been fishing in the Bay of Chaleurs?—A. No.

Q. What had the other vessels which were with you been doing?—
All of them, 40 or 50 in number, I should think, went in for a harbo

Q. Did you hear of vessels being seized for curing mackerel insh
that they had caught off shore?—A. I heard such a report on the fish
grounds; but that is not to my present knowledge.

Q. Did you hear of commanders of cutters levying contribution
some masters of fishing-vessels, compelling them to give from 5 t

| 20 barrels of mackerel, under pain of capture on refusal to do so ?—
I heard that this was the case; that was the common report among
fishermen in the bay at the time; but I have no personal knowledge
his regard,

). I have read from the 487th page of Sabine's report, which gives
details, although it does not mention any name.—A. I think that
master of the vessel that did so was Captain Darby.

). Those statements were believed by the American fishermen to be
e, whether this was the case or not?—A. We believed the stories,
I cannot say whether they were true or not.

). In 1867, the license-fee was raised to $1 a ton, and then three ves-
connected with your firm apparently took out licenses. Was the
ona your vessel?—A. Yes.

). And also the Winged Arrow and Alferetta?—A. Yes.

). You do not remember whether they took out licenses or not?—A.
I could not tell.

). Who had charge of the books of your first firm?—A. We had a
kkeeper, Mr. Jordan, who was also one of the partners.

). Did you take out any licenses in 1868?—A. I think not; I do not
w that we did so, but I would state, as chief owner of the vessels of
firm, that I did not wish them to take out licenses that year; still I
not say that in some instances they might [not] have been taken,
ugh I instructed the captains not to do so.

). Can you tell the result of the voyages of your vessels on the Ameri-
shore this year?—A. No, I have no statistics in this connection.

). How many vessels have you had engaged in mackerel-fishing this
r on our shore?—A. Only two.

). You do not know whether they have done well or poorly?—A. They
e done very well lately, but in midsummer they did not do much.
ey have, however, made very good catches during the last four weeks.

). How many barrels of mackerel do you think that a schooner must
e in a trip in the Gulf of Saint Lawrence in order to make the result
fitable to the owner?—A. Our best vessels are of about 75 tons; and
of them must take not less than 400 barrels, or between that num-
and 500, to make any kind of a paying voyage.

). During what length of time?—A. The season; a four months'
).

). This is a statement of the expenses connected with such a voy-
?—A. Yes; it is a statement of a suppositious fishing-voyage made
with the bills that would be necessary for such a trip to the Gulf of
nt Lawrence. It is based on the price which mackerel brought the
I came away from home and for which bay trips then sold.

). And on what catch is it based?—A. A catch of 400 barrels.

). Explain the items.—A. The vessel would land 200 barrels No. 1
ckerel, worth $16 a barrel, making $3,200; 100 barrels No. 2, worth
a barrel, making $1,000; and 100 barrels No. 3, worth $6 a barrel,
king $600. This is about the way in which such a trip would pack
—half ones, one-quarter twos, and one-quarter threes.

). You have given the actual prices of such mackerel?—A. Yes; the
ces which ruled the day I left home.

). That is without the charge of packing out?—A. Yes.

). What would be the result of the voyage?—A. $4,800 would be the
ue of the gross stocks.

). Show what the crew and captain would respectively get.—A. The
ls against the voyage, based on actual prices, are 40 barrels of porgy
t, worth $6 a barrel, making $240. I bought some bait a few days

before I left home at $6. Forty barrels would not be a large
for such a vessel. Then there would be 10 barrels of salt clam
$8 a barrel, making $80. That would not be a large quantity
for such a vessel on a 4 months' trip.

Q. It is a fair supply of bait?—A. Yes. The expenses per ba
for packing 400 barrels of mackerel, at $1.75 a barrel, would am
$700. That is the actual present charge this season for pac
made by all the firms.

Q. It includes the price of the barrels?—A. Yes. The stock
would hence amount to $1,020, and the net stock would consequ
$3,780, the crew's half amounting to $1,890; and this, divided a
hands, which number would be necessary on a vessel of that siz
leave $118.12 for each man.

Q. At what figure do you estimate the tonnage of the vessel?-
new measurement.

Q. Have you not got two more men than is usual?—A. No;
about a fair average crew for a vessel of that description.

Q. Is it economical and does it show good judgment to have
on such a vessel?—A. That would be about all the men that coul
alongside of each other and fish conveniently.

Q. And such a vessel would accommodate that many?—
about. The charterer of the vessel would pay the expenses of
age; and provisions and fuel, &c., for 16 men for 4 months would
cents a day per man, amounting in all to $700. We find by looki
our accounts last season that this was the usual cost in this r
40 cents a day for each man. Then there are 120 barrels of salt
the mackerel; it is worth $1 a barrel, making $120.

Q. Is that the actual price of Liverpool salt now?—A. Yes.

Q. And that is the right quantity of salt for such a vessel
consider so. A bait-mill would cost $15, and fishing gear $50.

Q. How long does a bait-mill last?—A. Two years, I suppose

Q. Then out of that $15 you might save $7.50?—A. Yes; with
such a mill might last two years.

Q. What is to be done with a bait-mill to keep it in order?—
teeth get out very frequently, and the mill has to be taken a
teeth inserted. Besides, there are some little charges connec
the clearing of the vessel, such as 8 cents per hogshead of salt fo
ing-fees, &c., which amount to about $15.

Q. You have given the price of salt in bond?—A. Yes; we
in fitting out vessels that we have to buy some fresh provision
bay, which cost from $50 to $100, and I have put down as the
ment for that purpose during the voyage $60.

Q. That is in excess of the 40 cents a day already mention
Yes.

Q. I suppose that in the course of a four months' trip the
the crew requires a supply of fresh vegetables, &c.?—A. The
have fresh vegetables, potatoes, &c., which they cannot alwa
with them on the voyage. I allow $250 a month for the chart
schooner, making for the four months $1,000.

Q. Is $250 a month a fair price for the charter of such a scho
A. That is about the usual price for a vessel of that size goi
Banks.

Q. What do you estimate such a vessel to be worth?—A.
$7,500.

Q. Is that a high price for a Gloucester mackerel-fishing vess
size?—A. It is not.

). Could one be built for less now ?—A. I think not. I had a vessel that size built last spring, and she cost me more money—she cost me $7,500, or more.

). Proceed with your statement.—A. I put down as insurance on the charter and outfits, including barrels, $104.20, which is based on 4 per cent. for the voyage; the rate we charge in our office for a voyage of that kind.

). You charge 4 per cent. for 4 months ?—A. Yes.

). For how much do you insure with these $104.20 ?—A. A little short of $3,000.

). Would it not be about $2,500 ?—A. I guess it would.

). What is embraced in the policy of $2,500 ? It does not cover the value of the hull of the vessel ?—A. No; but it includes the material on board of her for her voyage.

). And how much do these expenses sum up ?—A. $2,215.40.

). Is that a fair policy to take by the charterer of the vessel ?—A. Yes; I consider that it is.

). Is it a large or small estimate ?—A. It is not a large one; it only covers the actual outfit and charter for which he is liable to pay, whether the vessel returns or not.

). The charter of the vessel is to be paid for whether she is lost or not ?—A. This is the case up to the time when she is lost.

). Proceed to the next item ?—A. The charterer's expenses amount to $2,215.40 ; his half of the stock with which he has to pay these expenses is $1,890, and this shows a loss of $325.40.

). So that if a man had a vessel and paid $1,000 for her for four months, and got 400 barrels of mackerel, he would gain nothing for his time, but lose money ?—A. Yes; and there are some other expenses which I did not read ; there is the master's commission of 4 per cent. on the net stock, $3,780, and that amounts to $151.20.

). That is in addition to his share ?—A. Yes.

). Suppose that a man owned his own vessel, which was new, having cost $7,000, what would be a fair percentage to charge for depreciation right along from year to year ?—A. I have made it up, and put it down $300, as a fair amount for depreciation for a voyage of four months.

). How much would that be by the year ?—A. If we take it for a series of years, perhaps it would not be so much in proportion ; perhaps $500 might be a fair depreciation for a number of years. This statement which I have prepared is as follows:

NEW SCHOONER, CHARTERED. TONNAGE, 70 TONS.

For four months' mackerel-fishing in Gulf of St. Lawrence in 1877.

STOCK CHARGES.

bbls. of porgy bait, at $6	$240 00
bbls. of clam bait, at $8	80 00
expense for barrels and packing 400, at $1.75	700 00
Stock charges	1,020 00

OUTFITS AND EXPENSES.

provisions, fuel, &c., for 16 men, 4 months, at 40 cents per day each	$700 00
bbls. Liverpool salt	120 00
salt-mill $15, fishing gear $50	65 00
custom-house and port charges	15 00
fresh provisions bought in bay	60 00

Charter of schooner, 4 months, at $250...]
Insurance on charter and outfits, including with above—barrels $400, and bait
    $320—$2,605, at 4 per cent ....
Skippership or master's commission on net stock $3,780, at 4 per cent......

Total expense account, without interest.............................. ⁄

CATCH.

200 bbls. of No. 1 mackerel, at $16... $⁚
100 bbls. of No. 2 mackerel, at $10... ⁚
100 bbls. of No. 3 mackerel, at $6...

    Gross stock .... ⁚
Less stock charges..

    Net stock .... ⁚

Amount of charterer's half.. ⁚
Amount of crew's half.. ⁚

    Total net stock...

Crew's half...

Average share (16 hands)..

Charterer's expenses.. ⁚
Charterer's receipts .... ⁚

Loss, without 4 months' interest on outfits.................................

Dr.	VESSEL'S ACCOUNT.		
1877. To insurance on $7,000, four months, at 4 per cent.	$280 00	By charter	$⁚
Taxes on $6,000, four months, at $18 per thousand.............	36 00		
Interest on $7,000, four months, at 7 per cent. per annum	163 33		
Depreciation on vessel, four months	300 00		
	779 33		
Gain on charter........	220 67		
	1,000 00		

Q. Would 10 per cent. per annum be a fair charge for deprecia
a fishing-vessel ?—A. I think so; it would be under rather tha
actual depreciation during that time.

Q. Suppose a man owned a vessel and engaged in business w⁚
or chartered her, during how many months in the year can he e⁚
earn money with her; can he so earn during the whole twelve
months ?—A. She will have to be laid up for three or four month
year, sometimes longer or not so long; but, speaking generally, t
be the case for four months.

Q. Then a vessel that is chartered would not earn charter-m⁚
more than nine months in a year ?—A. This would not be the ⁚
over nine months and perhaps it would for less than that.

Q. Chartered at the rate of $250, a vessel would earn $2,250
What insurance would the owner have to pay to cover him on
worth $7,000 for nine months in the year, while under chart
About 7 per cent., I think.

For nine months?—A. Yes

For how much would he insure the vessel?—A. For seven-eighths
ir actual value, I think.

What would be the taxes levied in Gloucester on a vessel costing
)0?—A. Somewhere about $36, I think. Do you mean for the whole
?

Yes; I want to see how the owner who puts $7,000 in money into
ssel comes out. What percentage of the policy of insurance must
ise in order to recover value under the policy?—A. About 12 per
, on a vessel of that description. As a vessel grows older the rate
gher, and then it ranges from 12 to 20 per cent. on sails and rig-

That is the amount on the vessel which cannot be underwritten?—
'here has to be that amount taken off before the company holds
f responsible.

Do your policies cover the value of cables and rigging?—A. No;
is a total loss.

If the 400 barrels of mackerel were caught in less than four months,
igures would be altered and the expenses would be less?—A. Yes.

How would this be on the whole?—A. It would not be proportion-
' less, if outfits were taken for a voyage of that kind; but for a
t voyage the expenses might be something less.

How much must mackerel sell for a barrel to make the business a
essful one for the merchant?—A. Well, we consider the business to
est when the prices are low and the quantity offering large; such a
we consider to be the most favorable.

Why?—A. The mackerel are then more evenly distributed; all
ι portion; and we find that such years make the best years in the
ness. When mackerel are down to $9 or $10 a barrel, we make
ι successful voyages, but when high prices rule, we find that the
cet does not take a large quantity of fish.

Why not?—A. I do not know, save it be because the people won't
eat the fish.

Who eat the common mackerel; where do these go?—A. A great
ion of this quality of mackerel goes to the Southwest and West.

Are these eaten in the New England States?—A. They are used
ə very little, I think.

Mess mackerel, which is quite expensive, how large a quantity
ιat does the market take?—A. The demand is quite limited. It is
ι most on our large seaboard cities.

Now, at $20, supposing the mackerel are of the best quality, how
y barrels would be sold in your estimation?—A. I should judge
)0 barrels would be all that could be sold on the market at the price
20 or upward.

Have you had any experience in selling mackerel to merchants to
again, with reference to the effect of a high or the low price as to
ιmount that a dealer would take?—A. I have had considerable ex-
ənce in selling mackerel.

You sell mackerel to go how far West.—A. My customers are mostly
he New York Central Road to Chicago, Minnesota, some around
t Louis.

. You mentioned to me an instance of a customer who took a con-
rable quantity of you at last year's prices. I wish you would relate
ι to the Commission?—A. It was in Indiana. Last year he had
ə. During the season he had some 1,000 or 1,200 barrels.

. At what price?—A. $7 and $8.

Q. Poor mackerel?—A. Yes.

Q. What are they selling for this year and what does he ‹
They have been selling for $12 until recently, and then they con
to $10. He has been to my place recently, but he said he didr
whether he would purchase any.

Q. Will mackerel be taken for consumption at a price above
other staple articles of equivalent food value?—A. I don't thi
will in very large quantities.

Q. Now, what causes have been in existence interfering with
of salt mackerel during the past few years?—A. I think there ha
several causes. One is the facility of carrying our fresh fish i
tant parts of the country. That has materially interfered
Then there is the lake herring; during the months of Novem
December until May they are very plenty. They are now used
large quantities all throughout the West.

Q. What are lake herring?—A. A species of white fish, I thi
smaller.

Q. What do they sell for per barrel?—A. This party I refe
speaking of his trade, said that last year he used 30,000 packa
package is a half barrel.

Q. How are these put up?—A. Pickled. And he told me th
sold at $2 a package.

Q. You say these have interfered with the constancy of the der
A. I think, during the months we used to depend very largel,
consumption of our mackerel, the lake herring has been one gre
for the decline during these months in the market-value of mac

Q. As to the increased supply of fresh fish, and the extens
over which it can be distributed, what effect has that?—A. \
employ a very large fleet on the Grand Banks and other off shor
for halibut, and there have been of late years very large qu
taken, and the prices have been very low. They are going to ;
of the country, and I think that has had its effect. People will
salt fish when they can get fresh.

Q. How far West have you sent any halibut, or do you ku
being sent fresh in ice?—A. I have known instances where on
neighbors receives them up in Montana. I don't know in whai
ties. He ships them right direct.

Q. But as far as Mississippi does the fresh fish in ice go?-
along that section, I think.

Q. Taking such cities as Cincinnati, Chicago, Saint Louis
nothing of hundreds of smaller ones?—A. They are supplied w
fish in many instances. The cars take them right through.

Q. Now, I want to ask you something about the herring fisher
extensive is the herring fishery in the waters of the United Sta
Well, I haven't any statistics of the herring catch. There
large quantities taken there all along in the months of Septem
October, about six weeks in September and October, all a
shores.

Q. How are they taken?—A. All in nets.

Q. What becomes of them?—A. Generally the largest part
in our Western trade. Last year there was quite a large amc
was shipped to Sweden. I don't know what quantities. I she
some seven or eight barks or brigs loaded from Gloucester.

Q. Were they United States fish?—A. They were packed in
ter fresh.

Q. Where were they from?—A. They were caught around in the vicinity of Gloucester and Boston.

Q. Off the coast of Massachusetts?—A. Yes, off the coast of Massachusetts.

Q. Seven or eight barks you say. How many barrels to a bark?—A. I don't know what they took. I saw the vessels there. I can't say precisely the number. I should think they might probably have taken 5,000 barrels apiece.

Q. They went to Sweden?—A. Gottenburg, I believe.

Q. Have your vessels ever fished for herring in British waters or have you yourself?—A. I have been to the Magdalen Islands for herring. I have never fished there. I have been there for herring.

Q. How did you get them?—A. I bought them.

Q. From whom?—A. Provincial people.

Q. What did you do with the herring?—A. I carried them to Boston and used them for smoking purposes, as well as shipped them to the West Indies.

Q. Did you carry them fresh and frozen?—A. No; salted.

Q. Are they smoked after being salted?—A. Yes.

Q. When did you have anything to do with that Magdalen Island herring business?—A. (Referring to memorandum.) I was there in 1860, 1861, and 1862, I think. Those are the only years.

Q. What season?—A. During the month of May.

Q. Now, have you been to Newfoundland?—A. I have been there seven winters to buy herring.

Q. Beginning when?—A. I was there in 1857 the first year.

Q. Were you connected with Andrew Layton?—A. I was in company with him. We were the first ones to go there from our place for herring.

Q. Did you ever fish for any herring there?—A. I never did.

Q. How did you pay for them?—A. Partly with supplies, provisions, and the most in specie.

Q. Did you go prepared to fish for herring?—A. Never.

Q. Did you ever know a United States vessel that did?—A. I never heard of them.

Q. Now, do you know of any catching of herring prosecuted by United States vessels in any British waters anywhere?—A. I never knew of any. I have known them to go to Labrador in the summer for herring—some vessels.

Q. What is the price of herring? Give me some idea.—A. The price of herring varies very much. Magdalen herring are a very cheap fish, usually selling from the vessel at about $1.50 for 228 pounds, the way we sell them.

Q. At Gloucester?—A. Yes. Our shore herring is selling from the boats now, including the barrel, at about $3.00.

Q. What is the barrel worth?—A. Well, we consider it worth about a dollar usually.

Q. What would be the effect of a duty of a dollar a barrel on pickled herring, or five cents a box on smoked herring, upon the importation of herring from foreign countries—from the Dominion into the United States?—A. It would be prohibitory on the barreled herring, which is a cheap herring. I can't speak of the box herring, for I have no knowledge of it.

Q. Your business relations have brought you into contact with a good many of the business men and fishermen of the provinces, I suppose?—A. Very much. I have traded to all parts of the provinces.

Q. If you have the means of telling either from personal observation

or from information derived from others, I would like to know wl
the effect upon the provincial fishing interests of the termination
Reciprocity Treaty, that is the impostion of the duty in 1866
have no means of actual knowledge except that I have converse
people acquainted with the matter, the merchants of Canso; the
I have been intimately acquainted with in this way have said
very disastrous to their business. That is all. I had no personal
edge.

Q. During the continuance of the Reciprocity Treaty were '
good many fishing vessels from the provinces engaged in the
business ?—A. The last year of my fishing in these waters the
quite a large fleet from the West Shore, Chester, Lunenburg, au
that down. They built up a very fine fleet of vessels.

Q. Did they continue in the fishing business after Reciprocit
I have no personal knowledge only of some that told me this.
told me their business had very much run down. That is all the
edge I have of it.

Q. What effect, in your judgment, would the reimposition of
duties have upon the provincial fisheries ?—A. I think the effect
be the decline of these fisheries if there was a duty put upon the

Q. Then if they ceased to send their fish to the United States,
them in less quantities, how would the difference in the quantity
be made up ?—A. Well, I think it would naturally stimulate o
production. I suppose that would be the tendency.

Q. The operation of the duty, in your judgment, would be to
transfer of the business from the Dominion to the United State
I think it would stimulate the business to a greater amount.

Q. What branch of fishing is the chief industry of Glouceste
The cod fishery.

Q. What is the proportion, in your judgment, without stati:
the cod fishery to the mackerel fishery ?—A. Well, I can ans
myself. Within the last few years we, as curers of fish, cure
from 18,000 to 20,000 quintals of codfish in the season. We pack
3,000 to 6,000 barrels of mackerel.

Q. Well, give the proportion of your own business. How i
that is codfish, and how much is mackerel ? You have given it
tals, give it in fractions. Is the cod fishing twice or three t
great ?—A. About $100,000 for the codfishery, and, well, about o
as much for the mackerel fishery. Then we have other branch
fresh-halibut fishing.

Q. You are engaged in that fresh-halibut fishing ?—A. Yes.

Q. What do you do with the fresh halibut ?—A. We sell the
merchants, and they distribute them over the country.

Q. Where are they caught ?—A. Most of them catch them on
of the Banks in about 200 fathoms, where it falls off towards
Stream.

Q. How near shore to any place have you known of the halib
fished ?—A. 150 miles may be the nearest point.

Q. These are Banks, but haven't you known it to be done, or at
near shore ?—A. I have.

Q. Where have you known them ?—A. On the Labrador co
have caught them large near the shore. I have known them ca
in 30 miles or 25 miles, around Cape Sable. I fished there quit
ber of years—around Seal Island and Brown's Bank.

Q. How near land there did you ever fish ?—A. I have fishe
of land. I could see it.

Q. Did you ever fish within three miles?—A. No; I don't think any one could fish in there, because it is not a fishing ground.

Q. You don't know of any one?—A. No.

Q. You told me you had a vessel that strayed up into the Gulf of St. Lawrence for halibut. Give me an account of that.—A. I forget the year. I could tell by referring to a memorandum. I think it was somewhere about 1872. I am not precise, '72 or '73.

Q. Before the present treaty?—A. Yes.

Q. A long or a short time before?—A. 1 think it was about the time t went into action.

Q. Well, what was the name of the vessel, and what happened to her?—A. He was looking for halibut and trying close inshore. He didn't catch any. He was seized and carried to Quebec.

Q. Well, you got your vessel released, and there was no complaint?—A. Yes, we got her released. It was all satisfactory.

Q. I wanted to know whether you had known, excepting that instance, of any halibut fish there?—A. I know that about a week afterwards a vessel was doing the same thing up there. Our vessels go prospecting around to see where they can find fish, and he was looking for halibut, and was taken.

Q. Did these vessels catch any halibut?—A. I don't know of any catching any.

Q. Do you know of any American vessels fishing for halibut in the Gulf of St. Lawrence?—A. Nowhere, unless north and east of Anticosti—we call it Labrador shore—near Red Island, I think the place is called. I have heard of several trips caught there. It is down towards Belle Isle. That was some six years ago, I think. Two or three vessels caught parts of trips or their whole trips there. The one I have referred to is the only one I ever knew that was catching halibut inshore.

Q. Do you think the Canadian catch of mackerel that comes into the United States market has any perceptible effect upon the price of mackerel in the market?—A. Well, I don't think it has a great deal. It would, perhaps, have some.

Q. What is it regulates the price principally?—A. Well, the supply and demand would regulate the price up to a certain standard. When you get beyond that—I will illustrate it. This season there was a short supply of mackerel, and when they got up to a certain point—$12 a barrel or $14 a barrel—customers would not take them, and they dropped to $12, when they were bought a little more freely, but they didn't go off, although the quantity was small. When I came away, the mackerel were being taken at $10 quite freely. When they get to a certain point they seem to stop the consumption. Buyers say they can't handle them to profit. They say people will not eat them.

Q. You spoke of $1.75 as being the charge for packing out mackerel at Gloucester this year, including the cost of barrels. I want to ask you whether, when a mackerel schooner comes to wharf and her fish is packed out, she is charged wharfage?—A. No; in no instance do they charge wharfage. The mackerel are packed, the barrels found and coopered, they are salted and branded all at the expense of the packer; and for that he charges $1.75. This is a customary charge throughout the town.

Q. Then the mackerel packer owning the wharf gets his interest on the cost of his wharf, his rent for his wharf and buildings, in that $1.75?—A. Yes. Two years ago it was $2. This year it is $1.75.

Q. But the income for the wharf property comes out of that?—A. Yes.

Q. How much would these wharves cost, some of them ?—A
cost me $25,000. Some are more expensive than mine, and some

Q. Have you ever known any cod-fishing vessel go prepared t
mackerel as well as cod, or of any mackerel vessel going prepared t
cod as well as mackerel—mixed trips of that sort ?—A. I never l
any. They might catch a barrel.

Q. Your Gloucester halibut catchers go as far as Greenland or
sometimes ?—A. Not for fresh, but salted halibut.

By Mr. Davies :

Q. You spoke of the cost of your wharf as $25,000 ?—A. Yes.

Q. Is that an average ?—A. I don't think that is an average.
are some lower and some higher.

Q. Your business premises, I suppose, would in value involve
lay of a large sum of money besides that ?—A. There is nothi
nected with the business but the wharf.

Q. You do all your business on the wharf ?—A. That inclu
buildings on the wharf. Our store is just on the upland. We
that as part of our wharf.

Q. How many vessels are you interested in now ?—A. We ow

Q. As matters go, the world has smiled very favorably o
That is so, is it not ?—A. I have been considered one of the m
cessful ones at the place.

Q. What are the vessels worth apiece ?—A. To day ? It wou
very hard question to answer.

Q. I don't mean to say if you were to force them upon the i
But what do you value them at—$7,000 ?—A. That is one of t
ones. Many of them have been running some 12 years and h
down very materially in value—some down to $1,500.

Q. You built a new one in April ?—A. Yes.

Q. How many ?—A. Just one this year.

Q. What ones have been running 12 years ?—A. Well, we h
eral of them that have been 12 years and some that have been rur
years.

Q. You have of course your premises besides these, where
side ?—A. I have a place where I live.

Q. Your partner too, I suppose ?—A. He has not any house.

Q. I think you said that, in your opinion, the influx of C
mackerel did not very much affect the markets in the United
Do you say that ?—A. Well, not to any great extent.

Q. I just want to know if you have examined the statistics v
view to ascertain what proportion of the whole quantity of r
consumed in the United States comes from Canada ?—A. I hav

Q. Well, it would depend pretty much upon how you found th
tics what your answer would be ?—A. Well, not with regard to
catch ; the largeness or smallness of our own catch has made t
higher or lower more than anything else ; I have watched that.

Q. I quite understand that a large or small catch there would
less affect prices ; but supposing you examined the statistics ai
that one-third of the mackerel consumed came from Canadiau
would you then say that the importation of that quantity did no
ally affect the market ? I will put it at one-fourth.—A. It wou
it up to a certain point ; beyond that, I think, the market would
them.

Q. Well, would not the effect be to reduce the price ; the peo
take them if they went down low enough, wouldn't they ?—
mackerel gets at a low figure there is a great consumption.

Q. Would not the influx of a very large quantity of fish materially affect the price?—A. It would not materially affect it at the present market rates.

Q. Why?—A. Because the prices have got down now to where the market will take mackerel; at higher rates it would have effect.

Q. Do you mean to say that almost any quantity could be consumed at the present low prices?—A. Well, a large quantity.

Q. Well, I mean any reasonable quantity that could come in?—A. Well, year before last we had a very large catch, and the markets seemed to take them.

Q. Well, I will put my question in another way. Suppose one-quarter of the mackerel now supplied were withdrawn from the market, what effect would it have as to prices?—A. Well, I suppose the price would be somewhat higher, but the market would not take them beyond a certain point.

Q. Now, see. Take them at the prices now ruling. Supposing one-fourth of the quantity now in the market was withdrawn, would not the price of the three fourths remaining naturally and inevitably rise?—A. They would rise some.

Q. In consequence of the withdrawal of the one quarter?—A. I think it would affect it some; not more than 50 cents a barrel; I think it would to that amount.

Q. The reason I ask is that, examining your statistics, I find that the price of mackerel rises and falls more than any other commodity I know of, going sometimes from $22 down to $7. Is not that caused chiefly by the large quantity brought into the market?—A. It is not. If you will allow me to illustrate the case, I will take mackerel that sold for $22 some years ago, and after months of consumption, without any mackerel coming in, they went down to $6.

Q. What year was that?—A. I will not be exact. I think about five years ago I sold some for $22 in the fall, and afterwards they went for $6, and none came in.

Q. Are you sure about that?—A. I am sure.

Q. How do you know none came in?—A. I say no new catch.

Q. I fancy the year you and I refer to is the same. I will read from the annual report of the Chief of Statistics for 1871. I find that No. 1 mackerel in January were selling for $22 a barrel to $22.50; in February the same; in March the same; in April the same; in May they dropped to $18; in June they were $18. That is as the spring catch comes in in May and June.—A. There are not many come in May.

Q. Well, in June. I am told they go in April, and I assume that at the latter end of May some would come in.—A. Not many salt fish until June.

Q. Well, the fresh would be coming in to take the place of the salt.—A. I don't think many.

Q. Well, I will take June. Some would come in then.—A. The last of June.

Q. Very well. Then in July they dropped to $12; in August to $7.—A. I think those reports are based on the retail prices that they were in the market, not the Gloucester prices.

Q. Well, I am speaking of the market prices which the mackerel bring. I am reading from a statement showing the prices of staple articles in the New York market at the beginning of last month.—A. Well, the year I refer to I took our wholesale prices. I don't know what the Washington markets or any of those New York markets might have been charging.

Q. I selected that year because I thought it was the one you r
to.—A. I only knew the year we lost so much money in Glouce
mackerel was when mackerel was high in the fall and low in the

Q. I ask you this: Can you recall the year 1871 to your mind?
was the year of the Washington Treaty. Are you or are you no
that American vessels were admitted to the waters of Prince I
Island?—A. I have no knowledge about anything of that kind.

Q. Were not your vessels there?—A. I think I might have
them say that they were. I don't recollect.

Q. I find a rather curious coincidence that the price of macke
just about that time, and it struck me that the fact of their be
lowed to catch there might have something to do with it?—A
year?

Q. I speak of 1871.—A. My vessels don't show a very larg
that year.

Q. Your vessels, you say, have never fished near Prince I
Island, so that is quite consistent with my theory; but you v
knowledge, I think, and that is as much as I want, that ge
speaking the supply regulates the price.—A. To a certain exten

Q. To a material extent. Will you go as far as that?—A. V
to a certain point. If there was a very small quantity I don't th
market would take them. The trade will not take them beyon
tain limit. When the mackerel goes to $14 a barrel, or along t
$15, that is our own mackerel, they will not take them.

Q. They pay $25 for some.—A. That is men that have the m
pay, not poor people.

Q. But there is a class who will pay a large price for the bes
10,000 people you put it at.—A. I don't know exactly.

Q. Supposing the mackerel caught in colonial waters were ex
would it, or would it not, have any effect upon the price you
your fish? Supposing one-fourth of the quantity consumed
States was excluded, would it have any effect on the price of th
three-fourths?—A. I think some, not much. I think it would st
our home production.

Q. In what way would it stimulate it? By raising the pri
not?—A. Well, to a small extent.

Q. What do you mean by to a small extent?—A. Well, I thir
a certain point the market does not seem to take mackerel wh
go beyond a certain figure. At $15 and along there the macker
hard, even with a small quantity. It was surprising to me th
having mackerel to sell, that I had to look round to find buyer
when we have large quantities at low prices it seemed to me ev
wanted to buy.

Q. You are speaking of the Gloucester markets?—A. I
knowledge of any other market. I find my customers when the
a certain point will not take them.

Q. Well, then the effect of the British mackerel coming in is
consumer is able to buy it cheaper than he otherwise would?—
up to a certain point. The effect would be very small. There
large enough quantity. It is our home catch that affects it.

Q. I am putting what I conceive to be the fact, as I said, t
fourth of the mackerel consumed comes from the provinces. W
the exclusion of that naturally give you an enhanced price for t
three-fourths?—A. Well, I think it would to a certain extent, t
amount, I don't know how much.

Q. You made the same statement with regard to herring. I

your answer would be the same as to that, as it is with regard to the mackerel ?—A. I say that a duty up beyond a certain point would make them almost worthless.

Q. It would be prohibitory, you said ?—A. I think it would be on cheap herring.

Q. Would not the price go up ?—A. No. I don't think the market would take them at high figures, not that quality. I don't think they would go beyond $2.

Q. Two dollars a barrel is the outside limit they can be sold for. Now, if a large quantity comes in from a foreign market, must not the price naturally fall well below that outside limit ?—A. Well, I suppose it would fall some; when the fish goes down to a low price the market seems to take a very large quantity.

Q. That is just what I say. Now a word or two (before I come to the main question) about halibut. Have you been engaged practically in catching halibut since the year 1864 ?—A. I have not—not as a fisherman.

Q. You cannot speak of the places where halibut have been caught since that time from practical knowledge ?—A. No.

Q. Previous to 1864 you were engaged. How many seasons were you engaged catching halibut ?—A. I think some six or eight.

Q. When you were then engaged did you go into the Gulf of St. Lawrence at all for halibut ?—A. Never.

Q. Are you aware that there is a halibut-fishery around Anticosti ?— A. I never was aware of any.

Q. Well, the fact that two vessels were seized there while inside trying to catch would be some evidence that they believed the halibut were there ?—A. Well, they look for them everywhere.

Q. Don't you think they must have had reasonable grounds ?—A. I don't think it; they are in the habit of looking everywhere they may be.

Q. Do you stand by the full meaning of your answer, that you don't think they had reasonable grounds for believing the fish to be there ?—A. Well, a man might have reasonable grounds for believing they were in the water anywhere.

Q. Well, we have had evidence that the shores around Anticosti are well known as a halibut-ground, and that quantities are taken over at Gaspé too. Do you tell me you have never heard of those grounds being halibut-grounds ?—A. Not by our vessels catching them there.

Q. I do not care whether by your vessels or any other ?—A. I never heard them spoken of.

Q. What did you mean by answering me " not by your vessels catching them " ?—A. I meant that I never heard them spoken of.

Q. I wanted to know whether you were aware of persons fishing for halibut around those coasts ?—A. Never of their catching any.

Q. I did not ask you that.—A. I have no knowledge of it.

Q. Have you ever heard from those who have knowledge of the business whether halibut are caught around those coasts ?—A. I can't say I have.

Q. Will you say you have not ?—A. I don't know; I might have heard some one say they caught halibut there.

Q. Your evidence is that those two vessels, in your belief, went there without any previous knowledge that it was a halibut-ground, on pure, mere speculation ?—A. Certainly. We had vessels this year that went into three hundred fathoms of water, when they had no evidence of fish being there. They went there and tried. They had never any knowledge, or any one else.

Q. I dare say; but here are vessels going in and rendering them: liable to seizure, being, in fact, actually seized there; and you say went to those places on pure speculation, without any previous k edge?—A. Well, there was not any fish there, because it proved were not any there.

Q. You heard of one halibut?—A. Well, I might have.

Q. Who was the lucky fellow?—A. I did not say there was or might have heard of somebody catching a halibut. I can't say that.

Q. Now, when you were prosecuting that branch of the fisheries, were you accustomed to go?—A. To the George's Bank mostly; on Brown's Bank—that is off Cape Sable and on the Seal Island gr

Q. There is a difference between Cape Sable and Sable Island Yes.

Q. I want to ask you whether you fished off Cape Sable or the is —A. Cape Sable.

Q. I wish you would go to the map, because there is a little di ancy between your statement and that of a gentleman here before (Witness goes with counsel to map.)

Q. (Pointing to Sable Island.) Was it near Sable Island?—A I never fished there. I fished at Seal Island and Tusket Light.

Q. Was it toward that direction?—A. I fished all the way arou

Q. Do you know a harbor there called Lobster Harbor?—A. I I never was in there much.

Q. Perhaps you never tried in close around Cape Sable Isla all?—A. Never within eight or ten miles. Probably I have tri eight or ten miles.

Q. You never tried in within three miles there for halibut?—A

Q. Of course, then, you don't know about it. We have som dence that there have been fish caught in there, and as you have tried you won't, of course, contradict it?—A. No; I will not.

Q. You don't know anything about it. Now, you submitted a ment, and I understand it to be not the result of an actual voyag just a statement made up out of your own head as to what you would be the probable result of a voyage?—A. I have had a many years' experience, and I take that as a supposed voyage. not an actual voyage.

Q. It is a mere fancy statement. I don't mean in any improper It is not made as the result of any actual voyage. And you s loss on the catch of 400 barrels of some $325 to the charterer. remember when you were giving evidence and Mr. Foster aske what number of barrels should be taken to make a fair and voyage, you happened to say the very same number which yo by this account to have resulted in a loss.—A. I said 400 or 500 b

Q. You said 400 barrels, if I remember?—A. I didn't say 400 b did I?

Q. I understood you so?—A. I think I said 400 or 500.

Q. I think you began by saying 400. Then you said generall 400 to 500?—A. Well, between these two figures would be the of barrels that would make a paying voyage.

Q. Now, if $325 were lost upon 400 barrels caught, how reconcile the two statements?—A. It is made up by the charter vessel. My answer was on the vessel that was not chartered, by the owners; and the result there shows that the owner di some $220.

Q. You mean to say the owner would make, whereas the ch

ld lose ?—A. As a practical man of business I consider all these ges as charges that would be fair and just in making up the account. ike out that he would be a loser.

That is if he chartered ?—A. The party who owned the vessel would e money out of the charter.

He would make the charter, whatever it was; he would make the e of the charter, less the wear and tear of the vessel, less interest taxes. But do I understand you to say that the owner of a vessel ing her to the bay would make a. fair profit on 400 or 500 barrels, reas the charterer would lose ? Then there must be some particular ch in which the owner makes a profit, which the charterer has no intage of ?—A. In that case I have given, if the owner ran the ves-imself on that voyage, and got 400 barrels, he would not be much loser. If he got an advance on that, and was the charterer himself, ould have something left out of the voyage.

Must not he have the same expenses as a charterer would have ?—Vell, if he had an increased number of barrels he would make.

But with the same number of barrels and these expenses he would nake anything ?—A. He would get the interest on his money; he d earn that. The interest and taxes have gone into that account.

Well, you prove conclusively by this account that a man who ies 400 barrels loses $325.—A. If he is a charterer.

And if he is the owner he makes; now, where does the difference —A. If he is the owner he does not make.

I will see, now, if I can solve that difficulty, although I am only a in the business. You give certain charges here that are made ist the voyage; 40 barrels of pogie bait, $240, and 10 barrels of s, $80. That would have to be paid by the men who fitted her Expenses for barrels and packing 400, at $1.75, $700. Now, is not a very fair profit made out of that branch of the business ?—A. is not in connection with the vessel; that is with the business.

There is a handsome profit ?—A. There is a profit.

Could that business exist if the vessel didn't go on the voyage to the business ?—A. Well, it is part of the business.

Is it not a necessary incident which could not occur without the il going ?—A. Of course you have to have the vessel to get the iess.

Then I understand you to agree that there is a handsome profit upon that? And you have provisions, fuel, &c., for 16 men, four hs, at 40 cents per day each, $700. It struck me you put that very . What provisions do you supply them ?—A. I cannot give you all tems.

How many barrels of flour, for instance ?—A. Well, that is not my rtment, but we put aboard about 14 barrels of flour, 12 or 14.

You were so many years in the gulf that you must have known mány barrels you were accustomed to take. You can give the mission very near the exact quantity ?—A. I can give you the tity of large articles like flour and beef, but I could not give you ittle articles.

It struck me as being very high.—A. I would say in regard to that that is based on actual figures taken on our vessels year after . We have made up accounts to see what it costs per man. We e 40 cents is about what it costs a day for board.

That forty cents a day is made up and based upon the prices which charge the vessel for these goods ?—A. Yes.

Is there not a handsome profit made out of these ?—A. We consider if we have an outside vessel where the captain owns her himself that we make on this fitting about $75.

Q. Do you know what percentage that is? It is 10 per cent.—A. Well, we make up his account and settle with the crew.

Q. I am not complaining that it is exorbitant. I think it is very reasonable and fair paying business. Now there are 120 barrels of Liverpool salt, $120. Do you mean to say you pay $1 a barrel for Liverpool salt in bond. (I understood you to say that was taken out of bond.) We can buy Liverpool salt in Prince Edward Island cheaper than that.— A. Well, your vessels fetch it out as ballast.

Q. But does Liverpool salt in bond cost $1 a barrel?—A. Well, we take our salt. It is in the outside part of the town, in the storehouse. We have to send men to head it, and cooper it, and we have to pay for teaming it.

Q. You are explaining why you charge a profit upon it?—A. It is no profit. I am a dealer in salt, and import 50,000 hogsheads of salt. I think our Liverpool salt sells at $1.75 a hogshead.

Q. To whom?—A. Any dealers that wish to purchase.

Q. How many barrels to a hogshead?—A. We usually get down here two barrels.

Q. Is that all?—A. That is what we get. When we sell it, we call it three and a half bushels to a barrel.

Q. You charge the vessel about 15 cents more than the price?—A. We charge the vessel no profit on the salt. The vessel has to pay the extra charges there will be for cooperage, teaming it, and taking it to the vessel where she lies, and taking it in.

Q. Then you charge in addition to these things for the charter of the vessel $1,000, and then you charge insurance on the charter and outfits. You charge insurance upon the provisions you supply to the men. Do you, as a matter of fact, insure them?—A. Any man that charters that vessel has an insurable interest there. Any careful man will insure that interest he has there. There is nothing there that any business man would not call an insurable interest.

Q. What insurable interest have you in it?—A. I have no insurable interest. It is the man who has chartered her that has insured her. I think there are a good many things I haven't charged.

Q. Now, you have skippership or master's commission on net stock, $3,780, at 4 per cent., $151.20; and you make the total expense amount, without interest, $2,215.40. It is a very curious result. You think that is correct?—A. In my best judgment, that would be as fair as I could make it.

Q. I picked up a paper here on the table when you were giving your evidence, the Commercial Bulletin of Boston. That is well recognized as a commercial paper of standing, I believe. Now, in looking at the prices which you allowed this vessel for her mackerel, I find you are very much below the market prices quoted here. This is the extract; I will read it: "Prince Edward Island Number ones (I see that they specially quote the Prince Edward Island Number ones), from $18 to $19. Large Number twos $17 to $18; twos $12 to $14. Large Number threes $9 to $10. Medium threes $9 to $10. Now I have taken your prices. You give $16 for the $19 that they give. Where they quote $18 you give $10. Where they quote $9 to $10 for medium threes you give $6.—A. I have based that on the fish that were actually sold and were bought by Benjamin A. Baker. The prices he paid were these stated in that account.

Q. That cannot be extra mackerel?—A. Extra mackerel, mess mackerel, if a man had any, would be larger.

Q. Well, I understand that is a theoretical statement, and I want to test it in one or two ways. Now, if I take the prices as quoted in the extract I have read, I find they would make a difference of $1,325 in favor of the charterer; or, deducting the loss which you state of $325, there would be left a clear profit of $1,000, taking the Boston prices as quoted.—A. In my account I take the Gloucester rates, the wholesale Gloucester rates—actual sales which occurred at the time I came here, and which I can verify.

Q. What I say is, that if I made up the figures at these prices quoted, not the highest, but the average—for instance, instead of taking the large No. 2's at $18, I leave them out altogether and take the small ones at $14, and for the 3's I take the medium quality, not the highest—in this way allowing every charge that you put against the vessel, I have a clear profit of $1,000.—A. I have taken a trip of mackerel as I know they packed out. I would like to say one word more. There is a difference between the grades in different towns. One town will have a grade that will fetch more than another, and the brand does not guarantee that the quality is there. I don't know about Prince Edward Island. The grade may be very much higher, and the price may be much higher. I have taken the actual value as the fish sold.

Q. But this is your State inspection?—A. That paper does not say so.

Q. It says Prince Edward Island No. 1's. There is no inspection there at all.—A. That is the name of the mackerel. They are inspected there.

Q. No; they are not. Are not all mackerel that go into the United States inspected? Haven't they to submit to inspection by an officer of the State?—A. I think the buyers inspect them.

Q. Don't you know that they are all inspected by some official there?—A. I suppose they are. The buyers reinspect them.

Q. You are brought here as a man having an extensive acquaintance with this matter, dealing largely in fish, and owning vessels. Do you mean to say you don't know whether the mess-mackerel imported into the United States are inspected by an official of the United States?—A. I never had any knowledge as to the mackerel from the provinces.

Q. Do I understand that I could send mackerel in from the provinces and put them on the market without having an inspection at all?—A. I don't know anything about it.

Q. How did you do with the mackerel you got here; was there not an inspector of fish?—A. Yes.

Q. Did he not inspect them under a State law?—A. Yes.

Q. Are you not compelled to submit to that?—A. We do.

Q. Have you any doubt that that applies to all mackerel?—A. I suppose it does. I don't know what international law there may be with regard to it. There may be an international law that the fish, being admitted free of duty, are admitted without inspection. I know nothing about that.

Q. Now, we have had witnesses here to state positively, as I understood, that the mackerel which came from the bay and the mackerel which came from your shores were assorted and branded, and the same brands put upon both by the State inspector. I may be wrong, but I understood the evidence in that way.—A. I don't know that I understand you. Do you say that all qualities were branded alike?

Q. No; but that the mackerel are taken and assorted and marked and sent out with the official stamp as Nos. 1, 2, and 3.—A. That'i custom.

Q. I am not speaking of a custom but of a law to which you ha submit.—A. I would say here that mackerel coming from the Sta Maine are not reinspected; they are landed in our town from Port

Q. Are they not inspected in the State of Maine ?—A. They are. I think, not under any State law.

Q. Do you know ?—A. I don't know. how it is this year, for some they have a State law and sometimes they haven't.

Q. The mackerel imported into Maine are governed by the la Maine, and I suppose they haven't to submit to another inspection I am speaking of foreign mackerel. Do you mean to say the one State law for Gloucester and another for Boston ?—A. I l mackerel are landed by us and we have to make returns to th spector. In some cases of mackerel coming from the State of Mait don't.

Q. Of course not; you don't want to have them inspected twice But I don't know how it applies to provincial mackerel. I. handled any.

Q. I will just repeat the question. Do you mean to tell us now, ously—you have been in business all the semany years, engaged largely in the business—do you mean to say that you really don't whether there is a State law requiring the inspection of foreig imported into Massachusetts?—A. I don't know; I never investigat

Q. You have never dealt with those who catch these fish—witb vincial dealers ?—A. I never did.

Q. You never made the slightest inquiry ?—A. I never inquired

Q. Now, if you went into the market to-morrow, would you bu without the inspector's mark ?—A. I would buy them at the q they were by looking at them.

Q. Would you, without their having the inspector's mark ?— would if the quality suited.

Q. Could you sell them without having them inspected ?   Woul not be breaking the law ?—A. I could sell them anywhere in the without being inspected; but I could not send them out of the St

Q. Then there is no necessity for inspection at all ?—A. Not State of Massachusetts.

Q. Then, when you import your mackerel, you are not compel have them inspected ?—A. I have, in order to send them out State.

Q. If you don't intend to send them out of the State ?—A. I c them to my neighbors or any one around me by the cargo with spection.

Q. Well, can he put those mackerel into the market and sell t the person who consumes them, or to a trader to retail them; ea be done without inspection ?—A. I think they have to be inspect

Q. Don't you know ?   Have you any doubt at all ?—A. No; you me if I could sell them; I say I can.

Q. I am asking you for full information, not as to the means by the law can be evaded.   Do you believe there is a different law lating the inspection of fish in Boston from that which regulate Gloucester ?—A. I believe there is not.   But I would say in reg inspection that I have sold hundreds of barrels every year with spection.   I sold two cargoes this year without inspection.

Q. How much have you to pay for inspection ?—A. Two cents general inspector.

By Mr. Foster :

). That does not answer the whole question. How much does inspec-
i cost you ?—A. We receive ten cents a barrel for inspection from
purchaser.

). Of which two cents go where ?—A. To the general inspector.

). Where do the other eight cents go ?—A. To the deputy.

By Mr. Davies :

). There are no means of evading the payment of that 10 cents ?—A.

). Are you an inspector ?—A. I am. Every man is to a certain extent.
:ceive 8 cents.

). You are paid so much for inspecting the fish ?—A. I am paid by
charterer.

). And you inspect your own fish ?—A. Yes.

). Does the general inspector oversee it ?—A. He is supposed to.

). You are an inspector of fish in that State, and don't know what the
is ?—A. Our Massachusetts law ? I know the Massachusetts law in
ard to the fish I inspect. I don't know how it applies to fish coming
n other States.

). Did you ever read the law ?—A. I have read it frequently.

). Does it not apply to the whole State ?—A. It does, but I don't
w how it is as to fish imported from the provinces.

). What did you mean by telling me you did not know what the Bos-
law was ?—A. I did not say that.

). What did you say with reference to inspection in the Boston mar-
?—A. I said—I don't know just what the words were. We have had
siderable talk on this inspection business. I don't know what you
r to.

). I am satisfied I reported you correctly ?—A. I say it is just the
ie as it is with us as far as our home fish is concerned. I don't know
to Prince Edward Island mackerel, whether they are subject to in-
ction or not.

). Is it subject to inspection in Gloucester ?—A. I have no knowledge
:ther it would be liable to be reinspected or not—mackerel that has
e been inspected.

). I am speaking about foreign mackerel imported, which has not
n inspected.—A. I think all mackerel that has not been inspected
ild have to be inspected.

). Therefore Prince Edward Island fish would have to be inspected ?
.. Prince Edward Island mackerel are branded such and such a
nd. It is inspected.

). Where ?—A. In Prince Edward Island.

How do you know ?—A. Because your paper gives them as such.

). No such thing.—A. I have seen them branded as No. ones. I take
)r granted they were No. ones, because they were branded.

) Would you as inspector take it for granted and not inspect them
ou saw a vessel land them ?—A. I should take it for granted they
'e.

). And not inspect them ?—A. Without inspection.

).' And would you not charge your fee ?—A. I should not charge a
if I did not inspect them.

). Is that your practice ?—A. I have never had them.

[r. FOSTER (to Mr. Davies). Do you state as a fact that there is no
:ial inspection in Prince Edward Island ?

[r. DAVIES. Yes.

Mr. FOSTER. How is it in Nova Scotia and Cape Breton?

Mr. DAVIES. I don't know; I believe there is in Halifax.

Q. Now, one moment more. You say yourself you are in a pre position as the result of your fishing business?—A. I don't kn I said that.

Q. Well, I will ask you. At the time you ceased your fishing you went into business. Then you must have had some capit Well, I had some.

Q. Sufficient to justify you in entering into business?—A. W have said I have done as well as any one, or better.

Q. And you made money?—A. I had accumulated consideral

Q. Give us an idea.—A. I had some thousands.

Q. Now this statement of the result of a catch of 400 shows I find, however, that your average catch, although you have b largest in the bay, has only been 469, or between four and five during the whole time. So your average catch during that per only been about the number of barrels which you say would res loss?—A. I was the owner, which would make some difference. know that it is shown I did make a fortune in the bay.

Q. I take your statement as you gave it, that you had conside A. I never said that.

Q. You said that you had enough to justify you in going in ness.—A. I should not have gone into business if I had not th had enough.

Q. Now I ask you this: Can you produce instead of this a st copied from your books showing what your vessels actually did can; not to-day, because I have not the books with me. I wo however, my business was various. I was employed in a nu different branches of trade all those years.

Q. And incidentally the business connected with fishing is able one I believe, is it not, to those engaged in it; I mean su vessels?—A. In some instances.

Q. As a general rule?—A. Well, there is a profit in the busi

Q. It gives employment to a large number of hands?—A. Y or five men to a concern.

Q. It is in point of fact the staple business of Gloucester?— fishery.

Q. The fishery business?—A. Well, that is the main busines

Q. I see by the returns that two-thirds of the whole are coc one-third mackerel.—A. To the town?

Q. Of the whole fishing business of the town?—A. It has different years.

Q. The business gives employment to a large number of han Yes.

Q. Upon it, to a very large extent, the prosperity of Glouc pends?—A. I should say it did—to the fisheries.

Q. I find a Gloucester paper of August 31 comments on fact. I want to see whether you agree with it or not. It was at the time when the shore fishery threatened to be a failure. Ann Advertiser says:

What shall we do if the mackerel fleet do not get good fares, is now th many minds. The failure thus far makes money positively a scarce arti community, where usually at this season there are comparatively flush t proceeds of a hundred thousand barrels of mackerel scattered through a like this of ours give all classes a share, and this it is which we depend up business lively, pay up bills, and the like. There is a chance yet to catch t will be lively work to make up a season's work now, unless the mackerel

rge numbers, and the fleet are right on the spot to take advantage of it. Nothing
lat we know of in the way of good news, in a business point of view, would be more
elcome at the present writing than the intelligence that the Gloucester mackerel
set were coming in with "heavy decks." It would enliven everybody, and the fact
ould insure provisions and fuel for the coming winter to many a family who are now
ery anxious as to where their supplies are to come from.

Does that contain the substantial facts or not?—A. I should say
lat if 200 sail of vessels prosecute that business, and go to sea and get
o fish, the people do not get any meat or bread.

Q. There are a large number of people dependent on the success of
lat enterprise?—A. Yes; on all the business; that is one of the main
ortions of the business.

Q. You have said that lately the catch on your coast was better?—A.
; has been better during five or six years.

Q. Here is a paper of October 6, and I find, under the head of " Bos-
in Fish Market," the following :

Mackerel are arriving in sufficient supply from the provinces to meet all demands.
ood fish are most in demand, at full prices. Our home shore fleet is now near at
ind on the Middle Bank. It is probably the largest that has been together this sea-
n, over 300 sail. The first of the week they took a few fish with hooks, of better
te and quality, but during the past three days they have done nothing.

Q. Do you know of that? It refers to three days preceding 6th Oc-
iber.—A. I had vessels going—though I was not out fishing and could
ot tell personally—and I know they came in with very fair trips. That
the only knowledge I have.

Q. The editor of the Commercial Bulletin generally picks up his in-
rmation from those best qualified to give it?—A. I don't know where
e picks it up. He did not come to me for any.

Q. You are not the sole depositary of information, I suppose?—A. I
uld have given him some information about it. I could have spoken
: my own experience. The David Lowe, the day before I came away,
rought in 150 barrels, which had been caught two miles off the coast,
ld one-third of them were 1's. That was one item, which does not ap-
ear there, that I would have given him if he had called upon me.

Q. Could you tell whether any fish was caught during the three days
receding 6th October?—A. I could not tell.

Q. Mr. Foster asked you a question about blackmailing American
shing vessels on the part of the officers of the navy. Do you know
lything about the vessels?—A. I never had any personal knowledge.

Q. You have no reason to know it, except from common report?—A.
o.

Q. Which may or may not be true?—A. Yes.

Q. Were any of your vessels ever blackmailed in that way?—A. Not
i my knowledge. It was the common report that Captain Derby took
) barrels of mackerel from one vessel.

Q. In 1866 you were not fishing?—A. No.

Q. Nor in 1867 or 1868?—A. Not since 1864.

Q. You took out licenses?—A. Yes.

Q. During two years you took out licenses, and the crew had to pay
alf the fees?—A. It was made a stock charge. I am not positive about
, but I believe so. I would direct it to be done so, if I was there.

Q. They would therefore judge whether it was best to take out license
r not?—A. Yes; I suppose so.

Q. In 1868 your five vessels took only 625 barrels, and that year you
id not take out a license?—A. Yes.

Q. May not that account for the very small catch?—A. If the cap-
ins of those vessels had deemed it of great importance they would

have taken out licenses if the fish had been somewhere whe
could not take them without a license.

Q. They could not go inside to try?—A. Others could, ar
would know it, for it would be reported to them. If they k₁
fish were within the 3-mile limit, it would only have taken the ve
day to have got a license, and on board of the cutters themselves
could be obtained.

Q. You have said you did not take out licenses in 1868 beca
price had gone up?—A. Yes. •

Q. That was the reason?—A. Yes.

Q. It had nothing to do with the fish taken?—A. You aske
that was not the reason why they did not get more mackerel.
could have got mackerel in large quantities in that prohibited
by taking out licenses, I know that, though I had given directi
to take licenses, they would have taken them.

Q. Did you give directions not to take licenses?—A. I did, I

Q. You gave the captains directions not to take out licenses
think the matter was talked of, and it was considered that it w₁
pay, as the expense was too large.

Q. You gave instructions not to take licenses?—A. I think
don't remember exactly.

Q. And the five vessels took 625 barrels?—A. Those are th₁
figures taken from the books.

Q. Can you tell me, from the comparative statement of the l
shore trips, which you have given in, what is the length of tin
pied on the bay and shore trips, respectively?—A. The shore tr
prises the season for that vessel, though the catch is taken on d
trips, occupying different lengths of time.

Q. You are instituting a comparison between trips made in ₁
and off the shore, and unless we know the times occupied by the
no comparisons can be made?—A. The vessels would averag
four months or so each. The shore vessels land several trips eac
the bay vessels only make two fares.

Q. The shore vessels fish from early spring till fall?—A. Pe
part of the fleet went out on 1st June. I don't know that we l
go south in May, but we may have had one or two early in Jun

Q. And from then till November?—A. Yes.

Q. They fish late there?—A. About the same time as in t
sometimes a week later, but it depends on the weather.

Q. You think the mackerel are about as late in the bay as
own coast?—A. If the weather permitted. There may be a
ten days' difference—ten days, I should say.

Q. That opinion is different from what we have heard from
the other witnesses?—A. I say perhaps ten days if there is fair
Usually, after October, it is very boisterous, and our vessels ₁
much chance of fishing, and come away. There are often ₁
there, but there is not much chance to catch them. I have oft
mackerel there later than many of the vessels stay, but I had n
to catch them.

Q. You cannot tell me the exact time the vessels were occ
catching the trips?—A. Not the exact time.

Q. Are the mackerel you catch on your shore classed No. 3's
the spring?—A. They are mostly always threes till the middle
Along about then they begin to get some fat on them, but not

Q. They don't go beyond No. 3's?—A. We get some 2's.

Q. Any proportion?—A. Not a large quantity.

). I see the prices you have got for bay mackerel are very much
ger than that which you got for shore mackerel. For instance, take
8, you got $16 a barrel for bay and $11.87 for shore mackerel ?—A.
e bay mackerel of that year, or the mackerel caught at the Magdalen
inds, were all very large and heavy, and the average was very much
her because there were no poor or small mackerel among them. In
shore catch of that year many of the mackerel were caught early,
ze quantities in June and July, which made the average lower.
). You don't know that, because you were not fishing in 1868 ?—A.
now that from the reports of my captains.
). The next year the discrepancy is still greater. In 1869 you got
bay $16 and for shore $8.75, only about one-half. Is that on account
our catching 3's on your own coast and large mackerel in the bay ?—
No; not always. When our vessels went into the bay they got
ny No. 1's, and along our shore they caught smaller mackerel.
). I don't mean to say that No. 1's are taken round Cape Breton or
nce Edward Island, but I mean round at the Magdalen Islands did
y happen to be No. 1's ?—A. You may take that year or a series of
rs, they are always better there.
). Take 1870. You got for your bay mackerel $13 and for shore
31 ?—A. It is very true.
). That must show that the mackerel caught on your shores are in-
or to those got in the bay ?—A. Not always.
). As a rule ?—A. As a rule, I don't know that they are.
). Is it not so, according to your experience ?—A. The experience of
vessels and the mackerel they land proves that, on an average, No.
1ore mackerel was higher than bay. When bay was $18 shore was

). For Block Island mackerel ?—A. No ; for mackerel caught off our
st.
). I am speaking of the prices you got yourself. I will take the last
years ?—A. Take this year.
). I have not a return of this year here. In 1875 you got $11.33 for bay
$9.81 for shore. In 1876, $10.20 for bay and $5.80 for shore, nearly
ble the price for bay. It is a very curious thing that if the bay
kerel are not better you should get double the price. What is the
sou ?—A. No. 1 mackerel caught here are no better than those caught
re. Our vessels went in the bay later in the year, and consequently
r mackerel averaged a higher price. They went in at the season
en the mackerel were best. The vessels on our shore fished in the
y part of the season and caught poor mackerel, which makes their
rage lower.
). I understand that you did not catch mackerel around Seven Isl-
s or the shores of the river St. Lawrence during your actual fishing
rations ?—A. I never caught any of any account.
). Have you been up there and tried to fish ?—A. I have been up
und Bonaventure Island and along that shore.
). Did you ever fish at Seven Islands ?—A. I was there once.
). Did you try to fish there ?—A. I suppose we did try.
). How close to the shore did you try ?—A. When I tried there I
't know that I caught any fish, or that I threw bait; I was there for
t purpose. We tried close to the shore.
). How close ; within half a mile or a mile ?—A. Within half a mile.
). And the fish taken there are taken that distance from shore ?—A.
ard reports that mackerel were there, but I found none there.

Q. Did you ever fish round Bonaventure ?—A. I never caught there.

Q. You never tried there much ?—A. No.

Q. And I believe you tried only once in Bay Chaleurs ?—A. I cau on one trip 50 barrels in Bay Chaleurs.

Q. Where was those taken ?—A. Somewhere off Paspebiac.

Q. Upon the south side of Bay Chaleurs ?—A. On the north side

Q. You went in within three miles of the shore ?—A. I don't kr I was out in the bay ; I don't know where.

Q. You said at first you were not within three miles of the shor A. I don't know what distance I was from land ; I was out in the r dle of the bay. I don't know whether we were within the three-l limit or not. I don't know whether the bay at that point was ten n wide ; it might be six. I don't know and I had no reason to whether I was within the three-mile limit or not. It was in 1856, I th during the Reciprocity Treaty.

Q. The chances are, then, that you went inside ?—A. I don't k about that. I went where the fish were.

Q. Did you make Bay Chaleurs a resort ?—A. I never was there m I was there sometimes for a harbor.

Q. And when you were in for a harbor, you did not try to fish there A. I did not try to fish there ; I have seen others try.

Q. Did you fish down the west shore of New Brunswick much ?- I have fished there.

Q. Within three miles of shore ?—A. No.

Q. I think around Prince Edward Island you never fished wit three miles of shore ?—A. Not much around the island.

Q. Round Cape Breton you fished every fall, more or less ?—A. Mo every fall, more or less ; late in the fall.

Q. And you caught mackerel off Margaree, sometimes one mile sometimes three or four miles off ?—A. Yes.

Q. And every fall you got more or less off Cape Breton shore ?- A small portion I caught there. I might have caught in all my pic' perhaps one-tenth of all my mackerel there. One year, I think, last year I was there, I caught from 75 to 100 barrels there.

Q. I think you said you could not recollect what proportion ?— cannot tell positively ; I should judge I caught that proportion. I l no record.

Q. You have no record and it is fourteen years since you were tl Have you heard from the captains of your vessels whether the h: of the fish of late years have changed, and that they are now fi nearer the shore than they used to be ?—A. I have not heard that.

Q. Have you not heard it at all in any way ?—A. I never heard the fish had changed their localities.

Q. Have you ever heard in any way of late years that the fish in Gulf of St. Lawrence are found closer to the shores than they use be ?—A. I have not. I have two vessels there and I hear from l every week. They have not found any near the shore, or anywhere

Q. Some years you say you caught your fish everywhere and yoi not make any large catch ?—A. One year we had a very hard se: We were fishing all over the bay.

Q. Did you ever see a large fleet down at Port Hood ?—A. Yes.

Q. How many American vessels have you seen there ?—A. I l counted them. I should think I have seen 200 sail ; perhaps 150.

Q. They would be there on the same mission as you ?—A. usually come there when bound home ; they stop there.

Q. For the fall fishing?—A. Yes, for the end of the trip. They don't fish round Port Hood. When they come there with an easterly gale, they sometimes go off on Fisherman's Bank, and sometimes across to the Magdalen Islands.

Q. I notice you fishermen always state that the fish are taken off Banks; are the waters on those Banks shallower than the general waters of the gulf?—A. It is all fishing-ground on Fisherman's Bank.

Q. I take it that at Fisherman's Bank the water is shallower than that surrounding it?—A. I suppose that Bank implies there is shallower water there than that surrounding it.

Q. I want to know from you as a practical man if that is so?—A. Yes; there is always shallower water on Banks.

Q. On Banks Bradley and Orphan; are we to understand the water is shallower there?—A. When you come to Bank Orphan you find different depths of water from 40 to 300 fathoms. It is deep water down in the gulf and we don't look for mackerel in deep water. We always look for fish off soundings.

By Mr. Foster:

Q. You said you did not know of any market for mackerel except the Gloucester market?—A. Not any more than what I ship west in small quantities.

Q. Gloucester has become a great distributing center?—A. Yes, it is considered so.

Q. All the mackerel that comes into Gloucester, almost all, comes in American vessels, does it not?—A. I don't know of any other.

Q. Do you have any mackerel imported into Gloucester that is imported from the provinces and not in American vessels?—A. I don't know of any.

Q. All the imported mackerel comes to Boston?—A. I think invariably.

Q. Do you know any mackerel by the name of Prince Edward Island mackerel?—A. Nothing more than that I have seen it in print and on the wharves at Boston.

Q. You have seen it branded in that way?—A. Yes.

Q. And have you seen other barrels branded Nova Scotia and Halifax?—A. I think I have; Halifax mackerel and herring.

Q. But whether the Prince Edward Island mackerel is mackerel that is sold before it is inspected in the United States or not, you don't know?—A. I have no practical knowledge of it.

Q. Can you tell what reinspection of mackerel means?—A. I will tell you the practical part of reinspection. Mr. Franklin Snow has 1,000 barrels of island mackerel branded No. 2's and 1's. He takes those mackerel in his warehouse and reassorts them. Of the No. 2's he makes one-half No. 1's, and out of the No. 1's he makes one-half extras, and those extras are sold at $18 and $19, and No. 1's at $16, the prices I quoted.

Q. Is the insurance of outfit a common practice at Gloucester?—A. It is.

Q. In regard to Liverpool salt—you stated that the actual cost to the importer, out of bond, would be 87½ cents a barrel?—A. To the buyer from the importer.

Q. And that is in a bonded warehouse, some distance from your wharf?—A. Some half mile or so.

Q. And for the handling of it, teaming it, getting it on board the vessel, and for coopering, you have allowed 12½ cents a barrel?—A. I have allowed an amount that would cover the expense. The teaming is 10 cents a barrel.

Q. That is leaving $2\frac{1}{2}$ cents a barrel for coopering and putting board of your schooner?—A. Yes.

Q. The profit on packing out a barrel of mackerel, including all penses—what would it amount to, in your judgment? How much wo a man get, clear of what he pays out?—A. I think from 10 cents to cents a barrel, outside of the inspection. The inspection fee he rece from the purchaser. and it is 10 cents a barrel more.

Q. Out of that inspection fee 8 cents go to the deputy inspector?-That comes out of the consumer, I guess.

Q. Of the fee the deputy inspector gets 8 cents and the inspector-g eral 2 cents, and he appoints almost any one who will give him requisite bonds and pay him the 2 cents a barrel. The deputy ins tor is responsible for the quality of the mackerel?—A. He is respo ble to the purchaser.

Q. And he is liable, and his bonds are liable, for any deficiency?- The general inspector is really the party who is responsible, and looks to his deputy. If the purchaser thinks the fish are not what t should be, he calls on the inspector-general, and he calls on his dep and compels him to make it good or looks to his bonds to do so.

By Sir Alexander Galt:

Q. How does the inspector-general know what barrels each de has inspected?—A. The deputy has his name in full on the brand.

By Mr. Foster:

Q. The inspection mark guarantees that the contents of the cas barrel shall be up to a certain legal standard?—A. A certain num of pounds have to be there, and the fitness of the mackerel is all in judgment of the men who select the mackerel, and if the purch objects to them, as being not what they should be, it has to be left jury of inspectors to decide whether they are of the standard fitted the brand.

Q. You estimate that 40 cents a day is the cost of provisioning man in a crew?—A. We base that on actual statistics.

Q. For what purpose were the statistics prepared?—A. For cen nial purposes, by the different firms. The firms took their books got out amounts, and we found that 40 cents a day would simply p

Q. You were asked if it was not a supposed voyage of which have given an account?—A. That was a supposed voyage.

Q. No vessel has come back from the gulf with 400 barrels of m erel this year?—A. No one has brought back any such quantity.

Q. That is a larger quantity that is supposed than has come from the gulf this year?—A. I heard that the Gertie E. Foster days before I came away, had arrived with 300 barrels. I don't k the quantity packed out.

Q. And in regard to the price at which the mackerel is suppose be sold?—A. The price of mackerel is the market price the day I l what the trips were sold for.

Q. On what day did you leave?—A. Friday, 5th.

Q. So, whether between the 3d and 6th mackerel were caught— could not be very positive?—A. I could not tell. I know the came away one vessel got a good haul.

By Mr. Davies:

Q. What are the names of your vessels in the bay?—A. Margie S is one.

Q. Is the Etta Gott the other?—A. Yes; she has made one tri year.

Q. How many barrels did she get?—A. 220 barrels.

Q. She is on her second trip now?—A. She is out on the second trip at Canso.

Q. What has she taken on the second trip?—A. I have heard she was out in a gale of wind, and they had not seen any fish since the gale. The other vessel has got 60 barrels.

Q. The A. J. Franklin, which was seized on 15th October, 1870, for fishing within three miles of the shore, and condemned, was one of your vessels?—A. She was not seized while I was a member of the firm.

No. 57.

GILMAN S. WILLIAMS, of Gloucester, Mass., police officer, and formerly fisherman and master mariner, called on behalf of the Government of the United States, sworn and examined.

By Mr. Dana:

Question. You belong to Gloucester and have lived there?—Answer. I have lived there 21 or 22 years.

Q. You went into the gulf, as a fisherman, in 1859, I believe?—A. I did.

Q. How many years in succession were you in the gulf as a fisherman?—A. I was ten years in succession in the gulf.

Q. From 1859 to 1869?—A. Yes.

Q. During that time, excepting about the last three years, you were under the Reciprocity Treaty?—A. Yes.

Q. And you had the right to go where you pleased?—A. Yes.

Q. Did you make a trial of the inshore fishery?—A. I have tried inshore.

Q. During those 6 or 7 years, when you had the whole gulf free to you, how did you find the inshore fishing as compared with the outside fishing; that is the fishing within 3 miles of the shore and the fishing outside, and on the Banks and elsewhere?—A. I caught but very few inshore.

Q. How many did you you catch altogether in 1859?—A. About 240 barrels; I cannot say positively as to the quantity in that case.

Q. Were any of those caught inside of three miles from shore?—A. There might have been a few, a very few.

Q. Of the 240 barrels, how many might have been caught inside?—A. Perhaps 15 barrels.

Q. Take the whole time, from 1859 to 1869, when you gave up the regular gulf fishing; what proportion of your fish was caught within the three-mile line?—A. I should say less than one-tenth.

Q. In 1866, I think, the Reciprocity Treaty expired. Did you then take out a license?—A. I did.

Q. Do you remember whether you took out a license in 1867?—A. I think not.

Q. That is your impression?—A. That is my impression. I am not certain either way.

Q. You were in the bay in 1868 and 1869. Had you licenses those two years?—A. No.

Q. 1869, the last year—you feel sure about it for that year?—A. I had none then.

Q. In 1870 where did you fish?—A. I was on the Banks, cod-fishing.

Q. In 1871 were you on the Banks?—A. Yes.

Q. 1872 were you cod-fishing again?—A. Yes.

Q. 1873—what did you do that year ?—A. I was mackereling pa
the time.

Q. Did you go cod-fishing in spring ?—A. Yes.

Q. Then you went into the bay for mackerel ?—A. Yes.

Q. Then you had the freedom of all the shores ?—A. Yes.

Q. Do you recollect what your catch in the bay was?—A. 350 bar
I think.

Q. In 1874 did you again go cod-fishing in spring and mackerelin
the latter part of summer and autumn ?—A. Yes.

Q. In 1875 did you go cod-fishing?—A. Yes.

Q. And mackereling?—A. Yes; late in the fall.

Q. How many mackerel did you take?—A. About 80 barrels, I tl

Q. 1875 was your last year?—A. Yes.

Q. Have you since been in the fishing business at all ?—A. No.

Q. Taking all those years together, was the business profitab
you ?—A. I have just made a living—nothing more.

Q. You caught fish enough to enable you to keep fishing ?—A.
I had to keep fishing summer and winter.

Q. Taking your experience, has the mackerel fishery in the gul
creased or decreased ?—A. According to my experience it has
creased.

Q. And from what you know of the business at Gloucester, has i
creased ?—A. Yes.

Q. Which has been most valuable, in your experience, cod or m
erel fishing? Cod-fishing in spring or mackerel fishing at the latter
of the summer and the autumn, which is the best part of the year
it ?—A. I have made much more cod-fishing than mackereling.

Q. And from what you know of what is going on generally in G
cester, what do you think the relative profit between mackereling ii
gulf and cod-fishing ?—A. The general report among the fisherme
Gloucester is that they do best cod-fishing.

Q. When you have been cod-fishing, have you fished with salt
or fresh bait or both ?—A. I have fished with both, mostly with
bait.

Q. From your experience of both kinds of bait, salt and fresh, I
pose there is no doubt that fresh bait will draw fish quicker than
bait ?—A. Yes.

Q. As a commercial enterprise, either as owner of a vessel or o
the crew, which would be the more profitable, to use salt altogethe
stay on the Banks, or to go into Newfoundland or elsewhere and
themselves supplied with fresh bait ?—A. If I was going again I v
take salt bait.

Q. Taking not only your own experience but what you have l
from other people, do you think it would be more profitable to tak
bait and keep on the Banks or to run in for fresh bait?—A. I have l
quite a number of masters say they would never go in for fresh b
all, but would take salt bait.

Q. What are the objections to going in for fresh bait?—A. '
are several objections. A great deal of time is occupied in getti
They charge a very high price for ice to save the bait with in
cases. There is a great deal of difficulty with the crew getting
and disorderly and not attending to their business.

Q. As to the licenses. You said you took a license one year fo
tain, perhaps more; but you are not confident about that, for you
not examined into it. For what reason did you take a license whe
did take it? You say that though you have been there a great

ars, you found little benefit from the inshore fishing, that it does not
iount to much. The first year you took out a license what was your
tive?—A. I took it out to protect myself from the risk of my not
owing where the three-mile line was.

Q. Why could you not know?—A. Well, if a cutter overhauled me
e commander would decide instead of me. He would not allow me to
ve any voice about it.

Q. Was there any question as to how the lines were to be run?—A.
was a matter I did not understand. It was a matter of dispute. Some
d the line ran from headland to headland, and others said it did not.
lid not know how the cutters might decide on that.

Q. You had heard that different claims were made?—A. I had heard
it different claims were made, and that there were disputes.

Q. Except because of the disputes that might arise as to your being
ee or five miles or more out, or as to the manner in which the line
s to be run; as to the mere value of the fish to be caught, would you
ve given anything for the license?—A. But very little, if anything.

Q. How much would you have given?—A. A very small sum.

Q. Not as much as was charged?—A. No.

Q. Which would be most profitable to you as a fisherman or dealer in
1, to have the duty of $2 a barrel on again and be excluded from the
ee-mile limit, or to be admitted to within the three miles and have
duty off?—A. If I was going fishing again I would prefer having a
ty on and be excluded from the three miles.

Q. Suppose this three-mile line could have been marked to run, not
m headland to headland, but to follow the indentations of the coast,
some mark as intelligible as a fence on shore is between one man's
m and another, so that no question would be involved, would you
n give anything for the right to fish inside of that fence?—A. No.

Q. Do you know anything about the herring fishery off the coast of
United States?—A. I have often heard it spoken of, and I have seen
ring brought into Gloucester many times.

Q. Does Gloucester export herring?—A. It does.

Q. To what places?—A. Gottenburg is one place. I have seen ves-
s employed catching herring off the coast of Massachusetts.

Q. When did you last see them?—A. The last time I saw them was
Saturday last.

Q. You left Boston on Saturday in the steamer?—A. Yes.

Q. Where did you see the herring-vessels fishing?—A. Very near
ston light-house, in among some little islands called Brewsters.

Q. Perhaps the Graves?—A. Yes.

Q. Did you take the trouble to count the vessels?—A. I did.

Q. How many were there?—A. I counted 51; there may have been
o or three more perhaps; 51 were within range.

Q. You are sure there were 51?—A. I am.

Q. Has it been the custom for some years past for Gloucester and
ier places to send small vessels to fish for herring off Boston and
the bay there?—A. It has been for several years.

Q. Do you know whether it is a profitable business?—A. I have fre-
ently seen them after they have been gone two or three days, come
ck with their boats or vessels full.

Q. Do they always return to Gloucester, or do they sometimes run
o Boston?—A. They often go into Boston; they go into both places.

Q. They land the herring fresh?—A. Yes; and sell them fresh some-
es.

By Mr. Thomson:

Q. You commenced fishing in 1859 ?—A. Yes, as master of a ve

Q. Had you ever been in the gulf before that ?—A. Yes.

Q. How many years previous ?—A. One year.

Q. What year ?—A. Eighteen hundred and fifty-eight.

Q. How did you go there, as one of the crew ?—A. Yes.

Q. Had you any interest in the voyage except as one of the crew
A. No interest, other than in what I caught.

Q. Where did you fish then ?—A. At Magdalen Islands and E
Orphan.

Q. Did you fish anywhere else ?—A. Those were about all the pl;
where we caught the mackerel; we may have tried some other pl;
possibly.

Q. How many did you get that time ?—A. I think 258 barrels.

Q. Had you a license that year ?—A. I think not.

Q. Then you had a right to all the inshore fishing ?—A. Yes.

Q. Where did you try first, at the Magdalen Islands or Bank
phan ?—A. At Bank Orphan.

Q. You went through the Gut of Canso, I suppose ?—A. Yes.

Q. Did you run straight to Orphan Bank ?—A. From where ?

Q. Through from the Gulf of Canso ?—A. No.

Q. Where did you go to fish first ?—A. It would be a difficult tl
to run straight with a vessel.

Q. Did you go direct from Canso ?—A. We went directly there
fast as we could from the Strait of Canso to Bank Orphan.

Q. You went direct without fishing anywhere till you got to Orp
Bank ?—A. Yes.

Q. Where does it lie ?—A. To the southward of Bonaventure Isl;

Q. You passed Prince Edward Island ?—A. Yes.

Q. And went away to the northward and westward ?—A. To the nc
ward.

Q. Somewhat to the westward ?—A. No.

Q. Is it direct to the north ?—A. I cannot say to a point; it is so
near as I can recollect.

Q. I suppose you never heard of good fishing at Prince Edv
Island ?—A. I may have heard of it.

Q. And yet your captain never staid to try any place at the islan
A. We went to Bank Orphan.

Q. You passed by East Cape and North Cape ?—A. I don't know
we saw North Cape.

Q. You saw East Cape ?—A. I am not certain about it. I don't r
lect that we saw it.

Q. Did you pass within sight of the island at all ?—A. Yes; if it
been daylight we would have been in sight of it.

Q. Were you near enough to see the island ?—A. I don't recollect
I saw it.

Q. You went direct to Orphan Bank ?—A. Yes.

Q. How many mackerel did you catch on Orphan Bank ?—A. I
not tell you positively, but I think one-half of the trip we took the

Q. You got 240 barrels altogether ?—A. Yes, about that, as nigh
can recollect; I would not be positive of the exact amount.

Q. Why did you fix the amount at 240 barrels if you have no m
randum ?—A. It is as nigh as I can recollect.

Q. That is about 20 years ago. Have you no memorandum of
A. I think the vessel carried about 240 barrels, and she was full.

Q. Then you had a full cargo before you came home ?—A. Yes.

. At what time did you go into the bay ?—A. I think in July.

. And came out when ?—A. At the latter part of October, I think.

. Immediately after you got through fishing on Bank Orphan, did go direct to the Magdalen Islands ?—A. Yes.

. Did you take the fish inshore or off shore there, within three miles ie shore or off ?—A. I think both; partly off, more than three miles, partly inside.

. Was the larger proportion taken inshore or off shore ?—A. I can-answer that.

. What was the farthest distance from the Magdalen Islands you ·d ?—A. Perhaps twelve or fourteen miles some of the time.

. How far off was the nearest ?—A. We may have fished some within a mile, perhaps; I cannot recollect exactly.

. Cannot you recollect that, when you can recollect the number of els you had ?—A. No.

Well, then, you got your full fare without having any occasion to ,he inside waters at Prince Edward Island or the coast of Gaspé n Bay Chaleurs?—A. We fished our full fare at the Magdalen ids.

. You did not try within three miles along Prince Edward Island at —A. I think not.

. Neither did you try within three miles of the New Brunswick shore ong the Canada shore off Gaspé ?—A. No.

Did you try within three miles of Cape Breton shore ?—A. Per· ı we did ; I think we did.

Surely you can recollect ?—A. It is some time ago, and it is diffi-for me to remember every place at which we might have hove to ıty years ago.

Will you say you did or did not fish on the shore of Cape Breton ?— Ve caught but very few mackerel anywhere within three miles.

Did you fish within three miles of the shore at Cape Breton ?—A.

Did you fish anywhere within three miles of the shore, except at Magdalen Islands ?—A. No.

Why did you say you might have caught a very few inshore. I ıpeaking of 1858 altogether. What did you mean by saying you ht a small quantity inshore ?—A. I said we might have caught a few.

How is that possible if you did not fish within three miles ?—A. I say we caught nearly or quite all of our mackerel on Orphan Bank at Magdalen Islands.

You say you might have caught a small quantity inshore ?—A. I we might have caught a few near the shore of Cape Breton.

Within three miles ?—A. We might have caught a few within ꝫ miles of the shore of Cape Breton.

Did you fish within three miles of the shore at Cape Breton, wheth-ıu caught any or not ?—A. I am not able to say but what I caught ɔr two mackerel within three miles of Cape Breton shore.

I ask you, did you in fact fish within three miles of Cape Breton ꝫ ?—A. I say we might have hove to near Cape Breton Island and ht a very few mackerel.

Are you in doubt in your mind as to whether you fished within three ꝫ of Cape Breton shore ?—A. It is not possible for a man to recol· ,wenty years ago, whether he might have caught a very few mackerel hether he did not catch any——

162 F

Q. Have you in your own mind any doubt as to whether $\jmath$ within three miles of Cape Breton shore?—A. I don't recollect

Q. Have you any doubt? I don't ask you whether you reco I have forgotten whether we caught one mackerel within thre Cape Breton shore that year or not.

Q. You are serious, that you don't know whether you did or —A. Yes. I don't know whether we might have caught a few not, within three miles of Cape Breton shore.

No. 57.

THURSDAY, October 1

The Conference met.

Cross-examination of Gilman S. Williams, of Gloucester, Ma on behalf of the Government of the United States, resumed.

By Mr. Thomson

Question. When we adjourned yesterday we were speakii mackerel caught inside of three miles of the shore at Cape I suppose that was off Margaree, was it?—Answer. As I unde it referred to Margaree or thereabouts.

Q. That was in 1858. In 1859 you went into the bay and go rels—where did you fish then?—A. At Bank Orphan and Ba ley and Pigeon Hill grounds, the first trip.

Q. Did you make two trips in 1859?—A. Yes.

Q. Did you get 240 barrels each trip?—A. No.

Q. The aggregate of the two trips was 240 barrels?—A. In 1

Q. Was it your own vessel?—A. I was master of the vessel owner.

Q. Where did you get that memorandum?—A. Out of the the firm which owned the vessels.

Q. You don't recollect yourself?—A. Not so well; not so a as to give the figures.

Q. If you had not gone to the books, could you have recolle as far back as 1859, 18 years ago?—A. Yes, but not so accura

Q. You could not recollect the number of barrels taken?— nearly correct.

Q. Could you have recollected where you fished?—A. Yes.

Q. You went through the Gut of Canso?—A. Yes.

Q. Did you then go straight to Orphan Bank?—A. We v Magdalen Islands first.

Q. Without fishing anywhere?—A. Without fishing anyw

Q. Did you take a large proportion at Magdalen Islands did not get any the first trip at the Magdalen Islands.

Q. About what time did you enter the gulf?—A. Early could not tell the exact date.

Q. Then you went where?—A. As soon as we came throu we went direct to the Magdalen Islands, where we stayed a time, and went on Bank Bradley.

Q. Did you get many there?—A. Yes; nearly the whole.

Q. Where did you get the remainder?—A. On what I c Hill ground.

Q. That is off Gaspé?—A. No.

Q. In Bay Chaleurs?—A. It is farther to the southward th

Q. That would be Bay Chaleurs?—A. No.

Q. That is about southward?—A. No.

)id you take many at Pigeon Hill grounds ?—A. I think about
·els, to the best of my recollection.
)id that fill the schooner ?—A. Very nearly. We then worked
to the eastward on to Bank Bradley again, and there made up
yage.
'ou had then got a full fare ?—A. Yes.
Vhen fishing at what you call Pigeon Hill grounds, how near were
the shore ?—A. We were just in sight of Pigeon Hill on a clear
f it was a thick day we could not see it.
[ow far from the shore ?—A. I should suppose twelve miles, to
it of my knowledge.
'hen upon that voyage you never were within three miles of the
it all ?—A. Not whilst fishing.
'ou then went direct back to the States ?—A. Yes ; to Gloucester.
'ou did not fish any at that time on the shores of Cape Breton or
ree ?—A. Not any that voyage.
[ow many barrels did your schooner carry with a full cargo ?—A.
240 barrels is what we could carry conveniently.
'he next trip was made at what time ?—A. We got back to Mag-
[slands at the last of September.
[ow many did you get on that trip ?—A. 85 barrels.
ιre those all you got ?—A. Yes.
'hose quantities make 325 barrels for the season—not 240 ?   On
it trip your schooner, which could carry about 240 barrels, got a
e ?—A. I meant to tell you that in both trips we got 240 barrels.
)id you not tell me that you got a full cargo on your first trip ?—
)bably I did ; if I did, I made a mistake.
'hen, on your first trip you did not get a full fare ?—A. No.
[ay I ask you why, not having got a full fare on either Bank
y or Pigeon Hill ground, you did not try Bank Orphan ?—A. We
as long as we were able to try, on account of the lateness of the

am speaking of the first trip ?—A. I mean the first trip. We
as long as we had any provisions, it being late in the season.
Vhat do you call late in the season ?—A. We had only got time
,ome and get back again. As I have said, it was late in Septem-
:ore we returned for the second trip.
on got short of provisions ?—A. Yes.
,nd without waiting to get a full cargo, being short of provisions,
)ceeded home ?—A. Yes.
'ou did not think proper to try round the shores of Prince Ed-
sland ?—A. We had not time for one reason.
'ou had not time to try off Cape Breton ?—A. No, not on the first

[ow many barrels did you take on the first trip ?—A. About 130
, to the best of my recollection.
hat was not by 110 barrels sufficient to make a full cargo ?—A.

till you did not try within three miles anywhere, and that was at
when you were not prohibited from coming within three miles of
—A. No ; we could go anywhere.
Vas it not singular that you did not try within the three miles ?—
ιd not been accustomed to fish within three miles of the land at
ne.
'ake the next year, 1860. Did you go into the bay that year ?—

Q. Where did you fish then ?—A. I fished that year, the first t
Bank Orphan and Bank Bradley, and nearly the same ground
year previous.

Q. Except that the previous year you did not fish on Bank Orp
all ? You went straight from Canso to Magdalen Islands, and fai
find anything there, went to Bank Bradley, and from there to]
Hill ground, and came back to Bank Bradley, and went hom(
Those Banks are so nearly connected that we some days hardly
which we are on.

Q. Bank Orphan is a considerable distance to the north of
Bradley?—A. They are nearly connected in soundings and fishin

Q. Don't you know perfectly well when you are fishing on Bank
ley and Bank Orphan ?—A. Yes, if the weather is clear, so that (
see anything. We generally go here and there on various places be
those Banks, wherever we think we can get fish.

Q. You don't know whether in 1859 you fished on Bank Orpl
not?—A. I think we did.

Q. In 1860 you fished on Banks Orphan and Bradley ?—A. And
Hill ground.

Q. Did you go to the Magdalen Islands ?—A. Not the first triץ

Q. How many barrels did you get on the second trip ?—A. Th
in 1860. We got 225 barrels the first trip.

Q. What would have been a full fare ?—A. About 250 barrels.

Q. And you took 240 ?—A. Two hundred and twenty-five.

Q. During that time you did not fish anywhere along the c(
Prince Edward Island ?—A. No.

Q. Did you go into the Bay Chaleurs?—A. No.

Q. Or to Gaspé ?—A. No.

Q. You did not go within three miles of the shore anywhere
Not at Prince Edward Island or New Brunswick.

Q. Did you at Margaree ?—A. I think we did. I know we did

Q. How long where you fishing there ?—A. We stopped there |
home, and fished half a day or thereabouts.

Q. How many barrels did you get ?—A. I think we got three
barrels.

Q. Why did you not continue and fill up your vessel there ?—
account of scarcity of mackerel.

Q. There you were inshore, of course ?—A. Yes.

Q. You went home, and what time did you get back to the ba
I cannot tell you; but probably early in September—1st Septen

Q. Where did you fish then ?—A. At Magdalen Islands, mos
trip.

Q. Did you get your full fare there ?—A. Not quite.

Q. Where did you next go ?—A. After leaving Magdalen Isla

Q. Are you looking at any memorandum which shows you wl
went?—A. No; only the number of barrels.

Q. You went to Magdalen Islands and did not get a full fa।
many did you get?—A. I cannot tell you; about 100 barrels,
I am not certain.

Q. Was it the same vessel as you were in the first season ?—

Q. Where did you next go ?—A. To Port Hood.

Q. There you fished inshore ?—A. Yes.

Q. Did you get many there ?—A. A few; we fished across or
man's Bank, to the westward of Port Hood, between Cape Ge(
Georgetown.

Why did you run back to Port Hood instead of running across to
s Bradley and Orphan?—A. It was bad weather—windy weather.
Was that the reason you went away to Magdalen Islands?—A.

Do you think the Magdalen Islands a safe place?—A. It is in the
ner season, not when it gets windy.
What time does it become unsafe?—A. After 1st October it gets
very windy, and there are very few days when you can fish.
Do you call Magdalen Islands as dangerous as any place in the
—A. It is not so dangerous as to the loss of the vessel, but it blows
rd in October that it is difficult to fish there.
Why is it not dangerous if it blows so hard?—A. You can always
a lee under the islands.
Then there is no danger of the loss of life or vessel at Magdalen
ds?—A. I did not say there is no danger.
Comparatively small danger?—A. We can always sail to the lee-
of the islands, so that the wind will blow off the land.
Why did you not go to the leeward of the islands and fish?—A.
ws so hard we cannot fish very often.
Would not the water to the leeward be comparatively calm?—A.
uld blow so hard it would be impossible to fish; it often blows so
it is impossible to fish.
Yet you call that a safe place for a vessel?—A. Safe in regard to
nd property.
Do I understand that Magdalen Islands are safer or as safe as
ther place in the gulf in September and October?—A. As safe, I
:, in September.
And in October?—A. It is not as safe for property as some other
s.
Would you prefer, as a matter of safety, to be fishing off Prince
rd Island in October than off Magdalen Islands?—A. That would
id on what part of Prince Edward Island I was at.
Take the north part?—A. I should prefer Magdalen Islands.
Take East Point?—A. East Point is a long way from any harbor
y place to make a lee.
Souris Harbor is close by?—A. Souris Harbor is not a safe har-

Is there no safe harbor, as far as you are aware, on the north side
island?—A. Malpeque is a safe harbor if you can go in in the
ime and before the wind has been long blowing on shore.
How about Cascumpeque and Rustico?—A. Cascumpeque is not a
arbor.
Nor is Rustico, I suppose?—A. I never was in Rustico; I know
Gloucester vessels that go in there.
Have you been at Cascumpeque since the Dominion Government
pended money on the harbor?—A. I don't know that I have; it
or seven years since I was there, to the best of my knowledge.
You don't know that at Souris there is a large breakwater, which
60,000 or $70,000?—A. I have heard so; I have not been there
it was built.
On this trip in 1860 you did not fish inshore at all when you made
ip to Port Hood?—A. Only at Port Hood and near there; we
not have been exactly at Port Hood, but very near it.
How many did you get?—A. A few barrels at Port Hood.
Your whole cargo that time was how many?—A. Two hundred
wenty-five barrels.

Q. That year, then, you got over 450 barrels the two trips?—.
are speaking of the last trip, are you?

Q. If I understood you, the first trip you got 225 barrels?—/
is what I referred to now, when I spoke of 225 barrels; the last
got 160 barrels.

Q. On the last trip, did you fish anywhere on the shore of Prit
ward Island?—A. Yes; I hove to several times.

Q. Within three miles of the shore?—A. Yes.

Q. Where?—A. Between Souris and East Point.

Q. You did not get anything?—A. I should think one barrrel
to the best of my recollection.

Q. Nothing more than that?—A. Certainly not over five.

Q. What was that owing to—to your not staying there?—A.
to there not being any mackerel there.

Q. Then you went to Port Hood?—A. We had been to Por
before fishing there. We go from bay to bay.

Q. You did not fish on the north side of Prince Edward Islan
Not that fall.

Q. In 1861, were you in the bay?—A. Yes.

Q. How many trips did you make that year?—A. Two.

Q. Where did you go?—A. To nearly the same ground as the
ous year.

Q. And neither in 1861 nor 1862 did you go inshore at all?—.
are coming to 1862 now?

Q. Yes.—A. We went first to Banks Orphan and Bradley
Pigeon Hill ground, and got a fare of mackerel there.

Q. You did not fish inshore at all?—A. No.

. You did not even try?—A. No.

. You did not go to Magdalen Islands?—A. Not that trip.

. In the fall?—A. We went to the Magdalen Islands in the

Q. Were you successful there?—A. We got nearly our who
there.

. Q. How many barrels did you take?—A. 200.

Q. How many did you take on the first trip?—A. 230.

Q. All those were paying trips?—A. I never made much my
of mackerel.

Q. I mean paying to the owners of the vessels?—A. I shou
not.

Q. You think that each season would be a loss?—A. I owne
the vessel myself and lost money.

Q. In each of those seasons, did you?—A. In 1861 and 1862.

Q. Who furnished the supplies; were you one of the merc
furnish supplies?—A. No.

Q. Did your co-owners furnish the supplies?—A. Yes.

Q. Did they lose money?—A. I am not able to say.

Q. You did not ask them whether they made money?—A. I
over with them during the fall, when there came to be a settle
lost money myself.

Q. In 1860, 1861, and 1862, the prices of mackerel were ver
A. I think they were.

Q. What did you get a barrel for your fish?—A. I cannot
now.

Q. Are you not able to recollect what you got for your fish a
the number of barrels taken?—A. I cannot tell you, there are
years, and very different prices.

Q. Have you no idea how you happened to lose money? I

you would have lost money if you had had full fares, instead of full fares within 50 barrels?—A. There is other fishing connected with it. Some years there is a loss with other fishing connected with it—cod-fishing.

Q. A loss with cod-fishing as well?—A. Some years, at some times.

Q. As a practical fisherman, do you state that the inshore fishing at Prince Edward Island, Cape Breton, along the shore of New Brunswick and Quebec, are of no use to United States people?—A. Do you speak of Prince Edward Island in particular?

Q. I will take all the inshore waters of Cape Breton, Prince Edward Island, New Brunswick, and Gaspé, and along the south shore of Labrador. Do you say that those inshore fisheries are practically no use to United States fishermen?—A. I would not say they are no use to American fishermen.

Q. Do they make money by having access to them, or do they lose money—for if they lose money by them the fisheries are practically of no use?—A. From my own experience, they have never been much benefit to me.

Q. Have they been any benefit to you?—A. I have caught a few mackerel there occasionally. I might have caught as many somewhere else, perhaps, if I had been at another fishing-ground.

Q. I want your judgment as to whether those inshore fisheries are practically of any use whatever?—A. I should say they are very little benefit to me, if I was going fishing again.

Q. That is not the question. You are a practical man, and you seem a fair man, and I want your opinion as to whether you think that the privilege of fishing inshore, within 3 miles, is of any use to United States fishermen.—A. I think they were not any great use. That is as fair as I can answer your question.

Q. You admit they are of some use and benefit?—A. Yes. I have caught some fish there—a few.

Q. All the fish you admit having caught within the 3 miles amount to nothing. Half the time you did not try to fish inshore?—A. As a general thing I did not try to fish there. Some years I have tried to fish there.

Q. Tell me what practical use it is to the United States. Is it of any use at all?—A. Some other vessels may have fished there more than I did.

Q. Have you heard of any vessels being more fortunate than you in fishing within 3 miles of the shore?—A. I think I have heard of vessels which have taken more fish inshore than I have.

Q. Have you heard of American vessels taking large fares within 3 miles of the shore, not including Magdalen Islands?—A. I think I have heard of vessels getting considerable mackerel on the Cape Breton shore.

Q. You have not heard of them getting considerable mackerel along the coast of Prince Edward Island?—A. Not large fares inside of the 3-mile line.

Q. Then, practically, in your judgment, it is not worth while for the United States to make a fight about getting in there to fish? All the trouble is really sentimental. United States fishermen get on just as well with the right to fish in the gulf, keeping away from 3 miles of the coast?—A. I don't think it is worth while to make a great fight about it.

Q. You think it would not?—A. It would not.

Q. Are you aware whether these are the views of fishermen at Gloucester and Boston, that really the privilege of fishing inshore in

British waters does not amount to much ?—A. To the best of my kno
edge the Gloucester folks dou't consider the inshore fishing in the :
very valuable.

Q. Do they consider it of any value at all ?—A. I should think t
would consider it of little value.

Q. Would the Gloucester people who are engaged in cod-fishin;
able to employ their vessels all the year round except for the macke
fishing ?—A. Yes.

Q. And they would make more money by cod-fishing without m:
ereling ?—A. I did better myself cod-fishing than mackereling.

Q. About the general trade. Do you believe the Gloucester pec
could give their continuous attention to cod-fishing without macke
fishing ?—A. Without that of Bay St. Lawrence—I do.

Q. And without fishing for mackerel in Bay St. Lawrence they[wc
get along just as well ?—A. I think so.

Q. And make more money ?—A. I made more cod-fishing myself.

Q. What you have done, other people could do, I suppose. You
not account, under the circumstances, for the desire of American f
ermen to get the privilege of fishing within three miles of the shor
the gulf, can you ?—A. No; I don't know whether they do wish to
within the three miles or not.

Q. Do you mean to tell me they do not; if you mean it, say so ?-
I am not prepared to tell you they do not.

Q. Suppose they do, you cannot account for it ?—A. I can only
count for it, to the best of my judgment, by their not doing much wi'
three miles, as far as I know.

Q. Can you account for their wishing to get the privilege of go
within the three miles ; you would not wish to go within the three n
yourself ?—A. I would not give much for it myself.

Q. Can you account for anybody having that desire ?—A. I am
prepared to say in regard to other people.

By Mr. Whiteway :

Q. Are you now interested in any fishing-vessels ?—A. No; I
not.

Q. You have a thorough knowledge of the number of the ve
fitted out in Gloucester for the fisheries ?—A. I could not tell you
exact number.

Q. Could you give me an approximate number ?—A. To the be
my knowledge, about 500.

Q. Can you tell me how many are engaged in the cod-fishing busi
alone ?—A. No; I cannot.

Q. Can you give me the approximate number ?—A. To the best o
knowledge, I should say 200. I may not be correct.

Q. How many may be engaged in cod-fishing at one season and m
ereling at another ?—A. A great part of those which go mackerelin
cod-fishing early in the year.

Q. Then the greater number of the 500 vessels would go cod fis
and about 300 would go mackereling at one season of the year ?—
think so.

Q. You fitted out for cod-fishing, about what time ?—A. Many ve
fit out on 1st February, the greater part of them then.

Q. And they continue cod-fishing till when ?—A. About 1st Jul;

Q. Then they go mackerel-fishing in the gulf, till about what tim
A. We leave the gulf about 1st November.

Q. Are those vessels employed in any manner between the time ve off mackereling and commence cod-fishing ?—A. Many of them go ring voyages.

). Are the crews of those vessels engaged for the whole year, or are y engaged for the several distinct trips, cod, mackerel, and herring ages ?—A. Most of the crews leave Gloucester and go to their homes lifferent parts of the country.

). At what time ?—A. During the month of November.

). Those same crews are engaged in cod-fishing and mackereling, but on herring voyages ?—A. Not always. There are generally men ugh living in Gloucester to man the vessels that go on herring voy-s.

). You hire a distinct crew, as a general rule, for the herring voy-s ?—A. No; not exactly.

). Are the crew hired for the cod fishing and mackerel voyages to-her, and then when they return from the mackerel voyage is the w hired for the herring voyage ?—A. They will not be hired for the ring voyage till the vessel is ready to go. Vessels may lay up weeks, haps months, after leaving off mackereling, before going for herring.

). Is the same crew employed on the cod-fishing and mackerel voy-s ?—A. Not necessarily so.

). But generally is it not the same crew ?—A. Pretty generally so. :y may not have been in the same vessel, but in some other vessel.

). You have said you were fishing on the Banks between the years 0 and 1875, inclusive. Upon what Banks were you fishing ?—A. Sa-Island Bank or Western Bank, meaning all one; Banquero; also he Grand Bank at different times.

). How many years were you fishing on the Grand Banks ?—A. I e been parts of six years on the Grand Banks.

). That is between 1870 and 1875 ?—A. I was part of the time also)re 1870.

). Then you were engaged in Bank fishing prior to 1870 ?—A. Yes.

). As master ?—A. Yes.

). I understood you to say to Mr. Dana that from 1859 to 1869 you e engaged in mackerel-fishing in the gulf ?—A. Parts of the years.

). How many of those years, between 1859 and 1869, were you on the iks ?—A. Every year but one, I think.

). Then, in point of fact, between 1859 and 1875 you were every year he Banks fishing for cod, except one ?—A. I think so.

). You fit out for the Bank fishery about the beginning of February ?—Yes.

). Can you tell me the quantity of provisions you would put on board r vessel for a voyage of four months, with a crew say of sixteen men ?—Nine barrels of flour, not less; two barrels of pork, 25 pounds of tea, six rels of beef, ten bushels of potatoes, one barrel molasses, one barrel ar, one barrel beans, half barrel coffee, quarter barrel rice; also some ll articles which I have not mentioned.

. Do you supply the men with tobacco ?—A. No, they get that be-they leave port.

). They get it on their own account ?—A. Yes.

. Can you give me the prices at which those articles were charged, for 1875, the last year you were out ?—A. Flour, about $8.50 per rel; pork, $17 or $18 per barrel; tea, about 40 cents per pound; mo-es, 50 cents a gallon; rice, 15 cents to 16 cents per pound; potatoes, ents a bushel; beans, $3 a bushel; beef, about $16 a barrel; sugar, ents per pound.

. Are not those charges far in excess of the ordinary cash prices of

those articles ?—A. I don't think they are. I am not positive. I
not have been correct in the prices of those articles, but they are as
as I can tell.

Q. As an ordinary rule, are not the prices charged far in excess of
ordinary cash prices ?—A. I cannot say that they are.

Q. Can you say that they are not ?—A. They are not to my knowle

Q. There was a witness here the other day who said that 20 or 25
cent. was charged in addition to the ordinary cash price. Are you
pared to say that those prices you have mentioned were not muc
excess of the ordinary cash prices charged for those articles ?—A. I d
think they were; to the best of my knowledge they were not.

Q. How many gallons of molasses are there in a barrel ?—A. 5
believe, the way we fill a barrel.

Q. You have given the results of your mackereling voyages, o
least some of them; can you give me the results of your cod-fishing
ages, as regards the quantities taken, from 1870 to 1875 ?—A. It w
be rather difficult for me to do it correctly.

Q. You cannot do so ?—A. Not very accurately.

Q. But, upon the whole, the cod-fishing voyages were paying
ages ?—A. Yes, with me; I made more than I did mackereling.

Q. And does that same reply apply to all previous cod-fishing
ages from 1859 to 1869 ?—A. Yes, with me. I may have made some
voyages; I have made some poor voyages.

Q. But, upon the whole, the cod-fishing has been successful ?—A.
it has with me.

Q. Has not the cod-fishing fleet increased materially within the
two, three, or four years ?—A. Yes.

Q. Very materially ?—A. I believe it has.

Q. When did you begin to use fresh bait ?—A. From my first g
in 1859, we used fresh bait—going on Georges Bank from Gloucest
frozen herring.

Q. Did you continue to use fresh bait ?—A. Every year when I
to Georges Bank.

Q. And how long did you continue to go to Georges Bank ?—
have been there parts of nine winters, making one voyage each ye

Q. Where were you the remaining part of the year ?—A. I
down to the Western Bank, and the latter part of the season went t
Grand Bank.

Q. Then you made three voyages ?—A. The voyage to Georges
very short one, perhaps two weeks.

Q. Then you made three cod-fishing voyages nearly every year,
1859 to 1869 ?—A. Yes; and sometimes more than one voya
Georges.

Q. You stated, I think, that you had generally used fresh bait
I always used it when going to Georges.

Q. You said you had fished with both salt and fresh bait, but n
with fresh bait. As a general rule, you used fresh bait ?—A. Yes
general thing.

Q. Did you always fish with trawls ?—A. Not always, but p
for the last eight or nine years I did.

Q. Prior to that you used hand-lines ?—A. Yes.

Q. Do you find fresh bait as good for hand-line fishing as for
fishing; it is about the same, I suppose ?—A. It is better for har
fishing than for trawl-fishing, perhaps.

Q. Have you ever been to parts of the Dominion or Newfoun
for fresh bait whilst fishing on the Banks ?—A. Yes.

Q. Where have you been?—A. I have been to Prospect, which is not far from Halifax; to Whitehead, near the Strait of Canso; to the Strait of Canso; to Fortune Bay, Newfoundland; and St. Peter's on the coast of Newfoundland; and to quite a number of harbors on the coast of Newfoundland, not far from Fortune Bay.

Q. In what year did you commence to go into those places for fresh bait; what was the first year?—A. I was at Prospect 10 or 11 years ago. I think that was the first time I came into the Dominion for fresh bait.

Q. Have you continued to get fresh bait in different parts of the Dominion and Newfoundland from 10 or 12 years ago till 1875?—A. Not every year.

Q. But generally?—A. More than one-half of the time. Some years I have been unable to obtain it; after looking a month for it, I have not got it.

Q. You have come in for it every year?—A. I have come in nearly every year I have been to the Eastern Banks.

Q. For the last nine or ten years?—A. Yes; with one or two exceptions, perhaps.

Q. When was the first time you went into the coast of Newfoundland for fresh bait?—A. I think the first time I went to Newfoundland for bait was eight years ago.

Q. To what part did you go?—A. Into Fortune Bay.

Q. You went from Gloucester to Fortune Bay, and from thence to the Banks, I suppose?—A. We took bait at Gloucester, and used it on the Western Bank, and St. Peter's Bank, and then went to Fortune Bay, and got bait, and went from there to the Grand Bank.

Q. How long did it take you to go from St. Peter's Bank to Fortune Bay, and thence to the Grand Banks?—A. I have usually been one week, and sometimes two weeks, from the time of leaving St. Peter's, until we got bait, and reached the Grand Bank.

Q. Have you ever been in any harbor of Newfoundland between Cape Race and Conception Bay for bait?—A. No.

Q. Did you ever use caplin for bait?—A. I tried it, and gave it up.

Q. You have said you had some conversation with captains of vessels in reference to the use of fresh bait?—A. Yes.

Q. When had you those conversations?—A. At various times for the last eight or ten years.

Q. And they have at all these times expressed their strong disapprobation of going into ports for fresh bait?—A. They have very strong objections in regard to trouble with their crews, the time spent in obtaining bait, and sometimes the price of ice in which to preserve the bait.

Q. During eight or ten years these views have been expressed by you?—A. I have heard it spoken of in that way.

Q. Every year?—A. Perhaps not every year, but frequently.

Q. Generally?—A. Yes.

Q. Can you name any of the captains with whom you had the conversations?—A. I think I can name one or two.

Q. Name them—A. The last one who talked with me about it was William Williams, of Gloucester.

Q. Can you name any others?—A. I don't think I can without thinking some time.

Q. During the last three or four years, I believe, the great majority of the Bank fishing-vessels have come in for fresh bait, either into the

harbors of one of the provinces or into those of Newfoundland ?—
think they have done so.

Q. In fact, it is the general practice at this time for all cod-fi
vessels on the Banks to go in for fresh bait? I am not saying wh
it is advantageous or disadvantageous.—A. Many of them do.

Q. The great majority of them do; nearly all, in fact?—A. I
that more than one-half of them do. I refer to Gloucester vessels
I say that.

Q. Can you explain how it is, if the captains disapprove of going
those harbors for fresh bait, that the practice has grown until it h;
come almost universal?—A. I think it has been more difficult to o
bait and ice lately than it was years previously.

Q. You have not had any experience during the last two years
No.

Q. The practice being now almost universal of going into the ha
of the provinces, or the coast of Newfoundland, for fresh bait, hov
that the captains do so when you state that the practice is greatl
approved?—A. Vessels are very anxious to get fresh bait, if the
do so without too much disadvantage and time spent.

Q. It is considered so far superior that vessels are very anxic
obtain it, and make sacrifices to obtain it?—A. If one vessel is fi
with fresh bait and another vessel is fishing near with salt bait, th
with the salt bait will not do as much. I presume if they all fish
salt bait there will not be that difference.

Q. As a matter of fact, a salt-bait vessel has no chance when fi
alongside a vessel with fresh bait?—A. Not so good a chance.

Q. You cannot explain how it is that the practice has so incr
and become almost universal, when it is so disapproved?—A. P
are desirous of getting fresh bait.

Q. People are desirous of getting fresh bait?—A. Before they
in after this bait, I think the vessels did as well as they do now.

Q. Can you give any statistics in regard to vessels fishing wit
bait and fishing with fresh bait?—A. I am not prepared to do so

    By Mr. Dana:

Q. You were asked by last counsel (Mr. Whiteway) as to the re
prices at which articles were supplied you by the owners of the v
Without going into details, I would like you to state to the Comn
how the matter is generally managed in Gloucester. The suppl
the vessels usually charged to the crew are usually furnished, ar
not, by one of the owners, who acts as agent and purchases suppl
A. Usually.

Q. Is the practice universal? Is there any obligation to bu
the owners?—A. No; the crew are not obliged to do so. If a m
the money, and wishes to buy elsewhere, he is at liberty to do so

Q. Is Gloucester a place where there are few firms; or is it a
where there are a great many persons engaged in the selling of a
of outfits?—A. There are a great many.

Q. Is there any such thing as combination among them; or
petition greater than combination?—A. There is greater compet

Q. What class of persons make up, for the most part, the crews
sail from Gloucester? Is it or is it not the case that persons w
masters one day may be hands another day?—A. Yes; frequent

Q. Very much so?—A. Yes.

Q. You have among your hands a good many men who hav
masters themselves, and understand the business?—A. A good
men who have been masters, and are capable of going as master

Q. When they return from their trip they receive an account, do they)t, from the owners ?—A. Yes; and they are on the wharf to take ac-unt themselves of their catch.

Q. Do you know of anything like attempts to defraud them ? Would be a practicable thing ?—A. I never heard of such a thing being done.

Q. Would it be practicable ?—A. I don't know how it could be done.

Q. As a rule, crews are attentive to their settlements ?—A. The ma-rity of them are.

Q. And the number of persons employed on vessels is, of course, very rge. Do the men who go in Gloucester vessels change from one em-oyer to another ?—A. Yes; very frequently.

Q. Are there various habits among the different employers and out-ters, as to liberality or illiberality, as to closeness or generosity in aking up accounts and feeding the crews, and are these pretty well own in Gloucester ?—A. Perfectly well known among the crews.

Q. When the crew comes home the vessel's cargo is packed out. The ackerel are culled over when the crew are present. Is that an open a close transaction ?—A. They are supposed to be all there, and gen-ally are.

Q. They are present to see fair play ; they see the process of putting em into barrels and weighing ?—A. Yes; and one of the crew super-tends the weighing.

Q. So as to the culling; is there any objection made to the culling ?— . The crew are always there and speak of it.

Q. Is it sometimes the case that the owner of vessels, instead of fur-shing a fisherman with his outfit and clothing, gives him an order or dorses his bill on some shop where the fisherman buys ?—A. Quite equently gives the man an order to get his outfit and clothes at some her store.

Q. In that case the owner becomes responsible ?—A. Yes.

Q. If the fisherman is lost during the voyage and does not leave prop-ty behind him, the owner has to pay the debt ?—A. The owner loses e amount.

Q. And if the voyage turns out unprofitable, and the man has not e money to pay it, the owner must pay it ?—A. The owner has to y it.

Q. From your experience, do you know that, when an owner has a ore he retails articles out to his crews at retail prices, and buys ac-rding to his skill and sagacity at wholesale prices ?—A. Yes.

Q. What do you think, on an average, is the difference between the holesale price at which the owner is able to buy, and the retail price arged to the crew ?—A. Probably eight or ten per cent.

Q. You don't think it exceeds that ?—A. I do not.

Q. Is that a matter perfectly understood by the fishermen ?—A. Yes.

Q. Do you think the fisherman who has to take credit can do better an that, if he undertakes to supply himself ?—A. I don't think he can better than that.

Q. Is it not understood to be the business of the skipper to stand by d take accounts of all the weighing and other matters ?—A. Always.

Q. He has an interest like one of the crew ?—A. Yes ; and more than ey.

Q. And an account is made out of what is charged to the crew and hat to the master, and the same rate of charge is made to the skip-r as to the crew ?—A. Yes.

Q. There is a regular charge for the captain as well as for each mem-r of the crew ?—A. Yes.

By Hon. Mr. Kellogg:

Q. How many vessels of the mackerel fleet are there that d but fish for mackerel, that is to say, that have nothing to do fishing, the coasting trade, or West India trade, but lie up d winter? How many of the fleet are there that do nothing d winter, if there are any?—A. There are some, but I cannot te exact number.

Q. Is there a great proportion of the vessels engaged in o ness connected with cod-fishing?—A. Yes.

No. 58.

Maj. DAVID W. LOW, postmaster of Gloucester, Mass., call half of the Government of the United States, sworn and exan

By Mr. Dana:

Question. I think you were born in Gloucester?—Answer. I

Q. What age are you?—A. Forty-four years.

Q. Did you at any time go into the fishing business?—A. 1860.

. Did you go in as a partner?—A. I did.

. What was the name of the firm?—A. Sinclair and Low.

. How many years were you in it?—A. Three.

. In 1860, 1861, and 1862?—A. Yes.

. You were engaged in fitting out vessels, I suppose?—A.

. Did you ever make a fishing voyage yourself?—A. Yes.

. More than one?—A. Only one.

. What year was it?—A. Eighteen hundred and fifty-five.

. Did you go into the Gulf of St. Lawrence?—A. Yes.

. What was the vessel?—A. Austerlitz.

Q. Where did you fish?—A. In Bay Chaleurs and round Islands.

Q. Do you recollect what you caught?—A. One hundred a packed barrels; we got 205 sea-barrels, I think.

Q. You made but one trip?—A. Yes.

Q. Did you do any of that fishing inshore, within what you to be three miles of the shore?—A. Yes, some of it.

Q. You tried inshore and off shore?—A. Yes.

Q. What success had you with the inshore fishing?—A. V some fish.

Q. What proportion of your catch?—A. I should think we or 25 barrels inshore out of the whole trip.

Q. At that time the Reciprocity Treaty was in force; di the inshore fishery a fair trial?—A. Yes.

Q. In 1860, 1861, and 1862 you were partner in a firm fitting out vessels; how many vessels did you fit out in that Eight.

Q. Were you interested in those eight vessels?—A. I wa them.

Q. What voyages did they make?—A. They were cod George's Bank; trawling for halibut on the Western Bank; ereling in the Gulf of St. Lawrence and off the American co:

Q. During what months were these vessels employed in cod A. From January to June; one went for the whole season.

Q. And the others from January to June?—A. Yes.

Q. When were they employed trawling for halibut?—A. From Febuary to June.

Q. Where did they take the halibut which they caught?—A. They ok the most of it to Boston then.

Q. How was it preserved?—A. In ice.

Q. Was large or broken ice used?—A. The ice is broken up on board pack the fish in.

Q. Your vessels were not smacks?—A. No; smacks are not used in loucester at all.

Q. What bait was used by the cod-fishing vessels during this period?— . Herring and pogies, principally.

Q. Frozen herring?—A. Yes.

Q. Did any of your vessels engaged in cod-fishing run into any Doinion ports for bait?—A. No; not to my knowledge.

Q. During these three years, from 1860 to 1863, do you know, from e reports of the masters and inquiries and otherwise, where your vessls, as a general thing, caught their fish in the bay?—A. Yes; the agdalen Islands is the principal fishing ground which they have menned.

Q. Were the fish caught, according to the reports of the masters, and ur observation and knowledge, mostly outside or inside of what might called the three-mile line?—A. They were mostly taken outside.

Q. How many trips did your vessels usually make for mackerel after ey returned from cod-fishing? I suppose that some went for mackel?—A. Some made one trip and others two trips.

Q. Did they return to Gloucester when they made two trips?—A. es.

Q. In 1863 you gave up the business of fitting out vessels?—A. es.

Q. Were you in the war?—A. Yes.

Q. How long were you in the service?—A. About two years.

Q. To what rank did you rise?—A. Major.

Q. In what employments have you been engaged since the terminau of the war?—A. Since the war I have been employed surveying d conveyancing, and as town clerk in Gloucester, and from the town erk's office I went to the post-office.

Q. Apart from the duties of these posts, to what have you chiefly voted your time and attention?—A. When I was town clerk I made statistics with regard to our State, and I have done so since.

Q. Have you been very much engaged in the making up of statistics ith reference to the State and of Gloucester, and of the fishingisiness and population of Gloucester, &c.?—A. Yes; more or less.

Q. And those statistics have been incorporated into some volumes of imphlets?—A. Yes.

Q. Have you some of them here?—A. Yes.

Q. How many years of your statistics appeared in the report made the secretary of state to the legislature?—A. Those for the years .tending from 1868 to 1872 were contained in the reports returned to e librarian of the commonwealth from the town.

Q. Have they not been adopted and sent in as executive documents some instances to the legislature? Do you happen to know for what ars?—A. The law of Massachusetts requires the town clerks to return e town report of each year to the librarian of the commonwealth; d those reports I have returned.

Q. I think I saw some which seemed to be executive documents, giving the aggregates of property, taxes, &c., as assessed May 1st, compiled by the secretary of state of the commonwealth ?—A. Ye

Q. This was also the case for 1875 ?—A. Yes.

Q. And these are two specimen pamphlets ?—A. Yes.

Q. And they contain your Gloucester reports ?—A. These a them.

Q. Have you made up a column of statistics relating to Glouceste A. Yes; I first submit a statement with regard to its population. as follows:

GLOUCESTER, *August* 24, 1

The following is a true account of the population of Gloucester, in the cou Essex and State of Massachusetts, during the period
turns made by the census agents appointed for this purpose:

1850 ....
1855 ....
1860 ....
1865 ....
1870 ....
1875 ....
1877 (estimated at)..
  A true copy.
  Attested by—
                                    JOHN J. SOMES, *City C*

Q. The census is taken once every five years in Massachusetts; nately by the nation and by the State ?—A. Yes.

Q. The increase in the population of Gloucester seems to be very smaller for the last seven years than it was during previous perioc A. Yes.

Q. You have no doubt as to the correctness of that statement' No. I also beg to submit the following statement:

GLOUCESTER, *August* 23,

The following is a true and correct account of the valuation of Gloucester, county of Essex and State of Massachusetts, during the period mentioned, as from the assessor's books:

	1850	$1,
	1851	1,
	1852	2,
	1853	2,
Reciprocity..............	1854	3,
	1855	3,
	1856	3,
	1857	3,
	1858	3,
	1859	4,
	1860	4,
	1861	4,
	1862	4,
	1863	4,
	1864	3,
	1865	4,
Reciprocity terminated..	1866	5,
	1867	6,
	1868	6,
	1869	6,
	1870	7,
	1871	7,
Treaty of Washington ..	1872	7,
	1873	7,
	1874	8
	1875	9
	1876	9
	1877	9

  A true copy.
  Attested by—
                                    JOHN J. SOMES, *Cit*

· Q. The valuation in 1875 was $9,200,000 odd ; in 1876, $9,300,000 odd, and in 1877, $9,200,000 odd ; there seems to be no difference but rather a slight decrease, comparing 1877 with 1875 ; does that arise from any change of system of valuation, or is it, in your opinion, a correct valuation made on the same principle ?—A. It is a correct valuation made on the same principle.

Q. During the whole period from 1850 to 1877, do you know of any change in principle on which the valuations are made ?—A. Well, during the war there was an increased valuation put on, on account of the inflation of the currency.

By Sir Alexander Galt :

Q. Those are currency values, of course ?—A. Yes ; all are so.

By Mr. Dana :

Q. Since 1870, and from 1870 to 1877, after the more immediate effects of the war had passed away, was any change of policy or principle made in the mode of the valuation of property ?—A. No ; not to my knowledge.

Q. What is your next paper ?—A. It is a table showing the increase of the city of Gloucester, Mass., from 1850, when a town, in population and valuation ; it is as follows :

Table showing the increase of the city of Gloucester, Mass., from 1850 (when a town), in population and valuation. The census of 1840 gave the population 6,350.

Year.	Census.	Population.	Valuation.	Average valuation of each inhabitant.	Average increase of valuation of each inhabitant for each term of years.
1850	United States	7,786	$1,635,787	$210	....
1855	State	8,935	3,304,324	370	$160
1860	United States	10,904	4,332,740	396	26
1865	State	11,938	4,859,348	408	12
1870	United States	15,397	7,187,107	467	59
1875	State	16,754	9,238,265	552	85

Q. Have you made a careful inquiry so as to ascertain from the proper authorities information relative to the increase and condition of Gloucester as compared with some other towns of the county of Essex ?—A. I have.

Q. State these details for towns not engaged in fishing.—A. The statement is as follows :

1875. Population of Lynn, 32,600 ; valuation, $28,077,793 ; $861 to each inhabitant.

1870. Valuation, $20,927,115 ; increase in 5 years, $7,150,678.

1875. Population of Haverhill, 14,682 ; valuation, $10,497,132 ; $701 to each inhabitant.

1875. Population of Lawrence, 34,916 ; valuation, $24,117,373 ; $691 to each inhabitant.

1875. Valuation of Beverly, $8,545,125 ; in 1870, $5,563,050 ; increase, $2,982,075.

1875. Valuation of Marblehead, $4,058,610 ; in 1870, $3,115,300 ; increase, $943,310.

The above are all manufacturing places. Beverly and Marblehead were formerly large fishing-ports.

163 F

Q. Lynn is a place which has nothing to do with the f
ness?—A. Yes; it is a manufacturing town, and is engaged
business.

Q. Beverly has entirely ceased to be interested in the
ness?—A. Yes; almost. It has now gone into the shoe bu

Q. Marblehead was the first fishing-place in the United :
I think so; but it is gone now into manufacturing. Bever
blehead were formerly large fishing-places, but the towns
tioned are now all manufacturing places.

Q. Did you make up statistics in reference to the fishing
the Centennial?—A. I did.

Q. And you spent a good deal of time on them?—A. Yes

Q. And they were presented to the Centennial Commissiol

Q. Can you give us some statistics with relation to the fi
of Massachusetts, showing what the effect of this differel
fishing in the bay has been, as far as you can, on the fishil
of Massachusetts?—A. I have a table showing the valuatiol
cipal fishing-ports of Massachusetts other than Glouceste
follows:

Table showing the valuation of the principal fishing ports or towns of Mase
than Gloucester, in 1875, as compared with 1870.

Place.	Year.	Valuation.	De
Barnstable	1870	$2, 657, 180	
	1875	2, 614, 790	8
Chatham	1870	1, 007, 442	
	1875	770, 334	2
Provincetown	1870	1, 981, 161	
	1875	1, 844, 191	1
Brewster	1870	747, 849	
	1875	622, 104	1
Yarmouth	1870	1, 412, 017	
	1875	1, 402, 248	
Sandwich	1870	1, 405, 100	
	1875	1, 398, 950	
Dennis	1870	1, 478, 204	
	1875	1, 448, 587	
Orleans	1870	520, 621	
	1875	422, 364	
Wellfleet	1875	877, 149	
	1870	812, 849	
Total decrease in valuation, eight ports			
Gain in one port			

Q. You have taken every fishing town in that particula
Yes; every town which I knew had vessels engaged in fi
whole commonwealth, except Gloucester.

Q. Were these statistics made up by you before you kr
about the meeting of this Tribunal, and without any re
whatever?—A. These were made up here from the books
with me.

Q. And you made up your statistics for the purpose o
nial?—A. Yes; and I have also other statistics.

Q. You were very thorough in your preparation of then
tennial?—A. I tried to be so.

Q. The original ·census from which these statistics were obtained, were prepared without any reference to this Tribunal?—A. Yes.

Q. Have you ever made up any statistics relative to the shore and gulf fisheries, showing the difference between the American shore fishery and the Gulf of St. Lawrence fishery?—A. Yes, and the statement s as follows:

Number of fishing vessels in Gulf of St. Lawrence mackerel fishery and the American shore mackerel fishery.

	Barrels.
869.—194 vessels in gulf, average catch 209 barrels	40,546
151 vessels off shore, average catch 222 barrels	33,552
Mackerel caught by boats and some Eastern vessels packed in Gloucester	19,028
Mackerel inspected in Gloucester	93,126
875.—58 vessels in gulf, average catch 191 barrels	11,078
117 vessels American shore, average catch 409 barrels	47,853
	58,931

The average catch is based on the average catch of 84 vessels from 17 firms in 1869 ; nd 28 vessels in bay and 62 vessels off American shore from 20 firms in 1875. These rms have done better than the rest.

Q. You do not, I suppose, include in this statement any but vessels— : has nothing to do with boat-fishing?—A. No.

Q. Will you state from what source you have made up these statistics?—A. The information concerning the vessels which fished in the gulf, and those which fished off our shore, I obtained and tabulated for the information of Gloucester when I was town clerk, in 1869, and the eport for 1875 was procured for Centennial purposes—not by myself, ut by some one who did his work well.

Q. Can you say, as a matter of belief, that these statistics were made p for Centennial purposes and not with reference to this Tribunal?— l. Yes; I believe that is the case.

Q. From what sources were those for 1875, for instance, taken?—A. 'he catch was taken from the reports of the number of firms I mentioned.

Q. To how many firms do you refer?—A. These include the most successful firms, George Steele, &c.

· Q. Those are the firms that had been the most successful, whether on ur shore or in the Gulf of St. Lawrence; which are considered to be he most successful firms in Gloucester?—A. George Steele, Leighton & lo., Dennis & Ayer, and Smith & Gott.

Q. These are generally considered to be the most successful firms?—A. 'es.

Q. Were they all included in this return?—A. Yes.

Q. The tonnage of the vessels was somewhat larger in 1875 than it 'as in 1869?—A. I think not. I think it was about the same.

Q. In order that the Commission may understand whether these Gloucester merchants, when making their statements here, are guessing t what they say, or have absolute data to go upon and know what they re about, you have, at our request, made an examination of the books f one of the firms?—A. I have examined the books of the most successful firm engaged in the bay mackerel fishery.

Q. That is the firm of Mr. Steele?—A. Yes. I did this of my own ccord, because I wanted the Commission to see how these books are . ept.

Q. Will you produce these books?—A. I have the trip-bool
have numbered one, for the years since 1858 and 1859. Their
books were burned in the great fire at Gloucester in 1864. I
trip-books for the years extending from 1858 to 1876, inclusive

Q. What is the meaning of the term "trip-book"?—A. Thi:
with which the voyage is made up and settled with the crew, sh
parts which belong respectively to the vessel and the crew.
ages of all the schooners from 1858, as long as they were ru
drawn out. I have prepared an abstract from these books; a
mary of that abstract and an explanation of this summary.
summary of all the voyages made by the fishing-vessels
Steele from 1858 to 1877; it shows the time employed in th
halibut fishery, and those engaged in the mackerel fishery off
ican coast and the Gulf of St. Lawrence, giving the amount
of their catches, &c. (For summary of the voyages see A[
Evidence.)

Q. All this you were able to take from these books whic
kept for their own convenience?—A. Yes.

Q. What is that?—A. As you all well know, in Glouceste
ing-fleet meets with a great many disasters, and a great deal
has to be given in charity to widows and orphans of fisherme
for a few years back it has been the practice among vessel-
deduct, with the consent of the crews, of course, from the gros
of their vessels, one-quarter of one per cent. to be given to th
and orphans' fund.

Q. The owners contribute half and the men half?—A. Yes
is put in as a stock charge.

Q. Is it not the case that the number of widows and orph
sioned by disasters in the fishing business has been large?—
The statement continues:

The amount of the "stock expenses" is found on above summary by
vessel's share, which adds the crew's share, and taking that amount from
stock," this leaves the amount of the "stock expenses."

By dividing the "value of the catch" by the "barrels caught" (packe
the average value of the mackerel, exclusive of packing.

The number of "vessels employed" in each class of fishery, shows the
gaged in that particular fishery some part of the year, and the "number
the total number of vessels owned and fitted each year.

It will be found by the "summary of voyages," that from 1858 to 1865,
average catch of his vessels in the Gulf of St. Lawrence was 338 pack
mackerel, which sold, exclusive of the packing and barrels, for $11.10
200 pounds. From 1865 to 1872, inclusive, the average catch was 280 pa
sold for $14.40, average price per barrel. From 1872 to 1876, inclusive
catch was 223 barrels, sold at an average price of $10.01 per barrel, exclu
and packing.

The average time of each vessel employed in the Gulf of St. Lawre
fishery was 4 months 13 days by 6.3 vessels, yearly for 17 years. The
was 304 packed barrels, the average price sold for, $12 per barrel. The ve
the 17 years, $372.66 per month each; the average share to the crews, $24
each.

The average time employed in the cod and halibut fisheries was 6 m
each year, for 19 years, by 8.21 vessels. Average vessel's share per month

By Sir Alexander Galt:

Q. I thought that in your previous statement of month h
was $300 and something?—A. Yes; it was $372.66 in the g

Q. And what was it in the cod-fishing?—A. $352.21. Mr.
sels have been unusually successful in the Gulf of St. Lawr

By Mr. Dana:

Q. And the most so of any ?—A. Yes; that is a well-known fact. The statement continues:

Average share to crews, average 9.5 men, $38.12 per month.
The average time employed in the American shore mackerel fishery was 2 months 10 days each year for 9 years. The average catch per year for 2.3 vessels was 239 barrels of mackerel; the average price which was in years of low prices was $7.10 per barrel, exclusive of barrel and packing. Average share to vessels per month, $310.60. Crew's average share, $20.70 each per month.
The average time the vessels were employed in all the fisheries was 9 months 14 days by 9.1 vessels yearly for 19 years, for which time the average share for each vessel was 3,228.08, or $340.92 per month. The crew's shares, average share for each man, was 264.38, or $27.83 per month to 12.25 men, the average crew for each vessel.

Q. The cod fishery seemed in one respect to be superior to and more profitable than the mackerel fishery, and in another less so. The men's shares were more in the cod than they were in the mackerel fishery ?—A. The former is attended with a good deal less expense and requires fewer men.

Q. In the mackerel fishery a larger proportion of barrels is required ?—A. The proceeds of mackerel-fishing are to be divided among 5 men, while in the cod fishery these are to be shared amongst some 9 men.

Q. Will you select some one vessel from Steele's trip book and show in detail how it is kept ?—A. I have here the method of making up a voyage of a Grand Banker using fresh bait and a Grand Banker using salt bait. The statement for the former is as follows:

Schooner Pharsalia.

Sailed for Grand Bank May 29, 1875, arrived at Gloucester September 6, 1875. Time absent, 3 months 8 days.

1,685 lbs. large cod, at 2⅔ cents..................	$2,222 98
205 lbs. small cod, at 1⅝ cents	28 94
3,510 lbs. damaged cod, at 1 cent..................	135 10
6,100 lbs. fletches (halibut), at 4 cents............	244 00
95 galls. oil, at 45 cents.........................	87 75
number galls. blubber, at 0......................	00

	2,718 17	(Gross stock.)
Less stock charges	301 42	(Stock charges.)
	2)2,417 35	(Net stock.)
	1,208 67	
		Exd.
		(Examined by owner of vessel.)

Ledger page.	Crew's names.	Net shares.			
310	Samuel Aug. Keene (master)...........	$93 54			
335	Andrew Clark.......................	93 54			
	Michael Howlett	93 54			
378	Duncan McIaaac	93 54			
378	William Gosbee	93 54	2)$2,718 77	Gross stock.
	Levi Johnson.......................	93 54		
	William Albert Guptill ¼.............	23 39	12) 1,359 38	(½ Gross stock.)
417	Malcolm A. McKinnon ¾	70 15		
199	Charles Austin......................	93 54	113 28	Gross share.
418	John Welsh	93 54		
418	Barney Canivan.....................	93 54	Deduct	19 74	Expense.
56	George Somers	93 54		
468	Alex. McLoud ¾.....................	70 15	93 54	Net share.
469	Thomas Welsh ¼.....................	23 39		
	Crew's expenses	86 11		
	Balance	....		
	Total................	1,208 67		

Schooner Pharsalia.

5 tons ice, at $3, from Webster (bought in Gloucester for keeping bait)..	$15 00	
1 ton ice at St. Peter's, at $3.50, gold, at $1.15 (value of $1 in United States currency)	4 03	Cr. Keene (master
5 tons ice at Burene, at $15, gold, at $1.15 ($3 gold per ton)	17 25	Cr. Keene (master
2⁷⁄₂₀ tons ice at St. John's, at $21.50, gold, at $1.15 ($10 gold per ton)	24 73	
5¼ tons ice at Arichat, at $16.50, gold, at $1.15 ($3 gold per ton)....................................	18 98	Cr. Keene.
65 barrels bait at Fortune Bay, at $30, gold, at $1.15.	34 50	Cr. Keene.
55 barrels bait at Fortune Bay, at $55, gold, at $1.15.	63 25	Cr. Keene.
13 barrels caplin, at St. John's, $3.50, gold, at $1.15..	4 03	Cr. Keene.
20 barrels herring, at St. John's, $20, gold, at $1.15..	23 00	Cr. Keene.
12 pairs nippers, at 60 cents (worn on hands in fishing)	7 20	
Widows' and orphans' fund (¼ of 1 per cent. off gross stock)	7 00	
5 butts for oil, at $3	15 00	
5 iron-bound barrels for oil, $12.50....................	12 50	
Gauging-fee on oil, 75 cents; 2 hogshead tubs, $7 ...	7 75	
Wharfage, St. John's, $1.15; consul's fees, St. Johns, $3.18	4 33	
Entering and clearing at St. John's, $4.60............	4 60	
Commissions on bait-money at St. John's, $11.62	11 62	
Port charges paid by Keene at St. Pierre, $5, gold...	5 75	
Light dues paid by Keene at Fortune Bay, $17.54, gold..	20 17	
Telegram paid by Keene to Arichat, 63 cents gold...	73	
	2) 301 42	Stock charges.
¼ stock charges..	150 71	
Chronometer hire..	12 00	Cr., Sept. 10, 1875
4 dozen condensed milk....................................	14 00	
Towing, May 26, 1875......................................	5 00	paid Aug. 19, 187
Labor on ballast	23 50	
Gun, $2.50; caps, 60 cents; powder, $4.	7 10	
Tarring rigging	6 00	
Elwell, medicine chest	5 00	
1,500 barrels (gallons) water here	7 50	
2 feet wood, sawing and splitting	1 00	
Water at St. John's..	4 3	
Water paid by Keene (master)............................	64	Cr. Keene.
	12) 236 82	Crew's expenses.
Share of expenses...............................	19 74	(for each of crew

This copy was made from the trip-book of George Steele, of Gloucester, George F. Winter, bookkeeper, to show the method of settling the voyage of a " G Banker" that used fresh bait wholly. Abbreviations and other matters are expl in parentheses, thus ( ).

Attested.

DAVID W. LO

Q. Our men use nippers with their lines?—A. Yes; and some of hands are marked three-quarters, and some one-quarter; those are who pay only that proportion of the crew's charges.

By Sir Alexander Galt:

Q. What is the meaning of gross expenses, $86.11, following men's expenses in the book?—A. That is the amount of those expe on that side; several items which go to make up the sum tota thus included.

Q. Nothing is said about provisions?—A. No; the cost of provi

itered on the owner's ledger; this is a trip-book, showing the set-
ent of the voyages with the crew.

You have read from that statement that so many codfish of differ-
kinds produced the gross amount of $2,718; but there is no deduc-
mado from that which I notice.—A. There is $301.22.

For provisions?—A. That $1,208.67 is credited on the owner's
er, and the schooner has her share of the voyage.

And out of that comes the provisions?—A. The debtor side of the
er shows the cost of provisions and outfit.

By Hon. Mr. Kellogg:

I see that you divide that by 12 and 14?—A. There were on board
who paid only one quarter of a man's share of the expenses.

You have there charges for scraping and tarring, splitting wood,
Why are these charged to the crew?—A. Because in former times
rew did all that work themselves.

They came aboard the vessel and worked to fit her?—A. Yes.

They hoisted in and hoisted out, tarred the rigging, split the wood,
all that, themselves?—A. Yes.

They have dropped that on the understanding that they have to
for it?—A. Yes.

That has been the usage?—A. Yes.

Well understood?—A. Yes.

Before you leave that, I want to ask you in reference to an item
e, "damaged codfish."—A. 13,150 pounds of damaged cod, at 1
, $135.10.

Why should there be this damaged codfish? What is the cause
?—A. Well, I have my own opinion of the cause.

What do you believe to be the cause?—A. I believe the cause is
g in so much for fresh bait.

How should that damage the codfish?—A. My opinion is that the
rs salted it with the idea that they would not go in so much, and
't put so much salt on it. When she went into port so much, going
the warm water it heated.

So that if a vessel intends to go into harbor there ought to be a
different proportion?—A. Certainly.

That is coming out of the cold water on the Banks?—A. Yes.

By Sir Alexander Galt:

Before you leave this schooner, I would like to see what the result
at trip was to the vessel. I mean how much it cost the owners to
ision her, and how much they paid out of that $1,208.67 that went
e vessel's share.—A. I have made up a profit and loss account.
ourse, I had no such thing as a ledger to work from, but I had the
books, and I made up an account of Mr. Steele's trips in the bay,
the time they commenced in 1858 to 1876, for seventeen years.

What I wanted was, without going into the particulars of these
ges, to know what the actual-cash result was.—A. It is pretty
l to reckon that.

Of course, if you can say nothing more about it you need not dwell
it.—A. I cannot, because the manner of keeping the books does
show the particular voyages of any one vessel. The charges against
schooner are all entered on the debtor side and the result of the
ge on the creditor side.

By Mr. Dana:

Does not the book of original entries show what the charges in
ledger are made up of?—A. I have what the outfit of a mackerel
her cost.

Sir ALEXANDER GALT. No; not a mackerel catcher.

WITNESS. I have a Grand Banker, but not any particular voy

By Mr. Dana:

Q. Sir Alexander Galt asked you whether you had not the which you could make up an exact profit and loss account of th ticular voyage?—A. I could if I had time. I could make that the basis in making up such an account from facts which I carry mind in regard to the general course of the business.

Sir ALEXANDER GALT. That would not be exactly what I wor to have.

By Mr. Dana:

Q. That trip was in 1875?—A. Yes.

Q. Now, I suppose the object of Sir Alexander Galt's question ascertain what the cost of provisions was as one item.—A. I c that.

Q. From some other book?—A. From a paper I have. Not th ticular vessel, however.

Q. You haven't brought his ledger?—A. No, only his trip-boc

Q. You made this up after you arrived here?—A. Yes. Al statistics I made up since I arrived here. I had only those ma I didn't have time in Gloucester.

Q. If you were there it could easily be done?—A. Not for c ticular voyage.

Q. I suppose the provisions, being bought wholesale, are not c to any particular vessel?—A. Well, each vessel's outfit is c to her.

Q. But not when they are bought by the owners; that is me business?—A. No. That does not affect any one vessel. Whe are put aboard any one vessel they are charged to that vessel.

Q. That appears where?—A. In his day-book and ledger.

Q. Now, you have given the result of a cod-fishing voyage fresh bait. Have you a similar statement of a voyage where s was used?—A. Yes; I have. The following is the statement:

Schooner Madam Roland.

5 barrels slivers (porgie), at $8, including barrel from William Gardner	$40 00
5 barrels slack salted clams, at $11, including barrel from M. Knowlton	55 00
6 pairs nippers, at 60 cents (worn on hands in fishing)	3 60
1 butt for oil (hogshead)	3 00
Fee paid for gauging oil	1 20
12 oil-barrels	24 00
Widow and orphans' fund	6 90
11 water-barrels used up, at $1.50	16 50

2) 150 20

Crews expenses.			One-half stock charges
Bait	$3 96		12 gallons molasses for beer
Nippers	15		5 barrels hops
Oil-barrels	1 80		Half-barrel
Gauging	5		55 barrels Water
Widow and orphans	29		4 feet Wood, S. & S. (sawing
Beer	77		splitting)
Water	92		Towing, August 22, 1873
Wood	17		Towing, October 11, 1873
Towing	50		
	8 61		Crew's expenses
			Share of expenses (12 me

ands, all share alike, except .... 2) 2,758 27 gross stock.

Kaffery, who is on wages........................... 12) 1,379 13

50 per month, from August 15, 1873, to ....   114 92 gross share.
ber 15, 1873, 2 months, equal to $100..................   9 61 expenses out.

                                                  106 31 net share.

e above was copied from trip book of George Steel, of Gloucester, Mass., George inter, bookkeeper, to show the method of settling the voyage of a Grand Banker used salt bait, with what fresh bait they caught on the Banks. Abbreviations other terms used are explained in parenthesis, thus ( ).
test :

                                                 DAVID W. LOW.

Schooner Madam Roland.

iled for Grand Banks August 26, 1873. Arrived at Gloucester October 10, 1873. absent, one month fourteen days.

0 barrels large split fish (cod), at 2¼ $2,238 50
0 barrels small split fish (cod), at 1¾ 328 21
arrels fletches (halibut), at 7 ....   7 70

                                      2,574 41
;allons oil, at 58 cents 183 86

                                      2,758 27 gross stock.
stock charges 150 20

                                      2,608 07 net stock.

                                        1,304 03

r   Crew's names.

Millard F. Harris .... $106 31 paid.
John McIntire.. 106 31
John Reed 106 31
William Cummings..................................... 106 31
Stewart Hadley 106 31
Charles Scott.. 106 31
Charles Cogill... 106 31
Alexander Muise....................................... 106 31
Daniel W. Gerry....................................... 106 31

Charles Eruckson (no account) .... 106 31 } paid October 31, 1873,
                                                    on wages.

John Haffey... 106 31
Peter Green 106 31
Sundries, for beer..................................... 9 20
Water 11 00
Wood... 2 00
Towing 6 00
Balance 11

Total 1,304 03

By Sir Alexander Galt :

Have you in that account 12 oil-barrels, $24 ?—A. (Inspecting account.) No ; I am sorry to say I have omitted that.

By Mr. Dana :

One voyage is for four months and the other only one month and lf ?—A. Yes.

What appears to be the reason that the voyage on which fresh was used was so much longer than the one on which the salt bait used ? Were they fitted for voyages of different lengths or was it use of the time taken going in and out ?—A. That is the way I account for it. They usually fit for the same length of time.

Q. Now, we have had one voyage for cod with fresh bait and one salt bait; have you any other ?—A. I have a statement of a mac̄l catcher. It is as follows:

Schooner Oliver Eldridge.

55 barrels slivers (porgies), at $6 50, from Eclipse lot........	$357 50
7 barrels clams, at $6, from last year	42 00
Difference between skipper's account and wharf account (see explanation O)...	6 00
Harbor dues at Georgetown, Prince Edward Island, $1......	1 20
Widow and orphans' fund	8 86
	415 56 stock chs

Crew's expenses.			
Bait	$14 06	¼ stock charges	
Error, 21 cents; widow and orphans, 31 cents	52	4 dozen milk......................	
		Hoisting ballast	
Milk	98	Towing, November 3, 1875	
Towing	39	Rigging fly-jib	
Fly-jib	56	Taking off sails, &c............	
Sails	21	Scraping and tarring..........	
Scraping and tarring.......	57	Elwell medicine-chest.........	
Medicine-chest	44	Hoisting mackerel	
Hoisting	32	16 barrels water	
Water, 23 cents; wood, 7 cents...	30	2 feet T. and T. wood	
Cook..............................	8 48	Extra to cook	
		Cook's average, 16 shares	
	26 83		14¼ (

Cook has average share and half his fish and $10—14¼ shares.

Crew's names.	Mess No. 1.			Mess No. 2.			Mess No. 1.			Mess No. 2.		
	Barrels.	Pounds.	One-half value.	Barrels.	Pounds.	One-half value.	Barrels.	Pounds.	One-half value.	Barrels.	Pounds.	One-half value.
Wm. Crawley and John Hick..	....	....	......	....	....	......	30	43	$241 72	7	25	$42 75
Thomas Crawley, one-half	....	....	......	....	....	......	9	148	77 92	2	66	13 98
John Murphy, three-quarters.	....	....	......	....	....	......	6	168	54 72	2	126	15 78
John Collin	....	....	......	....	....	......	11	66	90 64	2	26	12 78
Maurice Hickey, one-quarter .	....	....	......	....	....	......	7	61	58 44	1	95	8 85
Mike Coughlan, one-half	....	....	......	....	....	......	5	159	46 36	1	99	8 97
Allan Cameron	....	....	......	....	....	......	15	82	123 28	3	137	22 11
Timothy Kelley	....	....	......	....	....	......	5	95	43 80	1	168	11 04
Thomas Green	....	....	......	....	....	......	12	118	100 72	3	19	18 5
Jos. Goslin, jr	....	....	......	....	....	......	11	39	89 56	2	142	
L. J. Dias, cook	....	....	......	....	....	......	10	192	87 68	1	97	8 9
Charles Cantrell	....	....	......	....	....	......	12	29	97 16	1	118	9 5
Nichola; J. O'Brien..........	....	....	......	....	....	......	14	50	114 00	2	97	
James Dooley	9	180	$99 00	....	160	$4 80	3	50	26 00	1	105	9 1
Michael Murray..............	9	183	99 15	5	40	31 20	....	2	8	....	90	2 7
John Barrett	5	32	51 60	1	100	9 00	....	....	......	1	90	8 7
Total.................	24	195	249 75	7	100	45 00	156	102	1,252 08	37	100	225 0

Schooner Oliver Eldridge.

Sailed for the Bay of St. Lawrence August 5, 1875. (Absent 2 months and 2 Arrived at Gloucester November 2, 1875.

Packg. off.

arrels, 195 pounds mess No. 1 mackerel, at 20	$499 50
arrels, 100 pounds mess No. 2 mackerel, at 12	90 00
arrels, 102 pounds mess No. 1 mackerel, at 16	2,504 16
arrels, 100 pounds mess No. 2 mackerel, at 12	450 00
97	3,543 66 (grs. stock.)
Less stock charges	415 56 (net stock.)
	2)3,128 10
	1,564 05

s-mackerel are mackerel with heads and tails cut off and scraped, losing in
.t 26 pounds on the barrel by the operation, but increasing the value of the mack-

Crew s names.	Net shares.
Villiam Crawley	$115 40
ohn Hickey	115 40
'homas Crawley, ¼	78 48
ohn Murphy	50 38
ohn Collin	76 59
Iaurice Hickey, ¼	60 58
Iichael Coughlan, ¼	41 91
.llan Cameron	118 56
'imothy Kelley, ¼	48 13
'homas Green	92 46
oseph Goslin, jr	78 99
.auriana J. Dias, cook	190 50
'harles Cantrell	79 87
Iicholas J. O'Brien	102 08
ames Dooley	112 12
Iichael Murray	106 30
ohn Barrett	42 47
filk, $14; ballast, 75 cents	14 75
'owing, $5; fly-jib, $8.10	13 10
ails, $3; scrp. and tarr., $8	11 00
Iedicine-chest, $6.20; hoisting, $4.50	10 70
Vater, $3.20; wood, $1	4 20
salance	8
	1,564 05

difference between skipper's account and wharf account is explained as follows:
:ipper or master keeps account as the different catches of his crew are weighed
f the account of the packed barrels, after they are rolled out on the wharf, dis-
with the skipper's, the value has to be charged or credited in gross stock, as it
hort or overruns.
"bay trip" was copied from Trip Book of George Steele, of Gloucester, Mass.
3 F. Winter, bookkeeper, to show the method of settling the voyage of a mack-
tcher. Abbreviations and other terms used are explained in brackets, thus ().
st :   DAVID W. LOW.

mess-mackerel are mackerel with the heads and tails cut off, and the mackerel
d; losing in weight 26 pounds on the barrel, but increasing the value of the
irel.

There is an item for difference between skipper's account and wharf
int. How much was it on that voyage ?—A. $6.

What does that mean ?—A. It means this: In weighing out the
erel the skipper keeps an account of the weight of each man's lot,
rhen the mackerel are rolled out on the wharf, if there is a discrep-
between the actual weight of it as rolled out and the footings of
kipper's account, of course they don't know on which one of the
it comes; so it is put in the gross stock account and divided among

all. If the balance is in the vessel's favor it is credited, and if the vessel it is charged in the stock account.

Q. What is the history of the cook's wages, coming out of the

A. In former times the crew had to take turns in cooking, and course, they had so many green cooks, and the fares were so p they made up their minds to have a cook.

Mr. DAVIES. Is there any special object in putting these in?

Mr. DANA. It is only to give a specimen of the manner of ma the accounts for each kind of a voyage.

Mr. FOSTER. It shows also the result of each kind of voyage.

By Sir Alexander Galt:

Q. I suppose the same remark applies to the calculation of sel's share in this case as in the other that you have given?— just the same. I have here a statement showing the method of up the voyage of a schooner to the Grand Banks.

By Mr. Dana:

Q. Is this codfish?—A. Yes; cod and halibut. We don't g halibut on the George's in proportion to the halibut caught by th go specially for it, and go into the deep water, where they ar likely to be found—about 200 or 300 fathoms. The statement is lows:

Schooner Howard Steele.

10 tons ice at $3, from Webster	$30 00
40 pounds bait at $1, bought by skipper, with cash carried ...	40 00
Widow and Orphans' Fund	1 61
	2)71 61 stock c

Crews' expenses.			
Ice	$1 36	½ stock charges	35 81
Bait	1 82	1 dozen condensed milk	3 50
Widow and orphans'	07	Scraping and tarring	5 00
Milk	32	12 barrels water	2 40
Scraping and tarring	46	1-foot wood (sawing and	
Water	22	splitting, &c.)	50
Wood	4	Cook's wages	29 34
Cook	2 67		11)76 55 crew's
	6 96	Share of expenses	6 96

	Fish.		White halibut.			Gray halibu
Crew's names.	Number.	One-half value.	Pounds gross, with heads.	Pounds net, without heads.	One-half value.	Pounds gross, with heads.	Pounds net, without heads.
Ed. Flagg	311	$25 61	66	57	$1 71		
James Madden	397	32 69	30	26	78	5	4
Thos. Kelly	375	30 87	64	55	1 65		
Ed. O'Neil	343	28 24	82	71	2 13	8	7
Dan. Donahue	305	25 11	18	15	45	30	26
John Egan	325	26 76	28	24	72	19	17
Nich. Johnson	315	25 94	39	33	99		10
Axel Obson	320	26 35	21	18	54	12	133
John Lewis	416	34 25	30	26	78	155	
D. Kennison	305	30 05	47	40	1 20		11
John Brien, cook	259	21 33	60	52	1 56	13	
Total	3,731	307 90	485	417	12 51	242	208

verage price of fish 16 46-100 cents each. Cook has average share, and half his fish
s one share of all expenses.
iled for George's Bank August 7, 1875. Arrived at Gloucester August 20, 1875
ent 13 days).

)5 lbs. large cod, at 2 5-8	493. 63
) lbs. small cod, at 1 5-16....................	85. 31
lbs. pollack, at 5-8	1. 62
gal. livers, at 15	29. 10
1 for sword-fish	4. 75
	614. 41
less heads)=417 lbs. white halibut, at 6.....	25. 02
" =208 lbs. gray halibut, at 3	6. 24
	145. 68 Gross stock.
stock charges.............................	71. 61
	2)574. 06 Net stock.
	287. 03 Amt. vessel or crew's share.

er page.	Crew's names.	Net shares.
386	Edwin Flagg	20. 36 cr
415	James Madden	26. 57 pd·
406	Thomas Kelly	25. 56 pd·
456	Edward O'Neil	22. 52 pd·
415	Daniel Donahue	18. 99 pd·
415	John Egan	20. 77 pd·
392	Nicholas Johnson	19. 97 pd·
392	Axel Olson	20. 08 pd·
435	John Lewis	30. 06 pd·
441	David Kennison	24. 29 pd·
o acct.	John Brien, cook	45. 44 pd·
	Milk	3. 50 pd·
	Scraping and tarring................................	5. 00
	Water...	2. 40
	Wood	50
	Balance	2
		287. 03

is trip or voyage was copied from " trip book " of George Stele, of Gloucester, Mass.,
ge F. Winter, bookkeeper, to show the method of settling the voyage of a George's
r fishing-vessel.
brevia'ions and other terms used are explained in parentheses thus ( ).
test.

DAVID W. LOW.

ι the Georges fishing each man's halibut, when he catches them, are
ked either. on the head or the tail with his private mark. The
ish are thrown together, but each one cuts out the tongue and throws
to a bucket. Then the skipper counts them up at the end of the
and sets down a memorandum of how many fish each man has
ght. The halibut are landed and weighed, and each man is credited
ι the number of fish he has caught in detail.

By Hon. Mr. Kellogg:
. That identifies the halibut, but how are the cod identified? They
vary from two to twenty pounds?—A. They make an average.

By Mr. Foster:
. What was the number of the crew in that trip?—A. Nine hands,
ink.

By Sir Alexander Galt:
. I want to ask you one question. I see this vessel took 40 barrels of
, and was out only thirteen days. Could she possibly use that?

What kind of bait is it?—A. Herring, or probably alewives. They ta money to buy bait, and go to Cape Cod or down east—generally to Ca Cod.

Q. They would not have it on board when they sailed?—A. No; th take money and buy it from a baiter outside if they come across a bait on the way, or if they don't they go down to Cape Cod.

By Mr. Foster:

Q. That quantity, if not used, would not be wasted?—A. No. They u hand-lines on the Georges, and are more liberal in the use of bait th the trawlers.

Q. You would not say, I suppose, that they would use up that bait that time?—A. I should say not. But they always look out to g bait enough, if they have a chance.

By Mr. Dana:

Q. Have you made out a table to show the cost of a new schooner the year 1875, fitted for each kind of business, or for the two kinds business—cod and mackerel? If you have, take one of them.—A. have. The first I take is as follows:

Cost of a new schooner, in 1875, at Gloucester, Mass., fitted for the mackerel fishery re for sea, with 17 hands, vessel 67 tons, for a three months' voyage.

Cost of hull, including spars, patent windlass, and patent steerer	$5,
Rigging, including sails, rigging, blocks, stove, tinware, 45 fathoms chain, 100 fathoms 8½-inch manila cable, and 2 anchors (1,060 lbs.)	2,

OUTFITS.

Bait, 55 bbls. of porgies and 7 bbls. of clams...................................	
Salt, 50 hhds. of salt	
Sundries—bait-mill, seines, hooks, adzes, and other articles used on deck.....	
Provisions, including fuel and oil for light for 3 months.......................	
Sundries—lanterns, horns, compasses, charts, bunting, spy-glass, log, sounding line and lead.....	
Barrels, 450 fish-barrels, unheaded and numbered...............................	
Total cost of vessel, with outfits	9,

FOR SEINING—ADDITIONAL COST.

Seine, length 200 fathoms (1,200 feet), depth 30 fathoms, 2½-inch mesh, fitted ready for use...	
Boat, seine-boat, fitted ready for use	
Dories, fitted ready for use..	
	1,
Less 50 bbls. bait, $325, and provisions for 3 less men 3 months, $125.........	
Total cost of seiner, with outfits......................	10

By Mr. Davies:

Q. Is that an actual case?—A. It is from the cost of an actual ves It was procured from an actual vessel fitted ready for sea. It was cured as a specimen for the Centennial.

By Mr. Foster:

Q. You did that yourself?—A. Yes; I went and procured the st ment from the owner, who bought the vessel and gave me the items

By Mr. Dana:

Q. You make a difference between the cost of a vessel for seining one for hand-lining?—A. Yes; the vessel fitted for hand-lining c

5, for seining $10,525. She has to be provided with a seine and boats and dories, which come to $1,200, but she does not carry so men or use so much bait, which makes a difference in her favor 25 against the $1,200 added, leaving a balance of $750 to be added : cost of a vessel fitted for hand-lining in order to fit her for seining. Now, can you give us a similar statement of the cost of a vessel awling halibut on the Banks, made out in the same manner for entennial ?—A. Yes; I have it. It is as follows:

a new schooner at Gloucester, Mass., in 1875, fitted for trawling halibut on the Banks-

el of 71 tons, cost $8,000. Vessel made 9 trips to Western and Grand Banks, be sea 302 days, with 12 men for crew, at the following expense, viz:

gear	$1,023 25
s expense account	1,822 25
ons, &c	1,426 03
l charges, ice, bait, salt, &c	1,135 50
	$5,408 64

Is that carpenters' measurement ?—A. No; that is new measure-

The carpenters build by their own old measurement, don't they ?— 's; they build by their own old measurement.
But this is the registered tonnage ?—A. Yes.

By Sir Alexander Galt:

I understand that this vessel cost $8,800, while the other cost ı ?—A. This is 71 tons.
Well, there is only a difference of four tons between this and the ou gave ?—A. I know that, but the $8,800 includes cost of rigging, the other is only the cost of hull.

By Mr. Dana:

I suppose there is a difference in the style of building ?—A. We t vessels built cheaper down East than at Essex, and some at Es- eaper than others. It is according to how they are built. The ing statement shows the cost of a schooner fitted for cod and hal- shing on the Grand Banks:

a new schooner, in 1875, at Gloucester, Mass., fitted for fishing on Grand Banks for h and halibut, the fish to be salted on board, fitted for four months' voyage, with 14

hull, 77.24 tons	$6,000
ı	2,550
ı, fitted ready for use	168
, 13,500 fathoms, fitted	607
	15
0 hhds	400
tons, for preserving bait	36
60 bbls	12
;,000 pogies, or herring	100
	34
ı, 2½ dozen pairs woollen	12
ons	800
'otal cost of vessel, with outfits	10,734

I have now a statement of a vessel fitted for the George's Banks for cod-fishing, ready for sea. It is as follows:

AT GLOUCESTER, MASS.

Vessel fitted for George's Bank cod-fishing, ready for sea, summer trip. Tonnage 80 tons, with 11 hands, 5 weeks.

Cost of hull	$5,200
Spars	400
Rigging	550
Sails	575
Dory	14
30 tons pebble ballast	50
Platforms, ice-houses, and other fittings of hold	75
Gurry-pens and other deck-fittings	30
230 fathoms 8¼ manila cable, weighing 3,304 pounds	450
3 anchors, of 500 pounds each	120
6 dozen 16-pound lines, 3 dozen gauging lines	10
Lanterns, horns, compasses, charts, bunting, spy-glass, log, &c.	100
10 tons ice, for preserving bait and halibut	30
40 barrels bait	40
Wood and coal	10
14 barrels water	3
Provisions for 11 men, 5 weeks	175
Total cost of vessel and outfits	7,862

Q. I believe that in the last but one of the accounts you read from the returns the small cod was put in. Is that now usually brought in?—A. Yes, it is saved and brought in.

Q. It used in former times to be thrown over?—A. Well, I don't know about that.

Q. Now they are brought in and have a market value?—A. Yes.

Q. The liver and other parts are brought in and saved?—A. Yes.

Q. Then the gurry-pen is the pen in which they throw the gurry?—A. Yes.

Q. That is kept and thrown overboard at the proper time and place?—A. Yes.

Q. Have you any memorandum there to show the amount of the importation into the United States from the Dominion fisheries in any one year, so as to show what value the privilege is to the people of the Dominion?—A. I have a memorandum of the importation last year.

Q. That is obtained from the custom-house?—A. It is obtained from a book that I saw in the room.

Mr. DAVIES. Let us have the book.

Mr. DANA. You need not mind that until we get the book. Will you take any other memorandum or table you have made?—A. I have a profit and loss account of George Steele's vessels in the Gulf of St. Lawrence mackerel fisheries for seventeen years. It is made up from his bay trip book, Gloucester.

By Sir Alexander Galt:

Q. Be kind enough to explain how you made it up?—A. I gave him credit for the number of barrels of mackerel he got, the gross catch of his vessels, and deducted from it the stock charges, making the net stock, and divided that by two, which gave the vessel's share for the whole period of seventeen years. Then I charged the outfits and expenses. I charged him for the charter what I supposed.

Q. Did you take this from his books?—A. No; it is an estimated profit and loss account, made up by me.

Q. He is the owner of the ship?—A. Yes.

♠ By Mr. Dana:

Q. Instead of trying to estimate a charge to be made for the use of the ship you call it "charter"?

Sir ALEXANDER GALT. I understand that one side of the account is made up from the books, and the other side is an estimate.

By Hon. Mr. Kellogg:

Q. Do you find in the book the actual sales?—A. Yes.

By Mr. Dana:

Q. You can go on with your statement.—A. It is as follows:

Number of vessels engaged during 17 years, from 1858 to 1876, inclusive, in the Gulf of Saint Lawrence mackerel fishery, excepting the years 1870 and 1871, when none were sent, by George Steele, of Gloucester, 107; average time employed yearly, 4 months 13 days; average number of hands employed yearly for 17 years, 15.

Stock charges, 17 years.		Catch, 17 years.	
For bait, &c.	$48,052 80	33,645 bbls. mackerel	$403,832 86
		Less stock charges	48,052 80
Outfits and expenses:			
Provisions for 15 men for 4 mos. 13 days; in 107 vessels, 15 x 133 x 107 x 40 cts. per day, for fuel, oil, and provisions.	85,386 00	Net stock	355,780 00
8,500 bbls. salt	8,500 00	Charterer for vessel's share...	177,890 00
107 bait mills, at $15	1,605 00	Crews' share	177,890 00
Fishing-gear for 107 vessels, at $45 each	4,815 00		355,780 00
Custom-house and port charges	2,140 00	Charterers' expenses	222,605 00
Charter of 107 schooners, 4 mos. 23 days each, at $200 per month	94,802 00	Charterers' share, or earnings of vessel	177,890 00
Insurance on charter, $94,802; barrels, $30,000; bait, $48,052; and outfits, $100,406; total, $278,160, at 4 per cent.	11,126 00	Loss	44,715 00
"Skippership," or master's commission, on "net stock," $355,780, at 4 per cent	14,231 00	Charterer's loss on each vessel.	418 00
		Each vessel's earnings, as per vessel account below	251 00
	222,605 00	Actual loss yearly on each vessel	167 00

DR.		VESSELS' ACCOUNT.	CR.
To insurance on 107 vessels, $535,000, at 4 per cent	$21,400 00	Charter	$96,802 00
interest on $535,000, at 7 per cent., 4½ mos	14,056 00		
taxes on $460,000, at $18 per year, for 4½ months	3,037 00		
depreciation on vessels, 4½ mos., 107 vessels, at $275 each	29,425 00		
	67,918 00		
Balance to 107 vessels	26,884 00		
	94,802 00		96,802 00

Net earnings of each schooner, $251.

Q. The first part of that statement, I understand, assumes that you are dealing with the charterer?—A. Yes.

Q. The latter part shows what would be the result to the owner if he would charter his vessels to some one else?—A. No. If the owner who owned the vessel kept his account as well as the charterer.

164 F

By Sir Alexander Galt:

Q. The man who charters the vessel would lose?—A. The one who chartered the vessel and fitted her for fishing loses $418, and the one who lets him have the vessel makes $251.

Q. Besides interest on his vessel?—A. Yes. Besides interest on the valuation of his vessel.

By Mr. Davies:

Q. Allowing for depreciation?—A. Yes.

Q. Ten per cent.? I did't hear you read the allowance for depreciation.—A. "Depreciation on vessels 4½ months, 107 vessels, at $275 each—$29,425."

Q. What rate is that?—A. I didn't reckon it any more than what, in my judgment, the depreciation would equal on one of our fishing vessels.

By Mr. Dana:

Q. From your experience, what do you take to be the depreciation in a new vessel the first five years? Have you any means of knowing that? Have you inquired into that?—A. Well, the depreciation the first year on a new vessel is more than any other time.

Q. What do you suppose to be the depreciation on an average of a well-built vessel, built at Gloucester or Essex, in the fishing business, when well taken care of? I don't mean incurring any extraordinary expenses, or suffering from extraordinary negligence, but with good ordinary care taken of her?—A. The first year she would depreciate $1,200. That is, supposing her to cost $8,000.

By Sir Alexander Galt:

Q. Why should she depreciate more the first year than the second?—A. Because everything is new, and if at the end of a year you want to sell a new vessel, she will not bring so much. All these articles have to be renewed at the end of two years at the most—sails, rigging, and everything of that kind.

Q. Then it would seem she should depreciate more the second year.

By Mr. Dana:

Q. A little of that depreciation must be fancy. It is just like the ordinary case where second-hand goods sell for much less than brand new goods, although, practically, they may in some cases be almost as good as new?—A. Yes.

Q. Do you think a merchant, having to make up a profit and loss account and wishing to know his exact position at the end of a year on that trip, would allow that amount?—A. I think he would strike off one thousand two hundred dollars.

Q. That is, in making up an account with himself, in which case he has no motive for misrepresenting the value. It is based on the theory that if he had to sell her under fair average circumstances he would lose that amount?—A. Yes.

Q. Now, what do you think the depreciation would be at the end of five years?—A. I think a vessel built for $8,000 at the end of five years would not be worth more than $6,000, kept, of course, in good running order.

By Sir Alexander Galt:

Q. That would only be $800 depreciation for the last four years.

● By Mr. Dana :

Q. Now, does the rate of depreciation diminish as you go on ?—A. Yes, sir.

Q. Is the depreciation for the second year as great as for the first ?—A. Not so much, but it is more than the third year, because at the end of the third year she has a new suit of sails.

Q. She gets a new lease of life almost ?—A. Yes.

Q. Then after that year I suppose she always has a proper suit of sails, and the depreciation diminishes on that vessel ?—A. Yes.

Q. The period of greatest depreciation is from the time she is brand new to the time when she is not brand new ?—A. Yes.

By Mr. Foster :

Q. How many months are these vessels employed per annum on an average ?—A. It is stated in that summary exactly.

Q. Mr. Steele's vessels would be about the average of the whole fleet ?—A. Yes.

Q. You have called the average $$75 for the depreciation on a trip of four and a half months ?—A. Yes.

Q. Then that would be $550 depreciation for the year ?—A. Yes.

Q. That would be an average for the course of her life ?—A. Yes.

Q. The cost is assumed to be how much ?—A. That average depreciation is based on an average cost of $5,000.

By Mr. Dana :

Q. Have you any other tables except the little one that we threw out ?—A. No other tables. I have a description of how a voyage for mackerel-fishing is conducted.

Q. We won't have that at present ?—A. I have a statement of the quantity of fish furnished to the Army during the war.

Q. You were active in getting fish put into the rations of the Army ?—A. I was.

Q. You may state, without going into figures, perhaps, what effect that had upon the fishing interests of Gloucester during the time the war lasted ?—A. I think it improved it. It made a better market for the fish and gave them higher prices.

Q. Do you think it had a sensible effect ?—A. It increased the demand.

Q. Do your statistics enable you to state to what extent ?—A. I can give you the number of barrels of fish used in the Army.

Q. I mean the quantity sent from Gloucester ?—A. No, I can't do that.

Q. What was the quantity used in the Army annually. Give us one year as a specimen ?—A. In the year 1864 they used 5,569,000 pounds of pickled fish, which cost $395,547.26, and 6,156,858 pounds of dried fish, which cost $451,025.

By Sir Alexander Galt :

Q. Where is that taken from ?—A. It is taken from a letter of the Commissary General of Subsistence of the United States Army in reply to a letter I wrote him.

Q. That might be the cost as delivered to the Army ?—A. That is what the United States paid for it when they bought it.

By Mr. Dana :

Q. They delivered it at their own expense to the troops ?—A. I presume so.

Q. Now I would like to ask you somewhat the same question I did to another witness, but I want to put it beyond doubt. You know they make up the voyages, and the details go into those books. Suppose a fisherman wants to know how much he is charged for his provisions, he has the means of knowing it from the books of the owners ?—A. There are no provisions charged to him in our books, unless he is on what is called winter-shore fishing.

Q. That I don't care so much about. But whatever the items are that are charged to him, he has the means of knowing by the accounts given him, and also by examination of the books, if he wishes it ?—A. Yes.

Q. And every owner of a vessel in Gloucester has to have a trip-book, doesn't he, and to have his accounts regularly kept ?—A. Yes. Some keep it on a sheet of paper and some in books. But all the trips have to be made up, so as to show to the master and crew.

Q. A sharesman is not obliged to take his share in money, is he ? He has a right to take it in fish ?—A. Yes, half his fish—that is, after he pays his share of the expenses.

Q. Of course he has to pay the incumbrances, but he has a right, instead of receiving their market value, to take them himself and do what he pleases with them ?—A. Yes.

Q. That is to say, he does not make a contract that he will take pay, but by his contract he may either take his fish or money ?—A. That is just it.

Q. Well, do they do that ever; that is, take their own fish ?—A. I have known instances where they took their own fish; where one of the crew was going home and he thought he could get more for the mackerel at home than it could be sold for there. (*See explanatory note below.*)

Q. Now, what class of men constitute the fishing crews generally that go from Gloucester ? Of course we know that there are some bad men, but how are they as a general thing ?—A. I think they are a very good class of men indeed.

Q. It is common, is it, for men to change from the post of master or skipper to a hand ?—A. Yes, I have known instances where several skippers have been aboard our vessel.

Q. Ex-skippers, I suppose, we would call them. There have been several, you say, on one vessel ?—A. Yes.

Q. Are the modes of doing business, the rates and charges and that sort of thing, well understood in Gloucester ?—A. I think they are.

Q. Well, is Gloucester a place where there is or can be any kind of monopoly or combination among the people who sell to the fishermen or furnish them or is it competition ?—A. Competition, decidedly so.

Q. Now, I need not ask you the question, but is Gloucester a place in daily and hourly connection by railway, telegraph, and newspaper with the rest of the country. They have the morning and evening papers from Boston every day, don't they ?—A. Yes.

Q. Now, I want you to tell me when a vessel comes in from her fishing—we have heard it in part, but tell me what is the course of business when she arrives at the wharf ? In the first place, the wharf belongs to the owner or to some owner ?—A. Yes ; the wharf belongs to the owner or fitter. A vessel may be owned by outside parties and come there to fit.

Q. There is no separate charge made for the use of the wharf in those cases ?—A. No.

Q. That goes into what the owner has to furnish ?—A. Yes.

Q. How is wharf property, high or low ?—A. Wharf property is very luable is Gloucester.

Q. I suppose that, like all property, it has decreased in value, owing the general depression. Is that so or not ?—A. Well, I don't know any wharves that have been sold in Gloucester.

Q. Well, it may be that wharf property has held its own more than operty in houses and land. How do you think that is ?—A. I think has not diminished so much as houses and lands up in town.

Q. I suppose there is a limit of available wharf property. You have ur harbor, and the wharf property must be cut out of that ?—A. Yes.

Q. Now, when the vessel comes to the wharf, what is the first thing ne ?—A. The first thing done is that the mackerel are hoisted out of e vessel to the wharf.

Q. By the crew ?—A. By the crew, with a hired horse.

Q. They have got beyond hoisting it themselves ?—A. Yes ; as soon it is landed each man knows his own fish by the private mark which s been put on the head of the barrel, and each stands by itself. The rrels are then unheaded by one of the crew and the fish pitched into e culling-crib, which is 2½ feet wide and 4 feet long. At each end ere is a culler—that is, a man who selects the mackerel as No. 1, 2, d 3. From this culling-crib they are thrown into the culling-tub, cording as the culler regards them as No. 1, 2, or 3.

Q. Who are those cullers ?—A. They are men experienced in that nd of business—men of good judgment, because you have to rely on e judgment of the culler, under our laws, in regard to the quality of e mackerel. It is left to his judgment.

Q. Well, the owner is bound by the act of the culler as well as the fisherman ?—A. Certainly.

Q. Have they ever been rejected ?—A. I have not known of it.

Q. These cullers are sometimes on one wharf and sometimes on another ? A. Yes. When these tubs are full enough, two of the crew take them ld lift them on the scales, where they are weighed by the weigher. As on as they are weighed he cries out "barrels one, two, three," as the se may be, and the captain marks it on his memorandum-book. Then 'o of the crew empty the tub into the packing-crib, and there the ew's part of it ends. Then at the packing-crib it is packed in barrels ld marked according to the grade. Then a half bushel of salt is put with it, and the cooper takes it, puts in the head, and gives it a roll the wharf. The barrel rolls down the wharf to where it is bored by e pickler.

Q. That is, he makes a bung-hole ?—A. Yes ; and then he puts a fun- ll in and pickles it. Then he allows it to stand awhile, and fills it up ;ain until it is full of pickle. Then he brings it up, sets it on end, and is branded with the deputy inspector's name and the grade of the fish. is then turned out ready for market.

Q. Are the crew usually present and taking an interest in this ?—A. es ; they are right on hand until it is weighed off, and then they don't re any more about it.

Q. Now, do the owners and outfitters of vessels keep shops for the le of clothing and such things ?—A. No ; there is very little if any pt by the outfitters. It used to be so.

Q. So these men who have clothes to purchase generally go to other aces ?—A. Yes.

Q. If they have cash or credit they make their own bargains ? If they ant the aid of the owner what do they do ?—A. They get an order on storekeeper.

Q. And the owner then becomes responsible ?—A. Yes.

Q. Then after the voyage is up what clothing he has had is char
on his private account ?—A. Yes.

Q. Now, what does the owner get for the risk ? He takes the ris
the life of the man and also of the catch not amounting to enou
What profit does he get for that ?—A. He gets a profit owing to
competition among the clothes-dealers. They allow a certain perc
age to the owner of the vessel for giving these orders.

Q. How much is that ? Is it based on the wholesale prices or as
bargain may be made ?—A. It is based principally on the whole
prices. They sell to the outfitter at the wholesale prices and charge
goods to the men at the retail prices at the store.

Q. The man knows what he will be charged on the outfitter's books
A. Yes.

Q. Now, would it be possible for those who have neither credit
cash to do any better than that ?—A. I think not.

Q. I suppose if they went without any credit or cash, or any on
become responsible in this way, they would hardly make a purchas
all ?—A. I think not. The risk is too great. As a general thing
storekeeper would rather have the order of the owner.

Q. Now, in case any of the crew thinks anything is going wrong,
does not get satisfaction, are there not plenty of lawyers ready to t
up their cases ?—A. It is to be assumed there are.

By Sir Alexander Galt :

Q. I did not understand him to answer the question as to the ou
ter's profit on the stores furnished on his credit ? The seaman gets
bill, with the rate put on the account to show him what he buys at ?—
Yes.

Q. That is what you call the retail rate. He can go from plac
place ?—A. Yes.

Q. Now, having got his bill at the retail rate, it is given to him on
understanding that before he gets the clothes the bill must be indorsed
A. He goes to the owner and says : "Here, I am going in your ve
and have no clothes. Give me an order on such and such a firm to
a suit of clothes or oiled clothes." He takes that order and goes
He knows what the clothes are worth, and will not pay extrava
prices.

Q. Now the question is what the outfitter gets as compensation fo
risk ?—A. He gets a profit out of the manufacturer, or rather the w
sale dealer. If he gives an order on Carter, a manufacturer of
clothes, Carter will sell them at the wholesale prices and charge t
on the account at the retail prices to the man.

Q. What is the percentage ?—A. I could not form any accurate
mate.

Q. As nearly as you can say ?—A. Some will pay more than ot
I don't think the average is more than 8 per cent., perhaps 10.

By Mr. Dana :

Q. What would the articles be that the men would buy at the d
ent stores ?—A. Clothing. Tobacco they would get at the outfi
store.

Q. The outfitter has tobacco ?—A. Yes.

Q. Do they buy anything but clothing in this way ?—A. I think
They only buy what they actually need to fit them out to go on
the vessel.

ßy Sir Alexander Galt:

case their families require assistance, is there any custom of sup-
,he families of the fishermen by the outfitters?—A. Yes; by let-
:m have supplies from the store and giving them cash.

that done upon half-pay orders, or anything of that sort?—A.
1ever had an order from a man that went for me. If his wife
,wn I always let her have provisions.

:y Mr. Dana:

> you think it is the custom to make advances either in cash or
-A. Yes, if they run up an account to more than the voyage
s, we check it.

; what rate are those goods charged?—A. I think the average
,e 10 per cent.

,u mean 10 per cent. on what?—A. I refer to the provision sup-
the families. I don't think they will average as much as that.

y Sir Alexander Galt:

ke, for instance, the case of a barrel of flour, or something of
t, what would the percentage be on that?—A. Well, a barrel of
1en I was in the business, was $8 or $10.

the percentage you name on which the goods are furnished a
,ge over the retail prices?—A. No, they could not go to the
and get it for cash avy cheaper than under this arrangement.

,w is the owner enabled to do that? You say they are furnished
, the same rate for which they would get those supplies, paying
A. Well, perhaps for a few months past the competition in gro-
,s been so great that for cash you could purchase at any price
se, and one grocer has gone up in consequence of that sort of

y Mr. Dana:

,t in fair average times the owners allow the families about the
: they could buy for with cash?—A. Yes.

here does the profit come from for the risk?—A. I do not be-
:y ever take that into consideration.

t, as a business transaction, they buy it at wholesale?—A.

en in these cases of goods allowed to the families is there any
ɔfit than the difference between wholesale and retail?—A. No;
hink there is, as far as my knowledge extends. I will not say
ιe firms in Gloucester. There have been many cases where gro-
,ve been sold in this way to the families of men who have never
ck.

ιe following day the witness requested leave to make an explan-
th regard to the right of one of the crew to take his share of
in place of its money value.. The explanation is to the follow-
ct: "The mackerel of the crew are all packed. If any one of
′ desires his share of fish instead of money, he can have it by
expenses, by requesting it of the agent of the schooner before
is sold.")

FRIDAY, *October* 12,]

The Conference met.

Examination of Major LOW resumed.

By Mr. Dana:

Question. Yesterday there was presented, but not explained
time, a history of 27 vessels; did you prepare this ?—Answer.
did.

Q. This gives a history, does it, of a series of vessels—twen
vessels—in a tabulated form. The first name is the Austerlitz, to
so much, number of hands so many; " fishing," I believe, mear
fishing ?—A. Yes; cod and halibut.

Q. The average hands fishing, 8; mackereling, 14. This gir
history down to 1868, when she was sold ? The statement also
what became of each vessel, whether sold or lost. The first o
gives the time engaged in cod and halibut fishing, the number of 1
and days each year, the time engaged in mackerel-fishing each ye
gross value of the catch each year, the vessel's share and the
share each year. The quantity of fish caught is put down in q
or barrels, according as it is mackerel or cod.

WITNESS. Might I be allowed to make an explanation regardin;
When I presented it yesterday, I intended to present it before tl
mary. The summary I presented in my evidence was a sumn
those abstracts.

Q. In the cost of a new schooner you gave yesterday, you h
item, " expense account." Have you the broadside that was 1
for the use of the Centennial ?—A. I can get it.

(The paper is produced, and explanation made that it cannot
into the case, as it was taken out of a frame, having been used
Centennial Exhibition, and brought here. It is a statement of t
of a new schooner, built in 1875, fitted for the mackerel-fishing
for sea, 67 tons.)

Q. This printed sheet was used at the Centennial ?—A. Yes ;
one of those framed and put around the tank in which we shov
models of fishing schooners.

Q. Are these the same vessels you gave in that paper ?—A.
made a slight alteration for the mackerel-catcher. That was v
show the cost of a schooner to fish off our own shores, and I
slight alteration to adapt it to the fishing in the gulf.

Q. Yes; and then you afterwards gave the difference betw
gulf-fishing vessels and a seiner on our own shores ?—A. Yes.

Q. I see you put the cost of fuel, light, and provisions at 40 cen
There has been some question whether that was not a large st
It is based on an actual voyage. I have with me the original doc
I asked different owners of vessels who had new schooners in tl
ent classes of fishing to furnish me with the cost of their schoo
such other information as they saw fit in relation to their sc
One of them gave me full details of the cost of running a schc
the whole season. I have the original papers that he handed n

Q. I suppose you would not like to part with them ?—A. I sh
like to, but, if required, I could put them in.

Q. Now take the items that make this 40 cents per day per n
Well, this vessel was engaged on the Grand Bank 302 days in t

)ut fishing with 12 men for a crew, and this is her bill for provisions
)02 days :

PROVISIONS.

tons coal	$115 00
cords wood	25 00
bbls. flour	168 00
" beef	214 50
" pork shoulders	89 25
" pork	84 00
bu. beans	10 00
lbs. rice	6 00
lbs. tea	35 50
bu. peas	5 00
gals. molasses	40 80
" vinegar	1 80
lbs. sugar	106 75
lbs. d. apples	19 00
lbs. cream tartar	8 50
lbs. saleratus	3 10
galls. kerosene	14 00
lbs. spice	10 00
lbs. soap	4 90
lbs. mustard	4 50
b. lbs. pept. sauce	50
Yeast cakes	2 50
Bread preparation	6 10
Lamp chimneys	4 00
Table salt	1 95
lbs. candles	1 50
doz. wicks	70
Bristol bricks	20
rolls stove polish	70
lbs. bread	12 00
lbs. coffee	7 75
bush. potatoes	66 40
bush. onions	12 00
bush. beets	3 00
bush. turnips	4 00
gross matches	12 00
lbs. lard	76 50
lbs. butter	147 00
lbs. fresh meat	31 30
Vegetables	30 00
bbls. water	40 00

1, 426 03

lave all the charges for that vessel that year.

They live pretty well on board these vessels ?—A. Yes; it is a well-
)n fact that they fare well on board the American schooners.

By Hon. Mr. Kellogg :

This is what the 40 cents per day is founded upon ?—A. Yes. I
observe that the peas seem pretty high, but they used split peas,
of them.

By Mr. Dana :

Now, is that a fair average cost for fitting out a vessel for that
?—A. I think it is ; because I know others have figured it up to 45
).

Now, how do you make out the 40 cents a day ? You haven't
) us that.—A. Well, it is got by dividing $1,426.03, the total cost,
)e number of men and the number of days. It is a fraction less
40 cents.

But there are some of those things that are not consumed. I sup-
they are destroyed. Of course there is more or less waste—such,

for instance, as chimneys for lamps.—A. Well, they are breakiṇ the time. There would not be much of that left when they got from their voyage.

By Sir Alexander Galt:

Q. That is a cod-fishing voyage?—A. Cod and halibut. It ᵥ apply to the Grand Banks or the Western Banks. All classes of vᵢ average about the same.

Q. Now, the trawl-gear is put down on this broadside as $1,00 a small fraction. Have you the items of that?—A. I have. The as follows:

Vessel 71 tons, cost $8,800. Fitted for trawling halibut.

TRAWL-GEAR.

Twine ....
8 baskets...
22 buoys ....
20 buckets...
46 files ....
1,483 pounds ground-lines...
346 pounds ganging-lines ....
26 knives ....
12 stones ....
32 staffs...
360 pounds buoy-line ....
4 dozen brooms..
52 gross hooks ....
23 pounds lobster-twine ....
5 dories..
Iron and copper tacks ....
4 shovels...
Anchors...
Oars and scoops...

1,

Any explanation in regard to this that may be required I can Some of the terms used are technical.

By Hon. Mr. Kellogg:

Q. There is a term ganging-lines.—A. That is the small line to the hooks are fastened.

By Mr. Dana:

Q. Now, you have here in this broadside the vessel's expense ac $1,823.85. Do they call that an expense account? Is that the waṣ entitle it on the books in making up the account?—A. No; it is ã in one account; all the things for the vessel are put in one ac These were separated for this special purpose.

Q. Now, you take this expense account; what period of time ₑ cover?—A. Three hundred and two days.

Q. Now, what are the items of the vessel's expense account They are as follows:

VESSEL'S EXPENSE.

Spunyarn ....
Parcelling...
Leather..
Jib hanks..
Nails..
Tinware, &c ....
1 anchor lost..
Topmast (broken)...
Paint and painting...

ʀay fee	$15 00
ꭇr	47 00
ᵼsmith	60 00
ꭋnter	65 00
ꞁaker's repairs	163 00
ꭋer for ice-house	43 00
ᴀnce	539 00
ꭋissions to skipper	465 00
ꭋs ballast	80 00
ꭋl gun	38 00
ꞃg rigging, &c	14 00
	1,823 85

Jib hanks are put in; they are part of the original furniture ?—
know; but they break some, probably, and have to be repaired.
You put in "Marine Railway"?—A. Well, all the vessels in Glou-
r are painted on the Marine Railway.
How many have you in town ?—A. Six.
They are hauled up there for repairs ?—A. Yes.
The insurance is for that period of 302 days ?—A. Yes.
They are insured in a mutual fishing-office ?—A. Yes.
I believe it was explained that that mutual office was got up by
rmen and owners for their own benefit, and conducted on principles
liar to themselves that were thought to be most beneficial. They
insure in the Boston offices ?—A. No, not now; the rates were too
for them.

By Sir Alexander Galt:
I understood this was an actual case for a particular vessel ?—A.
the name of the vessel is the Victor, belonging to Joseph O.
ᵼor.

By Hon. Mr. Kellogg:
Is the sum put in for insurance the actual sum paid ?—A. Yes.

By Mr. Dana:
Do you know how old a vessel she was ?—A. She was built in the
previous. I don't know what time of the year.

By Sir Alexander Galt:
This statement was prepared for the Centennial ?—A. Yes; it was
ꭇred for the Centennial, but we did not have room for it to go in
ꭋpace we had at the time at our disposal, and therefore we had to
ꞁ the abstract which is contained in the printed broadside.

By Mr. Dana:
You gave us your statement for the depreciation of the vessel ?—
es.
Did that include repairs ?—A. Yes, sir.
You put them into the depreciation ?—A. Yes, sir.
Now, that is considering the depreciation of the vessel to be the
ꞃnt laid out on her from year to year for repairs. But there will be
le more depreciation than that, would not there ? In point of fact,
ᵼ the depreciation of the vessel a little larger than the amount that
ꞁ be required to repair her ?—A. O, yes.
For instance, the substantial part of the ship, the hull from the
on all the way up, even if that does not require repairs, still if it
a certain number of years of age it will not sell as well as if new ?—
o, sir.

Q. Something lies in the fancy that a new vessel is worth more tha an old one?—A. There would be that.

Q. The next item here (on the broadside) is general charges, ice, bai salt, &c. These you have given us, haven't you?—A. No; they a called miscellaneous charges. They are as follows:

Miscellaneous charges.

200 tons ice	$600
Bait	354
Straw for bait	10
55 pair of nippers	27
Towage	50
75 lbs. powder	18
Medicine	25
Oil clothes, one man	15
18 hhds. salt	36
	1,135

Q. Can you give us the average life of a fishing-vessel? I don't mea how long she will remain a hulk, but take her from the time she is bui until she ceases to be fit to go.—A. I could not, right off, but I coul figure it out very shortly.

Q. Perhaps you don't care to give us a guess?—A. No.

By Sir Alexander Galt:

Q. I see you are leaving this item respecting the cost. I unders'o(him to say he would give us the result of the year's work of the vesse

By Mr. Dana:

Q. It is on that broadsheet, is it?—A. There is a recapitulation the on the broadside. (Reads.)

RECAPITULATION.

Trawl-gear	$1,023
Vessel's expense account	1,823
Provisions, &c	1,426
General charges	1,135
Total cost of running	5,408

By Mr. Davies:

Q. What was the owner's share?—A. $5,798.65, and the expenses that were $5,408.63. Then she made about $390.

By Mr. Dana:

Q. Now, you say that leaves a small profit to the owners?—A. Y

Q. Now, in making up the charges against the vessel, in the owne account, he credits himself with that $5,000, which is his share of catch after deducting certain expenses. You charge them enou against the ship to leave a small balance. You charge against it, course, the provision account, and the account for repairs?—A. Yes is all charged in one account without any division.

Q. Then, charging the repairs and charging the provision accou you leave that result, do you?—A. Yes, sir.

Q. Then, how do you include a fair compensation to the owner the use of his wharf and buildings and his own time?—A. That i profit he gets out of the fish after they are landed.

Q. There is no special charge made for them?—A. No; not to vessel.

Q. Well, is there any charge for depreciation on the vessel bey(

expenses of the repairs that are put upon her in that period of
e ?—A. No.

. You make no charge for depreciation, but you take it to be equal
he amount of the repairs ?—A. Well, I presume so.

By Mr. Foster:

. In the hypothetical case, yesterday, you allowed $550 for depreci-
n for the year; that $550, I understand, will have to pay for the
airs ?—A. Yes; I intended that to cover in the same proportion for
whole year.

. How much is charged for repairs in these items you give that
re up the amount,in the. broadside ?—A. It would seem that $100
ild be the amount included in that for repairs.

By Mr. Dana:

. Then it is perfectly understood that there is no special charge in
uection with the vessel for the use of the capital—what we call now
plant, the wharf and building which are his investment—but that he
s his compensation for all that in whatever charges are made for the
visions, fitting, &c. ?—A. Yes.

. Well, these men who are engaged in the fishing business in Glou-
er, are they workingmen themselves ?—A. Yes.

. Or are they men who put in their capital and let others take care
t ?—A. No; they are workingmen.

. In what sense are they workingmen ?—A. Well, most of them go
:he wharf and work just the same as a laborer on the wharf. They
to everything, and lend a hand when it is needed.

. Are they usually men who have had experience either in that busi-
s or as fishermen themselves?—A. They have.

. Now, would it be possible, do you think, from your long experience,
a man to make a living if he simply invested his capital, as a sort of
:y merchant, looking in at times to see how things went, if he didn't
e his personal attention to the business, and do a fair day's work
rseeing it ?—A. You mean whether he would get a living out of it?
.ink not.

. Are there any such cases down there?—A. You mean vessel-owners,
'esume ? No.

. Take the case of persons who don't themselves look after the work,
merely invest capital in the fishing and have others looking after it.
here such a thing as that known in Gloucester ?—A. No.

. It would not be an investment of any account if you undertook to
est your money and leave others to take care of it ?—A. I don't know
ut that. I don't know any instance where it is done.

. What is your opinion ? Have you a clear opinion ?—A. My opin-
1s that they would not make a great deal on their investments.

. What do you mean ?—A. Well, I mean that they would not get a
y large percentage.

. Do you think they would get anything ?—A. I think they would
a fair interest on it.

. Would they get more than that ?—A. No, I don't think they would.

. Perhaps you didn't understand me ; I don't mean where a person
i his capital to owners, because in that case they will pay interest ;
' suppose he was to invest his money in a fishing-vessel, simply pay-
for his share ?—A. As I understand, you ask whether the owners
l fitters of vessels in Gloucester make anything in their business ?

. No, because they incorporate skill and give their daily labor to the
rk. But take the case where a man simply pays for his share in a fish-

ing-vessel and gives no attention to the business. Take the cas
non-resident. For instance, suppose I should buy a tenth part of
sel and pay my proper share of the expenses, but put in no skill or
tion or time of my own ?—A. I think you would lose it.

Q. Are there any such cases now that you know of, at Glou
where people have simply invested in that way, incorporating no
attention, time, labor, or skill of their own ?—A. I don't know of

Q. Do you know of an attempt of that sort at Salem ?—A. I d

Q. How long ago ?—A. I can't exactly tell. It is within ten y

Q. What was it, a sort of joint-stock company ?—A. Yes. Tw
moved from Gloucester with their vessels and formed a stock cor

Q. Were they capable, competent men ?—A. Yes.

Q. There were no frauds you know of ?—A. No.

Q. Now, to show what the opinion is generally of the value of
these vessels, is it difficult or not to get money on mortgage
rates on a fishing-vessel ?—A. No; I think they would have to
extra rate of interest.

Q. Are there many such cases of mortgages of vessels ?—A. (
I presume so.

Q. Do you know what interest they have to pay ?—A. I don't.

Q. Now, as to selling vessels, is it an easy thing to sell a fishing-
if a man, for instance, desired to go out of the fishing business;
thing that can be depended upon ?—A. No; there is always a gre
rifice where vessels are sold at a forced sale.

Q. I don't mean a forced sale; but suppose he takes time enoug
gives notice, and sells at a fair open auction sale, is there a loss
ally ?—A. There is usually.

Q. And in settling up estates, how do vessels usually turn ou
As a general thing, poorly; during the war there were times wh
sel property sold to advantage.

Q. For paper ?—A. Yes.

Q. Now, is the reason of this that these vessels, being built sp
for fishing-vessels, they can't profitably be run except by person
will incorporate in the fishing business their own time and att
and skill ?—A. Yes.

Q. An outside purchaser does not want to buy them ?—A. No.

Q. Explain to the Commission how codfish are now packed and
—A. When the crew have been settled with, and the fish hav
weighed, they are pitched into a dory filled by one man from a
eight men wash the fish, and after they are washed they throw
into a wheelbarrow and they are wheeled into the fish-house an
ered there to a salter, who salts them, and he has one man to bri
the salt. They take four bushels of salt to a butt, and that ga
take care of fifty butts in a day; then they are kept in the bu
less than ten days, after which they are water-hawsed, by being
from the butts and piled up in piles about three feet high, to dr
pickle from them; this takes two men, and they were employ
days on the trips I have in my mind; fifty butts a day are tw
work.

By Sir Alexander Galt:

Q. How many quintals are there in a butt ?—A. There are abo
quintals to a butt. Then after they come from being water-haws
are spread on flakes to dry; it takes four men two days to whe
out, i. e., fifty butts. The flakes have three-cornered strips na
frames resting on horses, in such a way that the frames can b

ι and packed away; while they are drying on the flakes it takes men to tend them, and wheel them in and pile them up after they ry.

Now they are dried codfish. What is the custom now as to pre-ıg them for market? The merchants of Gloucester have made cester the distributing point. It used to be Boston?—A. Yes; send them to all parts of the United States direct. They take ι fish and cut the tails off, strip them of their skin, and take their .bone out. That is called boneless cod. Then some of them split ıgthwise, and others roll them up into rolls, cut them across the roll, ıtand them upon end in boxes. There are several different ways of ıging them in the boxes.

What is the usual size of those boxes?—A. They are 10, 20, 40, 60, ıd 100 pounds.

Now, they send those boxes all the way from 10 to 100 pounds. ıerly codfish were all sold whole, were they not?—A. Yes.

How long has this custom of trimming them and packing them in ι been in existence?—A. Since 1870.

Has it been found successful?—A. Yes; because it has opened up ater market for the codfish. Before that their bulk prevented their ; distributed so well. Now, being in a portable shape, they go all the Union. Anywhere they can transport a box of bread they can port a box of fish. It makes labor for a great many hands.

Now Gloucester has been, as we have seen by its statistics, with in fluctuations, a place of considerable pecuniary resources justify-considerable valuation. Will you be so good as to tell the Com-on what resources there are in Gloucester to account for the valu-of its property, besides what is traceable to the fishing business? ıe work of the merchants in connection with the handling of the ve allow to go in as a part of the fishing industry.—A. There are ıe railways.

I don't care about that. You say you have half a dozen perhaps, y supported by the fishing business.—A. We have others coming other places for repairs, which makes labor for calkers and painters. Then you have large vessels that go to the Mediterranean, Portu-nd the West Indies?—A. Some few; not much of that. We have tensive salt business.

Take the granite, for instance; what is the valuation of the granite ess of Gloucester?—A. The industrial pursuits of Gloucester pro-a million and a half per annum outside of the fisheries.

Granite is one of the principal ones?—A. Yes.

You have an unlimited supply of granite, I suppose?—A. Yes.

I mean something that you can cut, that lies in quarries?—A. Yes. ıaluation is largely increased by it.

In the first place there is a great deal of quarrying going on and ıt many men employed in quarrying stone?—A. Yes.

That stone is used for pavements in the cities and for house-build--A. Yes; it finds a good market.

A good many vessels are employed carrying it, or do you send it ıl?—A. No; it is sent by steamers and vessels.

Gloucester exports its granite as prepared from the quarries in the borhood?—A. Yes.

Are there any other reasons for the increase in the valuation?—A. summer residences bring in considerable.

You mean persons who do business and whose personal property

and investments are elsewhere?—A. Yes, and who have summ
deuces in Gloucester.

Q. That is because of the salubrity of the climate, and the
scenery? There has been a great deal of that?—A. Yes.

Q. Parts of Gloucester have been built up entirely?—A. Yes.

Q. Manchester and Magnolia?—A. Yes.

Q. Then down towards Eastern Point Light?—A. Well, there
or five summer boarding-houses there.

Q. Then you have summer boarding-houses, and the hotels in
depend to a large extent on summer boarders?—A. Yes.

Q. Now, has all that led to an increase in the value of lands?—

Q. The soil is not very fertile, I believe?—A. No. It is rock;

Q. And, as I recollect, there is not a great quantity of it?—A

Q. Its value, independent of what is given to it as a place of
residence, would be small?—A. I think it would.

Q. Now, do you recollect anything else besides what you have
tioned—granite, outside business, and summer residence? Ar
cases of men in Boston, whose business is in Boston, and who
bona-fide home is there, but who yet reside in Gloucester long en
pay taxes there?—A. Yes.

Q. In some cases, men of very large fortune?—A. Yes.

Q. A man died there the other day worth a couple of million
He was a manufacturer and general merchant living in Bo:
A. Yes.

Q. One question about insurance. Does that company whi
speak of insure to the full value of the vessel?—A. They do no

Q. Do you recollect to what proportion?—A. Yes.

Q. Do you recollect whether it is three fourths or seven-eigl
A. I won't say positively.

Q. But there is a portion that the owner has to pay himself?—

Q. Do they pay every loss, or only over a certain percentage
value?—A. Only over a certain percentage. I think it is 12 per

Q. At all events, whatever the percentage, there may be a
losses that the owner has to bear himself, that do not amount to
to make a partial loss.?—A. No. If they are run into, for instan
damaged by one another, they do not get anything, unless it i
certain percentage of the value.

Q. Have you a copy of the fishing articles of Gloucester fisher
A. No.

Q. Can you state from your own knowledge of their provi
how they have ever been construed, as to the legal right of the
take their own fish, subject to the incumbrances. Do you ki
that is?—A. No. The cases of fishermen wanting to take his
are very rare indeed. They are always satisfied with the se
they make with the owners.

Q. We should like to have the book which contains the b;
the insurance company; also, a copy of the cod-fishing arti
mackerel-fishing articles. That would be interesting.—A. I
them.

Q. There was a man named Joseph Campbell, of Souris, Pr
ward Island, examined as a witness. He was asked: "In 18
vessel did you go in?" and answered, "the Daniel McPhee."
asked: "Where did you go?" and answered, "We went to the l
landed and took dories and went up to Seven Islands again.
got 80 barrels at the same place as before. From that we wen
up to a place called Boubou, and got twenty or thirty barrels th

shore. We then crossed to the southern side to Griffin's Cove and
l up about twenty or thirty barrels there. We then crossed to
, then to Bay Chaleurs, picking up more or less every day. We
ine-fishing then. We gave up the boats after leaving Seven Is-
We went to North Cape, Prince Edward Island, to finish our trip.
ade only one trip and went home." Then he was asked: " What
ur catch ?" and answered, " We got 280 barrels; that was in 1860."
ie was asked: " Did you take them outside the limits ?" and an-
l, " We did some." Then to the question, " What proportion ?"
wered, " Sixty or seventy barrels at the outside." Now you have
equested to examine into this matter. Have you any personal
edge of the Daniel McPhee ?—A. I owned a portion of her in 1860.
You may state from your own knowledge what was the truth of
atter ?—A. To the best of my knowledge Joseph Campbell was
the schooner. She landed 17 barrels of mackerel, and was gone
three months.
'hat you state of your own knowledge ?—A. Yes.
You mean that was the whole trip ?—A. That is what she packed

Iave you looked to see whether this man was in the vessel ?—A.

'here was no such man ?—A. No, sir; I can give you the names
crew if you want them.
Io matter. Now, the same witness is asked, and answers as fol-

1861, what did you do ?—A. I was in the R. H. Oakes, Captain Nasen.
iat time did you come down ?—A. The 15th of July.
is that early ?—A. It is not early. It is a fair time. We did not find them bite
'e first fished, and we went up to Bay Chaleurs. We got about 120 barrels
,bout 90 barrels inside and the rest outside.
at would be 30 barrels outside ?—A. Yes, about that. We fished off Miscou
about 20 or 30 barrels off shore. We then came down the shore to Escu-
.nd picked up more or less every day along the shore.
,se in or off ?—A. Close in.
here did you get your next catch ?—A. We got 5 or 6 barrels along the shore to
'ard of the island (Prince Edward Island). There we got 70 or 80 barrels in
close in.
.thin the limits ?—A. Between two and three miles.
iat was the total result ?—A. One hundred and thirty barrels.
iat did you do with them ?—A. We took them back to Gloucester.
i you make only one trip ?—A. I made only one trip in her. I left her at Glou-

iat were fish bringing then ?—A. They were low. In 1861 mackerel brought
: to $13 and $14 a barrel. That was the year the war broke out.

low, can you tell us about the R. H. Oakes and this man Camp-
A. The R. H. Oakes in 1861 fitted about the last of June and
:d October 26. The vessel packed out 225¼ barrels of mackerel,
hich Campbell's share was $39.01.
[e was on board that time ?—A. Yes; the number ones of this
d for $7; number twos, $5 1/16; and the number threes at $3.
hen the same witness is asked, and answers as follows:

l you fish any more that year ?—A. I went home and fished on the home shore;
:he American shore, in the fall of 1862, in the Daniel McPhee.
iat did you catch there ?—A. We caught 40 barrels.

ow, what can you tell us about fishing on the American shore in
niel McPhee, in the fall of 1862 ?—A. In 1862 the schooner Dan-
'hee packed out on the fall trip, from October 4 to November 8,
rrels of mackerel.

165 F

Q. Whát do you make of his statement that it was 40 barrels ?. can't make anything out of it.

Q. Now, there is a man, Ronald McDonald. On page 396 of tl timony he is asked and answers as follows:

Q. Have you fished in American vessels ?—A. Yes.
Q. How many years ?—A. About seven summers.
Q. When did you first go in an American schooner ?—A. About 1859 or 1860.
Q. What is the name of the first vessel ?—A. Daniel McPhee, Gloucester, McPhee, captain.
Q. Where did you fish ?—A. We began to fish along the island toward Nortl Prince Edward Island.
Q. And you fished along at all the usual places ?—A. Yes.
Q. What did you catch that year ?—A. About 200 barrels for the season.
Q. How far from shore did you usually fish ?—A. We fished mostly all over t The principal part of the fish we got on the Canada shore and Cape Breton shc along the island. We caught a few on Bank Bradley, and some up northward Margaree. The principal part we got on the Cape Breton shore.

Now, can you tell us anything about this man in the Daniel Mc either in 1859 or 1860 ?—A. In 1859 she was on the stocks. .

Q. Did she afterwards go off under command of Daniel McPl A. Yes.

Q. To the gulf ?—A. Yes.

Q. With what result ?—A. The first trip was 17 barrels of. mac of which Ronald McDouald's share was 35 cents. On the secon she got 122½, and Ronald McDonald was not one of the crew.

Q. Now, there is a deponent named William H. Molloy, whos davit was put in on behalf of the British Government. He says:

The result of my last year's operations is as follows:
Total catch thirty-seven hundred quintals for the season, three Banking trips thereof about seventeen thousand dollars; expenses of wages, crew's share of ` outfit and provisions was about twelve thousand dollars, leaving a clear profi owner of about five thousand dollars. The owner derives a considerable profit al the difference between the prices he allows the crews for their share of fish, an it is worth to him in the market, by which he would gain on the quantity abov about eighteen hundred dollars.

What have you to say to that ?—A. I think that Captain Mullo not seem to understand his business. In the first place he exagg the number of vessels that are on the Banks from Gloucester, an he goes on and gives an account of the profits. Take his own ment. I have made up a little memorandum. The expenses of tl sel, he says, are $12,000; shrinkage and cost of curing 3,700 qu at $1 per quintal, is $3,700, which gives $15,700. It sells 30,13 tals, dry, for $4.80 per quintal, equal to $14,462.40, leaving a $1,237.60 instead of $6,800 gain.

Q. Then you say his own calculation does not produce the res A. Not what he states.

Q. In point of fact, has he made his statement correctly ? should say that 3,700 quintals of codfish caught by a vessel one was a very large catch, and to make three trips, and make a fu age each trip, is a remarkably successful year's voyage.

Q. Then he speaks of the difference between the price allow crew for their share of the fish, and what it is worth in the mark says the owner would gain on the quantity above stated about If he takes the value of the fish in the same state in which t landed they are worth no more to the owners than the crew ?—A

Q. Their superior value is the result of labor and skill afterw upon them ?—A. Yes. Fish are never bought in Gloucester knowledge, by the quintal from a vessel. The price of fish la was $2.75 per 100 pounds from the vessel, green.

By Mr. Whiteway:

Q. Is not that a quintal ?—A. 114 pounds are a quintal.

By Mr. Dana:

Q. He further says:

The owner in my case above cited settled with the crew at two dollars and seventy-five cents per quintal as weighed out of the vessel, the market value of which fish when cured was four dollars eighty cents per quintal ; the loss in weight, which is very trifling, and labor in curing, would not cost more than one dollar per quintal.

A. I took his own figures when I made my estimate.

Q. Is that a correct statement ?—A. I took his statement for that.

By Sir Alexander Galt:

Q. How do you think it is ?—A. I don't suppose it is a great way out of the way, taking into consideration the rent of the wharf and so forth.

By Mr. Dana:

Q. About $1 per quintal ?—A. I should think so. I have not figured it up to get it exactly, but he is not a great way out of the way.

Q. Is there anything else in his statement ?—A. He makes a comparison of two vessels; one under the Washington Treaty with the privilege of going into Newfoundland and buying fresh bait, and he reckons that that vessel would make three trips a season, while the vessel not under the Washington Treaty, and restricted from going in there, would only make one trip.

Q. What has the Washington Treaty to do with the right to go in there and buy bait ?—A. I don't know.

Q. Suppose it had, what has that to do with three trips ?—A. It is a fallacious statement in regard to three trips in comparison with one, because I think our vessels will make as many trips without the privilege of going into Newfoundland as they can with it.

By Mr. Davies:

Q. You have spoken of the statements made by Captain Campbell and Roland McDonald with regard to the vessel called Daniel McPhee ?—A. I have.

Q. Are you owner of the vessel ?—A. I was.

Q. And you have your books here ?—A. I have not.

Q. When were you requested to look up the accuracy of Campbell's statement—since you came here ?—A. No, in Gloucester.

Q. And what did you do in order to test its accuracy? I suppose, regarding that portion where he states where the fish were taken, you have nothing to say ?—A. No.

Q. You deny the accuracy of the statement that so many were taken ? —A. I do.

Q. Have you a statement of the names of the crew for the year ?—A. I have a statement of the crew's names on that first trip. The names are as follows: Daniel McPhee, master; Ronald McDonald, Michael McDonald, H. Sinclair, Alex. Cameron, George M. Reed, Joseph McDonald, Joseph McPhee, John Rogers, Joseph Silva, Daniel McIntire, William Wilder West, Thomas Johnson, Paul McNeil. She landed her dories when she returned with that trip.

Q. Having been requested to examine the accuracy of this statement, did you take the trouble to look at your books for more than one year to see whether there had been a mistake in the year ?—A. I did.

Q. What did you find ?—A. I did not find any.

Q. Will you give me a statement of the returns made by the vessel for the year preceding and following?—A. In 1861 he testified he was on the R. H. Oakes, another of my vessels.

Q. I ask you to give me the return of the vessel in 1861?—A. I don't understand what you mean by return.

Q. A statement of the number of barrels of mackerel landed?—A. I can give you the number of barrels of mackerel landed.

Q. And the names of the crew in her?—A. Yes.

Q. I observe you have your book with you?—A. Yes; my trip-book for 1861 and 1862, not for 1860.

Q. You did not bring the book for the year in regard to which we are speaking?—A. The book is not in existence.

Q. How did you get at this?—From my journal.

Q. Did you bring your journal?—A. I did not.

Q. You did not bring the book itself relating to the very year on which this man testified, and the correctness of whose testimony you dispute?—A. No.

Q. You brought a book relating to the following year?—A. The only trip-book I had.

Q. You brought a book for the following year?—A. For the following two years.

Q. Did it not strike you as a little curious that, when asked to dispute the accuracy of a man's statement, you should dispute it and bring a book relating to the following year to that in question, and leave the book at home that would settle the question?—A. I thought that my evidence and the list of the crew would be enough. I am on my oath.

Q. So was Campbell. Why did you bring the book for the next year? You were not asked to verify or dispute any statement for the next year?—A. No.

Q. Why did you omit to bring the book for the year respecting which you were asked to contradict Campbell's statement?—A. I brought the trip-book which shows the catches of mackerel.

Q. You say you lost the previous trip-book?—A. He was in another vessel of mine afterward.

Q. If you have lost that trip-book, how are you able to tell exactly what catch he made?—A. It is entered in my journal.

Q. Is each man's account transferred to the journal?—A. Yes.

Q. So that the journal would have done just as well as the trip-book?—A. It is a heavier and more bulky book.

Q. But it would have all the information?—A. I presume it would. I could have brought it, but I had Mr. Steele's books, which are very heavy.

Q. I notice that Capt. Joseph Campbell, of Souris, who was examined very nearly the beginning of this Commission, and Ronald McDonald, who was called toward the close, there being, I think, four or five weeks between the times at which they were called, testified on oath the facts respecting that vessel, and with the exception of the number of barrels spoken to by them, on which there is only a small difference, they agree with regard to the trip, the places where the mackerel were taken, and everything?—A. Yes.

must be a mistake about the year?—A. Here is the record for 1861. The vessel was not built in 1859.

Q. Campbell said:

We went to the bay. We landed and took dories and went up to the Seven Islands again. There we got 80 barrels at the same place as before. From that we went further up to a place called Boubon and got twenty or thirty barrels there close to the shore. We then crossed to the southern side, to Griffin's Cove, and picked up about twenty or thirty barrels there. We then crossed to Gaspé, then to Bay Chaleurs, picking up more or less every day. We were line-fishing then. We gave up the boats after leaving Seven Islands. We went to North Cape, Prince Edward Island, to finish our trip. We made only one trip, and went home.

Q. What light will the book for 1861 throw on the matter ?—A. It merely gives the names of the crew and what they caught. The vessel was not built in 1859.

Q. One of the witnesses stated that fishermen sometimes enter themselves under different names. Is that a fact within your knowledge ?—A. They sometimes do.

Q. It is possible Campbell may have entered himself under a different name in that vessel ?—A. That is true.

Q. Is this the return of the trips into the bay, or of the trips on your shore ?—A. The trips to the bay; on the other side is a return of shore trips.

Q. Are those Mr. Steele's books ?—A. No; my own.

Q. How are you able to state at this distance of time which refers to bay and which to shore trips, with the trips not divided ?—A. By the time of year.

Q. The shore trips will be after the vessels return in October ?—A. Yes.

Q. It seems by this that the vessel took 80 barrels on the shore. That is just what Campbell said :

Q. Only 40 barrels. That was in 1861 that you got 80 barrels there in the fall trip, and in 1862 you got 40 barrels ?—A. Yes.

That is right, within six barrels ?—A. In the fall of 1861 was he in the Daniel McPhee? Is his name among the crew for that shore-trip ?

Q. His name does not appear here (in the book). If he was there he must have been under another name ?—A. I don't think he was in her in the fall trip. Does he say he was with Captain Hunter ?

Mr. DAVIES. The preceding questions were the following :

Q. Did you fish any more that year ?—A. I went home and fished on the home-shore, that is, the American shore, in the fall of 1862, in the Daniel McPhee.
Q. What did you catch there ?—A. We caught 40 barrels.

By Sir Alexander Galt :

Q. Do you know Campbell ?—A. I don't remember him; I would know him if I saw him.

By Mr. Davies :

Q. Do you know whether the Daniel McPhee made more than one shore-trip in the fall of 1862 ?—A. In 1862, from July 27 to October 4, she was bay-fishing; from October 4 to November 8, shore-fishing.

Q. Do your vessels, fishing on your shore, make short or long trips ?—A. Sometimes short and sometimes long.

Q. If the vessel made two trips, his statement may be perfectly consistent with yours ?—A. She was only employed in 1862 one month and four days on the shore.

Q. He says about three weeks. . Is it not possible she may have made two trips ?—A. I don't know.

Q. Is Captain McPhee at Gloucester ?—A. He is dead.

Q. What is your impression with regard to the statements made by these two men, corroborating each other substantially, and made at different times ?—A. My impression is that they are mistaken altogether in regard to their catch and where they fished.

Q. How would you know where they fished; you were not tl
A. No.

Q. Therefore you cannot know personally; why, then, do yo
that statement ?—A. Because, in the fall of the year, on the
trip, they never got it at Seven Islands with dories, and she lan
dories when she came home on her first trip.

Q. Campbell says they commenced the trip at Seven Islands;
prepared to contradict that ?—A. I am.

Q. In what way ?—A. Because she returned home having caug
17 barrels.

Q. I am speaking regarding the places where the fish were ca
A. She left her dories at Gloucester after the first voyage. The
not get 280 barrels with her dories when they were on my wharf

Q. I am asking you with reference to places where they fished
say you can contradict Campbell's statement; how do you contra
—A. I cannot contradict it from personal knowledge.

Q. How can you state you believe it to be incorrect ?—A. Fr
dence I know is in existence in regard to it.

Q. To what evidence do you refer ?—A. I refer to a depositior
hands of counsel.

Q. You are speaking in regard to some deposition in the h;
counsel, and you base your evidence on that ?—A. I do not.

Q. That is the affidavit of another man; put that aside at j
From your own knowledge, can you pretend to say that Campbell
ment is not correct as to where he fished ?—A. I cannot believe i
when a man says he fished in a certain place, when he says they
one barrel here and eighty barrels there, and I know the vess
packed out 17 barrels; I cannot believe the statement to be true

Q. It is unfortunate that the trip-book for 1860 is not here,
regret it more than anything else. My little girl asked me last
a book, and I cut the leaves out, never supposing it would be

Q. Can you tell me of any other vessel in 1860 which return
a trip in Bay Chaleurs with 17 barrels or anything like that ?—
schooner Annah, another of my vessels, returned from the bay
barrels.

Q. What size was she ?—A. She was about 50 tons.

Q. What time of the year did she go into the bay ?—A. She v
July, and returned 12th September.

Q. What was the highest catch made by any of your vess
year ?—A. 336½ barrels.

Q. Will you explain to the Commission what this statement
to be ?—A. A table showing the voyages of my vessels duri
1861, and 1862.

Witness handed in the following statement:

Name of vessel	Year	Hands	Value of vessel	Halibut and cod fishing		To—	Value of catch	Vessel's share (Crew's same.)	First trip mackereling.	Hands	Barrels	Value.	1 Vessel's share.	Second trip mackereling.	Hands	Barrels	Value.
Schr. Cynisca	1860	10	$3,730	Cod-fishing and 10 trips trawling,	Feb.	Oct. 23	$2,522 45	$3,866 63	Oct. 26 to Nov. 18, 23 days, shore.	11	25½	$212 04	$61 2?				
Do	1861			Cod-fishing and trawling, 7 trips.	Mar.	Oct. 26		1,075 64	Oct. 26 to Nov. 11, 2 m. 1 d., Gulf St. L.		54	1,259 29	562 0?	Sept. 12 to Oct. 13, Am. shore.	13	208½	
Schr. C. C. Davis	1860		3,300	do	Jan.	July 5		1,633 35	July 10 to Sept. 11, 2 m. 1 d., Gulf St. L.				427 01	Oct. 26 to Nov. 29, shore.	12	34½	$299 75
Do	1861	10		Cod-fishing and trawling, 6 trips.	Jan.	July 11	2,918 23	985 19	July 11 to Oct. 24, 3 mos. 13 d., Gulf.	15	209½	1,259 29	936 37	41 3 to 41 18, shore.	12	132	590 87
Do	1862	9		Cod-fishing and trawling, 8 trips.	Feb.	July 11	3,977 67	1,793 22	July 11 to Oct. 2, 2 mos. 21 d., Gulf.	15	263½	2,018 57	270 7?	Sept. 14 to Oct. 8, shore.	12	32½	
Schr. Annah	1860	1	2,000	Cod-fishing, 6 trips Georges.	Mar.	July 1		689 56	July 5 to Sept. 17, 2 m. 7 d., Gulf St. L.	12	41	08	89 52	Sept. 12 to Nov. 19, Gulf.	14	129½	
Schr. Daniel McPhee	1860	3	3,500	Cod-fishing and trawling, 3 trips.	Mar.	June 2		1,047 76	June 13 to Sept. 12, 3 m., Gulf of St. L.	14	17		170 5?	Oct. 14 to Nov. 15, shore.	13	88½	645 18
Do	1861	10		Cod-fishing and trawling 9 mos. 4 days, 8 trips.	Dec.	Sept. 28	3,210 16	1,409 31	Oct. 9 to Oct. 14, 5 days, shore.	13	86½	496 56	869 8?	Oct. 4 to Nov. 8, sh rn.	14	230½	1,034 56
Do	1862	10		Trawling, 6 trips.		July 21	2,925 19	1,155 13	July 27 to Oct. 4, Gulf, 2 mos. 7 d.	14	244	2,164 34	1,529 55	Sept. 21 to Nov. 21, shore.	14	158½	1,061 79
Schr. Ella F. Bartlett	1860		3,600						June 1 (21) to Sept. 18, Gulf, 3 m. 27 d.	14	207		462 57	Sept. 27 to Nov. 13, shore.	14		
Do	1861	9		Cod-fishing and trawling, 4 trips.	Mar.	June 21	3,157 90	994 96	June 21 to Sept. 30, 3 mos. Gulf.	14	275	1,359 72	1,296 15				
Do	1862	9		Trawling, 7 trips.	Feb.	July 8	2,554 77	1,162 06	July 15 to Nov. 17, 4 mos. Gulf.	14	5	3,122 44	1,972 70	Nov. 3 to Nov. 27, shore.	16	65	1,471 27
Schr. Electric Flash	1860	6							May 10 (29) to Nov. 1, 5 mos. Gulf.	16	310	2,173 05	441 82	Sep. 9, Gulf, 2 m. 1 d.	15	259	2,950 11
Do	1861	7							July 10 to Sept. 5, 1 m. 25 d., Gulf.	17	396½	1,407 75	745 50	Aug. 28 to Oct. 18, Gulf, 1 m. 20 d.	16	366½	
Do	1862								June 16 to Aug. 28, 2 mos 12 d., Gulf.	15	385	1,658 75	31 96	June 21 to Oct. 26, 4 m. 5 d., Gulf.	16	255	1,471 27
Schr. R. H. Oakes	1861		4,200						May 11 to June 21, American shore.	14	57	188 75	1,137 6?		15		
Schr. I. G. Curtis	1862		6,500						Aug. 1 to Oct. 13, Gulf.	17	407½	2,975 44		Oct. 13 to Nov. 11, shore.	15	117½	892 35

Time fitting is included.

Table showing the vessels engaged in the cod, halibut, and mackerel fisheries in the years 1860, 1861, and 1862—Continued.

Name of vessel.	Year.	Vessel's share.	Third trip mackereling.	Hands.	Barrels.	Value.	Vessel's share.	Total number barrels Gulf.	Total number barrels American shore.	Total value Gulf catch.	Total value shore catch.	Total value vessel's whole catch.	Amount of vessel's credits for the year.	Amount of vessel's bills for the year.	Excess of vessel's share of catch over bills.	Deficit of vessel's share to pay bills.	Remarks.
Schr. Cynisca	1860											$3,866 62	$3,925 01	$3,275 43	$649 58		Vessel now in 1859 (&c.), 1861, &c., with all.
Do.	1861	$1,383 64			203½		$1,312 50	54	25½	$1,259 99	$212 04	4,136 89	1,186 64	1,900 88		$714 24	Lost, Dec., 1861, &c.
Schr. C. C. Davis	1860												3,505 10	2,273 30	1,231 80		
Do.	1861	99 93	Oct. 13 to Nov. 24, Am. shore.	11	145	$1,262 48	515 46	238½	34½	2,018 57	299 75		1,740 12	2,395 36		565 24	Peter Sinclair, owner and agent.
Do.	1862	349 83	Oct. 18 to Nov. 17, shore.		137½		929 92	263½	277		890 87						
Schr. Annah	1860	168 24	Oct. 8 to Nov. 22, shore.					41	170				1,713 09	1,662 32	50 77		
Schr. Daniel McPhee	1860	700 10						139	174½		1,141 74		2,116 14	3,225 00		1,118 86	Vessel now in 1860.
Do.	1861	242 85						944	134½	2,164 34	1,034 56		2,257 11	3,326 25	69 14		
Do.	1862	412 03						207	220½	3,638 86			2,446 41	3,221 99	224 42		
Schr. Ella F. Bartlett	1860	957 91						275	159½	1,359 72	1,061 79		2,744 91	3,328 60	416 22		Vessel now in 1860.
Do.	1861	390 66						325		3,123 44			2,657 66		83 69		
Do.	1862							310	65	2,173 05			2,141 35	2,145 29	338 39		
Schr. Electric Flash	1860	195 79								879 02			2,483 49				Jas. S. Ayer, owner and agent.
Do.	1861	892 42						565½	73½	638 86	573 66		550 07	805 40			Do.
Do.	1862	1,230 08	Oct. 18 to Nov. 15, shore.	14	72½	573 06	224 96	754½									Do.
Schr. R. H. Oakes	1861	518 11						255	57	1,471 27	188 75		1,521 60	1,189 16	332 44		Sold now in 1861, was lost on Newfoundland voyage.
Schr. L. G. Curtis	1862	356 48						407½	117½	2,975 44	356 48						
	8 vessels 3 years....							4,088	3,309½				36,331 04	37,746 73	3,387 31	2,742 81	
								Average, 291 barrels yearly.							2,742 81		584 50 in 3 years.

Q. When was it prepared?—A. It was prepared before I left home.

Q. What was the tonnage of the Daniel McPhee?—A. About 60 is, I think.

Q. You prepared this statement yourself?—A. Yes.

Q. From your own books?—A. Yes.

Q. Will you read the column of catches in which the 17 barrels appared?—A. 54, 230⅝, 263¼, 41, 17, 86¼, 244, 207, 275, 325, 310, 326½, 5, 57. They are shore and gulf mixed.

Q. Will you take out the shore?—A. 57, 86¼.

Q. The catches on your shore appear to be small compared with the iers?—A. The 86¼ barrels were caught in five days off our shores.

Q. But the small catches appear to have been taken on your shore; 300-barrel catches you have read were taken in the bay?—A. Not of them.

Q. I asked you to read those which were caught on your shores; you read them; were not the 300-barrel catches taken in the bay?—A. s; those were caught in the gulf.

Q. Don't you think it is more probable that, as your trip-book is lost, ich would be conclusive evidence on that point, you are mistaken as 17 barrels having been caught in the gulf on that trip, because Camp-l's name does not appear on the list of the men who were in the ves-when 17 barrels were taken?—A. No; I am positive he was not in vessel in the gulf that trip.

Q. Could he have deliberately coined the statement that he was in gulf and took that number of barrels? His name does not appear the list of the crew when the 17 barrels were taken?—A. It does'not pear in the list.

Q. You explained toward the close of your examination the right of aermen to take their fish and sell them elsewhere; when a vessel re-ns to Gloucester, does not the merchant, when the fish are landed, ck them?—A. Yes.

Q. That is a matter with which the fishermen, as fishermen, have thing to do?—A. Nothing to do with packing out.

Q. Therefore, if he were allowed to take his fish, he would have to y the merchant the packing charges?—A. Yes.

Q. They would amount to $2 a barrel?—A. That was the cost in cer-n years; it is now $1.75.

Q. So that practically it is never done?—A. No.

Q. It is also well understood that the merchant will have a lien on fish caught for any advances made the fishermen?—A. Yes.

Q. The practical working of the system is that the fisherman does take his fish elsewhere?—A. I don't know of any case where they l.

Q. One of the witnesses from Gloucester stated here that it was the stom for the ship-merchants to agree among themselves as to the price y will allow the fishermen for the fish when they pack out. Is it correct?—A. Not to my knowledge.

Q. How do the merchants arrange? Does one pay $10, another $11, l another $13, and are different prices paid to fishermen for their fish the same port?—A. For mackerel?

Q. Yes.—A. No; because trips are hardly ever sold at the same prices ee days running.

Q. I am speaking with regard to the price the merchant allows the aermen; whether the merchants agree among themselves to allow so ch?—A. The crew get the price at which the whole trip is sold.

Q. But the whole trip of mackerel may be held over for a yeai depending on the market?—A. The crew would hold over with l

Q. Do you mean to say that, if a crew came in in October, they not be paid when the packing out took place?—A. No.

Q. They might hold over till next spring?—A. If there is not ket for the fish the fish cannot be sold, so the crew cannot be with, and the cargo remains on the wharf till it is sold.

Q. Don't they agree on a price? Does not the merchant buy t from the men?—A. Sometimes they will settle in that way, a merchant will take them at a price.

Q. Did you ever know a case where a cargo has remained on a all winter waiting for a rise in price?—A. I do; I had several ve: 1860, the trips of which I kept over.

Q. And did not pay the men?—A. Not all of them; some o kept their fish in store, and I did not settle with them.

Q. How many of them did so?—A. I could not tell.

Q. Is it the general and invariable rule?—A. That was an exce} year. The usual rule is to settle the trips as soon as possible aft arrive.

Q. When they do settle, how do they arrive at the price; merchants agree on a price?—A. Nothing of the kind.

Q. It is so with regard to codfish; it has been so testified here the merchants agree on a certain price they will allow their fisl for green fish?—A. Yes.

Q. That is the rule with regard to codfish?—A. I cannot say i rule. They may do it; I don't know. I notice in Mr. Steele's be riations in price.

Q. I know they pay different prices in different years. Sup} vessels arrived to-day in Gloucester and packed out and paid th and the vessels were owned by eight or nine different persons, the men be paid different prices?—A. They would be; that, is il trips sold for different prices. If all arrived on one day, they we all settled with at the price of mackerel that day.

Q. Suppose the mackerel were not sold that day?—A. He se the market-price.

Q. At a sum they agree upon?—A. Yes. There is always a t price for mackerel, well understood.

Q. There is a market-price well understood at which the me pays the crews?—A. You misunderstand it. Let me explain Gloucester there is great competition for trips of mackerel, and five buyers come down as soon as a trip is in, after the trip of m: They will bid for the trip, and the one that bids highest takes it price. That is the usual way of selling mackerel at Gloucester. fitter and owner wants the mackerel himself to send to his custo} says he will take them himself at the highest bid.

Q. Is it offered at auction?—A. It is offered among the Sometimes there is great competition among them.

Q. Take such a firm as George Steele. When one of their

Q. Does he not pack himself?—A. Yes, he always packs.

Q. He would not sell the fish until they were packed?—A. Ne times he sells them as soon as they arrive. He says, "I will ; trip for so much after they are packed out."

Q. What is his practice; is it to sell to the buyers, or to pack chase it, and sell it himself?—A. To sell it to the buyers.

Q. There is a class of men known specially as buyers?—A.

Q. Is not Mr. Steele what you call a fish-merchant?—A. He is not a sh-buyer.

Q. Does he sell his own fish that his vessels have caught?—A. He oes.

Q. Upon the question of insurance, you explained that the insurers ould not be liable below a certain percentage. I did not understand hether you knew what the percentage was.—A. I do not. I believe it o be 12 per cent.

Q. I want to know positively. Do you wish that to go in your evience as your statement that it is 12 per cent.?—A. Not that it is, but hat I believe it to be so from hearsay.

Q. Does it differ from ordinary policies?—A. Yes, our risks are different.

Q. Do you know that your policies differ from ordinary policies about he percentage—about the percentage below which the insurer will not e liable?—A. I do not know that they differ.

Q. I understand that you don't wish to make a positive statement on hat point?—A. I don't wish to make a positive statement on anything don't understand.

Q. Do you know the percentage below which ordinary companies don't ay—is it 5 per cent.?—A. I don't know.

Q. In answer to Mr. Dana, you made what struck me as a curious tatement—that to raise money on mortgage on a vessel you had to pay very high rate of interest?—A. A higher rate than on real estate.

Q. What interest would you have to pay?—A. I know a mortgage on vessel would bring 8 per cent.

Q. That applies to all vessels, does it not?—A. Yes.

Q. Not specially to fishing-vessels?—A. I am talking about fishing-essels.

Q. With regard to other vessels, engaged in general trade, what vould be the rate of interest at which you could raise money on them?—. I don't know.

Q. For you know anything it may be the same as on fishing-vessels.)o you know or not that it is higher on general trading-vessels than on is hing-vessels?—A. No.

Q. In point of fact you don't know anything about it?—A. No.

Q. You don't know from practical knowledge that it is 8 per cent. ou ishing-vessels?—A. No.

Q. Your information on that is not such as will enable you to give vidence under oath?—A. It is not positive.

Q. You spoke in regard to the depreciation of those fishing-vessels, ind I understood your evidence to relate to all shipping?—A. To fishing-ressels generally.

Q. The same remarks you made with regard to the depreciation of ishing-vessels are applicable to all shipping?—A. I don't think so.

Q. Why not?—A. Because the wear and tear on fishing-vessels is nore than on any other class of vessels.

Q. I will limit the question to a vessel employed in the Gulf of St. Lawrence during the months when the fishery is prosecuted there—June, July, August, September, and October. Will the wear and tear of a ishing-vessel in the gulf during those months be more than the wear ind tear of a trading-vessel?—A. I should say it was.

Q. Give me your reason.—A. The Gulf of St. Lawrence in the fall is a very rough place.

Q. You will remember that the fishing months I gave you were from

June to November, not including November?—A. The greatest l
fishing vessels in the gulf was in August.

Q. The depreciation on a vessel engaged in fishing in the gulf d
those months is as great or greater than that of a vessel enga;
ordinary trade?—A. I think so.

Q. Can you give me your reason?—A. The reason is that the
is engaged in the fishing business and is on a dangerous route.

Q. You think the gulf is dangerous?—A. I do.

Q. What has the danger of the gulf to do with the wear and t
vessels?—A. The wear and tear of a vessel comprises injuries sh
receive in a gale or by being stranded.

Q. The stranding would perhaps come in another valuation. T
surers would most likely have to pay for that?—A. Perhaps s
perhaps not.

Q. Don't you think they would?—A. According to what th
would be. The insurance is 4 per cent. for four months. Why s
the rate of insurance be so high if there was no danger of wear an
to the vessel?

Q. I don't know. Do they insure the vessels for the season
trips?—A. For the trips. That is what they charge—4 per cent. i
gulf, one per cent. per month.

Q. What is the insurance of a vessel going to George's Bank?-
don't know.

Q. You were posted yourself in regard to it?—A. I never poste
self on that point.

Q. Take vessels fishing off your own coast. With regard to wea
tear, don't you think the wear and tear of vessels fishing off you
coast would be more than that of vessels fishing in the gulf durin
months they fish there?—A. I do not.

Q. Not in the winter season?—A. We fish on our shores all th
round.

Q. Is not the wear and tear greater on your coast than in th
during the summer months when they fish there?—A. I should
was.

Q. You spoke of the profits made out of fish, after they had
landed, by the fish merchants. Will you explain what the profits a
A. On mackerel all the profits are in the packing.

Q. And how much per barrel profit is there on that?—A. From
cents to fifty cents.

Q. A little higher than that, is it not?—A. No; I don't think i

Q. Have you ever packed yourself?—A. Yes.

Q. Much?—A. I packed during three years.

Q. So you are able to tell about packing.—A. Packing was the
at $1.15 per barrel. Now it is $1.75.

Q. Did it pay at $1.15?—A. Yes; barrels then were very much

Q. But it left a profit then?—A. Yes.

Q. Have barrels risen in proportion to the rise in the charge for
ing?—A. Yes.

Q. The same proportion?—A. About the same proportion, I th

Q. Then, do I understand that the increased cost of packing is
due to the increased cost of barrels? Is there not a larger profi
on packing?—A. I don't know but what they may make a larger
Prices went up during the war, and they remained so till, I thin
year, when they dropped.

Q. In what other ways have the merchants got profits up
visions furnished to the families of fishermen?—A. To the vesse

. Have you thought over since yesterday the question that was
ed you, as to the profits they charge on supplies furnished to the
ilies of the fishermen ?—A. I have not given it a thought since yes-
day.
. Perhaps you did not give it much thought before yesterday ?—A.
ıly gave it from my knowledge of the business.
. What would you be prepared to say to-day is the profit they make
supplies furnished to the families of fishermen ?—A. About ten per
t.
. Not more than that ?—A. It would not be over that.
. You know that sometimes they lose the supplies ?—A. I know
y do.
. And don't they make sufficient profit to cover all that ?—A. I don't
ık they do.
. You think they are not shrewd enough men to make the charge
icient to insure them against loss ?—A. They might.
. You don't know exactly. Have you examined their books and
es so as to be enabled to testify accurately ont hat point ?—A. No;
ıve not.
. You volunteer what you assume is correct ?—A. I give it from my
llection of my business in 1861 and 1862.
. I understand they agree with wholesale dealers, to have the goods
ished at wholesale prices, and the fishermen are charged the retail
es ?—A. Yes.
. The difference between the wholesale price and retail price you
't know ?—A. I don't know.
. The difference is the profit which the merchant makes ?—A. Yes,
takes the risk.
. You were town clerk of Gloucester for some time, and are ac-
inted, of course, with the valuations, more or less, of the different
chants ?—A. Yes.
. You spoke of two or three names as being leading men ?—A. Yes.
. What are those men assessed at ?—A. I could not tell; I don't
llect. As town clerk I would not know.
. You seem to have filled numerous offices, and, no doubt, filled
n efficiently ?—A. The assessors assess for taxes and keep their own
ks.
. From the knowledge you have gained in looking over the assess-
book, cannot you state what a man like Mr. Leighton is taxed for ?—
I guess he is taxed at——
. Take Mr. Leighton's firm.—A. I suppose it is assessed at $30,000.
. What is that on ?—A. That is on the valuation of his real estate
vessels.
. How does that compare with its value ?—A. In Gloucester they
at a little over three-fourths of the value.
. Of its cash value or ordinary market value ?—A. Of the ordinary
ket value, as it is considered. If you force such a property as Mr.
ghton's to a sale, it would not bring anything like its value.
. What other leading men did you mention ?—A. Dennis & Ayer.
. About what would be their valuation ?—A. I don't know.
. Take Mr. Steele; what would his firm be taxed at ?—A. Mr. Steele
robably taxed at $20,000.
. Would you put the four leading men in Gloucester down as worth
n $20,000 to $30,000 each ?—A. I don't think anybody in the fishing
iness in Gloucester is worth over $30,000.
. What are they assessed at ?—A. I don't know. I have not seen

the assessors' books for a good many years; I cannot tell. I formed my judgment from what I think they are worth.

Q. How many vessels is Mr. Steele running?—A. On an av nine vessels.

Q. They would range from what price?—A. They would av $5,000 each.

Q. What is his real estate worth?—A. About $10,000.

Q. What are the premises where he lives worth, another $10,0 A. I should think his house is worth $5,000; perhaps that is a high.

Q. Those amounts would reach $60,000; you told me he is put as being assessed at $20,000?—A. That may be.

Q. Why have you stated that you believed him to be assessed at $20,000?—A. I have stated his valuation, perhaps, high.

Q. Do you think there could be that difference between you an assessors?—A. There might be.

Q. Do you really think you could be, or the assessors could be, in error?—A. I should think George Steele is worth about $35,00

Q. You mean after paying all his debts?—A. I don't know wh debts are.

Q. You mean after paying his debts?—A. I mean the face va his property is $35,000. I don't know what his debts may be.

Q. How do you reconcile the statements?—A. I probably set value on his vessel property and other property.

Q. You have already put in the vessels at a valuation of $5,00 under the statement you made under oath yesterday.—A. I kn had some very expensive vessels.

Q. When you were making a statement of Mr. Steele's business, ing how much he had lost or gained, you put down the vessels as $5,000 each?—A. I did so. That is what I took as an average, b some cost $8,000 and some less.

Q. And in order to show what he gained or lost, you charged est at 5 per cent. on that amount?—A. Yes.

Q. Now, you may be all astray about the valuation?—A. No; say I am all astray. You asked me for the assessor's valuatio I could not give it, and I answered from my judgment.

Q. How do you reconcile the statements?—A. I can reconci this way: If Mr. Steele's property was sold to-day it would no more than $35,000; that is the face value of it.

Q. That is, if forced into the market to-day?—A. Yes; it wo bring more than $35,000.

Q. Don't you know that if a large quantity of any kind of pr not fishing property alone, is forced into the market the price is fall?—A. You want anything of that kind set at a cash value, don

Q. Suppose you force a lot of stock on the market, more than t lic want, will it not necessarily run the price down?—A. It wo low.

Q. I am not talking about forced sales, but of the assessed v sworn to by the assessors, and as you as a practical man would How do you reconcile the discrepancy between your statement of day, when you placed each vessel at $5,000, and that statement t do not believe the face value of Mr. Steele's property, irrespective he owns, is worth more than $20,000 or $30,000?—A. I took th age of vessels for 19 years. I did not take them at what they a to-day.

Q. I think you did. I think you allowed a large sum for depr

When you were making up the statement to show the fishing business, you took insurance 107 vessels, $535,000, that is $5,000 each vessel?— A. Yes.

Q. You charge insurance on those vessels at that rate, $21,000?—A. That is what he probably paid.

Q. You then charged against the earnings of the vessels the interest on that capital sum, $535,000 at 7 per cent?—A. Yes.

Q. You then charged taxes on $160,000?—A. One hundred and sixty thousand dollars for seventeen years.

Q. And then you charged depreciation on the vessels, $29,000?—A. Yes.

Q. So if you charge depreciation and interest you keep up the capital stock to where it originally was?—A. The depreciation is wear and tear to a large extent, and what are expenses of the vessel—sails and rigging, painting and repairing.

Q. I recall your attention to the fact that I asked you what was the depreciation of a vessel in one year, and you gave $1,200?—A. Yes.

Q. I ask you what would be the depreciation yearly for the next five years?—A. Probably not more than $800.

Q. You gave your estimate yesterday of Mr. Steele's worth and the value of his vessels—are you inclined to-day to withdraw it?—A. No, I hold to it.

Q. If you take off one-half of the principal the interest would be reduced one-half?—A. The value of the vessels would be $45,000—9 vessels averaging $5,000 each; and if the wharf was sold I think that it would bring $8,000, a fair valuation in my opinion.

Q. Did you not just now state that this wharf was worth $10,000?— A. I know I did; but his wharf is, together with another part, divided in the middle, and this would not make it so valuable as other wharf property.

Q. You change this valuation, then, from $10,000 to $8,000?—A. I should think that $8,000 would be a fair valuation, and then I should set down the house at $4,000.

Q. You are coming down on that valuation very much?—A. I said $5,000, but if it was put up at auction it would not bring that much.

Q. Does he own any other property besides the 9 vessels, the wharf, and the house?—A. That is all the property it shows on the face.

Q. Does he own stock of any kind?—A. I do not know.

Q. Has he no capital invested?—A. I do not know, but I presume that he owns ten shares in the Gloucester Bank. He is one of the directors, and he must have ten shares to qualify himself for being a director.

Q. I ask you frankly what do you believe; has he or has he not money invested in other public works in Gloucester?—D. I do not think so. I hardly think that he has.

Q. Does he own goods or anything else?—A. He has goods in his store, but our outfitters do not keep a large stock of goods in stock.

Q. What valuation would you put on this stock?—A. I should think that $1,500 would cover the value of the stock which he keeps on hand.

Q. Will you include the shares in your estimate?—A. I will do so.

Q. What would you put it at on the whole?—A. $45,000.

Q. How do you make that out?—A. Five times nine make $45,000. I make it $60,000, and three-quarters of it makes $45,000 as the cash value.

Q. Then this account which you have made up is not put down at the cash or real value, but at a fancy value?—A. It is put down at the

average value of his vessels, taken for the time that they ha
running.

Q. What right had you to charge interest and insurance on t
erty at an amount largely disproportionate to the real value'
you see that you reduce the profits immensely by that mode of
ing?—A. That is the face value of the property; if he pays int
more than he ought to, that is his loss.

Q. But you don't pretend to say that he is paying the inte
made up in this sum; this is your estimate?—A. Well, it is an
based on the original cost of the vessels, and the average cost.

Q. I will ask you frankly if you knew what his vessels wer
and what you ought to put down there? Is it fair to make up
and charge interest on $535,000?—A. I think so, because I have
nothing for losses.

Q. I beg your pardon; this does not allow the possibility
You have insured the capital invested, charged interest at the
per cent. on that capital, allowed 14½ per cent. for depreciation
sels, and charged insurance upon the charter and outfits, an
dead certainty?—A. That is true; insurance is charged on the

Q. There is a dead certainty and no possibility of risk?—A.
true, as the statement goes; yes.

Q. Do you think that is fair, when he is running no risk, to
to pay insurance on the value of the property far beyond wl
worth? In that way you reduce the profits down to nothing?—

Q. Suppose you readjust that sum, and make up the sum on
value of these things, and charge interest on the real value of
sels, and insurance and taxes on real value?—A. I should then
charge more for depreciation.

Q. Are you aware what percentage you charged for depreciati
I did not charge so much as it would be.

Q. Are you aware what percentage you charged in this accou
No; I did not reckon any percentage.

Q. It seems to me to look like 14½ per cent., at least?—A. Fo
ciation? Well.

Q. Do you think that 14½ per cent. is a large sum, or not, to
depreciation?—A. I do not think that it is a large sum.

Q. Why?—A. Because it is very expensive running a vessel

Q. But running a vessel has nothing to do with depreciati
Why not.

Q. Explain how it is. I cannot conceive of the connection?—
wear and tear of the vessel is an expense, and it costs something
her in repair and running order.

Q. That is for repairs?—A. Well, that is part of the depreci
count. Can you find repairs there anywhere?

Q. Part of it is depreciation account. It embraces both th
repairs and the actual depreciation which arises from the vesse
older?—A. That is it.

Q. You stated that the $800 is the amount of depreciation
first year for the following five years; do you still adhere to tl
Yes; that would be about right, I should think. If anything
be more, because Procter's vessel shows about $1,200 or $1,400
in this regard.

Q. That is in the statement which you have put in to-day?—

Q. I see in it that $79 is charged for tinware and $48 for an
but is that an ordinary expense? It is an extraordinary loss?
not often happen?—A. I have known vessels lose two anchor

I dare say, but is it ordinary wear and tear?—A. Why not? It is of the depreciation.

Is it an ordinary loss? Is it fair to charge the loss of an anchor 1 occurs during one year, as a general charge against a vessel for ear's depreciation?—A. No.

You have done it here.—A. How?

In this very statement, in which you make an expenditure of 3.—A. I did not call it $1,800, but about $1,200 or $1,400 for that l.

I find it marked down here as $1,823?—A. Yes.

And you think it would be about $1,400?—A. You misunderstand out this; insurance is set down at $539, and then there is another

Commission for skipper?—A. How large is that?

$465.—A. And then there is the cost of tinware.

But that is too large an amount for an ordinary charge. You do apply $79 worth of tinware every year or the tenth of it?—A. O,

Every year?—A. Yes.

How much would you take off from this item?—A. An owner l consider himself fortunate if an offer was made him to supply his l with tinware for $10 a year.

How much will you take off from the $79?—A. $60.

And how much from the lost-anchor item?—A. Not a cent.

You charge that every year as a part of the expenses?—A. Yes; ss that Steele's expenses average an anchor every year.

Then there are railway fees?—A. Yes; but that I don't take off.

You consider that a yearly expense?—A. Yes.

By Mr. Foster:

Explain what this is for.—A. It is for the marine railway for re-

By Mr. Davies:

You put down $63 for lumber for ice-house; is that required every ?—A. Yes; more or less.

Do you build new ice-houses every year?—A. No, not new; but expenditure is required in this relation yearly.

What do you think would be a fair allowance for that?—A. About alf; I will take $35 off from that item.

What do you do with ballast; does it remain in the vessel?—A. it is taken out.

Is this ballast expense incurred every year?—A. No; not the ß of it.

The sum of $80 is put down here for it?—A. Yes. I should say about $40 a year would be a fair estimate for ballast.

Is a new swivel gun required every year?—A. No.

In fact, this is not a depreciation account; it does not show the for depreciation and wear and tear?—A. Items are there for a charterer of a vessel would have to furnish.

By Mr. Foster:

But he would not supply a swivel gun?—A. Probably not.

By Mr. Davies:

The cost of ballast would never be charged for depreciation on vear and tear of a vessel?—A. I do not think so. It would be ged in the vessel's expense account.

Q There is a great difference between that and this account; these items in making up the sum total, and then tell us what age you charge for depreciation and wear and tear?—A. Those form part of the depreciation account.

Q. Do you really think that expenditure for ballast and a sw form part of the depreciation account? Do you honestly t major?—A. As to the swivel-gun, you can throw that out; it i ception to the general rule, because there are not many vesse carry such guns; but all those expenses, added to the depreci the hull of the vessel, go to make up that depreciation account.

Q. In making up this account you have included these items of it?—A. Yes.

Q. Even taking that method of making up and charging depr let me ask you to look at the return before you, showing as net for each schooner $251?—A. Yes.

Q. That would be for four and one-half months, half of the se A. Yes.

Q. That would be $500 for the season: this is for half of the and of course it would be the same for the other half of the s they were then employed?—A. Yes.

Q. Multiply that by 107, the number of vessels mentione sum?—A. Yes.

Q. What is the result?—A. Fifty-three thousand seven hunc fourteen dollars.

Q. That is not a bad profit for a man to make?—A. No.

Q. What percentage would that give on the capital employ You don't look above and see how the charterer stands.

Q. I will come to that directly. What percentage would $53,' on the capital invested; $535,000?—A. It would be a little she per cent.

Q. This is supposing that the owner of these 107 vessels wor run them without a shadow of risk, paying insurance upon tl receiving interest at the rate of 17 per cent—7 per cent. on hi being already included—paying taxes out of his profits, and h allowance of 14½ per cent. depreciation. If that is so, will yo explain what you meant by telling Mr. Dana that a person who his money in vessels and who did not bring skilled labor to be his operations could not make money?—A. I did so for the ve that George Steele's vessels are the most successful vessels in Gl

Q. But this is only a supposed state of things. What did by making that answer to Mr. Dana?—A. That is a well-know

Q. Unfortunately the facts and your evidence do not ag afraid. You have proved here pretty conclusively that a invests $535,000 on these vessels, employed in business, should per cent. on his money after paying taxes, insurance, and kee self perfectly safe. How do you reconcile that result with ment you made to Mr. Dana, that a person who invests his this business would be sure to lose?—A. You do not take int the loss, but you take it as being all profit.

Q. The owner would suffer no loss, though the charterer seems singular, does it not? You say this is where a man vessel?—A. Yes.

Q. In the first place, is George Steele a charterer of vessels'

Q. Then this statement, which assumes to relate to Georg business, as his name is mentioned as the charterer of the v not represent an existing state of facts, but is merely a the

put forth ?—A. I supposed I had mentioned on the account that it an estimate.

That is the real fact, is it not ?—A. Yes. The real fact is that I e a mere estimate in this regard.

George Steele does not charter vessels but owns them ?—A. Yes.

And this statement supposes him to be a charterer ?—A. Yes.

Though he is not one ?—A. Yes.

Have you had the opportunity of examining George Steele's books ? I have not.

How did you get these thirteen or fourteen trips ?—A. I saw the books. I asked Mr. Steele for permission to show them to the mission.

You then had the opportunity of examining his books ?—A. Yes, his trip-books, but not as to his ledger.

Did you ask for his ledger ?—A. I did not.

I suppose if you had done so you would have obtained access to -A. Probably I should.

Therefore you do not know what his books show as to actual profit loss sustained by him during this period ?—A. I do not.

And the actual state of facts may be at variance with the theory advance ?—A. I hardly think so.

Supposing that George Steele stands in the position you assume is statement, he would be bankrupt beyond all redemption ?—A.

You have proved him from theory to be bankrupt beyond all re- tion, when in fact he is a capitalist worth $45,000, which exhibits ifference between the practical statement and the theory?—A. Yes; e had capital when he went into the business.

Do you state that he brought it in with him ?—A. One-half of it made in the sail-making business.

Where was the other half made ?—A. In the fishing business dur- nineteen years, but that is only $1,000 a year, and he ought to make

The actual loss on each vessel, for 107 vessels, you place at $167 ?— es.

Will you make that up and tell me for how much he ought to be aulter ?—A. His loss would be $17,869.

And that is not consistent with the facts; he is not a defaulter to amount.—A. He has made it up in other parts of his business, but r as his vessels are concerned he has probably lost that sum.

You did not get access to his profit and loss ledger ?—A. No.

That would show exactly how it is, and this is an imaginary con- on ?—A. Yes. I could not make it up without the actual bills of ses for his vessels. I thought it was already understood that this maginary.

Turning to the credit side of that account, the catch is 33,645 bar- f mackerel ?—A. Yes.

Will you tell me where you got the values ?—A. From the trip-

And that shows the values at which he settled with his men ?—A.

Does it show the actual cash price which he received for these 5 barrels ?—A. Yes.

Will you explain ?—A. Remember that this is for the fish and the ng, which he receives when he sells the trip.

Does that trip on its face show the actual moneys which he received

for the barrels of fish and to whom they were sold ?—A. It
with the packing out.

Q. Will you turn up one of the trips and explain your meani
Here is a trip made between August and October in the
Marathon.

Q. It is a settlement between Mr. Steele and his crew ?—A. `
the settlement between Mr. Steele and his vessel for that trip.

Q. Does it show to whom the mackerel were sold ?—A. No.

Q. Does it show the price per barrel for which they were s
Yes; the packing out. The prices were $16, $12, and $6.

Q. Are not these the prices at which he settled with his m
Certainly, and the prices at which he sold the fish.

Q. Are you prepared to state that he never sold any of thos
any higher price than that which he allowed his men ?—A. I w
swear to that,,because I do not know.

Q. You do not know whether this was the case or not ?—
swear in this respect with regard to my own vessels.

Q. Are you prepared to state that Mr. Steele did not realize
price for the mackerel than that at which he settled with his cr
I do not actually know whether this was the case or not, but I
that it is the custom in Gloucester for the merchants to settle w
crews at the exact prices for which they sell their fish. The
settle with the crews for less than they get.

Q. Did not you tell me, major, that it was the invariable pr
the merchants to settle with their crews when the vessels pa
and that on a rise taking place in the market the former got th
of it ?—A. O, that is a different thing. If the merchant buys tl
erel of the crew and keeps the fish on hand for a rise, and o
that is his profit.

Q. So that the profit which Steele may have made with the
barrels of mackerel is a profit of which you absolutely know no
A. I know nothing about that.

Q. So this statement does not pretend to be an exhibit of t
profit which Steele may have made in this relation ?—A. N
know the custom of the city, and that is to sell the trip anc
the men the price then received.

Q. I merely want to show that the course of business is suc
experienced man can take advantage of a rise in the market a
a handsome profit of it ?—A. That is true; and on the other
may lose.

Q. At what rate per barrel do you credit these mackerel ?
average price, as I stated in my explanation of the summa
per barrel for the 17 years during which he had vessels in th
Saint Lawrence. That is the price which he actually receiv
mackerel.

By Sir Alexander Galt:

Q. Does that cover all descriptions of mackerel ?—A. Yes, a
tions that are packed from his vessel.

Q. And the average was as high as $12 ?—A. Yes.

Q. That was the actual result ?—A. Yes.

Q. That is without packing, of course ?—A. Yes.

By Mr. Foster:

Q. Do you mean to say that Mr. Steele's mackerel durin
averaged $12 a barrel, without packing-charges ?—A. Yes;
was very successful in his trips.

e took a large quantity of mackerel when currency prices were
ely high ?—A. When the price was low he sent his vessels cod-
and when they were high he sent them to the gulf.

Mr. Davies:

find that the average actual receipt of Mr. Noble, who has been
ed here for the three qualities of mackerel, were $15.34, so that
ou are a little below what I thought the price would be. These
rency values, I suppose ?—A. Yes.

ou charge against these catches of 17 years for bait, &c.,
.80 ?—A. Yes.

ividing that sum by 107 leaves $450 for each vessel ?—A. Yes.

notice that in a statement concerning an actual trip you put the
stock charges down at $415 ?—A. Yes.

howing a difference of thirty-five dollars between these items in
wo statements ?—A. That may be so.

Thy did you not charge this item as $415, as was the case with
arsalfa, concerning which the sample statement was put in here ?
f course I took the actual sum which was expended for stock
.

hen this expenditure for the Pharsalia was a little below the ordi-
in ?—A. Yes; it is below the average.

nd this item represents the actual expenditure taken from the
—A. Yes.

re the items for outfits and expenses put down also from actual
itures ?—A. No; they are estimates.

hey are suppositious ?—A. They are estimates; yes.

ou have already gone over the provisions to show that the item
ents a day in this regard was correct; that had reference to the
fishery ?—A. All other fisheries average the same.

ou think so ?—A. Yes.

t what figure do you estimate the percentage of profit which is
y the merchant who furnishes the supplies ?—A. I guess that it
e neighborhood of 10 per cent.

Tould you say that it is above ten per cent. ?—A. No; I think it
average about ten per cent.

hen on $85,386 spent for provisions a profit of about $8,530 would
le ?—A. Yes.

ou charge $1 a barrel for salt ?—A. Yes; that is the usual charge.

re there only two barrels in a hogshead of salt ?—A. There are
ind a half bushels, or two barrels in it.

urely there must be more ?—A. There are seven and a half bush-
wo barrels of salt.

o not two and a half bushels make a barrel of salt ?—A. No;
re three and a half bushels to the barrel.

Tould you not say that there are 5 barrels to the hogshead ?—A.
ould not say that.

Vhat would you put it at ?—A. 2.27 fish-barrels.

Vhat does it cost a hogshead ?—A. $2.

ou charge $8,500 for salt, for as many barrels at $1 a barrel;
lf of it would be profit, and that would leave $4,250 as profit ?—
Tes.

ou set down 107 bait-mills, one for each vessel, for the voyage ?—

o you mean to tell us that a vessel requires a new bait-mill on
voyage she makes ?—A. No.

Q. Would you reduce this item one-half?—A. I would reduce
quarter.

Q. Would not one bait-mill last two trips?—A. Yes; it would
4 months and 13 days.

Q. Would one last for 2 different trips?—A. These mills wear c
the teeth in one season, and these have to be renewed for the ne
The wood-work of the mill will last for 2 seasons.

Q. Then you charge the value of a new bait-mill for each
trip, and that is too much?—A. Yes; it should be ¾. As to sal
here mention that 50 hogsheads of salt will fill 115 barrels; the
heads contain about 3 barrels.

By Mr. Dana:

Q. How many bushels are reckoned to a hogshead of salt at
tom-house?—A. 8.

By Mr. Davies

Q. Do you mean to say that salt costs, wholesale, $2 a hogsl
A. I know that is the price charged for it.

Q. What does it cost, say, by the 100 or 1,000 hogsheads?
merchant for such a quantity pay $2 a hogshead?—A. No, proba
he would probably obtain it for $1.75 or $1.87½ per hogshead.

. Showing a difference of about 25 cents per hogshead as prol
Y.

Q. Would not the profit be more than 25 cents per hogshead
barrels of salt?—A. No.

Q. By the way, what portion did you take off the bait-mill ite
I took off one-quarter.

Q. Of what does the fishing-gear for these 107 vessels consi
Of hooks, and lines, and keelers.

Q. Are they not good for a second season?—A. Hooks and l
not, but the keelers may be so used.

Q. Do you mean to say that they throw away their hooks and lii
having been used for one season?—A. They are no good al
season.

Q. What else goes to make up this fishing-gear in this
$4,815?—A. The cost of the pewter is included, I guess.

Q. What proportion would you take off that for one season?—
a cent.

Q. What proportion of the money thus invested could be uti
the end of the season?—A. I do not think that a cent's worth
could be taken off this item. The keelers get pretty well used n
end of the season.

Q. Surely the pewter would be good at the end of the year?—
not think so.

Q. Do you say as a matter of fact that this fishing-gear, inclu
articles you have mentioned, is absolutely valueless at the en
fishing trip?—A. I do.

Q. Absolutely valueless, and treated so?—A. It is treated s
Q. Nothing can be realized from it at all?—A. Nothing at al
Q. Where did you get the custom-house and port charges fr
I obtained a good portion of them in the Dominion; 8 cents
head of salt is charged in Gloucester for weighing-fees; and
vessel has to clear from Gloucester.

Q. You think that this $140 is a fair charge?—A. Yes. M
paid a license on his vessel during those years.

Q. The next charge sets the charter of these 107 vessels

ı; you have made up this statement, I presume, to show, or to at-
, to show, the actual result in connection with fishing-vessels, but
he practice among the merchants who own vessels to charter them
ı others?—A. No.

Then this theory has no basis of fact to rest on?—A. There are
ns in Gloucester who sometimes charter vessels to go fishing.

But this is not the custom?—A. No.

Then of course it would be pretty difficult to arrive at a sum which
ıld be fair compensation to pay for a vessel; the merchants prefer
ı their vessels themselves?—A. Yes; they generally do so.

I suppose that there is not much insurance effected on charters in
ıester?—A. No.

Did you ever know any insurance to be effected on the charter of
ıel fishing in the gulf?—A. I do not know of anything of the sort,
is a customary charge on the charterer.

Is all the skipper's commission out of the net stock ($355,000)
ıed against the owner?—A. Yes.

The crew do not pay any part of it?—A. No.

Is it 4 per cent. or 3 per cent. that is thus paid?—A. It is 4 per

The master does pretty well, then?—A. O, yes.

What do you think would be the profit on the packing out of 33,645
ls of mackerel?—A. It would be 30 or 50 cents per barrel.

Taking 50 cents, that would make a profit of $16,825?—A. Fifty
is too high a figure.

What would be the result?—A. When I said that, I referred to the
ı which ruled during the war, when they got 50 cents.

Will you add up the different charges; I make them amount to
26; is that correct?—A. How many items have you?

There is $8,500?—A. That was reduced to $6,200.

How?—A. You reduced it, and you told me to set it at $6,200.

You calculated the rate at 10 per cent. of $8,500 odd, and I took
own figures, leaving $8,500; then there is $2,300 for profit on salt?
I did not say that; in round numbers the figures would be $1,750.
Then, from the bait-mill item you take off one-quarter, which
nts to $402?—A. Yes.

And the profit on packing is $16,825; add these items together.—
ıat makes $17,081.

I make it $27,000. Your sum shows a loss of $44,715, and deduct-
ıis from $27,800, what have you left; do the sum, as in the other
and tell me what profit is made on the whole transaction.—A. It
223.

Taking the whole transaction, what profit is made instead of the
loss you previously made out?—A. It is $9,233.

And that is after the insurance companies have been paid; this is
ıe season, mind.—A. Yes; it is on 107 vessels.

That is after the owner has received 7 per cent. for his money;
a depreciation of $29,000 has been considered; after the taxes have
paid; and after insurance has been obtained upon the capital
ted in these vessels' and upon the charter and outfits; and there
ıeen not one cent of the risk incurred while 7 per cent. has been
on the capital employed besides, and still you have this profit?—
here is $75 for each vessel.

I wanted to show this sum could be worked out differently with
own figures; this $9,000 profit is more consistent with the facts;
ık your figures are a little astray.—A. I am not satisfied about it.

Q. I suppose not.—A. From my general knowledge of the bu
of Gloucester I am not satisfied with that result.

Q. I find from your statements that after the Washington Trea
entered into, Mr. Steele withdrew his vessels from your shore i
and concentrated all his efforts on the bay; am I correct in m
that statement?—A. In 1870 and 1871 he did not send any ves
the bay.

Q. But in 1872 he commenced sending them to the bay?—A. '

Q. And he has sent them there ever since?—A. Yes.

Q. And he has since sent none to fish on your shore?—A. No.

Q. Since 1872 he has sent none to fish on your shore, but has s
his vessels to the bay?—A. Yes.

Q. What was the average price of the mackerel caught in the (
St. Lawrence realized by Mr. Steele between 1858 and 1865?
first place, what was the average catch per vessel made by his ves
the gulf between 1858 and 1865?—A. It was 338 packed barrels fo
years inclusive, and the mackerel sold for $11.10 per barrel.

Q. What was it between 1865 and 1872?—A. Two hundre
eighty barrels, which sold for $14.40, exclusive of the packing.

Q. And what was it between 1872 and 1876?—A. Two hundre
twenty-three barrels, which sold for $10.01.

Q. That makes an average catch per vessel of 304 packed b
which realized $12 a barrel?—A. Yes.

Q. What is the average catch of his shore vessels between 18
1865?—A. It was 191 barrels.

Q. As against 338 barrels for the vessels which he sent to th
What is the average price which he realized for these mackere
Five dollars and seventy cents per barrel. His vessels fished
shore for four years between those dates.

Q. As against $11 received for his bay mackerel. Now take the
period during which his vessels fished on the American shore.—
average time they were there employed was two months and
days each; their average catch was 239 barrels, and the averag
of their mackerel $7.10 a barrel.

Q. As against $12 per barrel which he received for his bay ma
What was the share per month of the vessels which were eng
fishing in the bay?—A. Three hundred and seventy-two dolla
sixty-six cents.

Q. What was such share for the vessels which fished on the A
shore?—A. Three hundred and ten dollars and sixty cents.

Q. What was the share for each man of the crews which fi
the bay?—A. Twenty-four dollars and eighty-four cents.

Q. And what was such share of the crews which fished on the
can shore?—A. Twenty dollars and seventy cents; but that i
fair average, because Steele's vessels were not engaged in fishi
rule on the American shore.

Q. Am I not taking the average for corresponding years in
and on your shore?—A. Yes.

Q. Does it not appear that Mr. Steele must have been losing
on your shore, and that after 1872 he transferred his fishing op
wholly to the Gulf of St. Lawrence, where he has entirely kept
sels since; is that a fact or not?—A. It is, because Mr. Steele's s
are more acquainted with gulf fishing than with fishing on ou
This has always been the case with them; they were always
customed to the bay branch of the fishery than to fishing on ou

Q. They knew where to fish there?—A. Yes.

MONDAY, *October* 15, 1877.

e Conference met.

e cross-examination of Major LOW was resumed.

By Mr. Davies:

iestion. I notice that in your examination on Friday, you said that comparison with reference to Steele's vessels might not be a fair with respect to the bay and shore fisheries, because they had been ged in fishing a longer time in the Bay of St. Lawrence than on American shore, and I want you to take the statement printed on 359½ and make the comparisons for corresponding periods which I indicate. In the first place, if you take the total number of vessels h were fishing in the Bay of St. Lawrence, how many would there —A. 107.

Can you tell me, from that statement, what is the average time vessel was occupied in fishing? Divide the total number of vessels the time so occupied, and give the result.—A. It is 4 months and ays.

Have you it already made up?—A. Yes; it is contained in my ination of the summary I filed.

How did you make it up?—A. I divided the time by the number ssels.

Try it again, and state the result.—A. It is $4\frac{45}{100}$ months, or 4 ths and 13 days. ´

Did you embrace the 75 days employed in the fitting out?—A.

Take it without this period and see what you make it, giving the al time consumed from the time when they left Gloucester until returned; I make it $3\frac{8}{10}$ months.—A. Yes; that is it.

Now, take the number of vessels engaged in the American coast ry and treat them in the same way, omitting the time employed in g out?—A. It is $2\frac{6}{10}$ months; I call the total period 59 months.

All of these vessels were mackereling?—A. One vessel was one there.

Having the average time which each vessel was so employed, I you to take the catch which each vessel made, and the receipts ined for those mackerel as you have them here; for instance, what the total gulf catch?—A. 33,645 barrels.

What did these 33,645 barrels of mackerel bring?—A. $12 a el.

And how much would that be in bulk?—A. $403,832.86.

How much did each vessel make per month?—A. $372,343.

No; I want to see how much was made per month.—A. It is all ed up here in the explanation of the summary on page 360.

You make it $372.66 for each vessel; then will you do the same for the period during the Reciprocity Treaty?—A. That is done, from 1858 to 1865 on page 360.

But that does not show what each vessel made per month. You given what the vessels made per month for the whole period of , and I want to see what it was during the Reciprocity Treaty. the gross catch, value it, and divide by the length of time they in the Gulf of St. Lawrence.—A. From 1858 to 1865, I make up umber as 60 vessels, and the value of the gross catch, $225,243.

. That leaves $3,754 for each vessel?—A. It is $401 13.

. You have misunderstood me. I want to find out for the period

from 1858 to 1865 what the earnings of each vessel per month we
A. They were $16,694.

Q. Per month for each vessel?—A. For each vessel per month
were $401.13.

Q. Add up the value of the catch for that period.—A. I did not
it up, but I added the vessel's share up.

Q. I am not asking you about that. I am taking the table and
paring one statement with another. I am asking you concernin
result for each vessel, and I want to see what the vessels' earning
month were.—A. But that won't give it.

Q. Yes; you either have to pay one-half of what you catch or w
I do not care which; the value of the gross catch is $225.238, and
were 60 vessels, thus leaving $3,754 for each vessel for the se
and as the average trip was $3\frac{8}{10}$ months, that would leave $1,00
month by my sum. Would this be the case or not?—A. The va
the gross catch is $225,243.29.

Q. And there are 60 vessels?—A. Yes; that makes $3,754.55 for
vessel.

Q. You divide that by the average number of months, $3\frac{8}{10}$?—
take the whole time that they were engaged fishing.

Q. What was the length of the average trip in the bay from 18
1865?—A. Eighty-three days was each vessel's average.

Q. For what period of time?— A. From 1858 to 1865; and this l
$98.80 per month.

Q. You are wrong; you say that you have $3,754 for each trip;
what is the length of time that each season occupied?—A. 3.8 mo

Q. Divide $3,754 by 3.8 and you will find that this will leave as
as possible $1,000 a month?—A. It leaves $998.

Q. Now do exactly the same sum for the same time on the Ame
shore. I only put you these questions because you answered previ
that owing to the difference in the length of time, a fair compa
could not be made between the vessels fishing on the American
and in the Gulf of St. Lawrence. Will you kindly read the catche
make them up?—A. The explanation of the summary which I have
up shows that the American shore fisheries realized less per month
the bay fisheries.

Q. I know, but I want to learn the amount exactly. The gulf f
realized $1,000, less $2, per month; now what do you make the
catch for the shore fisheries?—A. $12,713.20.

Q. I make it $12,434?—A. You will find that I am right.

Q. Then the number of the vessels is 12?—A. Yes.

Q. What will this give for each vessel?—A. $1,059.43.

Q. Take the average length of time—the average trip?—A.
were engaged in fishing for 19 months.

Q. Dividing the number of the vessels into the results, what
leave you?—A. $623.

Q. So that the average catch per month of the vessels emplo
the American shore fishery from 1858 to 1865 amounted in value to
while the average catch per month of the vessels engaged in the (
St. Lawrence fishery realized $998?—A. Yes.

Q. And the average value of the catch of the vessels engaged
gulf fishing for the same period of time was $998?—A. Yes.

Q. This refers entirely to the table you have put in with re
George Steele's vessels?—A. Yes.

Q. You put in another statement purporting to be a statement

the difference between the American shore and the Gulf of St.
rence fisheries ?—A. Yes.
. Do you think that this was a fair statement ?—A. A fair state-
t ?
. Yes.—A. Why not ?
. The counsel asked you if you had ever made up statistics relative
he shore and gulf fisheries, showing the difference between the
rican shore fishery and the Gulf of St. Lawrence fishery, and your
ver was: "Yes; the statement is as follows." Did you intend to
this statement as a fair statement, showing the relative difference
een these two fisheries ?—A. I explained what I meant right un-
eath, when I said :

e average catch is based on the average catch of 84 vessels, from 17 firms, in 1869,
28 vessels in the bay, and 62 vessels off American shore, from 20 firms in 1875.
e firms have done better than the rest.

. Was it your intention to show the relative catches made in these
fisheries ?—A. During these two periods; yes.
Did you intend that these periods should be taken as a fair repre-
ation of the catches usually made in these two fisheries ?—A. Those
e the actual catches made for those years by Gloucester vessels.
. I only want to know whether you intended that the Commission
ild draw from this statement the inference that it represented fairly
relative values of these two fisheries ?—A. I so intended it for those
's.
. But did you so intend it for any other years ?—A. No, I do not
v anything about any other years than those in this relation.
Did you never make up the catches for any other years save those ?
. No; those were the only years for which I ascertained the number
essels which had been fishing in the Gulf of St. Lawrence and off
American shore.
. How was it that you came to ascertain this for those years ?—A.
'as because in 1869 I was town clerk, and I then ascertained it for
information of the people of Gloucester; and in 1875 I obtained
information for Centennial purposes.
. You do not pretend to say that it shows anything like a fair repre-
ation of the relative values of the two fisheries ?—A. No, save for
e years. I show the number of barrels that was caught in that
od in these two fisheries.
. Is this result not directly opposite to the result shown by an ex-
iation of the catches of Mr. Steele's vessels ?—A. I do not consider
the catches of Mr. Steele's vessels show a fair criterion in this re-
t.
. But what is the actual result—you show in this statement that
shore fishery is very much better than the Gulf of St. Lawrence
ry for the two years 1869 and 1875 ?—A. Yes.
. Now taking the whole number of years that Mr. Steele was en-
d in the Gulf of St. Lawrence fisheries, is not the result directly
osite to the result you have shown in this statement ?—A. I know
it is.
. Then you did not intend that this statement should be taken by
Commission as a fair representation of the general value of these
fisheries ?—A. Yes, I did.
. For those two years ?—A. Yes.
. But nothing more ?—A. Nothing more.
. And this is directly opposite to the general result shown by the

catches of Mr. Steele's vessels in the bay for 17 years?—A. I c
think such is the general result.

Q. You said just now that it was?—A. Yes.

Q. To which statement do you adhere?—A. I adhere to what I
said: that the general average of Mr. Steele's vessels in the bay
a fair estimate, because he did not pay any attention to the Ame
shore fisheries.

Q. You said a moment ago that this was the case, and that it w;
the case; and I want to know which you really mean.—A. I mear
I say.

Q. You stated in your examination on page 359, that Mr. Steele'
was among the firms which were most successful, whether on your
or in the Gulf of St. Lawrence—that he was one of the most succ
on your own shore and in the gulf.—A. I beg your pardon. I
said that; or if I did say so, I did not mean to say that he was the
successful on our shore.

Q. The counsel put you this question :

Q. To how many firms do you refer?—A. These include the most successfu
George Steele, &c.

Q. Those are the firms that had been the most successful, whether on our ε
in the Gulf of St. Lawrence ; which are considered to be the most successful f
Gloucester?—A: George Steele, Leighton & Co., Dennis & Ayer, and Smith & '
Q. These are generally considered to be the most successful firms?—A. Yes.

A. I did mean to say that his firm was among the most su
ul firms on our shore. I did not clearly understand the quest
ftbe time.

Q. You did not mean to say that?—A. I did mean to say tha
included in the aggregate the most successful firms in Glouceste
I included George Steele as one of those firms; and I do consid
to be one of the most successful firms in the fishing business.

Q. You did not mean to say that his was one of the most succ
firms regarding the fishery on your coast?—A. No; but he was c
with the others.

Q. And if you are reported here as having said so, you wish
plain the matter in that way?—A. Certainly.

Q. I want to know whether, as an actual fact, the figures pro
by you concerning the periods of time for which Mr. Steele was er
iu the fishery on the American coast, and in the fishery in the C
St. Lawrence, do not show a result entirely opposite to that ma
in this statement relative to the years 1869 and 1876, which yo
put in?—A. That may be so.

Q. Is this the case or not? Is the result as to the relative va
the American shore fishery and the Gulf of St. Lawrence fishe
same in the statement you have filed for the years 1869 and 187
is when you compare the results of the whole 17 years during
Mr. Steele was engaged in these two fisheries?—A. The result
same as regards this statement.

Q. But does the result shown by the one statement exactly c
with the results shown by the other statement as to the relative
of the two fisheries, or does such comparison show that the bay
is far more valuable than the American shore fisheries?—A. Yo
by Mr. Steele's trips?

Q. Yes.—A. Taking Mr. Steele's statement alone it would shc
if you do not take into consideration any other consideration coi
with it.

Q. Taking Steele's statement as it appears here, does it not sh

Gulf of St. Lawrence fishery is far more valuable than the Ameri-
shore fishery ?—A. Yes.

And the other statement is put in to show that the American shore
:ry is more valuable than the Gulf of St. Lawrence fishery ?—A.

. But this latter statement only compares results for the two years,
) and 1875 ?—A. Yes.

. And the other statement covers a consecutive period of 17 years?—
I'his period is not consecutive.

Why not?—A. Because a good many gaps occurred between the
·s when his vessels were fishing.

. From 1858 it extends to 1875, omitting two years, I think?—A.
:ral more years are omitted. There were quite a number of years
u Mr. Steele's vessels were not fishing on the American shore,
reen 1858 and 1875. During a great many years they did not fish
he American shore at all.

. Taking the exact length of time he was engaged in the bay fishery,
not this show that it was much more valuable to him per month
1 was the American shore fishery per month?—A. Yes.

. You were asked whether some of these statements were not made
or the Centennial, and you stated that this was the case?—A. Yes.

. Some of these statements were not made up for the purposes ot
Tribunal at all. but for the Centennial?—A. Yes.

. And the motive for their preparation had no connection with this
)unal?—A. Yes—nothing whatever.

. What did you make them up for?—A. To show that Gloucester,
he fishing business, was the largest fishing port in the world.

. And what was your object in showing this?—A. It was to adver-
the place to some extent.

;. What end were you seeking to gain by advertising this?—A. I
1ted to make Gloucester more known, so that we might have a better
·ket for our fish; that was the idea.

;. And in order to have a better market for your fish, I suppose you
1ted to let capitalists know what a large business it carried on?—A.
·

;. And you proved it to be the third largest fishing port in the
ld?—A. I think that it so stands first.

;. I suppose you wanted to let people know that you carried on there
1rge fishing business which was profitable in a certain sense; you
not wish them to understand that it was an unprofitable business?—
Of course not. We wanted to show that this was the business of
ucester. I did not say, and I would not say, that the business of
ucester is unprofitable.

;. You desired to show that the fishing business was the business of
1ucester?—A. Yes.

;. And you re-affirm that here?—A. Yes; that it is the main busi-
s of Gloucester.

;. I suppose that this business has resulted in the building up of
1ucester?—A. Yes; to a great extent, of course.

;. There are industrial pursuits pursued incidentally by the popula-
1, but these are not the main pursuits of Gloucester?—A. No. I
1k, though, that, if anything, those other pursuits have brought more
1lth into Gloucester than the fishing business.

;. Do you think so?—A. Yes.

;. What makes you think that?—A. Well, the rich men that have

thus come there, and built and paid taxes, have helped out the val
tion of Gloucester.

Q. When did these rich men come there?—A. Some of them h;
been there for 10 or 15 or 20 years.

Q. Would you like it to go on record, as your opinion, that Glouces
owes her prosperity more to the mercantile business, and to other i
dental business, than to the fishing business?—A. I should not.   I c
sider the fishing business of Gloucester as the main business of
place.

Q. And the one to which she chiefly owes her prosperity?—A. Ye

Q. Looking up the files of the Cape Ann Advertiser, with refere
to the Centennial, I notice a statement relative to your fisheries, anc
the effect their prosecution has had on Gloucester, to which I would l
to call your attention, to see whether you agree with it or not.   I
contained in this paper of date November 12, 1875, and is as follows

In 1841 the fishery business of Gloucester had reached about its lowest ebb. (
about 7,000 barrels of mackerel were packed that year, and the whole product of
fisheries of the port was only about $300,000. In 1845 the business began to;revive,
Georges and Bay Chaleur tishery began to be developed, and from that time to
year, 1875, has been steadily increasing, until at the present time Gloucester's tonn
is 10,000 tons more than Salem, Newburyport, Beverly, and Marblehead united. Ne;
400 fishing-schooners are owned at and fitted from the port of Gloucester, by 39 fi
and the annual sales of fish are said to be between $3,000,000 and $4,000,000
distributed from here by Gloucester houses.

THE COMMERCIAL WHARVES.

The wharves once covered with molasses and sugar hogsheads, are now covered v
fish flakes, and the odors of the "sweets of the tropics" have given place to "the
cient and fish-like smells" of oil and dried cod; the few sailors of the commer
marine have been succeeded by five thousand fishermen drawn from all the marit
quarters of the globe; and the wharves that were the wonders of our boyhood d
are actually swallowed up in the splendid and capacious piers of the present day
much have they been lengthened and widened.

THE SALT TRADE.

For many years after the decline of the Surinam trade, hardly a large vessel
ever seen at Gloucester, and many persons thought that nevermore would a maj
ship be seen entering this capacious and splendid seaport. But never in the palm
days of Gloucester's foreign trade, were such immense vessels seen as at the pre
day. Ships of 1,500 tons (as big as six William and Henry's) sailed into Gloucester
bor from Liverpool and Cadiz, and came in to the wharve without breaking bulk,
also laid afloat at low water. More than forty ships, barks, brigs, and schooner
from 400 to 1,400 tons, laden with salt alone, have discharged at this port the pre
year, and also the same number last year. The old, venerable port never represe
such a forest of masts as can now frequently be seen; sometimes six ships and b
at a time, besides innumerable schooners.

THE CITY OF GLOUCESTER OF 1875 AND THE TOWN OF 1825.

What a contrast is presented as a ship enters the harbor now, with what was
sented in 1825. The little rusty, weather-beaten village, with two "meeting-hou
and a few dwellings and wharves gathered around them; two or three thousand
ple with $500,000 property, was all that Gloucester then was, as near as we can a
tain. Now the central wards, without suburban districts, contain 14,000 people, "
$9,000,000 valuation.

Was the valuation irrespective of the suburban districts that amoi
is this correct?—A. I could not say for certain. You have the va
tions to Gloucester for a series of years.

Q. Your valuation agrees with this; but the statement says that
valuation is irrespective of the suburban districts—you know as t
clerk whether this is so or not?—A. I was not town clerk then.

. Do you know whether this is the case or not ?—A. I know that whole valuation of the city does include the suburban districts.
. The article continues:

re banks with nearly $2,000,000 capital in them (including savings); and this in-
e has arisen, not from foreign commerce, but from the once despised and insignif-
i fisheries.
will be seen by a review of the history of Gloucester, that a foreign commerce did
mild the town up in population or wealth; that from 1825 to 1850, its increase
been very small; but from 1850 to 1875, it has grown from 8,000 to 17,000 inhabit-
and its valuation from $2,000,000 to $9,000,000! It is the fisheries that have
ly caused this great change; it is the success of that branch of industry that has
Gloucester harbor with wharves, warehouses, and packing-establishments, from
'ort to "Oakes's Cove." It is the fisheries that have built up Rocky Neck and
ern Point, and caused ward 3 (Gravel Hill and Prospect street) to show nearly all
:ain in population from 1870 to 1875.

you think that this picture is overdrawn as to the prosperity of icester or as to the cause to which this prosperity is attributed ?— Well, I think that it is a little overdrawn myself.
. You think that a little allowance ought to be made for the centen-year ?—A. Yes, I think so, in this respect.
. Do you think that we should make the same allowance with regard ie papers which you have put in concerning the cost of fitting out fishing schooners, &c., prepared for the centennial vear ?—A. No. ink that these are below rather than above the actual estimates; in I know that this is the case.
. Will you kindly tell me what your vessels cost when you were in fishing business ?—A. The Cynisca cost $3,730; the C. C. Davies, 00; the Anna, $2,000; the Daniel McPhee, $3,500; the Ella F. tlett, $3,600; the R. H. Oakes, $4,200; and the I. C. Curtis, $6,500; , is the whole valuation, but I only owned shares in them.
. That makes an average of $3,830 for each vessel ?—A. Yes.
. And that is the number of vessels in which you were interested ?— Yes.
ou have given the valuations and what they cost ?—A. Yes; what r cost.
. This, I suppose, represents about their value ?—A. Yes, at that).
. Do you not think that there is a very great difference between the ie of the vessels actually engaged in the fishery and the value of the ty vessels; the cost of which you sent to the Centennial ?—A. Fancy iels ? That was the actual cost of these vessels in 1875.
. What is the name of a vessel that cost so much ?—A. The Victor; cost $8,800.
. What was her size ?—A. 77 tons.
. Was she an ordinary vessel ?—A. Yes.
. Does she represent the ordinary class of vessels engaged in the eries ?—A. Yes.
. How is it that your seven vessels did not cost anything like so ch ?—A. That was before the war, when prices were on a gold basis.
. Is not the American paper dollar as good as gold now ?—A. Yes; y nearly.
. That reason cannot effect it; that has nothing to do with it. I it to know if your vessels were of an inferior class or were they a sample of the usual run of fishing-vessels ?—A. They were a fair iple of the vessels which were then engaged in the fisheries.
. We are to understand that this is about the average value of the sels engaged in the fisheries ?—A. Yes; at that time.

Q. That was when a dollar currency was worth a dollar in go the dollar currency is almost worth that now; do you mean to s the cost of building vessels now is dearer than it was then ?—A and it is a great deal dearer.

Q. Why ?—A. I do not know why; but it is due, I think, to creased value of labor and of material. I know that these do co now than they did then. They now cost double as much as t then.

Q. You stated that you were interested in 8 vessels and you ha named 7 ?—A. I only fitted out the schooner Electric Flash, but included her catch.

Q. You were not directly interested in her ?—A. No; save onl outfitter. She was a very successful vessel, and I merely mentio to show her catch in the gulf.

Q. Have you thought over the question of bait, since Friday, out whether or not the bait that is charged against a vessel. wl goes on a fishing-voyage, is generally all used ?—A. Yes; this case when they get a full trip.

Q. We know, as a matter of fact, that vessels do not genere full trips; now, suppose that a vessel gets only half a trip, and to Gloucester, is not the bait left from that which she took w when she went on her voyage still good bait ?—A. Yes.

Q. Therefore, that voyage could only be charged with the quantity of bait used ?—A. That is all she is charged with.

Q. What do you mean by that ?—A. What I say; that if any returned it is credited in the gross stock of her catch.

Q. I notice that, in the statement concerning the Oliver Eldrid charged that vessel with 55 barrels of slivers, pogies, at $6.50, fi Eclipse; was this not previously charged to the Eclipse ?—A. N

Q. How do you know that ?—A. These pogies came from the .

Q. What is she ?—A. A bait seiner.

Q. You also charge $7.50 for clams from last year ?—A. T credited back to a vessel last year.

Q. Was this credited in the trip-book ?—A. Yes.

Q. Will you get me the trip-book, and show me the entry ?— not know what vessel it was; but if I knew this I could show th

Q. You have the schooner Oliver Eldridge mentioned here must appear there ?—A. It is not credited from her trip last course.

Q. Surely you can tell by looking at the trip-book ?—A. I ca the trip-book where credit is given under the catch of mackere many barrels of bait returned; that is the way it is done be stock charges are taken out. The mackerel are credited first, pogies returned; the bait returned is credited under the macke added in, and then comes the stock charges, which are deduc both bait and mackerel.

Q. That may be so ?—A. It is so.

Q. The trip-book does not refer to any particular lot in this re A. No; the returned bait is simply taken out of the vessels an away.

Q. Show me the trip of the vessel where this is credited; a every vessel has a short fare, such an entry must appear in near account ?—A. This is not always so.

Q. Why not, if any bait is left ?—A. It is so if any is left.

Q. Every vessel not having a full fare must have something stock charges; and this will make a tremendous difference in ı ?—A. I see that Mr. Steele, in making up his voyages, has charged the bait used, but has not taken in all the bait they carried.

). How do you know that ?—A. Don't you see 27 barrels.

). Just tell me what there is to justify you in supposing that ?—A. ll, there was 27 barrels used in catching 219 barrels of mackerel ording to that. They will be likely to carry more bait than 27 barrels.

). But you find, I understand, that there is no credit to the stock rges in the books ?—A. I don't see any.

). You can find them ?—A. No.

). Now you assume he has only charged the bait actually used. But ant to know this. There is nothing on the face of the book ?—A. ; there does not appear to be on that book, but I think I have seen ɔmewhere on some books.

). What schooner was that ?—A. The George S. Loring.

). Now, you see if you go by that rule——A. You cannot go by any ɔ on bait.

). Well, here is the schooner. She took 226 barrels ; but she is rged with 55 barrels of bait ?—A. I know it.

). Would you assume from this that he had only charged what was ɪally used ?—A. I should presume so.

). Why ?—A. Because, in regard to using bait some vessels and some ɔpers use very much more bait than others. Some of the most suc-ɪful skippers are most liberal with bait.

). In other words, you just assume that what was there was actually d ?—A. Because I see no more, and from my judgment of the way ɪmackerel are caught. Here is a credit—schooner Charles Carroll ; was in Bay St. Lawrence in 1863 ; debtor 40 barrels slivers, 12 bar-clams, less 4 barrels slivers and 1 barrel of clams sold to schooner ɪame Roland.

). Madame Roland is another of his vessels that is in the commence-ɪt of the account. Well, we will take a vessel that is going to haul —A. There is the schooner Austerlitz. She had 8 barrels of clams, ɪs 1 barrel clams left." There is another where she ran short of ; and got it from another vessel. Here is the schooner Grenada.

). What year ?—A. 1863. Eighteen barrels slivers, 6 barrels clams, ɪrrels from schooner Altamaha in bay, less 7 barrels bait left.

). Well, in that other book we examined underneath your hand, I ɪld like to know if you could find any in that ?—A. No ; I don't see .

). So I presume there is none left ; either none left or none credited ?— If there was any left it was taken out of the bait before the bait was ɪred on the trip-book, because I know the bait is always accounted at the end of the voyage.

). Was Mr. Steele accustomed to take out licenses ?—A. He was.

). How are they charged ? In the trip-books ?—A. I think they are. ɪnk I saw them on the trip-books.

). You are sure of that ?—A. I am pretty certain.

. That they are charged on the trip-books against the voyage, part ɪtock charges ?—A. Yes.

. That would be then that the owner would pay half and the crew ɪ ?—A. What year were they ?

). 1866 and 1867. If they were charged in that way,` the owner ld pay half and the crew half?—A. If they are charged in that ɪ—yes.

. Can you give me the name of some one vessel that took a license ?—

167 F

A. [Refers to the book.] I find a fishing license was charged t Alhambra.

Q. I suppose when you made up the statement of charges they included in the custom-house and port charges you put in ?—A. I they are. They comprise a portion of that.

Q. So of course now that they are not payable, they could n charged for the years they are not payable ?—A. No.

Q. Now, in reading this book, "Fisheries of Gloucester," publ by Procter, but—before I refer to that, have you been looking int question of salt ?—A. Yes.

Q. What is the freight of a hogshead of salt from Liverpool ?— don't know.

Q. You can't tell ?—A. No; because I don't know.

Q. On page 75 of this book I find that there were imported in 20,136½ hogsheads of Liverpool salt, costing $8,673; of Cadiz salt 24 hogsheads, valued at $13,910. In 1875 the imports were 74,032 heads of Cadiz salt, and 20,480 of Liverpool, 10,966 of Trepani, Turk's Island, making a total of 108,486. The salt used was 1(hogsheads. The value of the salt, as appears there, would be fr to 47 cents per hogshead.—A. I don't know anything about th: know what it sold for.

Q. You are speaking of the price of salt as sold out. I am spe: of the value of the salt there.—A. That I don't know anything at

Q. What do you find it sold for—the wholesale prices ?—A. I know.

Q. Now one question. I understood you that in former yea: mackerel-fishermen and owners of mackerel-vessels used to insure vessels in Boston insurance offices ?—A. I think they did.

Q. But of late years they have found it more profitable to f(mutual company ?—A. Yes.

Q. That of course divides the losses among themselves, and th vide the profits, and really these 39 men who own all the fishing v of Gloucester are formed into a mutual insurance company ? It make $1,000 or $20,000, they get back their money in the shape o dends; so it is really like paying a duty and getting it back. I: drawback. Now, have you examined and can you tell me what] are made by this company ?—A. I cannot.

Q. You don't know ?—A. I guess the assessments come oftene: the dividends.

Q. Do you know so ?—A. Yes.

Q. Now I would like to know whether you are speaking at hapb because I have a statement under my hand.—A. Well, I haven't of late years acquainted with the working of the insurance comp but when I was in business I know I had to pay assessments.

Q. Were you a shareholder ?—A. Yes; all owners of vessels ar

Q. You have had to pay some calls. Now in this book, the "Fis of Gloucester," on page 73, a table of losses is given running fron to 1875. There was 333 losses, that is, an average annual loss of vessels for these years. For the past five years the average lo been greater, but that would be the total number. Now I have g the trouble of making up a little sum, and I think there must be : handsome dividend divided somewhere, if they pay 4 per cent. have said. You haven't made a statement yourself ?—A. No; b may rest assured, when I go home, I shall go into this insuranc< ness and know about it.

By Mr. Whiteway :

Iave you ever been personally engaged in packing mackerel ?—A.
.
;uring fish ?—A. Yes; I have.

\re you quite clear there is any salt used in the curing of fish
1aving been put into the waterhouse and washed out?—A. No,
,ere is none.

thought you were mistaken in your examination on that sub-
-A. I stated that there was salt put in before it was waterhawsed.

s there any before it is waterhawsed?—A. There is.

\re you clear on that?—A. Yes; there is about four barrels in a
hat is, eight quintals.

¯ou are quite clear on that ?—A. I am.

Iow, you gave us a statement of the operations of the Pharsalia
rand Bank voyage in 1875. That vessel was. out how long ?—A.
months and eight days.

n 1875 ?—A. Yes, sir.

¯ou took this from the trip-book?—A. I did.

Vell, now, what induced you to make the selection of this trip as
stration of the cost of a vessel using fresh bait and going to the
Bank ?—A. Because it covered so many ports which she entered,
e different rates charged for ice and bait.

s it not the most expensive trip that is in that book ?—A. I think

'urn up the other that is more extensive. See if you can find a
xpensive trip than that. What years does that event cover ?—A.
875, and a portion of 1876.

Iow is not this the most expensive trip made by any vessel using
,ait during these years ?—A. After referring to the book—it may
rom what examination I have made, I think it may be.

\s far as you have gone, you find it to be the most expensive
-A. Yes.

Iow, in contrast to that, you take the trip of a schooner—Madam
l—using salt bait, for the year, 1873, is it not ?—A. Yes.

;he fitted with salt bait?—A. Yes.

Iow, ou the other hand, the result of that trip was particularly
rous ?—A. No, sir.

¯or that year ?—A. For that year.

Iave you the trip-book ?—A. Yes, I have. (Reads from memo-
n as follows:)

Schooner George B. Loring.

,ook No. 9, page 32. Trip to Grand Bank, with salt bait, from June 8th to
30th, 1874—2 months 22 days—$2,835.97 net stock. Page 91. From Septem-
, to November 27th, 2 months 17 days, with fresh bait, $1,538.03 net stock.

Schooner Everett Steele.

,ook No. 9, July 21 to September 22nd, 1873. Salt bait, $3,756.25 net stock.

Schooner Madam Roland.

8, page 342, June 19 to Aug. 14, 1873, 2 months 5 days, with salt bait stocked,
) net stock. Aug. 26 to Oct. 10, 1873, salt bait, 1 month 14 days, stocked
7 net stock.

Iow, how do you know that these vessels used fresh bait as well
?—A. I presume they did; that bait was caught on the Banks.

Q. Didn't these vessels go into any port after leaving Gloucest
get fresh bait ?—A. No.

Q. You are certain of that ?—A. Yes.

Q. From what ?—A. From the trip-book.

Q. Can you rely always on the statements in the trip-book ?
can, because the bait is always charged to stock.

Q. You can always rely on the statements made in the trip-b
A. Yes.

Q. Now, turn to the trip-book of the Knight Templar in 1876.
does it appear that the vessel went in for fresh bait ?—A. She we
Bliss Island.

Q. Anywhere else ?—A. No, sir.

Q. Does it not say anywhere else ?—A. She went in for ice
Pierre.

Q. Didn't she get bait ?—A. Yes.

Q. Who was the captain of that vessel ?—A. Captain Gray, I

Q. Well, he swears that upon that trip he was into Hermitaç
and Bliss Island ?—A. Where is Hermitage Bay ?

Mr. Foster remarks that Captain Gray didn't say that he wei
Nova Scotia anywhere for bait, and that "Bliss Island" may be
print for Bois Island in Newfoundland.

Mr. WHITEWAY. I only refer to it to show that the trip-book
be implicitly depended upon.

Q. Do you consider that it is a fair criterion as regards the
tages either of salt bait or of fresh bait to take one trip in 1873 a
trip in 1875, one being a salt-bait trip and the other a fresh-ba
and draw conclusions as to the advantages of each respectivel
you consider it fair or not to take this as a basis ?—A. Let me e
in my answer. When I drew off this——

Q. I ask you a question. You can explain afterwards. (Q
repeated.)—A. I didn't draw any conclusions from that.

Q. I am asking the question whether you consider it fair upc
premises to draw a conclusion ?—A. No; I don't. I didn't draw
clusion on those two trips.

Q. Didn't you intend to show to the Commission by those tw
ments the advantages of salt bait and fresh ?—A. I did. With tl
catch of fish. They were the only two vessels I could get. I didr
to take two trips in vessels that were wide apart.

By Mr. Foster:

Q. Wide apart from what ?—A. Wide apart in the catch.
have taken extreme ones, but I wanted to give a fair average l
the two.

By Mr. Whiteway:

Q. Could not you find a fresh-bait one that stocked as muc
salt-bait ones you gave ?—A. No.

Q. Do you mean to say there haven't been many over and al
one you have given ?—A. I am not aware of it.

Q. You see Captain Malloy stocked with fresh bait 3,700,
didn't consider that a very large catch. Now, can you tell me
the Bank fishing for 1875 was a poor fishery, below the aver?
large fishery, above the average ?—A. I could not tell you.

Q. Have you never heard it was below the average; that is,
fore last, the Bank fishery ?—A. No; I have never heard it was b
average.

Q. Do you know what the Bank fishing was in 1873, wheth(

) or below the average ?—A. I don't know. I form my opinion from I saw on Steele's books.

Now, look at the trip of the Pharsalia, at which you were looking low.—A. I have it before me.

You see there is an item headed "damaged fish, at one cent a 1." You see that ?—A. Yes.

Will you find in the trip-book, which you presented here, another f a Grand Bank fishing-vessel fishing with fresh bait, where there has any damaged fish for these three years, 1874, 1875, and 1876 ?—A. chooner Knight Templar. (Reads items of outfit, among others m showing that she was on a salt-bait trip).

Then there is damaged fish on a salt-bait trip ?—A. Yes.

Now find another case on a fresh-bait trip. (Witness refers to)

I would like, if you have any doubt, if you would take time.—A. is a very small amount of bait to catch 226 barrels.

I don't think you will find any. You see fish may be damaged on a salt-bait vessel fishing on the Banks as well as on a fresh-bait —A. I see it.

Now, will you look, please, at the Pharsalia, on the next trip, after nded the cargo of which you put in an account ?—A. That was in was it not ?

No, 1875.—A. She foundered at sea.

Was she an old vessel ?—A. No.

What age was she ?—A. The abstract will tell exactly. I can't fter referring to abstract). She was brand new. She was lost on cond trip.

You stated in your examination-in-chief, in relation to the dam-) the Pharsalia's fish, as follows :

efore you leave that I want to ask you in reference to an item there—"damaged ."—A. 18,159 pounds of damaged cod, at one cent, $135.10.
Vhy should there be this damaged codfish ? What is the cause of it ?—A. Well, my own opinion of the cause.
Vhat do you believe to be the cause ?—A. I believe the cause is going in so much h bait.
low should that damage the codfish ?—A. My opinion is that the salters salted . the idea that they would not go in so much, and didn't put so much salt on it. she went into port so much, going into the warm water it heated.

you find there are damaged fish, as well with salt-bait fishing, as fresh ?—A. I do find it.

And it is upon that one case of damaged fish with fresh bait that arrive at this conclusion ?—A. I could not account for it in any way.

But it is this one case that you drew this conclusion from ?—A. Yes.

And you would lead the Commission to believe, then, that fish was to be damaged, because of vessels going in for fresh bait, because is one vessel on this one cruise ?—A. No, I don't now, I have seen other case.

You withdraw what you said before ?—A. I withdraw as far as s concerned.

Have you ever been on the Banks fishing ?—A. I haven't.

Then, you would not presume to put your opinion in contradiction opinion of experienced men who had been there six or seven years, y testified contrary to you ?—A. No, sir; of course not.

By Mr. Dana:

Q. Turning to page 367 of your testimony, you will find the fol
question and answer:

Q. Now, can you give us a similar statement of the cost of a vessel for
halibut on the Banks, made out in the same manner for the Centennial?—A
have it, as follows:

Cost of a new schooner at Gloucester, Mass., in 1875, fitted for trawling halibut on th

Vessel of 71 tons; cost $8,000. Vessel made nine trips to Western and Gran
being at sea 302 days, with 12 men for crew, at the following expense, viz:

Trawl-gear .... $
Vessel's expense account ....
Provisions, &c...
General charges, ice, bait, salt, &c...

Now, whose schooner was that?—A. Joseph O. Procter's.

Q. Now, take the vessel's expense account, $1,825,25; is that
from Procter's own account?—A. Yes, sir; he gave it to me.

Q. It was not anything you made up?—A. No, sir.

Q. Now, on page 374 the following questions and answers
ported:

By Mr. Dana:

Q. Now, you have here in this broadside the vessel's expense account, $
Do they call that an expense account? Is that the way they entitle it on th
in making up the account?—A. No; it is all put in one account. All the th
the vessel are put in one account. These were separated for this special purp

Q. Now, you take this expense account, what period of time does it co
Three hundred and two days.

Q. Now, what are the items of the vessel's expense account?—A. They a
lows:

Vessel, 71 tons; cost, $8,800.   Fitted for trawling halibut.

TRAWL-GEAR.

Twine ....
    8 baskets ....
    22 buoys...
    20 buckets ....
    46 files...
1,483 lbs. ground-lines...
    346 lbs. gauging-lines...
    26 knives ....
    12 stones..
    32 staffs ....
    360 lbs. buoy-line..
    4 doz. brooms ....
    52 gross hooks...
    23 lbs. lobster-twine ....
    5 dories...
Iron and copper tanks ....
    4 shovels..
Anchors ....
Oars and scoops...

VESSEL'S EXPENSE.

Spun yarn ....
Parceling ....
Leather..
Jib hanks..
Nails ....
Tinware, &c ....
1 anchor lost..

,ast (broken)	$12 00
; and painting	90 00
ray fee	15 00
)r	47 00
:smith	60 00
ةnter	65 00
،aker's repairs	163 00
)er for ice-house	43 00
ance	539 00
nissions to skipper	465 00
ıs ballast	80 00
٦l gun	38 00
ng rigging, &c	14 00
	1,823 85

Now many of those are actually consumable during the season, so at the end of the season what is left is of little account. But there ome items that may last over another year. Now, except in the of some large permanent expenditures, in making up this account ١ey charge an article that may last one or two years to the year in h it is bought, or do they undertake to distribute it over the time ٦hich it is likely to last ?—A. No ; it is charged to the vessel at the it is procured.

They don't undertake to distribute such things over the time they d probably be useful ?—A. No.

Would it be practicable to do that except where it might be re-٠d, as for instance in chancery proceedings ?—A. No.

ı Is that considered as giving a fair result in the end, charging the les as they are bought, although some of them may outlast the ٦—A. That is the way it is usually done.

Then you know this to be an actual account furnished by Mr. ،tor ?—A. Yes.

It is made up according to the usage ?—A. Yes.

If you were asked to make an equitable assessment of all these ges, for instance, if it was an estate that required to be settled, or were required to assign to each year the portion of the expenses would strictly fall to the account of that particular year, you would ι to make a differencei n the case of articles that lasted over this one ٦—A. Yes.

But that would not be the way the expense account is practically e up ?—A. No.

But this is the way they do the business ?—A. Yes.

And the statement you presented was the actual statement of the uses of that vessel for the year taken ?—A. Yes.

Have you ever put in an account of what would be the annual ex-.iture, supposing the cost of such articles to be distributed over the s during which they would last ?—A. No ; I have not.

Have you since prepared such a statement ?—A. I have ; it is ٰas ws :

١ge yearly expense of a Gloucester fishing vessel, engaged for nine months in the fisheries, the average life of the vessels being about 14 years.

١ and painting, twice yearly	$150 00
١e railway, fees for hauling out	30 00
١ew suit of sails (have to be renewed once in two years)	300 00
١ary expense for repairs and storage of sails	40 00
٠et standing rigging, $5 for junk	20 00
ning rigging, yearly (has to be renewed every 2 years)	125 00
٦ers, average yearly cost (overhauling rigging once in 4 years, $75)	18 75
٠230 fathoms 8½ inch cable every 3 years) $450	150 00

One anchor average loss yearly $45
¼ of calking (vessel has to be recalked once in 7 years for $140) $20, additional
   cost yearly besides, $15 35
Tinware and stoveware.. 20
¼ of cook's stove (renewed once in three years, for $30) 10
¼ of cabin stove (renewed once in three years, for $10).................... 3
Lanterns and lamp-chimneys.. 6
Stove-funnels, yearly 6

                                                             955

One-half for gulf fishing, 4½ months....................................... 479

Then I have the expenses of mackerel-fishing gear for a season of
months, in the Gulf of St. Lawrence, put on board of a Glouces
schooner:

Expenses of makerel-fishing gear for a season of 4½ months in Gulf of St. Lawrence,
on board of a Gloucester schooner. Average—

5 gross mackerel hooks, at 90c $4
7½ doz. mackerel lines, at $1.50..................................... 9
2 cod-fishing lines fitted, $5, less one returned..................... 9
12 bbls. block-tin, at 50c 6
2 doz. bait-knives, at $1.25 9
1 doz. splitting knives, at $1.25..................................... 1
1 clam-chopper, $2... 9
3 nests keelers, at $3.. 9
1 dozen scrub-brooms, at $3 3
1½ dozen buckets 4
½ dozen adzes, $3, less 3 returned, $1.50............................ 4
½ dozen flagging-irons, $3, less 3 returned, $1.50................... 4
5 pounds flags for barrels, at 40 cents 4
3 jig-molds, $1.50, less 1 returned, 50 cents 4
2 ladles, $1, worth one-half returned................................
½ dozen bushel-baskets, at $6....................................... 3
2 bait-boxes, $4, worth half returned...............................
⅓ dozen bait-heavers, at $3 1
15 mackerel-gaffs, at $1.50.. 2

                                                              65

Q. Is there any material change to be made in the general char
for provisions, trawl-gear, &c.?—A. I don't make any. I leave
statements I have put in just as they stand, because they are act
statements of the cost of those things on a particular vessel at
time shown in the statements.

Q. Charged in the way they charged them?—A. Yes.

Q. These statements you have made for your own information. I
not ask you to do so; but these statements you have just read sl
what the items would be if you had to make a nice distribution of
cost over the time during which they would last?—A. Yes.

Q. Well, then, when Mr. Davies treated the statement of expense
in before as being an exact equitable assessment on each year, that
not what you meant, was it?—A. Of course not.

Q. Now, I observe in Mr. Davies' cross-examination that he took
the Daniel McPhee. The evidence is reported as follows:

Q. When was it prepared?—A. It was prepared before I left home.
Q. What was the tonnage of the Daniel McPhee?—A. About 60 tons, I think.
Q. You prepared this statement yourself?—A. Yes.
Q. From your own books?—A. Yes.
Q. Will you read the column of catches in which the 17 barrels appeared?—A.
230, 263½, 41, 17, 86½, 244, 207, 275, 325, 310, 326½, 385, 57. They are shore and
mixed.
Q. Will you take out the shore?—A. 57, 86½.
Q. The catches on your shore appear to be small compared with the others?
The 86½ barrels were caught in five days off our shores.

Q. But the small catches appear to have been taken on your shore. The 300 barrel catches you have read were taken in the bay?—A. Not all of them.

Q. I asked you to read those which were caught on your shores. You did read them. Were not the 300 barrel catches taken in the bay?—A. Yes; those were caught in the gulf.

Now, that one column that Mr. Davies called for is of the first trips of all the vessels?—A. Yes.

Q. Now, does that give a fair indication of the relative value of the shore and gulf fisheries?—A. I don't think it does.

Q. Why not?—A. Because there was more fishing on the shore on the second trip than on the first.

Q. The question was confined to the first trip?—A. Yes; some made only one trip in the gulf.

Q. Now, on page 383, there is a question, "Is not Mr. Steele what you call a fish merchant?" and the answer is, "He is not a fish buyer." Is that correct as it stands? What does it mean?—A. We have men in Gloucester known as buyers aside from the merchants who carry on the business.

Q. They buy cargoes when they are brought in?—A. Yes.

Q. Do they prepare them for market after they have been salted and packed?—A. Yes.

Q. Well, they are the men that cut them up into strips?—A. Cod-fish, yes.

Q. They are buyers of codfish as well as buyers of mackerel?—A. Yes.

Q. Then Mr. Steele is not one of those, but sells? You are asked, "Does he sell his own fish that his vessels have caught?" and answer "He does." What do you mean by that answer?—A. I mean that he sells them to the buyers.

Q. He does not send them to market?—A. No.

Q. So he does not sell his own fish in the sense that he is a general seller, wholesale and retail, or jobber, but he sells to "buyers"?—A. Yes.

Q. In other words, he is a producer?—A. Yes.

Q. Now on page 182 you are asked and answer as follows:

Q. Take vessels fishing off your own coast. With regard to wear and tear, don't you think the wear and tear of vessels fishing off your own coast would be more than that of vessels fishing in the gulf during the months they fish there?—A. I do not.

Q. Not in the winter season?—A. We fish on our shores all the year round.

Q. Is not the wear and tear greater on your coast than in the gulf during the summer months when they fish there?—A. I should say it was.

Q. How did you understand that?—A. I supposed it to allude to the winter season.

Q. Now, comparing your wear and tear on your own coast during these 4½ months with the wear and tear in the gulf during the same period, which would be the greatest?—A. I should say in the gulf.

Q. What advantages are there on our coast apart from its being less boisterous?—A. Harbors more handy.

Q. Anything else?—A. Well, they have more facilities of seeing the storm signals to avoid danger.

Q. You have no doubt that for the same period of time our shore is less dangerous than the gulf. Now in autumn vessels are not permitted to go to the gulf. Is any vessel permitted to sail for the gulf from Gloucester after the 1st of November?—A. I think not.

Q. Do not the insurance companies go round and close up their business after the 1st November?—A. Yes; that is the general practice. It used to be the practice always to close up after the 1st November.

Q. The vessels then out were allowed to come in; they had thei cies renewed or extended?—A. Yes.

Q. At certain rates?—A. Yes; increased rates.

Q. Now, turning to page 384, you are asked and answer as fo

Q. What would you be prepared to say to-day is the profit they make on s furnished to the families of fishermen?—A. About ten per cent.

Q. Not more than that?—A. It would not be over that.

Q. You know that sometimes they lose the supplies?—A. I know they do.

Q. And don't they make sufficient profit to cover all that?—A. I don't thin do.

Q. You think they are not shrewd enough men to make the charge sufficien sure them against loss?—A. They might.

Q. What do you mean by that?—A. Well, I mean this, that might do it.

Q. Now, do they in point of fact, do the Gloucester merchants (interest on the cash they advance to the families of seamen?-don't think they do.

Q. Did you ever know an instance in which it was done?—A.

Q. It might be and you not know it, but your opinion is tha do not?—A. Yes.

Q. Why is it that they do not? Is the period long?—A. No; a general thing.

Q. And do you think they charge any more than the retail pric A. They do not.

Q. So as far as the families are concerned, the profits are the ence between retail and wholesale? Now is there any public o that bears on that sort of thing?—A. Yes; I think if any vessel was to take advantage of the families of the crew, he would n crews to go for him.

Q. The fishermen, of course, find out about it when they get hor A. Yes; they very soon know.

Q. They are not obliged to go for the same owners again?—A.

Q. It is for the interest of the owners, where there is so much petition, to treat the men well?—A. Yes.

Q. Now there is another inquiry:

Q. Would you put the four leading men in Gloucester down at worth from to $30,000 each?—A. I don't think anybody in the fishing business in Gloue worth over $30,000.

Q. Do you mean to include the money made outside the fishin ness?—A. No.

Q. Now as to Mr. Steele's property; it only goes to the value o opinion and does not affect your credit, but I want that put ri think you said Mr. Steele's property was taxed at $20,000. No what the assessment is based on according to Massachusetts law not on what property would sell at for cash?—A. Yes.

Q. Not sold on credit? It does not of course mean a forced sa with reasonable notice. Now, you speak of his having nine vesse ning and put them at an average of $5,000?—A. Yes.

Q. Now, do you think that is a proper sum to put in making account between Mr. Steele and his own vessels?—A. I do.

Q. What do you think those nine vessels or any one of them have sold for this year in cash, the sale being made at Gloucest reasonable time and notice? Would they bring anything like $5, A. No.

Q. It would be difficult to determine?—A. Yes.

Q. The number put on the market affects the price?—A. Yes.

. The vessels being designed solely for the fishing business, would
; sell as would other vessels ?—A. No.

. But suppose Mr. Steele was living and wanted to close up his
siness, but was in no hurry and could take his own time about it, and
ild sell them for cash or at credit, and could take them to any port
ere there seemed to be a demand—he might, by taking plenty of time,
rcise skill and judgment, and selling on credits, realize $5,000 each,
the vessels ?—A. Yes.

. In other words, is there any necessary connection between what
e fishing vessels would bring sold for cash on reasonable notice, not
ced, and the value which ought to be taken when settling between
self and his vessels as to the result of their voyages ?—A. I think
re is.

. Do you wish to alter your estimate that in making up those ac-
nts Mr. Steele's vessels should be entered at $5,000 each ?—A. No.

. You were asked a number of questions in regard to Mr. Steele's
able property. His taxable property you first estimated at $20,000.
n afterwards thought it would be $25,000, and you said you thought
would be worth $35,000. When you made your first estimate you
re asked what the firm was worth. Did you think at the time of in-
ding any personal property Mr. Steele might have, and real estate,
connected with the business ?—A. I did not.

. Do you wish to change your statement ?- Are you inclined to put
property at more than $35,000 ?—A. I think that is really the cash
ue.

. At the same time, you would not alter the mode of making up the
ounts ?—A. I think the vessels are worth $5,000 in his business.

. Those vessels, no doubt, all stand in his name, but do you know
ether he owns the whole of all of them ?—A. I don't know. I pre-
ne he does not.

. Why so ? He is a rich man.—A. Nearly every owner in Glouces-
has more or less shares of his vessels owned by his skippers.

. Is it for the interest of the vessel owner that his skipper shou d
interested in the ship ?—A. It is generally supposed so.

. What portion does a skipper generally own in a vessel in cases
ere he is not a capitalist ?—A. The owner generally gives him one-
irth.

. And he pays for it as he can ?—A. Yes.

. Do you know whether that is a matter of personal trade, or is the
tain's name entered at the custom-house ?—A. There is a bond some-
les.

. A bond between them ?—A. Yes. Sometimes a bill of sale is given
l a mortgage taken back.

. On page 387 of your evidence there is the following :

. You have proved him from theory to be bankrupt beyond all redemption, when in
: he is a capitalist worth $45,000, which exhibits the difference between the practi-
statement and the theory—A. Yes; but he had capital when he went into the
iness.

. Did you mean to say that $45,000 was his capital ?—A. I think I
rdly answered it in that way ; I might have said it, if it is so recorded.

. The evidence also reads :

. Do you state that he brought it in with him ?—A. One-half of it was made in
sail-making business.

. Then one-half of the capital he now has was made in the sail-
iking business ?—A. I should think so.

Q. And the rest in the fishing business during 19 years. You me
to say that he brought into the business the capital he had made a
sailmaker, and added to it from the fishing business during 19 years
A. Yes.

Q. On page 387 of your evidence there is the following :

Q. And that shows the values at which he settled with his men ?—A. Ye .
Q. Does it show the actual cash price which he received for these 33,645 barrels
A. Yes.
Q. Will you explain ?—A. Remember that this is for the fish and the packing wl
he receives when he sells the trip.

Explain what that means.—A. When he sells the fish the barrel is s
with it, so that the packing is included in the sale. In the books it
made up without charging the packing in the value of the fish ; ɛ
when he sells it, he sells it with the barrel.

Q. And when he settles with his crew the packing is taken out of
price?—A. Yes; that is customary.

Q. On page 388 of your evidence there is the following :

Q. Then his expenditure for the Pharsalia was a little below the ordinary run ?—
Yes; it is below the average.
Q. And this item represents the actual expenditure taken from the books ?—A. :
Q. Are the items for outfit and expenses put down also from actual expenditures
No; they are estimates.

Did you reckon there anything more than barrels packed out in m
ing your statement for the settlement of the crew ? There are m
sea barrels than packed barrels ?—A. Yes.

Q. What is the difference—about 10 per cent. ?—A. Yes.

Q. If barrel is exchanged for barrel do you make any allowance
10 per cent.?—A. I see by my reply I said they are estimates. D
that apply to the Pharsalia ?

Mr. DAVIES. That question related to the reason why you charg
$450, when in the sample statement it only showed $415 as being
pended.

By Mr. Dana :

Q. Did you mean to apply that to the Pharsalia ?—A. I did not.

Q. Have you any alteration to make that would add to the cost w
respect to the barrels? Might not the cost on them and interest on tl
be very fairly taken off ?—A. If I was going to make up the acco
again, I would make it up more clearly in my own mind by taking
the average cost of running and vessel's gear, and then I would m
a difference between sea and packed barrels. Those barrels had t
on board, and were part of the outfit, and the increased cost shoul
considered. Then, again, I did not calculate anything for the bar
the bait was in. The bait was charged in net stock there with the
rels taken out—only the bait. As the bait was taken out, the bar
could be used for holding mackerel.

Q. On page 388 of your evidence you were asked :

Q. You charge $8,500 for salt, for as many barrels at $1 a barrel; one-half of it w
be profit, and that would leave $4,250 as profit ?—A. Yes.

What does that mean ?—A. If I answered " yes," I answered it w
out thought, because there is no such profit as that on a barrel of

Q. What is about the rate of profit ?—A. I should not set down
profit on a barrel of salt at more than 12½ cents or 25 cents.

Q. There are eight bushels to a hogshead ?—A. Yes.

Q. A bushel of salt is a struck measure, and does not hold so n
as a bushel of other articles ?—A. Yes.

The following questions were put to you. by Mr. Davies, on 389:

find from your statements that after the Washington Treaty was entered into, eele withdrew his vessels from your shore fishery and concentrated all his efforts bay; am I correct in making that statement?—A. In 1870 and 1871 he did not ny vessels to the bay.
iut in 1872 he commenced sending them to the bay?—A. Yes.
.nd he has sent them there ever since?—A. Yes.
.nd he has since sent none to fish on your shore?—A. No.
ince 1872 he has sent none to fish on your shore, but has sent all his vessels to y?—A. Yes.

ve you any statement to show how Mr. Steele distributed his ves-
In 1858 how many vessels had he?—A. In 1858 he fitted 8 ners.
How were they distributed?—A. All 8 schooners went into the ind one went to the shore one day.
In 1859 how many vessels had he?—A. He fitted 10; all went to ay, and none to the shore.
In 1860?—A. Fitted 11; 8 to the bay, and three to the shore.
1861?—A. Fitted 11; 7 to the bay, and 4 to the shore.
1862?—A. Fitted 11; 5 went to the bay, 2 to the shore after they ied from the bay.
1863?—A. Fitted 9; 6 went to the bay, 2 to the shore for one i and 24 days, after returning from the bay.
1864?—A. Fitted 8; 8 went to the bay, none to the shore.
1865?—A. Fitted 8; 8 went to the bay, none to the shore.
1866?—A. Fitted 10; 10 went to the bay, none to the shore.
1867?—A. Fitted 10; 9 went to the bay, 1 to the shore for 18 days returning from the bay.
1868?—A. Fitted 10; 5 went to the bay, the rest went cod-fishing.
1869?—A. Fitted 8; 6 went to the bay, none to the shore.
1870?—A. Fitted 7; none went to the bay, 5 to the shore.
1871?—A. Fitted 6; none went to the bay, 3 to the shore.
Now comes the first year of the Washington Treaty. How many ls did he fit in 1872?—A. 10 vessels; 2 went to the bay and 2 to iore, and the rest went cod-fishing.
1873?—A. Fitted.8; 4 went to the bay, none to the shore, and 4 ihing.
1874?—A. Fitted 9; 3 went to the bay, the rest went codfishing.
1875?—A. Fitted 9; 3 went to the bay.
1876?—A. Fitted 13; 5 went to the bay.
Taking all those years together, do you see any striking difference 7-fishing before and after 1872?—A. I do not.
You find that many years long before the Washington Treaty he ot send any vessels shore-fishing. Did he ever do much at shore· g?—A. No.
Did he ever go into it fully?—A. No. I don't think he ever l a seiner.
Therefore he never tried seining on the shore?—A. No.
He did not much enter into the mackerel-fishing on our shores?— o.
His shore-mackerel business is no test of the general shore-mack- usiness?—A. No.
You know that the word chartering sometimes means hiring and imes letting. In speaking of chartering, did you mean to say that were no cases of chartering vessels either in the form of letting

or hiring vessels for fishing in Gloucester ?—A. There are cases of vessels for fishing.

Q. Who does it ?—A. It is generally done by outside vessels.

Q. Who hires them ?—A. Sometimes a successful skipper will c a vessel.

Q. You mean hire a vessel ?—A. Yes.

Q. Do Gloucester merchants, who are fitters-out and producers (let their vessels ?—A. No.

Q. Do they hire vessels ?—A. Some do, but it. is very seldom there are merchants who do not own vessels.

Q. The business of hiring vessels does not amount to anythir portant. Do you mean to say there is no such thing ?—A. No.

Q. What do you think is the average life of a fair fishing-vesse an extraordinarily good or unusually bad vessel ?—A. The avera of the vessels owned in Gloucester, in 1876, was 13.34 years.

Q. Do you make that out from documents ?—A. From an annua lication published by John S. E. Rogers, of Gloucester, Mass.

Extract handed in as follows :

The years are given in which 467 of the vessels in the list were built, the ! being boats of which no record is kept of their age. A comparison of them wi cate pretty nearly the depressions and prosperity of the fishing business dur last twenty-five years. The oldest vessel in the district is the schooner Ma Annisquim, which was built in 1837; the next oldest is the schooner Gilde, of Mi ter, built in 1839. The oldest vessel in Gloucester Harbor is the schooner Metec in 1844. Each year since 1844 has furnished one or more of the vessels whicl up our list, as follows:

Year.	No.	Year.	No.	Year.
1876	23	1864	5	1852
1875	38	1863	5	1851
1874	22	1862	2	1850
1873	12	1861	1	1849
1872	13	1860	24	1848
1871	22	1859	22	1847
1870	28	1858	16	1846
1869	30	1857	9	1845
1868	29	1856	4	1844
1867	35	1855	5	1839
1866	35	1854	5	1837
1865	14	1853	13	

Q. Do you suppose it to be correct on that point ?—A. Yes ; compiler is very accurate in getting up statistics.

Q. That is the average age of vessels existing at the time ?—A I may explain that this book gives the year each vessel was bui the number of vessels built in each year down to 1876.

By Sir Alexander Galt:

Q. Do you mean that the average life of a vessel would be al years ?—A. I think so.

By Hon. Mr. Kellogg:

Q. Do you mean that it is as long as the vessels can go a tri Of the vessels in the fishing business, owned in Gloucester, the a age was a trifle under 14 years.

By Mr. Dana:

Q. When a vessel is brought into Gloucester, not new, do the show where she was built ?—A. The table shows the year wh where built.

Q. Some vessels are pretty old ?—A. One vessel in the table w in 1837.

. You have said that Mr. Steele never did any seining on the Amer-
shore ?—A. I don't think he ever did.
. Seining has come into general vogue, has it not ?—A. Yes.
r. DAVIES. The years I took were the years of the Reciprocity Treaty
n there was no seining.

By Mr. Dana:

. As to insurance. Those merchants of Gloucester who own vessels
a company; that is really a sort of annual company ?—A. A com-
y formed every year.
. It closes up every year ?—A. Yes.
. The day it expires is 1st November ?—A. They have now organ-
it to continue the year round.
. But there is a new company once a year ?—A. Yes.
. All matters are closed up each year ?—A. Yes.
. If the vessel do not return by a certain date a sum is placed in the
ense account ?—A. Yes.
. They don't actually pay premiums and receive dividends ?—A. No.
. They give their notes, and at the end of the year there is an as-
ment ?—A. They are assessed from time to time.
. And at the end of the year, if necessary, there is an assessment ?—
here is a final assessment.
. There is no dividend paid ?—A. No.
. The crew have nothing to do with insurances ?—A. No.
. Do you know how the owner is able to assign to each vessel the
unt it ought to pay ?—A. Each vessel is charged with the amount
nsurance paid out during the year to the company.
. It is divided among different owners ?—A. Each vessel is put in at
rtain valuation, according to her age; the insurance amounts to so
:h, and each owner is charged with the insurance on that vessel.
. They don't actually pay out that insurance, do they ?—A. Yes; if
 not paid out in one season it is in another. They give their notes,
 when there is an assessment on the insurance they pay the amount.
. They are not charged on an ordinary note ?—A. They give a pre-
m note.

By Mr. Davies:

. If there is no assessment made, the premium note, I suppose, is re-
ned to him ?—A. I presume so.
. You have stated that the average age of fishing-vessels sailing out
Gloucester is fourteen years ?—A. Yes.
. Some of the vessels are, I suppose, twenty-five years old ?—A.
; some more than that.
. One nearly forty years old ?—A. Yes.
. I see by this book that 22 vessels were built in 1876 ?—A. Yes.
. 38 in 1875; 22 in 1874; 12 in 1873; 13 in 1872; 24 in 1860; 24 in
); 18 in 1858; 90 vessels were built previous to 1858, and would be
rom 19 years old to 40 years ?—A. Yes.
. In regard to packing; in the statement you made up of Mr.
le's vessels you told me you took the prices of his mackerel from
books ?—A. Yes.
. This statement you made up representing the voyages of 107 of
Steele's vessels does not include packing ?—A. No.
. You were asked a question about Mr. Steele's capital, and you
l about one-half had been made by him in the sail-making business,
. the other half since. Do you really know as a matter of fact what
Steele's capital is ?—A. I do not.

Q. It may be, for anything you know, $70,000, $80,000, or §
—A. It may be.

Q. You have no means of knowing what is his capital?—A
no means of knowing.

Q. You really don't know what Mr. Steele's capital is, and y
no means of knowing?—A. I do not. When you asked me that
previously I was entirely unprepared, and I gave you an es
value.

Q. You now say you really don't know what his capital is?—
not; only from my judgment, and from the common estimatio
valuation in the city. I never went to the assessor's books to s
his property was valued at.

Q. There is one answer which struck me as a little curious.
to a question by Mr. Dana you said the wear and tear of a v
your coast is less than the wear and tear of a vessel in Bay
rence?—A. I think so.

Q. The reason you gave was because their harbors were so ha
A. Yes.

Q. Is it not in evidence before this Commission that the gene
ing is from 15 to 100 miles off your coast?—A. I have referred
shore mackerel-fleet and the bay mackerel-fleet in my estimate.

Q. Does not the American fleet fishing for mackerel off you
fish from 15 to 100 miles off shore?—A. Yes.

Q. Is not Georges Bank one of the places where they fish?—A
times, but very seldom there.

Q. It is a very dangerous place?—A. Yes; in the winter seas

Q. Don't you know that the vessels fishing for mackerel in
Lawrence fish within 50, 40, or 20 miles of the shore?—A. That

Q. Therefore your reason cannot be correct, when your vessels
off your coast are further away from the harbors than vessels
bay?—A. Off the New England coast there is more sea-room
know that in Massachusetts Bay they have plenty of sea-room,
the gulf they have not.

Q. Do you mean to contend that the wear and tear of a vessel
off the American coast in November is not greater than the w
tear of a vessel fishing in the Bay St. Lawrence in August?
course not; it is not a parallel case.

Q. You mean only during the months they fish in the bay?—
the same months on our shore.

Q. But the months they fish off your shores when they canno
our shores, the wear and tear is greater than during the fishing
in the gulf?—A. For sails and rigging the wear and tear in th
just as much as fishing on our shores.

Q. How can that be?—A. Because in the gulf you are using
the time.

Q. Take a vessel fishing mackerel in November off your coa
the wear and tear of that vessel much greater than that of a n
fishing vessel in the bay in August?—A. I believe there was
gale down your coast in August.

Q. Take July?—A. Off our coast in November I should sa
decidedly rougher.

Q. Should you say that the wear and tear of a vessel was ∂
greater on your coast?—A. I should say it was somewhat grea

Q. You are not a practical fisherman now and have not bee
great many years?—A. No.

Q. You have no practical interest in ascertaining the prices?

iince you were here on Friday you have made up a statement dif-
somewhat in principle and also in some of its details from that
bmitted on Friday?—A. Yes.

'rom whom did you get the statement that the fishing gear of a
cost about $45?—A. I made it up from my own idea of the things,
hen I sat down and enumerated them I found they amounted to a
leal more than I had stated.

[he first statement you made was a hap-hazard one. Had you
ken the trouble to put down the items that made up $45?—A. I
»t put down the items. I took the cost of a seiner in 1875, the
; gear of which amounted to nearly $50.

[hen you took it from the highest cost we have had before us yet?
No.

s it not the Centennial one?—A. I allude to that one.

[he cost of the vessel was submitted to the Centennial Commis-
3?—A. Yes.

n this statement you make the cost much higher?—A. I do.

[ell me who did you consult with regard to the articles and prices
'riday?—A. I consulted myself as regards the articles.

Who did you consult with?—A. I did not consult with any one.

[ou made that up without consultation?—A. I made it up from
collection of the articles which went on board of a vessel.

)o you mean to say you made it up without consulting any prac-
ian?—A. I do. I asked in regard to the prices.

Whom did you consult?—A. With a Gloucester man who fits
}.

What is his name?—A. Mr. Wonson.

)f the prices, previous to consulting him, you had no knowledge?—
ad knowledge of the prices in 1860, 1861, and 1862.

[hat was 14 years ago?—A. The basis on which Mr. Steele's
es are made up is on an average for 19 years past.

What does this statement purport to be; is it the average of a
r of years?—A. It is an average of 17 years on which the
es of Mr. Steele's vessels were based.

thought it explained the mackerel fishery at the present time?—

Have you got a price list for each of the seventeen years the
of which Mr. Wonson gave you?—A. No.

He guessed the average price for seventeen years of each of those
s, or was it arrived at by a comparison of actual figures?—A. I
the prices of those articles, according to my recollection, in 1860,
ind 1862. I compared the prices of those years with the prices
o get at my estimate.

speak in regard to your conversation with Mr. Wonson. Did he
,ber the prices of each of the articles during the seventeen
'—A. Of course not.

Nor could you?—A. Of course not.

[herefore, if neither of you could recollect the prices, how could
ake up the statement?—A. I made it up according to the best of
lgment.

[he value of that would consist in the means of knowing. You
t possess price-lists for each year to ascertain the amount?—A.

[he second statement is $20 over the former statement?—A. Yes.

And that estimate was submitted to the Centennial Commis-

168 F

sion ?--A. $50 for a seiner, not for a gulf fisherman. Mackere
were an expense, and I did not take any account of them in the

Q. If you put half a dozen adze on board, will they not be an
at the end of the season ?—A. Yes, but they would not be wo
much, and they would not all come back.

Q. This statement is made up to the best of your judgment ?—A
I think you will find the facts warrant me in saying that it is far
the cost of those articles during seventeen years.

Q. It is fourteen years since you have been engaged in the busin
A. I know that the prices since I left the business have been a
deal higher.

Q. You cannot pretend to claim for your evidence on this po
same value as that of a practical man in business ?--A. Of cour

Q You would not have known how to make up the statement
for Mr. Wonson ?—A. I would, except the prices.

Q. You could not get the prices without Mr. Wonson ?—A. I co
get the prices to day. I had the prices for 1860, 1861, and 1862
mind.

Q. Those prices would not give you the average for sev
years ?—A. It would give the commencement.

Q. What was the price of buckets in 1872 ?—A. 25 cents apie

Q. You put them down in the statement at $3 a dozen ?—A. Y

Q. This other statement you have made up is also different fr
one you had put in ?—A.. Yes.

Q. Why did you make it different ?—A. Because that is the
amount.

Q. The expenditure on what vessel does it represent ?—A. It
sents any vessel.

Q. It is not an actual representation of any given vessel ?-
course not.

Q. It is a supposititious statement ?—A. You may call it so.

Q. I want to know whether you submit that to the Commissi
statement of actual expenditure incurred on a given vessel, or as
posititious statement ?—A. Not for any given vessel, but I subm
being, if anything, below the actual expenditure for any vessel r
out of Gloucester.

Q. What you suppose to be below ?—A. I think it is.

Q. You don't pretend to submit it as having been copied out
accounts of any vessel ?—A. No; it cannot be done.

Q. It was not taken from any given vessel ?—A. No.

Q. Nor from any practical man's accounts ?—A. No.

Q. It was made up out of your own head ?—A. Yes, the same
one estimating would make it up.

Q. The vessel's expense account which you submitted, you ex
you know nothing about, but that it was handed in by you fr
Procter ?—A. That is all. I know nothing about it.

Q. Mr. Procter was examined here ?—A. Yes.

By Mr. Whiteway:

Q. Turn to page 375 of your evidence, and you will find the fe
under the head of Recapitulation:

Trawl gear ....

Vessel's expense account ....

Provisions, &c..

General charges ....

      Total cost of running ....

lerstand that is the exact annual charge of a vessel during 302
was running?—A. I do.

der the miscellaneous charges, amounting to $1,135.50, there is
200 tons ice, $600. Do you mean to say that a vessel engaged
'ill use 200 tons ice in 302 days?—A. Yes.

1 you show me in your trip-book any such cases? Turn up the
ι.—A. That was a Grand Bank trip after Grand Bank codfish.
trip after fresh halibut. The cases are not parallel.

ιe a fresh-fish trawler and show me a consumption of 200 tons of
2 days.—A. Here are the items for the schooner Marathon: 25
ce, April to May, 1874; 23 tons, May 6 to June 14; 28 tons,
to July 31; 30 tons, August 4 to September 12; 15 tons, De-
nd January; total, 131 tons. Probably there are other vessels
more.

ιt is the highest quantity you can find?—A. No doubt I can
rallel case to that in the statement, because it is common. It
on how successful the vessel is in taking fish as to how much
:d. It is not an extraordinary occurrence to use 200 tons of ice

ɣ Mr. Davies:

ιderstood you to say that the abstracts you put in are correct?—
· I had prepared the abstracts, to make sure they were correct
ιlmost as much time in verifying them as I had in making them
ey agree within four cents.

ɣ Hon. Mr. Kellogg:

regard to bait used in mackerel-fishing; I suppose the quantity
ιken is not generally an exact indication of the quantity of bait
ι. No. Sometimes they will throw 50 or 75 barrels of bait and
:0 barrels of mackerel.

it need excite no wonder that a good deal of bait had been used
nall catch?—A. No.

Summary of the voyages made by the fishing-vessels of George Steele.

[Recapitulation of foregoing voyages, showing in condensed form the whole totals from 1858 to 1877; showing time employed in cod and halibut fishing, and American shore and Gulf of St. Lawrence mackerel fishery, with amount of catch, value, &c.]

Year.	No. of vessels. Cod and haddock fish'y.	From time of sailing, time employed.	Gross stock, or value of catch.	One-half of net stock, or vessel's share.	No. of vessels. Gulf mackerel fishery. Time employed.	Barrels caught. "Bay" mackerel.	Value of catch, or gross stock.	Time employed, from time of sailing.	Vessel's share, or one-half net stock.	No. of vessels. American shore.	Time employed.	No. of barrels caught.	Gross stock, or value of catch.	Vessel's share.	From time of sailing, total time employed.	Gross stock, or total value of catch.	Vessel's total stock. (Expenses are taken from gross stock)	Vessel or crew's share, or one-half of "net stock."	Remarks. Schooners fitted.	Remarks. Hands employed. Codfishing.	Remarks. Hands employed. Mackereling.
		Mos. Ds.						*Mos. Ds.*			*Mos. Ds.*				*Mos. Ds.*						
1858 ..	7	31 7	$15,170 68	$6,722 82	8	2,109¼	$23,159 37	33 22	$10,715 58	1	1	79	$277 62	$94 08	65	$41,607 67	$6,542 71	$17,532 48	8	9.	14.5
1859 .	8	33 9	22,037 59	9,026 11	10	1,923	24,727 61	42 13	10,457 41	....	......	......	....	....	75 22	44,765 20	5,798 1	19,483 52	10	9.	14.5
1860 ..	9	42 15	21,088 18	8,972 76	8	1,866½	20,295 91	33 18	9,178 75	3	7 24	1,098½	6,824 31	3,334 20	80 7	48,208 40	5,236 9	21,485 71	11	9.	14.5
1861 ..	9	55 3	19,989 75	8,708 33	7	1,809	10,446 87	22 3	4,469 73	4	6 14	688½	3,481 42	1,528 96	81 20	33,9[illegible]8 04	4,504 0	14,707 02	11	9.	14.6
1862 ..	8	59 8	32,074 32	14,460 22	5	1,360¼	10,363 77	14 16	4,719 50	2	2 27	239	1,267 99	556 73	76 21	43,706 08	4,233 1	19,736 45	9	9.	14.2
1863 ..	9	39 14	34,416 39	15,484 92	6	2,654	28,784 69	20 7	13,346 39	2	1 24	121	861 86	385 17	61 15	64,062 94	5,629 9	29,216 48	9	9.	14.2
1864 ..	8	37 6	32,711 49	15,122 36	8	4,319	52,751 83	27 25	22,010 83	....	......	......	....	....	65 1	85,463 32	11,196 94	37,133 19	8	9.1	14.5
1865 ..	8	26 24	48,142 00	22,403 83	8	4,246½	54,713 24	34 9	25,267 93	....	......	......	....	....	61 3	102,855 64	7,511 7	47,671 76	8	9.1	14.5
1866 ..	9	36 6	44,579 18	19,952 97	10	3,914	60,108 56	43 9	26,727 79	....	......	......	....	....	79 15	104,687 74	11,326 2	46,680 76	10	9.4	14.8
1867 ..	10	52 9	48,860 24	21,456 27	9	2,526½	35,667 11	34 13	15,970 47	1	18	23	235 03	82 37	87 10	84,762 38	9,744 1	37,509 11	10	9.4	14.8
1868 ..	10	66 6	71,543 22	32,327 30	5	1,712¾	13,437 01	17 16	5,276 94	....	......	......	....	....	83 22	84,980 23	9,771 75	37,604 24	10	9.4	14.8
1869 ..	8	48 21	60,777 09	26,564 49	6	105	19,133 87	19 3	7,498 88	....	......	......	....	....	67 24	79,910 96	11,784 2	34,063 37	8	9.5	15.
1870 .	5	37 26	36,689 00	15,338 06	.....	......	....	.....	....	5	17 18	1,702	17,045 71	7,511 79	55 14	53,734 71	8,035 01	22,849 85	7	9.5	15.
1871 ..	5	35 17	31,848 22	13,658 36	.....	......	....	.....	....	3	14 9	1,076	9,427 52	4,204 10	49 26	41,275 74	5,550 8	17,862 46	6	9.5	15.1
1872 ..	7	56 9	51,857 09	23,447 86	2	713¼	5,861 62	5 5	2,668 62	2	7 13	368	3,680 34	1,560 36	68 27	61,401 05	6,047 3	27,676 84	10	10.2	16.1
1873 ..	8	57 11	60,221 69	27,659 71	4	1,425	14,906 61	13 8	6,423 19	....	......	......	....	....	70 19	74,128 30	5,962 5	34,082 90	8	10.1	15.1
1874 ..	8	63 15	66,645 11	29,628 37	3	1,305	8,163 49	11 25	3,389 41	....	......	......	....	....	75 10	74,807 60	8,773 04	33,017 78	9	10.2	15.6
1875 ..	9	61 27	60,967 44	26,653 28	3	816	11,571 84	9 16	5,187 00	....	......	......	....	....	71 13	72,539 28	8,858 7	31,840 28	9	10.6	15.6
1876 .	10	74 11	55,897 25	26,938 65	5	840	9,739 46	17 21	4,081 61	....	......	......	....	....	92 2	65,636 71	11,596 1	27,020 26	13	10.5	16.
19 yrs.	155	915 4	813,515 93	360,526 67	107	33,645	403,832 86	400 29	177,390 03	23	58 28	5,394¾	43,101 80	19,257 76	1,369 1	1,262,431 29	146,159 4	558,135 90	174	180.5	283.4
		108 15	Time fitting.				Time fitting.	75 1							268 14	Time fitting vessels.			Average, 9.1 vessels yearly. Average, 9.5 hands fishing; 15 hands mackereling.		
	Av 8.21	1,023 19						476							1,637 15						

...ges made by George Steele's vessels is explained as follows: The 'time employed' is the actual time employed from the time she sailed on

[Tonnage, 94⅗ tons; average number of hands fishing, 8; mackereling,

Years	Time in cod and halibut fishing. Mos.	Days.	Gross stock or value of catch.	Vessel's share, or one-half of net stock; crew's same.	Time in Gulf of St. Lawrence mackerel fishery. Mos.	Days.	Number of barrels caught and packed out.	Value of catch.	Vessel's or crew's share of catch, one-half of net stock.	Time in American shore mackerel fishery. Mos.	Days.	Number of barrels caught.	Value of catch.	Vessel or crew's share.
1858	4	16	$2,214 39	$994 55	4	25	240	$2,690 50	$1,903 57	3	24	532	$3,516 00	$1,699 13
1859	4	20	2,746 33	243 92	4	8	175	2,245 67	913 83					
1860	4	14	1,978 05	637 47	3	5	218	1,273 55	528 02					
1861	5	6	1,797 80	738 90	3	11			528 16					
1862	9	18	5,529 07	470 38	3	26	539	5,339 69	3,207 59					
1863	4	20	4,536 60	105 38	3	9	699	5,384 78						
1864	3	12	3,412 62	1,608 96	4	10	564	7,256 61	3,443 92					
1865	4	9	6,420 57	3,041 65	4	12	366	3,831 26	1,653 05					
1866	4	8	4,354 17	1,907 00			218		920 55					
1867	1	13	3,118 51	1,384 96				9,822 09						
1868			1,932 38	880 96										
	50	29	38,040 11	17,013 35	32		2,919	33,844 15	14,838 69	3	24	532	3,516 00	1,699 13

Sold in spring of 1865.

Schooner Borodino.

Abandoned on Georges Bank, February 27, 1862.

[Tonnage about 59 tons (90 tons old); 9 hands fishing; 15 hands mackereling.]

Year.	Time in cod and halibut fishing. Mos.	Days.	Value of catch.	Vessel's share; crew's the same.	Time in Gulf of St. Lawrence, mackerel-fishing. Mos.	Days.	Barrels of bay mackerel caught.	Value of catch.	Vessel's share; crew's the same.	Time in American shore mackerel fishery. Mos.	Days.	Barrels of shore mackerel caught.	Value of catch.	Vessel's share; crew's the same.
1858	3	2	$1,689 38	$737 75	5	2	(2 trips. 386½)	$3,787 25	$1,765 57					
1859	2	24	2,856 58	1,313 97	5	7	(2 trips. 254½)	2,987 31	1,288 71					
1860	4	27	2,652 78	1,153 35						3	7	504½	$311 92	$1,559 06
1861	4	3	1,471 86	596 53						2	17	406	1,616 70	690 82
Four years	14	26	8,670 60	3,800 90	10	9	653	6,774 56	3,053 98	5	24	910½	4,728 62	2,249 88

SCHOONER ___.

[50 75-100 tons; hands employed cod and halibut fishing, 9; hands mackereling, 15.]

Years.	Time in cod and halibut fishing. (Mos. Days.)	Value of catch.	Vessel's share, net stock.	Time in Gulf of St. Lawrence, mackerel-fishing. (Mos. Days.)	Number of barrels caught.	Value of catch.	Vessel's share.	American shore mackerel fishery.
1858	4 17	$2,913 07	$1,018 97	2 trips. 4 11	383½	$4,929 91	$2,307 20	None.
1859	4 14	2,121 90	955 38	4 20	119½	1,643 69	676 97	
1860	4 19	1,779 14	763 10	3 trips. 3 28	166¼	1,780 58	741 34	
1861	4 29	1,603 65	683 06	3 11	256¼	1,329 94	581 87	
1862	5 24	2,538 54	1,148 73	3 27	263¼	2,311 39	1,049 69	
1863	4 21	4,041 86	1,815 16	4 trips. 2 4	458	4,908 57	2,165 58	
1864	5 5	3,756 06	1,787 13	3 21	540	6,631 68	2,706 91	
1865	3 16	6,349 04	2,931 39	3 trips. 2 30	539½	6,949 69	3,220 40	
1866	3 22	5,321 03	2,504 60	3 trips. 3 26	375	5,631 88	2,520 11	
1867	4 16	3,874 78	1,635 69	2 12	189¼	2,348 91	843 02	
1868	6 17	7,248 57	3,096 40	2 6	133½	2,307 39	956 29	
1869	8 10	9,112 59	3,955 26					
Total	62	50,161 53	22,234 87	41 6	3,426½	40,965 33	17,768 62	

Schooner Lodi.

[Average, 9 hands cod and halibut fishing; 14 hands mackereling.]

Years.	Time in cod and halibut fishery.		Value of catch.	Vessel's share.	Time in Gulf of St. Lawrence mackerel fishery.	Number of barrels caught.	Value of catch.	Vessel's share.	Time in American shore mackerel fishery.		Number of barrels caught.	Value of catch.	Vessel's share.
	Mos.	Days							Mos.	Days			
1858	4	9	$1,713 64	$729 71	Two trips 5 8	214	$2,456 38	$1,080					
1859	3	28	1,356 95	620 83	Two trips 6 7		3,483 05	1,922 48					
1860	5	21	1,888 51	853 25	3 21		1,546 45	773 22					
1861	5	22	1,276 86	538 12	Two trips 1	303	2,042 93	576 76					
1862	5	10	2,747 95	1,226 17	3 25	212	1,500 00	670 00					
1863	5	2	2,992 77	1,795 50	3 3	287	1,851 88	1,299 69	1	9	86	$617 59	$288 54
1864	5	1	2,908 99	1,315 84	3 16	453	5,334 75	2,135 13					
1865	3	21	5,852 68	2,716 61	Two trips 9 5	509		2,763 46					
1866	6	8	5,535 95	2,445 63	4 2	125	6,113 18	853 68					
1867	6	8	7,343 51	3,082 63			2,007 78						
1868	3	24	4,941 34	1,812 91									
Total	61	6	38,951 35	17,136 87	33	2,687	27,395 96	11,974 42	1	9	86	617 59	288 54

[About 85 tons, old; burnt at sea by bark Twoony June 22, 1863; 9 hands fishing, mackereling.]

Years.	Time employed in cod and halibut fishery.		Value of catch.	Vessel's share; crew's the same.	Time employed in Gulf of St. Lawrence mackereling.		Barrels of "bay" mackerel caught.	Value of catch.	Vessel's share.	Time in American shore mackerel-fishing.		Barrels caught of shore mackerel.	Value of catch.	Vessel's share.
	Mos.	*Days.*			*Mos.*	*Days.*				*Mos.*	*Days.*			
1858	5	9	$2,929 07	$1,304 22	3	8	194½	$2,133 12 Two trips.	$966 43					
1859	4	13	2,309 96	1,012 75	4	9	82½	1,162 68	423 59					
1860	7	22	5,098 35	2,260 13										
1861	7	21	3,492 59	1,508 54										
1862	9	13	6,194 36	2,819 15										
1863	3	11	4,665 10	2,053 32										
Total	37	29	24,616 36	10,958 11	7	17	277½	3,295 80	1,390 02					

Schooner Wm. Parkman.

Dismasted August 23, 1863, towed into Nova Scotia and sold.

[Tonnage about 80; hands employed cod-fishing, 9; mackereling, 14.]

Years.	Time employed in cod and halibut fishery.		Value of catch.	Vessel's share; crew's the same.	Time in Gulf of St. Lawrence mackerel trips.		Barrels of "bay" mackerel caught.	Value of catch.	Vessel's share; crew's the same.	Time in American shore mackerel fishery.		Barrels "shore" mackerel caught.	Value of catch.	Vessel's share; crew's the same.
	Mos.	Days.			Mos.	Days.				Mos.	Days.			
1858	3	17	$2,490 05	$1,120 21	One trip. 3	15	191¼	$1,942 84	$971 42					
1859	3	13	2,907 43	1,297 15	Two trips. 4	3	211¼	2,778 08	1,153 53					
1860	3	22	1,984 77	834 93	One trip. 3	17	181¼	1,810 47	753 71					
1861	7	19	2,391 38	1,043 77										
1862	8	20	5,594 11	2,579 52							24	34½	$295 76	$98 13
1863	3	17	2,954 57	1,289 38										
Total	30	18	18,322 31	8,174 96	11	5	563¾	6,531 39	2,878 66		24	31½	295 76	98 13

hands fishing; 14 hands mackerelin

Years	Time in cod and halibut fishery (Mos.)	(Days)	Value of catch	Vessel's share	Time in Gulf of St. Lawrence mackerel-fishing (Mos.)	(Days)	Number of barrels caught	Value of catch	Vessel's share	Time in American shore mackerel-fishing (Mos.)	(Days)	Number of barrels caught	Value of catch	Vessel's share
1858	5	27	$1,923 88	$807 41	2	21	149	$1,643 83	$270 29					
1859	4	29	2,099 26	903 98	4	1	166	2,208 80	961 15					
1860	4	26	1,467 99	568 01	3	27	108	1,993 02	842 76					
1861					3 trips. 6		304	1,418 07	548 40					
1862	1	19	712 32	972 38	3	28	299	1,635 11	758 68	2	5	177	$679 99	$373 73
1863	4	7	4,612 94	2,118 03	3	14	353	4,148 62	1,759 64		2	35	244 27	96 63
1864					2 trips. 3									
65	2	18	1,784 91	728 70	2 trips.		396	5,440 00	2,549 15					
66	3	9	2,559 63	1,112 56	5	10	465	7,181 33	3,402 41					
67	3	19	3,015 12	1,296 11	4	4	205	2,293 89	899 44					
68	3	7	2,682 96	1,199 42	4		85	1,653 97	617 01					
69	5	6	3,475 99	1,536 80	3	8	106	1,641 90	713 76	5	7	321	2,544 92	1,165 75
70														
71*														
Total	17		24,334 40	10,563 40	41	2	686	31,257 24	13,822 09	8	4	533	3,669 18	1,576 11

* Seized July 24, 1871, near Paraquet Island, Lower Canada, detained at Quebec until May, 1872, and released on payment of costs and charges of seizure; vessel sold in Quebec May 10, 1872.

Schooner Alhambra.

[New tonnage, 57 16-100 tons; 9 hands fishing; 15 hands mackereling.]

Years.	Time in cod and halibut fishery. Mos.	Days.	Value of catch.	Vessel's share.	Time in Gulf of St. Lawrence mackerel fishery. Mos.	Days.	Number of barrels caught.	Value of catch.	Vessel's share.	Time in American shore mackerel fishery. Mos.	Days.	Number of barrels caught.*	Value of catch.	Vessel's share.
1858						2 trips.	338	$3,575 54	$1,651 40		1	70	$977 60	$404 06
1859	4	18	$2,639 98	$1,678 83	4	20	253	3,538 57	1,551 28		23	62	196 39	76 01
1860	5	18	3,187 06	1,427 86	3	5	297	4,279 49	2,065 75					
1861	6	14	2,873 13	1,199 17	3	11	298	2,386 65	1,063 57					
1862	4	5	1,681 57	750 60	4	3	346	2,936 27	1,375 13					
1863	3	23	3,402 50	1,535 82	4	8	620	6,755 65	3,209 57		1½			
1864	4	17	4,965 42	1,918 50	2 trips.	8	525	6,672 21	3,010 31					
1865	2	16	3,480 24	1,753 62	4	26	519	6,993 63	3,212 98			23	235 03	82 37
1866	4	27	6,860 38	3,055 98	4	4	480	8,963 43	3,573 03					
1867	4	7	3,231 33	1,351 61	4	24	222	3,691 90	1,019 67					
1868	4	8	3,015 49	1,256 83	2	14	90	1,907 19	611 91					
1869	4	16	4,273 28	1,751 31	2 trips.	24	247	3,198 58	1,208 24	5	28	577	4,946 86	2,913 91
1870										5	29	370	3,809 94	1,905 61
1871										6	4	205	2,855 54	1,219 40
1872														
1873		12	3,842 66	1,582 77	3	3	297	3,401 60	1,478 48		13			
1874	1	25	3,114 58	1,379 69										
	55	21	47,295 92	20,741 49	49		4,550	57,002 71	25,050 00	19	13	1,316	11,411 38	4,980 14

* Porgies mostly.

[[Old tonnage, about 96 tons; 15 hands mackereling.]]

Years	Time in cod and halibut fishery. Mos.	Days.	Value of catch.	Vessel's share.	Time in Gulf of St. Lawrence mackerel fishery. Mos.	Number of barrels caught.	Value of catch.	Vessel's share.	Time in American can shore mackerel fishery. Mos.	Days.	Number of barrels caught.	Value of catch.	Vessel's share.
1859					2 / 8	159	$2,122 53	$936 41					

Schooner St. Cloud.

[About 120 tons; 17 hands mackereling.]

Years					Mos.								
1859					3 / 21	199	$2,556 93	$1,029 46					
					2 trips / 28	397	3,976 43	1,922 91					
1860					5 / 19	596	6,533 36	2,951 67					

Schooner Samantha C. Steele.

[About 120 tons; 17 hands mackereling.]

Years					Mos.				Mos.				
1861					2	161	$716 47	$390 11	2		154	$1,149 04	$569 05

Schooner Charles Carroll.

Old tonnage, 90 9-95 tons; new tonnage, 58 64-100 tons.—

[Average number of hands cod and halibut fishing, 9, mackereling, 14.]

Years.	Time in cod and halibut fishing.		Value of catch; gross stock.	Vessel's share; one-half of net stock.	Time in Gulf of St. Lawrence, mackerel fishing.		Number of barrels caught.	Value of catch.	Vessel's share or crew's share.	Time in American shore mackerel fishing.		Number of barrels caught.	Value of catch.	Vessel or crew's share.
	Mos.	*Days*			*Mos.*	*Days*				*Mos.*	*Days.*			
1860	6	10	1,904 98	823 51	6	x	166	1,802	732					
1861	5	9	2,401 42	1,067 40	2	29	161	1,278	551					
1862	6	29	4,692 72	2,141 12	1	23	250	1,921	846	1	22	62	388	183
1863	6	9	5,710 35	2,624 79	3	19	308	3,566	1,619					
1864	3	19	5,953 40	3,414 33	2	15	462	5,740	2,445					
1865	4	18	7,018 79	3,320 32	4	6	566	7,127	3,254					
1866	4	23	4,440 89	3,013 85	4	9	372	5,852	2,563					
1867	5	19	6,006 22	3,792 22	4	24	219	6,759	2,423					
1868	7	16	7,214 80	3,146 18	2	17	172	3,913	1,423					
1869	x	9	7,550 66	3,139 84	3		169	3,101	1,557					
1870	9	25	7,473 26	3,139 36						1	23	211	2,257	955
1871	9	13	6,517 45	3,499 47										
1872	9	12	9,009 17	4,003 14										
1873	5	11	9,664 46	3,718 00										
1874	7	28	8,411 86	3,129 50										
1875		4	5,704 47	2,325 95										
1876														
	106	10	97,024 73	43,027 98	35	29	2,845	36,399	15,968	2	15	273	2,645	1,138

[32 30-100 tons. 10 hands fishing; 15 hands mackereling.]

Years.	Time in cod and halibut fishery. Mos.	Days.	Value of catch.	Vessel's share.	Time in Gulf of St. Lawrence mackerel fishery. Mos.	Days.	Number of barrels caught.	Value of catch.	Vessel's share.	Time in American shore mackerel fishery. Mos.	Days.	Number of barrels caught.	Value of catch.	Vessel's share.
1860	7	26	$1,051 53	$494 76	3	18	329	$3,107 47	$1,347 76	1	3	94	$419 92	$170 96
1861	11	15	3,945 57	1,467 38										
1862	5	11	5,387 30	2,378 37	3	26	442	5,362 90	2,594 45					
1863	5	24	5,507 95	2,466 86	3	8	623	7,836 86	3,224 45					
1864	8	2	4,443 23	2,027 17	4	25	469	6,349 48	2,489 25					
1865	4	18	8,150 35	3,742 43	3	29	449	6,428 71	2,792 46					
1866	1	13	1,450 48	593 39	4	9	439	5,756 87	2,464 52					
1867	4	13	5,087 13	2,213 01	4	5	221	4,156 16	1,668 73	2	13	229	3,963 75	1,480 75
1868	4	5	4,602 15	1,973 90			212	3,306 54	1,191 74					
1869	6	12	5,471 82	2,377 56										
1870	8	22	3,450 11	1,319 08										
1871	10	22	7,171 32	3,044 79										
1872	10	20	10,197 07	4,781 08										
1873	9	4	12,010 79	5,896 22										
1874	8	16	10,139 11	4,418 13										
1875	9	13	3,574 87	3,574 15										
1876			6,562 59	2,639 23										
Total	113	11	102,342 37	45,397 51	32		3,184	42,364 99	18,113 36	3	16	323	3,683 67	1,651 71

Schooner Everett Steele.

[70 54-100 tons. Average, 10 hands codfishing; 16 hands mackereling.]

Years.	Time in cod and halibut fishery. (Mos.)	(Days.)	Value of catch.	Vessel's share.	Time in Gulf of St. Lawrence mackerel fishery.	Number of barrels caught.	Value of catch.	Vessel's share.	Time in American shore mackerel fishing. (Mos.)	(Days.)	Number of barrels caught.	Value of catch.	Vessel's share.
1864	2	6	$3,511 98	$1,721 94	Mos. 3 Days 9	664	$7,964 13	$3,133 06					
1865	3	10	7,742 11	3,675 70	Two trips.	694	8,490 65	3,925 49					
1866	4	9	7,118 98	3,161 14	4	18	391	6,016 50	2,710 90				
1867	6	3	6,586 52	3,026 66	Two trips. 3	26	310	4,070 51	1,591 22				
1868	10	25	14,726 73	6,873 56									
1869	9	16	16,406 94	7,479 06									
1870	5	21	6,619 98	2,821 06									
1871	5	27	7,133 43	3,107 07						2	7	364	$4,033 18	$1,757 08
1872	9	23	8,968 52	3,961 35						2	5	222	2,775 07	1,271 76
1873	10	3	8,877 10	4,128 79									
1874	11	21	10,981 69	5,071 61									
1875	8	18	8,108 02	3,457 77									
1876	9	27	7,836 85	3,264 97									
Thirteen years	97	29	115,018 75	51,757 61	15	23	2,049	26,541 79	11,360 67	4	12	586	6,808 25	3,028 84

Years.	Time in cod and [cod fishing].		Vessel's share.	Time in Gulf of St. Lawrence, mackerel fishing.		Number of barrels caught.	Value of catch.	Vessel's share.	American shore mackerel fishery.
	Mos.			Mos.	Days.				None.
1866	3		$1,853 33	2 trips	4 23	365	$5,394 31	$2,434 73	
1867	6		2,546 54		3 12	257	3,291 22	1,306 47	
1868	10		5,101 91						
1869	5		3,487 56		2 90	139	2,198 87	951 69	
1870	8		3,158 54						
1871	9		2,488 77						
1872	8		2,653 89	2 trips	4 98	387	3,806 77	1,674 68	
1873	5		1,150 73						
1874	9		3,810 72	2 trips	2 25	394	3,935 80	1,759 98	
1875	5		2,480 98		3				
1876	11		2,508 52						
Total	83		30,241 49		19 18	1,465	18,626 97	8,207 49	

Schooner *Franklin Snow.*

[Tonnage 66 34-100 tons. Average hands fishing, 11; mackereling, 16. Lost on Grand Bank with all hands, March, 1872.]

Years	Time in cod and halibut fishing.		Value of catch.	Vessel's share.	Time in Gulf of St. Lawrence mackerel-fishing.		Number of barrels caught.	Value of catch.	Value of vessel's share.	Time in American shore mackerel fishery.		Number of barrels caught.	Value of catch.	Vessel's share or crew's the same.
	Mos.	Days.			Mos.	Days.				Mos.	Days.			
1866	4	25	$6,563.55	$2,904.99	4	20	616	$9,501.76	$4,904.42					
1867	10	8	15,676.84	7,403.19	3	16	467	8,632.72	5,037.58					
1868	5	28	8,428.23	3,899.83										
1869	10	4	11,692.03	4,889.54										
1870		33	4,117.83	1,828.37	2	6	239	4,636.98	2,076.45	6	5	484	$3,752.51	$1,637.33
1871	2	18	1,227.87	571.48										
1872														
Total	34	24	47,106.35	21,467.40	10	12	1,322	22,761.46	11,338.45	6	5	484	3,752.51	1,637.33

1 tons. 11 hands fishing; 17 hands mackereling. Went ashore at Magdalen 24, 873.]

Years.	Time in cod and halibut fishing. (Mos. Days.)	Value of catch.	Vessel's share.	Time in Gulf of St. Lawrence mackerel fishery. (Mos. Days.)	Number of barrels caught.	Value of catch.	Vessel's share.	Time in American shore mackerel fishery. (Mos. Days.)	Number of barrels caught.	Value of catch.	Vessel's share.
1872	10 6	$15,997 40	$7,551 39	1 14							
1873	16 12	8,450 46	3,905 71	4 20	225	$2,048 54	$683 56				
1874				2 27	413	795 85	1,135 32				
1875	3 5	6,084 86	2,678 67	3 13	226	3,543 66	1,564 05				
1876	12 5	3,591 90	1,378 07		231	2,410 09	1,057 84				
Total	27	34,104 62	15,513 84	12 14	1,115	10,788 14	4,440 77				

Schooner Knight Templar.

(Bought in 1872.)

[Tonnage, 73 96-100 tons. Hands, 20 mackereling; 12 hands codfishing on Grand Banks.]

Years.	Time in cod and halibut fishing.		Value of catch.	Vessel's share.	Time in Gulf of St. Lawrence mackerel-fishing.		Number of barrels mackerel caught.	Value of catch.	Vessel's share.	American shore mackerel fishery.
	Mos.	Days.			Mos.	Days.				
1872	6	6	$7,660 24	$3,560 66	2	10	304½	$2,666 84	$1,232 33	
1873	6	12	10,729 74	4,952 71	3	13	381	2,193 25	809 59	
1874	9	2	8,691 01	4,003 33						
1875	6	23	6,983 65	3,213 57						
1876										
Total	28	13	34,064 64	15,730 27	5	23	685½	4,860 09	2,131 92	

Schooner Jamestown.

[69 tons. Mackereling, 17 hands.]

1876					3	19	196	$1,724 46	$737 30	

(New, December, 1873.)

[Tonnage, 96 43-100. 11 hands fishing; 15 hands mackereling.]

Years.	Time in cod and halibut fishery.		Value of catch.	Vessel's share.	Time in Gulf of St. Lawrence mackerel fishery.		Number of barrels "bay" caught.	Value of catch.	Vessel's share.	American shore mackerel fishery.
	Mos.	Days.			Mos.	Days.				
1874.........	11	2	$9,525 69	$4,147 81	One trip.		296	$4,099 38	$1,862 97	
1875.........	5	3	5,530 93	2,394 33	2	24	68	813 00	250 11	
1876.........	4	16	4,259 94	1,789 45	3	16				
	20	21	19,315 86	8,301 59	6	10	334	4,905 38	2,113 08	

Schooner H. A. Duncan.

(New in 1876.)

[87 70-100 tons. Mackereling, 18 hands.]

1876.........					3	19	192	$2,917 52	$946 71	

Schooner Monmouth.

(New, December, 1875.)

[Tonnage, 71 68-100 tons. Hands, 11, fishing.]

1876.........	10	16	$7,205 49	$2,831 99						

Schooner Plymouth Rock.

(New in 1876.)

[96 94-100 tons. 18 hands.]

Years.	Time in cod and halibut fishery. Mos.	Days.	Value of catch.	Vessel's share.	Time in Gulf of St. Lawrence mackerel fishing. Mos.	Days.	Number of barrels caught.	Value of catch.	Vessel's share.	Time in American shore mackerel fishing. Mos.	Days.	Number of barrels caught.	Value of catch.	Vessel's share.
1876	.....	.....	.....	.....	3	14	223	$2,574 39	$1,089 65					

Schooner George Steele.

[70 49-100 tons. 19 hands mackeroling in gulf; 16 hands "off shore." Lost January, 1877, on coast of Cuba.]

Years.	Time in cod and halibut fishery. Mos.	Days.	Value of catch.	Vessel's share.	Time in Gulf of St. Lawrence mackerel fishing. Mos.	Days.	Number of barrels caught. Part share.	Value of catch.	Vessel's share.	Time in American shore mackerel fishing. Mos.	Days.	Number of barrels caught.	Value of catch.	Vessel's share.
1872	.....	.....	.....	.....	2	25	399	$3,194 78	$1,436 20	1	9	163	$324 80	$340 90

Schooner Saratoga.

[74 96-100 tons. 9 hands codfishing. Sailed for Georges April 12, 1876, and did not return.]

Years.	Time in cod and halibut fishery. Mos.	Days.	Value of catch.	Vessel's share.	Time in Gulf of St. Lawrence mackerel fishing. Mos.	Days.	Number of barrels caught.	Value of catch.	Vessel's share.	Time in American shore mackerel fishing. Mos.	Days.	Number of barrels caught.	Value of catch.	Vessel's share.
1876	1	27	$1,791 65	$608 74	.....	.....	.....	.....	.....					

[60 37-100 tons. Average hands fishing, 10; hands mackereling, 14.]

Years.	Time in cod and halibut fishery.		Value of catch.	Vessel's share.	American shore mackerel fishery. Time in Gulf of St. Lawrence mackerel fishing.		Number of barrels caught.	Value of catch.	Vessel's share.
	Mos.	Days.			Mos.	Days			
1872	6	1	$2,600 94	$1,119 90					
1873	4	29	7,748 88	3,441 69	3	23	516	$5,649 70	$2,586 53
1874	4	8	4,994 56	2,129 70	3	22	491	3,184 39	1,354 50
1875	8	22	9,185 93	4,062 78					
1876	7	21	5,752 05	2,348 16					
Total	31	21	30,482 36	13,101 53	7	15	1,007	8,834 09	3,941 03

Lost November 25, 1876, on La Have Banks.

Schooner Pharsalia.

[76 96-100 tons. 12 hands codfishing.]

	Mos.	Days.	Value of catch.	Vessel's share.
1875	5	25	$4,421 20	$1,942 77

Sailed for Western Banks September 15, 1875, and never returned.

No. 59.

TUESDAY, *October* 16, 18

The Conference met.

ELIPHALET W. FRENCH, of Eastport, Me., fish merchant, calle behalf of the Government of the United States, sworn and examin

By Mr. Trescot:

Question. You are a native of Eastport, I believe ?—Answer. I a

Q. What age are you ?—A. Forty-one years.

Q. In what business are you engaged ?—A. In the wholesale fish iness and fitting out.

Q. How long have you been engaged in it ?—A. Twenty years.

Q. As in business for yourself, or as clerk, or how ?—A. I have in business for myself nineteen years last February; previous to tl was in a store with my father.

Q. What was your father's business ?—A. He followed the same ness.

Q. How long did he follow it ?—A. Nearly forty years.

Q. So the firm of which you are a member now, and which you resent, and the business in which your father was previously, ex over how many years ?—A. Something like sixty years in the same ness.

Q. Will you explain to the Commission what the business is ! Buying and selling fish and fitting fishermen.

Q. Buying fish whereabouts, as a general rule ?—A. From fisher

Q. From fishermen, where ?—A. At Grand Manan, Deer Island, pobello, Indian Island, and Beaver Harbor.

Q. Is it a matter of necessity in your business that you should a pretty good knowledge of the fishing at those places ?—A. Yes.

Q. You make or lose money according to the completeness and cision of your knowledge of that fishery ?—A. Yes.

Q. What is the fishery at Grand Manan and the Bay of Fundy erally ?—A. Codfish, pollock, hake, haddock, and herring.

Q. Are any of those fisheries entirely off-shore fisheries ?—A. Co is an off-shore fishery. Hake are taken off shore.

Q. Entirely or partially ?—A. Hake are entirely taken off shore

Q. Was it once an inshore fishery ?—A. Yes; it is only within or four years they have been taken off shore.

Q. Before that it was inshore ?—A. Inshore and out, both.

Q. How about haddock ?—A. Haddock is mostly an inshore fis

Q. Herring, of course, is an inshore fishery ?—A. Partly.

Q. Into what divisions do you mark the herring fishery ?—A. ' are smoked, pickled, and frozen herring.

Q. With regard to smoked herring, where is the market for sn herring that come from the Bay of Fundy, Grand Manan, and tl ands of the mainland ?—A. Boston and New York, principally.

Q. Are they sent to Boston and New York from Eastport, or do : go direct ?—A. They send most of them to Eastport. They are br(there in boats, and sent from there in steamers and sailing vessels Grand Manan they have three or four large vessels by which the them to Boston and New York direct.

Q. Are those American vessels or Grand Manan vessels own(Grand Manan people ?—A. I know one that is chartered is an Am(vessel, because it is my own vessel. I don't know in regard to o Q. Do they ship on account of Americans, or do they charter th(sels ?—A. They are chartered by Grand Manan people.

Have you any idea of what is the value of the smoked-herring ess at Grand Manan ?—A. I should place it at about $400,000.

Do you know by whom that fishery is conducted ?—A. It is con-
·d by the inhabitants of Grand Manan.

Entirely ?—A. Almost entirely. I understand there is a man at
›ort who owns part of a weir over there, or has an interest in some
ıu weirs there.

But, as a general thing, it is emphatically a native fishery ?—A.

With regard to the frozen herring, is that the same ?—A. Yes.

Have you any idea of the value of the frozen-herring fishery of
d Manan ?—A. I think about $40,000.

Is that exclusively a native fishery, or do Americans go and par-
ıte in it ?—A. Very few Americans do. Some small vessels at East-
go over there.

How many ?—A. Perhaps half a dozen.

Can you form any idea as to what proportion the value of their
. bears to the $40,000 you have mentioned ?—A. It would be a very
part, because Grand Manan owns perhaps twice as many vessels
ə Eastport people, and there are vessels at Campobello, Wilson's
b, and Deer Island.

As to the pickled-herring fishery, is that a special business, and
raluable ?—A. It is not so valuable as the others.

Is that conducted in the same way ?—A. Yes.

Are Americans engaged in catching and smoking herring on our
coast ?—A. Yes.

To any large extent ?—A. Yes.

Do you know what is the value of the Maine coast smoked-herring
·y by American fishermen ?—A. No ; but from the number of weirs,
uld think there are as many herring smoked on the coast of Maine
. the English side.

Do the herring smoked on the American side equal the British herin quality and bring as much in the market ?—A. Yes ; there is one
cular place at the town of Cutler and another at Manleybridge,
er on the coast of Maine. Manleybridge herring bring a better
than any other herring shipped to Boston and New York. Man-
idge is near Mount Desert.

Now, with regard to the remaining fisheries—cod, hake, and had-
. The cod fishery, you say, is an off-shore fishery ?—A. Yes.

Is the hake fishery an American or English fishery ?—A. It is an
ish fishery.

Is it both ?—A. It is almost entirely English. Those few vessels
ke of go over there hake fishing.

What is your estimate of the hake fishery ? Do you deal very
ı in hake ?—A. Yes ; I deal in them. I should think there might
been 25,000 quintals taken this season.

The large majority of those would be taken by British fishermen
n British waters ?—A. Yes. The boats fish near the shore, but the
ıls all fish outside.

Is the bulk of the fish taken outside, and is it considered to be an
de fishery ?—A. I think it has been for the last two or three years.

With regard to haddock, how is that ?—A. It is taken inshore
›ut, both.

Then with regard to the fisheries of the county of Charlotte, you
r pretty much what their extent is, do you not ?—A. Yes.

What do you estimate as the value of the whole fisheries of the county?—A. I should say the fishery at Campobello, Deer Island Indian Island would be about equal in value to what it is at Gran nan. Up the north shore I don't know so much about; it is not t extent; it may be half what it is at Grand Manan. I should $1,000,000 would cover the whole of the fishery.

Q. With your knowledge of that fishery and your dealings wit fishermen, and the necessity of knowing what the catch is, woul say that any appreciable portion is caught by American fishermen No; I should consider it an English fishery.

Q. Would you consider there was any possibility for the catch by American fishermen to be so large as to equal that amount $1,000,000 caught by British fishermen?—A. No; by no means.

Q. Is it possible that such a state of things should exist withou being acquainted with it?—A. No.

Q. Do you know Mr. James McLean?—A. I know him by sigh

Q. Do you know where he carries on business?—A. The firm business at Letite and Lepreau.

Q. I want to call your attention to some of his testimony with r to his estimates of the fishery of Charlotte County, and ask wl you think it correct, and, if not, how it should be reduced. The f ing is from Mr. McLean's testimony:

Q. Judging from your practical knowledge of the fishery, being an owner ing-vessels and dealing with the men who fish as you do, what do you say, a figure, would be the value of the fisheries and the actual worth of the fish cat British subjects between the points you mention, from Lepreau to Letite? would be a fair average value from 1871?—A. I should estimate the quan Charlotte County and the adjoining islands. We all fish; and it would be diff separate the two.

Q. You are acquainted with the catch of the island as well?—A. Yes. I visit Manan Island occasionally, and the adjoining islands often.

Q. What is the catch of the whole?—A. A low estimate for our fishery we $1,000,000 for each year.

That is about the estimate you made just now?—A. Yes.

Q. Then there is the following:

Q. For British subjects?—A. Yes.

Q. That is a low estimate?—A. Yes; I think I am under the mark; in fact no doubt of it all.

Q. And it may be a good deal more?—A. Yes.

Q. You have not a shadow of a doubt that it is at least a million?—A. No.

Q. And our American friends take a considerable amount more?—A. They many.

Q. They have more men and more vessels?—A. Yes.

Q. And they take at least as much?—A. Yes; fully as much as we do more.

Q. Have you any doubt that they do take more?—A. I believe that th more.

Q. You have no doubt of it?—A. No.

Q. That would make a million dollars' worth taken by them?—A. They mns million dollars' worth.

Q. That is the very least calculation?—A. Yes; I put it down as low as pos be safe and sure.

Q. They take at least as much as we do?—A. I believe that they take m they take as much any way.

Q. The American catch, as well as our own, on which you place an estim million dollars in value, is taken within three miles of the shore?—A. Yes confining myself to within the 3-mile limit.

Are you in a position to say whether that is true or not?—A. think it is true. I think he has made a mistake.

Q. Do you think your business is such that you would know t if it was so?—A. Yes.

That there could not be two million dollars' worth caught instead
million without you knowing it in your business ?—A. Yes.
f it is so, that would make a very good business for the merchants
tport, if they deal entirely with Grand Manan ?—A. Yes ; Campo-
Deer Island, and Grand Manan.
Vhat is the condition of things ? Is it such as to indicate very
rofits to the fishermen ?—A. No.
Vhat is the reason ?—A. There is not much money in the fishery.
'o the Eastport people, you mean ?—A. Yes ; and I have suffered
by it ; that is, in the fitting-out part, I mean. ·
Vhat do you say to this :

ong the coast of Maine, say from Eastport westward, there lives a large popula-
o fish entirely in our waters ?—A. Yes. They come from Lubec, Perry, Pem-
nd Eastport, and along by Cutler and Westward of Lubec, and still farther
an that.
d from Machias ?—A. I think so.
ey all come and fish in our waters ?—A. Yes.
d not in their own waters ?—A. I do not know of any fishing within the three-
it in their waters.
thin three miles of their coast there is no fishing of which you are aware ?—

d this is a population that lives by fishing alone ?—A. From Eastport and
ere they follow fishing for a livelihood, beyond question.
that a large body of American fishermen gain their whole livelihood in our
—A. Yes ; those that fish there do.

'hat is not so.
tate to the Commission what you know of the habits of those
—A. It speaks of the people being engaged in fishing only.
re engaged in farming mostly ; that is really their business, but
rry on both fishing and farming. There are only one or two or
r four vessels owned at Lubec, one or two at Machias, and one at
ort, that come down there.
find this, also, in Mr. McLean's testimony, speaking about St.
w's :

is sometimes called the Inner Bay of Passamaquoddy ?—A. I suppose that it is.
as not that at one time a great herring-ground ?—A. It was once a splendid
round.
ice the negotiation of the Washington Treaty, and since the Americans have
ere, what has become of it ?—A. It has been destroyed within the last two
It is now no good whatever.
w did the Americans destroy it ?—A. By bringing too many vessels there, and
ig too many nets. The water is quite rough there at times, the wind blowing
in from the northwest. Northwest winds prevail in winter, and three years
ad a very hard winter.

i know anything of the destruction of fish in St. Andrew's Bay ?—

'ou know something about the fishing there ?—A. Yes ; I know
re as many herring taken there as there ever were. A year ago
ring the catch was unusually large.
Ie says there is no fishing within three miles of the American
do you know of any fishing done not only by Americans but by
h fishermen on the American shore ?—A. The best fishing in St.
w's Bay is on the American side, from Dog Island, on Eastport,
erin's Cove, in Perry. There are other places of course, on the
:an shore. There are herring taken at Cross Island, near Machias,
bby Island, at the mouth of Machias River.
)o you know any fishing-vessels engaged fishing within the three
f the American shore ?—A. All vessels from the other side fish
Andrew's Bay on the American side.

Q. Do you know Walter B. McLaughlin ?—A. Only by reputatio keeper of a light-house.

Q. I want to call your attention to his testimony. There is the lowing:

Q. Now, in the spring are you not visited by the Grand Manan fleet from Glo ter ?—A. Yes; they used formerly to come to Grand Manan direct. Generally they go to Eastport and get the Eastport people to catch bait for them.

Q. When you say "formerly," do you mean after the Treaty of Washington Yes; they did not come before that much. It is since 1871 that they have come cipally. They will come down every spring.

Q. How long do they last ?—A. Sometimes a longer and sometimes a shorter ti

Q. How many years after the treaty did it commence ?—A. It has lasted down present time, for that matter. There has not been so many this last spring as b.

Q. I thought you said there had been a change in the practice ?—A. There h: been a change in the practice.of getting bait at our places, but in the mode of ge it. They generally come to Eastport and make that their place of departure. Eastport people are acquainted with our waters almost as well as our own people they come across and catch fish and sell to the Gloucester fishermen; that is the ority of the cases now.

Q. I understand that at first they came down themselves and bought ?—A. Ye

Q. And now they come chiefly to Eastport to employ Eastport fishermen, who the fish and bring them to them ?—A. The big vessels are not fitted out for he fishing. They take an Eastport vessel in company with them and come over an chor in our waters. They bring their own fishermen with them and anchor i waters, and get their bait there. They sometimes come in the fall for bait.

What do you know about that ?—A. I know that it is not so. I seen 40 vessels from Gloucester lying in the harbor of Eastport for and the boats would bring the .bait from the other side, and would them up.

Q. The boats would come from Grand Manan ?—A. From Campo and Deer Island. When I speak of the other side I mean the Br Islands.

Q. There is also the following:

Q. You are well acquainted with the fisheries of Charlotte County. Take the land fishing from Letete as far as Lepreau, is that a good fishing-ground ?—A. considered a good fishing-ground; I am not personally acquainted with it, and car say from what I have heard; my duties have never carried me there.

Q. But your practical knowledge extends there ?—A. Yes.

Q. What would be the value of the mainland fishery, the British fishery alone, t it from Letete to Lepreaux ?—A. My own fishery is, say, $500,000; Campobell West Isles must equal mine, and the mainland will certainly be more than half of if not equal to it.

Q. Well, then, you put Campobello and West Isles as about equal to Grand Man A. Yes; speaking as I do, not knowing exactly, I should say so.

Q. That would be half a million for those two islands, and half a million for (Manan—that makes a million; and you think the mainland is half as much as of those; that would be a fair estimate for the mainland ?—A. Yes; Charlotte C is a very important fishing county. In 1861 I was a census enumerator, and I the result of the fishery in that county nearly equaled that of all the other fisher the province, with the exception of St. John County.

Q. You put half a million of the catch of the British fishermen on the mainla the year, and, in your judgment, the American catch is the same ?—A. All I can ju by what I hear. They come down in their vessels. I think they have their ow on the north shore, very much more than on Grand Manan; I have a great (trouble with them there. But on the north shore I think they have things much as they want. I would say that they probably surpass our own catch.

You don't agree with that estimate ?—A. No.

By Mr. Thomson:

Q. I want to call your attention to the last paragraph read to y which you contradicted the evidence of Mr. McLaughlin. Mr. T read to you the following:

Q. You are well acquainted with the fisheries of Charlotte County; take the land from Letete as far as Lepreau, is that a good fishing-ground ?—A. I am n(sonally acquainted with it; I can only say from what I have heard. My dutie never carried me there.

you undertake to say that the fishing-ground from Lepreau to
e is a bad fishing-ground ?—A. No.
Then what made you contradict the statement?—A. I contradicted
remark he made in regard to American fishermen having their own

The whole passage was read to you and you contradicted it?—A.
:rred to the last part that was read.
Did you hear the whole read?—A. Yes.
Why did you not qualify your contradiction ?—A. I do so now.
You admit that if I had not called attention to it, your statement
l have gone as contradicting Mr. McLaughlin's testimony ?—A. I
·ed to the last part of what was read.
I call your attention to this:

Vhat would be the value of the mainland fishery, the British fishery alone,
; it from Letite to Lepreau ?—A. My own fishery is, say $500,000; Campobello
'est Isles must equal mine; and the mainland will certainly be more than half
t, if not equal to it.

u have said that Campobello and the West Islands would equal
d Manan ?—A. Campobello and West Isles would be, I think,
t the same as Grand Manan.
That is the statement made here by Mr. McLaughlin, and you con-
cted it.—A. I did not refer to that part.
| Mr. McLaughlin puts down that Campobello and West Isles would
|ual to Grand Manan. Do you contradict that ?—A. I admit it to
ue, so far as I know.
| You said in your answer to Mr. Trescot you did not agree to that.
| often have you been at Grand Manan for the purpose of inquiring
the value and extent of the fishery ?—A. I have never been there.
know is from the fish that come from there.
Never having been there, you yet presume to put your opinion
1st and contradict the statement of Mr. McLaughlin, who has been
: and has a practical knowledge of it ?—A. I know about it from
, I learn from the fishermen. I give my opinion of the value of the
ry.
You put your opinion against the oath of Mr. McLaughlin, who
1 practical knowledge of it ?—A. Yes, I put my opinion against his
10n.
Although you have never been there and never examined closely
the extent of the fishery ?—A. I know the fish that come from
:.
Do all the fish that come from there go to Eastport ?—A. I think
do.
Will you swear to that ?—A. No; because there are a few go to
ʼohn's—a very small quantity.
Will you swear that none are sent direct elsewhere than to St.
ı's and Eastport ?—A. I don't know of any.
Do you mean to say that American vessels which come down to
h fish off the main land take it to Eastport ? Do you not know that
take the fish direct to Boston, Newburyport, or other ports on the
rican coast ?—A. I do not know it.
Do you say that they do not ?—A. I never heard of vessels going
e.
. If American vessels have gone there and fished off the main land,
have never heard of it ?—A. No.
. If American vessels do go and fish there, would they not carry
r cargoes elsewhere than to Eastport ?—A. I don't think they would.

AWARD OF THE FISHERY COMMISSION.

• I think all the fish would come into Eastport, because all the
done in smaller vessels, from 10 to 20 tons.

Q. If vessels are sent down from Gloucester or Newbui
Machias, do you say they would necessarily call at Eastport af
a cargo in our waters ?—A. Machias vessels would, because t
Eastport.

Q. Do they always sell there ?—A. Yes.

Q. They never sell at Machias ?—A. I never knew them do

Q. How does that happen ?—A. Because Eastport is their

Q. Is there no market at Machias ?—A. Not to any extent.

Q. Did I understand you to say, in speaking of St. Andi
that the best fishing was on the American shore ?—A. Yes.

Q. And you further stated that Machias River ran into thi
A. No; I said there were herring taken at Cross Island.

Q. Did you not say when speaking of the fishing in St. Andi
that the best fishing was on the American shore, and went on
of the Machias River running into the bay ?—A. No; I will e:
statement. I say the best fishing in St. Andrew's Bay is
Island at Eastport to Lowerin's Cove in Perry, and there are al
taken at Cross Island, at Machias.

Q. What have Cross Island and Machias to do with St.
Bay ?—A. I was asked in regard to where herring are tak(
American shore.

Q. You say you have never been to the main land, and
therefore examined the fisheries, and yet you swear you don'
American vessels going there ?—A. I don't swear that. I kn(
a dozen vessels owned in Eastport.

Q. Do they go and fish there ?—A. Yes.

Q. Off the main land ?—A. Yes.

Q. What part of the main land ?—A. Off Lepreau; I know
in that vicinity. I don't know as much about the fishing there
Deer Island, Grand Manan and Campobello.

Q. Do you know where the fishing places on the main land
I know they fish off Beaver Harbor, Lepreau and Letite au
vicinity.

Q. Dont they fish at Back Bay ?—A. Yes, they fish there; i
in the winter.

Q. And at Mace's Bay ?—A. I have not heard of fish bein
Mace's Bay.

Q. You don't pretend to know where the fishing places a
main land ?—A. I have some general idea of them.

Q. Have you ever been to St. George ?—A. Yes.

Q. How long is it since you were last there ?—A. Several y

Q. Have you been there during the last ten years ?—A. I t

Q. Have you ever been in the adjoining parish, which bor(
bay, Pennfield ?—A. No.

Q. Or the next parish, Lepreau ?—A. I have never been t(

Q. Have you been along the inner bay of Passamaquoddy
shore ?—A. No.

Q. You have been to St. Andrew's, I suppose ?—A. Yes.

Q. How long is it since you were last there ?—A. A year (

Q. St. Andrew's is connected by a steamer with Eastport '

Q. It is easy of access ?—A. Yes.

Q. To St. George or St. Patrick, Pennfield or Lepreau you l
been, and you have been to St. George once, and that wi
ago ?—A. Yes.

Yet you put your opinion against that of a man who has been on 'round?—A. I make my estimate from vessels from Eastport which ow fish there, from the English fish which comes into Eastport from way, and from conversations with fishermen in regard to the fishing .

That is all?—A. Yes.

Did you have those conversations for the express purpose of find ut how many fish were taken along the British coast?—A. No; it was r mentioned.

You never had any object in finding out what the catch was?—A. I never inquired.

How often have you visited Grand Manan?—A. I have never been rand Manan.

Campobello, which is quite near to Eastport—you have been there, pose?—A. Yes.

Is there valuable fishing ground on Campobello shore?—A. They ip a good many smoked herring.

There is good fishing between Eastport and Campobello, within miles of Campobello shore?—A. Yes.

The fishing within three miles of Campobello shore is better than shing on the American coast, is it not?—A. The distance between port and Campobello is only one mile and three-quarters.

The fishing close up to the island is better than on the American ?—A. It is everywhere in the bay.

Is it not better close to the shores of Campobello than close to the rican shores?—A. It is pretty difficult to tell where the line runs .

Is not the channel much nearer the American shore than to the d of Campobello?—A. The place where they catch most of the fish tween Eastport and Campobello, and is called the Ledge. I think about half way between the two.

Is not the channel nearerer the American shore than Campo- ?—A. There is not any channel there; it is all deep water.

When the tide is out is there not a well-known channel there close ue American shore?—A. No; a vessel can anchor anywhere off port.

Don't you know that the British line runs close to the American e?—A. No; I don't know where the line does run, or anybody else.

And you don't know the channel close to the American shore?— Jo, I don't know it; I never heard any channel spoken of between port and Campobello.

Are there a large number of weirs round Campobello?—A. A good y.

Are there any on the Eastport side?—A. Yes.

Many?—A. A good many.

At Eastport?—A. Yes.

Are there many between Eastport and Lubec and along the e?—A. There are weirs at Perry, Lubec, and Cutler.

Which is nearest to Eastport, Perry or Lubec?—A. Perry adjoins port on the mainland. Lubec is about two miles opposite to East by water.

Along that shore, from Eastport to Lubec, are there on the rican shore many weirs?—A. I should think there were.

Do you know of your own knowledge that there are?—A. I know e is a large number.

What do they take?—A. Herring.

Q. And other fish?—A. No; there is a place at Treat's I there is an immense quantity of herring taken.

Q. Where is that?—A. It is part of Eastport, but it is a is owned by a man named Treat, who is a resident of Eas great many herring are taken at that island.

Q. Do I understand you to say that along the America can catch as many herring as they want?—A. If they foll business they could.

Q. Why do they not follow it?—A. A good many are farming. Those living at Eastport, where the weirs are, farms there, and do a great deal of farming besides.

Q. Are all the herring sold at Eastport? Is that the i Yes.

Q. Did I not understand you that when American vessel of late years men came over with herring from Grand Ma is a different kind to what is taken in weirs. The weir small herring.

Q. They don't use them for bait?—A. No.

Q. Don't you catch large herring on your coast?—A. winter.

Q. They do not take large herring in the weirs?—A. No tent.

Q. Then there are no large herring taken on your coas there are.

. Q. How many are taken?—A. There are large herring i of the coves at Eastport.

Q. Are they taken to any extent?—A. A good many.

Q. Are they used for bait?—A. They can use them for b are mostly taken in winter and frozen and brought into E shipped by steamer.

Q. At what season do the vessels which the fishermen bait come down to Lubec?—A. In the spring.

Q. If there are so many herring on your coast, why do n fishermen supply the vessels coming down in the spring fo cording to you the British fishermen go out and supply the though they have plenty on their own shores. How do yo it?—A. There are several reasons. One thing is they wou it from fishermen on the other side. The reason is becau Englishmen from Campobello on board those vessels and th will patronize their own people. I will give you an illust will allow me. Last March a gentleman from Gloucester, came to me to get up a quantity of herring to send to the ket. I had them put in barrels and sent to my place in E employed a man named Calder, of Campobello, to buy her After he got through there were so many small herring them that there was a loss on the enterprise, and the smal to be sold for smoking. The fishermen from the other si and wanted to sell, told him that Calder would not patr cept his own people at Campobello, and but for them, th sold him large herring. I don't know what there is in the give it as I got it.

Q. Do I understand that on board every vessel there ar who prevent the vessels from dealing with American fishe don't know that there are altogether. Every season a g from the other side up to Gloucester to ship in those vess

vessels on Grand Manan Banks are filled with fishermen from Campobello and Deer Island.

Q. Do I understand you to say that the majority of the crews are British or Americans of the vessels which come down?—A. At Eastport the majority of them are British subjects, fishermen from Campobello and Deer Island.

Q. Those are they who man the vessels?—A. Eastport vessels which go to the Banks.

Q. I am speaking of the vessels which come in the spring for bait?—A. I don't think the majority are.

Q. Though the majority are not English, the minority can control and make them buy of the British and not Americans. How do you account for that?—A. I account for it in this way, that those who are engaged in catching herring at that time are fishermen at Campobello and Deer Island, who come over to Eastport in their boats, and sell their herring to those vessels.

Q. I want to know how that happens, when there are plenty of herring on your own shore. Do you account for it by saying that the British on board control the Americans?—A. To some extent.

Q. It is a curious thing, which you are not able to explain?—A. I don't think any herring are taken at Eastport at the time those vessels come there for bait. I think the herring are taken on the other side altogether.

Q. You have never been to Grand Manan?—A. No.

Q. Do you undertake to say that there is not a large fleet of American vessels fishing in there every year?—A. I should say there is not. I should be likely to know it if there was.

Q. Not for herring alone, but for other fish?—A. Some vessels fish there for codfish.

Q. If such a thing happened you would have heard it?—A. Yes.

Q. You have heard of Mr. McLaughlin?—A. Yes.

Q. He is a respectable man?—A. Yes.

Q. He must have committed deliberate perjury in having stated that he saw American vessels there, you not having heard of any being there?—A. I don't say that.

Q. Do I understand you to say that you don't mean any American vessels come there for the purpose of fishing?—A. I don't say so. I say vessels do come there cod-fishing.

Q. For herring every year?—A. Not to any extent.

Q. You don't believe it?—A. No.

Q. Then if Mr. McLaughlin swore that they did, he was committing deliberate perjury?—A. I have nothing to say to that.

` Q. Mr. McLaughlin having sworn what he swore, and you having given the opinion that, in your judgment, those vessels were not there, I ask you if you can escape the conclusion that Mr. McLaughlin was telling what was false?—A. I think Mr. McLaughlin was right when he told somebody in Eastport that he would like to alter the testimony he had given here. I don't say anything as to whether Mr. McLaughlin told the truth or not.

Q. You, a man who has never been at the island, and consequently never saw what the fishing there was, put your opinion against that of a man who has been there and seen it?—A. I do; for I know from vessels which come from there to Eastport.

Q. Do you swear that a large fishing-fleet from Gloucester does not come down there and fish round the island, especially for herring?—A. I don't know that there is, only, as I said, for codfish.

170 F

Q. I want to call your attention to a statement made in the Cape Ann Advertiser; I suppose you are aware it is a fisherman's organ?—A. I know it is a paper published in Gloucester, that is all I know of it.

Q. I call your attention to a statement published in the issue of February 23, 1877. It is as follows:

From this humble beginning may be traced the success of the herring business, which has developed into a leading business industry, and employs many of the finest vessels of the fleet. For the first dozen years the business was confined to Newfoundland voyages; but of late years an extensive herring business has grown up with Grand Manan, and a few cargoes are brought annually from Nova Scotia.

Q. What do you say to that?—A. It refers to frozen herring.

Q. It says: "Of late years an extensive business has grown up with Grand Manan"?—A. I say that is true; I don't deny it. The vessels that come from Gloucester in the winter season go to Grand Manan first to buy cargoes of frozen herring.

Q. This article is headed "The herring business of Gloucester," and it says:

This herring industry enables our vessels to prosecute the Bank fisheries in February and March, when immense schools of fish resort thither, and the largest fares are brought in; it furnishes a valuable article of nourishing food for the New York, Boston, and other markets at a low price, and within the last year it has opened a profitable commerce with Sweden, from which the best of results are anticipated.

Another paragraph from the same article reads:

The export trade of the past season, and the improved demand for home consumption, gave an impetus to the various branches of the herring fishery the past season, and some thirty-nine vessels were employed in the Newfoundland herring trade, salt and fresh, while some thirty-six vessels made herring trips to Grand Manan and Nova Scotia on Gloucester account. Most of the fleet have completed their voyages, and besides keeping this market well stocked, eight cargoes from Newfoundland and five from Grand Manan have been forwarded to New York, three Manan fares have been sent to Philadelphia, and three Newfoundland and three New Brunswick cargoes have been marketed in Boston.

Do you believe those statements?—A. That refers entirely to the frozen-herring business, from the fact that it says they send them to New York and Philadelphia, and Gloucester vessels come down to Grand Manan and buy cargoes of herring, take them to Gloucester, and send them to markets at New York or Philadelphia.

Q. What is the practice round Grand Manan as to buying herring?—A. They pay so much per hundred for them.

Q. Do they fish for them themselves?—A. No; they buy them.

Q. You never have been there?—A. No.

Q. You swear positively that they don't catch them?—A. Yes.

Q. Do they employ the fishermen to catch herring for them?—A. The fishermen catch the herring, and they buy them and pay so much per hundred.

Q. They never catch a herring?—A. Not to any extent.

Q. To what extent do they catch them?—A. It is very slight. In fact, I think they have given it up altogether; a few vessels formerly brought down nets. The skippers of those vessels have told me it did not pay to catch the herring, and they would rather buy them. I know one particular friend of mine who did this last winter. Again, the fishermen about Deer Island won't let them catch herring, and cut their nets, saying that the fishing belongs to them.

Q. Although you were never at Grand Manan, you swear positively, that the Americans do not fish there?—A. I say they don't to any extent.

Q. That you swear to positively?—A. Yes.

Q. As a matter you are sure of ?—A. Yes; as far as I can be sure of anything by conversing with fishermen.

Q. Without any knowledge of your own ?—A. That is all the knowledge I have, and that ought to be enough.

Q. I want to call your attention to a statement in the Cape Ann Advertiser of January 26, 1877. Before I do so I wish to ask you if it is well understood there is a herring fleet that comes down there every season ?—A. Yes; there are a number of schooners that come down for herring.

Q. Is it called the herring fleet ?—A. I don't know whether it is or not. I know they come there to buy herring.

Q. This paper also says:

The number of fishing arrivals reported at this port the past week has been fourteen—ten from the Banks and La Have, and four from Grand Manan. The New Brunswick herring-fleet bring good cargoes, and the supply, being greater than will be needed to bait the fishing fleets, will be marketed in part in other markets.

That shows they go down to get bait ?—A. Yes; because it is frozen herring they get for bait. They bait the vessels for going on the Grand Banks.

Q. Is this true ? I am reading now from "The Fisheries of Gloucester from 1623 to 1876," published by Procter Bros., of Gloucester, in 1876:

The Newfoundland and New Brunswick herring fisheries, of comparatively recent origin, while not unattended with hardship and danger, became at once an important auxiliary of the Georges and Banks fisheries, and have been pursued unremittingly from the start.

A. I don't know anything about the Newfoundland herring fishery.

Q. Then about New Brunswick ?—A. I know they come there every winter.

Q. Do you deny that ?—A. It connects Newfoundland and New Brunswick. There may be hardships and dangers attending the Newfoundland fishery. I don't know about that.

Q. There is no hardship, in your estimation, about the Newfoundland fishery ?—A. No.

Q. You think the writer would connect New Brunswick with Newfoundland, and say there are hardships when he only meant it was in Newfoundland that hardships were incurred ?—A. I don't know what he meant.

Q. He says that in that enterprise there were dangers and hardships ?—A. It may be very well for a man sitting in his room to write such an article.

Q. Probably such a man could write this of the fisheries as a man living at Eastport could speak of the fishing at Grand Manan, when he had never been there ?—A. No; only he had not been engaged in the fishing business for 20 years, as I have been.

Q. You never did any fishing round Grand Manan and never saw it ?—A. But I have bought the fish and had conversations with fishermen.

Q. In the same article as I have read, it says further:

During the present season herring have been shipped hence to Sweden, at a good profit, and it is not impossible that this may prove the initial step toward the resumption of exportation of fish to foreign ports, an important industry of the port in the early days of its fishing enterprise.

Do you agree with that ?—A. That is correct; the herring are put up at Eastport.

Q. They are put up at Eastport and sent to Gloucester ?—A. Yes two or three different firms from Gloucester bought herring in Eastport last year. One I packed out, and another party was there buying them packed up in barrels.

Q. Do I understand that you wish the Commissioners to believe that the Gloucester fleet comes down for the purpose of getting herring round Grand Manan, goes down to Eastport and ships herring there?—A. Yes. These parties are from Gloucester.

Q. Does the New Brunswick fishing-fleet, the herring-fleet, take their cargoes into Eastport before they go to Gloucester?—A. They go down on the north side and buy herring and take them to Gloucester.

Q. It comes to this. You come here for the purpose of contradicting Mr. McLaughlin as to what took place on the island of Grand Manan, where you say you never were in your life. Is that true?—A. I did not come here to contradict Mr. McLaughlin.

Q. You have in fact contradicted Mr. McLaughlin?—A. I have told what I know.

Q. You put your opinion as to the facts respecting fishing round Grand Manan—though you have never been there in your life—against the opinion of Mr. McLaughlin, who has resided there all his life, and swears to certain facts. You do the same with regard to the main land, where you have never been, except once to St. George, and that ten years ago?—A. I consider I know as much about the fishing, buying fish at Eastport which comes from there, as Mr. McLaughlin, who keeps a light-house, knows about it.

Q. Are you aware that it is part of Mr. McLaughlin's business to go round to all the fishermen and ascertain exactly what the American catch was?—A. I understand he is fishery-warden there.

Q. Do I understand you to say you have as good a means of information in regard to Grand Manan as Mr. McLaughlin?—A. I think I have.

Q. Do you swear you have as good means of information as Mr. James McLean in regard to the mainland fishery, he living there and doing business there?—A. I think so. He is engaged there in buying fish, and I am engaged at Eastport buying it.

Q. Are you aware that he is engaged in fishing?—A. No; he is a merchant.

Q. Do you swear he does not send out any fishing-vessels and small boats?—A. He may send out some fishing-boats, but the principal part of his business is that of a merchant.

Q. If he swears that he sends out fishing-vessels and boats, do you mean to say the statement is untrue?—A. He may do that.

Q. You undertake to put your opinion against his?—A. Yes.

Q. Though you never have been there at all?—A. Yes.

Q. Mr. McLaughlin has said this.

Q. Now about how many American vessels fish on the coast during the season?—A. It would be hard to tell that; it has never been my duty to count them.

Q. They come in large numbers, and they generally outnumber ours?—A. Yes; our people at Grand Manan fish but little in vessels.

You contradict that?—A. I do.

Q. You say they fish a great deal in vessels and very little in boats?—A. I say very few American vessels come there to fish.

Q. Do you contradict the statement that Grand Manan people fish very little in vessels?—A. They have a dozen or twenty vessels over there.

Q. Do you contradict the statement or do you not?—A. I don't know what he calls small or large.

You swear that the Grand Manan people fish round their own
—A. Yes.

o you say that the American vessels do not outnumber the Grand
1 vessels?—A. I say they do not.

Though you had not been there at all?—A. I have not been there,
know.

ou swear positively that the statement is not true?—A. Yes.

Mr. McLaughlin also said:

o these vessels come in fishing within three miles?—A. At a certain time of the
n winter it is entirely within; the fall and winter fishing is entirely within.

you contradict that?—A. The most of those vessels fish on Grand
1 Banks.

hat is not the question. [Extract re-read.] What do you say to
A. I say that in winter perhaps half a dozen vessels owned in
ort may go over to Grand Manan fishing. They all fish inside
the herring are inside; within the last two or three or four years
rring have been outside, and they fished outside for them.

'o the statement is not true that the fall and winter fishing for
; is entirely inside?—A. It is not entirely inside.

s the bulk of it outside?—A. No; I don't know that the bulk is.

ou say that the fall and winter fishing is entirely outside?—A.
irely; I say to a great extent.

he larger portion is outside?—A. The boat fishermen of Grand
and the islands of New Brunswick are complaining that the
ich year are being set further off shore, and within the last year
or two or three years they have been so greedy, they say, that
ave put their nets four or five miles out.

Tell me a single man who has told you that the fishing in the fall
inter fishery is not within three miles of the shore?—A. I cannot
you the name of a Grand Manan man, but I can give you the
of a man who has been continually fishing there and in that
ty for twenty years. It is not only at Grand Manan but at other
; they are complaining.

Can you give me the name of any Grand Manan man who told
hat?—A. It was not a Grand Manan man who told me.

It comes to this: those men who are on the spot and ought to be
to know all about the fishing, you contradict, though you have
een on the spot?—A. I say my means of information are as good
eirs. I have been employed in business twenty years, and I have
accustomed to converse with fishermen.

Do you seriously swear before the Commission that your opinion
reference to the fisheries prosecuted on the main land and at
l Manan Island is as good as the opinion of those who have lived
all their lifetime?—A. I consider that my opinion and my means
ormation are as good as theirs.

By Mr. Trescot:

In giving your testimony before the Commissioners, you do not
to give it as a practical fisherman?—A. No; not at all.

You give it as a man representing a house which has been in the
ess for 60 years. You give your testimony, as I understand it, as
ton-buyer would give his experience of dealing in cotton. He
s the brands, the qualities, and the places from which the cotton
; and his views would be based on that sort of information. Now,
regard to this question about the fishery, you have expressed the
on that in winter it is not exclusively an inshore fishery, and Mr.

Thomson has submitted the opinion of Mr. McLaughlin as opp
this view; and I want to read the opinion of an overseer, Mr. C
ham, of the Inner Bay, and see whether it agrees with yours.
follows:

The winter herring fishery, I am sorry to say, shows a decrease from the
last year. This, I believe, is owing to the large quantities of nets—in fact
them—being set by United States fishermen all the way from Grand Mana
preaux, and far out in the bay by the Wolves, sunk from 20 to 25 fathoms, wl
the fish from coming into the bay.

As they are fishing far off shore, a week at a time, this destructive practi
followed with impunity and without fear of detection.

A. That is correct; that is what the fishermen are complainii
Q. With regard to what is called the Gloucester herring
which reference has been made here once or twice—are you a
not whether this fleet takes out licenses to touch and trade wh
come to buy herring at Newfoundland, or at Grand Manan,
Brunswick?—A. I do not know anything about that matter.

No. 60.

WILLIAM DAVIS, master mariner and fisherman, of Glouceste1
was called on behalf of the Government of the United State:
and examined.

By Mr. Foster:

Question. You are seventy-one years of age?—Answer. Yes.
Q. When did you first go fishing for mackerel in the Gulf of £
rence?—A. In 1838.
Q. And when were you last there?—A. In 1876.
Q. How many years were you there fishing in the interval
could not tell exactly; but I was there for a good many years.
Q. You have a list of them?—A. Yes.
Q. In what schooner were you there last year?—A. The B.
kins.
Q. How long were you there in her?—A. About three month
Q. How many barrels of mackerel did you then catch?—'
hundred.
Q. What was your share in money?—A. Twenty-six dollars.'
Q. For three mouths' work?—A. Yes.
Q. You were also there in 1872?—A. Yes.
Q. And you were there during a good many years between 1
1867?—A. Yes.
Q. Will you state to the Commission where you used to fis
those years, and where you caught your fish? I want you pai
to mention the places within the three miles of the shore where
to fish or try to fish?—A. I cannot name a great many plac
three miles of the shore.
Q. Where did you use to go to fish in the bay?—A. The fir
was there we caught what we did get, and that was not a gre
on Banks Bradley and Orphan.
Q. What were your principal fishing-grounds?—A. These we
Bradley and Orphan, and the Magdalen Islands.
Q. Where did you ever fish inshore in the bay within the 1
limit?—A. I so fished some little at Margaree, although I 1
fortunate enough to catch any mackerel there save very few.
Q. How near the main-land and how near the island did y

Did you ever fish in the Bend of Prince Edward Island ?—A. Yes,

When you did so, how far from the shore were you in the habit of
ig ?—A. Well, I have fished there 5 and 6 and 10 miles off shore,
do not think that I ever caught any mackerel there within the
-mile limit.   We were generally pretty shy of the bend of the island.
Why ?—A. On account of it being a rather bad place for getting
ht in with an on-shore wind.   It is a rather dangerous place.

By Mr. Davies:

Did you ever fish much on the American coast ?—A. Yes, in my
g days.
But of late years, and since 1855, you preferred to come down to
ay to fish ?—A. No; not always.
But generally was not this the case ?—A. Yes, I did prefer coming
e bay to fish with the hook and line.
Did you ever try in the Bay of Chaleurs ?—A. Yes.   I was in there

What was the average of the catches which you made since you
to the Bay of St. Lawrence to fish ?—A. I have not figured them
ut these catches were not very large.   I was not very lucky.
You have been rather unfortunate on your fishing trips ?—A. Yes.
And you never fished within 3 miles of land in the bay ?—A. I
d not say that.
You never caught any there to speak of ?—A. Yes.   I do not say
I did not catch anything within the three-mile limit, but I got very
here.
You fought shy of the Bend of Prince Edward Island ?—A. Well,
is so.

No. 61.

ILLIAM O. COOK, fisherman, of Gloucester, Mass., was called on be-
of the Government of the United States, sworn and examined.

By Mr. Foster:

lestion. How old are you ?—Answer. 48.
When did you first fish for mackerel in the Gulf of St. Lawrence ?—
n 1849, I think.
During how many years were you fishing in the gulf?—A. 7.
Which years were those ?—A. They are included from 1849 to 1861,
nk.
What was the course you usually took when fishing for mackerel
ie bay during this period ?—A. We usually first fished on Banks
ian and Bradley, and afterwards at the Magdalen Islands; from
ce we went and fished half-way across between the Magdalen Islands
the Cape Breton shore; this used to be our fishing-ground when I
went to the bay.
How long did you stay there ?—A. We used to cruise around there
g in October.
And where did you go in October ?—A. We then cruised on the
e Breton shore, keeping broad off from it.
Did you fish during any part of the autumn off the Bend of Prince
ard Island ?—A. O, yes, we have fished off there, but nowhere
in the three-mile limit.
Did you usually fish there ?—A. No.

Q. You say that in the autumn you usually went to the Cape ⸬
shore?—A. Yes.

Q. What was your harbor there?—A. Port Hood.

Q. When you made Port Hood your harbor, how long did you
the vicinity?—A. Sometimes a fortnight and sometimes three we

Q. When did you usually leave the Magdalen Islands to go o
the vicinity of Port Hood?—A. We usually left there about the
the middle of October.

Q. How near the main-land and how near Margaree Island we
in the habit of fishing when you were in the vicinity of Port Hc
A. I think that sometimes we fished near Margaree Island, but
the cutters used to be there we used to fish broad off.

Q. What is the greatest number of mackerel that you ever ⸬
within 3 miles of the shore, either of the island or main-land, a
garee?—A. As near as I can recollect, this was in 1856, when we ⸬
15 wash barrels about half-way between Mabou and Margaree I⸬

Q. Were you in the gulf when the cutters were there?—A. Ye⸬

Q. Do you remember any conversation taking place with th
tain of a cutter as to where you might fish?—A. He told us that we
fish three miles from the land.

Q. In what depth of water?—A. Twelve fathoms.

Q. What did he tell you about fishing in 12 fathoms of water?—
told us to stand off in 12 fathoms of water, and that we would t
clear of the land.

Q. Where was this?—A. Off New London Head.

Q. What was the name of this captain?—A. I do not remembe

Q. Do you remember the year when this took place?—A. It was
in 1851 or 1852—I forget which.

By Mr. Davies:

Q. I suppose that when you would be in 12 fathoms of water off
you would be about three miles from land?—A. I could not tell yo
I thought by the looks of it, this was pretty near in.

Q. And he told you to go off in 12 fathoms of water. I unde
you to say that at Cape Breton you used to make Port Hood yo
bor?—A. Yes.

Q. Did you stay there every night?—A. No.

Q. How often did you go in there?—A. When it was stormy w⸬
times went in there, and sometimes we anchored off Margaree Is⸬

Q. In the month of October, you did not fish near the Magda
ands at all?—A. O, I have been there late in October.

Q. Was this the case as a rule?—A. I do not know about a rul
have fished there in October.

Q. You stated in answer to Mr. Foster that when October ca⸬
cruised around the Cape Breton shore?—A. Well, that was during
October—not the 1st of October. During part of the month we

Q. When, as a rule, did you leave the Magdalen Islands to g⸬
Cape Breton shore?—A. I have staid around there until the 1⸬
the 15th of October.

Q. That was the extreme limit of your stay there?—A. I c⸬
say for certain, but that is the case as near as I can remember.

Q. When did you generally leave the Magdalen Islands and go '
the Cape Breton shore?—A. I think about the 10th or the 15th
tober.

Q. Do you state this to be the general time when you left the
Yes; we always were around there about the 10th, and someti⸬
5th and the 15th or the 20th of October.

Q. You left there from the 5th to the 20th of October?—A. Yes.

Q. And the remainder of the season you spent off the Cape Breton shore?—A. We did not spend the whole time there; we might start off and go somewhere else.

Q. Does the weather become blowy about the Magdalen Islands about that period?—A. Some years that is the case, and some years it is not.

Q. I suppose that during the years you were on our coast during the Reciprocity Treaty you fished inshore and off shore and everywhere?—A. There was nothing to stop us doing so, but we could not catch any fish inshore. There was nothing to catch inshore.

Q. Did you then take particular notice whether you caught your fish in or off shore?—A. I think we did.

Q. Why?—A. I do not know, but we talked the matter over among ourselves, as to how and where we caught our mackerel.

Q. Did you catch many mackerel near Margaree?—A. No; I do not think that we did.

Q. Do you mean to tell the Commission that the mackerel caught off Margaree are not caught within three miles of the island or within three miles of the shore?—A. I have caught mackerel inside of the three-mile limit off Margaree Island.

Q. When you had the right to fish in there, did you not go within the three-mile limit?—A. Yes; I say we did so.

Q. Was it not your habit and custom to fish within three miles of the shore during the Reciprocity Treaty?—A. No. We used to fish off shore.

Q. What, then, did you mean by telling Mr. Foster that you fished near Margaree, and that when the cutters were there you fished broad off?—A. And when the cutters were not there I fished inshore?

Q. That would be the inference?—A. I said that when the cutters were there, I fished broad offshore.

Q. I presume from this that when the cutters were not there, you fished inside the three-mile limit?—A. I do not know about that.

Q. Is that correct?—A. We always used to fish offshore, and inshore too.

Q. Did you take out licenses?—A. We did not.

Q. Were you in the bay during the license years?—A. Yes.

Q. During what years were you there? You said that you fished in the bay from 1849 to 1861—then you were not there during the license years?—A. No.

Q. What were your average catches in the bay?—A. 150 and 250 barrels; and some years 300 barrels; and one year our catch was 600 barrels; all of which we caught on Banks Bradley and Orphan.

Q. When was this?—A. In 1860.

Q. You do not know anything about fishing in the bay since 1861?—A. No.

Q. Or whether the fish have of late years been taken in their old haunts or not?—A. No.

Q. What was the size of the vessel in which you took that large catch?—A. 118 tons.

Q. Did you ever fish about Seven Islands?—A. No.

Q. And you never fished much about Prince Edward Island?—A. No, not a great deal; and I never fished any to the nor'ard of Banks Orphan and Bradley.

Q. Did you fish there outside of four or five miles from the shore?—A. We used to fish there so as just to see New London Head; and we fished from there to North Cape.

Q. And that would be in 12 fathoms of water?—A. We we pretty near in when in 12 fathoms of water.

Q. You did fish there off shore?—A. Yes; we did.

Q. But were you accustomed to fish there? Was it one of the grounds or haunts which you frequented?—A. No; we used t the Magdalen Islands to get big mackerel.

Q. And after they were done, and if you were not successfu you went to these other places?—A. We used to go to Banks] and Orphan, and to Bird Rocks.

Q. When you were not successful there do you mean to say tl did not try off Prince Edward Island?—A. We used to try br shore there—in sight of land.

Q. I am not speaking of the limits; but did you not try off Edward Island every year?—A. We fished there broad offshore.

Q. Never mind that; but every year you fished there?—A. I used to fish there so that we could see the land; we fished up an broad off the land; we would be about 25 or 26 miles off.

Q. Did you do so every year?—A. No; we did not. In 1860 we altogether off the Magdalen Islands and off Bird Rocks.

Q. That was for one year?—A. Yes; and in 1856 also we fishe altogether.

Q. With the exception of these two years, you fished every : Prince Edward Island?—A. Well, we used to fish there broad (so as to see land ; we did not like to go in.

Q. What then induced you to have a conversation with the of a cutter respecting the distance off shore, where and in what i of fathoms you should fish?—A. We did so because we wanted that out so as to satisfy ourselves.

Q. If you never fished off there save at a distance of 20 or 2 from land what earthly necessity could there be for making such an at all?—A. We had nothing to go by so as to tell what distance from land.

Q. Do you mean to tell the Commission that although you fi miles off shore there was any necessity to inquire of a captain o ter in how many fathoms of water you should fish, so as not within three miles of the shore?—A. If we fished in toward the we wanted to know when we would be safe.

Q. Why did you want to know the exact depth of water in v fish?—A. We saw the captain of the cutter when we were g and some wanted to heave to and fish, while others urged should ask him about it.

Q. And you never caught any fish inshore?—A. I did not we did.

Q. Why did you wish to know the exact limit?—A. I neve any fish inside the limit there; but I have done so on the Cape shore.

Q. Why did you want to know the exact distance at wl should fish off New London Head?—A. We wanted to sat minds and know where the limit was.

No. 62.

EDWARD HILL, fisherman, of Gloucester, Mass., was called of the Government of the United States, sworn and examined.

By Mr. Foster:

Question. How old are you?—Answer. I am 56.

Q. When did you first fish in the Gulf of St. Lawrence ?—A. In 1850.

Q. During how many years altogether have you fished for mackerel in the gulf ?—A. 14.

Q. When did you last fish there ?—A. In 1869.

Q. What were your principal fishing grounds when fishing for mackerel in the gulf ?—A. These were about the Magdalen Islands, and between them and Cape Breton, and on Banks Bradley and Orphan.

Q. Did you ever fish off the bend of Prince Edward Island ?—A. No; near North Cape and about 10 miles off was the closest in that I have been off the island ; but we never tried there.

Q. Where have you fished the nearest to the shore in the gulf ?—A. Off Margaree.

Q. When did you go there usually ?—A. In October.

Q. Were you in the gulf in October, 1850 ?—A. Yes.

Q. In what schooner ?—A. The B. H. Collis.

Q. Who was the captain ?—A. Llewellyn Reed.

Q. Did you come in contact with a cutter commanded by Captain Darby ?—A. We did while we were in Port Hood.

Q. I want you to relate that incident exactly as it occurred.—A. When we first got in the bay, on the first trip we went, it was in October ; about the 7th of October we went from Port Hood down to Margaree, and there was a man who came on board from another vessel, and says he. "There is a Rockport vessel which has been taken by Captain Darby.'

Q. Come right down to what was done by Captain Darby.—A. We caught about 25 barrels there, and then we got scared and went off shore. When we got to Port Hood we had a good deck of mackerel. We had them all salted on deck. Captain Darby came on board, and says he, "You have a fine lot of fish; I want to see your papers.' He took them on board the cutter, and said to the captain, "Come on board in about an hour's time; we will talk it over." The next thing, our captain came on board, and says he, "I have compromised with him by giving him 20 barrels of mackerel, and," says he, "a little pinkey will come alongside for them." We thought that this was in charge of the captain's brother, but I have heard since that this was not the case. We took the fish off our deck, and struck them down into his hold, and off he went; and he gave us permission to strike the mackerel down.

Q. What do you mean by striking them down ?—A. Heading them up and stowing them in the hold.

By Mr. Thomson :

Q. That was in 1850 or 1851 ?—A. It was in 1850.

Q. You had been fishing in Margaree Harbor ?—A. We had been fishing off Mabou.

Q. You had been fishing within three miles of the land ?—A. We then caught 25 barrels there.

Q. Within three miles of land ?—A. I do not know about that; the land is very high at Mabou, and it is hard to tell the distance exactly. No cutter was there, but only this little boat, which informed Captain Darby of it.

Q. Will you now undertake to swear that you did not catch those 25 barrels within three miles of the shore ?—A. Well, I am not certain about it; the distance off shore might have been three or four miles.

Q. Will you positively swear that you did not take them within three miles of land ?—A. No.

Q. How many barrels of mackerel had you then on hand ?—A 140.

Q. Where had you caught the rest?—A. Broad offshore, a
miles off; between that point and Entry Island, of the Magdalen

Q. Then you got frightened and ran off to Port Hood?—A.
our decks full and it breezed up and we had to run to Port Ho
harbor.

Q. Where were these 25 barrels lying?—A. On the deck alo
the rest.

Q. When you catch mackerel, do you not dress them and pi
at once into barrels?—A. No, not until we get all we can into the
and until they are fairly struck. We leave them for 24 hours g
and then head them up and strike them down.

Q. What do you call fairly struck?—A. Salted so that they
shrink.

Q. As soon as you catch them you salt them?—A. As soon as
them we let them soak in water for perhaps two or three hou
have good weather.

Q. You then open them?—A. We then dress them.

Q. How was it with these 25 barrels?—A. They were on dec
with the rest.

Q. Were these fish lying in water on deck?—A. They were a
when we reached Port Hood.

Q. And they were in barrels?—A. Yes.

Q. Were they headed up?—A. No.

Q. And you saw Captain Darby after you came to Port Ho
Yes.

Q. You were then in the harbor?—A. Yes.

Q. Was it foul weather when he came on board and took your
—A. He came on board and got the papers from the skipper,
then went back to his cutter and told the captain to come in a
hour's time, and he did so.

Q. Who was your captain?—A. Llewellyn Reed.

Q. Where is he now?—A. He is in Gloucester, working as a t

Q. Your captain went on board of the cutter?—A. Yes;
stopped there, I suppose, about half an hour, when he can
"Well," says he, "I have got the papers, and we have perm
head them up, and stow them down"; and says he, "I have go
him 20 barrels of mackerel to compromise for the papers."

Q. Then I understood you to say that Captain Darby came
your vessel, took away the papers, told the captain to come on
the cutter, and about half an hour after he went, your captain ca
and said he had compromised with Captain Darby, of the c
giving him 20 barrels of mackerel?—A. Yes.

Q. What kind of mackerel were they?—A. Number ones, a
ones—very good ones.

Q. Were these taken on board of the cutter?—A. They wer
board of the small pinkey; he had a little spy there, and he spie

Q. Was the pinkey the spy?—A. Yes.

Q. How much did this pinkey get?—A. I could not tell you
about how they settled her hash.

Q. What became of the fish?—A. They were put on boa
pinkey. Other vessels had to give him some. The Reindeer
buryport—I recollect it the same as if it had happened but yes
took 2 barrels alongside the cutter, but Captain Darby was so
on shore, or on board of some other vessel, at the time; they
Captain Darby was on board, and the answer was, "No"; the
mate, "What have you got?" "We have 2 barrels of macker

e us permission to stow our mackerel down." "Well," says the mate,
is is tall"; and they took on board the mackerel.

). As one of the crew, you were entitled to your share?—A. I lost
share of that catch. We did not know whose mackerel were taken.
do not put our private mark on them until they are headed up.

). How did you tell them?—A. We had them separated. I told the
)per not to mix them all up, but to take part of each man's catch.

'. How could you tell whose catch it was?—A. We have them all
arated, and a space left between.

'. Then you knew what barrels belonged to each of the crew?—A.
; because he mixed them all up—he was so agitated and scared.

'. That was before the cutter got hold of them at all?—A. We had
n all right before the cutter got hold of them.

'. Were they all headed up?—A. No; but they were in barrels, the
being piled up, and heaping over to a considerable extent, when
)tain Darby came on board.

). You mean that the barrels were full?—A. Yes; and heaped up.

. That was all done when you were running from Margaree to Port
d?—A. No; we proceeded to salt them in Port Hood. We had
n all in salt barrels; we were all night dressing them; and by the
e we got to Port Hood we had them all split, gutted, and in water;
then commenced to salt them; and when we had all but 2 barrels
ed we saw the cutter coming.

. To whom did these three barrels belong?—A. I could not tell.

. Had they been kept separate?—A. We had them all salted but
se.

. Do you know to whom these 2 barrels belonged?—A. No; I could
tell exactly.

). Did you know at the time?—A. No.

). Then the fish were all mixed up at that time?—A. We do not look
for each other's mackerel, but for our own; and I looked out for
e.

). Had any salt been put in these barrels at the time?—A. All my
i were then under salt.

). Were they in barrels?—A. Yes.

). You knew your own barrels?—A. Yes—if they have not been dis-
bed; I knew them as they were when I put them up, before they
re disturbed.

). How could they be disturbed when once in the barrels?—A. The
rels were shifted round. The skipper got excited.

). What were they shifted round for? Were they not shifted round
ause the officer of the cutter came on board?—A. After the skipper
e from the cutter he took anything and everytning, he was so ex-
ed.

). You mean that he slung the barrels about?—A. He took them as
y came and headed them up himself; that is, what Captain Darby
—the rest were not headed up.

). How many barrels of mackerel had you on board besides those
ich you gave to Captain Darby?—A. We had 140 on deck and in the
ld before we gave him any.

). If you had really been fishing within 3 miles of the shore, and
i cannot swear that you were not, he let you off pretty easily, instead
ting your whole cargo and your vessel besides?—A. He took just what
caught inshore.

). That was getting off pretty easily?—A. That was the first year I
s in the bay.

Q. You do not know what took place between your captain
tain Darby ?—A. No; I do not.

Q. You do not know whether your captain told him fairly en
he had caught 20 barrels within the limits ?—A. No; I could ↄ
to that.

Q. As you say, he just took the fish which you had caug
the limits. Now I will ask you fairly if that was not letting
great deal easier than you deserved, considering the fact that
forfeited the vessel and all that was in it ?—A. I do not kn
that; it was kind of hard.

Q. Would it not have been kind of harder if the vessel an
rest of the cargo had been taken ?—A. O, yes; of course.

Q. Now, were you not very glad to get off as you did; tha
pinkey, was too much for you ?—A. I told them that I would
my mackerel before I would give them up.

Q. That is the only experience you have had with the cut
Yes.

Q. I think that Captain Darby let you off wonderfully ea:
taking the fish which you had no business to catch, such as
ish subjects. During all these fourteen years it seems that you
nearer than within 10 miles of Prince Edward Island ?—A.
have been there myself within five and six miles of the shore.

Q. I thought that you never got nearer than within 10 miles ⸱
I took out a license once.

Q. When was this ?—A. In 1866; but it did not pay. Ther
mackerel inshore.

Q. Had you fished before 1866 within the limits ?—A. Well
have fished within four or five miles or so of the land; perhap
have done so, but I could not say. I caught them wherever I
them. I was, however, rather skittish about going in there, ⸀
owned the best part of the vessel myself, and I would not run

Q. But you did so sometimes ?—A. I thought I was outside

Q. Do I understand you to say that you never meant to g
in the three-mile limit at any time ?—A. Not when I owned
myself; only the year when I took out the license, I fished ⸀
had a mind to.

Q. You were afraid of the cutters ?—A. Yes; if I had lost
I had lost my all.

Q. And you would not risk it ?—A. No.

Q. During those years when you kept outside of the three.
did you get pretty good fares ?—A. Yes.

Q. Very good ones ?—A. Yes; very good indeed.

Q. How many barrels would your vessel take ?—A. One ⸀
take 267 barrels.

Q. In all these trips that you made, did you get full fares
all; in 1869 and in 1867 I did not get full fares.

Q. Before 1866, did you ever fish inshore ?—A. No; but I
barrels just in sight of Entry Island. I got my whole trip o
was never inshore at all during that trip.

Q. If in previous trips you had managed to get full trip
what induced you in 1866 to pay for a license ?—A. I wanted
of fishing inshore or offshore, as I might wish.

Q. What was your object in paying out money for a lice
viously you had got full fares outside ?—A. Sometimes the
Margaree fails, and sometimes there is a school of mackerel
I had been told, for I never saw them there myself. I dare⸀

Q. The fact of the matter is, that the mackerel are sometimes, according to your idea, out in the bay, and sometimes they school inshore; is it not then a privilege to be able to follow them inshore?—A. Yes.

Q. And the people who have that privilege are better off than those who have it not; the former have a better chance of securing fares?—A. Well, I do not know about that. I could not say that, because I found the mackerel more plentiful offshore than inshore.

Q. How much did you pay for the license?—A. 50 cents a ton.

Q. What was the tonnage of your vessel?—A. 49.

Q. Why did you pay $24.50 for a license, having no object for doing so?—A. I did it so that I could fish where I had a mind to, and so that if I found them inshore I could catch them there.

Q. And always before that you had found plenty of mackerel in the body of the bay?—A. Yes.

Q. You never previously fished within the limits at all?—A. Yes; I did so in 1851.

Q. Did you fish inshore in 1851?—A. Yes.

Q. Did you get good fares that year?—A. We caught, perhaps, 40 or 50 barrels inshore towards the last of our fishing.

Q. When were you last in the bay?—A. In 1869.

Q. I suppose that you have heard that the mackerel have kept inshore much more of late years than was formerly the case?—A. No; I do not know anything about it, because the vessels have not been doing anything. All the vessels say that they have not been doing anything at all.

Q. Have you heard that the mackerel have kept inshore of late years more than they did previously?—A. No; I have not.

Q. Then in all those voyages you never went inshore to fish, except in 1851 and in 1866, when you took out a license?—A. No; not inside the limits.

Q. You kept off shore all the time?—A. Yes.

Q. Did you get full fares all the time?—A. I did not get full fares in 1869 and 1867.

Q. And yet you did not try inshore at all?—A. No; because the vessels which went inshore did not get anything.

Q. And you would not try inshore?—A. I would not run the risk.

Q. Did you ever fish in the Bay of Chaleurs?—A. No; never.

Q. Have you never heard that good fishing was to be had on the northern shore of Prince Edward Island?—A. No.

Q. You never have?—A. No.

Q. Not from any one?—A. No. I went round the island once.

Q. You have never heard from anybody that there is good fishing along the northern shore of Prince Edward Island, within the three-mile limit?—A. No.

Q. Well, then, in your opinion the privilege of fishing within three miles of the shore along the British coasts is of no value at all to American fis e men?—A. It is not a great deal of value to them, I should think. h r

Q. Is it of any value?—A. I suppose it is some at times. I suppose there are times when the vessels themselves would benefit by it.

Q. Was it so in 1854 and before 1854? You recollect when the Reciprocity Treaty was entered into?—A. Yes.

Q. Was it a privilege then?—A. I was not in the bay then.

Q. You were there in 1850 and 1851?—A. Yes.

Q. Were you there in 1852 and 1853?—A. No.

Q. When were you next in the bay?—A. In 1855, I believe.

Q. Did you fish in the bay at all during the Reciprocity]
1854 to 1866 ?—A. Yes, I did so in 1858.

Q. Did you fish inshore then ?—A. We tried inshore and
rels of mackerel in August, off Cape George, with a seine.

Q. Where is Cape George ?—A. It is before you get to P

Q. Did you not fish along the shore of Prince Edward
year ?—A. No.

Q. Or off Margaree ?—A. No.

Q. Did you get a full fare then ?—A. No, nor half a fare.

Q. You then knew that you had a right to go inshore an
No, I did not know anything about it, nor did the captain.

Q. I understand you to say that you went there in 1858
know that you had a right to go and fish within three miles o
—A. I did not.

Q. You did not know that the Reciprocity Treaty was i
that it gave you a right to fish where you pleased ?—A. N
hand then.

Q. Did you understand from the captain that the reason
shore was because he was afraid of the cutters ?—A. No ;
afraid of the cutters.

Q. Why did you not go inshore ?—A. If he saw mackerel in
he would have seined them.

Q. You did not get a full fare ?—A. No.

Q. When did you enter the bay ?—A. About the last of .

Q. And when did you go out ?—A. The last of October.

Q. You only made one trip ?—A. Yes.

Q. Where were you fishing all that time ?—A. Broad off s
Bank Bradley.

Q. Broad off shore ?—A. Between the Magdalen Island
Breton.

Q. Were you fishing near East Point, Prince Edward Islar
we did not go near East Point, but we were off North Cape

Q. You were not broad off East Point at all ?—A. No ; b
was broad off between the Magdalen Islands and Cape Bre

Q. When was this ?—A. In 1858.

Q. And yet you did not know that you had then a right t
to fish ?—A. I did not mind anything about it.

Q. Why did you not suggest it to the captain since you w
ed in getting a full fare ?—A. I had nothing at all to say in

Q. You were a sharesman?—A. Yes.

Q. Why, then, did you not suggest to the captain to go
shore off Prince Edward Island ?—A. He might have told
my own business.

Q. But this was your business ?—A. If a man, while I
said anything like that to me, I would tell him to mind his o
and that I would attend to my own.

Q. Is it not the business of a sharesmán to do so ?—A.
on what we call half lines.

Q. Then, in 1858, although you had the right to fish ins
solutely kept out in the middle of the bay, only got hal
staid there from July to October ?—A. We tried insl
George, and we thought our luck would be the same at ot'

By Mr. Foster:

Q. Did you ever try seining in the gulf ?—A. Yes ; in 18
1860, in one vessel.

Q. With what success?—A. Very little indeed.

Q. Those were the years when you got these poor fares?—A. Yes; we each made about $75 the whole summer.

Q. What sort of seines did you use?—A. The purse-seine.

Q. Did you do so as early as 1858?—A. Yes; we had them on our shore.

Q. You were at Seven Islands?—A. Yes, with purse-seines, but got nothing. We stopped a good while there and we thus threw a great deal of our time away.

Q. You thus seined in 1858, 1859, and 1860?—A. Yes; we were at Seven Islands in 1858.

Q. What was the name of your schooner and the name of the captain?—A. The former was named the Potomac, and the latter, Nehemiah Adams.

Q. That was quite early for purse-seines?—A. We had purse seines for pogies and mackerel years before that at home; that is the way in which we catch pogies altogether on our shore. I have seen vessels belonging to this place at Seven Islands, which stopped until fall and came away without a barrel.

No. 63.

JOHN CONLEY, Jr., fisherman, of Rockport, Mass., was called on behalf of the Government of the United States, sworn and examined.

By Mr. Dana:

Question. What is your age?—Answer. It is 43.

Q. You have lived in Gloucester nearly all your life?—A. Yes; with the exception of 10 years, during which I have lived in Rockport.

Q. Is this place in a different customs district?—A. No; we have a deputy collector at Rockport, but we have to go to Gloucester to get our papers.

Q. When did you first fish in the Bay of St. Lawrence?—A. In 1854.

Q. What was the name of the vessel in which you were that year?—A. The C. C. Davis.

Q. You made one trip that year?—A. Yes.

Q. How many barrels of mackerel did you catch?—A. 175.

Q. Were they caught off or in shore?—A. They were taken offshore.

Q. All of them?—A. All with the exception of a few barrels, perhaps five, which were caught inshore.

Q. In what vessel were you in 1855?—A. The Racer. We made one trip.

Q. How many barrels did you catch?—A. 250.

Q. Where did you first fish?—A. On Bank Bradley.

Q. And then?—A. We next went down to the Magdalen Islands.

Q. How much of these 250 barrels did you catch at the Magdalen Islands?—A. We got almost the whole of them there.

Q. Where did you catch the rest?—A. Around East Point and scattered along the shore.

Q. In 1855 you had the right to fish where you liked?—A. Yes.

Q. And you knew that?—A. Yes.

Q. Did you attempt inshore fishing?—A. Yes.

Q. And you think that you gave it a fair trial?—A. Yes.

Q. What portion of your entire cargo did you catch inside of three miles of the shore that year?—A. Perhaps 15 barrels out of the 250.

Q. Were you in the bay in 1866?—A. Yes; in the Belvidere.

171 F

Q. How many barrels did you catch ?—A. 200.

Q. What portion of these were caught inside the three-mile
A. 7 or 8 barrels; we fished on Bank Bradley and along the E
shore, off the west coast.

Q. Were you in the bay or on our shore in 1857 ?—A. I wa
our shore.

Q. What were you doing ?—A. Seining.

Q. How many barrels did you take ?—A. About 500.

Q. That was the best business you had yet done ?—A. Yes.

Q. On what part of the American coast did you fish ?—A. Fro
Desert to Cape Cod.

Q. In what vessel were you in 1858 ?—A. The Sarah B.]
then made my first experience as master.

Q. How many trips did you make to the bay in 1858 ?—A.

Q. What did you catch ?—A. 130 barrels on the first and 17
on the second.

Q. Where did you catch the 130 barrels ?—A. At the Magdale

Q. Where did you make your second trip ?—A. At the]
Islands and at Margaree—broad off Margaree Island.

Q. How many of these 300 barrels do you think were caug
3 miles of the shore ?—A. Well, as well as I could judge, we mi
so caught 15 barrels.

Q. Were you in the bay in 1859 ?—A. Yes; in the Trenton.

Q. Were you mackerel or cod fishing ?—A. I was cod-fishing
and mackereling one trip.

Q. You were first cod-fishing ?—A. Yes.

Q. Where ?—A. On Banks Orphan and Bradley.

Q. Were you successful ?—A. Yes.

Q. Where did you make your second trip ?—A. In the bay, for
Q. What did you then catch ?—A. About 145 barrels.

Q. Where did you get them ?—A. We caught the most of
Cape George, on Fisherman's Bank.

Q. Did you catch any portion of them within three mil
coast ?—A. Yes.

Q. About what portion ?—A. 10 or 12 barrels, I should jue
were caught around Pomquet Island.

Q. What did you do in 1860 ?—A. I was banking.

Q. Cod fishing ?—A. Yes.

Q. Did you do well ?—A. Yes; very well, indeed.

Q. Did you go into the bay the same year ?—A. No; I did
go into the bay until 1862.

Q. In 1861 you were on the American coast ?—A. Yes.

Q. Mackereling ?—A. Yes.

Q. Seining ?—A. Yes.

Q. How many barrels did you take ?—A. 500, I think.

Q. Where were you in 1862 ?—A. In the bay, in the schoo
Williams.

Q. How many trips did you make ?—A. Two.

Q. How much did you get ?—A. 300 barrels each trip.

Q. Where did you catch them ?—A. Most of them at
Islands.

Q. Any portion of them inshore ?—A. Yes.

Q. What portion, do you think ?—A. Probably we got 20
shore.

Q. In 1863 where were you ?—A. On our shores. From th

to 1872, ten years, I was fishing on our shores—mackerel-fishing in small boats.

Q. Were not the 10 years from 1866 to 1876?—A. No.

Q. In 1863 what did you do?—A. I was in the Franklin F. Schauk.

Q. Where did you go first?—A. To the Grand Banks.

Q. Did you go into the bay at all?—A. Yes, in the fall.

Q. What did you catch?—A. 160 barrels of mackerel.

Q. Where did you catch them?—A. At Magdalen Islands and East Point.

Q. How many of those do you think you took inshore?—A. 15 barrels.

Q. Where did you catch them?—A. Right off Red Head, at Souris.

Q. Were you close in?—A. Yes.

Q. How did you catch them?—A. It was blowing fresh at the time, and we sprung up and caught them.

Q. In 1864 where were you?—A. On our shores.

Q. Cod-fishing?—A. Yes.

Q. How many trips did you make?—A. Our trips were short.

Q. How many pounds or quintals did you get for the whole season?—A. I made two trips and got 145,000 pounds each trip.

Q. Was that being very successful?—A. Yes.

Q. Take 1865—on the first trip did you go to the Banks or bay?—A. To the Banks.

Q. Did you do well there?—A. Yes.

Q. What else did you do that year?—A. I did not do anything.

Q. Did you catch any haddock?—A. I think we did a little haddocking, but nothing to speak of that year.

Q. From 1866 to 1876 you were on the American shore?—A. Yes.

Q. Did you go into the bay at all?—A. No.

Q. What were you engaged in?—A. In market fishing, for Boston market, for haddock or mackerel or any fish we could catch.

Q. You are out but a day or two?—A. We make short trips, sometimes two trips a week, sometimes one trip.

Q. For fresh fish?—A. Yes.

Q. You have never done any fishing with pounds and nets on shore?—A. No.

Q. During the ten years from 1866 to 1876 you were fishing on the American shore—were you successful?—A. Yes, successful.

Q. How did you succeed during the 10 years you were fishing on the American coast compared with the long period you were in the bay?—A. I think it was a little better than it was in the bay.

Q. You were in the bay from 1855 to 1865, during the Reciprocity Treaty, and there was nothing to prevent you fishing where you pleased. Do you think you gave a fair trial to the inshore fisheries?—A. Yes.

Q. What is the result of your experience during those 10 years you were in the bay as to the inshore fishing compared with the fishing outside?—A. As far as my own experience goes, I never reaped much benefit from the inshore fishing.

Q. And yet you tried it?—A. Yes, often.

Q. Taking the bay fishing as a whole, do you think the right to fish within three miles adds much to its value?—A. It did not to me, to my fishing.

Q. That is your experience?—A. Yes.

Q. You have been cod-fishing a good while?—A. Yes.

Q. Have you used fresh bait?—A. Yes.

Q. And fished with salt bait?—A. Yes.

Q. Take the result of your experience. Do you think it
more beneficial as regards the pecuniary results of the trips to
fresh bait or to take salt bait, and rely on what fresh bait you
at the Banks and stay out?—A. To stay out would be more
to me.

Q. You admit that fresh bait is better side by side than salt
Yes.

Q. Then what is the reason why you think it is better to sta:
salt bait?—A. On account of the time you lose in going in
money it costs to get it.

Q. To get it and keep it?—A. Yes.

Q. Did you find it pretty expensive?—A. I found it very e:

By Mr. Davies:

Q. For the last 'sixteen years you have been fishing on
shores, catching fresh fish for market?—A. Some parts of th
have.

Q. Have you been cod-fishing portions of the seasons?—A.

Q. Have you been on the Banks?—A. Yes.

Q. From 1866 to 1876 I believe you were off your own coasl
fresh fish for market?—A. Yes.

Q. So that for those ten years you know nothing of the mo
ing on the Banks from personal experience?—A. No.

Q. Previous to ten years ago, the system of fishing with fres]
not come into vogue, had it?—A. Yes, I think it had before
ago.

Q. Do you think that before ten years ago Bank codfisher
accustomed to take fresh bait or to run in to the coast for it?·

Q. Did you ever try it yourself?—A. Yes.

Q. Where did you go for fresh bait?—A. Round Cape £
round to a place called Pubnico.

Q. Did you fish on the Grand Banks of Newfoundland at
Not at that time.

Q. You never fished with fresh bait there?—A. No.

Q. You don't know anything about running into Newfour
fresh bait?—A. No.

Q. You were on Georges Banks?—A. Yes.

Q. Did you run in from Georges Bank for fresh bait?—A.

Q. Have you got any memorandum of the results of the v
A. No.

Q. You cannot remember them?—A. No; I did not think
essary.

Q. And you cannot tell, of course, what the results were?-

Q. And therefore you don't know whether one was better
other?—A. I remember going into Cape Sable for bait to go on
after halibut and codfish. I cannot remember the name of 1
where we went; it is a great place to go and get fresh bait.

Q. How many times did you run in for fresh bait from the G
A. About a dozen times.

Q. In one season?—A. In different seasons.

Q. Have you ever gone and fished on the Georges solel;
bait?—A. No.

Q. Or anywhere else—on the Grand Banks?—A. Yes, I h
Grand Banks.

Q. How many seasons were you on the Grand Banks?—
three.

Q. When was that ?—A. I don't remember the year; some time during the ten years. We made one trip there. We would go in the winter market fishing, and in the summer would make a trip to the Banks.

Q. During the last 14 years you have never been in Bay St. Lawrence fishing ?—A. I think I was there in 1873 in the Franklin S. Schank.

Q. That is a memorandum you made up from your memory ?—A. Yes.

Q. Refer to it again. You stated in answer to Mr. Dana that 1863 was the last year you were in the bay ?—A. Yes.

Q. Then for the last fourteen years you have not been in the bay fishing ?—A. No.

Q.. Then you know nothing about where the fish were caught during those fourteen years ?—A. No. I cannot answer it exactly, because my figures don't agree. My dates don't agree with my conscience. I have got it that I was there in 1873 in the Franklin S. Schank, and you have put it at 1863. I was in the Franklin S. Schank in 1873.

Q. Then you were not in that vessel in 1863 ?—A. No.

Q. Where were you in 1863 ?—A. I must have been on our shores. I took notes of the years when I was in the bay, but of the years when I was on our shore and at the Banks I did not.

Q. Could you from your memory state accurately what years you were in the bay ?—A. My memory fails me. I have not a good memory.

Q. You cannot tell from memory the years you were in the bay ?—A. No, unless I were to sit down and think it over.

Q. Irrespective of that one trip in the Franklin S. Schank in the fall ot 1873, you have not been in the bay for fourteen years ?—A. No.

Q. During all those years you do not pretend to say where the fish were caught ?—A. I do not.

Q. As to the Franklin S. Schank, what became of her ?—A. She was owned in Rockport.

Q. Was she not seized ?—A. Yes.

Q. In what year ?—A. The year she was built. I don't remember what the year was. She was seized and went to Quebec.

Q. Was she sold ?—A. Yes, and the parties bought her back.

Q. What was she condemned and sold for ?—A. For net fishing within the limits.

Q. She was sold and condemned ?—A. Yes; that was before I went in her.

Q. She was bought back and then you went in her ?—A. Yes.

Q. What time of the year did you come to the bay in her on the fall trip in 1873 ?—A. About the 15th of September we left home.

Q. I suppose you got down to the bay about the 25th ?—A. About 20th or along there.

Q. Where did you go ?—A. We went to the Magdalen Islands.

Q. Is it customary for vessels to go to Magdalen Islands after 25th September ?—A. It is.

Q. I understood they generally left about 25th September or 1st October ?—A. Some do not leave there till the weather blows them away.

Q. When is that ?—A. When the anchors won't hold on the bottom.

Q. When is that ?—A. About the last of November.

Q. Are you sure in stating that ?—A. Yes.

Q. That mackerel-fishing vessels remain there till the last of November ?—A. Yes; I staid myself.

Q. In what year ?—A. I don't remember the year.

Q. You have not been there for 14 years ?—A. I know I have not.

Q. Can you remember the name of the vessel you were in wh
staid till the last of November ?—A. Roger Williams.

Q. That was in 1862, was it ?—A. Yes; we went adrift. We
leave.

Q. Can you remember the time ?—A. I cannot remember the t

Q. Was it the last of November ?—A. It was somewhere abc
first.

Q. How do you mean you went adrift ?—A. We never stay in t
till the last of November. We always reckon to be out of the l
the 10th of November.

Q. You mean the last of October ?—A. Yes.

Q. Is it not the first of October they leave the Magdalen Isla
A. About the last.

Q. A witness (Mr. Cook) who preceded you said that from the
the 10th of October they left there. Where else did you fish th;
in the Franklin S. Schank ?—A. At East Point, Prince Edward

Q. How did you fish there; did you go inshore and drift ou
What we caught we caught to an anchor inshore.

Q. Did you try fishing and drifting off ?—A. Yes.

Q. Were there any vessels with you ?—A. There were not a
day we caught our mackerel. They were all in the harbor at Sc

Q. When you were fishing, drifting off the land, were there an
vessels there ?—A. Yes.

Q. Lots of them ?—A. Yes.

Q. How many would you say ?—A. 30 or 40 sail.

Q. All engaged in the same mode of fishing ?—A. Yes.

Q. Is there not a larger fleet generally found off East Point th;
40 sail ?—A. Sometimes there are more, and sometimes less.

Q. Sometimes a good deal larger ?—A. That was about an
that year.

Q. Can you remember, leaving out the Franklin S. Schank, wh
portion of the mackerel which you caught in the bay fourteen ye
was taken within three miles of shore ?—A. I think about one-nin
as near as I could judge from the little experience I had.

Q. Your experience was not much ?—A. No.

Q. Did you ever fish about Seven Islands ?—A. No.

Q. Nor in Bay Chaleurs ?—A. No.

Q. Nor along the west shore of New Brunswick, from Miscou
michi ?—A. Off shore I have a little.

Q. You have never tried within three miles of the shore ?—
not off that shore.

Q. Did you fish round the bend of Prince Edward Island ?—
I have tried there.

Q. Did you ever try within three miles of the shore, except
Point ?—A. Yes.

Q. Whereabouts ?—A. Off St. Peter's, New London Head,
along what we call the Sand Hills.

Q. Did you try many times there ?—A. Different times, yes.

Q. And you always tried by going in and drifting off ?—A.
wind would not always allow us to do that. Sometimes we wo
north and south. The wind would not always be right offshore
all depends on the wind. Sometimes we drifted along the shore
times from north and south; sometimes in and sometimes out.

Q. The fleet all pursued the same mode of fishing ?—A. Wh
trying along there I was always alone. I never happened to b
fleet when fishing there.

Q. You never saw anybody else doing so ?—A. I say I never tried with any fleet inside of three miles.

Q. Did you ever see any other vessels fishing in that way within three miles of the shore at the island ?—A. Yes.

Q. How could you see them ?—A. They were a distance off, trying along.

Q. There were vessels there besides you ?—A. Yes.

Q. What did you mean when you said you were always alone ?—A. Away from the fleet.

Q. Were there, or were there not, other vessels with you when you were so fishing ?—A. At a distance from me.

Q. What distance out ?—A. Perhaps five or six miles along the shore.

Q. How many would there be ?—A. Ten or twelve going and coming, some one way and some another. As far as my eye could see I would see vessels.

Q. You saw vessels more or less all the time ?—A. Yes.

Q. You always saw them when off the shore ?—A. Most generally.

Q. Is not the fleet accustomed to largely fish along there ?—A. When they strike mackerel they generally bunch up. When they cannot find any they go flying all around the shores.

Q. When they catch the mackerel schooling they bunch together, a good many of them ?—A. Yes.

Q. How many ?—A. As high as 105 sail.

Q. Round one school ?—A. Yes.

Q. Catching mackerel off the island ?—A. I did not say off the island.

Q. Did you not understand that my questions had reference to the north side of Prince Edward Island ?—A. I did not understand you to say within the three-mile limit.

Q. Did you understand me to refer to the north side of the island when you spoke about the vessels being scattered about at one time, and then being together in a bunch ?—A. I did.

Q. When you gave your answers to me you had reference to Prince Edward Island ?—A. I said I had seen 150 sail of vessels off the coast of the island.

Q. And every time you have been there, you have seen vessels more or less fishing off the coast ?—A. Sailing up and down and trying to fish.

Q. And have you known any fish caught there ?—A. Yes.

Q. As to distances from the shore ; is there much difficulty in telling the exact distance you are off shore ?—A. Yes, I should judge there was.

Q. A man might think he was three miles off when he was only two and a half, or he might think he was outside the limits when he was really very near the line of the limits, might he ?—A. Yes. The way I have always found it is this : if we thought we were a mile and a half off shore, and we pulled to shore, we would find it three or four miles.

Q. Where used you to harbor at the island ?—A. I have been into about all the harbors there. We used to anchor a good deal to a lee.

Q. Where ?—A. Off East Point.

Q. There is a good lee off East Point ?—A. Yes.

Q. You never had any difficulty in running round the point when the wind was from the northwest and getting a good lee ?—A. No.

Q. And when the wind was from the other side you slipped round the point ?—A. Yes.

Q. There is no difficulty about doing that ?—A. No.

Q. It is perfectly safe ?—A. No, it is not perfectly safe.

Q. Why not ?—A. Because when the wind comes to the eas[
have to get away. You have no lee when the wind is from the

Q. What harbors can you go into ?—A. Into no harbor wit[
east wind.

Q. You have not been there since the breakwater was bui[
have not been there since 1873.

Q. Do you know that a large breakwater has been built sinc[
A. They were commencing to build a breakwater then, but [
enough for two or three whale-boats.

Q. You have not seen the breakwater which has been buil[
an expense of $60,000 or $70,000 ?—A. No.

Q. How can you say it was but sufficient to cover three or f[
boats ?—A. It was not built when I was there.

Q. Did you ever fish much about Margaree ?—A. Yes.

Q. Within three miles of the shore?—A. No.

Q. Not off Margaree ?—A. I fished round Margaree, not wi[
miles of the shore.

Q. You did not try there ?—A. No; we were off shore.

Q. You are sure of that ?—A. Yes.

Q. Although it is sixteen years ago ?—A. Yes.

Q. Although you had the right to fish where you pleased dur[
of the years of which you have spoken. Did no other vessel[
A. No.

Q. How can you tell ?—A. We could not find any when we w[

Q. You swear you never went in to try within three mil[
shore; is that the fact ?—A. I don't recollect of swearing I n[
within three miles of shore to try.

Q. At Margaree ?—A. I don't remember it.

Q. Did you or did you not ?—A. I don't remember anything
I don't remember you asking me a question about Margaree I

Q. Did you or did you not ever try to fish within three m[
shore at or about Margaree?—A. I have.

Q. Where and when ?—A. In different years. Almost eve[
ever fished there we tried more or less.

Q. And the fleet tried more or less ?—A. Yes.

Q. Do many of the fleet go there in the fall ?—A. We we[
garee, Port Hood, and Cape George; some part of the fall w[
up and down that coast.

Q. Sometimes fishing within three miles of the shore and d[
—A. They cannot be always drifting off, because the wind is
blowing on shore.

Q. When the wind is favorable, is that mode of fishing [
A. Yes.

Q. And they tried it every year ?—A. Every year I have [

Q. When the wind is favorable they try within the limit[
off shore. That is the fact ?—A. They try more or less i[
drift off.

Q. What the results of the vessels' voyages were, you don[
A. No.

Q. You kept on trying every year within the lines ?—A. O[
we tried.

Q. Is there not round Margaree Island itself very excell[
ground ?—A. I never found it so.

Q. Have you heard other fishermen speak of it as such ?—[
heard of other vessels doing well there. It had been said

mackerel there, but when we got there we did not find any. I have heard from fishermen that they found fish there.

Q. You never were in Bay Chaleurs ?—A. No.

Q. You don't know anything about the fishing there ?—A. No.

Q. Did you try there in 1873 ?—A. We tried there.

Q. What did you catch there ?—A. Nothing.

Q. Did you ever try off Cape Breton shore ?—A. I never tried along the north shore of Cape Breton. We tried at the Magdalen Islands and Prince Edward Island. I understand you now refer to 1873.

Q. You went to Margaree ?—A. Yes.

Q. You tried once and did not catch any ?—A. Yes, and went away to Magdalen Islands.

By Mr. Dana :

Q. Your memorandum is made up for the bay voyages only ?—A. Yes.

Q. When did you make it up; before you came here ?—A. I made a kind of memorandum at home and copied it when I came here.

Q. Were you in the bay some time in 1855 ?—A. Yes.

Q. And in 1856 ?—A. Yes.

Q. And in 1858 ?—A. Yes.

Q. State what years you were in the bay.—A. In 1854 in C. C. Davis; 1855, Racer; 1856; Belvidere; 1858, Sarah B. Harris; 1859, Trenton; 1860, Trenton; 1862, Roger Williams; 1873, Franklin S. Schank.

Q. Do you think that during these eight years you gave a fair trial to the inshore fisheries ?—A. Yes.

Q. And you found them to be of little value; you tried them in various ways—drifting off sometimes, and anchoring and drifting off at other times, according to the wind ?—A. Yes.

Q. And you know of no other way of drifting ?—A. Yes.

No. 64.

JOHN C. KNOWLTON, fisherman, of Rockport, Mass., was called on behalf of the Government of the United States, sworn and examined.

By Mr. Foster :

Question. Rockport is a town adjoining Gloucester, and in the same maritime district ?—Answer. Yes.

Q. How old are you ?—A. I am 39.

Q. When did you first go fishing in the Gulf of St. Lawrence ?—A. In 1851.

Q. How many voyages in all did you make to the bay ?—A. Nine.

Q. In what year did you make your last voyage there ?—A. In 1874; 3 years ago.

Q. Were you sharesman or skipper ?—A. I was sharesman.

Q. Who was skipper ?—A. Donald McDonald.

Q. How many barrels of mackerel did you take ?—A. I think we landed 430 barrels at Canso, where I left the vessel, which went back to the bay, while I returned home.

Q. What became of her afterward ?—A. She came home, I think, with about 575 or 600 barrels, including the 430 mentioned.

Q. Was this not an unusually good catch for that year ?—A. No; there were vessels which did a great deal better than that.

By Sir Alexander Galt :

Q. When was this ?—A. In 1874; 3 years ago.

By Mr. Foster:

Q. Where were the mackerel taken which you caught?—A
we caught were taken close inshore at the Miramichi Bar,
words, I might say, close to the mouth of Miramichi Harbor
went to make a harbor.

Q. That is outside of Miramichi Bay?—A. Yes. Our fisl
it a harbor, where we can get round under the lee of the wi
can get round that bar and make a good harbor with the wir
tain direction.

Q. How many barrels of mackerel did you get there?—A.
like 30 or 40. I was then in the Grace L. Fears. We then c
off North Cape, and I think that we got some 60 or 70 barre
tween there and North Cape, broad off shore.

Q. At what distance from the shore?—A. Well, I think 10
likely, or 15 miles.

Q. Where did you go from there?—A. We fished down off.
and around there; we tried for one or two days, and then v
around West Cape and came back again. We principally fis
down the island.

Q. Did you fish up and down Prince Edward Island on
side?—A. We did so on the east side.

Q. What do you call the east side?—A. The part between
and East Point.

Q. How far from the shore did you fish off the bend of the
A. Well, with the exception of the time when we were con
Cascumpeque, we fish outside of the three-mile limit.

Q. How far from the shore?—A. From 12 to 20 miles, I s
or something in that neighborhood.

Q. Measured from where?—A. The main land.

Q. From the extreme bend of the island?—A. No; but fro
est land opposite where we were.

Q. You have told us the places were you fished that year v
miles of the shore?—A. Yes; with the exception of the tin
were coming out of Cascumpeque Harbor. We then got abc
barrels. I think we might have hove to somewhere about,
within the three-mile limit, outside the bar, among the fishin
drifted right off, so that, while doing so, we got about 60 w;

Q. Which was the next previous year when you were in f
A. 1872; I was then in the Waverley, Captain Tarr.

Q. How many barrels did you catch?—A. We brought h

Q. Where did you get them?—A. We caught part c
Prince Edward Island, between East Point and North C;
down the island—well, from New London up off North Cap
off the island.

Q. How far from the shore of the island did you usually
never was fishing within the limits with the exception of
and I caught very few mackerel there.

Q. To what voyage do you refer?—A. To the one I made
L. Fears in 1874.

Q. Where else besides off the island did you fish in 1872
erley?—A. Between East Point and the Magdalen Islands
Banks Bradley and Orphan; I also fished up and down th
15, or 20 miles up off North Cape.

Q. What was the next previous year when you were in tl
I will not be sure whether it was in 1868 or 1869.

Q. Who was captain of the vessel?—A. Mitchell.

You have brought no memoranda with you ?—A. No; I could not
up any, as far as that goes, for that voyage.
All you have done is to put down what your recollection enables
o state ?—A. Yes.
You have no books or anything to guide you in this regard ?—A.

What did you do while you were with Captain Mitchell ?—A. We
240 barrels of mackerel.
Where ?—A. On Banks Bradley and Orphan, and at the Magdalen
ds.
Did you get any of them anywhere else ?—A. No.
In what schooner were you in your next previous year in the bay ?
The Laura H. Dodd.
During how many years were you in her ?—A. Two; 1864 and

How many trips did you make during each of these years ?—A.

How many barrels of mackerel did you take in your two trips in
?—A. About 700, I think.
Where ?—A. At the Magdalen Islands.
Were any of them caught inshore, except at the Magdalen Islands?
No.
Whereabouts at the Magdalen Islands were they caught ?—A. At
Rocks, principally.
Is that true of both trips ?—A. Well, during both, and more es-
lly during the first trip, we got a great many barrels at the Bird
s.
Did you fish inshore anywhere ?—A. No.
The next year, 1865, you were in the Laura L. Dodd ?—A. Yes.
And you made two trips ?—A. Yes.
How many barrels did you catch ?—A. About 600, I think,
Where ?—A. On Banks Bradley and Orphan, and at the Magdalen
ds and off East Point; and a few were taken up and down the island.
How far from land did you fish off East Point ?—A. It might have
I should say, 15 or 20 miles.
How far from the land was it ?—A. We were outside the limits, and
10 to 20 miles off; no mackerel were to be got inshore at all. We
inshore.

By Mr. Thomson:
You have not fished since 1874 ?—A. No; not in the bay; but I
on our shore.
When was your last trip made before 1874 ?—A. In 1873.
And when was your next and previous trip made—in 1872 ?—A.

Did you not state, in direct examination, that you fished in 1872.
e bay?—A. I believe I did not—yes; I was in the Waverley in 1872.
I thought you said that you came here without memoranda ?—A.
not come with any; but I made a hasty sketch of my fishing ex-
uce the other night when I was coming down here on the steamer.
e nothing here that amounts to anything.
Do you recollect, in those memoranda, that you were in the bay in
?—A. Yes.
In what vessel ?—A. The Waverley.
If I understood you rightly, in 1874, your last year in the bay, you
ht over one hundred barrels inshore ?—A. Yes. I would not say

over one hundred, but it was somewhere in the neighborhood
hundred.   We caught fifty wash barrels off Cascumpeque.

Q. What do you mean by "wash barrels"?—A. A barrel of a
dressed just as we catch them, four or five buckets of water being
on the fish.

Q. Would that be equal to a barrel packed ?—A. No; it take
four wash barrels to make three packed barrels.

Q. When did you go into the gulf in 1874?—A. We left Glc
after the 4th of July—I think about the 8th.

Q. And where did you go after you passed through the Gut ?—
went over to Souris, where we put ashore a couple of ladies, a
we worked along the island.

Q. Did these girls belong to the island ?—A. Yes; we landed
Yankee Cove.

Q. Did you fish at Souris?—A. No.

Q. Why did you not try there ?—A. Because the mackerel the
not good for anything; they were small and poor.

Q. Were the boats fishing there ?—A. Some were, I think.

Q. Did you try there?—A. O, yes; while the boat was ashe
the girls we hauled the main boom out and threw over a little t
the mackerel we caught were not fat enough to grease the eye
a mosquito.

Q. But the boats were fishing there?—A. Yes.

Q. And still these mackerel were not fat enough to grease
brow of a mosquito ?—A. Yes.   We afterwards went north, and
better fish there and near Miramichi.

Q. How many mackerel did you catch at Souris?—A. About
sixty.

Q. What did you do with them?—A. I do not know; but
that we ground them up for bait.

Q. You would not put them in barrels at all ?—A. No; we
take any account of them at all.

Q. Were those the kind which the boats were catching ?—A.
they were.

Q. Are you sure of that?—A. I am not quite sure; but I gi
fish were all alike around there.

Q. Did you look at the fish which the boats were catching ?—
we did not stop there, but we saw the boats catching fish.

Q. On that occasion you lee-bowed the boats ?—A. O, no; a
boat which put the ladies ashore.

Q. Did you not go in among the boats which were fishing
shore ?—A. No; we ran in there.

Q. You ran in among the boats ?—A. No; but as we were goi
from Yankee Cove, down by East Point, we saw the boats off f

Q. Did you see what sort of fish they were catching ?—A.
could see them fishing, and I judge that they were catching
same fish as we caught.

Q. You threw bait over to catch poor fish ?—A. We threw a li
over and tried the fishing.

Q. And then you drifted off shore ?—A. No; as soon as the b
back we got under weigh; we threw bait over out of curiosit
out what kind of fish they were and to see if they would bite.

Q. And then you went on to North Cape ?—A. We went to
ard and worked up the island ; but we did not catch any fish.

Q. Did you try while going up ?—A. Yes; once in awhile
over a little bait.

Q. Was this within three miles of the shore ?—A. No.

Q. That was the only time that you caught any fish within three miles of the shore, until you reached Miramichi ?—A. Yes; then we fished off Miramichi Bar.

Q. That was close inshore ?—A. Yes.

Q. And there you got about 40 barrels ?—A. Somewhere about 30— between 30 and 40 barrels.

Q. It is as likely to have been 40 as 30 ?—A. Possibly the number might have been 40.

Q. These were good fish ?—A. Well, they were better than the first ones which they caught.

Q. You kept them ?—A. Yes; we salted them.

Q. They were fat enough to grease a mosquito ?—A. Well, yes; but not much more. The mackerel were very poor that year in the bay.

Q. The whole time that you were there ?—A. Yes.

Q. After that where did you fish ?—A. Across over to North Cape, off French Village, and around off North Cape.

Q. Close inshore ?—A. No; we never fished within the limits there.

Q. Why; were you afraid to do so ?—A. No.

Q. Why did you not fish nearer the shore ?—A. Well, we saw plenty of fish off shore. I do not know any other reason for not doing so. I was not skipper of the vessel.

Q. What was the size of your vessel ?—A. One hundred and ten or 120 tons.

Q. What was her full fare ?—A. About 550 barrels.

Q. How many did you actually take out of the bay ?—A. We landed 430 barrels at Canso.

Q. To what number was the catch afterwards made up ?—A. To somewhere about 600 barrels, I believe; I would not speak definitely on this point, but I believe they brought home about 600 barrels.

Q. On her next trip ?—A. This was the whole catch including what we landed at Canso.

Q. What was your object in landing them there ?—A. They wanted to get back to the bay again.

Q. You did not have a full cargo with 430 barrels ?—A. I wanted to get home myself, and if I had been skipper, I should have taken the vessel home.

Q. You did not have a full cargo then ?—A. Well, we had a very good fare for the time; if they had taken care, we would have had more— probably 100 barrels more.

Q. Why did the vessel not go straight home ?—A. I do not know; I was not skipper.

Q. You do not know why these fish were landed at Canso ?—A. I suppose that the captain thought, as I said before, that he would go back to the bay.

Q. Were you one of the sharesmen ?—A. Yes.

Q. You had then something to say about it ?—A. No, not at all; the captain generally does what he pleases in this respect.

Q. Does he never consult with the men ?—A. He does not do so very often.

Q. On this occasion did he consult with the men ?—A. No.

Q. Are you serious in saying that you do not know why you landed those fish at Canso ?—A. No, I do not know. I wanted to go home, as far as I was concerned, and I did so.

Q. And he wanted to get back to the bay at once ?—A. Yes, I suppose so.

Q. Was not that the reason?—A. Yes.

Q. Why did you not say so before?—A. I say I do not reason; there might have been other reasons. You might a son why I went home, and I would say, I suppose, it was wanted to.

Q. But that is your own business?—A. Yes.

Q. Do you not know that the captain knew he could make t transshipping his cargo at Canso?—A. Well, under some cir he could do so.

Q. And he could under those circumstances?—A. Yes.

Q. When the vessel came back in the fall with her secon she take the barrels.which had been landed at Canso on l Yes.

Q. She just landed and left them there?—A. Yes; until sl

Q. I suppose that this was of considerable service to you? I do not know of any service that it was, unless it aided th desire to get back to the bay.

Q. Does this not enable you to make two or three trips v wise you could only make one trip?—A. Well, sometimes it

Q. How long would it take you as an ordinary rule to run to Gloucester?—A. Well, I have gone home from there and again in eleven days.

Q. Is that the ordinary time consumed in this passage that is about two weeks.

Q. Are not these two weeks very important during the i son?—A. Well, that all depends on circumstances.

Q. If the circumstances are such that there is good fishing is it not important to be there as soon as possible?—A. No; last ten years, if I had been in the bay and got a trip of would have taken it home.

Q. Suppose there is good fishing in the bay, is it not ver: to get back there and save these two weeks?—A. No; th tear caused by leaving the fish round, and the leakage, ca percentage of them to be lost; and thus it is a disadvanta and leave them there. I would never consent to the landin of mine at Canso.

Q. Do I understand you to say that a large percentage of runs off there?—A. No; but it is bad for the fish to be l some cases.

Q. Was this the case with these particular fish in tha cargo?—A. I think it was with some of them.

Q. Will you swear that it was?—A. I will not swear that

Q. Why do you mention suposititious cases, unless this has place? What did you get for your mackerel that year? $6.50 for number ones, I think.

Q. Was that the ordinary price that year?—A. Yes; fo erel.

Q. You got the highest price that ruled for the season?—

Q. Then the fish were not injured in any way?—A. I (that they were.

Q. You stated that 600 barrels was not an extraordinar: year, and that others did better?—A. Yes.

Q. There was good fishing in the bay that season?—A. cially around the island.

Q. You mean inshore?—A. I mean around the island, off shore.

. Did you fish at all at Margaree that year?—A. No.

. Did you fish off Cascumpeque and Rustico, on the northern shore he island?—A. Yes.

. Did you fish there after you got back from Miramichi?—A. Yes; Cascumpeque we did.

. Inshore?—A. When we were coming out of the harbor—we ran here to make a harbor—we fished coming down.

. Did you get good fish?—A. We got better fish than we found down Souris.

. How many barrels did you catch there?—A. Somewhere about 50 0 wash barrels; I could not give the exact quantity.

. But they were good fish?—A. They were as good as any in the

. You have no respect as a rule for bay mackerel?—A. Oh, yes.

. Are there good mackerel in the bay?—A. Yes; some years they first rate and some years they are poor.

. I suppose this is the case everywhere?—A. Yes.

. As a rule there is good fishing in the bay?—A. It is not as good t is on our shore, as a rule.

. Do you catch mackerel within the three-mile limit on your shore?—Yes.

. Will you swear to that?—A. Yes; I so caught some myself this son.

. Is it a usual thing to catch them there within the three-mile limit, has this been the case during the last eight or ten years?—A. I do think that it is.

. Then you do not wish the Commission to understand that your re fishery is carried on within the three-mile limit?—A. No, not on whole.

. Your shore fishery is prosecuted from 10 to 15 and 50 miles from coast?—A. Yes; and 150 miles from it, off on George's Bank.

. That is what you call your shore fishery?—A. Yes.

. In point of fact no mackerel are caught as a rule within 3 miles of ir shore?—A. Oh, yes.

. Is there good mackerel-fishing there within the three-mile limit?—Yes.

. And this always has been so?—A. Yes; there is some nice fishing re.

. And the American witnesses who have testified here that there is fishing to speak of there within the three-mile limit are entirely mis-en?—A. Yes; I testify to my own experience.

. When were you fishing within 3 miles of your shore in a vessel?—Last summer, and for two days this summer.

. Where did you so fish last summer?—A. All up and down the st of Maine, and right in within 3 or 4 miles of Monhiggin.

. I am speaking of the three-mile limit.—A. It might have been 3 4 miles off shore.

. Do you not know that this is a very vague statement? Will you ear that you fished last year along your coast and caught mackerel hin 3 miles of your shore?—A. Yes.

. To any extent?—A. No, I won't say that.

. What proportion of your catch last year was taken within 3 miles your shore?—A. Well, a very small proportion. I was only so fish-t a very short time.

. The great bulk of the catch off the American shore is taken from to 50 miles out?—A. I do not know about that.

Q. You do not know whether this is the case or not ?—
know about that matter.

Q. What other time did you so fish along the American c
so fish, more or less, most every season, for a short time, eithe
or on our shore.

Q. Did you do so this year ?—A. Yes, for a little while ; a
night.

Q. In what vessel ?—A. In a dory and in a vessel of abou

Q. You did so in different vessels ?—A. Yes ; we went ou
cursion like.

Q. You were just out for a pleasure trip ?—A. Yes.

Q. Do you not know that this is a rather serious matter '
just got home, and being obliged to wait a while on a certa
I thought I would go out and catch a few fish.

Q. Just for recreation ?—A. Yes.

Q. How far did you go out ?—A. Well, not three gun-shc
rocks.

Q. Where ?—A. Off Cape Ann.

Q. What did you catch ?—A. Mackerel.

Q. How many ?—A. One day I struck a barrel myself an
the six of us got eight or nine barrels.

Q. What did you fish with ?—A. Lines and hooks.

Q. That was this year ?—A. Yes.

Q. Do you wish the Commission to understand that the m;
ery was first rate this year, off the American shore, within
the coast?—A. It was better inshore than off shore.   It has
poor year; our mackerel-fishing has been very unsuccess:
fishing there has been better inshore than off shore.

Q. Your fishermen have tried inshore this year ?—A. Yes

Q. And still they have been very unsuccessful ?—A. Ye
have tried off shore.

Q. And there the fishing was worst ?—A. Yes.

Q. That only shows that the mackerel have deserted your
inshore and off shore ?—A. It appears there are plenty of fi
are so small that the fishermen do not want to catch them.

Q. Do they catch them ?—A. They catch some, a certain
of them.

Q. With what ?—A. Lines and seines.

Q. As far as good fishing is concerned, there has been
along your coast at all to speak of this year ?—A. No ; br
fish have been caught on our shore this year.

Q. Then the American market has to be supplied with m;
the bay this year ?—A. I do not know about that, but I
small percentage, likely 25 per cent. of the mackerel in tl
market will come out of the bay ; I do not know that I w
swear it would be that.

Q. 25 per cent. will have to come in there from the bay.?-

Q. Then if the fishing has been very bad on your shore
the rest come from ?—A. From our shore.'

Q. And you say that there is no fishing at all on your sho
—A. Yes—where I say there is no fishing at all.

Q. And 75 per cent. will come in from your shore ?—A. '

Q. How many barrels of mackerel do you think have be
the American coast this year ?—A. I could not tell you.
estimate the quantity.

Q. Do you know how many have come in from the bay ?

Will you tell me how you estimate this—that about 25 per cent. of supply will come from the bay and 75 per cent. from your shore, ı do not know the number caught ?—A. I do not know definitely ; not say that 25 per cent. would come from the bay but it would be t that—25 or 30 per cent.

How is it possible to give a percentage if you do not know the ber of barrels caught ?—A. I have not made an estimate of the ber; I make up this estimate from what I have seen of vessels ng in from the bay and from the boat fishing.

Do you mean to say that you have come here to make this state-based on no certain knowledge of any kind, and that under these mstances you swear to the percentage that will come from the bay, ı you do not know the number of barrels of mackerel which have caught in the bay ?—A. No ; I do not confine myself to any per-ıge ; but I give the best estimate I am able to form in this relation.

Is it to make a statement concerning matters about which you do ¡now anything that you presume to come here and give the per-ıge that will come into the American market from the bay, and the utage that will come from your own shore, without knowing what atches have been in the bay, and on the American coast? Can any in his senses make a percentage without any basis for it ?—A. I t by inquiring from parties who had been there.

Tell me how many barrels did you learn from inquiry had been n on the American coast ?—A. I cannot tell you.

How many, did you learn from your inquiries, were taken in the —A. Well, a large portion of the mackerel which has been caught year in the bay has been taken by your boats, and they come into arket. When I speak about mackerel coming into our market ı the bay, I mean that your folks ship them.

. I want to find out how many barrels these people told you came ı the bay, so as to enable you to form an opinion as to the percent-!—A. Well, I would not confine myself to any rule about that mat-

. In point of fact, after swearing that 75 per cent. of the mackerel come from your shore, and 25 per cent. from the bay—— A. I beg ' pardon.

. I take it that in giving me an answer to any sort of a question, are swearing to such answer ?—A. I did not speak so precisely.

. You understand that you are answering questions under oath?— Ʋes.

Will you tell me what earthly basis you have for saying that only er cent. of your supply of mackerel would come from the bay, and er cent. from your own coast?—A. I say so from information that I ꜱ gathered from parties who have been there.

. What information is that?—A. It is that there has been a large h of mackerel taken by the boats, up and down and around the ıd ; it has been a very large catch, an exceedingly large catch, and nusually large catch. I do not know whether this is so or not; I ꜱ not seen the catch, but it is on that report that I base my estimate.

. And because there has been an unusually large catch in the bay, say that 25 per cent. of your supply would come thence ?—A. I a the catch by the boats—the small boats—and not by our fisher-
.

. And this mackerel goes to the American market?—A. Yes.

. You have heard this, and do you give that as a reason why only
172 F

25 per cent. of your supply should come from the bay, and 75 from your own coast?—A. Yes.

Q. I could understand it if you reversed the percentages?—saw 500 sail of seiners off Cape Ann, you would begin to t though they all got only 100 barrels apiece, still a great would be taken.

Q. Did all these vessels get 100 barrels apiece?—A. I do that they did; I say, if they did.

Q. Will you swear that 15,000 barrels of mackerel have be on your coast this year?—A. Yes, I swear so; I have not figures to make up statistics on, but I make them up on my o ment; yes, sir.

Q. Did you see the fish being taken?—A. No; only partial some taken.

Q. You are speaking at random altogether?—A. I have no

Q. Because you saw the seiners, you say that they must tak without any inquiry as to the facts?—A. I have seen them ta more or less.

Q. Do you swear that 15,000 barrels have been taken on y this year?—A. No; I would not swear that 15,000 barrels l taken.

Q. You will not swear what quantity has been taken?—A. to the best of my opinion 15,000 barrels have been taken.

Q. Do you know what quantity has been taken this year shore?—A. No.

Q. Do you know what quantity has been taken this ye: bay?—A. No.

Q. And all you know about the bay mackerel fishery is tl usually large catch has been made there this year?—A. Ye boats.

Q. And you admit that on your own coast this has been a season?—A. Yes.

Q. And, therefore, because you have heard that in the bay been an unusually large catch, and because on your own coasl been an unusually small catch, you think that your own coasl in 75 per cent. of the mackerel to your market, as against 25 from the bay?—A. I think so; that is my opinion.

Q. In what vessel were you in 1868?—A. The Veteran, I t

Q. Who was her captain?—A. Mitchell.

Q. How many barrels of mackerel did you catch?—A. Tw and thirty.

Q. What was her tonnage?—A. About 70, I think.

Q. What was her full cargo?—A. Three hundred or thre and twenty-five barrels.

Q. Then you got pretty nearly a full fare?—A. We obtaiı over two-thirds of it.

Q. Where did you fish?—A. Around the Magdalen Islaı Banks Bradley and Orphan.

Q. You did not attempt to go inshore?—A. No.

Q. And, although you had not a full cargo, you fished abou you have named, and did not go inshore to complete your carg you had a license?—A. Yes.

Q. Why did you take out a license?—A. We did not knov mackerel were when we got through the Gut of Canso, and so we would take out a license.

Q. Do I understand you to say that on coming into the b

1ow whether the fish would be inshore or off shore ?—A. No ; I saw the mackerel inshore until I made my last voyage there.

s it a fact, that you do not know when you enter the bay whether h are inshore or not ?—A. No.

'ou made your last voyage in the bay in 1874 ?—A. Yes.

nd that was the only time when you ever saw the fish inshore ?— s.

f that was the case, what induced you in 1868, six years previously, e out a license, when you did not want to go inshore at all ?—A. had been some trouble, and a license had been demanded once, I

Vhen you had only fished off shore ?—A. We did not know about ickerel being inshore.

s it not necessarily a privilege to be able to follow the mackerel they run inshore in the bay and wherever they may go ?—A. Yes.

f successful, is it not a privilege to be able to follow the schools ver they may go ?—A. Yes.

n that view of the matter, the right to fish inshore in the bay is nportant to the American people ?—A. Yes.

'ould they, in your opinion, successfully prosecute the fisheries in y without the right of going inshore to fish ?—A. As far as my ence goes, I think that this is not necessary. We always got the al part of our fish off shore ; and I think the off-shore fisheries could be prosecuted successfully.

id you not tell me just now that it was a great privilege for the ans to be able to follow the schools inshore ?—A. Yes ; that is a to a certain degree, I think.

id you not tell me that this was a great privilege ?—A. Well, it rivilege.

And a valuable privilege ?—A. Well, it is a privilege worthy of a n amount of consideration.

Is it or is it not a valuable privilege ?—A. It is valuable to a cer-xtent.

To what extent is this the case ?—A. Well, I could not say.

By Mr. Foster :

Have you seined in United States vessels off our coast ?—A. Yes.

When ?—A. Last year.

How many barrels of mackerel did you get ?—A. About 250, taken weeks ; we got about 100 in one haul.

You did not have very good luck ?—A. The vessel had not done ing previously.

Did you ever seine during any other year ?—A. Yes ; I did so the before, but 1 only seined a short time ; about four weeks.

You speak of seeing a large number of seiners together ; but where you seen as many as 500 vessels fishing at once with seines or off the American coast ?—A. I saw them in Gloucester Harbor ; had gone in there for a harbor.

Where do these vessels usually fish ?—A. I never saw that num-shing together ; they fish all scattered around the coast.

No. 65.

WEDNESDAY, *Octob*

The Conference met.

JAMES H. MYRICK, fish-dealer, of Boston, was called
the Government of the United States, sworn and examine

By Mr. Foster :

Question. Where were you born ?—Answer. At the t
castle, State of Maine.

Q. And your home is in the Dorchester district, Boston

Q. Where do you carry on your fishing business ?—A. (
nish, Prince Edward Island; that is the part of the bus
look after and represent.

Q. Who is your partner ?—A. Isaac C. Hall.

Q. Your firm's name is Hall & Myrick ?—A. Yes.

Q. During how many years have you constantly resided,
of the year, on Prince Edward Island ?—A. About 17.

Q. During how much of the year do you stay there ?
from three to six months.

Q. At what part of the island ?—A. Tignish.

Q. Where is Tignish situated ?—A. About eight mile:
Cape, Prince Edward Island.

Q. Describe the business which you carry on there.—
have a large retail store there, and we supply fishermen ai
occasionally vessels; we buy and cure fish, and ship fish.
duce and we ship produce, but the fish business is the p
ness which we carry on.

Q. How many fishing stages are there under your pe
vision, and where are they situated ?—A. Well, I have
season ; two of them are situated on the east side of Nor
two on the west side of it. We are near North Cape, and
or six miles across.

Q. How many boats do you employ ?—A. We have the p
of about 150 boats; we employ directly 50 boats, and, in
supply parties who own, perhaps, 100 boats, and obtain t
these boats.

Q. How many men are employed in these boats ?—A.
about three each; perhaps at some seasons of the year th
be a little larger.

Q. Over what extent of shore are these 150 boats locatec
30 miles.

Q. During the fishing season how often do you go
miles ?—A. I might say, I do so almost daily, so that I
distance along shore, that is during the busy season. I k
Tignish during the summer.

Q. And is your house there so situated as to command
water ?—A. Yes.

Q. How is your store there situated ?—A. It is directly n
edge, a stone's throw from the water.

Q. How many barrels of mackerel have been sent this :
part of the island and your stations ?—A. What I have
what I will ship, but has not yet gone forward, will an
4,600 or 4,700 barrels, for my part.

Q. That does not include what Mr. Hall, of Charlottet

ket?—A. No; this is just for these 4 stations, and what I gather
surrounding boats.

ow many barrels in all did you send from your own stations last
-A. A little over 2,000.

he catch is better this year than it was last?—A. Yes; very
etter.

ave you any vessels fishing?—A. Not from that point, anything
k of; we have, however, some very small vessels, which are little
han boats.

escribe the size and character of those boats of yours.—A. They
ry much; a small proportion of them are what I call large boats,
will go off for three or four days, or for perhaps a week; and on
the men can cook and sleep. They are open boats, but still large
to accommodate three or four men, for cooking and sleeping on
and salting fish. A small portion of them are of that character,
e size of the others varies from that down to small boats of 15 and
keel. Some of the boats go out and in perhaps two or three times
and others will go out and remain out a week.

escribe the way in which these boats of yours fish in the different
f the season; how far from the shore do they usually go to catch
el? Tell all you know about that, from what falls within your
al observation.—A. It is customary for these boats to start early
morning, and perhaps they will go off shore for a mile or 1½ miles,
me to try for mackerel, and throw out bait; and if they do find
rel there, why they stay there; but if they find few mackerel, or
ere, they go out farther. Some will scatter off, while one or two
sh within one or 1½ miles of the shore, another boat will go half a
rther out, and another half a mile farther still—they scatter in
ay. There is no uniform rule for taking up their places; but this
rally the way they do. Sometimes, when they find a school, all
its will gather in together; but if they merely pick up mackerel,
ay be half a mile, a mile, or two miles from the shore—stretched
ng the shore.

low far is the farthest distance from the shore to which these
usually go?—A. They will go out perhaps for 7—7 or eight miles;
, I should say, would be about the greatest distance, speaking for
nt where I am located. This varies in different parts of the island.
ne points on it they find the fish plentiful quite near the shore,
en, perhaps, 15 or 20 miles along the shore from that point, you
ve to go farther out to find them. I suppose that this depends
hat on the character of the bottom and of the curves and tides;
the way they fish. In the warmest weather, in midsummer, the
e nearer inshore in my experience, and towards the fall the fish-
have to go farther out for them. When the weather gets pretty
in the fall the small boats do not go out, but the larger boats go
ger distances.

low far out did the boats go during the past month?—A. During
st month I have not been aware of any fish having been caught
east side of North Cape, except 4 or 5 miles out; but on the other
North Cape, the west side, they were taken nearer inshore; this
ost always the case in the fall—on the one side the fish are then
at a longer distance off shore, while on the other side they are
handy. This depends on the wind; a west wind drives the fish
re on the one side and off shore on the other. They go with the
I think.

o these boats usually fish drifting or at anchor?—A. They almost

always fish at anchor, and very rarely drifting, unless i
moderate rate.

Q. Do these boats catch their mackerel from the botto
the water ?—A. They may sometimes have to take longer
from the bottom; and then again the fish may come fo
up to the surface. I think that this season—during the
it particularly—the men have fished nearer the surface;
come up, but they have been very delicate about biting
to make them bite any way; they came up around the hor
the bait that was thrown to them; but they did not like
hooks, and they avoided them.

Q. What bait do you furnish your boats with ?—A. B
and sometimes pogies and menhaden.

Q. Which is the better bait ?—A. Pogies.

Q. Why do you not use them altogether ?—A. They
pensive; we have to get them wholly from the States, an
expensive for boat-fishing; and then this is lighter bait,
surface. It is fatter, and it keeps the fish from going do

Q. You have seen, I suppose, the United States fishing
ing off your part of the coast ?—A O, yes.

Q. At what distance from the shore do they fish ?—A.
varies at different seasons; but as a general thing the ma
caught inshore are smaller than those which are taken
this season, I have known vessels come in, but not a gr
fish near the shore, within two or three miles off, fish aw
few mackerel, and on finding what their quality was, go
else; sometimes, however, they get better mackerel insid

Q. Do the United States schooners usually fish as ne
the boats ?—A. No; this is not the case at the point whei
—decidedly not.

Q. How is it that the boats can fish successfully wh
cannot do so ?—A. Well, a boat will go out and ancho
over bait and take it very leisurely, sticking perhaps in
all day, or for a good many hours, and pick up a few ma
vessel will come along, and finding the same kind of fi
think it worth while to stay there, but go off; then, a;
formation as to a great many instances of vessels comi
boats picking up mackerel pretty freely, and throwing
ing for half an hour or an hour and not catching any m
that has been my experience for a good many years. I
with the boats for half a day's fishing and seen it.

Q. Do the vessels ever fish from the bottom as the boat
often, but they will do so sometimes. When they cann
where else, they may come among the boats, put their
and spring up, as they call it, and catch a few macker
not make a practice of it, as a general thing. They ma
times.

Q. Taking the past few years, say the past four or fiv
extent have United States vessels fished under your obs
3 miles of the shore ?—A. Well, during the past four or
during the past three years particularly, the fleet of A
around the island has been quite small; this has been m
the case since the great storm. They have rather avoid
that part of the island since then.

Q. What do you mean by the great storm ?—A. I re

in 1873—the August gale, which wrecked so many American
rs about the island.

you have been on the island every year for something like sev-
·ears, you must have heard discussions as to the three-mile limit,
n?—A. Yes; I have heard a good deal said about it.

is your attention been drawn to estimate the distance from the
which the three-mile limit lies ?—A. Yes; I think that my judg-
pretty good on that subject.

iring how many months are your vessels employed in fishing ?—
l, cod and mackerel are caught for about 4½ months in the year,
·erage.

id how long are mackerel caught ?—A. For about 3½ months.

hat is a good catch of mackerel for one of your boats during the
—A. I consider 75 barrels a fair average; indeed, this is a very
tch for the average.

r three men ?—A. Yes.

id what would you regard as a good catch for a single day ?—A.
shall say two barrels, from 2 to 2½ barrels; and this is better
average.

here do all your fish go ?—A. To Boston and New York, but to
more particularly.

hat is the largest number of barrels of mackerel which ever went
ir port to Boston during one year ?—A. Something under 7,000,
6,800.

as that from you personally or from your firm ?—A. That was
personally; that was the catch for one year; but I do not think
ll went down the same season.

it it all went down earlier or later ?—A. Yes.

as the boat-fishing been increasing since you began to go to the
—A. Yes; it has increased very materially.

nd how has this been for the last few years, say since July, 1873?
has been increasing a good deal since then.

That kind of a year was last year for mackerel ?—A. The catch
y small and light.

or boats and vessels ?—A. Yes; for both.

id any vessels that came to fish in the gulf last year make any
at all ?—A. I made inquiries in the States, and the result of what
gather was that there was not a vessel which visited the bay
ir that made any money.

o you know how the vessel-fishing has been in the bay during
sent season ?—A. Well, I do somewhat ; as I stated before, a few
have been around the part of the island where I am located. I
en some vessels there, but the number has been small.

s far as you know, what has been the result of the vessel-fishing
bay this season ?—A. Well, I should think it has been light—
small catch.

ow has it been with the boats ?—A. They have made a very fair
his season ; this has been above the average considerably, I
think.

uring the Reciprocity Treaty, that is, prior to 1866, were many
ial vessels fishing for mackerel ?—A. Well, about Prince Edward
there was then quite a fleet of vessels.

fter the Reciprocity Treaty was abrogated, what became of
—A. Well, they gradually abandoned that business, so that at
sent time they have very few vessels of any considerable size fitted

out for mackerel-fishing in the gulf; that is, from Prince Edwar
I do not know how it is in this respect with Nova Scotia.

Q. And there are none now there?—A. The number of vesse
considerable size there is now very few.

Q. Do you know of any there?—A. Yes.

Q. Name them.—A. There is one, the Lettie, which my par
out at Charlottetown; she has always been engaged in that t
She goes fishing for two or three months in the year. I do not
any other, though I have understood that some others have be
out after this purpose.

Q. What view did you and your partner take with regard to
the fishery clauses in the Treaty of Washington?—A. Well,
very anxious to have free fish. My partner took a more activ
this relation; he had more opportunity than I had for doing so

Q. He went to Washington?—A. Yes.

Q. You did not?—A. No.

Q. What was the effect on your business of the terminatio
Reciprocity Treaty, and the imposition of a duty on Canadian
entering the American market?—A. Well, I cannot answer th
tion further than by saying that they had a very disastrous
our business.

Q. Did you begin to feel the full effect of it at once, or did t
some time?—A. No; during two or three years afterward we g
good quality of mackerel, for which we obtained pretty good p
that we could afford to pay the duty.

Q. Were these currency prices?—A. Yes. Prices then rule
high; that was a time when the price of everything was s
inflated.

Q. I suppose that you may say either that prices ruled high
currency then ruled low?—A. Yes; you can look at it either w
when we reached the year 1871, I think a good large catch
taken on the American shore, and a catch of poorer mackerel
island shore, and then matters turned the other way with us.
were very low, and we suffered accordingly.

Q. What became of your business, in view of that large catc
United States coast?—A. Prices went down very low, and we lo
very fast. Prices collapsed that year completely.

Q. What would be the effect upon the business of your firm o
back the former duty of $2 a barrel upon mackerel sent fron
Edward Island to the States? I would like you to explain y
in this regard particularly.—A. Well, I suppose, since we hav
business established there, and our buildings and facilities for
on the fishery, it would be difficult for us to abandon it altoge
we would then turn our attention more particularly to cod-fish
at any rate the mackerel season got well advanced and the
became fat, and if any would bring a high price it would be th
in the latter part of the season. We might catch some of t
we would not undertake to catch poor mackerel to compete w
caught on the American shore.

Q. Explain why not.—A. Well, No. 3 mackerel, which are p
erel, generally bring a good deal less price than fat mackerel,
do not catch any more poor mackerel than they do fat ones; t
catching them and of barreling and shipping them is the sa
the fat mackerel bring a better price. We could carry on the c
business irrespective of the American market; we could catch,
ship codfish to other markets—to the West India markets, and

make a fair business at that; but as to catching mackerel exclusively under such circumstances, it would not do to depend on it at all.

Q. How does Prince Edward Island mackerel compare in point of size and quality with those which are caught at the Magdalen Islands?—A. Well, in the reports I have heard of vessels fishing at the Magdalen Islands and at the point where the mackerel are sold, they speak of the Magdalen Island mackerel as being much better and larger; that is, for the greater number of years.

Q. Of late years, where have the best No. 1 mackerel been taken chiefly?—A. These are taken on the American shore; they suit the better class of customers and bring the highest price.

Q. Is there an inspector of mackerel on the island?—A. Yes.

Q. Are you a deputy inspector?—A. Yes; my name is on the barrels as deputy inspector and I pay my fees to the inspector general.

Q. Who is he?—A. His name is Frank Arsenault; he lives in Prince County.

Q. What do you pay him?—A. I think it is somewhere about 2 cents a barrel; it is not a very heavy fee.

Q. Mr. Davies says that you are mistaken about that?—A. My books show that we have paid it every year, whether it is a mistake or not. I obtained permission some years ago to act as deputy inspector, and I have paid my fees.

Q. Every year since?—A. Yes, every year since, I think. I think my books will show that I have paid the fees every year, for five or six years.

Q. You have paid two cents a barrel?—A. Yes, somewhere about that; between two and three cents.

Q. Is there any sort of doubt about your brand as inspector of mackerel?—A. No.

Q. Describe exactly what you put on the barrels.—A. The brand is circular; the first words are, " Prince Edward Island," and the next, I think, are, " Two Hundred Pounds—J. H. Myrick, Deputy Inspector." I think this covers the whole brand.

Q. Then you are deputy inspector *de facto*, whether there is law for it or not?—A. I do not know what the law is about it; but I know that I have paid my fees to the inspector-general. We have had a running account with this man, and we have given him credit every year, on the settlement, for his fees. I do not know that we are compelled to pay such fees; but I know that these have been paid; that he has had credit for them in his account every year, I think. He calls for the returns and we give them to him.

Q. Do you make returns of your mackerel?—A. Yes; to the general inspector, when he calls, and he generally calls in the winter time.

Q. To this same gentleman?—A. Yes.

Q. The fish go in that way to Boston?—A. Yes.

Q. Now, in point of fact, are a good many of your mackerel reinspected and culled after they are sold in Boston?—A. Well, I do not know about that, but this may be the case; that is a pretty difficult question to answer. I hardly know whether this is the case or not, because I am not there except in winter, and I do not know whether they go through another inspection or not. This is not necessary, but it may be done. A dealer may buy 100 barrels of mackerel and then put them in half barrels, and in that way have them inspected, but I do not think that he culls them.

Q. Some evidence has been given here as to imported mackerel being thus gone over, culled, and reinspected, so as to make them more sal-

able and the average better than they are when they com
foreign importation ?—A. I do not think that this makes th
more salable, but perhaps some dealer there may consider si
of mackerel, when number twos, good enough for number one:
them in half barrels and then have them branded number of

Q. In Boston ?—A. Yes. This may be done; I have no d
is done.

Q. For the very best mackerel, what they call mess macke
test and the best, how extensive is the market in the Unite
high prices ? How many barrels of mackerel, costing $20 a
from that upward, would the United States market take ?—/
take, I think, 6,000 or 8,000.

Q. No more ?—A. At $20 a barrel I should hardly thinl
would be taken.

Q. What becomes of it ?—A. Eight or ten years ago more
been taken, because a dollar more a barrel was not then look
the same light as at the present moment; but now that is n
moment

Q. Where do these high costing mackerel go?—A. To the ci
and hotels; some private families possibly take a few, but I d
that a very large proportion of them are used in New Englan
that a good many go to Pennsylvania, to Philadelphia; t
York City particularly.

Q. At high prices will the market take a large quantity
mon grades of mackerel, which are used not in the way of 1
for food ?—A. This would depend somewhat on the catch
and herring; a good many are used South; and these com
petition, I suppose, with the herring fisheries. I should su
at the rate of $7 or $8 a barrel, the market would take a 1
catch of mackerel, grades number twos and threes.

Q. At what point will the purchase on a large scale of com
erel cease for consumption ?—A. I should think that if t
grades of mackerel went in price above $10 a barrel, it woul
hard if any considerable quantity of them was taken.

Q. When you go to Boston in winter are you in the hal
about and making inquiries touching matters connected witl
ness ?—A. Yes, almost daily.

Q. You do not then have a great deal of business to do ?-

Q. What is it that fixes the price of mackerel in the Un
market?—A. O, well, of course it is the supply and deman
case with everything else. When there is a large catch of n
the American shore, prices rule low; this is a very sensit
If a fleet of 500, 600, or 800 vessels are fishing for mackere
interested get reports of the fleet doing anything, the mai
once; and this is the case particularly when prices are any v

Q. Has there been anything to interfere, during the las
with the demand for salt mackerel ? Has this been as great
as it was formerly ?—A. The universal opinion among dea
York and Boston and other places is that the demand for si
has fallen off a great deal. Of course, the number of inhal
creasing very rapidly, but the demand for mackerel has n
in that same ratio, and there must be some cause for it. P
catch of lake fish has interfered somewhat with this deman
ments of fresh fish by rail has been extending farther into
of late, besides.

Q. How far west are fresh fish sent ?—A. They are dispa
west as any one travels, I think, from what I have underst

Q. In what season of the year is the mackerel market most active ?—A. Well, my observation has been that during September and October and perhaps a part of August this is the case.

Q. How has it usually been of late years in winter ?—A. Of late years it has been very quiet, much more so than was the case formerly.

Q. You have had a long acquaintance with the fishing of vessels and boats; have you known trouble to occur frequently between them or not ?—A. Well, I have heard occasionally of vessels coming pretty near the boats, but the former very rarely ran foul of the latter; it has been several years since I have heard of any collisions of that kind, and any considerable complaint being made in this regard.

Q. How many complaints of that sort do you suppose you have heard during the 18 years you have been on Prince Edward Island ?—A. Many opinions prevail on this point among the boat fishermen; some will say, when they see an American fleet coming, that this is going to hurt their fishing, while others say that it may help them, owing to the throwing over of a large quantity of bait, which may attract the fish to the spot; others again say that the throwing over of a large quantity of bait drives the fish away. A great variety of opinions exist in this respect, and it is hard to form a correct judgment on the subject.

Q. Have you known mackerel seining to be successful in the gulf ?—A. No, not as a general thing. I have known vessels thus get a fare of fish, but, as a general thing, it has been a failure.

Q. What is the reason of this ?—A. Well, I think one reason for it is due to the clearness of the water in the bay, and another is because the water where the mackerel frequent is shallow, and too shallow to admit of the use of the large seines which the fishermen are in the habit of using on the American shore; then again the character of the bottom in the bay—it is rapid and rocky—is such that it catches the seines.

Q. It has been stated here that they could adapt these seines to shallow water. What is your opinion on this point ?—A. Well, I have heard that; but then again, I have heard it said that for mackerel, owing to its shyness, you want to be able to get a good way under them to thus bag them successfully; if they see the twine, they make a rush to get out from under it; that is the reason which numbers give for not trying their seines in the bay. These seines have been a great deal enlarged, and made larger and deeper in order to enable the fishermen to get around and under the schools without frightening and disturbing the fish.

Q. So these seines have grown longer and deeper instead of shorter and shallower ?—A. Yes, a great deal. I do not know but that they now have reached their maximum.

Q. Is any considerable quantity of mackerel sold in the British Provinces ?—A. In my experience, such sales have been pretty small. I have, however, sold a few in Canada.

Q. Have you tried the Dominion market ?—A. I have sold a few fish, but not many in it. I have shipped fish here, and had them reshipped to the States via the lakes.

Q. You have found that they could not be sold here ?—A. Yes.

Q. How far have you sent them in Canada ?—A. As far as Montreal.

Q. No farther ?—A. I do not remember of sending them any farther.

Q. Is there any market for fat mackerel, number ones' and twos, except in the United States ?—A. No; no considerable market; that is the market for mackerel, and particularly for fat mackerel. I suppose there is hardly a fraction of the whole catch that goes to any other market.

Q. Where do the poorest grades go ?—A. These are used in the West Indies; but the fat mackerel do not answer for the West India market; it does not stand the voyage. I suppose that is the reason why they do not ship the best qualities there.

Q. Suppose that the catch of mackerel in British waters suddenly ceased, and that none were there caught for a period of five years, what would be the effect thus produced in the United States market ?—A. Well, that would depend on how good a catch they would then have on the American shore.

Q. What would be the proportion ?—A. I should suppose that the proportion of the supply which is caught in British waters would be, perhaps, one-fourth of the aggregate catch.

Q. That is inshore, off shore, and everywhere ?—A. Yes; of the whole aggregate catch on the United States and Dominion coasts, perhaps one-quarter would be taken in British waters. Then, mackerel not being an indispensable article of food, I do not suppose that such cessation would have a very great effect; particularly in view of the fact that prices, in my opinion, could not be forced very high, even with a small catch.

Q. Which is the most important article of food in the United States, fresh or salt mackerel ?—A. I should say, fresh mackerel decidedly; there is a larger consumption of them; but then there are seasons in the year, as in winter, when people can get poultry of all kinds and fresh meats, when they do not care much about these fish. This is the complaint which fish-dealers make in this respect; farmers in particular prefer to use their own products to paying high prices for fish.

Q. One witness told us that every American family put down a barrel of mackerel and a barrel of pork to live on during the winter; does that statement correspond with any opinion which you have on this subject ? —A. I do not know as to how it may be outside of the limits of New England, but I think that very few New England families lay in a barrel of mackerel for consumption.

Q. Do you know what quantity of fish comes from the great lakes of the West ?—A. I do not; I have heard the quantity stated quite differently, but I have no data to speak from in reference to this matter.

Q. Have you had anything to do with herring caught at the Magdalen Islands ?—A. Yes; we have had a good deal to do with them.

Q. What did you procure them for ?—A. So far as I have obtained them, it has been chiefly for bait, but I think that a good many of these herring have been exported from Charlottetown to the West Indies and the States.

Q. Have you bought or caught them ?—A. I have done both.

Q. Did you send your vessels to the Magdalen Islands ?—A. Yes; with the means both for catching and buying herring.

Q. At what rate can you usually have Magdalen Island herring delivered on Prince Edward Island ?—A. Well, for $1, or $1.25 a barrel, without the barrel.

Q. Would the barrel be worth $1 ?—A. The barrel and the salt for packing would be worth about $1.

Q. At what price, furnishing the barrels, can you obtain these fish ?— A. We then pay about $1 for them.

Q. Do you furnish your own salt ?—A. They are all salted.

Q. And you can thus get them for that price ?—A. Yes.

Q. What would be the effect of a duty of $1 a barrel on pickled herring, as to the possibility of their being sent from the Dominion to the United States market ?—A. Well, if American vessels had no right to catch them at the Magdalen Islands, this might not affect their sale; but if they then came into competition with what the American vessels caught, these fish could not be sent there.

Q. Would this amount be a prohibition duty, in this respect ?—A. I should think so.

Q. How was the removal of the duties on mackerel and other fish, through the Washington Treaty, regarded by the inhabitants of Prince Edward Island ?—A. As far as my observation went, they were very eager to have this treaty, in this regard, go into effect; they thought that this would build up their business, and be of great benefit to them.

Q. What effect, in your judgment, would a return of these duties have ?—A. It would have a very bad effect unquestionably. It would hurt the fisheries there, because a great many of the fishermen, and the best fishermen we have now, would then at once go on board of American vessels, as they formerly did. A large number of the island fishermen formerly fished in American vessels; and a great many of them would under such circumstances go back, while they are now carrying on the boat fishery.

Q. In your boat-fishing you use herring more than pogies, because the former are cheaper than the latter ?—A. Yes.

Q. Can vessel mackerel-fishing be successfully prosecuted without pogie bait ?—A. I do not know but that it might; but they never use anything save pogies. As far as I have learned it is very rare when they do otherwise. I have in one or two instances heard skippers say that if they used herring, and a great deal more of them, perhaps they could get just as good trips as with pogies; but one might say that and a hundred might say the opposite.

Q. Have you the prices of mackerel with you ?—A. I have them for a few years—perhaps for the past five or six years.

Q. What are they ?—A. These are the net sales of mackerel in Boston market.

Q. Are they the actual result of your business derived from your books ?—A. No; I cannot exactly say that. This is merely an estimate.

Q. Mention the prices.—A. In 1876, last year, the average net value of mackerel at the island was about $9, as the result of sales in Boston.

Q. That is what you realized ?—A. This is about what we realized for the catch.

Q. Give the other prices.—A. In 1875 we make it about $11; in 1874, about $7.25; and in 1873, about $11.50.

By Hon. Mr. Kellogg:

Q. Are these the average prices for all grades ?—A. Yes.

By Mr. Foster:

Q. Continue the list.—A. In 1872 such price was about $8, and in 1871 it was about $4.10.

Q. What do you mean by net price ?—A. This is the result after the bait, freight, duties, commissions, wharfage, and other expenses are settled.

Q. The barrels and salt excepted ?—A. We do not take that. When we ship a barrel of mackerel it is all barreled up and ready for market.

Q. The mackerel catch of Prince Edward Island for last year, 1876, is estimated in the report of the Dominion commissioner of fisheries at 25,383 barrels, and the export of mackerel for the same year is estimated at 9,347½ barrels. Then, of course, 16,000 barrels must have been consumed at the island, if these figures are correct; and I want to know

how far this corresponds with your belief?—A. Well, I th
figures for the exports are not accurate, because I believ
mackerel were exported for which the figures have not fou
into the custom-house returns.

Q. What do you think that such exports from Prince E(
amounted to for 1876?—A. 11,000 or 12,000 barrels; I we
that they exceeded 12,000.

Q. Are you confident about that?—A. I feel very confid
but I cannot speak positively in this respect.

Q. Explain what your opportunities for obtaining knowl
subject are?—A. Well, taking this matter one way, I jud
number of boats which I have engaged in the mackerel fisl
number of boats which it is estimated is so engaged aroun
I take the average catch of the whole number of boats wh
mated to fish about the island, and from this calculation I
the exports of mackerel would not exceed 11,000 or 12,000

Q. I notice that, in his report, the aggregate product of
eries of Prince Edward Island is valued at $494,967.08, a
fish exports are valued at $169,714, leaving for consum
island, fish to the value of $225,253.08; what do you say
ures for 1876?—A. The consumption of fish on the island, t
erel, is pretty large; the island people consume a large qu
ring and a considerable quantity of codfish; but I shoul
these figures are rather astray.

Q. How much are they astray, according to your bes
What do you say to the aggregate yield of the fisheries o
ward Island for last year being valued at $494,967.08?—
best figures which I have been able to make, I should not
exceeded one-half of that amount.

Q. What do you say to the fish exports being valued at
A. Well, I do not know that this is far astray.

Q. Now as to prices; codfish in this report is valued at
dred-weight?—A. Well, that is not very far out of the wa
scarce and high last season, and that is about a fair figure

Q. The yield of the island herring fishery is estimated a
rels for last year; you say that there is a large consumpti
on the island?—A. Yes; but they do not use much poor l

Q. These herring are valued at $2.50 a barrel?—A. I
that was a large estimate.

Q. Mackerel are valued at $8 a barrel?—A. Well, that
the way; the price is small enough.

Q. The yield of hake is estimated at 14,862 hundred-w
at $2.50?—A. That is about what the market price was o

Q. The island yield of cod-tongues and sounds for las
mated at 594 barrels; what do you say to that?—A. Th
a mistake; I do not think that there were any produce
there last year—that is, any to speak of.

Q. The yield of fish-oil is estimated at 16,487 gallons
cents a gallon?—A. The price is about 15 cents too high.

Q. It is entered that 2,590 gallons of fish-oil were export
gallons produced?—A. That is too high a figure.

Q. Do they use 14,000 gallons of fish-oil on the island?
think so; at any rate, so many gallons of oil as is there
not produced on the island, unless the figure is made up l
from other places.

Q. The return of the number of fishermen on the islai

3,831; what do you say to that?—A. I do not know that this figure is out of the way. I did not suppose that there was quite so many, but this may be the case.

Q. According to those figures, each fisherman would get $128 worth of fish a year; what do you say to that? I notice that they are not so prosperous as the fishermen of New Brunswick, who are stated to have made a catch of fish valued in all at $1,953,088, and their number being 3,850, it seems that they would earn $510 a head.—A. I should think that the figures for the island were pretty high; $25 a month would be pretty good wages for fishermen there, for the season of four or four and a half months.

Q. What do you pay your fishermen?—A. I have men fishing in a variety of ways; but from the larger part of them I buy the fish fresh, paying them so much per hundred.

Q. That is for the men who fish in the larger portion of those 150 boats?—A. Yes. We own a few of the larger boats, and we receive for the use of these boats one-eighth of the catch, while they furnish their provisions and bait, and everything else they require, and we pay them so much per barrel for the fish when salted; then there are other boats from which we take the fish fresh and cure them, taking the fish round from the boats. These men find themselves, and we pay them so much per hundred for their fish through the season.

Q. How much do you pay them?—A. This season I paid them $1.35 per hundred mackerel; from the commencement to the end of the season, I did so.

Q. For any kind of mackerel?—A. Yes.

Q. That was fit to pack?—A. Yes; and I found the bait and boat.

Q. Did you find everything?—A. Yes; provisions excepted. I found the bait and boat, and paid them that amount.

By Sir Alexander Galt:

Q. How much did you pay when the men owned their boats?—A. Where they owned their own boats—these are mostly small and of moderate value—I paid them $10 or $12 a year extra for the use of their boats, but I have very few men of that description.

By Mr. Foster:

Q. But still you paid them the same price as the others for their mackerel?—A. Yes; we allowed them that amount for the use of their boats for the season.

Q. How many mackerel are there to a barrel?—A. They will average this year about 280, I should say; perhaps the number would be 260 or 280.

Q. Would the extreme points be 200 and 300 a barrel?—A. No; the highest number would be 350; this is for early mackerel when they are poor.

Q. And how many would there be of the biggest mackerel?—A. Not over a hundred.

Q. This would be of the very best?—A. Yes.

Q. The biggest average catch would be 240 or 250 to the barrel?—A. Yes; or 260.

Q. How good an average catch of mackerel can your fishermen and the fishermen of Prince Edward Island make?—A. There is a great difference in fishermen; some will make double the catch that others will at the same stage; some boats will earn double what others will make; some men understand the catching of the fish or the baiting of them better than others; for this or some other reason, at any rate, they

will catch many more fish than others; but the best men will
earn $125 or $130, while the lowest amount thus earned will be
$75 a season.

Q. Is this when they are furnished with boats ?—A. Yes,
bait, being subject to no expense save that of feeding themse
they live very cheaply.

Q. How long would be the fishing season during which th
earn $125 or $130 ?—A. Four or four and a half months.

Q. Is there any winter employment on the island ?—A. (
great many of the younger men leave the island in winter, and
to Mirimichi, N. B., and work in the woods, spending the win
and returning in the spring. Quite a number do so.

Q. If they stay on the island, can they earn wages in the v
A. A great many of these fishermen have farms, and in winter
out firewood while others get out cooperage-stock, hoop p
staves. They find something to do in winter, but they do n
great deal. Most of them have farms—some small ones and so
ones.

Q. What do you say about the value of mackerel swimmir
they are thickest ?—A. I do not think that my head is clear e
answer that question.

Q. Have you ever known any place where the fishermen as a
more than a bare ordinary living on the average ?—A. Son
fishermen are very well off; but then they have farms right
the fishing grounds.

Q. How good a chance have you where you are located of s
boats and vessels engaged in fishing ?—A. I am there all the
four or five months, and I have an opportunity of seeing th
from the time that I get up until dark ; I might constantly lo
the water during the day from where I am.

Q. Could any one with a pair of eyes have more constant op
of seeing the whole thing than you have for 30 miles' distanc
do not think that any one has a better opportunity than mysel
ing what is going on on the water for the four or five months t
there.

Q. I understand you to say that if the duty on mackerel
posed in the United States, your firm would, except for a sma
of the season, give up the mackerel business, and turn your
to something else ?—A. That is my opinion decidedly.

Q. If you could get rid of your property what would you c
event ?—A. If I could get rid of it at anything like reasor
value, I should then put it into the market, and go into somet

Q. If you were going to carry on the mackerel fishery in ves
Prince Edward Island, would you resort to the United States
all ; and, if so, why, and how ?—A. Well, I think I should t
favor, for a portion of the year at any rate, of trying the fishi
American coast, that is, if we could get captains and crews tl
like to follow that business; and I suppose that a great man
would do so.

Q. Do you mean with hooks and lines, or with seines, or wit
A. I do not know so much about it as to say. I should wan
up this question before deciding on that point, because I t
seining is getting rather played out, so they say.

Q. You think that it is ?—A. I think they have had p
enough of it, and I do not know how profitable it would be to
hook and line fishing there.

Q. Here is an account of a Portland schooner which got 1,265 barrels seining this year.—A. Yes; but I think that is an exception. I do not think that you would find a great many catches of that kind.

By Sir Alexander Galt:

Q. You know all about the quality of the fish taken on the American coast? You are well acquainted with this subject?—A. Generally speaking, yes.

Q. What proportion does the best quality of fish taken there bear to the poorer ones?—A. Well, this season, of the best quality, as I understand it, scarcely any have been taken; on that shore there has been a very small catch of very good mackerel this year; but this varies very materially different years. You will see by the reports of the inspectors, or by their returns, that a very large catch of number ones will have been taken one year, while perhaps the next year the catch may run very largely of number threes. The quality of the catch varies almost every year.

Q. We are told that the first caught early in the season, both off the American coast and in the Gulf of St. Lawrence, are poor?—A. O, yes; they are always poor in the spring, and then they gradually fatten up. Some seasons they fatten up more rapidly than they do during other seasons. Some seasons good mackerel are caught in July and August, and in other seasons this is not the case.

Q. Is the greater quantity of the fish that comes to market of the inferior or of the best qualities?—A. As I told you, this varies very much. Some years the larger quantity will consist of the best qualities, and other years, perhaps the very next season, it will be the direct reverse.

By Mr. Foster:

Q. Whereabouts on the American coast have the best mackerel been found?—A. Well, I see by the reports of this season that this has been at Block Island, and last year this was also the case, I think.

Q. For a few years past, which have sold for the highest price—number ones from the bay or number ones from the American shore?—A. O, their shore mackerel have been the best quality of fish.

Q. Some one the other day produced a Boston paper of recent date, in which Prince Edward Island mackerel—some of yours, I suppose?—A. Very likely.

Q. Were quoted higher than number ones shore mackerel; what does that mean?—A. This is because they have caught very few mackerel of good quality on the American shore this season, but I am not speaking about this season, but of other years; perhaps in that same paper, a few weeks ago, Block Island mackerel were quoted a good deal higher than bay mackerel; but this season has been rather an exception to the ordinary rule, and they have caught poor mackerel on the American shore, as I have understood.

Q. When is the time for the best catch over on the United States shore?—A. I think that it is over now, though they may get some good catches yet; but this is hardly to be expected.

Q. And the season is over in the Gulf of St. Lawrence?—A. Yes, substantially so.

Q. Of course, the spring mackerel are thin and poor wherever they are caught?—A. Yes.

Q. And very many more of them are caught off the United States coast than in the gulf?—A. Yes; they catch mackerel earlier there. A

173 F

large catch of mackerel is taken south before we have them in
at all.

Q. I suppose that the season during which there is mackere
both in the gulf and on the United States shore extends from
of June until the middle of October?—A. They commence fishin
bay about the 20th of June, I should say.

Q. When it extends from the 20th of June to the middle of (
how does the quality of the catch in the gulf compare with the
of the catch off the United States coast for the same months fr
to year?—A. Well, during the last five or six years, I think
quality has been taken, I think, on the American shore, but
known it to be right the reverse, and the very best mackerel to 1
in the bay.

Q. Where do the best mackerel in the bay come from?—A.
do not think that the mackerel taken at the different places va
in quality; sometimes the best mackerel are taken at the M
Islands, and sometimes they are got around the island; and so
away up about Gaspé the very best mackerel are obtained; an
times this is the case farther north.

Q. When you speak of round the island, do you mean with
miles of land, or farther out?—A. O, well, I do not know tha
either in view; speaking as a general thing, the larger mack
taken farther away from the shore.

Q. The collector at Port Mulgrave, in one of his returns f
says that "the most of these mackerel"—that is, the mackerel h
of as having been caught by 164 American vessels—"were caugl
Prince Edward Island, that is the smaller-sized mackerel; but
and largest were caught at the Magdalen Islands"?—A. Well, I k
one year, and perhaps more than one year, and during several
have heard it said by fish-dealers at Boston and other places tl
got the better quality of mackerel from the Magdalen Islands.

Q. I see that you are not going to run down Prince Edwar
mackerel?—A. No.

By Mr. Dana:

Q. I have understood that the mackerel as they grow fa
autumn leave the northeastern part of the gulf and go down thr
Gut of Canso, and around the other side, and pass along to tl
ward, and are to be found off Cape Cod and other parts of the A
coast for a short time in November and the latter part of Octo
very best condition; is that so?—A. I have heard that state
have known them to be taken around Cape Cod late in the sea
even later than the middle of November; but after November,
the water begins to get cold there, they begin to get thin.

Q. They then get thin again?—A. Yes.

Q. And those that come down from here and get there by tl
of October have been reported as being remarkably good, and
1st of November the fish are remarkably good; and then, for t
of fish, the market is not over in the United States?—A. Well
then over every year.

Q. In the middle of October?—A. They get them there in
so much with hooks. I don't think the mackerel take the hoo
are of the opinion that they are not the same kind of macke
different species. I have heard so.

Q. Some think the mackerel have been fattened up in th
come down, and others think it is not so. But at all events y

erel, so far as you have heard of the catch, have not increased?—A. They have not.

By Mr. Davies:

Q. Practically the fishing off the American coast for the season is now over?—A. I think so.

Q. There will be nothing more of any moment caught to affect the mackerel?—A. I should hardly think so. There has been such a thing, but as a general thing we don't look for mackerel after the middle of October.

Q. This year has been better than the average of years at the island?—A. I think it has.

Q. Has it not been a very excellent year?—A. I think that, considering the prices they have got and the quantity taken, it has been a very excellent year.

Q. As regards the quality of the fish taken, what is the quality of the fish taken at the island this year?—A. The quality of the fish has been poor. A very small proportion of the catch has been very good indeed; the rest has been poor, very poor.

Q. Can you tell me what price you obtained for your mackerel this year?—A. The prices in Boston in greenbacks are for 3's from $9 to $9.50; 2's, from $12.50 to $13; for 1's, so far as I have returns, from $16 to $18.

Q. Are you selling at those prices or holding for higher?—A. We are selling as fast as we can get them into the market.

Q. I suppose you find no difficulty in disposing of mackerel?—A. No. 1's go very hard. Early in the summer they were going pretty freely. The better grades of mackerel have gone very fairly, in consequence of the poor quality of the mackerel caught on the American shore.

Q. You say the mackerel market is a very sensitive market?—A. Yes.

Q. It is regulated almost entirely by the supply, of course?—A. Yes.

Q. If there is a large catch prices fall; and if a small quality of catch prices go up?—A. That is the fact. What I mean by a sensitive market is this: There is a large fishing fleet, and of course the dealers are watching the fleet very closely to see what the vessels are doing, and if the reports are that they are catching mackerel the dealers will not buy more than they can sell to-day, and if there is much stock in the market it will have to be held. That is what I mean by a sensitive market.

Q. Then every year when the mackerel season is about half over the dealers find out what the catch has been and is likely to be, and the prices are regulated by the conclusion they arrive at For instance, if the fleet have taken nothing half the season, and are not likely to catch many more, the prices will go up?—A. The dealers, I think, carry on the business differently from what they did ten or fifteen years ago. I don't think as a general thing they stock up anything like what they formerly did. I think they buy more from day to day. That is, I think their experience for the last five or six or six or eight years has been that it has been a losing business to stock up and carry mackerel.

Q. Taking the whole American catch, with the exception of those taken at Block Island, do you mean to say that Prince Edward Island mackerel do not compare favorably with them?—A. This year they do compare favorably.

Q. More than favorably?—A. More than favorably. What I mean to say is, that No. 1 mackerel caught on the American shore are very much preferred to mackerel caught in the bay. They are of a different species, apparently, to the bay mackerel, and they are whiter, cleaner,

and fatter fish. There are some localities where they won't 1
mackerel at all if they know it. That is in the State of Penns;
I heard a large dealer in New York say that his customers in Per
nia would not buy bay mackerel if they could get any other;
would not buy them at all.

Q. They prefer this different species?—A. It is a better fish.
better, whiter, and fatter fish.

Q. Your opinion is that it is not the same species as the ba;
erel?—A. I have almost come to that conclusion. I am rather ;
to think it is a different species of fish.

Q. You have examined them. What is the result of your e
tion? Would you say it is a different species?—A. I should t
One is larger than the other, and a whiter fish; what they feed
make the difference.

Q. If mackerel came down from the bay and staid two or thr
on the American shore, would they change in that way?—A.
very much whether they do that.

Q. Have you got any stages on the west side, from North Cap
to Miminegash?—A. None at Miminegash. Two on that side (
we call the Reef and two along the coast.

Q. The fishing at Miminegash is said to be very good this ye
Yes; particularly around Miminegash.

Q. There is a place sometimes called by the name French Vil
A. Yes.

Q. It has been very good there?—A. Not so good there as
west at Miminegash. It has been very good there, and it has be
fair further along.

Q. How has it been all around Cascumpeque?—A. It has be
poor comparatively.

Q. Your personal knowledge extends to that part of the islan
you never fished at East Point?—A. No.

Q. You know nothing about the eastern end of the island?—

Q. Nor about the mode of fishing there?—A. No; only fro
say.

Q. With regard to shore fishing. Where do your boats fish a;
Where is the bulk of the mackerel taken by boats?—A. I thin
side my store is on, off the east side of the island; that is, ne;
Cape; one-half of them are taken outside of three miles. On t
shore, I think more are caught within three miles. At Mimineg
ticularly the fish are very near.

Q. Are any taken outside?—A. Yes.

Q. Do small boats go out beyond three miles?—A. Yes; the;
frequently; but it varies in different years. The season of wha
the great catch, in 1874, I think the mackerel were caught clo
shore then as a general thing.

Q. Have you noticed if, during the last sixteen years, mack
been found closer to the shore than in 1855 and 1856?—A. W
think this year they have not been.

Q. During the last few years has there not been a tend
way?—A. I don't know but that there has. I should rather th
has been.

Q. That is the opinion of most of the fishermen?—A. Yes;
say so.

Q. You have noticed it sensibly so, I suppose?—A. We;
know that I should have noticed it without my attention ha
called to it.

Q. Now that your attention has been called to it, do you say so ?—A.
should say we catch more fish inside than we did five, six, or eight
ars ago.

Q. You don't know how far off shore the fish are taken at other parts
the island ?—A. I only judge from what I have heard.

Q. It is necessary in order to insure a fair catch to go inside with
ats ?—A. Yes; I suppose so.

Q. You would not like to carry on fishing and be excluded from com-
g within the three-mile limit ?—A. I should not.

Q. You would abandon it at once ?—A. Yes, I think so; that is, boat-
hing particularly.

Q. Has the Lettie been out fishing this year ?—A. Yes.

Q. How many barrels has she taken ?—A. At last accounts about 300
rrels altogether. She landed 175 packed barrels on the first trip, and
e was reported three weeks ago with 100 barrels. So I should say
ogether about 300 barrels. That is rather—considerably above the
erage.

Q. Would you prosecute the fishing in the bay if you were prohibited
m coming within three miles of the shore to fish ?—A. I don't think
would.

Q. Have you any doubt about it ?—A. I don't think I would. That is
I was compelled to come here. I might go to the Magdalen Islands
I had a right there.

Q. Suppose you could go to Magdalen Islands, and were excluded
m three miles of the shore everywhere else in the bay ?—A. I don't
ow, but I might try it, if forced to prosecute the fishery in the bay. It
es not take long to change berths.

Q. Suppose you were excluded from changing your berth and were
pt off shore ?—A. I would not want to carry it on. If I had vessels
hing on the American shore and found slim fishing there, it would not
ke long for them to come down to Magdalen Islands, try there, and go
ck again. Perhaps two weeks.

Q. Would you, under those circumstances, prosecute the bay fishery
a báy fishery, sending vessels there year after year to remain the sea-
n, and depending on it for the season's work ?—A. I don't think I
uld.

Q. Have you seen any large fleets of American vessels at your end of
e island ?—A. I have.

Q. What is the largest number you have seen ?—A. I could not un-
rtake to speak with accuracy, but I should say from 150 to 200 sail.

Q. At one time ?—A. I think I have seen 150 vessels at one time.

Q. Did they fish by coming in and drifting off ?—A. That is the prac-
e. Of course wherever they find the fish they go, but if they found
em near the land they would not undertake to fish in that way with
inshore wind. If there is a moderate wind off shore they come in,
row bait, and drift off, and work back again.

Q. You have seen them fishing in and out of the limits ?—A. Yes.

Q. Often ?—A. Yes. There have not been many vessels there for the
st two or three years, but previous to that I used to see them quite
equently.

Q. In fleets ?—A. Yes, 30 or 40 sail.

Q. Day after day during the season ?—A. I never saw them remain
ere a great while—perhaps one or two days. I don't remember them
maining over two days in succession.

Q. Then they would return again ?—A. Then they would go, perhaps to the other side of the island and keep going round the island, or per-haps go to Magdalen Islands or Bay Chaleurs or Escuminac.

Q. Would they come back again that season?—A. Very likely. They keep cruising round all the time, as a general thing. If they go to Magdalen Islands and have good fishing they hang round there.

Q. It is essential to the success of the vessels that they have the right to go wherever the mackerel are?—A. To make it successful I should say so.

Q. You were asked some questions with regard to the exports of the island and the provisions consumed and you said you thought they were much exaggerated. What means have you of forming an estimate of the catch of mackerel, say in Kings County?—A. It was in 1876 we were examining, I think. I know very nearly the number of barrels I caught and what I exported.

Q. I am not questioning your own catch; I am speaking with regard to the catch of the island. What means have you of knowing what mackerel, cod, or other fish were caught by the people of King's County, for instance?—A. I have not any means of giving an accurate state-ment.

Q. Were you there that year?—A. Yes.

Q. In King's County?—A. I was there but not for the purpose of making any special inquiries. The only knowledge I have is from what I heard and what I could gather as to the number of barrels the differ-ent localities had taken. I cannot say I give it accurately, but I ap-proximate it to the best of my judgment.

Q. In that judgment you may be astray?—A. Yes, I may be astray.

Q. You made a guess at it, judging it from your own business?—A. I did very much so, and from what I could hear.

Q. Do you know that there are fishery officers at Prince Edward Isl-and, and have been since confederation?—A. Yes.

Q. Take Mr. Samuel Clark, fishery officer of Prince County; is he a respectable man?—A. Yes; very much so.

Q. A man on whose judgment you could place some confidence?—A. In farming matters, yes; not in fishing matters.

Q. A man in whose veracity and integrity you would place confi-dence?—A. Yes.

Q. He stands very high in the county?—A. Yes; and is very much respected.

Q. Do you know that he made it his business to inquire at the differ-ent establishments what their catches were?—A. I don't know that he did. I don't know that he ever inquired at my place. He might have asked some of my men.

Q. He might have asked some of your head-men?—A. Yes.

Q. He would not willfully put down anything that he knew to be wrong?—A. I should not suppose so.

Q. He is not a man to do so?—A. No.

Q. In 1876 the exports are put down as of the value of $169,000?—A. Yes.

Q. That is probably below the mark, is it not?—A. I should think it was not above the mark.

Q. Quantities of fish leave the island, go to Shediac, and are shipped from there without being entered?—A. Yes.

Q. Do you know that as a matter of fact?—A. They always clear out the custom-house, but whether those quantities go into the returns at Charlottetown I don't know. We generally take clearances at Tignish, and sometimes when the vessels are half or three quarters loaded, and

rind springs up, they have to go, and they are as liable to run into
ediac as elsewhere and land their cargoes.

). Those cargoes do not appear in the returns ?—A. I should be in-
led to think they do not.

). You have stated that the people of the island consume large
ntities of fish ?—A. I should judge they consume very little mack-
l.

). You have no means of knowing accurately ?—A. No.

). They live largely upon fish ?—A. Yes.

). Have you examined the census to see how many families there are
the island ?—A. I should make a rough guess at 20,000.

). When you say this is an exaggeration, it is a rough figure ?—A.
t altogether. I know pretty nearly my own catch, and also what is
ight round that end of the island.

). I am not speaking of the catch ?—A. You have to get the catch
get the consumption. In knowing what my own place takes I have
ne better knowledge as to what the whole island takes than a person
o knows nothing at all about it.

). How many families do you say there are ?—A. 20,000; I don't
)w that that statement is correct, for they are pretty large families.
ierally. There ought to be that number with a population of one
idred thousand.

). What quantity of fish of all kinds do they consume per family ?—
They largely consume herring if they can get it. If they can get
ring they don't care much about any other fish. All of our fisher-
n—and there are a good many of them—pick up a few codfish and
ry home, and it amounts in the aggregate to a considerable quantity.
)ok that into account when I made my estimate. As a general thing
y use herring.

). But you are not prepared to say how much, or about how much,
ih family uses of all kinds of fish ?—A. No.

). I want to know how you get at your estimate ?—A. I get at it
m estimating what my own boats catch, and estimating the catch of
i island from that.

). Those prices which you give for the years, from 1871 to 1875, are
y not cash receipts which you put into your pocket after paying all
)enses ?—A. I make that as an estimate; that is not the exact figure.
nly gave it considerable thought between yesterday and to-day.

). You have a branch of your business at Boston ?—A. We have had.

). You carried on business there and sold fish ?—A. Yes.

). You bought fish on the island largely, and sold them there too ?—
Yes.

). Have you examined the statistics of the United States with a view
ascertaining how many mackerel are taken on their shores ?—A. I
/e every year obtained the returns of the inspector-general of Massa-
isetts.

). About how many are taken ?—A. I should say, on an average,
i Massachusetts inspection would average, perhaps, 234,000 or 240,000
rrels.

). Fish taken by American vessels ?—A. Yes.

). Altogether everywhere ?—A. Inspected in the State of Massa-
isetts. That is the total catch of Massachusetts vessels, and perhaps
ne vessels from Maine which come there and pack out. Those are
at are packed out by vessels in every district of Massachusetts.

). The mackerel fishing is in Massachusetts chiefly ?—A. It is the
ding State for mackerel fishing.

Q. What other statistics did you examine ?—A. Not tho other State.

Q. Does that return give you the quantity taken by those the American shore and the quantity taken on the British sl There is no distinction made; they are all put together.

Q. When you said that one quarter of the aggregate catch in British waters, what did you mean ?—A. I mean by that, t whole catch of mackerel in the State of Maine and Mas amounts to 280,000 barrels, and you add the Nova Scotia a Edward Island catch, which might amount to 40,000 or 50,0 that would be 330,000. I took one-fourth of that. It is mere mate.

Q. You don't know what proportion of the fish are taken and what in American waters ?—A. I can tell when a very comes into British waters and has poor success, that it w largely to the aggregate quantity.

Q. You understand me to be speaking of the whole gulf a the three-mile limit ?—A. I understand.

Q. When you say that one-fourth only of the aggregate catc in British waters did you mean to include the catch taken l people, or did you mean that the Americans themselves catch on our shores ?—A. I mean to say that aside from what are American vessels, what are caught at Prince Edward Island Scotia, which are the two principal places where mackerel ar their own people, amount as near as I can estimate without figures, to one-fourth of the gross aggregate catch.

Q. There is a little point regarding which I wish to put m before the Commission. I stated the other day here that the inspector of fish on Prince Edward Island. Now, have you p spector for the last two or three years since confederation ? very certain that every year I paid the inspection fee to the spector of Prince County.

Q. Since confederation ?—A. Yes. I talked the matter ov son with my bookkeeper as to whether it was best to pay t and he concluded it was.

Q. It enabled you to send your fish into Massachusetts deputy inspector and you put your brand on your mackerel a it is a benefit in that way to you ?—A. I consider it so.

Q. If it was not a benefit you would not continue it ?— think it is worth while to disturb the thing at all. I never was very reluctant to receive his fees.

Q. From your knowledge of the people of the United State engaged in fishing, are they anxious to have the right to waters—are the people greatly anxious to have it ?—A. I what the feeling is at the present time, but in former years, f sations that I have had with them, I should say that they wer have the right of fishing here, particularly those having ex sels here. They want full range of the whole waters of the and, of course, those who own expensive vessels do not wan disturbed by cutters.

Q. It was looked upon as a valuable privilege—the right the gulf and fish ?—A. Yes.

Q. Near the shores ?—A. Yes. There was a great differe ion among fishermen and among skippers of vessels about i not seem to care much about it and some did.

Q. That accounts for the fact that some of the witnesse

that they caught fish around Prince Edward Island and some did not ?—
A. A good many men fishing in American vessels, perhaps, were natives of the island, or natives of Nova Scotia, and familiar with those shores. Of course, those would fish where perhaps others, such as Cape Cod vessels, would not, for they did not care so much to come into the vicinity of the land.

Q. The island skippers would come close to the shores of the island, while others would keep out ?—A. Yes; those who were familiar with all the harbors and bays round the island, particularly those familiar with the harbors, for they would want to make for the harbors in a gale of wind. Those familiar with the harbors would not hesitate to fish round the shores, but a great many would hardly care to fish round the bend of the island at all.

Q. Those not acquainted with the place?—A. Yes.

Q. You have never fished at Magdalen Island yourself ?—A. No.

Q. You confine your operations to Prince Edward Island ?—A. Yes.

Q. Your fishing stages are round the island ?—A. Yes.

Q. You prefer to remain there ?—A. That is where the outlay has been made, and I would not care to extend it.

Q. You would not care to go to Magdalen Islands and start business there ?—A. I would not. I don't, however, pretend to know anything about Magdalen Islands. It may be a better place to fish, but any one who has made a large investment at a certain place would not care to extend it or change it. It takes a large amount of capital to get an extensive fishery started. You have to have a good many buildings, grounds, and wharves, and other accessories to make it a success.

Q. You were speaking about the effect of the United States imposing a duty on herring. The United States market is not the sole market for herring ?—A. No; by no means, though it is a very large market.

Q. So if they did impose a duty amounting to prohibition they would themselves suffer as much as anybody else ?—A. It would not destroy the fishing altogether, of course. It is very desirable, however, to have all the market you can get for your fish.

Q. And it is very desirable for the consumer to have all the fish coming in that he requires ?—A. Yes.

Q. What is the price of pogies ?—A. I think about an average price would be from $4 to $5 a barrel.

Q. Where; at the island?—A. In Boston.

By Mr. Foster:

Q. What are pogies worth in the island ?—A. The cost to bring them by steamer would be about 50 cents a barrel. If they charged for them $5 in Boston they would cost $5.50 landed at Charlottetown.

Q. Suppose the three-mile line marked out by a line of buoys so that every one could see when he was in and when out, and there was no danger of molestation outside, how important do you think United States fishermen would regard it ?—A. Well, I cannot say. I should suppose they would, of course, attach some importance to the privilege of coming inshore, but I don't think that it would stop their prosecuting the fisheries in the gulf.

Q. What was the real thing that made our people anxious about this? for you know. What was the real trouble that made them anxious about the removal of the restriction ?—A. Well, they want to come here without the expense of a license, and want to be free from annoyance from cutters, and, of course, they want to go where they please. They don't want to be restricted. If they find mackerel at any place, they want the privilege of catching them.

Q. Do you think the United States mackerel fleet could ?
a license-fee of $2 a ton, which was asked in the year
should not suppose they could.

Q. As a matter of money, was it worth that ?—A. I shou
it would be.

Q. When the license-fee was fifty cents a ton, did they n
it ?—A. I think they did.

Q. And when it was $1 per ton ?—A. I think some paid

Q. And when it was $2 per ton ?—A. I think they gener
risk, or else kept out to sea and did not frequent the limits

Q. Then, in your judgment, $2 per ton is a higher tar
privilege is worth in money ?—A. Most distinctly it is, taki
last years as a criterion.

Q. Go back to the years when it was put on.—A. I sl
give my own opinion, it would be prohibitory, even takin
range of the years; but for the three last years there has b
a vessel that has made any money, though having free acc
shores and bays.

Q. Now, if a man's vessel got seized, how much differer
make whether it was seized rightly or wrongly ?—A. If sei
tained for any time, it breaks up the voyage and the men
and it would be a great disaster to the owner in every way

Q. If he had every advantage ?—A. If everything was fa

Q. And supposing litigation in the admiralty courts of
and New Brunswick was not costly ?—A. Yes.

Q. Do you know about the sale of fresh fish in Charlott
firm sells it ?—A. Yes.

Q. Do you know how much mackerel they sell ?—A. Not
I am told the amount is very small, except fresh mackerel-
good many fresh.

Q. You were asked whether you would come to the gulf
fishing exclusively, if you were excluded from the three
Suppose you were located in the United States, and had t
fishing on the United States shore, would you send a mack
down here ?—A. I do not think so, from my personal know
matter.

Q. Your firm is established here, with a property that c
moved ?—A. It cannot be removed. It is a large inve
accumulation of many years.

Q. Are not United States mackerel schooners generally
the gulf fishery ?—A. It would seem so from the experien
few years; but they may take hold again. If mackerel s
in large quantities in the gulf, and there was a scarcity a
would come here again.

Q. Wherever there is a chance to make money, there er
be of course.—A. There have been seasons and sections o
haps years ago when mackerel were scarce and they ma
voyages.

Q. You spoke of the statistics of the quantity of macke
In Massachusetts there are accurate statistics of the numl
of mackerel inspected ?—A. They are supposed to be c
deputy inspector makes a return once a year.

Q. And that embraces all the salt mackerel that comes
States vessels ?—A. Yes.

Q. It also includes, does it not, all mackerel imported f

which chances to be reinspected?—A. I am not certain whether
overs reinspected mackerel or not, but I think it does.

he statistics of Maine are in pretty poor shape, I believe?—A. I
:now much about them. I only approximate to the catch of

want to see what your estimate was—how many barrels. The
ty varies greatly from year to year?—A. Yes.
mmensely?—A. Yes.
'o it is a difficult thing to make an average of?—A. Yes; one
was as low as 100,000 barrels, and another as high as 340,000
:.

Vhat was the average?—A. I think I said 240,000 or 250,000
).

hat did you estimate that to be—the quantity inspected in Mas-
etts?—A. The Massachusetts inspection.
hen there would be the Maine inspection?—A. Yes.
an you estimate that?—A. Maine has been falling off greatly for
t 10 or 15 years, and they have carried on the business much less
vely than formerly. A great many Maine vessels make their
arters at Boston and pack out there.
he whole business is centering in Gloucester?—A. Yes.
nd other fishing towns are dying out?—A. Yes; the Maine towns
larly have been dying for 20 years.
o that the salt-mackerel business is concentrating in Gloucester?—
.

ou say that 225,000 or 230,000 is the Massachusetts inspection;
t know whether you could hazard an estimate for Maine?—A. I
not.
You know, generally, whether it is 10,000 or 50,000 barrels?—A.
uld be more than 10,000 barrels; Portland alone would be more
l0,000. I would sooner say it would be 40,000 or 50,000 barrels.
Those quantities together make 270,000 or 275,000 barrels. In
ion to those there is what comes from the provinces, the British
; what do you estimate the British catch to be?—A. The average
h catch?
Yes.—A. I should say from 70,000 to 80,000 barrels.
And of that how much comes to the States?—A. I should say
than three-fourths.
To what port does that chiefly come?—A. Boston takes, I think,
reater portion; New York, of late years, has taken more than for-
.

Can you make an estimate of the quantity taken by New York?—
); but I know a good many more go to New York than formerly.
Those are about the only places?—A. Yes; I don't know but that
go to Philadelphia—not a great many.
You were asked with regard to your knowledge as to the quantity
t consumed upon the island; Mr. Howland is the gentleman who
s up statistics there?—A. I cannot say.
He estimates, I see, on page 77 of the British evidence, that there
i per cent. of the mackerel sold to go off the island that do not get
he exports; so his estimate would be that there are $92,000 worth
,ckerel that goes off the island. What do you say to that?—A.
akes that up for one year, does he not?
Yes. He was going on the basis of 1876, and was correcting offi-
tatistics?—A. I should think that was not very much out of the

Q. Then his estimate is that 25 per cent. of that amount w‹
consumed on the island—one-fourth of $92,000 ?—A. I think he
very much astray.

Q. His estimate is that one-fourth, which is $23,000, would
sumed on the island ?—A. I think he is very much out.

Q. You don't think the people of the island eat $23,000 wort
Not of mackerel. They eat very few mackerel; they eat more
of other fish.

By Mr. Davies:

Q. Some of the witnesses, who have been captains of Americ
sels, have said they caught nearly three-fourths, some one-half
one-fifth and one-eighth of their fish within three miles of the ‹
the gulf. You spoke, in answer to Mr. Foster, about the $2 d
ton being so large they could not pay it to go inside. As a m
fact, at the time when they did not take out licenses, did they no
on the preserves and come in and run the risk ?—A. Some vess
some did not.

Q. Because I find that for a vessel of 60 tons, at $2 per
amount would only be $120, and 10 barrels of mackerel at $12
would cover that.—A. But if they were just making both end
$120 would turn the scale.

Q. I have not found any witness who did not acknowledge he
some inside.—A. I am speaking in general terms. They wou
that cost into account in making up the voyage for the vessel, a
might very readily turn the scale. The owners might discuss t
tion whether they would send the vessel to the bay or on th
shores, and when they put down $120 that might determine the

Q. You don't know the proportion of the fleet that ran the ri;
I have not any means of knowing.

Q. I think I understand you to say that catching mackerel
ing injures the fishing ?—A. That is my opinion. Some other
would be able to give better evidence on that point. I can onl
from hearsay.

By Mr. Kellogg:

Q. You have had experience in the fishing business in the P
and also in Boston. It is said frequently that mackerel will br
a certain price in the American market, and that if they exce‹
tain price the people resort to other kinds for food. Have you
experience discovered whether they were any other kinds of
they resorted to, particularly when mackerel were a high price
so, what kinds of fish are they ?—A. The lake fish of late ye
been taken in large quantities and have supplied the markets
extent. A large amount of territory is covered by them, and
many like them and give them the preference.

Q. Any other kinds of sea fish ?—A. They use largely fresh
For instance, frozen herring are taken in very large quantit
Newfoundland and the Bay of Fundy.

Q. What I want to know is this; if, when mackerel are at
price, the people resort to other kinds of food that are chea
Yes.

Q. In regard to the market for fresh mackerel; when did tha
begin to expand, the fish going from the sea shore by the railw
the country ?—A. It has been growing very rapidly for the last
years, say for the last 12 years.

Q. Is it now growing or not ?—A. I think it is growing.

Q. How far do fresh mackerel go?—A. I don't know there is any limit.

Q. Do you know of any fresh mackerel being carried to California from our side?—A. I should think not. I don't know but they might carry it.

Q. They send lobsters canned?—A. And they send fresh salmon in cans from California here.

Q. According to your experience, how far up and down the Mississippi Valley does the fresh fish go?—A. It goes to Chicago and Milwaukee and other Western points.

Q. You have been engaged in the mackerel and cod-fishing at Prince Edward Island for a good many years, and you are located there. Have you ever attempted to cure codfish in the way they are cured for foreign markets, for warm climates, such as the West Indies?—A. I cure codfish almost exclusively for foreign markets in warm climates.

Q. Is that done very extensively by any except what are called Jerseymen?—A. It is.

Q. Have you always done it?—A. I have done it for 12 or 15 years.

Q. And always exported to foreign markets?—A. Yes, almost always.

Q. Did you ever find a market for that kind of cured fish in the United States?—A. For the large fish we do.

Q. Cured in that way?—A. Yes; for the large fish, but it is a small proportion of them.

No. 66.

CHRESTEN NELSON, of Gloucester, Mass., fisherman and sailmaker, was called on behalf of the Government of the United States, sworn and examined.

By Mr. Dana:

Question. What is your age?—Answer. 52 years.

Q. You are a native of what country?—A. Denmark.

Q. You now live at Gloucester?—A. Yes.

Q. And have done so for how many years?—A. For about 30 years.

Q. Do you recollect what was the first year you went into the gulf fishing?—A. 1851.

Q. Did you go cod-fishing part of the season?—A. Yes.

Q. Then you went into the gulf?—A. Yes.

Q. How many trips did you make that year?—A. Two.

Q. What did you catch the first trip?—A. The first trip we caught 300 barrels and the second 325.

Q. Did you catch those outside or inside?—A. The first trip we caught them entirely out of the limits; the second trip we caught as far as Margaree; I think we got a very few inside the limits.

Q. How many do you suppose, out of the 325 barrels, did you catch at Margaree inside?—A. I should think from 25 to 30 barrels.

Q. In 1852 were you cod-fishing in the early part of the season and afterward in the bay?—A. Yes.

Q. How many trips did you make?—A. One, and caught 350 barrels.

Q. Of those how many were caught inside?—A. I could not say very correctly, but I should say from 20 to 30 barrels.

Q. In 1853 what were you doing?—A. I went into the bay in July; I was not fishing in the spring; I was working at sail-making.

Q. And how much did you get?—A. 180 barrels.

Q. Where?—A. Off on Banks Orphan and Bradley. There were none caught inshore that year. We did not so catch any; and there were very few mackerel in the bay that year.

Q. Was this your last trip?—A. Yes.

Q. Now from your experience during those years, what do
of the inshore fishery in the bay for such vessels as are sent
Gloucester? What is the value, everything considered, of th
fishery in the bay for such vessels as are used in the State
should not consider it worth anything.

Q. What are your objections to it?—A. It is very dangero
inshore; our vessels are large and they want to be off shore
storm should come up.

Q. In your experience you found that there were plenty
shore?—A. Yes, except the last year; there were not any fi
bay that year save very few.

Q. You are a sailmaker, and in 1853 you went back to your
A. I went into business in the fall of 1853.

Q. And followed it up until when?—A. 1864.

Q. After that did you go into the fishing business, not as a
but as a dealer?—A. Yes.

Q. Had you a partner?—A. Yes; Sargent S. Day.

Q. What was the style of your firm?—A. Nelson & Day.

Q. How long were you in it?—A. From 1864 to 1869.

Q. Do you count 1864 and 1869?—A. Yes; that is, I came
fall of 1869.

Q. You are an outfitter and in the fishing business?—A. Y

Q. How many vessels did you usually manage?—A. We ha

Q. Were you interested in all of them?—A. Yes, I thir
except one.

Q. Some you owned?—A. Yes.

Q. And you were interested in all of them except one?—A.

Q. In these cases had your skippers shares in the vessels?-
they invariably held a small portion of them—one quarter or
like that.

Q. Is it customary in Gloucester for the skippers to take
vessels?—A. Yes.

Q. Is it to the interest of the owners to interest them in thei
in that way?—A. Yes; very much so.

Q. When the owner makes such an arrangement with a skipp
him a share in the vessel, one-quarter, one-eighth, or one-ha
they carry it out? Is the skipper entered at the custom-hou
owner? Has he a bill of sale?—A. In some cases this is don
in all cases. He sometimes receives obligations, to be given
sale when it is paid for.

Q. He sometimes has a bill of sale, and gives a mortgage
Yes.

Q. And sometimes a private agreement is made to give hi
sale when he pays for it?—A. Yes.

Q. While you were engaged in the fishing business during
or six years, were you cod-fishing as well?—A. I was some e
spring, but I was principally engaged in the bay fisheries, t
vessels were principally sent to the bay.

Q. Were you fishing off the American coast at all?—A. No,
except at George's Bank.

Q. How did your bay fishing turn out?—A. Very slim.

Q. Did you gain or lose by it?—A. We lost by it. In th
lost about all we had put into the concern.

Q. How much did you put in?—A. Somewhere in the
$15,000, I think.

Q. In what business had you made that?—A. I made it

lmaking, though this was not the case with the whole of it. I
some by doing other business attached to my sailmaking business.
You put in a capital of about $14,000 or $15,000 ?—A. Yes.
Did you lose it all ?—A. No, not the whole of it, but very nearly

To what was the loss due; the shore fishery, cod-fishing, or the bay
y ?—A. Well, it was due to the bay fishery. We sent our vessels
bay expecting to get something out of it, and we did not succeed.
Have you your books ?—A. No; what books I had were burned
t year when I was burned out.
During the time you were so engaged, how was your Bank fishing—
-A. Yes; it was fair.
How did your shore fishing turn out ?—A. That was very good.
Have you done anything in the fishing business since 1869 ?—A.

You then went back to your other business again ?—A. Yes.
How often does a fishing schooner need a new suit of sails on the
ge, if she is well handled and well managed ?—A. By good care a
suit of sails will last two years.
And this requires good care ?—A. Yes; I have known some cases
a new suit of sails was worn out in one year.
Does a suit of sails last a fishing vessel as long as a merchant-
—A. No.
A merchantman sails from one port to another, and furls her sails
she lies in port ?—A. Yes; and they are generally unbent when
essel goes into port.
While fishing vessels are at it all the time ?—A. Yes.
What did a new suit of sails cost during the war; not a fancy
out a foresail, a mainsail, and a couple of jibs ?—A. For a vessel
or 100 tons a suit of sails of that kind then cost about $2,100 or
).
How is it now ?—A. The same suit would now cost between $500
600.
While you were pursuing the business, how much have you paid
r suits of sails on the average ?—A. I guess they cost us, while I
the business, about $800 a suit on the average.
What will rigging—running and standing rigging both, with
s—delivered at the wharf, cost ?—A. From $1,000 to $1,200.
I suppose that some parts of the rigging wear out more rapidly
others ?—A. Yes.
Is the same material used in sails for fishing-vessels as for vessels
merchant service ?—A. They are made with the same materials,
ometimes they are not made out of the same materials. They are
out of hemp or Russia canvas.
Russia duck ?—A. Yes.
And not canvas ?—A. Not cotton canvas; they are made out of
and hemp canvas.
Is any better material to be had for sails for small vessels than
a duck ?—A. Yes; cotton is preferable.
Does it cost more ?—A. It did not cost much more during the war.
Cotton did not ?—A. No; but cotton cost the most during the

Your sails have been made since the war, and for many years past,
f Russia duck ?—A. No.
Out of what, then ?—A. Cotton.

Q. And that you think is the best material ?—A. Yes; for o
vessels.

Q. It wears the longest ?—A. Yes.

Q. And yet it won't wear over two years ?—A. No.

Q. You have had a good deal to do in fitting out vessels, &
would a well-built vessel now cost, as she is launched, and
such a vessel cost, say of 100 tons, built at Essex or Glouceste
average during the last five or six years ?—A. Without ri,
sails ?

Q. Rigged but without provisions—what would she co
tackled, with sails and rigging ?—A. Such a vessel would
$7,500.

Q. We will call it $8,000; suppose she cost this sum, what
depreciation be for the first year, if nothing extraordinary hap
if she is kept in good order, painted, and the rigging rove whe
was required; what would the depreciation on her market val
one year under such circumstances ?—A. If I set it at $1,0(
first year, that would be a very low sum.

Q. That would be one-eighth of her whole cost ?—A. Yes;
would be a very low figure.

Q. What do you think her fair average depreciation would
I should consider that a fair average would be $1,000 for
running from the time she first leaves the harbor; but it woul
that.

Q. It would more likely be more than less ?—A. Yes.

Q. What would it be after the first year, supposing she is kep
order all the while and suffers no extraordinary injury ?—A. I
might be $500 or $600 a year.

Q. What is considered among persons who deal in these ves
the average life of a fishing-vessel, supposing that she is well
well taken care of? You count her as a fishing-vessel dov
time when it becomes difficult to insure her, and so long as a
will take her as fairly qualified to make fishing voyages ?—A.
not know about this, but I have understood from the people in
ter, who have figured it up, that the average life of a fishing
fourteen years, but then I have never made it a study to fi
for myself.

Q. You take the current opinion in Gloucester on this p
Yes.

By Mr. Thomson :

Q. Do I understand you to say that fourteen years is th
period a Gloucester fishing-vessel lives ?—A. No. I think
are vessels which are a great deal older, but on the average
the case.

Q. How old have you known them to be run in Gloucester
twenty-five or thirty years, I think, and perhaps longer.

Q. For vessels accustomed to fish in the Bay of St. Lawr
Yes. I think it is likely they have fished there.

Q. According to you, a vessel worth $8,000 would deprec
a year ?—A. Yes, for the first year.

Q. And the next year she would depreciate in value $600
and I should think that would be a very low figure.

Q. And the next year how much would it be ?—A. Less.

Q. At what time would the depreciation stop altogether ?—
after a vessel has depreciated for 4 or 5 years, she does not
any more for a number of years.

Q. Does she get better after that?—A. I do not think she then gets any better, but she does not afterwards show depreciation so much.

Q. In what does the depreciation, which you are pleased to put down at $1,000 for the first year, consist?—A. Well, in sails and rigging and wear of the vessel.

Q. If she is properly fitted out, how does it happen that the loss is $1,000 the first year, and why the small amount of $600 afterwards?—A. She might not depreciate that amount, but any man knows that if she was put on the market the depreciation would amount to $2,000.

Q. In other words, she would not be considered a new vessel, and therefore she would not bring the same price as if she was just launched? —A. No.

Q. Would you undertake to swear that a vessel at the end of her first year would not be as good a vessel, for all practical purposes, if not better, perhaps, than when she was launched?—A. No; I would not swear any such thing.

Q. Would you swear that she then might be just as good?—A. No; there would be wear and tear of sails and rigging during that year.

Q. Would there be any wear and tear of the hull if she did not meet with any extraordinary accident?—A. I do not know that there would be any particular wear and tear of the hull if she was in good order.

Q. At the end of the first year, does not the rigging get set and does not the vessel then work generally better altogether than at first?—A. Well, I do not think so.

Q. Have you any experience yourself in this respect?—A. Well, I have had some—a little experience, but not a great deal.

Q. Do you wish to have the Commission understand that the usual value of the ordinary fishing-vessels which run out of Gloucester to fish in the Bay of St. Lawrence is $8,000?—A. Some are worth more than that.

Q. I mean on an ordinary vessel; is $8,000 the ordinary price for them?—A. I do not know that this would be the average value to-day of the vessels which come in to the Bay of St. Lawrence.

Q. I speak of 100-ton vessels; do you say that this would be the average value or the average cost of such vessels?—A. It would be the average cost of a new vessel.

Q. Do you speak of their cost as it was during the war, when built, rigged, and launched, or as it is at the present time?—A. I am speaking of the present time.

Q. Do you swear that an ordinary vessel of 100 tons, such as are used in Gloucester for fishing in the bay, now costs $8,000?—A. In the vicinity of that—yes; the cost would be $7,500 or $8,000.

Q. That is at the rate of $80 a ton?—A. Yes.

Q. Is not that an immense price?—A. I do not think so.

Q. Is that an ordinary price?—A. I think so; but I could not say. I have not bought any vessels by the ton.

Q. You see that if a 100 ton vessel costs $8,000, this would be $80 a ton?—A. Yes.

Q. Are you swearing as to the cost of vessels from your own knowledge or at hap-hazard?—A. Yes.

Q. Then you swear that a vessel of that description costs $80 a ton? —A. About that—yes.

Q. Did you ever build one yourself?—A. Yes.

Q. Is there anything extra about the building of these vessels?—A. Yes.

174 F

Q. What is it ?—A. Sometimes there is extra cost about think.

Q. But ordinarily I mean ?—A. They are all built as well as have them built.

Q. Is such a vessel copper-fastened ?—A. Yes.

Q. And coppered on the bottom ?—A. No.

A. What is there extra about her ?—A. This is the copper fa

Q. Does that cost very much ?—A. I could not say.

Q. Although you undertake to say that this is the common $80 a ton—you cannot tell whether copper fastening increases t materially or not ?—A. When we contract for a vessel we contr she shall be built with copper fastenings.

Q. And you cannot tell whether copper fastening increases t much or not ?—A. Well, our vessels are all copper-fastened.

Q. You cannot tell whether copper fastening increases the not ?—A. I could not say how much.

Q. Are you aware that vessels are now built in the States, w classed for 10 years, and sold for $60 a ton ?—A. I do not know

Q. Are you aware that 1,000-ton vessels are now built and for ten years, at that rate ?—A. I am not.

Q. Are you aware that this is not so ?—A. No, I could not s

Q. You are not familiar with this class of vessels ?—A. I familiar with that class of vessels.

Q. When you speak of the wear and tear of these vessels, time do they come into the bay ?—A. In July generally.

Q. And when do they go out ?—A. In the last part of Octob

Q. What do you do with them for the remainder of the seas They go winter fishing and shore fishing.

Q. On your own coast ?—A. Yes.

Q. How long do they fish there ?—A. During the winter pri

Q. During the whole winter ?—A. Principally, yes.

Q. Is not the whole or the chief part of this wear and tear s upon your own coast ?—A. I do not think that it is.

Q. Then you wish the Commission to understand that althou vessels are only in the Bay of St. Lawrence during the summer and the early fall months, all the wear and tear, or a large port takes place there; and that very little takes place in the winte on your own coast ?—A. I do not mean to say any such thing.

Q. What do you mean to say ? I ask you whether such wear is not chiefly sustained on your own coast when fishing in win I suppose that more wear and tear is suffered on our coast in wir would be the case in the Bay of St. Lawrence in summer; this the case.

Q. More than that—are not heavy snow-storms, and frost, and wind then encountered on your coast, and after they have does not the frost crack the sails ?—A. During a storm in w vessels generally seek a harbor.

Q. But before they get under cover do not the wind and sno affect the sails?—A. I do not think that it would injure the sail snow and ice on them.

Q. Then I understand you to say that sails which get we frozen are not injured by it ?—A. I do not think they are as lo are not used.

Q. Then the sails which are wet and frozen and thawed ou the winter are not injured by it, but they are injured by sum in the Gulf of St. Lawrence ?—A. They are injured a great in the Bay of St. Lawrence by fogs and mildew. They mildew in the bay in summer.

Q. Do you swear that it is foggy in the bay in summer ?—A. Yes.

Q. When is this the case ?—A. I have been there during three summers, and it was then foggy there for a great part of the time.

Q. For how many days on the average would it be foggy ?—A. That I could not say.

Q. How long would this be the case, taking the whole summer through ?—A. I would not pretend to say.

Q. You swear that the fog does more injury to the sails in the bay than the winter work on your own coast ?—A. I do.

Q. You swear that such fog does more injury to them than the rain and the ice and the snow on your coast ?—A. Yes.

Q. And the freezing and thawing out of your sails ?—A. Yes.

Q. And this does them more injury than the heavy gales which we all know prevail on your coast in winter ?—A. But they are not out in the gales ; if they are it would be different.

Q. I presume that they then are out?—A. Occasionally they might then be caught out.

Q. And you swear that more injury is done them by fog in the Bay of St. Lawrence than is done by all these other effects ?—A. This would not be the case but on our New England coast, and more injury is done them by fog in the bay than by use on our coast.

Q. What is the average duration of this fog in the bay in summer ?—A. I could not tell you.

Q. Suppose that it last for only three days during the whole season ; would you then swear that this would do the sails more harm than the winter fishing ?—A. No. I think there is more fog than that.

Q. You swear that there is more than that in the bay ?—A. Yes ; I can swear that there are more than 3 days' fog in the bay in summer.

Q. You swear this from your own experience ?—A. Yes.

Q. How long do you swear the fog continues ?—A. I would not want to swear to any particular number of days.

Q. How many days do you think that this is the case during the season ?—A. I think I might have been for a week at a time in a fog there.

Q. Where would you be fishing then ?—A. On Bank Orphan.

Q. Did you ever move off the Bank at all during this time ?—A. We jogged about there and fished on the Bank. We did not go off the Bank.

Q. Were you fishing during the fog ?—A. Yes.

Q. Were those the seasons when you did not come near the 3-mile limit?—A. Yes.

Q. If you could not see for a fog, how did you happen to know that you were not three miles from the coast ?—A. By soundings.

Q. Would the soundings necessarily indicate how near the coast you were ?—A. Yes ; most generally.

Q. Do I understand you to say that the water off Prince Edward Island shoals off exactly in the same proportion from one end of the coast to the other, and that all you have to do is to throw out the lead to know exactly how far from the land you are ?—A. I do not know as it does, but you can tell this pretty nearly.

Q. And when you have sworn that you did not fish within three miles of land, do you mean that the lead thus informed you as to the distance, and that you did not judge it from what you saw ?—A. This was not the case at that time. We were then off shore on the Banks.

Q. You were never inshore at all ?—A. Oh, yes.

Q. But you were never inshore in a fog ?—A. Yes; if we v in a fog we would go into a harbor.

Q. And you still adhere to your statement that this week do more harm in the mild summer weather in the bay than al and snows and rains on your own coast in winter ? ' Did you that the fog in the bay did more harm to the sails and rig vessels, and cause more wear and tear than all the wear i your winter work on your own coast? Did you not state tha and tear was caused by fog in the bay than by all the stor own coast ?—A. No; I did not say that.

Q. Did you not tell me so ?—A. I did not say in the wir said while fishing on the New England coast.

Q. I will put the question again: Do you say that there is age done the sails by summer weather in the bay than throu tear in winter on your own coast ?—A. I think not.

Q. Did you not tell me a little while ago that more wear a sustained by your vessels in the bay in summer than on you in winter ?—A. Well?

Q. Did you not say that ?—A. I did not understand you.

Q. Did you not say that ? Did you say so or not ?—A. I it so strong as that.

Q. Was that what you said or not ?—A. If I did say so I one week's fog in the bay would do more harm to a suit of would be done while fishing on our New England coast.

Q. By all your winter's fishing ?—A. I did not mean wiu but the same amount of time on our coast.

Q. That is to say that one week's fog in the bay would do than a week of winter weather on your coast ?—A. Yes.

Q. But suppose you then happened to have for a week sto: and rain, with frost, following each other, would this do more the other alternative ?—A. Perhaps it would, but I think no

Q. You think that more damage would be done on your c weather as that ?—A. I do not understand you.

Q. I understood you first to say that more damage would the bay to a vessel, taking the season through, than would your coast through all the storms of winter; and I under give as your reason for this that there might be a week's fog now you say you only meant that if a vessel was in a fog f the bay this would do as much damage as during a wee weather on your own coast; will you swear that a week's fo is as bad, or anything like it, as a week's storm of rain an frost and thaw following, one after another, on your own ter ?—A. Well, I do not know that it would. I do not t would.

Q. I am told that there is no such thing as a week's fo Tell me in what year you saw that fog ?—A. I saw it in 1853.

Q. You were there in 1851 and 1852 ?—A. Yes.

Q. And in 1853 ?—A. Yes.

Q. You only saw it in 1851 ?—A. And in 1853—yes.

Q. You did not see it in 1852 at all ?—A. Yes; we then

Q. You saw it in 1851 ?—A. Yes.

Q. During how long a time ?—A. I could not say.

Q. For a week ?—A. I think so, and more.

Q. More than a week ?—A. I think so.

)id you see it in 1852?—A. Yes; but I would not say for how

[ad you continuous fog for a week?—A. No; I do not mean that
d for a week through at a time.
ou mean separate foggy days during the season made up a
A. They made more than that.
ou never saw such a thing as a week's continuous fog in the
A. I could not swear that, but still in my mind it is very clear
e had over a week's fog.
'ontinuously?—A. I am not swearing positively to it.
Vill you swear that you saw anything like a week's continuous
1852?—A. No.
)r in 1853?—A. I should.
ou that year saw a week's continuous fog?—A. I think so.
Vhere?—A. Between Bonaventure and the island down toward
gdalen Islands—between the island and the Magdalen Islands.
)ut in the center of the gulf?—A. Yes; on Banks Orphan and
y.
nd that lasted a week?—A. I think so.
Zhat did you do all that time?—A. We tried for mackerel.
ould you tell where you were?—A. We could tell that pretty

ow far were you from the Magdalen Islands when the fog came
. I could not tell. I was then only a hand on the vessel.
ere you a sharesman?—A. Yes.
ow long is it since you left for Denmark?—A. Well, it is over
years ago.
'hat would be in 1847; and in 1851 you went fishing in the bay;
lid you do in the mean time?—A. I went to sea.
Where?—A. On foreign voyages.
suppose that, like most emigrants, when you came to America,
d not come with money of your own?—A. No, I do not think
did.
Vhatever money you made, you made in this country?—A. Yes.
n 1851, when you first went fishing in the gulf, you had not made
money?—A. No; not much, but I had a little.
Where did you learn your trade of sailmaking?—A. In the United

.
When?—A. I learned it during the winter in 1849, 1850, 1851,
and 1853.
Then you did not fish at all in winter?—A. No, but I fished
spring.
n 1853, when you left fishing altogether, and went into business,
apital did you bring into it?—A. I had but very little.
nto what kind of business did you go?—A. Sailmaking and
g.
And at this business you made your money?—A. Yes.
Did I not understand you to say that you went into the fishing
ss in 1853?—A. No.
When did you first go into the fishing business?—A. In 1864, I

And then you put $14,000 or $15,500 of capital into the busi-
—A. Yes.
And you had made this altogether by rigging?—A. Yes; rigging
ilmaking.
How many vessels did you send into the bay in the course of time

you were engaged in business?—A. We had four that went into the bay principally.

Q. Did you go with them yourself?—A. No.

Q. Did you send captains?—A. Yes.

Q. And were these captains part owners with you?—A. Yes.

Q. Do you know where those vessels fished?—A. I could not tell.

Q. You do not know whether they fished inshore or not?—A. No.

Q. Did you never inquire? Did they do a good business?—A. No; they did not do much.

Q. Did they get the same average catches which you obtained from 1851 to 1853?—A. Some years they did and some years they did not.

Q. Were the prices of mackerel then very low?—A. No; they were fair.

Q. Did those vessels in which you went into the bay in 1851, 1852, and 1853 make money?—A. No.

Q. Did they lose?—A. I do not think that they made anything.

Q. Will you tell me how it was that with the full knowledge which you had of the fishing business in the bay—it being either a losing business or one in which you did not make money—you were tempted to go into the business of sending vessels to the bay; you had had personal experience that the fisheries in the bay were good for nothing?—A. I had heard that a good many vessels had made money in the fishing business, and I went into it with the intention of making money, but I found that I was mistaken.

Q. You had heard that a good many vessels went into the bay and made money?—A. Yes, some.

Q. Although your experience personally was entirely against it?—A. Yes.

Q. In 1851, when you made two trips and caught 300 and 325 barrels, what was the size of the vessel?—A. I think about 80 tons.

Q. What would be a full fare?—A. 300 or 325 barrels.

Q. When you made those two trips, did you go both times back to Gloucester?—A. Yes.

Q. And you got full fares on both occasions?—A. Yes.

Q. In 1852, when you got 350 barrels, was it the same vessel?—A. Yes.

Q. That was a full fare?—A. Yes.

Q. You told me a full fare was 325 barrels?—A. We carried some on deck.

Q. Did you fish in 1853?—A. Yes.

Q. What was your fare then?—A. 180 barrels.

Q. The same vessel?—A. No.

Q. What tonnage was the vessel?—A. About the same tonnage, I think. Her name was Vienna.

Q. You did not get a full fare?—A. No.

Q. On that occasion you swear you only fished on Bradley and Orphan Banks?—A. On the first year I swear that.

Q. I speak of the last year, when you caught 182 barrels?—A. I do.

Q. That was not a full fare?—A. No.

Q. What time did you leave the bay?—A. I think about the 1st November.

Q. What time did you go into the bay?—A. In July.

Q. Though you only got 180 barrels, which was not a full fare by 120 barrels, you never, during the whole time, went inshore at all?—A. We went inshore.

Q. Did you go inshore?—A. We tried inshore.

here?—A. Coming out of Cascumpeque and Malpeque.
as that within the three miles?—A. Yes.
d you try in Bay Chaleurs?—A. Yes.
t Margaree?—A. Yes.
d you get any mackerel?—A. There were no mackerel there that
Ve tried, also, off Port Hood, and did not get any there.
en there were no mackerel at all inshore that year?—A. We
get any.
ere there any catches made in the bay that year?—A. Yes.
nd notwithstanding that cutters were in the bay you went in-
fish?—A. We tried coming out of harbors. I don't suppose the
saw.
hat did you go in for?—A. We went in for a harbor. I said
coming out of harbors we tried.
ll the trying you did was when you made for harbors, and tried
out?—A. Yes.
ou really did not try anywhere at all?—A. It is so long ago I
recollect.
et you recollect that in 1852 you caught 25 or 30 barrels at Mar-
—A. I recollect that because the cutter was coming down, and
under way and stood out.
hat was the reason you did not catch any more?—A. Yes; I
o doubt about it.
here was good fishing inshore there?—A. Yes; very good.
nd you went out of the bay because you could not fish inshore?
u try at Margaree in 1853?—A. There were no mackerel at Mar-
hat year.
id you try at the Magdalen Islands?—A. Yes; we caught a few
very few.
n answer to Mr. Dana, you said you only fished on Bradley and
Banks, and did not fish inshore?—A. That was where I caught
.
f you fished that year at Magdalen Islands, why did you not say
Ir. Dana?—A. We did not catch any mackerel there. I under-
Ir. Dana wanted to know where we took our mackerel, and I said
ks Bradley and Orphan. We tried toward Magdalen Islands and
garee and Prince Edward Island.
ou mean you did try at Magdalen Islands, but did not catch
A. Yes.
ow long did you stay at Magdalen Islands?—A. We might have
ere one or two days.
Vhat time of the year was it?—A. In September, I think.
Vhy did you go away from there?—A. It is no use to stay there
ackerel are there.
s it stormy round Magdalen Islands at all?—A. Yes.
o you consider it an unsafe place to fish late in the season?—A.

s it usually so considered among fishermen?—A. I believe so.
s it one of the most dangerous places in the bay?—A. I don't
r it half so dangerous as at Prince Edward Island.
Vhat part of Prince Edward Island is twice as dangerous as
len Islands?—A. In the bend of the island.
re there no harbors there?—A. Yes; there are harbors, but they
d harbors to get into.
ave you been there of late years to see if there are any harbors
ge there?—A. I have not.

Q. Are there not many more vessels lost at Magdalen Isla
Prince Edward Island ?—A. I think not.

Q. That is your idea ?—A. Of late years there may hav<
former years more were lost at Prince Edward Island.

Q. Do you mean to say that, excepting the year of the gr
can gale ?—A. I take that in.

Q. At what time of the year did that occur ?—A. I d<
whether in September or October. In October, I think.

Q. That is the season when few or no vessels are at
Islands ?—A. Yes.

Q. They would leave Magdalen Islands and go fishing at :
ward Island?—A. I don't know.

Q. Don't they fish around Prince Edward much later in
than around Magdalen Islands ?—A. Not at the bend of
Around East Point they do.

Q. Were not a number of the vessels lost at East Point ?
were lost there, I think.

Q. Then you swear that you believe Magdalen Islands to
place than Prince Edward Island ?—A. I would rather fish th<
are more chances for a vessel to get out.

Q. Why ?—A. There is a chance to go around the islands.

Q. Is there not a chance to go around Prince Edward Isl:
northeast or north end ?—A. If you are near either end tl
same; if you are not near one of the ends you have not m<
in a storm.

Q. Cannot you go into the harbors ?—A. Suppose a vessel
or 14 feet, she cannot go over the bars.

Q. If the bar has less depth of water, of course she canno
say the harbors have less than that ?—A. They had at that ti<
know what they are now.

Q. In answer to Mr. Dana, you stated that you believe 1
fishery is of no practical value to the United States ?—A. I
consider it so.

Q. And did you so consider it in 1851, 1852, and 1853?—<

Q. Was that the general opinion?—A. I think that is t
opinion of everybody.

Q. Amongst fishermen in 1851, 1852, and 1853, and ever
Yes; I think so.

Q. Did you ever hear any one among fishermen say to the <
A. I don't know I ever heard anybody.

Q. How do you account for their making such endeavors
right to fish inshore?—A. I did not know they made any en

Q. In your judgment they are good for nothing?—A. I
give one cent for the whole of them.

Q. And you think that is the opinion of all the fisher<
could not say what their opinion is. It is so, as far as I kn<

Q. And as far as you know is it the opinion of fish merc
I could not say.

Q. You were in that business yourself?—A. I am not
now.

Q. You have stated that in your opinion the inshore fish<
worth one cent, and that as far as you know that is the op:
fishermen ?—A. Yes.

Q. Is that the opinion of the fish merchants as well ?—A

Q. I suppose that is the opinion in Gloucester, Boston, a<
the coast of Massachusetts?—A. I think so.

nd if any person, either a United States fisherman or otherwise,
any trouble about getting the right to fish within the three miles
ir vessels, you think he is foolish ?—A. I think so.   I think they
fools to pay anything for it.

they can get the fishing without paying for it, they will not be
A. There are very few fish inshore anyway.

ven now that is so ?—A. I don't know.   I have not been there
I could not say.

ou don't know anything about it practically since 1853 ?—A. Not
ally.

ou seriously swear you would not give one cent for the inshore
s ?—A. At that time I would not.

hat is in 1854.   Have you heard that they have since been very
etter ?—A. I have not.

ould you rather have one cent in your pocket than the grant of
e fisheries ?—A. I think I should.

y Mr. Dana:

suppose you think, in that case, you would have to carry them
—A. Yes.

f you had a large number of vessels and you intended to send
o the bay to fish, would you send them if you had to pay for the
f inshore fishing ?—A. No; I would not.

nd the result of your experience is that it would not pay to send
to the bay to fish ?—A. No; as far as my experience goes.

bout sails.   Are there not great efforts made to procure some-
o prevent the effect of fog and mildew on sails ?—A. Yes.

t is considered a very serious evil ?—A. Yes.

lore so than ordinary storm and rain ?—A. Yes.

suppose seafaring-men, when they get into harbor, after a storm
d and rain, dry the sails?—A. Yes.

A few days of rain followed by sunshine would not hurt a vessel
h as long-continued dampness ?—A. No.

No. 67.

ES W. PATTILLO, of North Stoughton, Mass., retired fisherman,
on behalf of the Government of the United States, sworn and
ned.

By Mr. Trescot:

stion. How old are you ?—Answer. 71 years on 29th September

Zou have been a fisherman in your day ?—A. Yes.

And have fished a good deal ?—A. All the way along from 1834
3.

Were you fishing all that time ?—A. The best part of it; some
f the time I was not.

What were you doing when you were not fishing ?—A. I was agent
ars for the insurance company.

Whereabouts ?—A. Down at Cape Breton Island, at Port Hood,
g out for American vessels.

from 1834 to 1868, how often were you skipper ?—A. I was skip-
1838.

low many years ?—A. 1839, 1840, and all the way along pretty

Q. All the while from 1840 to 1868?—A. Yes, all the time I ᴠ
ter except two years, when I did not go to the bay.

Q. During that period of time have you been in the bay a go
—A. Some years I went to the bay two trips, some years but
and some years not at all.

Q. Have you done any fishing on the American coast as ᴠ
the bay?—A. I have.

Q. What sort of proportion does the fishing on the Americ;
bear to the fishing in the bay? Did you fish most on your
most in the bay?—A. I ·fished more in the bay than on tl
although I have·done fully better on our own shores in seasor
ever have in the bay.

Q. You say you went fishing first in 1834. Where did you
I did not go into North Bay in 1834. I fished on our own shor

Q. When was the first year you went into the bay?—A. In
the Good Hope.

Q. When was the last year you were in the gulf?—A. 1868.

Q. Did you find any difference in the fishing in 1868 from wh
in 1836, and, if so, what was the difference?—A. In 1836 we
little. We had a large vessel, Good Hope, with 13 or 14 men,
65 barrels. We proceeded there some time in July, and arrived
the latter part of September.

Q. How often after that did you go into the gulf? What is ᴛ
number of consecutive years you have been in the bay?—A. I hᴀ
there 21 trips.

Q. You have then got a pretty good knowledge of what the ᴀ
ing has been from 1836 to 1868. How does the gulf fishing
now with what it was when you first went there?—A. I have ᴀ
there since 1868, and of what has been done since I have littlᴇ
edge except what I have read.

Q. From 1836 to 1868, has there been a great change in the
ing, or was it pretty much the same?—A. In the gulf it used
Some years there would be pretty good fishing, and other years'
be pretty slim.

Q. Where was your general fishing-place in the gulf?—A. Ϲ
Orphan and Bradley, and at Magdalen Islands. At Magdaleᴎ
I fished mostly always, and I found better fishing 15 or 20 ᴍ
the land, on the north side of the Magdalens, and round Biᴙ
than anywhere else. I have caught·some mackerel along at Ᵽ
cou, in the range of North Cape, Prince Edward Island; but o
the mackerel we got at Magdalen Islands and round Banks Bᴙ:
Orphan.

Q. During these 21 years, how much fishing did you do wiᴛ
miles of the land?—A. To the best of my judgment, I will giᴠ
facts. I had the day and date for all the items, but in 1863
fire, and it was burned up, and therefore I will give you theᴅ
I can from memory. I never thought anything about it till a ᶦ
when I overhauled my memory, and I can give it to you. ᶦ
year, in the Good Hope, we got 65 barrels of mackerel; ᴛ
caught within the limits. I think we caught about 35 barrᴇ
day, about 8 or 10 miles to the northward of Magdalen Islanᵈ

Mr. THOMSON called attention to a memorandum from whiᶜ
was reading.

WITNESS said the paper was a memorandum he had made ᶦ
years he had been in North Bay and where he caught the mᴀ

Mr. THOMSON. If your books were lost and your memory does not serve you, how did you make up the paper?—A. From my memory.

Q. Why did you make up the paper?—A. I made it up to be accurate, and so that if I was asked questions, I might not mix up my voyages.

Mr. THOMSON. Then I understand you to state that you sat down and made up that paper from your recollection?—A. Yes.

Examination resumed.

WITNESS. The next mackerel we got was somewhere about 40 wash-barrels, about twenty miles broad off St. Peter's. That was all the mackerel we got to make up 65 barrels. Those were 65 sea-barrels, which we carried to Cape Ann. The second year, 1837, I was in the Mount Vernon, and we caught 300 barrels of mackerel. We caught 200 barrels broad off to an anchor within half a mile of the land; and 100 barrels we caught 10, 15, or 20 miles from the land.

Mr. TRESCOT. Where did you catch them?—A. At Margaree Island or Sea Cove Island. It was on 13th October, I remember it well, and we filled up. In 1838 I was master of the same Good Hope, and we got 270 barrels. I think, according to the best of my judgment, we got 50 barrels of them within three miles of the land, but I think, to the best of my judgment, the rest were taken in our own waters, 5, 10, 15 or 20 miles from the land. In 1839 I was in the Tiger, and got 75 barrels. We caught them all off shore, that is, without the three-mile limit. In 1840 I was not in the bay; I fell from the mast-head and broke my thigh. In 1841 I was in the bay twice in the Abigail. The first trip we got 250 barrels on Banks Bradley and Orphan. The second trip we got 75 barrels up at the bend of the island, making 325 barrels for the season. In 1842, 1843, and 1844, I was fishing on our shores in the Hosea Blue. In 1845 and 1846 I fished on our shores. In 1848 I fished on our shores in the Alexander. In 1849 I was at home. In 1850 I was in the Alexander on our shores. In 1851 I was in the bay in the Alexander, and made two trips; that was the year of the gale. On the first trip, I caught, between Point Miscou and North Cape, 314 barrels. I landed them at Arichat, with a member of the house named Martel, and he advanced me the money to fit out the second time. The next trip I got 214 barrels after the gale. To the best of my judgment I got from 75 to 100 barrels within the limits. We got them in two or three days after the gale. Some of them made out we were within the limits, so I went home; I thought it was no use to continue. Captain Derby was kind of chasing us, so I went home. I had to come to Arichat and get my 314 barrels. In 1852 I caught 335 barrels, and I caught them from the north part of Anticosti up to Seven Islands, right in the gulf, 15 or 20 miles from land. We were about in the range off from the northwest part of Anticosti to Seven Islands, and up the gulf. That was in the Alexander. In 1853 I had the schooner Highland Lass, and got 400 barrels. I caught them between Point Miscou, say 10 or 15 miles off Miscou, and up the west shore, 8 or 10 miles along, at Escuminac. I caught half of them to an anchor. It was the year when the vessel was new. Those are all sea-barrels. The next year, 1854, I got 300 barrels. In 1855 I had Christie Campbell, a new vessel. The Highland Lass was in the bay. A man named Samuel Chambers was in her; I know he did not do a great deal, but I don't know what he got. On the first trip I got 250 barrels on Banks Bradley and Orphan; on the second trip I caught 200 barrels at Magdalen Islands. In 1856 I got 285 barrels. I caught the principal part of them on Fisherman's Bank, between Cape George and George-town. I got about 100 barrels there at the last of the month; it wound

up my fare, on, I think, 19th October. In 1847 I was in the g₁
and got 330 barrels. I caught them at Magdalen Islands, off Bl
and some down round the Bird Rocks. We caught them rou
Rocks to an anchor, and the balance off Blackland, on the north
the Magdalens. In 1858 I was agent for the insurance compa
1859 I was at home. I had a man to go in her, so I staid at h₁
1860 I was again agent for the insurance company, looking after
can vessels. In 1861 I went to the gold diggings, down at Wi
bor, and bought an old claim for $60; but I did not get much g
1862 I was in the Rose Skerrit, and got two trips of mackerel. '
trip of 350 barrels I got off Blackland, at Magdalen Islands; th₁
trip I got 400 barrels, making 750 barrels in short of three mon
we went home and landed them. We caught the first trip in
days, and the second we took in twenty days. We got our
round the Magdalens, and perhaps half-way from Entry Island
Point.

Q. Did you get any within the three miles ?—A. Not one of th
1863 I went in Oliver Cromwell and got 940 barrels. I made
trip. I sent home 560 barrels, I think. I could not pretend to
barrel. I think I landed the first trip, 330 barrels, at Maguire
Gut, and the next trip we landed, making 560 barrels. That
best of my memory. Before we came home we made it up to 950

Q. Where did you catch those ?—A. I caught half of the first
tween Entry Island and Cheticamp, about half way. We ha
Island in sight, 25 miles off, and sometimes not quite so far. It i
to be a good fishing ground, and there we got one-half of our n
on the first trip. Of the rest of the mackerel, we caught som
the limits; I don't know just how many. I could not pretend t
my oath, but we got some. We got them in Georges Bay, betwe
George and Cape Patrick, in Antigonish Bay. Of these 940 ba
probably got 100 barrels within the limits; I think that is a la
mate of what we got there. I think it would be honest and fa
tween man and man, to say 100 barrels, which would be as mu
got inshore, to the best of my judgment. In 1864 I went in the
Scotland. She was 125 tons. We got 500 barrels that trip.
half of them on Banks Bradley and Orphan; some up off Poin
The next year, 1865, I went two trips in her. The first trip I
barrels; we got all of them on Banks Bradley and Orphan; a₁
second trip when we caught them, the east point of the island v
southwest of us 15 or 20 miles. We got a deck of mackerel th
dentally. We were becalmed and hove to and got 100 or 120 wa₁
there. We got half of the trip there, and we got the rest of
between East Point and Port Hood. In 1866 I was at home;
the Banks. In 1867 I was one trip in the Scotland and got :
barrels. I cannot tell you exactly, but I think not one barrel v
inshore. We caught them between Prince Edward Island a
Miscou. In 1868 I caught 450 barrels. I got them in the
caught 350 barrels on our own shore before I started. I made
on the Georges before I went to the bay. I went out and wa₁
days and got 130 barrels; I went again and got 220 barrels, m
barrels in, I guess, not over 25 or 28 days, and I got the bala
fall trip making 450, and also making 750 barrels for that yea

Q. Where did you get the 450 barrels ?—A. I got half of the₁
Entry Island and Prince Edward Island, and some to the north
Cape.

THURSDAY, *October* 18, 1877.

The Conference met.

The examination of JAMES W. PATTILLO was resumed.

By Mr. Trescot:

Question. I see you are stated to belong to North Stoughton; were you born there?—Answer. No; I was born in Chester, Lunenburg County, Nova Scotia, September 29, 1806.

Q. Without giving precise details of your catches during your 21 years of experience in the bay as a fisherman, will you tell me what proportion of the fish you caught during this period was taken within the 3-mile limit?—A. Possibly 10 per cent.—10 barrels out of 100; and I think that would be a large proportion, because during the 21 seasons I was in the bay the most mackerel I ever so caught was in my second year.

Q. Being a fisherman of that experience, what sort of advantage do you think it is to have the right to fish within the 3-mile limit in British waters; do you attach much importance to it?—A. Well, if I had to go in the bay I should not calculate that inshore fishing was worth anything at all. I would only go inshore to make harbors and dress fish. I would not give a snap of my finger for the inshore fisheries. When licenses cost 50 cents a ton I would not pay it. I would rather fish in my own waters, because I could do better there.

Q. You never took a license out?—A. I never did. I was for three years in the bay when they were issued, but I would not take one out. I did not want them.

Q. You were then master of your own vessel?—A. Yes; I owned the vessel and was master.

Q. And you ran the risk?—A. I fished in my own waters, 3, 4, 5, 10 and 20 miles off land, and I always did better there than inshore. I would not give a cent for the inshore fisheries. All I would go inshore for would be to make a harbor.

Q. You never had any trouble with the cutters?—A. No; save once when they chased me.

Q. But that was no trouble?—A. O, no; it was only for doing a kind act.

Q. Besides having fished for 21 years in the bay, did you fish much on our own coast?—A. I did.

Q. How does the fishing on our coast compare with the fishing in the bay?—A. I have myself always done better on our own shore, with the exception of one year, than I ever did in North Bay.

Q. During how many years did you fish on our shore?—A. I think I fished there 8 seasons, or somewhere about that; it was perhaps a little more, but I know I fished there 8 years.

Q. If you found the fishing on our shore so much better than the fishing in the bay, why did you go to the bay?—A. Well, there was just one principle on which we used mostly to go to the bay; the fact is that when we shipped a crew at Cape Cod, after we had been off for a fortnight or 3 weeks on our shore, men would leave the vessel; but when we got a crew and came to North Bay, they had to stay on board; there was then no back door to crawl out of. This was one of the chief reasons for coming to the bay, as we then had no trouble in the shipping of hands, good, bad, or indifferent; but when we were down on our shore, men would go off and we would have to secure new hands. Men would think they might do better, and they would go where the high line was; and we were then under the necessity of supplying their places. Another thing was, that by going to the bay, we got clear of the fog. On our

coast there is a great deal of fog, but when we reach North Ba,
clear of it.

Q. You say that in the gulf your fishing was done on the B:
toward the Magdalen Islands ?—A. Yes; we caught the he
mackerel invariably around the Magdalen Islands.

Q. As a fishing ground, taking it all in all, are the Magdale₁
much worse than Prince Edward Island ?—A. They are bet
Prince Edward Island.

Q. You did not fish much about Prince Edward Island ?—A
did a great deal. I tried around there, but I never caught n
there..

Q. You are sure that you never took a license out ?—A. Y
sure that I never took a license out. I never paid a red c
license.

By Mr. Thomson:

Q. You never took out a license ?—A. No.

Q. Where were you in 1866 ?—A. At home.

Q. Do you know of a vessel belonging to Gloucester called
land ?—A. Yes.

Q. Do you own her ?—A. Yes.

Q. Was she in the bay in 1866 ?—A. I do not recollect wh₁
was or not.

Q. How happens it, since you have given most extraordi
dence of having a good memory, recollecting not only what y₀
years ago, but the very days of the month when events occur
you do not remember where the Scotland was in 1866, and ₁
was then doing ?—A. I think that Captain Bartlett went in
year to the Banks, fresh halibuting—down at St. Peter's Bank

Q. And she did not go to the bay at all that year ?—A. I th

Q. Can you swear positively that she did not ?—A. No; I
but to the best of my recollection she did not go to the bay th:

Q. Did any of your vessels, when you were not in them,
licenses ?—A. Not that I know of.

Q. Can you swear that the Scotland did not take out a
1866, and did not fish in the Bay in 1866 ?—A. Well, she m₁
then been in the bay; I was not in her. I never paid for a
my knowledge in my life.

Q. I presume that the captain would not pay for a license
own pocket ?—A. Well, I cannot recollect paying for one. I I
I did not do so when I was in her myself.

Q. How happens it, if your memory is so good, that y₁
remember this ? You surprised me by stating as far back a
ago, not only what you did during a particular year, but also
did on the 18th and 19th of October ?—A. The 18th and 19th
ber ?

Q. I think so.—A. No; but I recollect catching macke
Mount Vernon, on the 11th, 12th and 13th of October, when w
barrels. I recollect that as well as if it had only happened
My memory serves me better concerning events which happ₁
40 years ago, than for those that have occurred somewhat rec

Q. That was in 1837 ?—A. Yes.

Q. Forty years ago ?—A. Yes.

Q. You not only recollect what you then did, but also the
of the month in this regard ?—A. That is true. I do so reco

Q. I do not mean to say that your memory is not quite
but it surprises me to find that with such an exceedingl₁

you fail to remember where the Scotland went in 1866 ?—A.
an recollect events that happened 40 and 50 years ago better
thing which happened yesterday. I had everything that
as I went along, until I was burned out; until then I had
ots referring to all my voyages and cruises, and everything
I did; and in this statement I have given the facts just as they
as well as my memory serves me. I give you the truth on
just as faithfully as I would if I were to die this very minute.
give you the exact truth.
n't dispute that.—A. That is it.
not charging you with making any willful mistake; but I wish
ether you are in error.—A. I may be in error.
say that all the memoranda which you kept concerning your
have been lost; why did you keep such written memoranda ?—
ys kept them, in order to know what I did, whereabouts I was,
much money I made, as I most always owned the whole of all
is I had, though I did not own the whole of the Scotland. I
ot such account further than concerned what expenses were
what balance belonged to me; and in this way I knew how
ade, after I had completed my voyage and paid all charges;
made $1,000, I thus knew that I made it such a year; and if I
000, I put that down for such or such a year, clear of living and
Sometimes it was more, and sometimes it was less; but such
I made a memorandum of it, to which I could refer and know
ly where I stood. I never went into debt, and I always paid

er you made such memoranda, you would have no occasion to
hem again ?—A. No; but I always could do so if any questions
dering it desirable.
I you occasion to refer back to them; nothing occurred to make
ssary until this occasion arose ?—A. No.
en did you last read them ?—A. I have not read any paper
g my voyages since I knocked off fishing, and my last year's
as in 1868. I have not thought of doing so.
esume that when you read the record of 1868, or of 1867, you
t have gone back to the extent of 30 years previously—to 1837,
Nothing had then happened to call your attention to such
—A. No; nothing has occurred in the fishing business in
have been in any way or shape interested, since I left off fish-
1868 was my last year.
868, when you made your last memorandum on the subject of
ing voyages, you had no occasion to turn over and read your
pts as far back as 1837 ?—A. Well, then I had no manuscripts
o.
you make memoranda concerning what you did in 1868 ?—A.
manuscripts were burned up, I never made any such memo-
all.
en were they burned up ?—A. In 1863 or 1864, I think.
n you did not make any such memoranda afterward ?—A. No.
ippose you made memoranda respecting what you did in 1863,
—A. They were burned up.
you do so in 1862 ?—A. I think so.
en you had done so, did you then have occasion to refer back
us entries as far back as 1837 ?—A. No.
er you had made an entry for any particular year, nothing ever
to call your attention back to those entries until after the books

which contained them were burned ?—A. No; I never referred to them, but often when we got together we would talk over what we had done such and such a year; we would talk over at the fireside what we had done in a vessel—say in 1836, 1837, or 1838—telling how many mackerel we got and how much money we made, and all that, in common talk. We would refer to these matters time and time again, telling who was high-line, and all what happened. We used to talk over these subjects in that way.

Q. Although you did talk over what you did in these different years, you never referred to this memorandum-book to verify your statements ?—A. No.

Q. Then it comes to this, that although you had a memorandum-book, you never referred to it at all to assist your memory ?—A. No; not a bit.

Q. With this extraordinary memory, the accuracy of which I do not dispute—recollecting not only what you did 40 years ago but the very days of the month on which certain events happened, yet you cannot tell me whether in 1866, 11 years ago, your vessel, the Scotland, went into the bay to fish or not ?—A. Well, she went halibuting that year.

Q. But she did not go into the bay ?—A. No; she went to St. Peter's Bank and the Western Bank.

Q. But that is not the Gulf of St. Lawrence ?—A. Well, she might have gone up above Seven Islands, where a good many halibut used to be got.

Q. That lies south of the coast of Labrador and north of the island of Anticosti ?—A. Yes.

Q. Did she go there to catch halibut ?—A. She might have done so; I was not in her. She was in charge of Captain Bartlett at the time.

Q. Your captain would surely tell you where he had been and where he had caught his fish ? This would be your first question ?—A. As long as he had halibut that was the chief thing I looked after.

Q. I do not think you would be content with merely knowing that? You would ask him where he had been and where he had caught his fish ?—A. Sometimes I might do so and sometimes I might not.

Q. Did you, in point of fact, ask and discover from him where he had been and what he had caught that year ?—A. I could not answer that question; I could not say whether I did so or not; I might possibly have done so, and I might not.

Q. Then I am right in stating that, notwithstanding your good memory, you do not recollect whether your vessel, the Scotland, went in 1866 into the gulf or not ?—A. Well, I am pretty positive in saying that she did not go there that year mackereling.

Q. Did she go there at all, for halibut or any other fish ?—A. Not that I know of; that is not within my recollection.

Q. You have no recollection of Captain Bartlett having taken out a license in the bay that year?—A. No.

Q. Do you recollect what the license-fee was that year ?—A. It might have been $1 for all I know, and it might have been 50 cents.

Q. What was the tonnage of the Scotland ?—A. 123, carpenter's measurement, and I think one hundred and something new tonnage. I think that I paid for 125 or 130 tons, when I bought her.

Q. Did they measure the tonnage by carpenter's measurement in levying fees ?—A. That I cannot tell.

Q. The fee would be at least $50, if they charged 50 cents per ton, or $120 if $1 a ton was charged.—A. Yes.

Q. That sum would not be paid by the captain ?—A. I suppose that it would come out of the common stock—the whole stock; one-half would be paid by the crew, and one-half by the owner. I suppose so—I do not know; but that is my impression.

Q. In the report concerning the issue of fishing licenses, for fishing inshore in Canadian waters, it is stated that in 1866 a license was taken out by the Scotland, J. W. Pattils, of Gloucester, Mass.?—A. There is no person of that name. James W. Pattillo is my name.

Q. The name entered here is J. W. Pattils—probably a misprint—and the tonnage of the Scotland is given as 78; that, I suppose, would be ordinary tonnage, not carpenter's measurement?—A. I suppose so.

Q. How many men did she carry?—A. Sometimes 14 and sometimes 15.

Q. She is represented here as having 16 men, and as having paid 50 cents per ton for the license, amounting in all to $38.50. There was no other Scotland, J. W. Pattils, of Gloucester, Mass.; and yet you see that she did take out a license that year?—A. How is that name spelled?

Q. Pattils.—A. My name is spelled Pattillo.

Q. There is no person that spells his name Pattils, that you are aware of, in Gloucester?—A. No.

Q. And your initials are J. W.?—A. Yes.

Q. Can you undertake to say that this entry is wrong, and that such a license was never taken out?—A. Well, I would not pretend to say that statement is wrong; but I have no recollection of this having been the case.

Q. At all events, if the captain took it in your absence, and without your knowledge, he had more respect for the inshore fisheries than you have now, apparently?—A. Well, I never paid a cent for a license to my knowledge, though I might have paid for that, but I do not recollect of having done so. I never considered inshore fishing in the bay worth 50 cents, nor yet would I pay 25 cents for the privilege.

Q. In answer to Mr. Trescot, you stated you thought that the fishing off the American coast was better than the fishing around Prince Edward Island and in the bay?—A. I think so.

Q. You spoke of the American coast as "our shore," and in the same breath you said you were born in Nova Scotia?—A. I have been naturalized; and I now call that our shore. I have become a citizen of the United States.

Q. When were you naturalized?—A. In 1836, I think; I have the papers to show.

Q. The oath you have thus taken is not merely, I believe, an oath of allegiance as a citizen of the United States, but also an oath of abrogation of allegiance to Queen Victoria and the sovereigns of Great Britain?—A. I think that when I was sworn, which was in open court, I swore to be true to the United States of America, and I also swore allegiance against Great Britain and Ireland and all Her Majesty's dominions.

Q. I thought so.—A. And I have tried to be loyal to the United States ever since.

Q. You came from Nova Scotia, and you say you swore allegiance against Nova Scotia when you took this oath?—A. Well, I wanted to have the right and privilege of any citizen, and I could not secure that without going through this preliminary.

Q. And after that you tried to keep your oath, and you have been heart and soul an American citizen ever since?—A. Yes; certainly.

Q. And you regard this question, which is now to be determined by

175 F

these Commissioners, from an American stand-point?—A.]
I do.

Q. And I suppose you take quite an interest in seeing
sioners award nothing, or as little as possible, against
States?—A. Well, I took no thought of it—good, bad, or
until I was invited to come down here; and that was a wee
day. I have tried to overhaul my memory the best I could
done the best I could. If anybody could could do it any b
like to have him try it. I have done the best I could, and i
wrong, I have not intended it. I would not lie for the
whether they give fifteen millions or not.

Q. Do not misunderstand me. I am not charging you
anything of that kind.—A. No; I would not do it.

Q. Tell me why, having this memory, and considering
your memoranda were destroyed, you wrote down memor
paper?—A. I could tell all the things just as they came
wanted to be accurate, and I did not know but they might
end or the other, and I wanted it to refer to.

Q. You have been examined before you came here?—A.]
talked it over.

Q. You had no idea of Mr. Trescot puzzling you?—A.
a word or two; but I did not then refer to any particular
bad, or indifferent.

Q. You had no idea of his entrapping you?—A. Well, I
but what you might catch me.

Q. You have stated you do not think that the inshore fi:
gulf are worth anything at all?—A. No; I do not.

Q. And you say that you never took out a license, but I
of your vessels took out a license; hence, her captain ente
ferent opinion from yourself in this regard; are you rea
saying that they are worth nothing at all?—A. No; they
fish of the sea, on any shore, are not worth anything.

Q. Then your idea is that these inshore fisheries ought
for by the United States, because the fish in the sea are
until they are caught?—A. That is it; I never thought
eries inshore were worth anything.

Q. For this reason, because they are not caught?—A.
one reason for it.

Q. You did catch fish inshore on several occasions;
than half one trip—100 barrels or upwards inshore?—A.
hand, and was along with William Forbes in the Mount
was a very poor year when very few mackerel were taken
bay.

Q. Even so, but you then caught one-half of your trip
We took two-thirds of it, 200 barrels.

Q. Inshore?—A. Yes; within half a mile of the isla
my second year fishing.

Q. The privilege of fishing inshore was worth somethin
A. We made a little out of it that time.

Q. If you could do that again, the inshore fishing w
something?—A. I have tried it a number of times, but I
anything of any account inshore.

Q. O, yes, you did afterward to some extent?—A. W
in the Oliver Cromwell I caught 940 barrels, and I think
rels of these were taken inshore. I did not go home wit
that year, but I sent fish home twice. I shipped from

I think, the first time, and 230 barrels, or thereabouts, the second and the rest I carried home.

Did you pack them out in Canso?—A. No; I only landed them .

Why?—A. I landed them because this was during the war, and 1en were afraid of being drafted, and if I had gone home, I would had to hire men for the purpose at Canso. Cruisers were burning ·thing up, and so I got a letter of marque and got all prepared. I ned a license from the Secretary of War over at Charlestown, and ed out my vessel with a six-pounder and shot and cutlasses, and ·thing necessary for us to fight our way; and I landed the fish and only one trip that season, because the men were afraid to return hey should be drafted.

You fitted out not against British but Southern cruisers, and your were afraid of being drafted into the northern army?—A. I fitted gainst any one who should trouble me anyhow; and I was deter-d, if necessary, to fight my way. If that bark had come across would have done my best to take her.

Which bark?—A. The one that burned the vessels about George's .

The Alabama?—A. No; but an old bark—the Tacony.

She was a Southern cruiser?—A. I do not know that, but I meant ve taken her if I could. The fact is, I was all cut and dried for The people of Halifax all came down to look at my vessel. I had ·pounder on board, and 24 rounds of round shot, and 24 rounds of , and bags of powder, and everything else required; while each had a cutlass and a revolver. I paid $800 for that outfit.

When was this?—A. It was in 1863.

Your men were afraid of going back to your coast lest they should rafted into the Northern army?—A. Yes.

And you were afraid of being captured by this Southern cruiser?—was not afraid, not a bit.

Well, lest you should be so captured, you armed yourself to show ?—A. Yes, I did.

You had no other object; you did not intend to fight any vessels pt Southern cruisers?—A. No, of course not. I intended to go z peaceably if I was left alone.

You told Mr. Trescot that, though the fisheries on your coast are ir than those in the gulf, you preferred to go to the gulf in order to your crews together?—A. That is so.

Was not that a great convenience to you?—A. Yes; and besides hus got clear of the fogs which prevail a great deal on our coast ig the summer. After we get through Canso, into North Bay, we , with little fog.

Have you any fog on your coast in winter?—A. Yes, sometimes; 1ot very often.

It is a stormy place to fish in winter, on your coast?—A. Some-s it is and sometimes it is not.

But taking the season through, it is a stormy coast?—A. All coasts stormy in winter; but our coast is not then so stormy as the coast nd the British Provinces and in the gulf.

A large portion of the gulf freezes up in winter?—A. Yes; but I , been in the gulf till near Christmas for produce on the north side rince Edward Island.

Without getting frozen up?—A. I did not get frozen up. I think t Malpeque on the 17th of November.

Q. Is not the weather on your coast in winter very hard
ging of vessels—on the sails, and so on ?—A. Yes.

Q. It is a good deal harder on them than is summer or fall
the bay, before the stormy season sets in ?—A. Certainly;
and tear is suffered in this regard in winter than in summer of

Q. You admit, then, that if it was not for the bay fishing in
you could not have kept the crews together, as you could n
your own coast ?—A. Well, that was one reason why I went
when we lost a man on our shore we could get another, bi
sioned loss of time.

Q. You could not keep your crews there ?—A. When we
one we could find another to replace him, but this caused lo

Q. And time is money ?—A. Of course.

Q. Therefore you made more money by taking your crews
than you could have made if you had fished on your shore,
replacing men the while ?—A. I suppose that sometimes we
make more money and sometimes we would not; we had to
of it.

Q. You saved yourself inconvenience and came to the
used to go there some seasons, when I had a mind to do so.

Q. Did you really send your vessels or come to the gulf k
you could thus make more money than if you fished on your
—A. I never sent a vessel into North Bay; I let the skipp
wished in this respect. He was his own guide, and he coul
gulf if he liked, or fish on our shore, according to his pre
was master of the vessel, and I fitted her out.

Q. Is that the rule of that particular trade, to allow the n
and fish where he pleases ?—A. As a general thing, yes.

Q. Without the owner controlling him at all ?—A. Well,
rule, at any rate, to do so. When I went for other people
where I had a mind to. I went just where I thought I co

Q. And the owner never attempted to control you in thi
A. No; if he had, I would have left his vessel.

Q. Was your practice in this respect the usual practice o
pers ?—A. I presume so, but I do not know that it was; I
ever, that I did. so myself.

Q. Have the skippers an interest in the vessels ?—A.
skippers of Cape Ann, for the last few years, have been pa
the extent of $\frac{1}{4}$ or $\frac{1}{8}$, or something like that, and the owner
will think that the captain would go where the most mo
made, or try to do so, and so the skippers are allowed to b
in this relation.

Q. Therefore it is to be presumed that the captains wh
to the gulf have done so because they could make more m
ing there than by fishing on your coast ?—A. Certainly;
reason why I went to the United States—because I could do
than here.

Q. You will admit, at all events, that coming to the bay
ience with respect to keeping the crews together? The g
an important fishery to the Americans ?—A. It was so for
years, but this is not the case at the present time, from
learned.

Q. You do not pretend to know anything about this matt
—A. I know the result of the fisheries from the figures
and I know what is going on at Cape Ann.

Q. But figures sometimes do not stand investigation ?—A. Figures, they say, always tell the truth; "figures cannot lie."

Q. By coming to the bay you also avoided the fogs in summer on your coast?—A. Yes.

Q. I believe that either there is no fog at all or very little fog in the Bay of St. Lawrence during the summer?—A. There is then very little of it.

Q. You have been there from 1837 ?—A. No, from 1836.

Q. Up to 1868, off and on, almost every year?—A. Yes.

Q. And during that time you saw very little fog in the bay ?—A. No, not a great deal.

Q. What was the duration of the longest fog you ever saw in the bay ?—A. I could not tell you. Sometimes the fog lasted for twelve hours, but I do not know that it continued longer than that; such is not to my knowledge, as far as I can recollect, but it might have been longer sometimes.

Q. It was of very rare occurrence that the fog lasted longer ?—A. I think so. We very rarely saw a fog after we were once in the bay; up by the island and past East Point and up on Banks Orphan and Bradley, and such like, you would have very little fog.

Q. Were you in the bay in 1851 ?—A. Yes; I then made two trips.

Q. You must have been in the bay most of that season ?—A. Well ?

Q. You were in the bay in 1851 and 1853; do you recollect of seeing any fog at all there during either of these years ? In 1853 you were in the Highland Lass ?—A. In 1851 I was in the Alexander.

Q. In 1851 you made two trips ?—A. I did not go home with my first trip; I landed it with Mr. Martel, at Arichat; I had not time to go home, and so I landed 314 barrels there, and he advanced me the money to fit out.

Q. In that season you were two trips in the bay, during the whole of the summer and fall; when did you go out in the fall?—A. I think I left home on the 7th of July; I usually left home on my fishing trips on the 7th of July, and I think that I arrived home about the 18th or the 20th of October.

Q. You were in the bay during all the summer and a large portion of the fall; do you recollect any one day during this period when you saw a fog in the bay in 1851 ?—A. Well, I cannot say that it was then foggy, but there was a most almighty smoke. It was so smoky that you could not see anything for three, four, or five days; and owing to this fact that year I got out of the mackerel, and getting behindhand, I had to land those mackerel and could not go home.

Q. Where did this smoke come from ?—A. From all round; from fires at Miramichi and on the West Shore, and up that way; the smoke was so dense that you could not see half a mile for three, four, or five days, all the way from North Cape over to Escuminac.

Q. I suppose that no person with eyes in his head could help knowing the difference between that and fog ?—A. Certainly; there was smoke but no fog.

Q. Did that smoke hurt your rigging in any way?—A. No; the only way in which it hurt us was by preventing us getting any mackerel.

Q. Do you recollect having seen any fog in the bay in 1853?—A. O, well, these are questions that I could not answer correctly, and I do not want to answer unless I can do so. We do not care anything at all about fogs, and though it might be foggy sometimes, we would not think anything about it, or remark it. There is nothing in a fog that would be thought of importance.

Q. You landed these mackerel at Arichat?—A. Yes.

Q. Did you afterwards take them away?—A. Yes; but n had taken to Gloucester the 214 barrels which I caught on r trip. I then returned to Arichat, took these 314 barrels on b charges, and came home.

Q. Did not the landing of these mackerel at Arichat enab come back to the bay and take another fare?—A. Well, it enal go back; but the heft of the vessels went home. I got out of erel on account of the smoke.

Q. The right of so landing cargoes, or the exercise of this really does enable you to make a second and third trip, as the be?—A. I think that if such landing was not practiced it money in our pockets; if we did not so land mackerel it would in the owners' pockets.

Q. Does it enable you to make extra trips, or more trips tl otherwise be the case?—A. Well, I should suppose that it w us a little more time in the bay.

Q. And more opportunity for catching fish?—A. It gives ι 10 days more. I have made the passage from Canso home again, and packed my mackerel, in 10 days.

Q. But you would not put that time forward as a specimen ᐟ A. No.

Q. How long would it take ordinarily to make this pas: Well, two weeks or fifteen days would give ample time to go back and pack the mackerel, and fit out.

Q. Would not a fortnight in the height of the fishing seasor important period, particularly if mackerel were then plen Mackerel might be plentiful in bad weather.

Q. I mean during good fishing, with all the circumstances for it?—A. If all the circumstances were favorable, I could l these vessels in five days.

Q. And those five days would then be very important?—⌁ five days I could fill up, if the mackerel were just as I wanted it would be pretty hard to get them in that way.

Q. Are not mackerel fish that move about the bay fror place?—A. Yes.

Q. Sometimes they go inshore and sometimes they go out ing the first part of the year they go to the nor'ard, but after they move right round and come to the southward, school aft that is their track, and the man who keeps the best run of tl gets the most of them.

Q. Can you swear that they come southward?—A. No; b the way in which they are caught. Say they are on Banks (Bradley, then the next thing they will be gone to North Cap they will perhaps be down square off East Point; and they ν in that way.

Q. There are no marks about mackerel by means of whic he distinguished?—A. Not a bit of it; they may be caugh' Cape day after day, and then sink, and afterward rise and leaving no sight of them anywhere; when they come up, w good day's work, 75 barrels or such like for perhaps two or and he who keeps the best run of their movements, will obt share of the fish.

Q. The mackerel which are caught on Banks Orphan and l are afterward lost sight of, you cannot pretend to say you ι the same fish, in the fish which afterward rise up off Nort

Cape?—A. Well, I cannot identify them as the same; but that is
ay in which we catch them, whether they are the same mackerel
t.

Can you undertake to say that there are not different schools of
erel?—A. Of course not. I cannot tell you that.

Did you ever take them early in the spring when they are very
?—A. Well, one year I went out in the Abigail for early mackerel
North Bay; but that is the only year I did so. This was in 1851. I
fished on Banks Orphan and Bradley.

You did not get into the bay that year until the middle of July?—
the Abigail?

In 1851 you said you left home on the 7th of July?—A. In some
ls I left home on that date; but I left in that vessel in June.

I think you told me that you made two trips to the bay that year?—
did.

And that you left home on the 7th of July?—A. I said the 7th of
here, but I did not say the 7th of July yesterday. I did not say
ing about the 7th of July, except to-day. I left on the 7th of July
e Rose Skerritt, and in the Oliver Cromwell, and for a number of
I left Gloucester on that date.

When was this?—A. I went out in the Abigail in June, 1851.

You told me previously that in 1851 you made two trips and
ed on the 7th of July?—A. Well, then, we will rectify that; I went
ue in the Abigail, and got my trip on Banks Orphan and Bradley;
ny second trip, 75 barrels, in the bend of the island.

That was very early?—A. I went very early for poor mackerel.

That is the season when the mackerel are thin?—A. Yes; we call
leather-bellies; they are full of spawn, and mackerel number threes
, but nothing except number threes.

You do not catch number ones during that part of the season?—
o.

The best mackerel are caught in the fall?—A. You can get as
mackerel along in the last of August and in September as at any

Did you ever look at the eyes of those fish which you call by that
nt and I dare say appropriate name, to see whether there was a
over them?—A. Well, a maxim is current among fishermen, that
the scale comes off their eyes they are apt to bite.

You do know of this, then?—A. I do not know that the film exists;
ve looked a number of times, but I could never perceive whether
cales were off or not.

How long is it since you first heard of their having scales on their
?—A. O, since I first went to the United States.

And as soon as these scales come off they are ready to bite?—A.
is the assertion which is made, but I do not know whether it is
ase or not.

Did any person ever start a theory to you, to give a reason why
should be scales over their eyes?—A. No; but I have heard old
Atwood, of Provincetown, speak about it, though I cannot say
her he knows much about it or not. I never paid much attention
s statements.

Do you think that Mr. Attwood is a little wild in his theories?—
do not know. I have often heard him speak about these things;
urse what he said might all be so, but from my experience I do not
it; what he said went in at one ear and came out of the other, for
art, and that is about the heft I got of it.

Q. How did the idea about these scales become current amoi
men ?—A. I suppose it was due to their talking the matter over
mackerel do not bite very well they will ask whether the scal
their eyes or not, and say that when the scales are off they wi
fair catch; and they are always very anxious to examine the fi
whether the scales are off.

Q. Could they see whether this was the case or not?—A.
know that they could.

Q. How do you suppose that the idea started ?—A. I could
you.

Q. This idea is general, at any rate ?—A. It was talked abou
the fishermen.

Q. And generally believed among fishermen ?—A. I cannot
I do not believe in it, for one.

Q. But you are not all the fishermen ?—A. Of course not;
not believe in it. I cannot speak in this regard for others. I kn
ever, that it was the general talk among fishermen, and I ha'
great many examine the fish to see whether the scales were
wait for this patiently, hoping to get a good deck of mackerel
scales come off.

Q. How many barrels of flour would you put on board of th
vessel with 16 men, leaving Gloucester?—A. Eleven or twelve

Q. What kind of flour would this be ?—A. It would general
best.

Q. What would it cost?—A. From $9 to $10 a barrel.

Q. That was during the war?—A. And before the war.

Q. You do not mean to say that this was the case before th
A. It was sometimes $8 a barrel. The price varied.

Q. Do you not know that the price was nearer $5 than $8 ?-
price might have been $5 here, but this was not the case up
The price has never been $5 a barrel since I have been in the

Q. Or $6 or $7?—A. I have paid $7, $8, and $9 a barrel f
so on; we do not buy poor trash, but the best flour. The best flo
the best bread, and is the cheapest in the end.

Q. How much does coal cost?—A. We did not use to take
us at all; but of late years it has been taken.

Q. What kind of coal is generally taken ?—A. Hard coal.

Q. What do you pay for it?—A. The price varies from $7 to

Q. That must surely have been the price in American curre
greenbacks were at a considerable discount?—A. Yes.

Q. Because the hard coal used in these provinces comes
States?—A. Certainly; we burn it mostly. I never took it wi
one or two years, and that was when I was in the Scotland.

Q. If we can get such coal here at $5 a ton, how is it that
of it in the States is $6 or $7?—A. It comes to us from Phila
freighters, and we pay $5, $6, and $7 a ton for it.

Q. Can it be possible that you pay more for this coal in
country than we do here?—A. Yes; this coal is worth $6 a
in the United States. I have paid $6 and $6.50, and $6.25 i
on which I have agreed for this winter's supply.

Q. How many tons of coal would you take on a vessel ?—A
than five, at any rate.

Q. Where have you obtained your wood?—A. Generally
we always made a point of doing so.

Q. Because it is cheap at Canso?—A. Yes.

What is it a cord there?—A. $3 for about seven feet; they call a cord down there.

During your experience in the bay, what was the highest price aid for a cord of wood?—A. $3 to my knowledge.

Did you ever fish very much within the limits in the bay, after the l of the Reciprocity Treaty, in 1866?—A. I have tried inshore, but I found that I could do anything there. I invariably did better off

Was this because you had to watch the cutters?—A. No; I did ave to watch them when we had reciprocity.

I am speaking of the time when this treaty was abrogated; from to 1868, did you fish a great deal inshore without licenses?—A. did not. I did not fish inshore while I was in the Scotland at all. the heft of my mackerel around the Magdalen Islands.

Do you mean to say that you never fished inshore at all?—A. I tried inshore, but I never got mackerel there of any account.

These three years followed the close of the American war?—A.

And then you were not obliged to be armed to the teeth as be—A. No.

Did any cutters ever seize or try to seize you?—A. In those ?

Yes.—A. No.

But previously?—A. Yes.

When?—A. In 1851.

Where were you seized in 1851?—A. I was not seized. I never seized.

Was any attempt made to seize you?—A. Yes.

Where were you then fishing?—A. It was at the last of my trip I got those 214 barrels.

Where were you fishing?—A. Wide off Margaree—between that Cheticamp.

Which cutter attempted to seize you?—A. A man named Cutler, Guysborough, was there in a little pinkey; he was a spy, and he to make compromises when vessels got a good deck of mackerel vhere and were dressing them inshore. He would take 20 or 10 els, making as good a bargain as he could. This Cutler was in this ey, and I was at anchor under Margaree Island at the time.

Were you lying close inshore?—A. I was at anchor and not ng.

Lying close inshore?—A. Yes, right close in under Margaree for er. He did not attempt to take me; if he had I would have given a clout, but he took another vessel, the Harp, Captain Andrews. pt a watch all night, but they did not come alongside; if they had, vould have given them grape-shot, I bet.

Had you grape-shot on board?—A. We had a gun loaded with s, or something of that sort.

In fact, then, you were never boarded by a customs or seizing er?—A. I was boarded by an officer who came for light-money, at e Canso, that same year.

Did you pay the light-money?—A. No.

Why?—A. Because this man was not authorized to receive it.

What did you do?—A. I hove him into his boat, of course, and cid of him.

You knew that the light-money was due?—A. Certainly; and I willing to pay it, had the right man come for it.

Q. Did he represent himself to be a custom-house officer ?—

Q. Did you ask him for his authority ?—A. Yes.

Q. And did he show it ?—A. No.

Q. And then you threw him overboard ?—A. I told him he leave, and seeing he would not go, I seized him by the naps of t and the breeches and put him into his boat. He was bound to because I had landed a poor girl.

Q. Was this girl contraband ?—A. Yes, I suppose they calle at any rate. I do not know that she is now in town, but she lawyer Blanchard's wife afterward. I merely took her on bo passenger, and landed her. Afterward I was fired at and ch three cutters.

Q. For putting this officer overboard ?—A. No. I did not overboard, but I put him into his boat.

Q. In lawyer's phrase, did you gently lay hands on him ?— him in his boat in the shortest way. He stripped off and said i take a man to handle him, but I made up my mind that he she stop, though I did not want to fight; still, I was well able to own part. I talked with him and told him that I had merely l poor girl with her effects, a trunk and a bandbox, &c.; but th not do him. When he came aboard he asked, "Who is maste vessel?" Says I, "I am for lack of a better." Says he, "I s vessel," and with red chalk he put the King's broad R on the m He wanted the jib hauled down in order to have the boat t board—we had not come to an anchor—but I told him that h have to wait a while. Finally he came down below and I took pers out of a canister; and being a little excited, of course, in off the cover a receipt for light-dues, which I had paid th dropped on the forecastle floor. He picked it up and said he wc me a receipt on the back of it. Says I, "Who are you ?" He a "I am Mr. Bigelow, the light-collector." "Well," says I, "w your documents ?" Says he, "I have left them ashore." "Then "go ashore, you vagabond, you have no business here." Says he, you pay me ?" "Not a red cent," says I; "out with you." He c "Put the helm down." Says I, "Put the helm up"; but he can near shoving us ashore, as we were within 10 fathoms of th Says he, "Who are you ?" I said, "I am Mr. Pattillo." Says h vagabond, I know the Pattillos." "Well," says I, "then y know me, for there are only two of us." Says he, "I will take how; I will have a cutter from Big Canso. There will be a ma there; and if there is not a man-of-war, there will be a cutter there is not a cutter I will raise the militia, for I am bound to ta I asked him if he meant to do all that, and he said he was just to do it. I seized him to put him back into his boat, and he str and told me that it took a man to handle him; with that I mad at him, and jumped 10 feet. If he had not avoided me, I wo taken the head off his body. I then seized him and chucked his boat. Then three cutters came down and chased me.

Q. But they did not catch you ?—A. No; that was the time chased me at Port Hood and around there, and fired 11 balls— ers—at me, one boring her right through and through. The flew about 6 feet over my head, through the mainsail; the r right under the bends, through a plank, cut the timber, and wen a sail and into the main-boom; the next struck on the port si a piece of about 5 or 6 inches out of the bulwarks, and striking chains; the next knocked a piece off the forward part of the n about 4 inches above the saddle of the main-boom; and the next struck in the windlass-bit; five shots struck us, and we were chased between 6 and 7 miles.

Q. When did you go to Newfoundland for bait?—A. I was there, in Fortune Bay, in the Tiger. I was on the first vessel that ever got herrings there.

Q. Did you get the fish right inshore?—A. Yes, we got them through the ice; I was frozen in.

Q. When was this?—A. I left Cape Cod on this trip in 1838, and I arrived home again in 1839.

Q. Did you stay during the winter at Fortune Bay?—A. Yes.

Q. You got a cargo through the ice?—A. Yes, up at the head of the bay.

Q. Inshore?—A. Yes, right inshore. An army of 30 men, all armed to the teeth, came there to take us—five men and a black boy; but I drove the whole calabash of them off.

Q. You succeeded in securing a cargo, and in getting safe home?—A. Yes.

Q. Did you sell any of your cargo before you left?—A. No.

Q. Did you lose your papers?—A. Yes; they were taken from me. I handed them to the man who came to see about it, when I went on the ice. He said his name was Gadin, and that he came from Harbor Briton, on my asking who he was; I then asked to see his documents, and he handed them to me. I then knew what I had to do, and I gave him my papers; but I was too honest; I ought to have kept possession of his documents until he had handed me back my papers, but did not do so. Finally, I requested him to give me my papers, but he went off with his army.

Q. You staid all winter there?—A. We stopped there as long as we could, and took herring out of the ice. We got out of the ice on the 17th of April and reached home on the 14th of May.

No. 68.

Prof. SPENCER F. BAIRD, assistant secretary of the Smithsonian Institution, Washington, and United States Commissioner of Fish and Fisheries, called on behalf of the Government of the United States, sworn, and examined.

By Mr. Dana:

Question. It is not necessary, of course, to ask this witness any questions to show his position or general acquaintance with and knowledge of the subject. I would like, however, to have you state, if you please, as I am going to give, by and by, some of the results of your inquiries—I would like to have you state particularly how you have obtained, and from what sources you have obtained, information respecting the fisheries of late, besides what you have studied in books.—Answer. I have been in the habit for five years past of spending from two to three months on the sea-coast, for the purpose of prosecuting inquiries into the condition of the fisheries, to determine whether, as alleged, the American coast fisheries have been decreasing, and to ascertain what steps, if any, might be adopted to remedy the difficulty, if found. I have, in pursuance of that work, established stations in successive years at Eastport, Portland, Salem, Woods Holl, on the south coast of New England, and at Noank. And I have had with me a force of experts, naturalists, and gentlemen interested in the biology of fishes, and have endeavored to

gather such information as I could, from my own personal obse
and that of my colleagues, as well as by inquiries from fishern
others whom I have met.

Q. How far have you prosecuted that personal inquiry of the
men and persons engaged in the fisheries?—A. I have, by the h
phonographic secretary, taken the testimony of many hundreds
ermen along the coast in reference principally to questions in the
history of fishes. The facts as to the statistics of the fisheri
come out incidentally, and were not the original object of my
I was interested more in determining what kinds of fish we ha
natural, physical, or moral causes influenced them, and what wou
ably be the result of these causes, and how any evil influences (
remedied.

Q. Then have you employed fishermen to examine and m
quiries?—A. I have had in my employ several men, some for tl
year, or several years in succession, and others for a part of tl
who have taken a series of printed questions that I prepared in
to the natural history of fishes and pursued these inquiries in
where I myself could not go conveniently, especially in the wintei
or in the early spring.

Q. Then you issued some printed circulars?—A. Yes; a grea
thousand blanks, inviting responses, and I have had a reasona
centage of returns, of which I consider a fair percentage more
reliable. But, as a general rule, as everybody knows, fisherme
less about fish than they do about anything else. That is to sa
know how to catch fish and the practical details of their busin
of their natural history they know very little. About such ques
the time of their migration, the rate of their growth, their sp
seasons, and other matters, only here and there will you find a n
has observed and noted the facts closely enough to be able to
your questions.

Q. You employed some such persons?—A. I have one man es]
a skilled fisherman, resident on the south coast of New Engla
whom I employ to visit the different fishing stations and gatl
tistics.

Q. Have you any of those circulars about you?—A. I have oi
cular produced.)

Q. (Reading circular.) There are something like nearly nii
ferent questions. Under one head you require the man's na
Then as to the distribution of fishes: what kind of fish he ha
neighborhood, their abundance, migrations, movements, food,
ships, reproduction, artificial culture, diseases, pursuits, captu
economical value, application, &c.—A. That circular was issued
I have issued a great many editions of it. Then I have another
which refers more particularly to the coast and river fisheries.
only issued this within the present year.

By Hon. Mr. Kellogg:

Q. Was that about the time, Professor?—A. Yes; the fir
I did was to distribute these questions in order to get as i
formation as I could. I have some eight or ten special circu
these are the ones I have most used. I have issued special circ
the cod and mackerel and menhaden, but of these I have no
with me.

By Mr. Dana:

Q. Here (referring to circular spoken of as issued during the year) you have the home fisheries, the river fisheries; they don't come directly under our cognizance.—A. These are the coast and river fisheries particularly.

Q. Not the deep sea?—A. Only incidentally. They are sea coast fish, but not outside. There is a schedule of the principal fish marketed in the Boston market. My object was to get the number of pounds of these fish taken in the vicinity of the person to whom the circular was given.

Q. You think these have been pretty fully answered?—A. I have a great many answers.

Q. And from your information, which you gather as you go about, from what is sent to you by the return of these circulars, and from the persons employed by you, it has been your business to make yourself fully acquainted with the subject?—A. Yes; I have, of course, used what published material I have found. I found a great deal of value in the reports of the Canadian fisheries. What little I know of the fisheries in Canada I have learned from these documents.

Q. Wherever there are documents published by the United States you have them?—A. Yes; I have them; and I have European documents, English, and Norwegian, &c. I believe I have everything.

Q. I will question you first about codfish. I want you to state what is your opinion about the cod as a fish for all sorts of commercial purposes, as compared with others.—A. I think the cod stands at the head of fish at the present day. There is no fish that furnishes food to so many people, the production of which is of so much importance, or which is applied to such a variety of purposes. The commercial yield is very great, and its capture is the main occupation of a large portion of the inhabitants of the sea-coast region of the Northern Hemisphere.

Q. Besides as an article of food, either fresh or salted, what other purposes does it serve?—A. Well, it is applied to a great many purposes by different nations. It is used, of course, as food in the different modes of preparation. Particular parts are used as food, other than the muscles. The sounds are used as food, converted into gelatine, and in the form of isinglass. They serve a great variety of purposes. The roes are used as food and bait for fish. The skin is tanned for leather and clothing. A great many nations dress very largely in the skins of cod and salmon. And the fish is dried and used as food for cattle in Iceland and Norway. The bones are used as fuel in some places; and, of course, the oil is used for medicine, and for the various purposes to which animal oils are applied. There is scarcely any part that is not valuable. The offal, in Norway, is converted into a valuable manure. Every part is called into play.

Q. The bones?—A. They are burned as fuel, as well as eaten by dogs, or converted into fertilizers.

Q. It is not, probably, applied in the United States to all the uses you have specified?—A. No; I don't think the skin is used as clothing in the United States, but it makes an admirable leather for shoes, and makes very nice slippers. We have in Washington quite a large number of articles made from the skins, as used in Alaska, the Aleutian Islands, and in Siberia.

Q. You think they can be used?—A. I have no doubt in the course of years the skin will be utilized very largely. In fact, I may remark, that at the late exhibition at the Westminster Aquarium, among the special articles exhibited were shoes made from leather of the codfish, furnished by an exhibitor from Christiania.

Q. You think it is the foremost fish?—A. I think it is. There is none

that furnishes so important an industry or which is so abund
widely disseminated.

Q. What is the geographical distribution of the cod?—A. T:
quite a number of species of the cod, some characterized by
peculiarities and some by others. The cod in the North Pacific
ent from that in the North Atlantic. Both are, however, codf
no one could mistake them for anything else but cod. In the .
the cod are found on the American side from the Winter Quarter
on the coast of Virginia; that is the most southern point I hav
it to; from that indefinitely to the northward. It is found eve
upon the coast, in the Bay of Fundy, the Bay of St. Lawre
Labrador and Newfoundland, on the Grand Bank, and man
places. The European species, although by some considered
from ours, probably have a geographical range equally extensiv
lieve they are not in Spitzbergen.

Q. What is the most important locality?—A. Probably the i
portant single locality that furnishes the greatest amount of fish
least possible labor in the shortest possible time is that in the
of the Lofoden Islands, on the northwest coast of Norway. 1
region where usually twenty-five millions of fish are taken
mouths by some twenty-five thousand men. The Dogger Banl
North Sea, is another European locality. In America the mo:
sive stores of cod are found, I suppose, on the Grand Banks
Georges. They are found, perhaps, also on the great banks off t
of Labrador, twenty or thirty miles off the coast, extending for h
of miles.

Q. Now give the Commission some notion of the abundance
fish.—A. Well, I have covered that point in my reply to the
question. It is found in the greater part of those regions at sc
tion of the year. It is usually more abundant in the spring or :
autumn or winter, in each locality, in numbers only to be meas
the ability of man to capture.

Q. What do you say of their migrations?—A. The cod is a
migrations of which cannot be followed readily, because it is a
fish and does not show on the surface as the mackerel and herr
so far as we can ascertain, there is a partial migration, at least
the fish don't seem to remain in the same localities the yea
They change their situation in search of food, or in consequen
variations in the temperature, the percentage of salt in the
some other cause. In the south of New England, south of C
the fishing is largely off shore. That is to say, the fish are off
in the cooler water in the summer, and as the temperature
proaching autumn, and the shores are cooled down to a certai
they come in and are taken within a few miles of the coast.
northern waters, as far as I can understand from the writing:
Hind, the fish generally go off shore in the winter-time, exce
the south side of Newfoundland, where, I am informed, they
their stay, or else come in in large abundance; but in the Bay
on the coast of Maine, and still further north, they don't remai
to the shore in winter as in other seasons.

Q. Take them as a whole, then, they are a deep-sea fish.
mean the deep sea as distinguished from the Banks?—A. A
fish? Well, they are to a very considerable extent. The large:
are taken off shore, and what are taken inshore are in speciall:
localities, perhaps on the coast of Labrador, and possibly off N

They bear a small proportion generally to what is taken outside, the conveniences of attack and approach are greater.

Now, what is known about the spawning-grounds of codfish?—A. ck positive information in regard to the spawning-grounds of this xcept that we know single localities. We know the Lofodon Isl- ire great spawning-grounds. We know that the fish come there t exclusively for the purpose of spawning. They are not there in dinary times of the year. They come in December and January,)awn in February and March, and are there in most overwhelm-)undance.

But on the coast of America?—A. We know there is one large ling-ground in Cape Cod Bay.

You mean Massachusetts Bay inside?—A. Yes; there is said to 're a long reef about 4 miles wide and about 20 miles long, and d go in there and furnish a very important winter fishery.

hen, I presume, there are similar spots along the whole Ameri- ast?—A. Probably they spawn at the Georges, and undoubtedly reat many localities in the Bay of St. Lawrence and on the Banks, igh I cannot speak of that, because I haven't had an opportunity)wing.

What are the relations of cod to other fish?—A They are friends nemies. They are warriors and victims. They are extremely ous, and devour everything that is small enough, without any f consideration, and in turn are consumed in all their stages by sh as can master them. The adult fish are principally interfered y horse-mackerel, the bluefish, the porpoise, and by sharks, and ing else big enough to swallow them, instead of being swallowed m. It is merely a question of size whether the codfish is the) or passive agent.

Now, what fish do they devour mostly?—A. They eat everything, ley live very largely on herring or mackerel, or any of the small)und on the sea bottoms. They devour crabs and small lobsters. tomach of the cod is one of the best dredges you can have. You here sometimes rare specimens that are never found elsewhere.

Do they digest the shells?—A. No, they digest the nutriment and throw out the shells. Sometimes you find the shells packed solid iside of another like saucers in a pile. The wonder is how they 7 them out.

But they do?—A. I suppose they must.

By Hon. Mr. Kellogg:

They devour them whole and then when the meat is digested they the shells?—A. The mouth is quite large, and the shell goes out ily as it goes in.

By Mr. Dana:

What do you think are the seasons for spawning on the American ?—A. I presume that, like many other fish, they may spawn over a range of time. But, so far as our own observation on the ican coast goes, their season is from November until March. In Cod Bay they spawn about December and January. I have no ;, however, that farther north, where the changes of temperature)t so abrupt, they may spawn more irregularly, and have only an ·al of a few months when there is no spawning.

Will you describe this spawn so as to show the prolific nature of ;h?—A. The cod is one of the brag fish in regard to spawning. is, we hear of ordinary multiplication of fish by that process, but

the cod has been found to contain from three to seven million
actual count. Turbot, I think, are one of the very few fish
beat it. They run up to twelve millions.

Q. We do not have the real turbot ?—A. No. From three to
lion might be considered a fair annual estimate of the eggs of
fish. From three to five millions of ripe eggs have been foun
ovary of one single cod, and more.

Q. What becomes of these eggs when discharged ?—A. The
of the spawning places for codfish has been one that was origina
uncertain. The researches of naturalists have shown that th
are discharged in the open sea on the Lofoden Banks. Some m
the shore they can be found floating at the surface, and can l
up by the bushel in towing nets. The eggs are very small, fi
twentieth to one-fiftieth of an inch in diameter, and they have
globule of oil to make them float.

Q. Now, do these eggs all produce fish unless they are injured
way ?—No; there are a great many contingencies. It is not like
very large percentage will be fertilized by the male. There is a
uncertainty about that. Then, as they are floating in the wat
fish that may be fond of that kind of sustenance devours th
greedily, and by the time they are hatched out, a large perce
destroyed in this way. Then, the young fry, while in a helple
are devoured in large numbers. I should think it extremely
that not one hundred thousand out of the three millions—pos
ten thousand—attain to a condition in which they are able to t
of themselves. It is entirely impossible to make any estima
know, however, from the analogy of other fish—from the facts i
to salmon, shad, and that kind of fish we can make an approx

Q. These eggs rise to the surface ?—A. They float at various d
from the surface down. Some are a little heavier and som
lighter. I mean that they are not attached to the bottom
specific gravity is very nearly that of the water. Of course v
water is cold they will float better, because the density is gre
when the water is warm they will sink.

By Hon. Mr. Kellogg:

Q. Before you leave this subject I would like to ask wh
spawn are visible in the ocean, that is, cod-spawn. What is the
A. It is transparent, with a little spot of oil in one corner. Y
not notice it under ordinary circumstances, but you might if
looking for it.

Q. The ocean might be full and a common man would not se
Certainly.

By Mr. Dana:

Q. Be kind enough now to tell us what are the principal
capturing cod ?—A. The modes of capture vary with the regi
commercial purposes, the fish are caught with hand-lines and
line, or long line as it should be called. It is taken very large
nets on the coast of Norway and in some other regions. I be
so taken on the coast of Labrador, but I don't think it is
quently on our own coast in nets.

Q. To what extent is the trawl-line used ?—A. It is used al
world. It is one of the oldest methods of catching fish.

Q. From your investigation, do you think the capture of
erally, or codfish, or other kinds, by some contrivance like t

is as ancient as any other ?—A. I know it is. The Indians, the Aleutian Islanders, have used them.

Q. That was not derived from us ?—A. No. Travelers have found them in use when the first white men came among them. We have specimens in great number of the trawl of the native savage. Ours have only been brought in within the last five or six years. I don't think it is possible to fix the date of the first use of the trawl. They have been traced back to such a period that there is no possibility of saying that it was introduced by this man or known to that one.

Q. What are the advantages of the method of trawl-fishing for cod ?—A. The alleged advantages, as far as I have heard them spoken of, are the larger yield of the fishery. The same number of men in the same time, and in the same locality, will catch a larger fare of fish with the trawl than with hand lines. Then they require less exposure of the fishermen. They can be set over night and left down through the day at times when the weather would be too inclement for hand-line fishing. Then it requires much less skillful fishermen to use the trawl than the hand lines. It is merely a matter of putting on the bait and throwing it overboard, and it does not require the delicate manipulation and skill that the hand-line fishing does, and therefore does not call into play to the same extent the functions of the practiced fisherman.

Q. Now, are there any disadvantages connected with the use of the trawl alleged or actual ?—A. There are a great many accusations brought, against it. How far these are valid it is impossible for me to say. The principal objection I suppose is that it tempts all kinds of fish. One objection is that it takes fish that are too small size. They use a smaller hook than the ordinary hand lines, and they say it takes a great many unmarketable fish, which affects the supply. Then another complaint is that the fish being longer in the water are liable to be destroyed by the depredations of sharks, dogfish, and fish of that class. Another objection is that after the fish are caught the marketable fish, owing to their weight, slip off from the small hook and float away and are lost. Another objection is that they catch what they call mother fish, that is the parent fish, which some fishermen think should be left to reproduce their kind.

Q. If they are taken after depositing their spawn you only lose one fish ?—A. Yes ; but it is probable, judging from the testimony of fishermen, that the fish can be taken during their spawning season with a trawl when they will not bite a hook. As a general thing very few will bite on the ordinary line, but the trawl bait is said to be attractive to them, and the fish are believed to be more likely to take the bait at that time from a trawl than from a hook on an ordinary line.

Q. Well, taking the reasons given both ways, what conclusion have you come to about the use of the trawl for cod-fishing ?—A. Well, it is just one of the wholesale modes of capture, which it is difficult to avoid, because the tendency is to centralize, to accomplish the same work by less expenditure of money and of human force.

Q. Do you think it is a case for prohibition or regulation ?—A. I don't see how it can be either prohibited or regulated. I hardly see. Of course I have had no practical experience. I may say that the trawl is used very much less on the coast of America than on the coast of England and of Europe generally, and I have failed to find anywhere in the English writers or in the testimony of the British Fishery Commission any complaint there such as occurs in America. There is a great complaint there against what is called the beam-trawl. When they speak of the trawl they don't mean what we mean. What they refer to is a trawl

176 F

such as we use in our steamer to capture flounders and such
Wherever you see the word trawl used by an English or Euro[
writer you must apply it to that large net that is dragged behind
vessel along the bottom of the sea. The word trawl is never applie
Europe to the line, and, therefore, there is a great deal of vagueness
error involved in the consideration of the subject unless you know w
the particular speaker or witness means by a trawl. But speal
of the long line, which is the general term, or bultow, I have faile
find in the reports of the British Fishery Commission any complain
anybody except three cases of complaint against the trawl-line or 1
line. One was that it destroyed the young fish, and the others were ·
they interfered with the nets. They complained that the trammel
especially, which is a particular kind used in England, was fouled
these lines and injured.

Q. On the other hand, the net was in the way of the trawl ?—A.
the trawl was in the way of the nets. The trawlers didn't care at
the net, but the net fishermen did complain of the trawl. But I t
looked carefully to find whether there was any complaint against ·
line, and I haven't found it. There may be, but I am quite confi(
it has not assumed anything like the antagonistic features and imp
sion of magnitude that it has in the United States and Ameriea ;
erally.

Q. We mean by the trawl a long line weighted or anchored w]
sinks to the bottom and has—— A. It has branches three feet l(
That is called a long line or bultow.

Q. Then at intervals there are buoys ?—A. Yes.

Q. To show the position. They are usually in a straight line ?—A
Europe there are generally several shorter lines united in one long]
so much so that on the coast of Great Britain they have a line of tr:
six or eight miles in length. In America the trawling on the Bank
generally by means of five shorter lines radiating from the vessel,
in England the trawling is done generally on a large scale, without
boats, directly from a vessel of forty or sixty tons, and the entire s(
of lines is united in one and sunk.

Q. They are hauled in from aboard the vessel, and not from a
at all ?—A. Yes.

Q. Now, what do they call that which we call a trawl, if it is us(
all ?—A. They call it a long line or bultow.

Q. What bait do you find to be the best for codfish ?—A. W(
can't say I find any bait to be the best, because I never caught r
fish, but I know that everything of an animal nature, and to som(
tent vegetable, has been used for the cod. Generally, in America
bait consists of herring, menhaden, mackerel, a portion of the off;
the fish, sea-birds of various kinds, clams, squid, and the various sp
of shells, and in fact anything that can be got hold of.

Q. Well, now, what are the methods of preservation of this bait ?
have heard of their using salt clams, &c. Has much attention
paid to the possibility of greater preservation of the bait than we
ever yet had ?—A. Yes ; the science of preserving bait, as well as (
preservation of fish on shipboard, is very low indeed, far below
can be applied, and I have no doubt will be applied, both in keepin[
for food and in keeping it for bait.

Q. Now, will you state what observation you have made respe(
the method of preserving fresh bait from the start all the v(
through ?—A. As a general rule it is now preserved, either by s:
or freezing. Of course they keep it as long as it will remain wi

spoiling, and when you have to carry it beyond that time, either ice it or salt it. Salting, of course, is a very simple process, but it alters materially the texture and taste to such a degree that fish or other bait that under certain circumstances is highly prized by the fish, is looked upon with a great deal of indifference when salted. Now, there are special methods of preserving the fish or bait by some chemical preparation, which preserves the fish without giving the saline taste. There are preparations by means of which oysters or clams or fish can be kept in solutions for six months without getting any appreciable taste, and without involving the slightest degree of deterioration or destruction. One process submitted to the group of judges of whom I was chairman, was exhibited by an experimenter who placed a great jar of oysters in our room prepared in that way. I think about the 1st of August those were placed in our room and they were kept there until the middle of September, for six weeks during the hottest portion of the centennial summer, and that was hot enough. At the end of that time we mustered up courage to pass judgment upon this preparation, and we tasted these oysters and could not find them affected. We would have preferred absolutely fresh oysters, but there was nothing repugnant to the sensibilities, and I believe we consumed the entire jar. And we gave the exhibitor, without any question, an award for an admirable new method. That man is now using that process on a very large scale in New York for the preservation of fish of all kinds, and he claims he can keep them any length of time and allow them to be used as fresh fish quite easily. I don't suppose any fisherman ever thought of using any preservative except salt.

Q. That is entirely experimental?—A. It is experimental, but it promises very well. Now, borax is one of the substances that will preserve animal matter a great deal better than salt and without changing the texture. Acetic acid is another preparation, or citric acid will keep fish a long time without any change of the quality, and by soaking it in fresh water for a little while the slightly acidulated taste will be removed. I don't believe a cod will know the difference between a clam preserved in that way and a fresh clam.

Q. Now, about ice. We know a good deal has been done in the way of preserving bait in ice. How far has that got?—A. It is a very crude and clumsy contrivance. They generally break up the ice into pieces about the size of pebble stones, or larger; then simply stratify the bait or fish with this ice, layer and layer about, until you fill up a certain depth or distance. The result is that if the bait can be kept two weeks in that method it is doing very well. They generally get a period of preservability of two weeks. The ice is continually melting and continually saturating the bait or fish with water, and a very slow process of decomposition or disorganization goes on until the fish becomes musty, flabby, and tasteless, unfit for the food of man or beast.

Q. Well, there is a newer method of preservation, is there not?—A. There is a better method than using ice. The method described by the Noank witness, by using what is equivalent to snow, allows the water to run off or to be sucked up as by a sponge. The mass being porous prevents the fish from becoming musty. But the coming methods of preserving bait are what are called the dry air process and the hard freezing process. In the dry air process you have your ice in large solid cakes in the upper part of the refrigerator and your substance to be preserved in the bottom. By a particular mode of adjusting the connection between the upper chamber and the lower there is a constant circulation of air by means of which all the moisture of the air is continually being

condensed on the ice, leaving that which envelops the bait or fi
fectly dry. Fish or any other animal substance will keep almost
nitely in perfectly dry air about 40° or 45°, which can be attaine
readily by means of this dry air apparatus. I had an instance of
the case of a refrigerator filled with peaches, grapes, salmon, a
mutton, and some beefsteaks, with a great variety of other subs
At the end of four months in midsummer, in the Agricultural Bu
these were in a perfectly sound and prepossessing condition.
would have hesitated one moment to eat the beefsteaks, and one
be very glad of the chance at times to have it cooked. This re
tor has been used between San Francisco and New York, and b
Chicago and New York, where the trip has occupied a week or te
and they are now used on a very large scale, tons upon tons of
and pears being sent from San Francisco by this means. I had a
of fish-eggs brought from California to Chicago in a perfect cor
Another method is the hard frozen process. You use a freezing r
of salt and ice powdered fine, this mixture producing a tempera
twenty degrees above zero, which can be kept up just as long
occasion requires by keeping up the supply of ice and salt.

Q. How big is the refrigerator?—A. There is no limit to the si
may be used. They are made of enormous size for the purpose
serving salmon, and in New York they keep all kinds of fish.
been in and seen a cord of codfish, a cord of salmon, a cord of
ish mackerel, and other fish piled up just like cord-wood, dry, ha
firm, and retaining its qualities for an indefinite time.

Q. Well, can fish or animals be kept for an unlimited period it
in that way?—A. You may keep fish or animals hard dried fro
a thousand years or ten thousand years perfectly well, and be a
there will be no change.

Q. Have geologists or paleontologists satisfied themselves of
actual cases of the preservation of animal substances for a long pe
A. Yes; we have perfectly satisfactory evidence of that. Abo
years ago the carcass of a mammoth, frozen, was washed out f
gravel of the river Lena, I think, one of the rivers of Siberia, a
in such perfect preservation that the flesh was served as food
dogs of the natives for over six months. Mr. Adams, a St. Pet
merchant, came along on a trading expedition, and found it nea
sumed, and bought what was left of it for the St. Petersburg A
of Science—the skeleton and some portion of flesh—which w
served first in salt and afterward in alcohol. Well, we know th
of time that must have elapsed since the mammoth lived in tl
circle must be very long. We know we can talk with perfect s
ten thousand years. The geological estimate of it is anywhe
fifty to a hundred thousand years; we cannot tell. There is n
measure; we know it must have been some hundreds of thousa
probably it would have remained in the same condition as muc

Q. Now, to come to a practical question, is this a mere m
theory or of possible use? For instance, could this method be
to the preservation of bait for three or four months if necessa
The only question, of course, is as to the expense. There is no
at all that bait of any kind can be kept indefinitely by that pr
do not think there would be the slightest difficulty in building
erator on any ordinary fishing-vessel, cod or halibut, or othe
vessel, that should keep with perfect ease all the bait necess
long voyage. I have made some inquiries as to the amount of
I am informed by Mr. Blackford, of New York, who is one of th

operators of this mode, that to keep a room ten feet each way, or a thousand cubic feet, at a temperature of 20° above zero, would require about 2,000 pounds of ice and two bushels of salt per week. With that he thinks it could be done without any difficulty. Well, an ordinary vessel would require about seventy-five barrels of bait—an ordinary trawling-vessel. That would occupy a bulk something less than 600 feet, so that probably four and a half tons of ice a month would keep that fish. And it must be remembered that his estimate was for keeping fish in midsummer in New York. The fishing-vessels would require a smaller expenditure of ice, as these vessels would be surrounded by a colder temperature. A stock of ten to twenty tons would in all probability be amply sufficient both to replace the waste by melting and to preserve the bait.

Q. Have you any doubt that some method like that will be put into immediate and successful use, if there is sufficient call for it?—A. I have no doubt the experiment will be tried within a twelvemonth. Another method of preserving is by drying. Squid, for instance, and clams, and a great many other kinds of bait can be dried without using any appreciable chemical, and can be readily softened in water. I noticed lately in a Newfoundland paper a paragraph recommending that, in view of the fact that the squid are found there for a limited period of time, the people should go into the industry of drying squid for bait, so that it would always be available for the purpose of cod-fishing. I think the suggestion is an excellent one, and I have no doubt it will be carried out.

Q. Now, what is the supply of bait for codfish on the American coast? —A. Well, as the codfish eats everything, there is a pretty abundant stock to call upon. Of course, the bait-fish are abundant, the menhaden and herring. The only bait-fish that is not found is the caplin. The herring is very abundant on the American coast, and the alewives enormously abundant. Squid are very abundant of two or three species, and, of course, clams of various kinds. Then we have one shell-fish that we possess. It is never used here, although it is very abundant; but it is almost exclusively the bait for trawling on the coast of Great Britain. This shell-fish is known as the whelp, or winkle.

Q. Is it a kind of mussel?—A. No; it is a kind of univalve shell (submits specimen), and is almost exclusively used for the capture of cod in England on deep-water trawl-liners. It is not used here at all.

Q. Why is it not used here?—A. I don't know except that they have other bait that they get at more readily, and they have not learned how to use this.

Q. But it is very abundant?—A. Yes; quite as abundant as it is anywhere. This is a rather small specimen. The advantage of this kind of bait is that it can be kept alive for a long time merely by moistening it or keeping it in water, so there is no question about salting it or using ice or any other application.

By Sir Alexander Galt:

Q. Is there any particular locality for that?—A. It is extremely abundant all through the northern seas. I am a little surprised that I have not seen more of them here. It is a northern shell. I presume it is very abundant in Newfoundland, and to the north. At any rate it is in any desired abundance in the Bay of Fundy, but not south of Cape Cod.

Q. From all you have learned, have you any doubt that, supposing the fishermen of the United States were precluded from using any bait ex .

cept what could be got upon their own coast, they could obtain
cient supply there ?—A. Well, unless the American fishery sh
expanded to very enormous limits, far in excess of what it is now
see that there would be any difficulty. I may refer to one bait
command, which is an excellent bait—salt liver. In some parts
considered an excellent bait. Of course each'part of the world
by its own particular bait. While the Cape Cod man swears 1
haden, the Newfoundlander by herring and caplin, and the Eng
by winkles, the Dutchman swears by salt liver.

Q. We could have that, of course.—A. Yes. Then the roes
are good for bait.

Q. What do you say about gurry ? We had a good deal abc
in the early part of this inquiry. Be so good as to tell what
you have or what conclusion you have come to about its use and
—A. It hardly applies to cod any more than to any other fish
at sea. The gurry is the offal, and that of course may be of sa
cod or haddock or mackerel. The practice of throwing overboar
is in many respects reprehensible, because in the first place it is
great waste of animal matter. The applicability of this offal to c
cial purposes is such that whenever it can be had in sufficient qu
it should be utilized. It is so on the coast of Norway. An en
number of pounds of fertilizer are made out of the gurry, and th
are dried and used for food for dogs and cattle. I presume yo
however, to the supposed influence of the gurry on the fishing ;
more particularly. Well, in the first place more of it can be us
In the process of hard freezing applied to cod it is brought in m
fresh fish. But a large proportion of what is thrown overboard
utilized. It can all be utilized, and it would be very proper, I tl
impose some penalty upon the waste of the gurry by throwing
board, in favor of securing its preservation and utilization.
course the question is as to what influence the gurry can exerci
the sea fishery supposing it to be abundant and to be throw
board. I have no practical experience in regard to that. I
great many persons testify that it is very objectionable. The
why I should be inclined to attribute very little importance to
jection is the readiness with which all such offal is consumed in
by the scavengers appointed by nature to destroy it. In the 1
seas, where codfish are most abundant and this gurry is in the
abundance, the waters abound with countless numbers of minu
taceans whose business it is to destroy animal matter. The
sea fleas are so active that if you take a fish the size of a cod
put it in a bag of net-work and put it overboard where it will be
for a tide in water, of anywhere from five to ten or twenty fath
will find, as a general rule, that next day you will have the bone
clean and a perfect skeleton without a single particle of flesh.
had thousands of skeletons (I may say literally so) of fishes a
and small quadrupeds prepared for museum purposes by simpl
ing them to the action of the sea fleas. I have put them in ba
rated with holes and left them at the edge of low tide for a tide
and the skeleton would be perfectly complete without a bit of n

Q. Well, these sea scavengers, are they usually at the bott
Everywhere, at the bottom and the top. Then there are the dog
small sharks, catfish, goosefish, sculpins, and the codfish them
variety of lobsters, and other inhabitants of the sea, that are
always ready and eager to seize anything of this kind and con
Then when the bones are exposed there are the sea-urchins, tl

a specialty of devouring them. Now, I cannot say but that this material, under certain circumstances, may lodge in the crevices of the rocks and remain there and become an offense to the surrounding fish, but I rather suspect that the trouble about the gurry is that it attracts the predatory fish. Where it is thrown overboard it tolls them from a long distance. The dogfish, the shark, and other fish are attracted and come to the place where this offal has been thrown overboard, and after they have consumed all that they turn their attention to the cod and other fish that may be there and drive them off.

Q. So that even throwing overboard the gurry there is a danger of defeating your own purpose?—A. Yes; certainly. That is the hypothesis given as to the supposed evil effect of throwing overboard the offal in the European waters. It prevents the fishing there as long as this state of things lasts, but whether there is an actual injury otherwise I cannot say. The general presumption is against the idea that these substances can have a lodgment for any length of time to produce any offense. It might do it in fresh water. In the lakes you may have such a condition where those scavengers are not provided. But it hardly seems to me that it can be in the seas, in the northern seas especially.

Q. What is the geographical distribution of mackerel?—A. The mackerel is a fish that has not so northerly a distribution as the cod, and perhaps extends somewhat further south; otherwise it is found over, to a very considerable extent, the same range. It is found as far south as the Azores in European waters, and as far as Spitzbergen and Norway to the north. On our southern coast we find it very rarely, and very few individual specimens have been taken in the vicinity of Charleston. It has never been taken in the West Indies; never in Bermuda, I believe; but it is found as far north as the Straits of Belle Isle, and how much further north I cannot say. The two species (American and European) are believed to be identical, and although they are constantly within a comparatively small number of leagues of each other, yet they do occur all the way across.

Q. What is the season for mackerel?—A. In America the mackerel season is in spring, summer, and autumn. In winter they are not found on our coast, and we don't get them, but we have them on our shores as early as the middle of April and as late as November.

Q. Now, as to the variation of seasons. What do you say about that? —A. It is very rarely they appear in the same abundance in two successive years, or, at least, it is rarely that the sum total of the experience of the fishermen gives about the same aggregate. Sometimes they are so scarce that the actual catch of one year will be much below that of other years, but we cannot say there are any fewer fish actually in the water. It may be that they take a different line; they may keep in different waters; they may show themselves less to fishermen; and may have other modes of variation; but we only know by the practical results of fishing that the catch in some seasons is much greater than in others.

Q. What do you think is known or what do you think is the best conjecture as to their migrations?—A. There have been a great many hypotheses on the subject of the migration of mackerel. At one time mackerel, as was supposed to be the case with cod and sea-herring, was believed to have an extreme range, that a large school traversed the coast of America or Europe, and swept over a range of thousands of miles, making a circuit that occupied one year in its completion. But the evidence at the present time tends to show that the mackerel comes in on the American coast as a great army, broadside, and appears within a

reasonable length of time, or very nearly the same time, on all that extent of coast.

Q. Do you think it strikes the coast a little later to the north and a
little earlier to the south ?—A. The left wing of the army, as we might
call it, strikes the American coast first, and the right wing strikes the
Bay of St. Lawrence last; but it comes in with a broad sweep, not moving along the coast but coming in broadside. When the quickening influence of the spring sun is felt on this great body of fish somewhere
outside, where I cannot say, they start, and the given temperature is
reached sooner at Cape Hatteras than at Bay St. Lawrence; but I do
not believe that the fish that enter the bay always skirt the American
coast, nor do I believe that the American fish go into the bay. They
come in a large number of schools, each school representing a family,
that is, they spawn together, and they may have a short lateral movement, and may move a limited number of miles along the coast till they
find a satisfactory spawning-ground ; but, as a general rule, they aggregate in three large bodies; one of those bodies is about Block Island and
Nantucket shoals, another is in the Gulf of Maine and Bay of Fundy,
and another in Bay St. Lawrence. There are connections between those
three bodies. You find them all along the coast; there are a certain
number which spawn and are taken all along the coast; they are
caught in weirs and pounds in spring and fall within one hundred yards
of the shore; but the mass, as far as I can learn from the testimony presented before the Commission, are aggregated in those three great bodies.

Q. Is anything known about their winter quarters ?—A. Nothing
definite. We miss them for several months, from the end of November
until March and April, and we say, we guess, we suggest they go into
the Gulf Stream. That they go somewhere where they can find a temperature that suits them and there they remain, is clear ; but it is a little
remarkable that they never have been seen schooling in the Gulf Stream,
that they never have shown themselves, that no fisherman, mackereler,
or steamboat captain has ever reported, so far as my information goes,
a school of mackerel in the winter season. If they were free swimmers,
one would suppose they would show themselves under such circumstances. There is a belief very generally entertained among fishermen
that they go into the mud and hybernate. That is an hypothesis I have
nothing to say against. It seems a little remarkable that so free a
swimmer as the mackerel should go into mud to spend its winter, but
there is abundance of analogy for it. Plenty of fish bury themselves in
mud in the winter time and go down two or three feet deep. There are
fish that are so ready to bury themselves in mud you can dig them out
of an almost dry patch as you could potatoes. The European tench,
the Australian mud-fish, and dozens of species do that. There is nothing
whatever in the economy of the mackerel or in the economy of fish generally against this idea, that it is an inhabitant of the mud. And the
fishermen believe that the scale, which grows over the eyes, according
to their account, in winter, is intended to curb their natural impetuosity
and make them more willing to go into mud and stay there in winter
and not be schooling out on the surface of the water. There are well-
authenticated cases of fish being taken from the mud between the prongs
of the jig when spearing for eels. That this has occurred off the Nova
Scotia coast, in St. Margaret's Bay and Bras d'Or, Cape Breton, and
parts of the Bay of St. Lawrence, I am assured is not at all doubtful.

Q. Do not fishermen mainly retain the old theory of the northern set
of the whole body ?—A. Very largely, but I think lately they are
changing their views.

By Hon. Mr. Kellogg:

Q. The fish were mackerel that were brought out of the mud?—A. When after eels they brought up mackerel out of the mud, in several instances, in January.

By Mr. Dana:

Q. What can you tell the Commission about the period of the spawning of mackerel?—A. Mackerel spawn almost immediately after they visit our shores. The earliest fish taken in the weirs, and pounds in Vineyard Sound and Buzzard's Bay are full of ripe spawn, so that when the fish are taken out of the pounds and put into boats to bring them to shore there are sometimes quarts and pecks of the spawn in the bottom of the boats. It runs out with the utmost freedom, as it does with any full-spawning fish. That period ranges from the middle of May on our coast, and from June and July in Bay St. Lawrence. Mr. Whiteaves says they spawn in Bay Chaleurs in June. The season extends from the early part of May to the beginning of July.

Q. Where do the mackerel deposit the eggs?—A. The mackerel, like all sea fish, with the exception of the herring, the tom-cod, and sculpin, has a free floating egg. The egg is discharged in the water wherever the fish happen to be, inshore or offshore, and it floats just under the same condition that the egg of the cod does. It has a small globule of oil as a buoy, and it floats on the surface or anywhere from that to half way down, or, perhaps, almost to the bottom, depending on the gravity of the egg and the specific gravity of the water.

Q. Is the mackerel supposed to be able to control the time when it will spawn?—A. When the egg is ripe it has to be discharged, whatever happens. The egg cannot be retained after it is overripe.

Q. How do the eggs of each mackerel compare in numbers with those of the cod?—A. The average of the mackerel spawn is about 500,000. They are very small, as you can imagine, for mackerel is not a very large fish. The eggs, when spawned, are only about one-fiftieth of an inch in diameter, about half the size of that of the cod. They vary in size, some being smaller and others larger, but they only vary within moderate limits.

Q. You say they spawned all along the American coast?—A. I presume they spawn in some numbers along the entire coast from the shore of Virginia to the coast of Labrador; formerly they spawned on the coast of Newfoundland, when mackerel were caught there, where they were very abundant a great many years ago, and also off the Bay of Fundy, when mackerel were abundant there.

Q. What is the food of the young mackerel?—A. The young mackerel, like the young of most other fish, feed on *diatoms* and other marine plants of low origin. They feed on the eggs of crabs and marine animals, probably on the small eggs of fish themselves, and as they grow they eat anything small enough to be swallowed. They don't bite as bluefish do, but they take everything at one mouthful and swallow it whole.

Q. And what is the food of the adult fish?—A: The adult fish feed very largely upon young fish, sand lantz and young herring, and probably upon the young of their own kind. They are cannibals, as all fish are. They feed very largely upon what is called bay-seed or cayenne; that is a minute kind of shrimp, which is so diminutive you require a microscope to separate it into its component parts. They feed also on large shrimps and on the young of large crabs. Its favorite food in summer is what fishermen have described as all eyes, that is, young fish which, so far as I can judge, must be young mackerel, because I do not know

any other fish that could be so abundant of that size at that s
the year. It is called all-eyes, because its body is perfectly tran
and when you see them swimming in the sunlight you can only
eyes, as two small, dark specks. That occurs in almost incredil
dance, covering miles square, and furnishing food for an euormc
of fish.

Q. With regard to its bearing upon the locations of mackerel
ask whether there is any particular place where the food of mac
to be found, or whether it is all along the coast where the r
come ?—A. The shrimp belongs to a class of crustaceans which
the high seas everywhere. We took them this year in great q'
in coming across from Salem to Halifax, at George's, La Ha
Brown's Banks, and in Halifax Harbor. We take them in F
Salem, and Portland Harbors, and, as far as I am advised, by
cialists who are associated with me, there is no part of the ocea
these small animals are not to be found in ample abundance, so
enormously aggregated and at other times less common. T
found at all depths of water, from the surface to the bottom.
them in our dredge and in our midway and surface nets. Th
the young of the large crabs are found under all circumstances
ditions.

Q. Then we take the common bait, pogies, or menhaden. '
mackerel bait, are they not?—A. Eaten by mackerel? I do n
they are, unless they eat them in the winter time.' As to the s
of pogies, we know nothing about it; we infer they spawn in w
the southern coast.

Q. Are not menhaden used as bait for mackerel by fisherm
The menhaden itself is taken all through the mackerel season
part of the American coast.

Q. Is it abundant within your observation ?—A. Yes; it is al
most abundant of our fish; indeed, it is a question which is mo
dant, sea-herring or menhaden.

Q. In regard to the catching of mackerel as affecting the su
the probable diminution or increase of mackerel, what have y
the Commission about the mode of taking mackerel?—A. The
is taken in a great variety of ways. At present it is taken by
and by the net in some form. Formerly it was taken by means
as we do for bluefish, sailing backward and forward in a boat
number of lines put from the vessel, and taking them when t
is under full speed. That method is still practiced on the coa
rope, where mackerel are still taken in that way. Then it w
that by keeping the vessel comparatively motionless and throw
or chopped meat overboard mackerel could be brought up to t
and that proved a much more efficient and thorough mode of
Nets were introduced, and many mackerel are now taken in
Seines, which are hauled to the shore, have been introduced
places on the coast of Nova Scotia, and a good many mackerel
in pounds and weirs, enormous quantities being taken in s
fall on the New England coast in that way. The purse-seine i
the most efficient and comprehensive method, and it is used b

Q. What is the proper depth of a purse-seine ?—A. Twenty
five, or thirty fathoms deep.

Q. To be successful it has to have that depth ?—A. It has t
but it must be shallower than the water, or it will get enta
torn.

Q. Do you know whether it is true that there must be that

order that the mackerel shall not discover it so quickly and escape ?—A. I could not say; that is a fisherman's theory, which I know nothing about.

Q. With regard to the preparation of mackerel, what have you to say ?—A. Nothing, except that they are used in increasing numbers fresh. The principal consumption in Europe is in fresh fish. The people there do not salt fish, or scarcely at all. They are put up in Europe, and I believe, to some extent, in Canada in cans; I do not think that is done in the United States.

Q. Of course, you have obtained information as to the manner in which the fish can be used by consumers; you have nothing to do with the mercantile side of the question ?—A. No.

Q. You have had it presented to you. Do you find that the demand for fresh fish of all kinds is increasing ?—A. I know the tendency at the present day is to substitute fresh fish for salt, in view of the improved methods of preparation and preservation, and the improved means of communication, railroads and steamboats coming to the shores and carrying away the fish and distributing it over an extent of thousands of miles and more in the interior, it bringing a much better price as fresh fish, and yielding a much better profit to the seller.

Q. Is that trade rapidly increasing ?—A. It is increasing with enormous rapidity. Every year witnesses a great extension of the methods and increased improvements in the mode of preparation and the size of the refrigerators and their number.

Q. In regard to herring, what have you to say ?—A. Herring is a fish of wide range. Though I cannot say it goes further north than cod—perhaps it does not—it goes scarcely as far south on the American coast. I have not found any evidence of it being taken south of Block Island. It is very abundant off Block Island and Narragansett Bay in winter, but whether it is found further south I am unable to say; it is found as far north as Labrador, and much further.

Q. It is found from Block Island to the shores of Labrador in great abundance ?—A. Yes.

Q. It is pretty fairly distributed all along ?—A. Yes; in some localities they are found in greater abundance at some periods of the year; but there is no part of the American coast, from Labrador to Block Island, where they are not found during a certain number of months.

Q. What are the movements of this fish ?—A. They present migrations not so extensive and demonstrative as that of mackerel, but more so than those of cod. They probably move from their ground from time to time in search of food, and generally have definite places for spawning, to which they resort at different seasons of the year at each particular coast. While the spawn is deposited, as a general rule, in certain localities, it is sometimes a matter of uncertainty. The destruction of herring has been less in America than in Europe, where it has been very marked. There are extensive regions where formerly the herring business was carried on, from which they have entirely disappeared, so much so that they import herring from Scotland and America.

Q. As to the egg of the herring ?—A. The egg is larger than that of the cod, and is about one-twentieth of an inch in diameter.

Q. What is the number to each fish ?—A. About 30,000.

Q. Do you think they have any particular spawning-ground ?—A. They have definite localities that are preferred by them. They spawn round the Magdalen Islands in great abundance, and in the bays of Newfoundland. The most extensive spawning-ground on the southern coast is round the southern end of Grand Manan, which is one of the most interesting and extensive spawning-grounds I know of. But they spawn also all along the reefs and rocky places of the New England coast as far as No Man's Land and Block Island.

Q. The yield of herring in New England, is it and can it be made very large?—A. I presume as many herring could be taken in New England, in seasons when they are able to be taken, as might be called for, if the price of them warranted it.

Q. Herring does not bring much in the market?—A. I believe not; they are taken in both spring and fall, but they are most abundant in the fall.

Q. I should like to put one or two questions to you bearing a good deal on this subject which the Commission has before it, respecting the kinds of fish which can be and are used in the United States. Leaving out cod, mackerel, and herring, will you tell the Commission what has been discovered regarding the kinds of fish that are used as a substitute for mackerel—salted fish, I mean?—A. There is a great variety in vast abundance of many kinds of fish all along the coast of the United States, from Saint John's River, Florida, and further south to the Bay of Fundy, and many of those could be utilized to very great advantage if there was a demand. They are taken in very large quantities and consumed as fresh fish, but they are not prepared in large quantities, with the exception of the Southern mullet.

Q. How far north is mullet found?—A. It straggles as far as Cape Cod; it is quite abundant at some seasons on the south side of New England, but not sufficiently so for marketable purposes, but off the coast of Virginia, and off the Carolinas, and all the way down to the extremity of Florida, the mullet is in quantities scarcely credible. They are taken and sold in great numbers; many thousands of barrels are put up, and if there was any speedy call for them they could be furnished. I presume I am safe in saying that one million barrels of mullet could be furnished annually from the south shore of Chesapeake Bay to the south end of Florida, if they were called for.

Q. How far has the mullet come into the market now?—A. The mullet does not come into the Northern market at all, but in North Carolina, South Carolina, and Georgia it fills the markets at the present time, excluding other kinds of imported fish. In former years there was a great demand for herring and mackerel, but the mullet is supplying the markets because they are sold fresher and supplied at much lower price, and they are considered by the Southern people a much superior article of food.

Q. Is it preferred to mackerel as a salted fish?—A. The persons familiar with mackerel and with mullet from whom I have made inquiries—I never tasted salt mullet—give the preference to mullet. It is a fatter, sweeter, and better fish, and of rather larger size. They grade up to 90 to a barrel of 200 pounds, and go down to three-quarters of a pound, and as a salt fish the preference is given by all from whom I have inquired to the mullet.

Q. Do you think the failure of the mackerel market in the Southern and Southwestern States is largely attributable to the introduction of mullet?—A. I cannot say that, but I imagine it must have a very decided influence.

Q. Can the mullet be caught as easily as mackerel?—A. More easily. It is entirely a shore fish, and is taken with seines hauled up on the banks by men who have no capital, but who are able to command a row-boat with which to lay out their seines, and they sometimes catch 100 barrels a day per man, and sometimes as many as 500 barrels have been taken at a single haul. The capital invested is only the boat, the seine, perhaps 100 or 200 yards long, the salt necessary for preserving the fish, and splitting boards and barrels.

Q. Can pounds be used ?—A. They have not been used, and I doubt whether they could be used. Pounds are not available in the sandy regions of the South.

Q. They are taken by seining ?—A. Yes, seines can be used. This work is entirely prosecuted by natives of the coast, and about two-thirds of the coast population are employed in the capture of these fish.

Q. Then the business has grown very much ?—A. It has grown very rapidly.

Q. When was it first known to you as a fish for the market ?—A. I never knew anything about it until 1872.

Q. Then it has been known during only five years ?—A. I cannot say; it has been known to me that length of time.

Q. During that time the business has very much increased ?—A. I am so informed; I cannot speak personally. All my information of it is from reports made to me in replies to circulars issued in 1872 and 1873. I have not issued a mullet circular since that time, when I issued a special circular asking information regarding the mullet.

Q. Then it is your opinion that the mullet has become, to some extent, and will become, an important source of food supply ?—A. It is destined, I suppose, to be a very formidable rival and competitor of the mackerel. I know in 1872 a single county in North Carolina put up 70,000 barrels of mullet, a single county of five States covering the mullet region.

Q. Repeat that statement.—A. I say 70,000 barrels of mullet were packed in Carteret County, North Carolina, in 1872—one county in the States of Virginia, North Carolina, South Carolina, Georgia, and Florida, where mullet occurs in great abundance during two or three months of the year. It is during the spawning season of the mullet that it is taken in this quantity, and mullet roes form a special delicacy over which every Southerner exults. It is a separate business, the roes being smoked and salted and sold in large quantities.

Q. Perhaps a reason—to get into the region of political economy— why mullet-fishing was not prosecuted formerly, was that the Southern people were not fishing-people under the slave system ?—A. They probably had not a proper method of taking them. They used more casting nets than seines.

Q. State to the Commission what mode of fishing and what kinds of fish are caught on the south of the New England coast, south of Cape Cod. Is it not a great region for fish ?—A. The variety of fish taken on the shores south of Cape Cod is very great, and constitutes a very important element in the food resources of the country. Many of them are fish of very great value as food, some selling as high as one dollar per pound, every pound of that fish that can be brought into market bringing never less than 60 cents, and up to one dollar per pound. Other fish range from 20 cents, 35 cents, and 40 cents per pound. Others from 20 cents to 25 cents, very few bringing less than 8 cents and 10 cents a pound as fresh fish.

Q. What kinds of fish are they which bring the high price of a dollar a pound ?—A. The pompano, which is the highest-priced fish.

By Sir Alexander Galt:

Q. To what size does it grow ?—A. Three pounds is the maximum. It is more generally one pound. The pompano brings one dollar per pound when it is freshly caught. Sometimes when it is brought to

New York and kept for a long time the price may come down.]
one occasion when it was sold at 10 cents a pound; but the fish w
marketable and should not have been sold. The next best
Spanish mackerel, a fish of remarkable excellence.

By Mr. Dana:

Q. In New York market at the proper season what does it br
A. I don't suppose it is ever sold under 25 cents per pound, and
that to 40 cents.

Q. Is that a mackerel?—A. It belongs to the mackerel famil
weighs about three pounds. There is the cero, a kind of Spanish
erel, which goes up to 15 pounds. Those are all found from Ca]
to Florida along the entire coast. There is the scup, which occur
Florida to Cape Cod in great abundance.

Q. The scup is found in great abundance off the south coast of
chusetts and Rhode Island?—A. Yes. There is also sea bass, w
one of the finest of the American fish, and is worth from 18 cent
cents per pound.

Q. How many pounds do they average in weight?—A. From
four pounds; three pounds is a large fish.

Q. They are found in abundance on the south coast of New En,
—A. Yes; very abundant. There is also the kingfish and the I
which is a very important fish.

Q. There is a fish of that character extending from Block Islan(
down to Cape Hatteras?—A. It is one of the same family. It '
up to five pounds. I have seen five thousand of those fish take
single time in a fishing-pound at Menemsha Bight. There is the
fish, which is the *piece de resistance.* There is the squeteague; o
fish I have seen 25,000 pounds taken at a haul.

Q. The bluefish is a great fish in the market?—A. It is the
pal fresh fish during the summer season on the coast of the
States from Cape Cod to North Carolina.

Q. Caught all along the shores?—A. All along the coast, bein
abundant in the summer season toward Cape Cod, and in wi
North Carolina.

Q. There is a great drift through Vineyard Sound?—A. Th
numerous catch.

Q. Are not the people on the southern coast of Massachusetts,
the coast of Rhode Island, now very much engaged in catchin
fish?—A. Very largely, taking them in pounds and gill nets, an
modes of capture.

Q. Is this a part of the development of the fresh fish mark
Yes. Since bluefish has come back to the coast it has constit
enormous element in the supply of fresh fish; it is not the con
element, but it is the largest single element, although combin
striped bass, squeteague, mullet, and scup, they considerably out
the bluefish. (Photographs of the fish referred to were exhibite

Q. What about tautog?—A. It is an important fish, but is not
immense abundance. While you talk of tautog being caught i
sands of pounds, you talk of others by hundreds of thousand
millions.

Q. Pounds are very common on the American coast?—A. It con
the principal mode of summer fishing from round Cape Cod as far
Long Island. Nearly all the fish taken on that coast are caugh
pounds. The small tunny is a fish which of late years has co
notice, and it is believed to have disturbed the mackerel and me

this year. It was never recorded till I found it in 1871 in Martha's Vineyard, where it was in enormous numbers. It is a fish weighing about 25 pounds, and it is something like the horse mackerel, but they never grow more than 25 pounds. Not unfrequently 500 or 1,000 of them are taken in a single night in one of the pounds, but the people make no use of them and consider them valueless. They sell the fish weighing 25 pounds for 25 cents. It is a coarse fish and very dark meat, but still it is a food resource when other fish are not taken. These fish are found in the Mediterranean, where they are very much looked after and bring very good prices, they being specially salted and put up in oil. The American tunny is undistinguishable from the European, though efforts have been made to separate them.

Q. The pound-fishing which has come into general use in the southern part of New England, what is its effect on the supply of fish?—A. That is a question which I think will require a longer period of years than we have had for its definite determination. In 1871 I made my first inquiries into these pounds, and satisfied myself then that they must have a positive influence upon the abundance of fish, in view of the concurrent enormous destruction of bluefish. I considered the bluefish was the greatest agency in the destruction of our food fishes. Its relation to scup and squeteague has long been established—that when bluefish are abundant the other fish are rare, and the moment bluefish diminish the other fish become enormously common. The squeteague in 1862 was unknown as a fish east of the waters of New Jersey except in small numbers, and was not found in Martha's Vineyard or Buzzard's Bay. In 1872, ten years subsequently, so plentiful were they that I know myself of 5,000 fish being taken at a single haul, averaging five pounds each fish. The bluefish then began to diminish, and from that time were much less abundant than in 1850 or 1860. Those pounds and the bluefish together I considered produced the decrease in the abundance of scup, sea bass, and tautog that has been so much complained of. I urged very strongly, and I still maintain my view, on the legislatures of Massachusetts and Rhode Island the propriety of exercising some sort of restriction upon the indiscriminate use of this apparatus. I recommended that one day and two nights, that is, from Saturday night, or, if possible, from Friday night till Monday morning, should be established as a close time during which those fish should not be taken by any of those-devices, thus giving the fish a chance to get into the spawning-grounds inshore, thereby securing their perpetuity.

I was quite satisfied in my own mind that unless something of this kind was done, very serious results would happen. Very much to my disgust, I must admit, the next year, even with all the abundance of those engines, the young scup came in in quantities so great as to exceed anything the oldest fisherman remembered, and thousands and tens of thousands of barrels of what was called dollar scup were sold. They were so thick in the pounds and so mixed with the fish that the owners could scarcely pick out the marketable fish, and consequently had to let large portions of the contents of the pounds go away. Since then scup has been very much more abundant than it was when I wrote my book and report.

Q. How do you account for this great increase?—A. I think those were scup, belonging to further south, which took a northern trip to northern waters and established themselves there. But I do urge in the most earnest manner the propriety of some restriction being placed on the pounds. I have not changed my views, although the evil has not arrived as I thought it would, and there are indications of some

other agency; whether it be the diminution of the bluefish which
mits the scup to increase or not I cannot say.

Q. Is it true the bluefish is diminishing?—A. It is not by any m
so abundant as it was, very much to the regret of all people who c
them, either for market or for sport.

Q. Can you remember the time when there was no bluefish on
American coast?—A. I cannot. I know we have the record of the.
and I know many persons who can remember it. Bluefish was ab
from the American coast for sixty years, during which time there
not a single bluefish to be found on the coast.

Q. You think the pounds should be dealt with as a matter for I
lation and not for banishment?—A. I don't think the market woul
amply supplied without them, and I don't think it would be expe
to prohibit them. I think a certain amount of regulation, such
have recommended, would be a great deal better for the fish an
fishermen. The disadvantage of the pounds is that they glut the
ket at times, so that there is no sale for the fish and fish are wa
and by the adoption of a close time not only will it secure proper sp
ing of the fish, but also equalize consumption.

No. 69.

WILLIAM J. MASS, of Chester, Nova Scotia, master mariner and
erman, called on behalf of the Government of the United States.

By Mr. Foster:

Question. You are 27 years of age, I believe?—Answer. Yes.

Q. And you were born at Chester, Nova Scotia?—A. Yes.

Q. Your wife is residing at Dartmouth?—A. Yes.

Q. You command the schooner Orinoco, sailing out of Gloucest
A. Yes.

Q. And you are a naturalized citizen of the United States?—A.

Q. To whom does the schooner belong?—A. John Pew.

Q. Where have you been fishing this summer?—A. I have been
ing in Bay St. Lawrence the latter part of the summer.

Q. About what time did you go into the bay?—A. About 20t
gust, I believe.

Q. When did you leave there?—A. Last Monday.

Q. How many barrels of mackerel did you take in that time
About 100 barrels.

Q. Sea barrels?—A. Yes.

Q. Where did you catch them?—A. At different places; some I
Magdalen Islands, Prince Edward Island, and Point Miscou—all roi
scattered.

Q. When you went fishing to the bend of the island, how far
the shore did you get your fish?—A. As near as I could tell we
outside of the limits; that is to the best of my knowledge, but w
not measure. I should think we were outside of the three miles.

Q. You have tried in and out?—A. Yes.

Q. You say you have got about 100 sea barrels; how have the sc
ers done that you have heard of?—A. The others have done very
Some vessels which were in at the first part of the season got some
erel, but I don't believe they will average 100 barrels all through,
and late.

Q. If you can remember any particular schooners, and the quai
they caught, name them.—A. The William S. Baker had about 1

believe she had been to the bay five weeks, but I could not tell

here is she from?—A. She belongs to Gloucester; her captain
ain Pierce.

ny others?—A. Capt. John Collins, in Helen M. Crosby, had
els. He had been there quite a month; I heard six weeks. He
ome to Gloucester. Capt. George Bass, in the Colonel Cook, of
ster, had about 80 barrels, and he had been in the bay eleven
I think they told me.

ny others?—A. The Rattler, belonging to Captain Leighton, had
rels, they told me. She had been in the bay over two and a half

ave you heard of any larger catch than that of the Rattler?—A.
nn H. Kennedy, of Portland, had 90 barrels.

that the largest catch you heard of?—A. No; Captain Knowles
rest Home had 210 barrels. That is the largest catch I know of.
here are other vessels with 12 or 15 barrels. The Serena Ann,
land, had 15 barrels; the Lizzie Ann, of Portland, had 14 bar-

want to know whether the mackerel-fishing of vessels in the
St. Lawrence has been a success or a failure this season, so far
know and from information given to you?—A. Well, so far as
wledge and information extend, it has been a failure this year—
two years.

By Mr. Davies:

What is the name of your vessel?—A. The Orinoco.
When did you come into the bay?—A. We went into the bay, I
, on the 20th or 22d August.
Was there much fishing around Magdalen Islands this year?—A.
las not been a great deal; there has been some mackerel there.
las the fishing there not been very bad?—A. Yes, very bad.
othing at all done there?—A. I cannot say nothing at all. One
vessels, out of 100 sail, have got a small share there; the rest
ot nothing, you may say.
t what would you put the whole fleet in the bay?—A. I could
exactly.
Would you say 250 sail altogether?—A. No; there were not that
his year.
ould you swear there were not?—A. I could not swear there
ot.
lad you any means of forming a correct opinion?—A. I don't
here were more than 100 sail.
Would you call it 200 sail?—A. It might be 200.
ou cannot swear that it is more or less?—A. I could not swear.
v lots of vessels, but I did not keep the run of them.
When you went into the bay, where did you first go?—A. We
om one place to another.
here did you go first?—A. To Port Hood and Cape George. We
ere close inshore, and we tried out. Inshore we did not raise
ig worth speaking of; we also tried off shore and got a few mack-
We tried two other days, and as there did not appear to be much
t of a catch, we went from there to Point Miscou.
lid you try at Magdalen Islands?—A. Yes.
lid you get any there?—A. Yes.
low many?—A. About 25 barrels. We stopped there about
days.
177 F

Q. Which was your main fishing-ground—Prince Edward Island?—A. Yes.

Q. Is that the main fishing-ground of the fleet this summer?—A. I could not tell you that. There are lots of vessels in during the whole year; they had tried in other places, but most mackerel had been got at Magdalen Islands.

Q. Name one vessel that has got mackerel at Magdalen Islands?—A. The Rambler, Captain R. Johnson, 200 barrels; he is high-liner.

Q. Where did you see him?—A. At Georgetown, two weeks ago.

Q. What was he doing there?—A. He was there for a harbor.

Q. Not there fishing?—A. He had come across from Magdalen Islands, having run short of outfit, and had to go to Canso to fit out.

Q. How far is it from Georgetown to Magdalen Islands—over 100 miles?—A. About 140.

Q. Could he not be running to Georgetown to fit, after fishing at Magdalen Islands?—A. I can tell you how he came to be there. He came from the Magdalen Islands, and was going to Canso to refit, and on the way, there came on a breeze of wind, and he went to Georgetown; he will go back to the Magdalens.

Q. He got 200 barrels?—A. Yes; about 200 barrels.

Q. You think he got them about the Magdalens?—A. Yes; and Bird Rocks.

Q. When you were fishing, how many vessels were about Prince Edward Island? Tell me where you were fishing?—A. We tried up and down. We did not get a great many at the island. We got some mackerel at Port Hood—a few mackerel.

Q. Did you not tell me that Prince Edward Island was your main fishing-ground?—A. We were there most of the time, but we did not get the most mackerel there.

Q. Where did you get most of your mackerel, if not at Prince Edward Island, Magdalen Islands, or Port Hood?—A. We did not get a great many anywhere. We got most of our mackerel off Port Hood.

Q. The first time you tried, you got none?—A. We went back afterwards.

Q. When fishing off Prince Edward Island, did you fish much off East Point?—A. We fished some there.

Q. You do not profess to say that you did not catch fish within the limits there?—A. I profess to say we did not catch many. I don't say we did not catch any, but that the number was very small.

Q. Are you prepared to say how many; or did you pay any attention to it?—A. No; it is pretty hard to tell exactly.

Q. You did not pay any attention to it?—A. No. I think we did not catch any worth speaking of.

Q. Did you pay any particular attention to the three-mile limit?—A. A man who has business on hand knows where he has done best, and calculates on going there again. If he does well at one place he always bears it in mind to go there again.

Q. Did you pay any particular attention to how far you were from land when you caught your fish?—A. I took notice always when we tried for mackerel, we tried for mackerel inshore and then out.

Q. You went wherever you thought you could find mackerel?—A. Yes.

Q. This year you went in and out irrespective of the limit?—A. Yes.

Q. Did you see boats fishing much there?—A. We saw some boats out in the bend of the island; a good many mackerel boats were there. We did not try much there. We went more round the Chapels.

That is where you fished chiefly ?—A. We were round there at
ent times, but we did not get many of our mackerel there. Some
ls got mackerel there.

You got mackerel off Port Hood ?—A. Yes; a good part of them.
You do not wish the Commission to understand that the low
es of vessels you have named are average catches ?—A. I gave you
ghest and the lowest catch.

Those are the lowest catches made in the fleet ?—A. They could
ell have any and have less.

You do not wish the Commission to understand that they were
ing like the average catch ?—A. I said that, so far as my knowl-
goes, they would not average over 100 barrels for the whole season.

Have you asked the captains of many vessels what their catches
been ?—A. Yes; we always found that out.

What is your own catch ?—A. It is about 100 barrels.

Cannot you tell me exactly ?—A. I could not tell you exactly; it
wed to be about 100 barrels.

Do you know what the catch of the Greyhound was ? She is re-
l to me as having caught 230 barrels. Is that correct ?—A. What
d was that she had 170.

Did you hear that from the captain himself ?—A. I never spoke
im.

When did you hear that ?—A. Two weeks ago.

She might have caught up to that number after that ?—A. No.

Did you hear it from the captain himself ?—A. I did not speak
he captain himself, but with the other men.

Your information, then, is third-hand ?—A. I did not get it from
out I got it pretty straight.

Do you know what the Moses Adams got ?—A. I could not tell ex-
The captain was on board of my vessel, but I never inquired.

He is reported to have got 270 barrels ?—A. I guess you will have
te a good many off that.

What did they tell you the Moses Adams had got ?—A. One hun-
and seventy barrels.

When was that ?—A. Just before he went home. He went home
r three days after that, so I was told. I know he did not catch
I know that from a vessel which spoke with him as he was going
, and he was bearing up for the Strait of Canso.

Do you know when he got to Canso?—A. I know pretty nearly.

How do you know, if you were not there? Might he not have
me at Margaree ?—A. The vessel saw him going by Port Hood;
s away this side of Margaree.

Do you know what the E. H. Horton got?—A. I don't know any
than what I heard.

What did you hear ?—A. One hundred and sixty barrels.

How was it you did not give the names of those vessels as being
g those in the bay ?—A. I could not think of all.

Do you know how many the John Gerard, of Newburyport,
t ?—A. I did not talk with her captain, but they said she had 150
ls. The Old Chad, of Newburyport, with nineteen hands—I know
ositively—got 120 barrels.

Do you know what the J. J. Clarke got?—A. I don't know ex-
You have got all the best there; there is not a poor one among

Do you know what the Cayenne got?—A. Is she an American
l?

Q. I presume so.—A. I never saw her; I don't know a vessel of that name.

Q. Do you know what the Frederick Gering, jr., got? She is reported with 330 barrels.—A. Then they have got a big spurt.

Q. You never heard of her?—A. Yes, I did; I heard she had 150 barrels.

Q. When did you hear that?—A. I should judge about two weeks ago.

Q. Were all of those vessels in the bay two weeks ago?—A. I did not see the vessels, but I have talked with the men.

Q. How many vessels were there in the bay when you left?—A. There were about 35 sail of vessels with us when we went out of Canso.

Q. How many did you leave when you came away?—A. I could not tell.

Q. Thirty-five or forty vessels?—A. I should estimate over that, but that number is of those we saw there.

Q. Do you know what the David F. Low got?—A. I could not tell positively; I have heard reports.

Q. How many seasons have you been in the bay?—A. About seventeen seasons.

Q. As master?—A. No.

Q. As hand?—A. As hand, except this last year, when I was in the bay as master.

Q. You must have been fishing in the bay ever since you went into the bay at all?—A. All but two seasons.

Q. Where did you fish then?—A. On the American shore; on George's, La Have, and Grand Banks, two years; I was master.

Q. What years were they?—A. Last year and the year before.

Q. During the years you fished in the bay, you fished both inside and outside the limits?—A. We tried all over.

Q. Inside and outside?—A. To the best of my knowledge we caught most of the mackerel off shore.

Q. You think you did?—A. I am positive of it; all the largest spurts. I have caught as high as 130 barrels with hooks off shore. We caught them about nine miles off Entry Island, to the southeast; we got 130 barrels from nine o'clock in the morning till half past four o'clock in the afternoon.

Q. Have you fished much about Margaree?—A. Yes; a great deal round Margaree.

Q. I believe in the fall nearly all the vessels fish there?—A. They used to do so years ago; these last years there does not seem to have been anything round there.

Q. What years do you speak of?—A. This year and last year. My brother was down in the bay last year, and he told me about it then.

Q. This year you did not fish about Margaree much?—A. We tried there, but did not take more than half a barrel.

Q. That is known as one of the best fishing-grounds in the fall?—A. It used to be counted the best.

Q. Up to the last two years?—A. It was when I was in the bay; that is, in the fall.

Q. Most of the fleet went to fish there in the fall?—A. There was a large part which did not fish there. I used to be in Nova Scotia vessels, and during the largest part of that time we saw very few American vessels.

Q. At the time when you catch them inshore it always happens you are in provincial vessels?—A. It is not that at all. Most of the vessels would not content themselves staying in; they would go away before

ourts would come at Margaree and Cheticamp, and we used to stop
was with my father, who owned a vessel called the Frank, which
for Halifax. We filled up two or three falls around Margaree.
few American vessels were there.
What time was that?—A. We caught 200 barrels, about 5th No-
er; I don't judge we were inside the three miles then.

By Mr. Foster:

How old were you when you first went into the bay?—A. Eight
.
You were with your father?—A. Yes; my first trip was in the
r.
When you fish round Margaree late in the autumn, how long do
tay—one week or two?—A. Sometimes one week, sometimes two.
times we have to lay there ten or twelve days and cannot get out.
perhaps one or two fine days will come, and we will get some
erel.

FRIDAY, *October* 19, 1877.

e Conference met.
e examination of Prof. SPENCER F. BAIRD, called on behalf of the
rnment of the United States, resumed.

By Mr. Dana:

estion. There were some matters with regard to herring, in regard
tich I did not ask you fully yesterday. Will you state to the Com-
on about the spawning-grounds of herring especially? I do not
for anything outside of the American coast.—Answer. The herring
n along the whole coast of the United States, from the Bay of Fundy
› Man's Land, which is a small island between Block Island and
ha's Vineyard. I have specimens of spawn from almost all the
ities between those two points, and I am informed they also spawn
id Block Island, but I have never seen any evidence myself.
But you know as to the fact?—A. I know it is so from testimony
eports.
Do the eggs of the herring lodge on the bottom?—A. The herring
iost the one—is, I think, the only one—of our important sea fish, the
of which are adherent; that is to say, when discharged, it falls to
oottom and adheres to the sea-weed, gravel, and rock. Generally
scattered, but not unfrequently a great part of the spawn of the
vill be aggregated into a mass of the size of a walnut or hickory
but more generally they are scattered and attached singly or by
and threes to sea-weed. I have here specimens of the eggs in the
rent form, some which I dragged up at the southern end of Grand
in.
Are the spawning-grounds extended along the coast all the way?
Yes; all the way.
And are very numerous?—A. There is no reason to suppose there
y part of the coast at which they are wanting. They are specially
dant about Cutler, in Maine, and about some of the islands off Pe-
cot Bay, about Cape Elizabeth, Portsmouth, off Newburyport, and
cularly along the edge of the coast from north and east of the en-
:e of Massachusetts Bay. They also spawn inside of Cape Cod
and all along the south coast of this region to No Man's Land, as

unlike the shad and mackerel, which spawn at a rising temp
The moment the water along our coast gets to a certain degree
perature, then the herring is incited to the act of spawning.
say in completion of this point that herring spawns in the spring
St. Lawrence and Newfoundland. It spawns in early summer at
Manan in July, August, and September. It spawns at the end
tember in Eastern Maine, and it spawns in October off Boston, a
not spawn till November and sometimes December at No Man's

Q. Making a difference of many months?—A. Yes, a differ
from six to eight months.

Q. Describe the modes by which herring are caught on the
the United States.—A. They are caught principally by weirs,
and gill-nets on our coast. They are caught with seines largely
St. Lawrence and Newfoundland, but the large, full-grown, sp
herring are usually taken in gill-nets on or near the spawning
A very large number are taken on the whole coast of Maine and
Bay of Fundy in weirs, but the great body of these are smaller
and are not used as fresh fish.

Q. How is it with weir fishing?—A. The weir fishing is g
conducted in Maine, and to some extent inside of Cape Cod to th
South of Cape Cod they are more generally taken in pounds, l
in gill-nets.

Q. How are they taken along the Massachusetts coast?—A
are taken, generally, in gill-nets in the fall. The regular pou
usually not down as late as the herring season, but in spring larg
bers are taken in the pounds.

Q. How do you feel sure that this statement about spawning
coast is correct?—A. By actual capture of the fish in the sp
season, and by dredging up their eggs from the bottom with ap
we use for such purposes.

Q. Is herring a very common fish on the United States coast
is exceedingly abundant. It is not utilized at all to the exten
capacity. The herring is not a very favorite fish, it is a cheap
as there are so many better fish on the coast it is not very ma
for food. It is sold in great quantities but at very low prices
used only by the poorer classes of the community. Of course it
for bait, but as fresh fish it is very seldom seen on the tables of t
to-do people.

Q. Is it dried and pickled?—A. They are pickled to some
Some are smoked, a great many are worked up in the form of l
and in this form it is very much sought after.

Q. You have been at the places where the business is carrie
A. I have seen 20 or 30 large boats, of a capacity of perhaps 500
or more, filled with herring, lying at the wharf at Boston at o
They are boats probably from 4 to 10 tons.

Q. Market boats?—A. They are open boats, known as herri
and the coast now is lined with the boats with gill-nets catching
for the fall trade.

Q. Have you anything to say about the predaceous fish, suc
shark and dogfish? Do you think they do a great deal of har
food-fish?—A. They constitute a very important factor in the
of the abundance of fish on our coast. They destroy enormous
and quantities of all the useful fish, and in proportion as they
in numbers the food-fish diminish and *vice versa*. They per
same function as bluefish; they are constantly in the pursuit
fish and destroying them.

There is no probability of changing that relation which fish seem to
to one another ?—A. They all have the relation of attack, defense,
,it, and flight.

But, notwithstanding that, I suppose they belong to what you call
,alance of nature ?—A. The balances of nature are such that it is
,mely difficult to say what will be the effect on the fisheries of de-
,ing or multiplying a particular stock of fish. The sharks, for in-
,e, are destroying great quantities of food-fish. A new enterprise
,ust been started, and will be opened in the course of a few weeks,
,ilize the sharks, porpoises, dogfish, and tunnies. An establishment
,ts to work up twelve million pounds annually of those fish, for
,h heretofore there has not been a market. They are caught in great
,tities on the shores, but not utilized, and now there is to be a mar-
,r them, and the parties offer the same price for them as they do
,enhaden.

Where is the company started ?—A. At Wood's Holl, Mass. The
,any expects to keep two or three steamers constantly traversing
,ast from Block Island to Penobscot Bay, or Bay of Fundy, and the
,any advertises that it will take all dogfish, sharks, porpoises, black-
,and other offal that may be offered to it, up to the amount, I think,
, or 25 tons a day. By a new process, the oil will be extracted with-
,eat, leaving the meat entirely free of grease, and, when it is dried,
,ll be ground up to make what they call fish flour, or meal, which
,e used for fertilizing purposes or food, as you please. The same
,tance is made from cod in Norway and is an article of food. It
,s a very nice form of food, and is used as fish-cakes and other prep-
,ons.

It can be made up like flour ?—A. Yes; and can be mixed up with-
,ny difficulty. The effect of the abstraction of twelve million pounds
,ose predaceous fish will undoubtedly be very great. Whether, as
, fish eat bluefish, it may not allow bluefish to multiply, and in that
,restore the balance again, it is impossible to say; but if it was to
,bluefish also, we would relax very largely the pressure on eatable
,and they would necessarily increase.

Is the philosophy of that substantially that when one kind of
,aceous fish becomes very numerous, and is destroying useful fish, it
,r disappears in time, or by what we regard as the regular course of
,re, and the work of man, that fish diminishes, or is exterminated,
,others take its place ?—A. After they have eaten up everything,
,will start out and go somewhere else. Whenever they have made
, favorite food scarce, they go somewhere else. So it is a very seri-
,question as to what had better be done, no matter what promise
,, mav be, in regard to altering the relations willfully and purposely
,een the different forms of the animals of the sea. If you take them
,,od, you allow the consequences to come as they may, but any ques-
,of protecting one kind of fish, or destroying or exterminating
,rs, should always be considered with a great deal of care, and from
,eat many points of view that do not strike the mind or attention at
,thought.

To undertake to regulate the relations of fish beyond shoal water
,re you can fish with nets, seines, and pounds, would be impracti-
,e ?—A. It would be very difficult, indeed, and the effect would prob-
,be very trifling.

, You spoke yesterday of the fish of the Southern States, the fish-
,, of which in the new order of things are being rather more de-
,ped by greater diversity of industry, and so forth ; can you mention

any other fish that are coming into use?—A. There are a gr
species, probably not less than fifty, all having a definite val
article of food, and all caught and consumed on the coast, c
limited quantities either to the Northern markets or to Cuba, th
be taken into consideration, but perhaps the capture of the fish th
the rank of fisheries relates more particularly to the mullet, me
striped bass, and bluefish. There is a very extensive fishery
fish on the southern coast. The bluefish, after leaving the
waters, spends a certain time on the coast of Virginia and No
lina, and by the time it gets back there it has attained enormou
sions, the fishes being generally from 12 to 15 pounds, at wl
they are found only casually and occasionally on the northern c
is not at all an uncommon thing for one fishery of a single lc
take 3,000 bluefish, averaging 12 pounds each fish.

Q. What do you mean by one fishery?—A. A single static
particular point, the fishing being controlled by one man or fi
enormous number of bluefish are sent late in fall and in earl
to the Northern markets.

Q. So that when bluefish leave the New England coast, the
disappear altogether from the American coast?—A. Not at all.
appears some time in February, and where it goes, we cannot t

Q. It disappears from the southern coast?—A. Yes. A sma
of bluefish is found all the year south to Florida, but the larg
of blue fish usually disappears in February, and, indeed, I may
never see it again. The fish, as they make their appearance ir
are smaller fish.

Q. Do they first appear on the south coast of New England?
first appearing on the coast of Carolina and Virginia, they
something like the mackerel, only they have a rather more c
travel, because they do not spawn on the northern coast.
the big bluefish go out somewhere to spawn, but what becomes
whether they spawn themselves out to a condition of nonentity,
say. We do not see them; they may go to Africa, or the Maur
bluefish are found all the world over; but whether they go to a
portion of the world from the United States, I cannot say.

Q. What have you to tell the Commission about menhade
South?—A. The menhaden is a very important fish on the sou
as an article of food. It is caught, salted, and pickled, and to
tent used in the country. There is quite a large export of men
the West Indies from the Southern States.

Q. Is it used fresh?—A. It is salted and pickled; it is also ea
very largely, and considered a very capital article of food.

Q. You have eaten it yourself?—A. Yes; it is a sweet fish
good as herring, but rather more bony; the bones are, howe
adherent to the skeleton. You can prepare menhaden by m
so that the greater part of the bones will stick to the vertebra
instead of being loose and lying about the muscular parts, as in

Q. Is it also salted in the South?—A. Yes.

Q. Is there now a large business in menhaden, or is there
be?—A. It is a business capable of almost any extension for wl
is a demand. There is no limit apparently, speaking in r
terms, to the number that can be taken, any more than there
North. There is nothing like the same quantity taken in the
as in the Northern waters. It is taken somewhat for the manu
oil. but the business is not fully developed.

Q. What other fish did you mention in the South?—A. T

aden, bluefish, and striped bass to some extent, but striped bass
re an estuary fish coming into brackish waters, and can scarcely,
propriety, be mentioned in this connection.

What have you to say about the drum?—A. It is a fish that can
ken in almost any desired quantity. It is obtained weighing up to
) 120 pounds, but it generally weighs from 10 to 20 pounds. There
| channel bass, which can be also taken in any desired quantities.
:ntirely a sea fish, and is caught in the rapid channel-ways between
ιores and islands on the coast.

|Especially, perhaps, in South Carolina?—A. Only stragglers come
e eastern coast, but it is found in enormous abundance from North
ina down to the southern extremity of Florida, and in the Gulf of
:o.

.Can the fish be salted for the market?—A. I don't think it has
been tried; it is worth almost too much as fresh fish.

|Is the fish called red snapper there?—A. Yes; it is very abundant
e coast of Florida. It is a large fish, of a blood-red color, as red
ildfish, and weighs from five to twenty pounds. It is caught in
| numbers in the winter season, and taken alive to Cuba. The Con-
:ut fishermen, after they have finished their halibut and cod sum-
|nd autumn fishing, go down to Florida, and spend two or three
hs catching red snappers and other fish and taking them to Cuba,
g them as fresh fish, alive. It is taken in the wells of vessels, and
d at very high prices in Havaua. Sometimes, on the return trip,
take a load to New York, and sell them in that market alive.

|In regard to pounds, they must be constructed in muddy ground?—
ι almost any ground, except sand, because the sand shifts.

|To construct a pound, you drive in piles or posts, and then make
ιight line of net-work right up?—A. Yes. (Diagram of a pound
)ited.) The stakes are driven right down with a pile-driver, and
stake to stake is extended a wall of netting, which extends down to
otton and makes a barrier for the fish. They are held down by a
ι. There is also the heart, bowl and pocket. The fish coming along
oast strike the wall of netting, and very naturally, in endeavoring
irt it, they turn seaward and go along till they get into this recep-
either way. A fish never turns a corner, and when it gets within
etting it swims round and round, but never goes back again. Then
ιally it is led into the inner inclosure, and the same process goes
he fish swim round and round, but never find their way out back
gh the opening. You may leave the pound for a week, and you
ιave there all the fish that have come in, except the striped bass,
ι is the only fish you cannot cheat in a pound; and you very
ι take them in that way. Then when they come to haul the pounds,
throw a gate of netting across the opening, and in the bowl the
ιg extends over the bottom and comes up the side. They gather
e end and haul it over the boat, and gradually concentrate the fish
corner, and turn them or throw them over into the permanent
:t, where the fish are kept until ready for market. Fish are kept
sometimes two or three weeks or more for a demand in the market;
ere is a glut in the market, they may keep perhaps 1,000, 2,000 or
fish in one of these inclosures.

How is the pocket formed?—A. It is a net-work, fastened down to
ottom by a chain, so that it will touch the bottom and not permit
o go under it. (Diagram of trap exhibited.) The trap is only used
ι waters of Rhode Island, and is used for scup, tautog, and sea-bass.
ι are no stakes used to the trap. It is a rectangular space of net-

ting, held at the corners by anchors. The fish go along the lead
pass into the receptacle. The trap requires constant watching
fish could go in and out. The moment a school of fish enter,
ting at the end is raised. They pursue the same mode of em
and turn the fish into the pocket, as with pounds.

Q. The difference is that in the case of pound, it is not necess
boats should be employed to visit them frequently?—A. In
weather you sometimes cannot get to a pound for a week. In
of traps they are visited three or four or half a dozen times a da

Q. When the boats off shore see a school of fish enter the tr
follow and take it whether large or small. [Diagram of weir ext
This weir consists of a small circle of brush or boards, with tw
and a spring. The fish come into the weir at high tide, and as th
falls they are left in a cavity inside the weir, and are taken out
nets. There are a dozen or twenty different forms of constructin

Q. What is the estimated cost of a pound?—A. $1,000 will
the construction of a very good pound, including the entire equ
A pound is managed by from two to four men, while a trap
two boats and about seven men.

Q. The trap is more expensive?—A. About the same cost
pound, because, although it has no stakes, yet it requires to be
considerable size and needs anchors. I should presume that t
cost of the two would not be very different.

Q. And what is the cost of a weir?—A. It is a simple thin
cost merely represents the lumber and labor.

Q. That is a permanent erection?—A. Yes; the others are a
up; the traps are only kept down six weeks in the year; the
are down for from two months to five, and at the end of the seas
use an apparatus to pull the stakes out of the water, and then pa
on shore for next season.

Q. What are the kinds of fish taken in the great lakes?—A.
a great variety of fish taken there, but the most important
matter of business, are the whitefish, lake herring, lake trout,
pike, maskalonge, sturgeon, and a variety of others. The mos
ant, however, are whitefish, herring, and trout.

Q. What are the methods of taking them?—A. They are ta
largely by pounds, which are constructed on a very large s
much more elaborate and expensive than on the coast. They a
by gill nets very largely, and by seines under certain circuu
At a certain time of the year, whitefish can be taken in great q
in seines, and kept in pounds until ready for market.

Q. Are those built and constructed to a great extent along
Canadian and American shores? -A. I presume they are used in
though I cannot say. I know they are on our own coasts.
quite a number of these pounds worked by Canadians on the
coast.

Q. Have you any statistics respecting the lake fishery for t
1876 and 1877?—A. I have only partial statistic. for 1877. I
the statistics in detail in my report for 1872, and I am no
statistics for 1877 collected, and will have them I suppose by t
the season.

Q. 1872 represents but faintly the present state of things.
tell us how it was in 1872?—A. In 1872 the American producti
in the great lakes was 32,250,000 pounds. That quantity of
taken, but how much more I cannot say. Those were mai
Buffalo, Cleveland, Chicago, and many other stations.

Q. Does that include the Canadian catch ?—A. I presume there is no Canadian catch in that amount. Those are the figures as they were obtained by my agents, from the fishermen and dealers.

Q. You obtained them from the dealers in the large cities ?—A. Yes, and the fishermen at the grounds. This year I have had every station on the American side of the lakes visited and canvassed.

Q. You have steady communication with and reports from the dealers ?—A. I have reports only when I send specially after them, as I did in 1872 and am doing this year.

Q. How far have you got in your inquiry this year ?—A. I have only a partial return from Chicago.

Q. What does that show ?—A. The total marketing of salted fish in Chicago up to the middle of October amounted to 100,000 half-barrels, with about 20,000 half-barrels expected for the rest of the season, or equal to 60,000 barrels of those fish for Chicago alone for the present year. The corresponding supply of barrels of fish in 1872 was 12,600 in Chicago, so that the Chicago trade has increased from 12,600 in 1872 to 60,000 in 1877, or almost fivefold—4 8-10. The total catch of fish in the lakes in 1872 was 32,250,000 pounds. If the total catch has increased in the same ratio as that market has done at Chicago, it will give 156,000,000 pounds of fish taken on the American side of the lakes for the present year.

Q. That, of course, cannot be a matter of certainty ?—A. No.

Q. What other large central markets for lake fish are there besides Chicago ?—A. Chicago and Buffalo are the most important. Cleveland takes a large quantity, but Chicago and Buffalo control the market. Detroit takes the fish to some extent, but it is not such a convenient shipping point.

Q. What proportion does that bear to the fish of Canada ?—A. I cannot say. I may say, in regard to this point, that on the same ratio the total product of the salt fish from the lakes in the American market would be 48,546,000 pounds. Of course, those figures are comparisons, and the estimates may be fallacious. Chicago may have a larger share of the lake trade in proportion, or may have a smaller share; other places may have crowded on it, or it may have gained on them.

Q. You expect to have full returns ?—A. I shall have them probably in the course of one month. I have not heard from my agent who is visiting all the Canadian stations and fishing points on the American coasts.

Q. You expect to ascertain the whole catch of the lakes for 1877 ?—A. Yes, with great precision. I have here an item which may perhaps be interesting in regard to the price of those fish. The ruling prices of fish on the 15th October, in Chicago, were $7.50 per barrel for whitefish, $5.50 for salmon trout, and $3.75 for lake herring. Those are the prices paid to the captors for the fish by the merchants; that is, before they are handled and any profit put upon them.

Q. In regard to the increase in the consumption of fish, are any as beneficial means being adopted in Canada to maintain the supply ?—A. Both Canada and the States bordering on the great lakes have striven very efficiently to prevent what would otherwise have been a great danger to the supply of an enormous amount of fish. They are hatching white-fish by artificial means to the extent of a great many millions annually. The two countries are not co-operating but concurring in this business, and probably this year they may introduce as many as 20, 30, or more millions of young fish into the waters, and that must necessarily have a very important influence on the maintenance of the fisheries.

They have not done anything yet in regard to lake herrin¿
fish, which is a much more valuable fish, is being carefully

Q. What States of the American Union are engaged in t
of whitefish ?—A. Ohio, Michigan, and Wisconsin.

Q. What has been the success generally of the fish-bree
by artificial means ?—A. It is now being practiced to such
Canada and the United States as to show it is a very effici
preventing the diminution of fish, and even of increasing the
has passed the region of experiment, and it is a positive fa
by the large appropriations made on both sides of the bo
purpose. It commands the respect and consideration of me
ies, and in our own country, at least, there is no difficulty i
appropriations that can profitably be expended to secure th

Q. It extends not only to the fish of the great lakes,
fish ?—A. To salmon, shad, striped bass, and alewives.

Q. You find as the result that a much larger proportion
are turned into fish than when left to natural exposures and
A. An ordinary estimate in regard to shad is that under nat
ing 995 out of 1,000 eggs perish without producing a young
feed for itself, and that you get five young fish which rea
of ability to feed for themselves; that is, after their. fins ¿
formed, and the fish is three-eighths of an inch in length.
then passed the ordinary perils of infancy, and are able to
themselves. With artificial spawning, a fish culturist wh
bring out 950 of 1,000 eggs to that state would be considered
of his business, except some unusual circumstance that c
controlled should come in to interfere.

Q. Can you tell the Commission how many traps and pou[
in the southern part of New England, Connecticut, Rhode¡
Massachusetts, at Martha's Vineyard, and all along to Ca[
There are 22 traps on the south side of Cape Cod, in the bay¡
about Chatham, 9 in Vineyard Sound, 30 at Buzzard's Bay
Island, 30 in Narraganset Bay. This year there have b'
and pounds on the southern coast of Rhode Island and M¿
exclusive of Connecticut. I have not the figures for Conn
This number represents the traps and pounds from Narr'
to the eastern end of Cape Cod.

Q. Have they been increasing ?—A. Yes; they are vei ¿
greater in number than they were when I made my first co

Q. Can you state the number of men who are emplo¿
traps ?—A. The number of men required to man the tra¡
traps requiring seven men each, taking 301.

Q. Your agent would know each of those traps?—A. I b
of the owner, and the catch of the greater portion of them

Q. Can you tell the Commission the catch of those traps
—A. I have here a table of the yield of that number of pc

Q. Give the result.—A. For some of the species, the fig
accurate, and for others they are estimated to some ex
estimate is essentially a record of the year, so far as they
it themselves, corrected by the personal observation of c
my men, who has taken a standard pound, and meted it e
self, and enumerated the catch and the kinds of fish. T
for 1876 included flounders, tautog, mackerel, Spanish n
peno, butter fish, squiteagle, scup, sea-bass, striped b
menblades, eels, cod, alewives, and herring. The total
year was 34,274,350 pounds. That is from Narraganse'

rn end of Cape Cod, on the south coast of Massachusetts and Rhode
d only.

Not the western part of Rhode Island?—A. It includes the whole
arraganset Bay. It does not include Long Island, where there are
at many pounds, or the most westerly part of Rhode Island.

Are all these pounds of fish capable of being used, and are used
od?—A. There is a large catch of menhaden in that 15 millions.

How many miles of coast-line does that catch represent?—A.
t 250 miles of coast-line.

Have you made up a calculation of the ratio of the catch per mile?
I have the ratio of 137,097 pounds of fish to the line or mile.

And to the men?—A. The ratio of the catch is 78,610 to each man.
otal value of the weir catch at the lowest wholesale rate is $847,900;
e lowest retail rate, $1,472,438; at a mean rate between the two,
h perhaps more exactly represents the value, $1,160,168. That,
ver, is the catch of that region only with traps and pounds; there
o a very large catch with hand-lines, gill-nets and seines. This is
or 94 weirs and traps. The aggregate catch of the entire fishery
e south coast of Rhode Island and Massachusetts is 45,917,750
ds, of the mean value of $1,875,840, which gives a ratio of 133,671
ds per linear mile, and equivalent to $7,504 to the linear mile. The
in the trap and pound fishery is over 78,610 pounds to the man, of
ney value of $2,661, being the product of each man's labor for an
age not exceeding four months. That sum, to bring it to the annual
nt, will have to be multiplied by three; each man thus would pro-
$8,000 worth a year by this mode of fishing.

You do not mean to say that each man makes that amount?—A.
but that is the ratio of fish to the man. Those pounds are gener-
owned by at least one of the men who run them, who sometimes
what additional assistance they require; perhaps, however, in half
e cases the owners manage the pounds and have no division of
ts.

Those statistics were prepared to show the amount of the fish, in-
ing the fresh fish as well as those salted?—A. None of these are
d except such of the salted menhaden as is for food. They do not
r into the returns of pickled fish. These fresh fish go almost exclu-
y to New York, very few to Boston.

It seems strange that you should be able to know the amount of
fish that passes into the great city and what is caught every day.
t method have you adopted to ascertain those facts?—A. The entire
-fish trade of New York is confined to nineteen firms which form
Wholesale Dealers' Association, to whose books and figures I have
access through and by the assistance of the large and retail dealer
ew York, Mr. Blackford, who has taken great interest in my inves-
tions and is a very hearty coadjutor. He has succeeded in interest-
those dealers, and I have just prepared a series of blanks in which
pe to have the dealers record all the catches of fish every day and
me the returns.

You have no doubt from your relations with the dealers who con-
the market that you know substantially the catch?—A. I cannot
I know the maximum catch on the coast, but I know I have reason
ly upon the figures of the fish that is actually marketed and comes
the hands of the wholesale men.

A large amount escapes notice?—A. Yes; all the local catch, the
h of fishermen which goes for their own benefit and is consumed on

the spot; the catch consumed in seaport towns and villages cann⟨
cluded in this enumeration.

Q. Are these caught within the treaty limits ?—A. All th⟨
which I have mentioned are caught east of Cape May.

Q. Northeast?—A. Yes; and all caught close to the shore, by ⟨
pounds, usually within 100 to 300 yards of the shore, or by gill-n
hand-lines, used by men also from the shore.

Q. The whole fishery, with pounds and nets, that goes on fr
shore, and with hook and line for market fish, all comes wit
treaty limits ?—A. Yes, of course, the mullet and winter blue⟨
south of the treaty limits ; but all the fish are practically wit
treaty limits.

Q. And in those fisheries the Canadians have the same rights a⟨
icans ?—A. The Canadians have the same rights there as we h⟨
does not include the fishery, not of Cape Cod Bay and round ⟨
port.

Q. Can you make any comparison of the corresponding ratio ⟨
or otherwise of the Canadian fisheries ?—A. I do not think I co
cause I believe the returns of the Canadian fisheries are not so 1⟨
they should be. I do not believe the Canadian returns are in pro
to the actual catch. I therefore think a comparative statemen⟨
be fallacious, and I would rather not make it.

Q. Some Canada tables have been published of the fisheries ⟨
including, perhaps, cod and herring?—A. Those relate to all t
eries. This estimate I submit is for weir-fishing on a limited co⟨

Q. The Canadian returns show a total amount of $11,000,000
think the total estimate of the Canadian fisheries for 1876 is ⟨
$11,000,000 and $12,000,000.

Q. If you put that of the United States at $50,000,000, would
a low or high estimate ?—A. I think we could figure up over $40⟨
without any difficulty; that is, for all the fisheries.

Q. Including the lake fisheries ?—A. Including hake, ring, an⟨
fish. Our oyster fisheries are worth $30,000,000 a year.

Q. That is nearly double the entire Canadian return ?—A. ⟨
There are $3,000,000 worth of oysters put in cans in Baltimore

Q. They are all included in the Canadian returns ?—A. I th⟨
Those industries with them are not so important as ours. Our o⟨
codfish, lake and river, shad, salmon, herring, lobster, crab, oy⟨
clam fisheries are included.

Q. Now, with reasonable legislation to limit certain methods of
is there in your judgment any danger of the existence of the
coast, and lake fisheries ?—A. I think that the lake fisheries wou⟨
been exhausted and greatly destroyed in a comparatively limit⟨
ber of years but for the timely warning taken by Canada and th⟨
States and the measures initiated in both countries for increas⟨
supply.

Q. You yourself have been very much engaged on the subje⟨
propagation of fish ?—A. Not so much in the lakes directly a⟨
rivers.

Q. You have shipped some of your fish by rail to Califor⟨
Yes.

Q. I remember reading an account of one of your large collec⟨
California being lodged in one of the rivers by a bridge breakin⟨
for which collection the State has never paid ?—A. Yes, a car of
which was being sent to California.

Q. In order to get some idea of the manipulation practiced in t⟨

tablishments, perhaps you will state whether steam machinery is
ow used?—A. That is a device we have adopted this year for the
ime in hatching shad, in which, instead of depending on the nat-
urrent of the river usually employed, we make the trays filled with
a move up and down in the water in a continuous alternation, and
t way hatching millions of eggs where formerly we could only hatch
ands.

You can state a case showing the result of one year's experiment?—
e had eleven millions of shad in Susquehanna River in about three
s in May and June.

Can you state to the Commission the result of some fish operations
tomac River?—A. The instance to which you refer is that of black
The black bass is not indigenous to the Potomac River, and none
in it. About two years ago half a dozen adult fish were placed in
ver, and it might now be said that the Potomac, with the excep-
f St. John's River, Florida, is the most prolific in black bass of any
n in the United States. Over an extent of one hundred miles, the
g for black bass both for market and sport is unrivaled anywhere.
Without claiming too much for our people, are not the ingenuity
ndustry of the American people in taking fish for consumption and
uses on the one hand, and in propagating them on the other, very
and very remarkable? How is that?—A. The methods of fish
re as practiced in the United States, and in Canada so far as they
the same ground, are, we think, better than those anywhere in the
World, and both countries hatch fish by millions where thousands
nsidered a large performance in Europe. The United States have
gle establishment in California at which more eggs are obtained
are gathered by all European hatcheries put together. This year
ive taken about six million eggs, and we have taken as many as
millions in a year. We have an establishment now on Columbia
where we expect to hatch twenty millions of eggs. Three millions
gs, I may say, in illustration of magnitude, would fill a hay-field cart
utmost capacity.

You have an estimate of the combined fishing of the United States
e year 1876, including the Bank fishing?—A. Yes. This is a table
product of the marine fisheries of the United States east of Cape
within the treaty limits. The total product of the inshore fisheries
at range, the fish taken by boats from the shore, that taken by
s, by traps, pounds, &c., amounts to 319,579,950 pounds, of a mean
of $4,064,484. The total fisheries of the United States, inshore and
ore within the limits, amount to 1,045,855,750 pounds, of the value
3,030,821. This is exclusive of any of the Southern fisheries, exclu-
f the lake fishery, of the whale, porpoise, and seal fishery, and of
lmon, shad, and herring fishery.

By Sir Alexander Galt:

Does it include the Grand Bank fishery and that at Georges?—A.

By Mr. Dana:

It is exclusive entirely of the fresh-water fish of the lakes and
, shad, herring, and salmon, of the whale and fur seal, of the oys-
obsters, and crabs. The total coast line on which the fisheries are
ed is 1,112 miles, from Cape May to Eastport, including the islands.
atio to the mile is 940,510 pounds, the ratio of value is $11,718.

Will you state how the returns are obtained?—A. The figures in
d to the herring, cod, and mackerel are obtained from the reports

of the Bureau of Statistics of the United States for 1876, the
ures are made up from a series of tables for each kind of fish.
estimate prepared of the production of each fishery, and tho
have been obtained partly from witnesses who have been here
partly from the books of dealers in Gloucester, Boston, New
and elsewhere, partly and very largely from the returns I have
through agents I have sent out, and from circulars I have di:
I have here an enumeration of all the different kinds of fish :
tity caught; it is simply a combined table from a great many s

Q. These tables you will put into the case ?—A. The tables
made up by me, but under my direction. They are put in by
piler under an affidavit.

Q. An examination will show they are very much in detail?—
tables, like all those of all nations, excepting, perhaps, those c
are imperfect, and are short of the true figures. I have no d
a large percentage should be added to the tables of both nati
New World. But they are accurate as far as they go; if they e
the direction of deficiency, not of excess.

Q. It is so on both sides ?—A. Yes.

Q. You are allowed a pretty large staff of persons to ass
writers?—A. I have all the clerks and assistants I require. B
many of those returns have been made to circulars. I have d
through the Departments of the Treasury and Post-Office, :
functionaries.

Q. In view of those vast resources of the country, and the
sea-fish of all kinds, the improved and increased methods of
the fish, do you think there is any one kind of fish, the entire
which would prove a very serious matter, such, for instanc
mackerel obtained in the Gulf of St. Lawrence ?—A. I do
that the entire failure of any kind of fish would affect the su
this would stimulate the fishermen to renewed efforts regar
other fish. If all the mackerel disappeared, their places wou
plied by the Southern mullet, which are more abundant than
erel, and which could be taken in twice the quantity, if not
every mackerel was destroyed the mackerel fishermen would g
the Southern coast, and take the mullet and pickle them.

Q. Your last statement applies only to fish caught nortl
May ?—A. Yes; it does not include any Southern fisheries at
catch of the same fish in Southern waters, such as the blue
mackerel.

By Mr. Foster:

Q. Is Cape May far north of the treaty line ?—A. It is dire
treaty line; this line cuts off Cape May and runs just at the r
of the coast there.

By Mr. Dana:

Q. So that these tables do not include the opening of
Bay?—A. No; but only the fisheries on the coast of New J
outer coast of New Jersey—and from that northward.

By Mr. Thomson:

Q. All this evidence which you have given, with refere
mullet becoming the fish of the future, is mere matter of spe
it not ?—A. It is nothing more than what I judge from the e.
this fish, the ease with which they are taken, and the ease

they are cured, and the extent to which it is practiced as a local fishery by the people of North Carolina and other Southern States.

Q. Has not that fishery been known for a great many years?—A. I cannot say. I have only known it since 1872 and 1873. It probably has been known as a fishery for some years.

Q. Persons have eaten these mullet 20 or 30 years ago down South?—A. Yes.

Q. And it has not progressed at all as food for Northern consumption?—A. It is not now used as a food-fish in the North; but it is a fish which occupies the place of Northern fish through a large portion of the Southern States.

Q. Do you know from definite personal knowledge of your own whether they would not rather have there one single salt mackerel than a whole barrel of mullet?—A. No, I cannot say anything about that—as to their preference.

Q. I was told that this was the case no longer ago than this morning by a lady who has lived there; and I wanted to know what your experience in this respect was.—A. I must to my shame confess that I have never tasted a salt mullet; but I propose, as soon as I go home, to get a barrel of them and I will send some to Halifax for the Commission. I hope they will make up their minds to try them; I will do it the very first thing after I reach home, and I hope you will all try them.

Q. Is it not a fact well known to those who are engaged in the sea-fisheries that Southern fish, or, in other words, fish taken in warm waters, are fish that will not bear transportation to Northern climates?—A. I cannot say anything about that at all; but I know the only peculiarity about mullet is, that it is a fall and winter fishery. It is a cold-water fishery. It begins in September, and lasts until November and December.

Q. You say it is a cold-water fishery; but the water is nothing like as cold there as it is in our waters during the same months?—A. No; but the water there is about as cold in winter—if not then quite as cold—as it is here in the summer time.

Q. Could cod, from your knowledge, live in the waters which are frequented by the mullet?—A. No; neither could the mullet live in the waters which are frequented by the cod.

Q. Are not the mullet also a fat fish?—A. Yes; they are very fat.

Q. Is not this fact also against transportation?—A. I do not know. I am not versed in the physics of transportation.

Q. How long ago is it since you first turned your attention to the fisheries at all?—A. I have done so since 1871.

Q. Previous to that time your specialties lay in another direction?—A. No; I have always been interested in fish as a branch of zoology for a great many years. I have been a specialist in icthyology, and I described prior to that date hundreds of new species.

Q. Speaking about the pounds established along the New England shore, how many of them did you say were there?—A. 94.

Q. In answer to Mr. Dana, you stated that this kind of fishing was open under the Washington Treaty to British fishermen; do you think that you are quite right in stating that?—A. Yes.

Q. Do you think that under this treaty we have a right to set down pounds upon American soil?—A. You can, subject to the consent of the owners of the shore—just the same as with respect to any fishery so prosecuted in the Dominion.

Q. Is it possible for any person to carry on the business of pound fishing, except he is a resident on the coast?—A. I see no reason why

178 F

any one from Canada could not go to Long Island Sound or to V
Sound, and prosecute this fishery.

Q. Then such a person must reside there?—A. No. Very
these pounds, and I think I may say that not one-half of th
fishing in Buzzard's Bay and Vineyard Sound, are prosecuted
zens of the State.

Q. A man must reside or remain there for the purpose of a
these pounds?—A. Yes; for two or three months in the year.

Q. He must be a resident of the shore for two or three m
order to attend to these pounds?—A. Certainly; he must be
ground, as any fisherman must be when fishing, in his boat.

Q. Practically and really this is a fishery which must be ca
by persons on the spot?—A. Of course; all fisheries must be
on on the spot; but they need not necessarily be carried on
dents of that region, or by citizens of the State. Most of these
in Buzzard's Bay are carried on by people who do not usuall
the spot.

Q. At all events, do you seriously state that under the prov
the Washington Treaty we have a right to put down pounds
American shore?—A. I think so, with the consent of the own
shore.

Q. That is another question.—A. Will you kindly read the
the Treaty of Washington in this relation?

Q. It is as follows:

It is agreed by the High Contracting Parties that, in addition to the liber
to the United States fishermen by the Convention between Great Britai
United States, signed at London on the 20th day of October, 1818, of takir
and drying fish on certain coasts of the British North American Colonies there
the inhabitants of the United States shall have, in common with the subje
Britannic Majesty, the liberty for the term of years mentioned in Article
this treaty, to take fish of every kind, except shell-fish, on the sea-coasts a
and in the bays, harbors, and creeks of the Provinces of Quebec, Nova Scoti.
Brunswick, and the colony of Prince Edward Island, and of the several isl
unto adjacent, without being restricted to any distance from the shore, wi
sion to land upon the said coasts, and shores, and islands, and also upon the
Islands, for the purpose of drying their nets and curing their fish.

A. Yes. I do not understand that any mode of fishing is p
under this treaty, unless it is so mentioned in express terms,
case with shad, salmon, and shell-fish. I do not understand
mode of fishing is prohibited to the citizens of the opposit
except what conflicts with the local law of the country.

Q. Can these pounds be put down without landing to make
tion for that purpose?—A. Yes, perfectly well. It is not a
necessary to go on shore at all to do it; indeed I know o
many pounds which do not touch the shore, but which are st
30, or 50 yards from the shore.

Q. Do you seriously contend that there are territorial right.
under the Washington Treaty because you recollect that th
down of poles in the soil is a territorial right?—A. Yes.

Q. Do I seriously understand you to contend that, under tl
rights are given either to the Americans on the one side or to
ish on the other, as to doing anything on the shores of eithe
except landing to cure fish and dry nets?—A. I understand t
wished to start a pound in Buzzard's Bay, you could go to
Island, owned by John M. Forbes, an eminent citizen of tl
States, and with his permission you can do so; and that you
permission in this regard either from the State of Massachus

Government of the United States; he has precisely the same right to give authority to put down a pound, I think, as has Ashby, who was a witness here and a native of Connecticut.

Q. That is to say that Mr. Forbes, who owns the land, could allow me to go and put down a pound there?—A. There is not the slightest question about it.

Q. Could he not do that before this treaty was ratified?—A. I do not know whether he could do so or not; I cannot say anything about that; that is a legal question.

Q. He could have given me that right previous to the treaty just as well as since?—A. I do not know what exact right the treaty may give in this relation; but that is no reason why this might not be done. I consider that this fishery is now perfectly open to Canadians.

Q. Has not the mode in which the rivers on the coast of Maine have been treated for a number of years back depleted the waters on that coast or on the New England coast of cod, for instance, which you say was once one of the most important fish found there?—A. The destruction of river fish, in my opinion, has had more to do with the diminution of inshore fish, such as cod and haddock——

Q. And mackerel, too?—A. No, not mackerel; this has nothing to do with them. Mackerel cannot be considered in that connection, because they do not depend on the fish of those rivers for food; but I think that such destruction has more than anything else to do with the decrease of these fish I have mentioned, inshore; and the result of the measures which are now being taken by the States of Maine and Massachusetts, in restoring the river fisheries, will bring back the original historical abundance of the sea-fish inshore.

Q. What this will do is as yet in the womb of the future; but at present are not those fisheries depleted?—A. The boat-fisheries for cod and haddock are now much inferior in yield on most parts of that coast to what was the case 50 or 100 years ago.

Q. You now allude to the coast-fisheries within the three-mile limit?—A. Yes; the fisheries carried on in open boats, which go out as far as a man can comfortably go in a day and come back again.

Q. Do you wish the Commission to understand that this system of treating the rivers has destroyed the food of sea-fish, and therefore that the bait or food is not there to induce the cod to come inshore, but that this has had no effect on the fish outside of the three-mile limit?—A. I cannot say how far out the effect extends, because some distance outside of the limits there are other fishes, such as herring and mackerel, and food of various kinds which they can get at.

Q. Is it possible that the inshore fisheries can be either destroyed or very considerably depleted within the three-mile limit and yet leave the fisheries just outside of this limit as good as ever?—A. I think so.

Q. And undiminished?—A. I think so, for the very reason that these fish naturally keep off from the shore. They are off-shore fish, and we find them largely inshore at certain seasons of the year because they then follow the fish that are coming inshore; and if you had an enormous number of shad and alewives and salmon, and especially of alewives and shad inshore, that involves their pursuit by an enormous number of predatory fish, such as cod and haddock and pollock, just exactly as the same fish follow the herring and caplin on the coasts of the Dominion and Newfoundland.

Q. Then I understand you to mean that, although the food which these fishes prey upon may be destroyed by reason of the depletion of the rivers, this will only affect the fishing within three miles of the shore and have no effect on the fishing beyond this limit?—A. I cannot say how far it will have effect.

Q. Will this effect stop short of the three-mile limit?—A. I think there are a great many concurrent agencies which affect the fish supply at different seasons on the different parts of the coast, and that while the inshore fishing of herring and shad, or other incoming fish, regulates that to some extent, it does not cover the whole ground.

Q. I want a direct answer: are you able to state that the destruction of bait, by reason of the bad treatment of these rivers, only affects the fishing along the coast to the extent of three miles from it?—A. I cannot say that; I cannot say how far such effect extends, and nobody can do so.

Q. It is reasonable to suppose that it extends for a considerable distance farther than three miles from the coast?—A. That I cannot say.

Q. Would this not more likely drive the fish to other coasts where the rivers are not so treated?—A. Fish certainly have to go where they can get food, and if they cannot procure it on one spot they have to go to some other spot for it.

Q. Is it not probable that they will go where the rivers are not so badly treated?—A. This depends on how far cod and haddock will migrate, under any circumstances. If they leave the shore, but can find an ample supply of food on Georges Bank or on Nantucket Shoals, they will probably stay there.

Q. Do cod migrate at all? Is this known for a certainty to be the case?—A. It is not certain that they have such migrations as we ascribe to the bluefish and mackerel; whether they traverse a mile of sea-bottom in search of food, or whether they go 100 miles for it, under any circumstances, I cannot say.

Q. I understood you to say yesterday that you could not trace their migrations at all?—A. No, I cannot.

Q. And you do not pretend to say that they do migrate? I rather understood you to say also that mackerel do not migrate?—A. They migrate, but they do not sweep along the coast—at least I do not think they do so, as was formerly supposed, for very many miles; but rather come direct from their winter grounds inshore.

Q. I understood you to say, your theory at present was that there was a vast body of mackerel which, forming one wing of their army, passed along the American coast; and that another wing directed their course into the gulf?—A. Yes.

Q. I see that in the Answer of the United States, page 10, the following language is used:

The migration of mackerel in the spring begins on the Atlantic coast from a point as far south as Cape Hatteras. The first-comers reach Provincetown, Mass., about May 10. Here they begin to scatter, and they are found during the entire season along the New England coast.

"Whatever may be the theories of others on the subject," says Professor Baird, "the American mackerel fisher knows perfectly well that in spring, about May, he will find the schools of mackerel off Cape Hatteras, and that he can follow them northward, day by day, as they move in countless myriads on to the coast of Maine, of Nova Scotia, and into the Gulf of St. Lawrence. They may be occasionally lost sight of by their sinking below the surface; but they are sure to present themselves, shortly after, to those who look for them farther north and east."

Do you now adhere to that statement?—A. I think that was not the most philosophical expression on that subject. My views in regard to the proper theory concerning mackerel have been modified since then, to the extent I have alleged.

Q. In fact, if I correctly understood you yesterday, you rather inclined

the theory which has been started here, that mackerel are not a
gratory fish at all, but hybernate in the mud ?—A. I cannot precisely
y ; but the evidence is quite strong in favor of hybernation of some
id, though I do not consider the case proven in this respect ; at the
me time I do not consider it philosophical to refuse to countenance its
ssibility.

Q. Will you tell me how, if possible, it could be otherwise, if it is true
at the mackerel have, in the spring, scales over their eyes, as has
en described by witnesses here, and, as I understand, you admit.—A.
annot say that this is the case; I have never seen it.

Q. If these scales are on their eyes they could not possibly do other-
se than hibernate?—A. I cannot say that; I am not a mackerel, and
ould not tell what they do or what they do not do.

Q. Is it certain that any fish, that you are aware of, hibernate in the
id ?—A. That is not certain, but it is believed to be the case.

Q. Do you know of any fish which certainly does hibernate?—A.
e eel does.

Q. Is its eyes protected against the mud by scales?—A. This is not
a case so far as I know. It has not been noted or reported.

Q. How has it become a theory if it has never been noted ? Is it the
nt of experience with reference to mackerel that you do not know
ether scales are found over its eyes or not?—A. I have never caught
ckerel in the critical period of the year when they are said to have
les over their eyes; but a specimen which I have preserved in alco-
l did have scales over its eyes, though the action of the alcohol on
e cornea of the eye always tends to make it opaque and destroys its
nsparency.

Q. Is there any period of the year when mackerel must be prevented
)m seeing, as far as you can judge from the specimen which you pos-
ss ?—A. No; I cannot say that.

Q. What are these scales for?—A. I cannot say. The theory of the
ihermen, however, is that it is to curb the roving habits of the mackel, and make it more ready to stay in the mud; and that otherwise
ey would not want to stay there; that is the hypothesis of the fisher-
en, and I give it for what it is worth.

Q. You do not assent to it?—A. No; it is not proven to be true.

Q. And it is not disproven?—A. All that is proven in this respect is,
at in winter we do not see the mackerel; they do not then school on
e surface, nor do they go to the West Indies, or to Bermuda, or to
orida; nor do they then appear on the surface anywhere as far as the
stimony has gone.

Q. With reference to the inshore fisheries in the State of Maine, and
the States of New England, generally, are they depleted or not?—A.
ie boat-fisheries there are not what they were 50 or 100 years ago;
at, I think, I am perfectly safe in saying; but whether there has been
iy decrease in them during the past few years I cannot say.

Q. I now quote from your own report, part second, for the years 1872
id 1873, page xi; it is headed "Conclusions as to decrease of cod-fish-
ies on the New England coast," and it states:

Of all the various fisheries formerly prosecuted directly off the coast of New Eng-
nd, north of Cape Cod, the depreciation in that of the cod appears to be of the
eatest economical importance. Formerly the waters abounded in this fish to such
. extent that a large supply could be taken throughout almost the entire year along
e Banks, especially in the vicinity of the mouths of the large rivers. At that time
e tidal streams were almost choked up with the alewives, shad, and salmon that
ere struggling for entrance in the spring, and which filled the adjacent waters
roughout a great part of the year.

As is well known, the erection of impassable dams across the streams, by preven the ascent of the species just mentioned to their spawning-grounds, produced a very g diminution, and almost the extermination, of their numbers, so that whereas in fo1 years a large trade could be carried on during the proper season, now nothing w be gained by the effort.

On page xii you say this :

It would, therefore, appear that while the river-fisheries have been depreciate destroyed by means of dams or by exhaustive fishing, the codfish have disappeared equal ratio. This is not, however, for the same reason, as they are taken only v the line, at a rate more than compensated by the natural fecundity of the fish. I well satisfied, however, that there is a relation of cause and effect between the pre and past condition of the two series of fish ; and in this I am supported by the opi1 of Capt. U. S. Treat, of Eastport, by whom, indeed, the idea was first suggested to Captain Treat is a successful fisherman, and dealer in fish on a very large scale, at the same time a gentleman of very great intelligence and knowledge of the m details connected with the natural history of our coast-fishes, and in this res worthily representing Captain Atwood, of Provincetown. It is to Captain Treat we owe many experiments on the reproduction of alewives in ponds, and the p1 bility of keeping salmon in fresh waters for a period of years. The general con sions which have been reached, as the result of repeated conversations with Cap Treat and other fishermen on the coast, incline me to believe that the reduction i1 cod and other fisheries, so as to become practically a failure, is due to the decreas our coast in the quantity, primarily, of alewives, and secondarily of shad and sal1 more than to any other cause.

It is well known by the old residents of Eastport that from thirty to fifty years cod could be taken in abundance in Passamaquoddy Bay and off Eastport, where stragglers are now to be caught. The same is the case at the mouth of the Penob River and at other points along the coast, where once the fish came close in to the sh and were readily captured with the hook throughout the greater part of the year.

A. Yes.

Q. Do you dissent now from that opinion ?—A. No ; I used that an impressive lesson to the State legislature to induce them to pass measures necessary to restore these river fisheries, which they are n doing very rapidly.

Q. Where is Capt. U. S. Treat, of Eastport, now ?—A. In Jap teaching the Japanese how to catch and cure fish.

Q. On page xiv of this Report you say :

Whatever may be the importance of increasing the supply of salmon, it is tri compared with the restoration of our exhausted cod-fisheries; and should thes brought back to their original condition, we shall find within a short time an crease of wealth on our shores, the amount of which it would be difficult to calc1 Not only would the general prosperity of the adjacent States be enhanced, but in increased number of vessels built, in the large number of men induced to devote t1 selves to maritime pursuits, and in the general stimulus to everything connected the business of the sea-faring profession, we should be recovering, in a great mea from that loss which has been the source of so much lamentation to political e1 mists and well-wishers of the country.

That you still adhere to ?—A. Certainly. I made that report as pressive as I could in order to produce the effect desired, which wa cause the legislature to pass a law in this regard, and it has had 1 effect. They have passed such laws, and I hope that this evil wil remedied in a reasonable number of years.

Q. It is not remedied yet ?—A. No.

Q. It takes a number of years to do that ?—A. I can give an inst where it has had such effect, if you like to have it. In Massachus the most has been done for the restoration of alewives and shad in Merrimack River; and the shore fisheries there have now increased very marked degree. At the present time it is perfectly possible f man to go out in a boat from the city of Newburyport and catch 4 pounds of codfish and bring them back the same night. This is the river in Massachusetts in which very great efforts have been mad restore these river fisheries ; and it is now possible to capture these

greater quantities than was the case 10 years ago; and this r
to the action of the State government with regard to the res-
of river fish.

)w many pounds did you mention ?—A. 4,000.

aght by a single man ?—A. Two men will do it; a man with a
id an assistant will go out in an open boat in the morning from
of Newburyport and come back at night, or go out at night and
1 the morning, and in the mean time take 4,000 pounds of cod.
the only point along there at which, at that distance from the
know that it is possible to catch cod in such numbers.

1st not a great lapse of time, or at least a very considerable
time occur, before the fisheries destroyed, as you have here de-
can be restored by the process you speak of ?—A. I think that
ends on the amount of time necessary for the restoration of the
ich run out to sea from the rivers. I think that if this year
'e no such fish as alewives, &c., to run into these rivers, and
next year a great army was to so run in, concurrent with that
1 army of cod and other fish would be there to prey upon them.
ee that in your Report for 1872 and 1873, referring to the lake
i say on page lxxxi :

itoration of food-fishes to localities originally tenanted by them, or their
) new waters, is, however, a question of time; and in the immense extent of
and lake systems, many years must necessarily elapse before the work can
)lished.

iat is a great number of years, certainly ; but that does not so
'fer to any particular river as to the aggregate rivers and lakes
d over the whole body of the United States.

)u say here that "many years must necessarily elapse" ?—A.
y.

hen did you commence this work ?—A. The actual process of
l propagation began, under my direction, in 1872.

) you refer to any term of years? I suppose that you mean a
)f 10, 12, or 14 years.—A. It might be more. The time of
lepends on the expenditure involved, and the concurrence of
legislation to protect the fish, and many other points.

)w many fish-breeding establishments have you in the States ?—
·ly every State in the Union has now a series of fish commis-
whose business it is to propagate fish within their borders.

iere is only one in each State ?—A. There is one State establish-
ind a certain number of private establishments in each, founded
)urpose of gain.

) you know how many there are in Canada ?—A. I know there
eat many. Canada is doing most admirably in this respect.

id very much more in proportion than the United States ?—A.
aink not: I think by far less in proportion.

proportion ?—A. Yes.

population ?—A. I do not say according to population. I shall
that statement by saying that what is done in Canada is done
ch less scale of magnitude than is the case in the United States.
that the aggregate of artificial propagation in the United States
greater than the aggregate in Canada ; but I would not take a
i think that both Canada and the United States are doing as
i they can in this regard, in the time that has been allowed for
)ose.

iuppose that Canada is doing a very large work in this connec-
A. She is doing most admirably—yes.

Q. She is expending large sums of money on it?—A. Certainl;
is doing most admirably. I am very happy to say that Canada :
United States are working concurrently in a great many direct
the line of artificial fish culture.

Q. Do you know the Canadian establishment on Detroit Rive
Yes.

Q. Is it doing a large business?—A. I don't know what it is
this year; but last year I understand that it did a very large bu

Q. It then hatched 10,000,000 eggs?—A. Yes, very likely.

Q. You say that cod cannot live except in cold water?—A. The c
inhabitant of the colder waters.

Q. Are you aware whether or not the Gulf Stream during th
mer months swings in at all more toward the American coast?-
does.

Q. For how many miles?—A. I cannot say.

Q. Would that have any effect in driving the cod away fr
American shores?—A. No; not the slightest.

Q. You think not?—A. Yes; it has not the slightest effect on
If you go down to a certain depth in the ocean, in the tropics
where else, you will find the water cold enough for cod; and '
nothing to prevent the cod being as abundant in tropical wate
off Brazil or the West Indies—as anywhere else; as far as temp
is concerned, it is cold enough there for them at a certain depth.

Q. Have they ever been caught there?—A. Not that I know ,
the water there is cold enough for them.

Q. Is it not very venturesome to state that there is nothing to
them staying there?—A. They may be there, but they have n
caught there. Nobody has fished at those great depths, for yc
got to go down from 6,000 to 15,000 and 20,000 feet to find that t
ture in tropical seas.

Q. Have you the slightest idea as to what sort of animals resid
there?—A. Yes. We have a very good knowledge of such sp'
can be taken up by the trawling line and dredge from those deptl
we know that an ample supply of food suitable for cod is to b'
there.

Q. Has any beam-trawl or dredge ever taken cod in those reg
A. No; you do not catch cod with small trawls any more than ,
so catch whales.

By Sir Alexander Galt:

Q. Would not the temperature in those waters interfere w
spawn of the cod, as this spawn floats?—A. I think that the wat
might be too warm for the development of codfish eggs in the a
but the effect would be to make them hatch out more rapidly tha
be the case in cold water. Of course it is a very serious que
decide whether, with the present constitution of the cod, its egg
develop in warm water, though whether it might not evolute and
into a warm-water cod I do not know.

By Mr. Thomson:

Q. On page 60 of your Report for 1872 and 1873, you use the
ing language :

It is in another still more important connection that we should consider tl
It is well known that within the last thirty or forty years the fisheries of cod, ha
hake along our coasts have measurably diminished, and in some places cease
Enough may be taken for local consumption, but localities which formerly
the material for an extensive commerce in dried fish have been entirely a

us causes have been assigned for this condition of things, and, among others, the
ed diminution of the sea-herring. After a careful consideration of the subject, how-
I am strongly inclined to believe that it is due to the diminution, and, in many
nces, to the extermination of the alewives. As already remarked, before the con-
tion of dams in the tidal rivers the alewife was found in incredible numbers along
ast, probably remaining not far from shore, excepting when moving up into
esh water, and, at any rate, spending a considerable interval off the mouths of
vers either at the time of their journey upward or on their return. The young,
fter returning from the ocean, usually swarmed in the same localities, and thus
hed for the larger species a bait such as is not supplied at present by any other
he sea-herring not excepted. We know that the alewife is particularly attract-
a bait to other fishes, especially for cod and mackerel.

Do I say mackerel?
Yes.—A. That is an inadvertence. I do not think that the ale-
is a bait for mackerel.
You say:

know that the alewife is particularly attractive as a bait to other fishes, espe-
for cod and mackerel.

Well, I should not have said that.
The alewives are the same as the fish we call gaspereaux in New
swick?—A. Yes.
You further say:

wives enter the streams on the south coast of New England before the arrival of
nefish; but the latter devote themselves with great assiduity to the capture of
ung as they come out from their breeding-ponds. The outlet of an alewife pond
ays a capital place for the blue-fish, and as they come very near the shore
h localities, they can be caught there with the line by what is called "heaving
auling," or throwing a squid from the shore, and hauling it in with the utmost
ity.
coincidence, at least, in the erection of the dams, and the enormous diminution
number of the alewives, and the decadence of the inshore cod-fishery, is cer-
very remarkable. It is probable, also, that the mackerel fisheries have suf-
in the same way, as these fish find in the young menhaden and alewives an attract-
it.

u see you say that twice.—A. That is an inadvertence.
You say:

probable also that the mackerel fisheries have suffered in the same way, as these
nd in the young menhaden and alewives an attractive bait.

This is the case on the northern coast probably.
It is hardly an inadvertence?—A. It is an inadvertence. It is a
lusion that is not justified by the fact.
Then you dissent from that opinion now?—A. Yes; I do not con-
that it has a bearing on the mackerel question.
All that goes to show that all these speculative opinions are enti-
to little weight; you see that you have changed your opinion in
respect?—A. Certainly; as the data vary the conclusions also vary.
I suppose you will admit that there is not the slightest reason why
in the next three years you may not have come back to the same
on which you now repudiate, or have then formed opinions totally
rent from those which you now express before the Commission?—
cannot say; that will depend entirely on the facts as they come.
After all, this is all the purest theory?—A. It is an hypothesis; it
t a theory.
Well, it is an hypothesis?—A. It is not a theory until it is abso-
y certified by the facts.
Then, of course, an hypothesis is more vague than a theory. You
in a mass of figures just now, which you state were made up by
assistant, based upon information which you have got from some

of the witnesses here, in answer to questions put them, and what
have I understood you rightly ?—A. Partly.

Q. And your assistant has verified them by his affidavit—have I
stood you rightly ?—A. Yes; they are verified by the affidavit
assistant who made them up.

Q. What sort of an affidavit is it? Does he state that these f
are correct, or simply that they are there ?—A. He certifies that l
compiled them, and what they represent.

(For this affidavit see No. 3, Appendix O.)

Q. In point of fact you cannot yourself swear that this statem
correct ?—A. I cannot swear that; but it is made up from the sta
of the Fishery Commission and investigations.

Q. Even to that I do not think you can swear ?—A. No mor
Mr. Whitcher or Mr. Smith can swear to the correctness of Can
statistics.

Q. You directed it to be made up by one of your assistants ?—A

Q. And you do not know whether it has been made up corree
not ?—A. No more than any man can swear to the accuracy of his
ant's work.

Q. As a fact, you have no personal knowledge as to its correctn
A. Certainly not.

Q. You directed it to be done ?—A. Precisely; it stands on the
footing as any table made up by a clerk.

Q. Did you directly take into consideration statements made t
nesses here ?—A. I have very largely taken into consideration in
made by Mr. Goode, my assistant, of witnesses here, according
same definite plan which I have adopted elsewhere.

Q. Inasmuch as we have not the results of what these inquiries
and since the Commissioners have not them before them, none of
inquiries which you made, and none of the information which yo
obtained, are before us, the papers being locked up in your des
They are all in the archives of the Fishery Commission.

Q. Then we have no means of testing the accuracy of those figu
A. No; not the slightest. They are there for what they are wo
present them with the affidavit which was made by my assistant

Q. You admit that you have not furnished us with any means
testing their accuracy ?—A. You must take them for what th
worth. They are of the same value as any table published by the
ery Department of Canada or the United States or anywhere els

Q. If I rightly understood your answer to Mr. Dana yesterda
rather think that the throwing over of offal amounts to nothin
No; I do not think that it does amount to anything.

Q. I thought you gave a rather interesting description of sea-
A. I merely say that it is a question whether it is or was injur
the food of fishes on the coast, as has been maintained. It is a q
as to which we have no definite proof that it injures the fishes;
am inclined to believe that it has more of a local and immediat
on the fish than it does injury to the fish.

Q. Would it not necessarily injure the spawn in its neighborh
A. No.

Q. You think not ?—A. No.

Q. Not if thrown over on the top of spawn ?—A. No; you
throw it over all day long and try to injure a load of floating spa
you could not do it. Nobody has ever suggested that gurry affe
spawn. By spawn I suppose you mean eggs.

Q. Yes.—A. No; nothing of the kind is to be thought of.

). You quoted yesterday Mr. Whiteaves's Report ; he says on page 11 :

n case Americans are allowed to fish in Canadian waters, the custom (said to be cticed by them) of splitting the fish caught at sea, and throwing the offal overboard, the fishing ground, should not be permitted.

\. I do not think that I quoted Mr. Whiteaves on that point, but :h regard to the spawning-time of mackerel in the bay.

). In your Report of 1872 and 1873, Mr. Milner is your assistant ?— Yes.

). On page 19 I find this language used :

HROWING OFFAL ON THE FISHING-GROUNDS.—It is the uniform testimony of all ermen that throwing offal or dead fish in the vicinity of the fishing-grounds is offen- ɔ to the whitefish, and drives him away. The whitefish is peculiarly cleanly in its tincts, and has an aversion for muddy or foul water of any description. Most fisher- n regard their own interest sufficiently to be careful in this particular, while many eless and shiftless men injure themselves and others by dumping offal and dead fish where in the lake where they find it convenient, reducing the catch in the vicinity several months.

\. Yes.

. It is also stated :

nsalable fishes are generally thrown overboard in the vicinity of the nets.

ou do not dissent from that opinion ?—A. No ; not at all. The es, however, are totally different. There are no scavengers in fresh ter as there are in the sea ; there are no sea-fleas, or sculpin, or lob- rs, or anything of the kind, to clean up offal in fresh water, as is the e in the ocean.

. In your opinion, are purse-seiners proper or improper agents for ;ing fish ?—A. I have not formed any opinion on the subject ; but I ɪ inclined to think, however, that this is not a destructive mode of hing. They destroy a good many fish, but I do not think that they minish the absolute number of fish in the sea.

By Sir Alexander Galt :

Q. Will you repeat that ?—A. I say I do not think that they affect ɔ total number of the fish in the sea materially, although they destroy d waste a great many fish. If you will permit me I would state my ɪson for this view ; it is this : Every school of mackerel has a large dy of predatory fish attendant upon it, such as dogfish, sharks, and her species, which are bound to have so many fish a day. They will t their one, two, or three fish a day, and if they cannot get them dead ey will eat them alive ; therefore, if a large body of young mackerel thrown out of these purse-seines, besides mackerel which are rejected d worthless, the predatory fish that are attendant upon the mackerel ll eat these dead fish, and if they do not find them dead they will ke them alive ; so it does not affect the number of fish in the sea.

By Mr. Thomson :

Q. Are you positive about that ; do you undertake to say that the edaceous fishes will, in preference to capturing live fish, which they n easily do, be content with dead ones ? — A. I think that is very :ely.

Q. There, there—you say " very likely " ?—A. I cannot say. I am t a predacious fish ; but I would prefer a live fish. 1 am pretty sure, wever, that these fish are quite ready to be saved the trouble of taking eir prey. It is on precisely the same principle that bait-fish, such as pliu and herring, are placed on hooks and cast overboard to catch the me fish, which follow and eat them in the natural way. I think this ay be inferred from that.

Q. You have something to do with the Annual Record of Scie
Industry, I believe ?—A. Something—yes.

Q. Do you agree with the language used in an article conta
page 473 of this journal for 1872 ?—A. I did not write that, bu
lished it.

Q. Have you in any article stated that you dissent from it ?—
It is not my business to do so. That article merely reflects the
of the writer. I would be very sorry to believe one-half of wha
lish in that periodical; but it expresses the progress of belief and
and I take it accordingly.

, Q. It is a matter of speculation whether dead fish are eaten,
say, by predaceous fishes; this is mere theory ?—A. I have no do
they are so eaten.

By Mr. Whiteway :

Q. You have stated that the largest quantity of codfish take:
shortest possible time was in the vicinity of the Loffoden Islan
Yes.

Q. You said that something like 25 millions were taken by
people?—A. Yes.

Q. In a very short time—in the course of three months ?—
and in a very small space.

Q. Where did you get your statistics from ?—A. From a repol
Norwegian Government.

Q. For what year ?—A. 1868, I think.

Q. Whose report was it ?—A. It is an extremely hard jaw-b
title; it is an abstract, prepared by Hermann Baars, of Bergen,]
It was an article prepared by him for presentation at the Paris
tion.

Q. You have not seen reports published since that time ?—A.
I have them much later.

Q. Did these later statistics correspond with the former as
the quantity ?—A. I know that the capture of cod in Loffoden Isl
1876, amounted to 21 or 22 millions; I have the figures here.

Q. Are you aware what quantity of codfish is caught on the
Newfoundland ?—A. No. I have been earnestly trying to get
tistics of Newfoundland in this respect, but I have not been ab
tain them as yet. I hope you will send them to me.

Q. You are not aware whether it is an inshore or deep-sea fii
that island ?—A. No. I know nothing about it.

Q. You say that fish are dried and used as food for cattle
islands and in Norway ?—A. Yes.

Q. What sort of cattle use it ?—A. Horses, oxen, and cows;
it with great avidity.

Q. What portion do they make use of ?—A. Any part, but m
erally the heads, which are offal; they make most admirable ni

Q. You say that a great many nations dress very largely in
of cod and salmon ?—A. Yes.

Q. Will you kindly tell me what nations these are ?—A. '
Tchuktchi, the Aleutian Islanders, the Norton Sound Esquima
natives of Alaska, and a few others.

Q. You say further that the most extensive resorts of col
Grand Banks and George's Bank; can you tell me the quanti
taken on these banks ?—A. No; I have not made any investi
tabulation in this regard.

Q. Then you really base that opinion upon no data ?—A.
base it on my general impression on that subject. I merely

as being the most prominent particular banks and localities which
d frequent. In speaking of the islands and other places in this
ction, I mentioned banks off the coast of Labrador, but I did not
o the great sweep of northern waters where the cod is found dif-
    I referred more particularly to the places that are known and
ly mentioned. What is not published in this regard I know noth-
out.
With reference to Labrador, can you answer whether the fish are
inshore—that is, within the three-mile range, or on the Banks off-
?—A. I am told, but I cannot say with what certainty, that at
ı seasons of the year the cod are there taken in great quantities
e from boats, but that the great bodies of the fish are on the Banks
e distance from the shore.
Are these Banks fished ?—A. That I cannot tell.
Vhere are these Banks ?—A. As far as I can learn, they extend
stance of some 15 or 25 miles, perhaps, along almost the entire
of the coast of Labrador.
Vill you pledge yourself to that statement ?—A. No; I know noth-
out it.
    rom whom did you get this information ?—A. From the published
ʒs of Professor Hind.
    think he indicates in these writings the exact position of these
ɛ ?—A. I think that probably he does. I may have located them
ar or too far from the shore. I speak merely in general terms.
I think that his report only indicates the existence of banks on
n portions of the coast of Labrador ?—A. Perhaps I may have
them too extensive.
You have referred to a bank on which codfish are taken, off Cape
ıbout 20 miles, I think, in length ; can you give me any informa-
s regards the annual product of this bank ?—A. I think you will
ıat given in Captain Atwood's testimony.
Can you give it ?—A. No; I know nothing of it, except from Cap-
ıtwood.
Is any report made in any public office in Massachusets or the
ı, from which you can gather information as regards the exact
ity of fish taken outside of the three-mile limit, and inside of this
—A. No.
In other words, is a report concerning the quantity of fish taken
ı and without this limit published ?—A. No.
Is nothing published in this relation ?—A. It is my business, or
lf-imposed mission to collect that information, and I am doing so
t as I can. I hope that my next report will contain a great deal
ɛ and other useful information.
How many vessels are engaged in this fishery off Cape Cod ?—A.
ıot tell you; but I have a great deal of information on this subject
· records, which, however, I do not carry with me, and I do not
my memory for anything.
I think you referred to the herring fishery as yielding a very great
ity of fish on the American coast ?—A. Yes.
On the coast of the United States ?—A. Yes.

Q. And in winter?—A. I do not think that they are caught ii
north of Cape Cod; I do not think so; but so little is know
biology and the natural history of herring that this might be the i
yet it be not known—I mean not known to the ordinary public.
entirely new to me five years ago that herring spawned on the
chusetts coast at all.

Q. Then there is no winter herring-fishery there?—A. The
fishery is a very small one; it is carried on around Block Isla
Narragansett Bay, but whether capabilities exist for prosecutin,
ter fishery elsewhere on the coast I cannot say.

Q. How do you account then for the fact that such a number
vessels come to the southern coast of Newfoundland for herring
are so prolific on your own coast?—A. That I cannot say. Wl
follows one line or direction rather than another I do not know
may not have appliances for catching them on our coast, and tl
not have the means of taking them in such quantities as is pos
Newfoundland; but it is certainly a notorious fact that herring a
more abundant on the coast of Newfoundland than they are on tl
of the United States; though whether the herring that are wa
the United States coast could or could not be had in the United
I cannot say; but I do think that herring are vastly more abun
Newfoundland and the Bay of Fundy than they are farther soui

Q. That accounts, then, for the number of your vessels that
Newfoundland for them, no doubt. Give us the number of i
United States coast along which fishing rights have been conc
British subjects under the Washington Treaty?—A. 1,112.

Q. Can you give the extent of the Dominion coast, including
Newfoundland?—A. Yes; the coast line of the Province of Ca
810 miles; of New Brunswick, 1,000 miles; of Nova Scotia, 39(
of Newfoundland, 1,650 miles; of Grand Manan, 30 miles; of
Edward Island, 285 miles; of the Magdalen Islands, 85 miles
Anticosti Island, 265 miles; the total length of the coast line (
ern British North America is 4,515 miles, four times that of the
States east of Cape Cod.

By Mr. Dana:

Q. Following the bays?—A. Following the large bays, but (
the smaller ones.

By Mr. Whiteway:

Q. In your statement regarding the annual product of the D
fisheries, you have not included the Newfoundland fisheries?—
I have only that of the Dominion of Canada.

Q. Are you aware that something like 1,500,000 or 1,600,000
of fish are caught in Newfoundland alone?—A. I think that
probable, but I do not know.

Q. Besides the large herring fishery?—A. I am very anxious
exactly what the Newfoundland catch is; I have made inquiries
ing it; but I have not been able to obtain any such public data

Q. You say that the depletion of the codfish on the coast
the result of the depletion of the river fisheries on the coast of
chusetts?—A. I gave that as presumably one reason for it. It
ably a very important element in the fishery.

Q. Then any act which may prove injurious to the bay fist
the coast would seriously affect the inshore fisheries by remov
which induced the cod to go on the coast?—A. Yes; it would
effect, I think. Possibly a very decided effect.

As a naturalist I would ask you to answer one or two questions.
do you mean by the term "fish"? Can you give us a definition?—
ell, a fish is a cold-blooded vertebrate, having a particular mode
)iration. It breathes through gills instead of lungs, and it has a
of a particular construction.
[will read the definition from a book published in New York by
·r Brothers, the Eucylopedia of Commerce, edited by ———
-. I presume that is an authority that can be relied upon (reads
,iou). I suppose that is a definition that can be relied upou?—A.
thiuk it cannot be relied upon at all. That would make anything
oats in the water a fish. So that the seal would be a fish and the
would be a fish.
[his is the Encyclopedia of Commerce. I suppose it is reliable.
n as an encyclopedia of commerce?—A. Well, I don't know. I
think it is quoted very much. It is probably a very good compi-
, There are a great many books of that class that one has occasion
k at without feeling that they are perfectly accurate.
Do you consider the seal a fish?—A. Not at all.
Why?—A. Because it is a warm-blooded mammal. It breathes
ans of lungs, &c.
[s not the whale the same?—A. The whale is no more a fish than
al.
[t is a mammal; it is a swimmer?—A. If you were to fall over-
in mid-ocean you would be a swimmer.
How is it with the walrus?—A. It is a mammal, not a fish.
So is the whale, is it not?—A. Yes.
How do you draw a distinction between the whale and the seal;
e you consider a fish and the other not?—A. I don't consider the
fish.
[thought you did. Now, don't you consider it a very unreasonable
on the part of the United States, the refusal to admit seal-oil as
l. Perhaps you don't care to answer?—A. I don't object to
r. I am not a politician. I am perfectly willing to answer the
on. I know that the penguin is considered a fish, commercially—
s, that penguin-oil is received in England as fish-oil.
[hat is a very important matter. I should like very much to have
en down that, as a commercial oil, the penguin-oil is considered a
l?—A. It is in London.
[s it not in the United States?—A. No; but as far as I am
ied the oil is classified in the London custom-house and trade
is as a fish-oil.
What is the quintal in weight?—A. 112 pounds in some localities,
some 100 pounds.
[t was given here as 114 pounds?—A. Well, it might be 114
s. It is simply my impression that the quintal is considered 112
s. I would not be positive. A practical fish-dealer would give
positive information than I could.

By Mr. Dana:

Here, on the 148th page of British Testimony we have a letter
Governor Hill to the Earl of Kimberly, taken from the journals
legislative council in Newfoundland. It appears here, in the
ace of Judge Bennett, as follows:

·   GOVERNMENT HOUSE,
                            Newfoundland, July 4, 1871.

LORD: I have the honor to inform your lordship that on the 1st
it I sent a telegram to your lordship, as follows, viz: "In reference

to terms of Washington Treaty, it is understood that fish-oil i
seal-oil. Explanation will oblige this government." And on
instant received the following reply, viz: "I am of opinion that
does not include seal-oil.—EARL KIMBERLY."

I have, &c.,

STEPHEN J. E

The Right Honorable the EARL OF KIMBERLEY,
&c., &c., &c.

Now you were asked a question what you thought of the exclu
that oil.

Mr. WHITEWAY. He didn't answer it.

Mr. DANA. You withdrew it, didn't you? Perhaps this letter o
to your mind.

The PRESIDENT. We suggested that the question had better b
drawn.

By Sir Alexander Galt:

Q. Before you leave, there are one or two questions I would
ask you. We have been told by a witness—I think it was your
that there was a difference in the appearance of the codfish tl
caught in certain waters. I would like to ask if you have notic
yourself.—A. Yes, there are a great many varieties of cod. Tl
as far as I believe, one species, but they assume peculiar variet
pending upon the particular bottom they are found on and tl
they consume. Experts will tell you from what Banks particu
are taken. For instance, inshore cod are nearly all red, while
cod are gray. Some have larger heads, some smaller, some hav
shoulders, and some are slender, but all these differences are lo
do not involve a distinction of species.

Q. Would not that, in your opinion, confirm the theory that
is not really a migratory fish?—A. It would. That is very go
dence that there is no great migration.

Q. There is another question I wished to ask you. You g
a very interesting account of a company that has been formed
purpose of catching these predaceous fish, and you seemed to t
would have the effect of materially diminishing their numbers.
if human means can reduce the predaceous fish, would you no
that the appliances that are being used by fishermen must be di
ing the edible fish?—A. I don't think that the amount captured
has any appreciable influence upon the supply of fish in the sea

Q. Well, that is what I understood you to say.—A. That w
effect is produced by waste or extravagance in the capture of th
itself so trifling, in proportion to the natural wear and tear of
that it may be thrown entirely out of account. The report of t
ish Fishery Commission is very satisfactory on that point.

Q. The only reason why I asked the question was that you
to think this company would succeed in reducing the number o
ceous fish.—A. Well, those are large and take a long time to
growth. You can imagine a limit to the abundance of certain
the shark, though you cannot to the other fish, such as the cod
mackerel.

Q. You are United States Commissioner. Are you cloth
authority respecting the several States of the Union?—A. No.

Q. Well, have you any authority?—A. I have none, except t
are all perfectly willing to have me spend all the money I will

s, and that they are willing to have me put as many shad, salmon, cod, and useful food-fishes as I think I can spare in their waters.

Have the United States collectively or the individual States the titutional control over their fisheries; that is, their inshore fisher- —A. The river fisheries are under the control of the several States, the question of the jurisdiction of the sea fisheries has not yet been ed. For the present it lies in the States. The general government exercised no control or authority on the inshore fisheries.

By Hon. Mr. Kellogg:

Referring to your hypothesis about the waters of the world being lied with one kind of fish as another leaves, what have you to say gard to the whale fishery; what is going to supply that ?—A. Well, ery diminishes to a certain extent until it does not pay, and then is doned. After being let alone it increases and again becomes a table enterprise.

Have any of the species of fish that were used in ancient times ppeared? They used fish in ancient times just as much as they do

Do you know of any tribe having actually disappeared ?—A. The kind of fish that has gone entirely out, so far as I know, is a kind ackerel that was formerly found, known as the chub-mackerel or ye mackerel. It was formerly well known. Thirty years ago it extremely common, a steady measurable article of the fish supply. ve been in search of specimens ever since I have been in my present of inquiry, and have a standing offer of $25 for a specimen, but it has been produced. There are many instances of the local abandonment ttensive shores. For instance, herring was formerly abundant on coast of Sweden.

Do you refer to a distinct species of mackerel ?—A. A totally dis- species. We had two species on our coast and now we have only I dare say there may be a few, but we don't find them as formerly.

No. 70.

OWARD M. CHURCHILL, of Rustico, Prince Edward Island, a ed States citizen, fish-merchant, called on behalf of the Govern- t of the United States, sworn and examined.

By Mr. Foster:

uestion. How long have you lived at Rustico ?—Answer. Nineteen s.

Have you been there usually through the winter ?—A. Most of the . Some winters I have been in Boston, and some in Charlottetown.

Most of the winters as well as summers you have been on the id ?—A. Yes.

What is your business ?—A. Fishing.

Explain how you carry it on ?—A. Well, we engage men in the ng. I do differently from most of them, I expect; I hire them by month.

To do what ?—A. To fish or to do anything else on shore, but the eral thing is to fish.

How many men do you hire ?—A. The average is about 45.

How do you hire them ?—A. I hire them by the month, feed and them and everything.

Do you supply boats ?—A. Yes.

How many boats ?—A. Eight.

Q. How many stages have you?—A. I only run one; I have c
but I only run one.

Q. Do you have a store also in connection with your business
Yes.

Q. What do you pay these men as wages. You say they are emp
by you?—A. The average wages are, I think, about $22 or $23 ea

Q. Do you find them?—A. Yes.

Q. For how many months in the year?—A. Very near four—thre
a half.

Q. Then you have the total produce of their catch?—A. Yes.

Q. What do they catch?—A. Fish—mackerel principally.

Q. Now, you have a house at Rustico?—A. Yes.

Q. You live there with your family?—A. Yes.

Q. What are your facilities for observing where the vessels and
fish off Rustico?—A. I can see. Of course we are not on a cap
we can see a few miles around.

Q. Your place of business and home are in sight of the harbo
the sea beyond it?—A. Yes.

Q. Now I would like you to tell the Commission where the boa
for mackerel off Rustico; how far out they go and how close in?—
is all distances, of course. In the spring and summer months th
ways fish in closer.

Q. How near is "close in?"—A. From a mile to three miles. L
the season they have to go out.

Q. How far?—A. As far as ten miles. The last month of thi
they were out ten miles. The average is eight or seven. They
so that you can't see the boats.

Q. What is the size of the boat?—A. Well, the boats are 27
feet keel.

Q. How does the size of the boats that are built for the last
three years compare with those that were used previously?—A
have built larger boats for the last two or three years. A fe
ago they used small boats altogether, about 15 or 16 feet keel.

Q. Are they being made bigger to enable them to go farther
A. Yes. It is fall fish we depend upon mostly. The small boat
like to go off for them.

Q. What do you mean by saying you depend mostly upon t
fish?—A. Well, the mackerel go off in the fall. They don't k
close in as they do in the spring and summer.

Q. Which part of the mackerel season is the most importa
earlier or the latter part?—A. The latter part, of course.

Q. Why?—A. Because the mackerel are larger and fatter late
season. They are growing. The first mackerel are always poor
last mackerel we expect to be fat.

Q. Has the mackerel season ended yet?—A. It is about ended
are hauling in the boats now.

Q. When did it begin?—A. The 10th of July.

Q. For boat-fishing, has this been a good year?—A. Yes; it ha
a fair, pretty good year.

Q. What has been the quality?—A. The average has been poo

Q. But the quantity?—A. The quantity has not been great, b
prices have been high. We haven't caught a great many.

Q. How was the year's business in 1867?—A. Poor, very poor

Q. What was the result of last year's business? Did you m
lose?—A. We lost.

Q. How much?—A. Over $3,000.

Will you make it up this year?—A. I wish I could; I will not do etter; I would be satisfied with that.

You have had an opportunity of observing, of course, where the d States vessels fish?—A. So far as there are any outside off ℃o.

You know where the mackerel fishers fish off Rustico?—A. Yes.

How far off do they go?—A. They are sometimes inside and some-outside. The last two or three years we haven't had any there to of. I think ten or a dozen is as high as I have seen within two ee years.

Usually, principally or chiefly, do they fish within or more than miles from land off Rustico?—A. It is very hard to say; I should bout three miles was where they fish. Sometimes you see the fleet le, and the boats run out to see what they are doing. It is a part island they don't care about staying in close.

Why, is there not a harbor?—A. There is no harbor; there is a r, but it is not fit for a vessel. A vessel can't come into Rustico.

Why not?—A. There is no water; it is a barred harbor.

What is the depth of water over the bar?—A. Eight feet of water.

With what tide?—A. With a good tide.

Do you know about how far it is from the land off Rustico to a ht line run from Cape North to East Point? Suppose you drew a ht line from Cape North to East Point, how long would the line m Rustico to meet that straight line at right angles?—A. I don't any more than I have heard. I have heard it stated as high as les. It is over 20. I never measured. I don't know anything it any more than I have heard.

You were on the island during the Reciprocity Treaty?—A. Yes.

You were there at the time when there was a duty on mackerel?—es.

You were there when the Washington Treaty passed, and have since?—A. Yes.

Now, I want to know what you regard the effect of the fishery s of the Washington Treaty to be upon the fishing interest of e Edward Island?—A. Well, so far as that is concerned, we would put our fish in free than pay $2 a barrel; that is all.

You know how you regard it; I want your opinion.—A. Well, is all; of course I look at the money; not anything else. We l rather not pay $2 than pay it.

Did you have to pay it when there was a duty on it?—A. Yes.

Didn't it come out of the people you sold the fish to in the States? If I hire men, I lose that.

You are satisfied of that?—A. I am sure of it.

Suppose the duty was to be reimposed on fish; what effect would e on your business?—A. Well, I don't know. Of course I could re men to begin with. If I did, I would have to hire them at less s. If I thought that really was to be the case I would not hire t all.

You would not hire men to fish for you at all?—A. No; I would em take their own risk.

What was the opinion of the people of Prince Edward Island, as you know?—A. When it was passed, of course it was against

What was?—A. That is to pay the duty. Of course when we t fish we had to figure the $2 in. If fish were selling for $5 in n, of course we had to take the $2 out of that.

Q. Suppose the Washington Treaty hadn't passed, and you ha~
along with the duty, how much longer would it have taken to
the business of selling mackerel in the United States from the isle
A. I don't know; it is pretty hard to tell that. We are in busines
cannot wind it up in a day or a year, especially the way I was sit
because I have to supply my men ahead all the time. If the dut;
to be $2 or $5 next year, I could not help it. They are supplied fc
year. The men I have are, two-thirds of them, men with familie;
ive right in Rustico. I have to supply them all winter.

Q. They are always indebted to you?—A. Yes.

Q. You are satisfied you had to pay the duty when it was paid
Certainly.

Q. Didn't you get it back?—A. Not I.

By Mr. Davies:

Q. You have been at Rustico before the Washington Treaty ar
ried on your business all the time the $2 duty was paid, and ha~
ried it on ever since?—A. Yes.

Q. Taking the last six years, have the fisheries largely increa
Prince Edward Island?—A. For the last six years? Well, I don't
think they have.

Q. What part of the island do you speak of when you sa,
haven't?—A. Just where I am.

Q. I don't mean your own business.—A. I mean in Rustico.
answer for anything else.

Q. Are not larger boats being built?—A. Yes.

Q. And more of them?—A. Yes.

Q. That is what I mean.—A. I thought you asked if the catc
been bigger.

Q. I mean that more people have gone into it?—A. Yes.

Q. And more money has been invested in it?—A. Yes.

Q. As to the catch, of course you can't tell what the catch was
No.

Q. I want to show that the fisheries increased, and more mon
invested and more people engaged, although a duty of $2 a barr
imposed.—A. At the time the duty was put on it was pretty blue

Q. And for the two or three years the duty remained on, do yo~
to say that more people didn't go into it?—A. I don't think it.

Q. Since then there have?—A. I think so.

Q. You don't know what the increase was then, or whether the
any?—A. No.

Q. Would you say there was none? Could you state that?—A
I could not.

Q. You have a strong interest in this $2 duty, haven't you?
have.

Q. Have you a large claim, about five or six thousand dollar
About half of that.

Q. I have the statement here from the petition in relation to th
is $4,999 marked against you.—A. I am glad it is so much; I t
it was about $3,000.

Q. When you applied to get the duty refunded, you felt th
should get it back?—A. Yes.

. Of course you naturally felt that that should be paid to yo~
Yes.

Q. Now didn't you buy fish as well as catch them?—A. Yes.

Q. Didn't you buy them with the knowledge that the duty w~
refunded?—A. Yes.

Q. And you paid $2 more than you otherwise would have done?—A. s. I didn't buy many.

Q. I refer to what you did buy.—A. Yes.

Q. Have you thought over this question of the duty, whether the con·mer pays it?—A. I gave it up long ago.

Q. Who do you think paid the duty on the potatoes we shipped last ar from the island?—A. It is no use to ask me that.

Q. Who do you think?—A. Potatoes are one thing and fish another.

Q. I want to see if the same principle does not govern both.—A. It merely guess-work, anything I should say.

Q. We got a price large enough to pay the duty?—A. Potatoes are ferent. There are a large fleet of American fishermen catching mack-d. What fish we catch is like a drop in the bucket there.

Q. Have you studied the statistics upon that point to see?—A. That my idea.

Q. Do you know what proportion of the whole quantity consumed by people of the United States comes from this country?—A. I don't ow anything about it.

Q. Then when you say it is a mere drop in the bucket you are speak-; at random?—A. I know it. I know there are 600 or 800 sail of ves-s. All I know is that when I send mackerel to the Boston market, it what the American fleet gets that governs our prices.

Q. You are getting high prices this year?—A. Yes.

Q. Has the failure of the American fleet anything to do with that?—Yes.

Q. When the price goes up beyond a certain point, who pays the duty n?—A. Well, that is what I think. If the American fleet catches a at many mackerel, we get a small price.

Q. I think you stated with reference to the vessel-fishing that it is ut three miles off they fish, and that they fish inside and outside?—Yes.

Q. That is what I supposed. Now, on the boat-fishing we are, I nk, a little at variance, that is, you and the witnesses I have called. u know Ross?—A. Yes.

Q. He does business alongside of you?—A. Yes; he is a good square n.

Q. A man of thorough integrity?—A. He is an honest man.

Q. A man you would believe?—A. Yes; a first class-man.

Q. Now, there is another point I want to refer to in this connection. u don't go in boats yourself?—A. No; I have never been out all nmer.

Q. So that men who actually do go would have a better knowledge the particular locality where the fishing was done than you could?—Yes; but I know where the boats are better than they do them-ves.

Q. How do you know that?—A. Because I am awake and they are eep half the time. Each one of them may know where he is himself, t I know where the whole of them are.

Q. And you think they don't know?—A. Each boat may know for nself, but I can see better than they can.

Q. You mean that, looking from the shore, you are apt to form a dif-ent opinion from those in the boats?—A. Yes.

Q. Don't you think that the man who goes out would have a better inion than the man on shore?—A. Not as to where they lie.

Q. Ross gives his opinion that nine-tenths of the mackerel caught by boat fishermen are taken within three miles?—A. I don't think it.

Q. Alexander McNeil, who is he ?—A. He is a good man.

Q. He is a justice of the peace ?—A. Yes.

Q. Of good standing and integrity ?—A. First class.

Q. Well, he has been fishing a good many years. He is a farm fisherman ?—A. Yes.

Q. He has been actively engaged since 1851, and he says tl caught by the boats are taken (see statement in evidence).—A. Th Cavendish.

Q. That would be correct there ?—A. He has a boat that is not than this table. They have nothing but dories and skiffs. The their boats on the beach on the rocks. We could not do that wil boats. We have different boats altogether. Those Cavendish mei down to Rustico and fish in our boats.

Q. Then he does catch fish in that close ?—A. Yes; I have no his statements are true as to Cavendish. It is bolder water, to with.

Q. How far from Rustico is it ?—A. Two or three miles.

Q. William J. McNeill, the member—you know him ?—A. Yes.

Q. He is a respectable man ?—A. He is a good man.

Q. He is of the same opinion. Now, I will take the months o and August—do you think the fishing is done within three miles in months ?—A. I do.

Q. Well within ?—A. Yes.

Q. Then, in the fall, the boats go out more ?—A. Yes.

Q. Is it not the fact that they catch both inside and outside (the fall ?—A. Certainly.

Q. Part is taken inside and part outside ?—A. Yes.

Q. You don't know the proportion ?—A. No; but generally tl out. They expect to go out in the fall.

By Hon. Mr. Kellogg :

Q. About the middle of September, for instance; is that a tim they go out or in ?—A. They go off then—off shore.

Q. Do they fish inside much about that time ?—A. Not much years are different; but they are always prepared to go outside.

No. 71.

ISAAC C. HALL, of Charlottetown, Prince Edward Island, an throp, Mass., fish merchant, called on behalf of the Government United States, sworn and examined.

By Mr. Foster :

Question. You are a citizen of the United States ?—Answer.

Q. You have a house in Charlottetown ?—A. A commercial yes.

Q. And you live part of the year at Charlottetown and parl year at Winthrop, Mass., near Boston, Suffolk County ?—A. Ye

Q. How old are you ?—A. Fifty-seven.

Q. How many years have you been engaged in the fishing busi Prince Edward Island ?—A. This is the twentieth year. It wi years next spring.

Q. Since the spring of 1858 what portion of each season ·h. spent on Prince Edward Island ?—A. I should think about 9 m(the year.

Q. Have you been there through the winter so far ?—A. I hav six years there pretty nearly all the time—part of the winter.

Where did you reside the first year on the island ?—A. Cascum-
e, or rather Alberton, Cascumpeque Harbor.

Since then you have resided at Charlottetown ?—A. Yes.

Now, you have been in the fishing business, how have you prose-
d it ?—A. I have been engaged, owning and fitting out vessels, and
-fishing, and I have been purchasing mackerel from the first.

Have you had any stages anywhere ?—A. Yes.

Where ?—A. You mean the firm ?

I don't want to ask you as to those that have been in charge of
partner, but how many have you had charge of yourself ?—A. I
had charge of three. One at Rustico.

How long have you had that ?—A. Seven years.

What others ?—A. One on Grand River, near Georgetown, about
miles east of it, on the south side of the island, and another at
George, Nova Scotia.

When you began to do business on Prince Edward Island, it was
t three years after the Reciprocity Treaty went into effect. Was
much fishing done then by the inhabitants ?—A. There was very
e. It was in its infancy.

Did they know how to take care of the fish they caught, to cure
n for market ?—A. No; it was sufficient to condemn fish in the
ton market, so far as bringing good prices was concerned, that they
from Prince Edward Island. That was the case previous to 1858.

. Do you know how many barrels of mackerel were sent this year
yourself and your partner to Boston ?—A. I don't know that I can
it exactly. I may approximate it. Only part of the catch has
shipped.

. Do you know what the catch has been of yourself and your part-
up to the present time—whether it is still in hand or going for-
d ?—A. Do you wish to ask what quantity I am shipping or what is
extent of the catch ?

. What number of barrels of mackerel do your firm take, in the first
e, and then what do they buy ?—A. The shipment will probably
unt this year to something like 7,000 or 8,000 barrels.

. How much last year ?—A. Can I refer to memoranda ?

. Certainly.—A. Our whole receipts last year were 4,534 barrels in
ton; about 300 were sent to Halifax; in all, 4,834 barrels.

. How much opportunity have you had to observe where the mack-
-boats fish off Prince Edward Island, and where the mackerel-ves-
fish ?—A. My observations this summer. I have been at Rustico a
t part of the time, and I have had a chance to observe the places
re they fish. and have taken some notice, more than I have hereto-
. I have been buying fish since I went on the island, more or less,
have a general idea, but nothing very accurate. In regard to boat-
ing in Rustico, they fish in the early part of the season quite near
shore, from one and a half to two and a half miles, and later in the
son, when the fish begin to move south, they have to go wide out for
m.

. What do you mean by "wide out"?—A. From four to eight miles.

. Take last month, run back to the middle of September or the first
k in September; within what distance from the shore were they fish-
?—A. We have been fishing wide out. We have caught no fish
hin four or five miles.

. You sent Mr. Davies some mackerel the other day; how far out
e those caught ?—A. I answered that question before.

. What has the quality of mackerel been this year at the island ?—

A. We have had some very fine fish—a few, but the majority have poor, very similar to 1874, when we got such a large catch.

Q. The boat catch has been how good this year?—A. It has good—more than an average.

Q. But the average quality has been poor?—A. Yes.

Q. Is that usually the case when the boat catch has been large? Well, we never get a large catch with boats unless they are poor; is a very large catch I am speaking of now. A very large catch inve small and poor fish. The average quality of the catch has not good this year, although the quantity has been large. I have at tico ten boats, and we have taken 1,250 barrels, that is, 125 to a' That is an average. Some of them have got 150, and some down to I think the first shipment amounted to 708 barrels. Over 650 of t were poor—number 3. I call all fish that will go to number 2 fat.

Q. You have a table?—A. I have a table of the percentage of fat poor mackerel from 1868 down to 1876. Shall I read it?

Q. If you please.—A. This is a table of the whole quantity that firm received:

Statement of mackerel received by Hall, Myrick & Co., Boston, 1868 to 1876, inclusi

• Year	No. 1.	No. 2.	No. 3.	Total.	Percentage, fat.	Percentage, poor.
1868	6,639	1,320½	2,229	8,188	97	3
1869	2,314½	3,657½	2,047	8,019	75	25
1870	2,885	3,770	779½	7,434½	89½	10½
1871	756½	4,635½	8,898½	14,290½	38	62
1872	2,029½	2,655	1,861	6,545½	71	29
1873	2,286	2,052	1,474½	5,812½	75	25
1874	3,439½	7,841	6,710	17,997½	63	37
1875	1,590	4,436½	4,129	10,155½	59	41
1876	1,827½	1,506½	1,200	4,534	73	27

Q. That table brings you to this year? Now, what proportion of t were taken in boats and what proportion in vessels?—A. It is p hard to make an estimate without going to the books. I haven't pared myself for it.

Q. You can explain how many vessels you have.—A. The gre number we fitted out was in 1871, when I had 8 vessels.

Q. How many have you had since that?—A. I don't think I have over two since then.

Q. You can tell in round numbers whether three-fourths or se eighths is about the vessels' catch?—A. Taking the whole time tog there may have been one-eighth vessel catch.

Q. But, of late years, since 1871, would more than seven-eight boat catch?—A. Yes, sir; nearly all. There have only been a few sels out since then.

Q. Have you been inspector of mackerel on the island?—A. Ye

Q. You inspect your own mackerel?—A. Yes.

Q. When your mackerel goes to Boston is it required to be inspecte A. No.

Q. It is repacked and reinspected?—A. To some extent the p who buy it put it in smaller packages to suit their own convenienc

Q. But it is not necessarily reinspected?—A. No.

Q. And unless it is reinspected in that way your mackerel woul go into the Massachusetts inspection figures?—A. No, they don' foreign mackerel into their report.

Now, I have asked you where the boats have fished; I want to ask so far as your observation extends whether the vessels fish in the e places as the boats or further out?—A. I think the vessels fish e off shore than the boats do.

Have you made any observations this year, or looked to see where vessels were fishing?—A. I have been watching the vessels since I e been at Rustico this summer.

You told me of some instances in which you made a count?—A. e was at Cape George. I was there, and from the house I counted the glass some 31 vessels fishing.

How far off were they?—A. Well, most of them were wide out. unted three, I think, that were as I considered inside of the three-limit.

Now, I see there is a Mr. Curry, a gentleman, on your island, I eve, is not he?—A. Yes.

He reports you as having estimated the catch of mackerel in the as being one-third inside of three miles and two-thirds outside. Did give any such estimate and under what circumstances; and does correspond with your present belief?—A. I recollect Mr. Curry com- n and asking me about the fishing in the bay, and I gave him my judgment.

When was that?—A. Several years ago, I think. My attention been called to it here. It was 1873, I think. I cannot recollect ex-
y.

What do you say about that?—A. I gave him my opinion to the of my judgment as I thought at that time. My opinion in regard istance is not of course equal to that of men who have been on the all their lives catching mackerel. I have merely been around the es and conversed with the captains who have been fishing for me.

Where do your captains belong?—A. To the island, most of them.

What do you now say as to the distance that the vessels fish from shore off the bend of the island? Do they fish in where the boats r further off?—A. They are sometimes in where the boats are, but erally further out.

Is the boat fishing and vessel fishing the same kind?—A. No.

Explain the difference.—A. The boat goes from the shore and gs the fish to the stage, and has them dressed on shore, as a gen- thing. Some boats go out and stay three or four days from the h part of the island. My boats make two trips a day in the sum- , and in the fall they make one trip, the men taking their dinners i them. The fish are all brought ashore and dressed ashore, and boats all fish on the half line or quarter line.

Now, can the vessels with a crew of 12 or 14 or 16 men get a prof- le catch of mackerel if they fish in where your boats do that make two s a day? What do you say about that?—A. I don't know that pinion would be worth anything on that point. I never had any ex- ence in the matter. There are some years I think they would. Other s they would not.

As a matter of observation, do they usually fish as far in as the s do?—A. They don't. They fish further out.

If you were to estimate again as to the proportion of mackerel ght within three miles of the shore by the vessels, would you con- r two-thirds a large or small estimate?—A. If I was to estimate by ersation with the men I have seen here from the States, I should ider that a very large estimate. If I took my estimate from those have been fishing for me, and have been giving testimony before

you here, I should say it was a very small one. I don't think n
ion would be worth much.

Q. You were in business on the island at the time the Reci
Treaty ended?—A. I was.

Q. What was the effect of the abrogation of the treaty upo
business?—A. The treaty was abrogated, I think, in 1866. We
pay duties on mackerel from 1866 down to 1870. From 1866 to
had a very superior quality of fish, as you will see by the estimate
given you here. The prices were high, and we got good fish, ar
enabled to do very well until the close of the year 1870 or the be
of 1871, when the market completely broke down and we lost ever
you may say. It was in 1870 that the raid was made on us the
the Dominion Government, and that, coupled with the fall of the
erel, was a very heavy loss to us. Then, in 1870 we had a vei
catch of mackerel, but of poor quality, and, having to pay dut
mackerel netted us very little. I have an estimate of the exact
of what they netted us that year. The net sales of No. 1 were
1871; No. 2, $4.81; and No. 3, which is the largest portion, $3.4
average for the year was $4.09, at which we sold 14,289 barrels.

Q. What caused that fall?—A. There was a very large catch
on the American coast, and the market completely broke down
close of the season.

Q. They had a pretty large catch the year preceding and a go
was carried over?—A. Yes. A large part of the catch of 1870 v
sumed before our fish came in in 1871. Our prices fell from $23
a barrel down to $7. We had very heavy stocks and it con
crushed us.

Q. What part did you take in getting the fishery clause of the
ington Treaty enacted?—A. Well, I had a very large interest in
course, I went on at the time the resolutions were being got
the city of Boston recommending that the bill should pass. I
free fish and free fishing.

Q. You met your Gloucester friends taking the other view
met Mr. Procter, who was one of the delegates from Gloucest
others. He had charge of them and seemed to be the leadir
There was a gentleman from Cape Cod. I labored with him
deal, and tried to have my view accepted.

Q. You finally beat him?—A. Well, I would not say I beat th
my plan was successful.

Q. What was the opinion of the people of Prince Edward I
to the effect upon their fishing interests of the clauses of the V
ton Treaty?—A. I have never seen any one that was interested
fishery, either actually engaged or otherwise, but what, so fa
fishing interest was concerned, looked upon it as a great boo
anything to the fishing business.

Q. After the repeal of the Reciprocity Treaty, and before the
clauses of the Washington Treaty took effect, were you able to
duty of $2 a barrel, or any part of it, to your fish, or did it con
you as a fish-seller?—A. I always supposed, and still believe,
to take it out of the fish. There was pretty good evidence of
1871; when it came out there was not much left.

Q. If the duty were reimposed upon mackerel going from th
to the United States, what effect would it have on your business
would have a very disastrous effect. We could not carry it
the ordinary price to make it a success.

Q. Explain that matter. Explain your views to the Commiss

, whenever there is a large catch of mackerel on the American
es, a thing which happens once in six or seven years, the prices go
n invariably. In 1870, owing to the large quantity of mackerel
ht on the United States shores, the prices went down.

By Sir Alexander Galt:

At what time of the year did the break in the prices take place?—A.
mmenced about the December of 1870. We had to meet that dis-
r, and the consequence was that in 1871 we had to sell our mackerel
ne-half of what it cost. In 1874 they had a great catch there, but
was after we had free trade, of course. We had to meet a very low
e, and not having the duty to pay, we sustained ourselves and made
cent thing of it. We caught a large quantity of fish. The largest
ntity ever caught was that year.

By Mr. Davies:

I think you are wrong about that year.—A. The catch on the
erican coast was in 1870, the great catch. But they also had a pretty
e catch the following year, and we had a large catch also. It fol-
s almost invariably that whenever they have a very large catch on
American shore we get a large part of those same fish the next year.
ollowed in the same way. Now, in 1874 they had a pretty large
h, and we had a very large catch. There was not as many mackerel
he gulf, but they were all inshore, and we made the largest catch
r made. In 1876, last year, our catch was very small. It was the
rest year we ever had. We had not only a poor catch, but poor
es, as we had to contend with a great catch on the American
re. We had a small catch and they had a large catch, and the re-
was that prices were very low, and of course it was a very disas-
is year for Prince Edward Island—as much so as any previous to
l.

By Mr. Foster:

. Now, how large a quantity of high-priced mackerel, say, No. 1's,
the United States market take in a year?—A. I can tell how many
1's.
. Take it at $20 a barrel, how many barrels would the United States
ket ordinarily take?—A. It is now very unlike what it was ten
rs ago; that is, the market for mackerel. Then we had a winter
le, now we have none. The fact is no business man has now any
h in a winter market.
. What becomes of the people who hold mackerel over usually?—
It is a losing business. It has been losing for several years. For-
ly it was not so.
. You say the market is very different; what has caused the differ-
e?—A. I have no doubt in my own mind it is the very large intro-
tion of fresh fish into the country, caught through the winter, and
great production of the western lakes. That is the principal thing.
. But of the fact there is, no doubt, that is, of the limitation of the
kerel market?—A. No doubt. It was easier to sell 200,000 ten
rs ago than 100,000 to-day.
. Now, you take No. 3 mackerel, what would be the effect of a duty
$2 a barrel in the United States market?—A. We could not catch
n and ship them there ordinarily unless there was a great scarcity
re, as happens this season.
. Practically what would become of your business of catching mack-
if the duty of $2 a barrel were reimposed?—A. Well, when a man
s his head against a post he must get around the best way he can.

Q. You are satisfied you could not add the duty to the price o
mackerel in the United States market?—A. No, it can't be done.

Q. How low must mackerel be to have a large quantity taken in
American market? At what price does the willingness to pur
begin to decidedly fall?—A. When No. 3 go up over $8 a barrel
No. 2 over $10, and No. 1 over $14, the market begins to drop.
consumption falls off very much indeed.

Q. Now, you didn't answer how many barrels of mess macker
very fine No. 1's, could be disposed of at $20 a barrel?—A. Well,
mackerel is a very small percentage, not more than 3 per cent. o
mackerel consumed. Looking at the papers to-day, I see we rece
from 1868 to 1876, of mess mackerel, including No. 1 and No. 2
mackerel, we received in nine years 3,097 barrels in a total recei
mackerel of 145,980.

Q. Can you sell this mackerel in Canada? Is there any Can:
market?—A. No. I went through Canada and went through al
cities and large places, and spent a long time one winter.

Q. How far west did you go?—A. As far as Toronto. I sold :
half barrels and kits altogether, a dozen to some parties. I thoug
could introduce them and I shipped them one or two different lots.
sold a few, a very few, and I finally reshipped them to Detroit
closed them up. The people didn't know much about them, and (
care much about them.

Q. The boat fisheries of Prince Edward Island have increase
flourished very much for the last few years?—A. Yes, very much.
have good reasons for it.

Q. What reasons?—A. A better class of fishermen. When w
started business we had, of course, to work with green hands.
every other business, it has to be learned, and men have to be pre
for it. Then when the duties were put on, the best fishermen le
and went aboard American vessels. They could ship from the i
or go to Gloucester and get good vessels and have their fish go in
United States and sell for their whole value. We had no other ma
and had inferior men. Now, since we have a free market, these
have been coming back. The character of the men and their abil
fish has increased very much. So much so that I honestly thin
can calculate the catch of the same number of men now at 25 to 3
cent. more than it was formerly.

Q. To what do you attribute this greater supply of boat fishe
and better quality?—A. These men find they can fish here. T
their home in many cases. A great many get boats and find the
do very well here now fishing, and they stock at home and fish fro
shore.

Q. Now, if the island were cut off from the United States ma
what would become of the fishermen?—A. Well, these fishermen '
probably go back to their old business. I would not want to fis
had to pay the duty on mackerel.

Q. Your codfish don't go much to the United States market, at
cut?—A. No. Very little.

Q. You cure them for the West Indies?—A. The small fish are
for the West India market, and the large fish are either consum
home or sent to Halifax.

Q. If you were going to pursue the vessel mackerel-fishing
Prince Edward Island would you require pogies as a necessary b:
A. We never think of sending a vessel without pogies.

Q. How is it that your boats get along with herring and mak

catches when the vessels can't?—A. Well, it has been somewhat of a mystery to us all, but we make it work.

Q. What is the difference between boat and vessel fishing?—A. Well, the boat goes off and comes to anchor and springs up, and they commence to throw the bait over.

By Mr. Dana:

Q. Springing up means coming broadside to the tide?—A. Yes. They throw the bait and the tide takes it away, and they keep feeding it out and gathering the fish around them all day; and although they may not have a large quantity of fish they make a decent business of it. Whereas a vessel can't do the same thing. They heave to most of the time and drift.

By Mr. Foster:

Q. If you were going to pursue vessel-fishing would you make any use of seines?—A. The seines don't seem to be as favorable with us as they were.

Q. Have seines been made successful in the gulf?—A. I have had two mackerel seiners there. One wore out, and the other half wore out and I sold it.

Q. To what do you attribute the fact that seining in the gulf does not seem to be a success?—A. To the shoal water and rough bottom.

Q. What do you say about making a shoal seine?—A. My seine was a shoal seine, made expressly for the bottom. Three times out of four you get foul of rocks and a hole is made, and away goes the mackerel.

Q. Suppose the three-mile limit were distinctly marked out by a line of buoys so that anybody could see it, and there was no danger of making a mistake as to it, would the right of fishing within three miles of the shore be worth to the United States vessels three dollars a ton?—A. Well, I don't think many would take it. There are very few vessels coming here now when they have free access to the shores. If they had to pay a dollar a ton I think it would be very seldom they would come. There might be times when it would be different, because they know by telegraph when there is a good run of mackerel, and when the gulf is full they might come down, but ordinarily they would not.

Q. To what do you attribute the apparently great importance of this three-mile concession?—A. I think the great importance of it is this: that when sometimes a man sends a vessel down here it is a valuable property, and they have to trust it to their captains. A mistake in regard to the line might involve them in any amount of trouble. Any captain of a vessel if he was four or five miles out would make out to sea if he was fishing and a cruiser came along, and it was unsafe to go even within that distance of shore, because you could not tell certainly as to the distance. No man can tell unless he has instruments. He may be 25 or 50 per cent. out of the way.

Q. Whether by mistake of the skipper, or by mistake of the cruiser, whether intentionally or unintentionally, if a man's vessel is seized what is the effect?—A. It does not make a great deal of difference whether he is guilty or not. It amounts pretty much to the same thing, so far as my experience goes. The business is broken up and the men thrown out of employment for the season. Everything is gone, and the vessel is laid up six months, eaten up by the worms. You might get your vessel back, but you would not get 60 per cent. of the value of her on the voyage.

Q. How much do you pay for mackerel to your fishermen?—A. Do

you mean my boats? I pay $1.50 a hundred for their portion of t
delivered on the stage. We dress them and do all the work.

Q. Let us have the biggest and lowest price you pay them
have paid within three or four years $2.00 to $1.25. $1.50 is th
age.

Q. You say that is for their part of the fish. What do you w
A. I find them the boat, lines, bait, provisions, and everything t
longs to the fishing. They have no expense. They catch their f
bring them into the harbor and we take account of them. W
him $1.50 a hundred for half the fish. The other half is our
wanted to know how many we take for the barrel.

Q. I didn't come to that. Have you a copy of the agreemer
(Produces and reads agreement.)

Q. That is before it is cured?—A. That is for fresh fish lande
stage.

Q. Now, being paid at that rate, how much can a man ea
month?—A. In a good season he will earn from $20 to $25; in
season from $12 to $15.

Q. I don't think I asked you about the size of the boats. If t
boats of different sizes that fish in different ways, I would like
tell?—A. We have large boats, with five men to a boat.

Q. How long are those?—A. From 22 to 25 feet keel.

Q. How long do they stay out? Do they stay over night?—
my boats. The men all sleep ashore.

Q. What is the size of the smaller boats?—A. A great mau
boats fish all round the island; some quite small, perhaps 12 or
keel.

Q. Are some owned by farmer fishermen?—A. Yes.

Q. Do you buy fish from them?—A. Yes. A great many of th
their own fish.

Q. Through you?—A. Yes, sometimes.

Q. And get the benefit of the market?—A. Yes.

Q. That is getting general. Is that a branch of industry t
been built up since the fishery clauses of the treaty went into e
A. It has been very much built up within the last few years.
been done by dozens of men that formerly sold us their fish.

Q. You have given us a description of what is called half-line
what is quarter-line fishing?—A. That is where the fisherman f
a specified sum per month, and gives the owner one-fourth of
for that sum; the owner thus receiving three-fourths of his cat

Q. You find them in food?—A. Yes, everything. They hav
pense, except for their own clothing.

Q. Do you mean that you board them for the month?—A. W
building for them, and have a cook-house. They sleep, eat, an
thing. They have no expense.

Q. Have you examined the Prince Edward Island statistic
request?—A. I have.

Q. Have you read the testimony of your partner, Mr. Myric
them?—A. I did.

Q. You know what he testified?—A. Yes.

Q. How does your judgment correspond with his in referenc
correctness or incorrectness of those island statistics?—A. I
is very nearly correct.

Q. Are there any particulars in which you would correct l
ment?—A. Well, I might if I had the details, but as a general
would not.

Q. Well, there is one particular in which, probably by an error either of the reporter or of the printer, there is a considerable difference between his statement and the one you gave me; what is that?—A. That is in regard to hake-fishing. It was placed on the list at $3.50 a quintal. That was a mistake of a dollar.

Q. Did you call his attention to that?—A. He said it was a mistake. He gave it, $2.50.

Q. Are there any hake sounds exported from the island?—A. Yes.

Q. There are no hake sounds down in the book?—A. They have got down cod sounds. There are 594 barrels of cod tongues and sounds down. He said he had no such thing.

Q. You say that is not correct?—A. Certainly not. I think it is intended for hake sounds.

Q. Are there that many hake sounds?—A. I don't think there is such a large amount.

Q. What become of the cod sounds?—A. They are thrown away with the offal of the fish. Our cod are mostly small. I never saw a barrel of cod sounds saved on the island.

Q. At what do you estimate the exportation of mackerel for 1876 from the island?—A. Not exceeding 12,000 barrels.

Q. Would there be consumed on the island as much more of mackerel?—A. We do not eat mackerel on the island.

Q. In regard to fresh fish: have you much of a market for fresh fish there?—A. We have a market in Charlottetown; we sell fifty barrels a year there.

Q. Has anybody else a market there?—A. No; farmers come in on market days and sell fish.

Q. How many inhabitants has Charlottetown?—A. About 9,000.

Q. And the only place where fish is sold, except from wagons on market days, disposes of fifty barrels a year. Farmers catch it for their own use, I suppose?—A. I think they do; they are not a mackerel-eating people. I do not sell on an average, in Charlottetown, five barrels of cured mackerel a year.

Q. Any estimate placing the production of salted mackerel at 20,000 for last year, you think, is absurdly erroneous?—A. It is erroneous; there is no question about it.

By Mr. Davies:

Q. How do you arrive at the quantity exported from the island; you have to make a guess at it?—A. We cannot get the exact amount because we have no statistics we can depend on; we have our exports to go by; so far as they go they are correct, but they do not cover the whole quantity; there is only 9,000 reported as exported.

Q. You think that is not a correct statement, and that it exceeds that amount?—A. I think there are about 2,000 barrels more exported.

Q. That is to say, you are guessing at the amount?—A. I cannot give the exact amount, but I can approximate very nearly to it; I know what we receive and what our neighbors receive; I know every man who does any mackerel business on the island, and as I know about the number of barrels they ship, I can get at it very nearly.

Q. You never set to work to make up such a statement?—A. Not to get it exactly to a barrel.

Q. You never attempted to do so?—A. I never attempted it.

Q. As to the quantity of mackerel consumed on the island: you never made any inquiry, I suppose, in the fishing districts to ascertain what quantity of No. 3's the people consumed, or whether it is not the habit

of the people to keep some portion of the mackerel for their ⟨
sumption ?—A. I know something about that because I am
with the fishermen on all parts of the island, and also the farm

Q. Fishermen and farmers ?—A. They use large quantities o1
and a considerable quantity of codfish in all parts of the island.
often heard them say they would rather have a barrel of herr
a barrel of mackerel.

Q. No doubt because herring is cheaper ?—A. They are acc
to eat herring, and not accustomed to mackerel.

Q. You would not put your statement against that of a pe1
had gone round and made an examination among the farmers ⟨
ermen as to the quantity consumed ?—A. If he went round an
people and farmers to inquire as to the quantity, I would not ⟨
general information would give me the idea that they do not
many mackerel.

Q. But not having made any inquiry for the purpose, you w⟨
place your estimate as against that of a man who had made a1
as to the quantity consumed ?—A. I don't believe any man co1
out what the quantity is.

Q. You have no doubt the sounds spoken of in the statistics ⟨
sounds ? We do not classify any sounds as hake sounds in t1
tics of the island ?—A. If so, though the price is enter⟨
barrel, and hake sounds are sold by the pound, being a very ˙
article. There cannot be any doubt but that is a mistake.

Q. When they put down cod sounds they meant hake soun
I don't know what they meant.

Q. Would you say they were cod sounds ?—A. No; but t
should not have been put in by the barrel. Hake sounds a
fifty cents, sometimes $1 per pound.

Q. Is the value stated correctly, or is it an undervaluation
they are cod sounds, it is a high value; if hake sounds, it i
small part of their value.˙

Q. You have already told the Commission that it is within you
edge they are not cod sounds, and I accept your statement as c⟨
A. Yes.

Q. If they are hake sounds they are undervalued ?—A. Und⟨
very much.

Q. You think that is a large number of barrels of hake soun
Rather large.

Q. They form a very valuable part of the fish, more valua
the hake itself?—A. Far more valuable.

Q. I did not quite understand you with respect to people n
distances. Do you think it is easy for a man to mistake the
he is from shore ?—A. My experience is that when we are app
the shore with a vessel we are very apt to think we are within
half a mile of the shore when we are more than a mile away. 1
difficult to decide the distance you are from shore from a vess⟨
That has been my experience, and I have heard a good m
express the same opinion.

Q. Is there not the same difficulty in looking out from the l⟨
Perhaps it would not be so difficult. Different phases of 1
would give different appearances. More experienced men wo
more about it.

Q. You are head of the fishing establishment of Hall & M
A. Yes.

Q. Your headquarters are at Charlottetown ?—A. Yes.

{. When you are on the island, do you not reside nine-tenths of your
ie in Charlottetown ?—A. I spend a large portion of the time there;
on't know about nine-tenths. That is my headquarters.

{. If I was to say you spend one day out of two weeks at Rustico,
uld I be wrong ?—A. I spent this summer half my time there.

{. But generally speaking ?—A. I spend all the Sabbaths and about
lf the week there.

{. Do you not generally live in Charlottetown when on the island ?—
I generally go to Rustico two or three times a week. I remain there
t a short time.

. Your opportunities of observation in regard to the fishing there
e limited compared with those of persons on the spot ?—A. Of course.

.. You would not pretend to give an opinion as to the distance the
its fished from the shore, as against the opinions of persons on the
t ?—A. I have only been there one season, but I have been round
island for twenty years.

{. Captain Chivirie is one of your captains ?—A. Yes.

{. And also Captain James McDonald ?—A. Yes.

{. Was their evidence put in your hands to read by Mr. Foster ?—A.
s.

Q. You read their statements ?—A. Yes.

Q. James McDonald is now captain of the Lettie ?—A. He is now.

Q. Is he out fishing this year ?—A. Yes.

Q. Is he a good fisherman ?—A. Yes, a good fisherman.

Q. He says :

hat two-thirds of the fish caught in American and other schooners are caught
hin a mile and one-half from the shore; the best-fishing is generally close to the
re.

You would not be prepared to contradict his statement ?—A. I have
it the same opinion he has. From what I know from conversations
th other men, and from my conversations with him in former times, I
ould not have such an opinion.

Q. I understood you to say, in answer to Mr. Foster, that your opinions
d been modified by conversation with American witnesses since you
me here ?—A. Not so much here; partly here and partly at other
aces.

Q. I understood you to say that, since you came here and conversed
th American witnesses, you had somewhat modified your opinion ?—
. If I had formed my opinion from conversations with them, it would
that not more than one-eighth or one-tenth of the catch was taken
shore; if from conversations with the other side, it would be that two-
irds, three-quarters, or nearly all was so taken.

Q. Did you ever converse with witnesses from the island about it ?—
. I have talked with them in various years oftentimes.

Q. You have no reason to doubt that James McDonald is a reliable
an ?—A. I have good reason to doubt.

Q. As to his veracity ?—A. No; I would not doubt any man's verac-
7, but the correctness of his opinion.

Q. You merely doubt his estimate ?—A. I doubt the estimate in re-
rd to the American fleet.

Q. Not his integrity and veracity ?—No.

Q. You spoke of seining; what was the depth of the seine with
hich you tried ?—A. I had one of 10 fathoms deep, and another of 12
thoms.

Q. You found they required to be so shallow in order to prosecute the
hing there ?—A. Yes.

Q. Did McDonald use the seine in the Lettie ?—A. No.

Q. Who used them, and on what part of the coast were they
A. The purse-seine I had with Captain Rogers, of Massachuse
fished along the coast, in the bend of the island, and back a
round the island shores. Afterwards I had a seine with Capt
shall.

Q. Did he fish round the island ?—A. The year he caught fish
them over at Gaspé Harbor.

Q. You say that in 1874 all the fish were taken inshore; I r
course, a very large part of them ?—A. I said the fish were ve
the shore in 1874, more so than I ever knew them.

Q. Some of the witnesses have stated that there has been a t
of the fish to frequent the shores of late years. Have you noti
the fish have been taken closer to the shore of late years than
or 1860 ?—A. I think the fish vary from year to year; I coulc
press a general opinion on that point. I believe the vessels of tl
fish nearer the island than the American vessels, and follow o
more closely; I believe that has led to the impression that the f
so much inshore.

Q. Were not Banks Bradley and Orphan formerly known ;
fishing places ?—A. They have not been able to take many fish at
during the last three years. The American fleet that has cou
has been a small fleet, and they have taken very few.

Q. Are not most of the American vessels furnished with sei
year ?—A. Pretty much all on the American coast.

Q. And here ?—A. A good many, a large number.

Q. You have stated that seining has not been a success with
It has not been profitable either to American vessels or those
from the island.

Q. But most of the fleet have seines this year ?—A. I could
the proportion of the fleet which has come to the bay with s
counted ten vessels with seines.

Q. Would you say that one-half of the vessels in the gulf
nished with seines ?—A. Perhaps one-third.

Q. I believe you have a claim against the American Govern
a refund of duties ?—A. Yes.

Q. It remains there yet ?—A. Yes.

Q. What is its amount ?—A. $30,700.

Q. You told Mr. Foster that if a duty was reimposed you wo
sider very seriously whether you would continue in the busin
Yes.

Q. You made that statement on the assumption that you
duty ?—A. Yes.

Q. I think it has been explained very clearly that the pri
depends almost altogether on the catch; this is the case to a
tent ?—A. To a large extent; yes. If there is a large catch of
prices rule low, and if there is a small catch they rule high.

Q. If the evidence given here on the part of British wit
correct, two-thirds of the fish taken by American vessels in t
may say, are caught inshore; and, assuming that two-thirds
whole catch in the gulf is taken inside of the three-mile limit,
American fleet, if they were excluded from fishing within t
prosecute the gulf fishery for the other third ; would this pay th
I think it would be a difficult business to do so, if that prop
correct.

Q. Have you any difficulty at all in answering this questio

they come to the bay to fish for one-third of their usual catch ?—A. I should not think that they could thus do a successful business ; it would be unsuccessful under such circumstances.

Q. You think it would not pay them then to come ?—A. Not if they caught two-thirds of their fish inside of and were excluded from the three-mile limit.

Q. Supposing that they catch that quantity within the limits, what would be the effect if they were excluded from this limit, and if, in consequence, two-thirds of the quantity which they caught were withdrawn from the market ?—A. That would depend upon the catch on the American shore.

Q. You gave one year, 1871, when a great catch was made on the American shore ?—A. Yes.

Q. Suppose that the catch on the American shore was not large, and that they were excluded from fishing within the limits in the gulf, where, we will assume, they get two-thirds of their fish, what would be the effect ?—A. If there was a large catch here they would feel it very much.

Q. Who ?—A. They would.

Q. Would the price then go up?—A. If there was a large catch here, and no catch there, this would be the case.

Q. Would the price go up under the circumstances I have mentioned, if the catch on the American shore was not a large one. What would be the effect of this on the fish caught by the island fishermen and forwarded to the States ?—A. That would most likely enhance the price.

Q. So the question as to who pays the duty depends almost altogether on the catch, and whether the Americans are allowed to fish within the limits in the gulf ?—A. Yes; the fact is that they take three-quarters of the catch, that is the trouble. Some years they have a large catch, and some years this is not the case.

Q. Take the average : you mean to say that, taking what the Americans catch in their vessels here and on their own coast, they take three-quarters of the catch ?—A. I mean to say that the inspection in the States shows that three-quarters of the fish are taken by American vessels.

Q. But you cannot state what proportion of this catch is taken in the Gulf of St. Lawrence ?—A. No ; no further than I hear, that this catch has been very small during the last three years.

Q. But how is it on the whole—no duty has been levied during the last three years ?—A. That does not make their catch any less. Of course, if there was good fishing in the gulf, and they had free access to the inshore fisheries, they would be more willing to come to the gulf than if licenses were required, or if they were excluded from these inshore fisheries.

Q. A number of American witnesses have told me that they desire duties put on our fish, because this would give them an enhanced price for their fish ; do you agree with that view ?—A. No.

Q. You think that all who state that opinion are in error ?—A. I think they are mistaken.

Q. You differ in opinion on this point from every one of them ?—A. I do. I think they are mistaken in supposing that the putting on of a duty would give them more a barrel for their fish. Taking it altogether, I think that this would not be the case.

Q. If you are correct in thinking that a duty would exclude our fish,

must it not necessarily enchance the price of their fish?—A. Not
sarily.

Q. What—if the supply is limited one-quarter, would not this
that effect?—A. If one-quarter of the supply was cut off, it would
some effect; but if there was a good catch on the American shor
would not enhance the price $2 a barrel.

Q. If the one-quarter thus lacking was made up, and the d
supplied, that would not be the case; but if one-quarter of the av
supply was taken out of the market, do you not believe that this
necessarily enhance the price?—A. It might have some effect u
but it would not enhance the price $2 a barrel.

Q. You think not?—A. No.

Q. Between what prices do mackerel vary in the market?—A.
$5 to $30 per barrel for the different qualities.

Q. What are the causes of these variations?—A. Partly the q
and partly the catch.

Q. The consumption remains on the average about the same
No; it does not. It is not now what it was 5 or 10 years ago.

Q. Has it been about the same during the last 5 years?—A. It
according to the price.

Q. What is the cause of the variation in prices?—A. The ca
great measure.

Q. Suppose that one-quarter of the catch was withdrawn,
the price then go up?—A. This would depend upon the catc
quality.

Q. If the catch fell off one-quarter, would not the price inevita
up?—A. It would have that effect, of course.

Q. Suppose that one-quarter of the catch on the American sho
off, compared with the average, would not the price then go u
It always goes up then.

Q. If the price goes up, who pays the enhanced price; is it
consumer?—A. Yes.

Q. And if the catch is large the price goes down; so it would
in some measure on whether the catch on the American or on o
shore was large, as to who would pay this duty?—A. Yes; and
quality of the mackerel.

Q. All these elements would have to be considered?—A. Som
there is no other market than the United States for mackerel,
course we have no other market for these fish.

Q. I think you left the impression on some minds, at least, t
imposition of the duty caused your disasters?—A. Yes.

Q. Was there not another cause for them, which accounted i
measure for the failure of your catch that year—the effect cons
on your vessels being seized?—A. They were seized in 1870.

Q. Had not that a great deal to do with your difficulties?
course. I lost money by these seizures, and, my business being
up, I was not able to trade in Charlottetown.

Q. Did not that materially contribute to your difficulties?—
would not have failed on that account. We were worth a
amount of property, and we could have stood a great many los
that.

Q. But this was one of the causes that contributed, and cont
largely to it?—A. A small percentage of it was due to that.

Q. Do you know whether purse-seining has been looked on by
men generally as a failure or not?—A. I think that it is not

upon as a failure altogether. Different opinions are entertained in this regard.

Q. Some think it is a failure and some think it is not?—A. I think that going into this seining is generally looked upon as a mistake.

Q. Why?—A. It is looked upon as an instrument that may be disastrous to the fishing in the future. A great many fish are lost in this mode of seining. A great many fish are thus caught which cannot be taken out, and they are hence altogether lost. I do not think that this has occurred here, but it has occurred on the American coast.

Q. What do you say your shipments of mackerel will be this year— 7,000 or 8,000 barrels?—A. Yes.

Q. What do you think the island shipments will amount to this year?—A. They will approximate between 20,000 and 25,000 barrels.

By Mr. Foster :

Q. You do not mean that this quantity has gone forward?—A. I mean the whole shipments. This is, however, a mere estimate.

Q. Mr. Davies has made the hypothesis that the United States vessels take two-thirds of their catch in the gulf within the limits, and he asked you what effect, under these circumstances, would their exclusion from these be, if they had a small catch on their own coast, and you say that this would tend to enhance the price, and of course it would. I would now like to know whether, on that hypothesis, prices would go up indefinitely, or whether there is a point where people would stop buying mackerel?—A. Mackerel will not be consumed in large quantities at high prices.

Q. What is the price at which they will stop buying, the quantity taken of mess mackerel, purchased as a luxury, excepted?—A. Large quantities of mackerel cannot be sold at prices over $8 for number threes, at about $10 and $11 for number twos, and about $12 or $14 for number ones.

Q. Do vessels which come to the gulf with seines, also bring hooks and lines?—A. Yes ; they do.

Q. Do you mean to say that no merchant can depend on mackerel continuing in demand at high prices?—A. No, he cannot. The business then falls off.

By Sir Alexander Galt :

Q. We have heard of a vessel called the Lettie, which fished on the American coast, of which, I believe, you are proprietor?—A. Yes.

Q. Can you tell me where she fished on the American coast, and whether she was successful?—A. She fished there one year for pogies, and was very successful. She got all she could bring..

Q. Did she fish close to the shore or off shore?—A. I think that she fished pretty near the shore sometimes.

Q. That is the only Canadian vessel which you know of as having fished there?—A. I am not acquainted with any other that has done so.

By Mr. Davies :

Q. How much do you pay the fishermen per barrel on shore for their mackerel?—A. I have paid them $1.50 per 100 fish.

Q. What is that per barrel?—A. $3.75.

Q. How much salt do you use for a barrel of mackerel?—A. It will take about 5 pecks to use a barrel and pack it.

Q. What does the salt cost you?—A. 25 cents a bushel.

Q. When you speak of paying them $3.75 a barrel, you mean all round—for ones, twos, and threes?—A. That would be for the average.

Q. What does the salt cost you ?—A. About 31 cents per barrel

Q. And what do the barrels cost ?—A. On the average, perha cents.

Q. What is the expense of pickling and packing, leaving out the of the barrel and salt ?—A. It would be very hard to tell that.

Q. They put the price of packing altogether in Gloucester at $2 they say that from 25 to 50 cents profit is made on that ?—A. In to cure our fish, we have to put a large gang of men, perhaps fr to 15, on shore, to handle the fish, and we have to pay them wage

Q. Would 30 cents per barrel suffice, besides the cost of the b. and salt, to cure a barrel of mackerel ?—A. No; that would not 1 to do it. That would probably take not less than $2 a barrel.

Q. In Gloucester they say they charge $2 for packing ?—A. T: merely for packing—a different thing entirely.

Q. That includes the barrel and salt ?—A. I understand that that is a different thing entirely. These fish, which are packed in cester, are already cured; they are merely packed, while our fish in fresh, and we have to split, gut, and rim them, soak and salt th hogsheads, and afterward, after they have lain long enough in the we have to pack them up.

Q. What would you think that you pack them for ?—A. I canno you an exact idea on that head ; but I would say that the whole ex would not be less than $3 a barrel.

Q. Including barrel and salt ?—A. That includes everything.

Q. And what is the cost of freight to Boston ?—A. About 85 or about 80 cents, actual freight. The cost of curing depends so on the catch, that you cannot form an idea with regard to the a cost. It costs as much to cure 700 barrels as 1,700, or there is very difference in this respect. The cost is about the same in eithe aside from the barrel and salt. If you have a gang of men to cur they are there, and you have to pay them wages; you must feed and when there is a small catch you have the same expense on hands as when there is a large catch. One year you may be succe and the cost will be small ; and another year you may not be succe and the cost will then be very high ; and so no estimate can be m this regard that would be correct.

By Mr. Foster:

Q. Your vessels were not seized for fishing inshore, but for trouble about registration ?—A. They were seized on the ground was a foreigner, who had a beneficial interest in vessels flying th lish flag.

Q. At what figure did you put the price for a bushel of salt About 25 cents.

Q. And how many bushels are there to a barrel ?—A. 3½, I . think, and 1½ bushels would cure a barrel, pickle and all.

By Hon. Mr. Kellogg:

Q. With regard to this conflict of testimony, which is very gr to the proportion of mackerel that is taken by American vessels of the three-mile limit—running, as you know, with witnesses fr E. Island, to the extent of two-thirds or three-quarters of their c: do you know whether that has always been the opinion of gent familiar with the fishing there on the island and the localities this fishing is prosecuted ?—A. I never supposed that it was. I think that this has been the case, but I cannot tell you what ha. the opinion in this relation farther than stating my own impress

ng it. I gave my impression from what I could hear from these
nd learn from my own observation, as you see, three or four years
and I gave it in good faith; but whether right or wrong, of course
as merely the impression which I received. The testimony given
by gentlemen of integrity and character from the States is very
ent from that; and the testimony of men from the island, and the
rs of my vessels, is right the reverse. I do not think that my
n on this subject is worth anything under the circumstances.

No. 72.

MONDAY, *October* 22, 1877.

Conference met.

LTER M. FALT, of Gloucester, Mass., fish merchant, called on
f of the Government of the United States, sworn and examined.

By Mr. Trescot:

stion. Where do you live?—Answer. At Gloucester.

How old are you?—A. Fifty-four. I am in my 55th year.

What is your business?—A. I carry on a fishing business.

What do you mean by that? Are you a fish merchant, or are you
ed actively in the fishing?—A. We have a firm, and send out
ls.

You have a firm, and are engaged in sending out fishing vessels
ir own?—A. Yes.

Have you been a practical fisherman at any time?—A. I was eleven
half years a master, and other years as a hand.

What fishing did you prosecute?—A. Principally cod-fishing and
it. George's fishing in the spring, and halibut fishing for the
nder of the year.

You haven't been doing anything very much in mackerel?—A. I
tried that since I was a master, but a month at a time was the
st at any time, and hardly that.

How many vessels have you?—A. 18 now that we handle.

They are engaged in what sort of fishing?—A. Mackerel, fresh
it, George's, salt fishing.

What proportion of your vessels are engaged in the mackerel fish-
-A. We send ten in the business.

Where do they go generally?—A. In the spring, generally south,
off New York, and to the southward, then they follow this way;
s, on our western shore.

Do these ten vessels go into the gulf?—A. We had five there this

Have you been sending very long to the bay?—A. Well, this is
st year we have had so many for the last three years. We dwindled
until we had only one; that was last year.

Have you any knowledge, or are you able to form any opinion
your bay fishers go?—A. Well, they generally go northward to
auks Bradley and Orphan, up that way and across to the Mag-
s.

Have you been able to form any knowledge, from what you
what proportion of the catches are made within the three-mile
in the bay?—A. In all my practice, and what I understand from
ssels, they practice outside of three miles on Bradley and Orphan,
t the Magdalens.

Well, in the course of your experience, with your vessels going
coast and to the bay, have you been able to form any comparison

in your own mind as to the relative value of the two fisheries ?—
found, since I have been in the business, that our business ha
more profitable on our own coast.

Q. Do you know what has been done, on the average, in the b
mean per vessel ?—A. Well, I guess you have the account here
firm.

Q. You are a partner of Leighton ?—A. Yes.

Q. Well, now, with regard to the halibut fishery, how many
have been employed, and what has been your knowledge of it yo
How long have you been at it ?—A. I followed that, I say, elev
a half years, from the first of April to the last of November;
what I practiced myself when I followed the water, to the mi
November or so.

Q. And where have you caught your halibut ?—A. On what
the Seal Island ground, Brown's and Lahave, and in the Bay of Fu
far as Grand Manan, Marblehead Bank, and so on.

Q. In your experience, what sort of fishing is it, off shore or wi
A. Well, you can't get any halibut within three miles, nor on th
miles.

Q. Will you point out what course you ran when you were l
fishing, and how near it brought you to Cape Sable Island ?—A.
to map and points out fishing-grounds.)

Q. You know the waters from Seal Island toward Cape Sal
Cape Sable Island ?—A. Yes.

Q. Have you ever known in your experience in that fishing,
fishing for halibut within three miles ?—A. No. It can't be got.

Q. Let me call your attention to the testimony of a gentleman
name of William B. Smith, residing at Cape Sable Island. It is
lows (Reads evidence of William B. Smith, page 439 of the
evidence, from the question: "With regard to halibut-fishing. I
any halibut-fishing carried on near Cape Sable Island ?" To th
tion: "Do they take the halibut they catch to market salted or
and the answer, inclusive): Now, with your knowledge—you
have yourself fished for eleven and a half years—do you think
any possibility of that being true?

Mr. THOMSON. Is that a general answer to the whole question

Mr. TRESCOT. Well, I will ask them severally.

Q. "With regard to halibut-fishing, is there any halibut-fish
ried on near Cape Sable Island ?—A. Not by British people; th
icans fish there."—A. That is not the case.

Q. "Every year ?—A. Every year, regularly."—A. They a
to be found there in any such depth of water; not so near.

Q. "What is the number of the fleet which comes there to
halibut ?—A. I have seen as high as nine sail at one time. I
suppose there was from 40 to 60 sail."—A. There never was tha
in the business in the world.

Q. You have some knowledge of the matter ?—A. I have.
every root and branch of it; and when it was at the most it
those years that I was going. That was the most that ever w
on those grounds.

Q. How many halibut vessels from Gloucester are there do y
pose ?—A. We ran at the most of any time 31 sail. These don'
to these grounds whatever. They resort to Grand Bank, Wester
Quero, and all such as that.

Q. What proportion of that fleet would be fishing about Seal

n the neighborhood of Cape Sable?—A. None at all. No one
iced that business since I left it.
"Are the vessels cod-fishers at other times of the year?—A. I
they are. During the latter part of May and June they fish for
ut; then they fish for cod until October, and then for halibut."
t do you say to that? Do you know of any of the American fleet
g for halibut in May and June?—A. No.
And then for cod until October, and then for halibut?—A. No.
Now you can answer the question whether a man can see a fleet
ing them from his door.—A. That man never saw them.
I notice, in another portion of this same gentleman's testimony, he
sked this question: "You used to catch halibut in weirs?" and
ered, "Yes, in our traps." You don't know of halibut being caught
irs as a practice?—A. Well, he might be just as likely; just as a
e would go into a harbor, or a black fish, once in a hundred years.

By Mr. Thomson:

Did you go into the Bay St. Lawrence when you went aboard your-
—A. When I was master? No.
You never were there at all?—A. I was there as a hand.
What years?—A. 1851, 1853, 1854, and 1855.
In 1851, where did you fish?—A. We went up to the northward,
the Banks, and across to the Magdalens.
You never fished within three miles?—A. We didn't practice that,
use the cutters were around.
Was that the reason you didn't fish within?—A. And also, our
er that I was with, it was the first he was there, and he was more
ous probably.
Was that the reason you did not fish inshore?—A. Yes.
What was your catch?—A. We brought home 240 barrels.
What was your tonnage?—A. Fifty-five tons; it was what they
pinkey.
What was her full cargo?—A. That was all she brought.
What time did you go into the gulf?—A. The latter end of July.
And what time did you come out?—A. We came out somewhere
the last of October.
During all that time you never fished within three miles?—A. We
when we came down from the northward, after the big gale. We
across to Margaree, and fished to make up somewhere about 20
ls.
What time did you go to Margaree?—A. After the big gale, ten

What time was the gale?—A. In October.
You were ten days in at Margaree?—A. I say we were at Souris
ek, and then came across between the island and what we call
aree, fishing across that way.
Where were you during the big gale?—A. Up to the island.
What part of the island?—A. We came out of Gaspé that morn-
he gale come on.
It was a northeast gale?—A. Yes.
You were north of the island, on that coast, when you came down
Gaspé?—A. I say we came out of Malpeque.
You said Gaspé?—A. I did not mean Gaspé; I mean Malpeque.
came out of that on a Friday morning, and Friday night the gale
on. It was moderate, and the wind hauled to the eastward, so we
uded we would go back, but it shut down so thick that we had to
off.

Q. Were you out in the bay all the time?—A. Yes.

Q. With Prince Edward Island forming a lee coast?—A. Yes.

Q. You rode out the gale?—A. We were under sail—the sa if it were to-night; in the morning we wore and laid her head southward and eastward until half past twelve o'clock, and then at half past five that night, and continued to make our way do island.

Q. What time was the storm over?—A. Not until Saturday ni

Q. And notwithstanding this great storm, you came down alo windward of Prince Edward Island without being wrecked?—A sir.

Q. Then you went over to Margaree?—A. Then we went to and repaired our damages, and came out and went across toward garee and finished up the balance.

Q. There you went within three miles?—A. We caught some f

Q. You did go in?—A. We had the heft of our fish before we w

Q. You did go in and fish, didn't you?—A. Well, I suppose anchored under the island we were in.

Q. What objection have you to mention the fact?—A. I ackno we went inside.

Q. You took fish in there?—A. Yes.

Q. How many?—A. I can't tell exactly. It might tote up 1! might be 20.

Q. It might be 25 or 30?—A. I didn't say that.

Q. But can you say it and tell the truth? If you did say 30 w be true?—A. No. I guess we didn't get that many there.

Q. How many do you say you did get?—A. From 15 to 20.

Q. Do you swear you didn't get more than 20?—A. I wou swear, because I could not bring that to my recollection perfectl

Q. Those you took close inshore?—A. Well, yes, the same rest of our vessels did.

Q. Were there many besides your own in?—A. I could not ca to my recollection. There might be one or two or there might l a dozen.

Q. Were there or not?—A. I could not say.

Q. Did you see any?—A. I say I could not bring it to my re tion. I know there was some there.

Q. Did you see any?—A. Yes.

Q. Did you see them also fishing within the limits?—A. I cou call that to my recollection, who they were. There was Engli American vessels there.

Q. Will you undertake to swear, or will you undertake to den there was a number of American vessels fishing around you at th time, and fishing within three miles?—A. I could not say that.

Q. You will not swear there was any? Have you any doubt ever that a number of American vessels were fishing around you three miles; that they were there, and that you saw them?—A are just as likely to be in the same position as myself, three, or f five miles.

Q. Do you say your vessel was three, or four, or five miles?— was to and fro, yes.

Q. You admit you took those 20 barrels?—A. I say from 15 to

Q. You took those within three miles?—A. I won't say we did them.

Q. You said you took 15 or 20 barrels within three miles. No o say you did not?—A. You asked me if I was there at Mar-

asked you how many you took within the three-mile limit, and
1 from 15 to 20. Now you say you didn't do anything of the
-A. I don't say I didn't.
idn't you tell me just now you took those within three miles?—
ight have answered that.
id you tell the truth when you did say so?
'RESCOT. I wish to enter my respectful protest against the style
s examination.
'HOMSON. I enter my counter-protest against the witness evad-
in questions.
idn't you tell me just now, within the last ten minutes, that you
from 15 to 20 barrels within the three-mile limit off Margaree?—
ated that we caught from 15 to 20 barrels while we were there.
ght have been, I have said, inside of three miles.
ave you any doubt about it?—A. I have no doubt we were in-
2 limits.
'hen you took the 15 or 20 barrels?—A. We might not have
hem all.
ow many do you swear you took inside the limits?—A. I could
whether we were all the time inside the three miles.
don't care whether you were all the time or half the time; but
any barrels will you swear you took within the limits?—A. I
ly.
'ill you swear to five?—A. Yes.
'ill you swear to ten?—A. No.
hen you swear positively it was between five and ten, and noth-
r?—A. I would not swear positively over that.
ow many did you get?—A. I will swear to five barrels.
ive is as high as you will go, after telling me you caught 20 bar-
hin three miles?—A. No; I said around that place.
'ill you swear you caught one single barrel outside the limits
Margaree?—A. I could not say that we were at the time three
ff all the time or three miles in.
hen your evidence is this, if I understand you: You swear posi-
hat you took five barrels within the limits; and you won't swear
u took one single barrel outside the limits. That is the extraor-
testimony you give now. I ask you, will you swear that you
single barrel outside, and you say you will not?—A. I say I can

idn't you tell me—I asked you if you would swear that you
a single barrel outside, and you said you could not?—A. I didn't
and you.
'hat was your answer?—A. I said yes, sir.
idn't you answer that you could not undertake to say?—A. I
nean it if I did; not by any means.
ow, your next trip was when?—A. 1853.
'here did you fish then?—A. On the same grounds.
'ere you master then?—A. No; I was a hand. All my time in
: I was a hand.
id you fish then within the three-mile limit?—A. We fished in
on the same grounds, at Margaree and Cheticamp.
o you mean to say those were the only places you fished within
its—that is, Cheticamp and Margaree?—A. We fished up the
on Bradley and Orphan and at the Magdalens.

Q. Do you call that fishing within the limits ?—A. No.

Q. Then I come back to your fishing on Margaree and Che Do I understand you only fished within the limits at Marga Cheticamp ?—A. Yes.

Q. How many did you take ?—A. Probably about 40 barrels.

Q. Now you understand my question, how many barrels did y at Margaree and Cheticamp within the limits ? Your answer is rels. Is that right ? Did you take off Margaree and Cheticam side the limits, any fish ?—A. When we worked across from th dalens we fished across outside the limits.

Q. You just took 40 barrels within the limits ?—A. To the bes knowledge.

Q. Those you certainly did take within the limits ? On that o were there a number of American vessels fishing around you could not tell you the number, whether there were more or less.

Q. I want to know whether there was a number of American around you. There were vessels ?—A. Yes.

Q. Can you give me any idea how many ?—A. I cannot.

Q. Over ten ?—A. I could not say.

Q. Could you say there were not twenty ?—A. Yes.

Q. Will you swear there were five ?—A. I should think there i the time we were fishing.

Q. They were also fishing, were they ?—A. Yes.

Q. Now what was the tonnage of your schooner on that occa A. About 90 tons, carpenters' measurement.

Q. She carried a cargo of 400 barrels ?—A. No, 275.

Q. Was that a full cargo ?—A. No, she carried about 300 bar

Q. Now during all that time you did not fish anywhere aro coast of New Brunswick, Bay Chaleurs, or Prince Edward Islan No.

Q. Why didn't you fish within three miles ?—A. All our fishi on the Cape Breton side.

Q. Why didn't you fish along the Prince Edward Island sho Because we were not on that coast.

Q. You were on the coast if you were on the Orphan Bank. a very little distance from the coast; why didn't you fish inshore t A. We didn't resort there.

Q. Why ? Were you afraid of cutters ?—A. Yes: the large there, and the small one, too, and the sailing-schooners.

Q. What time did you leave the bay that year ?—A. In the lat of October.

Q. And you didn't get a full cargo ?—A. No.

Q. Do you know anything about the inshore fisheries, of y knowledge, at all, except at Margaree and Chetticamp ?—A. N

Q. You never have fished inshore except there ?—A. That is

Q. Never at any time ?—A. No.

Q. What time did you go next into the bay ?—A. 1854.

Q. After the Reciprocity Treaty ?—A. Yes.

Q. Then you had the liberty of fishing inshore ?—A. Yes.

Q. Do you swear that you never tried inshore, although you liberty ?—A. We had the liberty then of going in to get water.

Q. And to fish too ?—A. We took the opportunity, as we can the harbor, or anything like that, to try as we went off.

Q. Didn't you know you had as good a right as the Britis men ?—A. Yes.

Q. Didn't you try ?—A. Yes.

You say you only tried when you were driven in?—A. I say when me out of the harbor.

This was the common practice, whether you had the right or not? es; that is our practice on our own coast.

Didn't you ever go in and try what the inshore fisheries were like you had the privilege; there was no cutter then?—A. All my wo years there was.

I am speaking now of 1854. You said you did not go in there, want to know why?—A. Wherever we could find them most we

Did you or did you not fish inshore?—A. Yes.

Along the whole coast of Prince Edward Island?—A. Wherever uld find fish, the same as off East Point, off Malpeque, and such s that.

Did you fish within three miles?—A. You can get a few.

Why did you tell me that at the time you were in the gulf you fished within the limits except at Cheticamp and Margaree, when w turns out——A. I mean that time I was there in those sea-

What seasons?—A. 1851 to 1853.

I did not ask you that. I asked you generally. You told me you fished inside except at Margaree and Cheticamp. There is no ke about that?—A. That is all correct, but I didn't intend any-more than that year.

Very well, then, I will take 1855. Did you get a full cargo in ?—A. No.

What was the vessel's size?—A. The same size—90 tons.

How many did you get that year?—A. 275.

Was that a full cargo?—A. She would probably carry 350 barrels, packages and all.

Then you hadn't a full cargo?—A. No; no year I was there.

Didn't you fish along off Cascumpec at all?—A. No; we never t any.

Didn't you fish at the Magdalen Islands at all?—A. We were s there.

Did you catch many there?—A. Some.

Now, take 1855; where did you fish then?—A. On the same ids.

What do you call the same grounds? Do you mean that you l along inshore that year?—A. It was inshore at Magaree and camp.

Anywhere else inshore?—A. No.

Did you get a full cargo?—A. No.

Then, although you did not get a full cargo, you never tried the g inshore?—A. No.

Why did you keep away?—A. Wherever we found most fish we ted.

Now, didn't you get your full cargo?—A. No.

Then why didn't you try inshore?—A. We tried inshore when we winding up in the fall.

Where?—A. We tried inshore at Margaree and Cheticamp.

Why didn't you try inshore at the island?—A. Because nobody aught any.

You discovered that others had tried and failed?—A. Yes.

Who did you inquire of?—A. We came with the fleet.

Did you inquire of the vessels that did fish in there, and find that they didn't catch any?—A. Yes. If they had, we wot tried too.

Q. I ask you, did you ever inquire of other vessels that ha in there and got nothing?—A. We never practiced inside thi or two miles of the shore.

Q. Now, don't you know that is an evasion of my question. you if you ever inquired of any captains whether they had f side and whether they had got any inside, and you say you ne' ticed inside. I will put my question again. Did you, on that (in 1855, meet any single American vessel that had fished inside miles along the coast of Prince Edward Island, and learn from there was no inside fishing?—A. I didn't particularly——

Q. Then, although——

Mr. TRESCOT. Let him answer.

Q. Do you want to say anything else?—A. When we are among our vessels, we speak and say this: "Did you find such and so?" And they say "No." Of course we don't go th

Q. Well, I presume you don't say "such and so." You give t of the place?—A. Yes.

Q. Now, I ask whether you put the question whether t fished at any place around the coast of Prince Edward Island?-

Q. Then, without finding from a single captain that he had f side on that coast and caught no mackerel, you came away w of a cargo, and didn't try inside, although you had full liber When we came away, we were on the Cape Breton Island side.

Q. From where?—A. We were at Chetticamp and Margaree. in the end of the season, and the mackerel gave out, and we can

Q. Now you have given the lie to William B. Smith. Do y' him?—A. No.

Q. According to you there is no fishing along Seal Island at Not so close in.

Q. Have you been there?—A. I have passed to and fro.

Q. Have you ever fished there?—A. No.

Q. Then, as to a ground on which you never fished, you are to swear that a man has committed perjury——

Mr. TRESCOT objects.

Q. You are pleased to swear that he has said what was not tr he said he caught fish there. You swear that his statement i untrue, although you never tried it yourself. You don't spea of opinions, but you have sworn to it as a fact——

Mr. TRESCOT. The witness referred to (William B. Smith) say that he caught fish there, but that he saw them caught.

By Mr. Thomson:

Q. Now, why, if you have never tried that ground, do you u to say that halibut could not be caught there?—A. Because in that depth of water.

Q. What is the depth of water within three miles or two mil coast there?—A. I guess you can't find anything more than nine fathoms there.

Q. You will swear to that? Do you know that from exper A. Yes.

Q. Have you sounded?—A. Yes.

Q. You have sounded there and found it to be only seven fat A. I say nine.

Q. Now I hold in my hand Admiral Bayfield's map with sound

Mr. TRESCOT. What chart is that?

THOMSON. This is a survey by Andrew P. F. Shortland, assisted
·eutenant Scott and others. It is one of the admiralty charts.
TRESCOT. What is the date?
THOMSON. It is 1855.
FOSTER. We have one corrected from the latest surveys, in 1876.
THOMSON. The soundings will not have changed since then.
FOSTER. They may have been more correctly taken, though.

By Mr. Thomson:

Here is Green Island, where that man said he lived; here are,
a two miles of the land, soundings running up to 14, 17, and 18
ms; and here, within half a mile, is a depth of 10 fathoms. All
are in the very place where the witness said he saw the vessels
g. He gives the bearings about southwest by west. Now, you
sworn that it was impossible for this man to see these vessels,
ι he swore were one and a half miles and two miles away from him.
don't undertake to say, now that I have shown you the distance
Green Island—you don't undertake to say that from that distance
·uld fail to see them if they were fishing there?—A. I say this,
was never that many to be seen.
Although you were not there, you undertake to say "that man
saw them"?—A. I have been around the ground. I have been
; the place enough to know whether there was that many there.
Now, have you followed the business?—A. I followed it from the
pril to the middle of November.
And you have taken soundings. I thought you told me just now
idn't fish there?—A. I know there was not that many fishermen
n the business. I am perfectly satisfied of it.
How long since you were there last?—A. Seven years ago this
o.
Of course, you are aware that Smith was speaking of the last year
·o, while you hadn't been there for eleven years?—A. Why I
;——

I don't want to know your reasons; I ask simply whether you
that Smith was speaking of what happened a year or two ago,
you admit you never were there for the last eleven years?—A. I
I was not there.
And you knew Smith was speaking of what took place a year or
,go?—A. I know there is not that many in the business. I sup-
ι he was speaking of what was transacted in the fishing business.
Did you suppose he was speaking of what was within a year or
,go?—A. No; I understood that he had been speaking of what
·ened to and fro for years.

By Mr. Trescot:

Just explain that. You are asked whether you understood that
ι was speaking of what he had seen in 1874 and 1875, and whether
lenied that he saw those vessels there then, or whether you sup-
ι he was referring to the fishing generally?—A. That is what I
·ed to. I supposed he referred to what had been transacted in
·ess for years to and fro.

No. 73.

ARLES H. PEW, of Gloucester, Mass., called on behalf of the Govent of the United States, sworn and examined.

By Mr. Foster:

estion. You were born in Gloucester?—Answer. Yes.

Q. How old are you ?—A. 42 years old.

Q. You   a member of the firm of John Pew & Sons, foun
your father—when ?—A. In 1849.

Q. I believe it is the largest firm in Gloucester ?—A. I guess i
largest in the States.

Q. What is your business ?—A. Owners and fitters of vessel
dealers in fish and salt.

Q. How many vessels have you owned or controlled within t
fifteen or twenty years ?—A. About 20 ; we have averaged abou

Q. By the way, your father started the firm in 1849 ; when d
go into it ?—A. I went into it when I was 16 years old as a clerk.
as a partner when I was 20. He shortened my time.

Q. Did you have a brother also in it ?—A. Yes.

Q. He retired from it in 1861, I am informed ?—A. Yes. Th
younger brother came in two or three years after that. He is in

Q. I thought you had a brother that retired about the end of th
—A. That is my elder brother.

Q. Who compose the firm now ?—A. My father, myself, a
younger brother. William A. Pew retired at the beginning of th
My father, previous to the establishment of the business, went
himself as a little boy.

Q. Now, what is the principal business of the firm ? What bra
A. Well, all are about equally important. We are largely enga
dealing in codfish. Probably codfish is the larger part of the bu
We deal largely in mackerel and herring, and also in salt.

Q. Can you give us a statement of your mackerel business in t
and on the coast of the United States for the past few years ?
can. It is as follows :

Year.	Mackerel. Total number of barrels, bay.	Total number of barrels, shore.	Caught in waters off British coast. Bay mackerel. No. 1.	No. 2.	No. 3.	Value.	Caught off American shore. Shore mackerel. No. 1.	No. 2.	No. 3.	Value.	Codfish, &c. Pounds of boneless.	Quintals.	Value.
1870	981	2,396	657	284	40	$17,011 04	343	2,008	45	$30,355 79	....	10,360	$66,428 39
1871	2,336	2,592	602	1,253	381	19,645 61	1,219	758	545	32,251 97	....	13,788	69,949 91
1872	690	3,341	435	146	39	7,254 52	1,415	1,962	664	37,911 01	....	16,748	85,966 09
1873	1,564	3,678	864	545	155	19,193 66	1,745	1,478	655	55,965 13	....	32,739	114,777 22
1874	1,006	5,542	395	420	191	6,935 55	2,349	1,304	1,889	63,205 96	66,720	32,084	113,154 17
1875	383	2,380	282	89	2	6,249 46	541	411	1,428	30,649 38	325,142	20,444	108,991 10
1876	167	3,823	137	26	3	1,685 38	*500	*2,823	*500	30,995 00	1,000,000	*30,000	144,306 22
Total for 7 years	6,957	23,882	3,372	2,773	811	77,985 22	8,112	10,044	5,726	271,333 54	1,391,862	136,163	702,873 10

* Estimated.

Total value of fish production in 7 years, as above:
Bay mackerel $77,985 22
Shore mackerel 271,333 54
Codfish, &c 702,873 10
Total 1,052,201 86

These figures give what our vessels caught. They don't give what we purchased outside of what the vessels caught.

Q. When you speak of the catch of your vessels, have they been in the habit of buying mackerel here?—A. No.

Q. But your firm has bought mackerel in Gloucester?—A. Yes.

Q. Which has been the most profitable to your firm, the bay fishing or the fishing of the United States shores?—A. On the United States shores.

Q. Have you any statement of the result there carried out—the proceeds?—A. No.

Q. Will you give me some illustration of the amount cleared by your vessels on our shores? You gave me one remarkable instance?—A. There was one schooner in 1874, I think it was. She cleared $8,000, which was divided among the owners.

Q. After the crew was paid?—A. After all expenses.

Q. What did the sharesmen get that year?—A. The sharesmen made, I think, over $900 each.

Q. It was done within what time?—A. The latter part of June, July, August, and the early part of September.

Q. Where was that mackerel caught?—A. The large part of it was caught off Jeffrey's Bank, just in sight of Gloucester, something like 12 or 14 miles off.

Q. How many barrels of mackerel realized that amount?—A. I think somewhere about 1,400 or 1,500.

Q. What was the quality?—A. Very fine.

Q. You gave me the amount of the last haul that vessel made in that year?—A. It was about 400 barrels in one haul of 10 days, I think. A few barrels short of 400.

Q. This was seining?—A. This one vessel was.

Q. Most of these catches on our shores have been made by seining?—A. For the last four or five years, from 1872, the largest part has been seining.

Q. How many vessels had you in the bay this year—1877?—A. We had 5 go seining, and 4 of them were at one time in the bay.

Q. Did those which went into the bay go equipped with seines and hooks and lines?—A. Yes.

Q. Were they successful seining in the bay?—A. Not as yet.

Q. Have you ever known cases of successful seining in the bay?—A. No.

Q. Can you give the catch of your own vessels in the gulf this summer?—A. We have only had one home, I think, and she has packed somewhere about 200 barrels; and we have one on her way home, which has about 100 sea barrels, and will probably pack about 90 barrels.

Q. Have you heard from the third vessel?—A. We heard from the two others, and they were reported having somewhere about 70 or 80 barrels apiece.

Q. And they were both equipped with hooks and lines?—A. Yes.

Q. Were their fish in the bay caught by seines or by hooks?—A. I should think that the larger part of them were taken with the hook. The statement for the trip is as follows.

Q. How many vessels had you in the gulf in 1876?—A. One.

Q. What did she do?—A. Nothing; she only took 167 barrels.

Q. What was the profit and loss resulting from that voyage?—A. The loss on that trip was $369.96 to the owners of the vessel. The statement for this trip is as follows:

SCHOONER GENERAL GRANT.

1876.

DR.

it, viz—

hhds. salt; 151 lbs. Manilla; 238 lbs. sugar; 68 qts. beans; 85 lbs.
iried apples; 58 gall. molasses; 13 gall. kerosene; 68 lbs. coffee; 25
bs. tea; 54 lbs. lard; 191 lbs. butter; 1 bbl. pork; 8 doz. mackerel
ines; 18 bbls. flour; 6 bbls. beef; 2 feet wood, and other simil'r stores,

tc	$663 91
yds. $2 O. C. duck, at 31c	50 22
al	12 75
wing, $4; railway bill, $27.90	31 90
cks, etc., $5.55; stores, etc., in bay, $42.30	47 85
pense on trip, $20.67; skippership, $66.06	87 23
ilway bill, $22.75; anchor, etc., $2.30	25 05
cksmithing, $9.14; rigging, $20.85	29 99
king, $7.25; sailmaking, $194.58	201 83
ware, $17.03; painting, $56.09	75 12
armaker's bill, $8; teaming, $11.83	19 83
	1,245 68

CR.

r sold on trip	$30 00
f trip	832 09
s (split wood, tar'g and scraping, etc)	13 63
trip	369 96
	1,245 68

In making this up, did you include anything for the captain of the
?—A. Yes. We make up the loss as is done in corporations; that
captain, whether interested or not in the vessel, has his share and
, which are always charged in. This is a separate account from
f the voyage, altogether.

When you say that a vessel has lost so much, do you include in
oss, interest on the cost of the vessel?—A. No. That simply in-
the cost of running the vessel for the trip, with regard to outfits
atstanding bills.

Is insurance included?—A. No. We never insure save very little.
nnot afford to do so.

What number of vessels had you in the bay in 1875?—A. Two.

What number of barrels of mackerel must a vessel take in order
ke a voyage to the Gulf of St. Lawrence paying?—A. Do you mean
vessel not employed in other fishing?

Yes. If you decide to send a vessel to the gulf, how many barrels
she bring home in order to make the trip profitable?—A. That
vary some. I have known vessels that got 600 barrels which did
y their bills; and then I have known vessels which got 300 barrels
lid pay them; I should think that it would take about 400 barrels
the bills of a vessel.

Without any compensation to the vessel owners?—A. That would
fore the vessel paid any profit as a vessel.

What is that reckoning the mackerel to sell for?—A. Well, ones
have to sell at $15, twos at $10, and threes at $8—$7 or $8, or
bouts.

Generally speaking, how much value do you attach to all the fishin the Bay of St. Lawrence as a business to be pursued—I mean
heries anywhere off the British coast?—A. I do not think that any
m are of any value at all.

Which costs the most—the mackerelers that go into the gulf or those that fish on our shore ?—A. The latter generally are 1 expense.

Q. I suppose that a seiner is more expensive than a hook vessel ?—A. The gear of it is; the gear is what costs most— vessel.

Q. What costs the most, the manning of a seiner or of a b line vessel ?—A. The seiner costs the most, owing to the valt seine.

Q. Does the extra cost of the seine used on the shore make u extra cost of the bait used in the gulf ?—A. The seine costs the m the bait; but taking the trips on the average, going to the g the most.

Q. Can an average vessel be run so that a person buying a her will get interest on his capital—considering this matter fo ber of years ?—A. Do you mean taking such a share haphazar way ?

Q. Not haphazard; but take an outside owner who buys an in a vessel; can he make money by buying such property ?— cannot get outside owners to buy such shares now.

Q. Why ?—A. Because they have most always lost what tl put in.

Q. How has the business of companies which have gone into ing business prospered ? I do not refer to Gloucester fishing fir how have corporations, which have gone into the fishing busin ceeded ?—A. They have been unsuccessful.

Q. You gave me an illustration of one ?—A. That was in £ think they called it the Chincoteague Fishing Company. Thi institution got up to assist people to go into the fishing busine lem by Gloucester people who moved up there.

Q. In hopes of restoring the fishing business of Salem ?— wished to build the place up, and they represented that by carı their scheme, money would become plentiful in their streets, t stores would flourish, &c.; but they failed completely in thei taking.

Q. Gloucester people up there started a corporation in co with the fishing business ?—A. Yes.

Q. What became of it ?—A. I think they subscribed, anc $30,000 and bought parts in several fishing-vessels—that is, that went into the affair bought the vessels, and the outside ov in $30,000, and took parts in some five or six or eight differen I think that when they divided up they got back about 25 pe what they had put in, without deducting interest or taxes or else.

Q. On the winding up of the business ?—A. Yes.

Q. Did they have intelligent and decent people to carry on ness ?—A. They were successful in Gloucester, and were men ried with them when they went up there $15,000 or $20,000 o cash capital, or capital so represented in vessels and material.

Q. How are your Gloucester vessels, which are run by fish owned ?—A. Firms as such cannot own them, save as individ ners.

Q. The registration has to be made in the names of the i members of the firm ?—A. Yes.

Q. Do the skippers usually have an interest in the vessels ? as a rule, but a great many of our skippers own shares in our

Q. Do you keep a separate profit and loss account for the

he result of running her as distinct from the rest of the busi-
-A. Yes.
hen you know whether your vessels, as such, make money or
-A. Yes.
How is this?—A. Our own vessels up to this last year have gen-
paid.
Do you mean up to 1877?—A. Up to 1877; yes. In 1876 they
hough not very much, but up to that time they have paid as ves-

What has been about the percentage on the average?—A. Some-
they have paid very largely. I hardly know how to answer that
on, but some years I know they have paid 25 per cent.
What was that doing?—A. That was during the years of the war.
In what business?—A. They were employed in different branches
business—cod-fishing and mackereling.
You have imported salt very largely?—A. We were for many years
ly salt dealers there, and we have imported salt for 20 years.
That has been a very large part of your business?—A. Well, no,
large part, but we have done the larger part of the salt business
We have sold on the average perhaps 600,000 or 800,000 bushels
.
Have you obtained the prices of salt for a series of years?—A. I
since 1860.
Will you give them?—A. In 1860, the average price was $2 a
ead.
What prices are these?—A. Those at which we sell.
To anybody that comes for a barrel?—A. No; but wholesale. In
the average price was $2 a hogshead, measuring 8 bushels; we
weigh it, but we measure it. In 1861 and 1862, the price was also
$2 a hogshead; in 1863, it was $2.25; 1864, $3⅝; 1865, $6.50; 1866,
; 1867, $4; 1868, $3½; 1869, $2⅞; 1870, $2⅞; 1871, $2⅞; 1872,
; 1873, $2¼; 1874, $2.25; 1875, $2; 1876, $1.75; and 1877, $1⅗;
ig an average price of $2.76, for these 18 years, for a hogshead of
sured bushels; that is, in American currency.

By Mr. Davies:
Including the duty?—A. There is no duty on it; it is in bond.
ig the years from 1860 to 1866 the prices include the duty, which
ik was taken off in 1866 but this did not go into operation until
though we had the privilege of procuring our salt on board of the
s in bond, while salt obtained on shore was charged the duty.

By Mr. Foster:
During the last two years, the price of salt has been very low?—
es; it is low now.
Your firm have been large buyers of fish?—A. Yes.
It has been the larger part of your business—buying fish from
is?—A. We have bought more than we caught.
Do you buy mackerel?—A. Yes.
Describe how you buy them on the American coast when a vessel
is in with a trip?—A. We go to the wharf and buy the fish as the
uns, paying different prices for the different numbers.
Is there competition in this respect between the different firms?—
here is between the different buyers; the competition generally
s from outside firms. The firms which have vessels generally pack
mackerel.
This is after packing?—A. No; not always. It depends on the

state of the market. We sometimes buy ahead, and somet
arrive, and I have known mackerel lay on the market for 2
sometimes.

Q. How large a quantity of mackerel costing, say, $20 a barre
will the market of the United States take? How large a m:
there for high-priced mackerel?—A. This is very limited. I she
say that over 5,000 or 6,000 or 8,000 barrels of this mackerel w
so taken; the quantity might perhaps go as high as 10,000 barr
I would be afraid to hazard that number as a calculation. The
will only take a very limited quantity of this quality.

Q. Where is it taken?—A. Principally by the leading hotels
taurants, which have it on their bills of fare.

Q. At what figure must the prices of the other grades range
to secure free consumption of them?—A. Well, they have to be
article of food, and range lower than all other fish and other p
of the United States which come into direct competition with th

Q. What must the prices be per barrel?—A. When the price
ber two mackerel, for instance, which is a staple article, gets v
a barrel, it sells hard; and we find that the trade do not then

Q. What must number one be sold at?—A. If their price wa
large amount of this quality could not be sold.

Q. We notice a very large range of prices in the price-list fc
erel; what do you say to that?—A. I do not know as I unders
It is owing probably to quality, some.

Q. It is a speculative article with respect to price?—A. Yes;
it is. I think that the prices of mackerel are as much influe1
speculation as by the catch.

Q. You think so?—A. Yes; I do. I think I can prove that a
an illustration of it.

Q. Let us have it.—A. I think that in the year 1870, if I mist
we had the next to the largest catch we ever had in one State;
pression is that the catch that year was over 300,000 barrels—
or 320,000; and I think that prices were higher that year th
have ever been any year that there has been a small catch.
this was owing to the fact that in 1869, 1868, and 1867 there was
catch; prices had ruled pretty high, and there had been a cons
demand; and in 1870, when there was a very large catch, the spe
just operated in them and kept prices up.

Q. Were these high prices maintained?—A. No. 1 think th
bay mackerel, in the fall, were bought by us at $22.50 and pil
over winter; and I think that the next May and June they were sc
as low as $4, $5, and $6 a barrel, the same fish; and I think th
mackerel, which had sold as high as $24, were then sold for a
same price. Prices had been carried above what the people wc
and they would not take them.

Q. Of late years can mackerel be carried beyond the autumn
without loss?—A. No. The way the demand has now turned,
the best demand the time they are caught; that is to say, Augu
erel will sell best in August, September mackerel in Septem
October mackerel in October; and when you get through that j
come on to the next year, the demand almost ceases. The m
this respect, is entirely changed to what it used to be.

Q. And through the winter and spring there is hardly any c
—A. Well, when you get into April and May and June there
mand, and holders then get rid of their fish in the best way t
From 1855 up to 1865 it used to be the direct reverse. We use

the best demand in the summer months and June. I have bought old mackerel in July and August that were caught the year preceding, but to pay very high prices for mackerel now from the commencement of the year would be throwing money away.

Q. Is the demand for salt mackerel as good now as it was years ago ? —A. No, not nearly so.

Q. To what do you attribute that ?—A. To the inland fisheries.

Q. Such as what ?—A. The white and siscoe or lake herring fisheries. Whitefish have formed the largest element in the destruction of the demand, of late years.

Q. To what regions has salt mackerel gone for consumption ?—A. To those near and in the large cities on the sea-coast, such as Boston, New York, and Philadelphia, and to Baltimore, to a limited extent; and then they have gone inland.

Q. What quality do the cities take ?—A. Always the best quality, with the exception of Baltimore, which always takes the poorest quality.

Q. Owing to a large negro population ?—A. No; they are sent thence to the markets south of it, where they take small mackerel, which will number out better than number ones. The price in Baltimore for medium threes is as large, I think, as for threes, and I do not know but as large as for twos, or, at all events, there is very little difference between them. Mackerel threes sell better there than ones.

Q. Retail ?—A. I mean wholesale. Number one mackerel have been, of late years, almost unknown in the Southern market, where 10 or 15 years ago there used to be a large trade for them ; in the New Orleans market, for instance, a great many of them used to be sold.

Q. You spoke of inland fisheries ; what do you say with respect to fresh fish from the sea ?—A. That trade has been developed very much lately, and people will buy fresh fish before they will salt fish, codfish excepted. I do not think that the codfish trade has been affected so much in this direction as the mackerel business. The codfish trade seems to hold its own ; the demand for this fish has, I think, really increased.

Q. It has held its own ?—A. The demand for cod has increased.

Q. Which do you regard as the more important article, the fresh or salt-mackerel ?—A. They are about equal; there is not much difference between them.

Q. How far west do fresh fish go ?—A. They go all over the whole country. In fact, before I came up here they were making arrangements to take fresh halibut and mackerel in refrigerated cars over the United States in summer. I think that a very large trade in fresh fish could be developed.

Q. And they do go as far west as the Mississippi ?—A. Yes; and to California. I have known halibut shipped to Omaha and all round those sections of the country.

Q. What do you say with reference to the catch of herring on our own coasts ?—A. Well, the catch of herring there has not been very large, and the price has been very low. I should say, excepting the annual catch during the last 5 or 6 years, 100,000 barrels a year would not be very far from a right estimate.

Q. It has been cheaper to buy, than to catch them ?—A. Well, yes.

Q. Is there a large supply of herring on our own coasts ?—A. I think that at the present time the largest supply is off our own coasts.

Q. You told me this morning something about the comparative price of a kind of herring you called round- herring ?—A. Yes, round shore herring.

Q. What do you mean by round shore herring ?—A. This term
in contradistinction to the term split herring; these are split do
belly, and the round are salted just as they come out of the wate

Q. You have compared with me the price of them in the United
and the price here in Halifax; what do you say about that?—A.
are very few of them in the Halifax market, and they are askir
$4 a barrel for them. The Halifax round herring differs from the
round herring; the gills of the former are taken out and a small
the entrails, and to do this costs about 25 cents a barrel. The
ring are quoted at $4 a barrel; and we calculate to retail them
States at $4; but we do not consider them at all.

Q. Their price current in Halifax is higher than the price at
they can be bought in Gloucester ?—A. It is higher than we c
them at to the retail trade.

Q. Have your vessels been in the herring business ?—A. Yes, n
less.

Q. Where have they gone for them ?—A. To Newfoundland, th
dalen Islands, and Grand Manan.

Q. Have they ever caught them in Newfoundland ?—A. No.

Q. Have they gone there prepared to catch them ?—A. No.

Q. They have bought them ?—A. They have always carried
there to buy them.

Q. How many vessels have you had go to Grand Manan for bi
—A. We have always had 2 or 3 go there in winter for them sin
or 1870. I am not sure which, but I think since 1870.

Q. Have they bought or caught them there ?—A. They have
taken from $1,500 to $2,000 in American currency, to get a carg
3 or 4 hands. They have carried no fishing gear and they were
supposed to have bought the herring. They always rendered a
of them as being bought.

Q. They went there without preparation to fish ?—A. They
them undoubtedly.

Q. And they left money behind them ?—A. They carried mon
that they used it on their voyage I have no doubt whatever.

Q. You have no more direct knowledge in this respect ?—A.
their bills, which come from the men down there, who made
receipts.

Q. What has been the cost of the herring which you have bo
Newfoundland and Grand Manan ?—A. When they first went t
foundland, which was, I think, in 1860, to Fortune Bay, they used
6 shillings or $1.20, in gold, a barrel. We used to have them cal
gold and part trade—that is, we used to fit out vessels to go the
we used to estimate the price at $1.50 a barrel, and take trade
to amount to $1.50 a barrel, and always gold enough to reach th
figure. We used to use trade if we could, and otherwise we use

Q. They cost $1.20 a barrel ?—A. That is $1.20 in the first pla
over $2 during the last few years. Last year I think that the pr
$2 or $2.50 per barrel—10 or 12 shillings.

Q. Have you bought herring which were caught on the United
coast ?—A. Yes.

Q. How has the quantity which you have purchased there co
with the amount which you bought in Newfoundland and at
Manan ?—A. It has been smaller than the quantity which we have
in Newfoundland and at Grand Manan and Magdalen Islands.

Q. Have you purchased both frozen and salt herring ?—A. Y

Q. You have also been in the cod-fishing business?—A. That has been the principal part of our fishing.

Q. If you compared your cod and mackerel fishery, what proportion would you say is cod and what proportion mackerel?—A. I have the figures. Well, the mackerel would be a very small part of it.

Q. Are the figures on the table which you have put in?—A. Yes.

Q. About what proportion would be cod, and what mackerel?—A. The cod is over two-thirds of it.

Q. Which has been the more profitable?—A. The cod always.

Q. What do you say about the comparative expediency of fishing for cod with fresh or with salt bait on the Grand Banks?—A. That is a pretty hard and difficult question. I can only answer it from our experience with our own vessels.

Q. I only want your general idea respecting it?—A. Well, I think that if the vessels do not use fresh bait, and do not make a practice of it, they will do just as well with salt bait; but if part of them used fresh bait, the whole of them have to do so; that would be my judgment.

Q. I meant to have asked you, before we passed from the herring business, whether anything is done in the exportation of herring from the United States?—A. We made one shipment, I think.

Q. Where?—A. To Gottenburg this last spring.

Q. Others began the business in 1876?—A. Yes; the year before.

Q. Are the herring which are exported caught on the United States shore?—A. They are caught both there and in British waters. I should say that one-half of those which are exported are caught in British waters.

Q. We have had some testimony as to the running expenses of vessels; what does it cost to run cod-fishing vessels that go to Georges Bank, by the year; and in the first place during how many months of the year are they there?—A. This varies a great deal; cod-fishing vessels would probably be for 9 months at Georges Bank, or 8 months would perhaps be a fair average.

Q. What would the running expenses be for a vessel which is there 8 or 9 months, for the year?—A. Well, I think that our vessels there have cost us on the average $2,300 or $2,400, not including interest or taxes, or, for the larger part of the time, insurance or depreciation.

Q. You mean money actually paid out?—A. I mean that is the amount of the actual bills of the vessel, nothing else.

Q. What is the yearly expenditure per vessel for anchors?—A. These entail very large bills.

Q. How much are they on the average?—A. I do not know, but the largest bill in this respect is entailed in the cod fishery at the Georges Bank.

Q. How many anchors would you lose per year?—A. Well, the number varies. Vessels which do not lose more than an anchor a year would be considered very fortunate.

Q. Have you had occasion to purchase any mackerel from a provincial vessel this summer, caught while fishing off our coast?—A. Yes.

Q. What was her name, what did she do, and what did you buy?—A. She had been seining, and I think her name was the Harriet. She belonged somewhere about Shelburne or Lockport, or somewhere about there. She was seining on our shore, and we bought mackerel.

Q. Where was this at?—A. At Gloucester.

Q. She brought them there?—A. Yes, and landed them at our wharf. We bought them before she landed them.

Q. What does an anchor cost?—A. This year they cost six c pound, and an anchor will average 600 pounds for a vessel, witho stock. The price for an anchor has this year been $38, and the has been as high as fifteen cents a pound. Some years the anchor has cost $90.

Q. That is for the anchor and chain part?—A. It is for the a and stock, and for nothing else.

Q. What does a cable cost?—A. About $2 a fathom this ye think that a cable of 250 fathoms would cost this year as near $ could be calculated.

Q. How many cables have you in your vessel?—A. We gen have one spring cable of about 250 fathoms in length.

Q. How often has it to be renewed?—A. They are not renewed over once in two years. We generally have to buy from 100 t fathoms of cable every year for a vessel that is following the f right along.

By Hon. Mr. Kellogg:

Q. Where are they made?—A. In Boston. They are spun a made of manila. We do not use chains at all.

By Mr. Foster:

Q. Your business expenses cover the period when there was a as when there was not a duty on fish? You did business previo during, and subsequent to reciprocity, and since the Treaty of ington, and I want to know whether, in your judgment, if the d $2 a barrel were reimposed on mackerel coming from the provinces the American market, it would come out of the provincial fishermen out of the people of the United States?—A. It would come out provincial fishermen, I should say.

Q. How near prohibitory would a duty of $2 a barrel, put grades of mackerel, be found?—A. I should think it would destr the profit and make their business unprofitable. It would ten way.

Q. What would be the effect of a duty of $1 a barrel on pro' herring?—A. That would be total prohibition. Herring do not times sell in the market at over $2.50 a barrel.

Q. What has been the effect of admitting herring from the pro under the treaty as to the herring business? To what extent h business of sending herring from the provinces to our market up since the duty was removed?—A. I think it has increased.

Q. Was it very large or was there any of it when the duty was A. I think it was then very small—there was hardly any of it a time.

Q. Have you vessels engaged in the halibut fishery?—A. Ye only incidentally. The vessels that fish for cod on George's Bank bring in more or less of halibut.

Q. Fresh or salt?—A. Fresh; the salt halibut comes from the

Q. This has never with you been an exclusive fishery?—A. No

Q. How many vessels go from Gloucester to catch halibut?—A fleet this year, I think, numbered 31 vessels.

Q. From your own knowledge you do not know where those go; but, speaking from report, where have they gone?—A. C years they have gone off into deep water off the western edge Grand Bank and to the southern part of Saint Peters's and Q Bank as it falls off toward the gulf. The fishing firms always where the vessels fish, in order to know where they go and to keep watch of the voyages.

Q. Have you known of any considerable number of them going in the vicinity of Cape Sable or Seal Island?—A. I never heard of any going there.

Q. What does it cost to build a fishing-schooner at Gloucester by the ton?—A. I think that a schooner of 100 tons, old tonnage, would cost about $7,000 or $7,200.

Q. Old tonnage is carpenter's measurement?—A. 100 tons old tonnage would average from 66 to 70 tons register.

Q. You think it would cost over $70 a ton?—A. Yes; we built three vessels this last season, and I think that they cost us about that.

Q. What do you include in the cost of the vessel?—A. Everything, exclusive of the fishing-gear—cables, anchors, and all those things.

Q. Can anybody get this done any cheaper than yourself?—A. I do not know about that.

Q. No one has more facilities for getting it done cheaper, of course. How does the character of the vessels built in Gloucester for the Gloucester fleet compare with the fishing-vessels built in the provinces?—A. The former are better than the latter in every way.

Q. Explain in what particular?—A. They are better built and better modeled, and their material is better.

Q. And what material is so used up here?—A. I do not know, but it is some soft wood or other. I never inquired much about it.

Q. Could you estimate the difference a ton between what you should suppose it would cost to build a mackerel-fishing schooner here and such cost in Gloucester? I do not mean built here; but suppose a vessel was built in Gloucester as they are built here, what would this cost here?—A. I do not know. That would be a pretty hard thing to tell. I do not think that you could get a man there to build a vessel in that way.

Q. What has been the conditions of fishing towns in Massachusetts, aside from Gloucester?—A. I think their business has decreased.

Q. Name these towns as they occur to you?—A. I think that Manchester, the town nearest Gloucester, a great many years ago, had from 12 to 13 vessels which went to the Banks, but now none are owned there. Beverly used to have, I think, about 50 vessels, which number is reduced to about 26 or 28. Marblehead used to be a very large fishing place; I think that at one time from 60 to 70 vessels were owned there; I think that originally this was the largest fishing place in Massachusetts; but now its fishing business has almost entirely gone.

Q. What is Marblehead doing now?—A. It has gone into the shore business. Plymouth used to be a very large fishing place, owning from 60 to 70 vessels; but this number now has fallen off down to 20 or 30, I think. The business of these towns has decreased all round, with the exception of Provincetown, which has held her own; they have there made fishing their principal business altogether. I think that Provincetown has held her own, but all along the other smaller towns have lost about all their fishing business, which has become centralized mostly in Gloucester.

Q. Has the fishing business of Wellfleet increased?—A. No; she has lost her cod-fishing business, and now only follows the mackerel business.

Q. You mean by fishing business, anything?—A. Yes; anything in the shape of fishing.

Q. Both cod and mackerel?—A. Yes.

Q. The general result is that as Gloucester has increased th
fishing places have decreased ?—A. Yes.

Q. If you cannot make money in the fishing business in Glou
is there any place on the continent where it can be so made ?—*
if it cannot be made there, then it can be so made nowhere.

Q. You have all the appliances nécessary in this connection ?—*

Q. And you know your business ?—A. Yes.

Q. You have said that your vessels have done well up to thi
and that sometimes they have made as much as 25 per cent.;
would like you to state more fully the business which your vessel
done and the way in which they have made money.—A. We
with my father, went anywhere except on our own shores; :
always, I think, from the time he commenced business, made a
deal of money in the fishing business; but we only went on o
shore exclusively, and have only taken the bay fishery and the
erel fishery as incidental. We have done very well, for the reaso
we have been on our own shore when other vessels were in th
when the bay fishery was followed more largely than is the ∢
present.

Q. Your firm is undoubtedly the most prosperous and the larg
Gloucester ?—A. I would not say that.

Q. Is there any doubt about it; there is no doubt about it ?—
are called so.

Q. Did you have a brother who went out of business a few
ago ?—A. Yes; he went out in 1865, I think. He was the or
went out of our firm in 1861, when our firm dissolved; he ther
into business by himself, and was in business in 1862, 1863, and
and I think he went out in 1865.

Q. Was he by himself ?—A. Yes; he was for four years by h
and then he retired altogether.

Q. I want to know whether you, yourself, would not have been
off at the present time if you had followed your brother's examp
retired in 1865 ?—A. Yes; I would then have been better off to-

By Mr. Davies:

Q. What did your brother retire on, or withdraw from busines
A. When he retired from our own firm ?

Q. Yes.—A. I think on something like $25,000 or $30,000, or
abouts.

Q. What share had he ?—A. One-third of the profits of the bi

Q. Exclusive of vessels ?—A. Yes; he owned part of the vess
of which were mackerelers, and he took his stock.

Q. During how many years had he been in the business ?—A.
he went into it in 1853.

Q. And he retired in 1861 ?—A. From our firm; yes.

Q. Worth $30,000 or $25,000 ?—A. Yes.

Q. Your firm owned about twenty vessels ?—A. Yes.

Q. What would be the average price of these vessels ?—A. Th

Q. Well, yes.—A. Values have gone down so much that it is
impossible to select an average value right along; but this yea
vessels would be worth, perhaps, a little less than $5,000—
$4,500 or $4,800.

Q. All round ?—A. Yes; that would be their average value.

Q. This would be about $100,000 ?—A. They cost us more.

Q. Did they cost you $150,000 ?—A. I think so.

Q. I suppose that you have large establishments there besid
Yes.

Wharves, &c. ?—A. We have four wharves.

I suppose you have a quarter of a million invested in them ?—A. would be a large estimate.

Would $200,000 be a large estimate ?—A. I think they cost us y that.

You spoke of a number of vessels engaged in the mackerel busi- I understood you to mean that they were exclusively halibuting ?— es; what we call fresh halibuting.

I understand from the evidence we have had that there are other ls which are engaged partially halibut and partially cod-fishing ?— hose are vessels which go cod-fishing and catch halibut on their es, in Bank vessels.

The number 31 you mentioned does not include these other vessels a fish for halibut and cod promiscuously ?—A. No.

You could not give any idea as to how many are engaged, more or in halibuting ?—A. Catching them on their trips ?

Yes.—A. Well, about 100 sail do so.

You, of course, never went halibuting yourself, and you do not r where they catch their fish ?—A. I suppose we have accurate mation on the subject.

You personally never went on a halibut-fishing voyage ?—A. No; once, when I was a little boy and did not know much about it.

Mr. Foster asked you a few questions about the losing of anchors, as to whether this ought to be charged to their voyages; George's t, I understand, is the place where most of the anchors are lost ?— lost of the anchors are lost there at certain seasons of the year; More are lost there in February and March than is the case any- e else.

And a great many vessels would be there in February and March ?— es; from 100 to 125 sail would then be there.

And when they lose anchors they lose cables too ?—A. You can- ose an anchor unless you lose some cable, of course, with it.

Are not more lost on George's Bank than in all the rest of the fish- put together ?—A. No.

Where else are they lost so largely ?—A. On the Grand Banks; lso lose them very largely in the bay.

Whereabouts is this the case in the bay ?—A. We lose them around Magdalen Islands, where our vessels usually fish.

You were speaking of a vessel from which you bought some mack- this year ?—A. Yes.

What is her name ?—A. I am about sure that it is the Harriet.

You do not know, of course, where they caught these fish ?—A. , it was south off the coast of Long Island, and off that way.

How do you know that ?—A. The master told me so. I bought l myself.

Where is she registered ?—A. In the provinces.

Did she take these fish off shore ?—A. She took them off Long Island, went south fishing; she came to my wharf to be fitted out.

You do mean to say that she caught them near the shore ?—A. No; nk she got them from 8 to 10 miles from the shore, where our ves- usually fish.

You have expressed an opinion about the duty; are you a pro- onist or a free trader ?—A. I am protectionist.

Is the free admission of fish into the United States an injury to fishermen ?—A. Yes; I think that it is.

Q. Why is it so ?—A. I think that it develops the Nova Scotia
ery, and makes for us a rival here.

Q. That is a benefit to us; but why is it an injury to you ?—£
cause if your fishery is kept down, the men engaged in it will có
from the provinces and go in our vessels. I think that the large:
of your best skippers learned their.trade in American vessels.

Q. Is that the only injury it is to you?—A. Well, the only in
yes; only to have a rival in business is always an injury. If a m:
a clear field, he always does better than if he has a rival.

Q. Why ? Does this affect the price at all?—A. What do you
by price ?

Q. The price you obtain for your fish when you sell them ?—A.
not much. I do not know that it affects the price a great deal. .

Q. Then it does you no injury ?—A. Yes; if it builds up an
sitiou trade, it has such an effect.

Q. How can it, if you get the same prices the while ?—A. Yes
then we have to catch more fish.

Q. The free admission of fish does not effect the catch ?—A
tainly it does. If you increase the product of fish in any particu
rection, of course it has that effect.

Q. I cannot see how the free admission of fish can affect your ca
A. For instance, we go to the Grand Banks, and you now fit out v
to go there; and to all the places where our fishermen go, your
go.

Q. As to vessels mackerel-fishing, we are withdrawing from it
You have built up a mackerel-fishing fleet?

Q. The evidence is the other way ?—A. During reciprocity, ;
stance, quite a large fleet of vessels was built up along Lunenbur
about there; and when the Reciprocity Treaty was abrogated,
that quite a number of vessels were left on the stocks, if I am n
taken, and were not built and finished for one or two years after
though when they were commenced they were intended to be
vessels.

Q. You are giving your impressions, I suppose; you do not
to intimate that you know this to have been the case?—A. Well,
it as well as I know Nova Scotia to be down here.

Q. Were you then there present?—A. Parties that were the
me of it.

Q. You have it from hearsay ?—A. Parties owning them, or wh
having them built, told me so.

Q. I am speaking of mackerel-fishing vessels; and the eviden
the effect that our mackerel-fishing fleet instead of increasing h.
decreasing in number ?—A. That is the case everywhere; it is g

Q. Is the number diminishing very largely ?—A. Yes; it is so
own coast.

Q. So the free admission of fish does not develop our fisheries
respect; 10 or 12 years ago we had 30 or 40 vessels from Prin
ward Island engaged more or less in the fisheries, and now w
hardly any vessels so engaged; that seems to point the conclu.
the opposite direction ?—A. That is because the business is not
able.

Q. But, so far from that being the case, the business has doubl
quadrupled 10 or 20 times over ?—A. The mackerel business ?

Q. Yes.—A. Where ?

Q. We have 20 times the capital engaged in it now than was t

10 years ago on Prince Edward Island?—A. Well, it requires 10 or 20 times the capital to get the same amount.

Q. Do I understand you to state that the free admission of fish caught in British waters into your markets does not affect the price?—A. I do not think that it affects the price to any extent; indeed I do not think that it does so at all. I do not think that this affects the price a grain.

Q. You differ a good deal from most of the witnesses we have heard.—A. I will tell you why I think so. It is because the price for consumer does not change at all. I do not believe that the price of mackerel, to the man who eats them, has changed a cent for the last ten years. I consider that the price of mackerel depends to a great degree on the manipulators—the dealers in them. I do not think that the question of duty on or duty off makes one fraction of difference as to the price; this is, however, influenced by many things. If you took the duty off one year and put it on again the next year, I do not think that it would alter the price one fraction, though some other influence might come in and do it. If there was a change in this respect every year, I do not think that it would affect the price one grain. We took the duty off potatoes, which were brought from Prince Edward Island, for instance, during reciprocity, and instead of having cheap potatoes in consequence of this, during that ten years potatoes were higher in the provinces and all over the States than was previously the case. I think they were sold here in the provinces at the rate of $1 a bushel.

Q. What is your opinion concerning the price of mackerel in this regard?—A. It is that a duty would not change the price one fraction.

Q. I understand you to mean that if the catch was one-half below the average, and if the demand could not be supplied by the catch at all, or if, putting the case in an extreme light, the catch fell to one-eighth, and there was not enough fish to meet the demand, still the price would remain the same.—A. It would not then vary save very little. We have an illustration of it this year. Now, the catch of mackerel this year has been smaller, I think, than has been the case for a great many years. The price of No. 2 mackerel, for instance, for a time went up to $10 and $11 a barrel. They were bought up, and the price the fishermen asked for them was given, but still the consumption almost stopped and decreased with no catch on the market; and I have known a man with 20 or 30 barrels on the market, when I have some-times bought 10,000 barrels in one day, hunting round for a buyer.

Q. Was not the year 1874 a year remarkable for a very large catch?—A. In 1874 there was an average catch, I think. It was nothing more than an average, I think. If I am not mistaken, the catch for 1872 and 1873 was small.

Q. Do you remember it sufficiently to state whether this was the case or not?—A. My impression is that there was about an average catch in 1874.

Q. We have the evidence of several witnesses who state that the catch that year was very large.—A. Still it was large, compared with the catch of 1875; but taking the catches for a series of years, this was not the case.

Q. How was it in 1873?—A. In 1872 and 1873 the catch was small compared with that of 1870.

Q. It was larger in 1874 than it was for the year immediately preceding?—A. Yes.

Q. How were prices that year?—A. In 1874 prices were about fair.

Q. Are you sure of that?—A. Yes.

Q. I know that the catch for Prince Edward Island was very l
that year, with very low prices.—A. Well, the island fish are poor

Q. That may be, but that is not the question at all; I am asking
whether the catch was large that year or the price small?—A.]
mostly all say that the catch in 1870 was the largest catch but one
we ever had, and the price that year was the largest we have had;
cannot form a calculation that will work uniformly from year to y

. Q. I understand your evidence to be that no matter what the catc
the price will remain about the same?—A. No; I did not say that.

Q. What did you say?—A. In 1870 we had the largest catch but
which we ever had, I think, in Massachusetts; it numbered, I th
318,000 barrels, and No. 1 mackerel ruled that year, I think, at $:
barrel; while in the next year, 1871, there was about an average ca
and yet the price was then from $4 to $5 lower than it was in 1870, ·
a very large catch; and in 1872 and 1873 there was a small catch,
mistake not, and I think that the prices were that year about the s:
They did not vary, save very little, from 1872.

Q. The catch does affect the price, in your opinion?—A. I sa
does some; but then I say there are a great many things which i
ence the price, such as the manipulations of operators, and all t
things.

Q. Is the rise or fall in the price more owing to the manipulatio
operations than to other causes?—A. I do not say that; but all t
things operate.

Q. To what extent do you think that the catch affects the price
not the price of mackerel, like that of every other article, governed
the laws of supply and demand; if the supply fails, does not the p
go up?—A. That would be the case if the selling price was alway
governed; that would be the case if the price to the consumer was
ways governed by the selling price; but this is not so in the cas
mackerel.

Q. You say then that the price to the consumer always remains
same?—A. The price to the man who eats them does not vary, |
very little.

Q. That is not affected by the catch at all, in your opinion; the |
to the consumer remains the same?—A. It has been the same for
last ten years.

Q. You think so?—A. I know so.

Q. You do not know it; your evidence does not agree with other
dence.—A. I know that is so, because I have had experience .in
trade.

Q. You say that the price is uniform, and that, in your opinion,
catch is not affected by it?—A. The catch does not affect the |
which the consumer pays; that has not affected it one fraction du
the last ten years. I mean this is the case as regards the man
eats and buys them.

Q. The catch, in your opinion, would not affect that price?—A. It
not done so during the last ten years.

Q. Would it do so, in the course of trade, in a long period of tim
A. If competition was sharp, it might reach that point, but it has
done so as yet.

Q. If the catch was reduced to one-eighth, would the consume
your opinion, then pay exactly the same for his mackerel which he w
pay were it otherwise?—A. They would not pay any more for then

Q. He would pay the same?—A. I think so; the price is gene
fixed at the highest price that will be paid.

he demand for fresh mackerel has increased a good deal of late
—A. It doubles and quadruples every year.

considerable portion of the catch on the American shore is sold
fresh state ?—A. Well, yes; I should say that a large portion of
sold, and it is increasing.

nd that necessarily opens the door for the sale of salt mackerel ?—
ink it shuts the door.

o you think that the consumption of fresh fish takes place in the
in the West ?—A. No; it does not go West.

thought you said fresh fish were carried as far as California ?—
, fresh sea-fish.

hat is what I am talking of, fresh mackerel; it is a sea-fish ?—A.

its consumption spreading all along the railways ?—A. Yes.

nd through all the towns ?—A. Yes; at certain seasons of the

he necessary result is that this takes up a portion of the catch on
erican coast. You said a large portion of it was consumed in
h state ?—A. Well, it is. You mean to say that the catch of
ackerel, which is a large portion of the whole catch, affects the
f fish off the American coast.

understood you to say that a large portion of the catch is con-
in the fresh state ?—A. Yes; it is, however, not the greater, but
part of the catch which is so consumed.

'as this statement which you have put in made up by you per-
?—A. It was made up by my brother.

he in your firm now ?—A. Yes.

'hat is his name ?—A. John J.

this his handwriting ?—A. No.

that the handwriting of Mr. Low, who was here the other
A. Yes.

len it was not made up by your brother, but by Mr. Low ?—A.
at is a copy of what was made up by my brother. I do not know
e the original in my pocket, but I have it all on one sheet.

this the form in which your brother made it up ?—A. Yes. I
keep the other one.

ou do not know how he got at the values, do you ?—A. They
en from the stocks of fishing-vessels; that is, when the stock of
is netted; that is, deducting the packing and other expenses.
the net stock which is divided among the crew and owners.

lis is the valuation at which you settle with the crew ?—A. Yes;
what is divided among the owners and crew.

lis does not purport to be the value at which the fish were after-
ld in the market ?—A. That is part of the price we would obtain
larket as dealers.

lis does not purport to be the price at which you sold the fish ?—
as dealers; no.

s Pew & Sons ?—A. It is the price at which the fish would be sold
ey were sold at the time to a person outside.

does not include the packing-out at all ?—A. No.

does not show what you got for them ?—A. I do not know that it does, as ſ. That.

~hether tᵇou feel any satisfaction in drawing the distinction between mostly all ¹ in that case and as dealers, do so.—A. There is a marked ᵣₑ ₐ-ₐᵤₜᵢₒₙ between these two positions.

Q. Is the packing out included in this statement ?—A. No.

Q. How could it come out if this is the valuation which you settled with the men; I understand that this does not represent in the slightest degree what you got for the fish, but that it represents the fixed figures at which you settled with the crews, and does not embrace the packing out at all, or what you got for the fish; am I right in making that assumption ?—A. No; it is an assumption, just as you say.

Q. Then I am right in it ?—A. It is an assumption, because you say it is the price of settlement.

Q. Am I right in saying that you settled with the crew at that price?—A. Yes; of course.

Q. Where, then, am I wrong in that assumption ?—A. You say that is the price which we would fix, and at which we would settle with the crew, without regard to anything we got; and I say, in that respect, it would not have any regard to what we got in our separate business, as dealers and retailers; it relates to the packing of the trip, the selling of it wholesale, and the paying of the crew, the highest wholesale price, which the fish would bring at time, if sold to anybody, per trip. We then take the trip and sell it at the price which would be brought by the disposal of it in small packages to different parties in the retail trade; this is a separate business.

Q. This represents, of course, the price at which you settled with the crew for the mackerel ?—A. Yes.

Q. And it is not the price at which you sold the mackerel in the market ?—A. Not as a retailer or dealer.

Q. As Pew & Sons, carrying on the fishing business in Gloucester, this does not represent the money received for mackerel when sold ?—A. As dealers, no; there is a distinction between the two positions. You judge it as if we settled with the crew at one price and obtained another price, thereby acting dishonestly.

Q. Not at all.—A. It would be so understood.

Q. Where would the dishonesty lie ?—A. You say that this is the price you fixed and at which you settled with the crew, without regard to the price you got; and unless that was explained the men would say we did not obtain the price we ought to have secured; and I want the matter set right.

Q. Some of these are mere estimates ?—A. They are actual figures.

Q. Some of them are mere estimates ?—A. Only one of them is an estimate on the different numbers; the aggregate number is correct.

Q. Can you tell me the length of time each of these vessels was in the bay, and their length of time in the shore-fishing ?—A. Well, the average——

Q. Hold; I do not want the average; you have given a list of vessels, 5 in number, which in 1870 were in the bay, and of 8, which were the same year fishing on your shore, and I desire to ascertain the exact time which was spent by these 8 vessels on your shore ?—A. It would be about the same—about 4 months.

Q. You say generally, about; was the time occupied in the bay about the same as was the case on your shore ?—A. Certainly.

Q. What was the tonnage of these 8, compared with these 5 vessels ?—A. It was about the same; they were, perhaps, the same ves

ı went one year on our shore and the next year into the bay,
their voyage. They were the same vessels precisely ; some
our shore one year and the next year in the bay.

etimes vessels going into the bay make very short trips, and at
es this is not the case ; there is no particular average for their

he bay ?—A. Of late years the mackerel fishery has been
d longer on our shore than was previously the case ; this has
uce we commenced seining. The vessels during this period
ı south to fish.

ıld that be about an average of the trips in the bay and on
e ?—A. Yes ; I think that is the exact time which they are
ɔne.

ers make 3 trips ?—A. I should include all the trips in the one.

are not able to name the actual vessels which went, and the
iod of time for which they were gone ?—A. No ; not now.

ıd you do so ?—A. Yes.

hin a reasonable time ?—A. I could do so in a week's time.

as during the war you made the highest interest on your in-
?—A. Yes.

t was during the Reciprocity Treaty ?—A. During the latter

customary to charter vessels in Gloucester ?—A. It is not a
ıstom ; it is done occasionally.

e you ever done it ?—A. Yes, I have chartered vessels.

ı Gloucester ?—A. From Gloucester people.

ing-vessels ?—A. Yes.

ıt did you pay per month ?—A. When we chartered a vessel,
ı some time ago, I think we paid $250 a month.

you get the vessel already fitted out for that sum ?—A. Yes.

ıat chartering a usual or an unusual thing ?—A. It is an un-
g.

ı unusual ?—A. It is not customary ; it is not the general

ı was a fishing-vessel you chartered ?—A. I think for a fishing
ı have chartered herring vessels to go to Newfoundland.

chartered vessels to go down and buy frozen herring in New-
?—A. To go in winter.

speaking of mackerel-fishing. Do you know of any vessel
tered for that fishing ?—A. Yes, a vessel has been chartered
er.

except ing that vessel, have vessels been so chartered during
ı years ?—A. They are chartered more or less every year.

nackerel-fishing ?—A. Yes.

system has been kept up ?—A. It is not a common practice,
the 300 or 400 vessels, some years perhaps three or four would
ıd and other years one or two ; it is a small number.

ı you were fishing for herring at Newfoundland and Grand
w did you enter them in your market ?—A. As merchandise.

merican herring ?—A. No ; we went under a register, and
ım as British products.

ıou pay any duty on them ?—A. No ; fresh fish for immediate
ın are admitted duty free always

By Mr. Whiteway:

Q. Have you ever carried on herring-fishing yourself on th
coast of Newfoundland ?—A. No ; vessels we own have gone

Q. When did you commence the business of sending the
herring?—A. In 1860 or 1861 ; 1860, I think.

Q. In what month did you send them ?—A. They start
last of November and come back as quickly as possible, usual
home in the early part of February.

Q. Between 1860 and the present time, how many vessels, (
age, have you been in the habit of sending there every w
Usually two or three every year, right along from year to ye

Q. Have any of your vessels taken nets to catch herring ?—

Q. You employed the people to catch herring for them
bought them from the people.

Q. Those are frozen herring you refer to ?—A. They we
as I understand, and the vessels froze them.

Q. What do you do with the herring ?—A. They take the
York and sell them retail in the markets as fish-food, and so
for bait. Some are also sent to Philadelphia and sold for foc

Q. What proportion do you say goes to New York—
whole ?—A. I should say New York and Philadelphia, on a
take two-thirds of them—the larger part of them.

Q. What did you pay the people of Newfoundland for h
winter ?—A. I think up to 6, 8, 10, and 12 shillings ; the price
for herring was scarce. Not more than two-thirds of the
loads, consequently they forced the prices up to $2.50 per ba

Q. Have you not bought them as low as 50 cents and 75 cents
A. They have never been bought so low. The first year th
vessels went there they were bought for 3 shillings or 4 shill

Q. What is the lowest price paid by you ?—A. One dollar

Q. As far back as 1860 ; are you sure about that ?—A.
clear on it.

Q. The lowest price you paid was $1 ?—A. Yes ; I am
that.

Q. You have heard of others having paid 80 cents ?—
year the business was started I think they were bought a
cents ; as soon as American vessels commenced to go the
went up to $1 and $1.20.

Q. Has it been a profitable trade with you ?—A. Profi
early part ; unprofitable at the last.

Q. But still you keep sending the same number of ves
man does what he has usually been doing.

Q. Have any of your vessels fishing on the Grand Ban
Newfoundland for bait?—A. Yes ; they have made a pra
years to go in.

Q. When did they commence that practice ?—A. My i
in either 1874 or 1875. I am not certain which year, but
years ago.

Q. The difference between the twenty vessels and tho
gone to the bay, have been employed on the Banks cod-
Mostly off our own shores, on the Georges, cod-fishing.

Q. How many have been on the Grand Bank ?—A. I tl
vessel I had on the Grand Bank was in 1870 or 1871. W
from one vessel up to 6, which number we have there this

Q. I believe you said that cod-fishing with you had been,
very prosperous ?—A. It has been the best part of our bus

Have you any bills or accounts with you as to what you paid for
n the coast of Newfoundland ?—A. No.

How many times on an average each year would a vessel go in for
—A. I should say that some of our vessels would go in once and
3 three times in one trip. I should think they would go in almost
times on an average.

What bait have they got ?—A. Herring, squid, and I am not sure
ier they got caplin or not.

Can you say as to what was the amount paid by each vessel for.
or the year ?—A. It would be an estimate. I have the drafts with
at I paid this year.

Have you made up an average ?—A. No.

Judging from your knowledge, can you approximate the amount ?
I think I can. I should say we paid from $2,000 to $2,500 this
it year.

Was that for baiting vessels ?—A. Yes.

Was that all paid for bait or did it include other articles ?—A.
irge part of it was for bait.

What proportion ?—A. There is only an amount paid for light-dues
wfoundland.

Were there any other supplies purchased by you ?—A. No; we
s fit out the vessels ourselves with the necessary supplies.

Do you buy everything for cash ?—A. Always for cash.

You will barter anything ?—A. Never. They draw sight drafts on.

By Mr. Davies:

I think you said you did not think the British fisheries were of any
?—A. I think they are of very little value.

Then if you were excluded from the bay, it would be of little mo-
to you ?—A. Yes, if your people were kept from our shores and
:ts.

Without considering the question of market; if American fisher-
'ere excluded from the bay, it would be very little injury to them ?—
would be very little.

Do you wish that to go on record as your opinion ?—A. Yes.

Can you then explain the previous anxiety displayed by them to
e inshore fishery in the bay ?—A. No; that is something I should
imebody else to explain. I never could understand why our people
id it. In 1863, 1864, and 1865, which were the most prosperous
in the bay and when our vessels did the best they ever did there,
issels on our own shores could make three dollars where they made
ollars in the bay; and yet the men wanted to go in the bay. They
s used to go ashore at Prince Edward Island, have a dance and a
time.

You think it was due to the attractions of the island ?—A. I think so.

The loss on the voyage in 1876 you place in the statement at $369 ?—
iat is a statement of the trip copied from the book.

By Mr. Foster:

Was the license fee of $1 per ton, in your judgment, as much as
kerelman going into the Bay of St. Lawrence could afford to pay
e privilege of the inshore fishery in the best years ?—A. I think it
iore.

You have been asked as to the longest of the trips. You have
the results in the bay and the results on the shore from 1870 to
inclusive. I want to know whether this represents the case of
ls which fish through the whole mackerel season in the respective

places ?—A. Yes; it does.   There are vessels that were fish
gether on the shore, and vessels that were in the bay all the 1
were mackereling, with the exception of last year.

· Q.   Does it represent from June to October in the bay, and ·
the length of the season was on our own shore ?—A.   Yes;
they were in the bay, and the length of the season on our sho
haps ·the vessels did not go in the bay till July.   It has only
or three years since the time has varied on our shore and in th

Q.   You did not put vessels which had fished four or five m
our shore against vessels which had been in the bay for 60 d
No; it represents the whole bay fishery of the vessels.

Q.   In those seven years you have had from Bay St. 1
$77,995.22 worth of mackerel, and from our shore $271,333.54
A.   Yes.

Q.   You have been asked about the settlement with the shar
the end of the mackerel voyage.   How is the price at which t
erel is taken by your firm determined ?—A It is determine
highest market price paid at the day of settlement.

Q.   If there is any dispute about it, how do you get at th
price ?—A.   We always take the highest price paid; it is deter
the sales at the place.

Q.   Do you not have a chance to cheat the captain and shar
A.   No.

Q.   Why not ?—A.   Because it is publicly known what the sa

Q.   The right of packing is reserved by your firm ?—A.   The 1
made after they are packed.

Q.   Reserving the right of packing to your firm, if your fir
give as much for the mackerel when packed as others will, 1
any right to give only part of the price ?—A.   No; we are com
give the market price.   When one master wishes to keep a tri
of an advancing market, then in that case the judges decide
trip should be valued at on the day the fish were ready for sale
crew will be settled with at that rate.   If the market is dul
crew insist on a settlement, the owner has the privilege of ta
crew's half, putting them on the market and selling them, an
price the crew will be settled with.

Q.   In regard to bay and shore mackerel, how have they
for two years past ?—A.   Ever since I can remember, with the
of two or three years, the shore mackerel have always been
and brought the highest price.   Those two or three years we
tional, and bay mackerel then brought a higher price.

Q.   You are a mackerel buyer ?—A.   Yes.

Q.   Have you bought mackerel in the provinces ?—A.   I ha
provincial mackerel, but not in the provinces.

Q.   When there was a duty on provincial mackerel, and a ma
mackerel at Halifax, would he have to pay the price of that sa
erel in the United States, or would you pay $2 less ?—A.   J
always buy at $2 per barrel less.

Q.   Have you bought any mackerel since you have been he
have tried to buy some.

Q.   As to this matter of the corner-grocery prices of mac
say that the retail price to the man who eats mackerel has 1
for the year, however the price in the market has fluctuate
has not varied for mackerel or codfish, materially.

Q.   A man who wants to buy mackerel for his family does
barrel ?—A.   Perhaps one or two pounds, or one or two fish.

nd the retail price for that quantity is still the same?—A. Yes.
suppose if I buy a salt codfish to make fish-balls for my family
stay at the same price to me for a good many years, notwith-
g extreme fluctuations in the market?—A. It will hardly vary.
he retailer may make or lose money?—A. The jobber generally
e difference.
he man selling me cannot raise the price on me much, unless
i a long-continued advance?—A. It would not make much differ-
two pounds of fish whether there was an advance of one or two
per barrel.
hen if the price goes down what is the effect to the retailer?—A.
s not make as much money.
r. Davies, I think I understood you say that you had vessels
vent fishing for halibut and cod indiscriminately—catching them
:uously. Explain.—A. I meant that we have 20 vessels which
ng for halibut exclusively; those are what we call fresh-halibut
. We have vessels which go to the Georges for salt codfish, and
k of those in pursuing their salt-fish voyages will get 10, 8, 5, 6,
0 or 200 pounds of halibut, and they bring them home fresh.
o great part of the vessels going to the Georges fish for halibut
as cod?—A. A very small part. I have vessels which have not
iugle halibut.
Then you spoke of paying $250 a month for chartering a vessel,
ike of her being all fitted out. Did you mean fitted out with
nd lines and seines?—A. No; I had reference to the vessel only.
ou did not include outfit?—A. No.

By Mr. Davies:

id I understand you to say that this statement of a voyage is
from the record in your books of an actual voyage?—A. Yes.
ave you a similar account opened for each schooner in your
—A. Yes.
hat represents the charges against the trip; not only the marine
t painting, calking, and supplying it with anchors?—A. Yes,
that voyage; we want those things.
ou don't presume to say that those are properly chargeable against
ntity of mackerel taken on that trip?—A. Yes; they are charges
me out of the trip, that are incidental to that trip. They ought
irger.
Thy?—A. Because the vessel had been in the winter to New-
nd, in the spring to the West Indies, and was ready to go on a
voyage.
moug the items, $162 is charged for duck?—A. That would pro-
je for a stay-sail.
nd fairly chargeable against one trip?—A. Certainly, the vessel
have to have it.
here is sail-making, $194?—A. Yes.
spar-making bill, $8. Do you think these charges fairly represent
rges against a vessel for the trip?—A. They vary somewhat.
ire actual charges made against the vessel on that trip.
Tould not the account be made up at the end of the year?—A.
:ount is made up for the voyage. There might be in the sail-
s bill some charges which ought to go in the spring trip, and
xpenses paid in another year should be charged against this trip.
ary a little always.
hen it does not represent truly the charges that ought to be

against this trip to see whether the trip was *bona fide* a profit or
A. No, because they might be greater or less.

Q. In your capacity as dealer you make a profit on the
out ?—A. Yes.

Q. So, though there is nominally loss, yet practically you
sustain a loss?—A. Yes, we did. We packed out on that
barrels. If you find the packing charge, it is, I think, $175,
could not possibly make more than $30 or $40 out of the packii

Q. From the other trips made during the year the charges ag:
vessel would be reduced, and consequently at the end of the :
result might show a profit?—A. Against the trip to Newfo
there was charged a quantity of duck, and I know we had t
that were used in the bay trips. Part of the sail-maker's
should go against the bay trip.

By Mr. Foster:

Q. There seem to be $1,245.68 charged on the debit side
account, and $661.94 as an offset for certain items, though they
carried out. That was the actual cost of the articles ?—A. Th
were taken from my books, under my direction.

Q. That account for each vessel is kept in order that you m
how your business is going on?—A. Yes.

Q. The suggestion has been made that it does not accurate
sent the precise results of the particular voyages, becau
expenses are charged here which would not always be charged
course that is true. But how much is the variation? Run y
over the items, and let us know to what extent the amount w
likely to vary, taking a number of years?—A. This account (
be larger.

Q. Explain what you mean.—A. I mean to say that the ve
partly fitted for the trip when she went in. For instance,
painted on deck, and her rigging was in perfect order, and she l
of her stores on board, which had been paid for on preceding
This account is a smaller account than it would actually l
vessel had not gone previously anywhere else.

Q. If Mr. Davies will send anybody to Gloucester, he c
access to examine your books?—A. Yes; and I shall be very g
will come and take some shares in our vessels.

By Sir Alexander Galt:

Q. You have mentioned the year 1870 as one of very high p
mackerel and at the same time a very large catch?—A. Yes.

Q. In 1871 prices were exceedingly low?—A. Yes.

Q. Do you know that 1871 was the year when the Washingto
was made? Do you think that would have any effect in redu
prices?—A. Not a great deal.

Q. Your opinion is that notwithstanding the large supply of
came in in 1870, and the readmission of Canadian fish provid
the treaty, it did not really affect the change in the price?—/
lay it altogether to speculation in the article. I know that, be
got very badly bitten.

By Mr. Foster:

Q. What was the date of the break in the prices?—A. They
ried along till about April or May, 1871.

By Sir Alexander Galt:

Q. Mr. Hall told us that the prices broke in December, 1870?-

d that year 50,000 barrels of mackerel and held them right along
e high prices—at the prices they were nominally on the market;
o sales were made after January or February.

Did you not expect the prices to fall when British fish were ad-
d ?—A. I did not consider the British fish at all.

By Mr. Dana:

In keeping an account for a vessel either by the trip or month, you
e to that month or that trip the expense that has been incurred
a that period; of course, the benefit may extend over the next
—A. Yes.

For instance, in this account the spar-maker's bill is very small,
the sail-maker's bill is rather large; in the next trip the accounts
be reversed ?—A. The accounts of our other vessels all through
hole year, and the profit or loss on the vessel, will not be deter-
l till the end of the year. This, however, was a vessel of which
aster owned half, and he had his voyage always made up when it
ompleted, whether from the Banks or Newfoundland.

In keeping an account of a vessel, it would be difficult and too
a matter of speculation to distribute the cost of a jib or jib-boom
two or three trips, and calculate the percentage ?—A. Yes.

To keep such an account would be an impossibility ?—A. It would
ry difficult.

So you charge to each trip the expenses incurred on that trip ?—
e usually go over the debit and credit accounts as they stand in
dger about three times a year. There is no settlement made, but
certain the condition of the vessels, for instance, in May, August,
October, and we take that into account in our future calculations.

You make those inquiries for your own benefit ?—A. Yes; in the
gement of our business.

By Mr. Foster:

Did you look over Major Low's account of Pharsalia ?—A. No.

By Hon. Mr. Kellogg:

In regard to the register of vessels and ownership, I did not quite
stand you. For instance, a corporation and partnership, as you
on are obliged to have your vessels owned by individuals, in order
ve them registered ?—A. The partnership business is a business
we are on equal terms. The vessels we own are registered by us
ners.

Do you own them individually ?—A. We each own parts of differ-
essels. All three own parts in the same vessel; but my father
more vessels than I do, and I own more vessels than my brother.

I thought they were owned separately. The company owns them,
iey are registered by the individual partners ?—A. The company
not own them as a company, but they are owned by us as indi-
ls.

The register is in individual names ?—A. Just as they are owned.
egister shows the owners.

By Hon. Mr. Kellogg:

Q. Is there any difference in the cost of building the same ves
your port and in the ports of the provinces ?—A. No. I should
it will cost fully as much, and perhaps more, to build in the pro
as good a ship as we build. It will cost fully as much, at any rat

Q. In regard to halibut-fishing by cod vessels. Are those h
caught on their way to fish for cod, or do they fish specially for the
A. No.

Q. You spoke in regard to salting halibut; do you often salt the
A. We do always on the Grand Banks. Our vessels for salt cod a
catch more or less halibut, which they put into salt. One vessel o
of its trips brough₁ back one-fourth of its fare as flitched halibut
the Grand Banks.

By Mr. Foster:

Q. Do you say you could not build a vessel of the same kind
provinces cheaper than at Gloucester ?—A. You mean that tak
white-oak vessel you ask me whether they can build it cheaper i
provinces than we can.

By Hon. Mr. Kellogg:

Q. Is there any difference in price in building vessels in our por
there ?—A. There are different kinds of vessels.

Q. Is there any difference in the cost of building vessels ; tak
same vessel ?—A. No ; very little. It is only a question of the
and that is a very small amount. There is a shipbuilder in Main
claims he can build them cheaper than they can be built in the
inces.

By Mr. Foster:

Q. That is quite contrary to what we had supposed to be the c
would like you to justify the opinion.—A. They have not the ma
in the provinces to build what we call a first-rate ship. They ha
any white oak.

Q. Where do you get your white oak ?—A. Our white oak w
from New Hampshire and Massachusetts. Our hard pine come
the Southern States.

Q. Take such vessels as are built in the provinces, are they be
less expense than those at Gloucester ?—A. They are cheaper-buil
ing-vessels. They use a cheaper-built fishing-vessel in the pro
than we do; but for the same vessel, I have my doubts whether
be built cheaper in the provinces than in the States.

By Mr. Davies:

Q. Do you make that statement with regard to the present time ?
sels built, say last year, and those now building, are they inferic
sels to United States fishing-vessels ?—A. Yes.

Q. Do you know what vessels have been built at Shelburne an
mouth during the last two years ?—A. I have seen them.

Q. And you still say they are inferior vessels ?—A. Yes.

Q. You wish to be understood as referring to the vessels thems
—A. I understand you take what I call a vessel—the quality
wood, and the workmanship put on the vessel. Those vessels I
consider so good as ours.

itness handed in the following tables:

Schooner General Grant.

[Sailed June 8; arrived October 27, 1876, $4\frac{1}{2}$ months.]

6-200 barrels mess mackerel, at	$17.00	$328 61
6-200 barrels No. 1 mackerel, at	14.50	1,713 61
0-200 barrels No. 2 mackerel, at	7.00	185 50
0-200 barrels No. 3 mackerel, at	6.00	15 00
7-200 barrels rusty mackerel, at	3.75	4 81
8 barrels slivers, at	2.00	16 00
Bait sold on trip		29 00
9-20		2,292 53

EXPENSES.

ng 167 159-200 barrels, at $1.75	$293 65
rels slivers, at $3.50	108 50
rel slivers, at 5.00	50 00
rel clams, at 4.25	42 50
rel slivers, at 3.00	90 00
rels water, $3.30; 2 feet wood, $1	4 30
ng and scraping	10 00
r, James Bowie	1 35
ing 175 barrels	2 63
ws and orphans	4 22
	607 15
17 men's shares	853 29
Schooner's half	832 09
	2,292 53

JOHN PEW & SONS.

Retail price of salt at Gloucester, from 1860 to 1877.

1860	$2	per	hhd. of 8 measured bushels.
1861	2	"	"
1862	2	"	"
1863	$2\frac{1}{4}$	"	"
1864	$3\frac{5}{8}$	"	"
1865	$6\frac{1}{2}$	"	"
1866	$4\frac{1}{4}$	"	"
1867	4	"	"
1868	$3\frac{1}{8}$	"	"
1869	$2\frac{7}{8}$	"	"
1870	$2\frac{7}{8}$	"	"
1871	$2\frac{3}{8}$	"	"
1872	$2\frac{1}{4}$	"	"
1873	$2\frac{1}{8}$	"	"
1874	$2\frac{1}{4}$	"	"
1875	2	"	"
1876	$1\frac{3}{4}$	"	"
1877	$1\frac{5}{8}$	"	"
18	$49\frac{7}{8}$		

2.76 average price for 18 years.

O. E.

JOHN PEW & SONS,
Gloucester, Mass.

No. 74.

Q. You never were a practical fisherman, I believe ?—A. No;]
went fishing.

Q. When did you actually go into the fishing business on you
account ?—A. On my own account in 1855.

Q. Previous to that you had been a clerk, or otherwise, in a f
house ?—A. I had.

Q. How many years ?—A. Six years.

Q. In what fishing house ?—A. J. Mansfield & Sons.

Q. Was that one of the largest firms in Gloucester?—A. Yes; ;
time it was one of the largest houses. It had been engaged in th
eries 70 or 80 years.

Q.—In all kinds of fishing ?—A. General fishing.

Q. You began with one vessel, I suppose ?—A. Yes; a small in
in only one vessel in the bay. fishery.

Q. Do you recollect what she made ?—A. About 200 barrels of

Q. In 1856 how many vessels had you ?—A. One vessel.

Q. In 1857 ?—A. I had one vessel, West Gleam, fitted out for se
and I sent her into the North Bay.

Q. Purse-seining ?—A. It was a seine adapted to either pursi
drawing on shore, as we make them sometimes.

Q. What luck had you with purse-seining in 1857?—A. I m
very successful voyage. The vessel packed 520 barrels, I think.

Q. Have you done anything like it since ?—A. No.

Q. What did you do in 1858 ?—A. In 1858, from the fact of I
made a successful voyage in the previous year, I fitted out three
vessels with seines for the same business.

Q. What did the different vessels take that year?—A. One [
273 barrels, another 270, and the third 47 barrels.

Q. Were those, in fact, taken by seines ?—A. They were not.

Q. How was the seining ?—A. It was not successful; very fev
taken. They were mostly taken with hooks.

Q. Then, so far as seining was concerned, the trips were a tot
ure ?—A. I consider so.

Q. How were those vessels commanded ?—A. One was comm
by the same man who was successful the previous year, anoth
commanded by his son, and the third by a competent man who ha
a witness here, Ezra Turner, of Isle of Haut.

Q. The fish that were obtained were taken by hooks ?—A. N
them, as I have reason to believe; a small portion may have beer
with seine.

Q. Were those taken with hook taken inshore or offshore ?—A.
sonally have no information on the subject.

Q. Do you happen to know from the reports of the masters ?—/

Q. How was it ?—A. The report from two of them was that the
round the Newfoundland coast, and to the Magdalen Islands, and
most of the mackerel there. As regards the third man, I have no
lection as to where he caught his mackerel.

Q. In 1859, did you send out a seiner ?—A. I sent two of thos
vessels into the bay. One of them caught 182 barrels, and the
of the other was nearly a failure; it caught very few mackerel;
barrels.

Q. Were those 180-odd barrels taken by hook or seine ?—A.
with hooks; I am not positive.

Q. In 1860, how many vessels did you send to the bay ?—A
one.

Q. How was she fitted out ?—A. With a seine and small boats

)se of fishing inshore round Prince Edward Island. I had been
and had become acquainted with the boat-fishing there, and I sent
essel there for the express purpose of fishing inshore.

What sort of a seine did she have?—A. A small seine adapted to
boal waters of the island.

Do you think a fair trial was given to that experiment?—A. I was
ɣs a little doubtful of it. The captain did not remain, I think, as
as he should have remained in order to make a successful voyage.
ʾent there, and his report was that, seeing no prospect, he sailed
t and went to Seal Island.

Did he get any mackerel at Prince Edward Island in his boats and
l seine?—A. I think not, from the fact that he returned with but
few mackerel in September.

Do you remember how many barrels he obtained?—A. I have
wn in my memorandum at 26 barrels.

Did he catch them off from the island?—A. I have no means
lowing. From his statement, he caught no mackerel at the island;
ught them in the bay generally.

You think that if he had staid longer, he might have perhaps done
r?—A. I did not approve of his leaving as soon as we did.

But still his judgment may have been best?—A. Certainly.

Where did he go when he left Prince Edward Island?—A. He ined me he went to Isle Sable. I believe 20 or 25 years ago fisher-
occasionally obtained some very large mackerel there, and he had
dea he might procure some and he went there; but he got practi-
nothing there, and his voyage was a failure.

From the experience obtained in those several voyages of seining,
, was the difficulty experienced, and why did it not succeed in the
?—A. The principal reason I can assign for that is that our seines
led the bottom, and the shores about the gulf are of sandstone,
ing a rough bottom, something like coral, and the fishermen do not
eed in pursing them as they can in deep water. Another reason is
the mackerel, in order to be successful at seining, must school—
to the surface of the water and show themselves—which they are
io likely to do in North Bay.

That is the whole reason?—A. I am not enabled to determine that.
ow what I have said has been the case.

Did you yourself go to Prince Edward Island and establish a busi-
?—A. I did, in 1858; in connection with those vessels I went to
sland, and since that time I have been engaged in shipping pro-
, and connected a little with the fisheries.

From 1858 you have been connected with the island as a mer-
t?—A. More or less to the present time.

What is the principal business you have been engaged in at the
d?—A. My principal business at the island has been the shipment
ɔtatoes, and in some cases cargoes of oats. I have also shipped
ɔes to the West Indies of the general products of the island, includ-
ive stock.

Then your business on the island has been dealing in the products
e island, and sending them to the West Indies and elsewhere?—A.
; principally to the markets of the United States, and occasionally
ie West Indies.

And at the same time you have kept up some connection with the
ng?—A. A little, occasionally.

Have you had an interest in a vessel or two every year?—A. I
;, passing over some two or three years. Along about 1863, 1864, and

1865, I was interested in the charter of some English vessels and (
two American vessels in connection with other parties at the isla
which I have no account here. I am unable to give the results of
voyages exactly.

Q. In 1862, did something happen which obliged you to perso
stay at the island?—A. My agent, who was down there, died, :
passed a portion of the season there, during 10 or 12 years—durin
time of navigation being opened, from spring till December.

Q. Did you have charge of a fishing stage at Rustico?—A. I dic
ing one year, in 1862. The man in charge was drowned, and I p
a portion of the year there, and superintended the business of the s

Q. You went into the boat fishing?—A. Yes.

Q. To what extent?—A. We had, I think, 6 or 8 large boats empl

Q. Was it a paying business to you or not?—A. Not sufficiently
induce me to stay another year. We caught 600 barrels of macke

Q. With all your boats?—A. Yes.

Q. You had to support the men and furnish supplies?—A. Tc
port the men in the ordinary manner, and we bought their fish.

Q. After one season you gave that up?—A. Yes.

Q. Were you engaged in the produce business and freighting, fr¢
ing for other people besides yourself?—A. Yes.

Q. But you still fitted out every year at least one vessel for fisl
—A. Yes, down there I did.

Q. Were those vessels you fitted out down there fitted with sein
hooks and lines, or both?—A. They were fitted with hooks and
and with seines as accessories; I had the seines on hand, and]
them as instruments to use in case of the mackerel schooling a
opportunity being offered of catching them.

Q. How long were the boats you used when you were engaged in
fishing?—A. The boats were, I think, from 25 to 30 feet in length
were designed with the object of being good boats and able to sai
to the wind. I should say that at first the boats were smaller, ar
had larger ones built and increased their size and sea-worthines:
adaptation to the business.

Q. How far out did the boats go to catch mackerel?—A. They
as far as they had occasion to find the fish, it depending on the v
Sometimes the fish were in round the headlands, within one mile (
shore; sometimes within half a mile; and frequently the boats
out so that I could just see them as specks with a glass, say 7 :
The men used to tell me they went seven or eight miles out, if the 1
erel happened to be there.

Q. You spoke of their being near inshore off the headlands; did
keep nearer shore there than at the bend of the island?—A. Yes;
the fact that the water is deeper at the headlands.

Q. I think you did not send any vessels to the bay this year
No.

Q. Did you send one there last year?—A. I did. I had one ves
North Bay in 1873.

Q. Take all those attempts you have made, with hand-lines and ¡
adapted to the coast, has it been a profitable or unprofitable busi
—A. On the whole, I can say with safety I have not made any ı
in the business on the aggregate revenues. Of course, in the firs
I made a very profitable voyage.

Q. That was in 1863?—A. In 1857.

Q. Do you think that voyage produced an effect on you?—
stimulated me to further action.

But your faith has given out?—A. A little, and I am getting a old.

Did you leave the island in 1873?—A. 1873 was my last visit to land.

During the time down to 1873 were you called to all other parts of land on business?—A. I was.

In your business connected with produce and fishing?—A. Yes; rchasing fish and products.

Thus you kept yourself informed?—A. I was necessarily compelled so on account of my general business.

During all that time have you seen many American vessels fishing :he bend of the island?—A. I have not. I have occasionally seen ican vessels, but of course, from the land, I had not a very good tunity of seeing many vessels fishing.

In so far as your observation went, you had not seen many Ameri- essels fishing?—A. I think not many.

Why had you not an opportunity of seeing them—because they not there?—A. Because I was not there much of the time.

From what you did observe, what conclusion did you come to— American vessels fished to a great extent within the line of three in the bend of the island?—A. I can only say that I saw but few ls fishing what I considered within the three-mile limit.

How about the distance from the headlands? Were they nearer eadlands than the bend of the island?—A. Necessarily so, because eadlands project more out into the sea.

Have you taken any pains to enable yourself to ascertain the ice from the land of vessels?—A. I have only done so in our own r, when the distance can be measured from one shore to another. e made a little observation in regard to the hulls of vessels appear- oove the shore line at that distance.

You have made observations with glasses and with your eyes?— erely incidentally, not with any particular reason or object; but g vessels out from what we call three miles in Gloucester Harbor, d see how they appear on the horizon.

So you have a substantial judgment as to the distance a vessel is hen you know the size of the vessel?—A. I have had some ex- ice, because I have had the experience of 50 years in vessels, hav- ad vessels myself, and from general observation.

Have you had occasion to observe how far out the boats went; I mean merely your own boats, but other boats?—A. I have; it art of my duty. I was interested in boats, and when there were tions of a storm or night was coming on, I would take a glass and ow the boats fared, for they might want assistance from the shore.

And what distance out did you often find the large boats that owned there and engaged in day fishing?—A. I have said before he fish were sometimes very near the shore, and other times if the ier was fine and the mackerel were playing off the coast, they l at a distance of 6, 7, or 8 miles from land.

Do you know Malpeque very well?—A. Yes.

What do you think of it as a place to run to?—A. I think Mal-

never measured it; but I have loaded vessels which have dra
feet.

Q. Do they go out except with a high tide and favorable wind
That is left discretionary with the master, of course; he goes wh
is prepared to go, but the presumption is he does not go out in a :

Q. What kind of place is it in case of an impending storm ?
instance, the tide is low, or the sea has begun to feel the effect (
gale, is it a safe place ?—A. I should think it would be unsafe,
prudent man would go round North Cape, and try and make a h
on the other side of the coast.

Q. Is the bar a constant one, or shifting one ?—A. I do not
from personal observation; but from general information it is li
sand-bars—changeable. I have had occasion, from year to year,
quire into the depth of water at the bars on the north side of the i:
in anticipation of sending vessels there. It depends on the act
the storms. In some cases the water is deeper one year than an
owing to the action of gales on the sand, as it is with all barrec
bors.

Q. Does the bar shift ?—A. It usually shifts somewhat by the :
of the sea.

Q. Do you know about Cascumpeque ? What sort of a bar is t
—A. I have loaded vessels at Cascumpeque frequently. It is a
harbor, and safe when you get inside. It is another barred harbo
is not considered quite as safe as Malpeque; it has not quite so wi
entrance, and has not quite such deep water.

Q. It has not so good an entrance as Malpeque ?—A. I don't coi
it so.

Q. In 1868, what had you in the bay ?—A. The schooner Rebec
Mathews.

TUESDAY, *October* 23, 1:

The Conference met.

The examination of GEORGE W. PLUMER was resumed.

By Mr. Dana:

Question. Yesterday you spoke about having fitted out a larg
sel in 1868; was her crew American ?—Answer. Yes.

Q. Did they sail under the American flag ?—A. Yes.

Q. Did you purchase a license ?—A. I think so. My attentio
yesterday called to a memorandum which I had in my possessio:
that is the only evidence I have of that fact.

Q. Your impression is that you purchased a license ?—A. I thi

Q. How long was your vessel gone on the voyage ?—A. Some
months, according to my impression.

Q. What did she take ?—A. About 70 barrels of mackerel.

Q. How much did you lose on that voyage ?—A. My estimate
on the return of the vessel to Charlottetown in October was
$2,200 or $2,300.

Q. After 1868 did you do any more fishing in the gulf ?—A. I
not, until 1873; but I had some vessels employed on our shore (
the interval. In 1873 I had a vessel in the bay.

Q. Had you any vessels on the American coast in 1869, 1870
and 1872 ?—A. Yes.

Q. How many ?—A. For a portion of the time, two only.

Q. Where were they fishing ?—A. On the coasts of Massach
and Maine; they went as far south as Cape Henry during that t

What was the result ?—A. I can only give it in general terms ; it atber unsatisfactory. I have not the figures with me.

How did it compare with the result you obtained in the gulf ?—A. -orably, except as to the first large catch I had.

Unfavorably, with respect to which fishery ?—A. The provincial.

Which was the best fishery ?—A. We were rather more successful r own shore than we were in the bay.

Did you again try fishing in the gulf in 1873 ?—A. Yes.

How many vessels had you then there ?—A. I have only a memum of one.

How many trips did she make ?—A. One ; she shipped home mack-on the 5th of August I received 128 barrels, and in December 53 ls. This vessel was lost in the gale of that year, in October, I , off the Magdalen Islands. Her entire catch was 181 barrels.

Did this pay ?—A. It probably would pay the expenses.

How many vessels had you fishing in the gulf in 1874 ?—A. One

What did she take ?—A. I have 186½ barrels down for her—the quantity we packed.

What number of vessels had you in the bay in 1875 ?—A. One, got during the season about 240 barrels.

What was her first catch ?—A. The first sent home was 179 bar-

Were those fish caught with hooks, or the purse-seine ?—A. A . portion of them was caught, I am informed, with the seine, and a large proportion with the hook.

Have you any information as to what proportion ?—A. I think in the vessel which I sent out in 1873 they obtained, probably, than 100 barrels with the seine, but in 1874 and 1875, when the ls had seines, I am not aware of them so securing any.

What did you do in 1876 ?—A. I then dispatched one vessel to ay, and she sent home 47½ barrels ; she was lost in a gale at Port i in October, when she went ashore.

Did you then give up fishing ?—A. I have done nothing at it this

What can you tell us about the menhaden fisheries in the United :s ?—A. I have had some general experience in that business; I employed vessels in the menhaden fishery for bait.

Where did they bring their cargoes of menhaden ?—A. To Glouces-

Were any part of them shipped to Prince Edward Island ?—A. I frequently sold bait to be shipped to Prince Edward Island and ·trait of Canso, and I have myself shipped them there.

Do you know whether orders are received at Gloucester from the d and other places in the provinces for menhaden ?—A. Yes, from act that I have very frequently received them myself, and have so menhaden almost every year more or less. This present year I sold some to go there.

Have you been engaged in the business of buying frozen herring ? Yes

Q. At what other places have you bought them?—A. I have d in the Bay of Fundy.

Q. During this whole period of 20 years, have you ever heard w your vessels fished for or bought herring?—A. In one instance I out the schooner Rebecca M. Atwood, which went seining in th in 1868, in October, to go on a voyage to Newfoundland; and sl cured a cargo of herring. On her return I was told by the maste a portion of these herring were seined by them. I sent a seine boat for seining with her. I also gave instructions to purchase, bu succeeded, as I was told, in getting a portion of this cargo by sei

Q. When was this?—A. In 1868.

Q. This vessel excepted, have you during these 20 years ever (herring?—A. No; that was the only instance when I ever caught

Q. With the exception of this one vessel, have you ever kno heard of American vessels which did catch herring there?—A.] I, with Ezra Turner, who was before the Commission, I understan I was interested with him in some of his enterprises there—ser for the purpose of catching fish ourselves; but not being success abandoned it.

Q. How often did you try this?—A. Only once, I think.

Q. Is that a different case from the one you have mentioned Yes; it was a different voyage, made to the Bay of Fundy inst Newfoundland.

Q. Then, in the course of these 20 years you have known of on vessel that caught a portion of her cargo in Newfoundland, and a which went to catch herring in the Bay of Fundy?—A. Yes.

Q. How long ago was this?—A. The first trip was made in 186 the other about 20 years ago.

Q. You have never been engaged in the herring business in any wise than purchase, and you have never known any American v obtain them, save by purchase, with those exceptions?—A.] have known of one vessel which was reported to have been fitte from Gloucester expressly to catch herring in the Bay of Fund was an American vessel, with an American crew, and with nets.

Q. How long ago was this?—A. Three or four years ago.

Q. What became of her?—A. The result was that they obtaine herring, but, on the whole, it was not a paying business, and s abandoned it; so I was informed by the captain.

Q. In the course of 20 years you have only known of two instances and heard of a third?—A. Yes; that is all.

Q. You are now living at Gloucester?—A. Yes.

Q. What is the condition of the trade in salt mackerel now, cor with what it was in times past?—A. I think that there has decline in the consumption of mackerel, and also a falling off catches and in the trade generally within the last 15 years.

Q. What are the causes of the falling off in the demand?— course that is a matter of conjecture. I have no facts to establ opinion, but my idea is that this is caused by the greater abund fresh fish, or rather the greater facilities for the transportation o fish into the interior of the United States by railroads divergin different points, and affording better facilities for transportation also due in a very large measure to the increase in the catch western-lake fisheries. Another reason I would give for this is lows:. I think there has been a great deal of fraud practiced own packers, and the quality of the fish packed has hence deteri

in consequence of this fact, people have been deceived, and have not got a good article. This has been a great weight on the trade.

Q. The quality of the fish has been marked too high?—A. Yes; the packers have not kept up the standard character of their fish.

Q. Do you know how it is with reference to the South and the Southern Middle States? Is there now a demand for mackerel from there as used to be the case?—A. I am informed, and my own experience is, that this demand is not so large as it was formerly.

Q. What do you think has caused the demand to slacken up there particularly? Is anything there used as a substitute for mackerel?—A. I can only account for it by presuming that the Southern fisheries may have been developed; and I have been informed that they have been somewhat; however, I have no personal knowledge in this matter farther south than Chesapeake Bay.

Q. What is the principal fishery which they have developed for use South?—A. It is what they call a herring fishery, though I should consider that these fish were more similar to our Northern alewives; and the mullet fishery. Whitefish from the lakes are also sent there.

Q. Do you know the extent to which the lake fish have been introduced into common use in the market?—A. I know nothing on this head from personal experience, and all I know about it is derived from general information which I have obtained on that subject from parties who are in the business.

Q. Do you know how much they put up for the market in Chicago?—A. I only know what I have been informed in this regard.

Q. Have any fish merchants left Gloucester to go to the Western States to engage in the lake-fish business?—A. Yes; I recollect one who did go.

Q. What is his name?—A. John J. Clarke.

Q. Was he a man who could not do anything in Gloucester, or was he a man of capital, enterprise, and high standing?—A. He was a man of good standing, with capital enough to carry on his business.

Q. He has gone to Chicago?—A. Yes; he abandoned business in Gloucester and now resides in Chicago.

Q. Is he largely engaged in the lake-fish business?—A. I am told so, and I have had some trade with him myself.

Q. Do you happen to know how much business he did last year?—A. I do not; but was informed by his brother while speaking of the matter incidentally that he packed some 26,000 or 28,000 packages himself.

Q. Of large fish?—A. Yes; whitefish.

Q. You have been to Prince Edward Island, and you have observed operations there carefully; what is the great business of this island, fishing or agriculture?—A. Agricultural pursuits form their principal occupation; on the sea-coast the farmers fish for a portion of the time; but I consider agriculture their principal pursuit.

Q. Fishing with them is incidental?—A. Yes.

Q. Do you remember a time when they used vessels fishing?—A. I do; at one time, some 12 years ago, I know they fitted out quite a number of vessels at the island.

Q. What was the effect of the Reciprocity Treaty on the fishing interest of the island?—A. I think that its tendency was to develop their fishing business somewhat. They fitted out, as I say, more vessels for this business, and there was quite an increase in the number of their fishing-boats, which were then made of a better style, and provided with better facilities than was previously the case.

Q. How was it with the island fishermen who had been engaged fish-

ing from Gloucester; did they return to the island to any ext
engage in fishing?—A. Well, that is a difficult question to
Many of our men come during the summer and return home ir
tumn from Nova Scotia, Prince Edward Island, and all parts of
North America; and they may return and they may not. Many
do return, and some of them take up their permanent resides
us. A large portion of our fishing people are from the province

Q. What was the effect of the termination, of the expiratio
Reciprocity Treaty which took place in 1866, on the fishing in
Prince Edward Island, this being followed by the restoration o
a barrel duty?—A. I have not had very much personal know
the fishing about the island since.

Q. Since you withdrew from it?—A. Yes. My last experien
was previous to that, in the boat-fishing. My experience in boa
was in 1862 and 1863, and principally, I think, in 1862.

Q. But you have remained, engaging in other business?—A
for a portion of the time, up to the last three or four years, a
still engaged in it somewhat. I have not been very largely so e
personally, but I send vessels there occasionally. I am conse
hardly competent to give an opinion on that subject.

By Mr. Weatherbe:

Q. In 1860 I think you said you were engaged in the boat-fi
the island?—A. I think it was in 1862.

Q. In 1862 you went down and took charge of a stage where ;
had been drowned?—A. Yes; that was my first experience in t
fishery.

Q. I think you sent a vessel there with seines and boats in 18
Yes.

Q. You stated that the captain did not then give that fishir
trial?—A. I think so. I consider that he did not. I requeste(
remain there until I met him myself, and I started home to 1
rangements, but he meanwhile went away. His excuse was
could not find any fish there, and hence he abandoned the voy;
I think myself that he did so too soon; I was not quite satis
his conduct.

Q. Previous to that you had not engaged in the boat-fisher
—A. No; I had, however, been there, and my attention havi
called to it, I thought it might be profitable; hence I fitted
vessel.

Q. You thought you would have been successful?—A. I t
was warranted in the undertaking.

Q. But previous to that, during the 3 preceding years, you h
sels engaged in the vessel mackerel fishery?—A. Yes.

Q. And they were not very successful?—A. They were not.
the result of their trips.

Q. Generally speaking, they were not successful?—A. Two
made very fair voyages; but one, to which I refer particularly,
did not do so.

Q. The one which was not successful made her voyage in 1{
Yes; she got some 47 barrels; and the one which, in 1860, we
island with the boats, only got a few fish.

Q. I think you said that the vessel which was not very succ
1858, from information that you got, fished outside of the t
limit?—A. I am not aware of having made any such statemen
nection with those voyages.

Q. Are you able to say now from information you received

g that season the fishery was carried on inside or outside of the
-mile limit ?—A. They fished I understood, as far as I could have
nformation on the subject, principally at the Magdalen Islands,
n the fall, off shore; and they did not succeed in getting fish early
: year.

During that year, as far as you could learn, this vessel was engaged
g at the Magdalen Islands and off shore at other places ?—A. I
that these vessels went with seines in the gulf where they were
ssful the year before; but they then failed to procure their fare
and they abandoned their seines; but during the autumn they
eded in getting the quantity which I gave.

I am speaking of 1858 altogether; how many barrels did your ves-
tch that year ?—A. I have stated that one vessel took 273 barrels,
er 270, and the third about 47 ; these are the approximate quanti-
s near as I could get them.

Did you seek information regarding the vessel which caught the
rrels, from the captain, as to where they had fished ?—A. Yes;
ese vessels were to go and fish on the north shore of the gulf—
vas the intention—where one of the captains had succeeded in
ing a cargo the year before.

Where did the captain of the vessel which caught the 47 barrels
·ou he fished ?—A. In the St. Lawrence, near the mouth, on the
shore.

Was that north of Anticosti ?—A. Yes; and west of Anticosti, in
icinity of Seven Islands, and to the west of it, up to the places
l St. Nicholas and Godbout.

That is where they fished and failed?—A. That is where all three
.ls went early in the season for the purpose of seining mackerel.

And they all fished there ?—A. They all went there early in the
)n.

Were you informed as to whether they fished inshore or not ?—
To ; they went there to seine.

That is where they fished ?—A. That is were they attempted to
but did not succeed in getting mackerel during the summer with
:s.

You stated that two of them fished on the Newfoundland coast and
e Magdalen Islands?—A. On their return, after having abandoned
herring voyages, I was informed that they had gone down the coast
ewfoundland to Anticosti and the Magdalen Islands.

For mackerel ?—A. Yes.

That is were they fished?--A. Yes; as I am informed.

In 1858, you had no vessels engaged in the mackerel fishery ?—A.
358, I had three vessels so engaged.

In 1858, you were yourself engaged in shipping potatoes and oats
P. E. Island ?—A. In 1858, I went there and made some arrange-
.s for loading these three vessels in the fall with produce.

Then, in 1862, you went to take charge of a fishing stage at Rus-
!—A. Yes.

So that was your first personal experience in the mackerel fish-
—A. That was my first experience in the boat fishery.

Were you personally engaged in the fisheries previously to that?—
never personally went fishing.

You have had no personal experience in fishing yourself?—A. No,
it all; I have never been a practical fisherman.

You never even had so much personal experience in connection

with the fisheries as you obtained at the fishing stage until y
and took charge of it?—A. No.

Q. Did you oversee the stage and take charge of it personal
Yes; I had general supervision of it that summer.

Q. You had six or eight boats employed?—A. Yes.

Q. And you caught 620 barrels?—A. I think so.

Q. Were these boats manned by persons who resided on the i:
A. We had four men from Gloucester, and the remainder of t:
were island men.

Q. Was this the first experience of these four Gloucester men
fishing?—A. I think that is probable, but they were experien
ermen.

Q. And the others you picked up on the shore?—A. They we
men.

Q. Were they fishing on shares?—A. Yes.

Q. Recently, you say, you have observed that the boats
creased in size on the island?—A. I think I said I have bee
formed. I have had no personal knowledge, or very little, in thi
since.

Q. Have they largely increased in number as well?—A. I on
on this head from information which I have received from othe

Q. How many boats have you heard they have?—A. I am u
say anything about the number.

Q. You say that the vessels fish nearer the headlands than tl
tations in the shore?—A. I had particular reference to the
making that statement.

Q. Do you know where the vessels fished?—A. I have ve
personal knowledge with regard to the vessels.

Q. You have very little personal knowledge as to where they
Yes; very little indeed.

Q. Do you know where your vessel fished the year when th
was obtained?—A. I do not; but I asked the sea-master about
days before I left home, and he told me that they fished that yea
pally on Banks Orphan and Bradley.

Q. And he failed there?—A. Yes; they only got a few mack
year—about 70 barrels, I think.

Q. Did you direct him to go there and fish?—A. I had no con
that matter.

Q. Did you give him any advice as to where he should fish?—
the captain had control of the voyage.

Q. In fact, you have never had a vessel fish within 3 mile
shore of Prince Edward Island?—A. Not that I am aware of,
exception. I think I had only one vessel there for the purpose
fishing.

Q. With that exception you have had no experience in this re
A. No; not within the three-mile limit.

Q. Do you mean to say that less mackerel are now used 1
formerly the case?—A. That is my impression; certainly.

Q. Can you give me any statistics regarding the quantity of 1
consumed in the United States?—A. I presume that the whole
taken is either exported or consumed.

Q. Where?—A. In the United States.

Q. Is the whole quantity caught off the United States coast c
there?—A. No; I think that the poorer grade of mackerel.
three, is exported to the West Indies.

Q. Are the mackerel caught in the Bay of St. Lawrence chi

·d in the United States ?—A. I should say that this is the case with
·ge portion of them.

Do you know how many barrels of mackerel are caught and con·
·d in the United States ?—A. I do not know how many are there
umed.

Can you give us any sort of an idea as to how many barrels of
·erel are consumed annually in the United States ?—A. I should
· that fully three-quarters of the entire catch are there consumed.

How many is that ?—A. I cannot give the catch for last year.

The largest number of barrels ever consumed in the United States
·ry small compared with the population ?—A. Yes, somewhat so.

Very little of this kind of fish is consumed there in comparison
the population ?—A. I think so; the catch some 15 years ago was
360,000 to 350,000 barrels; and last year it was only 180,000 bar·

I am now giving the figures for the State of Massachusetts alone.
·e years the catch has been as high as 300,000 barrels.

Those were caught in that State?—They were packed in that
·e.

Does this number include what was caught in the bay and packed
·at State ?—A I presume so.

During what years was the catch 300,000 barrels ?—A. I cannot
·on. I am now only speaking in general terms.

You spoke of a decline in the catch ?—A. In 1863 and 1864 we
a very large catch of mackerel.

. Can you give any sort of an idea as to the extent of such decline ?
. It has gone down from the quantity mentioned to 180,000 barrels
ast year; and this year the catch will be less.

What was it previously ?—A. I have no figures which would enable
to give such a statement.

. You cannot tell us what it was previously ?—A. I cannot give you
figures.

·. We were told yesterday by Mr. Pew that the custom now was to
·fresh mackerel into the interior?—A. It is so shipped very largely.

. Fresh mackerel ?—A. Yes; packed in ice.

. I understood you to say that the decline in the mackerel trade
·owing to existing facilities for sending fish into the interior ?—A.
ink that to a certain extent is a cause for it.

. But if they send this very fish in the interior in the fresh state,
·can that cause a decline in the mackerel trade? Would this not
·er cause an increase?—A. I was speaking up to the present time of
mackerel entirely.

. Then you admit that fresh mackerel are being sent into the inte·
·in the fresh state ?—A. Yes.

. And that trade is increasing ?—A. I think so; the trade in all
ls of fresh fish is increasing.

. Those fish are caught on your own coast ?—A. The fresh mack·
·; yes

. Do you not think that this would increase the demand for mack·
very greatly?—A. It would increase the demand for fresh mackerel.
·) not think that the one branch has any influence at all over the
·r; that is my impression. There is only a limited demand for
·kerel.

. And only a limited quantity of mackerel is caught?—A. Certainly.

. Do you not think that the demand for fresh fish, which is increas·
in the interior, opens an increased demand for salt mackerel ?—A.
at all.

Q. Since there is a limited supply altogether ?—A. I think tha
sons who wish to eat fresh mackerel would never eat salt mackere

Q. You think they give up the use of salt mackerel altogether ?
Not altogether, but to a certain extent.

Q. How is it with regard to codfish ?—A. Cod are also shipped ?

Q. Is the demand for salt codfish declining ?—I think not. I
that the demand for salt codfish is increasing. I think that thes
taken in preference to mackerel as an article of food, as they are,
lieve, obtained in better condition, as an article of food, than is the
with salt mackerel.

Q. You gave us to understand that one man who carried on the
ing business in Gloucester went West; did he do a very large bus
in Gloucester ?—A. He had quite a number of vessels—six or ei;
think, employed in the business.

Q. I suppose that the fish sent West are sent to him in large qu
ties ?—A. I think that he is not a buyer of fresh sea-fish—at least
not aware of it; I think that he deals in salt sea-fish.

No. 75.

JAMES A. PETTES, fisherman and hotel-keeper, of Grand Manan
called on behalf of the Government of the United States, sworn
examined.

By Mr. Trescot:

Question. You live at Grand Manan ?—Answer. Yes.

Q. How long have you lived there ?—A. Since I was 7 years of

Q. Where were you born ?—A. In Boston.

Q. What is your present occupation ?—A. I am a hotel-keeper ;
fish in winter.

Q. Do you fish yourself, or buy fish, or fit out fishing-boats ?—
fish and I buy fish.

Q. How long have you been keeping an hotel there ?—A. I coul
say exactly, but I have done so for 10 or 15 years. I live at ?
Head, Grand Manan.

Q. What is the population of Grand Manan ?—A. It is somev
about 2,000; it is now some time since the census was taken.

Q. What proportion of its people would you say are engaged ir
ing ?—A. I should think less than one-fifth of the population do ;
350 people.

Q. What fisheries are prosecuted there ?—A. The cod, hake, po
and herring fisheries, besides haddock; but very few of them are t;
and smoked herring are put up, and frozen herring in winter, and
few pickled herring.

Q. With regard to smoked and frozen and pickled herring, wk
the fishermen employed to catch them ? Where do they come fro
A. These are mostly natives of the island.

Q. Is there any large proportion of Americans employed in fi
there ?—A. No; not a large, but a very small proportion is so eng

Q. In your long experience in the island, how many American v
go there for the purpose of fishing ?—A. Of vessels, scarcely any
there; but small open boats, of something like from 3 to 5 tons,
there occasionally from Eastport and Lubec.

Q. Then the herring fishery is exclusively a fishery in whic
natives are engaged ?—A. Yes; nearly altogether.

Q. Do you know whether the bulk of the smoked herring is sent there ?—A. It mostly goes to Boston and New York. This year I think that it nearly all has gone there.

Q. How do they get to Boston and New York ?—A. Vessels owned at the island are employed in this trade. I think that four vessels owned there are constantly running to those points, and occasionally a vessel is chartered in this trade.

Q. What sort of a trade, in the way of smoked herring, is done between Eastport and Grand Manan ?—A. Small vessels and little vessels run over there from that place occasionally; and some of the smaller fishermen, perhaps, take their fish over in small boats.

Q. You know something about Eastport and its neighborhood ?— A. Yes; I ran a packet there for four years.

Q. Do you know of any body of people—Americans—living along that coast, which depend for their livelihood on fishing in British waters? —A. No; not to depend on fishing in British waters; I do not.

Q. Have you been able to form anything like an estimate which you think is a just one concerning the value of the whole Grand Manan herring fishery, including the hake and pollack fisheries ?—A. I should know this pretty well, as I am among the fishermen constantly.

By Mr. Thomson :

Q. What is that paper which you have now in your hand ?—A. It contains some notes which I have taken down.

Q. From where ?—A. For Grand Manan.

Q. From what ?—A. They concern the quantity of fish taken there.

Q. What did you take them from ?—A. My own observation, and from the amount of fish shipped, and the quantity of hake sounds taken.

Q. When did you make them up ?—A. Since I came here.

By Mr. Trescot :

Q. Can you make your statement without using this paper ?—A. Yes. There are about 10,000 quintals of hake taken, and about 8,000 quintals of codfish ; about 400,000 boxes of herring are smoked on the average ; about $17,000 worth of frozen herring are shipped in winter ; about 4,000 barrels of pickled herring—this is a large estimate—are shipped ; and the catch of herring which are sold for bait, and other kinds of fish, such as lobsters, haddock, and pollack, &c., would aggregate in value probably to $10,000.

Q. To the best of your judgment, what do you think that the Grand Manan fisheries are worth annually ?—A. Well, to the natives alone ?

Q. Yes.—A. I should say that $150,000 a year would be a large estimate for the native fisheries.

Q. Do you know anything about the fisheries prosecuted on Campobello and Deer Islands and from thence to the main-land, and from Letite to Lapreau ?—A. Of course I am not so intimately acquainted with this fishery as with the Grand Manan fishery; but I should say that the Campobello and Deer Island fishery would probably equal ours in value, and the fishery on the north shore, say from Letite to St. Andrew's, would probably come to something near the same sum.

Q. Suppose I were to tell you that in this fishery, from Letite and Lepreau on the mainland, and over at Grand Manan, there were caught annually fish valued at $1,500,000 by British fishermen, and fish valued at $1,500,000 by American fishermen, all in British waters, would you think that it would be a correct statement ?—A. No; I would not.

Q. Have you any idea that such a thing could be true ?—A. I think that the man who made that statement must have been mistaken.

Q. Do you know anything about Gloucester vessels coming down

stopping at Eastport, and going over to Grand Manan with I
fishermen and seines prepared to fish?—A. I never knew of a
that kind in my life.

Q. Have you had some opportunity of knowing whether such
the case?—A. Yes; because I am myself engaged in this fis
winter. I have known them, however, bring some boats from
bello in one or two instances.

By Mr. Thomson:

Q. I suppose that you are not an American citizen?—A. I v
in Boston, and I have not been naturalized.

Q. Then you went when quite young to live at Grand Manan
think I was about 7 years old when my parents moved there.

Q. And you have lived there ever since?—A. Yes; I have be
ever, in vessels on short trips.

Q. I suppose that your dealings are chiefly with the America
No; I ran a packet for 4 years between Grand Manan and St. A
that was up two years ago.

Q. But your fishing transactions are mostly with America
Yes; we deal mostly with them when selling our fish.

Q. The people who live on Grand Manan are ordinary whit
and British subjects; you call them natives?—A. We call
They compare favorably, I suppose, with the fishing populatio
ally in New Brunswick.

Q. You say that all the smoked herring which are caught c
to New York?—A. Yes, and to Boston. Boston, probably, ta
larger share.

Q. How are they shipped?—A. In our own vessels mostly; 4
owned on the island, run constantly to those ports.

Q. Is there any particular trade between Grand Manan and E
in these fish?—A. Yes; there is a small trade carried on by th
class of fishermen, with their small boats; they get more money
fish by taking them to Eastport.

Q. And the better class of fishermen are engaged in the smo
frozen herring business, and shipped directly to the States?—A
are not shipped by the natives; Gloucester vessels generally con
and buy them.

Q. Why do you persist in calling the inhabitants of the is
tives?—A. I will call them either way to suit you. I call them
because they are born there.

Q. What other fish are shipped by the inhabitants?—A. H
shipped.

Q. What about pickled fish?—A. There are not very many pic
shipped anywhere; there are not very many put up.

Q. I understood you to say that a quantity was put up?—.
4,000 barrels.

Q. What are they worth a barrel—$3, I suppose?—A. When
the cost of barrel and salt, the cost may come pretty well up t
these fish are generally sold fresh, and what is considered will
barrel then brings $1.25.

Q. I am speaking of these herring when put up: 4,000 b
pickled herring are put up at Grand Manan?—A. Yes.

Q. These must be worth at least $3 a barrel?—A. Yes, when
barrel and salt.

Q. I am speaking of them barreled as you sell them?—A. We
is a large average price for unpickled fish.

these herring sent to New York or Boston, or where ?—A.
sent all round the country more or less.

ere are they sent?—A. Some few go to Boston; I know of
ving been sent there this season; and some go to St. John,
nswick, and up to this year some have gone to Yarmouth,
tia.

many sent to Eastport ?—A. Very few go there.

nderstand you to say that from Grand Manan itself very few
y kind are sent to Eastport, save a few caught by the poorer
A. It makes in the aggregate, however, quite a considerable
oney in value, because there are quite a number of poor fisher-

at is the value of fish thus sold ?—A. I could not tell you ex-

t you come up to give the value of these fisheries ?—A. I have
u the value of the fisheries, but I cannot go into the details;
an.

v do you make up the aggregate value without knowing the de-
. I can make up the aggregate as to the fish caught. Take
·instance; I know the number of hake sounds which were
there this year, and the number of quintals of these fish that
n taken; I know the number of sounds which so many quintals
·ill make.

you know the number of quintals or quantity of fish that have
en by poor people to Eastport ?—A. I should say that not more
-quarter of the fish that has been caught there has been taken
ort.

ive 40 quintals been so taken ?—A. I say not more than one-
of the whole quantity.

ill you swear to one-quarter ?—A. No, I would not.

ill you swear that one-quarter does go there ?—A. I give that as
estimate.

d you ever heard attention called to this matter at all before you
re ?—A. No, not particularly; but I ran a packet there, and
sed to carry a good many fish as freight.

there is so little trade between Eastport and Grand Manan,
ld a fish merchant in Eastport know, by reason of the business
what the extent of the trade of the island was ?—A. Well, if
intimately acquainted with Grand Manan fishermen he would
y ask them from time to time about it, as he saw them.

r information only ?—A. Probably so.

Eastport fishermen stated that the great bulk of the fish from
lanan passed through Eastport hands, would that be true ?—A.
not the case.

anything like it ?—A. No; of course not.

u put the value of the whole catch around Grand Manan at
). I do not see how you get that, according to your figures.
down 10,000 quintals hake; what are they worth ?—A. About
quintal, as they are taken from the water; that price includes

Q. Then there are $10,000 worth of herring (used for bait) a
cellaneous fish ?—A. Yes.

Q. Then there are $17,000 worth of frozen herring ?—A. Yes.

Q. What else is there ?—A. The pickled herring.

Q. These 4,000 barrels would be worth, at the outside, $12,00
They are only estimated to be worth $1.25 when sold fresh.

Q. What are the 400,000 boxes of smoked herring worth ?
cents a box would be a large estimate this year; that is rathe
the regular price.

Q. That makes $156,000 ; and you put down $150,000 as the
the whole catch of the island ?—A. Yes; and I think it is a lai
mate.

Q. A very large estimate ?—A. I did not say very large, but

Q. You are making allowances, are you not ?—A. I think tl
large estimate for the season.

Q. And you undertake to say that the Campobello and Dee
fishery is worth about the same, though you know nothing abo
A. I did not say so.

Q. You said you were not very well acquainted with it. I
ever ascertain what their catch was ?—A. I have been aroun
islands considerably, and been among their fishermen, and I kn
they are not more successful than our fishermen.

Q. They may have a better catch ?—A. I do not think it.
that the heft of their fishermen come a great deal over to Grand
for fish.

Q. You say that no American vessels come to Grand Manan t
A. Very few indeed do so.

Q. When do they come; in the spring ?—A. Well, they do n
at any particular season. When they hear of a school of fis
Grand Manan, a few vessels from Lubec and Eastport will run

Q. There is no such thing as a Gloucester fleet that comes dov
in the spring or fall ?—A. I never saw one. I never knew one v
come there from Gloucester and fish inshore.

Q. Where do they fish there ?—A. Off on the Banks, and at ι
places.

Q. You have seen them fishing on the Banks ?—A. They coι
and get bait, and that is the last we see of them.

Q. They come to the Banks and get bait ?—A. They come tl
get bait.

Q. Where ?—A. From there they go we do not know where.

Q. Where do they come for bait ?—A. To Grand Manan.
not catch the bait, but buy it.

Q. They never fish around the island, within three miles
shore ?—A. I have never seen any so fish.

Q. You have never known this to be done in your life ?—A.
never known a Gloucester vessel fish around Grand Manan.

Q. You never saw American vessels fishing around the island
life ?—A. Within three miles of the shore; no.

Q. Although you have lived there since you were 7 years o
Yes.

Q. How old are you ?—A. Forty-one.

Q. During all this time, 34 years, you have never seen an Aι
vessel fishing within the three-mile limit ?—A. I never saw o
myself.

Q. I suppose that you never heard of one doing so ?—A.]
know as I ever did—that is, a Gloucester vessel.

ie boats do sometimes, I suppose, come over from the American
o fish there?—A. Yes, but very few; these have always been
ipen boats, with cuddies.

ien the American people who live along the shores about East-
d Lubec, and away on towards the westward, you say, do not
iats over there at all?—A. I did not say that they did not send
t all.

ut you say very few do so?—A. Small boats come over there
fferent places; there is not a very large fishing population on
ast.

7hy do they send boats over there, if they have good fishing on
ru coast?—A. I do not know that they have; I did not say so.

o you think that they have good fishing on their own coast?—A.
ain seasons they may have a considerable herring fishery up that
i the fall.

i your judgment, is the herring fishery better on the American
ian it is around Grand Manan?—A. It is not so long. There is a
f herring which comes on the sea-coast along from Mount Desert
3 Cod, to spawn, late in the fall; this is a very heavy body of fish,
iy do not last a great while.

hey come on the American coast altogether?—A. They come on
ierican coast.

a the neighborhood of Eastport?—A. No.

3 there any good fishing at Eastport, and westward of Lubec?—
iir fishing, I should think, is very poor there.

Vith respect to all kinds of fish?—A. Yes; from Mount Desert
tport.

a this quarter fishing of all kinds is poor?—A. Yes.

'ou only put down 400 people as engaged in the Grand Manan
?—A. I think that is a large estimate—400 men engaged in fish-

[as it been your special business to find out how many quintals,
, and boxes of fish are taken at Grand Manan?—A. I judge in
jard by former years. I used to trade considerably. I bought
all the hake every season.

.re the results of former years a good guide when the fisheries
every year?—A. We can tell that this year—5,000 pounds of
have been prepared.

io you buy the sounds?—A. No; but I am acquainted with the
at buy them, and I know how many pounds they buy.

Vhere did you get the figures which you have on your paper,
-A. I took them down from my memory.

Vby did you so put them down, if you took them from your mem-
A. I did so to refresh my memory.

Vhat object could you have in refreshing your memory, if it can
you to put such figures down without looking at any papers?—
ion examine the papers, you will find that I have made no mis-

Vhat did you take them down for?—A. To refresh my memory.

Q. Is he a respectable man ?—A. Yes; very.

Q. He is fish warden there ?—A. Yes.

Q. He goes around and collects information from the inhabit
to the quantity of fish taken ?—A. I have heard of him doing so i
past.

Q. Is he a truthful man and well spoken of where you are ?—
never told me a lie that I know of.

Q. Have you ever been on the mainland at all ?—A. I have.

Q. Have you ever been in the neighborhood of where Mr. Ja
McLean carries on business ?—A. I have been up there occasio1

Q. How long since you last were there ?—A. I came by ther
steamer the other day.

Q. I don't mean coming by in the steamer, but when were you t
A. I don't know that I have been there for two years on shore.

Q. Were you ever at his place of business ?—A. Never, I thir

Q. Where is his place of business ?—A. Letite and Back Ba}

Q. How long since you were last at Back Bay ?—A. I nev
ashore in Back Bay in my life.

Q. Were you ever ashore anywhere from St. George to Lep1
A. Yes.

Q. Where ?—A. I have been ashore at Beaver Harbor.

Q. Is Beaver Harbor a large fishing place ?—A. They hav
vessels.

Q. How long would you stay there ?—A. I went into harbor

Q. You went into harbor ? Is that the extent of your know:
the mainland ?—A. No. I am acquainted with McLean and with
ber of fishermen that belong over on that shore.

Q. From your personal knowledge ? Have you any personal
edge apart from what you may have acquired talking to these pe
A. I have quite a knowledge of how many are engaged in the
and I know they are not more successful than our own fisherme

Q. How long since you last were there on the mainland ?—A
it has been, I suppose, two years.

Q. You know McLean ?—A. I know McLean, not intimately
acquainted with him. I have met him at Eastport, and at our ow
this summer.

Q. Did you ever talk to him ?—A. Yes.

Q. I suppose it is possible he is as well informed as to the valu
fisheries on the mainland as you are?—A. He may be.

Q. Probably better ?—A. He probably has his idea and I hav

Q. That is not the question. I ask you whether he is any bet
to give an opinion as to the value of the fisheries on the mainla1
you ?—A. He may be better able.

Q. Have you any doubt that he has better means of informati
you ?—A. I don't know that he has better means.

Q. Although he resides there and carries on business the
Well, there is a large extent of coast. He is located at one pl;
he is as far from the extremes as I am.

Q. What part of the coast of the mainland have you any acqua
with there ?—A. Deer Island and Campobello.

Q. Do you call Deer Island a part of the mainland ?—A. V
Andrew's; I have run a packet there three or four years.

Q. And running a packet would give you a knowledge of the
business, you think. When did you stop running the packet
have not run it for two years.

Q. How long were you running it before that ?—A. Four yea

'or the last two years you have stopped?—A. Yes.

ınd the only means of information you have as to the fisheries at
drew's is that you have run a packet between Grand Manan and
drew's?—A. Yes; and bought fish while I was running.

Vhat other places have you knowledge of?—A. What other places
want a knowledge of?

want you to tell me what knowledge you have. I should want
have a knowledge of the whole mainland before you come here
radict other witnesses.—A. Do these witnesses have a knowledge
whole mainland?

'hose who have given evidence have. What other places do you
)etween St. Andrew's and the headwaters?—A. With the whole
Croix River I am more or less acquainted. St. Stephen.

't. Stephen is not a fishing place at all.—A. If you will name
rticular place.

f you have a knowledge of the mainland, you are better able to
hem than I.—A. I have told you I was not very well acquainted
ack Bay.

ıre you acquainted at all with the fisheries at Back Bay?—A. I
uainted with the fishermen.

hen you put your opinion as regards the mainland fisheries against
)inion of James R. McLean, do you, or Mr. Lord?—A. I have
ıg to do with Mr. McLean's opinion whatever. I give my own
ın. I did not come here to come in conflict with any other man's
n, but simply to give my opinion for what it is worth, to the best
kuowledge.

And you admit that your means of knowledge can't possibly be so
ıs those of a man who is engaged in business on the mainland?—
ıey are as to Grand Manan.

I don't mean that.—A. Why do you confine yourself to the main-

Because that is part of what you spoke of, and I cannot refer to
dozen things at once. I will come to Grand Manan in a minute.—
lidn't give the mainland so accurately. I said I thought it was so.
You said a person was mistaken if he would undertake to say——
ıay that if he would undertake to say it was so large he was mis-

You put that opinion against men who have been engaged on the
ınd?—A. If I had time I could prove it.

Do you swear that your means of information in reference to the
ınd fisheries are as good as the means of information of persons
ed on the mainland in these fisheries?—A. I don't know that I
ıuy business to swear to any such thing at all. I didn't come here
ıt.

If any person came here to swear that the fishery around Grand
ı was worth $500,000, or $350,000 more than you put it at, that is
d all reason according to you?—A. Well, I can't figure it out where
ꞅet it.

Do you say it is beyond reason?—A. I should say it was.

ꓕ   it is beyond all reason to put it at $500,000?—A. I do

fully stating what is false, or else has not the means of informat
A. I have nothing to say of anybody else's statements.

Q. Did you see that some of the American fishermen had ther
put it at five hundred thousand dollars a year?—A. No.

Q. Wouldn't it have altered your views if you had?—A. ꟾ
views are fixed.

Q. They were fixed before you came?—A. I didn't come to ma
mistatements.

Q. Where did you read the evidence?—A. Some of it in thꞁ
room.

Q. Whose evidence did you read?—A. McLaughlin's and Mc
and part of Fisher's.

Q. Did you read Lord's?—A. No.

Q. Have you read Fisher's?—A. I read part of it.

Q. Now, Fisher says, in answer to Mr. Trescot—I suppose hꞁ
knowledge of the island, has he?—A. He should; he has fished
considerable many years.

Q. He is asked, "What would be the annual value of the fis
Grand Manan, taking the opposite coast, and taking the neighb
generally, from your experience as a man of business with some
cal acquaintance with the operations yourself as a merchant?
would be the annual value, including Grand Manan and the coa
Letite to St. Andrew's and Lepreau?" And he answers: "I
set the value of the fish caught at Grand Manan at not over $4
They might go $500,000, but I think if I had $500,000 I woul
some left."—A. I should think he would.

Q. You see he puts it at $500,000?—A. He says "not over $4ꞁ

Q. He says it might go $500,000. Do you mean to say that hꞁ
state it was not over $400,000, and it might go $500,000, wher
only $150,000? Would he cover that meaning with those word
I have nothing to do with any other man's statement here. If
say conflicts with any other man's statement it is not my fault.

Q. You won't give any judgment upon that point?—A. I haꞁ
ing to say.

Q. Well, why did you answer Mr. Trescot when he put quesꞁ
you as to other persons coming here and making particular statꞁ

Mr. TRESCOT. I did not do it.

Mr. THOMSON. You said you would not give him any particular
but if persons came here and swore that such and such was tꞁ
you asked him if that would be correct.

Mr. TRESCOT. Quite so.

By Mr. Thomson:

Q. Then Mr. Fisher is entirely astray according to you?—
statement is large. .

Q. What is the extent of your business? You say you kept
during the summer and fished in the winter. Where did you fisꞁ
ever you went?—A. For herring?

Q. Yes. What is the extent of your catch?—A. Well, I coꞁ
say exactly—I never kept any minutes—but I might have gꞁ
worth for my share.

Q. Is that the extent of your fishing?—A. Yes.

Q. Now, there is Mr. Lakeman. Do you know him?—A. Yes
well acquainted with him.

Q. This question is put to him:

Q. How much do these several totals make?—A. $133,450.

Q. Think a little, and think what you meant by telling us a few minutes ꞁ

opinion, the value of the catch of the fisheries of Grand Manan Island only
ed to $50,000 or at the most to $60,000 ?—A. $500,000 I meant; did I say $50,000?
, that was a slip of the tongue, and if I said $60,000 I meant $600,000.
at is the annual proceeds of the Grand Manan fisheries?—A. No; the value
ake-sounds is yet to be considered.

uts it down at $500,000 without the hake sounds. You think
quite wild?—A. I think you must have confused him.
Vo. This was Mr. Trescot examining him?—A. I think his head
t clear.
Ie was entirely wrong about that?—A. I think the statement was
heu he says $500,000 or $600,000.
TRESCOT. Didn't he try afterward to give the items and find that
ld not bring them over $160,000?
THOMSON. Did you bring this gentleman to show that Lakeman
tirely wrong?
Then you say you catch $200 worth in the course of a year? Do
y any?—A. I am not engaged in buying at present. I have
t.
Iow long since you were last engaged in buying?—A. When I
nning a packet I bought more or less.
'or the purpose of cooking in your vessel?—A. No; to sell again.
Iow many would you buy?—A. I never kept any minutes of what
ht or sold. I don't know what bearing it has on this subject.
ust this. That you were pleased to state in answer to Mr. Trescot
u engaged in buying and selling. I want to see to what extent
ught and sold. You got two or three barrels of fish and sold
t St. Andrew's?—A. No; we sold them at Eastport. It would
e market at St. Andrew's.
)o you make the statement that two or three barrels would glut
arket at St. Andrew's? That is a town of 3,000 or 4,000 inhab-
and yet you say it would glut the market?—A. I say we sold
t Eastport.
Iow many did you sell?—A. I never kept any record of what I

an you swear to 50 barrels?—A. I can't swear to any particular
ty.
Vill you swear you sold as many as 50?—A. I will swear I have
many as that.
And what did you catch those herring for, those you fished your-
-A. I caught them to sell.
When you say you fished in winter, did you make a business of
.. We went fishing in winter.
Tou say "we." Are you speaking of yourself personally?—A.
nerally fish in company there; two or three boats fishing.
And your share amounted to $200, probably, a year, and with this
ence you come and say that the fishery is only worth $150,000,
at you have lived there 34 years, and yet during all that time
ver saw an American vessel fishing around Grand Manan.—A. I
Gloucester vessel.
put the question to you whether you had seen an American ves-

it.—A. I said Gloucester vessels. You asked me if there w
large fleet of Gloucester vessels.

Q. I asked you as to American vessels.—A. As I underst
referred to the Gloucester fleet; if there was not a large Glouce
that came down.

Q. Then I understand you now to admit that American ve
from Gloucester, do come?—A. I said a few small vessels and

Q. What do you call a few small vessels? Just exclude '
from your mind altogether.—A. Well, perhaps there might be
There might be a dozen vessels from Lubec.

Q. At one time?—A. Yes.

Q. Fishing?—A. Fishing off and on. Sometimes they woul
for bait and go away off.

Q. Would they fish within three miles?—A. They would no
within three miles.

Q. That is an evasion. Who asked about cod-fishing?—.
they set their nets inshore and took bait.

Q. Would they fish within three miles?—A. No; they we
set their nets for bait to catch line-fish.

Q. That is what the Gloucester vessels did, didn't they?—/
never knew Gloucester vessels set nets to catch bait for thems

Q. How many Gloucester vessels come down to catch bait?-
hard to average. Some years more and some years less.

Q. What season is it that they come down?—A. Along ea
spring they begin to come, after the frozen season is over, a
through the winter occasionally a vessel.

Q. How many would come down at one time?—A. I may l
ten vessels lying at one time—never more than that that I rec

Q. Will you swear you have not seen as many as 25 or 3
would be quite safe in swearing so, I think.

Q. Is ten the largest number you are certain of?—A. Ten is t
number I think.

Q. How long would they remain?—A. It depended upon th

Q. Did they come in and give their orders for bait?—A. T
in and tried to engage a boat.

Q. Did they tell each fisherman or a number of fishermen l
barrels they wanted?—A. Yes.

Q. And then these fishermen tried to catch bait for them?-

Q. They would come down in fleets of ten at a time?—A. :
was as many as I had seen.

Q. And their place would be supplied with ten more when
away?—A. Well, it might happen once in the year that there
I said they came down quite early in the spring.

Q. Didn't you tell me a while ago that you never heard of
cester fleet coming down there at all?—A. No; I said not to 1

Q. You didn't swear to me that you never heard of the (
fleet coming down to Grand Manan?—A. I said fishing.

Q. Is there not a certain fleet that comes down there a
known to come down there?—A. I have known as high proba

Q. Do they come down every year?—A. They come do
year.

Q. Is that known as the Gloucester fishing-fleet among the ii
of Grand Manan?—A. It is known as the Gloucester fleet a
goes.

Q. And these vessels come in, and the skippers engage the ii
to fish for them and supply them as fast as possible?—A. Ye

w much do they pay a barrel?—A. So much a hundred gen-

No. 76.

H ROWE, of Gloucester, Mass., called on behalf of the Govern-
the United States, sworn and examined.

y Mr. Foster:

ion. Your name is Joseph. There is a Samuel Rowe in Glou-
—Answer. Yes; he is a brother of mine.
ou belong to the firm of Rowe & Jordan?—A. Yes.
n were born in Gloucester?—A. Yes.
w old are you?—A. Fifty-two, come December.
early life you were a fisherman for a good many years?—A. It
ays my business, fishing, from a boy.
hat was the first year you were in the Gulf of St. Lawrence?—

w many years have you been there, in all, for mackerel?—A.
one.
hen were you first a skipper in the gulf?—A. In 1848.
om 1848 how many continuous years did you go as skipper in
?—A. Sixteen.
nding in what year?—A. 1864.
1864 you ceased to go to sea?—A. Yes.
hat firm did you go into?—A. Rowe & Smith.
ow long were you in that?—A. Three years.
en in 1867 what did you establish? Your present firm?—A.
uld be 1868.
ow many vessels has your firm usually had?—A. We have had
ght to thirteen.
elieve when you were in the gulf you were one of the successful
A. Well, yes; I always got a good voyage.
ke the last year you were there; how many mackerel did you
A. One thousand one hundred barrels.
two trips?—A. Well, we went two trips; we sent home one of
nd took the other home ourselves.
here were those 1,100 caught?—A. They were all caught at the
ens, except 100 barrels, or a little over 100—103, I think.
here were those caught?—A. At Margaree, and from Margaree
u.
ow long were you taking these 103 barrels?—A. One day.
ow near shore?—A. Well, we commenced about three miles,
as I can recollect; but we went nearer than that, not over a

iat day's fishing was inshore?—A. All inshore.
hat month was it in?—A. In October.
w, without dwelling in detail upon your seventeen years' ex-
as skipper, I want to know where your chief fishing-grounds
ring those seventeen years?—A. My chief fishing-ground was in
gdalens, although I have got trips in the bend of the island, and
zone on the Banks Bradley and Orphan. Early trips always on
and Orphan, and poor mackerel.
o you mean early in the summer?—A. Early in the spring.
here did you get the best mackerel?—A. The best mackerel in
er years was at the Magdalens, although I have caught as good
end of the island as I have ever caught anywhere, and I have
as good at Cape Breton as ever anywhere.

Q. At what particular place at the Magdalens did you ge
mackerel ?—A. Bird Rock, I believe, was the best I would say ;
I suppose Bird Rock mackerel were a little ahead, but not a
of these mackerel are caught there.

Q. What mackerel are there anywhere that compare with
Rock mackerel ?—A. Block Island mackerel are the only m
ever saw.

Q. But, except that, Bird Rock is as good as you have eve
A. There is but very few of that kind anywhere, but there wer
Block Island than at Bird Rock.

Q. Now, explain as to your fishing in the bend of the islan
much fishing have you done there, and at what distance from
have you generally fished ?—A. I don't remember ever cat
mackerel of any account nearer than from six to seven miles,
I might have caught a few. We always went in and came o
bors, but I never thought of heaving to and trying for then
were six or eight miles off.

Q. What is the difficulty fishing within three miles of the
the island with a vessel ?—A. Well, I never found any difficul
ing in, if the mackerel were there, but the mackerel is scatter
there is there. There is no body of them. There are more on

Q. How far out do you go to get a body of mackerel large ,
make it pay a vessel to fish ?—A. From six to fifteen miles.
miles just the rise of the land, so that you can just see Nev
Head. That is a better fishing ground than anywhere else an
island. We always made New London Head our mark.

Q. How high is the land at New London Head ?—A. Not v
but it shows more prominently than the other land around.
see that further than the land on each side of it.

Q. Well, how many years do you suppose of the sixteen or ;
you were skipper did you fish in the bend of the island ?—A
never fished the whole year through. I suppose I fished m
there for six or seven years. I could not say just the number

Q. Have you ever fished up Bay Chaleurs ?—A. No; I nev
ten barrels there in my life.

Q. Have you been up there ?—A. Twice only.

Q. Did you try for fish ?—A. I tried both times I went.

Q. But unsuccessfully ?—A. I never thought much of it.

Q. Have you ever fished up the Gulf of St. Lawrence,
Islands, so called ?—A. I have been there one year.

Q. When was that ? Do you remember what year it was ?—
I think it was in 1862.

Q. What did you succeed in doing up by the Seven Islands i
A. I caught 180 barrels. We were off Fox River, on the opp
on the south side of the gulf.

Q. How near inshore ?—A. We caught 80 barrels within a
a mile of land.

Q. The rest, how far out ?—A. The others fifteen miles off
into the gulf; that is, I think about that. The land is very l
might have been further, but we were wide out.

Q. What is the width across there ?—A. I think it is about
judge, sixty or seventy miles.

Q. From Seven Islands across to what point ?—A. To F
(Witness consults map, and points out the places where the
caught.)

:aught any there.

what places in the gulf, so far as you know, are the most mack-
;ht within three miles of the shore?—A. About Cape Breton,
my experience goes.

ir what point?—A. From Mabou to Margaree is the best place.
what part of the season do they catch these there?—A. I never
re to fish until October.

w long did you ever stop there?—A. Never long at one time.
:kerel strike there; they may be plenty to-day and gone to-

it is where you got your 103 barrels in 1864?—A. Yes; that
up.

w many mackerel, on an average, must a Gloucester vessel take
ere is a profit to the vessel? I understand that this is a ques-
does not admit of a definite answer, but I want to draw out
uion.—A. It is hard to determine. There is some difference in
is.

, there is a difference in the price and quality.—A. There is also
ice in the bills; but if we don't get 400 barrels we don't calcu-
ire going to do much.

u were in the Gulf of St. Lawrence most of the time during the
;ity Treaty, and you were there a number of years before. I
you knew about the cutters and the driving off of the fisher-
t came within 3 miles?—A. Yes.

u were not there during the license seasons, because you left in
ow, what is your view as to the importance of the restriction
fishing within 3 miles to the United States fishermen?—A.
as that?

w much consequence, in your judgment, is the prohibition to
in the 3-mile limit to the United States fishermen?—A. Well,
going myself, I should not consider it anything worth paying
; as I am situated now, I think I should be willing to pay, per-
cents a ton.

hat is the difference between going yourself and sending your
?—A. We have skippers that sometimes go in and try when
no occasion for it. If they try and are taken, it is just as bad
;y caught fish. If I went myself, I would not be running that

iu think you could fish successfully without going within 3
-A. I do.

w, your present firm, organized in 1868, has had about how
essels fishing for mackerel; did you say?—A. Well, we had
ars more and some years less.

ive you a statement? By the way, I want to know if you
any books from home?—A. No.

iy memoranda that you have made up here?—A. I have only
nda for the last two or three years in the bay. In 1874 we had
he bay.

hat did they do?—A. They got 1,847 barrels.

w many had you on our shore?—A. Five.

hat did they do?—A. They got 3,044.

 on to 1875.—A. We had one in the bay and got 153 barrels.
four on our shores, and got 3,784 barrels. In 1876 we had none
ay. On our shore we had five, and got 5,578.

ere those seiners?—A. All seiners.

Q. In 1877 how many have you had in the bay ?—A. We
four.

Q. Now, tell me how you happen to have sent them to the
year after your better experience on our shores and poor exp
the bay for the two previous years ?—A. Well, our vessels w
early in the season to run fresh mackerel to New York. The
were plenty, and they expected a big catch ; but in June, when
to have caught them, we caught none, and reports came dow1
mackerel were plenty this way. We therefore supposed they h:
into the gulf.

Q. What do you mean by reports coming ?—A. Well, we
from the strait. We had no letters, but we always hear, and
ter of fact there was mackerel here in June, and those that c;
early got trips of mackerel, poor mackerel. But when our
down they were gone, and they have been scarce ever since.

Q. Let me see what your vessels have done this year.—A. 1
M. Crosby took eight barrels. She was in something over a
She had gone in and tried all around the bay and found there
ing ; came out and fished on our shores.

Q. Did she have any better luck there ?—A. Yes ; she pack(
barrels before I came away, besides what she got in the bay.

Q. What other schooner ?—A. The Golden Hind. She can
before I came away, with 75 barrels.

Q. How long was she getting these ?—A. About eight weel

Q. What other vessels ?—A. The Herbert M. Rogers and t
couta. They are not at home. I heard the Barracouta had
the other 215.

Q. How long has the Herbert M. Rogers been in the gulf
wrote the day before the breeze. They had a gale down there
it was the 22d of September.

Q. How long has she been in the gulf ?—A. I think about fi

Q. Has she got back ?—A. No ; she hadn't got home when
at last accounts she had a little over 200 barrels.

Q. Now, are the seines successful in the gulf ?—A. They ne
been. I don't think they can seine there to make it pay.

Q. Did these vessels of yours go prepared to seine ?—A. 1
M. Crosby and the Herbert M. Rogers carried seines. The E
Rogers never set hers at all. That is, the skipper by lette
seine was no good, and he went down to Souris and landed it

Q. And caught his fish with hook and line ?—A. Yes.

Q. Why are not seines successful in the gulf ?—A. Well, th
shoal and the bottom rough. There are several causes. If ;
in deep water on Bradley or Orphan there are a great many he
get mixed up with the mackerel. They mesh in the seine, ar
so long to pick them out. They die and sink the seine.

Q. Something has been said about making shoal seines, to a
to the gulf fishing.—A. Well, they can catch a few that way
pretty hard to catch mackerel in a shoal seine, that is, the pu

Q. How much importance do you attach, as a man engag
fishing business, to the mackerel fisheries in the Gulf of St.
now ?—A. Well, I don't think much of it. It has gone down.
to be worth something once, but of late years we don't think
of it at all. We could do about as well without seining there

Q. What proportion of your business is mackerel and what (
is codfish ?—A. Well, I should say one-third of the proceeds is
and two-thirds codfish.

money value ?—A. Yes.

ve you ever sent to Grand Manan vessels for herring ?—A. We
it once or twice.

l they go to catch fish, or how did they get them ?—A. They
ought them. We always sent the money.

d they go with any preparation for fishing ?—A. Not any at all.
er thought of such a thing.

ve you ever been yourself or sent a vessel to Newfoundland
ng ?—A. I have been once myself and sent some two or three

w were the herring procured there ?—A. They were always
We never made preparations to fish.

ell, were you ever personally engaged in halibut fishing ?—A.
used to go to the George's Banks a good many years.

w far are the George's Banks from Seal Island ?—A. 70 miles,
as I can recollect.

w near Seal Island can you go ?—A. I have been two or three
ien I could just see the light, on a clear night. Right on the
the ground, right on the falling-off, there is where the halibut
be taken when I was there. But I don't think there is any
w. It was broken up. It didn't last but three or four years
was there.

ien you don't consider it a fishing ground, even 15 miles from
nd Light ? Did you ever fish within three miles for halibut ?—
er.

w many halibut fishers are there from Gloucester ?—A. 28, I
The number shifts a little. I think two or three more have
ded.

w recently have you built a fishing schooner in Gloucester or
built ?—A. We had one built last winter.

hen was she completed ?—A. In April, I think.

w what was the size, and what was the cost ?—A. She was 74
w measurement.

gister, 1 suppose ?—A. 110 carpenters'.

hat did she cost ?—A. A little over $7,200.

bargaining for building a schooner, you bargain to pay by car-
measurement ?—A. Yes.

w much a ton, carpenters' measurement ?—A. Well, it differs ;
47 a ton.

it you must have paid more for this ?—A. You have to rig it
rds. That is simply for the hull. We paid $4,950 for her. We
ckon by the ton. We give the dimensions, what we want, and
e us the figures what they will build her for.

hat does that include ?—A. The hull and spars.

as that as low as a vessel that size, first class, could be built
r in Gloucester ?—A. Yes, sir ; it was. They might since that,
, build for a dollar less on the ton. Perhaps a difference of $200
e made in the whole cost. They might build a vessel that size
$7,000.

von know the quality of the schooners built here in the prov-

vessels; of course they have soft-wood vessels, too. They
beech or birch.

Q. What are the Gloucester vessels built of?—A. White oa
and gray oak.

Q. How much difference in the tonnage would you estima
cost of a Gloucester and a provincial vessel, such as you hav
to?—A. I suppose a provincial vessel, in the best way it could l
we always calculate one of our vessels twelve years old is a
one of theirs new of the same tonnage, and I guess every one
sel owners that know, will say the same. I don't know.

Q. What do you say about the demand for salt mackerel in
ket within the past few years, compared with what it used to
It has fallen off a great deal.

Q. Why?—A. Well, there are different opinions, different
Some lay it to the lake-fishing, the whitefish.

Q. What do you know about the quantities of these?—A
don't know anything by experience only what I hear said by th
out there. They tell me, those that have gone out there from
and are in the business, that a great many are caught and that
sold cheap, and take the place of mackerel unless mackerel ar

Q. At what price per barrel can a large quantity of salt ma
disposed of freely in the market?—A. Well, they don't go ver

Q. Until they are down to $7?—A. Well, that is a large am

Q. Sold from where?—A. From our place. That is about w
ranged last year, and they went off very well. This year the
to $12, and were very scarce, and the market dragged. Fin
went down to $9.50.

Q. Why will not the people buy them at the high prices?—A
know any reason unless they get these lake fish cheaper.

Q. What quantity of high-priced mackerel, extra No. 1's, me
erel of the very best quality, costing $20 a barrel, can be disp
the United States markets?—A. Well, I have no way of kno
I should not think over from 8,000 to 10,000 barrels. I don't
that many. I could not tell how many.

Q. Where is the market for the consumption of the very be
erel, the highest priced, chiefly?—A. Philadelphia takes the b
erel, most of them.

Q. In what direction do the poorer qualities go?—A. I coul
I have never sent any. We always sell our fish at home. I
they scatter all over the country and in the Western countrie

Q. How do the sales of fresh mackerel compare of late y
what they used to be?—A. That has increased. It increases ev

Q. What would you estimate to be the annual value of
mackerel consumed in the United States?—A. I don't know th
give a very good estimate. Somewhere from three to four
thousand barrels, I should think.

Q. How is it about salt codfish?—A. That has improved. T
more fish and they go off readily at fair prices.

Q. Do you know how far West the fresh fish from the seabo
—A. Well, I don't know. I have no way of knowing, but I tl
send them to Chicago in the winter season; as far as that.

Q. We have evidence of their going further than that.—A
never shipped any fresh fish.

Q. Taking the corresponding qualities of bay and shore
which, for the last few years, has sold at the higher prices?—
our shore mackerel has brought the best price for the last n

The mackerel has been poor in the bay, poorer than it used to
e last four, five, or six years.
at effect in your judgment would the imposition of a duty of
rel on all grades of mackerel imported from the provinces have
market in the United States?—A. Well, I suppose it would
effect of lowering them some. It is pretty hard to determine.
now that I should say. Of course you put so many more mack-
the market they would not fetch so much.
o would have to pay the duty? Would it come out of the
at eat it or out of the provincial sellers?—A. I should say out
ovincial sellers.
hy—what makes you think so?—A. We take the most mack-
our mackerel determines the price.
n't you think they could raise the price of theirs and yours all
—A. No; I don't think it could be done, because we have the
.
ll, if a duty of a dollar a barrel were imposed on herring, do
k it could be imported?—A. No; I don't think it could. It is
ced fish.
ve you ever known mixed trips of cod and mackerel where a
ent out to catch whichever it could and brought back part of a
each kind?—A. Well, I don't know that I ever knew. I have
some tell about going some years half and half, but I guess it
iounted to much.
s any such thing happened from Gloucester?—A. I haven't
one for a great many years.
iat has been the course of their fishing down in Massachusetts
d with Gloucester; have they increased or decreased?—A. They
creased.
e business has concentrated in Gloucester?—A. Yes.

y Mr. Davies:
e you a protectionist or free-trader in principle?—A. A free-

you believe in free trade?—A. I do. I think there ought to
rade all over the world.
u think so?—A. Yes; I would like to see it so.
your own country are you a free-trader or a protectionist?—A.
far as fish goes?
; generally.—A. Well, I am a protectionist, if that is the case,
would be all over the whole world.
otice in your statement that the prices of the mackerel seem to
a great deal. Last year it was $7. This year it was $12 for
n explaining that you said it was on account of the catch being
ill this year?—A. Yes.
ippose the price is governed by the catch, whatever the catch
That is it.
ll, for this year, I saw a statement in the Monetary Times yes-
orning that the whole catch this year did not amount to 50,000
n your coast. Is that correct?—A. I have no way of knowing,
uld not think it was that much, if I was going to guess on it;
essels have been coming in since.
ll, that is a very small catch, indeed?—A. Yes; that is small
years.
w, I suppose if a large catch was made in the bay, and if your
rere excluded altogether from the best fishing-grounds in the

bay, and the catch on your coast was very small, as it is this
an exceptional case like that the duty would be paid by the co
because the price would go up ?—A. Well, if you had all the m:
of course.

Q. Well, if the statement was true that three-fourths of the m
that are taken out of the gulf are taken within the limits, that
have an appreciable effect upon the question who paid the duty
think it would.

Q. It is just a question of fact ?—A. Yes.

Q. Now, you say a Gloucester vessel twelve years old is as go
provincial vessel new. How long do those vessels last ? Th
last a very good length of time.—A. Well, we lose a great many
have vessels thirty and forty years old.

Q. I suppose thirty years old would not be beyond the average
she ought to last ?—A. If she was not lost. Yes, sir ; they will l:
time and longer.

Q. You said, of late years there were no vessels fishing cod a
but promiscuously, but it used to be so ?—A. I said fishing c
mackerel promiscuously.

Q. A gentleman said yesterday there was about 100 vessels
cod-fishing fleet that were accustomed to take m re or less hal
think it was Mr. Pew. He said 31 vessels devoted themselyes
sively to halibut-fishing, and a hundred of the cod-fishers too
sioual catches of halibut ?—A. This is right. They go with ice a
and get both.

Q. On the Seal Island ground you have never been in fishing
the shore ?—A. No.

Q. You can't tell what is taken there ?—A. I could not tell a
about it; but we never knew anything about its being a fishing-
Never thought of such a thing. I could not say there was non
there was I could not tell where any came from.

Q. I presume they came from the sea?—A. I mean the vessel

Q. How many years since you have been there ?—A. I have
there since 1852 or 1853, 1854 and 1855. I was only there on
trips, but before I left the halibut all broke up there.

Q. I think you would not care about saying what the fact is
A. No; any more than that I know where our own vessels go.

Q. You don't profess to know where the 31 halibut-fishers g
year, do you ?—A. Yes; I know where the other vessels go as
my own.

Q. Well, do you know where the 100 that catch both cod and
go ?—A. Yes; they go to the Georges.

Q. I am not speaking of what your general belief is, but 1
are giving evidence as to your knowledge.—A. Well, we send
the Georges, and they come back and say they have been to the (
and tell me what part of the Bank they have fished on, in h
water, and all that. I am as familiar with the Bank as they ar

Q. Do you know anything of the New London vessels ?
know where they go ?—A. No, I don't know anything about th

Q. I just want to know if you would contradict a witness w
on the spot where we say the halibut is caught and who said
them caught there ?—A. No.

Q. You haven't been personally in the Newfoundland herring
yourself ?—A. No. Only one trip.

Q. You have given a statement of what vessels you have ha
bay last year as compared with the shore. I notice a great

:atements have been made up referring to late years. Can you
a statement of what your vessels have done in the gulf during
tinuance of the Reciprocity Treaty, what the catch was, and
ssels you have had, and a similar statement as to your shores
period ?—A. No, I haven't got it.
ould you say, as an experienced man, that the catch on your
vas as great during the Reciprocity Treaty as in the bay ?—A.
because there was not so many vessels went into it. There
ie some years.
ike them through, from '54 to '66, the catch in the bay during
ears you acknowledge to be larger ?—A. I think it was. I think
ere more vessels went there.
ould not you give me a statement of the returns of your vessels ;
ou make it up and send it to me ?—A. Yes; I could take it from
ks at home.
'hat was your average catch during Reciprocity ?—A. Well, I
it been fishing since 1864.
ou went before that. What years have you statements for ?—A.
from 1848 down to 1864. In 1854 I made two trips and got 500
; in 1855, about 500 barrels—I can't recollect what we took the
p; in 1856, 450 barrels; in 1857, 900 barrels in three trips ; in
!5 barrels; in 1859, 470 barrels; in 1860, 325 barrels; in 1861,
rels.
ou have omitted some years ?—A. No.
ive me quantity for 1862.—A. I gave you 1861 last. In 1862
450 barrels; in 1863, 1,140 barrels; in 1864, 1,100 barrels. That
· last trip. That was in the bay.
n the whole you were a successful fisherman during those years,
dging from the evidence we have had, you must have made
Your catches were large.—A. Yes, I always had a good

l 1849, by this (referring to memorandum), you were in your
ore ?—A. Yes.
ow, you don't give the result in this paper ?—A. No; I did not
lown.
'hat was it ?—A. I think between 800 and 900 barrels. That
;ood year. I was high-liner. I did well. I went on the shore
ar, till the 10th of October. I made one trip in 1850, I think it
There was mackerel on our shore the first of the year and didn't
i be any in the fall. I went down late into the bay.
hen, after 1864, you retired and went into business ?—A. Yes.
ow you say you never fished much in the Bay Chaleurs ?—A.
out twice.
ou know it of course as a fishing-ground to which the fleet reat times ?—A. Yes, I have heard of fish being caught there.
requently heard ?—A. Yes. I knew it was a fishing-ground, but
never a fishing-ground for me.
i was not for you personally. Now, you never resorted to the
Islands ?—A. I went as far as there, but there didn't seem to be
ig.
o you know how far off they fish there ?—A. No, I don't know
ig about it.
ou have also heard about that ?—A. Yes, as a place of resort.
ou know that what mackerel are taken there are taken close in ?—
I don't know anything of the kind.
ou haven't heard it ?—A. No.

Q. Some of the witnesses have said they anchored right in cl
took them in dories?—A. I don't know anything of it.

Q. You fished close on the south shore of the river St. Lawre
A. Yes.

Q. That was well inshore?—A. We got 80 barrels very near i

Q. That was the only time you fished there?—A. Yes; I neve
there before that.

Q. You have fished about Prince Edward Island six or seven
—A. Yes, off and on.

Q. What time of the year did you go there fishing generall
Well, after July. We came in about the middle of July, or aft
any time till October.

Q. What port did you make headquarters?—A. I never ma
port unless we would want water. Then we went to Cascumpe
Malpeque.

Q. You didn't go to Souris much?—A. We never fished that

Q. You would fish of course as you went out and when going
A. Well, if we thought there was any fish we would fish any
but if we came out of harbor we would never think of heaving
we got 7 miles out.

Q. I am speaking of the time you had a right to fish there?—A
any time.

Q. Have you seen the fleet fishing?—A. Yes.

Q. How many?—A. Perhaps 200 sail, scattered about in all dii
sometimes, and sometimes bunched up near together. They sc
there some years quite plenty. When they school they are wi
than that.

Q. We have a good deal of evidence on that point.—A. Well,
as far as my experience goes.

Q. Do you know whether the habits of the mackerel have cha
late years, and whether they are now found nearer than they
be?—A. No, I could not say.

Q. Have you heard that?—A. Well, in my experience, I thi
when the mackerel are scarce it is more inshore than when ple
think that when they are scarce, like this year, there will be more
inshore than when they are plenty.

Q. But have you heard from any of your experienced fisherm
the mackerel are taken of late years more inshore than they used
—A. I haven't asked; I haven't had many going in.

Q. When you fished at Margaree, it was inshore?—A. What I
was inshore there, all but once.

Q. Then you took them outside?—A. Well, in the year of t
the water was stirred up, and the mackerel didn't come in ui
water was still.

Q. So you went outside?—A. Yes.

Q. But except that you took them inside. Now, in the fall
year the fleet generally make a dash at the Cape Breton shor
they, to finish up?—A. I think they do. They look to that pla
Cheticamp to Margaree, a good many of them. A great many o
will not go there.

Q. As a rule, they generally manage to get a good many fis
Well, I don't know about that. I have known a good many tha
get many.

Q. What is your personal experience of that? You caught o
dred barrels there one time?—A. I never caught a great m
there. I caught some in 1851; I caught, I think, eighty barrels

e only two years I recollect catching any of any importance—
u't recollect any big take.

course, one hundred barrels in a day is an enormous take?
'ou caught one hundred barrels in one day?   Were there any
;els there at that time?—A. I think there were six or eight.
they get equally good catches?—A. No.
' was it that you got a full fare?—A. We got all we could.
)3 barrels and had only 50 barrels to put them in.   We get all
for we were alone in the evening.   We came over from East
;he night, leaving the fleet at East Point, and in the morning
it we were in the cove at Margaree.
ppose you had been fishing at East Point?—A. We had been
ire.
were trying at East Point with the fleet and shipped away
id at Margaree first.   Did the fleet follow you the next day?—
ir six were there the next day.
;had not actually depleted the water of fish?—A. I know there
vessels there; four were from La Have, and two others.
; they got fish?—A. They all caught fish.
quantities, I suppose, you do not remember?—A. I don't know
i.   They all caught fish; they could not help it.
fish were so thick?—A. They were plentiful.
egard to Bird Rock and Block Island mackerel; how many of
ses of mackerel are caught?—A. From 300 to 500 barrels at
t.   I think 1,500 barrels were taken at Block Island last year.
at is about the average catch at Block Island?—A. During the
ir three years more have been caught.
at has been the catch at Block Island this year?—A. I could
500 or 600 barrels have come into Gloucester, and some have
oston, but how many I cannot say.
they caught with hook-and-line or seine?—A. This year they
tly caught with hook; last year mostly with the seine; they
t both ways.   In one trip last year a vessel took 200 barrels;
i taken with the seine.   They were all large fish, running 128
rel.
say you sent your vessels to the bay because there was no
on your own shores.   Were only two of them seiners?—A.
a M. Crosby.   The Golden Hind was a seiner at home, but her
left ashore when she came to the bay.
Helen M. Crosby was a seiner?—A. Yes.
tried for two weeks in the bay?—A. Yes.
was not successful with the seine?—A. No; nor with hooks.
uly 8 barrels.
only staid for two weeks?—A. That was all.
ing is not successful in the bay?—A. I don't think it is.
water in which the mackerel are taken is too shallow?—A.
)w and rough bottom.
ere did the captain of the Helen M. Crosby try to use the
i.   He did not try it at all, because he did not see any fish.
know where he went?—A. I think he told me he went to

Yes; I suppose he did. I could not say. He did not say :
about that.

Q. You don't know?—A. I do not know whether he went wi
three miles. If I was going to the island, the first route I wo
would be 7 or 8 or 10 miles off the land, and if I did not find fi:
I might go in nearer or farther out.

Q. Would it surprise you to hear that nearly all the boat-fi
done inside of the three miles?—A. It would not surprise m
because I know that it is inshore this year.

Q. The fish are mostly in there?—A. They are scattered
boat with two or three men picks up a barrel before night c
But to go in there with a vessel, the crew would be almost st:
death, for they would get nothing among 16 men. I know it
I have seen so much of it.

Q. You have not been there for 14 years?—A. I don't say
every time; there might be one or two trips made; but that is :
acter of the inshore-fishing.

Q. You told the Commissioner you always went from six
miles off, and you were so particular you did not try coming o
harbor?—A. I think I said he might have hove to and tried, ar
have caught some mackerel. We did not reckon to heave to th
general thing. If I said so I did not mean it, for we hove to a go
times in and out, but I never recollect catching mackerel ther
account inshore, not inside of three miles.

By Mr. Foster:

Q. Speaking of halibut-fishing, do you not know where the
fishermen go to catch halibut?—A. Yes, I know. I don't go w
to see where they anchor, but I know it the same as I know a go
other things.

Q. Cannot an experienced man tell from the characteristics of
where the halibut were caught?—A. The Georges halibut is a
white fish, while that taken on the Grand Banks in deep w
coarse, heavy fish. We do not get any such fish on the George
they are all plump and white. The Seal Island halibut, when
to get them there, is also a plump, white fish, but I have not
any halibut having been taken there for a series of years.

By Hon. Mr. Kellogg:

Q. You have spoken in regard to seeing vessels 15 miles fr
Hood. Suppose a man is standing at the edge of the water, hov
you see him, in view of the roundness of the earth?—A. I cannot

By Sir Alexander Galt:

Q. You have said that a large portion of your business is co
Have you fished with fresh or salt bait as a rule?—A. With f
altogether. Most of our cod-fishing is on the Georges, and
fresh bait altogether. While banking we have used fresh bait

Q. That is on Grand Banks?—A. Yes, but it does not pay
last vessel that came home is the last one I want to go after fi
She went in four times and brought home 75 quintals; the ve
only a little over a month on the Banks. I will have no more f
at that rate—costing over $400 for the four bait trips.

By Mr. Davies:

Q. It has been stated here that, so long as a portion of the
with fresh bait, you are compelled to have it?—A. Yes, if on t
ground. The Grand Banks are, however, large, and they

m the fleet and get their fares, because the best fares, or equally
es, have been caught with salt bait.
ould you be inclined to send vessels to fish with salt bait when
ortion of the fleet are using fresh bait ?—A. Yes. I would have
with salt bait, if they would do it, and go away from the rest of
on the Grand Banks, and fish by themselves. If they would go
m the fleet and fish on their own ground, they would get fish
t bait.
is it ever been done in your experience ?—A. Yes ; Province-
ssels use nothing but clams. I was talking with a man the other
uses salt bait, and he said he gets his fare of from 1,200 to
intals. But though we have used fresh. bait, we have not had
stul trip to the Grand Banks.
u don't know if the captains would consent ?—A. If the captains
o, I would like to send them in that way and let them use salt

you know anything about halibut-fishing on the eastern shore
osti ?—A. I know that several years ago some vessels caught
hree trips there ; but it was afterwards given up. I don't know
el that has been there for two or three vessels.

y Mr. Whiteway :
ive you ever been on the Grand Banks fishing yourself ?—A.

u had only a vessel there one year ?—A. We had one this year,
 year.
le three past years include all your experience of fishing on the
3anks ?—A. For the last five years we have had from one to two

u have had no experience personally of the advantages of either
 salt bait ?— A. Not on the Grand Bank ; all I get is from talk-
l men who fish with salt bait.
) you indorse the opinion that where fresh bait is used it is use-
idopt salt bait ?—A. I think it is ; but the vessel with salt bait
:o a different part of the ground.
s far as regards the actual time necessary to go i ito the coast of
ndland or Cape Breton and get fresh bait, you cannot judge ?—
ink I can. I have been told—I always asked in regard to it—
hey could get bait readily after they go in, it would take from
 days ; about 10 days, I should judge, from what they told me.
y do not always get bait readily ; sometimes they have to go to
:r's for ice and down to Conception Bay for bait.
ay they not waste their time occasionally ?—A. I have no doubt
 sometimes.

No. 77.

R W. WONSON, of Gloucester, Mass., fish merchant, called on
f the Government of the United States, sworn and examined:

3y Mr. Dana:

Q. And have been in it ever since?—A. Yes.

Q. How many vessels do you think you have run on an ave cluding these you owned and those you managed for other peol About twelve annually. I have ten at the present time.

Q. Starting from 1860, how many vessels had you in the bay A. I think I had one. I had from one vessel to five vessels mo time.

Q. How long have you been engaged in sending vessels to th A. Twenty years.

Q. Do you think you have given the bay a fair trial?—A. so.

Q. What is your experience in the bay during those twenty far as regards pecuniary results?—A. It has not been so profit us to send vessels there as on cod-fishing.

Q. Taking the bay mackerel fishery alone, has it been a profita ness?—A. I think not.

Q. Have you given up bay fishing?—A. Not wholly. We there this season.

Q. What is the name of the vessel?—A. The Russler.

Q. Have you heard from her?—A. We heard about two w that she had got eighty barrels. A gentleman who has come bay has since told me she had sixty barrels.

Q. The vessels you have sent down have been less in num those sent elsewhere?—A. Yes.

Q. You have had one or two in the bay each season?—A. five there one season. We never had more than three, exc season.

Q. How many vessels have you usually sent to the Bank should think they would average about six each season; that i ing those to George's Bank.

Q. What has been the result of you rbanking business?—A been profitable. That is to say, not a large profit, but it has be profitable than mackereling in the bay.

Q. Have you employed vessels in fishing at the South for and off Massachusetts and Maine?—A. Yes.

Q. What proportion of your vessels had been there mackere more or less every year?—A. Three or four. South a numbe sons, and about five on our coast.

Q. Those which go South only remain a short time?—A. Ye

Q. Fishing on our coast, they prosecute it the whole seasor have good luck?—A. Yes.

Q. Until this year, when we know the fishing was poor on o except during the first part of the season, what has been youi in fishing on the American coast?—A. We have done very well it has been very profitable.

Q. Have you also been engaged in the herring fishery?—A. frozen-herring business.

Q. When did you go into that?—A. In the winter of 1868.

Q. And followed it up to this time?—A. Yes.

Q. Is it to buy or catch herring?—A. To buy, except in one when one of our vessels caught a small cargo.

Q. What year was that?—A. The winter of 1873-'74.

Q. How many vessels do you send on an average to buy he A. Five.

Q. Where mostly?—A. On what we call the North shore, fr port to Beaver Harbor—Deer Island mostly.

many at Grand Manau ?—A. We have had three cargoes from
year as I can recollect.

.e on an average, or altogether ?—A. Three altogether.

gard to mackerel-fishing on the American coast, how was the
is year ?—A. The vessels did very well South, but when the
came up from the South they could not be found.

in Massachusetts Bay ?—A. No.

it intelligence did you get in Gloucester from the gulf when
not find mackerel in Massachusett's Bay ?—A. Reports were
ers, and posted up, that there were plenty of mackerel down
that vessels were doing well.

e you influenced by that at the time ?—A. Yes.

know pretty well what has been the result this year ?—A.

'on think it is probable there were signs of mackerel at first ?—
mackerel were seen there at the early part of the season ;
. Some vessels that went into the bay first got some mack-

e then ?—A. They have done poorly ; they have found scarcely

h regard to the herring business : with the exception you men-
you know any Gloucester vessel which has gone down to
swick and caught herring ?—A. That is the only cargo I know
a Gloucester vessel.

e you ever yourself on that coast looking after the herring
—A. Yes ; I have been there on an average about two months
er for four winters.

hat part of the coast were you ?—A. From Eastport to Beaver
ostly ; I have been to Grand Manan two or three times.

to Deer Island ?—A. About Deer Island mostly.

; is your personal experience ?—A. Yes.

re there did you ever see any Gloucester vessels catching
-A. I don't recollect seeing any.

'ou know how it is about boats fishing at Eastport and Grand
d so forth ?—A. I have seen a few Eastport boats fishing there
w Brunswick boats.

e you ever seen New Brunswick boats on the other side of the
No ; I don't think so. We do not catch many herring on the
; some are caught round Eastport ; not very many.

' do not mind the boundary-line much there ?—A. I don't
' do.

ild the herring business of Gloucester be considered as one
ig or buying herring ?—A. Of buying herring ; we don't pre-
tch any.

.e common speech among Gloucester merchants, dealers, and
, if anybody spoke of the herring fleet off Gloucester, what
understood by it ?—A. Those that go down to purchase her-

ere anything else to which they could allude ?—A. No.

' many American vessels do you suppose you have seen at one

that. I suppose it would affect the market for awhile, but not a grea while, I should suppose.

Q. Would it affect it very severely even for a while?—A. No; I shoul not say it would.

Q. Suppose the American market should lose the fish taken by Amei ican vessels within three miles of the Canadian coasts, would it have sensible effect on the American market?—A. I don't think it would.

By Mr. Thomson:

Q. In regard to the herring fishing; there is a fleet which goes dowi in the neighborhood of Grand Manan and Eastport, from Gloucester every year, to get bait—herring—is there not?—A. To buy bait; yes.

Q. Do they go down with appliances to fish?—A. Not except in th one case I have mentioned.

Q. One of your vessels went down and caught a cargo?—A. Yes.

Q. Where did she fish?—A. In St. Andrew's Bay she caught nearly the whole of them.

Q. In what year was it?—A. In the winter of 1873-'74.

Q. Did she get a full cargo?—A. Yes; it was a small vessel.

Q. What time do you send your vessels down?—A. About 20th No vember.

Q. Do you send them down in the spring, too?—A. Not to buy t freeze for the market.

Q. Do you not send them down to get bait?—A. Yes.

Q. They want the bait for fishing there?—A. On Western Bank usually.

Q. Where do they get the bait when they go down?—A. I don't kno in the spring. I have never been there in the spring and cannot tel personally, but somewhere on that coast.

Q. Do they go down in the spring with fishing appliances?—A. No that I know of; I never saw any.

Q. Do you send any of your own vessels?—A. Yes.

Q. You send them down entirely without fishing appliances?—A. We don't put any on board.

Q. Are you aware that your captains get bait at either Grand Manai or the north shore?—A. In that vicinity.

Q. The practice of your men is to go down and give notice to the fishermen that they want bait, and the fishermen will get it for them?— A. As soon as vessels go in fishermen come on board and see if they want bait.

Q. They then make a bargain?—A. Yes.

Q. And the fishermen go and get bait for them?—A. Yes.

Q. Are the persons who go on board American citizens or Britial subjects?—A. I have seen them go on board from Eastport, and we suppose they are American citizens there.

Q. They are American citizens who go over and get bait in British waters?—A. I think that most of the herring are caught in British waters.

Q. I think we have had some evidence that of late years Gloucester vessels have gone down and employed Americans to get bait for them, is that so?—A. I don't think they have employed Americans. I could not say.

Q. Is it not well known that the Gloucester fleet has gone down in spring and fall, in the fall for frozen herring, and in the spring for the purpose of getting bait?—A. Yes.

Q. You have mentioned that you saw 60 vessels at one time, where

:y lying ?—A. I saw.them from Eastport, down what we call
h Shore, between Eastport and Beaver Harbor. They come to
, first, usually.
· the North Shore you start at Letite ; you don't call Eastport
:h Shore ?—A. It is on that side. It is from Eastport down
call North Shore.
you include the islands in the North Shore ?—A. Deer Island
Vorth Shore.
u don't mean the north shore of the mainland ?—A. Not wholly.
)uld you include Grand Manan in your idea of the North Shore ?

Campobello ?—A. No.
ly Deer Island ?—A. Yes.
cause that lies nearer Letite.?—A. Yes.
d from that all along the main shore you call the North Shore ?
s.
at is where your vessels chiefly got their bait and frozen herring ?
at is as to frozen herring. I don't know where the fishermen
1 in the spring.
ere is a large fishing population at Eastport and along the shore
d to Lubeck, and toward Mount Desert, is there not ?—A. I
ink there are a great many fishing people from Eastport to
)esert.
from Eastport to Lubeck ?—A. Yes.
great many persons are engaged in fishing around Eastport ?—
in herring fishery—in Bank fishery.
nean in bait fishing ?—A. There are very few at Eastport com-
ith what there are across the line.
1 Eastport boats or fishermen go over into British waters and
L. Yes, I think they do, what there are of them.
l American fishermen go over and fish on the shores of the
—A. Yes. I think they do.
:her at Deer Island, Campobello, West Isles, or Grand Manan.
rself have no personal knowledge of the north shore or main
suppose ?—A. From Beaver Harbor to Letite. I have been in
)ors all along there.
ere is a great deal of fishing round that coast ?—A. Yes.
great many American vessels come in there every year ?—A. I
t say a great many; I have seen a few.
n't they come in and get bait ?—A. A lot of American vessels
,er bait.
large number come in and fish themselves ?—A. I have only
:w from Eastport.
large number come in and get bait ?—A. Yes, buy it.
ey give notice to the fishermen that they want bait, and the
u go and get it for them ?—A. Yes.
u said the fisheries of the gulf are very bad. State the number
your vessels have been in the gulf fishing ?—A. I could not tell
ore 1870. We have had one in every year, since 1870, till last
1en we had not any.

Q. They may have taken the whole catch, for anything you know, within the 3-mile limit?—A. I never heard them say that they had taken them inshore. They may have done so.

Q. Did you ever hear from them that they did not take them inshore?—A. No.

Q. Then, for anything you know, they might all have been taken within the 3 mile limit or all outside?—A. Yes.

Q. Some of the years were profitable?—A. I think two or three years we might have done very fairly, as far as I can recollect.

Q. Since 1870 how many vessels have you had in the bay?—A. From one to three, except last year, when we had not any.

Q. Had you made money in the gulf fishing up to 1870?—A. No; I do not think we had.

Q. Had you lost money?—A. I could not say for certain. I don't think we made any; but I could not say for certain we lost any. I don't think it was profitable.

Q. You had not lost any money up to that time?—A. I could not say we had.

Q. At all events, notwithstanding the character of that fishing—good or bad—you sent to the gulf after 1870 every year until last year?—A. Yes.

Q. Have you lost money since 1870?—A. Yes; we have.

Q. A large sum?—A. No; not very large.

Q. How much have you lost?—A. I could not say. I have not the figures, and have not examined the books.

Q. Cannot you tell how much you have lost?—A. I cannot you.

Q. You sold supplies to the vessels?—A. Yes.

Q. You charged a profit on all the supplies you put on board vessels?—A. Yes.

Q. Putting that business and the fishing business together, do you say you have lost money since 1870?—A. We have on bay fishing.

Q. Taking the profit on outfit on the fish after they are repacked and in other ways, have you lost money?—A. We have made a shrinkage.

Q. You sell the fish, or take them at a price?—A. We sell them for the benefit of the voyage.

Q. You allow the men so much for their share?—A. We don't buy mackerel ourselves. We sell them to the buyers and speculators there.

Q. You don't speculate at all yourselves?—A. Not in mackerel.

Q. Do you in other fish?—A. Yes; in codfish.

Q. What do you do with the vessels which are in the gulf in summer and early fall?—A. They go cod-fishing in spring, or to the South for mackerel; cod-fishing, chiefly.

Q. Then you want the bay fishery for the purpose of filling up their time?—A. We send them there to catch some fish if they can.

Q. Why do you keep them there every year?—A. We don't keep many there; we used to have five; we have only one there now.

Q. Why do you keep one in the bay?—A. In the hope it will do better.

Q. Are you serious in saying you don't think the gulf inshore fishery is worth anything?—A. Yes.

Q. Suppose the inshore fishery was taken away from you, and the rest of the gulf fishing was left to you, and the fishing at the Magdalen Islands, would it do you any injury?—A. I think not.

Q. Practically it is of no value to you?—A. I think not.

Q. Is that the opinion of Gloucester fishermen generally?—A. I could not say.

Q. Surely you must know the general opinion of Gloucester people, when you are a Gloucester man?—A. It is a matter I do not bear discussed much, and I could not say what the general opinion is.

Q. Do you think the opinion you hold is one in which no one else agrees with you?—A. I have heard my partner mention it.

Q. Do you say you know so little about the public opinion of Gloucester that you cannot tell whether that is the opinion of the people there?—A. Well, I think it is; I have not heard much about it.

Q. Some witnesses so have stated that Boston is the great center of the fish trade in the United States; is that your opinion?—A. I think it is, in certain kinds.

Q. Do you know what is the general opinion in Boston in regard to the right of fishing inshore in the gulf?—A. I do not.

Q. Does not the board of trade there represent the opinion of Boston in matters of trade?—A. I suppose it does; I don't know what its opinion is.

· Q. I want to call your attention to a report of the government of the boston board of trade presented to the board on 17th January, 1855. At page 1 it says:

The government of the Boston Board of Trade have the pleasure of placing before the members an account of proceedings upon the principal subjects which have engaged their attention since the organization of the board.

At the regular meeting in November, a report was made embracing many of these subjects, and the short time which has elapsed since has furnished them with but little new to communicate at the present time.

They deem it proper, however, on the occasion of the annual meeting, to review what has been done, and to give you some idea of the plan which it is proposed to pursue, in order to accomplish the end for which our board was incorporated.

At page 10, there is the following passage:

The people of Nova Scotia are differently employed, according to the districts in which they reside. In the agricultural portions of the province they are all farmers; on the seaboard they are ship-builders, fishermen, and sailors, the latter engaged in coasting and the carrying trade of the world, in vessels of their own build, wherever they can find employment.

In New Brunswick the population is about equally divided between farming, lumbering, and ship-building, with a small portion engaged in the fisheries.

It will thus be seen that the pursuits of the people are various, and that while in some particulars their interests are identical, in others they are antagonistic.

The inward and outward trade of the five British North American colonies amounts to about eighty millions of dollars annually. The ships inward and outward, to and from foreign ports, exclusive of local trade, amounted in 1853 to near four millions of tons, and the aggregate of tonnage owned and registered in these colonies now amounts to five hundred thousand tons. They built and sold in England in 1853, one hundred and fifty thousand tons of new shipping. These ships are employed on every ocean and the character of colonial ships is rapidly rising; they nearly equal the first-class American and British ships, and the improvement in intellectual and moral character of colonial ship-masters and seamen is fully keeping pace with their improvements in naval architecture.

The British North American colonies, though separated from us by several thousand miles of frontier, are geographically united to us, and the free exchange of merchandise in countries so situated is almost inevitable. Their present population is rapidly increasing and they are increasing in *material* wealth.

Some of the mutual advantages which the present treaty presents in *our own* particular relations with these provinces may be at once seen.

It opens another source from which to draw our breadstuffs, cattle, lumber, and fuel, and our thickly-settled manufacturing districts offer to the provinces the best market in our country for the consumption of their products; while, on the other hand, all our manufactures being admitted to the provinces on as favorable terms as those of Great Britain, or of any other country, we have a wide field open wherein to dispose of our surplus products, and offer them the important advantage of supplying themselves from first-hands. The value of our exports to the provinces is already one

and a half millions a year, made up of stoves, iron, and wooden-wares, and
Yankee inventions; and this amount, under free intercourse, will greatly in
The foreign imports into this district have increased in the last fifteen
fourteen to forty-six millions of dollars, and our market now offers, or sho
we are true to ourselves, every inducement for the inhabitants of the provin
ply themselves here with foreign dry-goods, teas, groceries, or whatever else
need.

In connection with this, your directors cannot refrain from mentioning, in
the great increase which is seen in the amount of goods sent in transit by w
ton to the Canadas within the past few years—from twenty-five thousand
1849, to over five millions in 1854; nor from referring to the great facilities
our harbor, by the improvements at East Boston, and the line of railway by
our roads from Boston may be united—as eminently calculated to augmeu
mercial relations, for export as well as import, with the British North Amer
inces, and with our whole Western countries, and as of almost incalculable
to our railroads, if they only show themselves capable of doing the business

But, in connection with the Reciprocity Treaty, it is to the importance
eries that your directors wish at this time particularly to call your attentio
per cent. of the tonnage employed in the whale, cod, and mackerel fishe
United States belongs to Massachusetts, and Boston is the business center.

By colonial construction of the Convention between the United States
Britain, of 1818, we were excluded from not less than four thousand miles
ground. The valuable mackerel fishery is situated between the shore and a
from the St. Croix River, southeast to Seal Island, and extending along tl
coast of Nova Scotia, about three miles from the coast, around Cape Bret
Prince Edward Island, across the entrance to the Bay of Chaleur; thence
Island of Anticosti to Mt. Joly, on the Labrador coast, where the right of sh
commences. The coasts within these limits, following their several indent
not less than four thousand miles in extent, all excellent fishing-grounds.
mackerel fishery began to be closely watched and protected, our vesse
swarmed on the fishing-ground within the spaces inclosed by the line ment

Each of these vessels made two or three full fares in the season, and some
of valuable cargoes were landed every year in the United States, adding
our wealth and prosperity.

A sad contrast has since existed. From Gloucester only one hundred a
vessels were sent to the Bay of Saint Lawrence in 1853. Of these, not mo
in ten made the *second* trip, and even they did not get full fares the first tri
a second time in the hope of doing better. The principal persons engaged
ness in Gloucester, estimated that the loss in 1853 amounted to an average
sand dollars on each vessel, without counting that incurred from detent
and damages from being driven out of the harbor and from waste of tim
It was agreed by all parties that if their vessels could have had free access
ing-grounds, as formerly, the difference to that district alone would have b
four hundred thousand dollars.

In 1853, there were forty-six vessels belonging to Beverly; thirteen of th
the bay in 1852, but owing to the restrictions their voyages were wholly u
and none of them went in 1853.

At Salem, only two mackerel licenses were granted in 1853, and at Marb
six.

At Newburyport there are ninety fishing-vessels; seventy of these went
for mackerel in 1853, but almost all of them, it is said, made ruinous v
Boston, only a dozen licenses were granted for this fishery in 1853, and ver
one hundred vessels belonging to the towns of Dennis and Harwich, on
two-thirds of which are engaged in the mackerel fishery, went to the bay f
last year, because of the ill success attending the operations of the year pre
of their vessels of one hundred tons burthen, manned by sixteen men, wa
in the bay in 1853, and returned with only one barrel of mackerel.

Unless some change had taken place beneficial to the interests of our h
men, the Northern fisheries would have been wholly ruined, and in all prob:
entirely ceased, except on a very limited scale on our own shores. The c
and fifty thousand tons of shipping employed in those fisheries would have l
to seek employment elsewhere, and the product of the fisheries themselves,
to three or four million dollars annually, would have been lost to us.
treaty opens to us again all these valuable fisheries, and our thanks are du
tinguished statesmen who have labored in bringing it to a successful termi:
your directors are most happy to make mention of the services of Israel
esq., a gentleman whom we hope to have the pleasure of meeting to-d:
worked most assiduously for the last four years in collecting and furni:
valuable reports almost all the information possessed on the subject, and wi
exertions, it is hardly too much to say, the treaty would never have been

ıt is the opinion of the Boston Board of Trade. Do you dis-
ı that opinion ?—A. I don't think they know so much about the
nsiness as Gloucester people do.
1853, were Gloucester people doing a flourishing business in the
rere they losing money ?—A. I could not say.
ı Boston board of directors state that "it was agreed by all
hat if their vessels (Gloucester vessels) could have had free
the fishing-grounds as formerly, the difference to that district
uld have been at least $600,000." Do you dissent from that
—A. Yes.
ow call your attention to a speech delivered by Mr. Erastus
lelivered at New York on May 28, 1874. He says:

lic documents show, first, in 1862, we had over 203,000 tons of shipping in
es, off what are now the Canadian coasts, with 28,000 seamen; the returns
ly exceeded $14,000,000.

ı agree or dissent from that opinion ?—A. I don't know any-
ɔut it.

says:

ıin three years from the abrogation of the treaty depriving our fishermen of
privileges under the treaty, our tonnage in the trade fell to 62,000 tons—a
ɔer cent.

ı dissent from that statement ?—A. Yes. I don't think it fell
much; it fell off considerably; I could not say how much.
further says:

reconcession of these shore privileges, under the Washington Treaty, has
ıbled the tonnage of our fishing-fleet from what it was in 1869.

ı dissent from that ?—A. I should not think it was a true state-
ough I could not say.
uppose you know as a fact that the tonnage did fall off after the
on of the Reciprocity Treaty ?—A. Yes.
d you know that, after the Treaty of Washington, in 1871, your
began to increase, and has increased ever since?—A. I don't
has.
ən you think this statement is not correct ?—A. It has fallen off.
ıce 1871 ?—A. I think so.
eu Mr. Brooks is wrong ?—A. It has been falling off all the

ıce 1861 it has not increased ?—A. I don't think it has.
is statement, then, is a misstatement?—A. I think it has been
ff all the time.
ıomson put in the following paper:

[New York Evening Express, May 28th, 1874.]

Produce Exchange.

CALL UPON THE GOVERNMENT—SPEECH OF ERASTUS BROOKS—RECIPROCAL
COMMERCIAL TREATY.

 og of the members of the exchange was held this afternoon, to consider t'ıe
restoring reciprocal commercial relations between the United States, Cau-
lewfoundland.
V. Floyd, vice-president, presided. The secretary read the following:
ırd of managers of the New York Produce Exchange having learned that
ns are now pending between the United States and the Dominion of Canada
oundland for the renewal of reciprocal commercial relations between the
ries, it is therefore
, That this exchange earnestly desires to impress upon the Government of
l States, and upon the Senators and Representatives of this State in Congress,

the great importance of the consumma'ion of such a treaty at the earliest
ticable.

Resolved, That a committee of 7 members of the produce exchange be ap
the president, who shall take snch action as in their judgment may be deel
sarv to carry out the objects of this meeting.

The president then introduced the Hon. Erastus Brooks, who spoke in su
follows:

Mr. Brooks said: The more freedom there is in trade the better for the c
its producers, for its consumers, for the merchant, and for the carrier; and
the just conclusion that the fewer restrictions imposed upon trade and cor
Federal or State laws, the better for the people at large. However muc
these propositions may be disputed, the truth of history will sustain this po
rare are the exceptions or qualifying circumstances that the main facts v
stand good.

The subject before us is the proposed restoration of the Reciprocity Tres
much freedom of trade as is practical for two governments to agree upon.
the States the fundamental law of the land wisely compels this freedom.
equal States, with equal rights for all citizens and all kinds of trade, wh
practice, is the natural and legal right of all; and but for unjust combi
selfish men for selfish purposes there would never be any departure from 1
maxim.

It is now proposed that, as between the United States and Canada, there
1. The waiver of money compensation by the United States for fisheries
Washington Treaty.
2. That the Canadian canals, from Lake Erie to Montreal, be enlarged
years at the cost of Canada, so as to admit the passage of vessels 260 feet
and 45 in breadth, and with a depth equal to the capacity of the lake harbo
3. That during the treaty all the Canadian canals, and the Erie, Whit
Sault St. Marie, and Lake St. Clair canals shall be open to vessels and boa
countries and on the same terms.
4. That the free navigation of Lake Michigan be put on the same terms '
navigation of the St. Lawrence River.
5. That the navigation of the St. Clair flats be maintained at the exper
countries in proportion to their commerce thereon.
6. That the productions of the farm, forest, mines, and water, and als
meats, and products of the dairy, be admitted into both countries duty f
provided in the Treaty of 1854.
7. This list may possibly include agricultural implements, manufactures
steel and of wood, minerals, oils, salt, and a few other articles.

This is opposed because, as alleged, it will interfere with protection and
Canadians to none of the benefits of American citizenship.

The answer to this assertion is that all the facts are against the objecti
1821 to 1833 the average annual traffic between the United States and C
$3,500,000, and from 1832 (sic) to 1845, $6,500,000, and from 1846 to 1853, .
This traffic rose in twelve years of reciprocity to a purchase by the colonie
States commodities to the gold value of $359,667,000, and the purchase by 1
colonies of products to the value of $197,000,000. There was a balance in g
of the United States during ten years of nearly $96,000,000, and in these t
the United States exports to Canada equaled in value all on r exports to
zil, Italy, Hayti, Russia, Venezuela, Austria, the Argentine Republic, Den
key, Portugal, the Sandwich Islands, Central America, and Japan; whil
with these governments showed that we imported from these countries over $
in excess of our exports other than gold. While thus the balance of trade
ada was nearly $96,000,000 in our favor, of our exports to Canada $151,000,(
manufactures.

THE FISHERY RIGHTS, LUMBER, ETC.

Our public documents show—
1. In 1862 we had over 203,000 tons of shipping in the fisheries off what a
Canadian coasts, with 28,000 seamen, and the returns considerably exceeded .
2. Within three years from the abrogation of the treaty, depriving our ti
the shore privileges under the treaty, our tonnage in the trade fell to 62,000
of 70 per cent.
3. The reconcession of these shore-privileges, under the Washington
already doubled the tonnage of our fishing-fleet from what it was in 1869.
4. As to the benefits of reciprocity, our official returns show that from 1
in which latter year the treaty went into operation, the provinces bought fr
chandise to the value of $167,216,709, while we bought from them but $67
cash balance in our favor of nearly $100,000,000.
5. In the years from 1854 to 1863, in which the treaty was in operation, th

purchased from us $255,282,698. while we purchased from them $193,269,153; a balance is our favor of $62,000,000. From July 1, 1863, to June 30, 1-66, our returns show that we imported from them a value of $132,000.000, while their returns show only $81,000,000 exported to us; a discrepancy of $50,000,000, which the Canadians allege must have originated from our war prices and inflated currency.

7th. If the United States returns are correct, the provinces in these three years had a large balance of trade in their favor; if the province returns are correct, the balance was in our favor.

8th. Canada asserts, as to a large portion of the articles received from her free of duty under the treaty, that our importations have been annually increasing since the repeal at greatly enhanced prices.

8th. While the treaty was in operation we purchased over $29,000,000 of lumber, or an average of $3 000,000 per annum, but in the seven years that have elapsed since the repeal, we have purchased nearly $59,000,000 of lumber, or an annual average of over $8,000,000.

9th. The cash price of clear lumber in Toronto is $26 per 1 000 feet, or double what it was ten years ago, and its price now in Portland, Me., is double the present price in Toronto.

Our great international interests relate chiefly to the several subjects involved in the above-named propositions. It is a good rule to judge of the future by the past, and, judging from the past, here are the advantages derived from the treaty when it existed. The Canadians quote against us our own official records to prove that in the old treaty we had all the advantage.

The British North American Provinces purchased from us merchandise to the value of $69,286,709, and the United States purchased from the provinces $67,749,426, leaving a balance in favor of the United States of $99,428,282. In the first ten years of the treaty we had a balance in favor of the United States of $62,013,545.

Since the abrogation of the old treaty, eight years since, articles that were free now pay an average duty of 25 per cent., while the more important articles formerly free were animals, breadstuffs, grain and flour, lumber, timber, coal, butter and cheese, wool, fish, and fish products. All these are necessities, and contribute to the food and clothing and shelter of the people.

But Canada and the United States are not the only parties in interest. Take the Province of Newfoundland. Our average imports from there amounted under the treaty to $300,000 annually, while the exports of pork and flour footed up $2,250,000 per annum. So in 1862, under the treaty, New Brunswick sold goods to the United States of the value of $890,000, and purchased $2,000,000, paying the difference in cash, while Nova Scotia, in the same year, sold $2,000,000 of codfish, &c., to the United States, and purchased goods to the amount of $3,800,000.

EFFECT OF THE REPEAL ON NEW YORK.

The repeal of the treaty has injured the commerce of this port to a great extent. One of the firms engaged in the tobacco trade says that his house sold $2,000,000 annually to Canadian buyers during the treaty, but that he has done comparatively nothing since 1866.

The butter and cheese trade of the country, representing $500,000,000 of its production, has had the same experience. This is also the experience of nearly all our business men, and it is this class who urge the restoration of the treaty. Of course, such a treaty must be reciprocal in fact as in name. It is said that under the treaty which expired "Canadians were ready to interchange free commodities, but on goods subject to duty they placed such exorbitant tariffs as to prohibit purchases in the United States. The result was loud and constant complaints and demands for the termination of the treaty. The benefits were mainly with the Canadians, the burdens with us."

The facts here given do not bear out this record, but if they were true the American Government would, of course, modify the treaty. The fact is, that while the old treaty existed, over 52 per cent. of the entire trade of the provinces was with this country, and since its abrogation our portion of the trade amounts to less than 35 per cent.

The conclusions from all these facts, whatever the country opinion, is that the repeal of the Reciprocal Treaty has lost the country many millions of dollars, and that its restoration in spirit, not necessarily in form, is most desirable to all general interests and detrimental to none of them. In the Dominion of Canada there are now over 4,000,000 of people with a debt considerably less than the debt of the city of New York. The commerce of the Dominion last year was 60 steamships, 446 sailing vessels, and 152,226 tons of shipping; and 11,089 sea-going ships, with a tonnage of 3,032,476 tons, arrived at Canadian ocean ports, and 18,960 lake and river vessels, with a tonnage of 2,094,484 tons, at Canadian inland ports, and this makes the Dominion, after England and the United States, next to France as the shipping country of the world.

The imports into Canada last year were valued at $138,961,231, of which $60,000,000

were without duty. Shall we repel a people and a trade so inviting as this ?
own and the general interests of the city I hope not. It was said in the days
Roman Empire that all roads lead to Rome. In the commerce, capital. credit
and the general thrift of the new world it may be said that all roads lead
York. We have but to do our whole duty, fairly aided by the general governme
only to secure property for ourselves, but to contribute largely to the prosp
others.

Mr. Archibald Baxter spoke of the importance of the treaty, and of the adva
of the old one, the abrogation of which did not remove any disadvantages
which the United States then labored. He insisted that nature intended t
countries to reciprocate commerce; we had only to look to their contiguity a
facilities provided to promote it. The speaker urged an emphatic demonstra
the meeting in favor of maintaining the treaty.

The resolutions were then unanimously adopted.

Q. I will now read you the following from the Cape Ann Adve
of October 18, 1877 :

THE TONNAGE OF GLOUCESTER.—The statement of the tonnage of the dis
Gloucester for the quarter ending September 30, 1877, shows a total of 523
aggregating 34,743½ tons, an increase during the quarter of 6 vessels and 1,375.5
4 are under permanent registers, 1,189.34 tons ; 1 temporary register, 533.67 to
permanent enrollment, 29,873.08 tons ; 6 temporary enrollments, 2,525.58 t
(less than 20 tons) under licenses, 698 83 tons ; 5 vessels, 1,653.01 tons, are empl
foreign trade ; 91 vessels, 9,013.22 tons, in the coasting trade ; 3 in yachting
tons ; and 417 vessels, 22,994.80 tons, in the fisheries. During the quarter, 2
158.83 tons, have been built in the district ; and 2, 109.97 tons, have been lost a
Cape Ann Advertiser.

Is that true, or do you dissent from the statement ?—A. I :
think it is true.

Q. That does not show the decrease you have just spoken of ?-
understood that you were speaking of fishing in Canadian waters
you mentioned the decrease.

Q. You do not then dissent from the statement that after the
was passed the tonnage increased to that extent, no matter wher
went fishing ?—A. The tonnage has been increasing in Glouceste
since I can remember.

Q. The tonnage of the fishing fleet fell from 1866—the time
Reciprocity Treaty—to 1869 to 62,000 tons ?—A. I thought you
me about the tonnage in Canadian waters.

Q. Did it not fall after the abrogation of the Reciprocity Treaty
There was not so much tonnage in Canadian waters.

Q. Did the tonnage fall ?—A. I don't think it did in Glouceste

Q. Did the whole American tonnage fall after the abrogation
Reciprocity Treaty ?—A. I cannot say, except as regards Glouce

By Mr. Dana :

Q. Do you know anything about the Boston Board of Trade 2:
ago ?—A. No.

Q. Had it anything to do with the fishing business ?—A. Not
know of.

Q. Did you ever know any member of the Board of Trade wl
anything to do with the fishing business ?—A. No.

Q. Was Boston or Gloucester the representative of the fishin
ness, or even now, as regards the ownership and employment
sels ?—A. Gloucester.

Q. Was there any ownership or employment of vessels with whi
Boston Board of Trade had anything to do ?—A. Not that I kno

Q. Has not the whole business of cod and mackerel fishing ch
since that time ? At that time, 22 years ago, was seining or tr
practiced by the vessels ?—A. Seining was not, and I do not think
ing was to any extent.

ˈou had an extract read to you from the report of the Boston
of Trade. Had it rather a swelling auctioneering style with it?
lid it strike you?—A. It may be true, but it does not appear to

t speaks of the colonial construction of the Treaty of 1868. That
nstruction which keeps us out of the great bays?—A. Yes.
)o you know how the colonies constructed the Treaty of 1818?—
on't recollect exactly.
f that report attributes the falling off in the gulf fishery, which
has been pretty steady, to the inability to fish within three miles
shore, is that a correct statement?—A. I could not say about

Ias the falling off of the gulf fishery from Gloucester been irre-
ˑe of the dates and times at which treaties have gone into opera-
nd has it been on the whole steady and uniform?—A. I think it
ˑen steady.
[f anybody did in 1855 form the opinion that our fishermen would
ˑr vastly if they could fish within the three miles and would go to
f they could not, has it or has it not turned out to be an entirely
ous opinion?—A. I think so.
s it true of the fishing tonnage, that during the three years after
rogation of the Reciprocity Treaty, the tonnage fell from 203,000
l00?—A. I think not.
s that anything within reason?—A. I think not.
he fishing clauses of the Washington Treaty had not been in
ion in Prince Edward Island more than two years, and in other
not more than one year, when the speech was made. Mr. Brooks

ˈhe reconcession of the shore privileges under the Washington Treaty has already
d the tonnage of our fishing fleet from what it was in 1869.

ˈve you any idea of such a thing having happened?—A. No.
Has the amount of tonnage employed in the bay fishery increased
uinished within the last six years?—A. It has diminished.
And there has been no marked change in its favor since the Wash-
a Treaty went into operation. The fishing in the gulf has not
ısed, but has diminished, without reference to the Washington
y?—A. The fishing in the gulf—yes.
You have not seen this speech, made by Mr. Erastus Brooks, be-
—A. No.
The extract from the Cape Ann Advertiser, which has been read,
ˀ an increase of six vessels during the quarter. Four of these are
ˈ permanent registers. Those, I suppose, are not bay fishing ves-
—A. No; I suppose not.
They would be trading vessels?—A. Yes.
Has the tonnage of Gloucester engaged in trading with the West
s and Europe and other parts increased?—A. Yes, and the coast-
ˀade.
Taking all the fishing—the home fishing for cod, haddock, and
at, on all the banks, and fishing in the gulf—has it, on the whole,
ısed or diminished?—A. I think it has increased somewhat.
But the increase has been in what branch of the business?—A.
y in the coasting trade. Perhaps our fishing has increased some-

Has the cod-fishing increased or decreased?—A. It has increased.
And the bay fishing has decreased?—A. Yes.

By Mr. Thomson:

Q. You stated, in answer to Mr. Dana, that you did not kno
person belonging to the Boston Board of Trade in the fishing bus
Do you know the members of the Board of Trade who framed
report in 1853?—A. No.

Q. Then you did not mean the Commissioners to understand i
composed by gentlemen who had nothing to do with the trade. D
know a single man who composed the report?—A. No.

Q. Then you cannot undertake to say that there was no man wh
not engaged in the fishing business?—A. I know there is no Glou
man.

By Sir Alexander Galt:

Q. Is the falling off in the fishing, in the Gulf of St. Law
attributed by you to its being less profitable of late years?—A. Y

Q. And more profitable on your own coast?—A. Yes.

Q. You say that this year the mackerel were reported to be
abundant in the bay and that induced you to send more of your v
to the bay?—A. That induced us to send what we did. We di
intend to send any—we sent one.

Q. Would it be your opinion that, if the mackerel should be as
tiful in the bay as they were in former years, the fleet would aga
as they did before?—A. If they were scarce on our coast, they m

Q. Under similar circumstances, they would go back. Do you
they did not go to the bay because they found fishing on the Ame
coast rather more profitable than in the bay?—A. Yes.

By Mr. Dana:

Q. And cod-fishing?—A. Yes.

No. 78.

WEDNESDAY, *October* 24, 1

The Conference met.

FITZ J. BABSON, collector of customs of Gloucester, Mass., cal
behalf of the Government of the United States, sworn and examin

By Mr. Trescot:

Question. Are you collector of the port of Gloucester?—Answer.

Q. How long have you been so?—A. Eight years.

Q. Is it your duty as collector to issue papers to all vessels goin
of Gloucester?—A. It is.

Q. What is the character of the papers you issue?—A. Three ki
domestic and foreign—a register fishing license and coasting licen

Q. Does the register or fishing license include the privilege to
and trade, or is it a special issue?—A. The privilege to touch and
is simply what is connected with the fishing license by application
upon the part of the captain or owner.

Q. Explain what it is.—A. A vessel taking a fishing license and
desirous to touch and trade as part of the trip or the whole of it, a
at the office for a permit to touch and trade, which is a paper tha
connection with the fishing license, and gives the same power fo
one voyage as a register.

Q. Then, as I understand it, a fishing-vessel sailing from Glou
with the intention to buy bait at Newfoundland, or to buy frozen he
would take out, besides a fishing license, a permit to touch and tra
A. It would.

'hat is the difference either in cost or in advantage between
out a permit to touch and trade, and taking a register?—A. A
to touch and trade would simply cost 25 cents. In case a vessel
, fishing license wishes to take a register it has to give up the
and take out a register, which would cost $2.25. The other
itures to which the vessel would be liable under a register would
inage tax of thirty cents per ton, and also a hospital tax of forty
er mouth on each individual member of the crew for the time she
; register.

nder a register the vessel would have to enter and clear at every
id that is a certain additional cost?—A. Yes.

ake a Gloucester vessel that is going fishing and she thinks she
int to purchase bait, or, at all events, to go and fish and purchase
herring; if she takes a register, when she returned with the cargo
uld have to enter and clear, and if she went out fishing she would
, enter and clear every voyage?—A. Yes.

7hereas, if it takes out a fishing license with a permit to touch
de she could go and come without any further entries?—A. Cer-

hen those vessels pay none of the duties you refer to?—A. With
g license, with permit to touch and trade, no duties are exacted.
/ith regard to the hospital tax. That is paid on every entry?—A.
ry entry of a vessel under a register. No hospital tax is exacted
ir fishermen.

. vessel under a register would have to pay the hospital tax at
t of entry without she had paid it at the port from which she
?—A. At every new entry.

hen a vessel going out of Gloucester, which takes a permit to
ud trade, would be considered as going on a trading voyage?—
it certainly, it takes it for that purpose.

/ith regard to Gloucester vessels that go to buy frozen herring,
;, as a general rule, take a license to touch and trade?—A. They

, gives to the voyage, in the eye of the law of the United States, a
character?—A. Most certainly.

'o you mean that all Gloucester vessels that go fishing, say for
el, take out permits to touch and trade?—A. No, only those that
zen herring. We have never had occasion to issue permits to
ind trade to other vessels. The mackerel-fishing is conducted
a general fishing license.

ocs the permit to touch and trade confine them to purchase her-
· does it authorize them to do a general trade?—A. It allows
, trade in the products of any country, wherever they may be on
es, or to which they may go; otherwise they would be liable to
ition and seizure for trading under a fishing license.

hen, as far as the permit goes, a vessel goes out under it, say
el-fishing?—A. Yes.

nd when it buys frozen herring it is in the way of trade?—A.
commercial voyage.

, there a drawback allowed on salt used in the fishing business

Q. Is it allowed to mackerel fishermen ?—A. It is allowed to a ermen.

Q. Can you form an estimate of the amount of drawback allo Gloucester ?—A. About $50,000.

Q. Are you able to say what portion of that $50,000 was allov the mackerel fisheries as against those of cod and other fish ?—. cording to the best of my judgment about one-fifth. It would be a ing to the catch ; sometimes it would exceed that a little.

Q. How are you able to ascertain that ?—A. On the cancella the bond given on a withdrawal entry of salt the parties are obli take the amount of fish taken by the vessels, and where the sa taken. We have a general standard by which we average that r The quantity of fish would show very nearly the amount of salt rec and upon that oath the bond is canceled.

Q. Have you any idea what proportion that $50,000 would b the general drawback on salt allowed in the United States ?—A. not. I have no data on which I could fix any sum.

Q. Can you tell me from any information you have, what the a would be, either in quantity or value, of the mackerel fisheries at cester; and, if so, state how you arrive at the information ?—A quested one of my inspectors to take the amount from their bo owners and fitters, for the last ten years, of the amount of ma taken by Gloucester vessels, not only on our own shores, but a the Gulf of St. Lawrence, involving the whole catch of the place, I have here, with his affidavit that he has attended to this dut he makes the report in that form.

Q. This is an official report by your inspector to you ?—A. Yes

Q. I don't understand, however, that it is a part of your official c make this inquiry ?—A. Not in this special case. We make a of the estimated fisheries for the benefit of the Bureau of Sta about June 30, the end of the fiscal year, which, of course, is a mate, because there is no return at that season from which to the table.

Q. You have examined this return ?—A. I have looked it ove ally.

Q. Without reference to any other information, have you come y to any conclusion from that return ?—A. My conclusion would b comparative statement relating to the value of the bay fishery and fishery, that in 1866 and 1867 there is but little doubt our cato the bay per vessel exceeded those on our own shores, but in succ years, including 1876 and not including 1877, there is but little our catches have constantly increased until the catches of our ves our own shores have doubled if not trebled those caught in the G St. Lawrence.

Q. Is it the duty of your office to report to the Treasury Depa the loss of Gloucester vessels and the cause of loss ?—A. It is.

Q. Have you prepared a list of the vessels lost and the cause I have a report here which embodies a portion of the losses a causes.

'itness handed in the following table :

Species of vessel.	Name of vessel.	Value.	Men lost.	Home port.	Date.	Where lost.
Schooner..	Amazon	$2,000		Gloucester..	1830	Bay Chaleur.
	Friendship	2,500		....do	1832	Cape Sable.
	Adrian	1,500		....do	1837	St. John's.
	Gentile	3,000		....do	1838	Margaree Island, Bay St. Lawrence.
	Mary and Elizabeth	2,000		....do	1840	St. Peter's, Bay St. Lawrence.
	Henrietta	1,000		....do	1843	Bay St. Lawrence, at sea.
	Branch	1,500		....do	1843	Do.
	Only Daughter	1,500		....do	1845	Off Cape Causo.
	Enchantress	1,000		....do	1849	Cape Sable
	Flirt	4,000	14	....do	1851	Bay St Lawrence, at sea.
	Princeton	3,000	10	....do	1851	Do
	Jubilee	900		....do	1851	Bay St. Lawrence, run down at sea.
	Daniel P. King	3,500		....do	1851	Cape Breton
	Red Wing	1,400		....do	1851	Cheticamp.
	Garland	4,000		....do	1851	Malpec.
	Powhattan	1,500		....do	1851	Bay St. Lawrence, at sea.
	Eleanor	4,000		....do	1851	Malpec.
	Eyrean T. Colby	5,000		....do	1852	Cascumpec.
	John Gerard	4,000		....do	1852	Bay St Lawrence, at sea.
	Atlanta	3,400		....do	1852	Souris, Prince Edward Island.
....do	Ocean Star	4,000		....do	1852	Do.
....do	Hannibal	2,600		....do	1852	Do.
....do	Augusta Parker	2,800		....do	1852	Do.
....do	Rio del Norte	2,800		....do	1852	Do.
....do	Leader	1,000		....do	1852	Do.
....do	Champion	1,800		....do	1853	At sea.
....do	Mary Jones	2,500		....do	1855	Prince Edward Island.
....do	Alpha	700		....do	1856	Canso
....do	Lioness	1,200		....do	1856	Bay Chaleur, at sea.
....do	Itaska	3,800		....do	1856	Bay St Lawrence, at sea
....do	Samuel Jones	3,800		....do	1856	Do.
....do	Arbutus	3,800		....do	1856	Do.
....do	Hosea Ballan	1,200		....do	1857	Do.
....do	Mary Hart	3,000		....do	1857	Cape Breton.
....do	Montezuma	2,300		....do	1857	Do.
....do	Village Belle	3,700	16	....do	1858	Bay St. Lawrence, at sea.
....do	Three Sisters	500		....do	1858	Do.
....do	Premium	800		....do	1858	Do.
....do	Geranium	800		....do	1858	Do.
....do	John Franklin	4,500	14	....do	1858	Prince Edward Island.
....do	Alexandria	4,000	6	....do	1858	Newfoundland.
....do	Queen of Clippers	4,000	6	....do	1858	Do.
....do	Ethelinde	4,500		....do	1859	Ragged Island, Newfoundland.
....do	Henrietta	4,000		....do	1859	Do.
....do	Pilot	1,600		....do	1860	Cheticamp, Nova Scotia.
....do	Mohenie	3,450		....do	1861	Cape Sable.
....do	Coquette	3,200		....do	1861	Port Hood.
....do	E. K. Kane	3,400		....do	1861	Liverpool, Nova Scotia.
....do	Republic	2,500		....do	1861	Ragged Island, Newfoundland.
....do	Narragangus	2,000		....do	1861	St. Mary's, Nova Scotia.
....do	R. H. Oakes	6,000		....do	1861	Louisburg Bar.
....do	Ella Osborne	3,200		....do	1861	Cole Bay.
....do	Ocean Traveller	4,000	10	....do	1862	Newfoundland.
....do	Alpalpa	2,500		....do	1863	Do.
....do	Mary E. Hiltz	7,500	1	....do	1864	Do.
....do	Kossuth	12,000		....do	1864	Owl's Harbor, Newfoundland.
....do	Fearless	5,500		....do	1864	Newfoundland.
....do	Fleetwing	6,500		....do	1864	Bay St Lawrence, at sea
....do	Orizimbo	8,000		....do	1864	Cheticamp.
....do	Northern Chief	9,000	6	....do	1865	Cape Sable.
....do	St. Lawrence	3,500		....do	1865	Ragged Island, Newfoundland.
....do	Minerva	3,500		....do	1865	Near Pictou, Nova Scotia.
....do	Colonel Allen	12,000		....do	1865	Near Louisburg, Cape Breton.
....do	George F. Marsh	*31,000		....do	1866	Magdalen Islands, with fares.
....do	M. C. Rowe	10,500		....do	1866	Newfoundland.
....do	General Sheridan	12,000	4	....do	1866	Cape Canso.
....do	Martha and Eliza	4,200		....do	1866	Magdalen Islands.
....do	Arcola	2,300		....do	1866	Port Hood.
....do	Fashion	4,500	12	....do	1867	Bay St. Lawrence, at sea.
....do	Water Spirit	9,075		....do	1869	Cheticamp.

* With fares.

No.	Species of vessels.	Name of vessel.	Value.	Men lost.	Home port.	Date.	Where l
71	Schooner..	Abby H. Fraser.....	$6,000	.....	Gloucester..	1869	Cape Negro.
72	... do	Pocumtuck	3,000	.....	....do	1870	Ship Harbor, N
73	...do	George. R. Bradford	7,500	6	....do	1870	Newfoundland.
74	.. do	Dauntless...........	8,000	12	....do	1870	Bay St. Lawren
75	....do	Exchange...........	1,300	.....	....do	1871	Cow Bay, Cape
76	....do	Lizzie A. Tarr	7,300	.....	....do	1871	Manitou, Labra
77	... do	Elaineur	1,700	.....	...po	1871	Argyle, Nova S
78	...do	River Queen........	7,900	.....	....do	1871	Nova Scotia.
79	...do	Samuel E. Sawyer...	6,760	.....	....do	1871	Magdalen Islan
80	...do	Thorwaldson........	7,800	7	.. do	1873	Newfoundland.
81	.. do	Southern Cross	7,000	.....	....do	1872	Do.
82	.. do	Tana H. Burnham..	7,500	.....	....do	1873	Sable Island, N
83	....do	Charles E Dame....	7,000	18	..do	1873	Bay St. Lawre
							Cape, Princе
							Island.
84	... do	Angie T. Friend ...	4,700	12	...do	1873	At sea.
85	... do	Royal Arch.........	6,500	14	...do	1873	White Head.
86	... do	Samuel Crowell	6,500	15	...do	1873	At sea.
87	...do	James G. Tarr	6,400	18	... do	1873	Do.
88	...do	Eldorado	1,300	7	... do	1873	White Head, N
89	..do	Mary T. Hind......	3,000	.....	...do	1873	Cape Canso, No
90	...do	Far West..........	2,200	.....	....do	1873	Port Mulgrave,
91	.. do	Centenion..........	1,000	.....	....do	1873	Ship Harbor, N
92	...do	Typhoon	3,780	.....	....do	1873	Harbor De Bar.
93	...do	D. H. Mansfield	2,100	.....	...do	1873	Magdalen Islau
94	...do	William Y. Dale	5,800	9	....do	1873	Newfoundland.
95	... do	Tana A. Dodd......	7,000	.....	....do	1874	Do.
96	....do	Mary Y. Dennis....	6,500	.....	....do	1874	Passage from
							land.
97	....do	Carry Francis	7,500	.....	.. do	1875	Malpeque Bar.
98	...do	Bloomingdale	2,500	.....	....do	1875	Woody Island, C
99	.. do	Monadnock	7,900	.....	....do	1875	Magdalen Island
100	.. do	Hattie M Lyons....	4,900	.....	....do	1875	Cape Hogan, Ca
101	....do	John M. Dodge	3,000	.....	....do	1875	Old Man's Ledge
							Scotia.
102	....do	Earl Ellsworth......	5,500	.....	... do	1876	Magdalen Island
103	....do	Reliance	3,600	.....	.. do	1876	Canso.
104	....do	Fisher	1,755	.....	....do	1876	Louisburg.
105	...do	George Peabody ...	2,100	.....	....do	1876	Bay St. Lawrenc

GLOUCESTER, *May 1*

The above list comprehends the names of the vessels lost, their valuation number of men lost, from the district of Gloucester, from 1830 to January 1, 1 *vessels were mostly engaged in the Bay of St. Lawrence fisheries and in the immed borhood of the British Provinces.* It does not include partial losses, or single, in or personal loss or injury to business, etc.

F. J. BABS
Collector District Gl

Q. It is taken from the official reports of your office?—A. I may say that for about all the report you may see in the variou cations regarding Gloucester, the information is derived from toms office.

By Mr. Davies:

Q. That does not show the vessels lost on the American shc No.

By Sir Alexander Galt:

Q. How far back does the return go?—A. To 1830.

By Mr. Trescot:

Q. The returns show where each vessel was lost?—A. Whei lost was reported at the office.

By Mr. Thomson:

Q. It is not a comparative statement of the losses in the gulf your shores in the same period?—A. No.

y Mr. Trescot:

om your official records can you tell me whether the tonnage of er has increased or diminished from 1869, and in what branches ess?—A. I have here a copy from the books of the tonnage of er from 1869 and number of vessels employed in the different s of business.

ss read the following statement:

t of the tonnage of the district of Gloucester, June 30, of each year.

vessels licensed for fisheries	24,891.04
vessels licensed for coasting	2,777.80
vessels licensed for foreign trade	1,416.09
Total	**29,084.93**
vessels licensed for fisheries	24,946.96
vessels licensed for coasting	3,433.71
vessels foreign trade	1,900.19
Total	**30,280.86**
vessels licensed for fisheries	24,274.81
vessels licensed for coasting	4,318.36
vessels foreign trade	1,196.24
Total	**29,789.31**
vessels licensed for fisheries	22,174.57
vessels licensed for coasting	4,475.90
vessels foreign trade	1,093.42
Total	**27,743.89**
vessels licensed for fisheries	21,364.59
vessels licensed for coasting	7,110.01
vessels foreign trade	507.71
Total	**28,982.34**
vessels licensed for fisheries	20,421.32
vessels licensed for coasting	7,947.00
vessels foreign trade	407.04
Total	**28,775.36**
vessels licensed for fisheries	20,646.44
vessels licensed for coasting	8,531.51
vessels foreign trade	555.31
Total	**29,733.26**
vessels licensed for fisheries	22,408.31
vessels licensed for coasting	11,121.50
vessels foreign trade	1,051.46
Total	**34,581.27**
vessels licensed for fishing	22,424.55
vessels licensed for coasting	9,148.00
vessels foreign trade	1,795.41
Total	**33,367.96**

By Mr. Davies:

Q. Have you produced a statement from the custom-house books of Gloucester showing the number of vessels engaged in the fisheries during the Reciprocity Treaty?—A. I cannot say that I have directly. I don't know whether I have furnished it or not to Mr. Foster under the certificate of the office.

Q. You have not put it in your evidence?—A. Not at the present time.

Q. Can you produce it for me now?—A. I cannot without referring to the books of the office.

Q. Are the books of the office in Halifax?—A. No.

Q. Did you bring down with you any such statement?—A. No; I did not.

Q. When you say the statement might have been given to Mr. Foster, you mean you might have given it to him in Boston?—A. I gave him in Boston a number of statements relating to the business of Gloucester, and there might have been a statement of that kind among them. I cannot give a statement of that kind to-day, because I cannot remember what classification I made for him with regard to vessels.

Q. This statement you have submitted only commences with 1869?—A. Yes.

Q. Why did you take that year to begin with?—A. I had no special reason.

Q. Is it not curious you should have commenced with that year?—A. It is nothing very curious.

Q. What special benefit was there in a paper showing the tonnage from 1869 to 1877? Does it cover a period of years which would enable any one to form a fair idea of the trade of Gloucester?—A. It would simply show the business of Gloucester in the years from 1869 to 1877. It covers a period embraced by the Washington Treaty, and a period when there was no Reciprocity Treaty in operation.

Q. It is of value only as showing the actual tonnage during those specified years?—A. That is all. I think there have been reports in Gloucester papers by which it appeard that the tonnage was 30,000 tons, and the impression was conveyed that it was all engaged in the fisheries. I culled that statement to show where the gain has been for the past few years.

Q. Those vessels that are classed in the statement as coasting vessels, what are we to understand they are engaged in?—A. Perhaps you will allow me to explain how we come to have a larger tonnage. A few years ago three-masted schooners were a specialty with our people, more especially for the carrying of coal from the State of Pennsylvania, and two, three, or four vessels of larger tonnage were built for that purpose; and, of course, we have a large number of vessels carrying stone from Rockport. That embraces about all our coasting trade. The large gain is principally in the three-masted schooners.

Q. Do you wish the Commission to imply from this statement that the fisheries of Gloucester have decreased?—A. I have no wish in the matter, except to put the plain facts before the Commissioners, and they may draw their own inferences.

Q. Is that your own mind, your own impression?—A. I have an impression that the number of vessels is decreasing; the tonnage is very nearly the same. The vessels that are being built are of large tonnage, and more able to prosecute the different branches of the fisheries.

Q. Does not the statement show an increase in the number of vessels?—A. Not to a very great extent; it does for the last two years.

Q. Compare 1869 with 1877. In 1869 the tonnage was 29,084, and in

1877 33,367 tons, which is an increase, though not a very large increase?—A. You will observe that in 1869 24,000 tons were engaged in fishing as against 22,000 tons in 1877. The gain is on the coasting.

Q. I suppose I would be correct in saying that in an equal number of years, immediately preceding 1869, the tonnage had largely increased. For instance, from 1859 to 1869?—A. I could not say about that without referring to the books.

Q. Does it not strike you as curious that you have come here to give statistics to the Commission, and yet do not produce from your books statistics showing what the tonnage was at the time of the commencement of the Reciprocity Treaty?—A. I am perfectly willing to produce them. My only object is to place the facts as nearly as I can before the Commission.

Q. There were some statements put in by you. You know nothing about them?—A. Not personally.

Q. Who handed them to you?—A. They have been sent to me since I have been here.

Q. Have you read them?—A. I have looked them over.

Q. You know nothing about them?—A. Not of my own personal knowledge.

Q. You did not prepare them?—A. No.

Q. You had nothing to do with their preparation?—A. No.

Q. You cannot speak of the correctness of the preparation?—A. Other than I can vouch for the fidelity of my own officer.

Q. Those papers were put in your hands, and you handed them to the Commission?—A. They were sent to me.

Q. It appears from the affidavit that those papers were furnished to Mr. Blatchford by certain firms in Gloucester, and were not made up by him?—A. Not made up by him, but he went to the firms direct.

Q. And asked them for the statements, and they gave them to him?—A. Yes.

Q. Those statements are not under oath?—A. No; they are not sworn, except so far as Mr. Blatchford's affidavit covers them.

Mr. DAVIES asked if it was intended to put in the statements in regard to the business done by the Gloucester firms.

Mr. FOSTER said that Mr. Davies, in cross-examining one of the Gloucester witnesses had expressed a desire to have a statement of the business of all the firms in Gloucester, and accordingly he (Mr. Foster) sent down to Gloucester and had that statement obtained. He put it in for whatever value may be attached to it. It bore a somewhat striking resemblance to the return of the catches made by the collector at Port Mulgrave, printed as an appendix to the British Case, except that these contain the catches from 1869 to 1876 or 1877, while the collector at Port Mulgrave gave them for 1873, 1874, and 1877, omitting 1875 and 1876.

Mr. DAVIES said he asked for a statement covering the period of years during which the Reciprocity Treaty was in force, and these statements did not cover that period, but, on the contrary, covered a period of time which he did not ask for and did not want.

Mr. FOSTER said he did not hear anything about the period of the Reciprocity Treaty until a few days ago, and he had told Mr. Davies that if a counsel was sent to examine the books of merchants of Gloucester, they could have access to them.

Mr. DAVIES submitted that there was an important difference between the submission of the Port Mulgrave returns and these returns. The former were embodied in the British Reply, while the latter they could not cross-examine upon, because the witness said he knew nothing

about the contents, and they must be accepted by the Commiss
out cross-examination.

Mr. FOSTER said he put in the statement to resist the exl
appeared on the appendix E, " Documents filed with the sec
the Halifax Commission, and read at the sitting held on the 30
July, 1877, in support of the case of Her Britannic Majesty's
ment," being a " return of United States mackerel-fishing ves
their catch in 1873, as reckoned at port Mulgrave, N. S., by
lector of customs at that port," and a similar return for the n
At the end it was signed David Murray, collector of PortMulgr
ruary 9, 1875.

Mr. DAVIES said the statement from the collector at Port I
had been before the American counsel almost since the comme
of the sittings, and they had had ample opportunities of ascerta
truth and cross-examining witnesses on it. The papers now s
be put in were not verified in any sense whatever. They a
however, to show a comparison of the catches on the Americ
and in the bay, and yet omitted the time during which the ves
employed in their respective trips. It would be remembered
always cross-examined on that point, holding that the value of
parison depended on the length of time the vessels were emplo

Mr. FOSTER said he thought such a position should not be
gentlemen who had introduced hearsay evidence from the beg
the end of the case, and who on 30th July put in those Port I
statements for selected years, omitting the years 1875 and 18
it was well known the fisheries failed in the gulf, and refused t
the returns for the years upon his request, which he put on th
book, that there might be no mistake about it. If an appeal v
to him with regard to the evidence, he thought the evidenc
proffered was quite as good as the statement put in from the co
Port Mulgrave. But if what the British counsel really wante
formation on the subject, let them accept the offer that had be
and send some one to Gloucester and have the whole retur
The statement he submitted stood like all statistical evidence
which was based upon the oath of the original source.

Mr. THOMSON cited the rules regarding notice to produce, and
by the notice given by Mr. Foster he required them to produce
tive evidence, and if he had been right he might have requirec
give any evidence he thought proper. As to the statement o
lector of Port Mulgrave, it was put in with the British Reply.
ish counsel had not time to test the accuracy of the statement
been tendered. In the former instance it was not put in as p
evidence, but was filed as part of the case in reply; but in
the statement was put in as evidence.

Mr. FOSTER said the British counsel had, hundreds of times
evidence what somebody told somebody else.

Mr. THOMSON said they had given hearsay evidence beca
admitted originally, and the American counsel commenced it tl
by cross examining on hearsay statements. In this inquiry
possible they could carry it on without giving to a very gr
hearsay evidence; but the moment a tabular statement was l
verified by no one, and not coming in as part of the answer on t
can side, they had the right to refer to the rules to see whet
with the evidence to be admitted. He held it did not. Moreo
put in on the very last day.

Mr. FOSTER. Whose last day ?

Mr. THOMSON. Yours?

Mr. FOSTER. Certainly.

Mr. KELLOGG asked to what rule the British counsel referred.

Mr. FOSTER said the British counsel put in their statistics, a mass of them, on the last day of their evidence.

Mr. THOMSON read the eleventh rule.

Hon. Mr. KELLOGG said that a modification of the rule in regard to affidavits had been assented to. Aside from that, no question could arise except that of relevancy. If the agents or counsel on either side assured the board that, in their view, that evidence was relevant to the hearing, he would be very slow himself to refuse its admission. It happened that it was late in the hearing, but all evidence had to come in some time or other.

Mr. THOMSON read the affidavit of Mr. Blatchford, and said it was to the effect that he went and asked the gentlemen to give him those statements, and he swore that they were copies of the statements which they were pleased to furnish him.

Mr. FOSTER said the British counsel put in a statement from George Murray, he being the collector of Port Mulgrave, of United States mackerel fishing vessels for 1873 and 1874. Mr. Murray stated the number of United States vessels, the number of barrels; and in regard to where they were caught, stated: "The most of those mackerel were caught about Prince Edward Island, small size mackerel; the best and largest were caught at Magdalen Islands. This may not be a true number of barrels; only gathered this from the vessel men; they call them that quantity; it is not much out of the way either way." When he found those statements he called for similar statements for the two following years, 1875 and 1876, and he had kept reminding the counsel about them. One of the English counsel in cross-examining one of the United States witnesses, did so from a paper which they said was Mr. Murray's statement of what American vessels had caught this year, whereupon he (Mr. Foster) called for it, and got it in as part of the cross-examination.

Mr. WEATHERBE asked if the paper was not an official report made by Mr. Murray to the department.

Mr. FOSTER. No.

Mr. WEATHERBE said if the paper was of the character of one prepared since the treaty went into operation, and to be presented before the Commission, the rules should be conformed to, and it should be presented under oath.

Mr. FOSTER said the paper was extracted from the cross-examination. It was called, "Account of American Mackerel Catches in North Bay, 1877."

Sir ALEXANDER GALT said he did not remember that the statement was put in as evidence.

Mr. FOSTER said it was not put in as independent evidence, but, after ascertaining what it was on which the witness was cross-examined, he had stated that he was entitled to have the paper put in.

Sir ALEXANDER GALT said the question was as to which side put in the paper.

Mr. FOSTER said that by the twenty-fourth article of the Treaty of Washington the Commissioners "shall be bound to receive such oral or written testimony as either government may present." He had called upon an official of the Government of the United States to obtain statistics with regard to this matter, and, in pursuance of that call, he had done so. The statistics came certified from the office, and, on behalf of

the Government of the United States, he (Mr. Foster) present
as evidence *quantum valuit.*

Mr. THOMSON said that hearsay evidence, though it was not
admitted by judicial tribunals, was admitted of this descript
dence of information parties had obtained in the course of c
tion in regard to the particular matter in hand, at a time, in nir
ces out of ten, when they had no reason to know of this p
tribunal or inquiry, and the persons, therefore, had no object
reach. That was not the character of the evidence now offer
consisted of hearsay evidence obtained from different firms in
ter, for the especial purpose of affecting this tribunal, and ma
person under oath. If the official had visited the different st
asked the different persons to show him their books, and i
sworn on examining those books the statements submitted w
copies, then it would be evidence. But here were people under
but knowing well that an inquiry was going on in which their
was interested, who gave to the official just what they though
True, he might state that he believed the statements true cop
the books, but unfortunately the Commission had no knowled
fact. That was the difference between the testimony which
admitted and that now offered.

Mr. FOSTER said he understood from the secretary that the]
grave statement had not been printed as part of the evidenc
peared in the cross-examination, which was as follows:

Q. Do you know anything about other vessels ? Some have got as many
rels, from that down ? I will read from the returns: (Reading the names
and catches.) These are gathered from the returns reported by them.
Mr. FOSTER. Do you submit that to our inspection.
Mr. DAVIES. Certainly. I would not have read it otherwise. (Explain
to Mr. Foster that these are returns of vessels that have been in the ba
home, as they reported themselves at Canso.)
Q. Now, have you heard of any of these vessels that made any of these re
I have heard of some of these vessels writing home.
Q. Have the returns you have heard accorded with those I have read ?—.
think not.
Q. You don't know whether these returns are correct or not ?—A. I don't
they are.
Q. If they were would you be inclined to modify your statement as to the
the gulf ?—A. No ; I would not.
Q. You still persist in the statement you made ?—A. I don't anything abc
Q. But supposing it correct, if it turns out to be correct, from comparison
lished returns in Gloucester papers ?—A. Well, that might perhaps have
information upon which that is based.
Q. You would consider the reports in Gloucester papers to be incorrect ?—
say any such thing.
Q. Would you place reliance upon them ?—A. As a general thing I would
Q. What did you mean by saying that the Gloucester papers might hav
information as that I have read ?—A. The crews sometimes report more
actually catch.
Q. Then we cannot believe the reports we see in those papers ?—A. Wel
difference between sea barrels and packed barrels. Perhaps the mackerel
short.
Q. That is by the difference between sea barrels and packed barrels ?—A
Q. But could not any person easily allow for that ?
Hon. Mr. KELLOGG asks if the returns just read are official.
Mr. DAVIES explains that the returns are those which the vessels make ;
through the Gut of Canso—that they are not official, but that the informat
ered by persons engaged by the inspector to ascertain the catch from the ci

If this had not gone in with the evidence, he proposed to pi
a paper on which the witness was cross-examined.

Mr. DAVIES said that when cross-examining a witness, wi
to the number of American vessels in the bay, and the numb
rels they caught, he held up a paper in his hand and asked wh

ught such a quantity. Mr. Foster asked him if it was a return, Mr. Davies), said it was a return, and explained that it was in an official one. Mr. Foster asked him, at the close of the ex- on, if he would let him see it, and he gave him the document. however, only part of what he had held in his hand; it was in no official record; it did not purport to be such, and was not read as such; but was only used by him for the purpose of cross- tion.

OSTER said, if the other part was produced, he would put it in.

LEXANDER GALT said he did not think Mr. Foster could put in of the other side.

OSTER reread the cross-examination referred to, and said it the paper.

LEXANDER GALT asked whether Mr. Foster or Mr. Ford put in rn, for some one must put it in and be responsible for it.

OSTER said a paper forming a subject matter of cross-examina- s at the disposal of the counsel on both sides of the case, and if sel opposed to the one who cross-examined, calls for the paper, be produced. When produced and inspected, he had the right t in as he pleased, not as independent evidence of his own, but of the subject matter of the cross-examination. That question in courts frequently in this way. A counsel cross-examines a as to the contents of a letter the witness is said to have written, letter is introduced by the cross-examining counsel by way of con- ng the witness, but it is incompetent to be introduced as substan- lence on either side. Then, as there has been cross-examination witness upon it, the party has the right to have the letter read ase.

LEXANDER GALT. Who puts the return in ?

OSTER. I put it in, not as substantive evidence on my side, but er drawn out from the other side, which the mode of their cross- ation entitles me to have in the case.

HOMSON said there was no such rule of evidence known to Brit- rts as that laid down by Mr. Foster. Counsel may for the pur- cross-examination produce a paper and ask a witness whether written a certain statement at variance with those he was then ; but before counsel could do that he must have the written nt in his hand and submit it to the judge, and satisfy him that not attempting to frighten the witness by an imaginary paper. tness was then requested to state whether such a statement was y him in writing; but that gave the opposing counsel no right the paper. It remained entirely with the counsel as to what use ild make of it afterward to contradict the statements of the wit- ring the examination ; if the witness admitted that he had made written statement, then he might be asked as to how he recon- e testimony he had given with the written testimony he had given time. Such a rule as that mentioned was unknown to any British that the fact of a counsel cross-examining a witness on a paper, ie control of the paper to the opposing counsel. He had never f such rule in any American court, though, of course, he would empt to place his opinion regarding the rules of United States against those of Mr. Foster. If Mr. Foster, as agent of the States, intended to take the paper and put it in evidence by of it having been in the hands of one of the British counsel for pose of cross-examination, he must take it and put it in as part vidence, vouching for its authenticity, and being responsible for ectness.

Hon. Mr. KELLOGG asked what .was the motion in regard
paper.

Mr. THOMSON said he understood Mr. Foster was offering it
dence.

Mr. DANA said he did not so understand it. A question aros
whether the paper was or was not in evidence. The Secretary t
it was not put in, and the Agent of the United States though
in. If it was in, no motion could be made for withdrawing it; i
not in, the question was not whether they should now put it
whether it was not an error that it was not in. Their position w
the paper went into the case from the nature of the cross-exam
and if there was a mistake made in not handing the paper to t
retary, or in the Secretary not understanding it was put in, the
rectify it now, not as testimony offered by one side or the other si
but as something that heretofore should have been in the case.
was no very great difference in the common law as administered
United States, Great Britain, and the colonies. It was all four
reason. Suppose a cross-examining counsel asks a witness whe
wrote a certain paper, then on that paper being produced by h
as evidence on his own side, but to contradict or impeach the ch
of the witness, or to diminish the weight of his testimony, and
per is made the subject-matter of cross-examination, that cross-
ation goes on the record, if the proceeding is by record, and pas
the hands of the jury, if the proceeding is at common law, an
sential part, in order that the cross-examination may be unders
the paper. It counsel produced a paper and cross-examined a
upon it, and had the cross-examination entered on the record, a
thought it would suit him better to have the paper on which th
examination was based in his pocket and put it there, in what
would the witness stand on the record? Any judge, reading th
examination, would say that he could not understand the wit
form an opinion as to the value of his testimony unless he
paper. In such cases it is considered an essential part of the c
amination, and counsel cannot withdraw it and put it in his
The jury has the right, in order to understand the testimony of
ness, to see the paper on which the questions were founded. In t
ent case, Mr. Foster had read the cross-examination of the witn
the paper produced for the purpose of his cross-examination. The
tion simply was that the paper was an essential part of the cros
ination, or was a sufficient part of the cross examination to a
either party who desired it to put it into the case that the cross
ation might be understood. The party who produced it might p
not as original testimony to prove his case, but as something wh
der the oral statements of the witness, affects the witness. If th
ments of the witness went into the record without the paper o
he was cross-examined, he was affected unfairly. The court
no doubt, declare that as counsel had seen fit to cross-examine
ness on the paper, in order that everything may be understo
justice done to the witness, the paper must go in with the cross
ation. Mr. Foster had supposed the paper was already in the c
(Mr. Dana) could not say he did so, for he had forgotten the
tion. He thought Mr. Thomson had referred to some other poin
could not be held that counsel could cross-examine a witnes
paper, and say to the court and opposing counsel, " I insist on
swers of the witness going down, but I also insist upon putt
paper into the fire."

Mr. THOMSON said that no witness could be cross-examined on

·use referred to by Mr. Dana, except in regard to a paper of
· had personally given evidence, or else in regard to a paper
· himself. It was impossible for a witness to be cross-examined
er, except under such circumstances—either as regards a paper
ich he had volunteered to give evidence and undertaken to hold
orth as having a personal knowledge of it, or in a case where a
ias written a paper and holds himself responsible for the con-
Vhen counsel holds up a paper, which it is not pretended is an
·turn, and asks questions from it, how does that prejudice the

He has the privilege of stating whether certain things are
ilse, and his answers are recorded. Counsel might have all the
id information down in his brief, and how was the witness in-
such a course? It had been said that the court could not under-
· testimony unless the paper was put in. The testimony stood
ugh. Mr. Davies had read what he pleased from the paper
d the witness if such was correct or incorrect; that was all.
·r was said by Mr. Davies, and the answers of the witness to
:ion, were taken down. He did not wish to throw any difficulty
y, and was quite prepared to discuss the question as if it had
the time of the cross-examination. If the American counsel
right on that day to take·the paper out of the hands of Mr.
ind put it in evidence, they had the right now. Mr. Davies
he paper over at the request of Mr. Foster, but he was not
do so unless he pleased. Mr. Foster could not have put in the
less Mr. Davies had been pleased to give it to him, and no court
ve obliged him to do so. That paper having been handed over
oster as a matter of courtesy, if he chose to offer it in evidence,
not object, but he could not put it in as a matter of right, and
part of the British evidence. If Mr. Foster offered it in evi-
iey would treat it as American evidence wholly.

ANA said that in Massachusetts, and he thought the United
enerally, counsel were not permitted to cross examine a witness
iaper.

Mr. KELLOGG said he recollected the circumstance very well,
iad understood from what had then passed between Mr. Davies
Foster, as to whether the paper should be admitted or not, that
iven to Mr. Foster, as he supposed, in the view of having it put
id not, however, know what the intention was.

OSTER said that a large part of the paper was read in evidence.

.LEXANDER GALT inquired what was the value of the return.

OSTER said that if the counsel had been pleased to cross exam-
chapter out of the book of Job, after he had done, he (Mr. Fos-
ld have been entitled to have that chapter placed before the
sion, as the basis of his cross-examination. Mr. Thomson had
t they could not cross-examine on a paper in that way, but the
:o this was, that the counsel had done this; and this being the
w in the world could he be deprived of the benefit of it?
.d supposed it was understood, that this paper was entered to be
with other matter; and wanting a copy of it, he had obtained
i the Secretary that night. Certainly, he had supposed that
ir was in, else he would certainly have renewed the controversy
t morning. Having deliberately cross-examined on this paper
i view of forcing the witness to say that it was correct, and that
d not dissent from the statement, the inquiries "Are you going
ih enough to disagree with these written statements?" and "Will
ture to say that this Mr. Murray, of Port Mulgrave, has not
ipportunities than you have of knowing how these matters stand?"

were to be read between the lines in Mr. Davies's questions. Th
purported to be a return; they might call it official, non-official,
official, he did not care what, but it was presented to induce the
to agree to the statements read to him; and this being the case
did not bring it into the case, as part of the cross-examinati
he was completely mistaken.

The PRESIDENT. The decision of the Commission is that th
shall be put in.

The return in question is as follows:

Account of American mackerel catches in North Bay.

Date.	Name.	Barrels.	Date.	Home or refitted.	Remark
1877.			1877.		
July 2	Macleod	170	Sept. 19	Refitted	
9	Flying Cloud	205	Sept. 4	Home	
10	Alice	235	July 25	....do	
10	Hyperion	240	Aug. 17	....do	
10	C. C. Davis	90	Sept. 7	Refitted	
11	J. J. Clarke	240	Aug. 16	Home	
11	Ceyenne	300	Aug. 19	....do	
12	Alice M. Lewis	200	Aug. 21	....do	
14	Marion Grimes	150	Aug. 30	....do	
14	Frederic Gerring, jr	330	Sept. 22	....do	
14	George B. Loring	250	Sept. 17	Refitted	
17	Fleetwood	90	Aug. 24	Home	
17	Falcon (supposed)	60	Aug. 23	....do	
17	Eastern Queen	120	Aug. 10	....do	210. Back on seco 28.
17	Amos Cutler	180	Aug. 25	....do	
17	Rambler	270	Sept. 22	Refitted	
18	Harvest Home	235	Sept. 13	....do	
18	Martha C	170	Aug. 24	Home	
19	E. A. Horton	235	Sept. 22	Refitted	
21	Gertie Lewis	127	Aug. 23	Home	
21	John Wesley	190	Sept. 2	....do	
21	Idela Surall	150	Sept. 13	Refitted	
21	Flash	85	Sept. 4	Home	
21	Onward	117½	Sept. 2	Refitted	
21	Miantinomah	101	Aug. 25	Home	
21	David F. Low	220	Sept. 12	Refitted twice	
23	Nettie Moore	70	Aug. 10	Home	
26	Lilly Dale	130	Aug. 24	Refitted	
27	Ellen Dale	88	Aug. 23	Home	
27	Seth Stockbridge	None	Aug. 24	....do	
27	F. L. Mayo	150	Sept. 8	Refitted	
27	B F. Some	160	Sept. 12	....do	
28	Maggie Power	90	Aug. 16	Home	
28	Clara L Dyer	90	Sept. 8	Refitted	
28	Ocean King	110	Aug. 30	....do	
30	Eunice P. Newcombe	85	Sept. 4	Home	
Aug. 2	Oasis	60	Aug. 23	....do	
2	Challenge	170	Sept. 24	Refitted	
2	Helen M. Crosby	30	Aug. 21	Home	
2	Lizzie E Hopkins	150	Sept. 24	....do	
6	Etta Gott	226	Sept. 14	Refitted	
6	Rattler	170	Sept. 20	....do	
7	M. J. Elliott	60	Aug. 24		To repair fores back.
7	Edmund Burke	230	Sept. 21	Home	
7	A. C. Newhall	140	Sept. 24	....do	
7	Roger Williams	80	Aug. 31	....do	
7	Lillian M. Warner	120	Aug. 21	....do	
7	Vidette	125	Sept. 19	Refitted	
7	Wm. A. Penn	160	Sept. 25	Home	
8	Lizzie Poor	150	Sept. 20	Refitted	
8	Lady Woodbury	220	Sept. 24	Home	
8	Martha A. Brewer	150	Sept. 20	Refitted	
9	Geo. B. McClellan	150	Sept. 24	Refitted	
9	Waterfall	85	Sept. 20	Home	
14	Grey Eagle	16	Sept. 4	....do	
16	Madawaska Maid	None.	Aug. 24	....do	
17	Cyrena Ann	50	Sept. 10	....do	
17	Alice M. Gould	None.	Aug. 21	....do	
21	Fred. P. Frye	5	Aug. 25	....do	
21	Eleanor B. Conwell	85	Sept. 24	Refitted	
	Total	8,365½			

This list is from vessels being in for supplies and going home, not including what is in
Only one supposed trip in the lot. Captain would not tell how many he had.

D. MUF

Codfish-trips.

Name.	Quin-tals.	Date.	Home or refitted.	Remarks.
		1877.		
.da K. Damon........	1,375	Aug. 28	Home	Time, 4 months ffom Banks.
en. T. Crockett......	1,400	Aug. 30	....do	2.9 months ffom North Bay.
ogus	1,100	Sept. 4	....do	2½ months from North Bay.
annuel Ober........	900	Sept. 7	....do	2.13 months from North Bay.
ucknow	1,100	Sept. 7	....do	3.17 months from North Bay.
liver Cromwell	900	Sept. 17	....do	3.23 months from North Bay.
okana..............	900	Sept. 19	....do	3.22 months from North Bay.
lavilla.............	1,000	Sept. 21	....do	4 1 months ffom North Bay.
riola	1,100	Sept. 21	....do	4 4 months from North Bay.
. Payne	1,000	Sept. 24	....do	4 0 months from North Bay.
reemont...........	900	Sept. 24	....do	4 3 months from North Bay.
loomer	1,200	Sept. 24	....do	4 6 months from North Bay.
londel	910	Sept. 24	....do	4.6 months ffom North Bay.
en. Scott	900	Sept. 25	....do	4 8 months ffom North Bay.
andelia	800	Sept. 25	....do	4.4 months from North Bay.
ulian	800	Sept. 22	Lost at Port Hood	
rcola	800	Sept. 25	Home............	4 0 months from North Bay.
eo. Water	900	Sept. 13	....do	3 20 months ffom North Bay.
	16,600	Quintals codfish ffom North Bay on trawls.		
	2,000	Quintals codfish on trawls, small trips.		
Total............	18,600	American vessels.		

ere a fleet of small vessels which went home ffom early trip before the boat was out. This
nerican vessels only. Have these figures from captains and crews.

D. MURRAY, Jr.

ER 25, 1877.

y Mr. Davies:

hen you were examining the books for the purpose of making
return of vessels lost, did it occur to you to compare the proof vessels lost in the bay with that lost on George's Bank?—A.
did not examine them for that purpose. I did not have a return
point.

ow was this return prepared; you say, I see, in some cases, that
els were lost "at sea"?—A. You will observe, with regard to the
tion of reports of that kind, that we get from the owners the
ormation they can give in this respect; they report every vessel
ost. I could not swear to the exact accuracy of every report;
ports are prepared in the same manner as all custom-house busi-
usually done.

this information obtained from the owners at the time of the
vessels?—A. Yes, as nearly as possible, as a general thing. I
tell in this regard for my own term of office. We have always
this information as soon as vessels are lost.

I went to the books of your office, would I find the statement
ed in this return on their face, about the time these vessels were
you have it copied out here?— A. You would find some of them
end of the year when we collect the information—when we are
to make up the list of vessels; and we drop from the list those
ve cannot carry over into the next year.

me I would find there?—A. Yes.

nd some I would not find?—A. For previous years you would
m at the end of the year.

ould I find them all there?—A. Yes, all we carry over; we have
vessels for 1876; and at the end of the year, in January, we
p a new list and transmit it to the department—in which we put
ressels owned in the district and how they are disposed of, stat-
ether they have been sold out of the district or whatever way
iy have been disposed of, or lost, or wherever they may have

been transferred—we make up a report showing exactly where th gone.

By Mr. Dana:

Q. Annually?—A. Yes; annually. We make up special re this relation.

By Mr. Davies:

Q. Is this compilation taken solely from your books?—A. Th clerk's report, prepared in the usual manner in which such thi done.

Q. Did your clerk compile this statement solely from the b your office?—A. Yes.

Q. Did he make any inquiries outside, in order to make it v I think he took it from the books of the office.

Q. Did you examine the books to see whether this was the not?—A. No, I did not.

Q. Is this in your handwriting?—A. Yes; he gave me the n the vessels as they came along, and I put them in.

Q. Is there a report made by the owner to your office at th vessel is lost?—A. This has always been the case since I have l office.

Q. Since when has that been?—A. Since 1869, 8 years ago.

Q. And do you not know whether this was done previous to A. For the time previous to that, we took what was in the book

Q. You cannot tell what was the practice previously in this res A. No.

Q. You cannot tell how the clerk made up the statement for t previous to your term of office?—A. I cannot tell; of course n derived his information from the books.

Q. You cannot tell whether this was taken solely from the you have not examined the books?—A. No; as I said before, t did this. My business is simply executive, and I do not perfo cal work myself.

Q. Suppose that a vessel starts from the St. Lawrence and heard from; how is it entered?—A. The owner gives the best inf that he can on the subject.

Q. It is entered, lost at sea?—A. Yes.

Q. This statement embraces the year of the great gale?—. cludes all the years back, until 1831.

Q. How did you arrive at these valuations?—A. We got th the office.

Q. At the time the vessels were lost?—A. As near the time . ble.

Q. During the years in which these occurred, at any rate?— a direct report is now required of us regarding every vessel that as soon as we know that a vessel is lost, we are obliged to make embracing the facts.

Q. Did that rule extend to 1831, when this list commences? those values were taken simply from the yearly returns.

Q. These are approximate values?—A. They must be so, I t a general thing, except within the last 8 years.

Q. How did you obtain the valuation of the Amazon, the sel?—A. That was probably the owner's report at the time made the report to the custom-house.

Q. You have never examined the books to see?—A. No, no personally. I made it up from my clerk's return.

ee that some vessels in the first part of the list are charged as if
the Bay of Chaleurs; are you aware that formerly the Bay of
ence was called the Bay of Chaleurs?—A. Yes.
hen it speaks of the Bay of Chaleurs, I suppose that somewhere
ulf is meant?—A. Yes.
is list embraces Newfoundland too?—A. Yes.
id the Banks?—A. If on the Banks, I suppose, offshore here.
that all the places are designated as nearly correct as possible.
e they all fishing, or are some trading vessels?—A. I think
y are about all fishing-vessels.
e lost vessels, Alexandria and Queen of Clippers, are charged
to Newfoundland; are you aware whether any fishing-vessels
nt to Newfoundland?—A. In 1858?
es.—A. O, yes; I think they did. I think that the Newfound-
zen-herring business has been pursued for some time in Ameri-
sels.
ou do not accurately remember the first year when they went
—A. No. The statement simply covers, as far as my memory is
ed, my own term of office. I was away previous to that time.
there an entry in your books giving, for instance, the value of
sel, the Alexandria, lost in 1858 at Newfoundland?—A. I pre-
, from the report made by the clerk to me; that paper was pre-
the same manner as was the case with these other papers.
o you know what the total number is when added up—is it 105?—
nk it is about 105.
own to the end of 1875, 101 vessels were lost in the Gulf of St.
ce and Newfoundland fisheries, according to your return?—A.
the coast of Nova Scotia, I suppose.
is return embraces all the British provinces?—A. Yes.
course they may have been lost on their way up from Glouces-
.. Yes; I cannot say as to that.
find in Procter's book concerning the fisheries of Gloucester,
as been quoted here so frequently, a table giving the losses of
vessels from 1830 to 1875 inclusive, the total number being 333 ves-
id the difference between your return and this return would
it vessels lost in fisheries other than those mentioned in your
—A. Of course.
ne hundred and one during this period were lost in our fisheries,
2 in yours?—A. I would say that most of those statistics are
p from our office.
ave you made up a statement to show the percentage of loss?
ntion is called to a statement written at the foot of this compi-
n which you say, "Said vessels were mostly engaged in the Bay
awrence fisheries, "Then evidently some of these vessels were
aged in those fisheries?—A. Most certainly.
ley were traders probably?—A. They were engaged in other
s probably; they might have been engaged in the Bank fishery
I have been lost on the coast of Nova Scotia.
nere is also added, "And in the immediate neighborhood of the
provinces"?—A. You are to understand that our vessels fish
British provinces, and their losses are reported to us by their
for the different points wherever the vessel may have been lost,
ly as can be ascertained. I suppose that is the idea which they
convey.
hen you wrote "were mostly engaged," you had in your mind
that some of them were engaged in other pursuits than those

which are specially mentioned ?—A. I meant that they were eng
fishing at other points besides the Bay of St. Lawrence about th
ish provinces; that is intended to cover the whole of the Nova
and Newfoundland shores. They go in in case of storms.

Q. Have you never had occasion to ascertain the percentage
of your fishing-vessels ?—A. Myself ?

Q. Yes.—A. No, I have never made that a subject for specific
tics at any time.

Q. Do you know whether this loss exceeds 2½ per cent. ?—A.]
entire fleet ?

Q. Yes.—A. I could not ascertain that without going into the f

Q. And you never have ascertained it ?—A. No.

Q. Have you ascertained, in conversation with leading men, w
it has been more than 2½ per cent. ?—A. Not in that form.

Q. In what form have you done so ?—A. We always understa
we lose from 10 to 15 vessels and from 100 to 150 men every yeai
general fisheries.

Q. That does not show what the percentage is ?—A. Not
means.

Q. What percentage is this loss; for instance, would 2½ per c
surance cover all such losses ?—A. You mean whether 2½ per
the whole fleet is lost ? I suppose that the loss would fully equ

Q. And you think it would not be more ?—A. I know that i
not be a great deal more than that.

Q. And the difference between that and what was charged fo
ance would represent the profits made ?—A. I do not know wl
mean.

Q. I want to ascertain the value of the vessels that leave Glo
to pursue the fishing-business, and whether 2½ per cent. of that va
would cover the loss that is incurred here ?—A. Allow me oné u
I did not understand that question as applying to insurance. I 1
you asked whether the loss amounted to 2½ per cent. of the who
ber of the vessels.

Q. That is just the way in which I put it.—A. But as far as in
is concerned, that is a matter of which I have no knowledge wl

Q. I want to ascertain what percentage of the fishing-vessel
leave Gloucester is lost ?—A. Well, we generally lose from 1(
every year, out of nearly 400 vessels.

Q. In the annual report of the Bureau of Statistics of the
States for 1876, on page 15, under the head of Trade with Cana(
ing the year ending the 30th of June, 1876, I find a table of
which had been omitted in the returns of the United States c
officers on the Canadian border, as appears from an official st:
furnished by the Commissioner of Customs, amounting to $10,
as against $15,596,224 for the preceding year : now, the fish e
from the United States into Canada by railway do not appea
return, do they ?—A. That is a thing with which I have never k
thing to do.

Q. I thought you might know something of this trade, and be
explain the discrepancy between the United States and Cana
turns ?—A. That is a matter entirely beyond my jurisdiction; th:
by the Grand Trunk Railway, I think.

Q. You do not know whether they make any return of fish
or of trade that is thus carried ou ?—A. We have no experience
kind at our office.

Mr. Trescot :

enever you give an order to a clerk to make such a report as
·garding the loss of vessels, you expect this to be done from
·m·house books and papers, and from nothing else ?—A. Of

Sir Alexander Galt:

he return concerning lost vessels, do the coasters include the
shing vessels ?—A. No. The herring-fishing vessels all run
·ing licenses, with permits to touch and trade; these are papers
·m our office, allowing vessels to pursue any business under the
he United States. The coasting paper and the fishing license
ent papers, confining, of course, those who run the vessels to
r them, and to do such business as is specified in these licenses.
vessels which take out fishing and trading licenses frequently
·eir business ?—A. They cannot do so; they are not allowed to
·ey can only pursue the business for which they take out a
A permit to touch and trade is given only for one voyage.
· vessel goes to Fortune Bay with a fishing license, and a touch
· license, and returns to Gloucester, can she go out again with-
·ing her license to touch and trade ?—A. A fishing license is
·one year; and a touch and trade license for a voyage; and at
·f such voyage, the vessel surrenders that permit. This permit
liar paper, intended for that business only.
·STER. Unless I have made some accidental omission, may· it
e Commissioners, the case of the United States is now closed,
exception of the case just spoken of, to wit : I propose, if per-
· put in, in case they come within a week, detailed reports from
ctor-general of the State of Massachusetts, showing the number
· of mackerel which have been packed in the State of Massachu-
·ing a long series of years, ·which I think may be valuable, going
fact, I do not know how far. I understand that the fisheries
·l books of the British provinces are in the case.
·OMSON. Yes.
·STER. That is all.

APPENDIX M.

No. 1.

[CONFIDENTIAL.]

ЛS RESPECTING THE FISHERIES TO BE PRO-
ED TO —— —— ON BEHALF OF THE UNITED

is your name and age, and in what town and State do you
·eeman Hodgdon; age fifty-two years, I reside at Boothbay,
 line.
opportunities have you had for becoming acquainted with
an and Canadian Atlantic sea-fisheries, and the value of the
different kinds of fish? I pursued the business for twenty
lave been in all the waters frequented by American and
shermen.
·u give the names of other persons in your neighborhood who
ad the opportnity of obtaining similar information? If so,
some such name. Yes. Thomas Berry has had more ex-
the fishing business than any other man on our coast. John
Joseph Maddocks.
· of the treaty between Great Britain and the United States,
ne Treaty of Washington, is hereto annexed. Will you ex-
es 18, to 22 inclusive, and state that you have done so? I

kinds of fish frequent the waters of your State, especially
ι are to be thrown open to the Canadian fishermen under the
f the Treaty of Washington? Cod, Mackerel, Hake, Hallibut,
d many others of less importance.
·u give a statement of the kinds and quantities of fish taken
· the coast of your State from the years 1854 to 1872, in-
f you can do this, please do so; and if not, please state where
ation can be procured. The quantity is very great. I do
xactly.
are able to do so, will you state the amount and value of the
sheries which are to be thrown open to Canadian fishermen
rovisions of the Treaty of Washington? Please state them
· · · · ˈɪ̈ˈ·̈·̈̈t kinds of fish and the value of each

by American subjects and that caught by British subjects
equal.

9. Do Canadian fishermen procure bait or supplies in the
your State; and if so, to what extent and value? They do
extent.

10. What is the probable annual value to Canadian fisherme
able to procure bait, to land and dry their nets, and to repacl
their fish on the coasts of your State, without any other restri
that contained in the Treaty of Washington? I cannot tell.

11. Will the admission of Canadian fishermen to our in-shor
cause any detriment or hinderance to the profitable pursuit of
eries by our own fishermen; and if so, in what manner, an
extent annually? I think not.

12. What number of Canadian vessels and boats are engag
fisheries of your State, and what are their tonnage and valu
number of men employed upon them? I do not know.

13. Of the fisheries pursued by American fishermen off th
coasts of the British North American Provinces, what propc
sists of the deep-sea fisheries, and what proportion of the in-
eries? Nearly all are deep-sea fisheries. Occasionally they
vantageous to fish in-shore for mackerel, but they can usuall
outside, even for mackerel.

14. For what description of fish do American fishermen
in-shore fisheries? Mackerel and Herring chiefly, and some
fish.

15. If you state that the inshore fisheries are pursued wholl
for mackerel, please state what proportion of mackerel is tal
the in-shore limits, and what proportion is taken outside of th
limits? Much the larger part are taken off shore. There
many years when the in-shore fisheries for mackerel were wort
fish played off-shore the whole season.

16. Is not much the larger quantity of mackerel caught by
fishermen off the coasts of British America taken outside tl
limits; and in the summer season especially are not mackerel
found on the banks, in the Gulf of Saint Lawrence, and not wit
The larger part are taken outside of the in-shore limits. Ma
found in the Gulf in summer and not in-shore.

17. Are Colonial fishermen injured by permitting American
to fish in Colonial inshore waters? Perhaps the inshore
Mackerel is injured somewhat. But the great quantity of b
over by American fishermen inshore tolls the fish in, and so m
more convenient for Canadian fishermen.

18. Are not more fish caught by Colonial fishermen, when
shore, alongside a fleet of American fishing-vessels, from w
quantities of bait are thrown out, than when fishing alone
they are.

19. What is the best bait for the mackerel, and where is it
taken? How much of it is taken within three miles of the
what is the annual value to the United States, or to the Bri
inces, as the case may be, to take such bait within three m
shore? Porgies. It is all taken on the American coast. No
on the Provincial coasts. The principal part is taken within
of shore.

20. Please state as to each class of fisheries carried on from
or district, the cost of fitting out, equipping, furnishing, and
vessel for carrying it on, estimating it by the average leng

State, as far as possible, in detail the elements which go to
the cost of taking and delivering a full cargo and of returning
ne port. To fit out a hundred ton cod-fisherman costs from, *from*
to $3,000.00, and they make two trips per year, usually. It
little less to fit a vessel for Mackereling. Our vessels are all
upon the shares.

ien you have fully answered question 20, please answer the
stion as to vessels fitted out, equipped, furnished, and manned
Dominion of Canada, including Prince Edward Island, so far
e able to do so. If you state that there is any difference be-
cost of the Canadian and the cost of the American vessel in
pects, explain what the difference is, and the reason for it.
e the advantage of us in the cost of vessels, and in cost of
hat the difference amounts to I cannot tell; but it is consider-
eir favor.

e you acquainted, and for how long, and in what capacity, with
ies on the coasts of Nova Scotia, New Brunswick, Quebec, or
dward Island, or with either, and if either, with which of these
' I was master of a fisherman some twelve years, and fished
oasts of Nova Scotia, New Brunswick, and Prince Edwards

iat kind of fish frequent the waters of those coasts which are to
ii open to American fishermen under the provisions of the
' Washington ? Cod, Mackerel Herring and Hallibut. Princi-
l and Mackerel.

ase state in detail the amount and the annual value (say from
872 inclusive) of the fisheries which are so to be thrown open to
o fishermen; also the amount and the annual value of the
the adjacent waters which are more than three miles distant
shore; please state these facts in detail. I cannot answer
litely.

American fishermen procure bait in the waters within three
the coast of the Dominion of Canada? If so, to what extent,
t is the value ? But very little if any.

not the American fishermen purchase supplies in the ports of
inion of Canada, including bait, ice, salt, barrels, provisions,
ous articles for the use of the men engaged in the fisheries ?
what ports, and to what extent? And, if that is the case, is
advantage to the ports of the Dominion to have the fishing-
f the United States in their neighborhood during the fishing
Explain why it is so, and estimate, if you can, the money-
that advantage. They do, at the ports of Charlottetown,
the straits of Canso. The trade is quite extensive, but I can-
its extent.

ve you any knowledge of how many United States fishing
early engage in the fisheries off the Atlantic coasts of the
North American Provinces, (excluding Newfoundland,) both
ind within the three-mile limit ? If so, state how many vessels
gaged, what is the value of their tonnage, what is the number
mployed annually on such vessels, what sorts of fish are taken
iat is the annual value of all the fish so caught, and what is
ortion, or probable proportion, in your judgment, of the amount
atch taken within three miles of the British coast, and of the
aken outside of the three-mile limit ? I cannot tell.

iat percentage of value. if any, is, in your judgment, added to
s of a voyage by the privilege to fish within three marine miles

of the coast; whence is such profit derived; and in what does it
It is impossible for me to tell. Sometimes the advantage might
siderable: in other cases it would be nothing.

29. Do the American fishermen gain under the Treaty of Was
any valuable rights of landing to dry nets and cure fish, or to
them, or to transship cargoes, which were not theirs before; if
are those rights, and what do you estimate them to be worth a
in the aggregate? I do not know how valuable the privileges
by the Treaty of Washington may prove.

30. Is not the Treaty of Washington, so far as the fishing cla
concerned, more, or quite as, beneficial to the people of the Britis
American Provinces as to the people of the United States? I
is more beneficial to the people of the Provinces.

31. What is the amount and value of colonial cargoes of fis
descriptions which are annually shipped to the United States
not know.

32. For all No. 1 and No. 2 mackerel, for the larger part of
herring, and for all No. 1 salmon, does not the United States af
only market? I think it is the principal market.

33. If you know what amount of duties is annually paid to the
States on fish and fish-oil imported from Canada, which are to
free under the provisions of the Treaty of Washington, plea
them annually, and by classes, from 1854 to 1872, inclusive?
know.

FREEMAN HODG

Sworn to and subscribed before me this tenth day of June, 18
ORRIN McFADDEN, Collector of Cu

No. 2.

[CONFIDENTIAL.]

QUESTIONS RESPECTING THE FISHERIES TO BE
POUNDED TO —— —— ON BEHALF OF THE U
STATES.

1. What is your name and age, and in what town and State
reside? Thomas Berry, age sixty-three, I live at Boothbay M

2. What opportunities have you had for becoming acquaint
the American and Canadian Atlantic sea-fisheries, and the
the catch of the different kinds of fish? I have been a fishing
Banks and on the coasts of the British Provinces for fifty-one

3. Can you give the names of other persons in your neighborh
have also had the opportunity of obtaining similar information
please give some such name. Charles Reed.

4. A copy of the Treaty between Great Britain and the Unite
known as the Treaty of Washington, is hereto annexed. Will
amine articles 18 to 22 inclusive, and state that you have don
have examined the treaty.

5. What kinds of fish frequent the waters of your State, e
those which are to be thrown open to the Canadian fishermen
provisions of the Treaty of Washington? Principally Porgies a
erel, would be sought for by the fishermen of the Provinces.
also cod haddock hake, Hallibut, and many other kinds.

6. Can you give a statement of the kinds and quantities of fi
annually off the coast of your State from the years 1854 to 18

'ou can do this, please do so; and if not, please state where
iation can be procured. I cannot tell. The amount is very
e quantity taken on our coast by American Fishermen greatly
э quantity taken on the coasts of the Provinces.

are able to do so, will you state the amount and value of the
fisheries which are to be thrown open to Canadian fishermen
provisions of the Treaty of Washington? Please state them
showing the different kinds of fish, and the value of each
n not able.

quantity and value of each kind of fish are annually taken
in fishermen, and what by American fishermen, in the waters
its which are to be thrown open to competition by the Treaty
gton? The people of the Provinces take as many codfish I
ie people of the States. Of Mackerel we take far the larger
irobably three times as many. They take the greater part
ring.

inadian fishermen procure bait or supplies in the waters of
:? and, if so, to what extent and value? They get a great
iir bait from this State. They catch some and buy some.

it is the probable annual value to Canadian fishermen in being
icure bait, to land and dry their nets, and to repack and cure
in the coasts of your State, without any other restriction than
lined in the Treaty of Washington? It is a great privilege.
э bait which they procure from this State is far better tan
for taking Mackerel.

the admission of Canadian fishermen to our in-shore fisheries
detriment or hindrance to the profitable pursuit of these fish-
ar own fishermen; and if so, in what manner, and to what
iually? I think it would injure our fishermen very little.
iuld our fishing on Canadian coasts injure theirs.

it number of Canadian vessels and boats are engaged in the
if your State, and what are their tonnage and value, and the
men employed upon them? I cannot tell. It is not large.

ihe fisheries pursued by American fishermen off the Atlantic
the British North American Provinces, what proportion con-
deep-sea fisheries, and what proportion of the in-shore fisheries?
three-fourths are deep sea fisheries.

what description of fish do American fishermen pursue the
sheries? Mackerel and Herring.

on state that the in shore fisheries are pursued wholly or
mackerel, please state what proportion of mackerel is taken
in-shore limits, and what proportion is taken outside of the
mits? The off-shore fishery has been the most valuable for
irty years.

ot much the larger quantity of mackerel caught by American
off the coasts of British America taken outside the in-shore
d in the summer season especially, are not mackerel generally
he banks, in the Gulf of Saint Lawrence, and not within shore?
larger quantity is taken outside the in-shore limits. Mackerel
illy found on the banks. When we can catch Mackerel off
· are of superior quality to those caught in-shore.

Colonial fishermen injured by permitting American fishermen

quantities of bait are thrown out, than when fishing alone ?   T|
The small fishermen of the Provinces are in the habit of follow
American fleet.

19. What is the best bait for the mackerel, and where is it pri
taken ?   How much of it is taken within three miles of the sh‹
what is the annual value to the United States, or to the Britis
inces, as the case may be, to take such bait within three mile‹
shore ?   Porgie Bait.   Taken on the coasts of this State.   The
part is taken within three miles of shore.   The United States fi‹
take none on the coasts of the Province.   The fishermen of the P|
will derive great benefit from the privilege of taking Bait on ou|
as they have none on their own.

20. Please state as to each class of fisheries carried on fro
State or district, the cost of fitting out, equipping, furnishing, a|
ning a vessel for carrying it on, estimating it by the average h
the cruise.   State, as far as possible, in detail the elements whi‹
make up the cost of taking and delivering a full cargo and of re
to the home port.   It will cost to fit a vessel of one hundred to|
$2,000 to $3,000 for a codfishing cruise.   For a mackerel crui
$1,200 to $1,500.

21. When you have fully answered question 20, please ans
same questions as to vessels fitted out, equipped, furnished, and
from the Dominion of Canada, including Prince Edward Island, ‹
you are able to do so.   If you state that there is any difference |
the cost of the Canadian and the cost of the American vessel
respects, explain what the difference is and the reason for it.   I
cost less.   Salt, cordage, lines, and nearly all their fishing tack
less.   And they can build vessels for much less than we can.

22. Are you acquainted, and for how long, and in what capaci·
the fisheries on the coasts of Nova Scotia, New Brunswick, Qu
Prince Edward Island, or with either, and if either, with which |
fisheries ?   I am acquainted with the cod and Mackerel fishery. |
been skipper of a fisherman for the last thirty years.

23. What kind of fish frequent the waters of those coasts wl
to be thrown open to American fishermen under the provision‹
Treaty of Washington ?   Mackerel chiefly.

24. Please state in detail the amount and the annual value (s
1854 to 1872, inclusive) of the fisheries which are so to be thro‹
to American fishermen ; also the amount and the annual value
catch in the adjacent waters which are more than three miles
from the shore ; please state these facts in detail.   I do not kn‹

25. Do American fishermen procure bait in the waters withi
miles of the coast of the Dominion of Canada ?   If so, to what
and what is the value ?   They do not:

26. Do not the American fishermen purchase supplies in the
the Dominion of Canada, including bait, ice, salt, barrels, pro
and various articles for the use of the men engaged in the fisher
so, in what ports, and to what extent ?   And, if that is the c‹
not an advantage to the ports of the Dominion to have the
vessels of the United States in their neighborhood during the
season ?   Explain why it is so, and estimate, if you can, the mon‹
of that advantage.   They do in the ports of Canso, Charlotteto‹
Hood and Halifax.   They do this to a large extent ; and will do
more under the Treaty of Washington than ever before.   Ves
now refit there.   The advantage of this trade to the people of tl
inces will be very great.

ave you any knowledge of how many United States fishing-ves-
ly engage in the fisheries off the Atlantic coasts of the British
American Provinces, (excluding Newfoundland,) both without
in the three-mile limit? If so, state how many vessels are so
, what is the value of their tonnage, what is the number of men
d annually on such vessels, what sorts of fish are taken there,
the annual value of all the fish so caught, and what is the pro-
or probable proportion, in your judgment, of the amount of such
ken within three miles of the British coast, and of the amount
tside of the three-mile limit? I cannot tell how many: it is a
ge fleet. The proportion which would fish within the three-mile
very small.
hat percentage of value, if any, is, in your judgment, added to
ts of a voyage by the privilege to fish within three marine miles
oast; whence is such profit derived; and in what does it con-
t is not worth over five per cent. We used to buy a license to
ore when we could buy them for fifty cents per ton. After the
as raised we could not make it pay to buy license.
o the American fishermen gain under the Treaty of Washington
able rights of landing to dry nets and cure fish, or to repack
r to transship cargoes, which were not theirs before; if so, what
e rights, and what do you estimate, them to be worth annually,
ggregate? I do not think they do.
not the Treaty of Washington, so far as the fishing clauses are
ed, more, or quite as, beneficial to the people of the British North
an Provinces as to the people of the United States? It is more
al to the people of the Provinces.
What is the amount and value of colonial cargoes of fish of all
ions which are annually shipped to the United States? I do
w. They ship all their fat mackerel to the United States.
or all No. 1 and No. 2 mackerel, for the larger part of the fat
, and for all No. 1 salmon, does not the United States afford the
arket? Yes.
you know what amount of duties is annually paid to the United
on fish and fish-oil imported from Canada, which are to be made
der the provisions of the Treaty of Washington, please state
nnually, and by classes, from 1854 to 1872, inclusive. I do not
The amount must be large.
you know what amount of duties is annually paid in Canada
and fish-oil imported from the United States, which are to be
ee under the provisions of the said Treaty, please state them an-
and by classes, from 1854 to 1872, inclusive. There has been
tle exportation of these articles to the Provinces during the last
rs.
he object of these inquiries is to ascertain whether the rights in
of fishing, and fishermen, and fish, which were granted to Great
by the Treaty of Washington, are or are not a just equivalent
rights in those respects which were granted by said treaty to
ited States. If you know anything bearing upon this subject
you have not already stated in reply to previous questions, please
as fully as if you had been specially inquired of in respect of it.
e that the priveleges of bringing their fish to our markets free of
nsidering that they can catch them cheaper than we can will stim-
eir fishing industries much more than the prevelege of fishing
will stimulate ours. I also think that the increased trade which
rue to the Provincial towns on the coast will of itself compensate

for all the detriment that can result to their fishermen from o
fishing.

THOMAS]

Sworn to and subscribed before me this tenth day of June
ORRIN McFADD
Collector of

No. 3.

[CONFIDENTIAL.]

QUESTIONS RESPECTING THE FISHERIES TO BE PR(
ED TO ——— ——— ON BEHALF OF THE UNITED S'

1. What is your name and age, and in what town and Sta
reside? (William Eaton) (58) Castine, Maine
2. What opportunities have you had for becoming acquai
the American and Canadian Atlantic sea-fisheries, and the va
catch of the different kinds of fish? Have been employed in
ican and Canadian, Cod and Mackerel fisheries, sixteen years
3. Can you give the names of other persons in your nei
who have also had the opportunity of obtaining similar inf
If so, please give some such name. Capt. Joseph Stearn
Maine, also Capt James Torrey Deer Isle Maine.
4. A copy of the treaty between Great Britain and the Unit
known as the Treaty of Washington, is hereto annexed. W
amine articles 18 to 22 inclusive, and state that you have do
have examined the above-named articles
5. What kinds of fish frequent the waters of your State,
those which are to be thrown open to the Canadian fishermen
provisions of the Treaty of Washington? Cod, Halibut, Hake,
Menhaden Pollock and Herring
6. Can you give a statement of the kinds and quantities of
annually off the coast of your State from the years 1854 to 1
sive? If you can do this please do so; and if not, please st
that information can be procured.
7. If you are able to do so, will you state the amount and va
American fisheries which are to be thrown open to Canadian
under the provisions of the treaty of Washington? Please sta
detail, showing the different kinds of fish, and the value of
8. What quantity and value of each kind of fish are annu
by Canadian fishermen, and what by American fishermen, in
off the coasts which are to be thrown open to competition by
of Washington?
9. Do Canadian fishermen procure bait or supplies in the
your State? and if so, to what extent and value? They pro
bait and Menhaden, mostly by purchase.
10. What is the probable annual value to Canadian fisherm
ing able to procure bait, to land and dry their nets, and to r
cure their fish on the coasts of your State, without any other
than that contained in the Treaty of Washington?
11. Will the admission of Canadian fishermen to our in-sho
cause any detriment or hinderance to the profitable pursui
fisheries by our own fishermen; and if so, in what manner, an
extent annually?
12. What number of Canadian vessels and boats are enga

s of your State, and what are their tonnage and value, and the
of men employed upon them?
f the fisheries pursued by American fishermen off the Atlantic
of the British North American Provinces, what proportion con-
the deep-sea fisheries, and what proportion of the in-shore fish-
The in-shore and deep-sea fisheries, in my opinion are of about
alue
or what description of fish do American fishermen pursue the in-
isheries? Mostly Mackerel & Herring, but considerable quan-
f Cod Halibut Hake & Haddock are caught in shore
f you state that the in-shore fisheries are pursued wholly or chiefly
kerel, please state what proportion of mackerel is taken within
shore limits, and what proportion is taken outside of the in-shore
One third in, and two thirds off shore.
s not much the larger quantity of mackerel caught by American
en off the coasts of British America taken outside the in-shore
and in the summer season especially, are not mackerel generally
on the banks, in the Gulf of St. Lawrence, and not within shore?
the larger quantities are taken outside the inshore limits
Are Colonial fishermen injured by permitting American fishermen
in Colonial inshore waters? They are benefitted by the inshore
by reason of the fish being "tolled" inshore by the large quan-
bait thrown by the fishermen
Are not more fish caught by Colonial fishermen, when fishing, in-
alongside a fleet of American fishing vessels, from which large
ties of bait are thrown out, than when fishing alone? There is
ly more fish caught
What is the best bait for the mackerel, and where is it principally
? How much of it is taken within three miles of the shore, and
is the annual value to the United States, or to the British Prov-
as the case may be, to take such bait within three miles of the
Clam bait and Menhaden is the principal bait, taken mostly on
ist of Maine and Massachusetts
Please state as to each class of fisheries carried on from your State
rict, the cost of fitting out, equipping, furnishing, and manning a
for carrying it on, estimating it by the average length of the
State as far as possible, in detail the elements which go to
up the cost of taking and delivering a full cargo and of returning
home port. It will cost for a vessel of 100 tons for a 4 months
$5,000, in the cod fisheries A vessel of the same size could be
and manned for a mackerel cruise for about $3,000 for the same

When you have fully answered question 20, please answer the
uestions as to vessels fitted out, equipped, furnished, and manned
he Dominion of Canada, including Prince Edward Island, so far
are able to do so. If you state that there is any difference be-
the cost of the Canadian and the cost of the American vessel in
respects, explain what the difference is, and the reason for it.
ist of vessels fittings and maning &c would not be so much be-
the custom house fees on salt are not so much, the pay of crews
also the cost of bbls, cables, anchers, and some kinds of provis-
e less. Their vessels cost about one third less than ours.
Are you acquainted, and for how long, and in what capacity, with
heries on the coasts of Nova Scotia, New Brunswick, Quebec, or
Edward Island, or with either, and if either, with which of these

fisheries? I am, or have been for a period of 15 years in
Master of vessels engaged in the cod and mackerel fishiries

23. What kind of fish frequent the waters of those coast;
to be thrown open to American fishermen under the provisi
Treaty of Washington? principly cod, and mackerel.

24. Please state in detail the amount and the annual valu
1854 to 1872 inclusive) of the fisheries which are so to be t
to American fishermen; also the amount and the annual v
catch in the adjacent waters which are more than three m
from the shore; please state these facts in detail.

25. Do American fishermen procure bait in the waters v
miles of the coast of the Dominion of Canada? If so, to v
and what is the value? Not to a great extent. Some cape
and alewives are taken.

26. Do not the American fishermen purchase supplies in
the Dominion of Canada, including bait, ice, salt, barrels,
and various articles for the use of the men engaged in th
If so, in what ports, and to what extent? And, if that is
it not an advantage to the ports of the Dominion to have
vessels of the United States in their neighborhood during
season? Explain why it is so, and estimate, if you can,
value of that advantage. They do obtain the articles menti
in Port Hood Cape Canso, Charlotte Town, Port Mulgrave ?

27. Have you any knowledge of how many United St;
vessels yearly engage in the fisheries off the Atlantic cc
British North American Provinces, (excluding Newfoun
without and within the three-mile limit? If so, state how n
are so engaged, what is the value of their tonnage, what is
of men employed annually on such vessels, what sorts of fi
there, what is the annual value of all the fish so caught, and
proportion, or probable proportion, in your judgment, of tl
such catch taken within three miles of the British coast;
amount taken outside of the three-mile limit?

28. What percentage of value, if any, is, in your judgme
the profits of a voyage by the privilege to fish within three
of the coast; whence is such profit derived; and in what do
In my experience the advantage has been very little.

29. Do the American fishermen gain under the Treaty of
any valuable rights of landing to dry nets and cure fish,
them, or to transsbip cargoes, which were not theirs before
are those rights, and what do you estimate them to be wo
in the aggregate? Drying and curing don't amount to
priviledge of transshipping cargoes is of some advantage.

30. Is not the Treaty of Washington, so far as the fishin
concerned, more, or quite as, beneficial to the people of the;
American Provinces as to the people of the United States?
ion the advantage is in their favor.

31. What is the amount and value of colonial cargoes of
scriptions which are annually shipped to the United State;

32. For all No. 1 and No. 2 mackerel, for the larger p
herring, and for all No. 1 salmon, does not the United Sta
only market.

33. If you know what amount of duties is annually paid
States on fish and fish-oil imported from Canada which a
free under the provisions of the Treaty of Washington, ple
annually, and by classes, from 1854 to 1872, inclusive.

'you know what amount of duties is annually paid in Canada on
fish-oil imported from the United States, which are to be made
.er the provisions of the said treaty, please state them annually,
classes, from 1854 to 1872, inclusive.

he object of these inquiries is to ascertain whether the rights in
of fishing, and fishermen, and fish, which were granted to Great
by the Treaty of Washington, are, or are not a just equivalent
rights in those respects which were granted by said treaty to the
States. If you know anything bearing upon this subject which
·e not already stated in reply to previous questions, please state
ly as if you had been specially inquired of in respect of it.

WILLIAM EATON.

CASTINE, July 5th, 1873

nally appeared the above named William Eaton, and on oath
at the foregoing statement by him signed is true to the best of
wledge and belief.
·e me

WM. H. SARGENT, Jus. Pea.

No. 4.

[CONFIDENTIAL.]

IONS RESPECTING THE FISHERIES TO BE PRO-
NDED TO ——— ——— ON BEHALF OF THE UNITED
rES.

hat is your name and age, and in what town and State do you
    L. G. Crane; Gouldsborough Maine.
hat opportunities have you had for becoming acquainted with
.erican and Canadian Atlantic sea-fisheries, and the value of the
f the different kinds of fish? Have owned fishermen, and have
.hing.
.n you give the names of other persons in your neighborhood
.ve also had the opportunity of obtaining similar information?
lease give some such name. Hadlock & Stanley.
copy of the treaty between Great Britain and the United States,
as the Treaty of Washington, is hereto annexed. Will you ex-
.rticles 18 to 22, inclusive, and state that you have done so? I
ramined them closely.
.hat kinds of fish frequent the waters of your State, especially
.hich are to be thrown open to the Canadian fishermen under the
ons of the Treaty of Washington? Codfish, Mackerel, Herring
., Halibut
.n you give a statement of the kinds and quantities of fish taken
ly off the coast of your State from the years 1854 to 1872, inclu-
If you can do this please do so; and, if not, please state where
formation can be procured? Could not answer correctly.
you are able to do so, will you state the amount and value of the
.an fisheries which are to be thrown open to Canadian fishermen
.he provisions of the Treaty of Washington? Please state them in
.showing the different kinds of fish, and the value of each kind.
ot answer this correctly.
7hat quantity and value of each kind of fish are annually taken
.adian fishermen, and what by American fishermen, in the waters

off the coasts which are to be thrown open to competition by the Treaty of Washington? I think that both nations are on equal footings.

9. Do Canadian fishermen procure bait or supplies in the waters of your State? and if so, to what extent and value? They do procure their mackerel bait. Bait for a vessel of 12 hands will cost three hundred dollars

10. What is the probable annual value to Canadian fishermen in being able to procure bait, to land and dry their nets, and to repack and cure their fish on the coasts of your State, without any other restriction than that contained in the Treaty of Washington?

11. Will the admission of Canadian fishermen to our in-shore fisheries cause any detriment or hinderance to the profitable pursuit of these fisheries by our own fishermen; and if so, in what manner, and to what extent annually? I think they would.

12. What number of Canadian vessels and boats are engaged in the fisheries of your State, and what are their tonnage and value, and the number of men employed upon them? There never has been any, but probably will be equal to our own.

13. Of the fisheries pursued by American fishermen off the Atlantic coasts of the British North American Provinces, what proportion consists of the deep-sea fisheries, and what proportion of the in-shore fisheries? Seven-eighths of our fishermen use the offshore fisheries.

14. For what description of fish do American fishermen pursue the inshore fisheries? Mackerel altogether.

15. If you state that the in-shore fisheries are pursued wholly or chiefly for mackerel, please state what proportion of mackerel is taken within the in-shore limits, and what proportion is taken outside of the in-shore limits? One-eighth inshore

16. Is not much the larger quantity of mackerel caught by American fishermen off the coasts of British America taken outside the in-shore limits; and in the summer season especially, are not mackerel generally found on the banks, in the Gulf of Saint Lawrence, and not within shore? Much the largest quantity taken outside the three mile limit.

17. Are Colonial fishermen injured by permitting American fishermen to fish in Colonial in shore waters? Not any.

18. Are not more fish caught by Colonial fishermen, when fishing in shore, alongside a fleet of American fishing-vessels, from which large quantities of bait are thrown out, than when fishing alone? If it was not for the American fishermen the Canadian fishermen would be unable to get any fish in their small boats.

19. What is the best bait for the mackerel, and where is it principally taken? How much of it is taken within three miles of the shore, and what is the annual value to the United States, or to the British Provinces, as the case may be, to take such bait within three miles of the shore? Porgies & Clams procured on the Coast of Maine—seven eighths within three miles of the shore.

20. Please state as to each class of fisheries carried on from your State or district, the cost of fitting out, equipping, furnishing, and manning vessel for carrying it on, estimating it by the average length of the cruise. State, as far as possible, in detail, the elements which go to make up the cost of taking and delivering a full cargo and of returning to the home port? A vessel of one hundred tons manned by fifteen men for three months voyage. Barrels $5,00. Salt five hundred bushels at $2.20 per Hhd. Bait $500. Victualling the vessel $300.

21. When you have fully answered question 20, please answer the same questions as to vessels fitted out, equipped, furnished, and manned

ninion of Canada, including Prince Edward Island, so far
le to do so. If you state that there is any difference be.
st of the Canadian and the cost of the American Vessel in
.s, explain what the difference is, and the reason for it. The
essel is not more than one half as much, and the outfits are
re than half as much as our Vessels.
u acquainted, and for how long, and in what capacity, with
on the coasts of Nova Scotia, New Brunswick, Quebec, or
ird Island, or with either, and if either, with which of these
   own fishermen and fitted out fishermen, and have been
lf for 20 years more or less. The principal fishing in the
Cod fish & Mackerel, and the greatest portion taken on the

kind of fish frequent the waters of those coasts which are
) open to American fishermen under the provisions of the
'ashington ? Cod & Mackerel.
) state in detail the amount and the annual value (say from
  inclusive) of the fisheries which are to be thrown open to
shermen; also the amount and the annual value of the catch
ent waters which are more than three miles distant from the
se state these facts in detail.
merican fishermen procure bait in the waters within three
; coast of the Dominion of Canada ? If so, to what extent,
, the value ? They do not.
)t the American fishermen purchase supplies in the ports of
on of Canada, including bait, ice, salt, barrels, provisions,
i articles for the use of the men engaged in the fisheries?
at ports, and to what extent ? And, if that is the case, is it
intago to the ports of the Dominion to have the fishing-ves-
Jnited States in their neighborhood during the fishing sea-
ain why it is so, and estimate, if you can, the money-value
antage. We sometimes procure barrels and bait and fresh
n Canso and many ports on Prince Edwards Island and at
's.
, you any knowledge of how many United States fishing-
cly engage in the fisheries off the Atlantic coasts of the Brit-
merican Provinces, (excluding Newfoundland,) both without
the three-mile limit ? If so, state how many vessels are so
bat is the value of their tonnage, what is the number of men
nnually on such vessels, what sorts of fish are taken there,
annual value of all the fish so caught, and what is the pro-
probable proportion, in your judgment, of the amount of
taken within three miles of the British coast, and of the
en outside of the three-mile limit ? Five hundred Vessels,
lue $7,000 each; seven eighths without the three-mile limit.
; percentage of value, if any, is, in your judgment, added to
)f a voyage by the privilege to fish within three marine miles
t: whence is such profit derived; and in what does it con-
e
ie American fishermen gain under the Treaty of Washington
le rights of landing to dry nets and cure fish, or to repack .
transship cargoes, which were not theirs before; if so, what
ghts, and what do you estimate them to be worth annually,
egate ? None at all
t the Treaty of Washington, so far as the fishing clauses are
more,· or quite as, beneficial to the people of the British

North American Provinces as to the people of the United States? I think it is more

31. What is the amount and value of colonial cargoes of fish of all descriptions which are annually shipped to the United States?

32. For all No. 1 and No. 2 mackerel, for the larger part of the fat herring, and for all No. 1 salmon, does not the United States afford the only market. Yes

33. If you know what amount of duties is annually paid to the United States on fish and fish-oil imported from Canada, which are to be made free under the provisions of the Treaty of Washington, please state them annually, and by classes, from 1854 to 1872, inclusive.

34. If you know what amount of duties is annually paid in Canada on fish and fish-oil imported from the United States, which are to be made free under the provisions of the said Treaty, please state them annually, and by classes, from 1854 to 1872, inclusive.

35. The object of these inquiries is to ascertain whether the rights in respect of fishing, and fishermen, and fish, which were granted to Great Britain by the Treaty of Washington, are or are not a just equivalent for the rights in those respects which were granted by said Treaty to the United States. If you know anything bearing upon this subject which you have not already stated in reply to previous questions, please state it as fully as if you had been specially inquired of in respect of it. I think it is of a great deal more value to the Province than it is to the American fishermen, and eventually will be a great injury to the interest of the American fishermen.

L G. CRANE,
Keeper Seguin Light Maine

Sworn to before me this 2d day of July, 1873

E. S J NEALLEY,
Collector.

No. 5.

[CONFIDENTIAL.]

QUESTIONS RESPECTING THE FISHERIES TO BE PROPOUNDED TO —— —— ON BEHALF OF THE UNITED STATES.

1. What is your name and age, and in what town and State do you reside? Henry E. Willard—35 years old—Reside in Cape Elizabeth.

2. What opportunities have you had for becoming acquainted with the American and Canadian Atlantic sea-fisheries, and the value of the catch of the different kinds of fish? I have been a fisherman for twenty-four years—master of a fishing vessel 9 years.

3. Can you give the names of other persons in your neighborhood who have also had the opportunity of obtaining similar information? If so, please give some such name. Geo W. Willard, Caleb Willard, John F. Lovitt Morris Cobb, Isaac Cobb, & others

4. A copy of the Treaty between Great Britain and the United States, known as the Treaty of Washington, is hereto annexed. Will you examine articles 18 to 22 inclusive, and state that you have done so? I have examined articles 18 & 22 of the "treaty of Washington"

5. What kinds of fish frequent the waters of your State, especially those which are to be thrown open to the Canadian fishermen under the provisions of the Treaty of Washington? Cod & Haddock, Mackrel, Pollock Herring, Pohagen, Halibut &c.

give a statement of the kinds and quantities of fish taken
the coast of your State from the years 1854 to 1872 inclu.
an do this, please do so; and if not, please state where that
an be procured. Cannot state.

re able to do so, will you state the amount and value of the
ieries which are to be thrown open to Canadian fishermen
visions of the Treaty of Washington ? Please state them
wing the different kinds of fish, and the value of each
ie kinds named in answer to question 5, which may be
it value to the Canadian fishermen, as they are now to
iermen.

iantity and value of each kind of fish are annually taken
fishermen, and what by American fishermen in the waters
which are to be thrown open to competition by the Treaty
n ? I cannot say.

adian fishermen procure bait or supplies in the waters of
and, if so, to what extent and value ? They do obtain con-
t in the waters of this State.

is the probable annual value to Canadian fishermen in
o procure bait, to land and dry their nets, and to repack
eir fish on the coasts of your State, without any other re-
l that contained in the Treaty of Washington ? Will de.
it extent the Canadian fishermen may pursue the fishing
ur waters.

ie admission of Canadian fishermen to our inshore fisheries
etriment or hinderance to the profitable pursuit of these
ur own fishermen ; and, if so, in what manner, and to what
lly ? Will open a competition for winter and early fishing
; American markets.

number of Canadian vessels and boats are engaged in the
our State, and what are their tonnage and value, and the
en employed upon them ? Cannot tell.

fisheries pursued by American fishermen off the Atlantic
British North American Provinces, what proportion con-
leep-sea fisheries, and what proportion of the in-shore fish-
one-fourth are caught in-shore. Chiefly caught out-side
iat description of fish do American fishermen pursue the
iries ? Mackrel—sometimes Herrings

state that the in-shore fisheries are pursued wholly or
ackerel, please state what proportion of mackerel is taken
-shore limits, and what proportion is taken outside of the
ts ? Not one-fourth of the mackerel caught are taken in-
fly taken out side.

much the larger quantity of mackerel caught by American
the coasts of British America taken outside the in-shore
a the summer season especially, are not mackerel generally
banks, in the Gulf of Saint Lawrence, and not within shore ?
en chiefly out side the in-shore limits—on the banks and in
Saint Lawrence.

lonial fishermen injured by permitting American fishermen
nial in-shore waters ? I should think no material injury.
t more fish caught by Colonial fishermen, when fishing inside a fleet of American fishing-vessels, from which large
' bait are thrown out, than when fishing alone ? Yes for
efly on the bait thrown over by American fishermen.
s the best bait for the mackerel, and where is it principally

taken ? How much of it is taken within three mile
and what is the annual value to the United States, o
Provinces, as the case may be, to take such bait withii
the shore ? Porgies are used chiefly for Mackrel Bait
taken on the Coast of Maine almost exclusively withir
the Shore.

20. Please state as to each class of fisheries carried on
or district, the cost of fitting out, equipping, furnishing
a vessel for carrying it on, estimating it by the averag
cruise. State, as far as possible, in detail the element
make up the cost of taking and delivering a full cargo a
to the home port. For a season—of say three trips—Ma
(two mouths to a trip.) Will cost $2,500, for Bait, Sali
& Eleven men at $40 per month—6 mos—$2,640 in a
lines, Hooks &c., $1,500.—Making $6,640 for 45 ton vesse
—or $2,210 per trip, *without* reconing cost of Vessel.

21. When you have fully answered question 20, plea
same questions as to vessels fitted out, equipped, furnishe
from the Dominion of Canada, including Prince Edware
as you are able to do so. If you state that there is an
tween the cost of the Canadian and the cost of the Am
these respects, explain what the difference is and the
Canadian Vessels are built of Soft woods & cheaply
cost I think, much more than half as much as Americai
not provision as expensively as American fishing Vessel

22. Are you acquainted, and for how long, and in wha
the fisheries on the coasts of Nova Scotia, New Brunsw
Prince Edward Island, or with either, and if either, witt
fisheries ? Am acquainted with Nova Scotia & Prince
fisheries—have fished there for four seasons.

23. What kind of fish frequent the waters of those c
to be thrown open to American fishermen under the p
Treaty of Washington ? Mackrel Herring, Pollock, Coo

24. Please state in detail the amount and the annual
1854 to 1872 inclusive) of the fisheries which are so to
to American fishermen; also the amount and the annu
catch in the adjacent waters which are more than thre
from the shore; please state these facts in detail. Can

25. Do American fishermen procure bait in the wate
miles of the coast of the Dominion of Canada ? If so,
and what is the value ? Occasionally Herring for Codf
valued at 10$ a season for each vessel.

26. Do not the American fishermen purchase supplie
the Dominion of Canada, including bait, ice, salt, ba
and various articles for the use of the men engaged in tl
so, in what ports and to what extent ? And, if that is t
an advantage to the ports of the Dominion to have th
of the United States in their neighborhood during th
Explain why it is so, and estimate, if you can, the mon
advantage. American fishermen do procure the above
Canso, Charlottetown P. E. I. Pictou N. S. Port-Hood
ports, & this trade must be of considerable value to
ports.

27. Have you any knowledge of how many United S
sels yearly engaged in the fisheries off the Atlantic co
ish North American Provinces, (excluding Newfoundlai

he three-mile limit ? If so, state how many vessels are so
at is the value of their tonnage, what is the number of men
mually on such vessels, what sorts of fish are taken there,
annual value of all the fish so caught, and what is the pro-
robable proportion, in your judgment, of the amount of such
within three miles of the British coast, and of the amount
.e of the three-mile limit ? Should think that 175 to 200
ing at 45 to 50 tons, averaging eleven men each, go annualley
h Provinces for Mackrel & will average, I should think, 180
el each for the seasons catch—of which, more than ⅜ are
de of the " three-mile-limit."
percentage of value, if any, is, in your judgment, added to
f a voyage by the privilege to fish within three marine miles
; whence is such profit derived ; and in what does it consist ?
nk it more profitable for a vessel *not* to go within three miles
—more fish would be taken, but the restriction is an annoy.

ie American fishermen gain under the Treaty of Washing-
nable rights of landing to dry nets and cure fish, or to repack
transship cargoes, which were not theirs before ; if so, what
ghts, and what do you estimate them to be worth annually,
egate ? I do not think the gain of any great advantage to
'ishermen.
; the Treaty of Washington, so far as the fishing clauses are
more, or quite as, beneficial to the people of the British North
Provinces as to the people of the United States ? I know
the Reciprocity treaty, that several persons—citizens in the
so (Charlottetown Port Hood) & other places got wealthy
rican fishing trade. & since its repeal those persons have
; trade—which I have no doubt this treaty will restore in a

; is the amount and value of colonial cargoes of fish of all
s which are annually shipped to the United. States ? Cannot
ill No. 1 and No. 2 mackerel, for the larger part of the fat
d for all No. 1 salmon, does not the United States afford the
t. · the only foreign market for Canadians
u know what amount of duties is annually paid to the United
sh and fish-oil imported from Canada, which are to be made
the provisions of the Treaty of Washington, please state
lly, and by classes, from 1854 to 1872, inclusive.
                                                H E WILLARD

y and truly swear that the foregoing statements by me sub-
true according to my best knowledge and belief. So help me

                                        H E WILLARD

fore me this sixteenth day of June A. D. 1873.
                        M. N. RICH (SEAL.)
                        Dep. Collector of Customs.

No. 6.

[CONFIDENTIAL.]

QUESTIONS RESPECTING THE FISHERIES
ED TO ——— ——— ON BEHALF OF THE

1. What is your name and age, and in what tow
side? Name Albert T Trufant Age, 39 years ¿
of Harpswell
   Q. What opportunities have you had for beco·
the American and Canadian Atlantic sea-fisheries
catch of the different kinds of fish? I have been
ing & Cureing Fish for the last 13 years and ha
Lawrence a Fishing
   3. Can you give the names of other persons in y
have also had the opportunity of obtaining simila
please give some such name.
   4. A copy of the Treaty between Great Britain
known as the Treaty of Washington, is hereto a
amine articles 18 to 22 inclusive, and state that y
   5. What kinds of fish frequent the waters of
those which are to be thrown open to the Canadi·
provisions of the Treaty of Washington?
   6. Can you give a statement of the kinds and ·
annually off the coast of your State from the ye
sive? If you can do this please do so; and if
that information can be procured.
   7. If you are able to do so, will you state the
the American fisheries which are to be thrown o]
men under the provisions of the Treaty of Wasl
them in detail, showing the different kinds of fisl
kind.
   8. What quantity and value of each kind of f
by Canadian fishermen, and what by American f
off the coasts which are to be thrown open to con
of Washington?
   9. Do Canadian fishermen procure bait or suppl
State? And if so, to what extent and value?
state to What extent
   10. What is the probable annual value to Can·
able to procure bait, to land and dry their nets,
their fish on the coasts of your State, without ar
that contained in the Treaty of Washington?
   11. Will the admission of Canadian fishermen
cause any detriment or hinderance to the profita
cries by our own fishermen; and if so, in wh:
extent annually? I think it will as they can Br
Duty and they can Fit & have their Vessels at
   12. What number of Canadian vessels and b
fisheries of your State, and what are their tonі
number of men employed upon them?
   13. Of the fisheries pursued by American fis
coasts of the British North American Provinc·
sists of the deep-sea fisheries, and what propor
cries?

ιat description of fish do American fishermen pursue the
ιries? for mackerel
state that the in-shore fisheries are pursued wholly or chiefly
, please state what proportion of mackerel is taken within
limits, and what proportion is taken outside of the in-shore
Iy Opinion their is not one Eight taken within the Shore
Three Miles.
much the larger quantity of mackerel caught by American
' the coasts of British America taken outside the in-shore
.n the summer season especially, are not mackerel generally
e banks, in the Gulf of Saint Lawrence, and not within
γ are
lonial fishermen injured by permitting American fishermen
onial in-shore waters? they are not
ιt more fish caught by colonial fishermen, when fishing inside a fleet of American fishing-vessels, from which large
f bait are thrown out, than when fishing alone? they are
is the best bait for the mackerel, and where is it principally
w much of it is taken within three miles of the shore, and
annual value to the United States, or to the British Prov·
ι case may be, to take such bait within three miles of the
ιhaden and I should Say that Seven Eights are taken within
of the Shore as to the Value I cannot State but it is of
ι value as it is the Prinsable Bait used for Mackerel
ι state as to each class of fisheries carried on from γoυr
trict, the cost of fitting out, equipping, furnishing, and maⁿ·
ιl for carrying it on, estimating it by the average length of
State as far as possible, in detail the elements which go to
ι cost of taking and delivering a full cargo and of returning
port. the Prinsaple Class of Fishing presude from Maine is
ckerel Fishery the relative cost of Fitting for Cod Fishing
.0 3,000 as to sise of Vessel and the length of the time
from 4 to 12 Weeks and the Principle Cost is Provisions
As for Mackerel Fishing it Cost less than for Cod Fishing
Vessells and their everage length of time to complete a
ιm 8 to 12 Weeks the Cost for Fitting for a Mackerel voyge
to 2000 as to beam & sise of Vessel.
ι you have fully answered question 20, please answer the
ιons as to vessels fitted out, equipped, furnished, and manned
ιminion of Canada, including Prince Edward Island. so far
ιble to do so. If you state that there is any difference between
the Canadian and the cost of the American vessel in these
:plain what the difference is and the reason for it. As for
ι Manning Vessells from the Provinces they can be Fitted &
less cost than from the States in the first place there is no
ι as it takes from 1 to 2 Weeks each why to get to the
rounds and they can build their Vessells at a less cost than
ιates as timber and all Material is Cheaper and also labor
ιan presue the Fishing Business at a less cost than the Ves-
ιhe States in every respect.
you acquainted, and for how long, and in what capacity,
ιheries on the coasts of Nova Scotia, New Brunswick, Que-
ιnce Edward Island, or with either, and if either, with which
ιheries?
ιt kind of fish frequent the waters of those coasts which are

to be thrown open to American fishermen under the provisions of the Treaty of Washington ?   Cod & Mackerel

24. Please state in detail the amount and the annual value (say from 1854 to 1872 inclusive) of the fisheries which are so to be thrown open to American fishermen; also the amount and the annual value of the catch in the adjacent waters which are more than three miles distant from the shore; please state these facts in detail.

25. Do American fishermen procure bait in the waters within three miles of the coast of the Dominion of Canada ? If so, to what extent, and what is the value ? They do Procure Bait sometimes within 3 Miles of the Shore but the Value is but of little importance as it is Mostley Herring Fish and of but little Value except for Bait

26. Do not the American fishermen purchase supplies in the ports of the Dominion of Canada, including bait, ice, salt, barrels, provisions, and various articles for the use of the men engaged in the fisheries ? If so, in what ports, and to what extent ? And, if that is the case, is it not an advantage to the ports of the Dominion to have the fishing-vessels of the United States in their neighborhood during the fishing season ? Explain why it is so, and estimate, if you can, the money-value of that advantage. They do Procure suplies and also Ice, Salt Barrells &c and it is of great advantage to the Provinces to Sell to the American Fishing Vessels they Buy in evry Harbor of any note in the Dominion of Novascotia Prince Edwards Island Cape Briton & the North Shore of the Gulf of Lower Canada I canot State the Vallue but it must be a Large Amount

27. Have you any knowledge of how many United States fishing-vessels yearly engage in the fisheries off the Atlantic coasts of the British North American Provinces, (excluding Newfoundland,) both without and within the three-mile limit ? If so, state how many vessels are so engaged, what is the value of their tonnage, what is the number of men employed annually on such vessels, what sorts of fish are taken there, what is the annual value of all the fish so caught, and what is the proportion, or probable proportion, in your judgment, of the amount of such catch taken within three miles of the British coast, and of the amount taken outside of the three-mile limit ? I cannot State What Number of Vessels ar yearley engaged in the Fisherey of the British Provinces but should from 2 to 300 and they are Mostly Fishing for Cod & Mackerel the everage Crews Consist from 7 to 12 or 15 Men as to sise of Vessels and I should say that but one eight of the Fish are caught within the 3 Miles limets of the Shore

28. What percentage of value, if any, is, in your judgment, added to the profits of a voyage by the privilege to fish within three marine miles of the coast; whence is such profit derived; and in what does it consist ? I should say that I do not consider 10 per cent is added to the privalige of Fishing within the 3 Miles limets and that consist of Mackerel & Bait taken within the limets

29. Do the American fishermen gain under the Treaty of Washington any valuable rights of landing to dry nets and cure fish, or to re-pack them, or to transship cargoes, which were not theirs before ; if so, what are those rights, and what do you estimate them to be worth annually, in the aggregate ?

30. Is not the Treaty of Washington, so far as the fishing clauses are concerned, more, or quite as, beneficial to the people of the British North American Provinces as to the people of the United States ? I should consider it of More advantage to the Provinces as regards the Fishing interest than to the United States

t is the amount and value of colonial cargoes of fish of all
s which are annually shipped to the United States ?
ll No. 1 and No. 2 mackerel, for the larger part of the fat her-
>r all No. 1 salmon, does not the United States afford the only
, does
u know what amount of duties is annually paid to the United
sh and fish-oil imported from Canada, which are to be made
the provisions of the Treaty of Washington, please state
lly, and by classes, from 1854 to 1872, inclusive.
u know what amount of duties is annually paid in Canada
fish-oil imported from the United States, which are to be
under the provisions of the said Treaty, please state them an-
l by classes, from 1854 to 1872, inclusive.
object of these inquiries is to ascertain whether the rights in
ishing, and fishermen, and fish, which were granted to Great
the Treaty of Washington, are or are not a just equivalent
its in those respects which were granted by said Treaty to the
tes. If you know anything bearing upon this subject which
ot already stated in reply to previous questions, please state
is if you had been specially inquired of in respect of it.

ALBERT T. TRUFANT.

STEPHEN PURINTON.

lly appeared the within named Albert T. Trufant & mad
he within instrument by him signed is true. Before me,

STEPHEN PURINTON,
Justice of the Peace.

No. 7.

[CONFIDENTIAL.]

NS RESPECTING THE FISHERIES TO BE PROPOUND-
ON BEHALF OF THE UNITED STATES.

1 G. Willard make answer to the several questions propound-
on behalf of the United States, as follows.
t is your name and age, and in what town and State do you
Enoch G. Willard,—reside in Portland, Maine—am 50 years old.
t opportunities have you had for becoming acquainted with the
and Canadian Atlantic sea-fisheries, and the value of the
he different kinds of fish ? I have been in the business of buy-
lling fish for over 20 years, and furnishing supplies and outfits
nen, and have been an importer and dealer in Salt, Pur-
er $400,000 worth of fish last year.
you give the names of other persons in your neighborhood
also had the opportunity of obtaining similar information ? If
give some such name. S. B. Chase of the house of Dana, &
rge Trefetheren, Henry Trefetheren, John Conley, Emery
A. G. Sterling, Geo. F. Lovett and others.
py of the Treaty between Great Britain and the United
own as the Treaty of Washington, is hereto annexed. Will
ine articles 18 to 22 inclusive, and state that you have done so.
amined articles 18 to 22 inclusive of the Treaty.
t kinds of fish frequent the waters of your State, especially
ch are to be thrown open to the Canadian fishermen under the
s of the Treaty of Washington. Cod, hake, haddock, macke-
g, porgies, are the principal.

6. Can you give a statement of the kinds and quantitie
annually off the coast of your State from the years 1854
sive? If you can do this, please do so; and if not, pleas
that information can be procured. The kinds are stated i
swer. The value of the fish purchased at this port, inclu
oil is about $2,200,000. Of the fish purchased here pro
twentieth part are caught on that part of the Canadian
open by the treaty,—but what portion of the nineteenth-tw
caught are taken upon the coast of this State, I am not
with anything like accuracy, nor do I know who can—
half.

7. If you are able to do so, will you state the amount an
American fisheries which are to be thrown open to Canad
under the provisions of the Treaty of Washington? Ple:
in detail, showing the different kinds of fish, and the valu
It is not within my power to give any definite answer or :
should feel certain about; to the first question I will stat
fish caught on the coast of Maine which by the treaty w
the Canadian fishermen. 1. Mackerel—this fishery is la
able, and may be made so to the Dominion fishermen if t
avail themselves of the opportunities offered. These fisł
the coast of Maine before they reach the coast to the eas
sent to the Southern markets. It is now a valuable fisher
fishermen, and will be opened to Dominion use. 2. The l
is large and important—especially on the Eastern coast.
fishery is very large. The most important district on the
Maine. The pogie taken here is fatter than any other an
oil. When the fishery is thrown open under the Treaty
fishermen will be at liberty to take pogies upon the coas
and enter into a large and profitable trade. Also to catc
the winter) cod and other fish for sale fresh in the Ame
in competition with American fishermen, and to catch
before they reach the Dominion waters, thus affording
the vessels and fishermen of the Provinces at times whe
upon their own coast.

8. What quantity and value of each kind of fish are
by Canadian fishermen, and what by American fishermer
off the coasts which are to be thrown open to competitio
of Washington? Cannot say.

9. Do Canadian fishermen procure bait or supplies ii
your State; and, if so, to what extent and value?
amount of bait is supplied from this State to Canadian fi
say how much.

10. What is the probable annual value to Canadian fish
able to procure bait, to land and dry their nets, and to r
their fish on the coasts of your State, without any other i
that contained in the Treaty of Washington? Canno
depend upon the enterprise of the fishermen.

11. Will the admission of Canadian fishermen to our in
cause any detriment or hinderance to the profitable pursı
eries by our own fishermen; and if so, in what manne
extent annually? Undoubtedly to some extent. Ther
competition in winter for our markets for fresh fish, ar
early in the season.

12. What number of Canadian vessels and boats are

'our State, and what are their tonnage and value, and the
ien employed upon them ? Don't know.

, fisheries pursued by American fishermen off the Atlantic
, British North American Provinces, what proportion con-
leep-sea fisheries, and what proportion of the in-shore fish-
) than nine tenths—perhaps nineteen-twentieths are out-

iat description of fish do American fishermen pursue the
aries ? Mackerel chiefly—Some herring.
state that the in shore fisheries are pursued wholly or chiefly
l, please state what proportion of mackerel is taken within
limits, and what proportion is taken outside of the in-shore
t over one fourth are taken within the inshore limits—three
iore outside.
much the larger quantity of mackerel caught by American
f the coasts of British America taken outside the in-shore
in the summer season especially, are not mackerel generally
ie banks, in the Gulf of Saint Lawrence, and not within
s. More than three-fourths. Mackerel in the Gulph of St.
re usually found on the Banks.
olonial fishermen injured by permitting American fishermen
ilonial in-shore waters ? I think not.
ot more fish caught by Colonial fishermen, when fishing inside a fleet of American fishing-vessels, from which large
f bait are thrown out, than when fishing alone ? Practical
an answer better than I.
, is the best bait for the mackerel, and where is it principally
iw much of it is taken within three miles of the shore, and
annual value to the United States, or to the British Prov-
a case may be, to take such bait within three miles of the
gie. Nearly all the mackerel bait is taken on the coast of
in three miles of the shore.
e state as to each class of fisheries carried on from your
itrict, the cost of fitting out, equipping, furnishing, and man-
sel for carrying it on, estimating it by the average length
State, as far as possible, in detail the elements which go to
ie cost of taking and delivering a full cargo and of returning
a port. A vessel of 60 tons costs $2,500 to 3,000 per an-
itting, furnishing &c., and makes usually three cruises a

n you have fully answered question 20, please answer the
ions as to vessels fitted out, equipped, furnished, and manned
ominion of Canada, including Prince Edward Island, so far as
ie to do so. If you state that there is any difference between
the Canadian and the cost of the American vessel in these
xplain what the difference is and the reason for it. The cost
iut, &c., in the Dominion is not so large as in the United
annot state the precise difference. Our fishermen generally
ie difference I think to be not less than 25 per cent. in favor
ninion. Reasons our vessels cost more—cost more to supply
, are less.
you acquainted, and for how long, and in what capacity, with
es on the coasts of Nova Scotia, New Brunswick, Quebec,
Edward Island, or with either, and if either, with which of
ries ? I am as a fish dealer as before stated with most or all
sheries.

23. What kind of fish frequent the waters of those coa
to be thrown open to American fishermen under the pro'
Treaty of Washington? Mackerel, herring and pollock.

24. Please state in detail the amount and the annual va
1854 to 1872 inclusive) of the fisheries which are so to be
to American fishermen; also the amount and the annual
catch in the adjacent waters which are more than three
from the shore; please state these facts in detail. I hav
formation at hand that would enable me to state with ac
catch in outside waters is of many times the value of the
as before stated.

25. Do American fishermen procure bait in the waters
miles of the coast of the Dominion of Canada? If so, to
and what is the value? They do sometimes, but not to a

26. Do not the American fishermen purchase supplies in
the Dominion of Canada, including bait, ice, salt, barrel
and various articles for the use of the men engaged in the
so, in what ports, and to what extent? And if that is the
an advantage to the ports of the Dominion to have the fish
the United States in their neighborhood during the seas
why it is so, and estimate, if you can, the money-value o
tage. They do, and will more largely when the Treat;
Will also buy fish by the cargo and in smaller quantity.
ble trade to the Provinces

27. Have you any knowledge of how many United State
sel yearly engaged in the fisheries off the Atlantic coasts c
Provinces, (excluding Newfoundland,) both without an
three-mile limit? If so, state how many vessels are so e
is the value of their tonnage, what is the number of men
nually on such vessels, what sorts of fish are taken there,
annual value of all the fish so caught, and what is the
probable proportion, in your judgment, of the amount of suc
within three miles of the British coast, and of the amou
side of the three-mile limit? I have already stated the sorts
those taken within the three mile limit would not be or
taken in those waters.

28. What percentage of value, if any, is, in your judgm
the profits of a voyage by the privilege to fish within thre
of the coast; whence is such profit derived; and in what de
Only for two months in a year is there any advantage, an
confined to catching the per cent of Mackerel before state

29. Do the American fishermen gain under the Treaty o
any valuable rights of landing to dry nets and cure fish
them, or to transship cargoes, which were not theirs befor
are those rights, and what do you estimate them to be we
in the aggregate? American fishermen do not repack fi
arrive home—the other rights except transhipping car
value.

30. Is not the Treaty of Washington, so far as the fishi
concerned, more or quite as beneficial to the people of the
American Provinces as to the people of the United Sta
have no doubt of it a large portion of fishermen and fish c
that without the repeal of the duty the former would ga
the latter, but with the repeal, the opinion is nearly if no
sal among intelligent and practical men that the balance
is with the people of the Provinces.

t is the amount and value of colonial cargoes of fish of all
ıs which are annually shipped to the United States ? Cannot

ıll No. 1 and No. 2 mackerel, for the larger part of the fat
d for all No. 1 salmon, does not the United States afford the
:t. Yes, the only market foreign to the Provinces.
ʹou know what amount of duties is annually paid to the
ıtes on fish and fish oil imported from Canada, which are to
ee under the provisions of the Treaty of Washington, please
ɑ annually, and by classes, from 1854 to 1872, inclusive.
ʹ.
ou know what amount of duties is annually paid in Canada
ɩ fish-oil imported from the United States, which are to made
the provisions of the said Treaty, please state them annually,
sses, from 1854 to 1872, inclusive.
object of these inquiries is to ascertain whether the rights in
fishing, and fishermen, and fish, which were granted to Great
the Treaty of Washington, are or are not a just equivalent
hts in those respects which were granted by said Treaty to
ɩ States. If you know anything bearing upon this subject
ı have not already stated in reply to previous questions,
e it as fully as if you had been specially inquired of in respect

ʹmnly, sincerely & truly swear that the foregoing Statements
correct to the best of my knowledge & belief. So help me

E G. WILLARD

o before me
ʹ RICH *Dep. Collector of Customs* (SEAL.)
72

No. 8.

[CONFIDENTIAL.]

ʹNS RESPECTING THE FISHERIES TO BE PRO-
ʹED TO ⸺ ⸺ ON BEHALF OF THE UNITED
S.

ɩ is your name and age, and in what town and State do you
꙼eo Trefethen, age forty-three. Portland Maine
ɩ opportunities have you had for becoming acquainted with
can and Canadian Atlantic sea fisheries, and the value of the
he different kinds of fish ? I am a wholesale dealer in Dry &
ıve been in the business twentyone years in Portland previ-
.ch worked at curing fish from my youth up. Am an owner
ing Schoones and have owned more or less for twenty years,
has been in the business sixty years
you give the names of other persons in your neighborhood
also had the opportunity of obtaining similar information ? If
give some such name. W. S. Dana, A. G. Sterling, C & H
E. G. Willard and many others
py of the Treaty between Great Britain and the United States,
the Treaty of Washington, is hereto annexed. Will you ex-
cles 18 to 22 inclusive, and state that you have done so ? I,

5. What kinds of fish frequent the waters of your State, especially those which are to be thrown open to the Canadian fishermen under the provisions of the Treaty of Washington? Mackerel Codfish Pollock Hake Haddock & Porgies

6. Can you give a statement of the kinds and quantities of fish taken annually off the coast of your State from the years 1854 to 1872, inclusive? If you can do this please do so; and, if not, please state where that information can be procured. I cannot state definately, and do not know where the information can be obtained

7. If you are able to do so, will you state the amount and value of the American fisheries which are to be thrown open to Canadian fishermen under the provisions of the Treaty of Washington? Please state them in detail, showing the different kinds of fish, and the value of each kind. I think the most valuable fisheries to be thrown open by the Treaty is the Porgie, which I should estimate to be worth a Million Dollars to the State of Maine And which we have now entirely as the fish follow the coast and are taken almost wholly within the three mile limit the next in importance is the Mackerel, which perhaps is realy of more value but is not confined to the shore so closely, a large portion being taken outside the limit Codfish are mostly taken outside the three miles on our coast.

8. What quantity and value of each kind of fish are annually taken by Canadian fishermen, and what by American fishermen, in the waters off the coasts which are to be thrown open to competition by the Treaty of Washington? I cannot State

9. Do Canadian fishermen procure bait or supplies in the waters of your State; and if so, to what extent and value? They do, but cannot state to what amount. Porgies for Mackerel Bait has been quite largely shipped to N. S. from this State

10. What is the probable annual value to Canadian fishermen in being able to procure bait, to land and dry their nets, and to repack and cure their fish on the coasts of your State, without any other restriction than that contained in the Treaty of Washington? I cannot tell. It will be owing entirely to how far they avail themselves of the priviledges opened to them

11. Will the admission of Canadian fishermen to our in-shore fisheries cause any detriment or hinderance to the profitable pursuit of these fisheries by our own fishermen; and if so, in what manner, and to what extent annually? If they should take advantage of our winter fishing, I think that they injure our fishermen by over stocking our markets with fresh fish, and thus reduce the price

12. What number of Canadian vessels and boats are engaged in the fisheries of your State, and what are their tonnage and value, and the number of men employed upon them? I do not know, but think it is very limited at present, confined to a few Mackerel fishermen in fall of the year

13. Of the fisheries pursued by American fishermen off the Atlantic coasts of the British North American Provinces, what proportion consists of the deep-sea fisheries, and what proportion of the in-shore fisheries? All of the Cod are taken off shore and a large proportion of the Mackerel, say three quarters to seven eights. Herring are mostly taken in shore, also Pollock

14. For what description of fish do American fishermen pursue the in-shore fisheries? Mackerel principly, and will for Herring after the treaty takes effect

15. If you state that the in shore fisheries are pursued wholly or

ıckerel, please state what proportion of mackerel is taken
-shore limits, and what proportion is taken outside of the
s? I should say three quarters to Seven eights outside and
a qarter in shore

much the larger quantity of mackerel caught by American
the coasts of British America taken outside the in-shore
ı the summer season especially, are not mackerel generally
banks, in the Gulf of Saint Lawrence, and not within
in the summer, say from June 1st to Sept 1st our fishermen
.ter off shore, but in the fall after the 1st of Sept the Mack-
lay in shore, and the weather being rough it is safer to be
r
ılonial fishermen injured by permitting American fishermen
ılonial in-shore waters? I should say not, except in rare

ıt more fish caught by Colonial fishermen, when fishing in-
ıde a fleet of American fishing-vessels, from which large
bait are thrown out, than when fishing alone? I do not

is the best bait for the mackerel, and where is it principally
w much of it is taken within three miles of the shore, and
annual value to the United States, or to the British Prov-
case may be, to take such bait within three miles of the
gies is the best bait for Mackerel, and is taken only on the
ıe and Massachusetts, and is all taken within three miles

ı state as to each class of fisheries carried on from your State
he cost of fitting out, equipping, furnishing, and manning
carrying it on, estimating it by the average length of the
te, as far as possible, in detail, the elements which go to
ı cost of taking and delivering a full cargo and of returning
ı port. For Bank cod fisheries we use vessels of about 60
from seven to ten thousand dollars, we usually fit and pro-
for a voyage of two to four months with a crew of ten men.
120 to 140 hhds Salt cost 300$ Bait 40 Bris. Clams, 320$
ç Hooks 180$ Provisions 500$ total $1300,—to which we add
in dories which the most of the fishermen do late years
ries total 1600$. this for the first or spring cruise, if $1600
ısualy last two months the second cruise will cost less,
000$ for two months if codfishing. if for mackerel in $1000
wrence 800$. third cruise for Mackerel usualy cost $600
refore if the vessel makes two Cod fish cruises and one ——
will cost about 3200$ if One Codfish and two Mack- $3200
in rare instances we get a fourth trip, but as often only two.
ı you have fully answered question 20, please answer the
ions as to vessels fitted out, equipped, furnished, and manned
ominion of Canada, including Prince Edward Island, so far
able to do so. If you state that there is any difference be-
cost of the Canadian and the cost of the American vessel in
cts, exPlain what the difference is, and the reason for it. I
te what it costs to fit out a vessel from the Provences, but
ıs understood that it cost them much less. In the first place
cheeper vessels. And not so well provided and Provisioned.

wn and run their vessels, and are satisfied with poorer pro-
n our people are, and many articles cost less in Nova Scotia

than in the States, vessels can be built for less, because
is cheeper. Salt is cheeper than any other articles

22. Are you acquainted, and for how long and in wha
the fisheries on the coasts of Nova Scotia, New Brunsw
Prince Edward Island, or with either, and if either, with
fisheries? only as a dealer and buyer of their fish

23. What kind of fish frequent the waters of those coas
be thrown open to American fishermen under the provisio
of Washington? Herring, Mackerel, Cod, &c.

24. Please state in detail the amount and the annual
1854 to 1872 inclusive) of the fisheries which are so to l
to American fishermen; also, the amount and the annu
catch in the adjacent waters which are no more than t
tant from the shore; please state these facts in detail.

25. Do American fishermen procure bait in the wate
miles of the coast of the Dominion of Canada? If so,
and what is the value? they do. Herring princap:
fishing which they purchase of the inhabitants and will (
chase, as the inhabitants can sell for less than our fishe
them I do not know the amount, but should estimate
sand dollars or more

26. Do not the American fishermen purchase supplies
the Dominion of Canada, including bait, ice, salt, barr
and various articles for the use of the men engaged in th
so, in what ports, and to what extent? And if that is
not an advantage to the ports of the Dominion to ha
vessels of the United States in their neighborhood dur
season? Explain why it is so, and estimate, if you ca
value of that advantage. they do to some extent in
Port Mulgrave & Port Hood, C. B., Charlotte town &
P. E. I., and other Ports of less note, and will after tl
effect to a *large extent*. It must be a decided advanta
those Ports to be able to supply our vessels with Fr
Potatoes &c and I know that they felt it to be a sad
when the former Treaty was abrogated, and I have be
parties in trade at Halifax, Port Mulgrave and Charlott
my vessels to them for supplies, and have done So

27. Have you any knowledge of how many United
vessels yearly engage in the fisheries off the Atlantic coa
ish North American Provinces, (excluding Newfoundlan
and within the three-mile limit? If so, state how man
engaged, what is the value of their tonnage, what is the
employed annually on such vessels, what sorts of fish a
what is the annual value of all the fish so caught, and v
portion, or probable proportion, in your judgment, of the
catch taken within three miles of the British coast, and
taken outside of the three-mile limit? I have no statisti
but should estimate the number to be Five or Six hun
some Two hundred and fifty Thousand dollars, manned
Six thousand men, Cod and Mackerel, should estimate tl
Million Dollars in round numbers, and should estimate tl
inshore or within three miles at not more than ten pe
hundred thousand, and I do not believe that it will exce
after the Treaty takes effect.

28. What percentage of value, if any, is, in your jud
the profits of a voyage by the privilege to fish with

coast; whence is such profit derived; and in what does it
lo not think that I would pay one-tenth of One per cent
ilege, in fact all the benefit that any vessel that I own in
e, would be in being allowed to fish for about a month inside
Mackerel   When the Dominion Govt granted permits to
ne three mile limit to our fishermen, by the payment of fifty
vessel, some of our fishermen, payd that amount for the
it when the next year the Dominion Govt raised the amount
lred Dollars, very few if any, would pay it, none that I was
id.
, American fishermen gain under the Treaty of Washington
e rights of landing to dry nets and cure fish, or to repack
ransship cargoes, which were not theirs before; if so, what
;hts, and what do you estimate them to be worth annually.
gate ?   None for the right to land and dry their nets and
hey may gain something in rights to land and transship
t I think the benifits to the people, where they are landed
ped would be fully equal to the benifit we derive.
t the Treaty of Washington, so far as the fishing clauses
ied, more or quite as beneficial to the people of the British
rican Provinces as to the people of the United States ?   I,
decidedly in favor of of the People of Provinces, the right
eir fish to our market free of Duty is worth more to them
y give is worth to us.
, is the amount and value of colonial cargoes of fish of all
s which are annually shipped to the United States ?   I do

ll No. 1 and No. 2 mackerel, for the larger part of the fat
d for all No. 1 salmon, does not the United States afford the
t ?   It does, and also a large part of the Large Codfish.
t know what amount of duties is annually paid to the United
sh and fish-oil imported from Canada, which are to be made
the provisions of the Treaty of Washington, please state
ally, and by classes, from 1854 to 1872, inclusive   I do not

i know what amount of duties is annually paid in Canada on
h-oil imported from the United States, which are to be made
the provisions of the said Treaty, please state them annually,
sses, from 1854 to 1872, inclusive.   I do not know.
object of these inquiries is to ascertain whether the rights in
ishing, and fishermen, and fish, which were granted to Great
the Treaty of Washington, are or are not a just equivalent
its in those respects which were granted by said Treaty to
States.   If you know anything bearing upon this subject
have not already stated in reply to previous questions, please
fully as if you had been specially inquired of in respect of it.
e in this connection that I have in my employ a number of
Nova Scotia, who now say they shall return to N. S. as by
and with the privilege of sending their fish to our market
can prosecute the business more profitably there than here.
ly, sincerely & truly swear that the foregoing statements
correct to the best of my knowledge & belief.   So help me

GEORGE TREFETHEN.

efore me this 12th day June 1873   •   (Seal.)
         M N RICH Dep. Collector.

No. 9.

[CONFIDENTIAL.]

QUESTIONS RESPECTING THE FISHERIES
POUNDED TO ——— ——— ON BEHALF OF
STATES.

1. What is your name and age, and in what town an
reside? John Conley. Portland, Me. age, 69 years.

2. What opportunities have you had for becoming
the American and Canadian Atlantic sea-fisheries, and '
catch of the different kinds of fish? I have been in the F
ness for the last thirty years.

3. Can you give the names of other persons in your nei
have also had the opportunity of obtaining similar infor
please give some such name. E. G. Willard; Geo. T1
Henry Trefethen & Sons; Emery Cushing; A. G. Sterli

4. A copy of the Treaty between Great Britain and th
known as the Treaty of Washington, is hereto annexed.
amine articles 18 to 22 inclusive, and state that you ha
have.

5. What kinds of fish frequent the waters of your S
those which are to be thrown open to the Canadian fishe
provision of the Treaty of Washington? Cod; Hake; C
Mackerel; Pollock; Herring; Menhaden, or porgies a
kinds.

6. Can you give a statement of the kinds and quantiti
annually off the coast of your State from the years 185'
sive? If you can do this please do so; and if not, ple
that information can be procured. The kinds of Fish are
The value of fish and fish-oil is about two million dollar
Portland sales.

7. If you are able to do so, will you state the amount
American fisheries which are to be thrown open to Can
under the provisions of the Treaty of Washington? P
in detail, showing the different kinds of fish, and the va
I cannot state the amount Mackerel in large quan
also Codfish; Hake, Haddock, Pollock, Herring & Pogie
importance and profit to the Canadian fishermen.

8. What quantity and value of each kind of fish are
by Canadian fishermen, and what by American fisherme
off the coasts which are to be thrown open to competiti
of Washington? I cannot say.

9. Do Canadian fishermen procure bait or supplies
your State? and if so, to what extent and value? Th
quantities of bait and supplies; value not known.

10. What is the probable annual value to Canadian fis
able to procure bait, to land and dry their nets, and to
their fish on the coasts of your State, without any othe
that contained in the Treaty of Washington? I cann
it very valuable.

11. Will the admission of Canadian fishermen to our
cause any detriment or hinderance to the profitable pu
eries by our own fishermen; and if so, in what man
extent annually? I do not think it will, to any grea

hance to compete with our winter fishing, which is very

umber of Canadian vessels and boats are engaged in the
ur State, and what are their tonnage and value, and the
n employed upon t em? I do not know.
fisheries pursued by American fishermen off the Atlantic
British North American Provinces, what proportion con-
ep-sea fisheries, and what proportion of the in-shore fish-
t three quarters of the fishing is deep-sea fishing.
at description of fish do American fishermen pursue the
ries? Mackerel and herring, principally.
ate that the in shore fisheries are pursued wholly or chiefly
please state what proportion of mackerel is taken within
limits, and what proportion is taken outside of the in-
  Should think that less than one fourth part are taken
shore limits.
much the larger quantity of mackerel caught by American
the coasts of British America taken outside the in-shore
the summer season especially, are not mackerel generally
banks, in the Gulf of Saint Lawrence, and not within shore?

lonial fishermen injured by permitting American fisher-
Colonial in-shore waters? Do not think they are.
t more fish caught by Colonial fishermen, when fishing in-
ide a fleet of American fishing-vessels, from which large
bait are thrown out, than when fishing alone? Cannot
ld think there would be.
s the best bait for the mackerel, and where is it principally
w much of it is taken within three miles of the shore,
he annual value to the United States, or to the British
, the case may be, to take such bait within three miles of
The best bait is pogies; nearly all the mackerel bait is
coast of Maine and within three miles of the shore.
state as to each class of fisheries carried on from your State
le cost of fitting out, equipping, furnishing, and manning
carrying it on, estimating it by the average length of the
e, as far as possible, in detail the elements which go to
cost of taking and delivering a full cargo and of returning
port. Salt, Lines, Provisions, etc. varying from One thou-
lollars to three thousand (3000) dollars. They usually make
three trips per year.
you have fully answered question 20, please answer the
us as to vessels fitted out, equipped, furnished, and manned
minion of Canada, including Prince Edward Island, so far
ble to do so. If you state that there is any difference best of the Canadian and the cost of the American vessel in
ects, explain what the difference is and the reason for it.
k the cost of the Canadian would be much less than the

ou acquainted, and for how long, and in what capacity, with
on the coasts of Nova Scotia, New Brunswick, Quebec, or
ard Island, or with either, and if either, with which of these
I have been acquainted with the Nova Scotia and New
fisheries for about twenty years.
kind of fish frequent the waters of those coasts which are

to be thrown open to American fishermen under the provisions of the Treaty of Washington ? Cod and Pollock principally.

24. Please state in detail the amount and the annual value (say from 1854 to 1872 inclusive) of the fisheries which are so to be thrown open to American fishermen; also the amount and the annual value of the catch in the adjacent waters which are more than three miles distant from the shore; please state these facts in detail. Do not know.

25. Do American fishermen fish within three miles of the coast of the Dominion of Canada ? If so, to what extent, and what is the value ? Should think not to any great extent or value.

26. Do not the American fishermen purchase supplies in the ports of the Dominion of Canada, including bait, ice, salt, barrels, provisions, and various articles for the use of the men engaged in the fisheries ? If so, in what ports, and to what extent ? And, if that is the case, is it not an advantage to the ports of the Dominion to have the fishing vessels of the United States in their neighborhood during the fishing season ? Explain why it is so, and estimate, if you can, the money-value of that advantage. They do purchase supplies in most all the ports on the fishing coast, and is consequently of advantage to the inhabitants of the different ports.

27. Have you any knowledge of how many United States fishing-vessels yearly engage in the fisheries off the Atlantic coasts of the British North American Provinces, (excluding Newfoundland,) both without and within the three-mile limit ? If so, state how many vessels are so engaged, what is the value of their tonnage, what is the number of men employed annually on such vessels, what sorts of fish are taken there, what is the annual value of all the fish so caught, and what is the proportion, or probable proportion, in your judgment, of the amount of such catch taken within three miles of the British coast, and of the amount taken outside of the three-mile limit ? Cannot state how many vessels are employed or the amount of fish taken.

28. What percentage of value, if any, is, in your judgment, added to the profits of a voyage by the privilege to fish within three marine miles of the coast; whence is such profit derived, and in what does it consist ? Only a small part of the fish are taken within three miles of the coast, and the profit not large compared with the outside fishery.

29. Do the American fishermen gain under the Treaty of Washington any valuable rights of landing to dry nets and cure fish, or to repack them, or to transship cargoes, which were not theirs before; if so, what are those rights, and what do you estimate them to be worth annually, in the aggregate ? Do not think they do, to any great extent.

30. Is not the Treaty of Washington, so far as the fishing clauses are concerned, more, or quite as, beneficial to the people of the British North American Provinces as to the people of the United States ? I consider the advantage fully equal and beneficial.

31. What is the amount and value of colonial cargoes of fish of all descriptions which are annually shipped to the United States ? Cannot say.

32. For all No. 1 and No. 2 mackerel, for the larger part of the fat herring, and for all No. 1 salmon, does not the United States afford the only market. I think it does to a large extent.

33. If you know what amount of duties is annually paid to the United States on fish and fish-oil imported from Canada, which are to be made free under the provisions of the Treaty of Washington, please state them annually, and by classes, from 1854 to 1872, inclusive. Cannot state.

you know what amount of duties is annually paid in Canada,
and fish-oil imported from the United States, which are to be
ee under the provisions of the said Treaty, please state them
y, and by classes, from 1854 to 1872, inclusive.
he object of these inquiries is to ascertain whether the rights in
of fishing, and fishermen, and fish, which were granted to Great
by the Treaty of Washington, are or are not a just equivalent
rights in those respects which were granted by said Treaty to
ited States. If you know anything bearing upon this subject
you have not already stated in reply to previous questions,
tate it as fully as if you had been specially inquired of in re·
f it?

nnly sincerely & truly swear that the foregoing Statements are
correct to the best of my knowledge & belief—so help me

JOHN CONLEY

u to before me this 14th day June 1873
M N RICH
Dep Collector.   (SEAL.)

No. 10.

[CONFIDENTIAL.]

TIONS RESPECTING THE FISHERIES TO BE PRO-
INDED TO ——— ——— ON BEHALF OF THE UNITED
.TES.

Vhat is your name and age, and in what town and State do you
? / O. B. Whitten; 34 Portland Maine
Vhat opportunities have you had for becoming acquainted with
nérican and Canadian Atlantic sea-fisheries, and the value of the
of the different kinds of fish? Have been in the fish business ten

an you give the names of other persons in your neighborhood
ave also had the opportunity of obtaining similar information? If
ase give some such name. T. C. Lewis Abel Chase C. M. Trefe·
R. T. Sterling
A copy of the Treaty between Great Britain and the United States,
n as the Treaty of Washington, is hereto annexed. Will you ex-
 articles 18 to 22, inclusive, and state that you have done so?
examined the articles referred to above
What kinds of fish frequent the waters of your State, especially
which are to be thrown open to the Canadian fishermen under the
sions of the Treaty of Washington? Cod—Haddock Pollock Hake
erel Herring and Pohagen
Can you give a statement of the kinds and quantites of fish taken
ally off the coast of your State from the years 1854 to 1872, inclu·
 If you can do this please do so; and if not, please state where
information can be procured. Unable to state
If you are able to do so, will you state the amount and value of the
rican fisheries which are to be thrown open to Canadian fishermen
r the provisions of the Treaty of Washington? Please state them
etail, showing the different kinds of fish, and the value of each kind.
1ot say

189 F

8. What quantity and value of each kind of fish are annually taken by Canadian fishermen, and what by American fishermen, in the waters off the coasts which are to be thrown open to competition by the Treaty of Washington? Do not know

9. Do Canadian fishermen procure bait or supplies in the waters of your State? and if so, to what extent and value? A very large proportion of the bait used by the Canadian mackerel fishermen is taken from the warters of this State

10. What is the probable annual value to Canadian fishermen in being able to procure bait, to land and dry their nets, and to repack and cure their fish on the coasts of your State, without any other restriction than that contained in the Treaty of Washington? Cannot say

11. Will the admission of Canadian fishermen to our in-shore fisheries cause any detriment or hinderance to the profitable pursuit of these fisheries by our own fishermen; and if so, in what manner, and to what extent annually? As the Canadian fishermen can build fitt and man their vessells at an exceedingly less cost than American it would be a detriment to American fisheries because they could not compete with them

12. What number of Canadian vessels and boats are engaged in the fisheries of your State, and what are their tonnage and value, and the number of men employed upon them? Do not know

13. Of the fisheries pursued by American fishermen off the Atlantic coasts of the British North American Provinces, what proportion consists of the deep sea fisheries, and what proportion of the in-shore fisheries? Most of the large fishing vessels of this State pursue the deep sea fishing off the Coast of British North American Provinces for nearly five months and then a large proportion of the same vessels pursue the mackerel fishing

14. For what description of fish do American fishermen pursue the in shore fisheries? Mackerel

15. If you state that the in shore fisheries are pursued wholly or chiefly for mackerel, please state what proportion of mackerel is taken within the in-shore limits, and what proportion is taken outside of the in-shore limits? Should judge that seven eighths of all the mackerel caught are taken out side of the in-shore limits

16. Is not much the larger quantity of mackerel caught by American fishermen off the coasts of British America taken outside the in-shore limits; and in the summer season especially, are not mackerel generally found on the banks, in the Gulf of Saint Lawrence, and not within shore? Yes

17. Are Colonial fishermen injured by permitting American fishermen to fish in Colonial in-shore waters? No

18. Are not more fish caught by Colonial fishermen, when fishing in-shore, alongside a fleet of American fishing-vessels, from which large quantities of bait are thrown out, than when fishing alone? It requires a continual throwing of bait to catch mackerel with a hook consequently vessels in the fleet do better than they would by fishing alone

19. What is the best bait for the mackerel, and where is it principally taken? How much of it is taken within three miles of the shore, and what is the annual value to the United States, or to the British Provinces, as the case may be, to take such bait within three miles of the shore? Pohagen—and all taken in American waters and most of it within three miles of the shore

20. Please state as to each class of fisheries carried on from your State or district, the cost of fitting out, equipping, furnishing, and man-

for carrying it on, estimating it by the average length of
State, as far as possible, in detail the elements which go
e cost of taking and delivering a full cargo and of return-
ne port.   It will cost to build and fit out a vessel of 100
shing to be absent the average time—say three months
mackerel fishing $11550

of Vessel	9500	Mackerel fishing, cost of Vessel				9500
" Provisions	1200	"	"	"	" Provisions	1000
" Salt	450	"	"	"	" Salt	150
" Dories	350	"	"	"	" Bait	300
" Bait	500	"	"	"	" Barrels	600
	$12000					$11550

you have fully answered question 20, please answer the
is as to vessels fitted out, equipped, furnished, and manned
inion of Canada, including Prince Edward Island, so far
le to do so.   If you state that there is any difference beit of the Canadian and the cost of the American vessel in
s, explain what the difference is, and the reason for it.
aat Canadian vessels can be built and fitted for nearly one
in American—material for building is less—They use a
of vessels and provision them at a very small expense
u acquainted, and for how long, and in what capacity, with
on the coasts of Nova Scotia, New Brunswick, Quebec, or
ird Island, or with either, and if either, with which of
es?   Acquainted with the cod and mackerel fisheries—
ars both curing cod-fish and inspecting mackerel
kind of fish frequent the waters of those coasts which are
open to American fishermen under the provisions of the
ashington?   Mackerel mostly
state in detail the amount and the annual value (say from
inclusive) of the fisheries which are so to be thrown open to
hermen; also the amount and the annual value of the catch
nt waters, which are more than three miles distant from
Please state these facts in detail.
erican fishermen procure bait in the waters within three
coast of the Dominion of Canada?   If so, to what extent,
the value?   Sometimes the American fishermen take bait
miles of the coast of the Dominion of Canada but to a very

, the American fishermen purchase supplies in the ports of
n of Canada, including bait, ice, salt, barrels, provisions.
articles for the use of the men engaged in the fisheries?   If
orts, and to what extent?   And, if that is the case, is it
itage to the ports of the Dominion to have the fishing-ves-
nited States in their neighborhood during the fishing sea-
in why it is so, and estimate, if you can, the money-value
atage.   They do purchase supplies in the ports of the Do-
nada—American fishermen frequently land their cargo of
1 ship them to American ports—then they are obliged to
, outfit, and it is a great advantage to have the trade of the
ls
you any knowledge of how many United States fishing-ves-
ngage in the fisheries off the Atlantic coasts of the British
ican Provinces, (excluding Newfoundland,) both without
he three-mile limit?   If so, state how many vessels are so
at is the value of their tonnage, what is the number of men

employed annually on such vessels, what sorts of fish are taken there, what is the annual value of all the fish so caught, and what is the proportion, or probable proportion, in your judgment, of the amount of such catch taken within three miles of the British coast, and of the amount taken outside of the three-mile limit?

28. What percentage of value, if any, is, in your judgment, added to the profits of a voyage by the privilege to fish within three marine miles of the coast; whence is such profit derived; and in what does it consist?

29. Do the American fishermen gain under the Treaty of Washington any valuable rights of landing to dry nets and cure fish, or to repack them, or to transship cargoes, which were not theirs before; if so, what are those rights, and what do you estimate them to be worth annually, in the aggregate? They do not

30. Is not the Treaty of Washington, so far as the fishing clauses are concerned, more, or quite as, beneficial to the people of the British North American Provinces as to the people of the United States? A far greater benefit to the people of British North American Provinces than to the people of the United States

31. What is the amount and value of colonial cargoes of fish of all descriptions which are annually shipped to the United States?

32. For all No. 1 and No. 2 mackerel, for the larger part of the fat herring, and for all No. 1 salmon, does not the United States afford the only market. Yes

33. If you know what amount of duties is annually paid to the United States on fish and fish-oil imported from Canada, which are to be made free under the provisions of the Treaty of Washington, please state them annually, and by classes, from 1854 to 1872, inclusive.

34. If you know what amount of duties is annually paid in Canada on fish and fish-oil imported from the United States, which are to be made free under the provisions of the said Treaty, please state them annually, and by classes, from 1854 to 1872, inclusive.

35. The object of these inquiries is to ascertain whether the rights in respect of fishing, and fishermen, and fish, which were granted to Great Britain by the Treaty of Washington, are or are not a just equivalent for the rights in those respects which were granted by said Treaty to the United States. If you know anything bearing upon this subject which you have not already stated in reply to previous questions, please state it as fully as if you had been specially inquired of in respect of it.

I solmnly sincerely & truly swear that the foregoing statements are true & correct to the best of my knowledge & belief. So help me God.

O. B. WHITEN

Sworn to before
      M N RICH
      Dep Collector

No. 11.

[CONFIDENTIAL.]

QUESTIONS RESPECTING THE FISHERIES TO BE PRO-POUNDED TO S B CHASE ON BEHALF OF THE UNITED STATES.

1. What is your name and age, and in what town and State do you reside? Stephen B Chase reside in Portland Main am 67 years old

'hat opportunities have you had for becoming acquainted with
ıerican and Canadian Atlantic sea-fisheries, and the value of the
ıf the different kinds of fish? I have been in the buisness of re.
; and Delvering fish for the last twentyfive years
an you give the names of other persons in your neighborhood who
lso had the opportunity of obtaining similar information? If so,
give some such name. E G Willard George Trefetherin Henry
herin John Conley Emery Cushing A G Sterling George F Lovett.
. copy of the Treaty between Great Britain and the United States,
ı as the Treaty of Washington, is hereto annexed. Will you ex.
articles 18 to 22 inclusive, and state that you have done so? I

Vhat kinds of fish frequent the waters of your State, especially
which are to be thrown open to the Canadian fishermen under the
ions of the Treaty of Washington? Cod Hake, Cusk Haddock
ırel Herring Pogies are the principle
Jan you give a statement of the kinds and quantities of fish taken
lly off the coast of your State from the years 1854 to 1872, inclu-
If you can do this please do so; and if not, please state where
ıformation can be procured. The kinds are statied in my last an-
The value of Fish purchase including Cod Liver Oil and the Oil
factured from Porgies is from $1800,000 to $2,000000.
f you are able to do so, will you state the amount and value of the
ican fisheries which are to be thrown open to Canadian fishermen
· the provisions of the Treaty of Washington? Please state them
ail, showing the different kinds of fish, and the value of each kind.
ıt give any answer to the first part of questions, the kinds of Fish
ıt on the coast of Maine which by the Treaty will be opened to the
adin Fisherman, 1st, Mackererll, which is large & valuable and may
ıid so to the fishermen of the Provinces if they choose to make them
they are taken earley in the season on our southern Cost and then
east untill Fall when they reach the English waters, this branch of
shing interest is large and vauable to Maine Fisherman, and will be
to Dominion fishermen 2d The Herring fishery is large and im-
ıt especially on the Eastern Coast 3d the pogie fishery is large
ıportant, especscaly to Maine, and by the treaty this branch is trown
to the Dominion Fishermen and will open to them a large and pro-
e buisness to them if they choose to themselves of it also the Fresh
buisness will be thrown open to them in the Winter season affording
ıument to men & vessels during the time they cannot be so em-
on their coast
What quantity and value of each kind of fish are annually taken
ınadian fishermen, and what by American fishermen, in the waters
e coasts which are to be thrown open to competition by the Treaty
ashington? Cannot say
Do Canadian fishermen procure bait or supplies in the waters of
State? and if so, to what extent and value? A large amount of
is supplied to Canadien Fisherman cant say how much . .
What is the probable annual value to Canadian fishermen in being
;o procure bait, to land and dry their nets, and to repack and cure
fish on the coasts of your State, without any other restriction than
contained in the Treaty of Washington? Cannot say
Will the admission of Canadian fishermen to our in-shore fisheries
ı any detriment or hinderance to the profitable pursuit of these fish-
by our own fishermen; and if so, in what manner, and to what ex-
annually? This will depend very much on the enterpris of the

Canadin Fisherman, as they will have a chance to competute for the winter fishing & earley mackerel Fishing

12. What number of Canadian vessels and boats are engaged in the fisheries of your State, and what are their tonnage and value, and the number of men employed upon them? Do not know

13. Of the fisheries pursued by American fishermen off the Atlantic coasts of the British North American Provinces, what proportion consists of the deep-sea fisheries, and what proportion of the in-shore fisheries? More than three qaurters perhaps Nine tenths are out side

14. For what description of fish do American fishermen pursue the in shore fisheries? Mackerel & Herring

15. If you state that the in-shore fisheries arepursued wholly or chiefly for mackerel, please state what proportion of mackerel is taken within the in-shore limits, and what proportion is taken outside of the in-shore limits? Should think one fourth part are taken within in shore limits

16. Is not much the larger quantity of mackerel caught by American fishermen off the coasts of British America taken outside the in-shore limits; and in the summer season especially, are not mackerel generally found on the banks, in the Gulf of Saint Lawrence, and not within shore? Cannot say

17. Are Colonial fishermen injured by permitting American fishermen to fish in Colonial in-shore waters? 1 think not

18. Are not more fish caught by Colonial fishermen, when fishing inshore, alongside a fleet of American fishing-vessels, from which large quantities of bait are thrown out, than when fishing alone? Cannot say

19. What is the best bait for the mackerel, and where is it principally taken? How much of it is taken within three miles of the shore, and what is the annual value to the United States,·or to the British Provinces, as the case may be, to take such bait within three miles of the shore? Pogies, nearly all the Mackerel Bait is taken on the coast of Maine and within three miles of shore

20. Please state as to each class of fisheries carried on from your State or district, the cost of fitting out, equipping, furnishing, and manning a vessel for carrying it on, estimating it by the average length of the cruise. State, as far as possible, in detail the elements which go to make up the cost of taking and delivering a full cargo and of returning to the home port. As near as I can ascertain from enquirey think the expence will will be from $2000 to $3000, and usualy make three cruses a year

21. When you have fully answered question 20, please answer the same questions as to vessels fitted out, equipped, furnished, and manned from the Dominion of Canada, including Prince Edward Island, so far as you are able to do so. If you state that there is any difference between the cost of the Canadian and the cost of the American vessel in these respects, explain what the difference is and the reason for it. Cannot tell

22. Are you acquainted, and for how long, and in what capacity, with the fisheries on the coast of Nova Scotia, New Brunswick, Quebec, or Prince Edward Island, or with either, and if either, with which of these fisheries? I am with the Nova Scotia and New Brunswic

23. What kinds of fish frequent the waters of those coasts which are to be thrown open to American fishermen under the provisions of the Treaty of Washington? Cod and Pollock and salmon.

24. Please state in detail the amount and the annual value (say from from 1854 to 1872 inclusive) of the fisheries which are so to be thrown open to American fishermen; also the amount and the annual value

in the adjacent waters which are more than three miles
the shore; please state these facts in detail. do not know
erican fishermen procure bait in the waters within three
oast of the Dominion of Canada; if so, to what extent,
he value? they do sometimes but to small extent.
the American fishermen purchase supplies in the ports of
1 of Canada. including bait, ice, salt, barrels, provisions.
rticles for the use of the men engaged in the fisheries; if
orts, and to what extent? And, if that is the case, is it
tage to the ports of the Dominion to have the fishing-vessels
l States in their neighborhood during the fishing season?
it is so, and estimate, if you can, the money-value of that
They do and will more largely when the treaty takes ef-
prove a valuable trade to the Province
-ou any knowledge of how many United States fishing-ves-
ngage in the fisheries off the Atlantic coasts of the British
can Provinces (excluding Newfoundland) both without and
three-mile limit? If so, state how many vessels are so en-
is the value of their tonnage, what is the number of men
nually on such vessels, what sorts of fish are taken there,
innual value of all the fish so caught, and what is the propor-
able proportion, in your judgment, of the amount of such
within three miles of the British coast, and of the amount
le of the three-mile limit? I have no knowledge of the
ressels employed or how many fish taken
percentage of value, if any, is, in your judgment, added to
f a voyage by the privilege to fish within three marine miles
whence is such profit derived; and in what does it consist?
hort time in the fall, and is mainly confined the per cent. of
fore stated
e American fishermen gain under the Treaty of Washington
, rights of landing to dry nets and cure fish, or to repack them,
hip cargoes, which were not theirs before; if so, what are
t, and what do you estimate them to be worth annually, in
ite? Americans do not repack fish until they arrive home
rhts excepting transshipping cargo is of no value
, the Treaty of Washington, so far as the fishing clauses are
nore, or quite as. beneficial to the people of the British North
Provinces as to the people of the United States? I have no
and in conversation with both class of Fisherman the Do-
nermen are better satisfied than our own with the Treaty
o there own statements
; is the amount and value of colonial cargoes of fish of all
s which are annually shipped to the United States? Cannot

all No. 1 and No. 2 mackerel, for the larger part of the fat
d for all No. 1 salmon, does not the United States afford the
t. . Yes.
n know what amount of duties is annually paid to the United
sh and fish-oil imported from Canada, which are to be made
the provisions of the Treaty of Washington, please state them
nd by classes, from 1854 to 1872, inclusive. Do not know
u know what amount of duties is annually paid in Canada on
h-oil imported from the United States, which are to be made
the provisions of the said Treaty, please state them annually,
sses, from 1854 to 1872, inclusive.

35. The object of these inquiries is to ascertain whether
respect of fishing, and fishermen, and fish, which were gran
Britain by the Treaty of Washington, are or are not a jus
for the rights in those respects which were granted by se
the United States. If you know anything bearing upon
which you have not already stated in reply to previous ques
state it as fully as if you had been specially inquired of in i

I solmnly sincerely and truly swear that the foregoing
are true & correct to the best of my knowledge & belief.   So l
                                                STEPHEN I

Sworn before me this 13th day of June 1873

                                                M N I
                                                Dep.

No. 12.

[CONFIDENTIAL.]

QUESTIONS RESPECTING THE FISHERIES TO
POUNDED TO ——— ———, ON BEHALF OF TH
STATES.

I, Marshall N. Rich, make the following answers to the s
tions propounded to me, respecting the fisheries on behalf c

1. What is your name and age, and in what town and S
reside? Marshall N Rich—reside in Portland Maine—an
age.

2. What opportunities have you had for becoming acqu
the American and Canadian Atlantic sea fisheriee, and the
catch of the different kinds of fish? I have been Secr
Board of Trade of this city for the past *ten* years—publishe
cial paper for seven years—in which capacities it has en
of my time in preparing & collating statistics and trade rep
also been Deputy Collector of Customs for this port fo
years, and am at this time,

3. Can you give the names of other persons in your i
who have also had the opportunity of obtaining similar
If so, please give some such name. W. S. Dana, E. G. Wi
Trefethen, Emery Cushing, Geo. F. Lovett, John Conley &

4. A copy of the Treaty between Great Britain and the U
known as the Treaty of Washington, is hereto annexed.
amine articles 18 to 22 inclusive, and state that you have
have examined Articles 18 and 22 inclusive of the "Tre
ington."

5. What kinds of fish frequent the waters of your Sta
those which are to be thrown open to the Canadian fishern
provisions of the Treaty of Washington? Cod, Pollock, Ha
Mackerel, Herring, & " Porgies" (chiefly.)

6. Can you give a statement of the kinds and quantities
annually off the coast of your State from the years 1854 t
sive? If you can do this, please do so; and if not, pleas
that information can be procured. Of the kinds of fish pi
merated, including Cod-liver Oil. The value of that purc
market, is not much short of two and a half million dollar
which, probably not one twentieth part are caught on tha
Coast to be thrown open by the "Treaty." I cannot state
formation asked can be procured.

u are able to do so, will you state the amount and value of the
fisheries which are to be thrown open to Canadian fishermen
provisions of the Treaty of Washington? Please state them
showing the different kinds of fish, and the value of each kind.
state with any practical degree of accuracy the amount and
the American fisheries to be open to the Canadian fishermen
.be provisions of the treaty. The kinds of fish that are caught
)ast of Maine are Mackerel—which is one of the most valuable
sful, especially early in the season before these fish frequent
; so-far Eastward as the Canadian shores, and would afford a
.tive business for the Canadian fishermen in supplying South.
ets early in the season, before these fish reach the more Eastern
the British Provinces. The "Porgie" fishery of Maine is prob-
next in importance to that of Mackerel—and the most valuable
ass, of the whole Atlantic coast, as the yield of oil is much
indant & better—than from any other source, this would open
inadian fisherman opportunities for an entirely new & remu-
business. The Herring fishery is also of considerable importance
.stern shores of Maine. "Winter Cod fishing," for supplying the
with *fresh* fish affords a large business to American fishermen,
i Canadian fishermen could compete under the provisions of the
f Washington.
at quantity and value of each kind of fish are annually taken
lian fishermen, and what by American fishermen, in the waters
)asts which are to be thrown open to competition by the Treaty
iugton? I cannot answer.
Canadian fishermen procure bait or supplies in the waters
State, and if so, to what extent and value? Canadian fishermen
.rge supplies of bait in the markets of this State.
hat is the probable annual value to Canadian fishermen in be-
to procure bait, to land and dry their nets, and repack and
r fish on the coasts of your State, without any other restriction
t contained in the Treaty of Washington? This will depend
o what extent the Canadian fishermen may avail themselves of
rtunities thus offered.
ill the admission of Canadian fishermen to our in-shore fisheries
y detriment or hinderance to the profitable pursuit of these fish-
our own fishermen; and if so, in what manner, and to what ex-
ually? The competition of Canadian fishermen will be likely
lerably reduce the profits of our own fishermen, especially in
er fishing.
hat number of Canadian vessels and boats are engaged in the
of your State, and what are their tonnage and value, and the
of men employed upon them? Can give no reliable informa-

the fisheries pursued by American fishermen off the Atlantic
the British North American Provinces, what proportion con-
:he deep-sea fisheries, and what proportion of the in-shore fish-
Chiefly deep-sea fishing, but a small proportion are in-shore

r what description of fish do American fishermen pursue the
fisheries? For mackerel chiefly.
you state that the in shore fisheries are pursued wholly or chiefly
.erel, please state what proportion of mackerel is taken within
ore limits, and what proportion is taken outside of the in-shore
I learn that probably not one quarter of the mackrel taken by

American fishermen are caught within the in-shore li⟩
than three quarters are taken outside.

16. Is not much the larger quantity of mackerel caugl
fishermen off the coasts of British America taken outs
limits ; and in the summer season especially, are not ma⟩
found on the banks, in the Gulf of Saint Lawrence,
shore ? Yes—from the best information I have.

17. Are Colonial fishermen injured by permitting Ame
to fish in Colonial in-shore waters ? I have heard Canadi
or coasters say, that it was rather an advantage in the ⟩
have American fishermen in their waters—than otherwise
not say.

18. Are not more fish caught by Colonial fishermen, ⟩
shore, alongside a fleet of American fishing-vessels, fr⟨
quantities of bait are thrown out, than when fishing al
say—from personal knowledge,

19. What is the best bait for the mackerel, and where
taken ? How much of it is taken within three miles of
what is the annual value to the United States, or to th
inces, as the case may be, to take such bait within thr
shore ? Porgies—principally taken within three miles ⟨

20. Please state as to each class of fisheries carried on
or district, the cost of fitting out, equipping, furnishin,
a vessel for carrying it on, estimating it by the averag
cruise. State, as far as possible, in detail, the eleme
make up the cost of taking and delivering a full cargo a
to the home port. Vessels of 60 to 70 tons costing ⟨
dollars are the prevailing class of craft employed by
ermen and to "fit out" for a mackerel cruise—compl
$2,500 to $3,000 per annum and they make three—someti
a year,

21. When you have fully answered question 20, pl⟨
same questions as to vessels fitted out, equipped, furnish
from the Dominion of Canada, including Prince Edwa⟩
as you are able to do so. If you state that there is a⟩
tween the cost of the Canadian and the cost of the Am
these respects, explain what the difference is and the
cannot state the cost of fitting & manning Canadian
think they must be very much less, as they are not so
vessels as those employed by American fishermen,

22. Are you acquainted, and for how long, and in wh⟨
the fisheries on the coasts of Nova Scotia, New Bruns⟩
Prince Edward Island, or with either, and if either, wit
fisheries ? Only from such information as I have acqu⟨
ness relations with the American fishermen & dealers
versation with Canadian Coasters,

23. What kind of fish frequent the waters of those ⟨
to be thrown open to American fishermen under the ⟩
Treaty of Washington ? Mackerel—Pollock, & Herrin⟨

24. Please state in detail the amount and the annual
1854 to 1872 inclusive) of the fisheries which are so to⟨
to American fishermen ; also the amount and the ann⟩
catch in the adjacent waters which are more than th⟩
from the shore ; please state these facts in detail. ⟩
answer intelligably,

25. Do American fishermen procure bait in the wa⟩

coast of the Dominion of Canada? If so, to what extent,
the value? Have heard that they do occasionally.

t the American fishermen purchase supplies in the ports of
on of Canada, including bait, ice, salt, barrels, provisions,
articles for the use of the men engaged in the fisheries? If
ports, and to what extent? And, if that is the case, is it not
e to the ports of the Dominion to have the fishing vessels
d States in their neighborhood during the fishing season?
7 it is so, and estimate, if you can, the money-value of that

Yes to some extent at Halifax Yarmouth—Cape Breton
es, and is an advantage to the ports of the Dominion, in
upplies, &c,

you any knowledge of how many United States fishing-ves-
engage in the fisheries off the Atlantic coasts of the British
rican Provinces, (excluding Newfoundland,) both without
the three-mile limit? If so, state how many vessels are so
at is the value of their tonnage, what is the number of men
nnually on such vessels, what sorts of fish are taken there,
annual value of all the fish so caught, and what is the propor-
bable proportion, in your judgment, of the amount of such
within three miles of the British coast, and of the amount
de of the three-mile limit? I cannot say how many U.
are yearly engaged or how many men employed—The
sh caught is previously stated—the portion caught within
he British coast is not over 10 per cent I think

t percentage of value, if any, is, in your judgment, added to
of a voyage by the privilege to fish within three marine miles
t; whence is such profit derived, and in what does it con-
aps ten per cent, as by such previledges, they can fish to bet-
ge near the shore for two months in the year.

he American fishermen gain under the Treaty of Washington
le rights of landing to dry nets and cure fish, or to repack
transship cargoes, which were not theirs before; if so, what
ights, and what do you estimate them to be worth annually,
egate? The fish caught by our fishermen are not repacked till
home. Transhipping cargoes will be of some value. There
other rights acquired by the treaty that I can now see.

t the Treaty of Washington, so far as the fishing clauses are
more, or quite as, beneficial to the people of the British North
Provinces as to the people of the United States? I should
Treaty" to be as beneficial to the British North American
in every respect as to the people of the United States—Smoke-
ll be established by American dealers at favorable ports of
in the British Provinces to secure the advantages of cheaper

t is the amount and value of colonial cargoes of fish of all
s which are annually shipped to the United States? Cannot

all No. 1 and No. 2 mackerel, for the larger part of the fat
nd for all No. 1 salmon, does not the United States afford the
et? Yes—so far as my knowledge goes,
ou know what amount of duties is annually paid to the United
fish and fish-oil imported from Canada, which are to be made
r the provisions of the Treaty of Washington, please state
ially, and by classes, from 1854 to 1872, inclusive. I cannot

34. If you know what amount of duties is annually paid in
fish and fish-oil imported from the United States, which are t
free under the provisions of the said Treaty, please state then:
and by classes, from 1854 to 1872 inclusive.

35. The object of these inquiries is to ascertain whether th
respect of fishing, and fishermen, and fish, which were grante
Britain by the Treaty of Washington, are or are not a just
for the rights in those respects which were granted by said
the United States. If you know anything bearing upon t
which you have not already stated in reply to previous questi
state it as fully as if you had been specially inquired of in re

I Marshall N. Rich do solmnly—sincerely & truly swear th
going statements are true & correct to the best of my knowl
lif—So help me God

                                        MARSHALL N

Sworn before me this 12th day of June 1873   (Seal.
                                        D MORT
                                  Dety Collr, Justice of

No. 13.

[CONFIDENTIAL.]

QUESTIONS RESPECTING THE FISHERIES TO
POUNDED TO ——— ——— ON BEHALF OF THI
STATES.

1. What is your name and age, and in what town and S
reside ? Noah Swett—47—Wellfleet Massachusetts.
2. What opportunities have you had for becoming acqu
the American and Canadian Atlantic sea-fisheries, and the '
catch of the different kinds of fish ? Have been engaged i
erel fishery 35 years. 15 years as catcher, 20 years as Inspec
have visited the Canadian waters.
3. Can you give the names of other persons in your neight
have also had the opportunity of obtaining similar informat
please give some such name.
4. A copy of the Treaty between Great Britain and the U!
known as the Treaty of Washington, is hereto annexed. '
amlue articles 18 to 22 inclusive, and state that you ha
Have examined the articles mentioned
5. What kinds of fish frequent the waters of your State
those which are to be thrown open to the Canadian fisherm
provisions of the Treaty of Washington ? Cod, Mackerel
den or Pogis are the Principal varieties of great value—
6. Can you give a statement of the kinds and quantities
annually off the coasts of your State from the years 185J
clusive ? If you can do this please do so ; and if not, pleas
that information can be procured. The Reports of the In:
eral will give the total catch of Mackerel for those years but
the foreign with the home catch, and it will be difficult I tl
separate statement of each. Am not aware that any pub
the catch of Cod on our shores has been kept.
7. If you are able to do so, will you state the amount and
American fisheries which are to be thrown open to Canadi:

rovisions of the Treaty of Washington? Please state them
lowing the different kinds of fish, and the value of each kind.
that an annual average catch of Mackl—to be 250.000 bar-
le New England States at $10 per barrel—the value would be
00 for such fish alone, the value of the Cod &, Porgy catch.
ell acquainted with
  quantity and value of each kind of fish are annually taken by
ishermen, and what by American fishermen, in the waters off
which are to be thrown open to competition by the Treaty of
on?
inadian fishermen procure bait or supplies in the waters of
? and if so, to what extent and value? I think the Canadian
have not only in exceptional cases procure Bait on our coast.
rocured it from second hands.
it is the probable annual value to Canadian fishermen in being
cure bait, to land and dry their nets, and to repack and cure
on the coasts of your State, without any other restriction than
ined in the Treaty of Washington? The privilege to procure
nable. so is the liberty to repack and inspect their mackerel.
ge relating to nets is not worth much to either side. they salt
and do not dry
  the admission of Canadian fishermen to our in-shore fisheries
detriment or hinderance to the profitable pursuit of these fishir own fishermen ; and, if so, in what manner and to what ex-
ily? Our home fleet is already too numerous for the pros-
the business.   If this Treaty causes the Canadian fishery
increase. the detriment to the Home vessel will be serious on
e difference in fitting. cost of vessel, &c enabling them to sell

at number of Canadian vessels and boats are engaged in the
f your State, and what are their tonnage and value, and the
men employed upon them? Am not aware that at present
any to make acct of
the fisheries pursued by American fishermen off the Atlantic
the British North American Provinces, what proportion con-
e'deep-sea fisheries, and what proportion of the in-shore fishery Largely deep sea fishery
  what description of fish do American fishermen pursue the
isheries? Mostly mackerel—
you state that the in shore fisheries are pursued wholly or
c mackerel, please state what proportion of mackerel is taken
e in-shore limits, and what proportion is taken outside of the
limits? My opinion is from what I can learn from what ex-
persons say that more than ¾ of the catch has been outside the
it in the Bay of St Lawrence. The American in shore fishery
iluable, especially early & late. for mackerel and fresh fishing
ter & spring
not much the larger quantity of mackerel caught by American
off the coasts of British America taken outside the in-shore
nd in the summer season especially, are not mackerel generally
the banks, in the Gulf of Saint Lawrence, and not within
Such are undoubtedly the facts
e Colonial fishermen injured by permitting American fishermen
Colonial in-shore waters? I look upon it as a very great ad-
to the Colonist
e not more fish caught by Colonial fishermen, when fishing in-

shore, alongside a fleet of American fishing-vessels, froi
quantities of bait are thrown out, than when fishing alon
the case that while fishing in shore the Colonial fishermen
American, so as to take advantage of her bait. to toll m
side

19. What is the best bait for the mackerel, and where is
taken? How much of it is taken within three miles of
what is the annual value to the United States, or to the
inces, as the case, may be, to take such bait within thre
shore? The Porgy is the almost universal bait used. and
Long Island to the Penobscot River. and is all taken wi
the annual value to one of our fishermen. is from $300 to

20. Please state as to each class of fisheries carried on fi
or district, the cost of fitting out, equipping, furnishing,
a vessel for carrying it on, estimating it by the average
cruise. State, as far as possible in detail the elements
make up the cost of taking and delivering a full cargo an
to the home ports For the mackerel Fishery—an averag
cost,...
Fitted with Barrels—..................................
    "   "   Salt.......................................
    "   "   Provisions..... ....
    "   "   Bait ....
    "   "   16 men—.................................

if she carries seine.................................

21. When you have fully answered question 20, plea
same questions as to vessels fitted out, equipped, furnishe
from the Dominion of Canada, including Prince Edwar
as you are able to do so. If you state that there is an
tween the cost of the Canadian and the cost of the Ame
these respects, explain what the difference is and the rea
American mackerel fleet is a fleet of Yachts calculate
and composed and constructed of the best materials,
fleet is far below the other in material and construction,
duties that the American pays are unknown to the Col
salt and Provisions are likewise lower and of an inferi
the habits of living on board are very much in favor of
judge that the inhabitant of the Dominion can furnis
Schooner at. ⅓ at least less cost than the American

22. Are you acquainted, and for how long, and in what
the fisheries on the coasts of Nova Scotia, New Brunswi
Prince Edward Island, or with either, and if either, \
fisheries? Have no personal acquaintance, but have oft
to those waters.

23. What kind of fish frequent the waters of those co
to be thrown open to American fishermen under the pr
Treaty of Washington? Mackerel & Cod——

24. Please state in detail the amount and the annual
1851 to 1872 inclusive) of the fisheries which are so to
to American fishermen; also the amount and the annu
catch in the adjacent waters which are more than thr

re; please state these facts in detail. For the ten pre-
our fishermen from Cape Cod especially have not fre-
ny great extent the Bay of St. Lawrence for years not
there from this town (Wellfleet) Our shore fishery proving
r and productive than that of the Bay Since seining has
pular Our hook fishermen are turning their attention that
 cruising on the same ground with the seiners
erican fishermen procure bait in the waters within three
:oast of the Dominion of Canada? If so. to what extent,
he value? Am not aware that they procur bait at all in
 Waters
the American fishermen purchase supplies in the ports of
n of Canada, including bait, ice, salt, barrels, provisions.
irticles for the use of the men engaged in the fisheries?
t ports, and to what extent? And, if that is the case, is
rantage to the ports of the Dominion to have the fishing-
e United States in their neighborhood during the fishing
plain why it is so, and estimate, if you can, the money-
t advantage. The Ports in Gut of Canso. Georgetown.
n Malpec & Cascumpec are largely indebted to the Ameri-
n for their custom. During the Reciprocity treaty these
hed from the gains derived from that source. Since that
:en cancelled those same places have suffered severely from
 to furnish supplies to American vessels
you any knowledge of how many United States fishing-ves-
ngage in the fisheries off the Atlantic coasts of the British
ican Provinces, (excluding Newfoundland,) both without
he three-mile limit? If so, state how many vessels are so
at is the value of their tonnage, what is the number of men
nually on such vessels, what sorts of fish are taken there,
annual value of all the fish so caught, and what is the pro-
probable proportion, in your judgment, of the amount of
aken within three miles of the British coast, and of the
:n outside of the three-mile limit?
percentage of value, if any, is, in your judgment, added to
f a voyage by the privilege to fish within three marine miles
; whence is such profit derived; and in what does it con-
urse it will be a convenience to fish in shore. When we were
privilege fishermen kept more at sea, did not frequent the
ften, and employed more time in business. deducting what
catch off shore during the time used in shore, and amt of
[think the privilege quite valueless.
e American fishermen gain under the Treaty of Washington
e rights of landing to dry nets and cure fish, or to repack
transship cargoes, which were not theirs before; if so, what
ghts, and what do you estimate them to be worth annually,
regate? Am not aware that the American will gain any
ght in this way that they do not now possess. '
t the Treaty of Washington, so far as the fishing clauses are
more, or quite as, beneficial to the people of the British North
Provinces as to the people of the United States? The fisher-
United States are a unit in deciding that the treaty is against

t is the amount and value of colonial cargoes of fish of all
s which are annually shipped to the United States?
ll No. 1 and No. 2 mackerel, for the larger part of the fat

herring, and for all No. 1 salmon, does not the United St
only market. They do. Fat fish will not keep in warm

33. If you know what amount of duties is annually pai
States on fish and fish-oil imported from Canada, which
free under the provisions of the Treaty of Washingto
them annually, and by classes, from 1854 to 1872, inclusi

34. If you know what amount of duties is annually pai
fish and fish-oil imported from the United States, which
free under the provisions of the said Treaty, please state
and by classes, from 1854 to 1872, inclusive.

35. The object of these inquiries is to ascertain whet
in respect of fishing, and fishermen, and fish, which w
Great Britain by the Treaty of Washington, are or are n
aleut for the rights in those respects which were granted
to the United States. If you know anything bearing up
which you have not already stated in reply to previous q
state it as fully as if you had been specially inquired c
it. I can only say that the universal opinion of those e
American fisheries both at sea and on shore is that th
treaty are decidedly against them, some have gone so fa
the total ruin of our own fisheries when brought in
with the Dominion fisheries. For the last 25 or 30 y
kee has been training the Colonist his business, ac
him his trade a large proportion of the fishermen of N
better acquainted on our shore than on their own. the
them many capable men who have only to fit out their
cheaply and enter the lists against their trainers and if t
the extent that Yankee enterprise would carry it were th
versed we may expect our business to decline and go in
so depressing an effect has this view upon the fisheries o
already this year we have sold 15 out of a fleet of 75 ves
none.

NO.

Then personally appeared the above named Noah Swe
edge the foregoing answers to be the best of his belief c

EBENEZER T. A
Justice

WELLFLEET June 17, 1873

No. 14.

[CONFIDENTIAL.]

QUESTIONS RESPECTING THE FISHERIES
POUNDED TO —— —— ON BEHALF OF
STATES.

1. What is your name and age, and in what town and
side? Chas. C. Pettingill, Salem, Massachusetts

2. What opportunities have you had for becoming a
the American and Canadian Atlantic sea-fisheries, and t
catch of the different kinds of fish? Have been in th
years past, most of the time in Gloucester

3. Can you give the names of other persons in you
who have also had the opportunity of obtaining similar i
so, please give some such name. Chas A Roper of Sal

' of the Treaty between Great Britain and the United
rn as the Treaty of Washington, is hereto annexed. Will
, articles 18 to 22 inclusive, and state that you have done so?
ined said articles
kinds of fish frequent the waters of your State, especially
are to be thrown open to the Canadian fishermen under the
f the Treaty of Washington? Menhaden, a fish which is
ally for Mackerel Bait, and the Provinces depend mainly
a supply. in my judgment it is quite a valuable considera-
a
u give a statement of the kinds and quantities of fish taken
the coast of your State from the years 1854 to 1872, inclu.
ou can do this please do so; and if not, please state where
ation can be procured. this information will come to you
) doubt.
are able to do so, will you state the amount and value of the
sheries which are to be thrown open to Canadian fishermen
rovisions of the Treaty of Washington? Please state them
owing the different kinds of fish, and the value of each kind.
nly, our advantage from the Treaty must come from the
ishery. I have always regarded free fishing for mackerel in
St. Lawrence quite important to our fishing interest, other
no particular value to us, which comes from the Treaty, with
in the Bay, which calls a large number of our vessels there
l large amount of trade from our fleet, which they have al-
led of much value to them. Add to that their fish free in
s, with the advantage of our Mackerel Bait which comes to
, I am inclined to think nearly if not quite balances their
ast us,
quantity and value of each kind of fish are annually taken
n fishermen, and what by American fishermen, in the waters
ts which are to be thrown open to competition by the Treaty
ton? These facts are contained in Reports which I presume
iable
nadian fishermen procure bait or supplies in the waters of
? and if so, to what extent and value? largely their Mack-
mes for our coast. Value could not say
t is the probable annual value to Canadian fishermen in being
cure bait, to land and dry their nets, and to repack and cure
a the coasts of your State, without any other restriction than
ned in the Treaty of Washington? Could not say
the admission of Canadian fishermen to our in-shore fisheries
letriment or hinderance to the profitable pursuit of these fishir own fishermen; and if so, in what manner, and to what
ally? Not very serious hinderance.
t number of Canadian vessels and boats are engaged in the
your State, and what are their tonnage and value, and the
men employed upon them?
e fisheries pursued by American fishermen off the Atlantic
ie British North American Provinces, what proportion con-
deep-sea fisheries, and what proportion of the in-shore fish-

what description of fish do American fishermen pursue the
heries? Mackerel chiefly.
u state that the in-shore fisheries are pursued wholly or chiefly
el, please state what proportion of mackerel is taken within

F

the in-shore limits, and what proportion is taken outside of the in-shore
limits? I think a very small portion of the catch, the past fifteen years
has been take within the limits. If our fishermen had felt secure and
free to fish always when three miles from land, their catch from year to
year would not have been much impaired. The trouble mainly has been,
a fear to fish within sight of land, whenever any Cutters were in sight,
knowing there was no redress when taken. here lies the great sacrifice
which our fishermen have had to bear in the past.

16. Is not much the larger quantity of mackerel caught by American
fishermen off the coasts of British America taken outside the in-shore
limits; and in the summer season especially, are not mackerel generally
found on the banks, in the Gulf of Saint Lawrence, and not within shore?
Yes.

17. Are Colonial fishermen injured by permitting American fishermen
to fish in Colonial in-shore waters? I think it has worked for their advantage rather than injury

18. Are not more fish caught by Colonial fishermen, when fishing inshore alongside a fleet of American fishing-vessels, from which large
quantities of bait are thrown out, than when fishing alone? this is
true

19. What is the best bait for the mackerel, and where is it principally
taken? How much of it is taken within three miles of the shore, and
what is the annual value to the United States, or to the British Provinces, as the case may be, to take such bait within three miles of the
shore? What we call Pogies, principally take on our coast, cannot
state quantity & value

20. Please state as to each class of fisheries carried on from your State
or district, the cost of fitting out, equipping, furnishing, and manning a
vessel for carrying it on, estimating it by the average length of the
cruise. State, as far as possible, in detail the elements which go to
make up the cost of taking and delivering a full cargo and of returning
to the home port. It cost about $2000. dollars to fit for a three month
cod fish Trip, and $1500. dollars for a three months mackerel trip, this
includes no wages or shares for the crew.

21. When you have fully answered question 20, please answer the
same questions as to vessels fitted out, equipped, furnished, and manned
from the Dominion of Canada, including Prince Edward Island, so far
as you are able to do so. If you state that there is any difference between the cost of the Canadian and the cost of the American vessel in
these respects, explain what the difference is and the reason for it.
Shoulld think they could save in fitting for the business at least 25 per
ct from our cost. Provisions, salt, cost of vessels, and all labor when
hired is much less than ours

22. Are you acquainted, and for how long, and in what capacity, with
the fisheries on the coasts of Nova Scotia, New Brunswick, Quebec, or
Prince Edward Island, or with either, and if either, with which of these
fisheries? 25 years

23. What kind of fish frequent the waters of those coasts which are
to be thrown open to American fishermen under the provisions of the
Treaty of Washington? Mackerel principally, other fish are little
sought for in the limits

24. Please state in detail the amount and the annual value (say from
1854 to 1872 inclusive) of the fisheries which are so to be thrown open
to American fishermen; also the amount and the annual value of the
catch in the adjacent waters which are more than three miles distant
from the shore; please state these facts in detail.

American fishermen procure bait in the waters within three
he coast of the Dominion of Canada? If so, to what extent,
s the value? Our Halibut Catcher often go in after fresh
always buy it, which is a good thing for them

ot the American fishermen purchase supplies in the ports of
ton of Canada, including bait, ice, salt, barrels, provisions,
as articles for the use of the men engaged in the fisheries? If
t ports, and to what extent? And, if that is the case, is it
vantage to the ports of the Dominion to have the fishing-ves-
) United States in their neighborhood during the fishing sea-
plain why it is so, and estimate, if you can, the money-value
ivantage. The amount of supplies bought by our Fishermen
e year must be quite large, while we had free fishing there.
vould be safe to say that the American fleet paid at: P. Ed
insoe, Port Hood & Halifax 250,000 dollas per year for sup-
l kinds

ve you any knowledge of how many United States fishing-
early engage in the fisheries off the Atlantic coasts of the
orth American Provinces, (excluding Newfoundland), both
nd within the three-mile limit? If so, state how many ves-
o engaged, what is the value of their tonnage, what is the
f men employed annually on such vessels, what sorts of fish
there, what is the annual value of all the fish so caught, and
ae proportion, or probable proportion, in your judgment, of the
f such catch taken within three miles of the British coast,
e amount taken outside of the three-mile limit?

iat percentage of value, if any, is, in your judgment, added to
s of a voyage by the privilege to fish within three marine miles
ast; whence is such profit derived; and in what does it con-
very small per centage of the fish will be caught within the
ill I think free fishing will add much to the value of the catch

the American fishermen gain under the Treaty of Washing-
valuable rights of landing to dry nets and cure fish, or to re-
oi, or to transship cargoes, which were not theirs before; if so,
those rights, and what do you estimate them to be worth an-
a the aggregate? I think none of any value. We have had
le in this respect of consequence

not the Treaty of Washington, so far as the fishing clauses are
d, more, or quite as, beneficial to the people of the British North
n Provinces as to the people of the United States? I have no
it

hat is the amount and value of colonial cargoes of fish of all
ons which are annually shipped to the United States? Reports
se facts

r all No. 1 and No. 2 mackerel, for the larger part of the fat her-
d for all No. 1 salmon, does not the United States afford the
:ket. this is mainly true

you know what amount of duties is annually paid to the United
a fish and fish-oil imported from Canada, which are to be made
ler the provisions of the Treaty of Washington, please state
nually, and by classes, from 1854 to 1872, inclusive.

you know what amount of duties is annually paid in Canada
md fish-oil imported from the United States, which are to be
ae under the provisions of the said Treaty, please state them
r, and by classes, from 1854 to 1872, inclusive.
ae object of these inquiries is to ascertain whether the rights in

respect of fishing, and fishermen, and fish, which were granted to Gre
Britain by the Treaty of Washington, are or are not a just equivale
for the rights in those respects which were granted by said Treaty to t
United States. If you know anything bearing upon this subject whi
you have not already stated in reply to previous questions, please sta
it as fully as if you had been specially inquired of in respect of it.
have no doubt that all the Provinces so far as the Fishing interest h
to do with it, will thrive and prosper, much better under the free fishir
durcing the ten years of Resciprosituty or free fishing, they prosper
much better than they have since, this is their own testimony, as I ha
heard it from very many of them, merchants as well as Fisherm
themselves.

CHAS C. PETTINGILL
Custom House, Salem.

Subscribed & sworn before me this twentieth day of June 1873.

CHAS. H. ODELL Collector

No. 15.

[CONFIDENTIAL.]

QUESTIONS RESPECTING THE FISHERIES TO BE PR
POUNDED TO ——— ——— ON BEHALF OF THE UNITE
STATES.

1. What is your name and age, and in what town and State do y
reside ? William H Nelson age 43. Plymouth Massachusetts

2. What opportunities have you had for becoming acquainted wi
the American and Canadian Atlantic sea-fisheries, and the value of t
catch of the different kinds of fish ? Have been engaged in the Co
fishery since 1851

3. Can you give the names of other persons in your neighborhood w
have also had the opportunity of obtaining similar information ? If
please give some such name.

4. A copy of the Treaty between Great Britain and the United Stat
known as the Treaty of Washington is hereto annexed. Will you
amine articles 18 to 22 inclusive, and state that you have done so
have examined it.

5. What kinds of fish frequent the waters of your State, especia
those which are to be thrown open to the Canadian fishermen under
provisions of the Treaty of Washington ? Mackerel Herrings & M
haden principally

6. Can you give a statement of the kinds and quantities of fish tal
annually off the coast of your State from the years 1854 to 1872,
clusive ? If you can do this please do so ; and if not, please state wh
that information can be procured. Mackerel fishery is carried on
Gloucester Provincetown Wellfleet Chatham Boston, Portland & ot
ports in Maine from which such information could be obtained

7. If you are able to do so, will you state the amount and value of
American fisheries which are to be thrown open to Canadian fisheri
under the provisions of the Treaty of Washington ? Please state tl
in detail, showing the different kinds of fish, and the value of each k
I cannot.

8. What quantity and value of each kind of fish are annually ta
by Canadian fishermen, and what by American fishermen, in the wa

f the coasts which are to be thrown open to competition by the Treaty
Washington? Cannot state but Gloucester should be able to give
is information.

9. Do Canadian fishermen procure bait or supplies in the waters of
ur State? and if so, to what extent and value? Bait is purchased
sent to their ports.

10. What is the probable annual value to Canadian fishermen in being
le to procure bait, to land and dry their nets, and to repack and cure
eir fish on the coasts of your State, without any other restriction than
at contained in the Treaty of Washington?—The Menhaden Bait which
e used principally for mackerel fisherman are taken wholly in Mass.
Maine and are valuable, to what extent I cannot say.

11. Will the admission of Canadian fishermen to our in-shore fish-
ies cause any detriment or hinderance to the profitable pursuit of these
sheries by our own fishermen; and if so, in what manner, and to what
tent annually? They will necessarily diminish the catch of our fish-
man as a large fleet is more destructive to schools of mackerel than
naller ones and any increase has that effect.

12. What number of Canadian vessels and boats are engaged in the
sheries of your State, and what are their tonnage and value, and the
umber of men employed upon them? I cannot say.

13. Of the fisheries pursued by American fishermen off the Atlantic
asts of the British North American Provinces, what proportion con-
sts of the deep-sea fisheries, and what proportion of the in-shore fishes? Mackerel fisherman are the only in shore fisherman and the num-
r Gloucester could determine as I am not engaged in it.

14. For what description of fish do American fishermen pursue the
-shore fisheries? Mackerel only.

15. If you state that the in shore fisheries are pursued wholly or chiefly
r mackerel, please state what proportion of mackerel is taken within
e in-shore limits, and what proportion is taken outside of the in-shore
nits? I cannot state from my own knowledge but only from the
atements made by the fishermen themselves some state it at about ½
hile others place the quantity much less and regard the inshore limit
of little or no value.

16. Is not much the larger quantity of mackerel caught by American
shermen off the coasts of British America taken outside the in-shore
nits; and in the summer season especially, are not mackerel generally
und on the banks, in the Gulf of Saint Lawrence, and not within shore?
hey are—

17. Are colonial fishermen injured by permitting American fishermen
fish in colonial in-shore waters? I should consider not

18. Are not more fish caught by Colonial fishermen, when fishing in-
ore, alongside a fleet of American fishing-vessels, from which large
antities of bait are thrown out than when fishing alone? I think it is
nquestionably so

19. What is the best bait for the mackerel, and where is it principally
ken? How much of it is taken within three miles of the shore, and
hat is the annual value to the United States, or to the British Prov-
ces, as the case may be, to take such bait within three miles of the
ore? Menhaden are the principal bait, and are caught usually in
ays & harbors. Vessels use from 20 to 60 Bs in season, and value is
om 5 to $8 per Bl

20. Please state as to each class of fisheries carried on from your
tate or district, the cost of fitting out, equipping, furnishing, and maning a vessel for carrying it on, estimating it by the average length of

the cruise. State, as far as possible, in detail the e
make up the cost of taking and delivering a full ca
to the home port. Cost of fitting & furnishing ve
exclusive of 1st cost of vessel & wages would be
$25 per ton of vessel engaged in deep sea fisheries
as a full one about 2.00 per Ql currency, not incl
which would vary considerably.

21. When you have fully answered question 20, pl
questions as to vessels fitted out, equipped, furnishe
the Dominion of Canada, including Prince Edward
are able to do so. If you state that there is any di
cost of the Canadian and the cost of the America
spects, explain what the difference is and the re
not state with any accuracy as to the cost of fittin;
dian ports, but it is much less on all articles of forci
as duties are much less on all such articles than
cost of their vessels is much less, not exceeding $\frac{2}{3}$
lar class of vessels built here their salt cost ther
quite an item in curing of fish and Lumber, chains
free of duty, costing not over $\frac{2}{3}$ of prices of such ar

22. Are you acquainted, and for how long, and in
the fisheries on the coasts of Nova Scotia, New B
Prince Edward Island, or with either, and if either,
fisheries ? I am not acquainted to any extent.

23. What kind of fish frequent the waters of th
to be thrown open to American fishermen under t
Treaty of Washington ? Mackeril & Herrings only

24. Please state in detail the amount and the an
1854 to 1872 inclusive) of the fisheries which are s
to American fishermen ; also the amount and the
catch in the adjacent waters which are more than
from the shore ; please state these facts in detail.

25. Do American fishermen procure bait in th
miles of the coast of the Dominion of Canada ?
and what is the value ? Not that I am aware of.

26. Do not the American fishermen purchase su
the Dominion of Canada, including bait, ice, sal
and various articles for the use of the men engagec
so, in what ports, and to what extent ? And, if
not an advantage to the ports of the Dominion t
sels of the United States in their neighborhood di
son ? Explain why it is so, and estimate, if you ca
that advantage. Supplies are purchased to a con.
the Ports of Prince Edward Island, Cape Breton ;
the trade must be of considerable value The ai
state.

27. Have you any knowledge of how many Uni
sels yearly engage in the fisheries off the Atlantic
North American Provinces, (excluding Newfour
and within the three-mile limit ? If so, state ho
engaged, what is the value of their tonnage, what
employed annually on such vessels, what sorts o
what is the annual value of all the fish so caught
portion, or probable proportion, in your judgm
such catch taken within three miles of the Br
amount taken outside of the three-mile limit ? I

number of vessels so engaged as the Gov't can easily
t from C. House returns. Gloucester chiefly is engaged
ries are prosecuted in those Waters and could furnish
ion.

ercentage of value, if any, is, in your judgment, added to
a voyage by the privilege to fish within three marine miles
whence is such profit derived; and in what does it con.
no value to any but mackerel fisherman

American fishermen gain under the Treaty of Washing.
ble rights of landing to dry nets and cure fish, or to repack
ransship cargoes, which were not theirs before; if so, what
its, and what do you estimate them to be worth annually,
ate ?   The American fisheman consider themselves as sur-
re than they receive and gain no rights in drying and cur.
1 they did not possess before

he Treaty of Washington, so far as the fishing clauses are
ore, or quite as, beneficial to the people of the British North
ovinces as to the people of the United States ? More so
s the amount and value of colonial cargoes of fish of all
which are annually shipped to the United States ?   I can.

No. 1 and No. 2 mackerel, for the larger part of the fat her,
all No. 1 salmon, does not the United States afford the only
loes the only market
kriow what amount of duties is annually paid to the United
and fish-oil imported from Canada, which are to be made
he provisions of the Treaty of Washington, please state
ly, and by classes, from 1854 to 1872, inclusive. I cannot.
know what amount of duties is annually paid in Canada
fish-oil imported from the United States, which are to be
der the provisions of the said Treaty, please state them an-
ny classes, from 1854 to 1872, inclusive. I do not.
ject of these inquiries is to ascertain whether the rights in
hing, and fishermen, and fish, which were granted to Great
ie Treaty of Washington, are or are not a just equivalent
ı in those respects which were granted by said Treaty to the
is.   If you know anything bearing upon this subject which
already stated in reply to previous questions, please state
if you had been specially inquired of in respect of it.   As
e stated the value of in shore fisheries accrues to the benefit
erel fisherman only, as the Codfishery is a deep sea fishery
y pursued on the Banks of Newfoundland, and the treaty
s fish & oil from the Provinces to come in free of duty
ly interfere with the value of our own catch in our own mar-
cannot with increased cost of outfits & vessels, compete
with these fisherman.   The mackerel fisheman feel that in
coast to their fisherman in procuring Bait and in supplying
with fresh fish and mackerel, which on our coast are supe-
y, is surrendering a greater value than any advantage which
ens up to our fisherman in the Bay of s't Laurence.   The
mackerel caught on our coast is much greater than that
eir coast and the price of mackerel of our coast catch will
ually 25 % per cent. more than that caught in Bay of st
The Fresh fish trade which has increased rapidly the past
d is now increasing by the opening up of Rail Communica-

tion is open to their fisheman by this treaty, and its valu
my opinion worth more to them than all the advantage we
back. The Codfishery interest here and in the vicinity wo
it in their power surrender our markets or open them free 1
man for all the rights they confer coupled with the paymen
to them as a compensation under the reciprocity treaty th
the ports of Barrington & vicinity numbered some 50 v
found a market for their fish in our ports since that time t
have declined in Barrington alone, to some 5 to 6 vessels o1
fisherman are pursuing the business in vessels from here
Some 12 entire crews coming from that section are employ
here this present season, the present treaty Will encourage·
and deprive us of men necessary to mau our vessels, whi
from Provinces.

                    Yours respectfully   ·

                                        W. H

COMMONWEALTH OF MASSACHUSETT

COUNTY OF PLYMOUTH

                                     TOWN OF

PLYMOUTH July 3, 1873

Then William H. Nelson personally appeared and made
statements by him made and signed, in the foregoing doc(
annexed, are true according to his best knowledge & belie
    Before me
        (Seal.)   JNO. J. RU:
                            Notary Public within & for si

No. 16.

[CONFIDENTIAL.]

QUESTIONS RESPECTING THE FISHERIES
    POUNDED TO ——— ——— ON BEHALF OF T
    STATES.

1. What is your name and age, and in what town and
reside? Asa W. Small; 33, Nantucket, Mass.

2. What opportunities have you had for becoming acqua
American and Canadian Atlantic sea-fisheries, and the val
of the different kinds of fish? I have been in the fishin
twenty years.

3. Can you give the names of other persons in your
who have also had the opportunity of obtaining simila1
If so, please give some such name.

4. A copy of the Treaty between Great Britain and the
known as the Treaty of Washington, is hereto annexed.
amine articles 18 to 22 inclusive, and state that you hav
have examined the articles from 18 to 22.

5. What kinds of fish frequent the waters of your S
those which are to be thrown open to the Canadian fisher
provisions of the Treaty of Washington? Cod, Macke
Pollock, Hake, Porgee, Bluefish, Herring, Shad, Striped-
& Halibut.

6. Can you give a statement of the kinds and quantiti(

the coast of your State from the years 1854 to 1872, inclu-
)u can do this please do so; and if not, please state where
ation can be procured.
are able to do so, will you state the amount and value ot
in fisheries which are to be thrown open to Canadian fisher-
the provisions of the Treaty of Washington? Please state
ail, showing the different kinds of fish, and the value of each

quantity and value of each kind of fish are annually taken
n fishermen, and what by American fishermen, in the waters
ts which are to be thrown open to competition by the Treaty
rton?
nadian fishermen procure bait or supplies in the waters of
! and if so, to what extent and value? They do not.
; is the probable annual value to Canadian fishermen in be-
procure bait, to land and dry their nets, and to repack and
ish on the coasts of your State, without any other restriction
ontained in the Treaty of Washington?
the admission of Canadian fishermen to our in-shore fisheries
detriment or hinderance to the profitable pursuit of these
· our own fishermen; and if so, in what manner, and to what
aally.
t number of Canadian vessels and boats are engaged in the
your State, and what are their tonnage and value, and the
men employed upon them? Not any at present.
ie fisheries pursued by American fishermen off the Atlantic
ie British North American Provinces, what proportion con-
deep-sea fisheries, and what proportion of the in-shore fish·

what description of fish do American fishermen pursue the in
ries? Cod, and Mackerel.
u state that the in shore fisheries are pursued wholly or chiefly
el, please state what proportion of mackerel is taken within
e limits, and what proportion is taken outside of the in-shore

)t much the larger quantity of mackerel caught by Americ'u
off the coasts of British America taken outside the in-shore
d in the summer season especially, are not mackerel gen-
id on the banks, in the Gulf of Saint Lawrence, and not within
he larger quantity are taken off shore.
colonial fishermen injured by permitting American fishermen
Colonial in-shore waters? I should say not.
not more fish caught by Colonial fishermen, when fishing in-
igside a fleet of American fishing-vessels, from which large
of bait are thrown out, than when fishing alone? Yes,—
been my experience.
at is the best bait for the mackerel, and where is it princi-
n? How much of it is taken within three miles of the shore,
is the annual value to the United States, or to the British
, as. the case may be, to take such bait within three miles of
? Porgee & Menhaden, principally taken from Long Island,
ie coast of Maine.
ase state as to each class of fisheries carried on from your
district, the cost of fitting out, equipping, furnishing, and
a vessel for carrying it on, estimating it by the average length
ise. State, as far as possible, in detail the elements which go

to make up the cost of taking and delivering a full
ing to the home port.

21. When you have fully answered question 2(
same questions as to vessels fitted out, equipped, fu
from the Dominion of Canada, including Prince E
as you are able to do so. If you state that there
tween the cost of the Canadian and the cost of th'
these respects, explain what the difference is and t

22. Are you acquainted, and for how long, an
with the fisheries on the coasts of Nova Scotia, New
or Prince Edward Island, or with either, and if e
these fisheries? I am acquainted with the fisherie
Prince Edwards' Island.

23. What kind of fish frequent the waters of th(
to be thrown open to American fishermen under t
Treaty of Washington? Cod and Mackerel.

24. Please state in detail the amount and the an
1854 to 1872 inclusive) of the fisheries which are s
to American fishermen; also the amount and the
catch in the adjacent waters which are more thai
from the shore; please state these facts in detail.

25. Do American fishermen procure bait in the
miles of the coast of the Dominion of Canada? I
and what is the value? They do not.

26. Do not the American fishermen purchase suj
the Dominion of Canada, including bait, ice, salt,
and various articles for the use of the men enga
If so, in what ports, and to what extent? And, if
not an advantage to the ports of the Dominion to
sels of the United States in their neighborhood
season? Explain why it is so, and estimate, if you
of that advantage.

27. Have you any knowledge of how many
vessels yearly engage in the fisheries off the
British North American Provinces, (excluding
without and within the three-mile limit? If so, s(
are so engaged, what is the value of their tonnag
of men employed annually on such vessels, what ,
there, what is the annual value of all the fish s
the proportion, or probable proportion, in your jud
of such catch taken within three miles of the Bri
amount taken outside of the three-mile limit?

28. What percentage of value, if any, is, in yot
the profits of a voyage by the privilege to fish witl
of the coast; whence is such profit derived; and
sist? Very little — or none

29. Do the American fishermen gain under th
ton any valuable rights of landing to dry nets a
pack them, or to transship cargoes, which were n
what are those rights, and what do you estimate
nually, in the aggregate? They do not gain any
in these days cure fish or repack, but return hon
their fares

30. Is not the Treaty of Washington, so far as
concerned, more, or quite as, beneficial to the
North American Provinces as to the people of t

,t the people of the British North American Provinces had by far—

the amount and value of colonial cargoes of fish of all hich are annually shipped to the United States?

No. 1 and No. 2 mackerel, for the larger part of the fat or all No. 1 salmon, does not the United States afford the It does.

now what amount of duties is annually paid to the United and fish-oil imported from Canada, which are to be made ie provisions of the Treaty of Washington, please state /, and by classes, from 1854 to 1872, inclusive.

:now what amount of duties is annually paid in Canada sh-oil imported from the United States, which are to be ler the provisions of the said Treaty, please state them . by classes from 1854 to 1872, inclusive.

ect of these inquiries is to ascertain whether the rights in iing, and fishermen, and fish, which were granted to Great e Treaty of Washington, are or are not a just equivalent in those respects which were granted by said Treaty to tates. If you know anything bearing upon this subject .re not already stated in reply to previous questions, please ly as if you had been specially inquired of in respect of it.

ASA W SMALL

:T, *ss.* *June 10th,* 1873.

mally appeared the above named Asa W. Small and made :uth of the foregoing statements by him signed, before me.

T. C. DEFRIEZ
Collector of Customs.

No. 17.

[CONFIDENTIAL.]

S RESPECTING THE FISHERIES TO BE PRO·
D TO ——— ——— ON BEHALF OF THE UNITED

i your name and age, and in what town and State do you

Smalley, aged 40, } Nantucket, Mass.
. Kenney aged 56, }

pportunities have you had for becoming acquainted with the d Canadian Atlantic sea-fisheries, and the value of the catch it kinds of fish ? Have followed the fishing business at Sea ars.

i give the names of other persons in your neighborhood who d the opportunity of obtaining similar information? If so, ome such name.

of the Treaty between Great Britain and the United States. e Treaty of Washington, is hereto annexed. Will you ex- s 18 to 22 inclusive, and state that you have done so ? We ed and read articles 18 to 22. inclusive.

:inds of fish frequent the waters of your State, especially are to be thrown open to the Canadian fishermen under the the Treaty of Washington ? Cod, Mackerel, Halibut, Had- ig, and Porgies.

i give a statement of the kinds and quantities of fish taken

annually off the coast of your State from the years 18
inclusive? If you can do this please do so; and if not,
where that information can be procured.

7. If you are able to do so, will you state the amount
the American fisheries which are to be thrown open to Can
men under the provisions of the Treaty of Washington?
them in detail, showing the different kinds of fish, and the
kind.

8. What quantity and value of each kind of fish are an
by Canadian fishermen, and what by American fishermen, i
off the coasts which are to be thrown open to competition b
of Washington?

9. Do Canadian fishermen procure bait or supplies in t
your State, and if so, to what extent and value? Canadi
do not purchase bait or Supplies in our State, to any exten

10. What is the probable annual value to Canadian
being able to procure bait, to land and dry their nets, an
and cure their fish on the coasts of your State, without
striction than that contained in the Treaty of Washington
is *nothing* in our estimation.

11. Will the admission of Canadian fishermen to our in
ies cause any detriment or hinderance to the profitable pur
fisheries by our own fishermen; and if so, in what manner,
extent annually? They will in this way; They can man
with less expense, consequently they can undersell us, and
their fish to our market they will do so, as there are no dut
and the result will be, our markets will soon be glutted,
low.

12. What number of Canadian vessels and boats are en
fisheries of your State, and what are their tonnage and v
number of men employed upon them? We do not
Canadian Boats or Vessels engaged in the fisheries, in *this*

13. Of the fisheries pursued by American fishermen off
coasts of the British North American Provinces, what pr
sists of the deep-sea fisheries, and what proportion of the
eries? In our estimation, Two Thirds consists of Deep sea
one third of Inshore fisheries.

14. For what description of fish do American fisherme
in-shore fisheries? Mackerel, Cod, and Porgies, chiefly M

15. If you state that the in shore fisheries are pursu
chiefly for mackerel, please state what proportion of macl
within the in-shore limits, and what proportion is taken
in-shore limits? More than two thirds of the Mackerel ar
of the *inshore* limits,—in our opinion.—

16. Is not much the larger quantity of mackerel caught
fishermen off the coasts of British America taken outsid
limits; and in the summer season especially, are not mack
found on the banks, in the Gulf of St. Lawrence, and not
We should say, The greater portion of Mackerel taken off
British America, would be outside the in shore limits, an
mer Season, Mackerel are generally found wide out on th

17. Are Colonial fishermen injured by permitting Ameri
to fish in Colonial in-shore waters? We should say they a
but benefitted in a measure.

18. Are not more fish caught by Colonial fishermen, wl
shore, alongside a fleet of American fishing-vessels, froi

f bait are thrown out, than when fishing alone? Should
olonial fishermen would be the gainers in the end by having
l baited up for them.

is the best bait for the mackerel, and where is it principally
w much of it is taken within three miles of the shore, and
annual value to the United States, or to the British Prov-
e case may be, to take such bait within three miles of the
e Porgie is considered the best bait for the Mackerel, is taken
e Shores & Rivers, Long Island Sound, Connecticut River,
ay, Boston Bay, off Portsmouth, Portland, and all along the
ore.

e state as to each class of fisheries carried on from your
trict, the cost of fitting out, equipping, furnishing, and man-
el for carrying it on, estimating it by the average length of
State, as far as possible, in detail the elements which go to
e cost of taking and delivering a full cargo and of returning
e port. For a Vessel of Seventy tons, manned by 10 men for
months to the Banks for Cod Fish

```
.......................................................  $700· 00
0.  Salt $350 ..........................................  ... 
ories $200 ............................................  400. 00
ads $50.  Sundries $100................................  100. 00
.......................................................  1,700. 00
.......................................................  $3,200. 00
```

n you have fully answered question 20, please answer the
ions as to vessels fitted out, equipped, furnished, and manned
ominion of Canada, including Prince Edward Island, so far
able to do so. If you state that there is any difference be-
cost of the Canadian and the cost of the American vessel in
cts, explain what the difference is and the reason for it.

you acquainted, and for how long, and in what capacity, with
s on the coasts of Nova Scotia, New Brunswick, Quebec, or
ward Island, or with either, and if either, with which of these

t kind of fish frequent the waters of those coasts which are
wn open to American fishermen under the provisions of the
Washington?
se state in detail the amount and the annual value (say from
72 inclusive) of the fisheries which are so to be thrown open to
fishermen; also the amount and the annual value of the catch
cent waters which are more than three miles distant from the
ase state these facts in detail.
American fishermen procure bait in the waters within three
e coast of the Dominion of Canada? If so, to what extent,
is the value? They do procure bait within 3 miles of the
st.
not the American fishermen purchase supplies in the ports of
nion of Canada, including bait, ice, salt, barrels, provisions,
s articles for the use of the men engaged in the fisheries? If
t ports, and to what extent? And, if that is the case, is it
lvantage to the ports of the Dominion to have the fishing-
the United States in their neighborhood during the fishing
Explain why it is so, and estimate if you can, the money-
that advantage. American fishermen do purchase supplies
alt, Bait, Ice, Barrels, and provisions &c in the Ports of the
of Canada.

27. Have you any knowledge of how many United States fishing-vessels yearly engage in the fisheries off the Atlantic coasts of the British North American Provinces, (excluding Newfoundland,) both without and within the three-mile limit? If so, state how many vessels are so engaged, what is the value of their tonnage, what is the number of men employed annually on such vessels, what sorts of fish are taken there, what is the annual value of all the fish so caught, and what is the proportion, or probable proportion, in your judgment, of the amount of such catch taken within three miles of the British coast, and of the amount taken outside of the three-mile limit?

28. What percentage of value, if any, is, in your judgment, added to the profits of a voyage by the privilege to fish within three marine miles of the coast; whence is such profit derived; and in what does it consist?

29. Do the American fishermen gain under the Treaty of Washington any valuable rights of landing to dry nets and cure fish, or to repack them, or to transship cargoes, which were not theirs before; if so, what are those rights, and what do you estimate them to be worth annually, in the aggregate? Do not consider it is any advantage to American fishermen, to dry nets or cure fish in any way, as by so doing, they injure themselves by the detention of getting their cargoes to market.

30. Is not the Treaty of Washington, so far as the fishing clauses are concerned, more, or quite as, beneficial to the people of the British North American Provinces as to the people of the United States? More beneficial to the people of the Provinces than to the people of the United States.

31. What is the amount and value of colonial cargoes of fish of all descriptions which are annually shipped to the United States?

32. For all No. 1 and No. 2 mackerel, for the larger part of the fat herring, and for all No. 1 salmon, does not the United States afford the only market. It does.

33. If you know what amount of duties is annually paid to the United States on fish and fish-oil imported from Canada, which are to be made free under the provisions of the Treaty of Washington, please state them annually, and by classes, from 1854 to 1872, inclusive.

34. If you know what amount of duties is annually paid in Canada on fish and fish-oil imported from the United States, which, are to be made free under the provisions of the said treaty, please state them annually, and by classes, from 1854 to 1872, inclusive.

35. The object of these inquiries is to ascertain whether the rights in respect of fishing, and fishermen, and fish; which were granted to Great Britain by the Treaty of Washington, are or are not a just equivalent for the rights in those respects which were granted by said treaty to the United States. If you know anything bearing upon this subject which you have not already stated in reply to previous questions, please state it as fully as if you had been specially inquired of in respect of it.

CHARLES. E. SMALLEY .
REUBEN C KENNEY

NANTUCKET, ss. June 9th, 1873.

Then personally appeared the above named Charles E. Smalley, and Reuben C. Kenney and made oath to the truth of the statements above signed by them—before me

T. C. DEFRIEZ.
Collector of Customs.

No. 18.

[CONFIDENTIAL.]

IONS RESPECTING THE FISHERIES TO BE PRO·
\DED TO —— —— ON BEHALF OF THE UNITED
!ES.

1at is your name and age, and in what town and State do you
  Elisha Crowell; Brooklyn. New-York. 59 Years
1at opportunities have you had for becoming acquainted with
  2rican and Canadian Atlantic sea-fisheries, and the value of the
  ' the different kinds of fish? Twenty five years experience in
  3, buying and selling fish
n you give the names of other persons in your neighborhood
  ve also had the opportunity of obtaining similar information?
  lease give some such name. Caleb Nickerson, Esq. Brooklyn.
)rk.
copy of the Treaty between Great Britain and the United States,
  as the Treaty of Washington, is hereto annexed. Will you ex·
  irticles 18 to 22 inclusive, and state that you have done so? I

hat kinds of fish frequent the waters of your State, especially
  /hich are to be thrown open to the Canadian fishermen under the
)ns of the Treaty of Washington? Mackerel. Herring. Codfish.
  :k. Hake. Bass. Shad. Porgies. Menhaden. Spanish Macker Eels
  rs. Bluefish. Sword & Week fish
1n you give a statement of the kinds and quantities of fish taken
  ly off the coast of your State from the years 1854 to 1872, inclu·
  If you can do this please do so; and if not, please state where
  formation can be procured.

ackerel	75.000 Barrels.	Menhaden.	500.000 Bbls.
)dfish	70.000 Quintals.	Haddock.	15.000 Bbls.
uefish	75.000 Bbls.	All other kind	300.000
)bsters.	10.000 Bbls.		Annually.
)rgies.	50.000 Bbls.		

you are able to do so, will you state the amount and value of the
  ;an fisheries which are to be thrown open to Canadian fishermen
  ,he provisions of the Treaty of Washington? Please state them
  il, showing the different kinds of fish, and the value of each kind.
  ate from waters in and adjacent to this state (N Y.) about Nine
  ion dollars in Mackerel alone. All other Kinds of Fish about
  )) Million dollars.
'hat quantity and value of each kind of fish are annually taken
  1adian fishermen, and what by American fishermen, in the waters
  coasts which are to be thrown open to competition by the Treaty
  ihington? Have no estimate.
o Canadian fishermen procure bait or supplies in the waters of
  tate? and if so, to what extent and value? Do not take bait
  ur waters, but purchase from the United States.
What is the probable annual value to Canadian fishermen in be
  le to procure bait, to land and dry their nets, and to repack and
  ieir fish on the coasts of your State, without any other restriction
  hat contained in the Treaty of Washington? About an equal
  except the priviledge of procuring bait from the United States.
Will the admission of Canadian fishermen to our in-shore fisher·

ies cause any detriment r hinderance to the profitable
fisheries by our own fishermen; and if so, in what man
extent annually? It will probably be a detriment to ou
amount of Twohundred Millions.

12. What number of Canadian vessels and boats are
fisheries of your State, and what are their tonnage an
number of men employed upon them? None.

13. Of the fisheries pursued by American fishermen
coasts of the British North American Provinces, what
sists of the deep-sea fisheries, and what proportion of
eries? fully Nine tenths ($\frac{9}{10}$) consist of deep sea fishe
tenth ($\frac{1}{10}$) in shore fisheries

14. For what description of fish do American fisherm
shore fisheries? Mackerel & Herring

15. If you state that the in shore fisheries are pu
chiefly for mackerel, please state what proportion of n
within the in-shore limits, and what proportion is take
in-shore limits? Nine tenths off shore. ($\frac{9}{10}$) One tentl

16. Is not much the larger quantity of mackerel caug
fishermen off the coasts of British America taken outs
limits; and in the summer season especially, are not m:
found on the banks, in the Gulf of Saint Lawrence,
shore? Yes. a very large proportion caught outside, s

17. Are Colonial fishermen injured by permitting Am
to fish in Colonial in-shore waters? No.

18. Are not more fish caught by American fishermen,
shore, alongside a fleet of American fishing-vessels, fi
quantities of bait are thrown out, than when fishing alc

19. What is the best bait for the mackerel, and where
taken? How much of it is taken within three miles o
what is the annual value to the United States, or to t
inces, as the case may be, to take such bait within th
shore? Menhaden taken from American waters all
Thousand dollars benefit to the British Provinces, annc

20. Please state as to each class of fisheries carried or
or district, the cost of fitting out, equipping, furnishing
vessel for carrying it on, estimating it by the average le
State, as far as possible, in detail the elements which g
cost of taking and delivering a full cargo and of retur
port. Menhaden, Mackerel, Codfish, Herring, Bluefis
gies, Haddock Hake, Halibut, Swordfish & Weekfish
$12,000 Fitting, equipping & furnishing for a cruis
$3,000

21. When you have fully answered question 20, p
same questions as to vessels fitted out, equipped, furnis
from the Dominion of Canada, including Prince Edwa
as you are able to do so. If you state that there is any d
the cost of the Canadian and the cost of the America
respects, explain what the difference is and the reason f
expense of Canadian Vessels one half of the same class
the United States, on account of the inferior Materials
also cheapness of Labor

22. Are you acquainted, and for how long, and ii
with the fisheries on the coasts of Nova Scotia, New
bec, or Prince Edward Island, or with either, and if e

·ies ? I am—for Twenty five years—having fished on their
,fish & mackerel.
:ind of fish frequent the waters of those coasts which are
open to American fishermen under the provisions of the
ıshington ? Mackerel, Herring, & Lobsters.
state in detail the amount and the annual value (say from
,nclusive) of the fisheries which are so to be thrown open
fishermen ; also the amount and the annual value of the
adjacent waters which are more than three miles distant
·e ; please state these facts in detail. No answer. See

ericau fishermen procure bait in the waters within three
:oast of the Dominion of Canada ? If so, to what extent,
,he value ? Do not procure any bait, not plenty in Cana-

the American fishermen purchase supplies in the ports of
n of Canada, including bait, ice, salt, barrels, provisions,
ırticles for the use of the men engaged in the fisheries ?
t ports, and to what extent ? And, if that is the case, is
antage to the ports of the Dominion to have the fishing·
: United States in their neighborhood during the fishing
plain why it is so, and estimate, if you can, the money-
advantage. They do at Halifax and in the ports of the
ıso & Prince Edward Islands. And it is a great advantage
ıion ports to have American vessels on account of trade &

ɣou any knowledge of how many United States fishing-ves·
ıgage in the fisheries off the Atlantic coasts of the British
can Provinces, (excluding Newfoundland,) both without and
ıree-mile limit ? If so, state how many vessels are so en·
is the value of their tonnage, what is the number of men
ınually on such vessels, what sorts of fish are taken there,
ınnual value of all the fish so caught, and what is the pro·
probable proportion, in your judgment, of the amount of
taken within three miles of the British coast, and of the
n outside of the three-mile limit ? About one hundred and
ıchooners. Valued at one Million five hundred thousand dol-
ying Fifteen hundred men—catching Mackerel and codfish
ıven hundred thousand dollars, one tenth ($\frac{1}{10}$) within three
ne tenths ($\frac{9}{10}$) outside the three mile limit
percentage of value, if any, is, in your judgment, added to the
ɣoyage by the privilege to fish within three marine miles of
ɣhence is such profit derived ; and in what does it consist ?
enth ($\frac{1}{10}$) when the fish lay in shore and cannot be taken off

e American fishermen gain under the Treaty of Washing-
ıable rights of landing to dry nets and cure fish, or to re-
or to transship cargoes, which were not theirs before ; if so,
ose rights, and what do you estimate them to be worth an-
ıe aggregate ? I do not consider it of any value to American

the Treaty of Washington, so far as the fishing clauses are
nore, or quite as, beneficial to the people of the British North
rovinces as to the people of the United States ? It is more
ıe Provinces, than the United states.
is the amount and value of colonial cargoes of fish of all

descriptions which are annually shipped to the United
to statistics.

32. For all No. 1 and No. 2 mackerel, for the larger
herring, and for all No. 1 salmon, does not the United St
only market. Yes, it *is the only* market

33. If you know what amount of duties is annuall
United States on fish and fish-oil imported from Canad
be made free under the provisions of the Treaty of Wasl
state them annually, and by classes, from 1854 to 1872 in
to Statistics in possession of the government.

34. If you know what amount of duties is annually ;
on fish and fish-oil imported from the United States, v
made free under the provisions of the said Treaty, ple
annually, and by classes, from 1854 to 1872, inclusive. I
any fish or fish oil being shipped to Canada.

35. The object of these inquiries is to ascertain wheth
respect of fishing, and fishermen, and fish, which were gr
Britain by the Treaty of Washington, are or are not a .
for the rights in those respects which were granted by
the United States. If you know anything bearing upc
which you have not already stated in reply to previous q
state it as fully as if you had been specially inquired of ;
I consider the Treaty of more value to the British Pro
the United States for the following reasons; First—for tl
fishing on the coast of the United States. Second.—the
shipping their fish free. Third—the furnishing our fishi
supplies.

ELISHA

STATE OF NEW YORK   }
CITY AND COUNTY OF NEW YORK } s. s.

Elisha Crowell, merchant of the City of New York, be
deposes and says, that the answers made by him to th
rogatories as above, have been duly considered by hin
same are based on his knowledge and experience of th
that the subject matter therein contained is true to his
and belief so far as the same can be ascertained.

ELISHA

Sworn before me This 18 day of June 1873

A. M. SARES
Notary Public.

No. 19.

[CONFIDENTIAL.]

QUESTIONS RESPECTING THE FISHERIES
POUNDED TO —— —— ON BEHALF OF
STATES.

1. What is your name and age, and in what town a
reside ? Caleb Nickerson, 48 years, Brooklyn, New Yo

2. What opportunities have you had for becoming
the American and Canadian Atlantic sea-fisheries, and
catch of the different kinds of fish ? Twenty years exp
ing, buying and selling fish.

3. Can you give the names of other persons in you

had the opportunity of obtaining similar information ?
ve some such name.　Elisha Crowell Esq. Brooklyn, New

the Treaty between Great Britain and the United States,
Treaty of Washington, is hereto annexed.　Will you ex-
18 to 22 inclusive, and state that you have done so ?　I

ds of fish frequent the waters of your State, especially
e to be thrown open to the Canadian fishermen under the
he Treaty of Washington ?　Mackerel, Herring, Codfish,
e, Bass, Shad, Porgies, Menhaden, Spanish Mackerel,
Blue fish, Sword and Week fish.
give a statement of the kinds and quantities of fish taken
ie coast of your State from the years 1854 to 1872, in-
ou can do this please do so ; and if not, please state where
on can be procured.

,000	Barrels	Menhaden	500,000 Bbls
,000	Quintals	all other kinds	300,000 "
,000	Bbls		
,000	"	Annually.	
),000	"	(The above estimate includes both *fresh*	
,000	"	& *salt* fish)	

e able to do so, will you state the amount and value of the
eries which are to be thrown open to Canadian fishermen
risions of the Treaty of Washington ?　Please state them
ing the different kinds of fish, and the value of each kind.
Million dollars in Mackerel alone.　All other kinds of fish,
nd Twenty five Million dollars.
antity and value of each kind of fish are annually taken
shermen, and what by American fishermen, in the waters
which are to be thrown open to competition by the Treaty
n ?
dian fishermen procure bait or supplies in the waters of
nd if so, to what extent and value ?　Do not take bait from
it purchase from the United States ; but can avail them-
privilege under the treaty.
i the probable annual value to Canadian fishermen in be-
ocure bait, to land and dry their nets, and to repack and
on the coasts of your State, without any other restriction
tained in the Treaty of Washington ?　About an equal
the privilege of procuring bait from the United States.
e admission of Canadian fishermen to our in-shore fisheries
triment or hinderance to the profitable pursuit of these
ir own fishermen ; and if so, in what manner, and to what
ly ?　It will.　Probably a detriment to our markets to the
ro Hundred Millions.
umber of Canadian vessels and boats are engaged in the
our State, and what are their tonnage and value, and the
n employed upon them ?　None
fisheries pursued by American fishermen off the Atlantic
British North American Provinces, what proportion con-
eep-sea fisheries, and what proportion of the in-shore fish-
nine tenths ($\frac{9}{10}$) consist of deep sea fisheries, about one
hore fisheries
at description of fish do American fishermen pursue the in-
s ?　Mackerel & Herring

15. If you state that the in shore fisheries are pursued wholly or chiefly for mackerel, please state what proportion of mackerel is taken within the in-shore limits, and what proportion is taken outside of the in-shore limits ? Nine tenths ($\frac{9}{10}$) off shore. One tenth ($\frac{1}{10}$) on shore.

16. Is not much the larger quantity of mackerel caught by American fishermen on the coasts of British America taken outside the in-shore limits; and in the summer season especially, are not mackerel generally found on the banks, in the Gulf of St. Lawrence, and not within shore ? Yes. A very large proportion caught outside

17. Are Colonial fishermen injured by permitting American fishermen to fish in Colonial in-shore waters ? No.

18. Are not more fish caught by Colonial fishermen, when fishing in-shore, alongside a fleet of American fishing-vessels, from which large quantities of bait are thrown out, than when fishing alone ? Yes.

19. What is the best bait for the mackerel, and where it is principally taken ? How much of it is taken within three miles of the shore, and what is the annual value to the United States, or to the British Provinces, as the case may be, to take such bait within three miles of the shore ? Menhaden—taken from American waters—all in shore. Fifty thousand dollars benefit to the British provinces.

20. Please state as to each class of fisheries carried on from your State or district, the cost of fitting out, equipping, furnishing, and manning a vessel for carrying it on, estimating it by the average length of the cruise. State, as far as possible, in detail the elements which go to make up the cost of taking and delivering a full cargo and of returning to the home port. Menhaden, Mackerel, Codfish, Herring, Blue fish, Lobsters, Porgies, Haddock, Hake, Halibut, Sword & Week fish. Cost of Schooner $12,000 Fitting, equipping, & furnishing for a cruise of Thirty days, or more $6,000

21. When you have fully answered question 20, please answer the same questions as to vessels fitted out, equipped, furnished, and manned from the Dominion of Canada, including Prince Edward Island, so far as you are able to do so. If you state that there is any difference between the cost of the Canadian and the cost of the American vessel in these respects, explain what the difference is and the reason for it. Estimated expense of Canadian Vessel, one half of the same kind or class of Vessel built in the United States. On account of the inferior materials and workmanship, also cheapness of labor.

22. Are you acquainted, and for how long, and in what capacity, with the fisheries on the coasts of Nova Scotia, New Brunswick, Quebec, or Prince Edward Island, or with either, and if either, with which of these fisheries ? I am, for Twenty years having fished on their Coasts for Codfish & Mackerel.

23. What kind of fish frequent the waters of those coasts which are to be thrown open to American fishermen under the provisions of the Treaty of Washington ? Codfish, Mackerel, Herring, Lobster.

24. Please state in detail the amount and the annual value (say from 1854 to 1872 inclusive) of the fisheries which are so to be thrown open to American fishermen; also the amount and the annual value of the catch in the adjacent waters which are more than three miles distant from the shore; please state these facts in detail. Uncertain as to correct figures. Question 27 seems to embrace some of the information sought.

25. Do American fishermen procure bait in the waters within three miles of the coast of the Dominion of Canada ? If so, to what extent,

e value? Do not procure any bait. The kind used are
ifficient numbers in Canadian Waters.
he American fishermen purchase supplies in the ports of
of Canada, including bait, ice, salt, barrels, provisions,
ticles for the use of the men engaged in the fisheries?
ports, and to what extent? And, if that is the case, is it
ige to the ports of the Dominion to have the fishing-ves-
ited States in their neighborhood during the fishing sea-
, why it is so, and estimate, if you can, the money-value
age. They do at Halifax, and in the ports of the Straits
?rince Edwards Island, and it is a great advantage to the
s' to have American Vessels, on account of trade and

u any knowledge of how many United States fishing-ves-
;age in the fisheries off the Atlantic coasts of the British
:an Provinces, (excluding Newfoundland,) both without
, three-mile limit? If so, state how many vessels are so
t is the value of their tonnage, what is the number of men
ually on such vessels, what sorts of fish are taken there,
inual value of all the fish so caught, and what is the pro-
obable proportion, in your judgment, of the amount of
.ken within three miles of the British coast, and of the
, outside of the three-mile limit? About One hundred
)f Schooners. Valued at one million five hundred thous-
imploying Fifteen hundred men, Catching Mackerel and
:d at seven hundred thousand dollars, one tenth $(\frac{1}{10})$ within
nit, and nine-tenths $(\frac{9}{10})$ out side the three mile limits.
ercentage of value, if any, is, in your judgment, added to
i voyage by the privilege to fish within three marine miles
whence is such profit derived; and in what does it consist?
nth $(\frac{1}{10})$ when the fish lay in shore and cannot be taken off

American fishermen gain under the Treaty of Washington
rights of landing to dry nets and cure fish, or to repack
ansship cargoes, which were not theirs before; if so, what
its, and what do you estimate them to be worth annually,
ate? I do not consider it of any value to American fish-

the Treaty of Washington, so far the fishing clauses are
ore, or quite as, beneficial to the people of the British North
ovinces as to the people of the United States? It is more
) Provinces than to the United States.
s the amount and value of colonial cargoes of fish of all
which are annually shipped to the United States? I

Barrels	Mackerel	valued at	....	$1,000000
"	Herring	, " "	....	5(0,( ))
Quintals	Codfish	" "	....	3(), ()()
"	Hake & Haddock	" "	....	1()(,()()
3bls.	fish oil		....	3(),()()
"	Alewives at $4½ per Bbl. say		....	5(),()()
)f fish			....	$2,410,()()

No. 1 and No. 2 mackerel, for the larger part of the fat her-
all No. 1 salmon, does not the United States afford the only
is, it is the only market.

33. If you know what amount of duties is annually paid
States on fish and fish-oil imported from Canada, which ɛ
free under the provisions of the Treaty of Washington
them annually, and by classes, from 1854 to 1872, inclusive
tical department of the Government can, perhaps, answe
only *estimate* based on answer to question 31, to wit:

Say on Mackerel.......................................
     Cod...
     Herring..
     Haddock ....
     Fish oil ....

       Aggregate..................................

34. If you know what amount of duties is annually paid
fish and fish-oil imported from the United States, which ɛ
free under the provisions of the said Treaty, please state t
and by classes, from 1854 to 1872 inclusive. I do not kno
or fish oil being shipped to Canada.

35. The object of these inquiries is to ascertain whethe
respect of fishing, and fishermen, and fish which were gr
Britain by the Treaty of Washington, are or are not a j
for the rights in those respects which were granted by ɛ
the United States. If you know anything bearing upo
which you have not already stated in reply to previous qu
state it as fully as if you had been specially inquired of in
I consider the treaty of more value to the British Provinc
United States, for the following reasons.

1st for the privilege of fishing on the Coast of the U. S
2d the marketing and shipping their fish free.
3d the furnishing of our fishing vessels with supplies.

STATE OF NEW YORK   } ss.
CITY & COUNTY OF NEW YORK, }

Caleb Nickerson of the City of New York being duly
and says, That the answers made by him to the several i
as above, have been duly considered by him, and that the ɛ
on his knowledge and experience of the subject of the fisl
he believes the same to be true so far as can be ascer
official statistical figures.

                   CALEB N]

Sworn before me
   This 13 day of June 1873.   (Seal.)
    I B GREGG *Notary Public.*

No. 20.

[CONFIDENTIAL.]

QUESTIONS RESPECTING THE FISHERIES 1
  POUNDED TO ——— ——— ON BEHALF OF '
  STATES.

1. What is your name and age, and in what town an
reside ? Horatio Babson; thirty six; Gloucester, Mass
2. What opportunities have you had for becoming ɛ

and Canadian Atlantic sea-fisheries, and the value of the
fferent kinds of fish ?　Have had sixteen years exp^eri^euce
business　Now own eleven vessels.
give the names of other persons in your neighborhood
) had the opportunity of obtaining similar information ?
;ive some such name.　John Pew & hundreds of others if

f the treaty between Great Britain and the United States,
Treaty of Washington, is hereto annexed.　Will you ex·
, 18 to 22 inclusive, and state that you have done so ?　I

nds of fish frequent the waters of your State, especially
re to be thrown open to the Canadian fishermen under the
the Treaty of Washington?　Mackerel, Halibut Codfish,
e, Menhaden, and many other kinds.
give a statement of the kinds and quantities of fish taken
he coast of your State from the yeass 1854 to 1872, inclusive?
) this please do so; and if not, please state where that in-
i be procured.　Would refer to the Genl Inspector's report
l catch of mackerel.　One hundred (120,000) and twenty
ls annually I should judge to be about an average catch
own coast most of which are caught inside of three miles
it. ·
re able to do so, will you state the amount and value of the
heries which are to be thrown open to Canadian fishermen
ovisions of the Treaty of Washington ?　Please state them
wing the different kinds of fish, and the value of each kind.
l fishery on our coast I consider more valuable than that on
oast.　As the quality of mackeral taken on our coast is far
hose taken on the coast of Nova Scotia and Bay of St. Law-
Menhaden fishery, the catch of which amounted to nearly
d thousand dollars off Gloucester last year are caught only
st, and have never been known to frequent British waters.
l other fisheries I regard as equal in value
uantity and value of each kind of fish are annually taken
i fishermen, and what by American fishermen, in the waters
s which are to be thrown open to competition by the Treaty
on ?　The quantity and value taken by Canadian fishermen
iue to them, than to our fishermen, as our American vessels
i anything but mackeral within the three-mile limit.
Jadian fishermen procure bait or supplies in the waters of
and if so, to what extent and value ?　I have known but
; instances of Canadian vessels taking bait within three miles
;, but they do purchase Menhaden for bait in large quantities.
is the probable annual value to Canadian fishermen in
o procure bait, to land and dry their nets, and to repack
eir fish· on the coasts of your State, without any other re-
in that contained in the Treaty of Washington ?· The value
ed there from is of equal value to Canadians as it is to our-
ild they improve the privilege as we do
the admission of Canadian fishermen to our in-shore fish-
any detriment or hinderance to the profitable pursuit of
·ies by·our own fishermen ; and if so, in what manner, and
ent annually ?　American fishermen can supply our markets,
caught by foreigners will have a tendency to injure our fish·

12. What number of Canadian vessels and boa
fisheries of your State, and what are their tonna
number of men employed upon them? I know o
time

13. Of the fisheries pursued by American fishe
coasts of the British North American Provinces,
sists of the deep-sea fisheries, and what proportio
eries? My opinion judging from the catch of
seven eighths of the catch is taken out side of th

14. For what description of fish do American fi:
shore fisheries? For Mackeral principally, and o

15. If you state that the in shore fisheries a
chiefly for mackerel, please state what proportion
within the in-shore limits, and what proportion i:
in-shore limits? During the last sixteen years I
gaged in the Bay of Chalieur & Bay of St Lawr
time I have questioned our Captains very partice
and I think I can truly say that about one eighth
are taken within three miles of the shore and se
the limits

16. Is not much the larger quantity of mackerel
fishermen off the coasts of British America take
limits; and in the summer season especially, are u
found on the banks, in the Gulf of Saint Lawr
shore? A large porportion, in fact about all the
catch are taken outside the limits, late in the Fall
shore.

17. Are Colonial fishermen injured by permittin
to fish in Colonial inshore waters? Only to a ve

18. Are not more fish caught by Colonial fishe
shore, alongside a fleet of American fishing-vess
quantities of bait are thrown out, than when fishi
quantity of bait thrown the more it tends to 'to
the catch will be larger.

19. What is the best bait for the mackerel, a
pally taken? How much of it is taken within th
and what is the annual value to the United St
Provinces, as the case may be, to take such bai
the shore? Pogies, sometimes called Menhade
Mackeral. They are caught only upon the Ne
tend inside of three miles. The value of Men
amounted to nearly ($800,000.00) Eight hundred

20. Please state as to each class of fisheries
State or district, the cost of fitting out, equippin
ning a vessel for carrying it on, estimating it by
the cruise. State, as far as possible, in detail th
make up the cost of taking and delivering a full
to the home port. The vessels are sailed on sl
half of proceeds. Average expense of a vessel f
thirty five hundred dollars for out fits Expense.
three thousand dollars making in all about sixt
for the voyage.

21. When you have fully answered question
same questions as to vessels fitted out, equipped,
from the Dominion of Canada, including Prince
as you are able to do so. If you state that thei

st of the Canadian and the cost of the American vessel in
s, explain what the difference is and the reason for it. Our
aermen cost about twice as much as the Canadian vessels,
eing better built from the best of white oak, and fitted with
·igging, sails &c., while the Canadian, Prince Edward Isl·
va Scotia vessels are built from soft wood (spruce) and are
itted in a very inferior manner compared with our vessels.
utfits for a Canadian fishing vessel to pursue a five mouths
d not be over one half of one of our American fishermen,
vessels to be of equal size
ou acquainted, and for how long, and in what capacity, with
on the coasts of Nova Scotia, New Brunswick, Quebec, or
ird Island, or with either, and if either, with which of these
With all the sea fisheries on the coast
kind of fish frequent the waters of those coasts which are
a open to American fishermen under the provisions of the
ashington? Mackeral, Herring, Halibut, Cod, Hake, Pol·
ae others of less importance.
state in detail the amount and the annual value (say from
inclusive) of the fisheries which are so to be thrown open
fishermen; also the amount and the annual value of the
adjacent waters which are more than three miles distant
ore; please state these facts in detail. I estimate the an·
luring the above years at about sixty thousand dollars per
fisheries inside of three miles. Outside of the three miles
of greater importance and depends all together on the en·
is made to catch the fish, The more vessels and men im·
greater the value.
merican fishermen procure bait in the waters within three
coast of the Dominion of Canada? If so, to what extent,
the value? Our vessels purchase large quantities of Her·
,keral for Bank fishing. I should judge we paid them one
d seventy thousand dollars annually in cash.
ot the American fishermen purchase supplies in the ports of
on of Canada, including bait, ice, salt, barrels, provisions,
articles for the use of the men engaged in the fisheries? If
ports, and to what extent? And, if that is the case, is it
antage to the ports of the Dominion to have the fishing·
he United States in their neighborhood during the fishing
Explain why it is so, and estimate, if you can, the money·
at advantage. I should judge the *profits* to be derived from
s which the Canadians receive from our vessels in purchasing
m them to be equal to one hundred thousand dollars annually.
you any knowledge of how many United States fishing·ves·
engage in the fisheries off the Atlantic coasts of the British
erican Provinces, (excluding Newfoundland.) both without
the three-mile limit? If so, state how many vessels are so
hat is the value of their tonnage, what is the number of men
annually on such vessels, what sorts of fish are taken there,
annual value of all the fish so caught, and what is the pro·
probable proportion, in your judgment, of the amount of
taken within three miles of the British coast, and of the
ten outside of the three·mile limit? I should judge about
dred and fifty sail, valued as near as I can judge at
.) seven million five hundred thousand. Each vessel will
velve men. Principal fish caught are Mackeral, Cod, Halibut,

and Herring. Annual value of fish caught, one and three-quar
lion dollars. Value of fish taken inside of three miles about sixt
sand dollars.

28. What percentage of value, if any, is, in your judgment, a
the profits of a voyage by the privilege to fish within three marin
of the coast; whence is such profit derived; and in what does
sist? I do not regard it of any value as far as profit is concerne
only benefit to be derived is freedom of Ports and free from ann

29. Do the American fishermen gain under the Treaty of Wasl
any valuable rights of landing to dry nets and cure fish, or to
them, or to transship cargoes, which were not theirs before; if s
are those rights, and what do you estimate them to be worth ar
in the aggregate? The value of the above privileg's I regard as
little importance.

30. Is not the Treaty of Washington, so far as the fishing clat
concerned, more, or quite as, beneficial to the people of the
North American Provinces as to the people of the United States
more beneficial to British subjects.

31. What is the amount and value of colonial cargoes of fish
descriptions which are annually shipped to the United States
not know the amount.

32. For all No. 1 and No. 2 mackerel, for the greater part of
herring, and for all No. 1 salmon does not the United States afl
only market. It does nearly all.

33. If you know what amount of duties is annually paid to the
States on fish and fish-oil imported from Canada, which are to k
free under the provisions of the Treaty of Washington, pleas
them annually, and by classes, from 1854 to 1872, inclusive. I
know the amount, but would refer to statistics

34. If you know what amount of duties is annually paid in Car
fish and fish oil imported from the United States, which are to
free under the provisions of the said Treaty, please state them ar
and by classes, from 1854 to 1872, inclusive. I do not know.

35. The object of these inquiries is to ascertain whether the r
respect of fishing, and fishermen, and fish, which were granted t
Britain by the Treaty of Washington, are or are not a just equiva
the rights in those respects which were granted by said Treaty
United States. If you know anything bearing upon this subjec
you have not already stated in reply to previous questions, plea
it as fully as if you had been specially inquired of in respect of
opinion is that England will derive more benefit from the t
Washington than the United States, and it is the opinion of n
who are engaged in the fishing business, that we have already
more privileges to the subjects of Great Britain under the treaty
shall receive. The admission of British fish into our markets
duty is a serious blow to the fishing interests of the United Stat
fishermen can supply our markets from the catch on our own c
the deep sea fisheries. Since the abrogation of the reciprocity
have kept about one half of my vessels employed off our coast, and
instance they have landed more fish and stocked more money th
that have been employed in the Bay of St Lawrence. When the D
Government authorized a system of licensing American fisher
which they charged fifty cents per ton for the privilege of fishin
the three-mile limit, freedom of their ports &c.—Our Captains
the first year took licenses (part of them) and the benefit they
from it they did not consider equal to the amount paid, and

n they went to the Bay the Dominion Government charged
r per ton for license. Our Captains declined taking licenses
ng the price too much for the benefit to be derived

HORATIO BABSON

GLOUCESTER *June* 21st 1873

ally appeared H. Babson and acknowledged the above to be
ct and deed and that these statements are true to the best of
ledge and belief.
me

AARON PARSONS *J P*,

les P. Mitchell, Captain of the American fishing schooner Mo·
Jeraulds have been engaged in fishing in the Bay of St Law·
ring the last fifteen years, Have read the questions and answers
anexed and I fully concur in them all.

CHARLES P. MITCHELL

JESTER June 21st 1873

·ge W. Lane, Captain of the American fishing schooner Adelia
well have been engaged in fishing in the Bay of St Lawrence
he last fifteen years, Have read the questions and answers
anexed and I fully concur in them all.

GEORGE W. LANE.

CESTER June 21st 1873

No. 21.

[CONFIDENTIAL.]

TIONS RESPECTING THE FISHERIES TO BE PRO·
JNDED TO ——— ——— ON BEHALF OF THE UNITED
.TES.

hat is your name and age, and in what town and State do you
Frank. W. Friend Gloucester, Mass
hat opportunities have you had for becoming acquainted with
erican and Canadian Atlantic sea-fisheries, and the value of the
f the different kinds of fish? Have been engaged in the Fishing
s as Owner and Fitter several years.
n you give the names of other persons in your neighborhood who
so had the opportunity of obtaining similar information? If so,
give some such name. Perkins Bros. Charles Parkhurst W. H.
& others.
copy of the Treaty between Great Britain and the United States,
as the Treaty of Washington, is hereto annexed. Will you ex-
articles 18 to 22 inclusive, and state that you have done so? I
ramined articles 18 to 22
'hat kinds of fish frequent the waters of your State, especially
rhich are to be thrown open to the Canadian fishermen under the
ons of the Treaty of Washington? Mackerel Herring Pogies

an you give a statement of the kinds and quantities of fish taken
ly off the coast of your State from the years 1851 to 1872, inclu-
If you can do this please do so; and if not, please state where
iformation can be procured.

7. If you are able to do so, will you state the amount and '
American fisheries which are to be thrown open to Canadia
under the provisions of the Treaty of Washington? Please
in detail, showing the different kinds of fish, and the va]
kind.

8. What quantity and value of each kind of fish are ann
by Canadian fishermen, and what by American fishermen, in
off the coasts which are to be thrown open to competition by
of Washington? Must be obtained from Statistics

9. Do Canadian fishermen procure bait or supplies in th
your State? and if so, to what extent and value? All their
is obtained from the U. S.

10. What is the probable annual value to Canadian fishern
able to procure bait, to land and dry their nets, and to repa
their fish on the coasts of your State, without any other rest
that contained in the Treaty of Washington?

11. Will the admission of Canadian fishermen to our in-shoe
cause any detriment or hinderance to the profitable pursu
fisheries by our own fishermen; and if so, in what manner, ;
extent annually? Nothing except cheaper vessels and mo
tion

12. What number of Canadian vessels and boats are eng
fisheries of your State, and what are their tonnage and val
number of men employed upon them? Uncertain

13. Of the fisheries pursued by American fishermen off t
coasts of the British North American Provinces, what pro|
sists of the deep sea fisheries, and what proportion of the in
eries? Nearly all the Fishing untill September is off sho
fishing

14. For what description of fish do American fishermen
in-shore fisheries? Mackerel principally

15. If you state that the in shore fisheries are pursue
chiefly for mackerel, please state what proportion of mack
within the in-shore limits, and what proportion is taken ou
in-shore limits? Think ¾ of the Mackerel caught before the
are caught outside the three-mile limit

16. Is not much the larger quantity of mackerel caught b
fishermen off the coasts of British America taken outside
limits; and in the summer season especially, are not macke
found on the banks, in the Gulf of Saint Lawrence, and
shore? They are, Bank Bradly & Orphan being the
grounds—in the summer season of Magdalen Island some .
caught

17. Are Colonial fishermen injured by permittting Ame
men to fish in Colonial in-shore waters? No In good sea.
much benefitted by American vessels fishing in their Wate

18. Are not more fish caught by Colonial fishermen, wh
shore, alongside a fleet of American fishing vessels, from
quantities of bait are thrown out, than when fishing alone

19. What is the best bait for the mackerel, and where is i
taken? How much of it is taken within three miles of th
what is the annual value to the United States, or to the
vinces, as the case may be, to take such bait within three
shore? Porgies, mostly taken on the shores of Massachus

20. Please state as to each class of fisheries carried on fro
or district, the cost of fitting out, equipping, furnishing, ·

carrying it on, estimatiug it b the average length of the
,te, as far as possible, in detaily the elemeuts which go to
a cost of taking and delivering a full cargo and of returning
port. Pogie Fishing requires a crew of 10 meu at a cost of
a month. Mackerel Fishing about the same exclusive of
es, Bank Fishing $400 a month this includes Barrels salt
ing Insurance &c—

i you have fully answered question 20, please answer the
ions as to vessels fitted out, equipped, furnished, and manned
ominion of Canada, including Prince Edward Island, so far
ible to do so. If you state that there is any difference be-
ost of the Canadian and the cost of the American vessel in
icts, explain what the difference is and the reason for it.
' the expense of fitting Canadian vessels but should judge
[have seen of their Vessels & fittings that they could be run
' of what American Vessels could

Sch Finance

son of 1872—
a Georges from Feb. 1 to July 15, then went to the Bay of
ce and stopped untill Sept. 20 and then followed Georges
till Nov. 15—

)res	1200	
	500	
rels	240	
uning the Vessel sails rigging &c—	900	
—	350	
	800	
	3990	
e	3900	$7890.00
60-000 w Codfish	5800	
20 Bll Mackerel	2400	
		$8200.00

s more than an average Season work—
you acquainted, and for how long, aud in what capacity, with
es on the coasts of Nova Scotia, New Brunswick, Quebec, or
ward Island, or with either, and if either, with which of these
Am well acquainted with them.
it kind of fish frequent the waters of those coasts which are
vn open to American fishermen under the provisions of the
Washington ? Mackerel mostly. Halibut & Cod fish in
itities.
se state in detail the amount and the annual value (say from
72 inclusive) of the fisheries which are so to be thrown open to
fishermen; also the amount and the annual value of the
ie adjacent waters which are more than three miles distant
hore; please state these facts in detail.
American fishermen procure bait in the waters within three
he coast of the Dominion of Canada ? If so, to what extent;
is the value ? As a general thing, the American fishermen
bait of the Canadians.
not the American fishermen purchase supplies in the ports of
nion of Canada, including bait, ice, salt, barrels, provisions,
as articles for the use of the men engaged in the fisheries ? If
it ports, and to what extent; and, if that is the case, is it not

an advantage to the ports of the dominion to have
sels of the United States in their neighborhood du
season; explain why it is so, and estimate, if you can,
of that advantage. Yes; during the Reciprocity Tr
whole American Fleet refitted in Canso & Charlottetowr
their Outfitts amounting to $1,500. I should think the
would average $600.

27. Have you any knowledge of how many Unite
vessels yearly engage in the fisheries off the Atlant
British North American Provinces, (excluding Newfounc
out and within the three-mile limit? If so, state how r
so engaged, what is the value of their tonnage, what i
men employed annually on such vessels, what sorts
there, what is the annual value of all the fish so caught
proportion, or probable proportion, in your judgment, (
such catch taken within three miles of the British
amount taken outside of the three-mile limit. About
annually engaged they average about 60 tons worth $6
000 employing 8,000 men.

28. What percentage of value, if any, is, in your jud
the profits of a voyage by the privilege to fish within th
of the coast; whence is such profits derived; and in v
sist? In case we are deprived of Fishing at the mout
the Fishey would be entirely valueless—

29. Do the American fishermen gain under the Treat,
any valuable rights of landing to dry nets and cure f
them, or to transship cargoes, which were not theirs be
are those rights, and what do you estimate them to be
in the aggregate? No, the Canadians are more benefi

30. Is not the Treaty of Washington, so far as the fis
concerned, more, or quite as, beneficial to the peop
North American Provinces as to the people of the Unit
more benefit to the Canadians than to the American F

31. What is the amount and value of colonial carg
descriptions which are annually shipped to the Unit
report of U. S. Statistics

32. For all No. 1 and No. 2 mackerel, for the larg
herring, and for all No. 1 salmon, does not the United
only market. No Fat Mackerel & Hering are ship
cept the U. S.

33. If you know what amount of duties is annually
ted States on fish and fish-oil imported from Canada
made free under the provisions of the Treaty of W
state them, annually and by classes, from 1854 to 187'
Report from Beaureou of Statistics

34. If you know what amount of duties is annuall,
on fish and fish-oil imported from the United State
made free under the provisions of the said Treaty, ple;
nually, and by classes, from 1854 to 1872, inclusive.
remission of Duties on Canadian Fish and the free ma
for their Mackerel, & other Fish, Saving of Expense.
the benefits of a large trade from the American Vess
to our coasts for Menhaden & Mackerel, will aggreg
of nearly $2,000,000 a year in gross amount—For t
privilege of persuing a fishery, which after deducting
nett to the American Fisherman $10,000 pr year—

The object of these inquiries is to ascertain whether the rights in
ct of fishing, and fishermen, and fish which were granted to Great
,in by the Treaty of Washington, are or are not a just equivalent
ie rights in those respects which were granted by said Treaty to
Jnited States. If you know anything bearing upon this subject
h you have not already stated in reply to previous questions, please
it as fully as if you had been specially inquired of in respect of it.
t we desire most by the treaty of Washington is to have accorded
merican Fishing Vessels, the same rights & privileges that have
been accorded to English Vessels in American Waters. If this
.esy is to be reckoned at the money value the Dominion may have
. claim, but if the in shore fishery is the only concession, barring us
right to fish at the mouths of the rivers, the U. States gets abso-
y nothing for the privilege of building up a Foreign fishery at the
nse of its own citizens.

FRANK. W. FRIEND
SIDNEY FRIEND
Of the firm of Sidney Friend & Bro

[E OF MASSACHUSETTS } ss. GLOUCESTER June 21st 1873
]OUNTY OF ESSEX S }

    Subscribed and sworn to,
Before me

DAVID W. LOW
Notary Public.

eal)

No. 22.

[CONFIDENTIAL.]

ESTIONS RESPECTING THE FISHERIES TO BE PRO·
OUNDED TO —— —— ON BEHALF OF THE UNITED
ΓATES.

What is your name and age, and in what town and State do you
de ?' George W. Plumer; Aged 55 yrs; Gloucester Massachusetts
  What opportunities have you had for becoming acquainted with
American and Canadian Atlantic sea-fisheries, and the value of the
:h of the different kinds of fish ? Have been familiar with the busi·
; for more than thirty years, and engaged in Mackerel—Herring and
ær fisheries fifteen years in American waters, also at Newfoundland,
.f of St Lawrence. P. E. Island &c &c
, Can you give the names of other persons in your neighborhood
) have also had the opportunity of obtaining similar information ?
;o, please give some such name. Andrew Leighton and hundreds of
ers if required
. A copy of the Treaty between Great Britain and the United States,
)wn as the Treaty of Washington, is hereto annexed. ·Will you ex·
ine articles 18 to 22 inclusive, and state that you have done so.
. What kinds of fish frequent the waters of your State, especially
se which are to be thrown open to the Canadian fishermen under the
visions of the Treaty of Washington ? Codfish. Halibut. Mackerel.
hagan. Herring and Pollock are most valuable. but many other kinds
ıld be mentioned
;. Can you give a statement of the kinds and quantities of fish taken
ıually off the coast of your State from the years 1854 to 1872, inclu-
e ? If you can do this please do so; and if not, please state where

that information can be procured. The kinds are those above named, but the quantity and value is so enormous that a long time would be required to ascertain from Statistics the actual fact, or a correct esti-mate

7. If you are able to do so, will you state the amount and value of the American fisheries which are to be thrown open to Canadian fisher-men under the provisions of the Treaty of Washington? Please state them in detail, showing the different kinds of fish, and the value of each kind. British vessels have had no occasion formerly to take fish in American Waters excepting to a limited extent. but under the Treaty of Washington they will have every facility that American fish-ermen have now or formerly enjoyed. and our markets being free will afford them a decided advantage over us from the fact of vessels being cheaper built and sailed than ours. I doubt if they ever improve these opportunities to any great extent. but if they choose to do so could employ one thousand Sail of Vessels in American fisheries, as well as Citizens of the United States

8. What quantity and value of each kind of fish are annually taken by Canadian fishermen, and what by American fishermen, in the waters off the coasts which are to be thrown open to competition by the Treaty of Washington? the quantity taken by Canadian and other British fishermen is very large and of great value to them. but to Americans of little value comparatively from the fact that the British takes mostly Codfish and Herring—while Americans seldom fish for Cod within three miles of land and only have occasion to take Mackerel and Herrings within the limits of three miles

9. Do Canadian fishermen procure bait or supplies in the waters of your State? and if so, to what extent and value? I have never known but one British vessel to take bait in the Waters of Massachusetts, but they do purchase Pohagan bait salted in considerable quantities

10. What is the probable annual value to Canadian fishermen in being able to procure bait, to land and dry their nets, and to repack and cure their fish on the coasts of your State, without any other restriction than that contained in the Treaty of Washington? This depends entirely on their improving these advantages as before stated. the privilege is as valuable to them as to us, if they make the best of it

11. Will the admission of Canadian fishermen to our in-shore fisheries cause any detriment or hinderance to the profitable pursuit of these fisheries by our own fishermen; and if so, in what manner, and to what extent annually? American fishermen can supply the Markets of the United States with all fish caught in our waters. so that all landed by foreigners are so much taken from our own fishermen

12. What number of Canadian vessels and boats are engaged in the fisheries of your States, and what are their tonnage and value, and the number of men employed upon them? None at this time June 1873

13. Of the fisheries pursued by American fishermen off the Atlantic coasts of the British North American Provinces, what proportion con-sists of the deep-sea fisheries, and what proportion of the in-shore fish-eries? I am of the opinion that more than nine tenths ($\frac{9}{10}$) of all fish caught by Americans in British waters are deep sea fish. or taken more than three miles from land.

14. For what description of fish do American fishermen pursue the in-shore fisheries? If at all only for Mackerel and Herring

15. If you state that the in shore fisheries are pursued wholly or chiefly for mackerel, please state what proportion of mackerel is taken within the in-shore limits, and what proportion is taken outside of the

nits? In answering this question I would state that having
iry of several competent Masters of vessels engaged many
Mackerel fishing in British waters, they all inform me that
y̆ few times in many years have they ever seen an opportunity
hin three miles of the shore, the difficulty has been they were
d to fish outside the three miles limit. being captured or au-
British Cruisers when five or six miles from land.
estion constantly arising of limitation. and in my judgment
rouble may come under the new Treaty of determining the
' Rivers, as Mackerel frequent the entrance of creeks and
obtain feed
ot much the larger quantity of mackerel caught by American
off the coasts of British America taken outside the in shore
d in the summer season especially, are not mackerel generally
he banks, in the Gulf of Saint Lawrence, and not within shore ?
coportion are off shore, but late in Summer and Autumn they
be mouths of Rivers and in shore for feed
Colonial fishermen injured by permitting American fishermen
Colonial in-shore waters ? Only to a very limited extent
not more fish caught by Colonial fishermen, when fishing in-
ngside a fleet of American fishing-vessels, from which large
of bait are thrown out, than when fishing alone ? The more
vn, and the better the quality the more Mackerel are taken, and
would have the advantage. our vessels using more bait
at is the best bait for the mackerel, and where is it principally
low much of it is taken within three miles of the shore, and
e annual value to the United States, or to the British Provin-
case may be, to take such bait within three miles of the shore ?
called "Pogies" make the best bait for Mackerel—and are
the New England Coast only—and usually within three Miles
my estimate of the value is ($750,000) three-fourths of a mil-
s.
se state as to each class of fisheries carried on from your State
, the cost of fitting out, equipping, furnishing and manning a
carrying it on, estimating it by the average length of the cruise.
ar as possible, in detail the elements which go to make up the
ting and delivering a full cargo and of returning to the home
vessels are usually sailed on Shares, the men receiving one-
oceeds of Sales of fish, but I should estimate the expenses and
f crews would average for the Mackerel Season of about five
iree thousand dollars ($3,000) to each vessel
en you have fully answered question 20, please answer the
itions as to vessels fitted out, equipped, furnished and manned
Dominion of Canada, including Prince Edward Island, so far
able to do so. If you state that there is any difference be-
cost of the Canadian and the cost of the American vessel in
ects, explain what the difference is and the reason for it.
een engaged in the fishing business at P. E. Island I should
the expense there at two thirds (⅔) for each vessel of that of.
s, for the reason that the vessels are built cheaper. the men
orer and of course at a lower rate there rate of duties on im-
ticles are less,
you acquainted, and for how long. and in what capacity, with
ies on the coast of Nova Scotia, New Brunswick, Quebec, or
ward Island, or with either, and if either, with which of these
In the Capacity of Owner for about fifteen years in Mackerel

F

and Herring mostly. at Gulf of St Lawrence Newfou
Fundy and particularly P. E. Island

23. What kind of fish frequent the waters of those c
to be thrown open to American fishermen under th
the Treaty of Washington ? Mackerel, Herrings- Cod, H
Haddock Hake and some other varieties

24. Please state in detail the amount and the annual
1854 to 1872 inclusive) of the fisheries which are so to
to American fishermen; also the amount and the annı
catch in the adjacent waters which are more than thre
from the shore; please state these facts in detail.

25. Do American fishermen procure bait in the wate
miles of the coast of the Dominion of Canada ? If so,
and what is the value ? They do obtain bait, and I est
at two hundred thousand dollars $200,000 which is 1
British fishermen.

26. Do not the American fishermen purchase supplies
the Dominion of Canada, including bait, ice, salt, bar
and various articles for the use of the men engaged in t'
so, in what ports, and to what extent ? And, if that is t
an advantage to the ports of the Dominion to have the
of the United States in their neighborhood during the
Explain why it is so, and estimate, if you can, the mon
advantage. Money value of this trade $500,000 Hal
do obtain supplies at all accessible British Ports. Say
Bay of Fundy Halifax and other ports in Nova Scotia, S
Sydney in Cape Breton Charlottetown and Georgetow
P. E. Island Bay Chaleur—and many other smaller plac

27. Have you any knowledge of how many United St
sels yearly engage in the fisheries off the Atlantic Coa-
North American Provinces, (excluding Newfoundland
and within the three-mile limit ? If so, state how many
gaged, what is the value of their tonnage, what is the
employed annually on such vessels, what sorts of fish
what is the annual value of all the fish so caught, and
portion, or probable proportion, in your judgment, of the
catch taken within three miles of the British coast, an
taken outside of the three-mile limit ? I estimate the n
so employed at Seven hundred, value at $3,000000 *three*
thousand men. fish taken are Cod, Mackerel, Halibut,
Haddock—Pollock. &c &c
Value of fish one and one half Million dollars and t
within three miles of land at fifty thousand dollars

28. What percentage of value, if any, is, in your juc
to the profits of a voyage by the privilege to fish wit!
miles of the coast; whence is such profit derived; and
consist ? Not over five per cent., and that from occa
Mackerel, and a small amount derived from taking He

29. Do the American fishermen gain under the Tr
ton any valuable rights of landing to dry nets and c
pack them, or to transship cargoes, which were not th
what are those rights, and what do you estimate the
nually, in the aggregate ? the value of drying Nets
are very small, and the right to land fish in transit we
or it has usually been done

he Treaty of Washington, so far as the fishing clauses are
)re, or quite as beneficial to the people of the British
:an Provinces as to the people of the United States ? more
British Subjects as all fat Mackerel and Herrings, and
nds of fat fish, are and must be marketed in the United
y will not bear heat to West Indies
; the amount and value of Colonial cargoes of fish of all
'hich are annually shipped to the United States ? Amount
, will be very largely increased with a free Market
No. 1 and No. 2 mackerel, for the larger part of the fat
:or all No. 1 salmon, does not the United States afford the
    Fat fish cannot be sent into hot climate as they melt and
iless, consequently the U. States consumes nearly all of
on
know what amount of duties is annually paid to the
; ou fish and fish-oil imported from Canada, which are to
under the provisions of the Treaty of Washington, please
nually, and by classes, from 1854 to 1872, inclusive. Am
sion of the Statistics to show a correct answer to this ques-
:now that they will be largely increased provided the Can-
:her British Subjects improve their opportunities, and in
)n I would say that the Canadian fisheries are controlled
:ent by Merchants of Wealth from the Island of Jersey,
very extensive establishments. and with all facilities at
e their Men and feed them as common Sailors.—-thereby
ing the Cost of Catching fish, while American fishermen
an double, and are fed and clothed better than the for-
'ing that if so disposed British Subjects can supply the
; with fish cheaper than we can do it ourselves
know what amount of duties is annually paid in Canada
sh-oil imported from the United States, which are to be
der the provisions of the said Treaty, please state them
l by classes, from 1854 to 1872, inclusive. Unknown.
ject of these inquiries is to ascertain whether the rights
.fishing, and fishermen, and fish, which were granted to
i by the Treaty of Washington, are or are not a just equiv'
rights in those respects which were granted by said Treaty
d States. If you know anything bearing upon this sub-
ou have not already stated in reply to previous questions,
it as fully as if you had been specially inquired of in re-
For reasons already given, and Many others that could
my opinion is that Great Britain has the best of the Treaty
.out any other Condition being granted,
g at liberty to express myself fully under this head, must
my judgement and in that of others engaged in the fish-
mistake of great importance has been made in excluding
Mouths of Rivers as Mackerel which are our most valuable
those waters where their natural feed is found and this
the case at points where the fresh and sea waters meet at
louth. and this question or line should be clearly defined.
the same trouble may arise in drawing the line, as grew out
mile question   G. W. PLUMER

'ER
June 1873

MASS } JULY 21, 1873
ESSEX SS. }

Personally appeared the said Geo W. Plumer and ma
these statements are true to the best of his knowledge and
Before me.

AARON PAR:

No. 23.

[CONFIDENTIAL.]

QUESTIONS RESPECTING THE FISHERIES TO POUNDED TO ——— ——— ON BEHALF OF TI STATES.

1. What is your name and age, and in what town and
reside? Harvey Knowlton & Edward A. Horton Glouces

2. What opportunities have you had for becoming acq
the American and Canadian Atlantic sea-fisheries, and the
catch of the different kinds of fish? Have been personall
practical Fishermen twenty two years, Fitted and owned
years We now fit out eight vessels.

3. Can you give the names of other persons in your neigb
have also had the opportunity of obtaining similar informa
please give some such name.

4. A copy of the treaty between Great Britain and the U
known as the Treaty of Washington, is hereto annexe
examine articles 18 to 22 inclusive, and state that you have d
have.

5. What kinds of fish frequent the waters of your St
those which are to be thrown open to the Canadian fis
the provisions of the Treaty of Washington? Mackerel
lock Menhaden

6. Can you give a statement of the kinds and quantities
annually off the coast of your State from the years 1854
sive? If you can do this please do so; and if not, pleas
that information can be procured. The reports of the Ins
Fish for the State of Massachusetts comprises the most a
ments. Think about 200,000 Bbls of Mackerel per year is
for Mass vessels

7. If you are able to do so, will you state the amount
the American fisheries which are to be thrown open to Ca
men under the provisions of the Treaty of Washington?
them in detail, showing the different kinds of fish, and the
kind. We consider the Mackerel fishery on our own coast
that on the British coast, the Codfishery in either case is
able The real difference is in the fact that the provinc
never have had the enterprise to avail themselves to any
of the benefits of this fishery

8. What quantity and value of each kind of fish are a
by Canadian fishermen, and what by American fishermen
off the coasts which are to be thrown open to competition
of Washington? If during reciprocity is meant, (within
the shore) our vessels took about 20000 Bbls Mackerel in
sons Our Mackerel and Menhaden fishery is valuable to
if they use them

Canadian fishermen procure bait or supplies in the waters of
ate? and if so, to what extent and value? They buy Menhaden
bait for Mackerel from the Americans The Menhaden fishery
y American. None have ever been known to frequent British

'hat is the probable annual value to Canadian fishermen in be.
) to procure bait, to land and dry their nets, and to repack and
ir fish on the coasts of your State, without any other restriction
at contained in the Treaty of Washington? That depends en.
1 their own enterprise They have never yet done much more
h of their own coasts.
'ill the admission of Canadian fishermen to our in-shore fisheries
ay detriment or hinderance to the profitable pursuit of these fish-
our own fishermen; and if so, in what manner, and to what ex.
aually? No
'hat number of Canadian vessels and boats are engaged in the
s of your State, and what are their tonnage and value, and the
of men employed upon them? We have seen some few of their
on our coasts for Mackerel say 20 vessels 250 men   •
if the fisheries pursued by American fishermen off the Atlantic
if the British North American Provinces, what proportion con-
the deep-sea fisheries, and what proportion of the in-shore fish-
⅘ of the Fisheries are deep sea fisheries At present all the Cod
)ut are caught on the Grand, Brown & Georges Banks
'or what description of fish do American fishermen pursue the
) fisheries? Almost entirely for Mackerel
f you state that the in shore fisheries are pursued wholly or chiefly
kerel, please state what proportion of mackerel is taken within
hore limits, and what proportion is taken outside of the in-shore
During the latter part of the season Mackerel tend in shore and
at 6 weeks the fishing is better in shore On a basis of 300 000
s the whole seasons catch for the Massachusetts fleet and allow-
) 000 Bbls to be taken in the Gulf of St Lawrence which is a
stimate ⅕, or 20 000 Bbls might under favorable circumstances
en within three miles but even during reciprocity less than
Bbls were taken one year both from British and American Wa-
the entire Mass fleet
s not much the larger quantity of mackerel caught by Ameri-
iermen off the coasts of British America taken outside the in-
mits; and in the summer season especially, are not mackerel
ly found on the banks, in the Gulf of Saint Lawrence, and not
shore?. Yes, Untill the 20th of Sept about all the Mackerel are
utside of three miles The Magdalen Islands afford good fishing
ast of the season
ire Colonial fishermen injured by permitting American fishermen
in Colonial in-shore waters? No. No. Every man that ever
a mackerel knows that the larger the fleet the better for all
ire not more fish caught, by Colonial fishermen, when fishing in-
alongside a fleet of American fishing-vessels, from which large
ies of bait are thrown out, than when fishing alone? Certainly,
proportion of the Canadian Fishery is carried on in small boats
ie shore, say within 20 miles, Our fleet, with their immense
ies of bait is of immense advantage to the Canadians
Vhat is the best bait for the mackerel, and where is it principally
How much of it is taken within three miles of the shore, and
i the annual value to the United States, or to the British Prov-

inces, as the case may be, to take such bait within thre
shore? Menhaden, which are taken for bait for their Oil
made into Guano worth 60 Dollars per Ton, The gros
this fishery for all purposes would not be less than four
it is entirely an American fishery.

20. Please state as to each class of fisheries carried
State or district, the cost of fitting out, equipping,
manning a vessel for carrying it on, estimating it t
length of the cruise. State, as far as possible, in detai
which go to make up the cost of taking and delivering a
of returning to the home port. The average cost for a s
eight months is about 3000 Dollars or 3,500, as including
visions, Trawls, lines. Gear & Boats insurance wear and

Time of 12 men 8 months

The average value of the entire fares from 5 to 8000 doll
This is when no losses are made.
Out of, a fleet of less than 500 Schooners at Glouceste
average loss has been for the last ten years over 10
sels yearly and 100 lives yearly The vessels and
are an entire loss as they are insured in the Mutual
ing office and all owners of vessels share in the loss

21. When you have fully answered question 20, ple
same questions as to vessels fitted out, equipped, furnish
from the Dominion of Canada, including Prince Edwar
as you are able to do so. If you state that there is an
tween the cost of the Canadian and the cost of the Am
these respects, explain what the difference is and the rea
American vessels cost 80 Dollars per ton present Gov't M
Canadian vessels cost from 30 to 35 Dollars per ton Th
fitting is in the price of Gear Boats &c and the Canadia
fed on Fish and potatoes principally while the Americ
meat, salt meat Pork Vegetables in fact as good as the

22. Are you acquainted, and for how long, and in wh
the fisheries on the coasts of Nova Scotia, New Brunsv
Prince Edward Island, or with either, and if either, wit
fisheries ? With all the fisheries on those coasts

23. What kind of fish frequent the waters of those c
to be thrown open to American fishermen under the p
Treaty of Washington ? Mackerel principally, some Co
but

24. Please state in detail the amount and the annual
1854 to 1872 inclusive) of the fisheries which are so to
to American fishermen; also the amount and the annu
catch in the adjacent waters which are more than thre
from the shore; please state these facts in detail. The
within three miles of the British coast would probably
the most favorable circumstances 15 to 20,000 Bbls of M
ly, worth 100000 Dollars net From this amount should
cost of catching (say 250 vessels, 6 weeks, together w
employed Bait salt &c, in fact the fish are worthless in
Gulf of St Lawrence Mackerel fishery probably produ
of Mackerel less than one fifth are caught within three n
The Statistics of Mass fisheries shows that when totall

isberies our vessels have caught more Mackerel than when
:ed to them, consequently the only advantage obtained is
of free ports and freedom from annoyance

nerican fishermen procure bait in the waters within three
coast of the Dominion of Canada? If so, to what extent,
the value? Yes, American Cod Fishermen buy large quan-
t from the Canadian shore Fishermen, Our vessels never
Bait always buy it some vessels pay as high as $1000,00
itish fishermen for Bait

t American fishermen purchase supplies in the ports of the
Canada, including bait, ice, salt, barrels, provisions, and
:les for the use of the men engaged in the fisheries? If so,
s, and to what extent? And, if that is the case, is it not
:e to the ports of the Dominion to have the fishing vessels
:d States in their neighborhood during the fishing season?
y it is so, and estimate, if you can, the money-value of that

Yes, 200 000 Dollars is yearly paid for Bait During Re-
:arly all the American fleet refitted in the Straits of Canso
f Prince Edward Island and Halifax At a cost of not less
00,00 This trade had grown to such dimensions that upon
on of the harsh measures adopted by the Canadian Govt
erican Fishermen there was a universal outcry on the part
hants and inhabitants of these ports.

you any knowledge of how many United States fishing-ves-
:ngage in the fisheries off the Atlantic coasts of the British
rican Provinces, (excluding Newfoundland,) both without
the three-mile limit? If so, state how many vessels are so
hat is the value of their tonnage, what is the number of men
nnually on such vessels, what sorts of fish are taken there,
annual value of all the fish so caught, and what is the pro-
probable proportion, in your judgment, of the amount of
taken within three miles of the British coast, and of the
en outside of the three-mile limit? The Codfishery on the
loy about 200 Vessels & 2400 Men The Mackerel Fishery
)0 Vessels 6000 Men Value of Vessels about 2000 000 Dol-
e of Mackerel about 700 000 Dollars Value of Codfish &
)ut 1 000 000 Dollars No *Codfish* or *Halibut* of any account
rithin three miles. About 15 or 20 000 Bbls Mackerel were
en in the best season during *reciprocity* within three miles,
sons much less,

; percentage of value, if any, is, in your judgment, added to
of a voyage by the privilege to fish within three marine
e coast; whence is such profit derived; and in what does it
:hat depends entirely on the amount of mackerel taken If
'e plenty, the price is consequently reduced and the mackerel
t all times precarious The whole matter is conditional and
:al The convenience of the ports, freedom from annoyance
: is the chief consideration, The Mackerel fishery may be best
coast for years, it may be better on the Canadian coast, the
ursue the fish wherever they may be is the main advantage in
e coast fishery, Statistics shows that our vessels have done
ur own coasts when totally excluded from the British fisheries
freely admitted to them
he American fishermen gain under the Treaty of Washington
le rights of landing to dry nets and cure fish, or to repack
transship cargoes, which were not theirs before; if so, what

are those rights, and what do you estimate them to be v
in the aggregate ? We never dry nets or cure fish on tl
idea applied when the fisheries were carried on in small bc
to transship cargoes to buy or sell is a right which every
sel has in English ports, as English Vessels have in Ameri
Dominion Govt under the clause in their law (*of prepa*
cluded every transaction of a commercial nature and p
rage after outrage on American Vessels, The American
never accepted the character of outlaws accorded them a
ity before the law with other citizens engaged in marine

30. Is not the Treaty of Washington, so far as the fish
concerned, more, or quite as, beneficial to the people
North American Provinces as to the people of the U
Where we shall receive one dollar's benefit they will rece
matter they have for sale is courtesy

31. What is the amount and value of colonial cargoes (
scriptious which are annually shipped to the United Sta
ume III 9th Census U States.

32. For all No. 1 and No. 2 mackerel, for the larger par
ring, and for all No. 1 salmon, does not the United St
only market ? Yes. Without the markets of the U St
fishery of the Dominion would be valueless, except for l
tion

33. If you know what amount of duties is annually pai
States on fish and fish-oil imported from Canada, which
free under the provisions of the Treaty of Washingto
them annually, and by classes, from 1854 to 1872, inclu
ume III 9th Census U States

34. If you know what amount of duties is annually
on fish and fish-oil imported from the United States,
made free under the provisions of the said Treaty, pleas
nually, and by classes, from 1854 to 1872, inclusive. C
ties will show this.

35. The object of these inquiries is to ascertain wheth
respect of fishing, and fishermen, and fish, which were g
Britain by the Treaty of Washington, are or are not a
for the rights in those respects which were granted by
the United States. If you know anything bearing up
which you have not already stated in reply to previous q
state it as fully as if you had been specially inquired of
Our vessels after the repeal of the Reciprocity Treaty
fee of 50 cts per Ton. This was the valuation placed u
fisheries by the Dominion Govt. We paid this more t
ance and capture on the slightest pretext and for the f
ports, than for the value of the fish, When it was incre
afterward 2 Dollars per Ton our vessels could not affo
it was universally repudiated, The Revenue derived
been over 10,000 Dollars and with all the advantages of
dom from capture and annoyance, we considered the pri
too high and the Dominion failed to obtain Customers
the repeal of the license system and the inauguration of
in its details we consider little better than *Piracy*. T
Dominion Fisheries depend entirely on the action of the
If admitted to free Markets in the United States their f
prosperous, and as they gain, our fishermen must lose
Markets of the United States their fisheries are valu

iption, and the fishermen of the U States can supply the
d of our own markets from our own shores and the deep
without being indebted to them for a single fish, 500 000
ly will not pay for the advantages they gain by the Treaty
on.

HARVEY KNOWLTON
EDWARD, A, HORTON

ASSACHUSETTS ⎱ ss.
OF ESSEX ⎰

'ER June 21st 1873. Then personally appeared the above
ey Knowlton and Edward A. Horton, and made oath that
its herein made including answer to Question 35. are true
f their knowledge and belief
e me
)

DAVID W. LOW
Notary Public

No. 24.

[CONFIDENTIAL.]

[S RESPECTING THE FISHERIES TO BE PRO-
:D TO ——— ——— ON BEHALF OF THE UNITED]

.s your name and age, and in what town and State do you
bion K. Peirce
opportunities have you had for becoming acquainted with
in and Canadian Atlantic sea-fisheries, and the value of the
, different kinds of fish? I have been to the Bay of St Law-
y years and also off our own coasts
ou give the names of other persons in your neighborhood
also had the opportunity of obtaining similar information?
e give some such name.
7 of the Treaty between Great Britain and the United States,
ne Treaty of Washington, is hereto annexed. Will you ex-
les 18 to 22 inclusive, and state that you have done so?

kinds of fish frequent the waters of your State, especially
i are to be thrown open to the Canadian fishermen under the
of the Treaty of Washington? Menhaden and Mackerel It
inderstood that in taking mackerel with the hook when we
l alongside biting well we may get our whole fare from that
if we were 5 miles from shore and the Cutters breaks up our
may not find a school ready to bite well again for a month.
re not like any other fish, one weeks steady catching would
sons work for us and if the mackerel should happen to tend
id bite well the inshore fishing would be useless to us, but if
iould get up a biting schooll say just 3 miles from the shore
.nce and breaking up of the fleets fishing would be the trou-
ime is spent by the fleet in hunting up the mackerel and find-
, that will bite than in the catching
ou give a statement of the kinds and quantities of fish taken
if the coast of your State from the year 1854 to 1872, inclusive?
do this please do so; and if not, please state where that infor-
i be procured.
i are able to do so, will you state the amount and value of the

American fisheries which are to be thrown open to Canadian fishermen under the provisions of the Treaty of Washington? Please state them in detail, showing the different kinds of fish, and the value of each kind. Menhaden are caught only on our coasts, the Canadians have to pay 6 to 8 dollars per barrel, ¼ of the Mackerel caught are caught within three miles of our own shores With the same enterprise on their part our inshore fisheries are of as much benefit to the Canadians as theirs is to us, the Menhaden are used at the rate of 6 Bbls to every 100 Bbls Mackerel

8. What quantity and value of each kind of fish are annually taken by Canadian fishermen, and what by American fishermen, in the waters off the coasts which are to be thrown open to competition by the Treaty of Washington? See Statistics

9. Do Canadian fishermen procure bait or supplies in the waters of your State? and if so, to what extent and value? They buy Menhaden bait that are caught by American fishermen and they will probably take their own bait under the treaty

10. What is the probable annual value to Canadian fishermen in being able to procure bait, to land and dry their nets, and to repack and cure their fish on the coasts of your State, without any other restriction than that contained in the Treaty of Washington? The Menhaden fishery is quite valuable and also the Mackerel fishery and the Canadians with the same enterprise would make our fisheries as valuable to them as theirs could be to us

11. Will the admission of Canadian fishermen to our in-shore fisheries cause any detriment or hinderance to the profitable pursuit of these fisheries by our own fishermen; and if so, in what manner, and to what extent annually? The competition of their cheap vessels and crews will lower the price of fish

12. What number of Canadian vessels and boats are engaged in the fisheries of your State, and what are their tonnage and value, and the number of men employed upon them? The most of their fisheries are carried on in boats and usually within 20 miles of the shore some of their vessels have been with our fleet on our coasts.

13. Of the fisheries pursued by American fishermen off the Atlantic coasts of the British North American provinces, what proportion consists of the deep-sea fisheries, and what proportion of the in-shore fisheries? The cod fishery is a deep sea fishery entirely. The Mackerel fishery is in the bay of St. Lawrence about ⅓ in 120,000 bbls are caught by American fishermen in-shore.

14. For what description of fish do American fishermen pursue the in-shore fisheries? Mackerel.

15. If you state that the in shore fisheries are pursued wholly or chiefly for mackerel, please state what proportion of mackerel is taken within the in-shore limits, and what proportion is taken outside of the inshore limits? Four-fifths are taken outside the three mile limits when the Fishery was free.

16. Is not much the larger quantity of mackerel caught by American fishermen off the coasts of British America taken outside the in-shore limits; and in the summer season especially, are not mackerel generally found on the banks, in the Gulf of Saint Lawrence, and not within shore? yes late in the season mackerel tend in shore, but our vessels do better off shore as the crews are kept on the vessels when if we were inshore they would be off half the time.

17. Are Colonial fishermen injured by permitting American fishermen to fish in Colonial in-shore waters? no.

not more fish caught by Colonial fishermen, when fishing in.
gside a fleet of American fishing-vessels, from which large
of bait are thrown out, than when fishing alone ? most cer-
rever the mackerel are fed they remain.

,t is the best bait for the mackerel, and where is it principally
.ow much of it is taken within three miles of the shore, and
e annual value to the United States, or to the British Prov-
ie case may be, to take such bait within three miles of the
lams & Menhaden mixed.

se state as to each class of fisheries carried on from your
strict, the cost of fitting out, equipping, furnishing, and man-
sel for carrying it on, estimating it by the average length of
  State, as far as possible, in detail the elements which go to
he cost of taking and delivering a full cargo and of returning
ie port. For a season's trip to the Bay, for Barrels, salt, pro.
surance, & wear and tear, 3,000..

en yod have fully answered question 20, please answer the
stions as to vessels fitted out, equipped, furnished, and
om the Dominion of Canada, including Prince Edward Island,
you are able to do so. If you state that there is any differ-
7een the cost of the Canadian and the cost of the American
these respects, explain what the difference is'and the reason
t more than one-half the cost of the American vessel The
  vessel stands about 100 Dollars per ton rigged and ready for
Canadian about $50. per ton Their men are fed principally
d potatoes. Our vessels have the best supplies the market

you acquainted, and for how long, and in what capacity, with
ies on the coasts of Nova Scotia, New Brunswick, Quebec, or
lward Island, or with either, and if either, with which of these
  all the fisheries
at kind of fish frequent the waters of those coasts which are
own open to American fishermen under the provisions of the
' Washington ? The Mackerell is all we take a a general

ase state in detail the amount and the annual value (say from
72 inclusive) of the fisheries which are so to be thrown open to
fishermen ; also the amount and the annual value of the catch
acent waters which are more than three miles distant from the
ease state these facts in detail.
American fishermen procure bait in the waters within three
the coast of the Dominion of Canada ? If so, to what extent
  is the value ? We buy all our bait for all fisheries on the
lue $200,000,00 which we pay to British fishermen.
not the American fishermen purchase supplies in the ports of
inion of Canada, including bait, ice, salt, barrels, provisions,
us articles for the use of the men engaged in the fisheries ?
that ports, and to what extent? And, if that is the case, is it
vantage to the ports of the Dominion to have the fishing-ves-
United States in their neighborhood during the fishing sea-
plain why it is so, and estimate, if you can. the money-value
lvantage. Yes, every vessel going to the Grand Banks and
banks stop for supplies and Bait at a cost of not less 800 Dol-
  The Mackerel fishermen under the Treaty will probably spend
nore, The Trade will amount to nearly if not quite a Million

27. Have you any knowledge of how many United State:
sels yearly engage in the fisheries off the Atlantic coasts o
North American Provinces, (excluding Newfoundland,) t
and within the three-mile limit? If so, state how many v
engaged, what is the value of their tonnage, what is the nu
employed annually on such vessels, what sorts of fish are
what is the annual value of all the fish so caught, and wha
portion, or probable proportion, in your judgment, of the am
catch taken within three miles of the British coast, and of
taken outside of the three-mile limit? About 7 or 800 Vess
value 2½ Millions. During Reciprocity about ⅛ of the M;
taken inshore, say 15 to 20000 bbls. We have done much l
own coasts, For Codfish & Halibut our vessels go to t
Browns Banks. All the Herring are bought from British F

28. What percentage of value, if any, is, in your judgme
the profits of a voyage by the privilege to fish within three
of the coast; whence is such profit derived; and in what do
The cost of taking any kind of fish fully equals their value
ducer all profits are made by the wholesale dealers, In asc
value if 20 000 bbls of Mackerel are taken worth $150 000
take from that amount the expense of 400 Vessels and 6000
for one months time in taking them. The whole valuation
fishery so far as profits are concerned is absolutely nothing

29. Do the American fishermen gain under the Treaty of
any valuable rights of landing to dry nets and cure fish, c
them, or to transship cargoes, which were not theirs before
are those rights, and what do you estimate them, to be wor
in the aggregate? No we think we had commercial righ
ports but have been denied them.

30. Is not the Treaty of Washington, so far as the fishin
concerned, more, or quite as, beneficial to the people of the
American Provinces as to the people of the United State
them.

31. What is the amount and value of colonial cargoes
descriptions which are annually shipped to the United Sta

32. For all No. 1 and No. 2 mackerel, for the larger pa
herring, and for all No. 1 salmon, does not the United Stat
only market. it does.

33. If you know what amount of duties is annually paid t
States on fish and fish-oil imported from Canada, which ar
free under the provisions of the Treaty of Washington,
them annually, and by classes, from 1854 to 1872, inclusi
the Treasury reports.

34. If you know what amount of duties is annually pai
on fish and fish-oil imported from the United States, whi
made free under the provisions of the said Treaty, pleas
annually, and by classes, from 1854 to 1872, inclusive. D
any American vessel ever carrying fish to Canadian ports.

35. The object of these inquiries is to ascertain whether
respect of fishing, and fishermen, and fish, which were gra
Britain by the Treaty of Washington, are or are not a ju
for the rights in those respects which were granted by s
the United States. If you know anything bearing upon
which you have not already stated in reply to previous que
state it as fully as if you had been specially inquired of in
The principal reason for satisfaction on the part of the fish

es is the relief from annoyance which the Treaty affords In
tion of the fishing business the liberty to take fish at all
e they may tend will scarcely afford them a living. The
hery is so variable and uncertain that we need all facilities
;hem wherever they are as a few days good fishing often
seasons work, Our own coast furnishes the best Mackerel,
e done better there than in the bay, but we like to have the
following the Mackerel, and the Canadians will be benefited
we are in coming on our coasts.

;ree (A. K. PIERCE, Master of Sch Wm. S. Baker.
)rse } GEO. BEARSE.   "   "   " Col. Cook.
irce) JAMES R. HAMILTON,   " Thorwaldsten.
ts. (JOHN McDONALD,   "   " Electric Flash.

and subscribed this 5th June 1873 before me,
ADDISON CENTER, *Dep. Collector.* (Seal.)

No. 25.

[CONFIDENTIAL.]

NS RESPECTING THE FISHERIES TO BE PRO-
ED TO —— —— ON BEHALF OF THE UNITED
i.

is your name and age, and in what town and State do you
ixty years, Geo. Norwood of the Firm Geo. Norwood & Son
Mass
opportunities have you had for becoming acquainted with
:an and Canadian Atlantic sea-fisheries, and the value of the
e different kinds of fish ? Have been engaged in the Fish-
; years.
ou give the names of other persons in your neighborhood
also had the opportunity of obtaining similar information ?
;e give some such name.
,y of the treaty between Great Britain and the United States,
the Treaty of Washington, is hereto annexed. Will you ex-
icles 18 to 22 inclusive, and state that you have done so ?

, kinds of fish frequent the waters of your State, especially those
to be thrown open to the Canadian fishermen under the pro-
:he Treaty of Washington ? Codfish, Mackerel. Menhaden.
:an give a statement of the kinds and quantities of fish taken
ff the coast of your State, from the years 1854 to 1872, in-
If you can do this please do so; and if not, please state where
mation can be procured. See Inspector Generals Report. on
ries of Mass. State House, Boston.
n are able to do so, will you state the amount and value of the
fisheries which are to be thrown open to Canadian fishermen
provisions of the Treaty of Washington ? Please state them
showing the different kinds of fish, and the value of each
.ckerel and Menhaden principally, Mackerel has a value
.tuates from $6.00 to $20.00 per bbl. With the same degree of
)on the part of the Canadians our Coast Fisheries, would be as
o them as what they possess would be to our Fishermen.
t quantity and value of each kind of fish are annually taken

by Canadian fishermen, and what by American fishermen, in the waters off the coasts which are to be thrown open to competition by the Treaty of Washington? That can be ascertained accurately only by Statistical Returns.

9. Do Canadian fishermen procure bait or supplies in the waters of your State? and if so, to what extent and value? They buy Menhaden Bait that are caught by American Fishermen in American Waters,

10. What is the probable annual value to Canadian fishermen in being able to procure bait, to land and dry their nets, and to repack and cure their fish on the coasts of your State, without any other restriction than that contained in the Treaty of Washington? The Canadians have never pursued any important Fishery on our Coasts. Their own shore Fisheries more than equal their Enterprize.

11. Will the admission of Canadian fishermen to our in-shore fisheries cause any detriment or hinderance to the profitable pursuit of these fisheries by our own fishermen; and if so, in what manner, and to what extent annually? The answer must be Comparitive. They can produce Fish at one half the expense of American Fisherman, and it would naturally affect the price of Fish

12. What number of Canadian vessels and boats are engaged in the fisheries of your State, and what are their tonnage and value, and the number of men employed upon them?

13. Of the fisheries pursued by American fishermen off the Atlantic coasts of the British North American Provinces, what proportion consists of the deep-sea fisheries, and what proportion of the in-shore fisheries? Cod-fishery & Halibut fishery are entirely a Deep Sea Fishery. The Mackerel Fishery is both a shore and deep Sea Fishery, About one filth of the Entire Mackel Fishery can be considered as a Shore Fishery.

14. For what description of fish do American fishermen pursue the in shore fisheries? *Mackerel.*

15. If you state that the in shore fisheris are pursued wholly or chiefly for mackerel, please state what proportion of mackerel is taken within the in-shore limits, and what proportion is taken outside of the in-shore limits? Under the Resprocity Treaty, the Entire British Shore free more than $\frac{4}{5}$ths were caught outside the 3 mile limits.

16. Is not much the larger quantity of mackerel caught by American fishermen off the coasts of British America taken outside the in-shore limits; and in the summer season especially, are not mackerel generally found on the banks, in the Gulf of Saint Lawrence, and not within shore? Yes.

17. Are Colonial fishermen injured by permitting American fishermen to fish in Colonial in-shore waters? No.

18. Are not more fish caught by Colonial fishermen, when fishing inshore, alongside a fleet of American fishing-vessels, from which large quantities of bait are thrown out, than when fishing alone? Yes: it is a well established fact founded on experience of over 40 years that in the Mackerel Fishery the larger amount of vessels in the Fleet the better for all.

19. What is the best bait for the mackerel, and where is it principally taken? How much of it is taken within three miles of the shore, and what is the annual value to the United States, or to the British Provinces, as the case may be, to take such bait within three miles of the shore? Clams & Menhaden mixed are the best, Clams are found on both American & English Shores. Menhaden are found only on the

hore. The value of the Menhaden Fishery is from 30? to
d dollars at Gloucester

e state as to each class of fisheries carried on from your State
.he cost of fitting out, equipping, furnishing and manning a
arrying it on, estimating it by the average length of the
ite, as far as possible, in detail the elements which go to make
of taking and delivering a full cargo and of returning to the
      $3000.00 for a season to the Bay including Bait, Barrels,
ince, Provisions and the Wear & Tear.

a you have fully answered question 20, please answer the same
s to vessels fitted out, equipped, furnished, and manned from
on of Canada, including Prince Edward Island, so far as you
do so. If you state that there is any difference between the
  Canadian and the cost of the American vessel in these re-
lain what the difference is, and the reason for it. Cost of
Vessels $100.00 per ton rigged. Cost of British Vessels from
Jost of running American Vessels per year from 3 to $4000.00.
3 12 Men each one year $3600.00. Canadian Vessels are pro-
ach cheaper than the Americans. their men living principally
l Potatoes ours on the best the Market affords

you acquainted, and for how long, and in what capacity, with
's on the coasts of Nova Scotia, New Brunswick, Quebec, or
vard Island, or with either, and if either, with which of these
  All of them.

it kind of fish frequent the waters of those coasts which are to
open to American fishermen under the provisions of the Treaty
gton ? The mackerel is the only available Fish to be caught
'an Vessels.

ise state in detail the amount and the annual value (say from
72 inclusive) of the fisheries which are so to be thrown open to
fishermen ; also the amount and the annual value of the catch
acent waters which are more than three miles distant from the
iase state these facts in detail.

American fishermen procure bait in the waters within three
1e coast of the Dominion of Canada ? If so, to what extent.
is the value ? The Fisherman do not catch any Bait them-
'hey buy all from the Shore Fisherman.

not the American fishermen purchase supplies in the ports of
inion of Canada, including bait, ice, salt, barrels. provisions,
is articles for the use of the men engaged in the fisheries ? It
it ports, and to what extent ? And, if that is the case, is it
vantage to the ports of the Dominion to have the fishing-ves-
; United States in their neighborhood during the fishing season ?
why it is so, and estimate, if you can, the money-value of that
e. American Vessels engaged both in the Deep Sea & Shore
off the Dominion Coast expend $1600.00 to $1000.00 each for
and Refitting amounting to about $400,000 00 in trade. Many
habitants of the Shores of the Provinces literally depend upon
'ican Fisherman for their Living.

ve you any knowledge of how many United States fishing-ves-
y engage in the fisheries off the Atlantic coasts of the British
nerican Provinces, (excluding Newfoundland,) both without and
le three-mile limit ? If so, state how many vessels are so en-
hat is the value of their tonnage, what is the number of men
l annually on such vessels, what sorts of fish are taken there,
he annual value of all the fish so caught, and what is the pro-

portion, or probable proportion, in your judgment, of the ¿
such catch taken within three miles of the British coast, a
amount taken outside of the three-mile limit ?   About 400 Vє
engaged in these Fisheries at the time of the Resprocity.   ⌐
under the restricted Policy many more American Vessels ɾ
Deep Sea Fisheries for Cod-fish & Halibut   since the introduc
for the preservation of Fish this business has been more pɾє
the Fish are sold fresh.   Vessels are worth from $60.00 to 8
ton.   The fish taken average about 2½ million dollars.   In
favorable season about $100 000 00 bbls are taken in the
Lawrence less than ⅓th of these are taken within 3 mile of t
This is the entire and only fishery used by Americans.

28. What percentage of value, if any, is, in your judgmє
to the profits of a voyage by the privilege to fish within thɪ
miles of the coast; whence is such profit derived; and in wl
consist ?   Any actual profit on the Fishing Business never hɑ
istance our Vessels have caught more Mackerel when entirelɟ
from the Inshore Limit,

29. Do the American fishermen gain under the Treaty of W
any valuable rights of landing to dry nets and cure fish, or
them, or to transship cargoes, which were not theirs before; i
are those rights, and what do you estimate them to be worth aɪ
the aggregate ?   No   We always had the right although depɪ
to land Fish or other merchandise in Bond to be transshipped
S.   In this as in all others Our Government have not protectɪ

30. Is not the Treaty of Washington, so far as the fishing c
concerned, more, or quite as, beneficial to the people of tl
North American Provinces as to the people of the Uniteɪ
Vastly more to the Provinces in every particular

31. What is the amount and value of colonial cargoes of
descriptions which are annually shipped to the United States

32. For all No. 1 and No. 2 mackerel, for the larger part
herring, and for all No. 1 salmon, does not the United States
only market ?   Most certainly Fat Mackerel shipped to warɪ
would have nothing left but the Bones before they were sold

33. If you know what amount of duties is annually p
United States on fish and fish-oil imported from Canada, w
be made free under the provisions of the Treaty of Washing
state them annually, and by classes, from 1854 to 1872, inclusi
to the Treasury Reports.

34. If you know what amount of duties is annually paid
on fish and fish-oil imported from the United States, whic
made free under the provisions of the said Treaty, please ,
annually, and by classes, from 1854 to 1872, inclusive.

35. The object of these inquiries is to ascertain whether th
respect of fishing, and fishermen, and fish, which were grantє
Britain by the Treaty of Washington, are or are not a just
for the rights in those respects which were granted by saiɪ
the United States.   If you know anything bearing upon tl
which you have not already stated in reply to previous questi
state it as fully as if you had been specially inquired of in rє
The simple Privilage of fishing within the In-shore limits of
ion has under any Circumstances a very small value.   The to
ception of the value and profits of the Fishing business held
not practically interested has given an assumed value to thє
in the Water,   The investments in the Fishing business, incl

arves, Ware-houses, Provisions, Lines, Nets, Sails, Rigging,
ilt, Barrels, and the time of the men engaged reckoned at the
es of pay as that obtained by regular Seamen or practical oper.
i the Land in any other business, has never yet or never will
ore than 6 per ct upon the whole amount. After paying 4 per
i investment of Capital and for the time of the Men and the
Tear and Depreciation of the Vessels, there will be no margin
.he purchase of Fish in the Water. It should be remembered
g with this subject that we should confine the value of Fish or
l in the hands of the Producer. That the values attached to
ippearing in Prices currant, are nearly double the value of the
their raw state before landing. What is cheifly the desire of
rican fisherman is to be protected from the continual annoy-
he danger of Capture upon the slightest reasons and the well-
iostility of the Dominion Government, from which they have
en afforded any protection, even from our own Government.
nties paid by the U. S. have been more than sufficient to estab-
antire Fishing interest. With these withdrawn and our Mar-
n to Canadian Fishermen free of duties who can produce the
ess than ½ the cost of American fisherman the Fisheries of the
i in danger of entire destruction.

GEO NORWOOD'

by endorse the above statements.

JAMES S AYER

'irm of Dennis & Ayer engaged in Fishing business 35 years

)F MASSACHUSETTS }
(NTY' OF ESSEX } ss.
CESTER June 21st
ribed and sworn to. Before me

DAVID W. LOW
Notary Public

No. 26.

[CONFIDENTIAL.]

IONS RESPECTING THE FISHERIES TO BE PRO-
IDED TO —— —— ON BEHALF OF THE UNITED
'ES.

iat is your name and age, and in what town and State do you re·
Andrew Leighton Aged 52 Gloucester Massachusetts.
iat opportunities have you had for becoming acquainted with
rican and Canadian Atlantic sea-fisheries, and the value of the
the different kinds of fish ? Have fished in Gulf of St. Law-
ring a period of twenty-eight years for Mackerel, also have been
in other kinds of fishing in the meantime, Since, for the last
:s, have carried on business as owner and fitter·
i you give the names of other persons in your neighborhood who
so had the opportunity of obtaining similar information ? If so,
i give some such name. Most of the members of firms (in the Fish·
ness) in Gloucester have been personally engaged in fishing in the
St. Lawrence. I would mention the names of Capt Benjamin
Capt Robert Reeves.
copy of the Treaty between Great Britain and the United States
)3 F.

known as the Treaty of Washington, is hereto annexed. Will you examine articles 18 to 22 inclusive, and state that you have done so? I
have examined the same.

5. What kinds of fish frequent the waters of your State, especially
those which are to be thrown open to the Canadian fishermen under the
provisions of the Treaty of Washington? Codfish Halibut. Haddock.
Polluck Hake—Menhaden. Mackerel, Swordfish &c.

6. Can you give a statement of the kinds and quantities of fish taken
annually off the coast of your State from the years 1854 to 1872, inclusive? If you can do this please do so; and if not, please state
where that information can be procured. Have never seen any estimates, the quantity is enormous, probably 300 000 Bbls Mackerel Mass
& Maine Menhaden probably 200,000 Dollars Cod haddock pollock,
1,500,000 Dollars

7. If you are able to do so, will you state the amount and value of the
American fisheries which are to be thrown open to Canadian fishermen
under the provisions of the Treaty of Washington? Please state them
in detail, showing the different kinds of fish, and the value of each kind.
see as above ————

Mackerel	$1 000,000
Menhaden	$2 000,000

8. What quantity and value of each kind of fish are annually taken
by Canadian fishermen, and what by American fishermen, in the waters
off the coasts which are to be thrown open to competition by the Treaty
of Washington? The only fish taken inside the three mile limit on the
Canadian coast, is Mackerel. The Herring taken at the Magdalenes are
already free to us.

9. Do Canadian fishermen procure bait or supplies in the waters of
your State? and if so, to what extent and value? They purchase bait
in large quantities for Mackerel.

10. What is the probable annual value to Canadian fishermen in being
able to procure bait, to land and dry their nets, and to repack and cure
their fish on the coasts of your State, without any other restriction than
that contained in the Treaty of Washington? This will be entirely
owing to their enterprise

11. Will the admission of Canadian fishermen to our in-shore fisheries
cause any detriment or hinderance to the profitable pursuit of these
fisheries by our own fishermen; and if so, in what manner, and to what
extent annually? Probably not. Except their vessels. costing less. they
could carry on the business profitably when we could not

12. What number of Canadian vessels and boats are engaged in the
fisheries of your State, and what are their tonnage and value, and the
number of men employed upon them? None that I know of at present

13. Of the fisheries pursued by American fishermen off the Atlantic
coasts of the British North American Provinces, what proportion consists of the deep-sea fisheries, and what proportion of the in-shore fisheries? Fully nine tenths of the Fishing is done outside the three mile
limit

14. For what description of fish do American fishermen pursue the inshore fisheries? Mackerel

15. If you state that the in shore fisheries are pursued wholly or chiefly
for mackerel, please state what proportion of mackerel is taken within
the in-shore limits, and what proportion is taken outside of the in-shore
limits? The advantage to us of being able to fish inside the three mile

are able to follow the Mackerel wherever we can catch
rtion cannot be accurately determined because it varys
   Should not think more than one tenth of the Mackerel
ore
ch the larger quantity of mackerel caught by American
ie coasts of British America taken outside the in-shore
ie summer season especially, are not mackerel generally
anks, in the Gulf of Saint Lawrence, and not within
true, yet late in the season they *sometimes* tend in shore,
of mackerel is usually found away from the shore.
ıtal fishermen injured by permitting American fishermen
al in-shore waters ? No they are not.
nore fish caught by Colonial fishermen, when fishing in-
; a fleet of American fishing-vessels, from which large
ıt are thrown out, than when fishing alone ? This is cer-
   it saves the Canadian boat fishermen a large sum as
oenefit of the bait thrown which otherwise they would
emselves
ıhe best bait for the mackerel, and where is it principally
ouch of it is taken within three miles of the shore, and
ıal value to the United States, or to the British provinces,
y be, to take such bait within three miles of the shore ?
t is best. Is taken on Coasts of Maine & Massachusetts.
ıen within three miles of shore. Do not know the aggre-
ık about $2 000,000
ate as to each class of fisheries carried on from your State
cost of fitting out, equipping, furnishing, and manning a
ing it on, estimating it by the average length of the cruise.
   possible, in detail the elements which go to make up the
and delivering a full cargo and of returning to the home
rage cost of running a fishing-vessel at Gloucester is from
rs per year for Salt Barrels Bait Ice Provisions &c   Crew
ə of Time, $3,600,00
ou have fully answered question 20, please answer the
ı as to vessels fitted out, equipped, furnished, and manned
nion of Canada, including Prince Edward Island, so far
e to do so. If you state that there is any difference be-
of the Canadian and the cost of the American vessels in
explain what the difference is and the reason for it. The
sels are not so well built more soft wood is used An
ing vessel cost new all rigged ready for sea 100 Dollars
dian not over 55 Dollars per ton Canadians live cheaper
toes We cannot get crews to go in our vessels unless
ood as the markets afford
acquainted, and for how long, and in what capacity, with
ı the coasts of Nova Scotia, New Brunswick, Quebec, or
d Island, or with either, and if either, with which of these
n acquainted as stated in article second with all the fish-

ind of fish frequent the waters of those coasts which are
ppen to American fisherman under the provisions of the
shington ? Mackerel.
state in detail the amount and the annual value (say from
nclusive) of the fisheries which are to be thrown open to
ermen ; also the amount and the annual value of the catch

in the adjacent waters which are more than three mile:
shore; please state these facts in detail.

25. Do American fishermen procure bait in the wa
miles of the coast of the Dominion of Canada? If s(
and what is the value? Our Cod & Halibut catchers b
to the Grand & Western Banks, buy bait on N. Scoti
shore to a considerable Extent say 200 000 Dollars per

26. Do not the American fishermen purchase supplies
Dominion of Canada, including .bait, ice, salt, barrel:
various articles for the use of the men engaged in the
in what ports, and to what extent? And, if that is the
advantage to the ports of the Dominion to have the
the United States in their neighborhood during the
Explain why it is so, and estimate, if you can, the mo(
advantage. They purchase supplies in large quanti
Gut of Canso, Halifax, also, at Charlottetown & Geo
The Mackerel Fleet usually purchase supplies, for ve
amounting from $300, to $600, each vessel.

27. Have you any knowledge of how many United S
sels yearly engage in the fisheries off the Atlantic coa:
North American Provinces, (excluding Newfoundlan
and within the three-mile limit? If so, state how ma
engaged, what is the value of their tonnage, what is th
employed annually on such vessels, what sorts of fish
what is the annual value of all the fish so caught, and
portion, or probable proportion, in your judgment, o
such catch taken within three miles of the British
amount taken outside of the three-mile limit? At
averaging 60 Tons & 14 men Costing from $100.00 to
New Measure *Mackerelling* 200 Bank Fishing

28. What percentage of value, if any, is, in your jud
the profits of a voyage by the privilege to fish within t
of the coast; whence is such profit derived; and in
sist? When mackerel are found inshore it is genera
of rivers or creeks, and unless we can go there to cat(
ilege is not worth much to us

29. Do the American fishermen gain under the Trea
any valuable rights of landing to dry nets and cure f
them, or to transship cargoes, which were not theirs b
are those rights, and what do you estimate them to b
in the aggregate? They will have no more rights tha
entitled to before.

30. Is not the Treaty of Washington, so far as the f
concerned, more, or quite as, beneficial to the people of
American Provinces as to the people of the United
to be the unanimous opinion of American Fishermen
the Treaty will be better for them than for us.

31. What is the amount and value of colonial carg
descriptions which are annually shipped to the Unite(

32. For all No. 1 and No. 2 mackerel, for the large
herring, and for all No. 1 salmon, does not the Unite(
only market. It does.

33. If you know what amount of duties is annually
States on fish and fish-oil imported from Canada, whi
free under the provisions of the Treaty of Washin
them annually, and by classes, from 1854 to 1872, inc

u know what amount of duties is annually paid in Canada
l fish-oil imported from the United States, which are to be
inder the provisions of the said Treaty, please state them an-
, by classes, from 1854 to 1872, inclusive.

object of these inquiries is to ascertain whether the rights in
ishing, and fishermen, and fish, which were granted to Great
the Treaty of Washington, are or are not a just equivalent
its in those respects which were granted by said Treaty to
States. If you know anything bearing upon this subject
have not already stated in reply to previous questions,
e it as fully as if you had been specially inquired of in re-

ANDREW LEIGHTON
WALTER M FALT

MASSACHUSETTS
  COUNTY OF ESSEX ss

GLOUCESTER, June 21st 1873

ed and sworn to,
            Before me

DAVID W. LOW
Notary Public

No. 27.

[CONFIDENTIAL.]

)NS RESPECTING THE FISHERIES TO BE PRO·
)ED TO ——— —— ON BEHALF OF THE UNITED
S.

; is your name and age, and in what town and State do you
W C Wonson of Gloucester Essex Co Mass
t opportunities have you had for becoming acquainted with
can and Canadian Atlantic sea-fisheries, and the value of the
he different kinds of fish ? I have been practically engaged
ing business for fourteen years   Am now conducting general
siness fitting eight vessels
you give the names of other persons in your neighborhood
  also had the opportunity of obtaining similar information ?
ise give some such name.
py of the Treaty between Great Britain and the United States,
  the Treaty of Washington, is hereto annexed. Will you ex-
icles 18 to 22 inclusive, and state that you have done so ? I

t kinds of fish frequent the waters of your State, especially
ch are to be thrown open to the Canadian fishermen under the
s of the Treaty of Washington ? Mackerel Menhaden Cod·
ck Haddock Hake Herring
you give a statement of the kinds and quantities of fish taken
off the coast of your State from the years 1854 to 1872, inclu·
  you can do this, please do so; and, if not, please state where
  mation can be procured. See reports of Ins General of the
ss
)u are able to do so, will you state the amount and value of the
. fisheries which are to be thrown open to Canadian fishermen
) provisions of the Treaty of Washington ? Please state them
showing the different kinds of fish, and the value of each kind.

Our Shore fisheries are worth some years more than
Mackerel are an erratic fish, our shore Mackerel are wo:
Bbls. more than the Bay Mackerel, The Menhaden f
shore fishery and are taken for oil Bait Guano &c is
$4000,000 00 Mackerel Fishery about the same though

8. What quantity and value of each kind of fish ar(
by Canadian fishermen, and what by American fisherm(
off the coasts which are to be thrown open to competiti(
of Washington ? See Canadian Statistics See U State

9. Do Canadian fishermen procure bait or supplies
your State; and, if so, to what extent and value ? I
tained by them by purchase

10. What is the probable annual value to Canadian
ing able to procure bait, to land and dry their nets, an(
cure their fish on the coasts of your State, without any
than that contained in the Treaty of Washington ? 1
the value of bait, say $75,000, but they do not do busin

11. Will the admission of Canadian fishermen to our i
cause any detriment or hinderance to the profitable
fisheries by our own fishermen; and, if so, in what
what extent annually ? Do not think it would affect us
will have cheap vessels, & there will be some competit:

12. What number of Canadian vessels and boats ar(
fisheries of your State, and what are their tonnage an(
number of men employed upon them ? Do not know u

13. Of the fisheries pursued by American fishermen
coasts of the British North American Provinces, what
sists of the deep-sea fisheries, and what proportion of t
eries ? Principally Deep Sea fishing until late in the fa
$\frac{1}{30}$ part would be taken in shore including all fisheries

14. For what description of fish do American fisher
in-shore fisheries ? Mackerel

15. If you state that the in shore fisheries are pu
chiefly for mackerel, please state what proportion of n
within the in-shore limits, and what proportion is tak(
in-shore limits ? Should not think that more than ou
taken within three miles of the shore.

16. Is not much the larger quantity of mackerel cau
fishermen off the coasts of British America taken out
limits; and in the summer season especially, are not m
found on the banks, in the Gulf of Saint Lawrence
shore ? Yes

17. Are Colonial fishermen injured by permitting An
to fish in Colonial inshore waters ? No

18. Are not more fish caught by Colonial fishermen,
shore, alongside a fleet of American fishing-vessels,
quantities of bait are thrown out, than when fishing :
The more vessels the better

19. What is the best bait for the mackerel, and when
taken ! How much of it is taken within three miles
what is the annual value to the United States, or to
iuces, as the case may be, to take such bait within t
shore ! Clams & Manhaden ; Manhaden are found on
can Shores,

20. Please state as to each class of fisheries carr
State or district, the cost of fitting out, equipping, fur

l for carrying it on, estimating it by the average length of
State, as far as possible, in detail the elements which go to
e cost of taking and delivering a full cargo and of returning
e port. Pogie Fishing requires a crew of from 10 to 15 men,
from 300 to 500 per month, Mackerel Fishing requires a
2 to 20 men, Cost about the same. Cod Fishing requires a
ut 13 men, Cost including salt fitting Insurance &c. about
onth.

you have fully answered question 20, please answer the
ons as to vessels fitted out, equipped, furnished, and manned
ominion of Canada, including Prince Edward Island, so far
ible to do so. If you state that there is any difference be-
ost of the Canadian and the cost of the American vessel in
cts, explain what the difference is and the reason for it. I
the expense of fitting Canadian vessels but should think that
be fitted and run at least one third cheaper than American
ld.

you acquainted, and for how long, and in what capacity,
sheries on the coasts of Nova Scotia, New Brunswick, Que-
nce Edward Island, or with either, and if either, with which
sheries? I am well acquainted with them.

t kind of fish frequent the waters of those coasts which are
vn open to American fishermen under the provisions of the
Washington? Mackerel Halibut & Cod fish,
se state in detail the amount and the annual value (say from
72 inclusive) of the fisheries which are so to be thrown open
n fishermen; also the amount and the annual value of the
ne adjacent waters which are more than three miles distant
hore; please state these facts in detail. Dont know

American fishermen procure bait in the waters within three
ne coast of the Dominion of Canada? If so, to what extent,
is the value? They sometimes buy their Bait of the Cana-
value of not less than $200,000.00.

not the American fishermen purchase supplies in the ports of
nion of Canada, including bait, ice, salt, barrels, provisions,
s articles for the use of the men engaged in the fisheries?
hat ports, and to what extent? And, if that is the case, is
idvantage to the ports of the Dominion to have the fishing-
the United States in their neighborhood during the fishing
Explain why it is so, and estimate, if you can, the money-
hat advantage. Yes. Our vessels often refit in the ports of
nion at an expense of from $100 to $600.

ve you any knowledge of how many United States fishing-
early engage in the fisheries off the Atlantic coasts of the
forth American Provinces, (excluding Newfoundland,) both
nd within the three-mile limit? If so, state how many ves-
o engaged, what is the value of their tonuage, what is the
f men employed annually on such vessels, what sorts of fish
there, what is the annual value of all the fish so caught, and
he proportion, or probable proportion, in your judgment, of the
f such catch taken within three miles of the British coast, and
ount taken outside of the three-mile limit? About 600 or 700
re annually engaged they average about 65 tons employing
00 men,

hat percentage of value, if any, is, in your judgment, added to
ts of a voyage by the privilege to fish within three marine miles

of the coast; whence is such profit derived; and in wh
sist? In case we are deprived of fishing at the moutl
the Mackerel Fishery would be rendered almost valueles

29. Do the American fishermen gain under the Trea·
ton any valuable rights of landing to dry nets and cur(
pack them, or to transship cargoes, which were not thei
what are those rights, and what do you estimate them
nually, in the aggregate? No the Canadians are more
we are.

30. Is not the Treaty of Washington, so far as the fisl
concerned, more, or quite as, beneficial to the people
North American Provinces as to the people of the Unit
is more benefit to the Canadians than to the American F

31. What is the amount and value of colonial cargoe
descriptions which are annually shipped to the United S

32. For all No. 1 and No. 2 mackerel, for the larger part of
and for all No. 1 salmon, does not the United States a
market. Yes. No fat mackerel are carried south of Ha·
all consumed in the Northern Middle and Western State

33. If you know what amount of duties is annually pai(
States on fish and fish-oil imported from Canada, which :
free under the provisions of the Treaty of Washington, pl·
annually, and by classes, from 1854 to 1872, inclusive.
will show think about from 200 to $300,000.00 The impo
be doubled by free markets.

34. If you know what amount of duties is annually pai(
fish and fish-oil imported from the United States, which
free under the provisions of the said Treaty, please state
and by classes, from 1854 to 1872, inclusive.

35. The object of these inquiries is to ascertain wheth
respect of fishing, and fishermen, and fish, which were g
Britain by the Treaty of Washington, are or are not a
for the rights in those respects which were granted by sa
United States. If you know anything bearing upon this wl
have not already stated in reply to previous questions, pl
fully as if you had been specially inquired of in resp(
United States should have claimed at least a half millio
fisheries that are to be affected depend solely on the U
for their value and we get no advantages except the rele:
ance. Our Mackerel fleet can take all the Mackerel tha
home consumption off our own coasts, and we are simpl
foreign fishery which is valueless without our markets f
of using British harbors, and giving them our trade wh
times more to them than any fisheries are to us.

WM. (

STATE OF MASSACHUSETTS ⎰
   COUNTY OF ESSEX   ⎱ ss

GLOUCESTER J

Then personally appeared the above named William (
made oath that the foregoing statements by him subscr
Before me
(Seal.)   DAVID ¥

No. 28.

[CONFIDENTIAL.]

JS RESPECTING THE FISHERIES TO BE PRO-
ED TO ——— ——— ON BEHALF OF THE UNITED

is your name and age, and in what town and State do you
eo Friend & Co. Gloucester Mass.
opportunities have you had for becoming acquainted with the
nd Canadian Atlantic sea-fisheries, and the value of the catch
rent kinds of fish ? Have caught them, cured them, & sold
prosecuting the fishing Business.
on give the names of other persons in your neighborhood who
ad the opportunity of obtaining similar information ? If so,
some such name. Could give the names of 40 Fishing
you have probably sent them these questions,
y of the Treaty between Great Britain and the United States,
the Treaty of Washington, is hereto annexed. Will you ex
les 18 to 22 inclusive, and state that you have done so ? We

kinds of fish frequent the waters of your State, especially those
to be thrown open to the Canadian fishermen under the pro-
the Treaty of Washington ? All Kinds that we have the
ke upon their shores, Mackerel & Menhaden in particular
ou give a statement of the kinds and quantities of fish taken
of the coast of your State from the years 1854 to 1872, inclusive ?
do this please do so; and if not please state where that in-
can be procured. Can get all the required information from
of the General Inspector, of our own and other fishing States,
are able to do so, will you state the amount and value of
can fisheries which are to be thrown open to Canadian fisher-
the provisions of the Treaty of Washington ? Please state
tail, showing the different kinds of fish, and the value of each
ckerel and Porgies are taken on our shores, the Porgie being
our own shore fishery, our shore Mackerel are worth, and will
e right along, than the Bay Mackerl. they seem to be a
everyway, and if there is any advantage it is in favor of the
fishermen almost in the proportion of 2 to 1.
t quantity and value of each kind of fish are annually taken
an fishermen, and what by American fishermen, in the waters
sts which are to be thrown open to competition by the Treaty
gton ? You had better consult the statistics of both countries,
ill learn the full quantity & value of the whole thing,
anadian fishermen procure bait or supplies in the waters of
? and if so, to what extent and value ? Only by purchasing
them Slivers or Porgie Bait, slivered ready for use.
at is the probable annual value to Canadian fishermen in being
ocure bait, to land and dry their nets, and to repack and cure
on the coasts of your State, without any other restriction than
ued in the Treaty of Washington ? same as their fisheries

Il the admission of Canadian fishermen to our in-shore fisheries
detriment or hinderance to the profitable pursuit of these

fisheries by our own fishermen ; and if so, in what manne
extent annually ?   We think it will injure our business a
their running cheaper vessels, & fitting cheaper can unde
time   Twill result in great loss to the American fisherme

12. What number of Canadian vessels and boats are e
fisheries of your State, and what are their tonnage, and '
number of men employed upon them ?   We dont think tl

13. Of the fisheries pursued by American fishermen o
coasts of the British North American Provinces, what prop
of the deep-sea fisheries, and what proportion of the in-s
$\frac{9}{10}$ are caught off shore, and some vessels dont take a
any kind.

14. For what description of fish do American fisherm
in-shore fisheries ?   Mackerel—Cod and Halibut.

15. If you state that the in shore fisheries are pursued w
for mackerel, please state what proportion of mackerel i
the in-shore limits, and what proportion is taken outside (
limits ?   The Mackerel which are taken inshore do not An
very small part of the vessels trips, they are only take
season and then about one half perhaps of our fleet are a
not return to the Bay.   Take off the annoyance of being
ters, and having to keep watch of an imaginary 3 mile
dont think our fishermen would care one cent wether
mackerel inside 3 miles.   We dont consider they are wor'

16. Is not much the larger quantity of mackerel caugh
fishermen off the coasts of British America taken outside
limits ; and in the summer season especially, are not macl
found on the banks, in the Gulf of Saint Lawrence, a
shore ?   Yes Thrible.

17. Are Colonial fishermen injured by permitting Ame
to fish in Colonial in-shore waters ?   Well we guess not
fitted a great deal.

18. Are not more fish caught by Colonial fishermen
in-shore, alongside a fleet of American fishing-vessels, fr
quantities of bait are thrown out, than when fishing alone
are twice as good.

19. What is the best bait for the mackerel, and where
taken ?   How much of it is taken within three miles of
what is the annual value to the United States, or to th
inces, as the case may be, to take such bait within thr
shore ?   Clams and Porgies, or Menhaden. Porgies are
our own shore.

20. Please state as to each class of fisheries carried on
or district, the cost of fitting out, equipping, furnishin
a vessel for carrying it on, estimating it by the averag
cruise.   State, as far as possible, in detail the elemer
make up the cost of taking and delivering a full cargo a
to the home port.   Pogie fishing not over 12 men, prin
ing about $500, per month,   Mackerelling, not over 20 n
age. 15 men.   Cost trifle more.   Cod—12 men   Cost
Porgie fishing.

21. When you have fully answered question 20, ple'
same questions as to vessels fitted out, equipped, furnish
from the Dominion of Canada, including Prince Edwar
as you are able to do so.   If you state that there is ar

cost of the Canadian and the cost of the American vessel in
ects, explain what the difference is and the reason for it. We
that Canadians can fit build and run their vessels cheaper
in, but how much cheaper we are unable to say. We think
. place the matter about right to say ¼ cheaper than we can
i and run our vessels. And we are confident we have placed
low.
you acquainted, and for how long, and in what capacity, with
es on the coasts of Nova Scotia, New Brunswick, Quebec, or
ward Island, or with either, and if either, with which of these
Well acquainted with all of them,
at kind of fish frequent the waters of those coasts which are
wn open to American fishermen under the provisions of the
Washington? Mackerel—Cod & Halibut.
ise state in detail the amount and the annual value (say from
i72 inclusive) of the fisheries which are so to be thrown open
:an fishermen; also the amount and the annual value of the
:he adjacent waters which are more than three miles distant
shore; please state these facts in detail. You must consult
again, for we cant give you the desired information.
American fishermen procure bait in the waters within three
.he coast of the Dominion of Canada? If so, to what extent.
is the value? Buy lots of Bait from them, and pay from ² to
l thousand dollars.
not the American fishermen purchase supplies in the ports of
inion of Canada, including bait, ice, salt, barrels, provisions,
ius articles for the use of the men engaged in the fisheries? If
at ports, and to what extent? And, if that is the case, is it not
tage to the ports of the Dominion to have the fishing-vessels
aited States in their neighborhood during the fishing season?
why it is so, and estimate, if you can, the money-value of that
;e. Our vessels often go in to their different Ports, refit. and
ything for the voyage, and pay the Dominion merchants all the
a $50 to $800, Have paid this Amt ourselves, for one vessel.
ive you any knowledge of how many United States fishing-
yearly engage in the fisheries off the Atlantic coasts of the
North American Provinces, (excluding Newfoundland.) both
and within the three-mile limit? If so, state how many vessels
igaged, what is the value of their tonnage, what is the number
imployed annually on such vessels, what sorts of fish are taken
iat is the annual value of all the fish so caught, and what is the
on, or probable proportion, in your judgment, of the amount of
.ch taken within three miles of the British coast, and of the
taken outside of the three-mile-limit? 600,—60 tons—8,000,
tatistics will give you the rest.
hat percentage of value, if any, is, in your judgment, added to
its of a voyage by the privilege to fish within three marine miles
oast; whence is such profit derived; and in what does it con-
fone whatever are added to the profits.
o the American fishermen gain under the Treaty of Washington
iable rights of landing to dry nets and cure fish, or to repack
to transship cargoes, which were not theirs before; if so, what
ie rights, and what do you estimate them to be worth annually,
ggregate? Canadian fishermen reap Double the benifit that the
in fishermen do.

30. Is not the Treaty of Washington, so far as the fishin concerned, more, or quite as, beneficial to the people North American Provinces as to the people of the United St same as Question 29

31. What is the amount and value of colonial cargoes descriptions which are annually shipped to the United £ say.

32. For all No. 1 and No. 2 mackerel, for the larger p herring, and for all No. 1 salmon does not the United Sta only market. Fat mackerel find a ready and about the o the U. S.

33. If you know what amount of duties is annually paid States on fish and fish-oil imported from Canada, which a free under the provisions of the Treaty of Washington, ple annually, and by classes, from 1854 to 1872, inclusive. show you the whole thing, we should think $250,000 wa And importations would more than dowble up by free ma

34. If you know what amount of duties is annually paid fish and fish-oil imported from the United States, which a free under the provisions of the said Treaty, please state t and by classes, from 1854 to 1872, inclusive. Dont know

35. The object of these inquiries is to ascertain whether respect of fishing, and fishermen, and fish, which were gra Britain by the Treaty of Washington, are or are not a ju for the rights in those respects which were granted by s the United States. If you know anything bearing upon which you have not already stated in reply to previous qu state it as fully as if you had been specially inquired of in Our impression in relation to fishing inside the three mile this. It will be a detriment instead of a benifit. One will be so is that our vessels would be likely to lie in tl Port Hood, and along their coast, when they ought to be ing ground. To take fish inside the three mile limit is o the American fishermen. It is only when our fishermen a say from 4 to 5 miles from the land, of being bored to dea sent out of their harbors when they seek them for she storms which frequent that coast, of not being permitte thing except wood and water, and hardly that that this lies. Our fishermen only want protection in this matter, erel they would take inside the three mile mile line. we w reputation, would not much more than pay for the Bait t

Attest to the foregoing.

GEO FRII

STATE OF MASSACHUSETTS
        COUNTY OF ESSEX s. s.

GLOUCESTER J

Then personally appeared John J. Somes and for himsel members of the firm of Geo. Friend & Co. made oath that statements subscribed in the firm's name are true Befo
(Seal.)   DAVID V

No. 29.

[CONFIDENTIAL.]

IS RESPECTING THE FISHERIES TO BE PRO-
ED TO —— —— ON BEHALF OF THE UNITED
3.

s your name and age, and in what town and State do you
ederic Gerring Gloucester Mass
opportunities have you had for becoming acquainted with
in and Canadian Atlantic sea-fisheries, and the value of the
different kinds of fish ? I have been practically engaged
ries 35 years & now conducting the general fishing business
e s
ou give the names of other persons in your neighborhood
lso had the opportunity of obtaining similar information ?
e give some such name. Alfred Low & Co, F. G. Wonson
nson 2d.
of the Treaty between Great Britain and the United States,
ie Treaty of Washington, is hereto annexed. Will you ex-
les 18 to 22 inclusive, and state that you have done so ? I

kinds of fish frequent the waters of your State, especially
are to be thrown open to the Canadian fishermen under the
of the Treaty of Washington ? Mackerel, Cod, Herring,

ou give a statement of the kinds and quantities of fish taken
f the coast of your State from the years 1854 to 1872, inclu-
ou can do this please do so; and if not, please state where
ation can be procured. I would refer you to the reports of
or General of the State,
are able to do so, will you state the amount and value of
an fisheries which are to be thrown open to Canadian fisher-
the provisions of the Treaty of Washington ? Please state
tail, showing the different kinds of fish, and the value of each
able to state
quantity and value of each kind of fish are annually taken
in fishermen, and what by American fishermen, in the waters
its which are to be thrown open to competition by the Treaty
gton ? Bureau of Statistics Washington D. C,
inadian fishermen procure bait or supplies in the waters of
? and if so, to what extent and value ? for all their Bait :
ckerel fisheries.
t is the probable annual value to Canadian fishermen in being
cure bait, to land and dry their nets, and to repack and cure
in the coasts of your State, without any other restriction than
ined in the Treaty of Washington ? unable to State
the admission of Canadian fishermen to our in-shore fisheries
detriment or hinderance to the profitable pursuit of these
y our own fishermen ; and if so, in what manner, and to what
ually ? No, except more competition
it number of Canadian vessels and boats are engaged in the
? your State, and what are their tonnage and value, and the
men employed upon them ? Should say about 15 vessels
he fisheries pursued by American fishermen off the Atlantic

coasts of the British North American Provinces, what pr
sists of the deep-sea fisheries, and what proportion of
fisheries? Should think about 80 per cent are deep sea fi

14. For what description of fish do American fisherme
in-shore fisheries? Mackerel late in the year

15. If you state that the in shore fisheries are pursu
chiefly for mackerel, please state what proportion of macl
within the in-shore limits, and what proportion is taken (
in-shore limits? *not one tenth* part of the mackerel taken
St. Lawrence are taken within the inshore limits

16. Is not much the larger quantity of mackerel caught
fishermen off the coasts of British America taken outside
limits; and in the summer season especially, are not mack
found on the banks, in the Gulf of Saint Lawrence, an
shore? YES

17. Are Colonial fishermen injured by permitting Ameri
to fish in Colonial in-shore waters? No.

18. Are not more fish caught by Colonial fishermen, wh
shore, alongside a fleet of American fishing-vessels, from
quantities of bait are thrown out, than when fishing alone

19. What is the best bait for the mackerel, and where is
taken? How much of it is taken within three miles of tl
what is the annual value to the United States, or to the l
inces, as the case may be, to take such bait within three
shore? Pogie or Menhaden, an American fish, taken off (
Value of this fishery about $1,000,000 yearly

20. Please state as to each class of fisheries carried (
State or district, the cost of fitting out, equipping, turnish:
ning a vessel for carrying it on, estimating it by the aver
the cruise. State as far as possible, in detail the element
make up the cost of taking and delivering a full cargo an(
to the home port. Pogie fishing, Crew 10 men cost of S:
visions &cc $400, *time 3 weeks mackerl fishing about the*
a voyage to Grand Banks of a Schooner of 80 tons about
term of 2 mos or 10 weeks

21. When you have fully answered question 20, 'pleas
same questions as to vessels fitted out, equipped, furnished
from the Dominion of Canada, including Prince Edward
as you are able to do so. If you state that there is any
tween the cost of the Canadian and the cost of the Ame
these respects, explain what the difference is and the
About one half what it costs to fit an American vessel

22. Are you acquainted, and for how long, and in w
with the fisheries on the coasts of Nova Scotia, New Br
bec, or Prince Edward Island, or with either, and if eith
of these fisheries? 20 years *all of them*

23. What kind of fish frequent the waters of those co
to be thrown open to American fishermen under the pr
Treaty of Washington? Codfish—Halibut & Mackerel

24. Please state in detail the amount and the annual v
from 1854 to 1872 inclusive) of the fisheries which are so
open to American fishermen; also the amount and the a
the catch in the adjacent waters which are more than tl
tant from the shore; please state these facts in detail. C
data required Should think that the Deep Sea fisher
from Shore were worth $2000,000 00 less cost of taking

ırican fishermen procure bait in the waters within three
ıast of the Dominion of Canada? If so, to what extent,
ıe value? Yes $200,000 worth a year

the American fishermen purchase supplies in the ports of
of Canada, including bait, ice, salt, barrels, provisions,
ıticle for the use of the men engaged in the fisheries? If
ırts, and to what extent? And, if that is the case, is it
ıage to the ports of the Dominion to have the fishing-ves-
ited States in their neighborhood during the fishing sea-
ı why it is so, and estimate, if you can, the money-value
tage. Yes, 10 years ago about all of the American fleet
Straits of Canso, N. S, and their trade was a great ad-
e natives there, say $500,000

ıu any knowledge of how many United States fishing-ves
gage in the fisheries off the Atlantic coasts of the British
ıan Provinces, (excluding Newfoundland,) both without
e three-mile limit? If so, state how many vessels are so
ıt is the value of their tonnage, what is the number of men
ınally on such vessels, what sorts of fish are taken there,
ınual value of all the fish so caught, and what is the pro-
obable proportion, in your judgment, of the amount of such
vithin three miles of the British coast, and of the amount
e of the three-mile limit? 700 Vessels, total tonnage,
costing about $60 per ton about 10,000 men employed and
the products of the fisheries of this district for the year
31, 1872 was valued at $3,437,000,—Gross.

ıercentage of value, if any, is, in your judgment, added to
a voyage by the privilege to fish within three marine miles
whence is such profit derived; and in what does it con-
uch, not over 5 per cent

American fishermen gain under the Treaty of Washington
rights of landing to dry nets and cure fish, or to repack
ransship cargoes, which were not theirs before; if so, what
hts, and what do you estimate them to be worth annually,
gate? no, I consider we had these right always

the Treaty of Washington, so far as the fishing clauses are
ıore, or quite as, beneficial to the people of the British
ican Provinces as to the people of the United States? Yes

is the amount and value of colonial cargoes of fish of all
which are annually shipped to the United States? No date

l No. 1 and No. 2 mackerel, for the larger part of the fat
for all No. 1 salmon, does not the United States afford the
. No, mey of their fish are exported direct to foreign coun-
han the U. S,

know what amount of duties is annually paid to the United
h and fish-oil imported from Canada, which are to be made
the provisions of the Treaty of Washington, please state
lly, and by classes, from 1854 to 1872, inclusive. Cannot

know what amount of duties is annually paid in Canada on
ı-oil imported from the United States, which are to be made
he provisions of the said Treaty, please state them annually,
ses, from 1854 to 1872, inclusive. Cannot Say
bject of these inquiries is to ascertain whether the rights in

respect of fishing, and fishermen, and fish, which were gr:
Britain by the Treaty of Washington, are or are not a J
for the rights in those respects which were granted by ı
the United States. If you know anything bearing upo
which you have not already stated in reply to previous qu
state it as fully as if you had been specially inquired of iı

GLOUCESTER, MASS.
  June 11, 1873,
    FRED. GERRING
      part owner of Six fishing Vessels, 20 years engaged
      business,

STATE OF MASSACHUSETTS } ss.
COUNTY OF ESSEX

  GLOUCESTER June 21st 1873 Then personally appea
named Frederic Gerring and made oath that the foregoi
by him subscribed, are true to the best of his knowledge
          Before me
  (Seal.)   ·   DAVID
                                   N

No. 30.

[CONFIDENTIAL.]

QUESTIONS RESPECTING THE FISHERIES T
  POUNDED TO ——— ———, ON BEHALF OF T
  STATES.

  1. What is you name and age, and in what town an
reside ? Frederick G. Wonson of Gloucester, Essex Co,
  2. What opportunities have you had for becoming ac
the American and Canadian Atlantic sea-fisheries, and tl
catch of the different kinds of fish ? Have been practi
both as Fisherman, and owner for the past twenty two
fitting fourteen vessels
  3. Can you give the names of other persons in youı
who have also had the opportunity of obtaining similar iı
so, please give some such name. F Gerring Walen & Cc
  4. A copy of the Treaty between Great Britain and the
known as the Treaty of Washington, is hereto annexed
amine articles 18 to 22 inclusive, and state that you hav
have examined articles 18 to 22
  5. What kinds of fish frequent the waters of your St
those which are to be thrown open to the Canadian fisher
provisions of the Treaty of Washington ? Mackerel, H
Codfish &c,
  6. Can you give a statement of the kinds and quantitie
annually off the coast of your State from the years 1854
sive ? If you can do this, please do so ; and if not, plea
that information can be procured. see Report Inspec
Fish State of Mass
  7. If you are able to do so, will you state the amount a
American fisheries which are to be thrown open to Cana
under the provisions of the Treaty of Washington ? Pl
in detail, showing the different kinds of fish, and the val

    Shore, Menhadn fishery $2,000,000.
    Shore, Mackerel fishery $1,500,000

:aught off the New England Coast have been worth from
iore per Barrel than the Bay of St Lawrence of the same

ntity and value of each kind of fish are annually taken by
rmen, and what by American fishermen, in the waters off
:h are to be thrown open to competition by the Treaty of
The Canadians have not engaged in the American fish-
ctent they have hardly had enterprise sufficient to take
· own waters.

lian fishermen procure bait or supplies in the waters of
id if so, to what extent and value ? Pogie Bait is ob-

the probable annual value to Canadian fishermen in being
a bait, to land and dry their nets, and to repack and cure
ie coasts of your State, without any other restriction than
in the Treaty of Washington ? Their own enterprise will

admission of Canadian fishermen to our in-shore fisheries
riment or hinderance to the profitable pursuit of these
r own fishermen; and if so, in what manner, and to what
ly ? Do not think that it would affect us materially other
have cheap vessels & there will be more competition ·
umber of Canadian vessels and boats are engaged in the
ur State, and what are their tonnage and value, and the
n employed upon them ? Do not know
isheries pursued by American fishermen off the Atlantic
British North American Provinces, what proportion con-
ep-sea fisheries, and what proportion of the in-shore fish-
ipally deep-sea fishing until late in the fall say ½⅞ is out-

s.
it description of fish do American fishermen pursue the
·ies ? Mackerel
tate that the in-shore fisheries are pursued wholly or chiefly
please state what proportion of mackerel is taken within
mits and what proportion is taken outside of the in-shore
ld not think that more than one fifth part are taken within
iit, or about from 12 to 20,000 Bbls
much the larger quantity of mackerel caught by Ameri-
a off the coasts of British America taken outside the in-
and in the summer season especially are not mackerel
id on the banks, in the Gulf of Saint Lawrence, and not
? Yes; on banks Bradly and Orphan, and around the
auds
lonial fishermen injured by permitting American fishermen
onial in-shore waters ? I do not think they are on the con-
ve they are benefitted
t more fish caught by Colonial fishermen, when fishing in-
ide a fleet of American fishing vessels, from which large
bait are thrown out, than when fishing alone ? There is
s the best bait for mackerel, and where is it principally
v much of it is taken within three miles of the shore, and
nnual value to the United States, or to the British Prov-
case may be, to take such bait within three miles of the
ies—which are taken on the New England shores only—
ue of the Pogie fishery cannot be less than two millions of

20. Please state as to each class of fisheries carried on from your State or district, the cost of fitting out, equipping, furnishing, and manning a vessel for carrying it on, estimating it by the average length of the cruise. State, as far as possible, in detail the elements which go to make up the cost of taking and delivering a full cargo, and of returning to the home port. Generally the crews of the Pogie catchers consist of about 10 men each—time about 3 weeks per trip—cost $400— Bank fishing $400 per month—this includes barrels, salt, cost of filling, Insurance, &c, Mackerel fishing

21. When you have fully answered question 20, please answer the same questions as to vessels fitted out, equipped, furnished, and manned from the Dominion of Canada, including Prince Edward Island, so far as you are able to do so. If you state that there is any difference between the cost of the Canadian and the cost of the American vessel in these respects, explain what the difference is and the reason for it. Should think that the Canadians Could prosecute th e fisheries at one-half the expense we could—owing to their much cheaper vessels— cheaper men and cheaper grub,

22. Are you acquainted, and for how long, and in what capacity, with the fisheries on the coasts of Nova Scotia, New Brunswick, Quebec, or Prince Edward Island, or with either, and if either, with which of these fisheries? Am acquainted with all kinds.

23. What kind of fish frequent the waters of those coasts which are to be thrown open to American fishermen under the provisions of the Treaty of Washington? Mackerel principally

24. Please state in detail the amount and the annual value (say from 1854 to 1872, inclusive,) of the fisheries which are so to be thrown open to American fishermen; also the amount and the annual value of the catch in the adjacent waters which are more than three miles distant from the shore; please state these facts in detail.

25. Do American fishermen procure bait in the waters within three miles of the coast of the Dominion of Canada; if so, to what extent, and what is the value? American fishermen buy bait of Canadians to a large extent, the value of which must be considerable, say $200,000.

26. Do not the American fishermen purchase supplies in the ports of the Dominion of Canada, including bait, ice, salt, barrels, provisions, and various articles for the use of the men engaged in the fisheries; if so, in what ports, and to what extent? And, if that is the case, is it not an advantage to the ports of the Dominion to have the fishing-vessels of the United States in their neighborhood during the fishing season? Explain why it is so, and estimate, if you can, the money-value of that advantage. They do purchase supplies to a great extent— should think the fleet would average each $500, at Charlottetown, P. E. I., Canso Strait, and others, and is of immense value to these places. During reciprocity nearly all the American fleets refitted at those ports, in some cases amounting to $1000 or $1500, each vessel

27. Have you any knowledge of how many United States fishing-vessels yearly engage in the fisheries off the Atlantic coasts of the British North American Provinces, (excluding Newfoundland,) both without and within the three-mile limit? If so, state how many vessels are so engaged, what is the value of their tonnage, what is the number of men employed annually on such vessels, what sorts of fish are taken there, what is the annual value of all the fish so caught, and what is the proportion, or probable proportion, in your judgment, of the amount of such catch taken within three miles of the British coast, and of the amount taken outside of the three-mile limit? Should think about 700

ngaged with a total tonnage 420,000 tons—about 60 tons
ibout $60, per ton—$2,520,000.

percentage of value, if any, is, in your judgment, added to
f a voyage by the privilege to fish within three marine miles
; whence is such profit derived; and in what does it con-
)t think the privilege to fish within 3 miles is of any value.
,yance is what we complain of

; American fishermen gain under the Treaty of Washington
> rights of landing to dry nets and cure fish, or to repack
:ransship cargoes, which were not theirs before ; if so, what
;hts, and what do you estimate them to be worth annually,
gate? I think we do not gain any rights of any value and
as will be greatly benefitted by the treaty.

the Treaty of Washington. so far as the fishing clauses are
more, or quite as, beneficial to the people of the British
ican Provinces as to the people of the United States? The
rill have the most benifit

is the amount and value of colonial cargoes of fish of all de-
'bich are annually shipped to the United States? Do not

ll No. 1 and No. 2 mackerel, for the larger part of the fat
l for all No. 1 salmon, does not the United States afford the
;. It does

t know what amount of duties is annually paid to the United
sh and fish-oil imported from Canada, which are to be made
the provisions of the Treaty of Washington, please state
lly, and by classes, from 1854 to 1872, inclusive. Cannot.
t know what amount of duties is annually paid in Canada on
t-oil imported from the United States, which are to be made
,he provisions of the said Treaty, please state them annually,
ses, from 1854 to 1872, inclusive. See U States Statistics
ibject of these inquiries is to ascertain whether the rights in
shing, and fishermen, and fish, which were granted to Great
the Treaty of Washington, are or are not a just equivalent
ts in those respects which were granted by said Treaty to
States. If you know anything bearing upon this subject
have not already stated in reply to previous questions, please
ully as if you had been specially inquired of in respect of it.
:s of the United States are the foundation of all the profits
terel fisheries to the Canadians Without them this fishery
s : The Fish caught by our vessels on the Ocean Banks are
ery large, These fish are larger than the shore fish caught
adian coast which are smaller and better fitted for the West
Mediteranean trade, The Georges Codfish always bring a
> than any other consequently the shore fisheries for Cod fish
le value If we are to be excluded from the mouths of
aking Mackerel the Mackerel fishery also will not amount to

FREDERIC G. WONSON, of John F, Wonson & Co

MASSACHUSETTS } ss
rY OF ESSEX }   GLOUCESTER June 21st 1873.

,ed and sworn to, by above named Frederic G. Wonson
                    Before me
                            DAVID W. LOW
il.)   Notary Public

No. 31.

I Charles H. Pew of Gloucester in the County of Essex and Commonwealth of Massachusetts, being duly sworn doth depose and say;

I am forty years old and have been engaged in the fishing business
ever since I entered my fathers store as a boy of fourteen years old.
Our firm is John Pew & Sons, my brother and myself are the sons—We
own twenty (20) fishing vessels and have averaged as many as that
number, their tonnage varies from forty (40) to one hundred (100) tons
each, they are exclusively engaged in the cod and mackerel fisheries.
Last year we had two vessels only engaged in the mackerel fishery in
the Canadian Waters and that not in fishing inshore.

Since the fishery clauses of the Treaty of Washington took effect viz ,
1872, we have had four years experience of the operation of the free
fishing clauses. During those years we have caught mackerel to the
value of $167,000$\frac{}{100}$ as shown by our sales in the United States waters
and $39,600$\frac{}{100}$ worth in British waters; of which $39,600$\frac{}{100}$ worth I
think hardly any were taken within three miles of the shore. Our vessels having chiefly fished at the Magdalen Islands. During the same
four years our catch of codfish &c has been $475,000$\frac{}{100}$ no part of
which was caught within three miles of the British shore but all in the
deep seas and on the coast of the United States. Seven eighths of the entire codfish catch has been off the coasts of the United States. Since 1872
the percentage of our catch of mackerel taken off the British coast has
decreased being in 1875 only $7,800 out of $156,014, total fish production. The shore fisheries of the United States are far more valuable
than those off the British coasts. The value of the fisheries on the
British coast has been steadily diminishing. The quality of the mackerel taken off the British coast has been growing poorer and that off the
United States coast has grown better for some years past.

The amount of bait bought by the vessells of our firm of the inhabitants
of the British Provinces was in 1874 about $500 worth in 1875 about
$800 worth, this bait was fresh herring for our vessels bound to the
banks of Newfoundland to fish for cod. We have never caught any bait
in British waters. Few if any United States vessels catch any bait in
their waters. All our mackerel bait consists of salted porgies taken off
the U. S. coast; this fish is not found in the British waters: they are a
warm water shore fish and are rarely found beyond Mt. Desert which
is considered their eastern and northern limit. The pogies are to some
extent bought by the Colonists as bait for mackerel, their only other bait
for mackerel is herring which is much inferior. The right to land and
dry nets or cure fish on shore is of no value to anybody, this practice
has become wholly obsolete, the whole mode of fishing to which this relates ceased more than a generation ago. All fish both cod and mackerel are brought home to cure the fishing vessels do not even cure their
own catch, but sell them green to be cured by fish dealers and packers.
The entire fishing fleet of Gloucester in August 1875 was in all 392 vessels, the number has been about the same for ten (10) years past though
the average tonnage has increased. In 1875 during the summer not
over 35 vessels entered the Bay of St Lawrence or any other British
waters for Mackerel, the rest fished off the coasts of the United States
alone; except about 100 on the banks of Newfoundland. As I have already stated the percentage caught in British waters has regularly decreased for five years past.

. The United States fishermen import nothing into the British Provinces, the provincial fishermen import into the United States all their

el and nearly all their poor mackerel Fat mackerel spoil
ed into southern latitudes and there is no market for them
he United States and there not south of Chesapeake Bay.
States also furnished the chief market for the large codfish,
here to better advantage than anywhere else, the small cod-
, by the provincial fishermen go to the West Indies, Spain and
ain.
ll the smoked herring from the provinces come into the
ates. The alewife fishery, salmon fresh and salt; large
f fish oils nearly all that is produced in the provinces come
nited States. The effect of free importations since the Treaty
gton has been very injurious to the fishing interests of the
competition caused by it has nearly ruined the profits of the

smuch as the cost of building and equipping a vessel in the
is much less than in the United States, from a third to a
ss—if there were as many fishermen in the provinces as in the
ates and they had equal capital, skill and energy the princi-
business would be transferred to the provinces.
ness experience is that the effect of the present treaty is and
former Reciprocity Treaty during its continuance, was, that
portation of fish from the British provinces is a great injury
ted States fishermen and far outweighs any benefit they may
n fishing inshore
e effect upon the prices of fish to the consumer of free importa-
r the treaty, there has not yet been any perceptable reduction of
he retail business although four years out of the ten named in
have already elapsed. In fact, the profits of the fishing busi-
o small that it is no exaggeration to say that a fish in the sea
ney value and that the cost of catching is so great that the
on capital invested in the fisheries is small and does not aver-
l as the returns from capital in other branches of business, the
ll made on shore by the curers and dealers who buy from the

CHARLES H. PEW

COMMONWEALTH OF MASSACHUSETTS

GLOUCESTER Dec 1875

ersonally appeared the abovenamed Charles H. Pew to me
nd made oath that all the foregoing statements by him sub-
re true to the best of his knowledge and belief—before me
DAVID W. LOW
Notary Public

d Mansfield of Gloucester of the County of Essex and Com
th of Massachusetts being duly sworn do depose and say—that
en engaged in the fishing business for the last 24 years. I am
r of the firm of James Mansfield & Sons—I have had in the
the two preceding fishing seasons frequent opportunities for
tion with intelligent and well informed Nova Scotia captains
rmen residing in the southern portion of Nova Scotia—that the
that region are now more extensively than ever turning their
to the catching of codfish both in their own immedeate waters
he more distant fishing banks—Attention is being attracted to
teries on the part of capitalists who previously have found in

other branches of marine business full employment for
have been unwilling to engage in a business paying so
the fisheries—

The Nova Scotians who have at their own doors what
mense source of wealth have been lacking an available
surplus product of their fisheries beyond that which the
supply, but under the existing state of affairs between the
and Great Britain this want is fully met—Since the aut
Grand Banks Codfishery has been as a whole unprodu
stocks of fish as the American vessels have produced
posed of without difficulty, but in the event of a large ca
fill all the markets of our own to overflowing the prese
amount of English fish thrown into the market on equ
our own and at greatly reduced cost of production from o
enabling them to be sold at a profit to their owners whe
would have to be sacrificed, would be a blow of great se
tire New England Codfishery—

At the present time there are in our market a greate
usual of English parties in pursuit of a cheap class of fis
and I have known within the past year of several instance
sels have been sold to parties from the Provinces to be
codfishing business—I consider that by means of the new
the United States and Great Britain the fishing interest
Provinces have received a most favorable and importan

ALFRED M

COMMONWEALTH OF MASSACHUSE1

Essex ss   Gloucester

Then personally appeared the above named Alfred
known and made oath that all the foregoing statemen
scribed are true so far as they depend upon his own kn
far as they depend upon information and belief he beli
true—

—before me—

DAVID ·

(Seal.)

No. 33.

I George Steele of Gloucester in the county of Esse
wealth of Massachusetts being duly sworn doth depo
and for the last 27 years have been engaged in the
owning and fitting out vessels for the cod and mackerel
North American coast. My vessels have been both on
British provinces and of the United States. I had last
vesseles.

The codfishery is wholly a deep sea fishery no cod a
three miles of the shore. The free fishery clauses of the
fore of no value to the United States fishermen engag
Nor do the cod fishermen catch their own bait, they c
home salt and fresh herring; they also to some extent
the provinces herring or squid.

The effect on the codfish business of allowing free i
the United States has been and must continue to be v
the provinces, for they find in the United States their

sh—their small codfish go to the West Indies and is con-
ome.

t on the codfisheries of the United States is to bring them
competition with the Canadians who by reason of the greater
of building and equipping vessells in which they have an
over us of from 25 to 50 percent could if they had equal
1 enterprise monopolise the business to the exclusion of our
nen.

kerel are the only fish caught at all in shore, the relative im-
f mackerel in the trade of the country has for some years
ily diminishing, they are much less used than formerly. In
rn States whitefish from the lakes are taking their place

lity of Mackerel caught off the coasts of the British provinces
ich poorer than formerly and the quantity taken much less.
nth of the mackerel caught in British waters are taken within
s of the shore.

the last three or four years the seine fishery for mackerel off
1 States coasts has been very successful. In 1875 the catch
tish coast was very small.

no doubt the free importation of mackerel into the United
a benefit to the provinces which far more than compensates
e United States can gain by fishing inshore. The United
the only market for fat mackerel and almost the only one for
grades.

d rather be subject to the restrictions formerly imposed and
owed to fish within three miles of the coast, if duties could be
osed on fish from the provinces.

GEORGE STEELE

COMMONWEALTH OF MASSACHUSETTS.

GLOUCESTER Dec 29th 1875

ersonally appeared the abovenamed George Steele to me known
oath that all the foregoing statements by him subscribed are
ir as they depend upon his own knowledge and as far as they
pon information and belief he believes them to be true.

DAVID W. LOW

e me—
Notary Public

No. 34.

mus Smith of Gloucester in the county of Essex and Common-
Massachusetts being duly sworn depose and say that I am
en years old and am a member of the firm of Smith and Gott,
ownes seventeen (17) vessels I have been engaged in the fish-
iess twenty eight years, seventeen years as master of a vessel
en years on shore fitting out vessels for the cod and mackerel
—Last year only two out of our whole fleet were engaged in fishing
anadian coast—No portion of all the catch last year was taken
—In 1874 we had five vessels in Canadian Waters and I should
out one eighth part of the fish caught were taken within three

of seines—fishing for mackerel with seines cannot be prof
on in Canadian Waters on account of the roughness of th
shoalness of the water, for this reason American fisher
most entirely ceased to use the Canadian mackerel fishery
used in mackerel fishing consists of menhaden or porgie
found off the coast of the United States, and which t
bought from the American fishermen to a great extent—
Treaty they have equal facilities with us for procuring it—
the Canadians herring and small mackerel to use on the I
bait; Our firm has paid as much as $2000.00 the past s
alone—We often repair and refit our vessels in the Provi
ing supplies &c and have paid as much as 500\frac{}{100}$ for on

I consider the right to land and dry nets cure fish &c on
shores as of no value—I have never had any of my ve
this purpose nor have I ever known of any other vesse
During the past season very few vessels from this town i
forty out of three hundred and fifty fished in the Gulf of
and these only for two or three months—

No fish are ever exported from the United States to
while all their large cod and the best quality of their mac
here; the only fish for which there is a market in the pro
small cod and poorer grades of mackerel—   .

I think that the fishermen of the United States will be i
Treaty of Washington—The Canadians can build ships
the Americans and by the free clause of the Treaty they
in some cases have carried their fish directly to the Ameri
sold them there—Under the old Reciprocity Treaty the Car
fleet increased largely but as soon as the repeal of the tre
their taking their fish into the United States free of duty
unprofitable that it was to a great extent given up and
they had begun building for the fishing business were left
the stocks—Since the present Treaty has taken effect, the
increased very largely in the Provinces—

I consider the inshore fisheries of little value, we ser
and they take few fish—All the value of the treaty to ou
the right to traid, buy bait &c unmolested and if we coul
in this, we should much prefer and desire the old tariff—
trade we have always claimed but it has been denied to u
been harassed in every way—

                                        SYLVAN

COMMONWEALTH OF MASSACHUSET

Essex ss   Gloucester D

Then personally appeared the above named Sylvanus
known and made oath that all the foregoing statemen
scribed are true so far as they depend upon his own kno
far as they depend upon information and belief he belie
true—before me—

          (Seal.)   DAVID V
                                         N

No. 35.

I, Morris Whelen of Gloucester in the County of Es
monwealth of Massachusetts, being duly sworn do depose
I have been twenty-two years engaged in fishing for mac

ter of a vessel for the last fifteen years. Most of the time I have
the Gulf of St Lawrence, I have in all this time caught very
within three miles of the shore—The fish in this Gulf are grow-
er each year, last season they were very scarce around Prince
Island—I have never caught any bait in Canadian waters, but
ays carried porgies from Gloucester to use for this purpose—I
er bought any supplies from the Canadians. The only thing
ve ever procured from the shore has been water.
e last few years many more fish have been taken off the Ameri-
es than in Canadian waters. I should think the proportion was
e I have generally fished off the Magdalen Island

MAURIS WHELEN

COMMONWEALTH OF MASSACHUSETTS

s GLOUCESTER Dec 29th 1875
personally appeared the above named Morris Whelan to me
nd made oath that all the foregoing statements by him sub-
are true to the best of his knowledge and belief

before me

DAVID W. LOW
Notary Public

No. 36.

mas Grady of Gloucester in the County of Essex and Common-
of Massachusetts being duly sworn do depose and say that I
en engaged in the Cod and Mackerel fishery since 1851 have
ster of a fishing vessel seventeen years—In 1872 fished off the
the United States for mackerel in 1873 and 1874 fished in Bay
awrence; in 1875 on the "Georges" Banks, Mackerel on the
n coast are much poorer and fewer than formerly and in conse-
fewer vessels from this port go there—The only bait for the
el is the pogie, which is only found in the United States and
be Canadians buy from us. I have in 1869 bought codfish bait
e Canadians for use on the Grand Banks—I do not think that
ing inshore would be any detriment to Canadian fishermen—I
r the Treaty of Washington of much more benefit to the Cana-
an to the fishermen of the United States.

THOMAS GRADY

COMMONWEALTH OF MASSACHUSETTS

GLOUCESTER Dec 28th 1875
ss
personally appeared the above named Thomas Grady to me
and made oath that all the foregoing statements by him sub-
are true to the best of his knowledge and belief—

Before me DAVID W LOW
tary Public

.) No. 37.

mes G. Tarr of Gloucester in the county of Essex and Common-
of Massachusetts being duly sworn do depose and say I am forty
ars old and have been engaged in the fishery business for the
fteen years—I am a member of the firm of J. G. Tarr and Brother,
the owners of fourteen vessels from fifty to eighty tons burden
which are engaged in the cod and mackerel fisheries—During

the past season only one out of all our vessels has been engaged in fishing off the coast of Canada—In 1866 we sent seven vessels out of a fleet of Eight sail to British waters; In 1867 the same number were sent there; In 1868 four vessels—In 1869 three vessels In 1870 four vessels, 1871 three vessels, 1872 only two vessels with an increase of fleet to ten sail—1873 four vessels, 1874 with an increase of fleet to twelve sail we sent only four vessels-

Since the Treaty we have used the inshore fisheries very little and our principal catch has been at the Magdalen Islands and on the Banks—For the last two years nearly all our vessels going to the Banks of Newfoundland for cod fish have touched at Colonial Ports and purchased herring bait there for use on the Banks, they also carry some salted bait from home for the codfishery—There is no inshore fishing for bait on the British Coast by United States vessels—I should consider seven eighths of all fisheries pursued by Americans on the Canadian shores consists of deep sea fishing, while only the remaining eighth inshore where only mackerel are caught.

I can conceive of no injury to Canadian fishermen that can be caused by our fishing in their waters side by side with them, but I should think that it would be a great benefit to them on account of the large amount of bait thrown overboard by American fishermen which attracts the fish—The only bait used for mackerel is the porgie or menhaden which is found entirely in the United States and which all the Canadians have to buy from the Americans in a salted state, this fish (the porgie) is not found in Canadian Waters and is almost the only bait used in the mackerel fishery; if the Canadians were unable to procure this bait, they would be compelled to use herring bait which is much inferior for the purpose—The bait which we buy from them for the codfishery consists of herring and some small mackerel—

For the last ten years our firm has averaged to pay the Canadians from $800—to 1000\frac{50}{100}$ a year for this bait—We are also in the habit of purchasing in the Provinces any supplies, ice &c of which our vessels may be in need our supplies thus purchased amount to about $500—a year on the average—In reference to the purchase of bait from the Americans by Canadian fishermen, I have known vessels to sail from this port with as many as three hundred barrels of porgie bait on board which was sold in Halifax and the Straits of Canso to Canadian fishermen.

I think the right of fishermen of either nation under the treaty to land dry nets &c on the shores of the other, amounts to nothing on either side, All fishing vessels are now in the habit of curing all their fish at the home ports—

During the period of the former Reciprocity Treaty and since the Treaty of Washington, the importations of fish into the United States from the Provinces have been very large and have materially interfered with the profits of our fishermen, this is especially the case with the mackerel almost all of which, that are caught by the Canadians are sent into the United States for sale—Also all their large codfish are sold in the United States as they have a market for the small cod only at home—All their fat herring and No. 1 salmon are sold in the United States—

I consider the Treaty of Washington of much more value to the Provinces than to the United States—I should prefer the old duty on fish and would be willing to give up all our rights of inshore fisheries under the Treaty, if the tariff could be renewed—This conclusion is the result of four years—experience under the Treaty of Washington and also un-

)le of the former Reciprocity Treaty As all vessels can be
)ped and manned in the colonies for a third less than in the
tes—consequently if there were as many colonial fishermen as
and they had equal skill and industry they could entirely
American fishermen out of the business—

JAMES G. TARR

COMMONWEALTH OF MASSACHUSETTS

GLOUCESTER Dec 22d 1875

rsonally appeared the abovenamed James G. Tarr to me
I made oath that all the foregoing statements by him sub-
, true as far as they depend upon his own knowledge and as
depend upon information and belief he believes to be true

before me

(Seal.)   DAVID W. LOW
Notary Public

No. 38.

E. Gorman of Gloucester in the county of Essex and Com·
, of Massachusetts being duly sworn do depose and say,
twenty six years old and have been engaged in the fish-
·ss for the last thirteen years during the last five years
en master of a vessel—I have been engaged in fishing for
in the Bay of St Lawrence every year but two, and since
7 has come into effect have been in the Bay each year—
uring the month of July I fished in shore to some extent
taken from 150 to 200 barrels out of 700 my whole catch
rip. In 1875 fished near the Magdalen Islands and caught
nshore—Out of my last three trips in which my whole catch
)arrells I caught not more than 200 barrels inshore—Most of
iken inshore are caught by the Canadians from small boats
from the shore and returning each day with their fish. They
ith profit this fishery where in many cases our large fishing
uld not go. This inshore fishery is f comparatively little
s, We would be much better off without this right and with
ity of $2 per barrel on fish imported from Canada—The Bay
s been steadily decreasing from year to year. last year of all
s from Gloucester engaged in the Mackerel fishery nearly four
n all only about 50 sail were in the Bay at any time. This is
the increase in value of the seine fishery on the coast of the
ates, in which most of the other vessels were engaged. This
ry is much more valuable and profitable than the fishing in
ith lines, the vessels make shorter trips. The seine fishery
tried to some extent in the Bay but was not profitable, the
too rough and the water too shoal—
in the Bay have diminished in number and deteriorated in
ry much within the last ten years. for instance last year
ls did not average more than 120 barrels each, while the best
s only 380 barrels, in 1874 my vessel caught 700 barrels and
s fleet averaged, as much as 300 barrels—
and pogies are the principal bait for mackerel, pogies are only
the coast of the United States and the Canadians buy it from
reat extent, I have sold them myself as much as ten barrels
:—The right to land &c as granted by the Treaty used to be
value in the old times when the Reciprocity Treaty was in

force, it was the custom then to tranship the fish and se
by freighters, but this is not done now each vessel carries
catch to Gloucester—American vessels purchase supp
Canadians to a great extent, furnishing supplies and ship
our vessels as hands for a fishing trip are the principal (
the people at Canso. Last year I spent $50.00 for supp
have probably averaged that amount each year—Canadi:
cute the fisheries in their waters with much less expense
they can build their vessels one-third cheaper, their cre\
in all Canadian vessels the skippers per centage is assess(
crew, while here it is paid by the owners—Now that
market is thrown open to them, they can undersell our 1
reduce their profits. Under the old tariff before the Trea
of the trips has been much less valuable—

JOHN. E.

COMMONWEALTH OF MASSACHUSETI

ESSEX ss   GLOUCESTER F
Then personally appeared the above named John G
known and made oath that all the foregoing statement
scribed are true upon his own knowledge and belief—
(Seal.)   DAVID W
A

No. 39.

I Nicholas Warren of Gloucester in the County of Es
monwealth of Massachusetts being duly sworn do depose :
have been engaged in the cod and mackerel fisheries for t
teen years have been in the Bay the last six years—I h
little inshore as I could not do so well there as further ou
ing vessels we cannot follow the mackerel so well as the
in their small boats come out from the shore—Last sum
very few fish in the Bay, this has been so for the last few
vessels engaged in fishing off the American coast have
ter fares than those which went to the Bay—Last season
more than forty Gloucester vessels in the Bay out of a fl(
dred, while ten years ago there would be as many as thre
Gloucester alone in the Bay at one time, This was befor
cry on our own coast became so valuable—I have known (
being tried in Canadian waters, but it has been unsucce
was shallow and the rough bottom tore their nets—I h
any bait to the Canadians but have known of its being (
extent, the bait used by us for mackerel is the menhad
found in Canadian waters and they have to use herrin(
and not nearly so good for the purpose—I have never
shipped any fish home by steamer and I do not conside
the treaty permitting this of any value, ten years ago it t
but not now Our trade is a great advantage to the C:
purchase supplies wood &c in great quantities, I have 1
$100.00 each year—

The free clause in the Treaty is of great benefit to the
has lowered our prices and diminished our profits — C:
have come to this town and sold their fish green here
market for them at home and the received much higher

The Canadians can build their vessels much cheaper t
also they pay their crew much less a man can be hired i

to $75 a trip, while we pay from $100 to $200 per man,
n under sell and make a profit where we could not live —

NICHOLAS WARREN

JOMMONWEALTH OF MASSACHUSETTS

GLOUCESTER Jany 26th 1876

sonally appeared the abovenamed Nicholas Warren to me
made oath that all the foregoing statements subscribed by
> as far they depend upon his own knowledge and as far as
upon information and belief he believes them to be true—

Before me—

DAVID W. LOW
Notary Public.

No. 40.

Hardy of Gloucester in the County of Essex and Common-
Massachusetts, being duly sworn do depose and say that I
ngaged in the fishery business for twenty one years, for last
ears master of a vessel—Since 1872 have been in the Bay
ery few fish were caught inshore not one eighth portion of
atch. This was in 1873 & 1874 last year did not fish inshore
ter outside—My principal catch has always been about the
slands—Last year there were about 125 vessels in the Bay
,rhaps 40 were from Gloucester. All most all the inshore bay
irried on by the Canadians in small boats from the shore, so
an use this fishery with profit where we could not, as they
,he fish closer to the shore—Fewer and fewer vessels go to
:h season as they can make more profit seine fishing on the
:oast I have tried to use a seine for mackerel in the Bay
no luck, the fish would not school there as the do in our
the water in many places is too shoal to permit of its being
y advantage—I think the free importation clause in the
great advantage to the Canadians, as they can carry on the
much cheaper than we can, There is a rebate of duty on all
ight by fishermen for their business and they can build boats
ien much cheaper—Many men have gone from here to the
where they can buy a boat for $50 and by going out from
atch there fish and carry them back at night, making more
a by going on fishing trips. Large Canadian fishing vessels
to Gloucester and sold their fish there green—Canadians use
·ring which they catch in their own waters but this is a poor
when they can they procure menhaden bait from us—Ameri-
s spend a great deal of money for supplies &c in Canada. I
mer paid out $2000.00 for refitting The merchants at Canso
.nd say that they have lost a great deal of money by the dim-
business caused by our vessels not coming to the bay as they
The only benefit under the treaty we receive is the right to
ors &c without molestation, we were troubled in every way
i away from the harbors on the ground that we were "pro-
fish." I have been chased several times by cutters when I
than seven miles away from the land and once in "Pirates
auso I was seized as a prize and my sails stripped off because
·t get away within the given time allowed me—All we want
lanadians are the rights in their harbors which are allowed to
essels except American fishing-vessels—

HENRY HARDY

COMMONWEALTH OF MASSACHUSETTS

Essx ss   GLOUCESTER Jan 25th 1876

Then personally appeared the abovenamed Henry Hardy and made oath that all the foregoing statements by him subscribed are true as far as they depend upon his own knowledge and as far as they depend upon information and belief he believes them to be true—

—before me—

(Seal.)   DAVID W. LOW
                                     Notary Public

No. 41.

I John E Saunders of Gloucester in the county of Essex and Commonwealth of Massachusetts being duly sworn do depose and say that I am forty seven years old and have been engaged in fishing since I was a boy for the last twenty five years I have been captain of a vessel I Have been in the Bay of St Lawrence every year from July to November. Since 1872 I have used the inshore fisheries very little, in all have not taken more than five barrels inshore—I can always do much better off shore —Last year there were very few Gloucester vessels in the Bay not more than forty, most of the others were engaged in seine fishing off our own coast which is very valuable and productive—The Bay catch has not been near so heavy for the last five years as before and for this reason we send fewer vessels each year to the Bay. The seine fishery has been tried in the Bay but has been unsuccessful the water is shallow and the mackerel do not school as they do off our coast—Canadians import men· haden bait from the United States to some extent, the menhaden is not found north of Cape Sable, fresh herring is used by Canadians some- what but it is an inferior sort of bait and they much prefer menhaden when they can get it. I never have used the right under the treaty to land and repack fish &c I do not consider it of any value—I have pur- chased supplies and refitted in Canadian ports, several times spent $250 —in one season and once paid $700—for refitting my vessel Americans are charged very high prices for every thing purchased—They can build their vessels much cheaper and by paying their crews much less they can carry on the business at much less cost and as by the treaty they can send their fish here free, they are enabled to make a profit where our fishermen could not live—

I consider the treaty of much benefit to the Canadians and of little value to us; The only use to us, is that we are allowed to buy pro- visions &c without hinderance, this right was always ours, but we were prevented and driven away on the ground that it was preparing to fish—

JOHN E. SAUNDERS

COMMONWEALTH OF MASSACHUSETTS

Essex ss   GLOUCESTER Jan 26th 1876

Then personally appeared the abovenamed John Saunders to me known and made oath that all the foregoing statements subscribed by him are true as far as they depend upon his own knowledge and as far as they depend upon information and belief he believes them to be true—

before me

(Seal.)   DAVID W. LOW
                                     Notary Public .

No. 42.

Hannan of Gloucester in the County of Essex and Com.
f Massachusetts being duly sworn do depose and say that
iree years old, have been on fishing trips ever since I was
e last eighteen years master of a vessell. Most every year
November have been mackerel fishing sometimes all the
ie last ten years have fished principally around the Magda-
have fished in the Bay both within and without three mile
re caught most fish offshore—Since 1872 I have used the
ries to some extent.   The catch inshore seemed much poorer
fished before inshore during the Reciprocity Treaty—The
has been very poor for last five years, the fish are few and
ce of Bay mackerel has been about $5 less than the Ameri-
el—only few Gloucester vessels from forty to fifty were in
year, ten years ago all the vessels fished there but by rea-
ewness of the fish they have left it and now fish on the
iores with a seine—I have seen vessels in the Bay fishing
but they had no luck and' tore or lost their seines—I have
len bait to the Canadians a few barrels each year, they im-
deal of this bait from the United States—now by the Treaty
ne here and catch this bait themselves, to my own knowl-
iave been two or three vessels here from Yarmouth or Argyle
to catch pogies for use in the Bay—I have bought cod bait.
: from the Canadians have paid $125—gold for codbait and
$500 for refitting my vessel in one summer—I have under
f the treaty,.landed mackerel transhipped it and sent them
iamer, but there is not any gain or benefit procured by doing
nse is much greater than if I had taken the fish home in my
[consider the right of the Canadians to send their fish in
. and sell them in the United States worth a great deal more
in anything we shall gain by the treaty I have known Cana-
i to land their small fish at home where there is a market for
hen taking the larger ones to the United States and selling
to more advantage—Canadians can use the inshore fishery
ire' advantage than we can, they go out in small boats from
id can fish near shore where our vessel cannot go—Prices of
ive been much lower during the past year than before and
irmen have lost money—The only benefit of the treaty to us
f the harbors without molestation and being permitted to
ons &c the inshore fisheries we cannot use to any profit—
, to send in fish free of duty is of much more value to the
than any rights we have received or will receive under the
s is my experience of four years under this and six under the
—

RICHARD HANNAN

COMMONWEALTH OF MASSACHUSETTS.'

GLOUCESTER, Jan 28th 1876

sonally appeared before me the abovenamed Richard Hanna
'n and made oath that all the foregoing statements by him
are true as far as they depend upon his own knowledge and
ey depend upon information and,belief he believes them to be
re me—
    (Seal.)

DAVID W. LOW
Notary Public

No. 43.

This is to certify, That the undersigned Stephen B. Morey **have** been engaged in the fishing business, for the past thirty years, at **Deer** Isle, and that since the Washington Treaty, so called, has been in effect, our vessels have been employed as follows: Namely since 1871

No. of Vessels employed five (5) 11 men to each Vessel

No. of Trips made six trips yearly each year

No. of Trips to Bay St. Lawrence ·········· 1872 1873 1874 1875 1876
·00   2   00   00   00.

No. of Barrels of Mackerel from Bay St. 1872 1873 1874 1875 1876
Lawrence 00   420   00   00   00

No. of Barrels of Mackerel caught within 3 miles of shore, not including Magdalene Islands
                None caught on Bradly Orphan & Magdalenes

Average value of Vessels each................................$3500
Average value of Outfits, Salt, Bait, &c........................$2400
Average value of Insurance........8 per cent on vessel & outfits yearly
Average value of Captains' and Crews' time, viz., wages per mo....$34
Average value of Commissions, &c........220$ to each Captain yearly
Average value of Wharves, Fish-houses, &c., for curing and packing, including expenses of Clerks, Proprietors and labor on shore....2300$

Number of Vessels lost

Value of Vessels lost, including outfits

Value of Fish lost

Number of lives lost

Total value of Fish taken, before curing, splitting, salting, &c. per cwt.
                85 cts

Total value of Mackerel taken, before curing, splitting, salting, &c., per bbl............ .... $2.20

Total value of Fish taken within three miles of British shores.nothing

Total value of Mackerel do ....nothing

Average market value of American Shore Mackerel.. No 1 No 2 No 3
$17 $13 $7.50

Average market value of Bay Mackerel..............$11.50 $8 $5.50

Average earnings of the operative fisherman per year $2.20

Average amount paid in British ports for bait, ice, and various supplies
                1200

Amount paid to British fishermen for herring $400

Amount paid to British fishermen as wages

Amount paid in British ports for repairs

Locations frequented by American vessels for Fish
                Grand Western Lahave Banks

Locations frequented by American vessels for Mackerel
                Cape Henry to Anticosta

Actual value of Fish in the water, before taking

Actual value of Mackerel in the water before taken

Facts as to changes in location and mode of conducting American fisheries

Early in going fishing I used the waters of the Bay of St Lawrence— Later in life in the same waters I used to go mackereling and made some fair Trips with the Jig. Since 1867 I have abandoned the fisheries of the Bay of St Lawrence only Sending there in 1873 and my vessels have been engaged in Fishing with trawls—and Seining mackerel on our Shore. So far as American fishermen are concerned our vessels have given up the Bay of St Lawrence—and regard it as an entire failure

                S. B. MOREY

n aud subscribed to before me, this eighth day of June 1877

THOMAS WARREN
Justice of the Peace

OF MAINE
COUNTY OF HANCOCK

STATE OF MAINE.

)CK, ss.

utson B. Saunders, Clerk of the Supreme Judicial Courts, in said
y, certify that Thomas Warren Esquire is and was at the date
Certificate an acting Justice of the Peace, in and for said County,
ommissioned and qualified to act as such, and that the signature
paper annexed, purporting to be his, is genuine, and that he is
,uthorized and empowered, by the laws of said State, to take ac·
edgment of Deeds, Assignments, and Powers of Attorney, and to
ister oaths.
:estimony whereof, I have hereunto set my Hand and affixed the
)f the ·Supreme Judicial Court, for said State, this eighth day of
in the year of our Lord one thousand eight hundred and seventy·

(Seal.) **HUTSON B SAUNDERS** *Clerk.*

No. 44.

is is to certify, That the undersigned Seth and C. H. S. Webb have
engaged in the fishing business, for the past Ten years, at Deer
Maine, and that since the Washington Treaty, so called, has been
'ect, our vessels have been employed as follows: viz. since 1871

)f Vessels employed	3, 15 men to each vessel
)f Trips made	five trips each year

	1871	1872	1873	1874	1875	1876
)f trips to Bay St. Lawrence	3	2	.0	0	0	0
)f Barrels of Mackerel from Bay St.) 1871 1872 1873 1874 1875 1876						
,wrence }	754	854	0	0	0	0

of Barrels of Mackerel caught within 3 miles of shore, not including
agdalen Islands all caught a Magdalens
rage value of vessels each $4000.
rage value of Outfits, Salt, Bait, &c $3000.
rage Value of Insurance 10% on vessel & outfits yearly
rage value of Captains' and Crews' time, viz., wages per mo..$37.50
rage value of Commissions, &c $175.
rage value of Wharves, Fish-houses, &c., for curing and packing
cluding expenses of Clerks, Proprietors and labor on shore....$2000
nber of vessels lost none
ué of Vessels lost, including outfits
ue of Fish lost none
mber of Lives lost
al value of Fsh taken, before curing, splitting, salting, &c. per cwt.
al value of Mackerel taken, before curing, splitting, salting, &c.,
er bbl $1.50
:al value of Fish taken within three miles of British shores..nothing
,al value of Mackerel do nothing
1 2 3
erage market value of American Shore Mackerel..$16.00 $12.00 $8.00
erage market value of Bay Mackerel $11.00 $7.00 $5.00

195 F

Average earnings of the operative fishermen per year..
Average amount paid in British ports for bait, ice, and
Amount paid to British fishermen for herring ....
Amount paid to British fishermen as wages
Amount paid in British ports for repairs
Locations frequented by American vessels for Fish
      Grand, Western La Have &
Locations frequented by American vessels for Mackerel
      Cape May to G
Actual value of Fish in the water, before taking......
Actual value of Mackerel in the water, before taken ..
Facts as to changes in location and mode of conductin
 eries

Had we not put seines on board our vessels, and se
shore, we would have been obliged to abandon the mac
tirely, for mackerel were scarce and of poor quality in t
were obliged to pay exorbitant prices at the British poi
and general supplies. so that it was impossible for o
their bills, It is now utterly impossible to ship a crew
on shares, for they cannot make a living. Mackerel a
good quality on our shore, and the risk and expence to t
much less than from the Bay, We consider the Bay fish
failure, None of our vessels used the inshore fisheries
as they could derive no advantage thereby.
          SE
          C.

Sworn and subscribed to before me, this eighth day
        THOMAS V
         Jus

STATE OF MAINE.

HANCOCK, SS.

I, Hutson B. Saunders, Clerk of the Supreme Judicia
County, certify that Thomas Warren Esquire is and
of this Certificate an acting Justice of the Peace, in and
duly commissioned and qualified to act as such, and tl
to the paper annexed, purporting to be his, is genuine
duly authorized and empowered, by the laws of said S
knowledgment of Deeds, Assignments, and Powers of
administer oaths.

In testimony whereof, I have hereunto set my Hand
Seal of the Supreme Judicial Court, for said State, thi
June in the year of our Lord one thousand eight hund
seven
 (Seal.)   HUTSON B SA

No. 45.

This is to certify, That the undersigned, John Stapl
gaged in the fishing business, for the past thirty years,
Maine, and that since the Washington Treaty, so ca
effect our vessels have been employed as follows: nam

No. of Vessels employed ....four (4) 13 m
No. of Trips made.......................five trips

s to Bay St. Lawrence

	1870	1871	1872	1873	1874	1875	1876
	none	none	none	2	none	none	none

els of Mackerel from Bay St. Lawrence....... · 1873 200 Bls

els of Mackerel caught within 3 miles of shore, not includ-
alene Islands................ ....all caught off Shore
lue of Vessels each .... 3000$
lue of outfits, Salt, Bait, &c..................... 2000$
lue of Insurance.....10 per cent on vessel & outfits yearly
lue of Captains' and Crews' time, viz., wages per mo....$33
lue of Commissions, &c.........240 to each Captain yearly
lue of Wharves, Fish-houses, &c., for curing and packing,
  expenses of Clerks, Proprietors and labor on shore...2400$
Vessels lost
essels lost, including outfits
sh lost
Lives lost
of Fish Taken, before curing, splitting, salting, &c., per cwt.
  80 cents,
of Macke el taken, before curing, splitting, salting, &c., per bbl.
  $2.00
of Fish taken within three miles of British shores···none
of Mackerel do ·····················none

	N 1	No 2	No 3
arket value of American Shore Mackerelo	16	12	8
arket value of Bay Mackerel··········	11	7	5

rnings of the operative fishermen per year.............240
nount paid in British ports for bait, ice, and various supplies
id to British fishermen for herring ·············nothing
id to British fishermen as wages
id in British ports for repairs
requented by American vessels for Fish
requented by American vessels for Mackerel
ne of Fish in the water, before taking
ne of Mackerel in the water before taken
:o changes in location and mode of conducting American

Started in the fishing business Some thirty years Since—all
aught on hand line & Mackerel on the jig—Early in my Send-
bay of St Lawrence my vessels made some fares that left a
:o to the owners—I kept sending to the Bay & sustaining
st Sent one vessel in 1873 and lost. The quantity fell off and
r was poor & unsaleable of Bay fish—Seines now are used for
& Trawls for fish—and I consider the right to fish inshore con-
nefit at all on American fishermen & no one here thinks of
the Bay   JOHN STAPLES

nd subscribed to before me, this sixth day of June 1877
                              THOMAS WARREN
                                   Justice of the Pea

STATE OF MAINE.

, ss.
on B. Saunders, Clerk of the Supreme Judical Courts, in said
entify that Thomas Warren Esquire is and was at the date of

his Certificate an acting Justice of the Peace, in and for said County, duly commissioned and qualified to act as such, and that the signature to the paper annexed, purporting to be his, is genuine, and that he is duly authorized and empowered, by the laws of said State, to take acknowledgment of Deeds, Assignments, and Powers of Attorney, and to administer oaths.

In testimony whereof, I have hereunto set my Hand and affixed the Seal of the Supreme Judicial Court, for said State, this sixth day of June in the year of our Lord one thousand eight hundred and seventy-seven

(Seal.)   HUTSON B SAUNDERS *Clerk.*

No. 46.

This is to certify, That the undersigned, composing the firm of Perkins Brothers have been engaged in the fishing business for the past Twenty years, at Gloucester Mass and that since the Washington Treaty, so called, has been in effect, our vessels have been employed as follows:

No. of Vessels employed..Nine (9)
No. of Trips made...........................Six trips to each vessel

                     1871 1872 1873 1874 1875 1876
No. of Trips to Bay St. Lawrence.......5   2   3   4   1   3
No. of Barrels of Mackerel from Bay St. Lawrence
                 3093 Bbls. in six years average 172 Bbls per trip.
No. of Barrels of Mackerel caught within 3 miles of shore, not including Magdalene Islands ....mostly at Magdalenes
Average value of Vessels each ....$5000.
Average value of Outfits, Salt, Bait, &c ....$3000, a year to each vessel
Average value of insurance......................................9%
Average value of Captains' and Crews' time, viz., wages per mo..$35.00
Average value of Commissions, &c.................$200. each vessel
Average value of Wharves, Fish-houses, &c., for curing and packing, including expenses of Clerks, Proprietors and labor on shore..$23,000.
Number of Vessels lost..one
Value of Vessels lost, including outfits.......................$4000
Value of Fish lost $1500
Number of Lives lost................................... ...none
Total value of Fish taken, before curing, splitting, salting &c. per cwt.
                                                75 cts
Total value of Mackerel taken, before curing, splitting, salting, &c., per bbl. $1.50
Total value of Fish taken within three miles of British shores......none
Total value of Mackerel do..$600.
Average market value of American Shore Mackerel
               No 1 $16.00   No 2 $12.00   No 3 $8.00
Average market value of Bay Mackerel
               No 1 $12.00   No 2 $8.00   No 3 $6.00
Average earnings of the operative fishermen per year.........$225.00
Average amount paid in British ports for bait, ice, and various supplies
                                     $800. a year
Amount paid to British fishermen for herring
Amount paid to British fishermen as wages
Amount paid in British ports for repairs ....$500. in five years
Locations frequented by American vessels for Fish
                                       Grand Banks Georgees

quented by American vessels for Mackerel
                From Cape May to Gulf of St Lawrence
of Fish in the water, before taking............nothing
of Mackerel in the water, before taken.........nothing
changes in location and mode of conducting American

f St. Lawrence fisheries have not proved remunerative, or
less our vessels have not paid their expenses consequencely
ine our vessels to our own shores for mackerel and to the
s for Cod Fish. We shall send no vessels to Bay of St.
iis year. We use the British waters only to procure bait
pplyes
       W H PERKINS   GEORGE PERKINS
       WM. H. PERKINS, JR.   GEORGE H PERKINS

l subscribed to before me, this thirty first day of May 1877.
                        DAVID W. LOW
                              Notary Public

OTHERS.   GLOUCESTER MASS—
of receipts &c from trips to the Bay for the last **four (4)**
ly caught at the Magdalenes

yer:
)ls No. 1 $12.50 $1679.30
' No. 2   9.50   356.75
' No. 3   7.00   10.05 $2016 10

bls No. 1 $15 $960.18
' No. 2 11   612.54
' No. 3   9   432.16 $2004 88

mpbell
bls No. 1 $12. $1601.35
less   17 (labor)   57.23
bls No. 2 8   29.22 $1637 85

mpbell
)bls No. 1 $12 $350.00
"   No. 2   8   907.00
"   No. 3   7.25   230.40
"   No. 4. 6.   82.36 $1569 86

mple
)bls No. 1 $9.75 $118.50
"   No. 2   8.   415.20 $533 70

ampbell
mess $12 (labor) $1123.40
bbls No. 1 8.   169.50
"   No. 2 6.50   137.07 $1429 97

ran
bbls No. 1 $8 $1332.90
"   No. 2   6   1026.10
"   No. 3   5   16 00 $2375 00

1875

    C. Campbell
        35 mess $21 ⎱ Labor on fish $678.95
        108 scraped   17 ⎰   1628.00
        46 bbls No. 1 15   605.50
        11 " No. 2 12   . 119.40
        5 ' " No. 4 7   29.30

WM. H. PERKINS   GEORGE PE]
    By W. H. P. Jr.   By W.
GEORGE H. PERKINS   WM. H. PERK
    By W. H. P. Jr.

No. 47.

This is to certify, That the undersigned, composing the
Pew & Son have been engaged in the fishing business
(1849-1877) 28 years at Gloucester Mass and that since the
Treaty, so called, has been in effect, our vessels have been
follows :

No. of Vessels employed—an average of................
No. of Trips made ....
No. of Trips to Bay St. Lawrence ....
No of Barrels of Mackerel from Bay St. Lawrence.......
No. of Barrels of Mackerel caught within 3 miles of shor
    ing Magdalene Islands
From general talk with our Skippers during the time. we
    understood all caught were outside of 3 miles—We ha
    knowledge that any were caught inside.
Average value of Vessels each.........................
Average value of Outfits, Salt, Bait, &c..............
Average value of Insurance ....
Average value of Captains' and Crews' time, viz., wages per
Average value of Commissions, &c......................
Average value of Wharves, Fish-houses, &c., for curing
    including expenses of Clerks, Proprietors and labor on
    of wharves. fish houses &c $75.000. Yearly expense ac
                                        ' partners
Number of Vessels lost.................................
Value of Vessels lost, including outfits ....
Value of Fish lost ....
Number of Lives lost..................................
Total value of Fish taken, before curing, splitting, salting

Total value of Mackerel taken, before curing, splitting, sal

Total value of Fish taken within three miles of British sho
Total value of Mackerel do ....
Average market value of American Shore Mackerel
                        No. 3   N
                        $8.00 $1
                        No. 3   N
Average market value of Bay Mackerel.......... $6½ $
Average earnings of the operative fishermen per year $30
    time though less at present.

)unt paid in British ports for bait, ice, and various sup-
....$600 pr year.
to British fishermen for herring ....$3000 "   "
to British fishermen as wages & shares
                                at least $15,000 yearly
| in British ports for repairs
quented by American vessels for Fish
e American coast, Sable bank, Quero St. Peters & Grand
                                          Banks
;quented by American vessels for Mackerel
[enry to Bay of Fundy & occasionally the Bay of St. Lawrence
, of Fish in the water before taking.............No value
, of Mackerel in the water before taken ....No value
hanges in location and mode of conducting American fish-
Cod fisheries have been those of greatest value. We fish
1e Banks off our own shores. and the past 5 years have sent
)er to the Grand Banks. The latter as a business investment
. We market all the product of our fisheries in the United
;re is no other market, of any value for Mackerel and none
except our own. The opening of our market to the Provin-
:n is very injurious to us. as they pay no duties while all we
ily taxed. The priviledge of their markets or their inshore
' no value compared to the priviledge of free entry to our

                    JOHN J PEW,
                    for JOHN PEW & SON.

l subscribed to before me, this thirtieth day of June 1877
                         DAVID W. LOW
)   *Notary Public.*

              No. 48.

certify, That the undersigned, composing the firm of Smith
,ve been engaged in the fishing business for the past ten
loucester Mass and that since the Washington Treaty, so
)een in effect, our vessels have been employed as follows :

els employed ·····································........6
s made·······························.56 per year
s to Bay St. Lawrence············1871—1 1873—2 1874—1
·els of Mackerel from Bay St. Lawrence···············1050
els of Mackerel caught within 3 miles of shore, not including
1e Islands·····························............Unknown
                                              ·········$5000.
.lue of Vessels each ·····················$3000 per year
.lue of Outfits, Salt, Bait, &c ·················
lue of Insurance..$4375, or 9 per ct on Vessell & outfits yearly
.lue of Captains' and Crews' time, viz., wages per mo
                                              $35. per month.
.lue of Commissions, &c··········.$300 each Vessell yearly
alue of Wharves, Fish-houses, &c., for curing and packing,
; expenses of Clerks, Proprietors and labor on shore
                                    $12,000, $5500=$17,500
                                    ·······························1
' Vessels lost·······································...$000
essels lost, including outfits························nothing
'ish lost·····························................17
   Lives lost ·········· ·····························

Total value of Fish taken, before curing, splitting, :
  cwt ....
Total value of Mackerel taken, before curing, splittin
  per bbl.... ....:....
Total value of Fish taken within three miles of British s
Total value of Mackerel do.............................
Average market value of American Shore Mackerel
                    No. 1. $16.00 No.'2 $1'
Average market value of Bay Mackerel
                    No. 1s $12.00 No. 2s $'
Average earnings of the operative fishermen per year .
Average amount paid in British ports for bait, ice, a
plies .... $100.00 each
Amount paid to British fishermen for herring $1700.00 pe
Amount paid to British fishermen as wages..........
Amount paid in British ports for repairs..... $25.00 per
Locations frequented by American vessels for Fish
              Georges to Grand Bank, Labrador I
Location frequented by American vessels for Mackerel
              From Cape May to Gd. Menan & B
Actual value of Fish in the water, before taking....
Actual value of Mackerel in the water, before taken.
Facts as to changes in location and mode of conducting
  eries

The Gloucester vessels fishing on Georges most of tl
up that branch of the business, commencing the last of
having given up by the last of June) and go to the Bay
for Mackerel but since the failure of the mackerel fishi
St Lawrence a larger number follow Georges fishing t
and others remain on this coast to catch mackerel, usi
of hook & line   Larger vessels are now used than fo
are engaged in the Grand Bank fisheries.

    PETER D SMITH   SMI

Sworn and subscribed to before me, this eighth day
(Seal.)   DAVID

No. 49.

This is to certify, that the undersigned, composing tl
& Allen have been engaged in the fishing business for
years, at Gloucester, Mass and that since the Wash
called, has been in effect our vessels have been employ

No. of Vessels employed ....
No. of Trips made ....Fou
No. of Trips to Bay of St. Lawrence ....
No. of Barrels of Mackerel from Bay St. Lawrence Ten
  Two bbls.
No. of Barrels of Mackerel caught within 3 miles of sh
  Magdalene Islands.....................Two hundi
Average value of Vessels each...................Six
Average value of outfits, Salt, Bait, &c..........One
Average value of Insurance.................Fifty-Tw
Average value of Captains' and Crews' time, viz., w

Average value of Commissions, &c............Three

ıe of Wharves, Fish-houses, &c., for curing and packing,
expenses of Clerks, Proprietors and labor on shore
                          Twenty Five thousand dollars

ʳessels lost...Five

ssels lost, including outfits......Eighteen thousand dollars

h lost

ives lost...None

of Fish taken, before curing, splitting, salting, &c. per cwt
                                 one dollar

of Mackerel taken, before curing, splitting, salting, &c. per
....Four dollars

of Fish taken within three miles of British shores

of Mackerel do................Three hundred dollars 6 yrs

ırket value of American Shore Mackerel
                         Eleven & $\frac{50}{100}$ per bbl

ırket value of Bay Mackerel....................$8 average

rnings of the operative fishermen per year.............$250

ıount paid in British ports for bait, ice, and various supplies
                          Twenty Five hundred dolls

ıid to British fishermen for herring
                   Twelve thousand in 5 years

ıd to British fishermen as wages

ıd in British ports for repairs

requented by American vessels for Fish
            Grand, Western, & Georges Bank, Seal Island &c

requented by American vessels for Mackerel
                   Mostly Magdalene Islands

ıe of Fish in the water, before taking............nothing

ıe of Mackerel in the water, before taking.........   "

ı changes in location and mode of conducting American fish-

our vessels are codfishing on the Ocean Banks and some of
ff our own shores mackerelling We send no vessels into the
Lawrence this year. Our experience is that the Mackerel
re is a failure. Last year we sent one vessel 150 Tons with
d she brought home as her seasons work 70 Bbls of mackerel.
ıery has been the last 5 years to pursue it would be ruinous.
ls enter British waters only for supplies & Bait for which we

                  MICHAEL WALEN

ınd subscribed to before me, this fourth day of June 1877
                  DAVID W. LOW
al.).   *Notary Public*

No. 50.

to certify, that the undersigned, composing the firm of Pettin-
ıningham have been engaged in the fishing business for the
teen years, at Gloucester Mass and that since the Washington
ı called, has been in effect, our vessels have been employed as
                                    Six

ıssels employed............from five to six each vessel yearly

ıps made................Six in five years

ıps to Bay St. Lawrence....................1200 Bbls

ırrels of Mackerel from Bay St. Lawrence..........

ırrels of Mackerel caught within 3 miles of shore, not includ
                                   300 Bbls

gdalene Islands......................................

Average value of Vessels each..................Five thous

Average value of Outfits, Salt, Bait, &c.

                 $1000 per Bay trip $3000 yearly

Average value of Insurance................∴...$300 per year

Average value of Captains' and Crews' time, viz., wages per

Average value of Commissions, &c ....$200 each v

Average value of Wharves, Fish-houses, &c., for curing ar

  including expenses of Clerks, Proprietors and labor on sh

Number of Vessels lost.......................................

Value of Vessels lost, including outfits ....

Value of Fish lost ....

Number of Lives lost ....

Total value of Fish taken, before curing, splitting, salting, &

Total value of Mackerel taken, before curing, splitting, saltir

  bbl............................ ....:.. ....

Total value of Fish taken within three miles of British shore

Total value of Mackerel do ....

Average market value of American Shore Mackerel .... $\frac{\$1}{1}$

Average market value of Bay Mackerel............$\frac{\text{No 1}}{\$12}$

Average earnings of the operative fishermen per year ......

Average amount paid in British ports for bait, ice and varic

                  500 each vessel or $

Amount paid to British fishermen for herring.............

Amount paid to British fishermen as wages............$

Amount paid in British ports for repairs ....

Locations frequented by American vessels for Fish

              Georges Grand Western L

Locations frequented by American vessels for Mackerel

              American Shores north o

Actual value of Fish in the water, before taking..........

Actual value of Mackerel in the water, before taken.......

Facts as to changes in location and mode of conducting An

  eries

For the last three years we have been obliged to send all
Bank Fishing putting into British ports for supplies &c   T
fishery in the Bay of St Lawrence falling off so much in q
quality as to make it impossible for American Vessels with
and equipment to pay their expenses.

                 CHARLES D PETT

Sworn and subscribed to before me, this fifth day of June
(Seal.)   DAVID W.

                        Not

No. 51.

This is to certify, That the undersigned, composing the fir
docks & Co have been engaged in the fishing business for t
years, at Gloucester Mass and that since the Washington
called, has been in effect, our vessels have been employed a

No. of Vessels employed...................................

No. of Trips made................. Three hundred & Six

No. of Trips to Bay St. Lawrence...................Twe

rels of Mackerel from Bay St. Lawrence
> Forty six hundred (4600)

rels of Mackerel caught within 3 miles of shore, not including
ne Islands
> more than one fourth ($\frac{1}{4}$) part of the Bay St Lawrence mack'l

alue of Vessels each.... Fort five Hundred ($4500) dollars
alue of Outfits, Salt, Bait, &c.y
> year or $700, Trip for each Vessel ($1200, for each Bay Trip).

alue of Insurance
> Four and one half pr cent pr year for Six Months

alue of Captains' and Crews' time, viz, wages per mo
> Capt $70 & Crew $25 each

alue of Commissions, &c ...... $300, for each vessel pr year
alue of Wharves, Fish-houses, &c., for curing and packing,
g expenses of Clerks, Proprietors and labor on shore
> Sixteen thousand ($16,000.00) dollars pr Year

f Vessels lost...................................Four (4)
Vessels lost, including outfits
> Seventeen thousand ($17000) dollars

Fish lost............ .....Thirty five hundred ($3500) dollars
f Lives lost...............................Thirty three (33)
ie of Fish taken, before curing, splitting, salting, &c. per cwt
ie of Mackerel taken, before curing, splitting, salting, &c., per
> bbl. But no fish and very few mackerel

ie of Fish taken within three miles of British shores
> Impossible to make correct estimate

ie of Mackerel do·········   "   "   "   "
narket value of American Shore Mackerel
> Eleven dollars pr Barrel

market value of Bay Mackerel....Eight $\frac{75}{100}$ dollars pr Barrel
earnings of the operative fishermen per year
> Two hundred & seventy five dollars

amount paid in British ports for bait, ice, and various supplies
> Three Thousand dollars pr. Year

paid to British fishermen for herring
> Two thousand dollars pr. Year

paid to British fishermen as wages .....Two thousand dollars
paid in British ports for repairs:..Twenty six hundred dollars
frequented by American vessels for Fish
Sable Island, and Grand Banks, & Gulf and Bay St. Lawrence
frequented by American vessels for Mackerel
> Atlantic Coast from Cape Hatteras to Eastport Me.

aine of Fish in the water, before taking ·············None
alue of Mackerel in the water, before taken ·········· None
to changes in location and mode of conducting American fish-

ployed a part of our fleet in the Bay St. Lawrence fisheries.
ie years of 1871-2-3, and found it to be a loseing business, and
3 we have employed our vessels in the Grand Banks & Georges
rican Shore fisheries with the exception of one Trip to the Bay
ence, in 1874, which did not pay one half the expenses of the
and we consider the Bay St. Lawrence fisheries entirely worth-
, and have so considered them for the past four or five years.
> B. MADDOCKS & CO.

MADDOCKS
and subscribed to before me, this fourth day of June 1877
> DAVID W. LOW

eal.)   *Notary Public*

No. 52.

This is to certify, That the undersigned, conposing the
Dennis & Co have been engaged in the fishing business for
years, at Gloucester and that since the Washington Trea
has been in effect, our vessels have been employed as follo\

No. of Vessels employed.................................-
No. of Trips...........................4 trips yearly
No. of Trips to Bay St. Lawrence
              1872—1 trip 1873—1 trip 1874—2 trips
No. of Barrels of Mackerel from Bay St. Lawrence
                          93 Bls — 94½ —
No. of Barrels of Mackerel caught within 3 miles of shore,
    ing Magdalene Islands..................................
Average value of Vessels each ....
Average value of Outfits, Salt, Bait, &c.................(
Average value of Insurance.... 200   9 per cts on Vesse
Average value of Captains' and Crews' time, viz., wages pc
                                                        1
Average value of Commissions, &c ....Three hun
Average value of Wharves, Fish-houses, &c., for curing a
    including expenses of Clerks, Proprietors and labor on
                                                  fifteen Th
Number of Vessels lost....................................
Value of Vessels lost, including outfits
Value of Fish lost
Number of Lives lost   .
Total value of Fsh taken, before curing, splitting, salting, &
                                                        (5
Total value of Mackerel taken, before curing, splitting, salt
    bb...
Total value of Fish taken within three miles of British sho
Total value of Mackerel do ....
Average market value of American Shore Mackerel......
                                                        &

Average market value of Bay Mackerel ....S
Average earnings of the operative fishermen per year
                                                Two hun
Average amount paid in British ports for bait, ice, and var
                              Each year   Eight hun
Amount paid to British fishermen
    for herring.. ....   "   Five   (
Amount paid to British fishermen as wages
                                8 men forty Dolla
Amount paid in British ports for repairs.. Twenty one hu
Locations frequented by American vessels for Fish
                                      Western Bank.
Locations frequented by American vessels for Mackerel
                                    Gulf of St Lawrence
Actual value of Fish in the water, before taking.........
Actual value of Mackerel in the water, before taken ....
Facts as to changes in location and mode of conducting A
    eries
        Lines & Trawls & Hand lines are used for taking fi

;sells are mostly confined to Ocean Banks for Fish. we do
any fish in British waters. the Bay St. Lawrence fisheries
7ed a falier in our experiance. Vessells sent their for the past
have not paid their expenses and to continue the Business in
ction would prove Ruinous.

GEO DENNIS
GEORGE TUCKER

and subscribed to before me, this 31st day of May 1877
DAVID W. LOW
l.) *Notary Public*

No. 53.

to certify, that the undersigned, Joseph O. Procter has been
in the fishing business for the past Thirty years, at Gloucester,
d that since the Washington Treaty, so called, has been in ef-
vessels have been employed as follows :

essels employed ....Thirteen
rips made ....Six yearly to each vessel—78

	1872	73	74	75	76
rips to Bay of St. Lawrence	5	13	11	5	1

arrels of Mackerel from Bay St. Lawrence
7.486 Bbls in 5 years or 211 Bbls per trip on the average.
arrels of Mackerel caught within 3 miles of shore, not including
alene Islands . , ...750
; value of Vessels each 5,000
; value of Outfits, Salt, Bait, &c. . $3.500.00 yearly to each vessel
; value of Insurance .... $300.00 yearly to each vessel
; value of Captains' and Crews' time, viz., wages per mo
$35. pr month
; value of Commissions, &c......... $200.00 pr Vessel per year
= value of Wharves, Fish-houses, &c., for curing and packing,
ling expenses of Clerks, Proprietors and labor on shore . $30,000,00
; of vessels lost ....Three
f Vessels lost, including outfits .... Fifteen thousand dollars
f Fish lost .... Four thousand dollars
r of Lives lost...Fifteen
alue of Fish taken, before curing, splitting, salting, &c. per cwt.
from 50 to $1.00.
alue of Mackerel taken, before curing, splitting, salting, &c., per
....Two dollars
alue of Fish taken within three miles of British shores...None
alue of Mackerel do ....$6,850, delivered at Gloucester
;e market value of American Shore Mackerel
No. 1, $16. No. 2=$12. No. 3—$8.00
;e market value of Bay Mackerel
No. 1—$12. No. 2=8, No. 3—$6.—
;e earnings of the operative fishermen per year
Three hundred dollars
;e amount paid in British ports for bait, ice, and various supplies
$1,800.—yearly
it paid to British fishermen for herring.........$900 each Season
it paid to British fishermen as wages ....Nothing
it paid in British ports for repairs
ons frequented by American vessels for Fish
Georges, Grand, Querau, St Peters and other Banks off Shore

Locations frequented by American vessels for Mackerel
From Cape Henry to Cape Northe.

Actual value of Fish in the water, be- ⎫ No value. C
fore taking ⎬ bring to catch,
Actual value of Mackerel in the water, ⎨ them for market.
before taken ⎭

Facts as to changes in location and mode of conductii
fisheries

Since the year 1870 the number of vessels using the Ba
rence for Mackerel catching has been gradually reduced f
to less than 60 vessels from the United States; the Macker
and in small quantity; while on our Shores Mack'l ha
plenty, of better quality, and a large fleet engaged from
Nov. 10th. *All* the Vessels on our Shore now use the Sei
the hook and line as formerly. Seining has not been su
ried on in the Bay of St Lawrence, the shoalness of the v
unevenness of the bottom, where the few Mack'l there ten
every voyage unsuccessful, and caused an abandonment of
There will probably be less Vessels in the Bay this Sea
season during the last Forty. Our Cod fisheries are *deep*
and outside of all local jurisdiction.

JOSEPH O. I

Sworn and subscribed to before me, this fifth day of Jui
(Seal.)   DAVID W. LO
                            No

No. 54.

This is to certify, That the undersigned, composing the fi
Haskell have been engaged in the fishing business for th
years, at Gloucester Mass and that since the Washingt
called, has been in effect, our vessels have been employed

No. of Vessels employed..................................

No. of Trips made..Seven & 8 trips yearly to each Vessel, t

	1872	1873	1874	1875
No. of Trips to Bay St. Lawrence..4	2	3	0	

No. Barrels of Mackerel from Bay St. Lawrence

1872	1873	1874
1100 bls	420 bls	383 bls to

No. of Barrels of Mackerel caught within 3 miles of shore,
Magdalene Islands ....

Average value of Vessels each................ five thor

Average value of Outfits, Salt, Bait, &c.... $2700 to each

Average value of Insurance................... $200 each

Average value of Captains' and Crews' time, viz., wages p
Captain $70 C

Average value of Commission, &c................... $20

Average value of Wharves, Fish-houses, &c., for curing
including expenses of Clerks, Proprietors and labor on

Number of Vessels lost......................
Value of Vessels lost, including outfits................
Value of fish lost ....
Number of lives lost......................
Total value of Fish taken, before curing, splitting, saltin

of Mackerel taken, before curing, splitting, salting, &c.,
.... $2,50 cts
of Fish taken within three miles of British shores.... None
of Mackerel do .... $1100 delivered at Gloucester
rket value of American Shore Mackerel
                         No 1. $16   No 2. $12,   No 3 $8
rket value of Bay Mackerel
                  No. 1 $12   No 2, $8   No 3, $6   I sold for $10,85
nings of the operative fishermen per year...$275 at my place
ount paid in British ports for bait, ice, and various supplies
            $200 each vessel yearly.   total $1200 yearly
d to British fishermen for herring..........$600 each year
id to British fishermen as wages.....................None
d in British ports for repairs.............. ....None
equented by American vessels for Fish
            Graud, Western, La, have, Georges Banks
equented by American vessels for Mackerel
            From Cape May to Eastport & Bay St Lawrence
e of Fish in the water, before taking..............Nothing
e of Mackerel in the water, before taken..........Nothing
changes in location and mode of conducting American fish·

t no vessels into the Bay of St Lawrence the last two
lay fishing does not pay the expenses. The last years I had
e in 73 & 74 they did not pay for their outfits   The Mack-
r worth ¼d less than shore mackerel it is a bad place to use
ng time is required for a trip and to pursue the Bay fishery,
one, would fail any firm in Gloucester. It is entirely & prac-
ess to us as a fishery. The Halibut and cod fishery are en·
fisheries owing no allegience to any Government
                                   SAML HASKELL

d subscribed to before me, this thirty first day of May 1877
                            DAVID W. LOW
.)   *Notary Public.*

No. 55.

certify, That the undersigned, composing the firm of Joseph
e been engaged in the fishing business for the past 40 years,
er Mass and that since the Washington Treaty, so called,
effect, our vessels have been employed as follows:

els employed 8.........................12 men each vessell
s made.........................6 to each Vessell
                              1872 1873 1874 1875 1876
                                4   3   1   0   0
to Bay St. Lawrence.........1872 1873 1874 1875 1876

els of Mackerel from Bay of St.
                              1500 1200 220   0   0
els of Mackerel caught within 3 miles of shore, not including
ie Islands...............................about one-tenth
lue of Vessels each........................6000, each
lue of Outfits, Salt, Bait, &c.............2000, do yearly
lue of Insurance ....9 & on vessels & outfits
lue of Captains' and crews' time, viz., wages per mo··.35 each
lue of Commissions, &c. ....200 each vessell

Average value of Wharves, Fish-houses, &c., for c[
  including expenses of clerks, Proprietors and labor
Number of vessels lost.......................one in
Value of vessels lost, including outfits.............
Value of Fish lost ....
Number of Lives lost..............................
Total value of Fish taken, before curing, splitting, saltii
Total value of Mackerel taken, before curing, split
  per bbl....................................
Total value of Fish taken within three miles of Britis
Total value of Mackerel do.......................

Average market value of American Shore Mackerel.

Average market value of Bay Mackerel ....
Average earnings of the operative fishermen per year
Average amount paid in British ports for bait, ice,
  plies......................................
Amount paid to British fishermen for herring ......
Amount paid to British fishermen as wages ....
Amount paid in British ports for repairs
Locations frequented by American vessels for Fish
                                        Grand
Locations frequented by American vessels for mackei
                              from Cape May 1
Actual value of Fish in the water, before taking ....
Actual value of mackerel in the water, before taken .
Facts as to changes in location and mode of conduct
  eries
    Years ago we sent meny, vessels to the Bay, of
Mackerel but for, the last five years the business has
able we cannot pursue it my, vessels are now confi
banks and our own shores intirely our shore Mac
superior in quality and being taken with Seins rea
then any, other Mackerel fishery my, vessels enter F
for. Bait suplies and Herring for, which I, pay, cash
                                        JO

Sworn and subscribed to before me, this first day
(Seal.)   DAVI

No. 56.

This is to certify, That the undersigned, composii
uel Lane & Bro have been engaged in the fishing b
thirteen years, at Gloucester Mass and that since the
so called, has been in effect, our vessels have been e

No. of Vessels employed ....
No. of Trips made...............................
No. of Trips to Bay St. Lawrence................
No. of Barrels of Mackerel from Bay St. Lawrence
No. of Barrels of Mackerel caught within 3 miles c
  including Magdalene Islands.................
Average value of Vessels each ....
Average value of Outfits, Salt, Bait, &c.........
Average value of Insurance.....................

of Captains' and Crews' time, viz., wages per mo.....$45
of Commissions, &c $175
of Wharves, Fish-houses, &c., for curing and packing,
expenses of Clerks, Proprietors and labor on shore.$27000
ssels lost...1
els lost, including outfits........ ....$8700
lost..none.
ves lost...12
f Fish taken, before curing, splitting, salting, &c. per
....$2
Mackerel taken, before curing, splitting, salting, &c. per
....$3
Fish taken within three miles of British shores......none
Mackerel do........ ....$300
cet value of American Shore Mackerel.............$12
cet value of Bay Mackerel....................$7 per Bbl.
ings of the operative fishermen per year....$400 per man.
unt paid in British ports for bait, ice, and various sup-
....$950 per Trip.
to British fishermen for herring $4300
to British fishermen as wages
         $8750 for mackl. caugh Bay St. Lwrence.
l in British ports for repairs $2500
quented by American vessels for fish
        none in Bay of St. Lawrence.
quented by American vessels for Mackerel
        P. E. Island—Magdalene Is—C. B. Is.
of Fish in the water, before taking.............no value.
of Mackerel in the water, before taken..........no value.
hanges in location and mode of conducting American fish-

year 1871 the Bay of St. Lawrence was some benefit to
lackerel Fishermen, but since then the-mackl have been
on the American Coast, therefore the Glou mackerel ves-
en growing less in no every year that formerly engaged in
it. Lawrence mackerel fishing and have tended the Amer-
th seines for mackerel. We consider Fishing in the Bay of
e of no value.

                SAML LANE & BRO

NE }
LANE }
l subscribed to before me, this first day of June 1877
             DAVID W. LOW
                Notary Public

No. 57.

certify, That the undersigned, composing the firm of George
been engaged in the fishing business for the past 25 years,
er Mass and that since the Washington Treaty, so called, has
et, our vessels have been employed as follows:
....average nine
els employed...........................350 in 6 year
s made ....19 " " "
to Bay St. Lawrence.................................
els of Mackerel from Bay
els of Mackerel caught within 3 miles of shore, not includ-
....none
alene Islands ....

Average value of Vessels each ....
Average value of Outfits, Salt, Bait, &c.................
Average value of Insurance................9% on value
Average value of Captains' and Crews' time, viz., wages
Average value of Commissions, &c...................$3
Average value of Wharves, Fish-houses, &c., for curing
   including expenses of Clerks, Proprietors and labor on
Number of Vessels lost ....
Value of Vessels lost, including outfits................
Value of Fish lost
Number of Lives lost..............................
Total value of Fish taken, before curing, splitting, sa
   cwt...
Total value of Mackerel taken, before curing, splitting
   per bbl ....
Total value of Fish taken within three miles of British sl
Total value of Mackerel do ....
Average market value of American Shore Mackerel ....
Average market value of Bay Mackerel...............
Average earnings of the operative fishermen per year ..
Average amount paid in British ports for bait, ice, ar
   plies ....$200. pe
Amount paid to British fishermen for herring
Amount paid to British fishermen as wages .... $50. pe
Amount paid in British ports for repairs. $750. per year f
Locations frequented by American vessels for Fish
                     Georges, Browns, Le Have &
Locations frequented by American vessels for Mackerel
                     from Cape May to Gul
Actual value of Fish in the water, before taking........
Actual value of Mackerel in the water, before taken. .
Facts as to changes in location and mode of conducting
   eries
Hand lining has about given way to Trawls and Seine
St. Lawrence fishing for Mackerel has not proved pr(
been gradually falling off for several years and vessels th
pay expenses. One vessel there last year for 3 mos wi
packed out 69 Barrels. Our vessels pursue the deep v
the Banks bordering the Gulf Stream and outside the
any nation.

                                        GEORG

Sworn and subscribed to before me, this second day of
(Seal.)   DAVID '

                     No. 58.

   This is to certify, That the undersigned, composing tl
ningham & Thompson have been engaged in the fishing '
past six years at Gloucester Mass and that since th
Treaty, so called, has been in effect, our vessels have be
follows :

No. of Vessels employed.............................
No. of Trips made ....Seven yearly
No. of Trips to Bay St. Lawrence.............Ten fr(

s of Mackerel from Bay St. Lawrence

Three thousand, $3,000

of Mackerel caught within 3 miles of shore, not including Islands...200 Bbls

e of Vessels each $6,500

e of Outfits, Salt, Bait, &c.

$1,000 for Bay trip. Average, $3,000 yearly

ie of Insurance..............9 per ct on Vessel & Outfits

e of Captains' and Crews' time, viz., wages per mo....$40

e of Commissions, &c.

4 pr ct ou gross stock about $200 each vessel.

e of Wharves, Fish-houses, &c., for curing and packing, in-

ienses of Clerks, Proprietors and labor on shore.

Appurtanences $22,000 Labor $5000 per Annum

essels lost........................... ....Three.

els lost, including outfits........... ....$18,000

lost.................................. ....$7,000

ves lost...Fifteen

of Fish taken, before curing, splitting, salting, &c., per

....75 cts

f Mackerel taken, before curing, splitting, salting, &c., per

....$1,00

f Fish taken within three miles of British shores....None

f Mackerel do......... ....$400

ket value of American Shore Mackerel

$15 No. 1 $12 No 2 $8 No 3

ket value of Bay Mackerel ..... $11 No 1 $7 No 2 $5 No 3

lings of the operative fishermen per year $250

ount paid in British ports for bait, ice, and various sup-

.....................................$250 to each vessel.

to British fishermen for herring.............$300 yearly

l to British fishermen as wages............. $150 per year.

l in British ports for repairs................$1000 yearly

quented by American vessels for Fish

Western, Georges, and Grand Bank

quented by American vessels for Mackerel

Long Island to Newfoundland

of Fish in the water, before taking.............No value

of Mackerel in the water, before taken......... No value

hanges in location and mode of conducting American fish-

iad no Vessels in the Bay of St. Lawrence since 1874 and at

e last 7 years have our vessels that went there paid their

e privelege of fishing within three miles of British shores

e whatever Over one half of our Fishermen are natives of

in employed by our Capital in our vessels and deriving

e therefrom, We consider the privelege of our free markets

iess of value of any concessions of shore fishing given by the

SYLVESTER CUNNINGHAM
WILLIAM THOMPSON

l subscribed to before me, this second day of June 1877

DAVID W. LOW
Notary Public

No. 59.

This is to certify, That the undersigned, composing the fir
& Ayer have been engaged in the fishing business for the
years, at Gloucester Mass and that since the Washingto
called, has been in effect, our vessels have been employed a

No. of Vessels employed.................................
No. of Trips made.............. Eighty per year for all o
No. of Trips to Bay St. Lawrence....................   S
No. of Barrels of Mackerel from Bay St. Lawrence
                           Eighteen h
No. of Barrels of Mackerel caught within 3 miles of shore, b
   Magdalene Islands.................................. ...
Average value of Vessels each................... Six thou
Average value of Outfits, Salt, Bait, &c......... One thou
Average value of Insurance................ ..... Five thou
Average value of Captains' and Crews' time, viz., wages pe
                                     T
Average value of Commissions, &c.... four per cent. to Ca
Average value of Wharves, Fish-houses, &c., for curing a
   including expenses of Clerks, Proprietors and labor on s
                               Forty thou
Number of Vessels lost......... ....
Value of Vessels lost, including outfits..... ..Eight thou
Value of Fish lost .... one thous
Number of Lives lost.... ....
Total value of Fish taken, before curing, splitting, salti
   cwt...
Total value of Mackerel taken, before curing, splitting,
   per bbl...
Total value of Fish taken within three miles of British sho
Total value of Mackerel do..................... ....
Average market value of American Shore Mackerel.....
Average market value of Bay Mackerel........ Eight do
Average earnings of the operative fishermen per year
                Two hundred & Sevent
Average amount paid in British ports for bait, ice, and
   plies .... Two hundred dollars per year fo
Amount paid to British fishermen for herring
             One thousand dollars per Year
Amount paid to British fishermen as wages.............
Amount paid in British ports for repairs.... one thousand
Locations frequented by American vessels for Fish
           Georges La Haven Western &
Locations frequented by American vessels for Mackerel
           Coast of the United States & Gulf
Actual value of Fish in the water, before taking........
Actual value of Mackerel in the water, before taken.....
Facts as to changes in location and mode of conducting
   eries

   Within last three years we have not had any Vesse
Fishing in British Waters either for Cod or Mackeral.
   The Mackl fishing being done on the Coast of the Unit
New Jersey to and along the Eastern Coast of Maine and
in Cod Fishing on Georgies Western Le Have & Grand Ba
ing to British Waters except to purchase Bait and occas

f of St Lawrence Fishery is so improftable that we consider
e failure.

S AYER.   DENNIS & AYER
G DENNIS

ind subscribed to before me, this 31st day of May 1877
                        DAVID W. LOW
                                Notary Public
                No. 60.

to certify, That the undersigned, composing the firm of
                                        have been
n the fishing business for the past
                        and that since the Washington
i called, has been in effect, our vessels have been employed as

ssels employed.............. ....Seven
ips made............................. .... Thirty five Yearly
ips to Bay St. Lawrence............. Two in 1873 none since
rrels of Mackerel from Bay St. Lawrence............ .. 400
rrels of Mackerel caught within 3 miles of shore, not including
lene Islands ....None
value of Vessels each..........................$5800,
value of Outfits, Salt, Bait, &c..................... $800,
value of Insurance................$4400, or about 9 per cent
    value of Captains' and Crews' time, viz., wages per
....$35, $200.00 each vessel
value of Commissions,&c..4 per cent on Gross Stock to Skipper
value of Wharves, Fish-houses, &c., for curing and packing,
ng expenses of Clerks, Proprietors and labor on shore..$18000.
of Vessels lost ....One
Vessels lost, including outfits.........................$6400
Fish lost..None
of Lives lost......................:...............Twelve
lue. of Fish taken, before curing, splitting, salting, &c, per
....75 cts
ue of Mackerel taken, before curing, splitting, salting, &c., per
....$1.00
ue of Fish taken within three miles of British shores····None
ue of Mackerel do.................. .. ..None
market value of American Shore Mackerel
                $14. for ones $12, for twos $8, for threes
market value of Bay Mackerel
                $11, for ones $8, for twos $6, for threes
earnings of the operative fishermen per year.... ....$250,
amount paid in British ports for bait, ice, and various sup-
....$400, Yearly
paid to British fishermen for herring
paid to British fishermen as wages·············· $220, Yearly
paid in British ports for repairs
s frequented by American vessels for Fish
                        Gr. Bank La Have Banks
s frequented by American vessels for Mackerel
                        Cape May to Bay St Lawrence
alue of Fish in the water, before taking.... ....Nothing
alue of Mackerel in the water, before taken·········Nothing

Facts as to changes in location and mode of conducting Ameri·
eries

The Bay of St Lawrence fishery has proved a failure in m‍y
ence my vessels not having paid their bills or expenses conseq
now confine my vessels to our own Shores for Mackerel and th·
Banks for fish   My vessels do not enter British Waters except
or supplies

WM. C. WO.

Sworn and subscribed to before me, this thirty first day of ‍‍
(Seal.)   DAVID W. LO‍
Notary

No. 61.

This is to certify, That the undersigned, composing the firm ‍
have been engaged in the fishing business for the past
         and that since the Washington Treaty, so called, ‍
in effect, our vessels have been employed as follows :

No. of Vessels employed.................................... ......
No. of Trips made.............231 Codfish trips.   17 mackeı
No. of Trips to Bay St. Lawrence.................. ....(11
No. of Barrels of Mackerel from Bay St. Lawrence....... .....
No. of Barrels of Mackerel caught within 3 miles of shore, not iı
    Magdalene Islands.............. ......Most caught off Maş
Average value of Vessels each ....
Average value of Outfits, Salt, Bait, &c ....
Average value of Insurance .... 9% on Vessel &
Average value of Captains' and Crews' time, viz., wages per
Average value of Commissions,&c................... $200 ea
Average value of Wharves, Fish-houses, &c., for curing and ı
    including expenses of Clerks, Proprietors and labor on shore
Number of Vessels lost.......................................
Value of Vessels lost, including outfits ....,
Value of Fish lost...
Number of Lives lost..
Total value of Fish taken, before curing, splitting, salting, &c

Total value of Mackerel taken, before curing, splitting, salting,
    bbl..
Total value of Fish taken within three miles of British shores
Total value of Mackerel do. ....
Average market value of American Shore Mackerel
$16 No 1's $12 no 2's
Average market value of Bay Mackerel
$11 75 no 1 $7.50 no 2 $5
Average earnings of the operative fishermen per year........
Average amount paid in British ports for bait, ice, and variouş
$10‍
Amount paid to British fishermen for herring
Amount paid to British fishermen as wages
Amount paid in British ports for repairs
Locations frequented by American vessels for Fish
Grand Bank—Georgeş
Locations frequented by American vessels for Mackerel
Cape May & Gulf St ‍
Actual value of Fish in the water, before taking ....

lue of Mackerel in the water, before taken .... nothing
o changes in location and mode of conducting American fish-
s
withdrawn vessels from Bay on acc of being unprofitable—
iness to pursue.
odfishing is pursued on Ocean Banks within no national Juris-
:ion
essels do not go in British water except to purchase Bait &
plies

EPES SAYWARD Jr,
GEO SAYWARD

and subscribed to before me, this thirty first day of May 1877
DAVID W. LOW
Notary Public

No. 62.

to certify, That the undersigned, composing the firm of Daniel
have been engaged in the fishing business for the past thirteen
Gloucester, and that since the Washington Treaty, so called,
in effect, our vessels have been employed as follows:

ssels employed....................... 7 to 5 seven to five
ips made .... 188 One hundred eighty-eight
ips to Bay St. Lawrence............ 12 Twelve in five years.
rrels of Mackerel from Bay St. Lawrence............ 2398.
rrels of Mackerel caught within 3 miles of shore, not including
.... 00
lene Islands ....
value of Vessels each..................... $6600. in 1871.
value of Outfits, Salt, Bait, &c·············· 800, " "
value of Insurance...................... 575, " "
value of Captains' and Crews' time, viz., wages per mo.
value of Commissions, &c.
value of Wharves, Fish-houses, &c., for curing and packing,
ng expenses of Clerks, Proprietors and labor on shore
$20000, " "
.... 3
of Vessels lost... .... $18000
Vessels lost, including outfits.......................
Fish lost 35
of Lives lost.............................
lue of Fish taken, before curing, splitting, salting, &c. per
.... 75 per hundred
lue of Mackerel taken, before curing, splitting, salting, &c., per
.... $1.50 per bbl.
lue of Fish taken within three miles of British shores....... 0
lue of Mackerel do.----------------------- 0
market value of American Shore Mackerel
No. 1 $16.   No. 2 $12.   No 3 $8.
market value of Bay Mackerel No. 1 $12. No. 2 $8. No. 3 $6.
earnings of the operative fishermen per year........... $225.
amount paid in British ports for bait, ice, and various sup-
.... $100, yearly
paid to British fishermen for herring
paid to British fishermen as wages
paid in British ports for repairs
as frequented by American vessels for Fish......Grand, West-
d George's Banks

Locations frequented by American vessels for Mackerel.....
   Shores & Bay St. Lawrence
Actual value of Fish in the water, before taking..........
Actual value of Mackerel in the water, before taken.... ...
Facts as to changes in location and mode of conducting
   fisheries

   My vessels have not paid their expenses for the last five ×
employed in taking mackerel at the Bay of St. Lawrence. ?
of the mackerel being poor, and the length of the trips maki
expensive that I cannot pursue this business to advantage.

   All of my codfishing business is pursued out on the ocean
side of the jurisdiction of any nation. Entering British wat
the purchase of bait and supplies.

DANIEL SA?

Sworn and subscribed to before me, this thirty first day of
(Seal.)   DAVID W. I
Nota

No. 63.

   This is to certify, That the undersigned, composing the firm
Parsons 2d & Co have been engaged in the fishing business t
Thirty years, at Gloucester Mass and that since the Washing
so called, has been in effect, our vessels have been employed

No. of Vessels employed.............................
No. of Trips made.. Five trips yearly each vessel, Total, 90 tri
1871 1872 1873 1874
No. of Trips to Bay St. Lawrence.. 3   3   4   2
Tota
No. of Barrels of Mackerel from Bay St. Lawrence......Tw
No. of Barrels of Mackerel caught within 3 miles of shore,
   ing Magdalene Islands..............................
Average value of vessels each ....Five thous
Average value of Outfits, Salt, Bait, &c....$2800 yearly to
Average value of Insurance ....$300 yearly to
Average value of Captains' and Crews' time, viz., wages per
Average value of Commissions, &c..........·.........$200
Average value of Wharves, Fish-houses, &c., for curing a
   including expenses of Clerks, Proprietors and labor on sl
Twenty thousand Do
Number of vessels lost........ ....
Value of vessels lost, including outfits..........Seven thous
Value of Fish lost..........................Two thous
Number of Lives lost.............................
Total value of Fish taken, before curing, splitting, salting, ¿
   per cwt...
Total value of Mackerel taken, before curing, splitting, salti
   &c., per bbl.....................................
Total value of Fish taken within three miles of British sho
Total value of Mackerel do................2500 in Glouc
Average market value of American Shore Mackerel
We sold fo
Average market value of Bay Mackerel
We sold for No 1 $10 No
   Average earnings of the operative fishermen per year
$200

amount paid in British ports for bait, ice, and various supplies
h vessel...................................$2800 yearly
paid to British fishermen for herring...........$1,000 yearly
paid to British fishermen as wages...................None
paid in British ports for repairs................five Hundred
frequented by American vessels for Fish
                    Georges Grand Western La Have Banks
frequented by American vessels for Mackerel
                    from Long Island to Newfoundland
alue of Fish in the water, before taking.............Nothing
alue of Mackerel in the water before taken..........Nothing
    to changes in location and mode of conducting American
s
e past eight years fishing in British waters has been a total
We have tried it thoroughly & completely—and our vessels
he Bay have not paid their expenses. American fishermen
ve been much better off never to have gone into those waters
las superseded the Hook & line fishing for Mackerel, the best
are off our own coasts nearer our markets, our vessels make
ps, the mackerel are in better condition, We have sent no ves-
ie Bay the last two years, No Codfish are taken by our vessels
British limits

> THOMAS L. PARSONS
> EBEN PARSONS 2d
> GEORGE PARSONS

and subscribed to before me, this 31st day of May 1877.
> DAVID W. LOW
> *Notary Public*

No. 64.

to certify, That the undersigned, composing the firm of Won-
)., have been engaged in the fishing business for the past twen-
ears, at Gloucester Mass and that since the Washington Treaty,
, has been in effect, our vessels have been employed as follows:

essels employed .... Ten (10)
rips made........·.................. five each vessel yearly
rips to Bay St. Lawrence.......... 1872 1873 1874 1875 1876
                                     2,   2,   2,   2,   1,
                              1872 1873 1874 1875 1876
arrels of Mackerel from Bay St. Lawrence 350, 400, 325, 300, 150
arrels of Mackerel caught within 3 miles of shore, not including
gdalene Islands   Mackerel caught at the Magdelena
                              5000
value of Vessels each. .... $3000 yearly each vessel
value of Outfits, Salt, Bait, &c......
value of Insurance..........9 per cent on Vessel & Outfits
value of Captains' and Crews' time, viz., wages per mo... $40
value of Commissions, &c. .... 200 each vessel
value of Wharves, Fish-houses, &c., for curing and packing,
ling expenses of Clerks, Proprietors and labor on shore
                              .... $20,000 yearly
of Vessels lost .... None
f Vessels lost, including outfits....................... None
f Fish lost
of Lives lost

Total value of Fish taken, before curing, splitting, salting,
  cwt...
Total value of Mackerel taken, before curing, splitting, salting,
  bbl...
Total value of Fish taken within three miles of British shores.
Total value of Mackerel do.......... ....
Average market value of American Shore Mackerel......　16
Average market value of Bay Mackerel...................　11
Average earnings of the operative fishermen per year....
Average amount paid in British ports for bait, ice,
  and various supplies...........................200 each vesse
Amount paid to British fishermen for herring
  　　　　　　　　$600 to $800 for 4 vessels eac
Amount paid to British fishermen as wages
Amount paid in British ports for repairs
Locations frequented by American vessels for Fish
  　　　　　　　　　　Grand Bank &
Locations frequented by American vessels
  　　　　　　　　Cape May to Bay St L
Actual value of Fish in the water, before taking..............
Actual value of Mackerel in the water, before taken...........
Facts as to changes in location and mode of conducting Americ
  eries
  Our vessels have been Cod fishing on the Banks & Mackerelin;
off our own shores, The Bay of St Lawrence fishery has constantl,
poorer Our vessels did not pay their expenses shall send no
there this year Our own Shore Mackerel are worth a third mo
Bay Mackerel, We are using Seines where we formerly used I
lines, The Cod fishery is pursued on the Banks bordering on
Stream many miles from any shores and within no National jur
  　　　　　　　　　　WONSON BROT

Sworn and subscribed to before me, this 31st day of May 18
  　　　　　　　　　　W. S. WONS
(Seal.)　　　　　　　　S G WONS

DAVID W. LOW
Notary Public

No. 65.

This is to certify, That the undersigned, composing the firm
Norwood & Son have been engaged in the fishing business for
Fifteen years, at Gloucester Mass. and that since the Washingtor
so called. has been in effect, our vessels have been employe
lows:

No. of Vessels employed......... ....
No. of Trips made....................... ....
No. of Trips to Bay St. Lawrence.................Sixteen s
No. of Barrels of Mackerel from Bay St. Lawrence
  　　　　　　　　　Thirty-Six Hundre
No. of Barrels of Mackerel caught within 3 miles of shore, not i
  Magdalen Islands....................................
Average value of Vessels each...................Six Thousan
Average value of Outfits, Salt, Bait, &c..........One Thousar
Average value of Insurance.....................Five Thousar

᠌ value of Captains' and Crews' time, viz., wages per mo

Thirty dollars

᠌ value of Commissions, &c.. four per cent. to Captain of Vessel

᠌ value of Wharves, Fish-houses, &c., for curing and packing,
ling.expenses of Clerks, Proprietors, and labor on shore

Twenty thousand dollars

᠌ of Vessels lost.................................. ......None

f Vessels lost, including outfits.

f Fish lost.

᠌ of lives lost...................... ....Four

᠌alue of Fish taken, before curing, splitting, salting, &c., per
....One dollar

᠌alue of Mackerel taken, before curing, splitting, salting, &c., per
....Two dollars

᠌alue of Fish taken within three miles of British shores...Nothing

᠌alue of Mackerel do........................... ....Nothing

᠌market value of American Shore Mackerel.Ten dollars per Barrel

᠌ market value of Bay Mackerel........Eight dollars per barrel

᠌ earnings of the operative fishermen per year

Two hundred & fifty dollars

᠌ amount paid in British ports for bait, ice, and various supplies

Two hundred dollars per year for each Vessel

᠌ paid to British fishermen for herring

᠌ paid to British fishermen as wages.....................None

᠌ paid in British ports for repairs..Four hundred dollars Since 1871

᠌ns frequented by American vessels for Fish

Georges, Grand, Western, & La Have, Banks

᠌ns frequented by American vessels for Mackerel

Coast of United States & Gulf St. Lawrence

᠌ value of Fish in the water before taking.-------------Nothing

᠌ value of Mackerel in the water, before taken----------Nothing

᠌s to changes in location and mode of conducting American fish-

᠌ave not had any Vessels engaged in British Waters fishing since

GEO NORWOOD
FREDERIC NORWOOD

᠌n and subscribed to before me, this thirty first day of May 1877

DAVID W. LOW

᠌al.)

Notary Public

No. 66.

᠌ is to certify, That the undersigned, composing the firm of Leon-
alen have been engaged in the fishing business for the past Ten
at Gloucester Mass and that since the Washington Treaty, so
has been in effect, our vessels have been employed as follows:

....Four

vessels employed..

Trips made.... Six trips yearly each vessel, Total, 24 each year

1872 1873

Trips to Bay St. Lawrence............................. 2   1

Barrels of Mackerel from Bay St. Lawrence ....900 Barrels

Barrels of Mackerel caught within 3 miles of shore, not including

dalene Islands ....None

ge value of Vessels each $7,500

ge value of Outfits, Salt, Bait, &c

$900 for Bay trip. ($3000 each vessel ye

Average value of Insurance.................... 300 eacl
Averege value of Captains' and Crews' time, viz., wages p
Average value of Commissions, &c 2
Average value of Wharves, Fish-houses, &c., for curing
  including expenses of Clerks, Proprietors and labor on
Number of vessels lost ....
Value of Vessels lost, including outfits.................
Value of Fish lost ... .
Number of Lives lost................................
Total value of fish taken, before curing, splitting, saltin

Total value of Mackerel taken, before curing, splitting
  per bbl...
Total value of Fish taken within three miles of British st
Total value of Mackerel do..........................
Average market value of American shore mackerel
                              No 1 $16 No 2,
Average market value Bay Mackerel
                              I sold for No 1 $12, No
Average earnings of the operative fishermen per year..
Average amount paid in British ports for bait, ice, and va

Amount paid to British fishermen for herring ....
Amount paid to British fishermen as wages ....
Amount paid in British ports for repairs ....
Locations frequented by American vessels for Fish
                        Grand Banks, Western, Geo
Locations frequented by American vessels for Mackerel
                  Long Island Sound to Bay St Lawre
Actual value of Fish in the water, before taking........
Actual value of Mackerel in the water, before taken.....
Facts as to changes in location and mode of conducting
  eries
  The Fisheries and the mode of taking has changed muc
formerly the shore fisheries were used when hand lines a
used now fish are taken on the Banks with trawls and
seines, Our vessels are the best that can be built and
on the Ocean Banks for fish the fish are met and taken
nearest the Gulfstream as they come on the Banks to s
of St Lawrence is entirely unprofitable to American fi
to the great expense of running the vessels and the po
quantity of fish & Mackerel there.
                              LEONAF

  Sworn and subscribed to before me, this thirty first d
  (Seal.)   DAVI

No. 67.

  This is to certify, That the undersigned, composing th
Jordan have been engaged in the fishing business for
years, at Gloucester and that since the Washington T
has been in effect, our vessels have been employed as fo
No. of Vessels employed.........................
No. of Trips made........ .... eight each yea
No. of Trips to Bay St Lawrence...................
No. of Barrels of Mackerel from Bay of St. Lawrence.

els of Mackerel caught within 3 miles of shore, not includ·
alene Islands........ .... none
lue of Vessels each
          fifty five hundred dollars at present time
lue of Outfits, Salt, Bait, &c.
          one thousand   "
lue of Insurance
          forty-eight hundred   "
lue of Captains' and Crews' time, viz., wages per mo.
          3900 each vessel
lue of Commissions, &c .... to Capt. $350 each,
lue of Wharves, Fish houses, &c., for curing and packing,
; expenses of Clerks, Proprietors and labor on shore. $30.800
vessels lost........................ six during live years
essels lost, including outfits...................... 45425
ish lost.................................... $7000
  Lives lost................................. twenty five (25)
; of Fish taken, before curing, splitting, salting, &c., per cwt.
000 lbs $39.000
; of Mackerel taken, before curing, splitting, salting, &c., per
, 21000 bbls $31.500
; of Fish taken within three miles of British shores. ·· none
; of Mackerel do..................................· none
iarket value of American Shore Mackerel··· thirteen dollars
iarket value of Bay Mackerel······ ····· ..... ten dollars
arnings of the operative fishermen per year··········· $275
mount paid in British ports for bait, ice, and various supplies
          $500 a year for each vessel
aid to British fishermen for herring
aid to British fishermen as wages
aid in British ports for repairs··················· ··· $1500
frequented by American vessels for Fish
      Grand Georges Western & Labave Banks
frequented by American vessels for Mackerel
   Coast of Maine & Mass Long Island & Bay St Lawrence
lue of Fish in the water, before taking············ nothing
lue of Mackerel in the water, before taken········   "
; changes in location and mode of conducting Amer-
ieries
the last four years the facilities for catching mackerl have in·
, that it does not pay to go for them from our own shores as
be taken in great abundance here & beside the chances of
iem in Bay of St Lawrence & adjacent waters seem to grow
all events the chances for getting either Mackerel or Cod Fish
uncertain that it is abandoned almost altogether, the vessels
ued it did so at a heavy pecuniary loss last year & the year

         JOSEPH ROWE.
         WILLIAM H. JORDAN.

and subscribed to before me, this 31st day of May 1877
         DAVID W. LOW
              Notary Public

       No. 68.

to certify, That the undersigned, composing the firm of Harvey
n Jr have been engaged in the fishing business for the past five

years, at Gloucestor Mass and that since the Washingto
called, has been in effect, our vessels have been employed a

No. of Vessels employed ....
No. of Trips made ....six each v
No. of Trips to Bay St. Lawrence ....five i
No. of Barrels of Mackerel from Bay St. Lawrence........
No. of Barrels of Mackerel caught within 3 miles of shore, n
   including Magdelene Islands...........................
Average value of Vessels each............................
Average value of Outfits, Salt, Bait, &c.... $3,000 each v
Average value of Insurance............... $300   "
Average value of Captains' and Crews' time, viz., wages per
Average value of Commissions, &c........... 250 each v
Average value of Wharves, Fish-houses, &c., for curing a
   including expenses of Clerks, Proprietors and labor on sho
Number of Vessels lost..................................
Value of Vessels lost, including outfits ... .
Value of Fish lost
Number of Lives lost...................................
Total value of Fish taken, before curing, splitting, salting, &
   per cwt..
Total value of Mackerel taken, before curing, splitting, saltin
   &c., per bbl...
Total value of Fish taken within three miles of British shor
Total value of Mackerel do..... ....
Average market value of American Shore Mackerel......$1

                                    No 1
Average market value of Bay Mackerel.. ....$12
Average earnings of the operative fishermen per year......
Average amount paid in British ports for bait, ice, and
   plies....................................$250 each
Amount paid to British fishermen for herring...........
Amount paid to British fishermen as wages.............$
Amount paid in British ports for repairs ....
Locations frequented by American vessels for Fish
                     Western Banks Grand Georg
Locations frequented by American vessels for Mackerel
                     American Shore Bay
Actual value of Fish in the water, before taking..........
Actual value of Mackerel in the water, before taken.......
Facts as to changes in location and mode of conducting A
   eries

    The Fisheries have changed from shore fishing to deep
fishing, The mackerel fishery has changed from the hand l
to use of seines The Bay of St Lawrence fishery has de
300 vessels yearly to 40 last year Not one of the vessels
the Bay of St Lawrence last year paid their expenses

                       HARVEY KNOW

  Sworn and subscribed to before me, this thirty first day
    (Seal.)   DAVID W.
                                  No

No. 69.

certify, That the undersigned, composing the firm of Sid.
& Co have been engaged in the fishing business for the past
Gloucester Mass and that since the Washington Treaty, so
been in effect, our vessels have been employed as follows:

iels employed.. 13
s made.................sixty per year—for all the vessels
s to Bay St Lawrence ....(4) four (or whatever)
:els of Mackerel from Bay St. Lawrence 1005
:els of Mackerel caught within 3 miles of shore, not includ.
;dalene Islands .... none
ilue of Vessels each........................... $6000, each
iiue of Outfits, Salt, Bait, &c

        about $700, per trip, or $2800, per year
ilue of Insurance....... ....$4500, each vessel
alue of Captains' and Crews' time, viz.,
r mo..... ... .$[[$35, per month
ihe of Commissions, &c

        3 per ct on gross stock—to Skipper
alue of Wharves, Fish-houses, &c., for curing and packing,
; expenses of Clerks, Proprietors and labor on shore
Establishment & $4400, for labor making
:lusive
Vessels lost.... . ... one
essels lost, including outfits................. .... $6000.
ish lost .... none
Lives lost..... 13
e of Fish taken, before curing, splitting, salting, &c., per
....75 cts
e of Mackerel taken, before curing, splitting, salting,
bbl .... $1.
; of Fish taken within three miles of British shore.. none
; of Mackerel do .... None
alue of American Shore Mackerel

        $15, for ones, $12, for twos $8, for threes
arket value of Bay Mackerel

        $12. for ones; $8. for twos; $6. for threes
irnings of the operative fishermen per year........... $250,
mount paid in British ports for bait, ice, and various supplies

        $200, each vessel.
iid to British fishermen for herring.................$300,
iid to British fishermen as wages....................$150,
iid in British ports for repairs....................$1.000,
frequented by American vessels for Fish

        Gd Bank, Le Have, Bradlee, Orphan
frequented by American vessels for Mackerel

        from Long Island to New Foundland.
ue of Fish in the water, before taking..............nothing
ue of Mackerel in the water, before taken..........nothing
:o changes in location and mode of conducting American

ibut & Cod fisheries are entirely deep-sea fisheries within no
irisdiction. The mackerel fishery has largely changed from
ine fishing to seine fishing—the American shore mackerel

bringing one third more in price than the Bay-mackerel on account of quality.

The Bay of St Lawrence fishery for mackerel has gradually deteriorated intill we cannot send vessels there at any profit whatever. Those vessels we have sent the past seven years have not paid their expenses We consider the Bay Fishery a failure and worthless to American fishermen.

SIDNEY FRIEND

Sworn and subscribed to before me, this first day of June 1877
(Seal.)   DAVID W. LOW
Notary Public

No. 70.

This is to certify, That the undersigned, composing the firm of David Low and Co have been engaged in the fishing business for the past twenty five years, at Gloucester Mass and that since the Washington Treaty, so called, has been in effect, our vessels have been employed as follows:

No. of Vessels employed . . . . .fourteen
No. of Trips made . . . . Six trips yearly each vessel

	1872	1873	1874	1875	1876
No. of Trips to Bay of St. Lawrence	5	5	2	1	0

	1872	1873	1874	1875	1876
No. of Barrels of Mackerel from Bay St. Lawrence	1250	750	440	200 bls	0

No. of Barrels of Mackerel caught within 3 miles of shore, not including Magdalene Islands

not one tenth

Average value of Vessels each . . . . .Six thousand dollars each
Average value of Outfits, Salt, Bait, &c
Seventeen Hundred dollars value each vessel
Average value of Insurance . . . . .nine per cent vessel & outfits
Average value of Captains' and Crews' time, viz., wages per mo
Thirty dollars each
Average value of Commissions, &c . . . . .Two hundred dollars
Average value of Wharves, Fish-houses, &c., for curing and packing, including expenses of Clerks, Proprietors and labor on shore
Thirty five thousand dollars
Number of vessels lost . . . . .one
Value of Vessels lost, including outfits . . . . .five thousand dollars,
Value of Fish lost
Number of Lives lost
Total value of Fish taken, before curing, splitting, salting, &c. per cwt.
fifty cts
Total value of Mackerel taken, before curing, splitting, salting, &c., per bbl . . . . .two dollars
Total value of Fish taken within three miles of British shores . . . . .none
Total value of Mackerel do . . . . .Six hundred dollars
Average market value of American Shore Mackerel
Sixteen, twelve, & eight
Average market value of Bay Mackerel . . . . .Eleven, Seven five
Average earnings of the operative fishermen per year
Two hundred fifty
Average amount paid in British ports for bait, ice, and various supplies
four thousand dollars yearly

d to British fishermen for herring

     Two thousand dollars yearly

d to British fishermen as wages

d in British ports for repairs..five hundred dollars yearly

requented by American vessels for Fish

     Grand Bank & Georgies

equented by American vessels for Mackerel

     Cape May to Bay of St Lawrence

e of Fish in the water, before taking..............nothing

e of Mackerel in the water, before taken ....nothing

 changes in location and mode of conducting American

, of July we used to send most of our vessels ten years
r of St Lawrence—but of late years that fishing proveng of
r vessels looseing money. we have confined them entirely to
res and the ocean banks. we send no vessels in the Brittish
sh or mackerel and only enter them for bait and Supplies
e pay cash. we consider the Brittish inshore fisheries a
lure   BENJAMIN LOW

l subscribed to before me, this first day of June 1877

     DAVID W. LOW

       Notary Public

No. 71.

certify, That the undersigned, composing the firm of Leigh-
ve been engaged in the fishing business for the past nine
oucester Mass and that since the Washington Treaty, so
een in effect, our vessels have been employed as follows :

els employed ....Eighteen

made..Averaging about Eight Trips yearly to each vessel

    1872 1873 1874 1875 1876

to Bay St. Lawrence··9 trips 14 Trips 4 Trips 1 Trip 1 Trip

    1872 1873 1874 1875 1876

ls of Mackerel from Bay St. Lawrence·2851 4273 1341 309 134

els of Mackerel caught within 3 miles of shore, not including
e Islands

   Not more than 450 Bbls. (Four Hundred & fifty)

lue of Vessels each....... .. ..$7500.00

lue of Outfits, Salt, Bait, &c

    $1500.00 for Bay Trips or Bank

h

lue of Insurance....... 9% per annum on Vessel & outfits

lue of Captains' and Crews' time, viz., wages per mo

     $35.00 per month

lue of Commissions, &c.................... ...$300.00

lue of Whaves, Fish-houses, &c., for curing and picking,

 expenses of Clerks, Proprietors and labor on shore

     $30.000. yearly

.....Nine

Vessels lost................................Averaging $8000.00

essels lost, including outfits............$1000.00 each

sh lost ....Seventy five

Lives lost....... .. .. per cwt.

of Fish taken, before curing, splitting, salting, &c.,

    Seventy five cts all kinds

of Mackerel taken, before curing, splitting, salting, &c, per

    Two Dollars

....

Total value of Fish taken within three miles of British shore
Total value of Mackerel do .... $900.00 (nine Hun
Average market value of American Shore Mackerel..$16.00
Average market value of Bay Mackerel............... 12.(
Average earnings of the operative fishermen per year..from
Average amount paid in British ports for bait, ice, and
   plies .... $400. per '
Amount paid to British fishermen for herring........... $6
Amount paid to British fishermen as wages........ about
Amount paid in British ports for repairs............ abou
Locations frequented by American vessels for Fish
                    Georges, Grand Banks also V
Locations frequented by American vessels for Mackerel
                    From Capes of Virginia to B;
Autual value of Fish in the water, before taking
                    Worth nothing in the water, value in the labo
Actual value of Mackerel in the water, before taken....the
Facts as to changes in location and mode of conducting A
eries We were once largely engaged in Mackerel fishery
Lawrence but this is now unprofitable owing to poor quali
in quantity of the Mack'l of late years All vessels sent
years returning largely in debt Our vessels now being
the banks for fish and on our shores for mack'l using seine
stead of Hooks for Mackl—and trawls mostly for fish
          ANDREW LEIGHTON)
          WALTER M.FALT   } LEIGH7
          GEORGE A. UPTON)

Sworn and subscribed to before me, this first day of Ju
(Seal.)   DAVID W
                                        N

No. 72.

This is to certify that the undersigned, composing the
Dodd & Tarr now James G Tarr & Bro have been engag«
ing business for the past twenty five years, at Gloucester.
since the Washington Treaty, so called, has been in effe
have been employed as follows :

No. of Vessels employed.......................
No. of Trips made ....Six trips yearly, to e;
                    1871 1872 1873 1874 18
No. of Trips to Bay St. Lawrence 4   2   4   3   (
No. of Barrels of Mackerel from Bay St. Lawrence
    1871   1872   1873   1874   1875   18;
    1287 bls 888 bls   672 bls   1124 bls 0   190
No. of Barrels of Mackerel caught within 3 miles of shore,
    Magdalene Islands .... about one-tenth, (Most ca
Average value of Vessels each ... .five The
Average value of Outfits, Salt, Bait, &c...$2,500 per year
Average value of Insurance......................... ...
Average value of Captains' and Crews' time, viz., wage.
                              Capt $75 Crew
Average value of Commissions, &c............. 200 yea1
Average value of Wharves, Fish-houses, &c., for curing
   including expenses of Clerks, Proprietors and labor on
                    ($31,000) Thirty one thousand 1

essels lost ....
sels lost, including outfits................. ......$24,000 Four
ı lost $3,000
ives lost .... thirty one
f Fish taken, before curing, splitting, salting, &c. per cwt.

One Dollar

f Mackerel taken, before curing, splitting, salting, &c., per
.... two Dollars
f Fish taken within three miles of British shores

None taken

f Mackerel do.................................$1300

               No 1   2   3
ket value of American Shore Mackerel $16, 12, 8
               No 1   2   3
ket value of Bay Mackerel 12   8   6
ings of the operative fishermen per year. $215 for past 6 years
unt paid in British ports for bait, ice, and
)plies............ $5,000 yearly total in six years $30,000
to British fishemen
................$4,100 yearly   " " " " $24,600
to British fishermen as wages............... hired none
. in British ports for repairs................ ....$1780
quented by American
Fish.......Gd Bank Georges Browns Lehave Bradelle &c
quented by American
Mackerel...........from Sandy Hook to Bay St Lawrence
of Fish in the water, be-
.... Nothing. as raw material valueless
of Mackerel in the water
:n.....................   "   " "   "   "
hanges in location and mode of conducting American fish-
g the last four years Mackerel in the Bay of St Lawrence
mparatively scarce. Seines have gradually been introduced
ent time hook fishing is nearly obsolete. Seine fishing in
it Lawrence & Chaleur is not practical and has proved a
aire and the business has been abandoned The Mackerel
ıfined to the American coast The Bay Codfishery has been
years not a dozen trips has been made from this port within
e depend upon the deep sea Banks entirely for Halibut &
employ the British shore boats and fishermen in taking Her-
them their price

                        DAVID TARR
                        JAMES G. TARR

. subscribed to before me, this 31st day of May 1877.
                  DAVID W. LOW
                       Notary Public

            No. 73.

o certify, that the undersigned, composing the firm of Smith
been engaged in the fishing business for the past 10 years,
ır Mass. and that since the Washington Treaty, so called,
effect, our vessels have been employed as follows:
.... Fifteen
ls employed............................ Six to each vessel yearly
made............ .... 1872 1873 1874 1875 1876

No. of Trips to Bay St. Lawrence 4   5   !
                                     1872   1873   18

No. of Barrels of Mackerel from Bay St.
   Lawrence......................... 1000   1000   7
No. of Barrels of Mackerel caught within 3 miles of shore
   Magdalene Islands .....most caught around the Mag
Average value of Vessels each ....
Average value of Outfits, Salt, Bait, &c...............
Average value of Insurance................ 9% on ves
Average value of Captains' and Crews' time, viz., wages
Average value of Commissions, &c.......................$
Average value of Wharves, Fish-houses, &c., for curing
   packing, including expenses of Clerks, Proprietors
   labor on shore...
Number of Vessels lost ....
Value of Vessels lost, including outfits...............
Value of Fish lost
Number of Lives lost ....
Total value of Fish taken, before curing, splitting, sal
   &c. per cwt..
Total value of Mackerel taken, before curing, splitting,
   ing, &c., per bbl...................................
Total value of Fish taken within three miles of British s
Total value of Mackerel do............ ....
Average market value of American Shore Mackerel....
Average market value of Bay Mackerel ....
Average earnings of the operative fishermen per year..
Average amount paid in British ports for Bait, ice,
   various supplies...................................
Amount paid to British fishermen for herring........
Amount paid to British fishermen as wages.........
Amount paid in British ports for repairs ....
Locations frequented by American vessels for Fish
                             Grand Banks, L
Locations frequented by American vessels for Mackere
                             Cape May to B
Actual value of Fish in the water, before taking......
Actual value of Mackerel in the water, before taken...

Facts as to changes in location and mode of conductin
   eries
     The fisheries have changed from hook and line fishing
and from line fishing to seining for Mackerel   We have
the St. Lawrence fishery, and find it is a failure, our ve
their expenses,   We shall send no vessels there this ye
ing is pursued outside of the jurisdiction of any natio
banks,

                 ADDISON GOLT Jr. SYLV.
                                   SM

     Sworn and subscribed to before me, this 31st day of
                                    DAV
(Seal.)

                         No. 74.

     This is to certify, That the undersigned, composing
& Somes have been engaged in the fishing business fo

Gloucester Mass., and that since the Washington Treaty, so
s been in effect, our vessels have been employed as follows:

ssels employed...Eleven
ips made...............(55 yearly) Five each vessel yearly
　　　　　　　　　　　　　1872 1873 1874 1875 1876
ips to Bay of St. Lawrence........ 4   4   2   0   1
　　　　　　　　　　　　　1872 1873 1874 1875
rrels of Mackerel from Bay St. Lawrence 812 680 300 0 60
rrels of Mackerel caught within 3 miles of shore, not including
lene Islands........ ...None of any consequence; not one tenth
value of Vessels each.................. Six thousand Dollars
value of Outfits, Salt, Bait, &c........... ....$2,500
value of Insurance................. 9 pr ct on Vessel & outfits
value of Captains' and Crews' time, viz., wages per mo....$40
value of Commissions, &c.................. $250 each vessel
value of Wharves, Fish-houses, &c., for curing and packing,
ng expenses of Clerks, Proprietors and labor on shore.$30,000
of Vessels lost
Vessels lost, including outfits
Fish lost
of Lives lost
ue of Fish taken, before curing, splitting, salting, &c. per
....50 cts
ue of Mackerel taken, before curing, splitting, salting, &c., per
....$1,50
ue of Fish taken within three miles of British shores....None
lue of Mackerel do $360
　　　　　　　　　　　　　　No 1 No 2 No 3
market value of American Shore Mackerel.. $16 $12 $8
　　　　　　　　　　　　　　No 1 No 2 No 3
market value of Bay Mackerel $11 $7 $5
earnings of the operative fishermen per year...........$250
amount paid in British ports for bait, ice, and various sup-
.... $3000 yearly
paid to British fishermen for herring...........$2500   "
paid to British fishermen as wages..................
paid in British ports for repairs........ ....
s frequented by American vessels for Fish
　　　　　　　　　Grand Banks Georges Western Bks
s frequented by American vessels for Mackerel
　　　　　　　　　Cape May to Gulf St Lawrence
alue of Fish in the water, before taking............Nothing
alue of Mackerel in the water, before taken..........Nothing
to changes in location and mode of conducting American fish-
Ve have formerly sent vessels to the Bay of St Lawrence from
1 to ½ of our fleet, but the constant reduction in quantity and
of the mackerel has rendered that fishery not only unprofitable
lutely ruinous to continue in it. Our shore mackerel are worth
oney are more readily taken are in better condition. Our sys-
eining cannot be applied in the Bay of St Lawrence as in shoal
le rocky bottom breaks the seine, and in deep water the Herring
seine and sink carrying the Mackerel with them. Our vessels
ritish Waters only to purchase supplies Ice Bait &c for which
cash

　　　　　　　　　　　　JOHN E SOMES
　　　　　　　　　　　　GEORGE CLARK Jr

Sworn and subscribed to before me, this 26th day of J
(Seal.)   DAVID V
                                                    λ

No. 75.

This is to certify, That the undersigned, composing 1
Munson & Company have been engaged in the fishing b
past twenty-five years, at Gloucester Mass and that sinc(
ton Treaty, so called, has been in effect, our vessels have
as follows :

No. of Vessels employed ....
No. of Trips made.......................Six trips yea
                                        1872   1873   18
No. of Trips to Bay St. Lawrence......   3   2   2
                                        1872   1873   18:
No. of Barrels of Mackerel from Bay
    St. Lawrence...................... 500   450   51
No. of Barrels of Mackerel caught within 3 miles of shore
    Magdalene Islands........................all caugh
Average value of Vessels each ....
Average value of Outfits, Salt, Bait, &c.
                    $1,000 for Bay trip $600 for
Average value of Insurance ....9 per ct on V
Average value of Captains' and Crews' time, viz., wages
Average value of Commissions, &c...................'
Average value of Wharves, Fish-houses, &c., for curing
    including expenses of Clerks, Proprietors and labor on
Number of Vessels lost ....
Value of Vessels lost, including outfits ....
Value of Fish lost
Number of Lives lost.................................
Total value of Fish taken, before curing, splitting, salting
Total value of Mackerel taken, before curing, splitting,
    bbl ....
Total value of Fish taken within three miles of British
Total value of Mackerel do ....
Average market value of American Shore Mackerel...
Average market value of Bay Mackerel ....
Average earnings of the operative fishermen per year..
Average amount paid in British ports for bait, ice, ai
    plies...
Amount paid to British fishermen for herring..6000 year
Amount paid to British fishermen as wages...........
Amount paid in British ports for repairs........ ....
Locations frequented by American vessels for Fish
Locations frequented by American vessels for Mackere
Actual value of fish in the water, before taking .. ....
Actual value of Mackerel in the water, before taken ....
Facts as to changes in location and mode of conductin
    eries

Trawls have taken the place of hand-lines for fish
mostly used for Mackerel. Shore off the coast of the U
ling is more profitable than any other shorter trips &
The Vessels we have sent to the Bay of St Lawrenc
their expenses We should have difficulty in shippin(
Bay We consider that fishery an entire failure The

ll and the great expense of the Bay trips makes it impossible
ϝ fishing there. None of our vessels use the inshore fisheries
ominion

> JOHN F. WONSON & CO
> JOHN F. WONSON
> FREDERIC G. WONSON
> ROGER, W. WONSON
> FRANKLIN A. WONSON.

and subscribed to before me, this 31st day of May 1877
DAVID W. LOW
Notary Public

No. 76.

MENT OF A. G. PROCTER, OF PROCTER, TRASK & CO.
LESALE FISH DEALERS, GLOUCESTER MASSACHU-
S.

way of information touching the value of Fish taken in Eng-
ers, I would state that our firm is extensively engaged in the
e of Herrings and Mackerel along the shores of the Gulf of St.
ce, Magdalen Islands and New Foundland. That we have pur-
of the British fishermen along these shores, during the past
n months, about Twenty thousand (20.000) barrels of Herrings:
, pay for the Herrings—delivered to our vessels at the Magdalen
by the British fishermen—Six (6) cents per barrel. These Her-
re caught in their own seines, and delivered from their own
and six (6) cents per barrel is the regular price charged for for
so delivered during the season. That for the Herrings caught
upper shores and along Anticosti Island we pay on an average
) cents per barrel. One cargo received by us during the past
consisting of Eighteen hundred (1800) barrels, cost in gold One
d eighty two ($182) Dollars. This was the actual cost of the
gs delivered, *fresh*, on the deck of our vessel, and includes the
the seines, nets and boats of the English fishermen and their
n securing and delivering. That the average cost of the New
and Herring taken at Fortune Bay, Boone Bay and Bay of
delivered to our vessels, fresh—is Fifty (50) cents per barrel.
ass of Herrings are all caught in *nets*, which method increases
t. The nets used cost about Twelve (12) Dollars each, and they
erage to wear only about two seasons; the price mentioned in-
all wear and tear of nets and gear, use of boats and labor in de-
g. Some of these Herrings are brought from thirty to forty
n boats to be delivered to our vessels. In all the Herring fish-
s far as our actual experience goes, in the British waters, my
ent is, that the cost to us of the product as delivered to our vessels
nore than equal to the value of the labor actually expended in
g and delivering them, including the cost and wear and tear of
terial used.

Mackerel caught in British waters, along the shores mentioned,
from Three (3) to Four (4) Dollars per barrel. This is for mack-
livered ready for packing from their boats, and includes the use
ensive gear, cost of splitting and labor, and cost of delivering.
abundance of Mackerel on our own shore for the past four or five
their superior quality and low price has made it more profitable
to purchase mackerel caught on our own shore, than those caught

in English waters; even at the low price at which the Englis
offered. We buy and dispose of $350,000. worth of fish ea
A G Pl

COMMONWEALTH OF MASSACHUSETTS.

ESSEX ss.   GLOUCESTER July {
    Then personally appeared the above named Addison G. I
made oath that all the foregoing statements by him subscrib
to the best of his knowledge and belief. Before me
(Seal.)   DAVID W. I
                                                    Nota

No. 77.

I Aaron Smith Master of the schooner Cora E Smith I w
North Haven. Maine do depose & say That I started from
on the 25th of April 1877 for a Mackerel voyage off Block .
absent one Month and took 200 Barrels Mackerel with seine
and worth Six Dollars per Bbl On the 8th of June 1877 s
trip for shore Mackerel and took 160 Bbls at round Pond Sta
These Mackerel were taken within 10 rods of the shore Mo
Mackerel were No 2 and brought 12 dollars per Bbl on an
have been 20 years engaged in fishing for Mackerel have l
seasons in the Bay of St Lawrence never done so well ther
own shores. I have assisted in taking over 3500 Barrels of
the Gulf of St Lawrence and of that amount not 200 Barrels
within 3 miles of the shore and so far as I know the same
will hold in the catch of other American Vessels. Ten year
we depended on the Hook fishing the Gulf of St Lawrenc
fishery could be pursued to advantage but since the intr
seines it cannot be pursued profitably
                                                    AARO.

STATE OF MASSACHUSETTS } ss.
    COUNTY OF ESSEX   }   GLOUCESTER Aug. 1
    Then personally appeared the above named Aaron Smit
oath that the above statement by him subscribed is true. I
(Seal.)   DAVID W.
                                                    Not

Also appeared Jerome B. Thomas one of the Crew of Sc
E. Smith who on oath, deposes and says that the above st
Aaron Smith Master is true. he also deposes and says
Master of Sch. David Brown Jr. in 1869 & 1870 and pro
Mackerel Fishery in the Bay of St. Lawrence that I did so
I left fishing as an occupation for several years and consider
erel Fishing with Seines on American Shores more profital
Bay fishing. My residence is North Haven in State of Mai
                                                    JEROME B '

STATE OF MASSACHUSETTS }
    COUNTY OF ESSEX   } ss.   GLOUCESTER Au
    Then personally appeared the above named Jerome B. '
made oath that the above statement by him subscribed is t
me
    (Seal.)   DAVID W.
                                                    Not

No. 78.

:o certify, That the undersigned, composing the firm of E.
lo have been engaged in the fishing business for the past 11
ewburyport Mass and that since the Washington Treaty, so
been in effect, our vessels have been employed as follows:

iels employed .... Six,
s made
iging from four to Six Trips yearly to Bay and home Fishing
          1872.   1873.   1874.   1875.   1876
is to Bay St. Lawrence ....   4.   4.   4.   3.   none.
          1872.   1873.   1874.   1875.   1876
rels of Mackerel from Bay
ence 1000   960   758.   555.   none
rels of Mackerel caught within 3 miles of shore, including
ne Islands
          560 Bbls. or about that, including Magdalene Islands
alue of Vessels each 7000
alue of Outfits, Salt, Bait, &c .... For Bay trip say 1000$
alue of Insurance .... 9 pr ct on schooners and outfits.
alue of Captains' and Crews' time, viz., wages per mo
                                        say Per Mo 35$.
alue of Commissions, &c .... 25$
alue of Wharves, Fish-houses, &c., for curing and packing,
g expenses of Clerks, Proprietors and labor on shore
                                        say 12000$
if Vessels lost ....one. (say 12000$)
Vessels lost, including outfits .... say 7500$
'ish lost .... say 3000$
: Lives lost .... none
ie of Fish taken, before curing, splitting, salting, &c. per

e of Mackerel taken, before curing, splitting, salting, &c. per
....Two dollars
ie of Fish taken within three miles of British shores, not any
ie of Mackerel do .... $1120. including Magdalene Isla
narket value of American Shore Mackerel .... 16$ 12$ $
narket value of Bay Mackerel .... 12$ 3$ 6$.
earnings of the operative fishermen per year
                                        from 140$ to 250$
amount paid in British ports for bait, ice, and various sup-
.... say 40$$ yearly.
iaid to British fishermen for herring
iaid to British fishermen as wages
iaid in British ports for repairs
                              according to damages by gales.
frequented by American vessels for Fish
frequented by American vessels for Mackerel
                      from Capes of Virginia to Bay Chaleur
ilue of Fish in the water, before ⎱ worth nothing in the water
                                  ⎰   Value being in the Labor
ilue of Mackerel in the water, be· ⎱ & Capital.
ien
io changes in location and mode of conducting American fish-

ssels. have always been in the Mackerel fishery, and were

formerly employed in the Bay of St Lawrence, but for the
years, owing to the small catch, and poor quality of the Fish, h
obliged to fish upon the American shore, using seines.   We
for two years seines in the Bay of St Lawrence, but they w‹
used there. and were put on shore and kept until the vessels
home in the Fall. making to us, an expense, for which we had ›
alent.

E. BUI

Sworn and subscribed to before me, this eighteenth day of :
(Seal.)   E. F. BARTLE
*Notar*₃

No. 79.

This is to certify, That the undersigned, composing the fir
Boardman and T. H Boardman & Co. have been engaged in t|
business for the past forty years, at Newburyport, Mass—and ⌡
the Washington Treaty, so called, has been in effect, our ves
been employed as follows :

No. of Vessels employed................................averag‹
No. of Trips made.................. averaging 5 to each ves

                      1872 1873 1874
No. of Trips to Bay St. Lawrence..........   12   9   5 —

                      1872 1873 1874
No. of Barrels of Mackerel from Bay St. Lawrence 3100 1756 124⌡
No. of Barrels of Mackerel caught within 3 miles of shore, not
   Magdalene Islands ....not exceeding
Average value of Vessels each......................
Average value of Outfits, Salt, Bait, &c......................
Average value of Insurance...................9 pr ct for ves
Average value of Captains' and Crews' time, viz., wages per m
Average value of Commissions, &c......................
Average value of Wharves, Fish-houses, &c., for curing and
   including expenses of Clerks, Proprietors, and labor on sho
                      say $14,
Number of Vessels lost ....
Value of Vessels lost, including outfits....................
Value of Fish lost......................................
Number of Lives lost.....................................
Total value of Fish taken, before curing, splitting, saltin
   cwt......................................Sevent.
Total value of Mackerel taken, before curing, splitting, sa
   per bbl.............................. one dollar &
Total value of Fish taken within three miles of British shores
Total value of Mackerel do...............................
Average market value of American Shore Mackerel..... $1(
Average market value of Bay Mackerel................ $11
Average earnings of the operative fishermen per year
                    from $1‹
Average amount paid in British ports for bait, ice, and vario
             about $350 pr v‹
Amount paid to British fishermen for herring........... $:
Amount paid to British fishermen as wages.............. $
Amount paid in British ports for repairs......... $400 yea
Locations frequented by American vessels for Fish Georges, G
        Western Banks Labrador & Newfoundl

ons frequented by American vessels for Mackerel
from Cape Henry to Bay Chaleur.
value of Fish in the water before taking..... nothing whatever
value of Mackerel in the water, before taken....... same value
as to changes in location and mode of conducting American fish-

y years ago, we were largely interested in the Mackerel Fisheries
quite a fleet of vessels and which were largely employed in the
St Lawrence fisheries: of late years owing to the scarcity of Fish
se waters, &.the poorer quality of them, we have gradually aban-
the Fishing grounds there, and have employed our vessels on our
hores in Hook Fishing. but mostly with Seines, at the present
we shall not send a single vessel to the Bay of St Lawrence for
tching of Mackerel, for our vessels in those waters have not, of
aid their expenses, the two vessels employed by us the past sea-
the Bay of St. Lawrence, with large crews and employed during
ole season, landing only 165 & 70 Bbls. respectively.

ISAAC H BOARDMAN for
T. H BOARDMAN & CO.

rn and subscribed to before me, this twenty ninth day of May

[Seal.]

E. F. BARTLETT,
Notary Public

to the liberty conceded by the "Treaty of Washington" to the
ican Fishermen, to take Fish within three miles of the shores of
rovinces, it is, practically, of little value, inasmuch as most of their
erel are taken by our Fishermen outside of that line, and in our opin·
he liberty so granted, is much more than overbalanced by allowing
rovinces to import Fish of all descriptions into the markets of the
d States, free of duties, thus competing successfully with our own
rmen, together with the right to fish on our shores for Mackerel,
iich occupation they now are employed in seining on our Southern
) together with all other kinds of Fish including Bait, on which
rovince Fishermen in a great measure depend for their supply
the United States.—In my opinion, (and I speak now from an ex-
nce of more than forty years,) and that of many American Fisher-
ind owners of Fishing vessels with whom I have conversed, the
inces have by far, in a pecuniary point of view, an overwhelming
ntage already by the terms of the Treaty. In fact, the concession
to our Fishermen is of little pecuniary value, the only real benefit
e avoiding of conflicts between the American Fishermen and the
d Cruisers of the Provinces, by the former fishing on or near an
inary line, and by the seizure and condemnation of American ves-
in some instances, solely by the preponderance in numbers of evi-
in some instances, solely by the preponderance in numbers of evi-
e by the larger crews of the cruisers, which have heretofore been
out and maintained at a large expence to the Provincial or British
rnments, and thus creating trouble and hostile feeling between
ontending parties, and the people of both nations.—

I. H. BOARDMAN

wburyport Mass. May. 1877.

No. 80.

is is to certify, That the undersigned, composing the firm of Ire-
& Trefethen have been engaged in the fishing business for the past

Twenty three years, at Newburyport and that since the W
Treaty, so called, has been in effect, our vessels have been en
follows :

No. of Vessels employed................................
No. of Trips made.......................... Six yearly to e

No. of Trips to Bay St. Lawrence...... 1876 1875 1874
                                1   1   1

No. of Barrels of Mackerel from Bay St. 1876 1875 1874
  Lawrence 200   240   360

No. of Barrels of Mackerell caught within 3 miles of shore, i
  ing Magdalene Islands.................... Caught all off
Average value of Vessels each...........................
Average value of Outfits, Salt, Bait, &c........ 1000 Dollar:
Average value of Insurance.............. 9 per ct on Vesse
Average value of Captains' and Crews' time, viz., wages per
  mo.... ... .
Average value of Commissions, &c................. $200 e
Average value of Wharves, Fish-house, &c., for curing and i
  ing, including expenses of Clerks, Proprietors and labe
  shore ....
Number of Vessels lost............................
Value of Vessels lost, including outfits.................
Value of Fish lost
Number of Lives lost
Total value of Fish taken, before curing, splitting, salting, &
Total value of Mackerel taken, before curing, splitting, saltii
  bbl.
Total value of Fish taken within three miles of British shore
Total value of Mackerel do............................
Average market value of American Shore Mackerel...... $1
Average market value of Bay Mackerel................ $1
Average earnings of the operative fishermen per year...... $
Average amount paid in British ports for bait, ice, and vario
Amount paid to British fishermen for herring
Amount paid to British fishermen as wages
Amount paid in British ports for repairs
Locations frequented by American vessels for Fish..George
Locations frequented by American vessels
  for Mackerel....................... Cape May to Bay S
Actual value of Fish in the water, before taking ....
Actual value of Mackerel in the water, before taken.......
Facts as to changes in location and mode of conducting Am
  eries

We have had vessels in the Bay of St Lawrence for pa
We have now changed our business to Bank fisheries for C
dock as the Bay of St Lawrence has proved a failure our
paying us any profit. One of our firm has personally been
fishery and in one of our vessels. The inshore fisheries of th
is entirely useless to us.

GEORGE W TREI
for the firm

Sworn and subscribed to before me, this eighteenth day o
[Seal.]   E. F. BARTL
                                      Note

No. 81.

is to certify, That the undersigned, composing the firm of R.
& Son have been engaged in the fishing business for the past
years, at Newburyport and that since the Washington Treaty, so
has been in effect, our vessels have been employed as follows :

Vessels employed.............Two (2) Mackerel One Labrador
Trips made....................Four   "   Two   "
Trips to Bay St. Lawrence ....Four
Barrels of Mackerel from Bay St. Lawrence.....Seven hundred
Barrels of Mackerel caught within 3 miles of shore, not includ.
Magdalene Islands..........Quantity unknown, very few if any
ge value of vessels each ....:....Thirty-five hundred dolls
ge value of Outfits, Salt, Bait, &c....Thirty-two hundred dolls.
ge value of Insurance,
                Four and one quarter pr. cent a year for six months.
ge value of Captains' and Crews' time, viz., wages per mo.,
                        Capt $75.   Crew $28 Each
ge value of Commissions, &c.
                Two hund & fifty dolls ea. vessel ea. year
ge value of Wharves, Fish-houses, &c., for curing and packing,
uding expenses of Clerks, Proprietors and labor on shore
                        Ten thousand dolls.
er of Vessels lost............... ....One
of Vessels lost, including outfits............Ten thousand dolls

of Fish lost ....Eight thousand dolls.
ber of Lives lost .... .None
value of Fish taken, before curing, splitting, salting, &c. per cwt.
value of Mackerel taken, before curing, splitting, salting, &c., per

value of Fish taken within three miles of British shores
                        No fish, cannot estimate Mack.
value of Mackerel do.   "   "   "
age market value of American Shore Mackerel
                Eleven & a quarer dolls pr. bbl.
age market value of Bay Mackerel.Seven & one half dolls. pr. bbl.
age earnings of the operative fishermen per year
                        Two hundred & fifty dolls.
age amount paid in British ports for bait, ice, and various sup·
es....................... ....Two hundred dolls
int paid to British fishermen for Herring.....Two thousand dolls
ant paid to British fishermen as wages...Fourteen Hundred dolls.
ant paid in British ports for repairs....Two hundred & fifty dolls
tions frequented by American vessels for Fish
                Gulf & Bay of St Lawrence and Labrador Coast
tions frequented by American vessels for mackerel ·
                        Cape Henry to Eastport Me.
al value of Fish in the water, before taking············Nothing
al value of Mackerel in the water, before taken·········Nothing
as to changes in location and mode of conducting American fish·
es
have employed our vessels in the Shore, Bay of St Lawrence and
ador fisheries during the past ten years and the business has
d so unremunerative and hazardous that we have abandoned it.

The Labrador fishery we consider very uncertain busines‹
very great more especially when the vessels are compelec
in the fall, as is the case most of the time in latter years
fill up if possible with herring, which have to be procured
dent fishermen

                                R. BAYLEY ‹

Sworn and subscribed to before me, this Twenty third
1877
                                J. T. BR
    (Seal.)   No₁

                        No. 82.

This is to certify, That the undersigned, composing the fi
O. Currier have been engaged in the fishing business for ₁
years, at Newburyport, Mass. and that since the Washingt
called, has been in effect, our vessels have been employed

No. of Vessels employed ....
No. of Trips made
No. of Trips to Bay St. Lawrence............................
No. of Barrels of Mackerel from Bay St. Lawrence.........
No. of Barrels of Mackerel caught within 3 miles of shore
    including Magdalen Islands ....
Average value of Vessels each.............................
Average value of outfits, Salt, Bait, &c...................
Average value of Insurance .. ..
Average value of Captains' and Crews' time, viz., wages per
                                                        $
Average value of Commissions, &c........... $250 pr yea
Average value of Wharves, Fish-houses, &c., for curing
    packing, including expenses of Clerks, Proprietors and ₁
    on shore ....
Number of Vessels lost
Value of Vessels lost, including outfits
Value of Fish lost
Number of Lives lost
Total value of Fish taken, before curing, splitting, salting,
Total value of Mackerel taken, before curing, splitting, sal
    bbl. ....
Total value of Fish taken within three miles of British sho
Total value of Mackerel do............................
Average market value of American Shore Mackerel
                        No 1 $17.00   No 2 $11.5
Average market value of Bay Mackerel
                        No 1. $11.00   No 2 $7.0
Average earnings of the operative fishermen per year....
Average amount paid in British ports for bait, ice, and
    plies ....
Amount paid to British fishermen for herring
Amount paid to British fishermen as wages
Amount paid in British ports for repairs...... $30.00 pr ₁
Locations frequented by American vessels for Fish
Locations frequented by American vessels for Mackerel
                From Cape May to Gd Menan & Bay
Actual value of Fish in the water, before taking
Actual value of Mackerel in the water, before taken

as to changes in location and mode of conducting American fish-

ccount of the uncertainty of the Bay fishing, most of the New-
rt Vessels gave up that fishing about twelve years ago, and en-
in the coast fishing, using Seines instead of hook and lines, doing
ousiness, while those who continued the Bay Mackerelling, have
losing business, and will mostly give up, and enter the Shore
;

　　　　　　　　　　　　　CHAS. O. CURRIER

rn and subscribed to before me, this twenty-first day of May

.l.)　　　　　　　　　　E. F. BARTLETT
　　　　　　　　　　　　　　　Notary Public

No. 83.

s is to certify, That the undersigned, composing the firm of Union
f Co have been engaged in the fishing business for the past Thirty
　at Provincetown Mass and that since the Washington Treaty, so
, has been in effect, our vessels have been employed as follows:

Vessels employed .... Seventeen
Trips made.. Sixty-Eight
Trips to Bay St. Lawrence .... Six since 1871
Barrels of Mackerel from Bay St. Lawrence
　　　　　　　　　　　　　　　　Twelve hundred bbls
f Barrels of Mackerel caught within 3 miles of shore, not includ-
Magdalene Islands...................... .... None
age value of Vessels each................. Five Thousand dollars
age value of Outfits, Salt, Bait, &c .... One thousand dollars
age value of Insurance..... .... Four thousand dollars
age value of Captains' and Crews' time, viz., wages per mo
　　　　　　　　　　　　　　　　　　Thirty dollars
age value of Commissions, &c.......... Four % to Caps of Vessel
age value of Wharves, Fish-houses, &c., for curing and packing,
ding expenses of Clerks, Proprietors and labor on shore
　　　　　　　　　　　　　　　Twenty five thousand dolls.
ber of Vessels lost.. .... One
e of vessels lost, including outfits.......... Five thousand dollars
e of Fish lost..................................... .... None
ber of lives Lost..................................... .... None
l value of Fish taken, before curing, splitting, salting, &c. per cwt.
　　　　　　　　　　　　　　　　　　One dollar
l value of Mackerel taken, before curing, splitting, salting, &c., per
bbl... Two dollars
l value of Fish taken within three miles of British shores... None
l value of Mackerel do .... None
rage market value of American Shore Mackerel........ Ten dollars
rage market value of Bay Mackerel............ Eight dollars pr bbl
rage earnings of the operative fishermen per year
　　　　　　　　　　　　Two hundred twenty five dollars
rage amount paid in British ports for bait, ice, and various supplies
　　　　　　　　　　　　　　　　　Fifty dollars
unt paid to British fishermen for herring.................... None
unt paid to British fishermen as wages.................. None
unt paid in British ports for repairs ....One hundred dollars

Locations frequented by American vessels for Fish
     Georgies. Block Island. Ea:
Locations frequented by American vessels for Mackerel
     Coast of United States & Gulf S
Actual value of Fish in the water, before taking ....
Actual value of Mackerel in the water, before taken........
Facts as to changes in location and mode of conducting Am
eries Within the last three years we have had but two
gaged in Fishing in British Waters and they for Mackerel &
Mackerel fishing being done on the Coast of the United St
along the Eastern Coast of Maine and on Georges Bank—n(
to British Waters at all. The Gulf of St Lawrence Fishe
profitable that we consider it a failure

    E M DYER
    B O GROSS
    A. T. WILLIAMS.
    LUTHER NICKERSON
         } UNION V

Sworn and subscribed to before me, this Eleventh day of]
(Seal.)   THOS. HILLI,
              Nota

No. 84.

This is to certify, That the undersigned, composing the firm
Wharf Co formerly R. E. & A. Nickerson & Co. & E. S. S
have been engaged in the fishing business for the past twen'
Provincetown, Mass. and that since the Washington Treat
has been in effect, our vessels have been employed as follow

No. of vessels employed
    Six to twelve (viz some years 6, other years u
No. of Trips made.................. five to seven yearly to |
No. of Trips to Bay St. Lawrence ....none
No. of Barrels of Mackerel from Bay St. Lawrence.....none
No. of Barrels of Mackerel caught within 3 miles of shore, n(
  Magdalene Islands any since 1873, but few inside of 3 mi'
            18'
Average value of Vessels each............ Forty five hun(
Average value of Outfits, Salt, Bait, &c..........2500$ to
Average value of Insurance ....
Average value of Captains' and Crews' time, viz., wages pe
         Captain 65.$
Average value of Commissions, &c.................. 200$
Average value of Wharves, Fish-houses, &c., for curing a1
 including expenses of Clerks, Proprietors and labor on sh
Number of Vessels lost ....
Value of Vessels lost, including outfits..................
Value of Fish lost ....
Number of Lives lost ....
Total value of Fish taken, before curing, splitting, salting,
           one dollar
Total value of Mackerel taken, before curing, splitting, &
 per bbl..
Total value of Fish taken within three miles of British shor(
Total value of Mackerel do .... $10. delivered at Provin
Average market value of American Shore Mackerel
        No. 1s $16. No 2 $

e market value of Bay Mackerel

No 1. $12. No 2. $8. No 3. $6. (our average in 1872. $10.20

e earnings of the operative fishermen per year

$225 at our place

e amount paid in British ports for bait, ice, and various sup.

i250 each Vessel including wages paid their—(total for 9 Vessels ald be 2250,$

t paid to British fishermen for herring ....none

t paid to British fishermen as wages ....100,$ per-year

t paid in British ports for repairs

thus far small repairs, but liable to large in case of accident

ns frequented by American vessels for Fish

Grand, Western & Georges Banks

ns frequented by American vessels for Mackerel

from Cape May to Eastport, and Georges Banks

value of Fish in the water, before taking..............Nothing

value of Mackerel in the water, before taken ....Nothing

s to changes in location and mode of conducting American fish-

ave sent no Vessels into the Bay of St. Laurence for Mackerel i73 and only two for Codfish, The facts are we do find the fish-iness, (more especially for Mackerel in the Bay of St Lawrence) , pay, that is our experience and is the only reason that we have wholy discontinued sending our Vessels their, and than again el takeing their are not as Valuable as those taken on our Coast, ing grounds are far distant, bad weather sets in much earlier an on our Coast, makeing it more hazardous, also as most of the el now are taken with Seines and we consider the Bay a very place for Seining. We consider the fishing grounds in Bay of rence inside of three miles from Shore (especially for Mackerel) lly useless to us, and would not fit a Vessel under any consider-)oking to that locality for the success of their Voyage

CENTRAL WHARF CO by A. NICKERSON

ATKINS NICKERSON
JAMES A. SMALL
ABNER B. RICH
NATHAN YOUNG
} Central Wharf Co.

:ribed and sworn to before me this ninth day of June A. D. 1877 al.) B. F. HUTCHINSON
Notary Public

No. 85.

is to certify, That the undersigned, composing the firm of H &. & Co have been engaged in the fishing business for the past five years, at Provincetown Mass and that since the Washing-aty, so called, has been in effect, our vessels have been employed ws :

7essels employed...Eight

[rips made................... one trip yearly total Eight Trips

[rips to Bay St. Lawrence One Trip in 1876 Cod Fishing (Failure)

3arrels of Mackerel from Bay St. Lawrence ....None

Barrels of Mackerel caught within 3 miles of shore, not includ-[agdalene Islands...None

98 F

Average value of Vessels each..................Five Thou

Average value of Outfits, Salt, Bait, &c..........$3,000 t

Average value of Insurance ....$248.0(

Average value of Captains' and Crews' time, viz., wages p
.   . $40)

Average value of Commissions, &c....... ....$50

Average value of Wharves, Fish-houses, &c., for curing ɛ
including expenses of Clerks, Proprietors and labor on
shore...........................$1.2.000 Twelve Thou

Number of vessels lost....................................

Value of Vessels lost, including outfits
$14,000 Fourteen Thou

Value of Fish lost...................$12,000 Twelve Thou

No. of Lives lost ....

Total value of Fish taken, before curing, splitting, salting,
cwt ....75 cts Seven

Total value of Mackerel taken, before curing, splitting,
per bbl.

Total value of Fish taken within three miles of British sho

Total value of Mackerel do..............................

Average market value of American Shore Mackerel

Average market value of Bay Mackerel

Average earnings of the operative fishermen per year.....

Average amount paid in British ports for bait, ice, and var

Amount paid to British fishermen for herring............

Amount paid to British fishermen as wages........... $(

Amount paid in British ports for repairs

Locations frequented by American vessels for Fish
From Long Island to ɴ

Locations frequented by American vessels for Mackerel

Actual value of Fish in the water, before taking ....

Actual value of Mackerel in the water, before taken

Facts as to changes in location and mode of conducting
eries

For the last fifteen years we have sent two vessels only
St Lawerenc Cod Fishing and both voyages proved a fail
past eight or ten years the fishing in the Bay St Laweren
no profit to us for neither Cod or Mackeral Fishing, and t
was nearly a Total failure. the Mackerel Fishing is carr
Seining and our vessels at Provincetown do better at
home, our cod Fishermen do not fish in British limits, a
pay for our Mackerel Fishermen,

H & S C

Sworn and subscribed to before me, this Ninth day of
(Seal.)   THOS. H
ɴ

No. 86.

This is to certify, That the undersigned, composing the
Freeman have been engaged in the fishing business for
years, at Provincetown Mass and that since the Washin‹
called, has been in effect, our vessels have been employe

No. of Vessels employed.......................... .....

No. of Trips made...................................

No. of Trips to Bay St. Lawrence........ ten in five ye

rels of Mackerel from Bay St. Lawrence..... ..... none
:rels of Mackerel caught within 3 miles of shore, not
g Magdalene Islands...:.......................... none
alue of Vessels each............................... $4,000.
alue of Outfits, Salt, Bait, &c..... $2000 Each vessell yearly
alue of Insurance................................ $150
·alue of Captains' and Crews' time, viz., wages per mo. $35,00
alue of Commissions, &c.............. 100 Each vessell yearly
·alue of Wharves, Fish-houses, &c., for curing and
, including expenses of Clerks, Proprietors and labor
Ə... $15,000
f Vessels lost...................................... none
Vessels lost, including outfits...................... One
Fish lost
f Lives lost
ιe of Fish taken, before curing, splitting, salting, &c.
.... $1,00
ιe of Mackerel taken, before curing, splitting, salting,
r bbl..................................... $2,00
ιe of Fish taken within three miles of British shores. none
ιe of Mackerel do............................... none

	No 1	No 2	No 3
narket value of American Shore Mackerel	$16,	$12,	$8,

	No 1	No 2	No 3
market value of Bay Mackerel..........	12,	$8,	$6,

earnings of the operative fishermen per year........ $200,
amount paid in British ports for bait, ice, and various
s.. nothing
)aid to British fishermen for herring................. nothing
)aid to British fishermen as wages.................. nothing
)aid in British ports for repairs.................... nothing
. frequented by American vessels for Fish
. Western and Grand Bank Georges & Block Island
, frequented by American vessels for Mackerel
American Shores Bay St Laurence
ιlue of Fish in the water, before taking............ nothing
.lue of Mackerel in the water, before taken......... nothing
:o changes in location and mode of conducting Amer·
ιeries
;heries have changed from shore fishing to deep sea and Bank
number of Vessels sent to Bay St Laurence from this port last
ng on Bank Bradley on Orphen and did not pay expenses
·t use the British wortes in side of thre miles for any fisherys

F M FREEMAN

and subscribed to before me, this ninth day of May 1877 Be·
ubscriber a Notary Public for the County of Barnstable
B F HUTCHINSON
Notary Public

No. 87.

to certify, That the undersigned, composing the firm of Free-
Hilliard have been engaged in the fishing business for the past

Twenty years, at Provincetown and that since the Washin,
so called, has been in effect, our vessels have been emp
lows :

No. of Vessels employed
No. of Trips made
No. of Trips to Bay St. Lawrence
No. of Barrels of Mackerel from Bay St. Lawrence
No. of Barrels of Mackerel caught within 3 miles of shore
    ing Magdalene Islands
Average value of Vessels each
Average value of Outfits, Salt, Bait, &c.
Average value of Insurance
Average value of Captains' and Crews' time, viz., wages p
Average value of Commissions, &c.
Average value of Wharves, Fish-houses, &c., for curing a
    including expenses of Clerks, Proprietors and labor on sl
Number of Vessels lost
Value of Vessels lost, including outfits
Value of Fish lost
Number of Lives lost
Total value of Fish taken, before curing, splitting, salting,
Total value of Mackerel taken, before curing, splitting, salt
    bbl.
Total value of Fish taken within three miles of British sho
Total value of Mackerel do.
Average market value of American Shore Mackerel
Average market value of Bay Mackerel
Average earnings of the operative fishermen per year
Average amount paid in British .ports for bait, ice, and
    plies
Amount paid to British fishermen for herring
Amount paid to British fishermen as wages
Amount paid in British ports for repairs
Locations frequented by American vessels for Fish
Locations frequented by American vessels for Mackerel
Actual value of Fish in the water, before taking
Actual value of Mackerel in the water, before taken
Facts as to changes in location and mode of conducting A
    eries

    For eight years last past we have sent our fishing vesse
seven in number to the Grand Banks. During this time
a vessel to the Gulf of St. Lawrence for fishing purposes,
that we have been unable to calculate upon any profit wh
sult from such voyages.
    N. D. FREEMAN ,
    J. D. HILLIARD   FREEMAN & I

    Sworn and subscribed to before me, this Eleventh day
    (Seal.)   THOS. HII
                                           N

                            No. 88.

    This is to certify, That the undersigned, composin
Crocker & Atwood have been engaged in the fishing bu
past fourteen years, at Provincetown and that since th

o called, has been in effect, our vessels have been employed as

essels employed..Five
ips made...................about five trips each vessel yearly
rips to Bay St. Lawrence...............................None
arrels of Mackerel from Bay St. Lawrence..............None
arrels of Mackerel caught within 3 miles of shore, not including
lene Islands..None
  value of Vessels each................Five Thousand Dollars
  value of Outfits, Salt, Bait, &c...$2500. on each vessel yearly
  value of Insurance.................$300. on   "   "   "
  value of Captains' and Crews' time, viz., wages per mo...$30.
lan per month
  value of Commissions, &c..........$250. each vessel yearly
  value of Wharves, Fish-houses, &c., for curing and packing,
ing expenses of Clerks, Proprietors and labor on shore..$3500.

of Vessels lost.......................................Two
Vessels lost, including outfits.....................$11,000.
Fish lost...$150.
of Lives lost...None
lue of Fish taken, before curing, splitting, salting, &c., per cwt.

lue of Mackerel taken, before curing, splitting, salting, &c., per
....2\frac{48}{100}$
lue of Fish taken within three miles of British shores....None
lue of Mackerel do....................................None
market value of American Shore Mackerel
market value of Bay Mackerel
earnings of the operative fishermen per year 0
amount paid in British ports for bait, ice, and various supplies
  paid to British fishermen for herring
  paid to British fishermen as wages
  paid in British ports for repairs
is frequented by American vessels for Fish
                    Massachusetts Bay and Nantucket Shoals
is frequented by American vessels for Mackerel
                    American Shores north of Cape May.
value of Fish in the water, before taking............Valuless
value of Mackerel in the water, before taken......... do
to changes in location and mode of conducting American fish-

essels being engaged in the Mackerel Seining business almost
ely and as they could not Seine fish in British Waters we were
to fish on the American coast.
                              CROCKER & ATWOOD

and subscribed to before me, this ninth day of May 1877
                              B F HUTCHINSON
l.)   *Notary Public*

No. 89.

s to certify, That the undersigned, composing the firm of E &
ok, having been engaged in the fishing business for the past
ars, at Provincetown and that since the Washington Treaty,
l, has been in effect, our vessels have been employed as follows:

No. of Vessels employed ....
No. of Trips made
No. of Trips to Bay St. Lawrence.........................
No. of Barrels of Mackerel from Bay St. Lawrence...........
No. of Barrels of Mackerel caught within 3 miles of shore, not
     including Magdalene Islands............................
Average value of Vessels each............................
Average value of Oufits, Salt, Bait, &c....................$8
Average value of Insurance.................$100 each vess
Average value of Captains' and Crews' time, viz., wages per
     mo..
Average value of Commissions, &c........................
Average value of Wharves, Fish-houses, &c., for curing and
     packing, including expenses of Clerks, Proprietors and labor
     on shore..
Number of Vessels lost ....
Value of Vessels lost, including outfits...................
Value of Fish lost......................................
Number of Lives lost...................................
Total value of Fish taken, before curing, splitting, salting, &c
     per cwt ....
Total value of Mackerel taken, before curing, splitting, salting
     &c., per bbl ....
Total value of Fish taken within three miles of British shores.
Total value of Mackerel do..............................
Average market value of American Shore Mackerel
                  No. $16.   no 2. $1 2   no 3. $
Average market value of Bay Mackerel. sold for no 1. $11.n
Average earnings of the operative fishermen per year ....
Average amount paid in British ports for bait, ice, and variou
     supplies
Amount paid to British fishermen for herring...............
Amount paid to British fishermen as wages...............
Amount paid in British ports for repairs ....
Locations frequented by American vessels for Fish..Banks i
     land Western & Georgies.
Locations frequented by American vessels for Mackerel...Lo
     Sound to Bay St Lawrence
Actual value of Fish in the water, before taking............
Actual value of Mackerel in the water, before taken.........
Facts as to changes in location and mode of conducting Ame
     ican fisheries

     The Mackerel Fisheries have changed very much during t
years   formerly the fish were caught with Line & Hook bu
universal way to take them is with Seins   The Cod fisheries
very materially changed   the Cod fish were formerly taken
line & Hook but Trawls are now mostly used.   Our Vessels
take their fish from the Banks of New Foundland we have
Bay fishing but with us it did not pay.   Our Mackerl fishe
them fish in American Waters for the reason that the Bay fi
not pay them. as the Mackerel are not near as plenty nor ‹
good a quality as they can find nearer home

                                            E. P

Sworn an l subscribed to before me, this tenth day of May
(Seal.)   THOS. HILLI
                                              Nota

No. 90.

to certify, That the undersigned, composing the firm of J & L
have been engaged in the fishing business for the past Sixteen
Provincetown Mass. and that since the Washington Treaty, so
is been in effect, our vessels have been employed as follows :

ssels employed... Seven

rips made..................One Trip yearly total Seven trips

rips to Bay St. Lawrence none $\frac{1871}{2}$ $\frac{1872}{2}$ $\frac{1873}{2}$ $\frac{1874}{2}$ $\frac{1875}{2}$ $\frac{1876}{2}$

                               total 6 yrs 12 vessels.

arrels of Mackerel from Bay St. Lawrence .... none
arrels of Mackerel caught within 3 miles of shore, not
ng Magdalene Islands .... none
value of Vessels each..................Four thousand dollars
of Outfits, Salt, Bait, &c.................$2000. to each vessel
value of Insurance......................$240. each vessel
value of Captains' and Crews' time, viz., wages per mo.. $35.
value of Commissions, &c .... $50.
value of Wharves, Fish-houses, &c., for curing and
g, including expenses of Clerks, Proprietors and labor
re.. $10,'000
of Vessels lost...................................... none
: Vessels lost, including outfits
'Fish lost .... none
of Lives lost.. one
lue of Fish taken, before curing, splitting, salting, &c.
rt .... 75 cts.
lue of Mackerel taken, before curing, splitting, salting,
er bbl
lue of Fish taken within three miles of British shores none
lue of Mackerel do .... none
market value of American Shore Mackerel
market value of Bay Mackerel
earnings of the operative fishermen per year........... $200.
amount paid in British ports for bait, ice, and various supplies
                     $200 each vessel $400. yearly
paid to British fishermen for herring................ nothing
paid to British fishermen as wages .. ..$400. yearly
paid in British ports for repairs .... $100.
is frequented by American vessels for Fish
m Long Island to Newfoundland including Bay of St Lawrence
is frequented by American vessels for Mackerel
value of Fish in the water, before taking .... nothing
value of Mackerel in the water, before taken
to changes in location and mode of conducting American fish-

le past Sixteen years we have sent two vessels to Gulf of St
ce. their voyages have not been as remunerative as those of
els that have fished in other localities The last year 1876. the
in the Bay of St Lawrence were almost a total failure. No fish
n by our vessels inside of British limits.

                              J & L N PAINE

l and subscribed to before me, this ninth day of May 1877 Be-
Subscriber a Notary Public for the County of Barnstable
)   B F HUTCHINSON
                            Notary Public

No. 91.

This is to certify, That the undersigned, composing the firᴅ
A Wborf have been engaged in the fishing business for the ᵱ
years, at Provincetown Mass and that since the Washington
called, has been in effect, our vessels have been employed as

No. of Vessels employed ....
No. of Trips made .... One average time fi
No. of Trips to Bay St. Lawrence
No. of Barrels of Mackerel from Bay St. Lawrence ....⸗
No. of Barrels of Mackerel caught within 3 miles of shore, not
  Magdalene Islands ......⸗.............................⸗
Average value of Vessels each ......:....................⸗
Average value of Outfits, Salt, Bait, &c.. $2,000 yearly pr e
Average Insurance.... On each vessel $1500, Outfits insuɪ
  amount
Average value of Captains' and Crews' time, viz., wages per m
Average value of Commissions, &c........ $ι00, Each vesse
Average value of Wharves, Fish-houses, &c., for curing anɩ
  including expenses of Clerks, Proprietors and labor on sho
Number of Vessels lost ....:................⸗
Value of Vessels lost, including outfits
Value of Fish lost
Number of Lives lost ....⸗
Total value of Fish taken, before curing, splitting, saltinɪ
  cwt..⸗⸗.........⸗
Total value of Mackerel taken, before curing, splitting, saɪ
  per bbl.......................⸗..................⸗ .
Total value of Fish taken within three miles of British shores
Total value of Mackerel do ....
Average market value of American Shore Mackerel...No 1
  $12, No 3s $8.
Average market value of Bay Mackerel....No 1 $12, No 2 $
Average earnings of the operative fishermen per year ......
Average amount paid in British ports for bait, ice, and vᶐ
  plies ....⸗
Amount paid to British fishermen for herring
Amount paid to British fishermen as wages
Amount paid in British ports for repairs
Locations frequented by American vessels for Fish
                              Western, and Gr
Locations frequented by American vessels for Mackerel
                         American shores Bay S
Actual value of Fish in the water, before taking............
Actual value of Mackerel in the water, before taken ....
Facts as to changes in location and mode of conducting
  fisheries

  .In my experience Bay fishing in British waters has been v
itable and in many cases tended with loss.both to owners
Our fishing consists largely of Western and Grand Bank fi
of the smaller vessels fishing around our own shores .
  Do not use the British waters inside of three miles ·

                                   P A

Sᴡorn and subscribed to before me, this ninth day of Ma,
(Seal.)   B F HUTCHIN
                               Nota

No. 92.

certify, That the undersigned, composing the firm of B. A.
have been engaged in the fishing business for the past
·s. at Provincetown and that since the Washington Treaty,
ıs been in effect, our vessels have been employed as follows:

els employed.......................................5
ı made.................................5 per year
ı to Bay St. Lawrence ....none for 7 years
els of Mackerel caught within 3 miles of shore, not includ·
alene Islands
lue of Vessels each....·.....................$3000.00
lue of Outfits, Salt, Bait, &c.............$2500,00 per year
lue of Insurance....................$400,00 " "
lue of Captains' and Crews' time, viz., wages per mo..$35.00
lue of Commissions, &c..................$250.00 per year
lue of Wharves, Fish-houses. &c., for curing and packing,
· expenses of Clerks, Proprietors and labor on shore.$8000.00
Vessels lost...None
essels lost, including outfits
sh lost
Lives lost.....................................One
, of Fish taken, before curing, splitting, salting, &c. per cwt.
ı of Mackerel taken, before curing, splitting, salting, &c., per

, of Fish taken within three miles of British shores
ı of Mackerel do.
arket value of American Shore Mackerel
arket value of Bay Mackerel
ırnings of the operative fishermen per year
nount paid in British ports for bait, ice, and various supplies
ıid to British fishermen for herring
ıid to British fishermen as wages
ıid in British ports for repairs
requented by American vessels for Fish.......Grand Banks
requented by American vessels for Mackerel
ue of Fish in the water, before taking
ue of Mackerel in the water, before taken
changes in location and mode of conducting American fisheries
ithin 7 or 8 years we sent vessels in St Lawrence bay for
Our experience was that vessels that went there done noth·
not pay their expences, So we sent our vessels seineing off
ıores and found they done much better, This is the expe-
ll who sent vessels for Mackerel in the bay from Provincetown
B. A. LEWIS

nd subscribed to before me, this tenth day of May 1877
THOS. HILLIARD
Notary Public

No. 93.

.o certify, That the undersigned, composing the firm of David
ave been engaged in the fishing business for the past Twenty
at Provincetown Mass and that since the Washington Treaty,
has been in effect, our vessels have been employed as follows:

No. of Vessels employed ....
No. of Trips made................................... o
No. of Trips to Bay St. Lawrence........................
No. of Barrels of Mackerel from Bay St. Lawrence........
No. of Barrels of Mackerel caught within 3 miles of shor
   ing Magdalene Islands.................................
Average value of Vessels each............. Forty five Hu
Average value of Outfits, Salt, Bait, &c. Two Thousand doll
Average value of Insurance.........Two hundred dollar
Average value of Captains' and Crews' time, viz., wages
Average value of Commissions, &c
                 One Hundred Twenty doll
Average value of Wharves, Fish-houses, &c., for curing
   including expenses of Clerks, Proprietors and labor on s
                 Fifteen thousand
Number of Vessels lost................................
Value of Vessels lost, including outfits ....
Value of Fish lost ....
Number of Lives lost..................................
Total value of Fish taken, before curing, splitting, sal
   cwt ....
Total value of Mackerel taken, before curing, splitting, sa
   bbl ....
Total value of Fish taken within three miles of British sh
Total value of Mackerel do ....
Average market value of American Shore Mackerel
                 I sold for $1
Average market value of Bay Mackerel...................
Average earnings of the operative fishermen per year. $150,
Average amount paid in British ports for bait, ice, and va
Amount paid to British fishermen for herring
Amount paid to British fishermen as wages
Amount paid in British ports for repairs
Locations frequented by American vessels for Fish
         Grand Banks La Have &
Locations frequented by American vessels for Mackerel
              Cape May t
Actual value of Fish in the water, before taking ....
Actual value of Mackerel in the water, before taken.....
Facts as to changes in location and mode of conducting
   eries

   In regard to Fishing in British waters for the past Seve
not (in general) been profitable, Codfish have been plenti
and the prices for new fish being better than for fish
time. I have keep my Vessels on the home grounds and
I have sent no vessels to the Bay of St Lawerance thi
neather have my Vessels taken Codfish or mackeral inside
British limets

                     DAVID

Sworn and subscribed to before me, this tenth day of
   (Seal.)   THOS. HIL
                          N

No. 94.

   This is to certify, That the undersigned, composing t
tral Wharf Company have been engaged in the fishing

teen years, at Wellfleet and that since the Washington Treaty,
has been in effect, our vessels have been employed as follows:

essels employed .... Thirteen 13
rips made .... 4 to Each vessel yearly

	1872	1873	1874	1875	1876
1ps to Bay St. Lawrence......	0	4	0	1	1
arrels of Mackerel from Bay St. Lawrence....	450	75		45	

1873 1875 1876

arrels of Mackerel caught within 3 miles of shore, not including
ilene Islands......................... all caught at Magdeline
value of Vessels each .... $5,500.
value of Outfits, Salt, Bait, &c...................... $2400.
value of Insurance........................... 711 Ea vessel
value of Captains' and Crews' time, viz., wages per mo
                                      $35. Pr Month
value of Commissions, &c.............. $200. to Each vessel
value of Wharves, Fish-houses, &c., for curing and packing,
ing expenses of Clerks, Proprietors and labor on shore..$15.000
of Vessels lost .... one vessel at Bay St. Lawrence
Vessels lost, including outfits....................... $7.900.
f Fish lost.................................... $2000.
of Lives lost....................................... One.
alue of Fish taken, before curing, splitting, salting, &c. per
.... 75 cts $2.00
ilue of Mackerel taken, before curing, splitting, salting, &c. per
.... $2.00
ilue of Fish taken within three miles of British shores·· None
ilue of Mackerel do................................. None
e market value of American Shore Mackerel.... 16.00 12.00 8.00
e market value of Bay Mackerel.............. 12.00. 8.00. 6.00
e earnings of the operative fishermen per year
                                  $125.00 at our place
e amount paid in British ports for bait, ice, and various sup‐
.... Nothing
t paid to British fishermen for herring.... .... Nothing
t paid to British fishermen as wages................. None
t paid in British ports for repairs.................... None
ns frequented by American vessels for Fish
                              Grand Banks & Georges
ns frequented by American vessels for Mackerel
                              From Cape May to Mt. Desert
value of Fish in the water, before taking............. Nothing
value of Mackerel in the water, before taken......... Nothing
s to changes in location and mode of conducting American fish-

he past ten years fishing in British waters has been unprofitable.
ifine our business to American waters entirely now. We could
cure an american crew to fish in Bay of St Lawrence. The res-
it have been sent there have made an entire failure and great
their owners & fitters. Our business is strictly confined to Mack-
hing. Our Shore Mackerel are of much better quality & bring
arger prices than the bay Mackerel.
PHEN YOUNG agt Cent Whf Co

n and subscribed to before me, this 10 day of May 1877
                              THOMAS KEMP
eal.)   Notary Public

No. 95.

This is to certify, That the undersigned, composing the firm
cial Wharf Co. have been engaged in the fishing business
Twenty five years, at Wellfleet and that since the Washir
so called, has been in effect, our vessels have been employe

No. of Vessels employed....................................
No. of Trips made...................................... Fc
No. of Trips to Bay St. Lawrence.................... Nor
No. of Barrels of Mackerel from Bay St Lawrence........
No. of Barrels of Mackerel caught within 3 miles of shore
   cluding Magdalene Islands............................
Average value of Vessels each ....
Average value of Outfits, Salt, Bait, &c.............. $20
Average value of Insurance......................... $7
Average value of Captains' and Crews' time, viz., wages per
Average value of Commissions, &c.......................
Average value of Wharves, Fish-houses, &c., for curing and
   cluding expenses of Clerks, Proprietors and labor on sh
Number of Vessels lost.................................
Value of Vessels lost, including outfits...................
Value of Fish lost..................... ....
Number of lives lost....................................
Total value of Fish taken, before curing, splitting, salting, &
   cwt..
Total value of Mackerel taken, before curing, splitting salt
   per bbl...
Total value of Fish taken within three miles of British sho
Total value of Mackerel do............................
Average market value of American Shore Mackerel.... 16
Average market value of Bay Mackerel.. ....
Average earnings of the operative fishermen per year......
Average amount paid in British ports for bait, ice, and vari
   plies..
Amount paid to British fishermen for herring...........
Amount paid to British fishermen as wages.............
Amount paid in British ports for repairs...... ....
Locations frequented by American vessels for Fish
                                        Grand Ba
Location frequented by American vessels for Mackerel
                                    Cape Hery &
Actual value of Fish in the water, before taking
Actual value of Mackerel in the water, before taken
Facts as to changes in location and mode of conducting A
   eries

By reasons of entire change in mode of Catching Mack
Hook and line to Seine, The Mackl fishing in the Bay of S
not prosecuted by our fishermen the waters of the Gulf are r
for Seining owing to shallowness and tendency of the fi
the shores, which entirely precludes the possibillity of ta
quantities

                                   NOA

Sworn and subscribed to before me, this 14th day of Ma
(Seal.)   THOS
                                      N

No. 96.

certify, That the undersigned, composing the firm of Mer-
arf Co have been engaged in the fishing business for the past
s, at Wellfleet and that since the Washington Treaty, so
been in effect, our vessels have been employed as follows:

sels employed.............................. Twenty (20)
s made....... .... 4 to Each vessel yearly

	1872	1873	1874	1875	1876
s to Bay St. Lawrence....	0 trips	4	0	0	0

els of Mackerel from Bay St. Lawrence............ 800 Bb
els of Mackerel caught within 3 miles of shore, not including
ne Islands.........None   caught near Magdaliu Islands
alue of Vessels each..................... .... $6500,
alue of Outfits, Salt, Bait, &c.............. $2500, Each
alue of Insurance....................... ..... $800, Each vessel
alue of Captains' and Crews' time, viz., wages per mo.. $35,
alue of Commissions, &c.............. .... $200 Each vessel
alue of Wharves, Fish-houses, &c., for curing and packing.
g expenses of Clerks, Proprietors and labor on shore. $48,000
Vessels lost... One
essels lost, including outfits....................... $9,000
ish lost.................................... ....None
Lives lost.................................. ....None
e of Fish taken, before curing, splitting, salting, &c., per
.... 75 cts
e of Mackerel taken, before curing, splitting, salting, &c., per
....$2.00
e of Fish taken within three miles of British shores.··Nothing
e of Mackerel do····························· ············Nothing

	16.00	12.00	8.00
narket value of American Shore Mackerel.···	1	2	3
	1	2	3
narket value of Bay Mackerel·············	12.00	8.00	6.00

arnings of the operative fishermen per year............$150.
amount paid in British ports for bait, ice, and various sup'
.... $200 since the Treaty
aid to British fishermen for herring················....Nothing
aid to British fishermen as wages················....Nothing
aid in British ports for repairs·····················.....None
frequented by American vessels for Fish
                                We send none fishing
frequented by American vessels for Mackerel
                                From Cape May to Mt. Desert
alue of Fish in the water, before taking.............Nothing
alue of Mackerel in the water, before taken..........Nothing
o changes in location and mode of conducting American fish-

ve sent no vessels to Bay of St. Lawrence since 1873, that year
our, they did not pay expenses.   We lost money on every vessel.
t time knowing that the business in Bay of St. Lawrence could
profitable we have confined our fishing business entirely to the
waters. The shore Mackerel being of better quality, bring
rices & we take them with *Seines*, seldom using hook & Lines.

We do not in future propose to use English waters for ou
ness. We could not ship an American crew for such a pur
JESSE H. FRE
Agnt Mercanti

Sworn and subscribed to before me, this 9th day of May
(Seal.)　　　　　　　　　　　　THOMA
N

No. 97.

This is to certify, That the undersigned, composing the
Nickerson have been engaged in the fishing business for 1
years, at Dennisport and that since the Washington Tre
has been in effect, our vessels having been employed as f

No. of Vessels employed ....
No. of Trips made.....................................
No. of Trips to Bay St. Lawrence ....
No. of Barrels of Mackerel from Bay St. Lawrence......
No. of Barrels of Mackerel caught within 3 miles of shoi
ing Magdalene Islands ....
Average value of Vessels each........................
Average value of Outfits, Salt, Bait, &c ....
Average value of Insurance.................... $625. 1
Average value of Captains' and Crews' time, viz., wages 1
Average value of Commissions, &c............... $250. 1
Average value of Wharves, Fish-house, &c., for curing
including expenses of Clerks, Proprietors and labor on sl
Number of Vessels lost
Value of Vessels lost, including outfits
Value of Fish lost
Number of Lives lost
Total value of Fish taken, before curing, splitting, salting
Total value of Mackerel taken, before curing, splitting,
per bbl......................................
Total value of Fish taken within three miles of British sl
Total value of Mackerel do ....
Average market value of American Shore Mackerel. $16.0
Average market value of Bay Mackerel..,..............
Average earnings of the operative fishermen per year..$15
Average amount paid in British ports for bait, ice, an
plies ....
Amount paid to British fishermen for herring...........
Amount paid to British fishermen as wages.............
Amount paid in British ports for repairs ....
Locations frequented by American vessels for Fish
Grand Ba
Locations frequented by American vessels for Mackerel
Cape May to
Actual value of Fish in the water, before taking.... ...
Actual value of Mackerel in the water, before taken....
Facts as to changes in location and mode of conducting
eries

For the past Eight years I confine my business to A
entirely.

HENRY N

Sworn and subscribed to before me, this Eleventh day
(Seal.)　　　　　　　SAMUEL S BAKER N

No. 98.

certify, That the undersigned, composing the firm of Nel
ɔw have been engaged in the fishing business for the past 25
ymouth and that since the Washington Treaty, so called,
effect, our vessels have been employed as follows:

els employed.. 4.
s made
s to Bay St. Lawrence............................... None
els of Mackerel from Bay St. Lawreuce............... None
els of Mackerel caught within 3 miles of shore, not including
ie Islands
ilue of Vessels each............................... $.3000
ilue of Outfits, Salt, Bait, &c............ 1550 for each Vessel
ilue of Insurance.................. 2000
ilue of Captains' and Crews' time, viz., wages per mo
                                      $35 to 40 per month
alue of Commissions, &c.
ilue of Wharves, Fish-houses, &c., for curing and packing,
ᵣ expenses of Clerks, Proprietors and labor on shore···.$5500
ᶻ Vessels lost .... None
essels lost, including outfits
ⁱⁱsh lost .... Noue
ᶻ Lives lost .... None
e of Fish taken, before curing, splitting, salting, &c. per cwt.
e of Mackerel taken, before curing, spliting, salting, &c.,

e of Fish taken within three miles of British shores···· None
e of Mackerel do································· None
ᵢarket value of American Shore Mackerel ············· $3500
ᵢarket value of Bay Mackerel
arnings of the operative fishermen per year
ᵢmount paid in British ports for bait, ice, and various sup⁻
.... $650 per year
aid to British fishermen for herring ················· 350
aid to British fishermen as wages ········in 6 years 20.000
aid in British ports for repairs ···············....... 5.50
frequented by American vessels for Fish
                              Banks of Newfoundland

frequented by American vessels for Mackerel
                              Chiefly on our own Coast & Banks

lue of Fish in the water, before taking
ᵢlue of Mackerel in the water, before taken
to changes in location and mode of conducting American

s
ssels from this place are with one or two exceptions wholly en-
Codfishing and their fishing grounds are the Banks of New-
l they resort to the Port in the Bᵣ Provinces for Bait and some
ᵣr supplies, a large portion of the crews are Bᵣ subjects and in
es the entire crews are from Nova Scotia.
a from this port are caught in Bᵣ Waters and We do not con-
ᵉe is any so valuable fishing grounds in their waters for Cod as
s of Newfoundland or any fishing ground for Mackerel as on
Coast and we never send vessels in the waters there or should

WILLIAM H. NELSON.

Sworn and subscribed to before me, this eleventh day of M₂
(Seal.)   ARTHUR LO
Notar

No. 99.

This is to certify, That the undersigned, composing the firm (
& Blackmer have been engaged in the fishing business for the
teen years, at Plymouth Mass and that since the Washington
so called, has been in effect, our vessels have been employed as

No. of Vessels employed ....
No of Trips made .... 1 Yearly to ea
No. of Trips to Bay St Lawrence
No. of Barrels of Mackerel from Bay St. Lawrence
No. of Barrels of Mackerel caught within 3 miles of shore, not i
   Magdalene Islands
Average value of Vessels each ....
Average value of Outfits, Salt, Bait, &c.... $1,200 yearly to ea
Average value of Insurance...................... ... $100 to ea
Average value of Captains' and Crews' time, viz., wages per n
                                         $35
Average value of Commissions, &c ..:.......... $80 pr vessel ⸱
Average value of Wharves, Fish-houses, &c for curing and pa₄
   cluding expenses of Clerks, Proprietors and labor on shore $7.0
Number of Vessels lost
Value of Vessels lost, including outfits
Value of Fish lost
Number of Lives lost
Total value of Fish taken, before curing, splitting, salting, &c.

Total value of Mackerel taken, before curing, splitting, salting
   bbl.
Total value of Fish taken within three miles of British shores
Total value of Mackerel do.
Average market value of American Shore Mackerel ⸱
Average market value of Bay Mackerel
Average earnings of the operative fishermen per year.........
Average amount paid in British ports for bait. ice, and various
                                      $5(
Amount paid to British fishermen for herring
Amount paid to British fishermen as wages
Amount paid in British ports for repairs   ⸱
Locations frequented by American vessels for Fish...Gra
   Georgies, Quero, St Peters and all banks bordering on Gulf
Locations frequented by American vessels for Mackerel
                       From Cape Henry to Newf
Actual value of Fish in the water, before taking............
Actual value of Mackerel in the water, before taking
Facts as to change in location and mode of conducting Ameri
   eries

In former years we used to send our vessels to the Bay of
rence: but not finding it successful we send now to deep wat₄
such as Grand, Georgies & Quero banks.
                   MANTER & BLACKM⸳
                       By PRINCE M

Sworn & subscribed, to before me, this sixteenth day of Ma
(Seal.)   ARTHUR LOW *Notary*

No. 100.

ᷓ to certify, That the undersigned, composing the firm of Abra.
Tower, have· been engaged in the fishing business for the past
ᴀrs, at Cohasset, Mass. and that since the Washington Treaty,
ᷓ, has been in effect, our vessels have been employed as follows:

essels employed..................................... Five
ʳrips made.......................... Six yearly, in all 30
rips to Bay St. Lawrence................................ None
ᴊarrels of Mackerel from Bay St. Lawrence............. None
arrels of Mackerel caught within 3 miles of shore, not including
ᴀlene Islands
ᷓ value of Vessels each................. Four thousand dollars.
ᷓ value of Outfits, Salt, Bait, &c.. Twenty five hundred dollars.
ᷓ value of Insurance.... Two hundred & fifty dollars per Vessel.
ᷓ value of Captains' and Crews' time, viz., wages per mo
                                         Thirty dollars
ᷓ value of Commissions, &c.... Two hundred dollars per Vessel.
ᷓ value of Wharves, Fish-houses, &c., for curing and packing,
ing expenses of Clerks, Proprietors and labor on shore
                                  Five thousand dollars.
 of Vessels lost.......................... .... None—
f Vessels lost, including outfits......................... 0—
f Fish lost... 0—
 of Lives lost....................... .... None.
ᴊlue of Fish taken, before curing, splitting, salting, &c. per cwt.
ᴊlue of Mackerel taken, before curing, splitting, salting, &c., per
.... two dollars
ᴊlue of Fish taken within three miles of British shores
                                Nothing, none taken
ᴊlue of Mackerel do................. ....   "   "
ᷓ market value of American Shore Mackerel
                                Eight dollars per Barrel
ᷓ market value of Bay Mackerel
ᷓ earnings of the operative fishermen per year
                                One hundred & fifty dollars.
ᷓ amount paid in British ports for bait, ice, and various sup-
.... Nothing
, paid to British fishermen for herring............   "
 paid to British fishermen as ᵥᵥᵃᵍᵉˢ................
, paid in British ports for repairs................   ..
ᴊs frequented by American vessels for Fish
ᴊs frequented by American vessel for Mackerel
                                Capes Delaware to Mount Desert.
ᴠalue of fish in the water, before taking
ᴠalue of Mackerel in the water, before taken········· Nothing
s to changes in location and mode of conducting American fish·

ᴊe last seven or Eight years our Mackerel fishermen have been
to the catch off the American Coast, owing to the Bay of St
ᴄe fishery being so very uncertain, as to offer no encouragement
ere—My vessels have not been there during that period—
                                ABRAHAM H TOWER

ᴊ and subscribed to before me, this Eighth day of May 1877
                                J Q A LOTHROP
                                Justice of the Peace

99 F

No. 101.

This is to certify, That the undersigned, composing the fij
Bates has been engaged in fishing business for the past
years, at Cohasset Mass and that since the Washington
called, has been in effect, our vessels have been employed as

No. of Vessels employed ....
No. of Trips made................................Six yeaɪ
No. of Trips to Bay St. Lawrence........................
No. of Barrels of Mackerel from Bay St. Lawrence........
No. of Barrels of Mackerel caught within 3 miles of sho
   cluding Magdalene Islands
Average value of Vessels each................ .Five thous:
Average value of Outfits, Salt, Bait, &c........Three ‚thous:
Average value of Insurance
                   Three hundred dollars yearly for ‹
Average value of Captains' and Crews' time, viz., wages per
                           Th
Average value of Commissions, &c.., ...$2(
Average value of Wharves, Fish-houses, &c., for curing an
   including expenses of Clerks, Proprietors and labor on she
Number of Vessels lost..................................
Value of Vessels lost, including outfits...................
Value of Fsh lost
Number of Lives lost...................................
Total value of Fish taken, before curing, splitting, salting, ‚&
Total value of Mackerel taken, before curing, splitting, saltiɪ
   bbl....................................... two dollar
Total value of Fish taken within three miles of British shor
Total value of Mackerel do ....
Average market value of American Shore Mackerel
                         eight dolla
Average market value of Bay Mackerel
Average earnings of the operative fishermen per year
                       one hundred &
Average amount paid in British ports for bait, ice, and v
   plies..
Amount paid to British fishermen for herring............
Amount paid to British fishermen as wages..............
Amount paid in British ports for repairs................
Locations frequented by American vessels for Fish
Locations frequented by American vessels for Mackerel
                   Cape Henlopen to M
Actual value of Fish in the water, before taking........ve
Actual value of Mackerel in the water, before taken...... ‹
Facts as to changes in location and mode of conducting Aɪ
   eries

For the last seven years mackerel have been so scarce
tain in the Bay of Saint Lawrence I have been obliged
the fishery in those waters

                          JOH

Sworn and subscribed to before me, this Seventh day o
             J. Q. A. LOTɪ
               Justice ǫ

No. 102.

certify, That the undersigned, composing the firm of
.s have been engaged in the fishing business for the past
years, at Dennisport, Mass—and that since the Washing-
io called, has been in effect, our vessels have been employed

ls employed .... Ten
made................ Six trips each yearly   total 60 trips
to Bay St. Lawrence...................... ....   none
ls of Mackerel from Bay St. Lawrence............   none
[s of Mackerel caught within 3 miles of shore, not including
ą Islands....................... .... none none
ue of Vessels each..Six Thousand Dollars each "average"
ue of Outfits, Salt, Bait, &c.
                           Three Thousand   "   "   "
ue of Insurance ....Four Hundred Dollars each
lue of Captains' and Crews' time, viz., wages per mo
                                          $40. per month
lue of Commissions, &c.......................$200. Each
ue of Wharves, Fish-houses, &c., for curing and packing,
  expenses of Clerks, Proprietors and labor on shore
                           Fourteen Thousand Dollars—
Vessels lost ....   none
ssels lost, including outfits
sh lost
Lives lost
of Fish taken, before curing, splitting, salting, &c. per cwt
                                    Fifty cts. pr cwt
of Mackerel taken, before curing, splitting, salting, &c.,
l..................................... two Dollars —
of Fish taken within three miles of British shores···· none
of Mackerel do·······························   none
                                              1   2   3
arket value of American Shore Mackerel········ 16—10—8
arket value of Bay Mackerel
rnings of the operative fishermen per year
                                  Two Hundred & Fifty
nount paid in British ports for bait, ice, and various supplies
id to British fishermen for herring
id to British fishermen as wages
id in British ports for repairs
requented by American vessels for Fish
requented by American vessels for Mackerel
                           Nothing East of Mt Desert —
e of Fish in the water before taking.............. nothing
ue of Mackerel in the water before taken
; changes in location and mode of conducting American fish-

5. years ago we sent our. last vessels to the Gulf of St Law-
sh the business being unprofitable. and vessels not Paying
ince which time we have found it much to our advantage to
r own shores—it is impossible to get a native crew to go to
St Lawrence fishing—one of our last trips there absent about
nly took twenty Bbls of fish valued less than two hundred
venteen men being employed—Seining has taken place of

Hand line fishing on our own coasts and we find that it is ?
advantage to fish nearer home. it being more advantage‹
fish being worth more than those taken in British wate!
quicker sales and much more profitable business.

BAKEF

Sworn and subscribed to before me, this 21st day of Ma
(Seal)   SAMUEL S. BA]
                                          N‹

No. 103.

This is to certify, That the undersigned, composing the
Eldridge have been engaged in the fishing business for the
years, at South Chatham and that since the Washingt‹
called, has been in effect, our vessels have been employed

No. of Vessels employed ·····························
No. of Trips made.................................3 t‹

	1872	1873	1874
No. of Trips to Bay St. Lawrence.......	0	0	0

No. of Barrels of Mackerel from Bay St. Lawrence ......
No. of Barrels of Mackerel caught within 3 miles of shore,
   Magdalene Islands...................................
Average value of Vessels each........................ ..
Average value of Outfits, Salt, Bait, &c.............. ·····
Average value of Insurance.....................$56
Average value of Captains' and Crews' time, viz., wages p

Average value of Commissions, &c................$175 t
Average value of Wharves, Fish-houses, &c., for curing ;
   including expenses of Clerks, Proprietors and labor on s!
Number of Vessels lost...............................
Value of Vessels lost, including outfits ....
Value of Fish lost....................................
Number of Lives lost.... ....
Total value of Fish taken, before curing, splitting, salt
   cwt...
Total value of Mackerel taken, before curing, splitting, sal
   bbl...
Total value of Fish taken within three miles of British sh
Total value of Mackerel do...........................
Average market value of American Shore Mackerel..$16.
Average market value of Bay Mackerel
Average earnings of the operative fishermen per year....
Average amount paid in British ports for bait, ice, and
   plies ....
Amount paid to British fishermen for herring...........
Amount paid to British fishermen as wages ....
Amount paid in British ports for repairs................
Locations frequented by American vessels for Fish
                                    Western Bank Quere:
Locations frequented by American vessels for Mackerel
                                    from Cape May
Actual value of Fish in the water, before taking........
Actual value of Mackerel in the water, before taken ....
Facts as to changes in location and mode of conducting ∠
   eries
   We think it is not profitable for us to send our vessels t

ー—we confine our business to American waters entirely our
s confined strictly to Shore fishing as it pays us we think much
in Bay fishing would

LEVI ELDRIDGE

and subscribed to before me, this Eleventh day of May 1877
SAMUEL S BAKER
Notary Public

No. 104.

to certify, That the undersigned, composing the firm of D. F.
lave been engaged in the fishing business for the past seven
So. Harwich and that since the Washington Treaty, so called,
in effect, our vessels have been employed as follows:

ssels employed . . . . average of three per, year
ips made . . . . 2 to banks and six to 8 Mackerel
ips to Bay St. Lawrence . . . . none
rrels of Mackerel from Bay St. Lawrence . . . . none
rrels of Mackerel caught within 3 miles of shore, not in-
; Magdalene Islands . . . . "
value of Vessels each . . . . Five thousand dollars
value of Outfits, Salt, Bait, &c . . . . Two thousand "
value of Insurance . . . . Six hundred "
value of Captains' and Crews' time, viz., wages per mo
forty dollars per Month
value of Commissions, &c . . . . . . Two hundred and Twenty five
value of Wharves, Fish-houses, &c., for curing and packing,
; expenses of Clerks, Proprietors and labor on shore
Six Thousand dollars
of Vessels lost . . . . Two
Vessels lost, including outfits . . . . ten thousand dollars
Fish lost . . . . fifteen hundred "
of lives lost
lue of Fish taken, before curing, splitting, salting, &c., per·
. . . . one dollar
ue of Mackerel taken, before curing, splitting, salting, &c., per
. . . . two dollars
lue of Fish taken within three miles of British shores . . . . . none
lue of Mackerel do . . . . none
market value of American Shore Mackerel $16. $12. $8.00
market value of Bay Mackerel . . . . none
earnings of the operative fishermen per year
about one hundred & fifty Dollars
amount paid in British ports for bait, ice, and various supplies.
nothing
paid to British fishermen for herring . . . . nothing
paid to British fishermen as wages
1870 1871 1872
$800. $600. $1400. nothing since
paid in British ports for repairs . . . . nothing
is frequented by American vessels for Fish
Grand bank Westirn & Georges
is frequented by American vessels for Mackerel
Cape May to Mt Desert
value of Fish in the water, before taking . . . . nothing
value of Mackerel in the water, before taken . . . . nothing

Facts as to changes in location and mode of conducting An
eries

The Bay St. Lawrence fishing entirely abandoned by th‹
in the fishing business here and all confine themselves to th
ing & Georges Bank for mackerel as the greater outlay an
used on the trips to the bay is so much that it is impossi‹
that fishing and from the present appearence of things our s
will be in the hand of British hands as their cheaper vessels, ‹
hire of crew's, and outfits enable them to place the fish in ‹
at a rate to us disasterous

            D. F. ↑

Sworn and subscribed to before me, this twelvth day of M
(Seal.)   SAMUEL S BA
              Not‹

No. 105.

This is certify, That the undersigned, composing the fir
Small have been engaged in the fishing business for the ‑p
seven years, at South Harwich Mass and that since the∙↑
Treaty, so called, has been in effect, our vessels have bee
as follows :

No. of Vessels employed..................................
No. of Trips made.......... one & two trips yearly 'to ea‹
         the Banks 8 or 10 trips Shore n
No. of Trips to Bay St. Lawrence.....................
No. of Barrels of Mackerel from Bay St. Lawrence.........
No. of Barrels of Mackerel caught within 3 miles of shore, n‹
 Magdalene Islands.................................
Average value of Vessels each............... Five Thous
Average value of Outfits, Salt, Bait, &c.....2500 to each v
Average value of Insurance ....
Average value of Captains' and Crews' time, viz., wages per
           Capt 70 Cre
Average value of Commissions, &c................... $200
Average value of Wharves, Fish-houses, &c., for curing an
 including expenses of Clerks, Proprietors and labor on sh
         $12000 Twelv
Number of Vessels lost...............................
Value of Vessels lost, including outfits ....
Value of Fish lost..................................
Number of Lives lost................................
Total value of Fish taken, before curing, splitting, salting, ‹

Total value of Mackerel taken, before curing, splitting, sal
 bbl...
Total value of Fish taken within three miles of British shor
Total value of Mackerel do ....
Average market value of American Shore Mackerel
        no 1 $16 no 2 $12 n
Average market value of Bay Mackerel................
Average earnings of the operative fishermen per year....
Average amount paid in British ports for bait, ice, and var
       years 1873 & 1874 $500 each year ‹
Amount paid to British fishermen for herring........ yea
Amount paid to British fishermen as wages.... Average $

nt paid in British ports for repairs.........................no
ons frequented by American vessels for Fish
        Western Bank Banqnereu Bank Grand Bank
ons frequently by American vessels for Mackerel
         From Cape Henry to Mt Desert Bank
l value of Fish in the water, before taking.............nothing
l value of Mackerel in the water, before taken..........nothing
as to changes in location and mode of conducting American fish-

re sent no vessels to the Bay of St Laurence for the last eight
excepting one vessel to Booue Bay for a load of Herrings in 1873
l not pay to send vessels to the Bay of St Laurence for mackerel
tch It is so uncertain and expence so large It is a Bad place to
fish on account of shallow water and foul Bottom The Cod fishery
entirely Bank fishery owing no allegince to any govenment The
ern Bank Quereaw and Grand Bank being from 100 miles to 400
from any land

                    CALEB SMALL

oru and subscribed to before me, this Twelvth day of May 1877
al.)   SAMUEL. S. BAKER
                         Notary Public

No. 106.

s is to certify, That the undersigned, composing the firm of Val·
e Doane have been engaged in the fishing business for the past
y Eight years, at Harwich Port and that since the Washington
y, so called, has been in effect, our vessels have been employed as
vs :

f Vessels employed..Seven
f Trips made..Cod fisherman 2 Trips Yearly macki fishern 8 to 10
f Trips to Bay St. Lawrence.....................noue Since 1862 —
f Barrels of Mackerel from Bay St. Lawrence·············· none
f Barrels of Mackerel caught within 3 miles of shore, not including
gdalene Islands.. none
age value of Vessels each........about 3,000 To .12000 dollar Each
age value of Outfits, Salt, Bait, &c..$3000 To Each Vessai yearly
age value of Insurance..$225
age value of Captains' and Crews' time, viz., wages per mo
                      Captn $08 Crews 30 Each
                                $120
age value of Commissions, &c......................................
age value of Wharves, Fish houses, &c., for curing and packing,
sluding expenses of Clerks, Proprietors and labor on shore
                    $11000 Eleven Thousand
iber of Vessels lost...Four
ie of Vessels lost, including outfits.....$4800 Each—Total $19.200
ie of Fish lost..$3,000
iber of Lives lost...Eleven—
l value of Fish taken, before curing, splitting, salting, &c. per cwt
                                $1,50
l value of Mackerel taken, before curing, splitting, salting, &c.
er bbl..1,80
l value of Fish taken within three miles of British shores ....none
l value of Mackerel do..none
rage market value of American Shore Mackerel
                    No 1. 17—No 10 No 3. 6.25

Average market value of Bay Mackerel ....None
Average earnings of the operative fishermen per year....... ..
Average amount paid in British ports for bait, ice, and varic
 plies................................. ... .
Amount paid to British fishermen for herring ....
Amount paid to British fishermen as wages ....
Amount paid in British ports for repairs....................
Locations frequented by American vessels for Fish
                            From Cape Charles to M¹
Locations frequented by American ves-
 sels for Mackerel..................   "   "   · "   "
Actual value of Fish in the water, before taking ....
Actual value of Mackerel in the water, before taken ....
Facts as to change in location and mode of conducting Americ
 eries
have Sent no vessels To Fish In British Waters for the Las
Years our Fishing since 1862 has wholly been done In American
as no American crews Would go To Fish In Bayst Laurance
British Waters those that have occasionally Tried made a fa
serious losses to owner & outfitters & crews—consequently our
is wholly carried on In American Waters.

                             VALENTINE. DC

Sworn and subscribed to before me this Ninth day of May 18¹
 (Seal.)   SAMUEL. S. BAKE
                                        Notary .

                      No. 107.

     This is to certify, That the undersigned, composing the firm
Baker have been engaged in the fishing business for the past
years, at Harwich Port and that since the Washington Treaty, s
has been in effect, our vessels have been employed as follows:
No. of Vessels employed ....
No. of Trips made..
No. of Trips to Bay St. Lawrence ....
No. of Barrels of Mackerel from Bay St. Lawrence............
No. of Barrels of Mackerel caught within 3 miles of shore, not
 cluding Magdalene Islands..................................
Averave value of vessels each... ....Six Thousand
Average value of Outfits, Salt, Bait, &c....Twenty five Hundred
Average value of Insurance....................Two do fif
Average value of Captains' and Crews' time, viz., wages per mo
                                    Thirty dollar
Average value of Commissions, &c....Two Hundred Twenty fiv
Average value of Wharves, Fish-houses, &c., for curing and ₁
 including expenses of Clerks, Proprietors and labor on shore
                                     Ten thousan
Number of Vessels lost.......................................
Value of Vessels lost, including outfits....................
Value of Fish lost..
Number of Lives lost.......................................
Total value of Fish taken, before curing, splitting, salting, &c.
Total value of Mackerel taken, before curing, splitting, salting,
 bbl ....Thre
Total value of Fish taken within three miles of British shores
Total value of Mackerel do..................................

$$1s \quad 2s \quad 3$$

market value of American Shore Mackerel...... $14 \times 9 \times 7$
market value of Bay Mackerel
earnings of the operative fishermen per year....Two Hundred
y five dollars
    amount paid in British ports for bait, ice, and various sup.
.... nothing
paid to British fishermen for herring................   "
paid to British fishermen as wages.................   "
paid in British ports for repairs.....................   "
s frequented by American vessels for Fish............   "
s frequented by American vessels for Mackerel
            Nothing east of Mt Desert
·alue of Fish in the water, before taking............. nothing
·alue of Mackerel in the water, before taken ....   "
to changes in location and mode of conducting American fish·

)nsidering fishing in British waters remunerative   Have sent no
to Bay of St Lawrence since have been in business
                        T. B. BAKER

and subscribed to before me, this 21st day of May 1877   ·
                    SAMUEL. S. BAKER
                            Notary Public

No 108.

s to certify, That the undersigned, composing the firm of V.
.r & Co. have been engaged in the fishing business for the past
·s, at Portsmouth N. H. and that since the Washington Treaty,
l, has been in effect, our vessels have been employed as follows:

Vessels employed....................... ....Ten
Trips made each season...............................Fifty
Trips to Bay St. Lawrence..............................None
Barrels of Mackerel from Bay St. Lawrence ....None
Barrels of Mackerel caught within 3 miles of shore, not including
aleue Islands ....None
e value of Vessels each ....Six thousand dollars
e value of Outfits, Salt, Bait, &c
            each season, including Boats & Seines: $2500. —
e value of Insurance.....Twenty-five Hundred dolls per season
e value of Captains' and Crews' time, viz., wages per mo
                            $390. for time employed
e value of Commissions, &c....Two Thousand dolls per season
e value of Wharves, Fish-houses, &c., for curing and packing,
ling expenses of Clerks, Proprietors and labor on shore
                            Nine thousand dolls per year
r of Vessels lost ....two
)f Vessels lost, including outfits .....Eighteen thousand dollars
)f Fish lost...Nothing
f of Lives lost...None
alue of Fish taken, before curing, splitting, salting, &c. per
....Nominal
alue of Mackerel taken, before curing, splitting, salting, &c.,
....One dollar
)bl ....
alue of Fish taken within three miles of British shores···Nothing
alue of Mackerel do·································Nothing

Average market value of American Shore Mackerel
Eight dollars per Bbl.

Average market value of Bay Mackerel .... None received

Average earnings of the operative fishermen per year
One hundred & fifty dolls per season

Average amount paid in British ports for bait, ice, and various supplies .... Five Hundred dollars

Amount paid to British fishermen for herring .... Nothing

Amount paid to British fishermen as wages
Twenty five Hundred dollars annually

Amount paid in British ports for repairs .... Two thousand dolls.

Locations frequented by American vessels for Fish
Grand & Western Banks

Locations frequented by American vessels for Mackerel .. Not acquainted

Actual value of Fish in the water, before taking .... Nothing

Actual value of Mackerel in the water, before taken .... Nothing

Facts as to changes in location and mode of conducting American fisheries.

But very little change in location on American Shores. A grand change made in mode of taking Mackerel, being: from hook & line, to, purse seining, largely increasing expense   The scarcity and poor quality of Mackerel in British waters. has induced parties fishing there, to transfer their fleet to our own shore fishing.   And it is not uncommon to see English vessels on this coast engaged in fishing with modern appliances, being found more profitable than their own Coast fishing and we have sold several cargo's of cured fish the past two years to go to Halifax N. S.

V. DOANE Jr & CO.

Sworn and subscribed to before me, this 31 day of May 1877.

(Seal.)   A. F. HOWARD
Notary Public.

No. 109.

This is to certify, That the undersigned, composing the firm of C. Morris Tredick have been engaged in the fishing business for the past five years, at Portsmouth N H and that since the Washington Treaty, so called, has been in effect, our vessels have been employed as follows:

No. of Vessels employed .... Fifteen

No. of Trips made .... Sixty

1875   1876

No. of Trips to Bay St. Lawrence 1   1

No. of Barrels of Mackerel from Bay St. Lawrence .. none, but Cod fish

No. of Barrels of Mackerel caught within 3 miles of shore, not including Magdalene Islands .... none

Average value of Vessels each .... Three thousand dollars

Average value of Outfits, Salt, Bait, &c ..... Twelve hundred dollars

Average value of Insurance 9%

Average value of Captains' and Crews' time, viz., wages per mo.
Thirty five dollars

Average value of Commissions, &c ..... one hundred and fifty dollars

Average value of Wharves, Fish-houses, &c., for curing and packing, including expenses of Clerks, Proprietors and labor on shore
Twenty thousand dollars

Number of Vessels lost 2

Value of Vessels lost, including outfits .... Seven thousand dollars

Value of Fish lost

er of Lives lost

value of Fish taken, before curing, splitting, salting, &c. per cwt.
                                                                                75c
value of Mackerel taken, before curing, splitting, salting, &c., per
....two dollars.
value of Fish taken within three miles of British shores....none
value of Mackerel do...none
ge market value of American Shore Mackerel..... $16. $12. $8.
ge market value of Bay Mackerel...................$12. $8. $6.
ge earnings of the operative fishermen per year
                                        Two hundred & fifty dollars
ge amount paid in British ports for bait, ice, and various supplies
                                        Six hundred dollars yearly
nt paid to British fishermen for ⎤
ring .... |
nt paid to British fishermen as } Three thousand dollars yearly
ges |
nt paid in British ports for re- |
rs   ⎦

ions frequented by American vessels for Fish
                                La Have, Grand & Western Bank
ions frequented by American vessels for Mackerel
                                Cape May to Bay St. Lawrence
al value of Fish in the water, before taking ....nothing
al value of Mackerel in the water, before taken...........nothing
ts as to changes in location and mode of conducting American
ies

thin last three years have not had any vessels engaged in Fishing
itish Waters either for Cod or Mackerel. The Mackerel fishing
· done on the Coast of the United States, and the Cod fishing on
d La Have and Western Banks, vessels resorting to British Wa-
nly for Bait and ice. The Gulf of St. Lawrence fishing of no ac-
·

                        C. MORRIS TREDICK.
orn and subscribed to before me, this 19th day of May 1877.
al.)   A. F. HOWARD
                                        Notary Public.

                        No. 110.

s is to certify, That the undersigned, James Frye have been en-
l in the fishing business, for the past twenty seven years, at North
n & Camden, Me. and that since the Washington Treaty, so called,
een in effect, my vessels have been employed as follows :

f Vessels employed.......................Five (5) 13 men each
f Trips made......................four trips yearly, each vessel
f Trips to Bay St. Lawrence ....none
f Barrels of Mackerel from Bay St. Lawrence ....none
f Barrels of Mackerel caught within 3 miles of shore, not includ-
Magdalene Islands.......................................none
age value of Vessels each $4000
age value of Outfits, Salt, Bait, &c......$2000 yearly each vessel
age value of Insurance.................................9 per cent
age value of Captains' and Crews' time, viz., wages per mo....$35
age value of Commissions, &c..................$200 each vessel
age value of Wharves, Fish-houses, &c., for curing and packing,
luding expenses of Clerks, Proprietors and labor on shore..$10,000

Number of Vessels lost
Value of Vessels lost, including outfits
Value of Fish lost
Number of Lives lost
Total value of Fish taken, before curing, splitting, salti
   cwt..
Total value of Mackerel taken, before curing, splitting, salti
   bbl...
Total value of Fish taken within three miles of British sho
Total value of Mackerel do..............................
Average market value of American Shore Mackerel.......
Average market value of Bay Mackerel
Average earnings of the operative fishermen per year.....
Average amount paid in British ports for bait, ice, and '
   plies ....
Amount paid to British fishermen for herring.............
Amount paid to British fishermen as wages
Amount paid in British ports for repairs
Locations frequented by American vessels for Fish
                           Grand & G(
Locations frequented by American vessels for Mackerel
                           Cape May t
Actual value of Fish in the water, before taking..........
Actual value of Mackerel in the water before taken..... .
Facts as to changes in location and mode of conducting An
   eries
   We have sent no fishermen to the Dominion Waters for t
years for the following reasons namely: the fish have b
quality & scarce and in all that have fished there from this
have paid their expenses   Mackerel on the American shore
and of good quality but the expenses are so high in catchin
we do not consider them worth anything in the water befor(
                                       JAMI

STATE OF MAINE
KNOX SS—

   Sworn and subscribed to before me, this second day of J
(Seal.)   J. F. STE
                                     No(

No. 111.

   This is to Certify, That the undersigned Geo. Tolman ha
gaged in the fishing business, for the past twelve years, a
Maine, and that since the Washington Treaty, so called,
effect, our vessels have been employed as follows : viz—sin

No. of Vessels employed......... 66 67 68 69 70 71 72

                                12 13 12 10 8 4 4
No. of Trips made................ 66 67 68 69 70 71 72

                                20 18 20 18 16 8 8
No. of Trips to Bay St. Lawrence... 66 67 68 69 70 71 72

                                16 17 15 13 9 8 6

No. of Barrels of Mackerel from Bay St. Lawrence ....
No. of Barrels of Mackerel caught within 3 miles of shore,
   the Magdalene Islands.....................................
Average value of Vessels each..................... ......

lue of Outfits, Salt, Bait, &c... ....2700 each yearly
lue of Insurance....................10% vessel & outfits
lue of Captains' and Crews' time, viz., wages per mo...$38.
lue of Commissions, &c........................ ...... $150.
lue of Warves, Fish-houses, &c., for curing and packing,
  expenses of Clerks, Proprietors and labor on shore 76000.00
penses including pack bill & value of premises
sels lost.. 4
essels lost, including outfits.................... $23,000,00
ish lost
Lives lost..................................... 17
  of Fish taken, before curing, splitting, salting, &c., per cwt
                                                .75 cts
  of Mackerel taken, before curing, splitting, salting, &c., per
....2.00
  of Fish taken within three miles of British shores.. Nothing
  of Mackerel do.............. .... Nothing

irket value of American Shore Mackerel..

	No. 1s	No. 2s	No. 3s
	$18.	$12.	$8.

iarket value of Bay Mackerel...........

	No 1	No. 2s	No. 3s
	$13.	$8.	$6.

ruings of the operative fishermen per year........ $250.
nount paid in British ports for bait, ice, and various supplies
                                                $2500
id to British fishermen for herring..........$1000. one year
id to British fishermen as wages..$5000.00 from 1866 to 1872
id in British ports for repairs........ .... $900.
requented by American vessels for Fish
                Grand. Western. La Have. Georges Banks
requented by American vessels for Mackerel
                Cape May to Gulf St. Lawrence
ue of Fish in the water, before taking............. Nothing
ue of Mackerel in the water before taken.......... Nothing
changes in location and mode of conducting American fish-

e of fishing has entirely changed since I commenced the busi-
wls have taken the place of hand lines. and there is hardly a
, is fitted with lines for mackerel. in fact all the vessels from
use Seines. I have lost thousands of dollars in sending ves-
r of St. Lawrence. I said in 1873 I would never send another
he Bay for fish. if I wished too I could not get a crew to go
tried the Bay fishing to long for our own interest, but every
went in again, on the promises made the fall before—Mack-
plenty on this shore, and so easily taken. that the Bay Mack-
e last few years have not been worth going there for—
                                        GEO. TOLMAN

nd subscribed to before me, this first day of June 1877

MAINE
OF HANCOCK   C. A. SPOFFORD
                                    Public Notary

No. 112.

to certify, that the undersigned, composing the firm of E G
ortland, Maine have been engaged in the fishing business for

the past Twenty-one (21) years, at Portland. Me. and
Washington Treaty, so called, has been in effect, our v
employed as follows: •

No. of Vessels employed ·············· ············
No. of Trips made····························· Av
No. of Trips to Bay St. Lawrence·················· ·····
No. of Barrels of Mackerel from Bay St. Lawrence ····
No. of Barrels of Mackerel caught within 3 miles of sh
    Magdalene Islands ··············· ········· ······
Average value of Vessels each············ ··· Forty five
Average value of Outfits, Salt, Bait, &c········ One 1
Average value of Insurance·······················
Average value of Captains' and Crews' time, viz., wage
                      Thirty Dollars per
Average value of Commissions, &c······· Three hund
Average value of Wharves, Fish-houses, &c., for curi
    including expenses of Clerks, Proprietors and labor 1
Number of Vessels lost ···················· ·········
Value of Vessels lost, including outfits········· Ten
Value of Fish lost
Number of Lives lost ·················· ···········
Total value of Fish taken, before curing, splitting, salt
                      Sixty
Total value of Mackerel taken, before curing, splitting
    bbl.
Total value of Fish taken within three miles of Briti
Total value of Mackerel   do ····················
Average market value of American Shore Mackerels
              $16—for ones—$12—for twoe
Average market value of Bay Mackerel
              $10—for ones $7—for two
Average earnings of the operative fishermen per year
Average amount paid in British ports for bait, ice, and
                    Five
Amount paid to British fishermen for herring
Amount paid to British fishermen as wages
Amount paid in British ports for repairs
Locations frequented by American vessels for Fish
                Western
Locations frequented by American vessels for Macke
              Bay St Lawrence &
Actual value of Fish in the water, before taking ...
Actual value of Mackerel in the water, before taken .
Facts as to changes in location and mode of conducti
    eries.

    Have abandoned the idea of sending My Vessels
Bay of St. Lawrence, and shall never send another V
as the whole business has been a failure as far as My
cerned. The Mackeral being very scarce there, and
pose of them when got, being so poor in quality.

STATE OF MAINE   }
CUMBERLAND CO. SS. }

    Sworn and subscribed to before me, this 21st day o
    (Seal.)   LEWIS

No. 113.

.o certify, That the undersigned, composing the firm of Jordan
ave been engaged in the fishing business for the past 30 years,
id Maine and that since the Washington Treaty, so called,
n effect, our vessels have been employed as follows:

ssels employed.................................... 40
ps made.. 8

	1872	1873	1874	1875	1876
ps to Bay St. Lawrence..........	0	0	1	0	0

'rels of Mackerel from Bay St. Lawrence........... 135
rrels of Mackerel caught within 3 miles of shore, not including
ène Islands...........................of Magdelenes
'alue of Vessels each.......................... $4000
'alue of Outfits, Salt, Bait, &..................... $1500
'alue of Insurance............................... 9 Per ct
'alue of Captains' and Crews' time, viz., wages per mo....$35
'alue of Commissions, &c.................$100 each vessel
'alue of Wharves, Fish-houses, &c., for curing and
:, including expenses of Clerks, Proprietors and labor
e... $25,000
if Vessels lost
Vessels lost, including outfits
Fish lost
if Lives lost
ie of Fish taken, before curing, splitting, salting, &c.
.
ie of Mackerel taken, before curing, splitting, salting,
r bbl.
ie of Fish taken within three miles of British shores.   None
ie of Mackerel do.....................................   "
market value of American Shore Mackerel.......$16 $12 $8
market value of Bay Mackerel..................$11 $7 $5
earnings of the operative fishermen per year........ $225
amount paid in British ports for bait, ice, and various sup-
....$100 yearly
paid to British fishermen for herring
paid to British fishermen as wages
)aid in British ports for repairs
s frequented by American vessels for Fish.............Jeffrys
s frequented by American vessels for Mackerel
                                       on American Shores
alue of Fish in the water, before taking.............Nothing
alue of Mackerel in the water before taken...........Nothing
to changes in location and mode of conducting American fish-

ve formerly had vessels engaged in the Bay of St Laurence
for Mackerel but finding it improfitable the vessels not paying
s we have entirely withdrawn our Vessels from the Bay fish-
confine them to our own shores for Mackerel and the Ocean
r fish. The British shore fisheries are worthless to us.
                                   LEVI C. BLAKE

rE OF MAINE,   }
BERLAND Co. ss   }
and subscribed to before me, this 29 day of May 1877
                       LEWIS B. SMITH
                              Notary Public.

No. 114.

This is to certify, That the undersigned, composing t]
Whitten & Co have been engaged in the fishing busi?
years, at Portland Maine and that since the Washin
called, has been in effect, our vessels have been employ(

No. of Vessels employed

1871	1872	1873	1874	1875	
17 in Bay	8 in Bay	8 in Bay	7 in Bay	6 in Bay	3
5 on shore	8 on shore	8 on shore	11 on shore	15 on shore	14(

No. of Trips made.................................
No. of Trips to Bay St. Lawrence
No. of Barrels of Mackerel from Bay St. Lawrence

1871	1872	1873	1874	1875
3189 Bbls.	1045 Bbls.	1474 Bbls.	1552 Bbls.	474 I

No. of Barrels of Mackerel caught within 3 miles of s[
ing Magdalene Islands
Average value of Vessels each.................Five 1
Average value of Outfits, Salt, Bait, &c..Six hundred (
Average value of Insurance,
          About two hundred dollars for th
Average value of Captains' and Crews' time, viz., wage
                       T]
Average value of Commissions, &c ....Two hun(
Average value of Wharves, Fish-houses, &c., for curin
   including expenses of Clerks, Proprietors and labor o
                      Twenty five
Number of Vessels lost............................
Value of Vessels lost, including outfits....Twenty five
Value of Fish lost................................
Number of Lives lost..............................
Total value of Fish taken, before curing, splitting,
   cwt ....not mor
Total value of Mackerel taken, before curing, splitting,
   bbl.......................... ....Not more than two d
Total value of Fish taken within three miles of British

Total value of Mackerel do.
Average market value of American Shore Mackerel

1871	1872
No. 1 — No. 2— 1s '	
$17½—$11½	$17¼—$
1874	1875
1s 2s	1s 2 :
$13—$9	$29—$16—$'

Average market value of Bay Mackerel

1871	1.
No 1s—No 2	1s
$15¼—$10	$16
1874	1875
1s 2	1s 2s
$12—$8	$18—$13½

Average earnings of the operative fishermen per year
                      Two hun

amount paid in British ports for bait, ice, and various sup.
.... About One thousand dollars per annum
paid to British fishermen for herring
paid to British fishermen as wages
paid in British ports for repairs
About Fifteen hundred dollars
s frequented by American vessels for Fish
Grand Banks—Western Banks & Georges
s frequented by American vessels for Mackerel
From Cape Henry to Bay of St Lawrence
alue of Fish in the water, before taking .... Nothing
alue of Mackerel in the water, before taken .... Nothing
to changes in location and mode of conducting American fish-

ve given the mackerel fishery in the Bay of St. Lawrence a *fair*
from the experience of the past three years we are fully satis-
it would prove ruinous to pursue it longer consequently we
send a vessel there this present season—The mckl. caught in
during the few past years have been very poor quality—and
scarce. There are now in this market two trips of Bay mckl.
nd packed last fall that cannot be sold on account of the poor
f the fish—Nearly all the mckl. are now caught in seines—A
ons ago we thought that seining might prove profitable in the
Lawrence—and fitted a vessel—but on arriving they found the
so rough—that they could not use the seine without a great
risk of loosing it—(and it cost one thousand dollars) so they
ed the voyage and returned home without any mackerel—so
all of our mckl. fleet will fish in American waters—One En-
sel has fitted here with a seine to fish in our waters.
                    T. C. LEWIS
                    O. B. WHITTEN
                    WM. H. WILLARD.

)F MAINE   }
LAND CO. ss)
and subscribed before me, this 23rd day of May, 1877.
                    LEWIS B. SMITH
                            Notary Public.

No. 115.

s to certify, That the undersigned, composing the firm of Charles
have been engaged in the fishing business for the past Ten years
nd, and that since the Washington Treaty, so called, has been in
ir vessels have been employed as follows :

essels employed .... Fifty
rips made ....Four Yearly
rips to Bay St. Lawrence ....None
arrels of Mackerel from Bay St. Lawrence ....None
arrels of Mackerel caught within 3 miles of shore, not including
lene Islands .... None
value of Vessels each
        Five large Class Valued at 5000 Each 45 1000 each
value of outfit, Salt, Bait, &c ....One thousand each
value of Insurance .... Three Thousand dollars
value of Captains' and Crews' time, viz., wages per mo.
                            Thirty Five

)0 F

Average value of Commissions, &c.... One hundred dolla
Average value of Wharves, Fish-houses, &c., for curing
　　including expenses of Clerks, Proprietors and labor on
　　　　　　　　　　　　　　　　　　　　　　．　Th
Number of Vessels lost................................
Value of Vessels lost including outfits.................F
Value of Fish lost....................................
Number of Lives lost................................
Total value of Fish taken, before curing, splitting, sal
　　cwt ....
Total value of Mackerel taken before curing, splitting, sa
　　bbl...
Total value of Fish taken within three miles of British sh
Total value of Mackerel do...........................
Average market value of American Shore Mackerel......
Average market value of Bay Mackerel................
Average earnings of the operative fishermen per year. ..
Average amount paid in British ports for bait, ice, and
　　plies ....
Amount paid to British fishermen for herring.... One Th
Amount paid to British fishermen as wages.... ....
Amount paid to British ports for repairs...............
Locations frequented by American vessels for Fish
　　　　　　　　　　　　　　　　Western Bank G
Locations frequented by American vessels for Mackerel
　　　　　　　　　　　　　　　American Shore Ba
Actual value of Fish in the water before taking.........
Actual value of Mackerel in the water, before taken.....
Facts as to changes in location and mode of conducting
　　eries
My Vessels are Mostly Employed in Mackerel Fisher
Vessel in English Waters for the reason that the fish are
American Mackerel that Vessels cannot pay their outfit
them My Vessels are Mostly engaged in seineing and
erel in American Waters I cannot find any one who is
Mackerel Catcher for Bay of St Lawrence Vessels that h
have fell in debt largely I paid an assessment of 232$ o
this Year on two Years fishing in English Waters 1874 a
　　　　　　　　　　　　　　　　　　　　　CHA

STATE OF MAINE　　　}
CUMBERLAND CO. S. S. }

　　Sworn and subscribed to before me, this 25th day of M
(Seal.)　　　　　　　　　　　　　　　　LEWIS B.
　　　　　　　　　　　　　　　　　　　　　　　N

No. 116.

　　This is to certify, That the undersigned W. S. Jord
been engaged in the fishing business, for the past thir
at Portland Me, and that since the Washington Treaty
been in effect, our vessels have been employed as follows
No. of Vessels employed............Twelve, averaging
No. of Trips made ....♪....................Four tr
No. of Trips to Bay St. Lawrence
　　　　　　　　　　　　　Average two each year, o

---

* This Sch was in the employ of C & H Trefethen of Port

rrels of Mackerel from Bay St. Lawrence

      Thirteen hundred and fifty in five years

rrels of Mackerel caught within 3 miles of shore, not including
.ene Islands

value of Vessels each............................... $2000.00
value of Outfits, Salt, Bait, &c.................... $800.00
value of Insurance......... .... 9 %
value of Captains' and Crews' time, viz., wages per mo..$30.00
value of Commissions, &c .... $120.00 to each vessel
value of Wharves, Fish-houses, &c., for curing and packing,
ng expenses of Clerks, Proprietors and labor on shore
)f Vessels lost..................... .... None.
Vessels lost, including outfits
Fish lost
)f Lives lost
ne of Fish taken, before curing, splitting, salting, &c. per cwt.
ne of Mackerel taken, before curing, splitting, salting, &c., per

ne of Fish taken within three miles of British shores.. None.
ne of Mackerel do
market value of American Shore Mackerel
      16$ for 1s 12$ for 2s 8$ for 3s
market value of Bay Mackerel 11$ for 1s 7$ for-2s 5$ for 3s
earnings of the operative fishermen per year....... $200.00
 amount paid in British ports for bait, ice, and vari·
)plies $200.00
paid to British fishermen for herring
paid to British fishermen as wages   Nothing.
paid in British ports for repairs   Nothing.
s frequented by American vessels for Fish ....Western Banks.
s frequented by American vessels for Mackerel Coast from Cape
) Gulf of St. Lawrence
alue of Fish in the water, before taking············ Nothing.
ılue of Mackerel in the water before taken·········· Nothing.
to changes in location and mode of conducting American fish-

 to the unprofitable returns from the bay of St Lawrence by
,ls sent there that branch of the business has been abandoned
s fitted by our house have not paid their bills, consequently
:ls are confined to our own shores for Mackerel and the Ocean
)r fish. British waters are not used by our vessels except as
for shelter and when necessity compels supplies

       WINTHROP S. JORDAN

)F MAINE, }
LAND CO. ss. }
 and subscribed to before me, this 29 day of May, 1877
       LEWIS B. SMITH
eal.)   *Notary Public.*

No. 117.

; to certify, That the undersigned, composing the firm of Geo
n & Co have been engaged in the fishing business for the past
oue years, at Portland, Maine and that since the Washington
so called, has been in effect, our vessels have been employed as

No. of Vessels employed..**Six**
No. of Trips made.................................Three, to, **four**
No. of Trips to Bay St. Lawrence.............One and occasionly **two**
No. of Barrels of Mackerel from Bay St. Lawrence
                              One, to three hundred per **Vessels**
No. of Barrels of Mackerel caught within 3 miles of shore, not including
    Magdalene Islands.........................Not more than one in **ten**
Average value of Vessels each..................four thousand **dollars**
Average value of Outfits, Salt, Bait, &c..........Seven hundred **dollars**
Average value of Insurance
Average value of Captains' and Crews' time, viz , wages per mo
                              Capt 60$ Crew 30$
Average value of Commissions, &c.
Average value of Wharves, Fish-houses, &c., for curing and packing,
    including expenses of Clerks, Proprietors and labor on shore
Nothing as we do not cure our fish, but pay one twelveth for curing dry
                    fish and about 1$ per Brl for **Mackerel**
Number of Vessels lost...two
Value of Vessels lost, including outfits..........Nine thousand **dollars**
Value of Fish lost................................two thousand **dollars**
Number of Lives lost..Eleven
Total value of Fish taken, before curing, splitting, salting, &c. per cwt.
do not consider fish of any, or at least of very little value when taken
                                            from the **water**
Total value of Mackerel taken, before curing, splitting, salting, &c., per
    bbl...the same as above
Total value of Fish taken within three miles of British shores......**none**
Total value of Mackerel do....do not consider fish swimming of any **value**
Average market value of American Shore Mackerel
            12 to 15$ No 1—7 to 8 for No 2—and 5 to 6$ No 3
Average market value of Bay Mackerel
                    No 1 — 10$ No 2— 7$ No 3 — 5$
Average earnings of the operative fishermen per year
                              two hundred **dollars**
Average amount paid in British ports for bait, ice, and various **supplies**
                              fifty dollars per vessel per **annam**
Amount paid to British fishermen for herring................**nothing,**
Amount paid to British fishermen as wages
                    Twenty five hundred dollars per year
Amount paid in British ports for repairs
Locations frequented by American vessels for Fish
                    Western Bank and Quero Bank
Locations frequented by American vessels for Mackerel
                              Gulf of St **Lawrence**
Actual value of Fish in the water, before taking..................**none**
Actual value of Mackerel in the water, before taken.............**none**
Facts as to changes in location and mode of conducting American
    fisheries
    Within the last few years the mode of taken Mackerel has change en-
tirely. from taken them by the Hook to seining, or netting, and for our
shore fishing it has become useless to send a vessel without a sein,
while in the Gulf of St Lawrence. our fisherman have been unable to use
them to any profit. owing to the rocky Nature of the bottom, and the
large quantities of small Herring. that fill the meshes of the seine, the
Mackerel are inferior to those taken on our own Shore, for these causes,
we have been gradually withdrawing from the Gulf of St **Lawrence**

ıst year sending only one vessel, and this year shall not send

GEORGE TREFETHEN
THOMAS S. JACK

.TE OF MAINE, }
ıBERLAND CO. ss }

nd subscribed to before me, this 31st day of May 1877
LEWIS B. SMITH
Notary Public.

No. 118.

to certify, That the undersigned, composing the firm of J. W.
Co, have been engaged in the fishing business for the past
ırs, at Portland Me and that since the Washington Treaty, so
s been in effect, our vessels have been employed as follows

ısels employed............................. ....Fifteen (15)
ps made ....Two each Vessel yearly
1872 1873 1874 1875 1876
ps to Bay St. Lawrence.......... 1 · 8 5 2 1
rels of Mackerel from Bay St. Lawrence.250. 975. 1000. 200—150
rrels of Mackerel caught within 3 miles of shore, not including
ene Islands
Mostly Caught at Magdalene Isls
value of Vessels each .... $5000.
value of Outfits, Salt, Bait, &c.......3000 yearly each Vessel
value of Insurance............9 per cent on Vessel & Outfits
value of Captains' and Crews' time, viz., wages per mo..$40.
value of Commissions, &c .... 175.
value of Wharves, Fish-houses, &c., for curing and packing,
ıg expenses of Clerks, Proprietors and labor on shore
1000. Yearly
f Vessels lost......................Two at Bay St Lawrence
Vessels lost, including outfits.. Seventeen ($17000.) Thousand
Fish lost ... .$2000 in mackerel
ıf Lives lost... none
ıe of Fish taken, before curing, splitting, salting, &c. per wt
cte 75
ıe of Mackerel taken, before curing, splitting, salting, &c., per

ıe of Fish taken within three miles of British shores·· None
ıe of Mackerel do................................. "
market value of American Shore Mackerel ......$16. 10. & 8
market value of Bay Mackerel....................$11. 8 & 6
earnings of the operative fishermen per year .... · $250
amount paid in British ports for bait, ice, and various sup-
....$200. each Vessl Yearly
ıaid to British fishermen for herring
From $3 to 500. three Vessles
ıaid to British fishermen as wages
ıaid in British ports for repairs
ı frequented by American vessels for Fish
Western & Grand Banks
ı frequented by American vessels for Mackerel
Cape May to Bay St Lawrence
ılue of Fish in the water before taken ....Nothing
ılue of Mackerel in the water, before taken ········ "

Facts as to changes in location and mode of conducting America
eries Our Vessels have been codfishing ou the Banks and n
eling mosty off our own shore. The Bay of St Lawrence fishi
constantly grown poorer our Vessels have not paid their ex
Shall send none there this Season. The shore mackerel are bett
bring a higher price. We use Seines where we formaley used h
lines. The Codfish are taken many miles from any Shore. and
No National Jurisdiction

J W. SAWYER
D L FERNALD
ROBT. H. SAWYEF

STATE OF MAINE.
CUMBERLAND CO. SS.

Sworn and subscribed to before me, this 21st day of May 1877
(Seal.)   LEWIS B. SMITF
                                    Notary P

No. 119.

This is to certify, That the undersigned, composing the firm of Th
Chase and Co have been engaged in the fishing business for tk
Twenty Eight years, at Portland Me and that since the Wasl
Treaty, so called, has been in effect, our vessels have beeen em
as follows :

No. of Vessels employed..
No. of Trips made.

No. of Trips to Bay St. Lawrence.. $\frac{1871}{6}$ $\frac{1872}{4}$ $\frac{1873}{4}$ $\frac{1874}{3}$ $\frac{187\ell}{2}$

No. of Barrels of Mackerel from Bay St. Lawrence
                    1871 1872 1873 1874 18
                    1200 600   600   350   2

No. of Barrels of Mackerel caught within three miles of shore
  cluding Magdalen Islands
                         most caught in round Magdalene|

Average value of Vessels each.................... Fifty-five H
Average value of Outfits, Salt, Bait, &c
                         Fifteen to Twenty hundred
Average value of Insurance.............................
Average value of Captains' and Crews' time, viz., wages per mo
Average value of Commissions, &c..........................
Average value of Wharves, Fish-houses, &c., for curing and p
  including expenses of Clerks, Proprietors, and labor on shore
                                        Twenty Thousand|

Number of Vessels lost.............................
Value of Vessels lost, including outfits....................
Value of Fish lost.............................
Number of Lives lost.............................
Total value of Fish taken, before curing, splitting, salting, &c.

Total value of Mackerel taken, before curing, splitting, salting,
  bbl..
Total value of Fish taken within three miles of British shores...
Total value of Mackerel do.............................
Average market value of American Shore Mackerel...$16 $12 $8
Average market value of Bay Mackerel...........$11 $8 & $6
Average earnings of the operative fishermen per year.........

ge .amount paid in British ports for bait, ice, and various sup-
s...$150 yearly
nt paid to British fishermen for herring
nt paid to British fishermen as wages
ut paid in British ports for repairs
ons frequented by American vessels for Fish
Bay of Fundy La Have & Grand Bank
ons frequented by American vessels for Mackerel
Cape May to Bay St. Lawrence
l value of Fish in the water, before taking..............nothing
l value of Mackerel in the water, before taken..........nothing
as to changes in location and mode of conducting American fish-
s.

Bay St Lawrence Fishing has been fallen off with me for the last
or eight years, so that it has got to be an impossibility for my
s to pay their expenses fishing in their waters for Mackerel. I
send no more vessels to the Bay of St Lawrence,

C D THOMES
W. H. CHASE

E OF MAINE,
UMBERLAND COUNTY ss,

orn and subscribed before me this 23rd day of May 1877.
LEWIS B. SMITH
al.)
Notary Public

No. 120.

s is to certify, That the undersigned, composing the firm of E. H
e have been engaged in the fishing business for the past 20 years,
ortland & Boothbay and that since the Washington Treaty, so
l, has been in effect, our vessels have been employed as follows:

f Vessels employed.............................Thirty-five
f Trips made.................. Four to six to each vessel yearly
f Trips to Bay St. Lawrence ·····

	1873	1874	1875	1876	1877
	7	5	4	2	none

f Barrels of Mackerel from Bay St. Lawrence

	1873	1874	1875	1876	1877
	1255	1000	870	360	none

f Barrels of Mackerel caught within 3 miles of shore, not includ-
Magdalene Islands Most Caught in around the Magdalene Islands
age value of Vessels each ·· $6500
rage value of Outfits, Salt, Bait, &c. ···························· 3000
rage value of Insurance 9%
rage value of Captains' and Crews' time, viz., wages per mo . $30
rage value of Commissions, &c.................. 200 Each vessel
rage value of Wharves, Fish-houses, &c., for curing and packing,
cluding expenses of Clerks, Proprietors and labor on shore..$40.000
iber of Vessels lost ·· one
ie of Vessels lost, including outfits........................ $12.000
ie of Fish lost .... None
iber of lives lost ....
l value of Fish taken, before curing, splitting, salting, &c, per
rt 50c
l value of Mackerel taken, before curing, splitting, salting, &c., per
bl.. $1.50

Total value of Fish taken within three miles of British shores....
Total value of Mackerel do.....................................
Average market value of American Shore Mackerel...... $16.
Average market value of Bay Mackerel..................... $1
Average earnings of the operative fishermen per year.........
Average amount paid in British ports for bait, ice, and vario
⚑ plies..... .... One Hundred eacl
Amount paid to British fishermen for herring........ $6000 ea
Amount paid to British fishermen as wages................. 2
Amount paid in British ports for repairs ....
Locations frequented by American vessels for Fish
Bay Fundy & Ca
Locations frequented by American vessels for Mackerel
to Bay St Lɛ
Actual value of Fish in the water, before taking.............. :
Actual value of Mackerel in the water, before taken.......... 1
Facts as to changes in location and mode of conducting Americ
eries

I shall not send any more vessels in British waters fishing;
been a failure with me. for the last four years the vessels have n
their expenses. The fish or mackerel caught ther last year by :
sels are still on my hands; I have been unable to sell them at aɪ
they being such poor Quality the dealers will not take them wh
can get our shore mackerel.
                                                      E. H. CB

STATE OF MAINE   ⎰
CUMBERLAND CO. SS ⎱

    Sworn and subscribed to before me, this 23rd day of May 1877
(Seal.)   LEWIS B. SMIT
                                                 Notary

                        No. 121.

    This is to certify, That the undersigned, composing the firm
H Trefethen have been engaged in the fishing business for the :
years, at Portland Maine and that since the Washington Treaty, s
has been in effect, our vessels have been employed as follows:

No. of Vessels employed ....
No. of Trips made..........One hundred pr year for all of the
No. of Trips to Bay St. Lawrence...... ....Nine si.
No. of Barrels of Mackerel from Bay St. Lawrence
                              Fourteen hundred seven
No. of Barrels of Mackerel caught within 3 miles of shore, not in
  Magdalene Islands ....
Average value of Vessels each ....Three thousand
Average value of outfits, Salt, Bait, &c ....Eight hundred
Average value of Insurance..............Twenty two hundred
Average value of Captains' and Crews' time, viz., wages per mc
                                                  Thirty
Average value of Commissions, &c.
                  Three per cent on net stock to Capts o:
Average value of Wharves, Fish-houses, &c., for curing and :
  including expenses of Clerks, Proprietors and labor on shore
                                          Twenty five thousand
Number of Vessels lost ....
Value of Vessels lost, including outfits ....Four thousand
Value of Fish lost

Lives lost......................................Fifteen
e of Fish taken, before curing, splitting, salting, &c. per cwt
                                                        On dollar
e of Mackerel taken, before curing, splitting, salting, &c., per
....Two dollars
e of Fish taken within three miles of British shores
e of Mackerel do.
iarket value of American Shore Mackerel........Ten dollars
iarket value of Bay Mackerel.................Eight dollars
arnings of the operative fishermen per year
                              Two hundred & seventy dollars
imount paid in British ports for bait, ice, and various supplies
            One hundred and fifty dollars pr year for each vessel
)aid to British fishermen ˙for herring
                              Two hundred dollars pr year
aid to British fishermen as wages..Thirty thousand since 1871
)aid in British ports for repairs
                Three hundred dollars since 1871
frequented by American vessels for Fish
        Western & Quereau Bank & Gulf of St Lawrence
frequented by American vessels for Mackerel
        Coast of the United States & Gulf of St Lawrence
lue of Fish in the water, before taking ....Nothing
lue of Mackerel in the water, before taken..........Nothing
o changes in location and mode of conducting American fish˙

e not had any vessels engaged in mackerell fishing in British
e past year. we consider that branch of fishing a failure as
Gulf of St Lawrence is concerned our mackerell fishing is all
he coast of the United States those engaged in codfishing go
    Western & Quereau Banks and occasionally to Gulf of St
, but the last named fishing ground has prooved almost a fall˙
ist year
                              C & H. TREFETHEN

OF ˙MAINE   )
RLAND Co. ss)
and subscribed to before me, this 26th day of May 1877
                    LEWIS B. SMITH
                              Notary Public.

                    No. 122.

to certify, That the undersigned, composing the firm of Chase
g this Company have been engaged in the fishing business for
hirty five years, at Portland Me and that since the Washington
o called, has been in effect, our vessels have been employed as

....Twelve
essels employed ....Everag three
ips made ....
                            1872 1873 1874 1875 1876
ips to Bay St. Lawrence...   4   2   2   3   2
                            1872 1873 1871 1875 1876

rrels of Mackerel from Bay   600   425   360   230   180
iawrence................
rrels of Mackerel caught within 3 miles of shore, not including
....None
dalene Islands ....

Average value of vessels each ....

Average value of Outfits, Salt, Bait, &c....1000 Bay trips 600 Sho

Average value of Insurance

Average value of Captains' and Crews' time, viz., wages per mo

Average value of Commissions, &c. ....

Average value of Wharves, Fish-houses, &c., for curing and p
    including expenses of Clerks, Proprietors and labor on shor

Number of Vessels lost

Value of Vessels lost, including outfits

Value of Fish lost

Number of Lives lost

Total value of Fish taken, before curing, splitting, salting,
    cwt...

Total value of Mackerel taken, before curing, splitting, salting,
    bbl.

Total value of Fish taken within three miles of British shores

Total value of Mackerel do.

Average market value of American Shore Mackerel ......16.

Average market value of Bay Mackerel ....10.

Average earnings of the operative fishermen per year ....

Average amount paid in British ports for bait, ice, and various

Amount paid to British fishermen for herring

Amount paid to British fishermen as wages

Amount paid in British ports for repairs

Locations frequented by American vessels for Fish

Locations frequented by American vessels for Mackerel

Actual value of Fish in the water, before taking..............

Actual value of Mackerel in the water, before taken..........

Facts as to changes in location and mode of conducting Ameri
    eries

    Senes are Moslley yousd for Shore fishing for Mackerling on
of New England   We Have No Seains in youse in inglish Wat
fishing for Mackerling in Bay Stlorece & Shelore Bay W
Abandend as a Lusing Buesnes

                                                    M M CHAS
                                                    EMERY CUS

STATE OF MAINE, {
CUMBERLAND, SS }·

    Sworn and subscribed to before me, this 21st day of May 187
                                            LEWIS B. SMI
                                                    Notary

                        No. 123.

    This is to certify, That the undersigned, William Maddo
been engaged in the fishing business for the past Sixty-Two
Southport. Me, and that since the Washington Treaty, so c.
been in effect, our vessels have been employed as follows:

No. of Vessels employed....................................

No. of Trips made..... ....
                                            1874

No. of Trips to Bay St. Lawrence.............. 1 only in

No. of Barrels of Mackerel from Bay St. Lawrence..........

No. of Barrels of Mackerel caught within 3 miles of shore, n
    ing Magdalene Islands ....

ge value of Vessels each................................$5,500

ge value of Outfits, Salt, Bait, &c......................2,500

ge value of Insurance.......................... ...9.0 per cent

ge value of Captains' and Crews' time, viz., wages per mo

[$50. per mo

ge value of Commissions, &c......................$200.00

ge value of Wharves, Fish-houses, &c., for curing and packing,

iding expenses of Clerks, Proprietors and labor on shore..$25.000

er of Vessels lost

of Vessels lost, including outfits

of Fish lost

er of Lives lost

value of Fish taken, before curing, splitting, salting, &c., per

....50 cents per 100 lbs

value of Mackerel taken, before curing, splitting, salting, &c.,

bbl...1.50 per bbl.

value of Fish taken within three miles of British shores.. nothing

value of Mackerel do................................. "

ge market value of American Shore Mackerel.........18. 12. 8.

ge market value of Bay Mackerel.............12. 8. 5. per bbl—

ge earnings of the operative fishermen per year.........$200.00

ge amount paid in British ports for bait, ice, and various supplies

nt paid to British fishermen for herring

nt paid to British fishermen as wages.........$500.—per annum.

nt paid in British ports for repairs...........$50 "   "

ions frequented by American vessels for Fish....Western Banks

ions frequented by American vessels for Mackerel

Cape May to Eastport.

l value of Fish in the water, before taking............nothing

l value of Mackerel in the water, before taken.......... "

as to changes in location and mode of conducting American fish-

s

nt one vessel to Bay St. Lawrence in 1874—and she lost $500 on

ip—

vious to 1870 we fitted a large fleet for the Bay—but could not

it pay, and consider that fishing entirely worthless. The fish

our vessels bring are caught on Banks many miles from the ju-

tion of any government   WM T MADDOCKS.

E OF MAINE

OLN S.S.

orn and subscribed to before me, this Twenty-Third day of May

G. B. KENNISTON

al.)   *Notary Public.*

No. 124.

is is to certify, That the undersigned, Freeman Orne have been

ged in the fishing business for the past Fifty years, at Southport,

e and that since the Washington Treaty, so called, has been in

:, our vessels have been employed as follows :

....Six—

f Vessels employed...................................Three

f Trips made ....1 in 1874 got 100 bbls mackeral

f Trips to Bay St. Lawrence......1 in 1874 got 100 bbls mackeral

f Barrels of Mackerel from Bay St. Lawrence.. 100 "

No. of Barrels of Mackerel caught within 3 miles of shore, not inclu{
    Magdalene Islands ....}
Average value of Vessels each.................................$8
Average value of Outfits, Salt, Bait, &c........................$8
Average value of Insurance.......................................
Average value of Captains' and Crews' time, viz., wages per mo....$
Average value of Commissions, &c $2
Average value of Wharves, Fish-houses, &c., for curing and pack
    including expenses of Clerks, Proprietors and labor on shore. $15.0{
Number of Vessels lost...
Value of Vessels lost, including outfits.............. ....$7.0
Value of Fish lost
Number of Lives lost
Total value of Fish taken, before curing, splitting, salting, &c.
    cwt.... ....5{
Total value of Mackerel taken, before curing, splitting, salting, &c.,
    bbl...$
Total value of Fish taken within three miles of British shores Not{
Total value of Mackerel do.............................. "
Average market value of American Shore Mackerel..........18. 1
Average market value of Bay Mackerel......................11.
Average earnings of the operative fishermen per year..........$2{
Average amount paid in British ports for bait, ice, and various
    plies...$5{
Amount paid to British fishermen for herring
Amount paid to British fishermen as wages....................$10
Amount paid in British ports for repairs........... $400.00 per an{
Locations frequented by American vessels for Fish
                    Western Banks & Orp
Locations frequented by American vessels for Mackerel
                    Cape May to Eastport.
Actual value of Fish in the water, before taking..............Not
Actual value of Mackerel in the water, before taken..........
Facts as to changes in location and mode of conducting American
eries
    We send no vessels to Bay fishing—It is abandoned so far as
selves—are interested.
    Shore Mackerel bring one third more than bay and the catch,
seine is surer—
    Our vessels catch fish on banks with trawls, many miles from an
tional jurisdiction—Our experience in Bay fishing has been ruinous
                       FREEMAN OR{

STATE OF MAINE
LINCOLN S.S.

    S   n and subscribed to before me, this Twenty. Third day of
187{ ~~ivor~~
    (Seal.)
                    G. B. KENNISTO{
                      Notary Pul

               No. 125.

    This is to certify, That the undersigned, composing the firm of {
E. Peirce & Co—have been engaged in the fishing business for the
Forty years, at Boothbay, Me. and that since the Washington T{
so called, has been in effect, our vessels have been employed as follo

. of Vessels employed .... Fifty
. of Trips made...average of Three

                      1872 1873 1874 1875 1876
. of Trip's to Bay St. Lawrence.......... 6   8   6   6   2

                      1872 1873 1874 1875 1876
. of Barrels of Mackerel from Bay St. Law-
rence..................................... 1200 800 1200 600 200
. of Barrels of Mackerel caught within 3 miles of shore, not including
Magdalene Islands......Did not fish in St. Le. but Modaline Islands
rerage value of Vessels each............................$5000.—each
rerage value of Outfits, Salt, Bait, &c.................$2000.—each
rerage value of Insurance........................ ....9 per cent
rerage value of Captains' and Crews' time, viz., wages per mo
                                $50.00 per mo.
rerage value of Commissions, &c.................................$250.00
rerage value of Wharves, Fish-houses, &c., for curing and packing, including expenses of Clerks, Proprietors and labor on shore.....$30.000
imber of Vessels lost...Three.
ilue of Vessels lost, including outfits......................$25.000
ilue of Fish lost
imber of Lives lost
ital value of Fish taken, before curing, splitting, salting, &c. per cwt
                                75 cents
ital value of Mackerel taken, before curing, splitting, salting, &c., per
bbl $200
ital value of Fish taken within three miles of British shores.·· Nothing
ital value of Mackerel do....................... ·············
verage market value of American Shore Mackerel·· 16. 12—8—per bbl.
verage market value of Bay Mackerel 11. 6. 4
verage earnings of the operative fishermen per year............$250
verage amount paid in British ports for bait, ice, and various supplies
                               $3.000 per annum
mount paid to British fishermen for herring··· ····$2.000 per annum
mount paid to British fishermen as wages..........$500 " "
mount paid in British ports for repairs·············$500 " "
ocations frequented by American vessels for Fish..................
          Grand & Western Braddelle & Orphan Banks
ocations frequented by American vessels for Mackerel
                  Cape May to St. Lawrence.
.ctual value of Fish in the water, before taking.............Nothing
.ctual value of Mackerel in the water, before taken.......... "
'acts as to changes in location and mode of conducting American fish-
ries
    Fishing business in my case has been changed from hand lining
) trawling seining—Can send no vessels to Bay of St. Laurence profit-
lly—business had so depreciated—Our vessels now fished on banks,
rithout national jurisdiction. My Mackerel have been caught chiefly on
ur own shores—for the bay fishing has been an entire failure—I cannot
hip a crew of good fishermen in this place to go to the bay
                              M E PEIRCE

STATE OF MAINE
LINCOLN.
    Sworn and subscribed to before me, this Twenty-second day of May
.877
    (Seal.)   G. B. KENNISTON
                                   Notary Public.

.No. 126.

This is to certify, That the undersigned, Stephen G. Hodgd
been engaged in the fishing business for the past Thirty (30) y
Boothbay—Me—and that since the Washington Treaty, so cal
been in effect, our vessels have been employed as follows:

No. of Vessels employed..
No. of Trips made............... ....Th
No. of Trips to Bay St. Lawrence...................1876 sent on
No. of Barrels of Mackerel from Bay St. Lawrence ....8(
No. of Barrels of Mackerel caught within 3 miles of shore, not in
   Magdalene Islands..
Average value of Vessels each ....
Average value of Outfits, Salt, Bait, &c.....................§
Average value of Insurance.............................10 ş
Average value of Captains' and Crews' time, viz., wages per mo..
Average value of Commissions, &c...............................
Average value of Wharves, Fish-houses, &c., for curing and p
   including expenses of Clerks, Proprietors and labor on shore..
Number of vessels lost ....
Value of Vessels lost, including outfits ....
Value of Fish lost
Number of Lives lost ....
Total value of Fish taken, before curing, splitting, salting, &c.,

Total value of Mackerel taken, before curing, splitting, salting, ҫ
   bbl ....
Total value of Fish taken within three miles of British shores..
Total value of Mackerel do.....................................
Average market value of American Shore Mackerel.......16.
Average market value of Bay Mackerel ....11. 7. 5—p
Average earnings of the operative fishermen per year ....
Average amount paid in British ports for bait, ice, and vari
   plies...$600. per
Amount paid to British fishermen for herring
Amount paid to British fishermen as wages ....$250. per a
Amount paid in British ports for repairs
Locations frequented by American vessels for Fish
                          Western & Quer
Locations frequented by American vessels for Mackerel
                         Cape May to Bay St.
Actual value of Fish in the water, before taking..............
Actual value of Mackerel in the water, before taken ....
Facts as to changes in location and mode of conducting Ameri
   eries

The Bay fishing is an entire failure in my experience. I sent
sel 1876 and she sunk $800. getting only 80 bbls—Shall send
—The fish are taken by my vessels on the banks named and fa
the jurisdiction of any government. Fish by trawls & senes.
                                 S. G. HOD

STATE OF MAINE
      LINCOLN. S.S.

Sworn and subscribed to before me, this Twenty second day
1877
   (Seal.)   G. B. KENNISTO
                                    Notary

No. 127.

s is to certify, That the undersigned, Allen Lewis of Boothbay
been engaged in the fishing business for the past Fifty years, at
ibay and that since the Washington Treaty, so called, has been in
, our vessels have been employed as follows:

f Vessels employed....................... .... .fifteen vessels—
f Trips made........................ ....Three trips each—

f Trips to Bay St. Lawrence...... 1872 1873 1874 1875 1876
                                     8   8   8   8   2

f Barrels of Mackerel from Bay St. Lawrence
                                  1872 1873 1874 1875 1876
                                  1000 1000   700 1.000   300

f Barrels of Mackerel caught within 3 miles of shore, not includ-
; Magdalene Islands .... Did no fish in shore—
age value of Vessels each........................... $4,000—
age value of Outfits, Salt, Bait, &c.................... $3,000—
age value of Insurance .... 9 per cent—
age value of Captains' and Crews' time, viz., wages per mo.. $40.—
age value of Commissions, &c $225.00
age value of Wharves, Fish-houses, &c., for curing and packing,
iluding expenses of Clerks, Proprietors and labor on shore
                                                       $25.000—
ber of Vessels lost..... ....none
e of Vessels lost, including outfits............ .... "
e of Fish lost .... "
ber of Lives lost .... "
l value of Fish taken, before curing, splitting, salting, &c. per
t ....70 cents
l value of Mackerel taken, before curing, splitting, salting, &c., per
l $200
l value of Fish taken within three miles of British shores.. Nothing
l value of Mackerel do................. .... "
rage market value of American Shore Mackerel 16. 12. 8 per bll
rage market value of Bay Mackerel......... 11. 7. 5 per bll
rage earnings of the operative fishermen per year......... $200.—
rage amount paid in British ports for bait, ice, and various supplies
                                                  $2.500 per annum.

)unt-paid to British fishermen for herring
)unt paid to British fishermen as wages........ $750 per annum—
)unt paid in British ports for repairs............ $400. per annum
itions frequented by American vessels for Fish
                                          Grand Bank & Western.

itions frequented by American vessels for Mackerel
                                 Cape May to Bay of St Laurence.
ual value of Fish in the water, before taking .... Nothing
ual value of Mackerel in the water, before taking........... "
ts as to changes in location and mode of conducting American fish-
ies
y method of doing fishing business has been totally changed within
year—We fish by trawls and seines— where we used formerly hand
s entirely—Our shore Mackerel bring much larger prices—and men
ine to be shipped for the bay if they can get other work—Our Bank
ermen take their fish many miles from any national jurisdiction.
                                             ALLEN LEWIS

STATE OF MAINE.

LINCOLN. SS.

Sworn and subscribed to before me, this Twenty second day 1877

(Seal.)   G. B. KENNISTO]

Notary j

No. 128.

This is to certify, That the undersigned, Albion P. Hodgd been engaged in the fishing business for the past Thirty five ; Boothbay Me and that since the Washington Treaty, so called, l in effect, our vessels have been employed as follows:

No. of Vessels employed.................................,.............

No. of Trips made...... ............---.--.-.......

	1872	1873	1874	187
No. of Trips to Bay St. Lawrence......	2	3	2	2

No. of Barrels of Mackerel from Bay St. Lawrence

average trips 150 b

No. of Barrels of Mackerel caught within 3 miles of shore, not ing Magdalene Islands...

Average value of Vessels each... ....

Average value of Outfits, Salt, Bait, &c.....................

Average value of Insurance...................................9

Average value of Captains' and Crews' time, viz., wages per mo

Average value of Commissions, &c...........................

Average value of Wharves, Fish-houses, &c., for curing and ₱ including expenses of Clerks, Proprietors and labor on shore.

Number of Vessels lost................................

Value of Vessels lost, including outfits.....................

Value of Fish lost...

Number of Lives lost

Total value of Fish taken, before curing, splitting, salting, &c.

50 cents per

Total value of Mackerel taken, before curing, splitting, salti per bbl..$1.5

Total value of Fish taken within three miles of British shores..

Total value of Mackerel do...................................

Average market value of American Shore Mackerel........18.

Average market value of Bay Mackerel.........11. 7— 5 p

Average earnings of the operative fishermen per year...$200.0

Average amount paid in British ports for bait, ice, and various $500.0

Amount paid to British fishermen for herring

Amount paid to British fishermen as wages..........$250. pe

Amount paid in British ports for repairs............$250. ‘

Locations frequented by American vessels for Fish....Wester

Locations frequented by American vessels for Mackerel

Cape May to Bay St.

Actual value of Fish in the water, before taking............

Actual value of Mackerel in the water, before taken..........

Facts as to changes in location and mode of conducting Amer eries

The fishing business is become almost wholly changed. fro lines to Trawling and seines for mackeral.

men cannot be had for Bay fishing and all our fish are taken on
is far from the jurisdiction of any Government. All vessels went
bay of St. Laurence for three years have not paid their bills and
iend no more—

A P HODGDON

OF MAINE—
N S.S.

i and subscribed to before me, this twenty-second day of May

G. B. KENNISTON—
Notary Public.

· No. 129.

is to certify, That the undersigned, Luther Maddocks have been
I in the fishing business for the past Fifteen years, at Boothbay
that since the Washington Treaty, so called, has been in effect,
sels have been employed as follows:

ressels employed..Thirteen
Trips made
Trips to Bay St. Lawrence................Nothing since 1872—
Barrels of Mackerel from Bay St. Lawrence...............none
Barrels of Mackerel caught within 3 miles of shore, not in-
ug Magdalene Islands............................/........ "
e value of Vessels each $5,000
e value of Outfits, Salt, Bait, &c................$2.500 each
e value of Insurance ....9% per cent
e value of Captains' and Crews' time, viz., wages per mo....$40
e value of Commissions, &c...........................$250
e value of Wharves, Fish houses, &c., for curing and packing,
ding expenses of Clerks, Proprietors and labor on shore.$30 000
r of Vessels lost.. Two (2)
)f Vessels lost, including outfits.................. $7.000 each—
)f Fish lost
r of Lives lost...................................... Fourteen
alue of Fish taken, before curing, splitting, salting, &c. per cwt.
                                                          —70 cents

alue of Mackerel taken, before curing, splitting, salting, &c per
.... $200
alue of Fish taken within three miles of British shores
                                                          none
alue of Mackerel do ....
ge market value of American Shore Mackerel. 16. 12. 8. per bbl—
ge market value of Bay Mackerel............ 11. 7—5 per bbl—
ge earnings of the operative fishermen per year
                                          $225—00 per annum.

ge amount paid in British ports for bait, ice, and various supplies
                                          $2.000 per annum—

it paid to British fishermen for herring..... $1.000— "
it paid to British fishermen as wages.......... $600 "
it paid in British ports for repairs........... $500— "
)us frequented by American vessels for Fish
                                  Grand, Western & Orpha Banks.

ons frequented by American vessels for Mackerel
                                  Cape May to Bay of St. Lawrence
                                                          nothing
I value of Fish in the water, before taking............ "
I value of Mackerel in the water, before taken..........

201 F

Facts as to changes in location and mode of conducting Amer
   eries
   Our Vessels were formerly wholly engaged in the cod and
fishery—but we were compelled to abandon the business & for
have been wholly engaged in the Menhaden & Mackeral fishe
own coast—The bay of St. Laurence fishery, proving, in my ex
a total failure and for that reason we have sent no vessels the
years—& have taken no fish of any kind within three miles of th
   STATE OF MAINE
   LINCOLN SS
         B   LUTHER MADE
   Sworn and subscribed to before me, this Twenty second da
1877—
   (Seal.)   G. B. KENNIST
                                    Notary

No. 130.

   This is to certify, That the undersigned, Levi Reed, have bee
in the fishing business for the past Forty years, at Boothbay,
that since the Washington Treaty, so called, has been in effec
sels have been employed as follows :

No. of Vessels employed ....
No. of Trips made ....
No. of Trips to Bay St. Lawrence. ....None within fiv
No. of Barrels of Mackerel from Bay St. Lawrence...........
No. of Barrels of Mackerel caught within 3 miles of shore, not
   Magdalene Islands..
Average value of Vessels each............,..................$
Average value of Outfits, Salt, Bait, &c.................. .
Average value of Insurance....... 1
Average value of Captains' and Crews' time, viz., wages pe

Average value of Commissions, &c................... $250]
Average value of Wharves, Fish-houses, &c., for curing and
   including expenses of Clerks, Proprietors, and labor on shor
Number of Vessels lost.... ....
Value of Vessels lost, including outfits....................
Value of Fish lost ....
Number of Lives lost.......................................
Total number of Fish taken, before curing, splitting, salting
   cwt...
Total value of Mackerel taken, before curing, splitting, saltin
   bbl $1
Total value of Fish taken within three miles of British shores
Total value of Mackerel do... ....
Average market value of American Shore Mackerel.........
Average market value of Bay Mackerel....................
Average earnings of the operative fishermen per year.......
Average amount paid in British ports for bait, ice, and
   various supplies.................................. 500]
Amount paid to British fishermen for herring........$1000
Amount paid to British fishermen as wages.... .... $400
Amount paid in British ports for repairs............. $200
Locations frequented by American vessels for Fish
                                          Grand Bank

s frequented by American vessels for Mackerel

Magdalen Islands —

alue of Fish in the water, before taking .... nothing

'alue of Mackerel in water, before taken.............. "

to changes in location and mode of conducting American fish.

ess has become so unremunative that I have been compelled to it, so as Bay St. Lawrence. Cath now with seners in ameri. rs. Never got fish within English jurisdiction but on banks shore.

LEVI REED

:ATE OF MAINE

:NCOLN S.S.

and subscribed to before me, this Twenty-second day of May

G. B. KENNISTON

Notary Public

No. 131.

s to certify, That the undersigned, Charles C. Blake have been in the fishing business for the past six years, at Boothbay, Me. ; since the Washington Treaty, so called, has been in effect, our iave been employed as follows :

'essels employed........ ....Two—

rips made..................................Two trips each—

1873 & 1874

rips to Bay St. Lawrence...........2, ——— ——— bbls only.

116   210

.arrels of Mackerel caught within 3 miles of shore,

cluding Magdalene Islands······················....not one tenth

e value of Vessels each······························.....$4.500

e value of Outfits, Salt, Bait, &c·······················....$2.500

e value of Insurance···························........10 per cent

e value of Captains' and Crews' time, viz., wages per mo.

$40—per month

e value of Commissions, &c·····················..........$200—

e value of Wharves, Fish-houses, &c., for curing and packing,

ling expenses of Clerks, Proprietors and labor on shore

Six thousand dollars.

of Vessels lost ······ ·····························............none

f Vessels lost, including outfits···························· ..... "

f Fish lost ············· ········· .... "

of Lives lost·······················.......... ....

alue of Fish taken, before curing, splitting, salting. &c. per

...................50 cents per 100 lbs.

··················· ·················· ....

ilue of Mackerel taken, before curing, splitting, salting, &c., per

·················· ········· ············$2.00 per bbl.

··················· ·················· ....

iiue of Fish taken within three miles of British shores

caught none

ilue of Mackerel do·····························.... " "

e.market value of American Shore Mackerel.......16. 12. 8.

e market value of Bay Mackerel············· 10—6—4. per bbl.

e earnings of the operative fishermen per year

Less than $200. per man.

Average amount paid in British ports for bait, ice, and variou
plies..... ....50 per ar
Amount paid to British fishermen for herring
Amount paid to British fishermen as wages
Amount paid in British ports for repairs
Locations frequented by American vessels for Fish
Western Bank | Quero
Locations frequented by American vessels for Mackerel.coast of
Actual value of Fish in the water, before taking...............N
Actual value of Mackerel in the water, before taken ....
Facts as to changes in location and mode of conducting Americ
eries
send my vesels to the banks as above—within no jurisdiction
government—Have sent two vessels to Bay St L. and. both ma
ures—Now seine for Meckerel off our own coast—
Shall never send vessels to the bay. as it does not pay.
C C BL

Sworn and subscribed to before me, this Twenty Third day ₁
1877
(Seal.)   G. B. KENNISTOⁱ
                                        Notary P

No. 132.

This is to certify, That the undersigned, composing the firm
Dougall & Race have been engaged in the fishing business for t
Twenty-Two years, at Boothbay. Maine and that since the Wasl
Treaty, so called, has been in effect, our vessels have been empl
follows:

No. of Vessels employed..
No. of Trips made................................... Three trips
No. of Trips to Bay St. Lawrence...... 1872   1873   1874   187
                                         20   15   10   10
No. of Barrels of Mackerel from Bay St. Lawrence
                                   1872   1873   1874   187
                                   5.000 2.000 1.500
No. of Barrels of Mackerel caught within 3 miles of shore,
   not including Magdalene Islands... ....not oi
Average value of Vessels each ....
Average value of Outfits, Salt Bait, &c.........................
Average value of Insurance.. 9
Average value of Captains' and Crews' time viz., wages per mo
Average value of Commissions, &c................................
Average value of Wharves, Fish-houses, &c., for curing and ₁
   including expenses of Clerks, Proprietors and labor on shore
                                        Fifteen Thousand
Number of Vessels lost ....
Value of Vessels lost, including outfits........... Thirteen T
Value of Fish lost ....
Number of Lives lost ....
Total value of Fish taken, before curing, splitting. salting, ₁
   cwt... .. 76 cents pe ₁
Total value of Mackerel taken, before curing, splitting, salti
   per bbl ....
Total value of Fish taken within three miles of British shores..
Total value of Mackerel do ....$300 pe

age market value of American Shore Mackerel.........18—12. 6.
age market value of Bay Mackerel.... ....11. 8. 6—per bbl—
age earnings of the operative fishermen per year........ $225. —
age amount paid in British ports for bait, ice, and various sup-
es...... .... $900—per annum —
int paid to British fishermen for herring..... $300 " "
int paid to British fishermen as wages.......$1,000.—" "
int paid in British ports for repairs
ions frequented by American vessels for Fish
　　　　　　　　　　　　　Grand — & Western Banks
tions frequented by American vessels for Mackerel
　　　　　　　　　　　　　Cape May to Bay St. Law.
al value of fish in the water, before taking......Less than nothing
al value of Mackerel in the water, before taken.. " " "
i as to changes in location and mode of conducting American fishes
e bave now dissolved partner ship—and the business cannot be
ably conducted. Fishing was profitable only during the excite-
of the war—Never caught any fish within the jurisdiction of any
rnment except American—
ihing is conducted now by trowling & with Seines.
　　　　　　　　　　　SIMON McDOUGALL
　　　　　　　　　　　JAMES L RACE

ATE OF MAINE—
VCOLN S.S.
orn and subscribed to before me, this twenty-second day of May

al.)　　　　　　　　　G. B. KENNISTON,
　　　　　　　　　　　　　　Notary Public.

the Bay of St. Lawrence in the years 1875 & 1876 the business of
ig was so unprofitable that we send none this year.
is impossible to get good fishermen to ship for such voyages—
　　　　　　　　　　　　JAMES L RACE

E OF MAINE—
OLN S. S.
rsonally appeared James L. Race on this Twenty second day of
A. D. 1877. and made oath to the truth of the above statement by
subscribed—
eal.)　　　　　　　　G. B. KENNISTON
　　　　　　　　　　　　　Notary Public.

No. 133.

iis is to certify, That the undersigned, composing the firm of S.
erson & Sons have been engaged in the fishing business for the
Eleven years, at Boothbay. Me. and that since the Washington
ty, so called, has been in effect, our vessels have been employed as
ws :
　　　　　　　　　　　　　　　　　　.... .Four.
of Vessels employed ····························
of Trips made ···················· average six trips each—

	1872	1873	1874	1875	1876
of Trips to Bay St. Lawrence.......	2	2	0	0	0
				1872	1873
of Barrels of Mackerel from Bay St. Lawrence.........				300	300

No. of Barrels of Mackerel caught within 3 miles of shore, n(
ing Magdalene Islands....................................

Average value of Vessels each..............................

Average value of Outfits, Salt, Bait, &c.....................

Average value of Insurance...............................(

Average value of Captains' and Crews' time, viz., wages per n
$40.0

Average value of Commissions, &c..........................

Average value of Wharves, Fish-houses, &c., for curing a
packing, including expenses of Clerks, Proprietors and labor
shore... ....

Number of Vessels lost.....................................

Value of Vessels lost, including outfits......................

Value of Fish lost..

Number of Lives lost.......................................

Total value of Fish taken, before curing, splitting, salting,
cwt................ ....75 cents—per 1(

Total value of Mackerel taken, before curing, splitting, salting
bbl.. $200

Total value of Fish taken within three miles of British shores.

Total value of Mackerel do.................................

Average market value of American Shore Mackerel
16. 12 & 8

Average market value of Bay Mackerel......................

Average earnings of the operative fishermen per year........

Average amount paid in British ports for bait, ice, and vari
plies . ...

Amount paid to British fishermen for herring ....

Amount paid to British fishermen as wages......$300.00 per

Amount paid in British ports for repairs......$300.00———p(

Locations frequented by American vessels for Fish
Grand Banks—Weste

Locations frequented by American vessels for Mackerel
now off our c

Actual value of Fish in the water, before taking.... ....

Actual value of Mackerel in the water, before taken........

Facts as to changes in location and mode of conducting
fisheries

The chang has been almost entire in our business—in a 1
Since 1873 we have sent no vessels to St. Lawrence after Ma
cause it does not pay.—none of our ve
fish within the limits of the Dominion—all are caught on t
many miles from any National Jurisdiction.

STEPHEN NICKERS
STEPHEN E. NICKI
ALONZO R. NICKEl

STATE OF MAINE }
LINCOLN S. S.   }

S o n and subscribed to before me, this Twenty second d(
187%v r

(Seal.)   G. B. KENNIST
Notar;

No. 134.

This is to certify, That the undersigned, composing the fir
McClintock & Co. have been engaged in the fishing busine

orty-Three years, at Boothbay and that since the Washington so called, has been in effect, our vessels have been employed as :

Vessels employed.........................:...................Eight—(8)
Trips made...................5 Trips each vessel yearly average.
Trips to Bay St. Lawrence.... one   "   "   "
av. each 1872 1873 1874 1875 1876

Barrels of Mackerel from Bay St.
rence.........................200 250 125 100 0 each—
Barrels of Mackerel caught within 3 miles of shore
no. including Magdalene Islands none except near Modeline la.
ge value of Vessels each.................. .....average $5 000
ge value of Outfits, Salt, Bait, &c.............. " $2,500
ge value of Insurance......................about 9 per cent
ge value of Captains' and Crews' time, viz., wages per mo
$40.00 per mo—
ge value of Commissions, &c ....$225.—
ge value of Wharves, Fish-houses, &c., for curing and packing,
iding expenses of Clerks, Proprietors and labor on shore
$20.000.—
er of Vessels lost ....Two—
of Vessels lost including outfits.....Fourteen Thousand dollars.
of Fish lost..$2.000—
er of Lives lost ....none
value of Fish taken, before curing, splitting, salting, &c. per
....70.c Seventy cents
value of Mackerel taken, before curing, splitting, salting, &c., per
....$5.00
value of Fish taken within three miles of British shores. nothing
value' of Mackerel do .... "
ge market value of American Shore Mackerel. 16. 10. 8—per bbl
ge market value of Bay Mackerel·........11. 8. 6—per bbl—
ge earnings of the operative fishermen per year.. ......$200.00
ge amount paid in British ports for bait, ice, and various sup'
..$1.000 yearly—
s............. ....
nt paid to British fishermen for herring........ $1.500 "
nt paid to British fishermen as wages..........$1.500 "
nt paid in British ports for repairs ....$500.—"
ions frequented by American vessels for Fish
Grand & Western Banks.
ions frequented by American vessels for Mackerel
Cape May to bay St Lawrence
il value of Fish in the water, before taking ....nothing
il value of Mackerel in the water, before taken.......... "
as to changes in location and mode of conducting American fish·
ES
have had vessells engaged in cod fishing generally and macker-
off our shore—The bay fishing has decreased in value each year
re years till it is now worthless—We sent none in 1876 & shall
none 1877. On this coast our vessells fish for mackeral using seines
ally since Mackeral caught here are worth 40 per cent more than
Mackeral—Our fish are taken on the Banks far from shore outside
y National jurisdiction   W G McCLINTOCK }
JOHN H McCLINTOCK }

STATE OF MAINE—
LINCOLN S. S.
Sworn and subscribed to before me, this Twenty second da
1877
(Seal.) G. B. KENNIST(
Notar

No. 135.

This is to certify, That the undersigned, composing the fi
chewl Stinson have been engaged in the fishing business for
twenty years, at Swans Island and that since the Washingto
so called, has been in effect, our vessels have been employed a:

No. of Vessels employed ....
No. of Trips made .... €
No. of Trips to Bay St. Lawrence .... none fo
No. of Barrels of Mackerel from Bay St. Lawrence
No. of Barrels of Mackerel caught within 3 miles of shore, not
  Magdalene Islands
Average value of Vessels each ....
Average value of Outfits, Salt, Bait, &c .... $200(
Average value of Insurance............................3(
Average value of Captains' and Crews' time, viz., wages mo..
Average value of Commissions, &c.... .... 20(
Average value of Wharves, Fish-houses, &c., for curing and
  including expenses of Clerks, Proprietors and labor on shore
Number of Vessels lost ....
· Value of Vessels lost, including outfits ....
Value of Fish lost.......................................
Number of Lives lost
Total value of Fish taken, before curing, splitting, salting, &c

Total value of Mackerel taken, before curing, splitting, salting
  bbl..
Total value of Fish taken within three miles of British shore
Total value of Mackerel do.

Average market value of American Shore Mackerel.... .....

Average market value of Bay Mackerel ....
Average earnings of the operative fishermen per year.... ..
Average amount paid in British ports for bait, ice, and variou
Amount paid to British fishermen for herring
Amount paid to British fishermen as wages
Amount paid in British ports for repairs
Locations frequented by American vessels for Fish .... Wes
Locations frequented by American vessels for Mackerel
Actual value of Fish in the water, before taking............
Actual value of Mackerel in the water, before taken........
Facts as to changes in location and mode of conducting Ame
  eries

Have formerly been largely engaged in Mackereling in Ba
rence say 8 years ago since have been seining off our o;
You left the Bay fishing because we could not pay our ex
not consider the Bay of St Laurence fishery of any value what
not pay for our out fits this is the experience of all fishermen

:annot ship a Crew to go to the Bay on Shares every vessel
t there 8 years ago lost money

MICHAEL STINSON

and subscribed to before me, this 15 day of May 1877

F T BABSON
Coll of Customs
Dist of Gloucester

No. 136.

, to certify, That the undersigned Lewis McDonald have been
in the fishing business, for the past Ten years, at North Haven
nd that since the Washington Treaty, so called, has been in
ir vessels have been employed as follows :

essels employed..........12, & fit 18 others engaged as below					
rips made.................					
	1872	1873	1874	1875	1876
rips to Bay St. Lawrence.....	4	4	3	1	0
arrels of Mackerel from Bay St.					
nce.......................	700	700	650	200	0

arrels of Mackerel caught within 3 miles of shore, not includ-
agdalene Islands ....Not one Barrel in Ten
, value of Vessels each $3,500
, value of Outfits, Salt, Bait, &c ....$2,000 each Vessel
, value of Insurance...................... .....9 per ct
, value of Captains' and Crews' time, viz., wages per mo ...$35
, value of Commissions, &c. ....$200 each Vessel
, value of Wharves, Fish-houses, &c., for curing and packing,
ing expenses of Clerks, Proprietors and labor on shore.$10,000
of Vessels lost   .
f Vessels lost, including outfits
f Fish lost
of Lives lost
ilue of Fish taken, before curing, splitting, salting, &c. per cwt
50 cts

alue of Mackerel taken, before curing, splitting, salting, &c.,
ol...... ....$3.50
ilue of Fish taken within three miles of British shores
ilue of Mackerel do
e market value of American Shore Mackerel... ....16. 12. 8
e market value of Bay Mackerel.....................11. 7. 5
e earnings of the operative fishermen per year...... ....$250
e amount paid in British ports for bait, ice, and various sup-
.... $1500 Yearly

t paid to British fishermen for herring
t paid to British fishermen as wages ....$500 Yearly
t paid in British ports for repairs
ns frequented by American vessels for fish......Western Banks
ns frequented by American vessels for Mackerel
Cape May Bay St Lawrence
value of Fish in the water, before taking............Nothing
value of Mackerel in the water before taken. ....   "
is to changes in location and mode of conducting American
ries
e not made it a paying business sending Vessels into the Bay of
rence for Mackerel. for the last 5 Years. Last year sent none

3210   AWARD OF THE FISHERY COMMISSION.

there the Vessels cannot pay expenses I have therefore
the Business at that point and confine my Vessels to the O
for fish and off our own shores for Mackerel using Seines & '
           LEWIS McI

Sworn and subscribed to before me, this 25 day of May 1:
(Seal.)   F T BABSON
              Collector of Cu
                Dist of (

No. 137.

This is to certify, That the undersigned O Wasgatt & Co
been engaged in the fishing business for the past Sixteen yea
Island Maine, and that since the Washington Treaty, so call
in effect, our vessels have been employed as follows: N
1866

No. of Vessels employed ....Ten (10) 14 men to
No. of Trips made ....five trips year
No. of Trips to Bay St Lawrence
     1866 1867 1868 1869 1870 1871 1872 1873 187
     6   00   00   00   1   00   00   00   00
No. of Barrels of Mackerel from Bay St Lawrence $\frac{1866}{900}$ Bl

No. of Barrels of Mackerel caught within 3 miles of shore,
   ing Magdalene Islands......None caught within three mi
Average value of vessels each ....
Average value of Outfits, Salt, Bait, &c. ....
Average value of Insurance ....9 per cent on Ves:
Average value of Captains' and Crews' time, viz., wages pe
Average value of Commissions, &c.........$225 to each Ca
Average value of Wharves, Fish-houses, &c., for curing a
   including expenses of Clerks, Proprietors and labor on s

Number of vessels lost
Value of vessels lost, including outfits
Value of Fish lost
Number of Lives lost
Total value of Fish taken, before curing, splitting, salti
   cwt ....
Total value of Mackerel taken, before curing, splitting, salt
   bbl...... ....
Total value of Fish taken within three miles of British sho
Total value of Mackerel do........................... ...
Average market value of American Shore Mackerel
                No 1s 16 No 2 1
Average market value of Bay Mackerel   "   " 11   "   "
Average earnings of the operative fishermen per year....
Average amount paid in British ports for bait, ice, and
   plies ....
Amount paid to British fishermen for herring...........
Amount paid to British fishermen as wages
Amount paid to British ports for repairs
Locations frequented by American vessels for Fish
                Cape May to Gulf of
Locations frequented by American vessels for Mackerel
Actual value of Fish in the water, before taking.........
Actual value of Mackerel in the water before taken......

to changes in location and mode of conducting American fish.

[, in the year 1861 became engaged in the fishing business, the
.. Lawrence was considered the best fishing ground for mack.
I sent my vessels there, but the business was not remunerative.
ring of 1867 I concluded I had lost enough money there. Since
none that I have controlled have gone there (One of which I
part went, I think, in 1870 but she did not pay her bill.) Since
ng the Bay of St. Lawrence the business has, with me, been re-
ve, I own four times the tonnage and value now that I did in
ot óne of our Captains or crews have to my recollection, even
a trip to the Bay within the last five years

                                        C WASGATT

and subscribed to before me, this Sixth day of June 1877
                        THOMAS WARREN,
                        ·   *Justice of the Peace.*

STATE OF MAINE.

K, SS. ·
son B. Saunders, Clerk of the Supreme Judicial Courts. in said
certify that Thomas Warren Esquire is and was at the date
ertificate an acting Justice of the Peace, in and for said County,
imissioned and qualified to act as such, and that the signature
per annexed, purporting to be his, is genuine, and that he is
horized and empowered, by the laws of said State, to take ac
gment of Deeds, Assignments, and Powers of Attorney, and to
er oaths.
timony whereof, I have hereunto set my Hand and affixed the
the Supreme Judicial Court, for said State, this Sixth day of
the year of our Lord one thousand eight hundred and seventy·

                        HUTSON B SAUNDERS *Clerk.*

No. 138.

s to certify, That the undersigned, composing the firm of James
· N London Conn have been engaged in the fishing business
past twenty years, at New London Conn and that since the
gton Treaty, so called, has been in effect, our vessels have been
d as follows :   Ten.
Vessels employed ·················· ················· ···Eight
Trips made ·················· ················ ···········none
Trips to Bay St. Lawrence·················· ·············none
Barrels of Mackerel from Bay St. Lawrence·············none
Barrels of Mackerel caught within 3 miles of shore, not including
alene Islands·················· ············ ··········
e value of Vessels each···············   Three Thousand Dolls
e value of Outfits, Salt, Bait, &c·········Two Thousand Dolls
e value of Insurance ···············   ······Nine per cent
e value of Captains' and Crews' time, viz., wages per mo
                                          Thirty five Dolls
e value of Commissions, &c·············Two Hundred Dolls
e value of Wharves, Fish-houses, &c., for curing and packing, in-
ng expenses of Clerks, Proprietors and labor on shore
                                        Twenty Thousand Dolls

Number of Vessels lost ....
Value of Vessels lost, including outfits .... Three Thous:
Value of Fish lost ....
Number of Lives lost ....
Total value of Fish taken, before curing, splitting, salting, &
Total value of Mackerel taken, before curing, splitting, salti
 bbl.
Total value of Fish taken within three miles of British shor
Total value of Mackerel do.
Average market value of American Shore Mackerel
Average market value of Bay Mackerel
Average earnings of the operative fishermen per year
        Two Hundred &
Average amount paid in British ports for bait, ice, and v
 plies.... .... yearly one Hu
Amount paid to British fishermen for herring
Amount paid to British fishermen as wages
Amount paid in British ports for repairs
Locations frequented by American vessels for Fish
       Georges & La
Locations frequented by American vessels for Mackerel
Actual value of Fish in the water, before taking ....
Actual value of Mackerel in the water, before taken.......
Facts as to changes in location and mode of conducting Am
 eries
 Our vessels are engaged mostly in the Halibut & Cod Fishe
of them have tried down to the Bay of Fundy & have prov
for this reason we confine our fishing to the American wa
Ocean Banks not using the British waters for any fishing w
           JAMES

Sworn and subscribed to before me, this 17th day of May
(Seal.)   C. G. SIS
            Note

No. 139.

 This is to certify, That the undersigned, composing the f
Weaver & Co New London Conn have been engaged in the f
ness for the past 35 years, at New London Conn and tha
Washington Treaty, so called, has been in effect, our vessel
employed as follows:

No. of Vessels employed.... ....
No. of Trips made.................................. ....
No. of Trips to Bay St. Lawrence.... ....
No. of Barrels of Mackerel from Bay St. Lawrence......
No. of Barrels of Mackerel caught within 3 miles of shore. n
 Magdalene Islands......... ....
Average value of Vessels each.... ....
Average value of Outfits, Salt, Bait, &c.............. ......
Average value of Insurance .... .n
Average value of Captains' and Crews' time, viz., wages per
Average value of Commissions, &c.. .... Fo
Average value of Wharves, Fish-houses, &c., for curing a
 including expenses of Clerks, Proprietors and labor on sh
         Twenty Th
Number of Vessels lost.................................

ssels lost, including outfits.....................$14000,—
sh lost .... 1200—
Lives lost. ....none
of Fish taken, before curing, splitting, salting, &c. per cwt.
of Mackerel taken, before curing, splitting, salting, &c.,

of Fish taken within three miles of British shores....none
of Mackerel do....................... .... "
irket value of American Shore Mackerel
irket value of Bay Mackerel
rnings of the operative fishermen per year
    Two Hundred & fifty doll
iount paid in British ports for bait, ice, and various sup-
....300 dollors yearley
id to British fishermen for herring
id to British fishermen as wages
id in British ports for repairs...............50 doll yearley
requented by American vessels for Fish
    Georges Browns Lahove & Western banks
requented by American vessels for Mackerel
ie of Fish in the water, before taking.............nothing
ie of Mackerel in the water, before taken ....nothing
changes in location and mode of conducting American fish-

alls are engaged mostley in the Halibut and Cod fisheries
nt our vessels in the the Bay of Funday the trips have
ilure in almost every trip for this reason we coufine our
 the oacean banks out side of oney national jurisdiction and
ores
     C A WEAVER & CO

id subscribed to before me, this 17th day of May 1877
     C. G. SISTARE
      Notary Public

No. 140.

o certify, That the undersigned, composing the firm of H A
)o of New London Conn have been engaged in the fishing
r Ten years at New London Conn and that since the Wash-
aty, so called, has been in effect, our vessels have been em-
follows :
sels employed .... Ten
ps made ....Eight
)s to Bay St. Lawrence ....None
rels of Mackerel from Bay St. Lawrence............None
rels of Mackerel caught within 3 miles of shore, not includ-
dalene Islands........................... . None
alue of Vessels each ....Four Thousand
alue of Outfits, Salt, Bait, &c...... .....Three Thousand
alue of Insurance.............................Nine per cent
ralue of Captains' and Crews' time, viz., wages per mo.
      Thirty five
alue of Commissions, &c ....Two Hundred Dollars
alue of Wharves, Fish-houses, &c., for curing and packing.
g expenses of Clerks, Proprietors and labor on shore.
     Twenty Thousand Dollars
f Vessels lost ....Five

Value of Vessels lost, including outfits........Thirty Thousa
Value of Fish lost
Number of Lives lost...... ....T\
Total value of Fish taken, before curing, splitting, salting, &\
Total value of Mackerel taken, before curing, splitting, saltin
    bbl
Total value of Fish taken within three miles of British shores
Total value of Mackerel do.
Average market value of American Shore Mackerel
Average market value of Bay Mackerel
Average earnings of the operative fishermen per year
                 Two Hundred & Fifty
Average amount paid in British ports for bait, ice, and va
   plies.......................... ....Two Hundr
Amount paid to British fishermen for herring
Amount paid to British fishermen as wages
Amount paid in British ports for repairs
Locations frequented by American vessels for Fish
              Georges Brown, La Have & Wester
Locations frequented by American vessels for Mackerel
Actual value of Fish in the water, before taking............
Actual value of Mackerel in the water, before taken.........
Facts as to changes in location and mode of conducting Ame
  'eries
    Our Vessels are engaged mostly in the Halibut & Cod
We have had our vessels go to the Bay of Fundy in some ca
has been unprofitable & we have discontinued it & confine o\
to the Banks outside of any National Jurisdiction and to our ‹
                       H A BROW

    Sworn and subscribed to before me, this 17th day of May
(Seal.)   C. G. SIS
                               Notar

No. 141.

Solemn Declaration of William Harvey concerning the Fisherie
can Canadian Waters

    I William Harvey reside at Aulds Cove Strait of Canso
    My name is William Harvey am fifty four years of age
engaged fishing since I was twelve Years old, have been emp
Eighteen to twenty Seasons in American Vessels fishing f\
Mackerel in the Gulf of St Lawrence and on the Atlanti
British America and two Seasons on the United States Coas
often fished alongside of an American Mackerel fishing fleet
ployed in Provincial fishing Vessels. the Catch of Mackere
nial Mackerel fishing vessels is not at all lessened on acco
American fleet being alongside of them the main reason fo
think is that more bait is thrown out
    Fully one half of the Crews of American fishing Schoon
the fishing grounds of Dominion of Canada are residents an
of the Dominion of Canada In case they are employed on S
Monthly Wages will average from thirty to thirty five Dollars
many get for the trip lasting for about three Months from on
and twenty to One hundred and fifty Dollars.
    They the American fishermen very seldom make use of ou
Curing their fish or drying Nets.

ackerel fishing during the last four or five Years has very much
', during that time the Average Catch has at most only been
ie half of what it was ten or twelve Years ago There is no boat
one by the Americans worth mentioning on these Shores I have
asionally a few American vessels the beginning of June arrive
shing grounds but the great body or heft of them don't arrive
ly

William Harvey aforesaid do solemnly declare that I consci.
7 declare that the Statements made in the foregoing declaration
and I make this Solemn declaration by virtue of the Act passed
7th Year of Her Majestys Reign entitled an Act for the Suppres
7oluntary and Extra judicial Oaths
, Cove, Nova Scotia June 11. 1877

WILLIAM HARVEY

sence of

JAMES G. McKEEN
Justice of the Peace.

No. 142.

d McEachren being duly sworn, says.

me is Donald McEachren I am fifty two years old I am a
Subject   reside at New Town Strait of Canso. have since Eigh-
adred and fifty been employed as a fisherman every Season with
eption of two on board of American fishing Schooners. about
welve summers I was shipped in the United States. the Vessels
oners in which I was employed fished for Mackerel and Cod on
st of Prince Edward Island. Cape Breton New Brunswick Prov-
' Quebec and the Magdalen Islands We often fished alongside
nial Vessels the American fleet being alongside of them did not
3 with the Catch of Mackerel or Cod by Colonial Vessels, on the
y, on account of the great quantity of bait thrown out by the
in fishermen the Mackerel stay longer on the surface of the
and bite better than they do when Colonial Vessels are alone
, the latter throw out much smaller quantity of bait. therefore
nial Vessels catch more Mackerel when alongside of an Amer
3t, the Colonial Vessels are in the habit of following the Amer·
ssels on the fishing grounds for the reasons stated during the
o Seasons the Americans have visited the Colonial Waters in
maller numbers than formerly because there own fishing grounds
come very productive that is they have always been very good
ate years they Americans have got into the habit of Seine fish
ch they may use in deep water and is the most profitable way
ing Mackerel. Mackerel is found in great abundance in deep
ou the American Coast.
dependent of the number of American fishing Vessels there will per.
a series of year when Mackerel will appear in great quantities
3 Shores, then almost disappear from these Coasts for another
of Years or Seasons and thereupon reappear in as great quantities
, the causes for that may be many but are not known. Mackerel
y uncertain in their movements
ng the last three years the average number of American fishing
in the entire Atlantic Provincial Waters excepting those of New-
nd have been about One hundred and fifty Sails this is, that Num.
engaged in Mackerel fishing during the last year there ware only
Seventy five Sail of American Mackerel fishermen in the fishing
s just mentioned during the five Years previous to the last

three Years the average number of American Mackerel fis]
was within the same Waters that I have just named betw
five hundred. The average tonnage of an American fis
is about Seventy five Tons

Codfishing is not carried on by the American fishing V
three miles from shore

I do not know what the expences are of an averaged si.
Seventy five Tons would be for another outfit received in tl
on proceeding again to the fishing grounds after having lat
in the Provincial Ports for reshipment but the average amou
by the American fishing fleet in the Provinces would be
hundred Dollars for Each Vessel per season independent of
of the fleet which land their Cargoes in the Provinces and
outlays in refitting for another trip or fare of Mackerel.

For Number one and two Mackerel and Number one Sa'
by Colonial fishermen the United States are the only Mark
may be said of fat Herring during the last few years. form
proportion of them went to Quebec and Montreal

The Americans do not use the Coast of the British Prov
Newfoundland for drying Net, or Curing fish

About two thousand Provincial fishermen have been
Season during the last ten Years on board American fis]
Among these are about five hundred from Prince Edward
others to the greater extent from Nova Scotia

The presence of American fishermen on our Coasts has in
been a great advantage to the people of the Provinces

And I Donald McEachren aforesaid do solemnly declare (
I conscientiously believe that the Statements made in tl
declaration are true, so help me God

DONALD McE

CONSULATE OF THE UNITED STATES OF AM
At Pictou, Nova Scotia, Port Hastings Agency Jun

I hereby certify that the foregoing and above Affidavit w:
before me on the 9th. day of June 1877 by the above na
McEachren and on said day signed and sworn to before m
said McEachern.

OSCAR MAL
U. S. Consu

No. 143.

*Solemn Declaration of Richard Jackman concerning the
Canadian and American Waters.*

Richard Jackman says that he resides near to Port Mul
West side of the Strait of Canso I am a fisherman by occ
thirty Six Years of age went fishing when I was ten ye
been engaged fishing on board of American fishing Vesse
fish and Mackerel about twenty one years and five Seasor
fishing vessels. I was Master of American fishing Vessel
and three Seasons Master of Colonial fishing Vessels. I u
first part of the Year Codfishing and the latter part Ma
went generally to the Grand Banks Western Banks au
Lawrence for Codfish and to the Gulf of St Lawrence
American Shore for Mackerel. I went in American fishi
the Georges Banks for Codfish Seven Winters

:rel first appear in the Spring about the first of April off the
,n Coast near Cape Henry where they are generally caught or
. Seines and from there they follow the American Coast East
,o Cape Cod and from there they scatter, part remaining around
:rican Coast and part going Eastwardly along the Nova Scotia
id entering the Gulf of St. Lawrence about the first of June
:rel are taken with Seines in large quantities on the American
ie last few Years formerly they were caught with hooks
.merican fishermen generally commence taking Mackerel in the
St Lawrence or other parts of the Atlantic Coast of British
.merica about the tenth of June and continue fishing until about
of November
than half the Mackerel caught along the Coasts of British North
ı during the last ten Years by both Colonial and American fish.
:els were taken outside of three Miles from the Shore
t ten Years ago there were upwards of three hundred American
Vessels passed through the Strait of Canso into the Gulf of
rence every season for the purpose of Catching Mackerel & Cod-
'e years ago there probably two hundred vessels Since that
ə number has been decreasing until last year when there only
∍venty Sail of American fishing Vessels in the Gulf of St Law-

verage size of American fishing Vessels is about Seventy Tons.
Vessel when new would cost to build and rig about Six to seven
d Dollars and a vessel of the same would cost to build and rig in
vinces about three thousand to four thousand Dollars
nly fish the American catch inshore on the Atlantic Colonial
re Mackerel The most of the American Mackerel fishermen now
fackerel on their own coast only
eve that the right to fish on the American Coast would be as val-
, the people of the British Provinces as the Colonial fisheries to
ıns provided our people had as good vessels and titted them out
and had as much enterprise as the Americans The presence of
ın fishermen in the Provinces is of great pecuniary gain and ad-
; to our people in consequence of said fishermen purchasing in
ts large supplies of Provisions Bait Salt and fresh Barrels Salt
ce and all kinds of fishermen's supplies and occasionally making
to their Vessels requiring Cables Anchors Canvas Cordage
:c. &c From my experience I believe that the average expendi-
American fishing Vessels in the British Provinces during the whole
would be upwards of Seven hundred Dollars
American fishermen make little or no use of the privilege of cur-
ir fish and drying their nets on the Coast of the Province
bait used for Catching Mackerel comes from the United States
; of Pogies and Clams and is taken almost entirely on the Amer-
ast Colonial fishing Vessels use the same kind of bait and ob-
from the United States, Pogies are taken nearly altogether in
and within three miles of the land
; born in the Strait of Canso and am a British Subject
I Richard Jackman aforesaid do Solemnly declare that I con-
usly believe that the Statements made by me in the foregoing
tion are true and I make this Solemn declaration by virtue of
; passed in the 37th Year of Her Majestys Reign entitled an Act
Suppression of Voluntary and Extra judicial Oaths

RICHARD JACKMAN

I the undersigned Notary Public Do hereby Certify that on '
day of June 1877 personally appeared before me the above nam
ard Jackman and then and there made and subscribed the at
foregoing declaration as Witness my hand and Seal of Office
Mulgrave the day and year above mentioned
(Seal.)   JAMES G McKEE
                                      Notary

No. 144.

Statement of Thomas Chas Smith of Port Hood Island concerning
made June 8th. 1877.

My name is Thomas Chas Smith, am about 55 years old, have
resided on Port Hood Island, I have been engaged in fishing
was a boy, have never sailed on American fishing schooners—m
has almost exclusively *boat* fishing between and along the Coasts
Breton & Pr. Edwr Island   the American fishermen have come
less during the last 5 years to these fishing grounds—I am co
that the presence of Am. fishing schooners has pecuniarily
benefited the people of this Province and that the American
fleet has never interfered with, that is, lessened the catch of
fishermen of mackerel or other fish on the contrary I believe
presence of the American fishing fleet on account of their throw
such a great quantity of best bait has attracted the mackerel
parts and that when the Americans were so much interfered
Dominion Revenue Cutters some years ago and thereby and
molestations partly driven away from these waters, the macker
to leave us to, not be able to obtain as much excellent food as w
Americans threw out so much bait.   Where from 8 to 10 years
before that time a hundred barrels of mackerel caught there
& have been during the last 3 years scarcely 10 barrels caug
Americans do not take to *boat* fishing, their way of mackerel
by schooners.   The American fishermen do not cure their fis
shores and but exceptionally dry their nets on our grounds.
of cattle and great quantities of all kinds of farm produce
during the season to the Americans while they were comin
great numbers and money circulated freely in consequence but
able to make an estimate of how much they spent on an averag
the season either per single vessel or in the aggregate.
                                      THOMAS .
Subscribed & sworn to before me June 8. 1877
                                      OSCAR MALMR
                                           U. S.

No. 145.

Solemn Declaration of Asberry Strahan concerning the Fisheries
dian and American Waters

Asberry Strahan says that he resides near Aulds Cove on
eru side of the Strait of Canso, am a fisherman by occupation
fifty years of Age, am a British Subject, my home has alway
Nova Scotia where I was born, I have been thirty seven Sum
ing, thirty two Summers of which, I was fishing in America
and five Summers in Colonial Vessels
The first few Years I went fishing in American Vessels, wa
fish, in the Gulf of St Lawrence, always outside of three i

then I went fishing for Mackerel in American Vessels, into the
St Lawrence, the last three years I have been engaged Seining
·el on the American Coast in United States Vessels, and found
·el plentiful, I was fishing on Shares as a hand on board, the
length of the fishing Season is about five months. the first
r I was Seining Mackerel, I cleared two hundred and fifteen Dol.
e. second season three hundred and Sixty two Dollars, and the
·son two hundred and sixty Dollars, averaging Each season two
d and Seventy nine Dollars or fifty five Dollars pr Month clear
·ding
bait used for catching Mackerel comes from the United States,
s of Pogies or Menhaden and Clams, and is taken almost entirely
he American Coast, Colonial fishing vessels use the same kind
as American fishing vessels, and obtain it from the United States,
are taken nearly altogether in Seines and within three Miles of
d,
to twelve Years ago about three hundred American fishing ves.
quented the Gulf of St Lawrence after Mackerel, and generally
·d good fares, taking from one to three fares each season, and
itly landing their first and second trips or fares in the Strait of
or in Prince Edwards Island for reshipment to the United States,
amer or Sailing Vessel, Mackerel have been getting scarcer in
lf of St. Lawrence every Year during the last four or five Years,
American Mackerel fishermen purchase large quantities of Supplies
Provinces, such as Salt, Barrels, Bait, Clothing, provisions, Wood,
Stores, and all kinds of fishing supplies, and occasionally require
utlays in repairs to their vessels, the average expenditure by
ierican Mackerel fishermen in the British Provinces during the
tive seasons would I have no doubt be upward of Seven hundred
s each pr Season which would in the aggregate amount to two
·d and ten thousand Dollars ($210.000) from the Mackerel fleet
on
Codfishing fleet of American vessels also purchase supplies largely
Provinces such as Ice, fresh Herring and Mackerel for baiting their
, Clothing, Wood, provisions, small Stores &c with occasional
, the average expenditure of the Codfishing fleet would be about
iundred and fifty Dollars to four hundred for each vessel pr sea·
ere are about One hundred American Codfishing Vessels calling
taining Supplies in the Strait of Canso. I cannot give an opin·
·he amount of Supplies they purchase in other ports of the British
ces,
éntire fleet of American fishing Vessels give employment on
their vessels to a great many of the people of this Province, I
say that during the last ten Years on an average that six to
hundred of our men found employment on board of American
Vessels yearly The presence of American fishermen in our
s of great pecuniary gain to our people, in consequence of the
imountts of Supplies they purchase in our Ports, and the great
r of our Men employed in American fishing Vessels
American fishermen make very little use of the privilege of cur·
i and drying nets &c on our shores,
n Mackerel were plentiful in the Gulf of St. Lawrence, they were
iearly all over the Gulf, Wherever bait was thrown Mackerel
generally appear on the surface, and more Mackerel were taken
· than inside three Miles from the Shore
ieve that the right to fish on the American Coast would be as

valuable to the Colonial fishermen as the Colonial fisheries t‹
cans, provided our people had as good vessels as well fitted an›
much Capital and enterprise as the Americans

And I Asberry Strahan aforesaid do solemnly declare tha
scientiously believe that the Statements made in the foregoing
tion are true and I make this declaration by virtue of the Ac
in the 37th. Year of Her Majestys Reign Entitled an Act for
pression of voluntary and extra judicial oaths

BERRY STR.

I hereby Certify that on the 9th day of June 1877   abov
Berry Strahan personally appeared before me and made and su
the foregoing Solemn Declaration As witness my hand & se
fice
(Seal.)   JAMES G McKEI
Notary

No. 146.

PORT HOOD ISLAND, C. B. June 7th

Statement of Nathaniel Smith of Port Hood Island.

I am 58 years old, have always lived on Port Hood Island
cod and mackerel fishing since I began to grow up—during tl
years the mackerels have much less frequented the Gulf of St l
their number has much decreased and during the last 3 years
of mackerel has been almost a failure—We hardly ever see tl
cans fish in boats. I don't think the catch of mackerel in thes
has decreased on account of the fishing of the American fi
The Americans as far as I know never land of the adjacent
cure fish and but seldom to dry nets—codfishing is not carr
the Americans within 3 miles from shore or at least extremel
I have never been employed as a fisherman on American ves
Americans while the catches were good put considerable m
circulation in this neighbourhood but I have no idea of the
amount or of the average expenditure of a single vessel. I
declare that the above statement of facts is correct and mak
laration conscientiously believing that said facts are true and
act of 37 Victoria entitled an Act for the suppression of volu
extra judicial oaths.

N

Port Hood Island June 7 1877

Declaration made and subscribed before

OSCAR MALM
U.

No. 147.

*Solemn Declaration by Hugh Cameron concerning the Fisheries
dian & American Waters made at Port Hastings Strait of C
this 5th day of June 1877*

Hugh Cameron says that he resides at New Town on the
the Strait of Canso, am a British subject fiftytwo Years o
quainted with the American and Canadian Atlantic Sea Fish

For the last three years there has been more or less of a fa
Catch of Codfish Mackerel and Herring in the Waters of t

urence no Codfish are Caught inside the Waters of the Atlantic
oast of the Dominion of Canada except in the Gulf of St. Laurence
lling off in the Catch of Codfish has been about in the following
rtion, that while it now takes a Vessel of Sixty Tons to catch a
ind Quintle of Codfish about ten Weeks it would take the same
l about Eight Weeks to Obtain the same quantity of fish ten years
bout twenty Years ago it would take six Weeks, and about thirty
ago about five Weeks to Obtain the same quantity of fish in the
sized vessel

Catch of Mackerel in the Gulf of St Laurence has gone down
two thirds at any rate from what it was before that time four
ago five years ago a vessel during the season would take in a fare
half or Cargo and half. ten years ago a vessel would take in
two Cargoes or fares about twenty Years ago about three Car-
or fares

ave been employed as a fisherman on board of American fishing
ls ever since I was Eighteen Years old with the Exception of three
ns when I did not go fishing. and another Season that I was on
a Colonial fishing Vessel I have never known American fishing
ls. curing fish or drying their Nets on shore. Except those re-
iking Herrings at the Magdalen Islands where they dry their
s on Shore The Americans do not use the inshore fisheries at all
ie Catching of Codfish There is more mackerel caught outside
iree Mile limit than inside, as near as I can judge about two thirds
Mackerel caught by Americans are caught from three to six Miles
Shore

ckerel fishing now begins off the Coast of New Jersey. fishing
ls follow the fish in their run Eastward to the State of Maine. and
e to the Coasts of the British Provinces about from two thirds to
quarters of the mackerel remain during their run North Eastward
New Jersey to the Gulf of St. Lawrence over three Miles from
, opposite the Southern Coast of Nova Scotia only a very small
in of the Mackerel during their course Eastward come nearer to
iore than six Miles for the purpose of playing during fine Weather
ring the Seasons when Mackerel and Codfish were plenty there
in the Course of the Season in the Gulf of St Lawrence about four
red American Mackerel fishing Vessels and about two hundred
fty to three hundred American Codfishing Vessels according to
at measurement the tonnage of American fishing Vessels referred
re from thirty to ninety Tons the average would be about fifty
o fifty Eight Tons—for an averaged sized Vessel for Codfishing
umber of the Crew would be about ten. and the number of Crew
Mackerel Catcher would be sixteen and the Crew of a Vessel of

ge size after Herrings would be about six hands
r about ten Years I shipped on board American fishing Vessels in
inited States generally during the month of April and continued
em until the close of the season about the 1st of November and
ther Seasons I shipped in the American Vessels at the Strait of
o. during these Seasons these Vessels were supplied in the Sev-
Ports of the British Provinces from Yarmouth all the way to Port
el in the Bay Cheleur with all kinds of outfits such as Provisions
Barrels Bait ice Clothing small Stores and occasionally with Rig-
Canvas Anchors and repairs to vessels spar booms &c. &c
om what I have seen and heard during my Experience I should
that the average expenditure of American fishing vessels in the
sh Provinces during the whole Season would be upwards of Seven

hundred Dollars out of every hundred Vessels frequenting th
St Laurence fishing about Seven or Eight would require mo
repairs the proper proportion of which is included in my Esti

In my opinion the coming of American fishing Vessels to o
has no influence whatever in lessening the Catch of Macke
Colonial fishing Vessels

The difference in fitting out and furnishing for a fishing V
American Vessel as compared with a Colonial fishing Vessel
about twenty five pr Cent. the American Vessel costing that n
than the other

I believe that the right to fish on the American Coast wc
valuable to the people of the British Provinces as the Colonia
are to the Americans provided our people had as good Ve
fitted them out as well and had as much enterprise as the Am

And I Hugh Cameron aforesaid do solemnly declare that I
tiously believe that the statements made in the foregoing do
are true and I make this declaration by virtue of the Act pas
37th Year of Her Majestys Reign entitled an act for the supp
Voluntary and Extra Judicial Oaths

HUGH CAN

In presence of:
  OSCAR MALMROS   }
        U. S. Consul   }

PORT HASTINGS NOVA SCO
June 7

Personally come and appeared before me the subscribing Jus
Peace for the County of Inverness, Hugh Cameron of New Tow
acknowledge before me that he Voluntarily made and subs
foregoing solemn Declaration

JAMES G. McK
Justice of t

No. 148.

Memorandum of remarks made by James Johnson concerning
Fisheries

James Johnson says that he resides at Port Hastings Cap
am a fisherman by occupation from 1853 to 1876 with the e
one season I have been employed as a fisherman on Board
fishing Schooners on or near the Coast of British North Ame
Atlantic British Coast   I went chiefly from Gloucester Mass,
once however from New London I have been mostly engage
erel fishing in the Bay of Cheleur, North Cape Prince Edwa
between the latter and Cape Breton

American fishermen generally commence taking Mackerel
of St. Laurence or other parts of the Atlantic Coast of Br
America about the 15th of June and continue fishing until al
of November, the average voyage being about six Weeks in

The Colonial fishermen when fishing inshore, alongside of
can fleet of fishing Vessels catch more fish on account of the
Vessels throwing large quantities of Bait   Fishing Vessels
size in the United States would cost about Sixty per Cent
Colonial built Vessels and the Outfit about one quarter more
Colonies, the only fish the Americans Catch in shore on t
Colonial Coasts are Mackerel. The most of the America
fishermen now Catch Mackerel on their own Coast only,

ut thirty sail of American Mackerel fishermen in the Gulf of
ence last season and the Gulf of St. Laurence comprises about
Iackerel fishing grounds

ve that the right to fish on the American Coast would be as
to the people of the British Provinces as the Colonial fisheries
icans provided our people had as good Vessels and fitted them
ell and had as much enterprise as the Americans
Iackerel fishery in the Gulf of St. Laurence has been much less
ve during the last six or Seven Years than formerly, formerly
il about ten years ago from two hundred to two hundred and
erican Vessels for Mackerel used to frequent the Gulf of St
e and obtain fair average Cargoes of Mackerel while in the sea
876 only about thirty Mackerel fishing Vessels came into the
d the greater part of these made broken voyages
resence of American fishermen in the Provinces is of great pe-
benefit to our people
any years past little or no use has been made of the privilege
g fish and drying Nets on our Shores by the American fisher-

g the seasons when the Mackerel fisheries were productive as they
years ago the American fishermen would get full Cargo within
ix Weeks they would then deposit or store at this or neighbor-
its on the Strait of Canso to be reshipped to the United States
ney would return once or twice more to the fishing grounds to
urther Cargo during such a season the average Expenditure of
ig sized Schooner (say 70 Tons) in the Provinces would be about
isequence of the lesser productiveness of the Mackerel fisheries
the last six or seven Years the American fishing Vessels have
taken over one Cargo of Mackerel in the season and frequently
ot been half filled and consequently the Expenditures in the
es have been proportionably reduced, very few Mackerel having
nded for reshipment to the United States
and always have been a British subject residing in the Province
i Scotia
[James Johnson aforesaid do solemnly declare that I conscien-
believe that the facts contained in the foregoing declaration are
d I make this declaration by virtue of the Act passed in the 37th
' Her Majesty's Reign Entitled an Act for the suppression of
ry and Extra Judicial Oaths.   JAMES JOHNSON.

Port Hastings Nova Scotia }
   June 5th 1877   }
eby Certify that on the 5th day of June 1877 the above named
Johnson personally appeared before me and made and Subscribed
egoing Solemn Declaration. As Witness my hand and Seal of

Seal.)   JAMES G. McKEEN
                                   Notary Public

No. 149.

*Declaration by Edward Fox concerning the Fisheries in Canadian
& American Waters*

ard Fox says that he resides at Fox Pond on the East side of the
of Canso, am a British subject twenty Eight Years old, have fol-

lowed the fishing business for twelve Years. always in Am‹
vessels with the Exception of one fishing voyage in a Nova

The Colonial fishermen as a rule catch more Mackerel wh‹
fleet of American fishermen which throw out large quan
the best and principal bait used for Mackerel is nearly all
American Coast and within three miles of the shore so ‹
ever seen, the bait referred to consists of Pogies and Cla
.the bait now used by Colonial fishing Vessels is the bait
tioned by me and is taken along the American Coast

For Number one and two Mackerel, Number One Salmon
rings the United States are the only Market with the E
small quantity that go to Canada, of the fat Herrings how‹
sent to Canada than of the Mackerel or Salmon

The average size of American Mackerel and Codfishing
gaged fishing on the Colonial Coasts is from sixty-five to
the Catch of Mackerel in the Gulf of St. Laurence during
or seven Years has been gradually decreasing, the Seaso
ing almost a failure in the Catch of Mackerel in Colonial ‹

Mackerel for some unknown reasons sometimes appear
Years on some Costs in great numbers and then again for
years will appear in decreasing numbers and finally alt‹
pear.

Ten Years ago and up to that time there were about tw
fifty to three hundred American fishing Vessels passing
Strait of Canso every season to catch fish in the Chelaur B
of the Gulf of St Laurence Six Years ago there were ab
dred vessels, since that time the number has been great
until last Year when the entire fleet of Mackerel fishing ‹
Gulf of St Laurence was probably not over fifty vessels

During the Seasons while the catch of Mackerel was ve
a quarter of the fleet of American Mackerel fishermen wo
one to three Cargoes of Mackerel in the Strait of Canso e
reshipment to the United States. A vessel of Seventy T
ple having landed a trip of Mackerel requires or usually
lowing supplies before going again to the fishing ground
Cargo viz about three hundred Empty barrels worth about
Each from Eighty to one hundred barrels of Salt worth a
lar and a quarter Each, twenty five to thirty barrels of Ba
five to six Dollars which with provisions and Small Stor
hundred and fifty Dollars would make in all for the fit ou
hundred and fifty Dollars and for a Second trip or fit out
dred Dollars worth of Supplies would be required,   The av
iture of those American fishing Schooners which visit o
out landing Cargoes of fish for reshipment amount to abou
Dollars each per season in our Provinces, the averag
therefore of the entire Mackerel fleet of American fishing
British Provinces during the productive Seasons would
hundred Dollars each pr Season

In consequence of the decreased Catch of Mackerel d
six or Seven Year in the Gulf of St Laurence the expend
can fishing Vessels in the British Provinces has been mu

The number of American Vessels engaged in the Codfi
the Colonial Atlantic Coasts has more than doubled with
Years about one hundred of these Codfishing vessels ca
or another in the Strait of Canso twice during the Seas‹
of ice fresh bait provisions &c the average expenditure f‹

ing for about ten Tons ice About thirty Dollars and for about a hun-
ed barrels of round Herrings or Mackerel about two hundred Dollars
hich with about one hundred Dollars for Wood Clothing occasional
pairs &c would make in all about three hundred and thirty Dollars
r each Vessel pr Season

For many years past little or no use has been made by the American
hermen of the privelege of curing fish and drying Nets on our shores
And I Edward Fox aforesaid do solemnly declare that I conscien-
ously believe that the Statements made in the foregoing declaration are
ue and I make this declaration by virtue of the act passed in the 37th
ear of Her Majestys Reign Entitled an Act for the Suppression of
oluntary and Extra judicial Oaths

THOMAS EDWARD FOX

Port Hastings Nova Scotia June 6. 1877
In presence ot :
    OSCAR MALMROS
        U. S. Consul

This is to certify that the above and foregoing Solemn Declaration
as duly made before me on the 6th day of June 1877. and subscribed
my presence by the above named Thomas Edward Fox

JAMES G. McKEEN
Justice of the Peace

No. 150.

I, William H. McAlpine do solemnly declare—that I reside at Louis-
urg, Cape Breton, where I am now and since the year 1866 have been
gaged in General merchandizing and of supplying American fishing
essels calling at this Port—that during the last six (6) years the num-
er of vessels calling as aforesaid has averaged at least 100 i. e. Ameri-
an fishing vessels one half of which number are codfishing and the
ther half herring fishing vessels—that these vessels are in the habit
f calling at different Ports of the Maritime Provinces before they call
t this Port and of buying supplies as them or at most of them—that
be amount expended at this Port by each of said vessels during said
eriod of six years has averaged at least twenty five dollars per season—
hat about one half of said vessels have been annually supplied by me
nd the other half by Mr Gardener of this Port and that the supplies
or which said expenses were incurred consist of ice, bait, small stores,
eef, mutton and occasionally other items to a small extent that I am
ot aware that the presence of American fishermen in the waters of the
Dominion of Canada is of any injury to the people thereof, but I think
hat their presence is of great pecuniary profit to the maritime Provinces
nd I make this solemn declaration conscientiously believing the same
o be true and by virtue of the Act passed in the 37th year of the reign
f Her Majesty entitled an Act for the suppression of voluntary and
xtra-judicial oaths

Louisburg C. B. July 17th 1877.
In presence of

W. H. McALPINE

UNITED STATES CONSULATE AT PICTOU, NOVA SCOTIA
LOUISBURG C. B. July 17th 1877.

I hereby certify that at said Louisburg on said July 17th the above
amed William H. McAlpine made before me and subscribed in my
resence the foregoing " Solemn Declaration."

    Attested :

OSCAR MALMROS
U. S. Consul

No. 151.

I, Joseph Townsend do solemnly declare—that I reside
C. B., that since 1863 I have been employed as Clerk and
of the Principal as the manager of the business of first M
Gardener of this place and afterwards of the " Louisburg
pany " to which Mr. Gardener transferred or sold his said t
said business from 1863 up to the present time has been i
supplying American fishing vessels calling at this Port, on
about being supplied by the above business in which I wa
ployed and one half by Mr Wm. H. McAlpine of this pl
number of American fishing vessels calling here has ave
the last 5 or 6 years at least one hundred, one half of the
the other half herring fishing vessels—that the average ex
vessel per season during said period has been about $25, p
more, at this port—that the American fishing vessels are
of calling at different ports of the Maritime Provinces be
and after they have called at this port and of buying sup
most of the Ports where they call—that the supplies purch
at our Port consist in ice, bait, small stores, beef, mutton an
in other items to a small extent—that I think that the prese
can fishermen on our coasts a great pecuniary advantage
thereof i. e. of the Provinces while I am not aware that i
presence of American fishermen on our coasts is in any re
to the interests of the Provinces, and I make this solem
conscientiously believing the same to be true and by virt
passed in the 37th year of Her Majesty's reign entitled a
suppression of voluntary and extra judicial oaths.
Louisburg C. B. July 17th 1877.

JOSEPH T

UNITED STATES CONSULATE AT PICTOU, NOVA
LOUISBURG C. B. Ju

I hereby certify that at said Louisburg on this 20th day
the above named Joseph Townsend made and subscribed
foregoing Solemn Declaration
Attested: OSCAR MA

No. 152.

I, James Peeples of Pirate Cove, Guysboro County do
clare: that I have been a fisherman for the last 33 years
employed during that time as well on American as on No
ing vessels, mostly on American vessels prosecuting the
ery in the Gulf of St Lawrence, for the last 5 or 6 years
said I have not been employed in fishing—according to
American fishing vessels make no use or but very little u
lege of drying their nets on the Coasts of the Dominion of
not at all cure their fish on these coasts—I do not think t
fishermen catch less fish on account of having a fleet of A
fishing along side of them I rather think the Provincial f
more fish by fishing alongside of an American fleet becau
of bait thrown keeps the fish on the surface of the water
in American fishing vessels prosecuting the fishery in the
rence that have spent from 1300 to 1500 dollars per season i
in case they had to refit after landing their first catch f

ɔ the States—I went this spring employed as cooper in an American
·hing schooner "Stagawa" from Gloucester catching herring at the
agdalen Islands and I know that her bill of expenses at Pirate Cove
nounted to about $600 $\frac{00}{100}$—during the last 6 or 7 years the mackerel
shery has much fallen off—I think that about one half only of the
ackerel that were caught from 10 to 12 years ago have been caught
uring the last 5 years—the last 2 years the mackerel fishery was a
retty bad failure—I know that very few if any vessel caught enough
sh to make more than one trip—I know that the American fishing
essels call at a great many Ports all along the coasts of the Dominion
nd expend much money in these Ports, formerly Yankee money was
ɔout all the money we saw—the presence of American fishermen on
ɪe Coasts of these provinces has been a great help to the people of the
'rovinces—they were in the habit of buying socks, mittens, all kinds of
egetables, mutton beef, store goods and supplies of all kind, their pres-
nce was certainly no injury to our people in any respect; I do not think
at much fishing will diminish the fish that annually visit the fishing
rounds—I rather think that feeding them by throwing out much bait
ttracts them—seine fishing may injure the fisheries, but the real reason
hy in some years mackerel are plentiful and in other years scarce is
ot known, I think that more than one half of the crew of American
shing vessels are natives and residents of the Canadian Provinces;
nd I make this solemn declaration conscientiously believing the same
o be true and by virtue of the Act passed in the 37th year of Her
Iajesty's reign entitled "An Act for the suppression of voluntary and
xtra-judicial oaths.

JAMES PEEPLES

Dated Pirate Cove July 20th, 1877.

UNITED STATES CONSULATE AT PICTOU N. S.
PIRATE COVE July 20th, 1877.

I hereby certify that on this 20th day of July 1877 the above named
fames Peeples before me, at said Pirate Cove voluntarily made and
ıubscribed the foregoing Solemn Declaration.

Attested :   OSCAR MALMROS,
U. S. Consul.

No. 153.

I, Samuel Peeples of Pirate Cove, Guysboro County do solemnly de-
:lare: that I have been for over 30 years a fisherman I have been
ɪearly every summer been engaged on American fishing vessels fishing
n the Gulf of St Lawrence, during the spring and fall I have been en-
ʒaged in boat fishing on my own account—during the last 8 or 9 years
.he mackerel fishery has much fallen off—during the last 6 years the
:atch has not averaged more than ½ of what it was 10 or 15 years ago
ınd during the last two years it has been almost a total failure—I do
ɪot think that Provincial fishermen catch any the less fish on account
ɔf fishing alongside of an American mackerel fishing fleet on the con-
.rary I think their catch is then greater; I have often seen Provincial
ïshermen in their boats come out to fish alongside of the American fleet
ɔecause they would catch a greater quantity by following the fleet than
;hey would by remaining in-shore—American fishermen make but little
ıse of the coasts of these Provinces for drying nets and none for curing
ïsh—I know that American fishermen call at a great many ports of the
Canadian Provinces and that they buy more or less at every port where
;hey call; they buy beef, mutton, all kinds of vegetables, store goods

of all descriptions, homespun cloth, mittens & socks &c ₹
opinion that on account of the money they spend they b
rially benefitted the people of these Provinces while I
that their presence on the coasts of the Dominion has
been injurious to the interests of its inhabitants—I thi
one half of the crew of the American fishing fleet is comp
and residents of the Maritime Provinces—All fat mack
know goes to the United States and I make this sole
conscientiously believing the same to be true and by vi
passed during the 37th year of Her Majesty's reign enti
the suppression of voluntary and extra-judicial oaths.

Dated Pirate Cove July 20th 1877.

SAMUEL P PI

UNITED STATES CONSULATE
PICTOU, NOV/
PIRATE COVE JU

I hereby certify that at Pirate Cove, County of Guysb
tia, the above named Samuel A. Peeples, on this 20th d
voluntarily made before me and subscribed in my prese
ing "Solemn Declaration.

Attested:

OSCAR M/

No. 154.

I, Isaiah Crittenden do solemnly declare that I am a
a native of Nova Scotia and living at Pirate Cove Gu
Nova Scotia I am 42 years old and have been employed
summer since I was 13 years old, during the last 27 s
always been engaged as one of the crew of American
the American fishing vessels hardly ever dry their nets
the Coasts of the Dominion of Canada about 40 to 50 A
fishing vessels have annually visited the coasts of the
Dominion of Canada their crew is about 7 or 8 men ea
catch per vessel has been about 600 barrels during the l
season—from 8 to 10 years back the American macke
consisted of from 300 to 500 sails per season in the Gulf
the mackerel fishing vessels average about 12 to 14
during the last 6 years and particularly the last 2 the
been getting very scarce the reason being according to
that of many old fishermen that the scarcity of bait fout
erel induced them to go to other grounds—the bait wa
the American fishing fleet had been driven away by th
enue Cutters during the fishery troubles of 1870 or I t
from that time the mackerel fishery began to fall off—
off took place when the Revenue Vessels of Great E
with the American fishermen about the years 1853
Americans in consequence resorted in but small numb
St Lawrence—during the last 5 years according to the
can form the American fishing fleet fishing for macker
St Lawrence has consisted of about 250 sails during th
if I strike an average of their number during that pe
can mackerel fishing vessels begin to arrive in the Gulf
about the beginning of June in each year in small
greater number arrive only after the first week in

be beginning of August—the herring fishing vessels arrive
agdalen Islands about the 1st of May, they remain there as
out 2 to 3 weeks unless the fish happen to be scarce there when
n go to the coast of Newfoundland—Generally the herring fleet
it one trip a season and after their return home fish off the
i coast for cod or mackerel or sometimes they go to the Gulf of
·nce—the American herring vessels have considerably benefited
le on this Strait, besides buying supplies of all kinds, they
l hire from two to three boats to go with them to the Magdalen
)aying about 30 dollars a trip for a man and his boat and ten
i boat without a man, the average number of the crew of
n herring fishing vessels when they arrive at the Strait consists
to 5 men and the hire the rest here paying about $20 a man
an to the Magdalen Islands and back—the mackerel fishing
?xpend likewise a great deal of money in the Maritime
s as they call at a great many ports and spend money in every
long as I can remember has the trade of the merchants on the
Canso principally consisted in selling goods of all kinds to
n fishermen and the people of the Strait of Canso would have
very little money if it had not been for the money spent by
n fishing vessels—On the whole I don't think that pro-
fishermen get a smaller catch of fish on account of the
of American mackerel fishing vessels in the Gulf of St
e—Generally and almost without exception the fishing of
n Mackerel fishing vessels up to the middle of August or be-
of September is done outside the 3 mile limit from shore and
t until the latter part of October they mostly fish inshore—the
iing prosecuted by American fishermen off the Coasts of the
)n of Canada is the herring, the mackerel and the codfishing,
ish is all caught outside the limits, off shore. During the times
iackerel fishing was still good the American fishing vessels
ihip from 300 to 350 men each season from the Strait of Canso
pe Bre'on I think that the crew of American fishing vessels is
)d of about ½ natives of the Maritime Provinces who continue to
i the Provinces and are British subjects—In my opinion the out-
f an American fishing vessel for the Gulf of St Lawrence costs
300 to $400 more than the outfitting of a fishing vessel of the
nnage in the Province of Nova Scotia; And I make this solemn
ion conscientiously believing the same to be true and by virtue
:t passed in the 37th year of Her Majesty's reign entituled An
the suppression of voluntary and extra judicial oaths.

l Pirate Cove July 21st 1877.

                                    ISAIAH CRITTENDEN

UNITED STATES CONSULATE AT
PICTOU, NOVA SCOTIA
PIRATE COVE July 21st 1877.

iby certify that on this 21st day of July 1877 at Pirate Cove,
ro' County, Nova Scotia, the above named Isaiah Crittenden
rily made before me and subscribed in my presence the above
?going " Solemn Declaration."
ted :

                                    OSCAR MALMROS,
                                       U. S. Consul

No. 155.

I, E. Aug. Crittenden at Pirate Cove, Strait of
declare that: I have followed the business of fishing 1
a British subject & have always resided in Nova S₀
the whole period of 44 years I have every summer
American fishing vessels   that during the last six y
fisheries in the Gulf of St Lawrence have much fall
ing those six years certainly been not more than one
was before ; the cause of this falling off is I think e₁
the annual number of American fishing vessels of ev
the Gulf of St Lawrence during the last 5 years ha
50 sails fifty sails while ten years ago or longer they ₁
to 500 sails—the average tonnage of an America₁
about sixty (60) tons, a vessel of this size is manned
14 men ; fully one half of the crew of the American 1
subjects of and residents of the Dominion of Cana₀
make hardly any use of the privilege of drying nets
the Coasts of the Dominion—I do not believe from ₁
the catch of Provincial fishermen is smaller when fi
an American fishing fleet   on the contrary I think ₁
brought to the surface and caught when a number
ing together—during the last two or three years the
fishing fleet in the waters on the coasts of the Do
bered about 20 to 25 a year, in former years it nun
50 sails—during the last 3 years the herring fishing
averaged per vessel about 400 to 500 barrels per vess
that is 8 or 10 years ago they averaged about one the
codfish caught by the Americans is all caught out₁
(3) miles from shore—the halibut or other fish caugh
the coasts of the Dominion of Canada is totally ins
worth mentioning—the American fishermen expen
money in the Provinces for beef, mutton, potatoes ₀
and supplies of every description as they are in th
many ports of the Dominion in succession from the t
American coast until they arrive on the fishing grou
whole season while they are in the Gulf of St Law₁
buying more or less at every port they call at—I thi
penditure of a seventy ton American fishing vessel i
of the maritime Province may be safely estimated
unless they land their fare for re-shipment to the S
the expenses for a re-outfit would be of course muc
vessel of a size which costs here about $500 would ₀
$1600 in the States and the outfit in the States is at
the cost of outfitting a fishing vessel of the same
Scotia—I think that the presence of American fishe
of the maritime Provinces is a great pecuniary bene
Provinces and not in any respect injurious to the in
ple of the Provinces ; and I make this solemn de
tiously believing the same to be true and by virtue
during the 37th year of her Majestys reign entitule₀
suppression of voluntary and extrajudicial oaths.
Dated Pirate Cove July 19th 1877.

E. AUG. + hi
ma

In presence of :
OSCAR MALMROS

UNITED STATES CONSULATE AT
PICTOU, NOVA SCOTIA
PIRATE COVE July 19th 1877

ereby certify that on this 19th day of July 1877 the above named
gustus Crittenden at Pirate Cove before me made and subscribed
regoing " Solemn Declaration."
ested :

OSCAR MALMROS
U. S. Consul.

No. 156.

benezer C Peeples of the County of Guysborough in the Prov-
f Nova Scotia Do Solemly declare that I am a British subject,
am by occupation a fisherman.   Have been fishing in American
g vessels for the last thirty six Summers during the Spring and
have often been engaged fishing in Boats inshore on my own ac-
the Vessels in which I was employed prosecuted the Mackerel
y in the Bay of St. Lawrence during the last five or six years
bout one fourth of the Mackerel were caught during the season
ere caught in former Years, say fifteen Years ago and prior to that
ording to my estimate three quarters of the Mackerel caught by
can fishing vessels are caught outside of the three Mile limit from
not more than one quarter being caught inshore
not think that the Catch of Provincial fishermen are any the less
se an American fleet are fishing in the same vicinity
cause why mackerel are very plentiful in some seasons and very
e in other seasons is not known
least one half of the Crews of American fishing Vessel are com-
l of Natives and residents of the Maritime Provinces of Canada
e American fishing fleet derive little or no advantage from the
lege of drying nets and Curing fish on our Coasts as they are not
habit of making use of the privelege, occasionally the may cure
significant quantity of Herrings at the Magdalene Islands
ring the last five Years the average number of American Mackerel
g vessel averaged about two hundred sail in the Gulf of St. Law-

average tonnage of these Vessels is I think about fifty Tons
presence of American fishing vessels on the Atlantic Coasts of the
nion has greatly benefited its people owing to the purchase by the
ican fishermen of supplies of every description and the Employ-
given on board these vessels to a large number of people belong-
the Provinces
number of the Crew of an averaged sized American fishing Ves-
about fourteen
Codfish caught by American fishing Vessels are taken entirely
le the three mile limit
average number of Crew on board Herring fishing Vessels are
Eight. the Herring caught by these American Vessels is nearly
ught on the Coast of the Magdalene Islands About fifty vessels
the United States go to the Magdalen Island for Herrings every
z. sometimes some of them go the Island of Anticosti and the
oundland shore when Herrings are scarce at the Magdalens. The
ge catch of these vessels have been for the last five Years about
hundred barrels Herring each Vessel
ckerel Herring and Codfish are the only fish that as far as I know
mericans are in the habit of catching in the Gulf of St Laurence

And I make this solemn declaration conscientiously
same to be true and by virtue of the Act passed in the 3'
Majestys Reign entitled an act for the suppression of
extrajudicial Oaths
Pirate Cove Strait Canso July 20. 1877
EBENEZER

UNITED STATES CONSULATE
PICTOU, NOVA
PIRATE COVE J

I hereby certify that at Pirate Cove on this 20th d;
before me and in my presence the above named Eben
voluntarily made and subscribed the foregoing " Solemn
Attested :
OSCAR M

No. 157.

I, Samuel Peeples of Port Mulgrave on the Strait (
emnly declare that I am 34 years old   that for 16 years
years I have been one of the crew of some American M
fishing vessel—that I am of the opinion that nearly t
thirds ($\frac{2}{3}$) of the crew of American fishing vessels are s
habitants of the British North American Provinces—tha
fishermen catch quite as many mackerel when fishing :
American Mackerel fishing fleet as they would catch in
no American fishing vessels on the Mackerel grounds
North American coasts—until within about the last 6 y
can Mackerel fishing vessels began to arrive on the fish
the Gulf of St Lawrence at the beginning of June but
5 or 6 years but very few arrived until after the 4th of J
the present season they have but just now arrived in an
reason why they have during the last 6 years arrived so
of St Lawrence is that the Americans have had a very
ing the early part of the summer season off their own
about the middle of July the mackerel in the Gulf are r
don't begin to fatten until about the middle of July—
entire catch of the American Mackerel catching fleet i
Lawrence is caught off-shore that is out side of the 3 mil
and only about $\frac{1}{4}$ is caught inside that limit—the codfis
American cod fishing vessels is all caught outside the
the grand banks of Newfoundland and other places on
the Americans do not dry their nets on the coasts of th
American Provinces or at least but very rarely and do
their fish on these coasts—I consider the presence of A
vessels on our coasts and in our ports as of the greate
inhabitants of the Provinces as they spend much money
where they call and they are in the habit of calling :
Provincial Ports in the course of the season in fact wl
the custom of the American fishing vessels in the Strai
is but very little business done of any kind and I make
laration conscientiously believing the same to be true
an Act passed during the 37th year of Her Majesty's I
Act for the suppression of voluntary and extra-judicial
Dated at Port Mulgrave July 21st 1877.
SAMUEL

UNITED STATES CONSULATE AT PICTOU, NOVA SCOTIA,
PORT MULGRAVE July 21. 1877

is to certify that at said Port Mulgrave on this 21st day of July
ove named Samuel H. Peeples voluntarily made before me and
ally subscribed the foregoing "Solemn Declaration.
ested:

OSCAR MALMROS
U. S. Consul

No. 158.

ames McNair do solemnly declare that I live at Port Mulgrave on
rait of Canso—that I am 48 years old—that ever since 1849 I have
shing every season except the two last seasons, mostly on Ameri-
ssels but sometimes also on vessels belonging to the Strait of
—the Americans do not make use of the coasts of the Dominion
nada to dry nets or cure fish except that the American herring
sometimes dry their seines on the Magdalen Islands—the cod-
g is carried on by Americans altogether off shore—the proportion
ckerel caught inshore by the Americans averages I think about ¼
ir entire catch—I do not think that the Provincial fishermen catch
ller quantity of mackerel on account of fishing alongside of an
ican fleet—I think that mackerel fishing by seines ought to be pro-
d as it breaks up the schools of mackerel and injures the fishing
few American vessels however fish with seines—indeed I do not
that fishing with seines is profitable as those at least that the
cans use can not be employed in shore to advantage—the Ameri-
ften land their seines because they find the fishing by hook more
ble—I think that at least one half of the crew of Am. fishing
s are natives of and reside in the several Provinces of the Dominion
ada—the mackerel fishery has very much fallen off during the last
s or so—the reason why the mackerel catch has been poor 2 sea-
go is that during that season the mackerel were very much chased
horse mackerel a fish from 5 to 8 feet long preying upon the mack-
the mackerels shift and take new routes during some seasons;
lo not regularly return to the breeding grounds like the salmon—
the mackerel were very plentiful, they say last season on the coasts
wfoundland while they were scarce in the Gulf of St Lawrence—
ly fish caught by Americans off the Atlantic coasts of the Domin-
ther in-shore or off shore are mackerel, codfish and herring, to a
extent however the Americans prosecute also the halibut fishing—
lo not employ more than from 6 to 8 vessels in halibut fishing and
generally fish off the Coasts of Anticosti And I do make this
n declaration conscientiously believing the same to be true and by
of the Act passed during the 37th year of Her Majestys reign en-
"An Act for the suppression of voluntary and extra-judicial oaths.
ed Port Mulgrave July 21.st 1877.

JAMES McNAIR

UNITED STATES CONSULATE AT PICTOU N. S.
PORT MULGRAVE July 21st 1877.

reby certify that the above named James McNair on this 21st day
y 1877, at Port Mulgrave, personally made before me and sub-
d in my presence voluntarily the above " Solemn Declaration.
ested:

OSCAR MALMROS
U. S. Consul

No. 159.

I, John Murray, do solemnly declare that I was born and a
been living at Port Mulgrave on the Strait of Canso ; that I a
of age—that since I was 19 years of age I have been enga
ing during the summer seasons—that with the excepti
seasons I have always shipped in American fishing vessels d
2 season I was in Provincial vessels—the Americans do no
nets on the coasts of the Dominion except occasionally for 1
nor do they cure their fish on these coasts—the crew is about ½ c
natives of the British North American Provinces who are st
in the Provinces and are of course british subjects—the Amer
all their codfish on the banks or off-shore. I do not think tb
cial fishermen catch any smaller number of fish on account
alongside of American fleets of mackerel fishers—the macke
has much fallen off during the last 5 years and especially (
last 2 years it has almost been an entire failure—the cause of
off of the mackerel fishery is not known—during the pres
mackerel promise to be in fair quantities in the Gulf of St
from all I have lately heard—the American fishermen i. e
fishers begin to come in June but of late years they don't ar
fishing grounds in any number until after the 4th of July—
erel are poor until after they have spawned that is about the
July—they are just getting fat now—the Americans catch
larger quantity of mackerel outside of the three mile line fro
should not think that the Americans catch more than one fou
entire catch of mackerel in-shore that is inside the 3 mile
cost of outfit of American vessels engaged in the fisheries is
bly higher that that of Provincial fishing vessels, their out
better too than that of the Provincials—fat mackerel and
caught by Provincial fishing vessels are nearly all sold in
States, and I make this solemn declaration conscientiousl
the same to be true and by virtue of an Act passed during tl
of Her Majesty's reign entituled an Act for the suppressiono
and extra-judicial oaths.

Dated Port Mulgrave July 21st. 1877.

JOHN M

UNITED STATES CONSULATE AT PICTOU,
PORT MULGRAVE July

I hereby certify that at Port Mulgrave on this 21st day
above named John Murray voluntarily made before me and
in my presence the foregoing " Solemn Declaration. '

Attested :

OSCAR MALM
U.

No. 160.

I, John H. Ingraham, of North Sydney, Cape Breton, M
Trader, do solemnly depose and say :

That I have been doing business as a trader and general
North Sydney, Cape Breton, for the last twenty years.

During that period the port of Sydney has been visited
a number of vessels engaged in prosecuting the cod and m
ery, belonging to the United States of America. Within

rs the average number of American fishing vessels frequenting this
t has been not less than fifty annually.

he expenditure of the said American fishing fleet with me as a mer-
nt during the last five years has been as follows:

1872, for Salt	121.
" Supplies	511.
	$632
1873 for Bait	15
" Salt	110.
" Supplies	2475
	$2600
1874, for Salt	83.
" Bait	12
" Sundries	2590
	$2685
1875 for salt	17·
" sundries	1980
	$1997.
1876 for salt	44
" bait	27.
" sundries	2100
	$2171

There are no fishing vessels employed at present out of this port, the
nery being entirely conducted by shore boats, and fishermen earn only
precarious living

According to my Experience nearly one half of the crews of Ameri-
1 fishing vessels frequenting this port are natives of Nova Scotia and
pe Breton.

I consider that the presence of American fishing vessels on our
ounds, is of great pecuniary benefit to this country.

Dated at North Sydney C. B. this 18th day of July 1877

JOHN L INGRAHAM

Sworn to before me

B. ARCHIBALD J. P

No. 161.

I. William H. Moore, of North Sydney Cape Breton, Merchant and
ader, do solemnly depose and say:

That I have been doing business as a trader and General Merchant
North Sydney Cape Breton for the last twenty years.

During that period the port of Sidney has been visited annually by a
mber of vessels engaged in prosecuting the Cod and Mackerel fishery,
longing to the United States of America. Within the last five years
e average number of American fishing vessels frequenting this port
s not been less than fifty annually.

The expenditure of the said American fishing fleet with me
chant during the last five years has been as follows:

In 1872, for Supplies...
" 1873 for Supplies........ 331
        " Bait & Salt.............................. 18
                                                          —
" 1874 " Supplies...
" 1875 " Supplies...
" 1876 " Supplies...

There are no fishing vessels employed out of this port. The
prosecuted to some extent at this port, but altogether by Sh
and fishermen make only a precarious living.

According to my experience nearly one half of the crews of
fishing Vessels frequenting this port are natives of Nova S
Cape Breton.

I consider that the presence of American fishing vessel
grounds is of great pecuniary benefit to this country.

Dated at North Sydney C. B. this 18th day of July 1877.

W. H.]

Sworn to before me.

B. ARCHIBALD *J. P.*

No. 162.

I Allan McDonald do solemnly declare that I was born and
about 1 mile from Cape Jack Antigonish County, Nova Sco
41 years of age—I have been mackerel fishing for about th
years partly in American and partly in Provincial vessels-
think that Americans dry their nets or cure their fish or but
the coasts of the British Provinces—the codfish caught by
vessels is caught on the banks or other places on the high se
rate they catch them but seldom in-shore—the only fish
Americans off the Coasts of British America are codfish, mac
but and herring—during good seasons the American macke
the Gulf of St Lawrence consists of about (500) ve hundre
during the last few years there were but few, the catch of mad
ing much fallen off—last year I don't think there were more
American Mackerel fishing vessels in the Gulf and I don't
they have averaged more during the last three years—the
herring fleet on the Atlantic coasts of the British Province
aged during the last 5 years from 30 to 40 sails a season—I
seen more than 10 to 12 sails of American halibut fishing ve
Coasts of the British Provinces the American codfishing fi
grand banks of Newfoundland is large, I have seen there a
four hundred vessels at a time—I have been codfishing, her
and mackerel fishing, we often go out early in spring codfish
ring fishing and afterwards mackerel fishing in the Gulf—I
my own experience that all these American fishing vessels t
mentioned are in the habit of calling each at different ports i
inces during each season and of leaving very considerabl
each port they call at—I think I have a pretty correct id
their expenses amount to and according to my estimate the
penses of an American fishing vessel in the several ports of
Provinces amount during the season to about three hun
hundred dollars—I should judge that about one half of the

American fishing fleet fishing off the Coasts of the British Provinces consist of natives who are at the same time residents of the Provinces and I do not refer to those who have removed their residence to Gloucester and other places in the United States—I do not think that the presence of the American fishing vessels in the Gulf of St Lawrence essens the chances of Colonial fishermen to catch fish on the contrary my experience has taught me that mackerel are more easily perceived when there are fishing vessels distributed all over the Gulf, then when hey rise at one place see it by their spy-glasses and join the vessels where the fish rise and all get their share of fish, when there are out few vessels on the fishing grounds they may not at all get to know it what spots to find the mackerel—the latter also rise better when more bait is thrown out than can be done by a few vessels—I have no doubt hat the presence of the American fishermen on the coasts of these Provinces has, been of great benefit to them, nearly half our fishermen might almost starve if it was not for the employment given them by the American vessels, And I make this solemn declaration conscientiously believing the same to be true and by virtue of an Act passed during the 7th year of Her Majesty's reign entituled an Act for the suppression f voluntary and extra-judicial oaths.

Dated Cape Jack July 24. 1877.

his
ALLAN + McDONALD
mark.

In presence of
JAMES G. McKEEN
OSCAR MALMROS

PROVINCE OF NOVA SCOTIA
COUNTY OF ANTIGONISH

I hereby Certify that the above named Allan McDonald voluntarily made and affixed his mark of hand before me at Cape Jack Settlement in Said County of Antigonish the foregoing solemn declaration

Given under my hand and Notarial Seal this 24th day of July 1877

(Seal.) JAMES G McKEEN
Notary Public

No. 163.

I, Donald McDonald (Duncan's son) do solemnly declare: that I am living about ⅞ of a mile south of Cape Jack Light House in Antigonish County, Nova Scotia—that I am 69 years old and have been fishing for the last 50 years with the exception of one summer and during that year I went out in the fall mackerel fishing—I have been on American and Nova Scotian fishing vessels mackerel and codfishing mostly however mackerel fishing—the American fishermen do not dry their nets or cure their fish on the coasts of the British Provinces—I think that about one half of the crew of the American fishing vessels fishing off the Coasts of the British Provinces are british subjects and residing in these Provinces—I think that Colonial fishing vessels catch pretty nearly as many mackerel when fishing alongside of an American mackerel fleet as when fishing alone or as they would do if there were no American fishing vessels in the Gulf—codfish is all caught by Americans off-shore on the banks of Newfoundland the in-shore fishing by American fishermen on the Coasts of these provinces has not been of any appreciable injury to Colonial fishermen—while the money expended by them on our coasts for beef, mutton, potatoes and other vegetables mittens, socks, homespun cloths and supplies furnished by our merchants has been of

great advantage to our people—that all the fat mackerel and the
quantity of the fat herring finds its only market in the United
some of the fat herring goes to Canada—And I make this solemn
ation conscientiously believing the same to true and by virtue
Act passed during the 37th year of her Majestys reign entitled
for the suppression of voluntary and extra-judicial oaths.

Dated Cape Jack July 24. 1877.

his
DONALD + McDONALD (Duncan's
mark

In presence of
OSCAR MALMROS

PROVINCE OF NOVA SCOT
COUNTY OF ANTIGON

I hereby Certify that the above named Donald McDonald (Du
Son) voluntarily made and subscribed by affixing his mark befo
at Cape Jack Settlement in said County of Antigonish the for
Solemn declaration.

Given under my hand and Notarial Seal this 24th day of July
(Seal.) JAMES G McKEEN
Notary I

No. 164.

I Michael Crispo do solemnly declare that I reside at
Bouché Antigonish County, Nova Scotia, that during about 20
have been engaged in the fishing business during that period
owned several fishing vessels during One time I owned 4
vessels—my principal business has been in mackerel but also to
extent in the codfishing business I have exported my fish to
New York, Philadelphia, Halifax and Montreal—the United Sta
the only market for No 1 and No two mackerel and most of the fat
is sent to the States—since the duty was taken off fish in the Sta
average profit in the fish business is from 5 to 8 per cent on th
tal and labor invested in the business—during the period of say
years preceding the taking off of the duty on fish in the Sta
experience has been that money and capital invested in the fishi
ness has returned hardly any profit, at the least the profit has
very insignificant one and I make this statement conscientio
lieving the same to be true and by virtue of an Act passed dur
37th year of her Majestys reign entitled " An Act for the supp
of voluntary and extra-judicial oaths

Dated July 25th 1877.

MICHAEL CR

In prsence of:
OSCAR MALMROS
U S Consul

PROVINCE OF NOVASCOTI
COUNTY OF ANTIG

I hereby Certify that the foregoing named Michael Crispo vol
made and Subscribed before me at Harbour Bouché in said Co
Antigonish the foregoing Solemn declaration

Given under my hand and Notarial Seal this 25th day of July
JAMES G McKEE
(Seal.) *Notary*

No. 165.

I Patrick Webb of Harbor Bouché do solemnly declare that I live
t said Harbor Bouché, Antigonish County, Nova Scotia, that I have
 een fishing for Mackerel for some years—I am now engaged in the fish
usiness, I own one fishing vessel myself exclusively and own an inter-
st in three other fishing vessels, I also supply a number of fishermen
nd they pay me after their trips by giving me their catch of fish at cur-
ent prices—The best estimate I am able to make at a rough calculation
· that the profits of the fish business during the last 5 years have aver-
ged about five per cent per annum on the capital and labor invested in
he fisheries I do think that Colonial fishermen catch about as many
sh when fishing together with american vessels in the Gulf as when
shing alone I know that the American fishermen in the course of the
eason call at many of the Colonial harbours and spend much money
nd I think that on the whole the presence of the American fisher-
 en on our Coasts has been a great pecuniary benefit to the People
f the Provinces And I make this solemn declaration conscientiously
elieving the same to be true and by virtue of an Act passed during the
7th year of Her Majestys reign entituled An Act for the suppression
f voluntary and extra judicial oaths

Dated at Harbor Bouché July 25th 1877.

PATRICK WEBB

In presence of
OSCAR MALMROS
U. S. Consul

PROVINCE OF NOVA SCOTIA
COUNTY OF ANTIGONISH

I hereby Certify that the above named Patrick Webb voluntarily
 ade and subscribed before me at Habour Bouché in said County of
Antigonish the foregoing solemn declaration

Given under my hand and Notarial Seal this 25th day July 1877

JAMES G. McKEEN

(Seal.)   *Notary Public*

No. 166.

I James Gillis do solemnly declare: that I am 67 years of age that I
 m living about ¾ of a mile from Cape Jack Light House, that for 37
 ears I have been mackerel fishing, two seasons I have been codfishing—
 I don't think that that Provincial fishing vessels catch a smaller quantity
 f mackerel on account of fishing alongside of an American Mackerel
 shing fleet—during some seasons the American fishing vessels can do
better in-shore at other seasons they can do better off shore that outside
the three mile limit from shore—taken one season with another I think
the Americans catch the greater portion of their mackerel outside of
the 3 mile limit from shore—I know that during the last 5 or 6 years the
mackerel fishery in the Gulf of St. Lawrence has very much fallen off
but can not give an estimate of how much that is in what proportion
compared with former years it has fallen off—According to my opinion
and experience I think that about ½ of the crew of the American fishing
fleet that comes to the Gulf of St Lawrence is composed of natives of
the British Provinces who are also living in these Provinces—some but
a few only of the American fishermen occasionally dry their nets and
cure fish on the coasts of these Provinces—I have no doubt that the
presence of American fishermen on these coasts and in our harbors is of
very great pecuniary profit to the Peoples of the Provinces on account

of the purchase by them of all kinds of supplies and count
and because they give employment to great many of our fish
other people—that No. 1 and No. 2 mackerel and most of the
caught by Colonial fishermen finds its only market in the Un
a part of the fat herring however is sent to Canada, and I
solemn declaration conscientiously believing the same to be t
virtue of an Act passed during the 37th year of Her Majesty
tituled an Act for the suppression of voluntary and extra-jud
    Dated Cape Jack July 24th 1877.
                                        his
                            JAMES + C
                                       mark
In presence of
    JAMES G. McKEEN
                            PROVINCE OF NOVA SC
                            COUNTY OF AN]
    I hereby Certify that the above named James Gillies volun
and Subscribed by affixing his mark before me at Cape Jack
in Said County of Antigonish the foregoing Solemn declarati
    Given under my hand and Notarial Seal this 24th day of J
    (Seal.)   JAMES G McK]
                                        Nota
                    No. 167.

    I, William Embree do solemnly declare: that I live at a p
Bear Island, on the Strait of Canso about 2 miles below Po
bury in the County of Richmond, Nova Scotia—that I am by
a fisherman—that I am 55 years old and have been out fishi
son since I was 18 years old—that I have never been empl
American fishing vessel—that I have been fishing in the Gul
rence around Sydney the Magdalen Islands and other pl
Gulf—that I have fished alongside of American vessels
A never thought that I caught a smaller number of fish on
fishing alongside of the American fleet—American Mack
vessels begin to arrive in the month of June in each year b
numbers only—they do not come as a rule before the first we
this year they are but just now beginning to arrive and I
that the bulk will arrive before August—the mackerel beg
up from about the middle of July—as far as I know the A
not dry their nets or but very rarely and do not cure their
coasts of the British North American Provinces—the Ame
their codfish all on the banks & other places on the high s
as I can come to it I think that about two thirds ($\frac{2}{3}$) of the
of mackerels by the American fleet in the Gulf of St Lawren
outside of the 3 mile line from shore and about $\frac{1}{3}$ in-shore—
between $\frac{1}{3}$ and $\frac{1}{2}$ of the crew of the American fishing fleet i
of natives and residents of the British American Province
age number of the crew of an American Mackerel fishing ve
13 to 14   the crew of an American herring fishing vessel av
8 men—the mackerel fishing in the Gulf of St Lawrence has
off—formerly that is ten or fifteen years ago there were as
to 800 Am. vessels counting each return of the vessels to
new vessel—fishing for mackerel in the Gulf of St Lawren
ing the last 6 years taking an average their number durin
has not I think been more than 200—I am convinced that
of American fishermen in the ports and on the coasts of t

is of great pecuniary advantage to the people thereof and in no respect an injury to the interests of the people of the Provinces—I do not think that the American fishing vessels have driven away the mackerel from our fishing grounds, because not only mackerel but herring have got to be very scarce in the Strait of Canso and all around the coasts of Nova Scotia and Prince Edward Island and yet the Americans have never fished here for herring; and I do solemnly declare that I believe conscientiously that the foregoing statement or declaration is true and that I make this declaration by virtue of an Act passed during the 37th year of Her Majesty's reign entituled an Act for the suppression of voluntary and extra-judicial oaths.

Dated July 23d 1877 Bear Island, N. S.

WILLIAM EMBREE

In presence of
    OSCAR MALMROS
        U. S. Consul

PROVINCE OF NOVA SCOTIA
COUNTY OF RICHMOND

I hereby Certify that the above named William Embree voluntarily made and subscribed before me at Bear Island settlement in said County of Richmond the foregoing Solemn declaration

Given under my hand and Notarial Seal this 23rd day of July 1877
    (Seal.)   JAMES G. McKEEN
Notary Public

No. 168.

I Charles Steward do solemnly declare—that I live at Bear Island Settlement about 5 miles below Hawkesbury on the Strait of Canso—that I am 46 years old—that I have been fishing ever since I was 12 years old and have followed nothing but that—about 7 or 8 years I have been mackerel fishing during the summer—in the spring I have always been net-fishing in boats—I was 3 seasons in American Mackerel fishing vessels—they generally come from home after the 4th of July and stay up to about the middle or last of September—the mackerel fishing has not been very productive during the last 5 or 6 years, the last 2 or 3 years the catch of mackerel in the Gulf of St. Lawrence has been very poor —while I was in the American fishing vessels they caught at least $\frac{3}{4}$ of their entire catch outside a line 3 miles from shore in fact most mackerel were caught by them from 6 to 7 miles from shore—the greater the fishing fleet is the more the mackerel are stirred up and brought to the surface of the water and I don't think that Colonial vessel catch any the less mackerel on account of fishing alongside of an American fleet—I think the seine fishing is injurious to fishing as it breaks up the schools of mackerel—there have been but few American seine fishers in the Gulf and they never succeeded very well in the Gulf—seine fishing ought to be prohibited—I think about $\frac{1}{4}$ of the crew of American fishing vessels is composed of natives of the British Provinces who continue to reside in the Provinces—The American fishermen do not, as far as I know dry their nets or cure fish on the Coasts of the British North American Provinces—during the last 6 years I should think the American mackerel fleet in the Gulf has not averaged over fifty sails a season —during the period of from 10 to 15 years ago the American mackerel fleet in the Gulf averaged I should think about 300 sails—the codfishing is prosecuted by the Americans exclusively outside the 3 mile limit from shore, mostly on the banks of Newfoundland—the American herring fleet during the last 10 years has averaged about 20 sails off the Coasts

of the British Provinces, they prosecute the fishery at the Mag
Islands from about the first of May and stay from two to three
when they return home—they make but one trip during the year—
average catch per vessel is about 1000 barrels I think—herrin,
and mackerel are as far as I know the only fish caught by Am
vessels off the Coasts of the British North American Colonies—
make this solemn declaration conscientiously believing the same
true and by virtue of an Act passed during the 37th year o
Majesty's reign entitled an Act for the suppression of voluntar.
extra judicial oaths.

Dated Bear Island Settlement July 23, 1877.

CHARLES STUA

In presence of:
> OSCAR MALMROS
> *U. S. Consul*

PROVINCE OF NOVA SCOTIA
COUNTY OF RICHM

I hereby Certify that the above named Charles Stuart volur
made and subscribed before me at Bear Island Settlement in said C
of Richmond the foregoing Solemn declaration

Given under my hand and Notarial Seal this 23rd day of July
(Seal.)

JAMES G. McKEEN
Notary P

No. 169.

I Edward Levanger do solemnly declare that I am living at E
Bouché that I am 31 years old—that for about eleven years I hav
a fisherman by occupation I have been Captain of a fishing ves
my own the "Winfield Scott" but I sold her this year—durin
fishing times I remember to have counted as many as 500 Americ
ing vessels between East Point on Prince Edward Island & the M
len Islands; the mackerel fishing has much fallen off during the
years I don't think that during that time half as many mackere
been caught that during 6 years preceding the period datin,
from 8 years ago—I think that Provincial fishing vessels catch q
many fish when fishing alongside of American vessels as they w
the Provincial vessel were by themselves provided they have a
bait as the Americans have which they sometimes however hav
during some years the Americans catch more fish inside a line
from shore at other years they catch by far the greater part outsi
line, striking an average I think that taken one year with anot
Americans have caught an equal portion of their entire catch of
erel inside a line 3 miles from shore and outside of that line—I thin
about one half of the crew of the American fishing fleet fishing
waters off the coasts of the Atlantic British Provinces are native.
British Colonies who still are residents of the Provinces—the Am
dry their nets or seines but very seldom on the coasts of the
Provinces and they don't cure their fish on the shores of the Col
the American herring fleet that comes to the shores of the Britisl
inces averages about 60 to 70 sails the season during the sprin
fish at the Magdalen Islands for about two to three weeks & t
home—in the fall they go about the last of September to the co
Labrador and Newfoundland—the average size of an American l
fishing vessel is about eighty tons and during the spring trip suc
sel would on an average catch a thousand barrels of herring
vessel going in the fall to the coasts of Labrador and Newfou

vould average during the winter trip a catch of about eight hundred
)arrels—all the codfish Caught by the Americans is caught outside the
' mile limits—the Americans to a small extent catch halibut off the
oasts of the Colonies—about 3 to 5 American halibut fishing vessels
ish on the coasts of Anticosti they make generally two trips during the
eason and each vessel averages per trip about fifty thousand pounds—
esides going to Anticosti the Americans don't fish for mackerel on any
ther places off the coasts the British Provinces except about 15
\merican vessels who go halibut fishing on the grand banks of New-
'oundland—the Americans don't fish for any other class of fish off the
:oasts of the British Colonies except those I have mentioned and I make
his solemn declaration conscientiously believing the same to be true
ind by virtue of an Act passed during the 37th year of the reign of her
Majesty entituled an act for the suppression of voluntary and extra-judicial oaths.

Dated Harbor Bouche July 25th 1877.

EDWARD LEVANGER

In presence of
OSCAR MALMROS
U. S. Consul

PROVINCE OF NOVA SCOTIA
COUNTY OF ANTIGONISH July 25, 1877

I hereby Certify that the above named Edward Levanger this 25th
day of July 1877 duly made and Subscribed before me the foregoing
solemn declaration freely and voluntarily at Harbour Bouché in said
county of Antigonish

Given under my hand and Notarial Seal the day and year above
mentioned

JAMES G. McKEEN
Notary Public

(Seal.)

No. 170.

I George Langley do solemnly declare that I am fifty four (54) years
old—that I live at Bear Island Strait of Canso and am a british subject—that I went first fishing when I was between 12 and 13 years old
and have been at it ever since, during the summer season I go in fishing vessels but during the spring season and late in the fall I go boat-
fishing in-shore—during three seasons I have been employed on American Mackerel fishing vessels during the other seasons I have been employed in Provincial Mackerel fishing vessels in the Gulf of St Lawrence—during the last 6 or 7 years the mackerel fishing has been getting
poorer every year and has been nothing like what it was say 10 to 15
years ago—I don't believe that the average annual catch during the
last 6 years has been over ¼ part of the entire annual catch of the period of from 10 to 15 years ago—my own experience in the American
vessels on which I have been engaged is that we caught during every
one of the three seasons all our mackerel many more than 3 miles from
any shore—during clear days the North Cape of Prince Edward Island
could just be seen—I can form no estimate of the proportion of mackerel caught by the entire American fleet inshore—from my experience I
don't think that Provincial fishermen ever catch a smaller number of
mackerel on account of having an American fleet fishing alongside of
them—I have never seen an American fishing vessel fish for bait inshore on the Coasts of the Dominion of Canada—the earliest I have
been in the Gulf of St Lawrence on an American fishing schooner was

the 20th of June—the big fleet of the American fishing fleet
until after the fourth of July—during the period of from 10
ago there were probably from 400 to 500 American sails
fishing for mackerel—during the last 5 years they did not av
than 70 or 80 sails annually—I think that fully $\frac{1}{3}$ of the
American fishing fleet in the Gulf of St Lawrence is compo
jects of the North American British Provinces who conti
dents of the Provinces. I think that the presence of Am
ermen on these coasts and in our harbours is of great pe
vantage to the people of the Provinces while I am not aw
injuriously affects any of their interests and I make this so
ration conscientiously believing the same to be true and t
an Act passed during the 37th year of Her Majesty's reign e
Act for the suppression of voluntary and extra-judicial oath

Dated Bear Island July 23d 1877.

GEORGE L

In presence of:
OSCAR MALMROS
U. S. Consul

PROVINCE OF NOVA
COUNTY OF RICH

I hereby Certify that the above named George Langley
made and subscribed before me at Bear Island Settleme
County of Richmond the foregoing Solemn declaration

Given under my hand and Notarial Seal this 23rd day of

JAMES G. McK

(Seal.) *Nota*

No. 171.

I Hugh McPherson of Bear Island, Strait of Canso, Richm
Nova Scotia do solemnly declare that I am a native of and
the Province of Nova—that by occupation I am a fisher
have been a fisherman during the last nine (9) years having
time been a seaman—during two seasons I have been empl
of the crews of American fishing vessels fishing for macke
that Colonial fishing vessels catch quite as many mackerel
alongside of an American mackerel fishing fleet as they w
case there were no American fishing vessels in the Gulf of
—the Americans catch their codfish outside the three mil
shore—I don't think that on an average the Americans catc
$\frac{1}{4}$th of their entire catch of mackerel within the 3 miles line
$\frac{3}{4}$th is caught outside that line—the catch of mackerel has
off during the last 5 or 6 years, during the 2 last seasons th
very few mackerel caught in the Gulf—last season there w
not over thirty American mackerel fishing vessels in the
Lawrence and the year before probably not over fifty or six
last year & the year before there were not over $\frac{1}{3}$d of th
Colonial fishing vessels in the Gulf of St Lawrence that visi
6 or 7 years ago—eight years ago according to a rough
should say there were about 300 to 400 American mackerel
sels in the Gulf—I don't think that the Americans anywh
on the Colonial coasts and I have not seen them dry their
shores—a small number of American mackerel fishing ves.
the Gulf of St Lawrence in June but the bulk of them don
July and August the presence of American fishermen is a
niary advantage to the People of the Provinces especial

atch of fish is good—they are in the habit of buying at a great num-
ер of Ports supplies of every description of the merchaut and the
armer and I don't know in what respect their presence would be dis-
dvantageous to the people of the Provinces and I make this solemn
eclaration conscientiously believing the same to be true and by virtue
f the Act passed in the 37th year of Her Majesty's reign entituled
' An Act for the suppression of voluntary and extra-judicial oaths.
Dated at Bear Island July 23d 1877.

HUGH McPHERSON

In presence of
OSCAR MALMROS
U. S. Consul

PROVINCE OF NOVA SCOTIA
COUNTY OF RICHMOND

I hereby certify that the above named Hugh McPherson voluntarily
nade and subscribed before me at Bear Island settlement in said County
f Richmond the foregoing Solemn declaration
Given under my hand and Notarial Seal this 23rd day of July 1877

JAMES G. McKEEN

(Seal.) *Notary Public.*

No. 172.

I Chandler Embree do solemnly declare that I have been born and
always living at Bear Island Settlement about 2 miles below Hawkesbury on the Strait of Causo—that I am 30 years of age—that ever since
I was 14 years old I have been employed in fishing in boats and vessels
ηhat during 4 summers I was employed on American fishing vessels in
the Gulf of St Lawrence—the mass of American Mackerel fishers arrive in the Gulf about the 4th of July—a few American vessels may be
there before that time—I do not believe that the catch of Colonial fishermen is lessened on account of an American mackerel fleet fishing alongside of them—the average crew of an American fishing vessel consists of
about 13 to 14 men—I think that fully one half of the crew of the American fishing fleet is composed of natives of the several British North
American Provinces who continue to reside in these Provinces—I think
that about ¾th of the entire catch of mackerel by the American fleet is
usually caught outside a line 3 miles from shore and about ¼th in-shore
—the Americans do not one in a hundred make use of the privilege to
dry nets and none to cure fish on the Colonial coasts as far as I know
—the outfitting of an American fishing vessel is much more expensive
than that of Colonial vessels of the same tonnage but I cannot say how
much higher it comes—The Americans do not fish for Codfish inside
the 3 mile limit from shore—I know although I have not seen them that
a few American vessels are engaged in halibut fishing of the coast of
Anticosti but I can not say how many—codfish, mackerel, herring and
halibut are all the fish that Americans catch off the coasts of British
North America—the average of herring caught annually by an averaged
sized American herring fishing vessel is about I should think 1200 bar-
—(1200 barrels)—I don't think that there have been over 7 seine fishing
mackerel vessels on an average during the last 5 years in the Gulf of
St Lawrence—they have to go into deep water to get their seines to
work—seine fishing is injurious to fishing as it breaks up the schools of
mackerel—the American seiners do not seem to have been successful
in the Gulf of St Lawrence the presence of American fishermen on
the coasts and in the ports of the several Atlantic British Provinces
has pecuniarily greatly benefited the people of the Colonies and as far

as I know not been an injury to them in any respect, and I do so
declare that I have made the foregoing declaration conscientiou
lieving the same to be true and by virtue of an Act passed duri
37th year of Her Majesty's reign entituled an Act for the suppi
of voluntary and extra judicial oaths.

Bear Island Settlement July 23d 1877.

                          CHANDLER EMB]

In presence of:
    OSCAR MALMROS
          U. S. Consul

                          PROVINCE OF NOVA SCOTIA
                          COUNTY OF RICHA

I hereby Certify that the above named Chandler Embree volu
made and subscribed before me at Bear Island Settlement i
County of Richmond the foregoing solemn declaration

Given under my hand & Notarial Seal this 23rd day of July 18
(Seal.)   JAMES G. McKEEN
                              Notary P

              No. 173.

I, Solomon Cahoon do solemnly declare that I have been enga
a merchant at Cape Canso C. B. for over 10 years—that I have l
the habit of trading with American codfishing vessels—that las
which in that respect was an average year, I traded with ab
American fishing vessels to the aggregate amount of, as near a
come to it, about $10,000—this amount represents the sum expen
them at this port and neighboring ports within about 3 hours s
supplies of all kinds including about $5000.00 advanced to t
purchasing bait at said ports—the Am. vessels, as a rule, buy
bait they obtain at these ports and adjacent waters, exceptionall
ever they themselves catch some squid for bait, this however is in
cant and hardly worth being taken into account—the vessels i. e. A
vessels, who call at this port for supplies, are in the habit of calli
at other ports in the Dominion to receive supplies of different d
tions during the same fishing cruise I can not estimate the su
pended by them in such other ports—the Americans do not ca
boatfishing in these waters and make no use of curing fish and b
little, if any, of drying nets or seines on the coasts of these Provi
for No 1 Salmon and No 2 Mackerel, caught by Coloni
sels, the United States are the only market and most of the fat h
although I do not know the exact proportion, goes to the United
a portion of the fat herring, I know, finds a market in the Provi
Quebec and Ontario—codfishing is carried on by the Am. vess
the high seas, they do not catch cod within 3 miles from sho
presence of American fishermen in the waters of these Provinc
far as I know in no respect injurious to the interests of the Pr
but of great pecuniary advantage to them, and I make this solen
laration conscientiously believing it to be true and by virtue of t
passed in the 37th year of Her Majesty's reign entitled an Act
suppression of voluntary and extra-judicial oaths

Cape Canso June 16th 1877.

                          SOLOMON. COH

Witness:
    OSCAR MALMROS

CONSULATE OF THE U. S. OF AMERICA AT
PICTOU, N. S., CAPE CANSO AGENCY
June 16th 1877.

This is to certify that before me, the undersigned, Oscar Malmros, U. Consul for Pictou N. S. and the dependencies thereof, personally appeared the above named Solomon Cohoon and on said 16th of June at pe Canso voluntarily made and subscribed the foregoing Solemn 'claration.

OSCAR MALMROS
U. S. Consul

No. 174.

I Thomas C. Cook of Cape Canso in the Province of Nova Scotia do lemuly declare that I now am and for the last Twenty years, have en a Merchant transacting business at this port, and am well acainted with the business transacted by American Codfishing vessels quenting this port, and to my knowledge American fishing vessels do t fish Codfish at all within three miles from the shores, and very rare ses if any mackarel by seines within that distance, and from the anges in the methods of fishing of late years, the inshore fisheries are ss important than formerly—

I am not aware that American fishermen make any use of the Shores the British Provinces for the purpose of drying nets or curing fish—

Fresh bait, fishing supplies, and outfits of all kinds are purchased at l convenient harbours on the Coasts of Nova Scotia to a large extent, this port and harbors within two three or hours sail—the amount pended for the above purpose reaches the aggregate Amount of wenty to Twenty Five thousand Dollars Annually—

The United States markets are now the only markets for the Number 'ne Salmon, Number One and Two Mackerel, and for nearly all the fat [errings produced by the fisheries of the British Provinces, a few only f the Herring of that Class being sent to Canada—

It is a fact felt and acknowledged by all engaged in the business that 1e in-shore fisheries of the British Provinces are less valuable than 'rmerly, the deep sea Codfishery being more advantageously fol-'wed—

American fishermen purchase annually at this port and adjacent har-ours—within two or three hours sail—fresh fish for bait—to the Amount f Twelve to fifteen thousand Dollars, and Catch no bait whatever ex-ept on rare occasions a few Squid which are not worth taking into ac-ount.

I would judge that about half or more of the crews of American fish-1g vessels are residents of the British Provinces.

While the presence of American fishermen in the waters of the British rovinces is in no respects injurious to the fishermen of said Provinces ; is of great pecuniary profit and and advantage to the people of the 'ominion of Canada—,

And I make this solemn declaration conscientiously believing it to be rue—and by virtue of the Act passed in the Thirty-Seventh Year of [er Majestys Reign Entitled An Act for the Suppression of Voluntary nd Extra judicial oaths,

Cape Canso June 16th 1877

THOS. C. COOK

COUNTY OF GUYSBOROUGI
CAPE CANSO

I the undersigned Justice of the Peace for the County of Guysb
do hereby certify that the foregoing Statement and declarati
made and Subscribed, before me by the before mentioned Tho
Cook

SOLOMON COHOON

No. 175.

I, Alfred W. Hart do solemnly declare that I have been a m
in Cape Canso during the last 16 years that I have been in the l
supplying American Codfishing vessels at this port—last yea
nished supplies to about 100 Am. fish'g vessels the supplies togetl
moneys furnished them to buy bait aggregating $10,000 or ov
year before was considerably better than last year but my trad
Am. fishing vessels during the last 10 years would average as n
can come about $10,000 a year—the same vessels that were supp
me no doubt got supplies, especially bait, at other points in th
dian Provinces besides that of Canso—Mackerel & herring fishing
are not in the habit of calling here—I am not aware of any injui
by Am. fishing vessels in the waters of the Provinces but am .
ion that their presence in the waters of the Colonies have been
pecuniary benefit to the people thereof—The only market for N
No 2 mackerel and No 1 Salmon is the United States—the A
fishermen do not engage in boatfishing, they catch cod over 3 mil
shore—the American buy nearly all the bait they obtain here
perhaps not quite $\frac{1}{20}$th part they may catch themselves the pre
Am. fishing fleets alongside of Provincial fishermen does not les
catch of the latter—I have never heard of American fishermen
made use of any of the shores of Nova Scotia or the Gulf of St L
for curing fish or drying nets or seines—I judge that fully on
the crew of Am. fishing vessels visiting the British Colonial
waters are British subjects residing in the Dominion of Canad
make this solemn declaration conscientiously believing it to be t
by virtue of the Act passed during the 37th year of her Majest
entitlued an Act for the suppression of voluntary & extrajudicia
Cape Canso C. B. June 16. 1877.

ALFRED W

In presence of:
OSCAR MALMROS   }
       U. S. Consul }

PROVINCE OF NOVA SCOTIA
GUYSBORO' COUNTY, TOWN OF CAPE

Be it remembered that on this 16th day of June in the Yea
Lord One thousand Eight hundred and Seventy Seven, perso
peared before me Thomas C Cook of Cape Canso in the Pr
Nova Scotia Notary Public, Alfred W. Hart, who made and su
the foregoing statement and declaration,

In testimony whereof I the said Notary have hereunto subsc
name, and affixed my Notarial Seal at Cape Canso in the Provin
said on the day and year aforementioned—

(Seal.)

THOS. C. COO
No

No. 176.

My name is James G. McKeen, I am a British subject, have resided at Port Hastings Strait of Canso for the last thirty five years, the greater part of that time I have been engaged Merchandising. I have had considerable dealings with fishermen a large part of my trade was with American Mackerel and Codfishermen, visiting the Gulf of St. Lawrence,

About ten Years ago when Mackerel were plentiful in the Gulf of St Lawrence, the American Mackerel fishermen purchased fishing supplies largely in the Strait of Canso, such as Barrels, Salt, Bait, Wood, Flour, Beef, Pork, Butter, Lard, Potatoes, Small Stores Clothing, &c. &c.

The trade from the American fishing Vessels in the Strait of Canso has been of very great pecuniary advantage to the people of this part of Nova Scotia, I have know American Mackerel fishing Vessels frequently purchase supplies here amounting to from one thousand to fifteen hundred Dollars pr Season Each, I believe that American fishermen have been in the habit of buying supplies in the several Harbours along the Coasts of the British Provinces and that they bought fishing supplies largely in Prince Edwards Island, but I cannot give any approximate idea of the Amount

The Codfishermen for Several Years past purchase also the ordinary supplies above named, to a large extent, and besides they purchase Ice and large quantities of fresh Herrings and Mackerel for bait all along the Coasts of the Provinces, this supplying of Ice and fresh fish for bait to American Codfishing vessels is becoming quite an extensive business, New Icehouses are being erected every Year around the Coasts of the Provinces. and larger stocks of ice are stored, to be sold principally to the United States fishermen, these fishermen after taking in a supply of ice go for fresh Herring or Mackerel, purchasing from forty to sixty barrels, wherever they are to be had along the Coast, and this "baiting up" as it is called is repeated two or three times each season, and oftener when Codfish are scarce, these Herring and Mackerel are sold to the fishermen at from one Dollar and fifty Cents to three Dollars and sometimes higher The American fishing Vessels both the Codfishing and mackerel fleet frequently make considerable expenditures in Ports of the Provinces for repairs to their Vessels and in the purchase of Anchors, Cables, Sails, Spars. &c. &c.

About ten to twelve Years ago from two hundred and fifty to three hundred American fishing vessels passed through the Strait of Canso yearly bound into the Gulf of St Lawrence for the purpose of catching Mackerel, but during the last four or five Years this number has decreased very much owing as I have understood from the scarcity of Mackerel in the Gulf of St Lawrence and the large catch of Mackerel on the United States coast, last Season there were probably not over Seventy American Mackerel fishing Vessels in the Gulf of St. Lawrence and the average Catch of these vessels was reported not to have exceeded one hundred barrels of Mackerel each

The bait chiefly used by American Mackerel fishing Vessels is Menhaden or Porgies. these fish are taken I believe entirely on the coast of the United States, and mostly in Seines within three Miles of the land, so I have been informed. British Mackerel fishermen use the same kind of bait principally and depend on the United States for the supply, clams are also used as bait for Catching Mackerel by both American and Colonial Mackerel fishing vessels, and they are obtained chiefly in the United States,

204 F

Nearly all the Numbers one, and two, and a large pa
ber three Mackerel, number one Salmon, and large quan
poor Herrings, caught by Provincial fishermen around
shipped to the United States for a Market, that being t
most the only Market for our fat and best fish

I am not aware that the American fishermen use to a
extent the shores of the Provinces for curing their fish

The American fishing Vessels employ large numbers c
ing to the Provinces on board their vessels every year
two thousand men yearly, these men go in Mackerel
generally on Shares and in Codfishing Vessels they ar
receiving fairly remunerative Wages, the employmei
men on board American fishing Vessels is considered a g
to our people in a pecuniary point of view

And I James G. McKeen aforesaid do solemnly decl:
scientiously believe that the facts contained in the fore
tion are true and I make this declaration, by virtue of t
in the 37th Year of Her Majestys Reign entitled an act 1
sion of voluntary and extra judicial Oaths

                                    JAMES (

I hereby certify that the foregoing statement was sigr
ence by James G. McKeen above named at Port Hastin
the 13th day of June A D 1877

                                    A B SE
                    Justice of the Peace for the County o

No. 177.

I George Bunker do solemnly declare that I am 31 ye
am living at Margaret Bay 24 miles from Halifax—I
ployed as a fisherman ever since I was a boy—for 10 seas
master of a fishing vessel fishing in the waters off the A
& those of Nova Scotia, the Gulf of St Lawrence & M
for cod and mackerel & herring—cod fish is not at all
Am. fishermen within 3 miles from shore—about ½ of the
by the Americans is caught within 3 miles from shore
mackerel in Provincials waters has much fallen off duri
6 years, of late years they are doing hardly anything in
ing in Provincial waters—the crew of American fishing
vincial waters consist of from ¼ to ½ of British subjects
Provinces—the monthly wages of the crew of these fishi
average about $30_{100}^{00} per man. The Americans buy a
obtain in the Provinces, they do not fish for bait here
American fishing schooner of say from 70 tons to 85 t
in the provinces from $200 to $300_{100}^{00} for bait, ice, fuel & p
if such schooner called only once during the season at a
iuces & did not land cargo for re-shipment—I do not
Canadian fisheries have sustained any injury on accou
of the Americans nor that that the catch of Provinci
been less on account of fishing along side of an Americ
It costs fully one third more to fit,—out man & furni
fishing vessel than a Provincial—The Americans mal
shores of the Provinces for curing fish and but very sel
pose of drying nets—codfish is not caught by Americal
from shore—the Americans fish for mackerel in the I

but very little before the month of July because up to that time the mackerel are poor and lean—I believe that if the Provincials had as much enterprise and invested as much capital in fishing & fishing vessels as the Americans that the privilege of fishing in Am. waters north of the 39th degree of latitude would be as valuable to them as the right to fish in Provincial waters is to the Americans There can be no doubt that the presence of American fishermen in the waters of the Provinces is of very great benefit to the People thereof as they expend a great deal of money for clothing, provisions & supplies of all kinds, and I make this solemn declaration conscientiously believing the same to be true and by virtue of an Act passed in the 37th year of Her Majesty's reign entituled "An Act for the suppression of voluntary and extra-judicial Oaths

Cape Canso June 16th 1877.

CAPT GEORGE BUNKER

In presence of
> OSCAR MALMROS
> > *U. S. Consul*

I Thomas C Cook of Cape Canso in the Province of Nova Scotia Notary Public do hereby certify unto all whom it may concern that the above and foregoing declaration and Statement was made and subscribed in my presence by the above named George Bunker on the day of the date thereof

In testimony whereof I the said Notary have hereunto subscribed my name and affixed my Notarial Seal at Cape Canso aforesaid this Sixteenth day of June in the Year of Our Lord One thousand Eight hundred and Seventy Seven—

> (Seal.)

THOS. C. COOK
Not. Pub.

No. 178.

Francis Marmeau of Arichat being sworn says : I have been engaged in Arichat in General Merchandising for about 22 years and am well acquainted with the general trade of this Port and with everything connected with the fisheries I have also been in the habit of supplying American fishing vessels calling at this Port—the average number of American fishing vessels calling at this Port during the last five years was about two hundred the year—they call for bait and ice and get the former at this place or on the coast of this Island i. e Isle Madame—take one with another and each vessel during that time has bought at each call about sixty dollars worth of bait—the bait consists in fresh herring and mackerel, the herring costs them in the spring about 50 cents a hundred and from the 1st of July the herring costs about 1_{100}^{00} a hundred—for mackerel they pay about 5 or 6 dollars a barrel—the Am fishing vessels never catch there bait here in the bay, they always buy it—for ice each vessel during said period has expended at this Port about from fifteen to twenty-five dollars at 2_{100}^{50} a ton for the ice—the American fishing vessels calling here in the spring and summer don't buy anything else here than ice and bait—about 10 Am. herring fishing vessels call here late in the fall on their way to the Newfoundland shore and at that time they do not buy any bait or ice but buy considerable quantities of beef pork mutton potatoes and country wollen cloth manufactured by the country people butter and other articles, each vessel expends here on an average for those articles in the fall before going to the fisheries for the winter trip fully five hundred dollars or over—the entire number of young fishermen who annually are engaged by the

American fishing vessels calling at this Port is part of the
American vessels during the season is fully 300 from I[
alone—these young men return to their homes after the
son—the presence of the American fishing fleet on our coast
pecuniary advantage to our people and does not injuriousl
of the interests of our people. The vessels i. e. Am vessels
plied for their fishing tour amount to about 5 or 6 vessels p
I have never seen or heard of American fishermen drying t
the coasts of these Provinces and of but one American fi[
have dried fish on our coasts.

FRS M/

Subscribed & sworn to before me this 28th day of July 1[
OSCAR MALM
U.

PROVINCE OF NOVA S(
ARICHAT, COUNTY OF I

At Arichat in said Richmond County on this 28th day (
the above named Francis Marmeau made and subscribed in [
the foregoing affidavit
    Given under my hand and Notarial Seal at Arichat afore[
(Seal.)   JAMES G McB
Not[

No. 179.

I, James L. Girrois do solemnly declare that: I am living
Isle Madame—the extent of the Island is 7 miles by 14 mile[
ter of the schooner Maggie of this Port (Arichat)—I am wel
with the trade of the Port having always lived here—from
American fishing vessels, mostly codfishing have called
average each season during the last five years—they take
and bait—each vessel buys bait here to the amount of abou
of mackerel and herring for the herring they pay about $1_{T}^{0}
and for the mackerel about 5_{100}^{00} a barrel the average cos[
barrel herring & mackerel will cost them about 2_{100}^{50} a
also take in each on an average about 5 or 6 tons of ice [
$2.50 to 3_{100}^{00} per ton—fully three hundred of the fisher
American fishing vessels from Isle Madame, going mostly
to Gloucester for that purpose—I am of the opinion that t[
American fishermen to our coasts to fish is a good thing f[
inces as they spend considerable money in our ports and
ment to a great many of our fishermen and I make this so[
tion conscientiously believing the same to be true and by
Act passed during the 37th year of her Majestys reign ent[
for the suppression of voluntary and extra-judicial oaths.
    Dated Arichat Isle Madame July 29th 1877.
JAMES L. GI[
Master S[

In presence of:
    OSCAR MALMROS
U. S. Consul.

PROVINCE OF NOVA [
WEST ARICHAT COUNTY OF [

At West Arichat in said Richmond County on this 29t[

7 the above named James L Girrois made and Subscribed the fore-
ng solemn declaration before me
Given under my hand and Notarial Seal at Arichat aforesaid this 29th
' of July 1877
Seal.)   JAMES G McKEEN
                                              Notary Public

No. 180.

Isidore Le Blanc do swear that I am a general merchant doing busi-
s at Arichat Isle Madame, almost the only or at least by far the prin-
al business of this place is the fishing interest—I don't think that
ital invested in fishing vessels owned in this Island (Isle Madame)
cleared during the last five years on an average over five per cent
fit I think that during the period just named about three hundred
erican fishing vessels have called per annum at this Port and bought
this Island on an average each about $200 worth of fresh bait, con-
ing in herring and mackerel and I think about $15 to $20,$\frac{0.0}{0.0}$ worth
ice per vessel although as to this latter article I am not sure—I know
t about 100 of our young fishermen go each year in April & May to
ucester to secure good berths on fishing, mostly codfishing, vessels—
y return to the Island after the end of the fishing season—they fish
shares and do well at it I think that the coming of American fish-
vessels to our coasts advances the prosperity of our people and does
interfere with any of its interests. So help me God.
ated Arichat July 29th 1877.   ISIDURE LE BLANC

    ubscribed & sworn to before me ⎱
          July 29th 1877   ⎰
OSCAR MALMROS
      U. S. Consul

                        PROVINCE OF NOVA SCOTIA
                      ARICHAT, COUNTY OF RICHMOND
At Arichat in said Richmond County on this 29th day of July 1877
e above named Isadore Le Blance made and subscribed in my pres-
ce the foregoing affidavit
Given under my hand and Notarial Seal at Arichat aforesaid the 29th
y of July 1877
                                          JAMES G. McKEEN
(Seal.)   *Notary Public*

No. 181.

I, Simon P. Le Blanc do solemnly declare that I am shipping master
West Arichat Isle Madam—I have lived here since I was born I
low that about one hundred American fishing vessels call annually at
e Ports of Arichat and West Arichat, besides a great number of
merican fishing vessels buy bait on the Island without entering any
rbor—on an average each Am. fishing vessel during the last five or
x years has bought bait on the Island to the amount of between twenty
'e and thirty barrels, sometime the same vessel will call three or four
nes during the same season and each time take in a similar quantity
bait, the price of the bait averages about between three and four
llars per barrel for the herring and about (7\frac{0.0}{100}$) for the mackerel
r barrel—they take mostly herring it being most common in the
ring but they prefer mackerel—each vessel takes about from five to
ght tons of ice, those who go halibut fishing take from 30 to 40 tons
ice—the price of ice here is from two to three dollars per ton—I think

that fully one hundred fishermen go every spring to Glouce
to go codfishing mostly in American fishing vessel, besides
able number are shipped during the season from this Is
fishing vessels — I am of the opinion that the presence of A
ing vessels on the coasts of the Province is of great pecu
tage to our people because they spend much money on our
give employment to many of our fishermen and I make
declaration conscientiously believing the same to be true a
of an Act passed during the 37th year of her Majestys r
An Act for the suppression of voluntary and extra judicial

S. P. I

Dated West Arichat July 29th 1877.

In presence of :
OSCAR MALMROS
U. S. Consul

PROVINCE OF No$_{VA}$ Sco'
WEST ARICHAT, COUNTY OF

At West Arichat in Said County of Richmond on this
July 1877 the above named S. P. Leblanc made and Subscri
going solemn declaration before me
Given under my hand and Notarial Seal at Arichat afore
July 1877
(Seal.)   JAMES G Mcl
No

No. 182.

I Simon Theriot do solemnly declare that I reside at W
Isle Madame, N. S., that I am engaged as a general trader
fish that I have been the owner of a fishing vessel engaged
on the grand banks of Newfoundland the vessel was out fis
and 1876 and made no returns for the capital and labor in
—many others were ready to engage in fishing and investi
fishing vessels but when I did not succeed they conclude
no use to try and do any business in that line—I know of n
invested capital in fishing vessels in this place and who di
not one—about 150 American fishing vessels have as far a
make a rough estimate visited Isle Madame each season on a
ing the last three years and bought bait each to the averag
hundred dollars; they the American vessels never catch any
coasts—I have never known them to dry their nets or c
on our coasts—each Am. fishing vessels on an average
Arichat about 6 to 10 tons of ice—last year they, the ice m
ice at $4\frac{00}{100}$ a ton, now they sell it at $2\frac{50}{100}$ a ton An
solemn declaration conscientiously believing the same to b
virtue of an act passed during the 37th year of her Maje
titled an Act for the suppression of voluntary and extra
West Arichat July 29th 1877.

SIMO

In presence of :
OSCAR MALMROS
U. S. Consul

PROVINCE OF NOVA S
WEST ARICHAT, COUNTY OF
At West Arichat in said County of Richmond on this 29

the above named Simon Terrio made and Subscribed the foregoing
mu declaration before me
iven under my hand and Notarial Seal at Arichat aforesaid this 29th
of July 1877

JAMES G. McKEEN
eal.) *Notary Public*

No. 183.

'VINCE OF NOVA SCOTIA }
OUNTY OF RICHMOND }

William LeVesconte of D'Escouse in Isle Madam Cape Breton
chant do declare as follows—

hat for the past twenty five years I have been engaged in the fishing
ness in this Island—supplying vessels and fishermen for the deep
and other fisheries—and from my knowledge and experience there-
do estimate that the number of fishermen who have left this Island
erve in American fishing vessels—returning to their homes at the
e of the season for the past five years—to average two hundred—
hat there has been a large amount of bait procured on this Coast
American fishing vessels but I cannot form any correct estimate as
uantity
hat the British fishing vessels have, in this locality, yielded a profit
t least twenty five per cent during the period above mentioned—
hat certain advantages have been derived by the resident fishermen
the calling of American vessels for bait and other necessaries to the
nt of the amount expended herefor—
hat I do not consider the interests of British fishermen on this coast
e been interfered with by those in American vessels to any extent—
d lastly I do not know of any American vessel curing her fish on
; coast and only in one instance of the fact of drying her nets
make the above declaration conscientiously believing the same to
true—

WILL^M LeVESCONTE.

ligned and declared to before me this 30th day of July AD. 1877. at
scouse

W. R; CUTLER
Notary Public

No. 184.

OVINCE OF NOVA SCOTIA }
COUNTY OF RICHMOND }

Charles Doyle of Rocky Bay in Isle Madam do declare as follows—
t I am a fisherman and have been engaged in that business regularly
the past thirty years—That a large quantity of fish are taken in this
ılity by nets and it is a great resort for American Bank vessels to
cure bait during the fishing season
'hat in my opinion at least one hundred vessels have on an average,
the past five years, been 'baited' in this Bay and adjacent harbors
the Island—and have annually purchased at least Twenty five hun-
d barrels of herring and mackerel for that purpose—paying therefor
the rate of three dollars per barrel for herring and six dollars per
rel for Mackerel—That most of those vessels are provided with ice
en they come here from ports outside of this Island—
'hat large advantages are gained by the fishermen from the fact of
ir vessels calling here for bait and supplies all of which are paid for
ash

That no interference is given to the British fishermen i
cution of their calling by the American vessels as they
sufficiently long to procure their necessaries and then leave i
for the Banks

That no American fishermen have set nets or dried the:
fish on this part of the coast within my knowledge—I mak
declaration conscientiously believing the same to be true

CHARLES

Signed and declared to before me this 30 day of July 187
Bay

W. R. CUTLEI
Notary I
No

No. 185.

PROVINCE OF NOVA SCOTIA }
COUNTY OF RICHMOND }

—I David Gruchy of Descouse in Isle Madam Cape Breto
do hereby declare that I have been thirty three years eng
fishing business of this Island— —that from my knowledge
ence therein I estimate the number of fishermen who ha
Island to join American vessels—and who return at the clos
—Averaging the last five years One hundred and fifty—th
years there has been far less than formerly—

That a large quantity of bait has been procured by Ameri
around the coast of this Island.

The British fishing vessels in this locality have yielded
over twenty per cent during the period above mentioned

That the resident fishermen have derived advantages fro
American vessels calling here for bait and supplies—to the e
sums paid therefor

That the interests of British fishermen on this coast ha
interfered with in my opinion to any extent

And lastly I know of no American vessels curing fish or
on this coast since I have been in the business here—

I make the above declaration conscientiously believing th
true—

D.

Signed and declared to before me at Descouse this 30th 。
W. R. CUTLE
· *Notary*
N(

No. 186.

John Grant being duly sworn says:

I am living at Hawkesbury on the Strait of Canso I am six
old—I am by occupation a fisherman and pilot—for 40 years
a fisheiman in over 20 American fishing vessels in the Gul
rence—during the last six years the mackerel fishing has muc
about 10 to 15 years ago the mackerel were very plentiful a
ber to have seen as many as 700 American sails in the Gulf
seasons. During those years there were only about 50 Prov
in the Gulf—during those years Provincial vessels went m
ing on the coasts of Labrador they had not the vessels fit for n
ing and did not understand the business of mackerel fishing 、

is about 15 years or 20 years ago—last year was the slackest fishing season I have seen; I think there were nearly one hundred american fishing vessels in the Gulf and about 10 Provincial vessels fishing for mackerel—I don't think that a single vessel made two trips during the year and not many of them had a full cargo, many in fact not over 50 barrels. During the four seasons preceding the last there were about 120 American sails on an average during each season in the Gulf fishing for mackerel and about 15 to 20 Provincial vessels but the vessels did not well during any of those years—when I was with the Americans, that is, employed on their fishing vessels, we caught most of the mackerel outside of line 3 miles from shore, we caught them outside of sight of land entirely on Bank Bradley and Bank   that is from 20 to 30 years ago. —Ten (10) to 15 years ago we caught the mackerel in the American vessels I was in off the East Point Prince Edward Island and off New London P. E. I. and off Cascumbec P. E. I. about 8 to 10 miles off and the same distance off the North Cape P. E. I.; during the last 8 years the Americans caught most of their mackerel on the North Side of Prince Edward Island about 5 to 8 miles off the coast—they have caught but a small proportion of their entire catch inside 3 miles from shore certainly not more than one fourth of their entire catch inside 3 miles from shore and they caught that portion in the fall of the year—the American fishing vessels make most of the business that there is in the Strait of Canso, when there are but few American fishing vessels in our waters trade in the Strait is slack and money is scarce; during many years the only money we saw was Yankee money they buy a great deal of country produce as beef, mutton potatoes, all kinds of other vegetables, homespun cloth, socks & mittens made by the country people and other things besides buying largely store goods of various kinds and they give employment to a very great many of our fishermen besides to coopers and other mechanics—particularly during the last 10 or 15 years a great proportion of the crew of the American fishing fleet is composed of Colonial people, I mean such as have not removed their place of living to the States. I think it is of great advantage to the people of these Provinces that the American fishermen should visit our coasts and fish there as much as they please they do no injury to our fishing and nearly half of our fishermen would be out of employment if the Americans did not employ them in their vessels.

                                        JOHN GRANT

Subscribed & sworn to before me this 27th day of July 1877.
                                        OSCAR MALMROS
                                              U. S. Consul

PROVINCE OF NOVA SCOTIA
PORT HASTINGS, COUNTY OF INVERNESS

At Port Hastings in said County of Inverness on this 27th day of July 1877 the above named John Grant made and subscribed in my presence the foregoing affidavit

Given under my hand and Notarial Seal at Port Hastings aforesaid the 27th day of July 1877
(Seal.)   JAMES G McKEEN
                                              Notary Public

No. 187.

Patrick Walsh being duly sworn says:

I am about 35 years old am living near McGuire's at Steep Creek Guysboro Co, Nova Scotia have been fishing in vessels, mostly Ameri-

can vessels during the 21 years next preceding last year,
last year because mackerel were too scarrce in the Bay—the
can fleet does not leave home until after the 4th of July
of St Lawrence to fish for mackerel mackerel don't begin to
til the middle of August—the bait used by both Provincial
can vessels is Pogies and clam & these come all from
States, exceptionally a Provincial vessel may use herring bu
a good bait—the average number of vessels fishing for
the Gulf during the rebellion in the States was about 300
about 30 to 40 (thirty to forty) Provincial vessels—during
years I was out mackerel fishing the Provincial vessels wer
tenth of the number of American vessels fishing for mac
Gulf—fishing alongside of an American mackerel fleet woul
the catch of Provincial vessels provided the latter had a:
and vessels as well fitted out as the Americans—the aver
of hands employed on an American mackerel catcher is ab
hands—during the last 6 or 7 years the mackerel fishery in
St Lawrence has much fallen off—I don't think that the av
during that period was more than one fifth part per year of
caught say ten years ago and during the ten years next p
season of ten years ago—I think that both Provincial vesse
American vessels catch more mackerel outside a line three
shore taking one year with another than they catch inside
never fished near land for codfish in the Gulf but always ou
land—their bait for codfishing in the North Bay they, the
buy mostly from Provincial fishermen along the British
mostly buy herring by the hundred paying about one dol
a hundred, this pays the Provincial fishermen much better
the herring and putting them in barrels—I think about one
crew of American fishing vessels in the Gulf are men
homes in the British Provinces—it is a great advantage tha
can fishing vessels come to our coasts as they leave much n
our people.

Steep Creek August 7. 1877

his
PATRICK +
ma

In presence of
JAMES G. McKEEN
OSCAR MALMROS

PROVINCE OF NOVA S
COUNTY OF GUY

I hereby Certify that the above named Patrick Walsh be
Oath to   subscribed the foregoing statement.

Given under my hand and Notarial Seal at Steep Creek i
of Guysborough Province of Nova Scotia this 7th day of
(Seal.)   JAMES G. Mc

No

No. 188.

George Critchet being duly sworn says: I am living at M
Guysboro County Nova Scotia—I am 37 years old from
until 4 years ago I have been out mackerel—and cod-fishi
American vessels—I left off fishing because the mackere
been poor for several years and is still; whenever macke
plenty again I will be out fishing in vessels I think that in

say from 10 years ago and longer the average number of the American mackerel fleet was upwards of three hundred during the season—during the same period about 30 or 40 Provincial vessels were in the Gulf of St Lawrence—the number of American vessels above referred to is intended as the number in the Gulf of St Lawrence—during the years previous to the last 10 years the average catch of mackerel was two trips for each vessel—during the last 6 or 7 years they have scarcely averaged one full cargo during the season—I think that mackerel go where they find the best and largest quantity of feed and that when the wind if off shore it drives the small fish on which mackerel feed into deeper water and the mackerel follow them and whenever there is a big fleet off shore and heave over much bait the mackerel will follow the fleet—during the years I was out fishing we did better outside a line 3 miles from shore than inside that line—on an average, I am of the opinion, about from $\frac{1}{2}$ to $\frac{2}{3}$d of all mackerel caught by vessels in the Gulf is caught outside of a line 3 miles from shore—I think that seine-fishing is very injurious to the mackerel fishery and ought to be prohibited entirely— I hope the Halifax Fishery Commission will recommend a treaty abolishing seine-fishing—it has never proved profitable in the Gulf of St Lawrence—the seines are about 25 fathoms deep and there are but few places in the Gulf deep enough for seine fishing—until the present season there were only two or three seine-fishers in the Gulf—the only bait used by mackerel fishers is clam and Porgies and that comes all from the United States—I have been out codfishing in the Bay i. e. Gulf of St Lawrence— the codfish caught by vessels in that Bay is all caught in deep water that is more than three miles from shore—the bait used for codfishing is herring and mackerel—this is mostely bought by American vessel from Provincial store-fishers—the spring-herring bait is bought per barrel at the rate of $1.50 to $2.00 each, fat herring is mostly bought by the hundred at the rate of about a dollar a hundred and $2.50 per hundred fresh mackerel (300 *spring* mackerel per barrel) generally it pays the boat-fishers better to sell the fish fresh to the codfishers than to salt and pack them—I don't think that Provincial vessels catch any less mackerel on account of fishing alongside of an American fleet—I don't think that the American fishermen dry nets or cure fish on the British coasts, at least I have never seen them do it—I think that about one third of the crew of American fishing vessels visiting the Gulf are men having their homes in the British Provinces. I think that the presence of American fishing vessels on our Coasts is of considerable pecuniary advantage to our people and does not in any way interfere with their interests.

Dated Middle Millford, Guysboro Co. Aug 7th 1877
GEORGE CRITCHETT

In presence of: }
OSCAR MALMROS   }

PROVINCE OF NOVA SCOTIA
COUNTY OF GUYSBOROUGH.

I hereby Certify that the above named George Critchett before me made oath to and subscribed the foregoing statement

Given under my hand and Notarial Seal at Middle Milford in the County of Guysborough Province of Nova Scotia this 7th day of August 1877

(Seal.)
JAMES G. McKEEN
Notary Public

No. 189.

I Christopher Carrigan do solemnly declare that I am t
old—am by occupation a fisherman and that I am living al
ford in the County of Guysborough in the Province of N
have been out mackerel fishing in the North Bay during t
next preceding the Summer of 1876—during the time I wa
the North Bay I think the American Mackerel fleet fishing
Bay would average about one hundred Vessels, the Vessel
was fishing during that time averaged per Season I thinl
about 200 barrels per Season. I think that during the 6 ye
the North Bay the Mackerel fleet from the Provinces fishing
Bay was about 20 vessels

Provincial Mackerel fishing Vessels would—catch as mai
side by side with American fishing vessels as if fishing by t
I do not know how many of the hundred American Vessels
above were Mackerel fishers and how many were Codfishers
in which I was Mackerel fishing used Porgies & Clams onl
have been two trip in the North Bay in Provincial Mack
Vessels and they also used only Porgies & Clams for bait.

As far as I know the Americans do not cure their fish or d:
on the Coasts of the British Provinces

I was out this spring & last spring in American Herring
sels to the Magdalens I think there were from 30 to 40 An
ring fishing Vessels there. Each Spring these Vessels Er
average two Men and two Boats from the British Provinces
an average for Each Man & Boat about 30 dollars for the
about 3 weeks this Spring the American Herring Vessels at
len Islands did not average a Catch of over 300 barrels
Spring they all had full fares averaging about one thousan

The presence of the American fishing Vessels during the s
the Coasts of the British Provinces is a great pecuniary a
the people of these Provinces from the large amount of mo
pend among us and the large number of our men they emp
Vessels

And (I do solemnly declare that) I make this solemn dec
scientiously believing the same to be true and by virtue
passed in the 37th Year of Her Majestys Reign entitled an
pression of Voluntary and Extra-judicial Oaths

Dated at Lower Milford County Guysborough this 8th da
1877

CHRISTOPHER. CA

In presence of:
OSCAR MALMROS

PROVINCE OF NOVA S
COUNTY OF GUY

I hereby Certify that the above named Christopher Car
tarily declared to and subscribed before me the foregoin
claration

Given under my hand and Notarial Seal at Lower M
County of Guysborough Province of Nova Scotia this 8th d
1877

(Seal.)   JAMES G McI
                                   No

No. 190.

William T. England being duly sworn says: I am fifty six years old, at middle Millford Guysboro' County N. S. since I was 11 years old o about 7 years ago I have been out fishing in fishing vessels, mostly erican vessels, that is I have been fishing in vessels for 40 years, ing the last 7 years I have been boat fishing and farming—as far as now the Americans don't dry their nets on the British Coasts nor do y cure their fish on them—the bait used for mackerel is Porgies and ns and these all come from the United States—herring is now but y rarely used for bait and never except by Provincial vessels—the t for codfish used by Americans in the Gulf of St Lawrence is mostly ght by themselves on the fishing grounds by the Americans and ght consequently in the deep seas—I have often sold bait to the ericans going to the grand banks of Newfoundland codfishing—the fishers going to the grand banks buy nearly all the bait they use, y use during the trip from 30 to 40 barrels of herring, buying it tly by the barrel, but often by the hundred—the hundred costs them m one dollar to one dollar and a quarter; it is much more profitable the fishermen to sell their fish to the Bankers for bait than to salt l pack them in barrels and sell them to the merchants—I don't think t Provincial fishermen catch any less mackerel on account of fishing ngside of an American fleet—during some seasons or rather series easons there are among the mackerel a great many old ones and n the mackerel keep much more off-shore in the deep seas, then fols a series of seasons when old mackerel are very scarce and almost have disappeared and during such periods the mackerel will keep ch more in-shore—those mackerel that are comparatively young vays prefer to keep more in-shore—I have never known as small an nerican cod and mackerel fleet in the Gulf of St Lawrence as during e last two years and especially last year because the catch of mackel was very poor. The American fleet, leaves every season, especially ien mackerel are plenty considerable money among us and are there·e and because they employ many of our men of considerable benefit our coasts and as far as I know they don't do any harm to any of r interest—all along the Strait of Canso the American fishing vessels at go to the Magdalen Islands herring fishing, about on an average (fourty) sails a season, hire boats and men—they each hire on an erage 3 or 4 boats with as many men for an average trip of from 3 to veeks—they pay as high as $30\frac{00}{100}$ to $35\frac{00}{100}$ for a man and boat—I yself went this spring with an American herring catcher to the Maglen Islands—I was three weeks away and got $35\frac{00}{100}$ for the trip— Dated Middle Millford Guysboro Co. Nova Scotia August 7th 1877

his
WILLIAM T. + ENGLAND
mark.

In presence of:
OSCAR MALMROS

PROVINCE OF NOVA SCOTIA
COUNTY OF GUYSBOROUGH

I hereby Certify that the above named William T. England voluntay made oath to and subscribed before me the foregoing statement Given under my hand and Notarial Seal at Middle Milford in the Co Guysborough Province of Nova Scotia this 7th day of August 1877 (Seal.) JAMES G. McKEEN

Notary Public

No. 191.

I, Martin Ryan do solemnly declare that : I am living at ?
ford, County of Guysboro'—I am 63 years old—have been
mackerel vessels over thirty years—about 7 years ago I le
fishing in vessels since that time I have been boatfishing and
the Americans do not as far as I know dry their nets or cur
on British coasts—Provincial vessels do not according to my
catch any smaller quantity of mackerel on account of fishin
of an American mackerel fleet in the Gulf of St Lawrence—'
out fishing in the Gulf the Americans, during the time th
privilege of fishing inshore as well as at other times when t
fish in limits, caught nearly all their mackerel outside the
from shore it was only an odd vessel that went in-shore and c
mackerel there—the mackerel during most of the years I
Gulf mackerel fishing kept mostly in the deep water and not
one fourth of the entire catch of the American vessels in v
was caught inside a line 3 miles from shore I have alway
American vessels with the exception of five seasons when I
in Provincial vessels—the bait used by the mackerel vessels
fished was Porgies and clams, we used no other bait—Porgie:
all comes from the United States—between one third to $\frac{1}{2}$ of
the American fleet of mackerel fishing vessels are men having
in the British Provinces—the Americans have much benefitec
here in the Strait of Canso—the American herring fishers
here in the spring give the first relief to our poor people at
not for the American fishing vessels on our coasts a very gr
of our laboring men would be without employment, the great
the American mackerel fleet come to the Gulf of St Law
about the 10th of July—the mackerel fishery has much fa
during the last three years the catch of mackerel has not be
one at all; during the last two years mackerel fishing has
a failure; and I do solemnly declare that I make this sole
tion conscientiously believing it to be true and by virtue of an
during the 37th year of her Majestys reign entitled an Act
pression of voluntary and extra-judicial oaths.

Dated Middle Millford August 7th 1877.

MARTI

In presence of:
OSCAR MALMROS

PROVINCE OF NOVA SCO
COUNTY OF GUYS

I hereby Certify that the above named Martin Ryan vo
clared to and subscribed before me the foregoing solemn de

Given under my hand and Notarial Seal at Middle Mi
County of Guysborough Province of Nova Scotia this 7th da
1877

(Seal.) JAMES G McL
. Not

No. 192.

I, Philipp Ryan do solemnly declare that: I am living at
ford, I am 42 years of age—I think I was about 16 years
went out fishing in the Gulf of St Lawrence in fishing ves.
mostly been mackerel fishing although some seasons I hav

ing in the Bay—I left off going in fishing vessels in 1872—the Amer-
n fishermen don't dry their nets nor cure their fish on our coasts as
as I know—during the last 8 or 10 years mackerel fishing has much
len off and during the last two years as far as I can hear mackerel
ing has almost been a failure—Porgies and clams as far as I know
universally used in the Bay as bait although a few Provincial vessels
y occasionally use herring—Porgies & clams get all from the States
far as I am aware—I should think that about one half of all the mack-
l caught by vessels is caught outside a line 3 miles from shore and ½
ide that line—I should say that of late years about one third of the
w of American fishing vessels was composed of men having their
mes in the British Provinces—I should say the cost of outfitting an
nerican fishing vessel is about ¼ greater than that of a Provincial
ssel of the same size—And I do solemnly declare that I conscien-
usly believe the foregoing declaration to be true and make this state-
nt by virtue of an Act passed during the 37th year of her Majesty's
gn entituled An Act for the suppression of voluntary & extra judicial
ths.
Dated Middle Milford August 7th 1877.

PHILIP RYAN

In presence of:
OSCAR MALMROS
U. S. Consul

PROVINCE OF NOVA SCOTIA
COUNTY OF GUYSBOROUGH

I hereby Certify that the afore named Phillip Ryan voluntarily de-
ared to and Subscribed before me the foregoing Solemn declaration
Given under my hand and Notarial Seal at Middle Milford in the
ounty of Guysborough Province of Nova Scotia this 7th day of August
377
(Seal.)   JAMES G McKEEN
                                                    Notary Public

No. 193.

I Andrew Lourie do solemnly declare that I am living at Lower Mil-
rd Guysboro County, Nova Scotia I am a fisherman by occupation I
ave been fishing in the Gulf of St Lawrence about thirty years up to
years ago—I am 56 years of age the American fishing fleet fishing for
ackerel begin to arrive in the North Bay about the middle of June
ut the greater number of mackerel vessels don't leave the States until
fter the 4th of July—Pogies and clams are the bait used for mackerel
shing, herring is only used as bait when the vessels are out of Pogies
; clams—herring is not as good a bait as pogies and clams—I have
ever seen American fishermen dry their nets or cure fish on the shores
f British Provinces—the fishing alongside of American mackerel vesels don't lessen in my opinion the catch of mackerel by Provincial vesels I think they catch quite as many when fishing side by side of American
essels—of late years I have heard that more mackerel are caught in-shore
ut when I went fishing the heft of mackerel that were caught were caught
utside a line three (3) miles from shore—I have also often been codfish-
ig in the Bay—the codfish is all caught outside a line three miles from
hore—the bait used for codfishing is herring mackerel, squid and clams
1 the spring—the American Codfishers in the Bay procure their bait
1 the spring at the Magdalen Islands from the shore fishermen and in
ummer they catch their own bait wherever they may happen to be fish-

ing—I think that the presence of American fishing vessels (
a pecuniary advantage to our people as they spend much n
employment to many of our people And I make this so
tion conscientiously believing the same to be true and b
Act for the suppression of voluntary and extra-judicial o:

Dated at Lower Milford August 8th 1877.

ANDREV

In presence of:
    OSCAR MALMROS

PROVINCE OF NOVA
COUNTY OF GU

I hereby Certify that the above named Andrew Low:
declared to and Subscribed the foregoing Solemn declara:

Given under my hand and Notarial Seal at Lower M
County Guysborough. Province of Nova Scoti a this 8th d
1877

(Seal.)   JAMES G M(
N

No. 194.

I Thomas England do Solemnly declare that I am liv
Milford, Guysborough County Nova Scotia, I am about 2
during the last 10 Years I have been out Mackerel fishi:
one of those 10 Seasons I have been also Codfishing in t
Lawrence—I have mostly been netfishing in the Spring an
during the summer—I suppose that Provincial vessels fisb
of American Mackerel Catchers would not on that acc:
smaller quantity of Mackerel that they would do other'
and Clams are the bait used by Mackerel vessels—occasi
vincial vessel may use a little herring as bait.—My ow
that more Mackerel are caught outside a line 3 miles fr:
inside that line—the Americans don't dry their nets o:
Coasts or cure their fish there as far as I am aware—the *
ing fleet especially when Mackerel are plenty leave consid
on Our Coasts and I think that their presence on these
great pecuniary advantage to our people

And I make this Solemn declaration Conscientiously
same to be true and by Virtue of an Act passed during
of Her Majestys Reign entitled An Act for the Suppres:
tary and Extrajudicial Oaths.

Dated at Middle Milford in the County of Guysboroug!
7, 1877

his
THOMAS ×
mark

In presence of:
    OSCAR MALMROS

PROVINCE OF NOVA
COUNTY OF GU

I hereby Certify that the above named Thomas Engla
and subscribed the foregoing solemn declaration before n

Given under my hand and Notarial Seal at Middle
County of Guysborough N. S. this 7th day of August 18:
(Seal.)   JAMES G M
*

No. 195.

m forty six years of age and a fisherman by occupation, I am liv-
t Lower Milford Guysboro County Nova Scotia I have been fish-
n the North Bay about 14 years up to and inclusive of the season
73 whenever I was not out fishing in vessels I have been boat-
ıg I have never seen American fishermen dry their nets or cure
n the shores of the British Provinces—I do not think that a Pro-
al vessel if well fitted out will catch a less quantity of mackerel on
ınt of fishing alongside of an American mackerel fleet—I should
: that fully one third of the crew of the American fishing fleet fish-
ff the Coasts of the British North American Provinces is composed
ıtives who are residents of these Provinces—the bait used for mack-
catching is clams and porgies and these all come from the United
es—herring is but rarely used as a bait for mackerel—the codfish
ht by the American vessels is all caught in the deep seas more than
es from land their bait consists in fresh herring or mackerel—in the
ıg they buy it from Provincial boat fishers on the coasts of the Brit-
rovinces and during the rest of the season they mostly catch their
ın nets on the deep seas where they happen to be for cod-fishing—
merican Mackerel fleet begins to arrive in the North Bay about the
lle of June but the greatest number of the American Mackerel fleet
ot leave home for the Bay until after the 4th day of July—About 7
years ago the mackerel fishery in the North Bay began to fall off
the last two years were particularly bad—ten years ago and up-
s the average catch of mackerel consisted in about 2 full fares for
vessel but during the last 6 or 7 years I don't think that mackerel
,els averaged one full fare during the season—I think that the pres-
: of American fishermen on our coasts has pecuniarily benefited our
ıle as they spend considerable money and give employment to many
ur men And I make this solemn declaration conscientiously believ-
the same to be true and by virtue of an Act passed during the 37th
: of Her Majesty's reign entituled an Act for the suppression of volun-
and extra-judicial oaths. Dated Lower Milford August 8th 1877
RUFUS CARRIGAN

PROVINCE OF NOVA SCOTIA
COUNTY OF GUYSBOROUGH

hereby Certify that the above named Rufus Carrigan voluntarily
ared to and subscribed before me the foregoing solemn declaration
iven under my hand and Notarial Seal at Lower Milford in the
nty of Guysborough Province of Nova Scotia this 8th day of August

ıeal.)   JAMES G McKEEN
                                    Notary Public

No. 196.

Edward Walsh do solemnly declare that I am living at Lower Mil-
, Guysboro County, Nova Scotia, I am by occupation a fisherman—
ten or twelve years I have been fishing in American vessels from
ıt 1853 to 1865 since that time I have been net-fishing except one
ıon 5 years ago when I was out fishing in a Nova Scotia vessel in
North Bay—the mackerel fishers from the United States begin to
ve in the North Bay about the 15th of June but the greater number
ımerican Mackerel catchers don't arrive until after the 4th of July—

205 F

during late years the mackerel runs closer into the land but formerly when mackerel were still plenty say 10 to 15 years ago about as many mackerel were caught both by Provincials and Americans outside a line 3 miles from shore as there were in-shore—the American Codfishers in the North Bay get their bait in the spring from the fishermen on the coasts of Nova Scotia and the Magdalen Islands; during the summer the American Codfishers in the Bay catch their own bait on the deep seas wherever they may happen to fish—I think on an average an American Codfisher in the North Bay buys about 30 barrels of herring on the coasts of the Provinces for bait—I think that the presence of American fishermen on our coasts of considerable pecuniary advantage to our people as they spend much money and employ many of our men. And I make this solemn declaration conscientiously believing the same to be true and by virtue of an Act passed during the 37th year of Her Majesty's reign entitled An Act for the suppression of voluntary and extra-judicial oaths   Dated at Lower Milford Guysboro County N. S. August 8th, 1877

EDWARD WELSH

PROVINCE OF NOVA SCOTIA
COUTY OF GUYSBOROUGH

I hereby Certify that the above named Edward Walsh voluntarily declared to and subscribed before the foregoing Solemn declaration

Given under my hand and Notarial Seal at Lower Milford in the County of Guysborough Province of Nova Scotia this 8th day of August 1877.
(Seal.)   JAMES G McKEEN
Notary Public

No. 197.

I, Charles Lowrie do solemnly declare that I am living at Middle Millford County of Guysboro Province of Nova Scotia—I am a fisherman by occupation, I am 45 years old ; about 20 years ago I went first fishing in vessels in the Gulf of St Lawrence and since that time I have been out in the Bay in vessels fishing for Cod and mackerel 10 or 11 seasons—the last season I was Bay fishing was that of the great August storm of 1873 when I was not fishing in vessels I have been boat fishing and I follow that now Some of the American Mackerel vessels come to the North Bay as early as about the 10th of June but the greater number of them don't leave home for the North Bay until after the 4th of July—I should think that the average size of an American Mackerel is about 60 to 65 tons new measurement—the crew of a mackerel vessel of say 60 tons is about from 15 to 17 hands—during the years previous to the last 10 years the American mackerel vessels in the Bay averaged I think 2 trips a season landing one trip in the Strait of Canso for shipment to the States sometimes however the American vessels went home with their fare and then returned to the North Bay for a second trip—On an average I should say that during seasons when mackerel were plenty as many of them were caught outside a line 3 miles from shore as inside that line both by Provincial and American vessels—Porgies & clams are the bait used for mackerel, some Provincial vessels occasionally use however herring but this is not considered as so good a bait—I do think that Provincial mackerel vessels catch as many mackerel when fishing alongside of an American Mackerel fleet as they do when fishing by themselves provided they are as well fitted out in every respect and have as good bait as the American vessels ; this is however often not the

e—the American codfisheries in the North Bay use herring and
ckerel as bait, the trawlers buy most of their bait from shore fisher-
n but the hook codfisheries catch their own bait on the deep sea
erever they may be fishing—the codfish is all caught by the Ameri-
ı vessels outside a line 3 miles from shore—the codfishers going to
. grand banks of Newfoundland buy nearly all the bait they use of
ıvincial fishermen they run in usually 2 or 3 times to bait up—some
their bait, especially squid, they catch themselves on the grand
ıks—it pays the boatfishers better to sell their herring and mackerel
the American Codfishers in the North Bay and on the Grand Banks
ın to salt and pack their herring and mackerel because the price they
. is usually the same and they save packing, salting and the barrels
don't think that the mackerel vessels in the North Bay during the
t 5 or 6 years have averaged per season one full fare the mackerel
ıery in the Bay having fallen off so much—The fleet of American
·ring vessels going to the Magdalene Islands averages I should say
to 16 vessels each spring, these hire on an average three men and
·ee boats each in this Province for their trip to the Magdalenes' last-
about 3 weeks paying for a man and his boat from $30 to 35\frac{00}{100}$—
ı spring while I was there, there were hardly any herring, last season
en I was there they averaged about 200 barrels a vessels and during
ıd seasons they will average fully 1000 barrels of herring each—the
er seasons while I was there that is about 5 besides the 3 mentioned
catch of herring was good—I think that about one half of the Crew
American fishing vessels fishing off the coasts of the British North
erican Provinces consist of men who have their homes in these
ovinces. I think the presence of American fishing vessels on our
ısts and in our harbors a great pecuniary advantage to our people;
ıd I make this solemn declaration conscientiously believing the same
be true and by virtue of an Act passed during the 37th year of Her
ajesty's reign entituled an Act for the suppression of voluntary and
trajudicial oaths.
Dated Middle Milford August 9th 1877.

CHARLES LOWRIE

In presence of:
  OSCAR MALMROS

PROVINCE OF NOVA SCOTIA
COUNTY OF GUYSBOROUGH N. S.

I hereby Certify that the above named Charles Lowrie declared to
ıd subscribed the foregoing Solemn declaration before me
Given under my hand and Notarial Seal at Middle Milford in the
ıunty of Guysborough, Nova Scotia this 9th day of August 1877
(Seal.)   JAMES G. McKEEN
Notary Public

No. 198.

Nicholas Nicholson says and deposes on oath as follows : I am living
: Port Hastings, Strait of Canso, am by trade a fisherman, have during
·e last six years been out fishing in American fishing vessels—my age
30 years, I was codfishing I meant to say six years besides having
·en fishing for mackerel during two seasons, that is, last summer and
ıe summer of four years ago—the codfish that is caught by the Amer-
ıns is all caught outside a line 3 miles from shore and of the mackerel,
ı far as my experience goes, fully two thirds is caught by the Ameri-
ıns outside a line 3 miles from shore and about one third inside that

line—towards the latter part of the season it is that mackerl is caught more inshore—the Americans do not dry their nets on our coasts but preserve them by salting them in hogsheads—I have often seen American mackerel fishing vessels and Provincial fishing side by side and my experience is that the vessels of the Provinces catch quite as many mackerel when fishing side by side with an American fleet as they do when not alongside of them—codfishers (American) in the Gulf of St Lawrence catch most of their bait, herring principally, and mackerel in the bay, in nets, much more than 3 miles from shore—the codfishers going to the banks of Newfoundland partly buy their bait at Provincial Ports, about enough to last them three weeks, partly they catch it on the banks, if they can get squids, they prefer it—I think that fully one half of the fishermen of the American vessels fishing off the Coasts of the British Provinces are natives of the British Provinces who continue to live in the Provinces—I think that the American fishing vessels on our coasts is a great benefit to our people because they spend much money among us and give employment to many of our men.

NICHOLAS NICHOLSON

PORT HASTINGS Aug 1st 1877.

Sworn to & subscribed before me } this 1st day of Aug 1877 }

OSCAR MALMROS
U. S. Consul

PROVINCE OF NOVA SCOTIA
PORT HASTINGS COUNTY OF INVERNESS

I hereby Certify that the above named Nicholas Nicholson voluntarily made and in my presence subscribed the foregoing affidavit

Given under my hand and Notarial Seal at Port Hastings aforesaid this 1st day of August 1877

(Seal.)

JAMES G. McKEEN
Notary Public

No. 199.

Duncan McEachren being duly sworn says: 1 am living at Craignish County of Inverness C. B.—I am about 45 years old—this is the 3d summer that I am at home not fishing, 3 years ago I was fishing for mackerel and ever since 1853 up to 3 years ago I have been mackerel fishing every summer mostly in American vessels, the Americans do not as far as I know dry their nets on our coasts nor do they cure their fish on the coasts of the Provinces—take one year with another and I should say that on an average the American mackerel fishing vessels take more mackerel outside a line 3 miles from shore than inside—all the vessels I ever was in got their bait from the States—when I was out fishing I always saw the Americans raise the mackerel first, they, the mackerel often seemed to follow the American fleet because they throw out much bait—I think that the Provincial fishing vessels catch as much mackerel when fishing side by side with an American fleet than they would or than they do when not fishing along side of the Americans—I suppose that all of two thousand men from the British Provinces that is men who have their homes in the Provinces are annually employed as fishermen in American fishing vessels—it is a benefit to the people of the Provinces that the American vessels visit our coasts because they expend much money in the coasts and give employment to many people.

DUNCAN McEACHERN

Sworn to and subscribed before me this 2nd day of August 1877

OSCAR MALMROS
U S Consul

PROVINCE OF NOVA SCOTIA
COUNTY OF INVERNESS

I hereby Certify that the above named Duncan McEachren voluntarily
made and subscribed in my presence the foregoing affidavit at Creignish
the said County this 2nd day of August 1877

Given under my hand and Notarial Seal at Cregnish aforesaid this
nd day of August 1877

(Seal.)

JAMES G. McKEEN
Notary Public

No. 200.

George Laidlaw, being duly sworn says: I am 39 years old; am by
ccupation a fisherman; I was out fishing in vessels, mostly American,
rom 1851 to 1872 inclusive—if fishing were good I would still go out
ishing and may do so next season in case mackerel are plenty—two sea-
ons or part of them I fished on the American shore—during the time I
ras out fishing the American fleet in the Gulf of St Lawrence fishing for
ackerel would average per year I think nearly 300 vessels—during the
rst year I was out the fleet of Provincial mackerel vessels in the Gulf was
arger than during any of the ten following years—I don't think that dur-
ng that entire time the Provincial vessels would average per year more
han fifty sails in the Gulf—the mackerel fisheries fell off much during the
ast 6 or 8 years—I don't think that during the last 6 or 8 years more than
ne quarter of the mackerel have been caught of the quantity caught per
season say 10 years ago—during the last 3 years there were not any
mackerel in the Gulf of St Lawrence worth going for—A long time ago,
about 18 years, the American mackerel vessels began to come to the
Gulf as early as the 5th of June and would come thick about the middle
of June—during the last 10 years the big American mackerel fleet did
not leave home until after the 4th of July—during some seasons mackerl will keep more in-shore during other seasons more off-shore—American and Provincial vessels, when the former have the privilege, fish
equally much in-shore and off shore—I think that when the Americans
are kept outside a line 3 miles from shore that most mackerel perhaps $\frac{2}{3}$
are caught outside by Provincial vessels because the Americans have a
heavy fleet and heave over much bait and the mackerel follow them—I
don't think it hurts the Americans much to be kept outside the 3 mile
limits,—they catch during the time they are kept *in* limits about as many
mackerel as when they are allowed to fish in-shore—I think about $\frac{2}{3}$ of
the mackerel I ever caught were caught outside of the 3 mile line—I
think that an American mackerel vessel averages about 70 tons or 75
tons old measurement—the bait for mackerel is Porgies and clam—it is
used alike by Provincials and Americans although occasionally the former use also herring but this is an exception—fishing alongside an
American fleet does not lessen the catch of mackerel by Provincial vessels, on the contrary the more vessels the more bait and mackerel—
I have been codfishing during two seasons or rather part of two seasons
fishing for mackerel afterwards—American codfish vessels average a
crew of from 10 to 12 hands—the codfishers going to the grand banks of
Newfoundland buy from Provincial people about 40 barrels of fresh herring on going to the banks and afterwards catch a small portion of their
supply of bait on the grand banks going again to the British coasts to

buy bait as they need it—codfish is caught outside the 3 mile line
once in a while when cod is caught inshore—the Americans a
mackerel catching goes have according to my estimate at all s
when allowed to fish in-shore, caught about ⅔d of their entire ca
side of the 3 mile line—the codfishers don't catch any of their
side 3 miles from shore except once in a while and not worth s
of—the American fishermen don't dry their nets on the British
they pickle their nets on their vessels in order to preserve them
they cure their fish on our coasts—the best two seasons I have ev
mackerel fishing were on the American shore and it is my opini
if the Provincial vessels were as well fitted out as the America
they employed as many of our most experienced fishermen as th
icans do and had as good bait that the fishery on the American
north of the Chesapeake Bay would be as valuable to Provincial
British Atlantic shores to the Americans—I think the presence o
ican fishing vessels on our coasts a considerable advantage to ou
because they leave a good deal of money

Dated Near Low Point Inverness County Aug 4th 1877
•
GEORGE LAID

Sworn to and subscribed before me this 4th day of August 18
OSCAR MALMRO
-    U S (

PROVINCE OF NOVA SCO
COUNTY OF INVE

I hereby Certify that the above named George Laidlaw vol
made and Subscribed in my presence the foregoing affidavit
Point in said County this 4th day of August 1877

Given under my hand and Notarial Seal this 4th August 187
(Seal.)   •   JAMES G. McKEE
Notary

No. 201.

I, Roderick McDonald of Low Point, N. S. do declare and say
as follows: I am living at Low Point Inverness Co. Nova Sc
over thirty years old, have been fishing for about 12 years un
years ago, when I knocked off because mackerel was scarce in
and it did not pay—the mackerel fishing has much fallen off durin
6 or 7 years—during these 6 or 7 years the average yearly catch
been over ⅓ of what it was 8 or ten years ago—during some
they will be much more off shore at other seasons more inshore
hot weather they will work more off shore—the best place for
I have ever seen is on Bradley Bank about twenty miles fro
Cape P. E. I.—sometimes the Americans when mackerel is pl
catch about ⅔d of their entire catch outside a line three miles fr
but striking an average I think that during season when ma
plenty Americans will catch about one half outside and the o
inside a line three miles from shore—the only bait American
vessels use is Porgies and clam and that is the bait nearly alw
by Provincial vessels but sometimes the latter use herring whi
a good bait and would not do at all to use as bait in fishing s
of vessels throwing out Porgies & clam—All the Porgies and c
as bait in the Gulf of St Lawrence comes from the United
think the Provincial fishermen catch as many mackerel fishin
side of an American fleet as they would do if no Americans we

ulf because a large fleet heaves over much bait and raises mackerel
:tter than a small number of vessels could do—I think that about half
' our fishermen from Cape Breton and on the Nova Scotia side of the
rait of Canso find employment in American fishing vessels and if they
ere not so employed they would have very hard times.   I think the
ming of American fishermen to our coasts is a great benefit to our
·ople especially when the American fleet in these waters is large.   So
·lp me God.

his
RODERICK + McDONALD
mark

Sworn to & subscribed in presence of
JAMES G. McKEEN

PROVINCE OF NOVA SCOTIA
LOW POINT INVERNESS COUNTY

I hereby certify that on the 3d day of August 1877 personally ap-
eared before me the above named Roderick McDonald and was by me
uly sworn to the above and foregoing Declaration which he subscribed
y affixing his mark at the foot of said declaration
Attested :   OSCAR MALMROS
U. S. Consul.

PROVINCE OF NOVA SCOTIA
COUNTY OF INVERNESS

I hereby Certify That the above named Roderick McDonald volunta-
'ly made and subscribed in my prence the foregoing affidavit at Low
. oint in said County.
Gived under my hand and Notarial Seal this 3rd day of August 1877
(Seal.)   JAMES G. McKEEN,
Notary Public.

No. 202.

I, Daniel McDonald do say on oath that : I am living at Low Point
nverness County Nova Scotia, am a fisherman by occupation, I have been
.shing mostly in American but partly also in Nova Scotia fishing vesels   I knocked off fishing about 4 years ago because the fisheries that
s mackerel fishing had so much fallen off that it did not pay to go fish-
ng; ever since the last 6 or 7 years the mackerel fisheries have been
:etting worse—10 or 12 years or longer there were about 400 or 500
\merican mackerel vessels in the bay of St Lawrence, during the
ame time there were about a hundred Provincial fishing vessels in the
3ay—the only bait used for mackerel, or almost the only, consists in
'orgies and clams and these all come from the United States whether
.sed by Provincials or Americans ; a few English vessels use also a lit-
le fat herring but this is used in quantities hardly worth mentioning
he Americans neither dry their nets nor cure their fish on the British
oasts—I don't think there were over fifty mackerel fishing vessels
ither Provincials or Americans in the Bay of St Lawrence—I have also
·een codfishing and know that the codfish caught by Americans is
ll caught more than 3 miles three miles from shore—during most
f th · seasons I went fishing by far the greater portion of mackerel
aught by the American fishing vessels were caught outside a line 3
iiles from shore, in some years the mackerel keep more outside in the
eep sea at other seasons they are found in greater numbers in shore—
f late years the mackerel have kept close to the shore—ten years ago

and for many years before that mackerel were much more p'
shore, say from 4 to 10 miles from shore and a large proport
caught still farther off from land—I think that the Provincia
in case they are as good and well fitted out as the America
catch as much mackerel and I don't think that fishing alor
American fishing vessels interferes with the catch of Provincia
I think they catch quite as many mackerel fishing side by side
Americans as they would do otherwise—I think that about on
the crew of the American vessels visiting the Gulf of St La'
composed of Natives of the Provinces who have their homes
Provinces. The American fishing vessels buy large quantities
etables, meal, and many other articles, they spend much mone
people and when the American fishing fleet on our coasts is sma
is scarce when there are plenty of American fishing vessels
coasts there is plenty of money among the people; and I do
swear that the foregoing statements now made by me are tru
ing to the best of my belief and knowledge; so help me God.
Dated Low Point Inverness Co. August 3d 1877.

his
DANIEL + McDO:
mark

Subscribed & sworn to before me Aug 3d 1877

OSCAR MALMR(
U. S.

PROVINCE OF NOVA SCOT
COUNTY OF INVE

I hereby Certify that the above namd Daniel McDonald vo
made and Subscribed in my presence the foregoing affidavi
Point in said County

Given under my hand & notarial Seal this 3rd day of Augu
(Seal.)   JAMES G. McKE
Notary

No. 203.

I, Dougald McKinnon of Long Point, Inverness County, No
say and depose on oath that: I am living at Long Point,
County Nova Scotia—I have been fishing for about the la
years partly in American partly in Provincial vessels, most
former and fishing for mackerel; for part of seven or 8 seaso
been codfishing in the Bay or on the banks of Newfoundland
wards fishing for mackerel—the crew of a mackerel fishing ve
ages 13 or 14 hands—the crew of American codfishing vessels
now from 10 to 12 hands—the average wages on codfishing v
from twenty five to fifty dollars a hand per month according
perience of each person in a crew—of late years most men go on
I should think that about from $\frac{1}{3}$ to $\frac{1}{2}$ of the crew of Americ;
vessels is composed of fishermen who are british subjects anc
the British Provinces—during the last 5 or 6 years mackerel fi.
very much fallen off—in this Bay i. e. the Bay of St Lawrence
has fallen off in my opinion over fifty per cent last year it w
an entire failure—during the times that mackerel were plen
before the last ten years much the greater quantity taken by
were taken outside a line 3 miles from the shore—but since
become scarce they have mostly been taken inside that lin
think that Provincial vessels catch any smaller quantity of m;

count of fishing along side of an American fleet—a large fleet of ves-
ls has a much better chance of finding the mackerel than a few vessels
themselves would have—I would rather take my chance in the Bay
ackerel fishing when there were 200 vessels in the Bay than when
ere are only twenty vessels—according to my estimate the average
penditure of an American fishing vessel in the several ports of the
itish Provinces during the season would amount to about $200 or
er, that is of a vessel making only one trip during the season—in case
vessel lands her cargo on these coasts for re-shipment to the States
should think that all her expenses including a complete re-outfit would
erage a thousand dollars or over—I think the coming of American
hing vessels to our coasts a greater advantage to our people, especi-
ly when the American fishing vessels come in great numbers. the
merican fishermen do not dry their nets or cure their fish on the coasts
the British Provinces—All the codfish caught by Americans is caught
itside a line 3 miles from shore—there are about on an average, taking
e last 10 years, from three to four American halibut fishers off the
oasts of the British waters, they, the halibut are as a rule caught out-
de a line three miles from shore ; it is an exception when they are caught
side that line—The bait for mackerel mostly comes from the States—
ere is no bait in the Dominion for mackerel fishers—The American
dfishers bring their bait partly from home, partly they buy it in the
rovinces or catch outside the 3 miles from shore.   And I do solemnly
clare on oath that according to the best of my knowledge and belief
e above and foregoing statements made by me are true.   So help me
od.
Dated Long Point, Inverness Co. August 2nd 1877.

DOUGALD McKINNON

Sworn to and subscribed before me this 2nd day of August 1877

OSCAR MALMROS
U. S. Consul

PROVINCE OF NOVA SCOTIA
COUNTY OF INVERNESS

I hereby Certify that the above named Dougald McKinnon volunta-
ly made and subscribed in my presence the foregoing affidavit
Given under my hand & Notarial Seal at Long Point County of Inver-
ess this 2nd day of August 1877
(Seal.)

JAMES G. McKEEN
Notary Public

No. 204.

OMINION OF CANADA
PROVINCE OF NOVA SCOTIA
HALIFAX SS
I Moses C. Morgan of Halifax in the County of Halifax in the Prov-
ice of Nova Scotia Merchant being solemnly sworn do make oath and
ay as follows :
1st I say that I am at present a fish dealer in the City of Halifax en-
aged in buying fish for export—and have been so engaged in the said
ity for about eight years.   I am intimately acquainted with the fish
rade and generally with all matters relating to the fisheries of Nova
cotia and Prince Edward Island.
I was formerly of Gloucester in the State of Massachusetts, where I
as connected with the fishery business aforesaid.
2nd.   I say that it has for several years been the practice for the Col-

onial fishermen, who have been engaged in the mackerel fi
the shores of Prince Edward Island and Cape Breton to pr
tion of their bait for so fishing from United States Fisherm
bait consisting of pogies or manhaden being brought from
States by the fishermen of that Country.

3rd The boat fisheries of Colonial fishermen are prosec
taking of Cod, haddock, hake, pollock, herrings, lobsters an
Of the fish so taken in boats by Colonial fishermen, the lar
is codfish, as is shewn by the fact that the product of the C
Nova Scotia in 1876 amounted to Two Millions five hundre
nine thousand dollars while the other descriptions of fish t
same year, exclusive of mackeral, amounted to two million
dred and forty two thousand dollars more.   The in-shore m
ery of Nova Scotia amounted that year, as appears *by th
the Canadian Fishery Commissioner, only to about seven b
fourteen thousand dollars constituting not more than about
of the aggregate product of the inshore Colonial boat fish
Scotia.

4th Of the Makeral caught inshore, that is to say, within
of the shore in boats by the fishermen of this Province no
one twentieth part of the aggregate catch is taken on that
Nova Scotia or Cape Breton Coast which is frequented b
fishermen from the United States and which is that part
lying on the Northern side of the Island of Cape Breton an
between the Strait of Canso and Sydney in said Island.

5th Cod and hallibut are caught by United States fisher
the deep sea or on the several off-shore fishing banks ou
three Mile limit.

6th The Mackeral taken by United States Fishermen
caught only around the shores of the Magdalen Islands
shores of Prince Edward Island on the east coast of Ne
lying in the Gulf of Saint Lawrence and the North Coast
ton extending from the Strait of Canso to Sydney.   All oth
caught by United States fishermen off the Coasts of British
ica are taken outside of the three mile limit in the Gulf of
rence.

7th The inshore fisheries are prosecuted by United Stat
on the Coasts of the British North American Provinces sol
eral and not in boats, but in vessels which only approach
fish during the months of July August, September and
other seasons they prosecute the mackeral fishery in the d
eries of the Gulf of Saint Lawrence outside of the three mil

8th The whole mackeral catch by United States fisherm
North American waters in the year 1876 I believe will n
value thirty thousand dollars, the reason for the catch be
was that for some years past the Mackeral fishery could b
more advantageously along the Coasts of the United States
coasts of British North America.   Last year was one of the
able and productive years on record for the mackeral fis
United States Coast.

9th. The in-shore fisheries, that is to say: the fisherie
three mile limit on the British North American Coast ar
cuted by United States fishermen for mackeral and in v
boats—

10th. The catch of Mackerel both inshore and offshore
fishermen constitutes only about one sixth of the aggreg

fish. Of the Mackerel caught by United States fishermen on the British North American Coast not more than one fourth are caught inshore or within the three mile limit. The rest are caught outside the three mile limit. All other descriptions of fish caught by United States fishermen are caught on the banks and constitute the great bulk of the fisheries.

The proportions which I have mentioned in this section of my affidavit are arrived at by taking an average of the results of fishing seasons through several years.

But little injury if any in my opinion can result to Colonial fishermen from United States fishermen coming inshore to fish for mackeral. The large quantity of bait thrown from United States fishing vessels Attracts the fish in large numbers and enables the Colonial fishermen in boats to prosecute the fishery much more successfully than they could otherwise do; and experience has shewn that the free access of United States fishermen to the inshore fishery has not diminished the Colonial boat fisheries, but that such boat fisheries have been steadily increasing since such free access was given and so far from its being found disadvantageous to fishermen to have a number of vessels fishing in company. It is quite usual and customary for large numbers of such vessels to be engaged fishing for a length of time side by side and the practical result of such a mode of fishing is that the fish are attracted by the bait thrown in large quantities from the vessels as aforesaid and the fishing of Colonial fishermen in boats is greatly facilitated thereby.

11th Another advantage which Colonial fishermen derive from United States fishermen having access to the British North American fisheries, is by the former procuring bait from the latter as deposed to in the second paragraph of this affidavit. A further advantage to the Colonial fishermen is that United States fishermen buy from the Colonial fishermen herrings for bait to prosecute the Bank codfishery. The United States fishermen do not catch herring in British North American waters but buy such quantities as they require for bait for the Cod fishery from the Colonial fishermen. And another advantage accruing to the Provinces from the United States fishermen having access to the British North American fisheries arises from the fact that the United States fishermen purchase from traders in the Colonies supplies, not only of bait, but of ice, provisions, clothing, barrels salt, nets, twines and many other articles. The purchases of bait and such other articles as are herein mentioned give employment to large numbers of persons and give a very important trade to a number of settlements along the coast, such as Prospect, Canso, Port Mulgrave and Louisburg. At Prospect alone about one thousand nets were set to catch herring for bait to be sold to United States fishermen last season. Ice to the quantity of seven hundred or eight hundred tons is usually bought there by the United States fishermen and in that place alone last season the purchases by the last named fishermen amounted from ten thousand dollars to fifteen thousand dollars.

The procuring of bait on the coasts of the Colonies by the United States fishermen is quite as beneficial to the Colonists as to those fishermen and the herring so supplied to them as bait is not used for mackeral nor for any fishery inshore, but for the Bank fishery. During the last ten or fifteen years very few of the United States fishermen use salt bait they formerly brought salt bait with them and caught fresh fish, as they could for fresh bait, but now most of them procure their fresh

bait from the Coast and keep it in the ice houses, with whi‹
their vessels are furnished.

12th. During the last few years the mackeral fishery in tl
Saint Lawrence has been almost abandoned by Colonial a⟩
States fishing vessels and is being almost entirely prosecute‹
by Colonial fishermen. The fishery on the American Coast h.
much more productive of late years as to attract many of t
formerly came to the Gulf; And the decline of that fishery ir
being such as to cause many of the Colonial fishing vessels tha
resorted there to be employed in other ways.

At the time of the treaty the mackeral fishery along the Brit
American coast was considered valuable and important to t
States fishermen, but at the present time the deep sea fisheri‹
fisheries on their own Coasts are principally relied on by ther

13th. A very large quantity of fresh fish, consisting of S‹
halibut and in the winter of frozen herrings caught by Color
men find a market in the United States probably from twe
thousand to two hundred and fifty thousand dollars worth of
mon alone being exported annually from the British Province‹
America to the United States. A large number of vessels loa‹
at Fortune Bay in the Island of Newfoundland with frozer
there caught by Colonial fishermen for the United States M
employment is thereby given and benefits received by large n
Colonial fishermen who are engaged in that branch of the
which is the principal means of support of a large part of
population during the winter season. At Grand Manaan an
also large quantities of herring are caught by Colonial fisherm
United States Market and these are largely shipped to the Uni
in Colonial vessels, and the same statement herein deposed
gards the benefits accruing to the population at Fortune Bay
that at Grand Manaan.

Although previous to the Washington Treaty fresh fish
enumerated were admitted to the United States Markets fre
yet their admission was subject to changes in legislation fr
time instead of the Markets being permanently open as at pi

14th. The United States afford the only markets for n
number one and number two grade all fat herring not consu
Dominion and of number one Salmon caught by Colonial
Such descriptions of fish find a market in the United States

15th In this affidavit the statements which I have made ir
ent tense apply to the state of things which has existed
seven years except where I have expressed a different mean

M. C. M

Sworn to before me at Halifax in the County of Halifax i
ince of Nova Scotia this 16th day of August A D 1877.
(Seal.)   W. D. HARRINGT

No. 205.

I Richard Beazley of Halifax in the County of Halifax
being solemnly sworn do make oath and say as follows:

1st I say that for forty years last past, I have been eng
fisheries of Nova Scotia, Labrador, Newfoundland Prin
Island, New Brunswick, Gulf of St Lawrence and Baie. d‹
besides the deep sea fisheries as a fisherman and dealer in fis

been for that time intimately acquainted with the condition of the said fisheries and the manner in which fishing has been carried on by Colonial and United States fishermen.

2nd The same kinds and descriptions of fish that are found on the coasts and shores of the British North American Provinces are to be found on the coasts and shores of the United States which are now made available to Colonial fishermen by the Treaty of Washington and on the coasts and shores of the United States several kinds of fish are procured which cannot be found on the coasts and shores of the British North American Provinces such as bass, porgies and other kinds,

3rd Nearly all the bait for mackeral used by Colonial fishermen is and must be procured by them from the United States fishermen who come to the coast of British North America under the provisions of the Treaty of Washington. The bait chiefly used for mackeral and the best bait are porgies which are all taken on the coast of the United States and generally within three miles of the shore. It is a great benefit to Colonial fishermen to be able to procure such bait from the United States fishermen.

4th The United States fishermen who come to the fisheries off the coast of British North America principally pursue the deep sea fisheries outside the three mile limit. About five sixths of the fish taken by United States fishermen off the British North American coast are taken outside the three mile limit.

5th The fish taken inshore by United States fishermen is almost wholly mackerel and not more than one fourth of the mackerel taken by them in the vicinity of the British North American coast is taken inside the three mile limit while about three fourths, taking the average of seasons is procured outside the three mile limit, The fishery in British North American waters is not carried on in boats by the United States fishermen but in vessels and when they are fishing inshore for mackeral it is principally around the shores of the Magdalen Islands and of Prince Edward Island and on the coast of New Brunswick, in the Gulf of St. Lawrence and on the north coast of Cape Breton. The Colonial fisher-men fish principally in boats,

6th Colonial fishermen are benefitted and not injured in the prosecu-tion of the fisheries by United States fishermen being allowed to fish within the inshore limits. By such permission being given the Colonial fishermen are enabled to purchase their bait from the United States fishermen which is a great advantage to the former and besides that the throwing of bait by United States fishing vessels attracts the fish and enables the Colonial fishermen fishing in boats to fish much more suc-cessfully than they could otherwise do. For this reason it is quite com-mon for a large number of fishing vessels and boats to be seen engaged in fishing for a length of time side by side such a mode of fishing being found advantageous to all but especially to those who are fishing in boats.

7th. The cost of fishing vessels and of the outfits for the same in the Brit-ish Provinces is at least twenty-five per cent lower than the cost thereof in the United States and as a consequence of this difference in prices a large number of United States fishing vessels procure their outfits in the British North American Provinces.

8th The United States fishermen use herring almost entirely for bait in the codfishery which they prosecute on the Banks and in the deep sea fishery outside the three mile limit and they procure almost all the herring and other bait which they use for that purpose from Colonial

fishermen. In addition to bait the United States fisherm
from the people of the British Provinces large quantitie:
barrels, provisions, clothing, nets, twines, and other article
prosecution of the fisheries. The trade with the United ?
men for such articles is of great benefit to the people ot
Provinces and is the principal trade of some of the ports ·
tia. Large quantities of fresh fish are also purchased by ⅃
some parts of the British Provinces for shipment to the Ꭲ
and such shipments are mostly made in Colonial vessels.

9th Of late years the drying and curing of fish by the Ꭲ
fishermen is principally done on the decks of their vessels ;
dom land to dry nets or to cure fish or to repack them or
cargoes.

10th The Treaty of Washington so far as the privileges ot
are concerned is I verily believe as beneficial to the people ⸋
Provinces as to the people of the United States, both wi
benefitted by its provisions being carried out.

11th For all number one and number two mackerel, foi
ring not consumed at home and for all number one salm
British Provinces the United States afford the only mai
duties paid on the exportation of such fish from the Briti⸳
before the Treaty of Washington amounted to a very l:
money annually and the opening of the United States mar
Treaty to such exportations has been a very great benefit
of the British Provinces.

12th For several years past the inshore fisheries of the ⸳
inces have not been so much resorted to by United States
they were formerly and they are being less and less reso
year by such fishermen, one reason for this fact is the c
modes of fishing pursued by such fishermen and another is
the mackerel fishery on the coasts of the British Provinces
eral years past been declining while it has been improvin
same period on the coasts of the United States.

13th The fisheries on the coasts of the United States w
nearly as valuable to Colonial fishermen as to the United
men if the former chose to avail themselves of the conc
Washington Treaty in that particular, and latterly they ɑ
to avail themselves of that fishery which is annually be
valuable.

14th In this affidavit the statements which I have mad
ent tense apply to the state of things which has existed fo
years except where I have expressed a different meaning.

RICHARD

Sworn to before me at Halifax in the County of Halifax t
day of June A D 1877
(Seal.)   WM McI
N

No. 206.

I John Glazebrook of Halifax in the County of Halifa
ince of Nova Scotia Fisherman being solemnly sworn do
say as follows:

1st I say that for forty five years last past I have be
the fisheries of British North America and have been for
mately acquainted with the condition of the said fisheries

ner in which fishing has been carried on by the Colonial and United States fishermen.

2nd The same kinds and descriptions of fish that are found in the fisheries mentioned in the last paragraph are to be found on the coasts and shores of the United States which are now thrown open to Colonial fishermen by the Treaty of Washington and also several other kinds such as Bass and pogies which are not to be found on the coasts and shores of British North America.

3rd The greater part of the bait used by Colonial fishermen in the mackeral fishery is procured from the United States and is furnished to said fishermen by United States fishermen who come to the coasts of the Provinces under the provisions of the Treaty of Washington. The best and most commonly used bait for mackerel are pogies which are taken from the coasts of the United States and generally inshore and the procuring of such bait is a great benefit to Colonial fishermen.

4th Much the larger proportion of the fisheries pursued by United States fishermen off the Atlantic Coast of British North America consists of the deep sea fisheries outside of the three mile limit. I believe that at least three fourths if not five sixths of the fish taken by United States fishermen off the shores of the British Provinces are taken outside the three mile limit.

5th The United States fishermen pursue the inshore fisheries almost solely for mackerel and of the mackerel taken by such fishermen on the coasts of British North America much the smaller part—in fact only about one fourth is taken inside while about three fourths are taken outside the three mile limit taking the average of seasons. The United States fishermen do not fish in boats when in British North American waters but in vessels. The Colonial fishermen fish principally in boats. The United States fishermen procure the mackerel which they catch in shore chiefly around the shores of the Magdalen Islands around the shores of Prince Edward Island—on the east coast of New Brunswick in the Gulf of Saint Lawrence and on the north coast of Cape Breton.

6th Colonial fishermen are benefitted and not injured in the prosecution of the fisheries by the United States fishermen being allowed to fish within the inshore limit—they are benefitted by being enabled to purchase bait as before mentioned and are enabled to take larger quantities of fish than they could do if fishing alone by reason of the fish being attracted by the quantities of bait thrown from the United States fishing vessels.

7th The cost of fishing vessels and of outfits therefor in the British Provinces is at least twenty five per cent lower than the cost thereof in the United States and as a consequence of this difference in prices a large number of United States fishing vessels procure their outfits in the British Provinces yearly.

8th The United States fishermen procure the herring which is almost the only bait which they use for the deep sea codfishery by purchase from Colonial fishermen—they make such purchases in large quantities buying all or nearly all the bait they need for that fishery from Colonial fishermen and they buy in addition from the inhabitants along the coasts of the British Provinces large quantities of ice salt barrels provisions nets twines cables clothing and all other articles used in the prosecution of the fisheries. This is the principal trade of some of the ports of Nova Scotia and is a great benefit to the inhabitants. Large quantities of fresh fish are also purchased by Americans in some parts of the British Provinces for shipment to the United States and such shipments are chiefly made in Colonial vessels.

9th Of late years the drying and curing of fish by United
ermen is principally done on the decks of their vessels and t
land to dry nets or to cure fish or to repack them or to trans-s

10th The Treaty of Washington so far as the privileges
ermen are concerned is I verily believe as beneficial to the p
British Provinces as to the people of the United States.

11th The United States afford the only market for all num
number two mackerel for all fat herring not consumed at h
all number one salmon from the British Provinces and the
on the exportation of such fish from the British Province
Treaty of Washington amounted to a very large sum of mone
The provisions of the Treaty of Washington by which said
made free are a very great benefit to the people of the Britisb

12th For several years past the inshore fisheries of the B
inces have not been so much resorted to by United States fi
they were formerly and they are being less and less resort
year by such fishermen. The change in the mode of fishing
such fishermen is one reason for this circumstance and ano
is that the mackerel fishery on the coasts of British North A
for several years past been declining while it has been impro
the same period on the coasts of the United States. The
the coasts of the United States would be as valuable to Col
men as to the United States fishermen if the former chose to
selves of the concessions of the Treaty of Washington in that

13th In this affidavit the statements which I have made in
tense apply to the state of things existing for the last six or
except where I have expressed a different meaning.

·

his
JOHN + GLAZE
mark

Sworn to before me at Halifax in the Province of Nova
20th day of June A D 1877 being first read and explained t
(Seal.)   WM McKER

Nota

No. 207.

1 William Hays of Halifax in the County Halifax fishe
solemnly sworn do make oath and say as follows :

1st I say that for forty years last past I have been engaged
eries of Nova Scotia, Prince Edward Island and Newfou
have been for that time intimately acquainted with the con
said fisheries and the manner in which fishing has been c
the Colonial and United States fishermen.

2nd The same kinds and descriptions of fish that are f
coasts and shores of Nova Scotia and Prince Edward Isla
found on the coasts and shores of the United States which a
available to Colonial fishermen by the Treaty of Washing
the coasts and shores of the United States several descrip
are procured which cannot be found on the coasts and sho
Scotia and Prince Edward Island, namely, Bass, porgies
kinds, .

3rd The greater part of the bait used by Colonial fishe
mackeral fishery is and must be procured from the Unite
is furnished to them by United States fishermen who come
of the Provinces under the provisions of the Treaty of
The best and most commonly used bait for mackeral are p

are all taken from the coasts of the United States and generally inshore, and the procuring of such bait in this way is a great benefit to the Colonial fishermen.

4th Of the fisheries pursued by United States fishermen off the Atlantic coast of British North America much the larger proportion consists of the deep sea fisheries outside the three mile limit. I believe that at least three fourths if not five sixths of the fish taken by United States fishermen off the said coast last mentioned are taken outside the three mile limit,

5th The United States fishermen pursue the inshore fisheries chiefly for mackeral and of the mackeral taken by such fishermen on the Coasts of British North America about one fourth is taken inside and about three fourths outside the three mile limit, taking the average of seasons. The United States fishermen do not fish in boats when in British North American waters but in vessels, the Colonial fishermen fish principally in boats, The United States fishermen procure the mackeral which they catch inshore principally around the shores of the Magdalen Islands, around the shores of Prince Edward Island, the East coast of New Brunswick and the North coasts of Cape Breton.

6th Colonial fishermen are not injured in the prosecution of the fisheries but benefitted by the United States fishermen being allowed to fish within the inshore limits, the facility thus given for the purchase of bait is a great advantage to Colonial fishermen and in consequence of the large quantities of bait thrown from a fleet of United States fishing vessels the Colonial fishermen fishing in the vicinity of such a fleet are enabled to take much larger quantities of fish than they could if fishing alone,—

7th The cost of fishing vessels and of the outfits for the same in the British Provinces is at least twenty five per cent lower than the cost thereof in the United States and as a consequence of this difference in prices a large number of United States fishing vessels procure their outfits in the British North American Provinces

8th The United States fishermen procure the bait which they use for the deep sea codfishery which bait consists of herring by purchasing the the same from Colonial fishermen, they purchase herring for such purpose in large quantities and in fact obtain all or nearly all they need in that way from Colonial fishermen and in addition to their purchases of bait the United States fishermen purchase from traders along the coasts of the British Provinces large quantities of ice, salt, barrels, provisions, nets, twines, clothing and all other articles used in the prosecution of the fisheries. The trade with the United States fishermen for such articles is of great benefit to the people of the British Provinces and is the principal trade of some of the ports of Nova Scotia, Large quantities of fresh fish are also purchased by Americans in some parts of the British Provinces for shipment to the United States and such shipments are mostly made in Colonial vessels.

9th Of late years the drying and curing of fish by United States fishermen is principally done on the decks of their vessels and they seldom land to dry nets or to cure fish or to repack them or to trans-ship cargoes,—

10th The Treaty of Washington so far as the priviliges of the fisheries are concerned is, I verily believe as beneficial to the people of the British Provinces as to the people of the United States, both will be equally benefitted by such privileges being given.

11th For all number one and number two mackeral for all fat herring not consumed at home and for all number one Salmon from the British

Provinces the United States afford the only market and the du
the exportation of such fish from the British Provinces before
of Washington amounted to a very large sum of money an
the opening of the United States Market by the Treaty of V
to such exportation has been a very great benefit to the pe
British Provinces,

12th For several years past the inshore fisheries of the Br
inces have not been so much resorted to by United States 1
they were formerly and they are being less and less resorte
year by such fishermen—one reason for this fact is the cha
modes of fishing pursued by such fishermen, Another is th
the mackerel fishery on the coasts of the British Provinc
several years past been declining while it has been improv
the same period on the coasts of the United States

13th The fisheries on the coast of the United States˙w
valuable to Colonial fishermen as to the United States fishe
Colonial fishermen chose to avail themselves of the concess
Washington Treaty in that particular and latterly they are
to avail themselves of that fishery which is annually beco
valuable.

14th In this affidavit the statements which I have made in
tense apply to the state of things which has existed for tl
years except where I have expressed a different meaning.

WILLIAM

Sworn to before me at Halifax in the County of Halifax in
ince of Nova Scotia this 13th day of June A D 1877

WM McKER]

(Seal.) Nota

No. 208.

*The Examination of Captain William A. Molloy of Great
Newfoundland taken before George Henry Emerson Attorr
Examiner*

The said witness being sworn saith—I am a native of Ne
and am 27 years of age. I have been engaged in the Fish
all my life. There is very little inshore-fishing done by Am
eimau within three miles of the Coast of Newfoundland
taking. There is no mackerel-fishing done on the Coast of
land by either American or British fisherman. There is no
done on the inshore by American fisherman I was eight y
out of Gloucester six years of which I was Master—I am tl
fectly acquainted with the American fishing in the Maratim
I have never known the American Fisherman avail thems
privilege of landing to dry nets, cure fish or use the shore f
purpose in this Colony except for obtaining Water The
Newfoundland benefit very materially by intercourse wit
fisherman both by traffic in bait, ice and fishing-stores an
by American-fisherman within the Colony, of their small
I think that the importance of the intercourse of America
with British fisherman cannot at present be estimated. I
can Fishing vessel that comes to Newfoundland cannot gt
an outlay of from sixty to seventy dollars for bait and ice.
fisheries for the past few years have been less productive a
tive to those engaged in them, than formerly. The shore

e inshore have been of very little value to those prosecutiug them
her from the States or Newfouudland for the past four years. The
hing by American fisherman in the Waters of the Provinces does not
sen the catch of American or British fisherman; and the presence
American Fishermen in the Provincial Waters improves the Status
the Provincial fisherman, who are much inferior to the American
herman, and are at least a century behind the age in the manner of
tching fish. If the British fishermen employed as much capital and
d as much energy and enterprise as the American Fisherman I believe
at the American Fishermen cannot compete on the Newfoundland
ast in catching fish. The only advantage derived by American Fish-
nan from the Treaty of Washington 1871, is the advantage of catch-
ʳ bait and obtaining ice which is also of great advantage to New-
ındlanders in the way of Traffic.

WILLIAM MULLOY

Taken before me at Saint Johns Newfoundland this 1st day of June
D 1877

GEO H.Y EMERSON Jʀ
Examiner—

No. 209.

ıe examination of Levi Griffin of Boston United States of America but at
ıresent of Saint John's Newfoundland taken before me George Henry
Emerson Jr Examiner—

This Witness being sworn, saith :—
I am a native of the State of Maine but at present am fishing in New-
undland I am thirty four years of age, and have been engaged in the
ıhery-business about twenty years. The American fisherman do not
ıe and have never used the inshore fisheries for cod fishing. There is
ı mackerel fishing on the Coast of Newfoundland. There is no boat-
ıhing done by Americans on the Coast of Newfoundland Even the
ank fishing has become less lucrative and important within the past
n years than it formerly was. To my knowledge there has been no
ıe made by the Americans of the privilege of landing on the Coast of
ewfoundland for curing the fish, drying the nets, obtaining their
ɔod. There is no object whatever to be obtained by such landing.
merican fisherman generally purchase whatever they require from the
ɪople of the Island. The value to all provincial fisherman especially
ı Newfoundlanders cannot be too highly estimated (and will no doubt
ɪ of greater value ın the future) of their intercourse with Americans.
very Fishing vessel that enters the ports of Newfoundland, belouging
ı Americans leaves at least Eighty dollars. Nearly all the American
ıherman purchase ice, bait and stores and supplies in large quantities
Newfoundland and this trade is increasing very largely every year.
have repeatedly heard the fisherman of Newfoundland assert that it
as a great benefit to them to have constant intercourse with Americans
housands of Barrels of bait would pass the shores of Newfoundland
ʳery year if the Americans did not come down to purchase them. This
ade with the fisherman of Newfoundland for bait and ice is of great
ınefit to the Island and generally recognized to be so except by the
rge Merchants of the Island. A great impetus has been given to the
ıhing-business in Newfoundland since the passing of the Washington
reaty 1871. The trade of Americans with Newfoundlanders has in-
eased at least *One hundred per. cent. per annum*, since the passing of
ıe Treaty and is steadily increasing with great advautage to all con-

cerned. It is the real opinion of the Inhabitants of the Mara
inces especially Newfoundland that the incidental advant
derived from the presence of American fisherman in British V
of great value to British Fisherman is very great, and that tl
on the Coast of Newfoundland do not suffer to any extent. ar
lessen in any way the catch of British fisherman. If the Br
man employed as much capital and had as much energy and
as American fisherman the American Waters would be of n
tance to Newfoundlanders than the British Waters are to .
especially as there are no mackerel to be caught on the New
coast
‣ The fishing-business as a rule does not make very large re
pared with other businesses, considering the Amount of C
time employed in its prosecution. It is a very precarious m
ing—and the "fisherman's luck" is almost as proverbial as tl
luck."

LEVI G

Taken before me at Saint John's this 2nd day of July A D
GEO. H.Y EMERSON
Ex

No. 210.

The examination of Henry A. Cobb a native Province Town X
at present of Saint John's Newfoundland taken before me Ge
Emerson, Examiner.

This witness being sworn saith: My name is Henry A. Cobl
years of age and have been engaged in the cod and other fish
life. I have been fishing on the Grand Bank for a period of
It is not true that American Fishermen use the inshore fis
three miles for cod-fishing. There are no mackerel on th
Newfoundland. There is not any boat-fishing done by Amer
men on the inshore fisheries except bait-taking, which is sel
as American Fishermen are rarely equipped for bait-catching
and are consequently driven to purchase from the Newfound
inshore fishing is of no value to American fisherman and
knowledge been of very little value to British-fishermen for
ten years I have never known, in all my experience, exte
ten years of American fisherman availing themselves of t
of landing on the Coast of Newfoundland to dry nets, cur
any other purpose. Since the Treaty of Washington the
American fishing-vessels has not increased on the coast of
land and the only advantage derived by American fisher
privilege of obtaining fresh-bait from Newfoundland fish
advantage derived from intercourse with American fisher
great to Newfoundlanders. American fishing vessels call a
ent ports on the South East and West of Newfoundland ar
ice, and fishing stores to large amounts and sell their small
Every fishing vessel entering a Newfoundland port expe
Seventy five dollars every trip before she leaves. This is
vantage to the Newfoundland people especially in the ou
the fisherman is generally very poor and very destitute. I
the British fisheries are much less productive and less v
they formerly were and the inshore fishery's on the coast o
land has been reduced about fifty per cent. in quantity and

ɔ past ten years. It is the opinion of most maritime provincial fish-
nen that the incidental advantages derived by them from intercourse
th American fishermen are very great; and that the presence of
nerican fisherman in British Waters is not detrimental to the interests
 British fishermen, either by depreciating the value of the fish by
mpetition, or decreasing the Catch of fish in the provinces. If the
·itish fishermen were more energetic and put more capital into their
heries and had the same class of vessels prosecuting the fishery that
ɔ Americans have, the Mackerel fishing of the United States would
 of inestimable value to them as they have no mackerel fishing in
ɔwfoundland.

I do not think there has been any advantage obtained by American
hermen by the Treaty of Washington except taking bait. The only
ackerel fishing that the Americans prosecuted in British Waters
fore the passing of the Treaty was at Bay Chaleur, and that has
iled from natural causes.

HENRY A COBB.

Taken before me at Saint Johns Newfoundland this 2nd day of Junə
D 1877.

GEO. H.Y EMERSON Jʀ
Examiner

No. 211.

*he examination of Cyrenius Brown of Trepassey in the Island of Newfound
land (formerly of the State of Maine U. S.) taken before me at Saint
John's Newfoundland,*

This Witness being sworn saith : —   ᵛ
I am a native of Bucksport in the State of Maine United States of
.merica but at present residing in Trepassey in the Island of Newfound
ɪnd. I am sixty nine years of age. I have been engaged in the Fishery
usiness about forty years. It is not true that American fisherman use
ɪe inshore fisheries within three miles of the Coast of Newfoundland
ɪr cod or other fishing. American fisherman fish either on the Grand
ɪank, St. Peters Bank or Banquero. There is no mackerel on the Coast
f Newfoundland. The inshore fishery is of little or no value to Amer-
ɪan fisherman. It is never prosecuted by American fishermen. I never
new American fishermen to land on the coast of Newfoundland for the
urpose of drying their nets curing their fish. This privilege is never
vailed of by American fishermen because they bring their fish to the
ɪtates in a "green" condition, which is more profitable than drying and
uring in Newfoundland, where the weather is much less suited for the
ure of fish than the climate of the United States.

I think the value of American "Bankers" visiting Newfoundland is
f great value to Newfoundlands. The American "Bankers" purchase
ɪrge quantities of Bait and ice in Newfoundland. This practice of vis-
ɪing Newfoundland for the purpose of obtaining Bait, which was hardly
nown ten years ago, is increasing rapidly and will be of more value to
ɪewfoundlanders in the future. This practice increases about *twenty*
er. cent. every year. Each American "Banker" spends about sixty to
ɪeventy dollars for Bait on her visit to Newfoundland. This Traffic is
f great value to Newfoundland. and the people of the country think it
, great blessing to be able to sell the Bait to the Americans, which would
ɪtherwise be useless and unprofitable to any one. Newfoundlanders
ɪenerally acknowledge that they receive a great deal more by free inter-

course with Americans in their fishery business than they do with either Canadian or Nova Scotian fisherman.

CYRENIUS BROWN

Taken before me at Saint Johns Newfoundland this 2nd day of July 1877.

GEO. H.Y EMERSON JR
Examiner

No. 212.

The Examination of William Fitzgerald of St John's Newfoundland taken before me George Henry Emerson Examiner.

This witness being sworn saith :—I am thirty nine years of age. I have been engaged in the Fishery-business over twenty years. I have been fishing out of the Port of Gloucester, United States, for the past ten years. I am well acquainted with the American fishing on the Coast of Newfoundland The Americans never did not do they now use the inshore-fishery within three miles for the purposes of cod or any other fishing except the taking of bait There is not any mackerel fishing on the coast of Newfoundland by either American of British Fishermen. There is no boat fishing by the Americans on the Coast of Newfoundland at all. American fishermen do not come prepared for inshore fishing. Inshore fishing would not be profitable to Americans as the inshore fish would not find a market in the United States owing to the smallness of the fish. Americans do not make use in any way of the privilege granted under the Treaty of Washington of landing on the coast of Newfoundland to cure fish, dry nets or procure wood and water. Americans buy their wood and water from the Newfoundlanders. The only advantage derived by Americans under the Above Treaty is the privilege of procuring fresh-bait and ice which they always, with few exceptions, purchase in the different ports of Newfoundland. I think that the presence of American fishermen in the ports of Newfoundland purchasing stores bait ice &c is of great advantage to the people of the Colony and is of great value to the fishermen of the provinces in the way of increased traffic and will be of more importance to the people in the future. I paid last year fifty cents per hundred to Newfoundlanders for Squids for bait and I purchased about 15,000 at that price. I consider that number of Squids small for a vessel to take. I have paid as high as ninety cents per hundred for squids on the Western Coast of Newfoundland.

I think great advantages will be obtained by Newfoundland in the future by the intercourse of American fishermen with Newfoundland fishermen, quite as much as the benefits derived by American fishermen by privileges granted under the Washington Treaty. The Mutual intercourse will improve the habits and customs of the Newfoundland fishermen especially in the manner of taking and curing fish and also in giving labour to Newfoundland fishermen; which they are not at all times able to obtain. Half the population of Newfoundland are thrown out of employment when the inshore fishery fails.

his
WILLIAM + FITZGERALD
mark

Taken before me at Saint Johns this 5th day of June A D 1877 ——

GEO H. Y EMERSON JR

No. 213.

I, Charles H Nute Master of Sch Edward E. Webster of Gloucester and formerly Master of Sch's Ben Perley Poore, Lightfoot, Ontario & O. B. Manning—all of Gloucester, was born in Gloucester, am 32 years of age & have been engaged in the fisheries for 20 years & continuously engaged in the Grand Bank fishery for the past twelve (12) years taking Cod & Halibut for the first nine years obtained my bait upon the Banks —usually carrying from home a few barrels of Pogie Slivers to procure the first fish & afterwards fishes-peas & other refuse parts of fish, also useing Bird-meat,—a large quantity being obtained by catching the Hagdon with a hook—for the last three years I have bought my bait of the inhabitants of Newfoundland paying cash for the same. the holding of bait by traps and pounds by the people of N. F. enables us to obtain our bait readily & is a source of income to them and convenience to us —the people will often chase us for miles for an opportunity to bait an American fisherman,—we meet their boats off St. Peters seeking for American vessels to sell them bait,—there being a very active competition in selling bait and supplies the Newfoundlanders carry this bait to St Peters to sell to the French vessels & we could easily procure this bait there, as there are thousands of barrels annually thrown overboard for want of a market & the only object in going to Newfoundland is to obtain the bait in its freshest state—I never have caught any bait at N. F. but have purchased it when I have got any at N. F.—I have never known any American vessel to catch bait at Newfoundland having uniformly purchased the same.

I paid on this last voyage, ending Aug 10. 1877, $271 to the inhabitants of N. F. for bait

I know that this trade is of great advantage to the inhabitants of Newfoundland, as our vessels leave from one to two thousand dollars some days, in some of the little Coves of the Coast—the Squid are entirely useless except for the purposes of bait, and the American and French fleet provide the only market—there is about 250 American vessels engaged in the Bank fishery—a portion—say one half—purchase bait at Newfoundland   I have never caught any Halibut or Cod within one hundred & fifty miles of the British shores the american Cod & Halibut fishery being entirely a deep-sea or ocean fishery and I knew of no American vessels taking Cod or Halibut within three miles of the shore—there is no American vessel engaged in the Codfishery that carries seines or nets to procure bait

CHARLES H NUTE

COMMONWEALTH OF MASSACHUSETTS

ESSEX ss.   August 13th 1877

Then personally appeared the above named Charles H. Nute and made oath that all the above statements by him subscribed are true to the best of his knowledge & belief before me

(Seal.)   DAVID W. LOW
                                          Notary Public

No. 214.

I, Joseph Oakley, Master of the Schooner Sarah P. Ayer of Gloucester do depose and say that I was born in Nova Scotia, am 29 years of age, have been continuously engaged in the fisheries—the last eight years of which being out of Gloucester & always to the Grand Banks.

I have read the statement of Captain Charles H. Nute of S
R. Webster, and in all its features and statements it accore
own experience & is perfectly true—on my last trip to Gra
took my bait at Newfoundland and paid $209,76 cash for
have never caught.fish or halibut while in an American ves
miles of the shore—the American Cod & halibut fishery is
deep-sea or ocean fishery. I consider the bait business of
land of vastly more profit to the inhabitants than convenien
to the Americans and I believe that were it not for this trad
supplies to the American fleet; the inhabitants would suffe
tress & poverty. as their stock in trade would be entirely u
it not for our fleet to purchase them,

JOSEPH C

COMMONWEALTH OF MASSACHUSETTS

ESSEX SS.   GLOUCESTER Aug. 1
Then personally appeared the above named Joseph Oakle
oath that all the above statements by him subscribed are
best of his knowledge and belief before me
(Seal.)   DAVID W. I
Nota

No. 215.

I, Mathew McDonald Master of the Sch Clara B. Chapma
sequently of the Sch Webster Sanborn was born in Prin
Island am twenty six years of age, have been engaged in t
from Gloucester for the past eight years — principally on
Banks, taking Codfish & halibut. I have used for bait prin
ring & squid in all cases purchasing the same of the inhabita
foundland & paying Cash for the same at the rate of $2.
Herring and 50 Cts per 100 for Squid — the people there be
to sell the same to the American fishermen — I have never
to catch any bait on the Coast of N. F. — am well acquaint
manner in which bait is obtained by the American fisherme
that all with which I am acquainted buy their bait — payi
the same,—have never known of but one case in which the bai
— one vessel taking a few Bbls of Squid at Conception Ba
have never fished for, Cod or Halibut on the British shore
know of any American vessel ever taking these fish within
three miles from the shore, the Cod & Halibut fisheries, as
by the American fishermen, is entirely a deep-sea fishery.

MATHEW McI

STATE OF MASSACHUSETS } SS.
    COUNTY OF ESSEX   }

GLOUCESTER Aug
Then personally appeared the within named Mathew McD
ter of Sch. Clara B. Chapman, and made oath that the withi
by him subscribed is true

Before me
(Seal.)   DAVID W.
Nota

No. 216.

The Examination of Patrick Walsh of St. John's Newfoundland taken before me George Henry Emerson jr Examiner—

This witness being sworn saith—

I am forty three years of age and have been engaged in the Fishery since I was fourteen years old. I am Master of a Newfoundland Steam Bait Skiff, a vessel belonging to the Honorable Ambrose Shea of St John's Newfoundland, and used by him for procuring bait for the Fishermen of Newfoundland.

I never knew the American fishermen use the inshore shore fishery for Cod or other fishing. We have no mackerel on the Coast of this Island. The American fisherman frequent our Harbors for the purpose of procuring bait to prosecute the fishery on the Banks of Newfoundland. They purchase always and do not catch it themselves. The fishermen of Newfoundland benefit by this traffic with the American fishermen in bait and ice. The Newfoundland fishermen can procure plenty of bait when it is impossible to catch fish, which bait the Americans purchase from him at the rate of 40 to 50 cents per hundred. This is of inestimable value to Newfoundlanders as the inshore fishery on this Coast for the past ten years has been very unproductive while there has been a great quantity of bait, which if it were not for the purchase by the American fishermen would be perfectly useless to any one.

his
PATRICK × WALSH.
mark.

Taken before me at Saint Johns Newfoundland this 4th day of June A D 1877

GEO. H. Y. EMERSON JR

No. 217.

Examination of Captain James Brown of Boston, Mass: at present of Saint John's taken before me George Henry Emerson, Examiner.

This witness being sworn saith —

I am thirty two years of age and have been engaged in the Bank fishery on the Coast of Newfoundland for the past fifteen years. The American fishermen do not use the inshore fisheries within three miles of the Coast of Newfoundland for either Cod or other fishing, except for taking bait. American fishermen always buy their bait on the coast of Newfoundland from the Newfoundland fishermen. The is no mackerel fishing on the Coast of Newfoundland. There is no boat-fishing by the Americans on the Coast of Newfoundland. I have never known American fishermen land on the Coast of Newfoundland to dry nets, cure fish or for any other purpose. There is no necessity of American Fishermen landing in Newfoundland except for the purpose of purchasing bait, Ice, and fishing stores. American fishermen always purchase bait. They never catch their own bait. The Americans never come prepared; and find it cheaper to purchase bait, than to bring nets and gear from the States, to catch it with, An American fishing vessel would want about fifty barrels of Herring for bait, or about twenty thousand squids. Herring average about forty dollars for fifty barrels of Herring, and about forty cents per Hundred for squids — I think that the traffic between the American fisherman and the Newfoundland fisherman is of great importance to the Newfoundlander, in putting into circulation among the people of the Western Coast a great deal of money and the facility of obtaining by the Newfoundlander from the Americans provisions at a cheaper rate than can be obtained from the Newfoundland Merchant, whose prices are exceedingly high. The intercourse of American and Newfoundland fisherman is also of great importance in improving the manners and habits of the Newfoundlander especially in the manner of catching fish and in improving generally the status of the Newfoundland fisherman who is at least half a century behind the age even in obtaining and curing fish which is his only means of support. I think the American fishermen leave about sixty thousand dollars a years in Newfoundland and all this money is spent among the fishermen and not among the merchants. This must be of inestimable value to the people of Newfoundland who are a very people and have very little money among them —   JAMES BROWN

Taken before me at Saint Johns aforesaid this 4th day of June A D 1877 —

GEO. H. Y EMERSON Jr
Examiner

No. 218.

I. John H. McKinnon a native of Cape Breton N. S. aged 28 years Master of Schooner Rutherford B. Hayes of Gloucester, Mass. on oath deposes and says that in 1875 he was Master of Schooner Mary Low of Gloucester Mass. and was engaged in the Grand Bank Fishing for Cod and Halibut, catching them with Trawls baited mostly with Herring purchased in Hermitage Bay Newfoundland, that I have never caught any bait myself but they the Newfoundlanders have asked my Crew to help them catch the bait, but I did not get it any cheaper on that account. *My* experience has been that no American Vessel has caught their own bait but occasionally as a favor or to get their bait quicker have aided the Newfoundland fishermen in catching it. paying in full for it. American fishermen do not carry Nets or anything to take bait with, except a few Squid jigs—I never took any Codfish or Halibut within three miles of the coast of Newfoundland or British Provinces while I have been in an American Vessel. and do not believe an American Vessel does it, except to get a fresh fish to eat. All their Cod & Halibut Fisheries are deep Sea fisheries. I have purchased Ice in Newfoundland for which nearly double was paid for it more than Ice sold for in Gloucester. All the supplies wanted for Vessel use is a great deal higher in Newfoundland and the Inhabitants are making money from their trade with American Vessels—In selling to American Vessels I consider it is worth much more to *them* than the privilege of buying is, to us, as the markets of the French Islands are open to us. and the bait would seek that Market were the Ports of Newfoundland closed to American Fishermen, and I think it is made a market for their bait now, to considerable extent.

I have been engaged in the Cod & Halibut fisheries for the past five years having been four years Skipper or Master.

JOHN McKINNON

STATE OF MASSACHUSETTS } ss
     COUNTY OF ESSEX   }

GLOUCESTER Aug. 13th, 1877

Then personally appeared the above named John McKinnon and subscribed and made oath that the foregoing statement is true. Before me
(Seal.)   DAVID W. LOW *Notary Public*

No. 219.

I. John Curzon a native of Pictou Nova Scotia. Master of Schooner Mist of Gloucester Massachusetts Aged 35 years on oath depose and say that I have been engaged in the fishing business, nine years, Cod & Halibut Fishing wholly, with exception of one trip after Mackerel, have fished on Grand Bank. and Georges Banks. In fishing on the Grand Banks I have bought my bait. paying cash have procured them in Fortune, Tar and Conception Bays in Newfoundland, paying from 20c to 75c per hundred for Squid and from $25 to $30 for baiting our Schooner for the voyage. I have purchased Ship Stores and Ice in Newfoundland always paying more than I could have bought for at home, they asking the highest prices for everything—I have never carried Nets or anything to catch bait and know of no vessel (American) that has. the trade with American vessels has been for three or four years past and they make money out of it I do not know what they would do without us for their Squid would be worthless without our trade. and their Herring would be almost wortless to them except what few they could sell at the French Islands. If prevented from purchasing bait and supplies in Newfoundland, American fishermen could go to the French Islands and get plenty, and their other supplies much cheaper.

That I consider that their chance to sell to American Fishermen is worth a great deal more to them than our privilege to go there and purchase. for dozzens are running after you to sell bait and if they think you want supplies and ice the Merchants or Traders solicit your trade.

JOHN CURZON

COMMONWEALTH OF MASSACHUSETTS

Essex ss.   GLOUCESTER Aug 13th 1877

Then personally appeared John Curzon, above named, and made oath that all the above statements by him subscribed are true. before me

DAVID W. LOW
Notary Public

(Seal.)

No. 220.

I, John G. Dennis of Gloucester in the county of Essex and Commonwealth of Massachusetts, being duly sworn do depose and say that I am forty years old, and have been engaged in the fishing business both as fishermen and in sending out vessels. for the last fifteen years I am now a member of the firm of Dennis and Ayer. I send on an average two vessels each winter to Fortune Bay Newfoundland for herring— Herring are purchased from the inhabitants of Newfoundland and are never caught by the Americans—The vessels that go to Newfoundland for herring are not prepared for fishing they purchase herring paying from one to two dollars per barrel partly in money and partly in goods, provisions, &c these vessels all make entry at the Custom-House and pay duties upon the goods with which they purchase the herring— American vessels leave from ($25000,00) twenty-five thousand dollars to ($40,000 00) forty thousand dollars Each year in the region of Fortune Bay—This is the only business the inhabitants of Fortune Bay have during the winter, and the only market for their herring and without it they would not be able to live—American vessels have never been ordered off or forbidden to purchase herring on the coast of New foundland—

I am also engaged in the cod fishery on the Grand Banks and my ves-

sels purchase bait on the Coast of Newfoundland herrin
principally used, my vessels bring some bait from the U
but when they are out of it they call at the various bays o.
land and purchase it there, No objection has ever been 1
chasing bait and supples on the Newfoundland coast, the
are glad enough to sell it to us as it is a very profitable trad
The Newfoundland traders in bait and ice advertise in th(
newspapers and send circulars to the various fishing firms
custom—Bait is also purchased at the French Islands fr
foundland jacks which come there to sell the herring bait t·
and American fishing vessels—I consider the herring fisl
foundland of no value to Americans, they never catch but o
the fish and pay the full value for them—American vesse
for cod or any other fish within three miles of the Coast o
land.

JOHN G.

COMMONWEALTH OF MASSACHUSETTS

ESSEX ss   GLOUCESTER July
Then personally appeared the above named John G.
made oath that all the foregoing statements by him sub
true to the best of his knowledge and belief
                    before me
(Seal.)   DAVID W.
                                                   No

No. 221.

I Andrew Leighton of Gloucester in the county of Es
monwealth of Massachusetts being duly sworn do depose
I am fifty-four years old, and have been engaged in the fis
both as fishermen and dealer for over thirty years, I h
gaged in the Newfoundland herring trade for eighteen yea
winter principally at Fortune Bay, The Method of doing
send vessels from here to purchase cargoes of frozen her
fishermen on that coast, which are then carried to the
and there sold. I have never caught any herring on the
foundland and I have never known of any American ve
as it is much cheaper to buy them from the inhabitants w
in small boats, than to catch them ourselves—No objec
been made by the Government of Newfoundland to our p
ring there to my knowledge. the inhabitants are glad e
to us as they depend for their living entirely during tl
the trade with the American vessels—

ANDREW

COMMONWEALTH OF MASSACHUSET

ESSEX ss.   GLOUCESTE
Then personally appeared the abovenamed Andrew
made oath that all the foregoing statements by him subs
to the best of his knowledge and belief, before me
(Seal.)   DAVID
                                                   N

No. 222.

I Robert J. Reeves of Gloucester in the County of Essex and Commonwealth of Massachusetts, being duly sworn do depose and say that I am thirty-nine years of age and am the Captain of the three-masted schooner William I Shepard of 475 tons burden, that I have been engaged in the Newfoundland herring trade for about eight years and during that time I made a voyage each winter to the coast of Newfoundland usually to Fortune Bay for the purpose of purchasing cargoes of frozen herrings of the inhabitants, that I have never fished for herring on that coast and have never known of any American vessels catching herring there. the usual course is for the American vessels to purchase their cargo from the fishermen paying them in gold from one to two dollars per barrel for the hering fresh, sometimes they pay for them in provisions but at the same rate as in money—Our vessels are not furnished for fishing and do not carry nets, they enter regularly at the Custom-house and when they cary goods with which to purchase the herring, they pay the duties—It is much cheaper for us to purchase the herring from the Newfoundland fishermen than to catch them ourselves, the inhabitants of the country around Fortune Bay depend during the winter for their living entirely upon the trade with American vessels and without it they would soon starve ; the American vessels pay on an average each from six hundred to one thousand dollars for the herring— No objection has ever been made to the Americans purchasing herring, to my knowledge, the inhabitants are glad to have Americans come as it is the only market they have for their herring during the winter—

ROBERT J. REEVES

COMMONWEALTH OF MASSACHUSETTS

Essex ss   Gloucester July 1877
Then personally appeared the abovenamed Robert J. Reeves and made oath that—all the foregoing facts were true to the best of his knowledge and belief before me—
(Seal.)   DAVID W. LOW
                                             Notary Public

No. 223.

Gloucester, Aug 18, 1877
I Wm H Kirby was born in Reddington, Berkshire, England, and am 37 years of age and on oath do depose and say that I have been engaged in the American Fisheries 19 years I have been Master of the Schooners Eliza K Parker, B D Haskins Amos, Cutter, Ocean Lodge Right Bower, Chas A Ropes Cornelius Stokem, of Gloucester & Salem State of Mass.
I have been engaged in the Bank Fisheries for Cod & Halibut & Gulf of St Lawrence for Mackerel & Newfoundland and Magdelen Island Herring fishery. The American Cod & Halibut fishery is entirely a deep sea fishery I always carried Clams and Porgie slivers and obtained the rest of my bait on the Banks viz (fishes peas & squid) I never took any Codfish or Halibut within three miles of the shore and none within 30 miles of land I went fifteen seasons in the Gulf of St Lawrence, occupying about 5 months each season My highest stock from the Gulf of St Lawrence was $ 6,400,00 and my lowest $2300,00
An American vessel manned and equipped for a season of five months

in the Gulf of St Lawrence must stock at least $6,000,00 to pa
Very few vessels have paid their bills for the last 4 years :
I carried no Seine but depended upon the hook & line   I di
one fifth of my Mackerel within three miles.   A purse seine a
cannot well be used inshore   I dressed most of my Macke:
whenever we dress inshore the fishing boats from shore come
Mackerel Gills and offal to bait their trawls with.   Most o
boats use trawls for fish.   The Nova Scotia North Cape fishe
is Schooners, get all the Mackerel offal they can to bait tt
This bait is the best for Cod fishing   Mackerel fit for the
worth too much to use for bait for Cod fish to any extent

   I have been Ten Winters to Newfoundland for Herring.
nets only one voyage and that was last winter.   I set my nets
the second night they were stolen.   I had ever before bougl
ring from the Newfoundland fishermen, paying at the rate of
per Bbl in gold   When I first went to Newfoundland the I
were very poor hardly owning a boat or net.   They had no
their Herring years ago except the Nova Scotia fishermen bu
advent of the Americans fleet the prices rose from 3 shillings
Shilling per Barrel.   The Merchants on the west side of Nev
send vessels to Fortune Bay for Herring and once had them a
price.   Now the American fishermen having raised the price
poor operative the British traders cannot have them at thei
and pay for them in trade consequently they the traders
of the Americans and would do anything to keep them away.
icans have absolutely raised up this population of poor opera
men from poverty and made them independent in their busi
the grinding and debasing influence of the trading capitalist,
ermen were in the hands of the traders they would keep t
Codfishery entirely and make them dependent on the trade
the fishermen can supply the American fleet with Herring ε
pendent and prosperous,   there has long been this state of f
and it has culminated in various acts of violence   Many of tl
fishermen now have good houses and own boats and nets wh
they had neither, except a log hut, and all this is derived fro
with Americans.

   The Magdalen Island fishery for Herring is carried on in t
manner.   The American vessels do not go prepared to cat
They go from Gloucester with 3 or 4 men and at Canso hir
Boats and men enough to handle it   They pay for use of Se
lars for a boat & man 40 Dollars for the trip generally hir
each vessel and about six men   The English fishermen ha
on shore with the Herring and the Americans, hire the herri
of in boats by the people of the Island and in case of packing
to dress and pack,   The whole operative portion of the v
done by the inhabitants and they being paid for it.   It is
and universal custom to pack them on the vessel as there are
and it would be very unhandy to do the work on the bea
knew of Americans being denied the right to seine Herring
dalen Islands   I have never paid any Port Charges at thes
Customs duties

   At Fortune Bay Newfoundland they make us pay dutie
and salt whether they are landed or not.

W. H

COMMONWEALTH OF MASSACHUSETTS

Y OF ESSEX SS.   GLOUCESTER Aug. 18th 1877
personally appeared the above named William H. Kirby and
ath that all the above statements by him subscribed are true,
best of his knowledge and belief   before me
l.)   DAVID W. LOW
                                                        Notary Public
                               No. 224.

                                                GLOUCESTER Aug 17, 1877
yron Hines do depose and say that I was born in Pubnico, N, S,
m 40 years of age   am now mastee of the Sch Grand Mastee of
co N, S,   am now engaged in fishing on the Grand Banks and
ring my fish at Gloucester Mass, have been engaged continously
Bank fishery mostly, for the past 25 years   am thoroughly acted with the manner of obtaining bait at Newfoundland & Nova
my experience has been that all vessels American English and
h have bought their bait and paid for it in Cash—a large part of
hing business of New Foundland is engaged in supplying this bait
s very profitable to those engaged in it, more so than any other
y pursued by them—the American fleet have not taken bait only
the last three years at Newfoundland—I have never caught any
here neither have I ever known any American vessel to catch
t Newfoundland—there are 50 vessels of from 25 to 40 tons each
ntly carrying bait from Newfoundland to the French Islands (St
& Mequelon) and the American fleet buy their bait largely at
places   We pay more for the bait, as such, than in other form in
it can be used, and other supplies in the same ratio. I have paid
r Bbl for sound Herring this spring at N, F, if we could not obtain
ait we could supply its place with porgies & clam, & I think to
lvantage—the Newfoundland vessels board American vessels miles
the Coast for the purpose of obtaining their trade and whole comes have been built up and are in a prosperous condition wholly by
rade,—in going in to these places for bait the vessel will often lose
nights time—with my experience as a Bank fisherman I should
at it would be better to go without this bait, if *all* would do so—
merican Cod and hœlibut fishery is wholly a Bank or deep sea
y and not a shore fishery in any sense
                                                        BYRON HINES

                COMMONWEALTH OF MASSACHUSETTS

X SS.   GLOUCESTER Aug 17th 1877
n personally appeared the above named Byron Hines and made
that all the above statements by him subscribed are true, to the
f his knowledge & belief—before me
al.)   DAVID W. LOW
                                                        Notary Public
                               No. 225.

illiam Greenleaf, Master of the Sch Chester R. Lawrence of Glou-
, & formerly master of Schr's John S Presson, F. W. Homans, Polar
, & Phœnix of said Gloucestee, born at Westport, Me. am 29 years
do depose & say that I have been engaged in the fisheries for the

past 18 years & master for the past 10 years. Have been con
Grand Bank fishery for the last eight years. I have read '
of Capt C. H. Nute * of Sch Edward R. Webster and acc
experience is true in every respect—the last voyage I made
land I paid $286, for bait the practice of buying bait at New1
only existed about three years—the inhabetants afording
and anxious for the trade,—& have never known any Amer
catch Cod or Halibut within three miles of the shore.

WILLIAM GR

(* See page 221.)

COMMONWEALTH OF MASSACHUSET1

ESSEX SS. GLOUCESTER Au1
Then personally appeared the above named William C
made oath that all the above statements by him subscribe
the best of his knowledge and belief, before me
(Seal.) DAVID W
N1

No. 226.

GLOUCESTER 1
I Harvey C Knowlton, born in Gloucester am 47 yee1
have been engaged in the fisheries, 25 years I was engag
Herring at Newfoundland in the four successive winters 1
1867, and 1868.

These Herring were frozen for bait and for the fresh fisb
York and other American cities, I paid from one Dollar
& seventy five cents per Barrel in gold, I bought the
fishermen direct who were very glad to sell them. I hav1
American vessels at one time taking Herring at Fortune 1
$1200,00 each for the Herring bought When I first v
Bay the people were very poor this was the first commen
Herring trade by the Americans most of them living in
subsisting on Herring and some potatoes. The prices o1
been increased largely by the American trade and at t
asked there can be no money made by buying them for
market. The American demand for Herring can be sup
Eastern shores of Maine and the Bay of Fundy the voy
dangerous and can be made more profitable. At the pr1
winter & spring fleet is largely supplied with Herring
being brought fresh by rail direct and at about the sa1
American fleet is not dependent on Newfoundland for bai
a convenience which they vastly overpay in the price paid
the present time Last Winter the Herring from Mai1
Menan completely glutted our Market and large quantiti1
overboard in the Harbor of Gloucester, being spoilt fo
tomers,

HARVEY KNO1

MASS }
ESSEX s. s. }

Personally appeared said Knowlton, and made oath
the above Statement.
Before me

AARON PA
Justice

No. 227.

GLOUCESTER Aug 17, 1877.

Dennis C Murphy was born at St Johns Newfoundland am 39 years
ige and on oath do depose and say that I have been engaged in the fish-
's 10 years from Gloucester on the Grand Banks and St peirre Bank
n thoroughly acquainted with the fisheries of Newfoundland. The
versal practice of the American Fishermen is to buy bait of the
iabitants and pay cash for it I have paid as low as one Dollar and
iigh as three Dollars in gold per Barrel for Herring bait at Newfound-
d and from eighty cents to two Dollars per Hundred for Squid. It
nly about 3 years since we have bought bait at Newfoundland I
ld buy bait at St peirres. I was the first Captain that bought bait
'onception Bay when I was in the Carrie T Dagle The Inhabitants
Newfoundland asked Ten Dollars a Ton for Ice and I would not pay
nd went up to 47° north and took some from an Iceberg. The Cus-
is authorities make us pay Water taxes, heavy pilotage, all the sup-
es are charged at the highest rates. This trade with the Americans
' made whole communities prosperous there is no other market for
i bait except the fishing vessels, and Herring and Squid are so plenty
t they are washed a shore on the beaches, there is a jealousy of the
erican fishermen because they are more successfull than their people
ave never caught any fish within three miles of the British shores.
e American Cod and Halibut fisheries are exclusively a deep sea fish-
within no national jurisdiction. I never knew of any American
sel selling fish at Newfoundland the small Codfish are just as good
strip up as the large, I never fished for bait on the British coast
d I know that every American Vessel that takes bait at Newfound-
id buys and pays for it in cash If we did not take bait at Newfound-
id we could use Porgie and clams, takeng them from the United States
d at no greater cost, I have been Master of the Schooners, James
iss, Harvey C Mackey Lizzie A Tarr, Frank A Williams Wachusett,
zzie K Clark, Carrie T Dagle, Centennial, all are engaged in the bank
heries. I have stocked as high as $17,000,00 a year in this business
d as low a $9,000,00 a year.

D C MURPHY

COMMONWEALTH OF MASSACHUSETTS

iSEX SS.   AUGUST 18th 1877

Then personally appeared the above named Dennis C. Murphy and
ide oath that all the above statements by him subscribed are true, to
e best of his knowledge and belief. before me
(Seal.)   DAVID W. LOW
                                           Notary Public

No. 228.

PROVINCE OF QUEBEC
DISTRICT AND COUNTY OF GASPÉ
GASPÉ BASIN
August 1st 1877

I, the undersigned, John S. Ascah,—of Gaspé Bay,—North—Master
the schooner " Seaflower " of Gaspé Basin,—do hereby solemnly de-
ire as follows viz—
That for thirty five years I have been engaged in the Whale—Cod—
207 F

and Mackerel fisheries—of the waters of the Gulf of St Le
the Coast of Labrador, in charge of a fishing schooner,—Wl
Straits of Belle Isle and to the Northwards—Codfishing in '
on the coast of Labrador—And taking Mackerel in the Bay
—In the years 1850 to 1856—I fished in company with Ame
men—and often had the use of their Seines to draw my ba
charge—willingly granted—and moreover always kindly as
required—and I know personally of valuable services rendei
them to a number of our Gaspé fishermen—I do not hesitate
I believe candidly—speaking—and unprejudiced Gaspé fishe
believe that the greater their intercourse—and dealings wit
fishermen in Canadian waters—the greater they profit b;
course : which is the experience of former years, for, Compa
few American fishermen have been seen in these waters for
years—I have not seen Americans curing fish or drying
shores of the Gulf waters.—Mackerel fishing—was their ch;
but for the last ten years—this fish has been disappearii
such an extent—that *now* I would consider—it, undoubte
risky enterprise to fit out a schooner, even from here,—to en
branch of the fisheries.

. If Canadian fishermen had the means—or were indepe
could take their fish and oil to markets in the United State
greater profits than American fishermen in their own por
obvious.   Our fishing and coasting schooners are about—f
seventy-five tons burthen ;—the larger size costing about fo
dollars :—wages to men are $16. @ $20 per month—and pr
much lower in price than in the United States.—It seems
prise—was wanting, that more fish is not taken to the Unite
Canadians—while it is exempt from duty.

JOHN

Declared and Subscribed to before me, this first day of A
at Gaspé Basin
(Seal.)   GEO: H. I
U

No. 229.

PORT OF GASPÉ
COUNTY AND DISTRICT OF (
PROVINCE O

I—Benjamin Asselin, Master of the British schooner '
Gaspé, do hereby solemnly declare, that I have been conne
fishery business of the Gulf of St Laurence for about twen
and that for the greater period of that time—the transpor
has been my chief employment ;—between the fishery sta
shipping ports ;—that my vocation has afforded me an exp
fisheries in the gulf, which is not excelled—if equalled—
that from my own personal knowledge, I am aware tha
fishery has been declining for several years past and I co
has now become so reduced and precarious as to offer no e
for the pursuit of that enterprise in these waters.

My occupation brings me annually,—during the fishin
the close vicinity of many of the principal fishery stations
and I am enabled to say that American fishermen have n
tomed to land on the shores to dry nets, cure fish &c—a
so far as I have been able to observe ;—in accordance with
granted to them by the Treaty of Washington of 1871.—

I am positive that the inhabitants of the coasts have derived much
nefit from the visits and intercourse of American fishermen formerly—
the improvement in their trade—by selling supplies and bait.
I further declare that I have given this subject much reflection and
em it right to freely express my belief as herein noted. The words
wenty-four years" added on the margin before signing
Gaspé June 18th 1877

BENJAMIN ASSELIN

Declared and subscribed to, this eighteenth day of June 1877. before
e at Gaspé
(Seal.)

GEO: H. HOLT
U. S. Consul

No. 230.

PROVINCE OF QUEBEC
DISTRICT OF GASPÉ
DOUGLASTOWN August 6th 1877.

I, the undersigned,—Luke M'Auley of Douglastown—in the Bay of
aspé do hereby solemnly declare as follows. VIZ—
That I have been fishing in and about the Bay of Gaspé for about
rty years—without intermission—during the fishing seasons—taking
incipally codfish and mackerel—That from the year 1866—until the
esent time, the Mackerel fishery has been very poor—I have had inter-
urse with a great many American fishermen during my life time,—in
e Bay of Gaspé—previous to the year 1866.—and very frequently have
ld them supplies—and often have received valuable assistance from
em on the fishing grounds, and I know of many of my neighbors who
ve also received benefits—without charge, at their hands—And my
rm opinion is that they are of far more benefit to our fishermen—in
iese waters—than detrimental to our successful pursuit of the fisher-
s—In fact they were always ready and willing to render assistance to
s fishermen when we needed—and I have heard many of my neighbors
xpress themselves to this effect—
I have never seen American fishermen cure fish or dry their nets on
iore—
My experience with American fishermen has been such that I would
e pleased to see them at all times in our waters—Many years and many
mes they have been to my house and spent hours with my family—and
have never seen them misbehave themselves.
Our vessels cost so much less than American vessels—and sailing
iem at so much less expense—there is no reason why Canadian fisher-
ien could not sell fish and oil at a greater profit in the markets of the
'nited States than American fishermen in their own ports—
There is no fishermen, now here, who has fished in the Bay of Gaspé—
inger than I have—or as long.

LUKE McAULEY

Subscribed and declared before me this sixth day of August 1877 at
'ouglastown

GEO: H HOLT
U. S. Consul

(Seal.)

No. 231.

PROVINCE OF QUEBEC
DISTRICT AND COUNTY OF GASPÉ
GASPÉ BASIN July 9th 1877

I, the undersigned,—John Howell—of Sandy Beach—Gaspé,—Mas-
er—(and part owner) of the Schooner "Undaunted"—of the Port of .

Gaspé; do—hereby declare solemnly that—I am now abo
years of age—that since the age of eleven years, I have be
engaged in the business of the fisheries,—both in fishing a
ing fish.—in the Gulf of St Lawrence along the Nortl
Natashquan to the Moisie river,—and off the North side
—taking codfish—only.—excepting Halibut when caught o
(but we do not fish for the latter purposely.—) We do 1
half of the quantity of fish we caught about eighteen ye
an average—The fisheries have evidently declined for a nu1
past—from what cause—it is impossible to say—

Mackerel fish are disappearing from their former ust
About eleven years ago—on the North side of Anticosti—
our boats—about two hundred barrels in one fishing seasc
that time the Mackerel have appeared there but once in n
we have had no other opportunity to make a haul of them—
right away again—immediately after showing themselves-
not tell where they go to.—American fishing vessels used to
in large numbers about fifteen years ago—but since that 1
only rarely seen—in our fishing waters—excepting near t
Islands,—& Prince Edward Island. In my experience of
seven years *on the water*—and coast, I cannot remember
American fishermen curing fish or drying nets on shoi
exception of one summer at Grande Grave, Gaspé Bay,-
ago. I consider that it is a great advantage to the people
—for American fishermen to buy bait,—supplies—&tc fro
they profit by the transactions—and get money—which th
otherwise get.—In the days when the Mackerel fishing w:
people did well—for Americans spent a good deal of n
coast. For the last twelve or fourteen years I have been
larly off the coast of Anticosti,—during the fishing seas
own vessel and crew, and am intimately acquainted with
around that island—my opinion is that Mackerel will never
at Anticosti as in former years—they are too long gone n

I believe that from the less cost of building,—equippi1
ning our fishing vessels, and being upon the spot—that
our fish *into* American ports—and undersell American fishe
own markets—if we possessed the energy to make the att

I declare solemnly to my belief in the truth of the fo1
ment which I have made with deliberation.

                                                  JOHN

Declared and subscribed to before me, this ninth day of
Gaspé Basin:
    (Seal.)   GEO: H

No. 232.

PROVINCE OF QUEBE
                           GASPÉ BASIN Ju1

I.—William Howell—of Sandy Beach—Gaspé Bay,—
emnly declare—that my occupation is that of a fisherman
fished in the bay of Gaspé;—off Island of Anticosti, and S
dor,—for Mackerel—Codfish and Whales—Herring &c—
twenty six years—on the best fishing grounds of the G
rence and adjacent waters.—In former years—say from 1:
I have been accustomed to take during the fishing seaso1

thirty barrels of Mackerel per boat with two men :—that previous to
at time the catch was about one third larger—but since the year 1865
e Mackerel fishery has been declining so that I have not been able to
tch more than from one to five barrels per boat—in the fishing seasons
in the bay of Gaspé—which in former years was considered the best
hing bay in northern waters—My catch for the last two years was
ıe half barrel of mackerel each year—I live on the shore of the fishing
ound and pay particular attention to the movements of mackerel espec-
lly,—I believe the fish come in about two thirds less than formerly to
ıe bay—but only to spawn—they won't bite and go out again—& I am
ell aware that they do spawn in our bay,—When we can catch any—
is only in stormy weather—Up to the year 1855. I have seen as many
· Sixty five sail of American fishing vessels—in the bay of Gaspé—
ling rapidly with Mackerel—at the same time.—Since then—the num-
·r of American vessels fishing in the bay has been annually decreasing
For the last few years—they have rarely appeared—Last year two
merican fishing vessels came in but did not succeed in finding fish.—I
ıve conversed with my neighbors—who are also fishermen, frequently,
ıd they agree with me in the opinion that the American fishermen in
ır waters have been of no detriment to our fisheries—but on the con-
ary have been beneficial to us by their intercourse in purchasing bait
ıd supplies—besides it is a known fact that we have caught more
ackerel when they have been in our proximity—Unfortunately for us
since they have acquired the right by the Treaty to the inshore fish-
ies—we have seen less of them than before—
The honest and candid belief and expression of the fishermen of the
ast is that the American fishermen have done no damage to the Ca-
adian fisheries—
The Fishery of the Mackerel in the Province of Quebec is only pur-
ued by catching by boats—and nets—No vessels fitted out for this fish-
ry—Canadian fishermen—in the Gulf do not fish for Halibut—but ·
ccasionally they are taken on the Cod lines—
My experience in the fisheries has been—as I have observed—of many
ears—and there are but few men on the Coast who do not know me as
, fisherman—
I Subscribe to this with a full knowledge of its Contents—

WILLIAM HOWELL

Declared and subscribed to before me this twenty third day of June
877, at Gaspé'Basin

(Seal.) GEO: H HOLT
U. S. Consul

No. 233.

PROVINCE OF QUEBEC
DISTRICT AND COUNTY OF GASPÉ—
GASPÉ BASIN July 28th 1877

I—the Undersigned, Charles Stewart—of New Carlisle—Gaspé—
ow—Master of the Schooner "IP. Palmer" of Gaspé—do hereby
olemnly declare—as follows—I am about fifty-seven years of age,—
or about thirty years I have been in command of a vessel employed in
he business of the fisheries of the Gulf of St Lawrence—and have had
mple opportunities to observe the yield of the various fisheries along
he Coasts and shoals of the Gulf for many years past.—It is many years
ince I have seen American fishermen—fishing for Cod fish near the
hore and in all my experience on the waters of the Gulf I have never

observed them (American fishermen) Curing fish, or dry
on shore—I have seen them buying bait and Supplies fror
of the Coasts—in former years;—and know of no Ca
these dealings they have given dissatisfaction—but on tl
believe that their presence in the vicinity of the fishing p
of advantage to the latter—and to be desirable—Since
have disappeared from their usual haunts, within a f
American fishermen have been rarely seen in the bay of Ga
one of the finest fishing grounds for Mackerel—

It is a well known fact that Canadians can build vesse
sail them at a lower cost, than Americans—and the fish
very doors—as it were— it is plain that Canadian fisher
able to carry their fish to American ports.—and make be
profit—the duty being off,—than American fishermen wh
so far from their own ports—

CHARLES

Declared and Subscribed to before me this twenty eigh
1877

GEO: B

(Seal.)

No. 234.

GLOUCESTER, Se

I, Christopher C. Poole, Master of the American schoon
do on oath depose and say, that I was born in Rockpor
been engaged in the fisheries for over 30 years. I have b
of St. Lawrence mackereling 30 seasons. My highest s
3,500 dollars for a season. Last year was my poorest se
only 200 dollars. I bought the *John Wesley* in 1866; du
she has been six years mackereling, and five years coast
to this she was owned at Cape Cod. She is 42 tons new
will carry 300 barrels. I always fished at the Magdalen
is the principal American fishing ground. I have take
mackerel on Banks Orphan and Bradley, and in my exp
never taken one barrel of mackerel in ten within the thre
have just arrived from the Gulf of St. Lawrence, and bro
barrels that I bought from the English boat fishermen.
to fish with my own vessel, but finding the prospect so
these mackerel and came home.

I bought my mackerel for two cents apiece out of the b
300 to a barrel.

I cannot save myself a dollar by this trip. I left the
September. I saw many American vessels at Port Hoo
and none of them had done anything. Some vessels lef
out having been able to take a single mackerel. This i
a season as I have ever witnessed in the Bay, and with
every vessel there will fail to pay their expenses.

CHRISTOPHER

COMMONWEALTH OF MASSACHUSETTS,
    ESSEX ss., GLOUCESTER, Sept. 21st, 1877.

Subscribed and sworn to by above named Christo
before me,

DAVID V

No. 235.

GLOUCESTER, Sept. 17, 1877.

I, Russell D. Terry, born in Nova Scotia, master of the American schooner *Addie R. Terry*, do on oath depose and say that I have just returned from a trip to the coast of Maine for mackerel, having been absent four weeks.

I landed 20 bbls. No. 1 Mackerel,
" " 130 " " 2 "
" " 62 " " 3 "

orth and sold for 2,376 dollars. The average catch during the time was there was 100 bbls, to each vessel.

I have been in the Gulf of St. Lawrence 17 seasons. My best stock here for a full season was 8000 dollars. My poorest stock for a full season was 500 dollars.

I caught the most of my mackerel around the Magdalens and some ; P. E. Island. I think including the years previous to 1870 that one fth of the mackerel I took were taken within the three mile limit cluding the Magdalen Islands.

I consider that to be a fair estimate for the other American vessels hat were in company with me.

CAPT. RUSSELL D. TERRY.

ESSEX, S. S., }
   GLOUCESTER, Sept. 17, 1877. }

Personally appeared the above named Russell D. Terry who subscribed and made oath that the above statement is true, before me.

ADDISON CARTER,
Justice of the Peace and Spec. Dep. Collector of Customs for
DISTRICT OF GLOUCESTER.

No. 236.

I, William Herrick, of Swan's Island, Me., on oath, depose and say, that I am master of Schooner *Cyanne*, of Salem, Mass. That I have ust arrived from the Gulf of St. Lawrence, from a mackerel voyage. The said schooner went through the Strait of Canso the 11th day of July, 1877. Between Cape George and Port Hood, we caught our first fish, 25 wash barrels, from 8 to 10 miles from shore. On the North side of East Point, of Prince Edward Island, we took 200 wash barrels, caught n four schools, the one nearest the land was over 3 miles off, the others, 3 or more miles off. This was the 17th or 18th of July. Two days afterwards, at same place, took 90 wash barrels, 60 of them from one school, over 4 miles from land, and 30 in another school within 3 miles from the land or shore. Took 15 wash barrels off Kildare, within three miles from shore, (about two and-a-half miles). The balance of my trip, I picked up on the hook, scattering from 4 to 10 miles from shore, cruising in Bay of Chaleur, down along the Island, and to Port Hood. Found no mackerel in Bay Chaleur, and very few anywhere. Spoke 25 sail of vessels in my cruise, who all reported mackerel very scarce. Finding nothing to stop for, and no prospect ahead of finding mackerel, I left for home, and arrived at Gloucester, Aug. 30th, 1877, with 320 sea barrels, and packed out about 300.

That I chartered my vessel for $225 per month, of Charles
of Salem, finding my own Seines and Gear.

Charter of Vessel, 2 months........................ ....
Seines, (2), Boat's Value, $2,000, 2 months use. ....
Outfits of Provisions, Lines, &c.............................
16 hands @ $30 per Month, 2 Months.....................
Captain's Wages, 2 Months ....
Insurance of Seines and Seine Boats..... ....
Salt................................... ....

RECEIPTS.

10 bbls.	No. 1's @	$ 16,		$
170 "	No. 2's @	10½,		1,'
120 "	No. 3's @	7½,		!

$2,(

STOCK EXPENSE.

25 bbls. Pogie bait,	$162
Packing 300 bbls., and Barrels, &c.,	525

$2,157

Actual loss by the voyage,

That this trip is the *best* one brought home from the Gul
rence this season. That my men were hired on shares, but i
estimate of the voyage, I have charged as wages what is paid
of the schooner *John Gerard*, of Newburyport, whose whole
wages, instead of shares.

I have been in the Gulf of St. Lawrence ten seasons, five
master. Have fished in all parts of the Gulf, and consider
posted in its fisheries. I was master of schr *Amos Cutter* t
previous to this. That I was in the Gulf four years ago.
barrels, not one fish of which, do I believe, we caught with
mile limit from shore. Was *gone two and a-half months*, and
where that mackerel are likely to be found in the Fall of th
out success. Six years ago, I was in the Gulf, in the schr
and took 260 barrels in a two months voyage, all of which,
tion of 20 barrels, were caught at the Magdalene Islands—th
were caught 20 miles from shore of Cape Miscou. This trip
dollars and fifty cents per barrel, and was a losing voyage.
five seasons in the Gulf as master, I have brought home 13
mackerel, not over 250 barrels were caught within three mi
shore.

In all my experience, during the ten years I have fished
of St. Lawrence, the vessel I was in myself, nor any vesse
or heard of, ever interfered with the boat fishermen in any
best of feeling always existing between the American and
ermen. When anchored inshore, they always come aboar
little bait; and I never knew, or heard of a fleet of Americ
running in among boat fishermen for mackerel, but have
boats a great many times run out among the fleet while fish

I have trans-shipped mackerel twice, the first time from Canso. The vessel was so long coming (four weeks) that we gained by it, mackerel rising in value. I was then in the *Barbara Fritchie*, and sent home 260 barrels. The second time, from Charlottetown, by steamer, sending home 150 barrels from same schooner, costing $1.00 per barrel to get them home. In the six weeks following, I only took 40 barrels of mackerel, which was all I did take for that trip, besides what had been sent home, and would have made money not to have trans-shipped any mackerel home, but have taken them home in the schooner.

All the years I have been to the Gulf, $100, in gold, each year, on an average, was paid to British traders for goods, for which we paid more than we could have procured them for at home.

The last three years I have been fishing off our American shores in schrs *Glad Tidings* and *Rebecca M. Atwood*. In the schr. *Glad Tidings* we landed 1750 barrels of mackerel, stocking $13,600—*net stock*. In the *Atwood*, two years ago, we landed 900 barrels of mackerel, stocking $10,300, *net*. Last year, in same schooner, (*Rebecca M. Atwood*), we landed 2700 barrels of mackerel, *net stock*, being $11,000.

That the mackerel being small here, the first of season, and hearing of large quantities of mackerel being in the Bay, I was induced to go there, much to my sorrow and regret now, for I found that I had been deceived by the stories told, and despatches published in the papers, to draw American fishermen to the Gulf of St. Lawrence this year. I feel satisfied, that had I remained on our own shores, I should have done much better. Our shore mackerel are better in quality than Bay.

WILLIAM HERRICK.

COMMONWEALTH OF MASSACHUSETTS,

COUNTY OF ESSEX, ss.   GLOUCESTER, Sept. 4th, 1877.

Then personally appeared the above named William Herrick, and made oath that all his statements above subscribed are true, to the best of his knowledge and belief, before me,

(L. S.)   DAVID W. LOW,
Notary Public.

No. 237.

GLOUCESTER, Aug. 28, 1877.

I, Thomas H. White, master of the schooner *Hyperion*, of Gloucester, Mass., do on oath depose and say :—

I was born in Margaree, Cape Breton; am 29 years of age; have been engaged in the fisheries for the past 17 years. I have been master of the schooners *John T. Tyler*, *Finance*, and my present vessel, the *Hyperion*.

I have just returned from a trip to the Gulf of St. Lawrence for mackerel. I brought home 225 sea-barrels of mackerel, mostly twos. I commenced to fit my vessel on the 1st of July, and sailed from Gloucester on the 5th; arrived in the Bay on the 12th of July. My first mackerel I took off East Point on the hook, (I had no seine) about 15 wash barrels 2 miles from the shore, and of the remainder of the trip of mackerel we took certainly one-half inside of the three mile limit and the rest outside.

The charter of my vessel is worth for two months	$500.00
My men's time is worth $30 per month; 14 men at $30, 2 months each	900.00
Outfits	600.00

Insurance .. ..
41 Bbls. Bait, $4 per bbl ....
Packing ....,..... ....
Lines, &c.. ....

.... 8

Receipts :
205 packed bbls. at $11½ .... $

Net profit.. ....

When I first arrived in the Bay I thought the prospect was a large catch, when I came away it looked altogether different. was about 100 sail of American vessels there and those that w would average from 25 to 50 barrels each. I have been in the St. Lawrence mackereling four seasons. My highest stock for season was $4,500. My lowest stock was $3,000. Any Ameri sel as they are now fitted must stock $4,500 for a seasons mac in the Gulf to pay their bills.

I have fished part of two seasons off the American coast for m I made on one trip 52 dollars in 3 weeks. I also made three trip two months time and made over 100 dollars. I have been boa from Margaree and it is the general practice to throw offal ov I never heard of such a thing as injury to the fish from this so this had been an injury there would not be any fish in the G The American cod and halibut fishery is a deep sea fishery From my experience in the mackerel fisheries of the Gulf of St. L the American vessels do not take more than one-third of their within three miles of the shore, that is not including the M Islands. There has been a good deal of trading by America which is an advantage to the people. I am of the opinion that knowledge of the people there is a strong prejudice against th can fishermen. I should say this sentiment has been fostered f pose. As a general thing heretofore the people on the coast h very friendly and never before have I heard any complaints by fishermen or traders of the American fishermen. The people we glad to have them come to trade with them and it has been a g in many ways to the people living near the shore to have the A fleet down there giving employment to the men and buying of ers and traders. Any other ideas I think must be born of pre any one disposed to be fair will say.

I know that the average catch of American vessels for the las in the Gulf of St. Lawrence is not over 350 barrels each. I h one trip to Newfoundland for herring. I bought my herring o ple and paid for it mostly in cash. It is of great advantage to th of Newfoundland to have the Americans buy their herring. Th almost be in a starving condition if it were not for this trade.

THOMAS H. W

COMMONWEALTH OF MASSACHUSETTS,
    COUNTY OF ESSEX, ss., GLOUCESTER, August 28th, 187

Then personally appeared the above named Thomas H. W made oath that all the above statement by him subscribed before me,

DAVID W. I
    Notary

(L. S.)

No. 238.

GLOUCESTER, Aug. 28, 1877.

I, Charles Lee, Master of the schooner *I. I. Clark*, of Gloucester, on ath do depose and say, that I was born in New York, am 40 years of ge, and have been engaged in the fisheries 20 years.

I have just returned from a trip to the Gulf of St. Lawrence.

I commenced to fit my vessel for this trip on the 1st of July, sailed rom Gloucester on the 5th of July, arrived in the Bay on the 12th of uly. I caught my first mackerel off the east point P E. Island, taking ne hundred barrels in the seine. This was outside of the three-mile imit; caught the rest of my trip—130 barrels—on the hook, about 12 o 15 miles from the shore of Prince Edward Island. We set our seine bout 20 times to take what mackerel we got in it. The entire time consumed in this trip is just two months. My vessel is nearly new; cost 9,000. She is 70 tons new measurement, carries 14 men. My two eines and boat cost me $1,500.

'he charter of my vessel is worth $250 per month	$500 00
'he wear and tear of seines, boats, &c.	200 00
Vages of 14 men two months, at $30 per month	900 00
ntfits, including provisions, brls. salt etc.	600 00
nsurance	100 00
acking	173 00
ines, hooks, etc.	25 00
Total cost of trip	$2,498 00

RECEIPTS.

230 barrels of mackerel, at $11½	2,645 00
Net profit	$147 00

With one exception, this is the best trip taken that I know of in the Bay this year. I spoke a number of American vessels when I came out of the Bay, and they would not average 25 brls. each.

I have been in the Gulf of St. Lawrence 13 seasons mackereling; about ten years as master of the vessel.

During that time it was necessary to stock 5,000 dollars in a season, in the Bay, to pay the bills. I have, as a general thing, done much better than the average of American vessels in the Bay. Most of the time I have owned my vessel. I have also fished for mackerel on the American shore, and I have always done better there than in the Bay; take ten consecutive years, and I have landed double the amount of mackerel from shore mackereling than from Bay mackereling, and the American shore mackerel are of better quality and sell for more money. In all the mackereling I have done in the Bay I have not taken one barrel in ten within three miles of the shore. The boat fishing from the shore is seldom, or ever, interfered with by the schooners, and I never knew of any boat being injured by our vessels. I have always found the people anxious for us to trade with them, and in the trans-shipment of mackerel a large portion used to be in British bottoms, before the steamer run.

I have been to the Magdalens this Spring for herring, in the schooner *Orient*, 94 tons. Took 652 brls. of herring for Boston. We calculated to take 1,400. We bought all our herring from the English seiners. We hired boats at Canso to take the herring from the seine to our ves-

sel; this is the universal custom of American vessels. All the
and profits of the taking is with the British subjects. There wa
50 sail of American vessels there, and some got no herring at all
no vessel while I was there got fully loaded. Both the herrin
mackerel fisheries are very uncertain.

In the Newfoundland herring fishery I have always bought an
for the herring in cash. The Newfoundland Customs Officers
American vessels to pay duties on barrels in which the herri
packed, although the barrels are never landed or leave the vesse
are carried down there and brought away without touching the
They also charge light dues, averaging 25 dollars to each America
sel; in fact, there are no fees neglected. The American cod an
but fishery is purely a deep-sea fishery. The few American vesse
go into the Gulf of St. Lawrence for codfish, take them 12 to 1!
from the shore, or on Banks Bradley or Orphan. The throwing
board of mackerel cleanings never injured the mackerel or fish.]
heard of such a thing.

CHARLES I

I, John F. Peoples, having been on this trip, this last two mon
the Gulf of St. Lawrence, hereby on oath declare that the statem
true in every particular.

JOHN F. PEEP]

COMMONWEALTH OF MASSACHUSETTS.

County of Essex, ss.   Gloucester, Aug. 28, 1

Then personally appeared the above named Charles Lee and J
Peeples, and made oath that all the statements subscribed to by sa
are true to the best of their knowledge and belief.

Before me,

(L. S.)   DAVID W. LOW.
Notary Pt

No. 239.

I, Joseph McPhee, of Gloucester, in the State of Massachusett
carpenter, on oath, depose and say, that I was born in Prince E
Island; that in the year 1860 I was with my brother Capt.
McPhee (now deceased) in sch. *Daniel McPhee*, of Gloucester, th
schooner fitted at the firm of Sinclair and Low, that on our first
the Gulf of St. Lawrence in the summer of 1860, we took dories. t
tried for mackerel at Seven Island's, found none, got a few off Ba
Cove, tried off Mount Louis and Madeline River and went h
September with sixteen or seventeen barrels of mackerel. That
Campbell was not in said schooner the trip above mentioned, r
he one of the crew the fall trip of said schooner in which we
most of our trip of 125 bbls. of mackerel off Magdalen Islands, b
10 and 15 miles south east from Entry Island. Some were cau
Malpeque and some off Margaree. That of said catch less th
tenth of them were caught within three miles from the shore;
took no dories on our second trip and did not go to the Seven Is

JOSEPH McPl

United States of America,
 Commonweath of Massachusetts,
County of Essex, s. s., City of Gloucester. }

Personally appeared before me, this twenty-first day of Sep
A. D. 1877, the above-named Joseph McPhee, to me well kno

ə solemn oath to the truth of the foregoing statement by him sub-
)ed.

CYRUS STORY,
Notary Public in and for said County.

No. 240.

William Parsons, 2nd, of Gloucester, in the State of Massachusetts,
ath depose and say, that I am senior member of the firm of William
ions, 2nd, & Co., owners and fitters of schooner *Gen'l Burnside*, that
schooner went to the Gulf of St. Lawrence from said firm only two
ons 1864 and 1865; that in 1864 I find in the crew list of said
ioner the name of J. McDonald whose share of the trip in said
ioner was $121.60; the vessels share was $2,242.84; that said vessel
engaged in making her one voyage in 1864, from August 1st to
ember 10th, and packed out 462 barrels ot mackerel.

WM. PARSONS, 2nd.

ImONWEALTH OF MASSACHUSETTS,
   ESSEX, SS., GLOUCESTER, Sept. 21st, 1877.

hen personally appeared the above named William Parsons, 2nd,
made oath that the above statement by him subscribed is true,
ire me,

DAVID W. LOW,
Notary Public.

No. 241.

, Solomon Pool, a resident of Gloucester, in the State of Massachu-
s, on oath, depose and say, that I was formerly of the firm of Pool
. Cunningham and part owner and fitter of the schooner *Daniel Web-
, that I have examined the books of said firm and find that said
ooner in the year 1859 made two trips to the Gulf of St. Lawrence
r mackerel, that she was engaged from the last of June till Novem-
23rd; that from her first trip was packed two hundred and fifty-one
one-half barrels (251½) only.   Her net stock amounting to $1,936.72,
half of which was shared among her crew.   That from her second
to the Bay, was packed twenty (20) barrels of mackerel only.   Her
stock amounting to $164.10, one half of which was shared among
crew.
hat I have looked for the name of James or Joseph Campbell on my
ks, and cannot find it neither name appearing on them.

SOLOMON POOL,

ubscribed and sworn to by above named Solomon Pool, this   day
September, A. D., 1877, before me.

DAVID W. LOW,
Notary Public.

No. 242.

GLOUCESTER, October 10th, 1877.

, Benjamin Swim of Gloucester, Mass., on oath depose and say, that
as born at Barrington, Nova Scotia, am 27 years of age, and am
r Master of schooner *Sarah C. Pyle*, of Gloucester, and have been
ie April of this year—have been engaged in codfishing during that
e, have landed 150,000 lbs. of codfish and about 3,000 lbs. of hali-
; and caught them all, both codfish and halibut, on Western Banks.

The nearest to the shore that I have caught fish of any kind
is at least forty miles.

BENJAMIN SW

Master of schr. Sarah

ESSEX SS.   GLOUCESTER, Oct. 1

Personally appeared the above named Benj. Swim, Maste
Sarah C. Pyle, who subscribed and made oath that the above
by him subscribed is true.   Before me,

ADDISON CART

(L. S.)   *Justice of the Peace and Deputy Collector of (*

No. 243.

GLOUCESTER, Aug. 1

I, Charles F. Carter, Master of the schr. *Falcon*, of Glouces
do on oath depose and say, that I was born at Steep Creek, in
of Canso, Nova Scotia, am 39 years of age, have been enga;
fisheries 28 years.   I have just returned from a trip from the (
Lawrence.   I commenced to fit my vessel on the 1st of July, 1!
from Gloucester on the 9th, arrived in the Bay on the 14th
barrels on the first day; caught them with a hook in Antig(
We caught them all of five miles from the shore.   Went do
East Point, P. E. Island; 10 miles from East Point took a su
in the seine; took 20 brls.   Afterward, cruised up the Gul
Bay of Chaleurs, to Bathurst; never got a mackerel, and neve
then run down to the Magdalen Islands; took 75 brls. on t
miles from Brine Island.   The remainder of my trip, or fare,
various places south of P. E. Island.   Took about five barre
not half mile off.   I brought home 132 sea barrels, mostly N(
The whole time employed in this trip is just two months.   1
seine-boat and two seines.

The Charter of my vessel is worth $250 per month.........
Crew of 14 Men—wages at $30 per month.................
Outfits ....
Two Seines and Boat—use and wear...... ....
Insurance ....
Lines, &c..

     Total cost....... ....
Inspection and Packing 115 barrels.....................

RECEIPTS.

115 packed barrels Mackerel, at $11.50 ....

     Actual loss.... ....

I have been seven seasons in the Gulf of St. Lawrence m
The highest stock I ever made there in a season was $4,2(
lowest stock is this year (that is so far), and I consider the pro;
hopeless for the rest of the year.   I have fished four years from
the shore boat—fishing, principally for codfish.
I never knew of any interference or injury from American
the English boats.   We always, in these boats, dressed ou

rowing the offal overboard. I never heard of such a thing as into the fish, in throwing over fresh offal. In all my experience in
·ican vessels, I never knew of any collisions with the boat fisher-
on the contrary, the best of feeling has ever been manifested, the
fishermen coming on board the American vessels for bait, and also
ind their bait in our mills. This last trip I gave away more than
, barrels of bait to the boat fishermen. I know that there is less
one fourth of the mackerel taken by the American fleet, taken
n three miles. Distance on the water is very deceptive, and look-
rom the shore any one would be liable to be deceived in the dis-
, a vessel was from the shore, especially when the water is smooth.
·e often to settle a question among the crew, put over the patent
and run, and invariably the distance supposed to be three miles
d tally over five miles. This will account for much of the mistaken
:ments of people on shore, as to distance on the water, especially
igh lands. I have been mackereling more or less on the American
₂ for nearly 20 years. I have stocked on one year's mackereling, off
American shore, $13,600.00, and my lowest stock in any one year
$7,200.00. I stocked on the American shore mackereling, last year,
)00.00.
iis year I have seen many of the fish called albicores in the Gulf, in
Bay of Chaleur, and all along the coast. I consider this fish as fatal
ie mackerel and menhadden, as wolves would be among sheep. I
₂ seen none of these fish for a number of years before this year, and
ι of the opinion, firmly, that the scarcity of mackerel in the Gulf,
on all the Atlantic coasts, is owing to their presence. There is a
ual convenience in the trading of the American fleet in the Gulf and
g the shore. There is really a great benefit derived by the inhabit-
, by this trade, and the absence of the American fleet makes a decay
usiness that is universally felt. The mackerel fishery at the best is
ry uncertain business, and the causes of their being plenty or scarce
beyond the computation of any man.
nd there is no such thing as making a safe estimate of value from
year to another, and all calculations based on so called certainties
Ɔ where the mackerel will be this year, or next, are chimerical.
have been master of the following vessels:—*Golden Eagle, Farragut,
Foam, Falcon.*

CHARLES F. CARTER.

COMMONWEALTH OF MASSACHUSETTS.

GLOUCESTER, Aug. 22th, 1877.

'NTY OF ESSEX ss.
hen personally appeared the above names Charles F. Carter and
le oath, that all the above statements by him subscribed are true to
best of his knowledge and belief. Before me,

DAVID W. LOW,

₂. S.)   *Notary Public.*

No. 244.

Winthrop Thurston, of Rockport, Mass., on oath, depose and say,
; I have been accustomed to reside at Grand Manan, N. B., every
:mer for the past fifteen years, and am personally cognisant with the
le and manner by which American vessels obtain their bait, which
one to great extent; and they uniformly buy their herring for bait

of the inhabitants, paying the cash. Therefore, this custom is of advantage to the inhabitants, who are very desirous of securii trade.

WINTHROP THURS1

CUSTOM HOUSE, GLOUCESTER,
Oct. 3, 1877.

Personally appeared the above named Winthrop Thurston, who oath, that the above statement subscribed by him is true, before
ADDISON CAR1
Deputy Collector of Customs and Justice of the P

No. 245.

I, James A. Colson, of Gloucester, Mass., on oath, depose an that I have been engaged in fishing for the past six years, and 1 past 3 years in the Bank fishery. Have been one of the crew of 1 lowing vessels, all of Gloucester, which vessels have been into Manan or vicinity for bait:—*Schr. D. D. Geyer, Schr. Schuyler* < *Schr. George S. Boutwell, Schr. Hyperion.* Five or six times I hav there, and have usually taken about 50 bbls. of herring at each b paying, therefor, from $1 to $2 per barrel. Have never caught ar ring, but have uniformly bought them. Have never known any. can vessel to catch their herring.

JAMES A. COLS

CUSTOM HOUSE,
GLOUCESTER, Oct. 2, 18

Personally appeared the above named James A. Colson, wh scribed, and made oath, that the above statement is true.
(Seal). ADDISON CARTER.
Deputy Collector and Justice of the F

No. 246.

Henry G. Coas, of Gloucester, Mass., on oath, depose and sa was born in Gloucester, am thirty-six years of age, am now ma schr. *John S. McQuin*, of Gloucester, have been master for nine y the schr. *Charles H. Hildreth*, of said Gloucester, have been in < St. Lawrence seven years of that time mackereling; 1867 I was Bay the whole season, took 200 bbls in all, caught them off Bradl Bonaventure, caught none of them within 3 miles of the shore; i was in the Bay, and caught 220 bbls on the first trip, (the secoi we caught only 6 bbls)—I caught the 220 bbls about 8 miles fron off Muscow, none within 3 miles; in 1869, was in the Bay of S rence, was there the whole season, and caught 130 bbls ma caught them all over the Gulf, not 10 bbls, however, were caught three miles of the shore; in 1870, was not in the Bay, went on (Bank until August, then went off our own shore mackerelir caught 375 bbls on coast of Maine, Middle Bank, and off Cap we caught them in 4 trips—the quality of these macke very good, and we got twice as much for them as for Bay macke we made a good year's work; in 1871, I was engaged in fisl Georges Bank the whole year; in 1872, was in the Gulf of S rence for mackerel, 2 trips, and caught 270 bbls the first trip, a

the second trip, caught them all but 30 bbls at Madeline Islands,
ı trips), the 30 bbls we caught around the Island of P. E., about
of these 30 bbls. I caught within 3 miles of the shore—we got for
ȝ mackerel $13 per bbl., and were all mostly No. 1s, our shore mack-
were worth then, I recollect, $20 for ones; in 1874, was in the Gulf
. Lawrence for mackerel, and caught 260 bbls. the first trip, and
ıbls on the second trip (sea bbls.), the first trip we caught off P. E.
d, and should judge that we caught half of them within 3
· of the shore—the second trip we caught 75 bbls. at Madeline
ıd, and the rest at P. E. Island, 6 or 8 miles from the shore, (none
in 3 miles); in 1875, was in the Bay of St. Lawrence, and caught
ıbls, all of which were caught within 3 miles of shore at Madeline
ıds, and was all our season's work; in 1876, was at Georges all the
. All the above years I have been master ofther schr *Charles H. Hil-*
ı—this year, 1877, I have been master of the schr *John S. McQuin,*
have just returned from the Gulf of St. Lawrence, and off our own
e, with 107 barrels of mackerel, 3 barrels of which we caught in the
after being there a week, trying for mackerel, off Cape George, P.
. etc., caught 104 of the 107 off the coast of Maine, for which we
:9.50, the 3 barrels caught in the Bay sold for $10 per bbl. In the
er time, I have been accustomed to go to Grand Manan for herring,
been there for last seven winters, with exception of 1873, when I
at Newfoundland for herring, generally making two trips to Grand
an. I have always bought my herring, paying the cash at from 50
5 cents per 100—last year, for my two trips, I paid $1,875, for
eraged about $1000 for each cargo.
l of the herring brought from Grand Manan by the Americans have
bought of the inhabitants, have never known anything to the con-
y in my experience. In my trip to Newfoundland, in 1873, I was in
Membrino Chief, we bought 2200 barrels of herring, for which we
ȝ $2200, gold; never knew of any American vessels to get herring
ewfoundland, except by buying them of the inhabitants, they being
ıys very anxious to sell to you, and the inhabitants depend on this
ic with Americans as the principal means of support, and must be
ıcalculable advantage to them.

HENRY G. COAS.

GLOUCESTER, Oct. 2d, 1877.

ersonally appeared the above named Henry G. Coas, who subscribed,
made oath, that the foregoing statement is true, before me,
eal). ADDISON CARTER,
Justice of the Peace, and Special Deputy Collector of Customs.

No. 247.

Joseph J. Tupper, of Gloucester, Mass., on oath depose and say, that
ıs born in Liverpool, N. S., am thirty-seven years of age, have been
ng over twenty years, am now master of schooner *Madawaska Maid,*
Hloucester, and have been master of said vessel for the past nine
·s; have been in the Gulf of St. Lawrence mackereling, with excep·
of the past three years, every season. The past three years have
ı engaged in fishing on the American shore,—seining for mackerel
ng the summers, and in the past seven winters have been to New
nswick for herring. I have now just returned from the Gulf of St.
rence on a mackerel voyage,—sailing from Gloucester about the 8th
ıugust, and seined 30 barrels of pogie slivers for bait, on the coast

20ᵒ F

of Maine,—arrived at Prince Edward Island about the 18th of
having tried unsuccessfully at Margaree; and not finding ma
Prince Edward Island, I went to the Magdalen Islands, and t
for one week, with pleasant weather, catching only 10 barrels al
Spoke many vessels, both American and British, all telling
story, "that mackerel was very scarce." Being dissatisfied
prospect, I sailed for home, with a number of others equally d
I omitted to state that previous to going to the Gulf of St. La
caught thirty-five barrels of shore mackerel off Block Island.
sold for $24 per barrel; the 10 barrels of Bay mackerel I sol
per barrel, which is one dollar more than the regular price, as 1
me one dollar more for them, in order to secure the shore ma
have been in the Gulf of St. Lawrence mackereling thirteen sea
averaged 300 barrels each year; and I have no hesitation in say
not one-tenth part were caught within three miles from the sho
those I caught at Magdalen Islands. I did not take a license d
years of exclusion. I never knew or heard of any injury to ;
boats by the American fleet, and this very trip I have given
these boats bait, which they solicit. I never heard that macke
ings were injurious in any way to the fishery; on the contrary,
grind it with the other bait. I have known of times when I l
solicited by farmers in St. Mary's Bay to save my offal for t
they would send a boat for it,—they wanting it for their farm:
tilizer, and not on account of any injury to the fishery by bein
overboard. The reason I did not take out a license during the
exclusion was because I did not fish within the three-mile l
therefore was of no value to me. The cost of my late fishin
fallows:—

Charter of my Vessel, per month, $250 . ...
13 Men at $30 per month ....
Captain's Wages ....
Seine and Boat, use of. ....
Outfits, Provisions, Bbls. Salt Bait ....
Insurance, Packing and Inspection ....

RECEIPTS.

35 Bbls. Block Island Mackerel, @ $24... ....
10 "   taken in Gulf of St. Lawrence @ $13..............

RECAPITULATION.

Cost of Voyage ....
Receipts from Voyage.....................................

Amount lost by Voyage ....

During the winters for the past seven years, I have be
Brunswick for herring, averaging 2 trips during the winte
uniformly bought my herring, paying the cash, and have
average, $2500 a year, with the exception of last winter, w
three trips, and paid them $3600. I usually pay from th
ninety cents per hundred, taking 500 to the barrel. The her
men there have often told me that they could not realize 1

0, if it were not for the American vessels coming for them, and they
ve no other market for them to any extent.

While I was engaged in the Bay fishing, my highest stock was $4,000
· any one season, while my lowest was $2,000. On this American
ore, the highest stock I ever made was $10,000 for any one season,
d my lowest, including this year, so far, including the 12 barrels
ught in the Gulf of St. Lawrence, is $3500.

I went one trip to Newfoundland for salt herring, in, I think, 1869,
d also one trip in 1870, both of which trips we bought our herring,
ying one dollar in gold per barrel. The first voyage, we bought 850
rrels, and the second voyage, we paid for 2,000 barrels. I never knew
any American vessels catching herring in nets or seines at New-
undland or New Brunswick.

JOSEPH J. TUPPER,
Master of Schr. Madawaska Maid.

COMMONWEALTH OF MASSACHUSETTS,

UNTY OF ESSEX, SS. GLOUCESTER, Sept. 3d, 1877

Then personally appeared the above named Joseph J. Tupper, and
ade oath, that all the above statements by him subscribed, are true,
fore me,

DAVID W. LOW.
Notary Public.

No. 248.

I, Hanson B. Joyce, of Swan's Island, Maine, on oath, depose and say,
iat I am Master of Schooner *Alice*, of Portland, have been engaged in
ie Fisheries eighteen years, and have been master for the last seven
ears—have been master of the *Alice* the past two years—have been
iackereling the whole of this season, first going south on our shore up
) the 20th June, and caught 900 barrels, and netted $4,000.

I went into the Bay of St. Lawrence, arriving at Canso, July 10th,
nd fished midway between Cape George and Port Hood, and caught in
vo days 140 bbls. with seine not less than three miles from the shore,
nd one day fished off the north-end of P. E. Island, and caught 30 bbls.
ith seine, catching them not less than seven miles from the shore. We
ien fished between Cape George and P. E. Island, and about the east
nd of the Island, and caught 37 bbls. altogether, one-half of these 37
ith seine, and not any within four miles from the shore. After the pros-
ect not being favorable enough, we started for home and arrived Aug.
4th, having been in the Bay about a month, and getting what packed
nt, 188 bbls., which sold for $1,917. We were gone, considering the
oing and coming, a month and a-half, and the owners of the vessel re-
eived three hundred and forty-two dollars, which is less than I would
e willing to charter the vessel for that length of time at this season of
ie year by $200. After packing out from the Bay, went mackereling
n this (the American) shore, and caught up to this time, 365 barrels,
hich will average at least $9 per barrel, $3,285. Having caught, dur-
ig the whole season, on this shore, 1,265 barrels, and in the Bay 207.
[he above are sea-barrels).

I chartered the schr. *G. W. Reed*, in the Winter of 1872, and went into
rand Manan, or rather Point Lepreau, N. B., for herring, and loaded
er with 150,000 frozen herring, for which I paid $375. At this time,
iere were at least 30 sail of American vessels at this place, and in the
icinity, engaged in the same business, and they all invariably bought

their herring. I have never known of but four instances i
attempted to catch them.

In the season of 1868 and 1869, I was engaged iu a smal
tons for about a month of each season, in catching herring
of Maine, and caught 250 barrels each season. This busin
very extensive, were it profitable enough to induce the ir
engage in it, as the herring are very numerous on the sh
and Massachusetts, so much so, that they interfere with (
fishing considerably.

HANSON B. J(
Master of ,

GLOUCESTER, O(

Personally appeared the above named Hanson B. Joyce, :
schr. *Alice*, who made oath, that the above statement is tru
(L. S).   ADDISON CA]
Justice of the Peace, and Special Deputy Collector

No. 249.

GLOUCESTER, MASS., Oc

I certify that I have this day personally visited the i
enumerated below and have ascertained from them and th
vessels belonging to Gloucester engaged in the mackerel
have arrived from the Bay of St. Lawrence or British watei
year and up to this date (Oct. 15th, 1877) and the number
mackerel caught by each while in the Bay, or British wa
they were caught, whether within three miles of the sho
amount of money realized from the sale of said mackerel.
that the following list of vessels are all the vessels belong
cester engaged in the mackerel fishery that have as yet re
the Bay of St. Lawrence or British waters.

ADDISON CA]
Spec. Dep. Collector for District of

NAMELY :

Sidney Friend & Bro.—Sch. *Hyperion*, packed out 215½
for $2400—supposed to be caught off East Point, P. E.
Clark packed 229½ barrels; sold for $2250—don't know wh

Leonard Walen—Sch. *Martha C.*, packed 159 barrels; so
caught about one-half of them at Madeline Islands, one-
garee, one-sixth up north.

Dennis and Ayer—Sch. *Mary Fernald*, packed out 13(
sold but will average $15; total $1950—don't know where

Wonson Brothers—Sch. *Madawaska Maid*, packed 9 barr
$16 per barrel, caught at Madeline Islands. Sch. *John*
caught no mackerel in the Bay.

James G. Tarr & Bro.—Sch. *Amos Cutter*, packed 150 b
caught off St. George Bay. Sch. *Flash*, packed 150 ba
caught at Madeline Islands all but 20 barrels, caught at St

Harvey Knowlton—Sch. *Edward A. Horton*, packed
$2534.50; caught off West Cape; about 20 barrels su
caught inside of 3 miles.

George Dennis & Co.—Sch. *Helen M. Dennis*, packed :
sold; average $13 per barrel; caught off Madeline Islands

e, caught nothing in the Bay. Sch. *Seth Stockbridge*, 80 barrels, raging $10 per barrel; don't know where caught.

owe & Jordan—Schr. *Ellen M. Crosby*, packed 8 barrels, at $10—$80.

r. *Golden Hind*, packed 70; not sold; where caught not known.

ohn Pew & Son—Schr. *Eastern Queen*, packed 210 barrels—$2,145; re caught not known.

amuel Lane—Schr. *Moses Adams*, packed 85 barrels, average at $11— 5; where caught not known.

eighton & Co.—Schr. *Falcon*, packed 107¾ barrels—$1,250.93; caught ladeline Islands—40 barrels at East Point.

oseph Friend—Schr. *William S. Baker*, packed 10 barrels, at $11— 0.

IcKenzie, Hardy & Co.—Schr. *Vidette*, packed 133 barrels—$1,629.25; ght principally at Madeline Islands.

). C. & H. Babson—Schr. *Marion Grimes*, packed 137 barrels—$1,635; ght at Madeline Islands.

'lark & Somes—Schr. *Frederic Gerring, Jr.*, packed 343 barrels— 531; don't know where caught—vessel is away.

enj. Haskell & Son—Schr. *Colorado*, pickled 85 barrels—$860; caught Rustico—about quarter within 3 miles of shore.

ames Mansfield & Son—Schr. *William A. Pew*, packed 140 barrels— 300.75; not known where caught—vessel out.

ohn H. Gale—Schr. *Alice M. Lewis*, packed out 199½ barrels—sold $2,476; seined 10 miles off the Island.

certify that the foregoing statement is true.

ADDISON CARTER,
Spec. Dy. Collector.

James G. Tarr & Bro.—Schr. *Davy Crocket*, Capt. Charles Osier, will ɔk out 218 barrels mackerel, caught one-half at Madeline Islands, and ʒ-half off Prince Edward Island; did not catch one-eighth of whole ount within the three-mile limit. The foregoing is the statement of pt. Charles Osier. (Arrived the 16th Oct., 1877.)

Pettingell & Cunningham—Schr. *David M. Hilton*, Capt. Daniels, ,h 200 sea-barrels of mackerel, from the Bay; caught 90 barrels at deline Islands, and 110 barrels off Prince Edward Island; not more ιn 50 barrels of the whole were caught within three miles of the ɔre. The foregoing is a statement of Capt. Daniels.

Cunningham & Thompson—Schr. *Gwendolen*, Capt. William T. Gray, ived from Bay of St. Lawrence on the 16th inst. Packed 225 bar-ɜ mackerel, one-third of which were number ones, the remainder num-′ twos. About one-half were caught at Madeline Islands, the re-inder off and around P. E. Island; not more than one-eighth were ιght within the three-mile limit. This is the statement of Mr. Thomp-ι, of the above firm.

Henry Friend, owner—Schr. *David J. Adams*, Capt. Danl. Rackliff, m Bay of St. Lawrence, arrived on the 18th inst. (having been in the y over two months), with 50 barrels of mackerel,—one-third ones, and ι rest twos; 40 barrels were caught around P. E. Island, and 10 bar-ɜ caught near Port Hood; nearly all caught within three miles of the ɔre.

CUSTOM HOUSE, GLOUCESTER, Oct. 19, 1877.

certify that the foregoing statement concerning schooners *David* ɔckett, *David M. Hilton*, *Gwendolen*, and *David J. Adams*, have been orted to me as true, by the master or owner of the said vessel; and ιt these, together with a former certified list, sent to Capt. F. J. Babson

at Halifax, are all the vessels belonging to Gloucester th
from the Bay of St. Lawrence with mackerel this season,
ing of Oct. 19, 1877.

(L. S.) ADDISON C

No. 250.

I, Joseph McLean, a naturalized citizen of the Unit
residing at Cape Negro, in the Province of Nova Sc(
sworn, do depose and say, that I am the Captain of the
pion, of Gloucester, in the State of Massachusetts, and t]
engaged in fishing for mackerel in the Gulf of St. Law
17th of August, 1877; and I came out of the Gulf the 2
That during that time, my vessel took seventy sea-barre
that I came into the Harbour of Halifax last evening
expect to leave this morning. As nearly as I can learn, t
in the Bay did not average more than half a trip, and th
ery in the Gulf for the present year, as regards the Uni
been a complete failure. I have heard of two vessels o
three hundred barrels—the *George S. Low*, and the *Et*
heard that the *Herbert M. Rogers* took two hundred, an
Crosby six barrels—the *William S. Baker*, three bar
which I have named have left the Bay, except the *Etta*

JOSEP.

Sworn at Halifax, this 23d day of October, A. D., 187
L. W. DesB
J

No. 251.

Statement of the number of barrels of mackerel ins;
Goodwin, Deputy Inspector of Fish, Port of Newburyp
ing the years 1865, 1866, 1867, 1868, 1869, and 1870,—

Date.
1865
1866
1867
1868
1869
1870

A. E

UNITED STATES OF AMERICA, STATE OF MAS

COUNTY OF ESSEX, SS.

Before me, E. F. Bartlett, a Notary Public, within and
of Essex, duly commismissioned and qualified, personall;
named A. E. Goodwin, well known to me as an Inspe(
whom I believe to be a man of truth and veracity, and

ing statement, and made oath that the same was true and correct
best knowledge and belief.

ness my hand and Notarial Seal at Newburyport, in said County
ex, this Twenty-Fourth day of September, A. D., 1877.
3.]   .   E. F. BARTLETT,
Notary Public.

No. 252.

ement ot the Number of Barrels of Mackerel Inspected by George
arlow, Inspector of Fish, for the Port of Newburyport, Mass., dur-
e years 1873, 1874, 1875, 1876:

Date.	American waters. Number of barrels.	British waters. Number of barrels.
....	948	2,130
....	2,687	2,371
....	1,347	843
....	2,005	....
	6,987	5,344

GEORGE D. THURLOW.

'ED STATES OF AMERICA, STATE OF MASSACHUSETTS,

TY OF ESSEX, SS.

'ore me, E. F. Bartlett, Notary Public, duly commissioned and
led, personally appeared the above named George D. Thurlow, per-
·y known to be an inspector of fish, and whom I believe to be a
·f truth and veracity, and made oath that the foregoing statement
n subscribed was true and correct, to his best knowledge and
.

tness my hand and Notarial Seal, this Twenty-Fourth day of Sep-
·r, A. D., 1877.
(L. S.)   E. F. BARTLETT.
Notary Public.

No. 253.

· following is a statement of the number of barrels of herring
·t by the several firms in Gloucester during the year 1876; said
·g having been caught by the inhabitants on the shores of the
ed Stat·s:—

Number of Barrels.	Name of Firm.
15,733	D. C. & H. Babson.
7,500	Gloucester Fish Co.
450	James H. Stetson.
2,000	Geo. P. Trigg & Co.
2,500	Geo. Perkins.
1,500	Simon Merchant.
6,000	Proctor, Trask & Co.,
1,492	John Pew & Son.
700	Clark & Somes.
37,975	

GLOUCESTER, O

I certify that the above figures are a true statement of tl
enumerated, as stated to me by them.

BENJ. F.
Inspector

No. 254.

AUG

Arrived at Gloucester British schooner *Harriet*, Capt
from Shelburne, N. S.

British schooner *Gertie*, from Lockeport, N. S., arrived
July 11th, 1877.

British schooner *Avon*, from fishing, arrived May 24t
and July 23rd, 1877.

I certify that the British schooner *Harriet* and *Gertie* :
Port as above stated, and fitted for seining. Also, that
(British) *Avon*, has been engaged in fishing on this coat
the fish at this place since May 5th, 1877.

BENJ. F. BLATCH
Boarding Officer, Glouc

No. 255.

GLOUCESTER, Se

I, Thomas E. Roberts, Master of the British schooner *i*
on oath do depose and say that I was born in Guysb
Scotia, am 31 years of age, have been engaged in freighti
Scotia to Boston 4 years. I have brought up this trij
mackerel, 503 of these are English maçkerel. I get 50 ce
freight from Canso to Boston.

Last trip before this, I bought herring at 50 cents per b
that the expense on a barrel of mackerel or herring brou
is at least one dollar per barrel to Gloucester. I have
last four years 700 barrels of American mackerel. The fr
about the same.

It is the universal fact, that one dollar is no more than
I was part owner, and master of the schr. *Dusky Lake,*
was in the Gulf of St. Lawrence mackereling in 1869—g
four weeks ; and not doing so well as I ought to, I aband
ery, and went onto the ocean Banks for fish. I have nev
ereling since, but I now go freighting.

THOMAS

COMMONWEALTH OF MASSACHUSET'

COUNTY OF ESSEX, SS.   GLOUCESTER, Sept

Then personally appeared the above named Thomas
made oath that the above statements by him subscr
before me,

DAVID W
N

No. 256.

I, J. Warren Wonson, of Gloucester, in the County of
Massachusetts, on oath, depose and say, that I was p
agent of schr. *Tragabigzanda*, of Gloucester, of which
Molloy was master, that in the season of 1876 said vessel
trip to the Grand Banks for cod-fish, the first trip said v
for sea March 21st, 1876, and returned Aug. 23rd, 187

nt 4 months and 28 days. Said vessel's trip was weighed off, and
unted for as follows:—

65,300 lbs Large Cod,	@ 2½c	$1,632.50
7,440 " Small "	@ 1¼	95.00
110 Gals. Oil	@ 45	49.50
108 " "	@ 50	54.00
20 " "	@ 40	8.00
Fish sold by master,		239.68
620 lbs, Flitched Halibut, @ 2c.,		12.40

	$2,091.08
Less Stock Expenses,	296.31

	2)1,794.77
Vessels,	897.38½
Crew,	897.38½

	$1,794.77

Stock Expenses as follows:—

Bait,	$230.20
Ice,	11,60
Water,	3.20
Port Charges,	38.81
Towing,	8.00
6 Barrels,	4.50
	296.31

12)897.38

Crew's Share,   74.78 each for 4 month and 28 days.
further depose, and say, that on her second trip, she went to the
stern Bank and Cape Sable. Sailed on or about the 28th day of
gust, and returned Nov. 24th—absent about 2 months and 26 days.
weighed off as follows:—

21,743 lbs Large Cod,	@ 3 c	$652.29
3,625 " Small "	@ 1½	54.37
Fish sold by Master in Prospect,		280.50
220 Gals. Slivers, @ 15c.,		33.00

	$1,020.16
Stock Expenses,	256.43

	2)763.73
	381.86½
	381.86½

	$763.73

Stock Expenses as follows:—

Bait,	$184.22
Ice,	47.55
Water,	7.22
Custom House,	4.46
Pilot,	8.88
Telegram,	1.10
Towing,	3.00

	$256.43

Crew's Share, (12 men), for 2 months and 26 days, $31.82.

I further depose and say, that said schr. *Tragabigzanda* d
running expenses during the year 1876 by Two Thousand
That said Molloy was discharged from our employ as '
untrustworthy, and to the best of my belief, is now a res
foundland, where he came from.

In presence of CYRUS STORY.)   J. WARREN

I, Joseph Adams, a resident of Gloucester, County of
of Massachusetts, on oath depose and say, that I was on
of schr. *Tragabigzanda*, of Gloucester, in 1876, on her seco
Banks. That we fished on the Western Banks and off Ca
that said schooner did not go near Newfoundland. All b
having been bought at Shelburne and Prospect, Nova Sco
                                                        b
                                        JOSEPH >
                                               m:
(In presence of FRANK E. SMOTHER & CYRUS STC

UNITED STATES OF AMERICA, COMMONWEALT
                SACHUSETTS.

COUNTY OF ESSEX ss.   CITY OF GI
Know all men by these present,—that on this twentieth
ber, A. D., 1877, before me, Cyrus Story, a Notary Public, d
and sworn in and for the County of Essex, aforesaid, person
J. Warren Wonson and Joseph Adams, before named, wl
to the truth of the foregoing statements by them signed.
whereof, I have hereunto set my hand and affixed my Not:
day and year last above written.
(L. S.)   CYRUS S
                                              N

                    No. 257.

                          GLOUCESTER, S
I, Charles Martin, Master of the schr *Martha C.*, of Glo
oath depose and say, that I was born in Halifax, Nova
years of age, have been engaged in the fisheries for 30
just returned from a trip to the Gulf of St. Lawrence fo
commenced to fit my vessel for this trip July 3rd, 1877, a
Gloucester the 9th, arrived in the Bay on the 17th; to
the coast of Maine. Took my first mackerel in Antigoni
15 barrels on the hook, within three miles of the shor
between Cape George and East Point, we went around I
Island, could not find any mackerel; tried in the midd
between Cape George and East Point again; caught 80
hook, from six to eight miles from shore. Afterward we
and Chittigong; took 80 barrels there, close into the sh
all we got. We then cruised all around the Island ar
North, and did not find any mackerel. We then went t
and refitted, and then went into the Bay again, and foun
neither could I find any vessel that had seen any. I g
couraged and left the Bay, and came up on the Nova Sc
found no prospect of mackerel there, and came home; fo
doing anything. I arrived home the 1st of September.
40 barrels number ones, and 110 barrels of number tw
rels threes. My mackerel were worth $1,920.00.

vessel is a new, first-class one, 79 tons.
arried a seine-boat and seine.

The charter of my vessel is worth $250 per month,	$500 00
Wages of 14 men, at $30 per month,	840 00
Captain's wages, two months,	140 00
Outfits,	600 00
Packing and inspection,	120 00
Insurance,	100 00
Use of seine and boat,	150 00
Cost of trip,	$2,450 00
Receipts—160 barrels mackerel, at $12,	$1,920 00
Loss,	$530 00

have been in the Gulf of St. Lawrence 14 seasons for mackerel. I
there in 1875, and brought home 70 barrels; was gone over two
ths. The mackerel fishery in the bay is a failure, compared with
er years. The mackerel do not stay there as formerly. I do think
the large amount of bait, thrown by American vessels, formerly
the mackerel in the Bay. There is no feed at all for the mackerel
e Bay now. I have seen no brit or shrimp there this year. Some of
mackerel I took had small smelt in them; this is unusual. I never
any smelt in mackerel in the Bay before. I have never caught
y mackerel inshore, except at the Magdalen Islands. I have caught
e inshore this trip than any I have been. My best judgment, from
experience, as fair and candid, is, that not more than one-sixth of
mackerel taken by American vessels, are taken within three miles
e shore.
have taken many whole trips without going inside of five miles.
en a large fleet of vessels are throwing bait, they can keep the mack-
off shore five miles without any trouble.
have trans-shipped my fare of mackerel once, from Canso. The ex-
se, landed in Gloucester, was one dollar per barrel. I never heard
oats being injured, nor any complaint whatever. Never heard or
v of mackerel gurry hurting the fisheries; in dressing mackerel the
will follow the vessel to get the gurry thrown over.
have seined off the American shore for mackerel two seasons. The
erican shore mackerel are much better than the Bay mackerel in
ity and price.
have stocked as high as $7,000 in one season in the Bay, eight years

y lowest stock for one season in the Bay was $600.
n American vessel, as they are now fitted, must stock $5,000 in the
, to pay her bills. I have been the two last winters to Newfoundland
erring. Bought all my herring of the people on shore. Paid on an
age eight shillings per barrel, or $1.60; paid for some $2. There is
ray that the people there can realize so much for their herring as
sale to American vessels. The American trade there for herring
he chief support of the people, and is a source of great profit to
a.
have been master of the schooners *Quickstep, Belvidere, Seaman's
le, Enterprise, D. A. Bunham, Fred. Gerring, Charlotte Augusta, Mary
Daniels, Joseph Chandler, Martha C.*

CHARLES MARTIN.

COMMONWEALTH OF MASSACHUSET͵

COUNTY OF ESSEX, SS.   GLOUCESTER, Se͵

Then personally appeared the above named Charles Ma͵
oath, that all the statements by him above made, are true
his knowledge and belief, before me,

DAVID W.
(L. S.)   N͵

No. 258.

I, William Parsons, 2nd, senior member of the firm of
sons 2nd & Co., on oath depose and say, that I am part ow
with others of said firm, of the schooner *Pescadore (Pes͵*
have examined the books of said firm and find that James
two trips in said schooner, in the year 1867; that said sc͵
out 463¾ barrels of mackerel; that the shares of said vess
that said Howlett's shares was $224.37.

I further depose and say that I have also examined the
firm in regard to Daniel McPhee, in schooner *Messina,* and
as one of the crew, in 1865 only, he not having been i
Said schooner packed out in 1865, when said McPhee w
hundred and sixty barrels of mackerel (260 bbls.), his sh͵
to $98.21; the vessels' share was $1,745.19.

WM. PAR

COMMONWEALTH OF MASSACHUSET͵

COUNTY OF ESSEX SS.   GLOUCESTER, Se͵

Subscribed and sworn to by above named William ͵
before me,

DAVID W.
(L. S.)   N͵

No. 259.

I, Solomon Jacobs, of Gloucester, Mass., on oath, depos͵
I am Master of the schr. *Moses Adams,* of Gloucester, ͵
arrived from a mackerel voyage to the Gulf of St. Law
caught 190 bbls. of mackerel on the trip, one-third of th
on Bank Orphan, the rest at different places, and ab͵
within the three mile limit. I am very sure that the n
within three mile limit will not exceed 25 barrels. I sho͵
150 of the 190 bbls. are number ones, as they are good-s͵
having caught the most of them well up north in the G
yet sold, but expect to get $16 for 1's, $10.50, and $7.0͵
have been two months on the trip.

The cost of the trip is as follows:—

Charter, @ $500 per Month $1,000
Provisions, &c., ...   300
Barrels, Inspection, &c., @ $1.75   330
Captain's Commissions, @   4.00 per cwt.   106
                                           _____
                                           $1,736.00
Owner's Profit.... ....   1,278.25
                                           _____
                                           $457.75 lost

) bbls No. 1s @ $16.00.....	$2,400.00
5 " " 2s @ 10.50.....	262.50
	$2,662.50
iptain's Commissions	106.00
	$2,556.50
ew's Half	1,278.25
vner's Share	$1,278.25

This is my first trip to the Bay for mackereling, and I think it will be e last, and would have done a great deal better on our own shore. I ve, for the five years previous, fished on our own shore, and always ne a great deal better than I have this year. In the year 1872, I was aster of the sch'r *Sabine*, and fished off this shore, starting late in the ason, and caught 650 bbls., which sold for $18 and $20 per barrel; id in 1873, I was master of the schooner *S. R. Lane*, of Gloucester, id caught 1,600 barrels off this shore (the American); in 1874, I was aster of same vessel, and caught 1,200 barrels, averaging $10 a barrel; 1875, I was master of same vessel, and caught 1,800 barrels of mack- el off the American shore, and stocked $11,000.

I would state that previous to going into the Bay this year, I was ackereling on this shore, and caught 800 bbls., for which we stocked 5,200.

SOLOMON JACOBS,
Master of Schr. Moses Adams.

CUSTOM HOUSE, GLOUCESTER, }
Oct. 4th, 1877. }

Personally appeared the above named Solomon Jacobs, master of hr. *Moses Adams*, who subscribed, and made oath, that the above tatement is true, before me,

ADDISON CARTER,
Special Deputy Collector and Justice of the Peace.

No. 260.

I, Albian K. Pierce of Gloucester, Mass., on oath depose and say that am master of schooner *Wm. S. Baker* of Gloucester, and have been ngaged in mackereling during this season, and fished off the American hore the first two months of the season, and caught 350 barrels, by hich we stocked $1,950. From dispatches and favorable reports I as induced to go to the Bay of St. Lawrence, and sailed for Bay haleur the 18th July, and was in the Bay 14 days, and tried for mack- rel all the way from P. E. Island to Gaspe and other places, inshore nd out, and caught three barrels only. I then came home and fished n the coost of Maine, and caught 160 barrels at that place, from which he ne, stock amounted to $1,455. I consider in my trip to the Bay his year I lost $2,000. Last year, 1876 I was master of the same ves- el, and fished on the American coast, and caught 1,420 barrels, and tocked $11,000 net. In 1875 I was master of the same vessel. I fished n this shore and landed 1,000 barrels of mackerel up to middle of July; nd on the 16th July we started for the Bay and tried hard at P. E. sland and Madeline Islands for ten days. but finding no mackerel of any onsequence, we started for home, having caught nine barrels of No. 2's

during all the time in the Bay. We then fished on the Am
and caught 600 barrels, making 1,600 barrels of good mack
on this shore during the year, from which we stocked $13,3(
I was master of the same vessel, and fished for mackerel
season on this (the American) shore, and caught over 1,]
from which we stocked $9,000. Previous to 1874, I had 1
habit of going to the Bay mackereling, and some years we (
others poorly. Over one-half of all the mackerel caught
years were caught off Madeline Islands, and, excepting a
Islands, not one-tenth part were caught within the three-mi

I have been employed during the winter for the past sev
going to Newfoundland after herring, and for the past thr
loaded ten vessels at that place. I hired the inhabitants tc
and left with the inhabitants $24,000, for 20,300 barrels
loaded into the ten vessels which I superintended. During
winters the owners of this enterprise have lost $8,000 by t
tion of this business. Previous to the last three winters I
tomed to go there for herring for myself alone, and was
winters in succession, and always got a cargo, paying $1 pe
them. This business is very extensive and of great import
inhabitants. I have seen at one time over twenty sail o
vessels there buy herring, and all of them buy their he
have never known an American vessel to catch their her:
place, always invariably buying them of the inhabitants.
Bay, the inhabitants rely almost entirely upon this trade w
sels, and without which they would be very destitute. In tl
1876, when I was there, the herring were very scarce,—almo
—and occasioned great destitution and suffering among the
of Boone Bay; so much so, that I was obliged to give away
of flour to them,—and Mr. Curling, minister at that plac
me as many more, and other stores, which he distributed
poor people.

ALBION K. PI

GLOUCESTER, Oct.

Personally appeared the above named Albion K. Pierce
oath that the above statement, by him subscribed, is true, I
ADDISON CARTER,
Justice of the Peace, Spec. Dep. Collector of District of

No. 260 A.

GLOUCESTER, Sep{

" I, William Elwell, master of the schr. *Isabella*, born in
have been engaged in the fisheries 20 years. I have been
of St. Lawrence 12 seasons for mackerel. My best stock in
$2000, my poorest $1200. I left, off going there 8 years a{
could do so much better on the American coast. I have fish
erel on the American coast the past 8 years—5 years us
My best stock mackereling on the American coast was
months fishing.

My poorest stock in any season was $4,500.

When in the Gulf of St. Lawrence I took the most of my
the Magdalens. The American fleet usually fish the most
not get more than one barrel in ten inside of three miles.
the Bay when in large bodies or masses are most always o!

miles, and when we find them there we get large decks of them.
ckerel on the American coast are from the rocks to thirty miles

sider the American fishermen are not at all compensated by free
within three miles of the British coasts in lieu of the imposed
$2 per barrel on British mackerel.

WILLIAM ELWELL.

)UCESTER, MASS.,   }
s. s., Sept. 17, 1877. }

)nally appeared the above named Wm. Elwell, who subscribed to
.de oath that the foregoing statement was true before me.
.)   ADDISON CARTER,
          Justice of the Peace, and Special Deputy Collector
                    of Customs, for District of Gloucester.

No. 261.

)ter Sinclair, master and owner of the American schooner *C. B.*
ıg, was born in the Orkney Islands, am 58 years of age, and have
ngaged in the fisheries nearly 50 years. I am now seining off the
:an shore for mackerel.
ve been seven seasons mackereling in the Gulf of St. Lawrence.
not been there since 1873. The highest stock I ever made in the
f St. Lawrence mackereling was $7,000.00 (1859.) My poorest
stocked $150.00 (one hundred and fifty dollars), gone six weeks;
ıs in 1860. Any American vessel, over 50 tons, with 12 or 14 men,
tock at least $5,000 for a full season's work in the Gulf of St. Law-
nackereling, to pay her bills. Of all the mackerel I have taken in
ılf of St. Lawrence, not more than one-third were taken within
uiles of the shore, including the Magdalen Islands; and the larger
et of vessels in the Bay, throwing bait, the longer the mackerel
)p in one place. The action of the mackerel is largely influenced
movements of the fleet. Four years ago, when I was in the Bay,
ackerel fishery there was a partial failure, and since then the
can shore mackereling has been much more successful and profit-

the last six years the American shore mackerel have been of much
uality, and brought better prices than Bay mackerel of the same

mackerel feed on shrimp and a red seed that floats on the water;
ver we find them we usually find mackerel. This food is generally
)lenty on the American coast than in the Gulf, and I have found
rel with young mackerel inside of them, having eaten them for

ver knew that throwing over mackerel cleanings would hurt the
ackerel; on the contrary, I have always noticed the mackerel to fol-
e vessel while we were dressing, and eat all we threw overboard. 1
knew of any American vessels interfering with the shore boats in
ay, except in cases where the boats got blowed off, to pick them up
)w them in, and in some cases to take men from the bottom of the
that had been upset, and save their lives; and I have often given
at fishermen bait and also lines and hooks. I do not consider the
·ge to fish inshore of any real value whatever, and the duties re-
l on Canadian fish and mackerel is vastly in excess of compensa-
)r what is of little value to our fishermen. The only advantage
l by the inshore concession is security from annoyance, heretofore

practiced by the Canadian marine force, the object of seizure be
lated by one-half of the prize money being divided among the
the cutters. The inshore fisheries of the Gulf of St. Lawrer
and halibut is a matter belonging to the past. No American
now fishes inshore for either. I have fished out of Gloucest
and halibut 27 seasons, and I never took either fish inside of t
of the English shore. The American fishery now is absolutely :
a deep-sea fishery for cod and halibut.

The first fresh bait bought in Newfoundland by American
was about 22 years ago, and brought to Gloucester to bait th
men. It is about 8 or 9 years since the Grand Bankers an
Bankers began to buy bait at Newfoundland; for centuries t
had used salt bait and the other bait and refused fish tak
Banks; they also used to buy bait at St. Peirre. Now they
tune Bay for it; they pay cash for this bait. It costs $150
for a Grand Bank fare. The people there have got well off by
this bait; they are rich, and every dollar left there by Ameri
is clear gain to them, as there is no other use or market where 1
use these herring they sell to American vessels.

I have owned and run more than thirty vessels, and in th
branches of the fisheries pursued by American fishermen, I ha
much experience as any person now living; and I know th
the different fisheries by actual experience in practical fishir
department, and the scale of values by actual sales. In th
trade for the first eleven years, it was profitable to those eng
but for the past eleven years there has been more lost than ;
a fair average.

I have lost myself $1,500 on one voyage, and $1,100 on a
never made over one thousand dollars on any one herring voya
known vessel after vessel to throw overboard her cargo of her
harbor of Gloucester, and to have given them away in Ne
manure.

                                        PETER SIN

COMMONWEALTH OF MASSACHUSETTS,

COUNTY OF ESSEX SS.   GLOUCESTER, Sept

Then personally appeared the above named Peter Sinclair.
oath that all the above statements by him subscribed are t
me,

                                        DAVID W. L
(L. S.)   Notar
                        No. 262.

                        GLOUCESTER, Septembe

I, Wm. T. Rowe, Master of the schr. *B. D. Haskins*, of Glo
on oath, depose and say, that I was born in Gloucester, am
age, have been engaged in the fisheries 25 years.

I have just returned from a trip to Block Island, and the
off Monhegan, Maine.

The mackerel taken off Block Island are very large and fa
mackerel to a barrel. We set our seine once off Monhegan,
barrels No. 1s and 2s. We came home to refit and are goi
ately to the Eastern shore. There is now a great body of mac
from close into the rocks to 25 miles off. The *Maud Mul*
bbls in her seine at one haul. The *Fairy Queen*, of Portla

at one haul. The *Volunteer* took 100 barrels in 3 hauls. All the
ls the day we left, took all the way from 20 to 60 bbls. The *Cor-
Trim,* of Swan's Island, is in with 210 barrels No. 1 and 2 mackerel,
1 on the hook. She took from 10 to 15 barrels each day. This is
best prospect we have had this year, and it indicates a good fall
on our shores. The owners of some of the vessels now in the Bay
. Lawrence have sent by telegraph for them to come home and go
hese shore mackerel. I have been in the Gulf of St. Lawrence 7
ns, mackereling. The early trips in the Bay the mackerel were
1 offshore, later in the Fall the mackerel were inshore.

1851, we took all our mackerel inshore, that is, from one mile to
in 1854, we never took a mackerel within ten miles of the shore;
not been there since 1854. I have been shore seining for mackerel
, every season. I have shared $241 to a share in six weeks' mack-
ng in the Bay of St. Lawrence; I have shared $241 to a share in
lay's fishing on our own shores. The average difference in the two
erel fisheries is, as two dollars for the Bay to five dollars for our
shores. I have been master of the schr. *Mary Elizabeth,* 4 years;
mfield, 2 years: *David Osier,* 2 years: *Farragut,* 5 years; *Belle,* 2
; *Elihu Burritt,* 1 year; *A. M. Dodd,* 1 year; *B. D. Haskins,* 1

                                                    WILLIAM T. ROWE.
CESTER, Sept. 1, 1877.

        Sworn and subscribed before me,
. S.)   ADDISON CARTER,
    Justice of the Peace, and Deputy Collector of Port of Gloucester.

No. 263.

                                        GLOUCESTER, Aug. 29, 1877.
Oliver F. Howard, master of the late schooner *Coll Ellsworth,* of
cester, do on oath depose and say that I was born in Deer Isle,
ie, am 53 years of age, have been engaged in the fisheries 32 years.
have been in the Gulf of St. Lawrence 28 seasons mackereling, and
horoughly acquainted with all the fisheries. The highest stock I
made in the Bay mackereling was $5,000, and my lowest stock was
0, and an American vessel must stock certainly $4,500 in the Bay
kerel fishery to pay her bills. I have mostly fished for mackerel off
Magdalen Islands, and of all the mackerel I have taken in the Gulf
t. Lawrence, not one-fourth were taken within 3 miles. I have never
any interference with the shore boats, never heard any complaints
rowing over offal or mackerel gibs. My experience in this respect
at the mackerel cleanings is first-rate food for codfish, as they swarm
nd the vessel and eat it voraciously. As master and owner of my
vessel I have not made any money in the Bay mackereling. I have
e a living and that is all. I should say that a fair average during
last 20 years would be 300 sail of American vessels in the Gulf, and
a full knowledge of the facts, I should say that 300 barrels is a
average catch for each vessel. I have been in the herring business
easons. Invariably the herring are bought from the British fisher-
and paid for in cash. The only demand for these herring is from
ericans or for the American market, or for bait. Without this mar-
the herring would be entirely useless to the British people.
know that this herring trade has been of great advantage to the
ibitants of the English coasts. The Winter trade supplies them with

the only fishing they have at that season, and they '
other employment if it were not for the herring trade.
cod and halibut fishery is entirely a deep sea fishery, i
fish of this kind taken less than 12 miles from the shoi
of them are taken on the ocean banks. I have just retu
of St. Lawrence in the yacht *America*. The prospect th∢
for a large catch of mackerel. Last year I was in the I
rence mackereling, and it was the poorest year I had ev∢
I observed a great many Albecores, sometimes called I
Benitos, which are deadly foes to the mackerel, driving t
every locality where these fish are found. In coming al
coast and the American shores in the yacht *America*, w
quantities of these fish, and in my opinion the presence
fatal to the mackerel fishery while they remain in any lc
   The albecore is a fish about 3 feet long, formed like
large fin erect on the back. They are extremely vora
smart I have not seen any before for 8 years, and thei
my mind the reason of the mackerel being so scarce i
along the British and American shores. The vessels I hɛ
are as follows : *Pocahontas, E. P. Howard, C. C. Davis, Tyj
Coll Ellsworth.*

OLIVER F. HO

Master Schooner C

COMMONWEALTH OF MASSACHUSE7

GLOUCESTER, ∤

COUNTY OF ESSEX, SS.
   Then personally appeared the above-named Oliver
made oath that the above statements by him subscribed
best of his knowledge and belief, before me,

DAVID W. LOW, ∤

No. 264.

GLOUCESTER, ∤

   I, Joseph W. Collins, master of the American schr. *H*
cester, on oath do depose and say :—That I was born in
38 years of age, have been engaged in the fisheries 2ξ
just returned from a fishing voyage to the Western Bank
nearly every year partially on the Grand and Western Bɛ
Have purchased bait at Newfoundland and Nova Scotia.
modes of keeping fish taken on these Banks : One met!
ice for a fresh halibut trip ; the other we use salt for a fɪ
carry some bait from home. We also take a few barrels
from Nova Scotia and after the first set of our trawls w
fish taken on our trawls for bait for halibut, which is all
purpose. I never caught any bait inshore and I never
can vessel to get bait there other than by purchase.
   The average amount of fresh bait taken at Nova Scot
rels of herring to each vessel for a fresh trip for hali
trip for codfish we buy bait along the coast of Nova Sc
foundland. From 20 to 40 barrels baiting each on the l∢
to the Grand Banks. We bait from 3 to 4 times usua
land, averaging about 200 dollars for the whole trip.
   I have taken several whole fares without leaving the

bait squid, taken on the Banks and refuse fish. The buying of bait on the shores of Newfoundland is a convenience rather than a necessity, the whole profit of the transaction resting with the Newfoundlanders. We also buy ice of the people, paying $2½ to $3 per ton in gold for it. We also use ice from the icebergs. The only market for their ice is the ice used by American fishermen to preserve the bait fresh and it is only within three years since this manner has been adopted by them. For centuries this fishery has been pursued successfully without this convenience of iced bait.

When our vessels go into Newfoundland for bait they are delayed often a fortnight, which of course is a loss to them. My trip in July, 1876, I was delayed a fortnight. The inhabitants are very eager for our trade, coming out to meet us in boats to solicit our patronage. The men who furnish bait are operative fishermen. Since the advent of the American fleet these men have become independent of the coast traders and there is some feeling on the part of the traders on that account. The operative fishermen were formerly employed by the traders and paid out of the store mostly, but the American trade in herring paying money for them, has changed the relations largely.

There is no fishery on the shores of the Dominion, or Newfoundland, used as a shore fishery for halibut and codfish by American fishermen. Their fisheries are wholly and purely deep sea fisheries.

I have been in the Gulf of St. Lawrence for mackerel part of 22 seasons.

My highest stock was $8000 whole season.
" lowest " " $1800 " "

An American vessel manned and equipped as the Bay-men are, must at the least stock $5000 for a season to pay her bills. In my experience not more than one-fourth of the mackerel taken were taken within 3 miles of the shore. I never heard such a thing as mackerel cleanings or offal affecting the fish unfavorably, when thrown overboard. Often times after dressing and throwing the fresh offal overboard, we have found the mackerel attracted by it and caught good decks of mackerel that had apparently come in to this as in to our throw bait. We use it often to extend our bait. The British boat fishery is pursued near the shore and the schooners will not venture in where they are, especially if the wind is on shore owing to the shallowness of the water. The boat fishery is one thing, the schooner fishery another and different thing. I never knew of but one boat injured by the fleet and that was done by accident. The boat fishermen often come on board our vessels for favors which are cheerfully granted, and in the case of injury, above mentioned, the owners were well remunerated for the loss. The idea that fish offal thrown overboard can be detected by the smell after it has sunk is nonsense. I have trans-shipped my mackerel in one instance, putting them on board a British vessel for freight home. The advantage of trans-shipment at present is of no value whatever, as few or none of our vessels obtain a full trip, and the Bay mackereling has been a losing business the past 4 years and this year bids fair to be worse than any.

JOS. W. COLLINS.

COMMONWEALTH OF MASSACHUSETTS,)
  COUNTY OF ESSEX, S. S.,   }
    GLOUCESTER, Aug. 28th, 1877.)

Then personally appeared the above named Joseph W. Collins and made oath that all the above statements by him subscribed are true to the best of his knowledge and belief, before me.

[L. S.]   DAVID W. LOW, *Notary Public.*

No. 265.

GLOUCESTER, .

I, John Glenn, was born in York, Maine; am 39 year
oath do depose and say, that I have been engaged in
ness twenty years. I have been mackereling in Gulf £
10 seasons, mostly from Gloucester. The best stock
$5,000 in any season;. was in the *Abba H. Swasey*, of Gl
a license for fishing inshore. We fished mostly aroun
Islands, and about all our mackerel were taken there.
highest stock I ever made in the Gulf of St. Lawrence,
in the *Abba H. Swasey*. We did not have occasion to
We were also on Bank Bradley. My lowest stock was
An American schooner for a full season's fishing from
October in the Gulf of St. Lawrence, must stock $5,000
I never knew of any American vessel damaging the B1
on the contrary, have often had them come to us to grin
favors.

This present season we went from York, Maine, to (
rence, codfishing, in schooner *Anna F. Mason*, 30 tons
Commenced to fit the 1st of July; took no bait from he
in the Gut of Canso; paid $3 per ton for it; went up o
caught our bait on the grounds,—*i. e.*, that is, 15 miles
in nets; the bait was herring, and commenced fishing v
there a fortnight; took 25,000 lbs. split fish; threw r
overboard. There were 10 other American vessels fisl
place; saw 20 Nova Scotia vessels up and down P. I
for codfish using hand lines. They throw over the
Never knew of over 30 sail of American vessels in the
I should say there were 100 sail of American vessels
know that while I have been in the Gulf of St. Lawre
tenth part of the whole American catch of mackerel
three miles of the shore. We have always thrown o
gurry, and I never have noticed any diminution of fish
The American fleet fish in 20 fathoms of water, and
their gurry in this deep water. We bought some sup
home. I know of no inshore fishery for codfish now pt
can vessels in the Gulf of St. Lawrence. The vessels
tain any quantity of porgie slivers and clams for bait
cheaper to catch the bait on the Banks. Bait was s
on the fishing grounds. We could have obtained bait
shore fishermen at about the same price as it would co
home; but we prefer to take the chance of getting
ground. There used to be quite a number of vessels
sue the codfishery in the Gulf of St. Lawrence, but of 1
fallen off greatly.

The fishermen have put their vessels into the Amer
erel fishery, which has been very much more profital
This present trip my crew shared $30 each; time emp
I have been master of the schooners *Joe Hooker*, *Me*
Mason.　　　　　　　　　　　　　　　　　JOH」
Master of Schooner A. H. M

GLOCESTER,

Personally appeared the above named John Glenn
the above statement by him subscribed, is true, befor
ADDISON CARTER, *Just*

No. 266.

GLOUCESTER, August 31, 1877.

John P. Hutchinson, master of the schr. *Robert T. Clark*, of Bridge-
, Connecticut, do, on oath, depose and say, that I was born in New
k, am 54 years of age, and have just returned from a voyage to Got-
)urg, Sweden. I started from Gloucester, the 21st of April, 1877,
went to the Magdalen Islands for herring. I carried no nets from
acester, but in the Straits of Canso, I hired one seine and two boats,
4 men, all British subjects. At the Island, the seine, manned by
owners, and some 6 others that I hired there, took about 400 barrels
erring. All the labor of taking, packing, etc., was done by British
ects, and their service paid for in cash. I also bought 200 barrels
erring from other British fishermen, paying about 25 cents per bar-
lauded on board my vessel. Not being able to get as many herring
wanted at the Magdalens, I started on the 20th of May for Fortune
. There were 30 American vessels at the Magdalen Islands after
ing, buying and hiring the herring caught, the same as I was. Ar-
d at Fortune Bay on the 25th of May, and bought 1,300 barrels of
ing from the people on shore, paid 80 cents per barrel in gold.
eft Fortune Bay the 18th of June, and arrived at Gottenburg on the
of July, herring in good order, and sold slow, and at prices that will
more than pay the expenses of the voyage. I found the people at
tune Bay very desirous to sell.
[Y voyage was as much a commercial voyage, as if I were buying po-
es or any other product of the Dominion; and all of the herring
n by other vessels, so far as I could observe, were bought and paid
in the same manner as I bought. I carried 2,000 bbls from Eastport
ch were never landed at Fortune Bay, but I was obliged to pay du-
on them. I also paid light dues, $45.
have never been in the fishing business, and as far as my observa-
goes, the trade with the American vessels at Newfoundland and the
rdalens is a source of profit, and large gains to the people there.
he *Joseph Wilder*, an American vessel, was at Gottenburg when I
, and her cargo of herring was half rotten. Taking the whole of the
opean trade in herring, sent from this side, I should say, on the
le, that there has been no money made in it by Americans. This
le is experimental, and the full results are, so far, not very satisfac-
.

JOHN P. HUTCHINSON.

COMMONWEALTH OF MASSACHUSETTS,

JNTY OF ESSEX, SS.   GLOUCESTER, Sept. 1st, 1877.
hen personally appeared John P. Hutchinson, above named, who
ie oath, that all the above statements by him subscribed are true,
he best of his knowledge and belief, before me,
L. S.)   DAVID W. LOW,
                                              Notary Public.

No. 267.

GLOUCESTER, Aug. 31, 1877.

, James McIsaac, Master of the schooner *Lais*, of Port Hawkesbury,
va Scotia, on oath do depose and say, that I was born in Port Hast-
s, Strait of Canso, am 42 years of age, that I have been engaged in

the fisheries for 18 years, just arrived from Grand Banks a
St. Lawrence from a codfish trip. I brought in 80,000 lbs. c
took 60,000 lbs. on Grand Banks; the vessel sprung a leak, :
to run in home. I, after my vessel was repaired, went (
Bradelle, in the Gulf of St. Lawrence, where I took 20,000 m
fish, 25 miles from shore. I caught my bait for this trip
Edward Island, about three miles off from shore; the bait
mackerel. It is the usual custom of the vessels from N(
bound to the Banks codfishing, to buy bait from the shor
Newfoundland and Nova Scotia; the average price of herrin
$2 per barrel. I have paid as high as $3.50 per barrel.

The market of the fishing vessels buying bait of the shore
very profitable one for the shoresmen, as they get more fo
ring, selling them fresh, than any other way they can dispo⟨
I have been to Newfoundland, to buy fresh herring, seven s⟨
when I first went there the people hardly had a net or a boa
were living very poorly; but now, owing to the herring tra⟨
American and other vessels, they are prosperous and are liv
style. They own boats and nets, and all of this prosperity
owing to this trade. There is no other market for these h
they would be useless if it were not for the market this tr
On the Banks, for a fresh trip, we first use herring to start u,
after the first fish are caught, we use the refuse fish for ba
caught four trips on the Banks without having any herring, an⟨
on the Banks, and these squid, with the refuse, was all I use⟨
say that if all the vessels would carry salt bait they would do
as they do now with herring. I think using fresh bait ma
dainty. The Provincetown vessels this year have done as well
sels with fresh bait; they using clams. I have never heard of
the Bay being injured before the talk this year; but I have
boats to flock around the American vessels to get the bene
bait, so that the vessels could not get a line into the water.

I have been in the Gulf of St. Lawrence 10 seasons mac
American vessels; never with seines; always with the hoo⟨
season's work I ever made in the bay was $400 to a share.
season was $200. I have not been in the bay for four years.
we get more inshore; some years get more offshore. I sho⟨
one-half of the mackerel are, in my experience of bookin⟨
shore, viz: within three miles. I never heard or knew of ⟨
as fish cleanings hurting the fish; that is a new idea.

The American seiners have made a great deal of mone⟨
mackerel off their own coast; this I know, being where I co⟨
this fact.

The American cod and halibut fishery is a deep-sea fisher
Years ago a few trips were made up around Anticosti, b⟨
ing to the great sea-fishing. Now they take all their fish o⟨
off shore; none less than 12 miles off, and some 300 miles ⟨

JAMES ⟨

COMMONWEALTH OF MASSACHUSETTS

COUNTY OF ESSEX, ss.   GLOUCESTER, Au⟨

Then personally appeared the above named James McIsa⟨
oath that the above statement, by him subscribed, is t⟨
me,

(L. S.)   DAVID ⟨

No⟨

No. 268.

GLOUCESTER, Aug. 28, 1877.

ohn S. Jameson, master of the schr. *Henry Wilson*, of Gloucester,
th, do depose and say : That I was born in Guysboro, Nova Scotia,
years of age, have been engaged in the fisheries for 30 years.
ive just arrived from a trip to Greenland for halibut. I brought
120,000 lbs. of halibut and 30,000 lbs. of codfish. We caught our
5 miles from land. I have been 10 years in the Western and
1 Bank fisheries. We usually take 15 bbls. of porgie slivers for a
·om Gloucester, and either go to Nova Scotia or Newfoundland for
bait. We always buy this fresh bait and pay cash for it. We
n an average about 1½ dollars per barrel for this bait, taking 45
·o a trip, usually two trips a year. Sometimes we go in for bait 4
to a trip, taking 45 bbls. each time. The bait costs us about 200
·s for the full trip. If there was no demand for these herring the
e would not catch them at all. The American fisheries on the
s has absolutely created a new business for these people. I have
it a number of trips of fish without getting any fresh bait from the
, using my slivers and refuse fish. The Grand Bank fisheries has
pursued for centuries, the first beginning of this shore fresh bait
ess is within 10 years. It is entirely to the advantage of the shore
e of Newfoundland and other places to sell this bait, as they realize
sums from what would otherwise be of no value whatever to them.
ere is nearly a half million dollars paid to the English people for
ng by Americans, including the winter fresh herring trade. This
d be entirely worthless to them except for the American trade.
American cod and halibut fishery is entirely a deep sea fishery.
centuries of fishing on the sea Banks and for centuries throwing
offal there is no real diminution of fish there. The use of fresh
ias made the fish dainty and on the whole it has been an injury to
.shing there using this bait. If all the Bank fishermen would use
·ait it would be better for the whole.
ave been in the Gulf of St. Lawrence for mackerel 10 years or sea-
Not more than one-fourth of the mackerel are taken within three
of the shore by the Americans. . American vessels in the Bay will
verage more than three hundred barrels of mackerel each for a
·ns mackereling there, this is a fair average for 10 years.

JOHN S. JAMESON.

COMMONWEALTH OF MASSACHUSETTS.

ITY OF ESSEX, s. s.   GLOUCESTER, Aug, 28, 1877.

en personally appeared the above named James S. Jameson and
) oath that all the statements by him subscribed are true before me.
S.)   DAVID W. LOW,
                                         Notary Public.

No. 269.

GLOUCESTER, September 3, 1877.

James L. Anderson, Master of the American schr. *Seth Stockbridge*,
loucester, Mass., do, on oath, depose and say, that I was born in
lle Millford, Straits of Canso, am 37 years of age. I have been en-
d in the Gulf of St. Lawrence mackerel fishery for 24 seasons.
iave just returned from a trip to the Gulf of St. Lawrence for mack-

. I began to fit my vessel for this trip on the 11th of July, 18
from Gloucester on the 14th; went down to the coast of N
seined porgies for bait; took 30 bbls of slivers; I arrived in t:
St. Lawrence on the 28th of July; caught our first mackere
Point, 4 miles from shore; took 15 barrels; then went up the
of Prince Edward Island, as far as New London, tried all th
and got no mackerel. We then ran down the Island to Secon
and took 10 barrels of mackerel there, inside of three miles.
down to the Magdalen Islands, and took 45 barrels in four da
hook, off Brine Island, over three miles from shore. I then
to P. E. Island, fished there for a week, and did not get 10
mackerel. We then went to the whole northern side of Cap
tried all the way for mackerel, and got nothing. Again w
Magdalen Islands, tried there 4 days, and got 5 barrels of 1
went back to P. E. Island again, tried all round the north,
south sides, and found nothing. I then fished off Port Hood,
George, took 10 barrels of mackerel, and being completely dis
I left the Bay on the 24th of August. We could find no
neither had any vessels we saw, seen any mackerel to spea
fortnight. I know that the mackerel fishery in the Gulf of St.
is a thorough and complete failure this year, and cannot he
great loss to American owners and fishermen, in having th
go there at all. I think the mackerel went out of the Bay, fo
son that there was nothing in the water for them to eat.
that the large amount of bait formerly thrown by the Amer
when fishing with hooks, had a great effect in keeping the m
the Bay. Since the vessels have ceased to go there in large
this bait has not been there to keep them in. Each Ameri
used to throw, on an average, 90 barrels of bait in a seas
from 4 to 6 dollars per barrel.

My present trip from the Gulf of St. Lawrence packed out
of mackerel, mostly No. 2s, a few No. 1s and No. 3s.

The time consumed from the date of fitting, to final settl
be just two months.

My vessel is a new, first-class vessel, rating 90 tons, ne
ment. I had a seine boat and seine, partly used, worth 750

My vessel's charter is worth $300 per Month, for 2 months
The use of seine and boat for 2 months,
Sixteen Men's Wages, at $30 per Month, for 2 Months,
Captain's Wages at $75 per Month,   "
Outfits, including Provisions, Bait, Salt Barrels, &c.,
Packing and Inspection,   .
Insurance,

      Total Cost,
                    RECEIPTS.
Ninety Barrels of Mackerel, at $12,

      Actual Loss,   .

In 1875, I was in the Gulf of St. Lawrence, and cruised
and found no mackerel at all.

I have been in the Gulf of St. Lawrence for the last 20 y
year, except 1873, 1874, 1876.

I did not go there last year, as all the reports showed tha
no mackerel there.

ı all my experience in taking mackerel in the Gulf, not more than
fourth are taken within three miles of the shore. I have taken
le entire trips with not a single mackerel of them taken within five
s of the shore.

have seined off the American shore parts of five years. I have
ked in a single season, seining mackerel there alone, reckoning no
r fish, seven thousand six hundred dollars in a season.

he best stock I ever made in the Gulf of St. Lawrence mackerel
ery in one whole season, was six thousand seven hundred dollars.
se figures are taken from my books, and are correct. My poorest
k in the Gulf of St. Lawrence mackerel fishery was in 1875, when I
1 all over the Gulf, and could not raise a mackerel. Of course, I
ked nothing.

uring the past 10 years, the American shore mackerel have been
atly superior to the Bay mackerel of the same brand in texture, qual-
and price.

n the American shore, we take mackerel sometimes close in, and
are sometimes taken on Georges Banks 100 miles off.

have been some trips to the Western Banks for cod-fish, and we
ght our fresh bait of the shore people of the Dominion of Canada,
ays paying cash for it.

he people make more than double the profit selling herring to the
erican fishermen, than in any other manner that they can dispose of
m. I have caught a whole trip on the Banks, entirely by the use of
bait, carried from the United States.

ish offal, when thrown overboard in very shoal water, has a tendency
eep fish away until the water clears; but in deep water, there is no
ceptible effect on the fish. I never knew of the shore boats being
erfered with, or injured by the vessels. The American schooners are
y particular not to trouble the boats; and it is a universal fact that
schooners never can get any mackerel on the grounds inshore, in shoal
ter, where the boats usually fish. I never took 10 barrels of mack-
l on the boat's fishing grounds in all my fishing in the Bay.

[have "hove to" this year near where the boats were fishing and
ting some mackerel, and we could not catch a mackerel. In most of
places where the boats fish, my vessel could not go in, as they
ı in from two to four fathoms of water, and my vessel draws 12 feet
water; and this fact applies to most of the American schooners.

have been to Grand Manau for herring, to carry to Gloucester, to
t Georges men, and paid from 65 cents to one dollar per hundred for
sh herring, and the same herring for any other purpose or market was
worth to the people who took them 25 cents a hundred to salt. The
re people always catch the herring.

have had but one trip of mackerel sent home from the Bay by trans-
pment, and that trip cost just one dollar per barrel to get them to
ucester by a sailing vessel. This was in 1861.

have been master of the following schooners:—The *Morning Light,*
cador, Ida *Thurlow, Benj. Haskell, George S. Low, Seth Stockbridge.*

CAPT. JAMES L. ANDERSON.

COMMONWEALTH OF MASSACHUSETTS.

GLOUCESTER, Aug. 4, 1877.

UNTY OF ESSEX, SS.

Then personally appeared the above named James L. Anderson, Cap-
n, and made oath, that all the statements by him subscribed, are true,
the best of his knowledge and belief, before me,

L. S.)   DAVID W. LOW, *Notary Public.*

No. 270.

GLOUCESTER, Aug. 2'

I, Jesse Lewis, Master of the American schr. *Alice M. Lewis*
cester, on oath do depose and say, that I was born in Kitter
am 48 years age, and have been engaged in the fisheries 35
have just arrived from the Gulf of St. Lawrence from a mackere
I commenced to fit my vessel for this trip the 1st of July, 1877.
from Gloucester the 5th of July, arrived in the Gulf of St.
about the 14th of July. Was fitted with a purse seine and
one small seine. The first mackerel I took two miles off East
the seine,—about 100 brls., mostly twos; from there went
Miscou and Gaspe; got no mackerel there; came back to Princ
Island; caught 50 brls. on the hook near the shore. We afterv
to the Magdalen Islands, and caught about 50 brls. on the ho
the shore. The average of these mackerel were twos, worth :
per bbl. Our trip packed out 175 bbls., and brought 2,100 dol
My trip will consume just two months' time, for vessel and

The charter of my vessel, at $250 per month,	$500 (
Wages of 15 men, at $30 per month,	900 (
Outfits, viz., provisions, salt, barrels, etc.,	500 (
Insurance,	100 (
Packing,	131 :
Expense of seines, wear and mending and use,	200 (
Hooks and lines,	25 (
Total cost,	$2, 356 :
Total receipts,	$2, 100 (
Actual and real loss,	$256

I have been in the Bay 28 seasons,—24 mackereling and 4 c
My average stock for the whole of the seasons in the Bay i
season. Not over one-third of the mackerel I have taken t
taken within three miles of the shore. We always throw
the cleanings of the mackerel, except what we save to use as t
The fish come eagerly after this offal. I never heard of any being
by it; but they swarm to get it. I never heard any fishermen
as I have seen them this year, the British boats throwing all
overboard. This is the universal practice of all fishermen, Am
English.

The practice of lee-bowing is universal, both by English a
can vessels. I never knew of any British boats being injur
American schooners. The American and British mode of f
entirely different, as the boat fishing is a shore fishery, and
American schooners cannot, on account of the depth of v
where the boats generally resort. The boats obtain many f
the American vessels, such as using their mills to grind bait
giving them salt and bait. The boat fishermen, as a class, h
been jealous of the American fishermen. I have this year
to a number of their boats. The years that our fishermen v
excluded from the inshore mackerel fishing by the cutters,
the best fares. That is my personal experience. I know of
codfishery pursued by American vessels in the Gulf of St.
I never caught a codfish there inside of 15 miles from the
ever knew any American vessel so doing.

There are more British than American vessels engaged in the codfishery of the Gulf of St. Lawrence; they all throw their offal overboard, including the shore boats. I went to Newfoundland 19 years ago, for herring; have been 15 trips since. I never caught a herring there, but invariably bought them, and paid the inhabitants for them. When I first went there I paid one dollar per bbl.; they are now worth from $1.50 to $2. The American trade in herring has kept the people from starvation, and raised whole communities from poverty to comparative affluence. I have known $60,000 to be paid for herring in Fortune Bay alone, by the American fleet, in one single winter, and there would have been none sold otherwise, as there is not any demand for these herring, except by Americans, for the American market. I think there are about 100 sail of Americans in the Bay this year. The average number of American vessels in the Gulf of St. Lawrence the past 20 years is not over 250 vessels, taking one year with another. Out of the fleet this year there is not over a dozen that have taken as many mackerel as I have, and a large proportion of the fleet are leaving the Bay entirely discouraged. The *Wm. S. Baker* has arrived in Gloucester, within two hours, from the Bay of St. Lawrence with only five barrels of mackerel.

I have been master of the schooners *Susan E. Brown, Hattie Lewis, Ida May, Two Forty, Theron F. Dale, Alice M. Lewis.*

JESSE LEWIS.

COMMONWEALTH OF MASSACHUSETTS.

COUNTY OF ESSEX, SS.   GLOUCESTER, Aug. 27, 1877.

Then personally appeared the above named Jesse Lewis, and made oath, that all the above statements by him subscribed, are true to the best of his knowledge and belief, before me.

DAVID W. LOW.

(L. S.)   *Notary Public.*

No. 271.

GLOUCESTER, Sept. 3, 1877.

I, Samuel M. Farmer, master of the schooner *Maud Muller,* of Gloucester, on oath do depose and say, that I was born in Booth Bay, Me. I have just returned from a trip to the coast of Maine. I have been absent five weeks. I brought home 230 barrels of mackerel, making 40 barrels No. 1's and 190 barrels No. 2's. The No. 1's are worth $24 per barrel, the No. 2's are worth $15 per barrel. My whole trip is worth $3,810.

The charter of my vessel is worth $100 per month .	$125 00
Thirteen men	390 00
Bait	30 00
Outfits	150 00
Insurance	50 00
Packing and Inspection	172 00
Use of Seine and Boat	75 00
Cost of trip	$992 00
Receipts 230 barrels mackerel	3,810 00
Profit	$2,818 00

My vessel is only 45 tons. She took these mackerel 8 miles from Mount Desert Rock. The mackerel are schooling in every direction

there. I am going back immediately. I think the pros
for a large Fall catch on our shores. I have been in the
Lawrence three seasons for mackerel, in 1868, 1869, 1870—
1870 I made $66 for the season, the two years previous we s
each man for 5 months fishing. These were extra good y
Bay.

Of all the mackerel we took during the three years an
nearly 1,800 barrels, only 90 wash barrels were taken on Si
within three miles of the shore.

I have on the American shore made $500 to a share in a
least I ever made on this shore mackereling was $400, a ses
months. The Bay mackerel fishery for this and the two las
been an entire failure. I have been to Grand Manau one
herring. I bought my herring of the people on shore, payi
them. I paid from 60 to 90 cents per hundred. There is no i
no use to which these herring can be put that will begin to p
ple the amount of profit that this sale to American vessels p
have also been to the Western Banks fishing for cod. W
baiting at New Brunswick and one at Cape Breton, payir
per hundred at New Brunswick, and $1 per barrel at Cap
cash. At Cape Breton the herring remaining on hand v
overboard after we were baited, as there was no vessels th
them, they were worthless for any purpose for which the p
use them.

SAMUEL M. F

COMMONWEALTH OF MASSACHUSETTS.

GLOUCESTER, Sept

COUNTY OF ESSEX, SS.

Then personally appeared the above-named Samuel M.
made oath that all the above statements by him subscribed,
the best of his knowledge and belief, before me,

DAVID W. LOW, Not

No. 272.

I, Alexander McDonald, of Provincetown, in the Com
Massachusetts, being duly sworn, do depose and say that
years of age and am the captain of the schooner *Willie A. Jo*
in fishing for cod upon the Grand Banks and I have return
thousand quintals of fish—all taken on trawls. I have b
for cod for nine years and until this year have always use
for bait which I carried from home. This year I went to N
to purchase fresh bait for the first time. I arrived at the
about the eighteenth day of July to get fresh bait, with se
quintals on board, taken previously with salt clams and
on the Banks. I found no bait at Bay of Bulls and left for
finding no bait there either. Then went to Portugal Cove
Bay, where I had to wait five days before I could purchas
all. I then returned to the Banks with twenty barrels of sq
I paid about thirty cents per hundred, having been absent
ing grounds about two weeks. I caught one hundred qui
squid I had purchased at Newfoundland, the remainder
caught with salt bait at Newfoundland, and if I had not wa
time in going to Newfoundland after fresh bait I should

e fish on the Banks and have came home earlier. I have never fished
bait at Newfoundland but have always purchased it and if excluded
purchasing I certainly should not go to Newfoundland to catch it
elf. I consider the trade in bait to be of great advantage to the in-
itants of Newfoundland. While at Portugal Cove I paid William
k, the collector, sixteen 80·100 dollars ($16.80) for light dues, being
he rate of twenty-four cents per ton, and this due is collected from
American fishing vessels visiting Newfoundland.

ALEX. McDONALD.

worn before me at Halifax, this 29th day of September, A. D.
7.

N. H. MEAGHER,
Notary Public for the Province of Nova Scotia.

No. 273.

Alonzo Covey, of Swampscott, in the Commonwealth of Massachu-
s, being duly sworn, do depose and say that I am fifty-three years
and am the captain of the *A. C. Newhall*, a fishing vessel of twenty-
(29) tons, at present in Halifax, Nova Scotia. I have been en-
ed in the fishing business, both as captain and hand, for twenty-five
rs. I have just returned from a trip to the Bay of St. Lawrence,
kerel fishing. I left Swampscott the 28th day of last July, and ar-
d in the Bay the 7th of August. I first fished near Port Hood, and
k four barrels of mackerel six miles from the shore. I then took
nty-five barrels twelve miles broad off Mimnigash. Then fished off
nneack from 5 to 15 miles from the land, and took the balance of my
there, with the exception of 14 barrels, which were taken between
t Cape and Port Hood. I took one hundred and twenty-five barrels
he Bay, all of which were taken more than three miles from land,
ept five barrels at North Cape taken inshore. This trip has not been
cessful. The share of the vessel will not more than pay the cost of
outfit. Before this season I have been engaged in fishing on the
ted States coast, and my trips there have been much more remuner-
'e than my present trip to the Bay. I do not consider the privilege
ishing within three miles of the Canadian coast of any value to
erican fishermen, and I should much prefer to be entirely excluded
refrom, and the former duty of two dollars per barrel to be imposed
he Canadian fish.

ALONZO COVEY.

worn before me in the City of Halifax, in the County of Halifax,
29th day of September, A. D., 1877.

ROBT. SEDGEWICK,
Notary Public.

No. 274.

Edward N. Wilkins, of Swampscott, in the Commonwealth of Mas-
husetts, being duly sworn, do depese and say that I am forty-two
rs old. I have been a fisherman for twenty-five years, and am now one
he crew of the schooner *A. C. Newhall*, Captain Covey, and have just
urned from the Bay of St. Lawrence. We caught 125 barrels of
kerel, all of which were taken more than three miles from the shore
h the exception of five barrels taken inshore between North Cape
Mimnigash, Prince Edward Island. Previous to this year I have
n in the Bay mackerel fishing twelve seasons, the last trip was in

1873 in the schooner *Knight Templar*, of Gloucester, we took 4ł
of mackerel, all of which were taken more than 3 miles from ɩ
except about 50 barrels taken inshore near Rustico.   In all m
the Bay I do not think that one-fifth of all the mackerel ta
caught within three miles of the shore.

EDWARD N. WD

Sworn before me, at the City of Halifax, in the County oɩ
this 29th day of September, A. D. 1877.

ROBT. SEDGEWICK, *Notary*

No. 275.

I, John S. Staples, of Swans Island, Maine, on oath depose
that I am master of the schr. *John Somes*, of Portland, Me.,
been engaged in catching mackerel during this season, comm
fishing off the American shore, and caught 450 barrels which
$10 per barrel.   The favorable reports from Canso induced
down the Bay of St. Lawrence and I accordingly sailed abouɩ
of July.   I was on the trip a little over a month, tried for ma
the way from Port Hood to New London Head, and from ther
dalene Islands and from there to Margaree Island, and suc
getting only eleven barrels which are worth $8 per barrel.
this trip to the Bay $1500, at the least calculation.   At Caɩ
visited by the officer who exacted one dollar from me for the ɩ
buoys—this is collected of all American vessels.   I arrived ɩ
the Bay about the 3rd Sept. and since that time I have cɩ
barrels of mackerel on this shore, which are worth $1400.   In
I was master of schr. *Joseph Story*, of Gloucester, was in
mackereling and caught 250 barrels, not over 10 barrels of w
caught within three miles of the shore.   In the year 1873 I w
of the same schooner and fished for mackerel off the Amer·
and took 900 barrels, from which we stocked $8,000.   In 187
the said schooner up to July 25th, when I left her on accou
ness, up to that time we took 650 barrels, from which we stoc
all this year the said schooner fished on the American shorɩ
left her the said schooner took 600 barrels.   In 1875 I was i
Rushlight and fished for mackerel on the American coast, and t
the season 900 barrels and stocked about $7,000.   In 1876 (ɩ
was in the schooner *John Somes*, and fished for mackerel
season on the American shore and took 1,600 barrels and stocl
I would state that previous to the years enumerated above,
Bay mackereling for 15 years and am confident that not on
part of the mackerel caught were caught within the three-mi
consider and regard the mackerel fishery on the American sl
more superior and valuable than the British Bay fishery.

In the Winter of 1870 I was in the schooner *Annie E.]*
went to Grand Manan for cargo of frozen herring, and boug
at the rate of 45 cents per 100.   There was at the time
vessels there after herring, all of which loaded with herring ɩ
them of the inhabitants—they carrying all the way from
400,000, at from 40 to 60 cents per 100.   This trade with the ɩ
of great importance to the inhabitants, as they would undoub
were it not for this trade as they get a great deal of mone
source, which is all clear gain to them, as they have no oɩ
for their herring.

JOHN S. STAP
Master of Schooner Jo

CUSTOM HOUSE, GLOUCESTER, Oct. 4, 1877.

rsonally appeared Capt. John S. Staples, who subscribed to the
'oing statement, and made oath that the foregoing statement was
, before me.

ADDISON CARTER,
Special Deputy Collector and Justice of the Peace.

No. 276.

GLOUCESTER, August 25, 1877.

Daniel McNeil, on oath depose and say, that I was born on Cape
on; am 34 years of age; have been engaged in the fisheries for 21
s, principally in the Bank fishing on Grand Bank, Western and
ro; have been master for five years; am now master of the schooner
ι *Parsons*, of Gloucester. Arrived from the Grand Banks this
ι. Have always bought my bait of the inhabitants of Newfound-
. I paid $80 for my bait on the last trip, and I did not get a full
ing. I have never fished for bait at Newfoundland, neither have I
 known any of the American fishermen to do so at Newfoundland,—
ιys invariably buying what they needed,—and, in fact, if they
ed to catch their bait they could not, for they are fitted with no
iances for the purpose. The inhabitants of Newfoundland are very
.ous for this trade, always coming on board, even before I can come
nchor, soliciting the sale of this bait; and though the American fish-
ɘn pay the highest price for their bait, ice and supplies, still I re-
it as cheaper to do so. This bait supply to the fishermen furnishes
ιpation to a large part of the inhabitants, and is quite lucrative to
se engaged in it. This trade has been patronized by the Americans
gaged in the Bank fishery) very generally for the last seven years.
ιvious to that time, it was the custom to catch our bait on the Banks.
h-peas, fish cut up, birds and squid constituted our bait. The in-
ιitants of Newfoundland find the only market for their bait in the
nch and American Bank fleet. I regard this traffic of vastly more
ιortance to the inhabitants of Newfoundland than to the American
ermen, as we could procure our bait, as heretofore, on the Banks. I
'e seen 20 sail of American vessels in a small cove at Newfoundland
bait, which they uniformly purchased. If prevented from purchas-
bait at Newfoundland, the Americans could procure this bait at the
nch Islands, where the French fleet of Bankers get their bait and
ιplies.

DANIEL McNEIL.

GLOUCESTER, Aug. 25, 1877.

Sworn to and subscribed before me,

ADDISON CARTER,
Justice of the Peace.

No. 277.

, Charles E. Parkhurst, of Gloucester, in the State of Massachusetts,
ιk-keeper, on oath depose and say, that schooner *Energy* was built
l owned by my father, Charles Parkhurst, and run by him in the fish-
' business until she was sold to go to California. That in 1868 she
s engaged in the Gulf of St. Lawrence mackerel fishery; that she
led July 18th, and returned Nov. 14th, 1868; was absent three months
l twenty-six days, making but one voyage. She brought home and
:ked out one hundred and thirty-three (133) barrels of mackerel,

which was all her catch for that season. The vessel's sha
That James Howlett was one of the crew of said vessel o
which was the only voyage he made in her after macke
share of said voyage was eighty-seven dollars and 71-1
trusteed and paid to Lawyer Perrin.

CHARLES E. PA

COMMONWEALTH OF MASSACHUSETTS, ⎱
      ESSEX, S. S.,
             Sept. 21st, 1877. ⎰

Then personally appeared the above named Charles E.
made oath that the above statement, by him subscribed,
me,

DAVID W.
N

No. 278.

COMMONWEALTH OF MASSACHUSET

ESSEX, SS.

I, Zebulon Tarr, of Gloucester, in said County of Es
monwealth of Massachusetts, do hereby certify that I
gaged in the herring business somewhat extensively in t
New Brunswick, in the harbors of Deer Isle, St. Andrew'
and other harbors at which herring are to be bough
Within the last ten years I have bought fifteen trips of h
ing two hundred and twenty thousand each, at a cost
and fifty cents a thousand, amounting to fourteen thousa
dred and fifty dollars. Two trips, three hundred thousa
dollars a thousand, amounting to three thousand dollars

Witness my hand, this seventeenth day of October, in
Lord eighteen hundred and seventy-seven.

ZEBU

COMMONWEALTH OF MASSACHUSET

ESSEX, SS.   ROCKPORT, Octobe

Then personally appeared the above named Zebulon 1
solemn oath to the truth of the foregoing statement by h
before me,

NATHANIEL F. S.
Justice

No. 279.

We have been asked to make a statement of the numb
herring caught in American waters on the coast of the
and the number of barrels of herring caught in Foreign
the last year handled by us, and to state the relative
barrel in its green state as it is when taken from the wa

We find upon examination of our books that we hav
business during the last year (28,208) twenty-eight thou
dred and eight barrels of herring.

(16,063) sixteen thousand and sixty-three barrels wer
coast of the United States, between Eastport, Maine, and
Massachusetts.

herring cost us for those caught on the coast of the United States
vo dollars and twenty-five cents to two dollars and seventy-five
ier barrel ; that is for the herring, not including the barrel, salt,
etc., etc.

45) twelve thousand one hundred and forty-five barrels were
on the coast of Newfoundland, Cape Breton, Nova Scotia, Mag-
slands, and Labrador, as follows :—

		Barrels.	
Caught at Fortune Bay, Nfld		8,587	
" " Port Hood, C. B		200	
" " Nova Scotia (coast)		348	12,145
" " Magdalens		510	
" " Bay of Islands, Nfld		2,500	

ie caught at Fortune Bay in-paid seventy-five cents, gold, per bar-
Port Hood, one dollar per barrel ; Nova Scotia, one dollar per
Magdalens, seventy-five cents per barrel ; and at Bay of Islands,
;wo dollars per barrel. These prices include what is paid for the
id does not include the barrels, salt, labor, etc., etc.
the herring which we put up in the Provinces as stated herein,
ight from the fishermen and paid them at prices as stated ; and
:ase whatever did we ever catch any in nets or seines, but always
.sed the fish from the natives.
above number of barrels does not include any herring which our
i brought in the Provinces during the year, for bait.
have taken from our books the number of barrels packed.
UCESTER, MASS., U. S. A., October 17th, 1877.

D. C. & H. BABSON.
NESS—CHAS. H. BROWN.

COMMONWEALTH OF MASSACHUSETTS.

October 17th, 1877.

, SS.

1 personally appeared the within named Horatio Babson, and made
o the truth of the within statement by him subscribed, in behalf
l firm of D. C. & H. Babson, before me.
ness my hand and official seal the day and year last above writ·

[L. S.]   JAMES DAVIS,
Notary Public.

No. 280.

iam Cogswell, of Salem, County of Essex, and Commonwealth of
chusetts, on oath, deposes and says, that since August 24th, A.
36, he has held, and does now, hold the office of Inspector-General
b, within and for the said Commonwealth ; the duties of which
fice, among other things, are to supervise, either personally or by
7, the packing and inspecting of all pickled fish put up within
ommonwealth, to keep an accurate account of the same, and to
  thereon in detail, as to the number of barrels, the quality
:iud of such fish, to the Secretary of the Commonwealth,
e is under bonds to the Treasurer of the said Commonwealth,
  sum of ten thousand dollars; that in the discharge of his du-
ie is assisted by some one hundred deputies, more or less, in
ifferent seaport towns of said Commonwealth, each of whom

210 F

are under bonds to him in the sum of six thousand
he has given especial attention to informing himself fr
sources of information, in what waters, and what coasts
has passed under his supervision since he came into his s
caught; that he has also required and received sworn re
vits from a large number of his deputies, many of whom
the fishing vessels; many of whom have been engaged ir
self, and all of whom have as accurate knowledge on the su
sible to be obtained, showing the number of barrels
within the three mile line of the coast of Her Britannic
minions in North America, during the fishing seasons of
inclusive, upon which said returns or affidavits, and upon
knowledge and belief, and upon his own reports as afores
follows:—That in the year ending December 20th, 1867,
spected in said Commonwealth, two hundred and eleven
hundred and ten barrels of mackerel, and no more; tha
vits as aforesaid, covering some ninety-seven thousand 1
mackerel, of which only some two thousand were caug
three mile line, or in other words, about two and one-sixte
which applied to the whole catch of that year, would gi
three hundred and sixty barrels of mackerel only that
within said line, in said year of 1867.

That in the year ending December 20th, 1868, there '
in said Commonwealth, one hundred and eighty thousan
barrels of mackerel and no more. That of this number
vits as aforesaid covering some one hundred and two the
of said mackerel and no more of which only some sixteer
rels were caught within said three mile line, or in other w
and one-half per cent. which applied to the whole catc
would give some twenty-seven hundred barrels of mac
were caught within said three mile line in said year of 1

That in the year ending December 20th, 1869, there we
said Commonwealth, two hundred and thirty-four thou
dred barrels of mackerel and no more, and that of this
affidavits as aforesaid covering some one hundred and t
sand barrels and no more of said mackerel, of which only
dred barrels were caught within said three-mile line, or
some one and one-third per cent. which applied to the
that year, would give some thirty-one hundred barrels o
that were caught within said three-mile line in said year

That in the year ending December 20th, 1870, there w
said Commonwealth three hundred and eighteen thousa
and twenty-one barrels of mackerel and no more, and th
ber he has affidavits as aforesaid, covering some one hund
eight thousand barrels and no more of said mackerel
some twenty-five hundred barrels were caught within
line, or in other words some one and one-eight per cent
to the whole catch of that year would give some thir
barrels of mackerel only that were caught within said tl
said year of 1870.

That in the year ending December 20th, 1871, there w
said Commonwealth, two hundred and fifty-nine thousan
and sixteen barrels and no more, of mackerel, and that
he has affidavits as aforesaid, covering some one hund
five thousand barrels and no more of said mackerel, of v
eighteen hundred barrels were caught within said three

words some one per cent., which applied to the whole catch of
·ear, would give some twenty-five hundred barrels mackerel, only
vere caught within said three-mile line in said year of 1871.

it in the year ending December 20th, 1872, there were inspected in
Commonwealth one hundred and eighty one-thousand nine hundred
ifty-seven barrels of mackerel, and no more; and that of this num-
e has affidavits as aforesaid, covering some one hundred and twenty-
thousand barrels, and no more, of said mackerel,—of which only
sixteen hundred barrels were caught within said three-mile line,
ι other words, some one and one-sixth per cent., which applied to
vhole catch of that year, would give some two thousand one hun-
and twenty-three barrels of mackerel only that were caught within
three-mile line in said year of 1872.

at in the year ending December 20th, 1873, there were inspected in
Commonwealth, one hundred eighty-five thousand seven hundred
forty-eight barrels of mackerel, and no more; and that of this num-
e has affidavits as aforesaid, covering some one hundred and forty-
thousand barrels, and no more, of said mackerel, of which only some
ty-four hundred barrels were caught within said three-mile line,—
ι other words, some one and three-eighths per cent.,—which, applied
e whole catch of that year, would give some twenty-eight hundred
·ls of mackerel only that were caught within said three mile line in
year of 1873.

at in the year ending December 20th, 1874, there were inspected
id Commonwealth, two hundred and fifty-eight thousand three hun-
and eighty barrels of mackerel, and no more; and that of this
ber he has affidavits as aforesaid, covering some one hundred and
ty-four thousand barrels, and no more, of said mackerel, of which
some eight hundred barrels were caught within said three-mile
.—or, in other words, some three-sixteenths of one per cent.,—which,
lied to the whole catch of that year, would give some eleven hun-
l barrels of mackerel only that were caught within said three-mile
in said year of 1874.

hat in the year ending December 20th, 1875, there were inspected in
ι Commonwealth, one hundred and thirty thousand and fourteen
rels of mackerel, and no more; and that he has affidavits covering
e ninety thousand barrels, and no more, of said mackerel, of which
ι some three hundred barrels were caught within said three-mile line,
ι other words, some one-third of one per cent., which applied to the
le catch of that year, would give some four hundred and thirty-three
·els of mackerel only that were caught within the said three-mile
in said year of 1875.

hat in the year ending December 20th, 1876, there were inspected in
ι Commonwealth, two hundred and twenty-five thousand nine hun-
l and forty-one barrels of mackerel, and no more; and that he has
davits as aforesaid, covering some one hundred and ninety thousand
rels, and no more of said mackerel, of which only some three hun-
d barrels were caught within said three mile line, or in other words,
ιe one-sixth of one per cent., which, applied to the whole catch of
t year, would give some three hundred and seventy-six barrels of
ːkerel only that were caught within said three mile line in said year
876. And said deponent doth further depose and say, upon his best
ζment, information and belief, that of the whole number of barrels
nackerel inspected in said Commonwealth, from 1867 to 1876, inclu-
·, amounting to nearly two million two hundred thousand barrels,
more than some twenty-three thousand barrels were caught within

the said three mile line. That of the whole number o
mackerel inspected in said Commonwealth from 1873 to 187
amounting to some eight hundred thousand barrels, not mor
forty-seven hundred and nine barrels were caught within sai
line. And that for the last four or five years preceding the
the catch of mackerel within said three mile line, and off tl
in the Bays along the coasts of Her Britannic Majesty's]
North America has been rapidly decreasing, the catch with
mile line as aforesaid, decreasing from twenty-eight hundre
1873 to eleven hundred barrels in 1874, to four hundred and
barrels in 1875, to three hundred and seventy-six barrels in
from his own personal knowledge, the fishing firms of sa
wealth, during the last four or five years as aforesaid, have s
given up as of but little or no profit what is known as the "]
and have confined their fishing vessels substantially to the s
and coasts within the jurisdiction of the United States of
  Witness my hand, at Boston, County of Suffolk, and Col
of Massachusetts, this ——— day of August, A. D., 1877.
WM. COGSW
Inspector-General of Fish for Mas

COMMONWEALTH OF MASSACHUSETTS

OFFICE OF THE SECRETARY OF THE COMMONWEALTH, SU
  This may certify that William Cogswell, of Salem, Cour
and Commonwealth aforesaid, has held the office of Inspec
of fish within and for this Commonwealth since Aug. 24, A.
does now hold the said office, and that on this twentieth da
1877, said Cogswell personally appeared before me and ma
the foregoing statement by him subscribed was true, acco
best judgement, information and belief. Witness my hand a
Seal of the Commonwealth of Massachusetts, the year and
written.

(L. S.)
HENRY B. PE
Secretary of the Com

APPENDIX N.

[COPY.]

OUNDLAND, }
No. 28. }

DOWNING STREET, 17th June, 1871.

—I have the honor to enclose herewith copies of the Treaty signed
ihington on May 8th by the Joint High Commissioners, which has
.tified by Her Majesty and by the President of the United States;
Instructions to Her Majesty's High Commissioners and Protocols
Conferences held by the Commission; of two notes which have
between Sir E. Thornton and Mr. Fish; and of a despatch of
ite, herewith, which I have addressed to the Governor-General of
ι, stating the views of Her Majesty's Government on these im-
: documents.

ι reference to that part of my Despatch to Lord Lisgar, which
ipon the proposed arrangement for the immediate provisional ad-
ι of the United States fishermen to the Colonial Fisheries, I have
irve that Her Majesty's Government are aware that under this
, as under the Convention of 1854, Newfoundland is placed in a
hat different position to that of the other Colonies interested, but
ould strongly urge upon the Government of Newfoundland, that
ist desirable for the general interest of the Empire that the same
should be pursued as in 1854, and that the application made by
ited States Government should be acceded to by Newfoundland,
ι American fishermen may be at once allowed, during the present
, the provisional use of the privileges granted to them by the

I have, &c.,
(Signed)   KIMBERLEY.
ιrnor HILL, C. B., &c.

ιmpliance with the request made by the Right Hon. Earl Kim-
in his despatch of 17th June último, to His Excellency the
ιor, it is agreed to accede thereto.

ect copy.
(Signed)
                              G. D. SHEA,
                                Clerk Ex. Council.

APPENDIX O.

'ATISTICS PRODUCED ON BEHALF OF THE UNITED STATES.

1.

stical Documents relating to the Fisheries and Trade in Fish between the United States and British North America.

I.

showing the importations into the United States of fish of all kinds from all countries

	Fresh for daily use.	Free.	Dutiable.	Total.
			1, 973, 170	1, 973, 170
			2, 316, 453	2, 316, 453
			2, 503, 924	2, 503, 924
	242, 429		1, 907, 688	2, 150, 117
	278, 921		2, 806, 336	3, 085, 257
	294, 837	1, 536, 390	1, 377, 300	3, 208, 527
	351, 889	1, 801, 217	855, 509	3, 008, 615
	271, 597	1, 503, 121	878, 530	2, 653, 248

II.

orts of fish and products of fish into the United States from British North America.

$2, 044, 629
989, 344
1, 505, 299
1, 398, 505
1, 383, 965
1, 400, 173
1, 690, 617
2, 104, 134
2, 348, 641
*1, 862, 797
) months, to March 31...... 1, 292, 616

imports into the United States from British North America in 1876 appear to have been equal to
rd of the total exports from British North America for that year, which are officially reported
1,221.

III.

Imports of fish into the United States from British North America.

IV.

FISH OF ALL KINDS.

Importations into the United States from British North America.

	Dutiable value.	Duty.
1845 to 1854. For the ten fiscal years before reciprocity Annual average..	$570,500 00	$113,128 3
1855 to 1866. During reciprocity. Annual average	1,462,875 36	
1866 to 1872 For the six fiscal years after reciprocity. Annual average	1,170,650 00	277,943 8
1873 (fresh, 278,707)...	1,340,714 00	331,843 0
1874 (" 294,815)...	1,639,488 00	....
1875 (" 351,889)...	1,815,698 00	....
1876 (" 271,597)...	1,506,896 00	....

V.

MACKEREL AND HERRING.—I.

Quantity and value entering into annual consumption in the United Sta

	Mackerel.		Her
	Quantity.	Value.	Quantity.
1868..	30,686 bbls.	$289,175	61,451 bbl
1869..	27,468 "	306,695	91,567 "
1870..	28,480 "	291,527	87,283 "
1871..	28,487 "	309,074	62,022 "
1872..	39,572 "	247,701	62,474 "
1873..	70,651 "	523,577	63,497 "
1874..	90,872 "	807,080	82,826 " 205,819 bo
1875..	78,132 "	587,349	98,190 bb 309,549 bo
1876..	76,599 "	695,917	107,319 bb 307,190 bo

VI.

MACKEREL AND HERRING.—II.

Annual importation into the United States.

	Mackerel.		
	Quantity.	Value.	
1872..	79,227 bbls.	$449,624	78,217 l
1873..	90,889 "	610,457	68,692
1874..	89,693 "	802,470	82,551
1875..	77,538 "	584,836	92,344
1876..	76,538 "	695,460	104,812

VII.

MACKEREL AND HERRING.—III.

Annual importation into the United States from British North America.

	Mackerel.		Herring.	
	Quantity.	Value.	Quantity.	Value.
....	77, 731 bbls.	$438, 410	64, 200 bbls.	$225, 144
....	89, 698 "	605, 778	53, 039 "	179, 377
....	89, 693 "	802, 470	63, 931 "	229, 522
....	77, 488 "	584, 353	72, 167 "	295, 924
....	76, 538 "	695, 460	87, 773 "	307, 384
nths to March 31.......................... }	37, 190 "	336, 582	53, 300 "	186, 955

VIII.

MACKEREL.

Imports into the United States from British North America.

	Value.	Duty.	Duty saved.
to 1854. seven fiscal years before reciprocity, annual average..	$429, 898 28	$85, 979 65	....
to 1866. reciprocity. Annual average........................ er reciprocity.	....	....	....
....	675, 986 00	155, 006 00	....
....	364, 429 00	83, 310 00	....
....	438, 410 00	155, 462 00	....
....	605, 778 00	179, 396 00	....
nnual average ...*	521, 151 00	143, 294 00	....
bls. 89,693...	802, 470 00	....	$179, 386 00
" 77,488...	584, 353 00	....	154, 976 00
" 76,538...	695, 460 00	....	153, 076 00
nnual average	694, 094 00	....	$162, 479 00

IX.

Mackerel imports into the Port of Boston from British North America.

	Canada			Newfoundland.			Prince Edward Island.			Total.		
	Value.	Duty.	Duty saved (estimated.)	Value.	Duty.	Duty saved (estimated.)	Value.	Duty.	Duty saved (estimated.)	Value.	Duty.	Duty saved (estimated.)
1845 to 1855	$2,657,865 74	$410,173 31										
1847 to 1855				$6,841 56	$1,366 31							
1849 to 1855												
1855 to 1866 free	3,001,038 00			25,079 00			$22,218 98	$4,443 69				
1866 to 1872	1,064,195 00	267,309 24		9,901 00	2,633 00		361,295 00	104,803 50				
1873........free	290,721 00	29,840 00					422,322 00					
1874........	334,889 00		} $252,500 00									
1875........	204,574 00			26 00	0 60	3,700 00	1,996 00					
1876........	308,461 00			14,213 00			85,580 00					
1873........free	214,024 00						251,403 00	261 00				
1875........free							141,219 00					
1873........							83,812 00					
1874........									143,000 00			
1875........												
1876........	$7,475,767 74	$707,222 55	$252,500 00	$56,060 56	$4,010 31	$3,700 00	$1,499,975 98	$109,508 19	$143,000 00	$8,941,804 28	$820,741 05	$399,200 00

ANNUAL AVERAGES.

	Canada			Newfoundland.			Prince Edward Island.		
1845 to 1855	$265,786 57			1847 to 1855	$855 00		1849 to 1855	$3,703 00	
1855 to 1866	272,821 00			1855 to 1866	2,280 00		1855 to 1866	32,845 00	
1866 to 1872	177,366 00			1866 to 1872	1,650 00		1866 to 1872	70,420 00	
1873 to 1876	205,487 00			1873	14,213 00		1873 to 1876	130,504 00	

X.

ATEMENT OF DUIY SAVED ON FISH OILS IMPORTED INTO THE UNITED STATES FROM
BRITISH NORTH AMERICA.

	Dutiable Value.	Duty Saved.
74	$91,944	
75	147,485	
76	72,438	

$311,867 —20 per cent., $62,373 40

Annual average $20,791 13

XI.

PORT OF BOSTON.

*Importation of fish of all kinds from British North America during the calendar years 1845
to 1876.*

	Value.	Duty.
45 to 1855. For ten years prior to the reciprocity treaty, fraction of year deducted. Annual average	$333 932 14	$67,533 31
mallest year, 1846	127,642 82	33,436 07
argest year, 1854	609,270 00	123,383 00
55 to 1866. During reciprocity. Annual average	853,914 63	
66 to 1875. For nine years after the termination of treaty, fraction of year deducted. Annual average	796,732 55	101,066 72
or the year 1876	654,366 00	

XII.

PORT OF BOSTON.

Importation of fish-oil from British North America during the calendar years 1845 to 1876.

	Value.	Duty.
845 to 1855. For ten years prior to the reciprocity treaty, fraction of year deducted. Annual average	$40,686 95	$8,152 72
mallest year, 1845	551 00	82 65
argest year, 1852	242,981 00	48,596 20
annual average, omitting 1852	18,209 83	3,659 01
855 to 1866. During reciprocity. Annual average	138,273 36	
866 to 1875. For nine years after the termination of treaty, fraction of year deducted. Annual average	110,014 00	17,468 21
or the year 1876	46,811 00	

XIII.

Export of fish from the United States to British North America.

	Domestic.	Foreign.	Total.
368	$51,789	$17,379	$69,168
369	20,387	11,944	32,331
370	23,353	17,218	40,571
371	47,602	39,764	87,366
372	38,077	86,006	124,083
372	31,043	37,050	68,093
373	13,672	66,053	79,725
374	32,089	51,736	83,825
375	41,740	25,131	66,871
376	150,251	24,648	174,899
377, 9 mos. to Mch. 31	120,235	1,029	121,264
			$948,196 92
Add for difference in returns in 1870			
			$948,288 3
Deduct for difference in returns in 1875			
			$948,285

XIV.

Exports of fish from the United States to the Dominion of Canada and to th
of B. N. America.

	Canada.			Other provinces, B.	
	Foreign.	Domestic.	Total.	Foreign.	Domestic.
1867					
1868					
1869	16, 311	19, 999	36, 310	907	3, 354
1870	38, 228	41, 423	79, 711	1, 476	6, 271
1871	84, 821	33, 564	118, 385	1, 185	4, 513
1872	34, 499	20, 467	54, 966	2, 551	10, 576
1873	63, 527	6, 452	69, 979	2, 526	7, 220
1874	48, 847	30, 286	79, 133	2, 889	1, 803
1875	18, 897	36, 591	55, 488	6, 231	5, 149
1876	24, 074	142, 901	166, 975	574	7, 350
1877, 9 months to March 31					

XV.

PRODUCT OF THE AMERICAN FISHERIES EXCEPT THE WHA

```
1870 ....................................................... 8
1871 ....................................................... 11
1872 ....................................................... 9
1873 ....................................................... 8
1874 ....................................................... 9
1875 ....................................................... 10
1876 ....................................................... 10
Annual Average ........................................... 9
```

XVI.

YIELD AND VALUE OF THE CANADIAN FISHERIES.

The following figures are taken from the annual reports of the Cana Marine and Fisheries.

```
1870 ......Estimate ........................................... $
1871...... do.* ...........................................
1872......Return ...........................................
1873...... do. ........................................... 1
1874...... do. ........................................... 1
1875...... do. ........................................... 1
1876...... do. ........................................... 1
```

* See report for 1871, page 60.

XVII.

Exports of fish from British North America.

```
1870 ................................................... $3, 608
1871 ................................................... 3, 994
1872 ................................................... 4, 348
1873 ................................................... 4, 779
1874 ................................................... 5, 292
1875 ................................................... 5, 380
1876 ................................................... 5, 501
```

MACKEREL.

1875, six months, ended Dec. 31.................................... 475

XVIII.

showing the statistics of the manufacture of menhaden oil and guano in the United States in the years 1873, 1874, 1875, 1876.

	1873.	1874.	1875.	1876.
factories in operation	62	64	60	64
sail-vessels employed	383	283	304	320
steam-vessels "	20	25	39	46
men employed in fisheries	1,009	871		
men employed in factories	1,197	1,567		
number of men employed	2,306	2,438	2,633	2,758
it of capital invested	$2,388,000	$2,500,000	$2,650,000	$2,750,000
fish taken	397,700,000	492,878,000	563,327,000	512,450,000
" " (estimated in barrels)	1,193,100	1,478,634	1,887,767	1,535,885
gallons of oil made	2,214,800	3,372,837	2,681,487	2,992,000
tons of guano made	36,299	50,976	53,625	51,245
gallons of oil held by manufacturers at nd of the year	484,520	648,000	125,000	264,000
tons of guano held by manufacturers at nd of the year	2,700	5,200	1,850	7,275
of oil at 37c	$819,476	$1,247,950	$992,140	$1,107,040
of guano at $11	$399,199	$560,736	$589,875	$503,695
value of manufactured products	$1,218,675	$1,808,686	$1,582,015	$1,670,735

d number of menhaden annually taken on the coast of the United States, estimate 750,000,000.
874 one company, on the coast of New Jersey, put up 30,000 dozen boxes of menhaden in oil, the name of "American sardines," the value of which was, at least, $90,000.
he coast of New England thirty-five decked vessels, and numerous small ones, engage in the bait , the catch of which approximates 100,000 barrels annually, worth from $100,000 to $130,000.

Hamilton Andrews Hill, of Boston, in the County of Suffolk and monwealth of Massachusetts, being duly sworn, do hereby depose declare that I was Secretary of the Boston Board of Trade from to 1873, and of the National Board of Trade of the United States its organization in 1868 to 1873, during which time I was contly engaged in studying the trade of the United States and other tries, and have had much experience in compiling statistics, and I have compiled the series of tables hereto annexed relating to the eries and the trade in fish between the United States and British th America, and that they are correct to the best of my belief. These es are numbered from one (1) to seventeen (17) respectively. Num (1) one to (8) eight and (10) ten and (13) thirteen to (15) fifteen, compiled from the annual volumes on Commerce and Navigation ed by the Bureau of Statistics at Washington, and from special es relating to the Fisheries and the Fish trade, prepared under the ction of Dr. Young, Chief of that Bureau.

umber nine (9), eleven (11) and twelve (12) were compiled from state ts made up at the Custom House in Boston. Number sixteen (16) made up from the Annual Reports of the Canadian Minister of Ma and Fisheries.

umber seventeen (17) is imperfect, and the figures which it contains e been taken from such Canadian authorities as I have had access nd from Official Reports furnished to the State Department at shington by the Consul General of the United States at Montreal, the American Consul at Halifax.

umber two (2) shows the annual importation of Fish and fish pro ts into the United States from British North America, from 1867 to 7. Number seventeen (17) gives partial returns of the Exports of same commodities from British North America to the United States. ill be noticed that in the corresponding years, the values returned he Canadian tables of fish exported to the United States are not the ivalent to those given in the American tables of fish imported from

Canada, as it might seem that they should be. This, however, concordance with what is usually observable in comparing the tra ports of any two countries with each other. The export returns one always vary from the import returns of the other, and usuall value of the former appears as less than that of the latter. The r for this is that the returns of exports are usually made up from manifests and similar documents, often hastily and imperfectly up; but on the arrival of a cargo at its destination, when it becon import, and perhaps liable to duty, it is carefully and specifically rep upon Custom House entries with complete invoice attached. T turns of the authorities in the importing country are generally acc therefore, as showing the true course of trade.

Number four (4) shows the amount saved in duties on fish imp into the United States from Canada, under the provisions of the T of Washington, to average annually for the three years 1874 to about three hundred and forty thousand dollars ($340,000.00.) figures are the result of careful estimates.

Numbers thirteen (13) and fourteen (14) show the American ex of Fish, of both domestic and foreign production to the Dominion o ada, and to the other Provinces of British North America, from to 1877. These returns will be found to vary from the correspo returns of Canadian import, (which do not appear at all in these t very much more than the American returns of imports vary fro Canadian returns of exports, to which reference has already been and for the additional reason that a very large part of the fish sen the United States into Canada, goes by rail, and is not reported at any American Custom House, while it is of course entered at a adian Custom House, as soon as it has crossed the frontier.

Numbers thirteen (13) and fourteen (14) show the value of fish out of bond in the United States to be exported to Canada, an which is shipped by vessels clearing at American ports. I have m with my name the several volumes and returns used in the prepa of these tables, and the same are certified to by Alfred D. F Notary Public, before whom my oath to this affidavit is made.

(Signed)   HAMILTON ANDREWS H

COMMONWEALTH OF MASSACHUSETTS,
Boston, June 8th, 1

SUFFOLK, S. S.

Then personally appeared the above named, Hamilton Andrew and made oath that all the foregoing statements by him subscrib true of his own personal knowledge, except so far as they depend information and belief, and those he believes to be true, before m

(Signed)   ALFRED D. FOSTER,
Notary Pu

II.   .

)ers and Tonnage of Vessels of the United States employed in the
Cod and Mackerel Fisheries from 1866 to 1876, inclusive.

APPENDIX O.

II.

TREASURY DEPARTMENT,
REGISTER'S OFFICE,
Washington, D. C., September 5th, 1877.

RSUANT to Section 886 of the Revised Statutes of the United
is, I, W. P. Titcomb, Acting Register of t he Treasury Department,
ireby certify that the annexed is a correct statement of the tonnage
e United States employed in the cod and mackerel fisheries in the
i indicated, as shown by the records of this office.
W. P. TITCOMB,
Acting Register.

i IT REMEMBERED, That W. P. Titcomb, Esq., who certified the
xed transcript, is now, and was at the time of doing so, Acting
ster of the Treasury of the United States, and that full faith and
t are due to his official attestations.

TESTIMONY WHEREOF, I, John Sherman, Secretary of the Treasury
ie United States, have hereunto subscribed my name, and caused
i affixed the Seal of this Department, at the City of Washington,
fifth day of September, in the year of our Lord 1877.

s.]
JOHN SHERMAN,
Secretary of the Treasury.

'EMENT shewing the number and tonnage of vessels of the United States- employed in
the cod and mackerel fisheries from 1866 to 1876, inclusive:—

Years.	Vessels above 20 tons.		Vessels under 20 tons.		Total.	
	No.	Tons.	No.	Tons.	No.	Tons.
ew adm't)	....	42, 796, 28	....	8, 343, 88	....	51, 140, 16
ld adm't)	....	....	....	503, 88	....	503, 88
....	....	36, 708, 62	....	7, 858, 04	....	44, 566, 66
....	1, 467	74, 762, 92	753	9, 123, 95	1, 220	83, 886, 87
....	1, 093	55, 165, 43	621	7, 538, 82	1, 714	62, 704, 25
....	1, 561	82, 612, 27	731	8, 847, 72	2, 292	91, 459, 99
....	1, 563	82, 902, 43	863	9, 963, 04	2, 426	92, 865, 47
....	1, 486	87, 403, 08	899	10, 143, 48	2, 385	97, 546, 56
....	1, 558	99, 541, 58	895	9, 976, 73	2, 453	109, 518, 31
....	1, 230	68, 489, 62	869	9, 800, 39	2, 099	78, 290, 01
....	1, 259	68, 703, 16	929	11, 503, 52	2, 188	80, 206, 68

III.

Statistics prepared by Mr. Goode.

III.

I, George Brown Goode, of the City of Washington, in the D
Columbia and United States of America, being duly sworn, d
and say that I am the Assistant Curator of the United States
Museum, and for the last eight years I have been engaged in
the natural history and habits of the fishes of the North Atlan'
and during the last six years I have been an assistant to th
States Fish Commission, and during that time it has been pa
employment to collect and arrange statistics as to the amou
fish taken on the coast of the United States,—that the tables b
nexed were compiled from statistics and returns made from t.
ent fishing towns of the Northern Atlantic States to the Unite
Fish Commission, and that the same are true to the best of m.
edge and belief; that the prices stated of the various kinds of
actual prices as paid for said fish in Fulton Market, New Yor]
that the table marked XVIII, (see Part I, Appendix O),
"Table Showing Statistics of the Manufacture of Menhadden
Guano in the United States, in the years 1873, 1874, 1875, 18
also compiled by me from the returns of the United States F
mission, and that the same is true to the best of my knowle
belief.

GEORGE BROWN GO

PROVINCE OF NOVA SCOTIA, }
    COUNTY OF HALIFAX, SS. }

HALIFAX, *October 10t*

Then personally appeared the above-named George Brown Go
made oath that the foregoing affidavit, by him subscribed, is tr
best of his knowledge and belief, before me,

L. G. POWE
Notary

ESTIMATED TOTAL OF AMERICAN FISHERIES FOR 1876.

Consolidated table of sea-fisheries east of Cape May.....................
Lake fisheries in 1872 (Milner)...
Products of whale fishery...

This is exclusive of all river fisheries; of the river fisheri
mon, shad, alewives and striped bass; of the coast fisheries
Delaware Bay (Mullet, Bluefish, Menhadden, etc.); of all th
coast fisheries, (salmon, cod, haddock, etc.); of the shell-fish
clams, etc.); of the Crustaceans (lobsters, crabs, etc.); of sp

		Men.
....		23	88
....		9	36
....		30	90
....		3	12
....		30	210
....	100	—	14
	100	9	14.436

PRODUCTS of Ma

	Pounds.	Price.	Wholesale Value.	Price.	Retail Value.	Price.
			INSHORE FISHERIES, Or Fisheries Conducted from the Sho			
Flounders and Flatfish.................	1, 827, 000*	4	73, 080*	8	146, 160*	(
Halibut (fresh)	....	...	....	...	....	...
" " New York..............	....	...	....	...	....	...
" (cured) Gloucester, &c., flitches	....	...	....	...	....	...
" fins	....	...	....	...	....	...
" napes...........	....	...	....	...	....	...
Cod (fresh) New York	5, 000, 000	5	250, 000	8	400, 000	(
" " Gloucester, Boston, &c.....	20, 000, 000*	3	600, 000	5	1, 000, 000	4
" cured	28, 4±0, 000	....				1
" roes.................................	80, 000	1	800	2¼	1, 800	1
Tomcod..................................	100, 000	3	3, 000	8	8, 000	²
Cunner	250, 000	3	7, 500	5	12, 500	4
Tautog	615, 550	8	49, 244	15	92, 332	11
Mackerel (fresh)..........................	3, 481, 000	8	278, 480	15	522, 150	11
" cured ...						
Spanish Mackerel........................	105, 000	25	26, 250	30	31, 500	27
Bonito	2, 200, 000	5	110, 000	8	176, 000	(
Pompano	5, 000	60	3, 000	100	5, 000	8(
Swordfish.................................	1, 500, 000	7	105, 000	15	225, 000	11
Butterfish, Whiting, White Perch......	50, 000	4	2, 000	8	4, 000	(
Sea Robins...............................	90, 000	2	1, 800	3	2, 700	2
Squeteague	1, 727, 600	6	103, 656	10	172, 760	8
Kingfish..................................	10, 000	15	1, 500	25	2, 500	20
Spot and Croaker	75, 000	5	3, 750	10	7, 500	7
Sheepshead	75, 000	15	11, 250	20	15, 000	17
Scup	7, 760, 000	05	388, 000	8	620, 800	6
Sea Bass	598, 500	10	59, 850	15	89, 775	18
Striped Bass	123, 200	15	18, 480	20	24, 640	17
Bluefish..................................	7, 068, 000	4	282, 720	8	565, 440	6
Smelt	400, 000	10	40, 000	15	60, 000	18
Menhaden	224, 834, 000					
Eels	250, 000	12	30, 000	18	45, 000	15
Sturgeon.................................	75, 000	5	3, 750	10	7, 500	
Sea Shad.................................	3, 770, 200	5	188, 510	7½	282, 765	
Salmon	40, 100					
Alewife...................................	7, 385, 000	½	36, 925	1	73, 8±0	
Herring	1, 604, 800	2	32, 096	4	64, 192	
" (cured)	....					
	319, 579, 950		$2, 710, 641		$4, 658, 864	
Ratio to mile of coast line....... (1, 112)	287, 392	....		....		

N. B.—The cured cod have been restored to their green weight (three times as much
mackerel have been restored to their green weight (one-sixth additional).

hern Atlantic States.

ds.	Price	Wholes'le Value.	Price	Retail Value.	Price	Mean Value.	Aggregate of Weights.	Aggregate of Values.	
		OFFSHORE FISHERIES, belies Conducted in large vessels, principally over Twenty Tons.							
							1, 827, 000	109, 620	
000	4	493, 560	15	1, 850, 850	9½	1, 172, 205	....	1, 172, 205	
	10	100, 000	15	150, 000	12½	125, 000	....	125, 000	
	2	169, 520	...	302, 500	...	236, 010	....	236, 010	$1, 546, 240
	5½	10, 500	7½	15, 000	6½	12, 750	....	12, 750	
C00	2½	250	3	300	2½	275	22, 025, 000	275	
	...	....	...	....	...	....		325, 000	
	...	....	...	....	...	....		800, 000	
700	...	....	...	....	...	3, 319, 182	214, 221, 700	3, 698, 915*	
	1	200	2¼	450	1⅛	325	100. 000	1, 625	
	...	....	...	....	...	....	100, 000	5, 500	
	...	....	...	....	...	....	250, 000	10, C00	
	...	....	...	....	...	....	615. 550	70, 788	
000	8	209, 200	15	392, 250	11¼	300, 725	6, 096, 000	701, 040	
900	...	....	...	....	...	....	35, 632, 900	1, 674, 222*	
	...	....	...	....	...	....	105, 000	28, 875	
	...	....	...	....	...	....	2, 200, 000	143, 000	
	...	....	...	....	...	....	5, 000	4, 000	
	...	....	...	....	...	....	1, 500, 000	165, 000	
	...	....	...	....	...	....	50, 000	3, 000	
	...	....	...	....	...	....	90, 000	2, 250	
	...	....	...	....	...	....	1, 727, 600	138, 208	
	...	....	...	....	...	....	10, 000	2, 000	
	...	....	...	....	...	....	75, 000	5, 625	
	...	....	...	....	...	....	75, 000	13, 125.	
	...	....	...	....	...	....	7, 760, 000	504, 400	
	...	....	...	....	...	....	598, 500	74, 812	
	...	....	...	....	...	....	123, 200	21, 560	
	...	....	...	....	...	....	7, 068, 000	424, 080	
	...	....	...	....	...	....	400, 000	50, 000	
500	...	....	• ..	....	...	....	703, 746, 500	1, 657, 790†	
	...	....	...	....	...	....	250, 000	37, 500	
	...	....	...	....	...	....	75, 000	5, 625	
	...	....	...	....	...	....	3, 770, 200	235, 637	
	...	....	...	....	...	....	40, 100	8, 020	
	...	....	...	....	...	....	7, 385, 000	55, 387	
	...	....	...	....	...	....	5, 604, 800 }	48, 144	
	...	....	...	....	...	....	22, 328, 700 }	459, 833*	
							1, 045, 855, 750	$13, 030, 821	
	...	....	...	....	...	....	940, 510	$11, 718	

* From Report of Bureau of Statistics.   † From official reports.

CUSTOM-HOUSE, BOSTON, ?
Collector's Office, October

Statement of the importations of mackerel into the port of Boston, January 1st, 18 tember 30th, 1877.

From.	Nova Scotia and New Brunswick.		Prince Edwar
	Bbls.	Value.	Bbls.
1877 January	3,867	$42,521 00	
February	858	7,685 00	
March	587½	5,720 00	
April	5½	39 00	
May	517¼	3,188 00	
June	4,730	28,696 00	60
July	5,972½	31,235 00	611
August	6,151½	44,375 00	7,517
September	13,886½	114,952 00	6,361½
	36,576	$278,341 00	14,549½

No importations of mackerel from Newfoundland.

BOSTON CUSTOM-H
Collec:or's Office, Octobe

I hereby certify the foregoing statements to be true, as appearing upon the records of thi
[L. S.]   J. M. FISKI
Asst. Dept.

IV.

Statement taken from the Books of Gloucester Firms,—produce Babson,—filed by Mr. Foster on October 24, 1877, and objected British Counsel as not being properly verified, and therefore ina as evidence, but admitted by Commissioners for what it may be

I, BENJ. F. BLATCHFORD, an Inspector of Customs, for trict of Gloucester, on oath, do depose and say, that at the re Hon. Dwight Foster, I visited the fishing firms of this city, quested from them a statement, *taken from their books,* of the n vessels employed in the Bay of St. Lawrence mackerel fishe the number of Bay mackerel packed by them each year, from 1877. Also the same statistics in regard to the United Sta mackerel fishery, and annexed I send a true copy of their se ports made to me marked A, B, &c.

BENJ. F. BLATCHF

MASSACHUSETTS, ESSEX, SS.

Personally appeared, said Blatchford, who made oath to the the above affidavit. Before me,

AARON PARSON
Justice of the

David Low & Co.'s statement.

Years.	No. of vessels at bay.	No. of vessels off shore.	Bbls. of bay mackerel packed.	Bbls. of shore mackerel packed.	Total.
....	5	3	1,249	1,379	2,628
....	4	2	1,068	929	1,997
....	6	4	917	835	1,752
....	9	8	1,867	2,463	4,330
....	7	7	1,203	3,610	4,813
....	4	6	1,096	2,726	3,822
....	3	4	460	1,493	1,953
....	8	3	1,944	1,338	3,282
....	4	3	1,328	2,977	4,305
....	1	4	205	2,258	2,463
....	0	4	None ...	4,775	4,775
....	2	4	310	1,983	2,293 to Oct. 18

ified to as correct. Before me this 19th Oct., 1877.

ADDISON CARTER,
Special D. C.

A.—*Leighton & Co.'s statement.*

They fit 18 vessels.

Years.	No. of vessels at bay.	No. of vessels off shore.	Bbls. of bay mackerel.	Bbls. of shore mackerel.
....	5	5	1,330	953
....	7	9	2,075	1,945
....	6	6	1,616	2,474
....	10	6	3,105	2,177
....	6	4	2,465	1,917
....	11	5	4,657	1,634
....	3	5	1,345	4,180
....	1	4	308	1,450
....	1	5	134	5,589
....	5	10	107	1,604
	55	59	17,142	24,620

B.—*Pettengell & Cunningham's statement.*

They fit 6 vessels.

Years.	No. of vessels in bay.	No. of vessels off shore.	Bbls. of bay mackerel.	Bbls. of shore mackerel.
....	6	4	1,200	1,800
	4	4	900	850

C.—*Wm. Parsons, 2d, & Co.'s statement.*

They fit 14 vessels.

Years	No. of vessels in bay of St. Lawrence.	No. of vessels off shore U. S.	No. of bbls. of bay mackerel.
1866	10	1	3,087
1867	9	2	2,676
1868	6	2	1,263
1869	6	2	1,109
1870	5	5	1,058
1871	4	4	907
1872	2	2	562
1873	4	1	952
1874	1	3	430
1875	....	3	....
1876	....	4	....
1877	....	0	....

D.—*Alfred Mansfield's statement.*

They fit 9 vessels.

Years.	No. of vessels in bay.	No. of vessels off shore.	Bbls. of bay mackerel.
1866	1	9	105
1867	3	10	570
1868	1	11	
1869	0	10	None..
1870	0	13	None..
1871	2	7	28
1872	0	7	None..
1873	5	4	1,12
1874	3	5	1,23
1875	1	4	8
1876	0	2	None..
1877	2	2	....

E.—*B. Maddock's statement.*

[They fit 10 vessels.]

Years.	No. of vessels in bay.	No. of vessels off shore.	Bbls. of bay mackerel.
1866	....	....	....
1867	10	2	3,20
1868	7	10	1,00
1869	5	6	1,80
1870	4	5	1,50
1871	8	5	2,00
1872	2	4	50
1873	5	2	1,50
1874	1	2	11
1875	0	2	None..
1876	0	2	None..
1877	3	1	None date.

F.—*D. C. & H. Babson's statement.*

[Thèy fit 13 vessels.]

Years.	No. of vessels in bay.	No. of vessels off shore.	Bbls. of bay mackerel.	Bbls. of shore mackerel.
....	9	1	3, 246	356
....	6	3	1, 629	834
....	3	5	475	916
....	6	3	964	587
....	3	8	500	3, 115
....	3	6	887	1, 429
....	1	3	380	1, 005
....	4	3	1, 110	1, 395
....	1	5	270	2, 043
....	3	5	642	1, 288
....	0	6	....	3, 977
....	1	4	138	679

G.—*Statement of Perkins Brothers.*

[They fit 9 vessels.]

Years.	No. of vessels in bay.	No. of vessels off shore.	No. of bbls. of bay mackerel.	No. of bbls. of shore mackerel.
....	.....	.....	.....	.....
....	.....	.....	.....	.....
....	.....	.....	.....	.....
....	1	6	203	3, 712
....	5	6	326	2, 350
....	2	3	409	440
....	3	4	435	1, 315
....	3	4	1, 035	2, 596
....	1	3	205	1, 082
....	3	2	211	1, 655
....	0	2	None....	520

H.—*Statement of Hardy & McKenzie.*

[They fit 6 vessels.]

Years.	vessels in bay.	vessels off hore.	of bay ckerel.	of shore ckerel.

I.—*Statement of William C. Wonson.*

[He fits 8 vessels.]

Years.	No. of vessels in bay.	No. of vessels off shore.
1866	0	4
1867	0	3
1868	0	2
1869	2	4
1870	0	5
1871	0	5
1872	3	4
1873	2	2
1874	0	0
1875	0	0
1876	0	2
1877	0	2

J.—*Statement of George Sayward.*

[He fits 5 vessels.]

Years.	No. of vessels in bay.	No. of vessels off shore.
1866	2	1
1867	2	1
1868	3	2
1869	3	0
1870	1	1
1871	2	3
1872	1	1
1873	2	0
1874	2	0
1875	1	0
1876	0	0
1877	1	0

K.—*Statement of Daniel Sayward.*

[He fits 4 vessels.]

Years.	No. of vessels in bay.	No. of vessels off shore.
1866	2	3
1867	4	2
1868	3	4
1869	5	3
1870	3	6
1871	6	3
1872	4	3
1873	2	2
1874	2	2
1875	1	1
1876	0	0
1877	2	0

L.—*Statement of Frederick G. Wonson.*

[He fits 11 vessels.]

Years.	No. of vessels in bay.	No. of vessels off shore.	bls. m rel. b	Bbls. of shore mackerel.
....	4	5		1,156
....	4	9		1,391
....	6	6		1,202
....	5	7	1,411	1,746
....	5	8	740	3,883
....	6	8		4,460
....	2	7		3,168
....	4	6		3,332
....	3	12		7,270
....	2	10		3,129
....	0	12		6,213
....	1	11	....	....

M.—*Statement of Samuel Haskell.*

[He fits 5 vessels]

Years.	No. of vessels in bay.	No. of vessels off shore.	Bbls. of bay mackerel.	Bbls. of shore mackerel.
....	0	0	0	0
....	0	0	0	0
....	2	3	550	339
....	1	2	145	435
....	2	3	335	604
....	2	3	540	675
....	0	3	0	1,294
....	4	1	672	512
....	2	2	790	1,143
....	0	1	0	710
....	0	1	0	1,226
....	1	1	0	308

N.—*Statement of Smith & Oakes.*

[They fit 7 vessels.]

Years.	No. of vessels in bay.	No. of vessels off shore.	Bbls. of bay mackerel.	Bbls. of shore mackerel.
....	3	2	500	580

O.—*Statement of Samuel Lane & Bro.*

[They fit 8 vessels.]

Years.	No. of vessels in bay.	No. of vessels off shore.	Bbls. of bay.
1866	3	......	
1867	4	1	
1868	4	0	
1869	3	2	
1870	0	3	
1871	1	3	
1872	2	2	
1873	4	1	1
1874	3	2	1
1875	3	3	
1876	0	3	
1877	3	3	

P.—*Statement of Shute & Merchant.*

[They fit 11 vessels.]

Years.	No. of vessels in bay.	No. of vessels off shore.	Bbls. of bay.
1867	11	3	3
1868	3	8	
1869	6	5	1
1870	2	8	
1871	3	6	1
1872	3	5	1
1873	4	5	1
1874	2	6	1
1875	1	6	
1876	1	4	
1877	1	4	Not riv
	37	60	6

Q.—*Statement of Walen & Allen.*

[They fit 13 vessels.]

Years.	No. of vessels in bay.	No. of vessels off shore.	Bbls. of bay.
1870	1	4	
1871	3	4	
1872	0	4	
1873	2	2	
1874	1	3	
1875	1	2	
1876	1	2	
1877	0	3	
	9	24	

R.—*Statement of Dennis & Ayer.*

[They fit 12 vessels.]

Years.	No. of vessels in bay.	No. of vessels off shore.	Bbls. of bay mackerel.	Bbls. of shore mackerel.
....	13	8	5,370	733
....	13	6	3,393	307
....	12	14	1,873	1,758
....	11	13	2,372	1,914
....	12	14	2,559	2,466
....	8	12	2,585	2,491
....	8	5	2,287	1,150
....	8	8	2,504	1,199
....	7	6	2,455	1,519
....	1	4	116	2,210
....	1	5	136	3,251
....	0	4	0	433

S.—*Joseph O. Procter's statement.*

Years.	Vessels in bay fishing.	Vessels shore fishing.	Bbls. of bay mackerel.	Barrels shore.	Total.
....	7	1	3,127	128	3,255
....	7	3	1,977	403	2,380
....	8	2	1,099	192	1,291
....	3	5	637	1,535	2,172
....	2	7	458	3,392	3,850
....	3	8	712	2,138	2,850
....	5	3	1,324	807	2,131
....	9	2	2,701	1,188	3,889
....	7	2	2,456	359	2,815
....	5	1	815	231	1,046
....	1	1	190	445	635
....	1	1	....	167	....

T.—*Statement of James G. Tarr & Bro.*

Years.	No. of vessels in bay.	No. of vessels off shore.	Bbls. of bay mackerel.	Bbls. of shore mackerel.
....	9	3	2,913	758
....	5	4	1,312	956

U.—Statement of Clark & Somes.

Years.	No. of vessels in bay.	No. of vessels off shore.	Bbls. of hav
1866	No data. {	....	....
1867		....	....
1868		....	....
1869		....	....
1870		....	....
1871	6	2	i
1872	9	2	i
1873	7	2	i
1874	4	1	
1875	0	2	....
1876	1	4	
1877	1	2	

CLARK &

V.

Years.	No. of vessels in bay.	No. of vessels off shore.	hav
1866	8	3	
1867	9	4	
1868	8	4	
1869	4	8	
1870	4	10	
1871	1	12	
1872	1	4	
1873	1	5	
1874	1	8	
1875	....	9	....
1876	....	10	....
1877	2	5	....
	39	82	1

I certify that the above is a true statement from the books of Joseph Friend and
A. CAR

W.—Statement of George Norwood & Son.

Years.	No. of vessels in bay.	No. of vessels off shore.	
1866	....	....	...
1867	....	....	...
1868	....	....	...
1869	....	....	...
1870	....	....	...
1871	4	9	...
1872	2	5	...
1873	5	2	...
1874	....	4	...
1875	....	3	...
1876	....	3	...
1877	....	....	...

GEO. NOR

X.—*Statement of George Friend & Co.*

Years.	No. of vessels in bay.	No. of vessels off shore.	Bbls. of bay mackerel.	Bbls. of shore mackerel.
....	0	0	0	0
....	0	0	0	0
....	0	0	0	0
....	0	0	0	0
....		4	....	1,567
....	3	5	622	2,173
....	2	3	506	971
....	Not in business.			
....				
....				
....				

GEORGE FRIEND & CO.,
By JOHN J SOMES.

Y.—*Statement of Cunningham & Thompson.*

They fit 11 vessels.

Years.	No. of vessels in bay.	No. of vessels off shore.	Bbls. of bay mackerel.	Bbls. of shore mackerel.
....	0	1	No return	1,100
....	1	2	No return	500

CUNNINGHAM & THOMPSON.

:ESTER, Oct. 16, 1876.

Z.—*Statement of George Dennis & Co.*

Years.	No. of vessels in bay.	No. of vessels off shore.	Bbls. of bay mackerel.	Bbls. of shore mackerel.
....	Not in business.			
....				
....				
....				
....	1	1	93	203
....	2	....	368	....
....	1	3	270	1,712

AA.

Years.	No. of vessels in bay.	No. of vessels off shore.
1866	9	1
1867	8	2
1868	5	1
1869	4	2
1870	5	1
1871	5	0
1872	4	1
1873	3	1
1874	4	5
1875	1	4
1876	0	5
1877	4	{ 5 early. 3 since Sept. 10th. }

The above does not include fresh mackerel sold, which would probably amount to s
taken on this shore, but includes salt sold out of pickle, which accounts for the differe
and our inspection returns

ROW1

BB.—*Statement of Leonard Walen.*

Fits 5 vessels.

Years.	No. of bbls. of bay mackerel.	No. of bbls. of shore mackerel.
1866	215	1,100
1867	182	940
1868	210	1,300
1869	None	....
1870	None	....
1871	480	880
1872	None	....
1873	None	....
1874	200	1,600
1875	None	....
1876	170	860
1877	159	900

Oct. 17, 1877.

LEON

CC.—*Statement of William S. Wonson.*

Years.	No. of vessels in bay.	No. of vessels off shore.	Bbls. of bay mackerel.	Bbls. of shore mackerel.
....	0	0	....	....
....	0	6	....	767
....	2	4	972	490
....	2	7	841	1,061
....	1	4	155	1,132
....	3	3	547	363
....	0	1	....	261
....	2	7	923	927
....	2	3	885	266
....	1	1	156	450
....	0	7	....	2,873
....	1	6	9	1,200

WM. S WONSON.

V.

ment of Mackerel inspected at Portsmouth and Newcastle for the years 1869 to 1877, inclusive.

V.

.CKEREL INSPECTED AT PORTSMOUTH AND NEWCASTLE, N. H.

ending May 1, 1869......................................	157 Barrels.
" " 1870..............................	3,700 "
" " 1871..............................	2,071 "
" " 1872..............................	1,878 "
" " 1873..............................	2,398 "
" 1874..............................	5,519 "
" " 1875..................:...........	3,415 "
" " 1876..............................	5,351 "
" " 1877..........:..................	643 "

9) 25,132

Average 2,792

E OF NEW HAMPSHIRE,
  Secretary's Office, Concord, Sept. 4, 1877.
ereby certify that the above statement is taken from the Reports
spection made to His Excellency the Governor by the several In-
ors for the years therein named.
testimony whereof, I have hereunto subscribed my official signa-
and affixed the Seal of the State.

A. B. THOMPSON,
Secretary of State.

VI.

STATE OF MAINE
OFFICE OF SECRETARY OF S?

I hereby certify, that the following is a correct summary of th
Returns of the Inspector General of Fish for the State of Main
several years hereafter written, so far as relates to mackerel j
by him, viz. :

1866	45,407	barrels.	1870	51,(	
1867	33,676	do.	1871	48,	
1868	26,876	do.	1872	22,	
1869	36,031	do.	1873	22,	

No return was made for the year 1874.

In testimony whereof, I have caused the seal of the State t(
unto affixed. Given under my hand· at Augusta, this ninth d
·tober, in the year of our Lord, one thousand eight hundred anc
seven, and in the one hundred and second year of the Indepe1
the United States of America.

S. J. CHADBOURN
Secretary o

VII.

Summary of Returns of Mackerel inspected in the State of N
setts for several years past.

A.—Analysis of reports of inspectors of mackerel for the Commonwealth of Massachusetts, showing the number of barrels inspected each year at each of the undermentioned districts.

	Boston.	Gloucester.	Newburyport.	Rockport.	Hingham.	Cohasset.	Barnstable.	Yarmouth.	Dennis.	Harwich.	Chatham.	Wellfleet.	Truro.	Provincetown.	Nantucket & Dartmouth.	Other places.	Total.
1850	52,856	49,993	22,929	3,916	14,536	15,346	6,065	5,891	20,395	14,839	5,764	17,615	8,570	27,865		5,062	242,573
1851	40,738	81,627	21,203	9,240	23,863	22,712	6,182	7,537	16,220	21,835	9,923	33,477	10,985	20,488		4,642	399,242
1852	39,893	48,013	11,906	5,345	13,134	11,017	3,900	3,225	10,290	12,471	5,769	11,367	2,540	18,264		1,184	198,198
1853	33,398	37,891	10,393	4,523	6,874	7,603	2,484	1,050	6,664	7,464	2,039	8,723	298	8,357		1,119	133,340
1854	28,600	41,332		3,278	5,327	7,592	580	1,192	8,731	8,907	2,365	13,018	250	8,731		139	135,350
1855	43,987	73,135	8,071	3,740	5,451	8,773	447	1,399	8,366	11,736	3,156	20,838	5,511	6,966		769	212,015
1856	54,140	68,094	13,940	6,513	9,014	7,954				10,030	4,413	20,595	2,339	9,528		469	214,312
1857			12,131														168,706
1858	35,547	56,489	9,089	4,153	3,007	3,130		398	2,112	3,719	1,904	5,335	1,644	5,985		86	131,692
1859	32,923	59,664	6,852	3,004	3,500	2,344		291	2,608	3,196	508	7,758	1,119	5,877		358	99,716
1860	32,128	90,516	6,405	5,562	11,774	11,940		653	7,094	9,890	4,514	27,250	986	19,350		302	235,706
1861	19,471	116,538	7,180	4,990	9,925	9,273		407	7,605	10,917	3,458	14,118	220	16,596		982	194,984
1862	29,324	153,892	7,378	4,100	11,396	11,454		435	11,077	10,342	6,455	26,431		22,753			960,865
1863	30,550	154,938	6,982	5,671	14,344	15,852			10,658	13,666	6,946	27,086		25,337		1,218	306,943
1864	23,356	141,576	7,608	4,970	4,970	9,028			6,009	6,711	7,049	28,775	16	17,923		1,118	974,357
1865	38,399	112,856	8,543	5,746	5,701	8,722			4,009	5,893	4,131	17,536		17,403	895		956,996
1866	46,133	103,918	7,460	7,363	5,411	7,434		92	3,391	6,530	2,946	15,834		14,893	2,064	1,206	231,510
18..	18,441	75,517	5,196	5,260	5,915	9,758			3,489	5,702	2,314	17,592		17,592	3,908	2,901	
1868	30,289					4,990			5,219	7,149	2,456	11,356		20,856	2,977	15	180,056
1869	34,135	93,127	6,209	5,962	6,526	9,632			7,773	9,853	3,659	27,375		23,998	3,088	2,371	324,901
1870	42,766	129,595	7,395	6,800	7,200	10,766			7,461	17,642	8,148	41,353		22,889	3,067	4,479	318,531
1871	43,016	107,009	6,146	6,941	2,288	5,518			8,927	11,996	6,908	32,871		25,375	731	4,391	259,417
1872	35,455	67,396	3,621	3,679	1,651	5,016			5,816	10,516	3,413	23,740		16,719	1,092	3,733	181,957
1873	36,505	63,439	3,058	3,084	1,200	4,145			4,187	12,167	3,988	23,877		15,996	7	3,989	185,748
1874	25,572	118,313	2,202	4,196	1,457	4,268			4,698	16,802	4,544	34,833		12,030	19	3,561	258,380
1875	36,364	51,040	3,981	1,742		4,968			1,526	10,340	1,802	18,406		10,189		2,978	130,064
1 56		95,421		5,610		6,988			2,175	13,934	4,884	38,381		16,931		1,759	225,941

212 F

B.—*Statement showing the number of barrels of each quality of mackerel, (being*
United States vessels,) submitted annually for inspection within the Commonwealth
chusetts, from 1850 to 1876.

Years.	No. 1 barrels.	No. 2 barrels.	No. 3 barrels.	No. 4 barrels
1850	88, 401	44, 909	87, 604	21, 65
1851	90, 763	102, 467	135, 598	41
1852	84, 026	67, 075	44, 815	2, 21
1853	49, 016	24, 583	39, 897	19, 84
1854	39, 595	46, 242	55, 133	3, 38
1855	29, 202	91, 122	90, 199	1, 45
1856	89, 333	76, 819	47, 981	17
1857	84, 519	45, 218	38, 257	71
1858	75, 347	21, 930	32, 333	1, 85
1859	61, 330	12, 060	22, 207	11
1860	58, 828	122, 837	50, 579	3, 44
1861	70, 877	100, 286	22, 486	63
1862	81, 903	78, 388	100, 011	56
1863	67, 985	136, 075	102, 602	26
1864	103, 383	137, 747	32, 213	1
1865	153, 923	63, 562	39, 266	24
1866	150, 329	36, 319	44, 784	26
1867	123, 616	46, 284	41, 189	45
1868	93, 091	42, 262	44, 077	65
1869	72, 914	92, 019	65, 717	3, 53
1870	66, 046	189, 423	63, 019	3
1871	105, 187	85, 867	68, 323	4
1872	71, 867	54, 371	55, 603	11
1873	83, 687	63, 889	37, 795	37
1874	112, 972	71, 442	73, 966	....
1875	33, 106	19, 270	73, 426	4, 26
1876	30, 869	96, 773	93, 481	4, 81

C.—*Statement showing the number of barrels of each quality of mackerel, (bein*
of other than United States vessels,) submitted annually for reinspection within t
wealth of Massachusetts, from 1850 to 1876.

Years.	Barrels No. 1.	Barrels No. 2.	Barrels No. 3.	Barre No. 4
1850	11, 143	8, 356	2, 069	
1851	5, 722	6, 192	1, 553	....
1852	9, 420	7, 048	3, 304	....
1853	5, 173	3, 562	2, 927	....
1854	Not	given.		
1855	"	"		
1856	"	"		
1857	"	"		
1858	"	"		
1859	14, 681	7, 242	10, 083	2,
1860	Not	given.		
1861	6, 062	6, 420	3, 143	
1862	7, 414	5, 959	3, 393	
1863	9, 508	7, 333	5, 580	
1864	13, 046	11, 729	7, 537	
1865	24, 272	19, 304	7, 727	
1866	14, 654	4, 986	4, 491	..
1867	49, 007	11, 063	6, 712	
1868	14, 327	3, 627	2, 122	
1869	9, 927	9, 052	6, 713	
1870	9, 206	17, 526	7, 149	..
1871	11, 051	13, 047	6, 692	..
1872	15, 757	17, 189	15, 734	..
1873	12, 933	14, 813	9, 592	..
1874	19, 887	15, 211	10, 574	..
1875	14, 444	16, 215	13, 112	
1876	11, 257	13, 934	11, 835	

NOTE.—The re-inspection of foreign mackerel is confined mainly to Boston

D.

1851.

llowing statistical information is obtained through the returns
that purpose by the deputy inspector of fish to the inspector-
f fish for the Commonwealth of Massachusetts, for the year 1851,
efore may be relied upon as being correct, showing the extent
litics of the mackerel fishery; the number of vessels owned in
usetts and in other States engaged in that branch of industry,
we packed their fish in this State; the amount of tonnage, and
ber of men and boys employed on board those vessels, viz:

Where owned.	No. of vessels.	Tonnage.	Men and boys.
....	7	596	85
....	12	761	97
....	28	1,918	339
....	4	259	47
l...	2	74	14
....	19	1,346	230
....	44	2,885	561
....	1	117	16
....	47	3,096	585
....	3	170	23
....	1	71	10
....	241	13,639	2,326
....	48	3,231	577
....	37	2,492	491
....	4	187	33
....	1	45	8
....	1	30	5
ineyard	6	421	65
....	3	168	30
rt...	67	4,343	707
....	5	336	54
....	6	561	65
rn	61	4,322	688
....	42	1,537	283
....	1	80	9
....	13	715	119
..*..	4	305	48
....	52	3,626	581
....	79	5,411	852
....	14	990	169
in Massachusetts...	853	53,712	9,117
....	47	3,019	446
hire..	8	515	84
d...	7	479	71
;...	23	1,551	255
....	2	141	25
	940	59,417	9,998

1851.

int of mackerel inspected in Massachusetts in 1851 in barrels ·············   329,242
ere caught at Bay Chaleurs or in British waters······················   140,906
hores of the United States or in American waters·····················   188,336

           329,242

                    CHAS. MAYO,
d)   *Inspector-General of Fish.*

1852.

int of mackerel inspected in Massachusetts in 1852 ··············· 198,127 barrels.
nount were caught in the Bay of St Lawrence in American ves·   38,000
American waters..   160,127

           198,127

              CHARLES MAYO,
d)   *Inspector-General of Fish.*

E.

Statement of the vessels owned in Massachusetts, employed in the mackerel fi
1853.

Where owned.	No. of vessels.	T
Boston	8	
Beverly	12	
Barnstable	30	
Brewster	4	
Charlestown	2	
Cohasset	37	
Chatham	18	
Dartmouth	1	
Dennis	48	
Eastham	3	
Essex	1	
Gloucester	259	
Harwich	60	
Hingham	30	
Lynn	6	
Manchester	1	
Marblehead	1	
Martha's Vineyard	6	
Nantucket	3	
Newburyport	57	
Orleans	5	
Plymouth	6	
Provincetown	65	
Rockport	50	
Salem	1	
Scituate	7	
Salisbury	4	
Truro	49	
Wellfleet	86	
Yarmouth	15	

(Signed)　　　　　　　　　　　　　　　　PAYNE G.
　　　　　　　　　　　　　　　　　　　　　　I.

APPENDIX P.

No. 1.

In the Court of Vice Admiralty.

gment of His Honor Judge Hazen in the case of the "White Fawn."

he following is a copy of the decision recently pronounced by His Honor
e Hazen in this case.

the last sitting of this Court, Mr. Tuck, B. C., Proctor for the
n, applied, on behalf of Sir John A. McDonald, the Attorney-Gen-
of the Dominion, for a monition, calling upon the owners of the
oner and her cargo, to show cause why the *White Fawn* and the
les above enumerated with her tackle, etc., should not be consid-
as forfeited to the Crown for a violation of the Imperial Statute 59,
rge III., Cap. 38, and the Dominion Statutes 31 Vic., Cap. 61, and
'ic., Cap. 15.

he *White Fawn*, as it appears from her papers, was a new vessel of
ons, and registered at Gloucester, Massachusetts, in 1870, and owned
qual shares by Messrs. Somes, Friend, and Smith, of that place;
hat she was duly licensed for one year, to be employed in the Coast-
Trade and Fisheries, under the laws of the United States;
hat by her "Fishery Shipping Paper," signed by the master and ten
i, the usual agreement was entered into for pursuing the Cod and
er Fisheries, with minute provisions for the division of the profits
ing the owners, skipper, and crew. These papers and other docu-
its found on board, are all in perfect order, and not the slightest sus-
on can be thrown upon them. The Seamen's Articles are dated 19th
'ember, 1870:—On the 24th Nov., 1870, she arrived at Head Harbor,
aall Bay in the eastern end of Campobello, in the county of Char-
e, in this Province.

aptain Betts, a Fishery Officer, in command of the *Water Lily*, a ves-
in the service of the Dominion, states that on the 25th November he
lying with his vessel *at* Head Harbor. Several other vessels, and
ing them the *White Fawn*, were lying *in* the harbor; that he went
board the *White Fawn:* He states a number of particulars respect-
the vessel from her papers, and adds that the said vessel, *White*
in, had arrived at Head Harbor on the 24th Nov., and had been
aged purchasing fresh herrings, to be used as bait in trawl fish-
; that there were on board about 5,000 herrings, which had been
iined and taken on board at Head Harbor; also 15 tons of ice, and
the materials and appliances for trawl fishing, and that the master
itted to him that the herring had been obtained at Head Harbor by
. for the purpose of being used as bait for fishing. There are then
ie remarks as to the master being deceived as to the fact of the cut-
being in the neighborhood, which are not material; and, that de-
ent further understood that persons had been employed at Head
'hour to catch the herring for him; that he seized the schooner on the
i, [sic], and arrived with her the same evening at St. John, and de-
red her on the next day to the Collector of the Customs.

'o reason is given for the delay which has taken place of more than

two months in proceeding against the vessel, which was sei
alleged by Captain Betts, for a violation of the terms of the Con
and the Laws of Canada; her voyage was broken up, and h
dispersed at the time of the seizure.

By the Imperial Statute, 59 George III., cap. 38, it is declared
any foreign vessel, or person on board thereof, " shall be foun
fishing, or to have been fishing, or preparing to fish within s
tance (three marine miles) of the coast, such vessel and cargo s
forfeited."

The Dominion Statute, 31 Vic., Cap. 61, as amended by 33 Vi
15, enacts: " If such foreign vessel is found fishing, or preparing
or to have been fishing in British waters, within three marine
the coast, such vessel, her tackle, etc., and cargo, shall be forfei

The *White Fawn* was a foreign vessel in British waters;
within one of the Counties of this Province when she was seizec
not alleged that she is subject to forfeiture for having enteree
Harbour for other purposes than shelter or obtaining wood anc
Under Section III, of the Imperial Act, no forfeiture but a pen:
be inflicted for such entry. Nor is it alleged that she committ
infraction of the Customs or Revenue Laws. It is not stated t
had fished within the prescribed limits, or had been found fish
that she was "preparing to fish," having bought bait (an ar
doubt very material if not necessary for successful fishing) fr
inhabitants of Campobello. Assuming that the fact of such p
establishes a "preparing to fish" under the Statutes (which I
admit), I think, before a forfeiture could be incurred, it must b(
that the preparations were for an illegal fishing in British
hence, for aught which appears, the intention of the Master m:
been to prosecuting his fishing outside of the three-mile limit
formity with the Statutes; and it is not for the court to impu
or an intention to infringe the provisions of our statutes to any
British or foreign, in the absence of evidence of such fraud.
right, in common with all other persons, to pass with his vessel
the three miles, from our coast to the fishing grounds outside, '
might lawfully use, and, as I have already stated, there is no
of any intention to fish before he reached such grounds.

The construction sought to be put upon the statutes by th
officers would appear to be thus:—"A foreign vessel, being in
waters and purchasing from a British subject any article wh
be used in prosecuting the fisheries, without its being shown t
article is to be used in illegal fishing in British waters, is liab
feiture as preparing to fish in British waters."

I cannot adopt such a construction. I think it harsh and un
ble, and not warranted by the words of the statutes. It woul(
a foreign vessel, which might be of great value, as in the pres
to forfeiture, with her cargo and outfits, for purchasing (while
pursuing her voyage in British waters, as she lawfully might d(
three miles of our coast) of a British subject any article, howe\
in value (a cod-line or net for instance) without its being sh(
there was any intention of using such articles in illegal fishing i
waters before she reached the fishing ground to which she migh
resort for fishing under the terms of the Statutes.

I construe the Statutes simply thus:—If a foreign vessel is fo
having taken fish; 2nd, fishing, although no fish have been tak
" preparing to fish," (i. e.), with her crew arranging her nets, 1
fishing tackle for fishing, though not actually applied to fi

British waters, in either of those cases specified in the statutes the forfeiture attaches.

I think the words "preparing to fish" were introduced for the purpose of preventing the escape of a foreign vessel which, though with intent of illegal fishing in British waters, had not taken fish or engaged in fishing by setting nets and lines, but was seized in the very act of putting out her lines, nets, etc., into the water, and so preparing to fish. Without these a vessel so situated would escape seizure, inasmuch as the crew had neither caught fish nor been found fishing.

Taking this view of the Statutes, I am of the opinion that the facts disclosed by the affidavits do not furnish legal grounds for the seizure of the American schooner *White Fawn*, by Captain Betts, the commander of the Dominion vessel *Water Lily*, and do not make out a *prima facie* case for condemnation in this Court, of the schooner, her tackle, &c., and cargo.

I may add that as the construction I have put upon the Statute differs from that adopted by the Crown Officers of the Dominion, it is satisfactory to know that the judgment of the Supreme Court may be obtained by information, filed there, as the Imperial Act 59, George III., Cap. 38, gave concurrent jurisdiction to that Court in cases of this nature.

No. 2.

[Extract from the Halifax Daily Reporter and Times, Dec. 7, 1870.]

In the Vice Admiralty Court at Halifax.

The "Wampatuck."—Case No. 254.—Sir William Young, Judge.—6th Dec.,
1870.

This is an American fishing vessel of 46 tons burthen, owned at Plymouth, in the State of Massachusetts, and sailing under a fishing license, issued by the Collector there on the 25th of April last. On the 27th of June she was seized by Capt. Tory, of the Dominion cutter *Ida E.*, for a violation of the Dominion Fishery Acts of 1868 and 1870, and her nationality and character appear from her enrolment and other papers delivered up by her master, and on file in this Court. A monition having issued in the usual form on the 27th of July, a libel was filed on the 10th of August, and a claim having been put in by the owners with a bond for costs, as required by the Act, they filed their responsive allegation on the 18th of August. The fish and salt on board at the time of seizure being perishable, were sold under an order of the Court, and the proceeds, with the vessel herself, remain subject to its decree. The evidence was completed early in September, but the case, being the first of the several fishing cases, that has been tried, was not brought before the Court for a hearing till the 26th ult., when it was fully argued, and stands now for judgment. Although it presents few or none of the nicer and more perplexing questions that will arise in the other cases, now also ripe for a hearing, it will be regarded with the deepest interest by the community and the profession, and on that account demands a more cautious and thorough examination than it might require simply on its own merits.

"An attempt was made at the argument to import into it wider and more comprehensive inquiries than properly belong to it. I am here to

administer the law as I find it, not to determine its expediency
justice, still less to inquire into the wisdom of a Treaty delib·
made by the two Governments of Great Britain and the United
and acknowledged by both. If the people of the United States
vertently, as it is alleged, or unwisely (which I by no means
renounced their inherent rights, and ought to fall back on the Tr
1783, rather than abide by the existing Treaty of 1818, that is a
for negotiation between the two contracting powers—it belongs
higher region of international and political action, and not to th
bler, but still the highly responsible and honorable duty now in
on me, of interpreting and enforcing the law as it is.

"By the first Article of the Treaty of 1818, after certain pri
or rights within certain limits conceded to American fisherme
declared, that "the United States hereby renounce forever any
heretofore enjoyed or claimed by the inhabitants thereof, to tak
or cure fish, on or within three marine miles of any of the coasts
creeks, or harbors of His Britannic Majesty's dominions in Ameri
included within the above mentioned limits. Provided, howeve
the American fishermen shall be admitted to enter such bays or b
for the purpose of shelter, and of repairing damage therein, of pr
ing wood, and of obtaining water, and for no other purpose wh.
But they shall be under such restrictions as may be necessary to p
their taking, drying, or curing fish therein, or in any other manner
ever abusing the privileges hereby reserved to them.

"Every word of this Article should be studied and underste
the people of these Provinces. They perfectly appreciate the va
their exclusive right to the inshore fishery, thus formally and
recognized, and they must take care temperately but firmly to pr
and guard it. It was argued in this case, that the restriction a
only to fishing vessels; that is, vessels fitted out for the purp
fishing—that it did not extend to other vessels which might find
venient or profitable to fish within the limits. But that is not t
guage of the Treaty nor of the Acts founded on it. The United
renounce the liberty enjoyed or claimed by the inhabitants, not
by the fishermen thereof, and any vessel, fishing or otherwise,
the limits prescribed by the Treaty, is liable to forfeiture.

"Extreme cases were put to me at the hearing, and I have see
frequently stated elsewhere, of a trading vessel or an American
catching a few fish for food or for pleasure, and the Court wa
whether in such and the like cases it would impose forfeituras
alties. When such cases arise there will be no difficulty, I t
dealing with them. Neither the Government nor the Courts
Dominion would favor a narrow and illiberal construction, or sar
forfeiture or penalty inconsistent with national comity and usa
with the plain object and intent of the Treaty. The rights of a
as of an individual, are never so much respected as when they a
cised in a spirit of fairness and moderation. Besides, by a claus
Dominion Act of 1868, which is not to be found in the Imperial
1819, nor in our Nova Scotia Act of 1836, which formed the
rules and regulations under the Treaty of 1818, with the same
His Majesty, the Governor-General in Council, in cases of seizur
the Act, may, by order, direct a stay of proceedings ; and, in
condemnation, may relieve from the penalty, in whole or in pa
on such terms as may be deemed right. Any undue strainin
law, or harshness in its application may thus be softened or rec
and although I was told that little confidence was to be placed

on of Governments; it is obvious that confidence is placed in
authorities and by the people of the United States; and it is
norable to both parties, that the naval forces employed on the
rounds in the past seasons, have acted in perfect harmony, and
ut the provisions of the Treaty in good faith. The organs of
)inion, indeed, in the United States, of the highest stamp, have
d open and deliberate violation of the Treaty in terms as de-
we ourselves could use.

) considerations have prepared us for a review of the pleadings
e evidence taken in this case. The libel contains six articles.
sets out in the briefest possible terms, the first article already
he Treaty of 20th Oct., 1818. The second gives the title of the
Act 59 Geo. 3, chap. 38. The third that of the British North
n Act 1867, the 30th and 31st Vic. chap. The fourth, those of
inion Acts of 1868 and 1870, the 31st Vic., chap. 61 and the 33
p. 15. The fifth alleges that on the 27th of June last, the
uck, her master and crew, within the limits reserved in the
ere discovered fishing at Aspy Bay in British waters, within
rine miles of the coast, without license for that purpose, and
vessel and cargo were thereupon seized by Capt. Tory, being a
fficer in command of the *Ida E.*, a vessel in the service of the
1ent of Canada, for a breach of the provisions of the Conven-
f the Statutes in that behalf, and delivered into the custody of
ipal officer of Customs at Sydney, Cape Breton. The conclud-
le prays for a condemnation of the vessel and cargo, as forfeited
rown.

responsive allegation admits the Convention, and the several
as pleaded, raising no question thereon. It admits that the
uck, being an American vessel, left the port of Plymouth on a
/oyage to the Grand Bank, beyond the limits of any rights re-
)y the Convention of 1818, and alleges that she was not intended
n the coasts or in the bays of British North America; that on
day of June, while pursuing her said voyage, becoming short
r, she ran into Aspy Bay for the purpose of procuring a supply
and for no other purpose whatsoever; that the master, with
he crew, rowed ashore to get a supply of water as aforesaid,
:cted the crew on board to work the vessel inshore to a con-
distance for watering, and that the master and crew were not
·ed fishing within three marine miles of the coast as alleged.
,h article, repeating the same allegations, proceeds to state fur-
1at ' as the owners are informed, while the said master was on
, aforesaid, the steward of the said vessel, and being one of the
the same, while the said vessel was lying becalmed in the said
with a fishing-line, being part of the tackle of the said vessel,
,ven codfish for the purpose of cooking them, then and there, for
l of the crew of the said vessel, and not for the purpose of
)r preserving them, as part of the cargo of the said vessel;
, said fish were so caught without the knowledge, against the
l in the absence of the master of the said vessel and part of
r,' and for this offense only the vessel and cargo had been seized.
serve that this last allegation was repeated in an affidavit of
he owners on file, and, as we must infer, was consistent with his
t the time, and probably led to the claim being put in under the
1 12th sections of the Act of 1868. Had the evidence sustained
ase would have assumed a very different complexion; but, as

we shall presently see, it is utterly at variance with the acts
admissions of the parties on board.

" It is a remarkable circumstance that neither the master no₁
the vessel have been examined, nor any evidence adduced on
fense, although a Commission was granted on the 7th Septe₁
that purpose. At the hearing, indeed, two papers were tend
the Defendant's counsel—one an *ex parte* examination of F₍
Rollin, one of the crew, taken on the 27th September, in the
Maine; the other, a deposition of Daniel Goodwin, the mast₍
on the 2nd of July—neither of which I could receive by the r₁
govern this Court, and neither of which I have read. The l₍
deed, had never been filed, nor had the deponent been subj
cross-examination.

" The case, therefore, was heard solely upon the evidence for ₁
ecution, consisting of the depositions of Captain Tory, Martin ₅
his second mate, and five others of the crew of the *Ida E.* Fr₍
it appears that the latter entered Aspy Bay about 10 o'clock
morning of June 27th, and was engaged all day in boarding th₍
lying there; and what seems very strange, but is plainly sho'
her presence and character were known to the master and cre·
Wampatuck, and as one would have thought, would have ma·
cautious in their proceedings. She had entered the Bay on t
morning, and remained hovering about the shore all that day,
or 5 miles from the *Ida E.* Gibson, one of the crew, states that
Tory and four of his crew, including the witness, left the *Id₍*
tween 6 and 7 o'clock in·the evening to go to the *Wampatuc*
latter vessel was then about 1½ miles or a little more from tl
When they reached her they saw several cod-fish about 15 o
deck, very lately caught—some of which were alive, jumpin₍
deck. They also saw some codfish lines on deck, not wound u
ently just taken out of the water. Captain Tory states that s
the crew were engaged in fishing codfish—that they saw severa
unsplit, very recently caught, on her deck, some of which we
In his cross-examination he says that he saw three or four
lines overboard, apparently in the act of fishing, and that th
more than 8 or 10 newly caught fish on the deck,—he judged fr
20. Graham states that they saw several codfish very recentl₍
on the deck, some of which were alive,—saw also several codfisl
deck, and one of the crew of the *Wampatuck* haul a line in—t
5 or 6 men on board of her at the time. These statements are ₍
confirmed by the other four witnesses, and being uncontradict
no doubt of the fact of a fishing within the reserved limits, fo₁
pose of curing and not of procuring food only, as was averred.

" The admissions of Captain Goodwin are equally emphatic.
on board immediately after the seizure, and Sullivan heard hin
he could not blame Captain Tory,—his crew was so crazy to ₍
that they would not stop. Graham heard Captain Goodwin s
knew he had broken the rules and was inside of the limits, an
vessel was a lawful prize, that Captain Tory had done no mor
duty, that he could not blame him. This witness, in his cross
tion, says that about an hour after Captain Goodwin came on
heard him say that he told the crew not to catch fish inside wh
away, but it was no use to talk, that fishermen would catch
ever they would get them to bite. The same witness says that
the crew, as they knew it was the cutter's boat coming, wh₍
not throw the fish overboard, and one of them said they m

done so, but it did not come in their minds. Captain Tory testifies that Captain Goodwin repeatedly admitted to him that he was aware that their fishing in shore was a violation of the law, and pleaded that he would not be severe on him. In his cross-examination, Captain Tory says that at the time of such admissions he does not recollect Captain Goodwin saying that the fishing was done without his knowledge or against his orders. Captain Tory does not think that he said so, as witness believes the Captain was aware the *Wampatuck* went out from the harbor to fish, and that he saw her within the limits. Gibson also testifies that on their way across the Bay he heard Captain Goodwin tell Captain Tory that he could not blame him—it was not his fault—that he blamed himself, and that he knew he had violated the law.

"This mass of testimony having been open to the inspection of the defendants and their counsel since the beginning of September, it is very significant that they produced no witness in reply, and that it stood at the hearing, wholly uncontradicted. As neither want of ability, nor of zeal, can be imputed to the counsel, the necessary inference is, that the facts testified to are substantially true.

"Two or three arguments were urged at the hearing, which it is incumbent on me to notice.

"It was said that there could be no forfeiture, unless an intent to violate the law were clearly shown on the part of the prosecution. The answer is, that the intent was shown by the admissions in proof, and that, independently of the admissions, where acts are illegal, the intent is to be gathered from the acts themselves.

"It was next said that the captain of the *Ida E.* ought to have notified the master of the *Wampatuck*, but it was admitted in the same breath that notice was not required in the Statute, the Act of 1870 being somewhat more stringent in that respect than the Act of 1868, while the private instructions to the captain of the cutter were not in proof.

"The main objection, however, was, that the fishing having been done in the absence and without the authority of Capt. Goodwin, the vessel was not liable to forfeiture. Now, it is to be noted that there is no evidence, nothing under oath, of the master having prohibited, or been ignorant of, the fishing. I have stated his disclaimer as accompanying, or qualifying, his admissions; but if the prohibition or want of authority would constitute a defence, it should have been proved. It is to be observed, too, that under the shipping paper, showing a crew of nine persons in all, seven besides the skipper and salter, the men were not shipped by wages, nor by the thousand of fish caught, but were sharesmen having an interest in the voyage, and whose acts as fishermen, necessarily compromised the vessel. They were inhabitants of the United States, fishing in violation of the Treaty, and the Act of 1870 declares that if any foreign ship or vessel have been found fishing, or preparing to fish, or to have been fishing (in British waters) within the prescribed limits, such ship, vessel or boat, and the tackle, rigging, apparel, furniture, stores and cargo thereof, shall be forfeited. But supposing the doctrine as between master and servant, or as between principal and agent, to apply, for which no authority was cited, it would not avail the defendants. The last point, as to agency, was examined thoroughly in the Supreme Court of this Province, in the case of Pope vs. the Pictou Steamboat Company, in 1865, and was decided against the principal. And as to the analogy of master and servant—the responsibility of the master for the act of the servant, where, as in this case, the servant was acting within the scope of his employment, I would content myself with citing the decision of the Exchequer Chamber in the case of Limpus vs. the General Omnibus

Company, 7 Law Term, Reports, N. S., 641, where the rule is
by Blackburn, J., in these words :—'It is agreed by all that a
responsible for the improper act of his servant, even if it be wi
less or improper, provided the act is the act of the servant in
of his employment, and in executing the matter for whic
engaged at the time.'

"These objections, therefore, having failed, and the fishing b⟩
within the reserved limits having been abundantly proved, t
condemns the *Wampatuck*, her tackle, apparel, furniture, s
cargo as forfeited under the Dominion Acts, the vessel to b
public auction, and the proceeds to be distributed, along witl
ceeds of the cargo, as directed by the Act of 1868."

No. 3.

[Extract from the Halifax Daily Reporter and Times, Feb. 11, 18⁊

In the Vice Admiralty Court, 10th Feb'y, 1871.

*The "A. H. Wanson," Fishing Vessel.—Sir William Young, ⱼ
Admiralty.*

"This is a schooner of 63 tons burthen, belonging to Glo⟨
the State of Massachusetts, sailing under an enrolment of
1868, and a fishing license of 27th June last.   On the 3rd Sep⟨
seized by Capt. Carmichael, of the *Sweepstakes*, one of the
cutters, for fishing within three marine miles of the coast of Ca
at Broad Cove, and was libelled therefor in the usual form o
On the 19th her owners put in their responsive allegation,
same time her master and four of her crew were examine
For the prosecution there were examined by the 30th Sept., th
the first officer, three of the other officers, and ten of the c
Sweepstakes; and on the 21st and 22nd October there were
under commission at Canso, the master and two of the sea
Dusky Lake, a fishing schooner belonging to Margaree.   A⟨
nesses on both sides in these 23 depositions were subjecte
examination, and the evidence, as was perhaps to be expec⟨
flicting.   The case, as it will be perceived, was ready for t
end of October; but the intervening terms of the Supreme
the incessant engagements both of Judge and Counsel rend
possible to bring it on for a hearing until the 4th inst.   The le
ples applicable to the case having been fully discussed in t
Wampatuck, the argument was confined to the effect of the
and the decision will turn solely on questions of fact.

"On the 2d of September, the cutter, a sailing vessel, an
distinguishable from the usual class of fishing craft, arrived
Cove about ten o'clock at night, and next morning a littl
o'clock, according to Captain Carmichael, who is confirmed i
tial particulars by his officers and crew, he discovered a
vessels, some say as many as 70, fishing close to them, a⟨
under their mainsails.   Some of these were American, and
boatswain, says he saw the captain of the American vessel
them stand on the house and wave his hat to the other vesse
hand, and they immediately hoisted their jibs and made off f

these were caught; but Captain Carmichael discovered the
anson about a third of a mile distant. She was hove to under
sail, with her rail manned, and fishing on the starboard side,
g to the established usage. The morning was clear, and he
the men on her deck distinctly, casting their lines and throw-
; he also looked at her through his spyglass, and described
narks on her to his men, that they might easily distinguish and
r. He then steered in the direction of the *A. H. Wanson*, and
out fifty yards of her, hoisted his colors, and fired a blank car-
The vessel then showed American colors, and Nickerson, the
er, and boat's crew, went on board.
erson testifies that he also distinctly saw the men casting and
in their lines, and throwing bait, until the cutter was within
ndred yards of them. He observed them at this work for about
inutes. After going on deck, he observed four lines over the
e water, on the starboard side; he saw several of the hooks
vith fresh bait; he saw the bait on the lines in the water after
uled in; he also saw scales of fresh mackerel on the deck, and
inside of the strike barrels then on the deck; also two bait-
rith fresh bait in them—pogies and clams. He then signalled
aptain of the Cutter, who came on board, and asked some of
why they did not get under weigh when they saw his vessel,
iad plenty of time to get off. Some of them replied that they
see him; they were not thinking of Cutters, only of Steamers,
arrived only the evening before. The vessel was then in 17
of water, by the lead, less than two miles from Cape Breton
nd Sea Wolf Island bearing about North by the compass.
eized she was drifting, with mainsail guyed off, in the direction
Volf Island, forging a trifle ahead.
ould be a waste of time to go through the depositions of the
ficers and crew of the Cutter, which are more or less affirmative
none of them contradict the above. Jones says he saw one man
of the main rigging throw a scoop of bait into the water. This
med by five others—Grant, Langley, Cleas, Evans, and Heu-

e says that the crew ceased casting their lines about a minute
he *Sweepstakes* rounded to. The *A. H. Wanson* was then inside
niles from Cape Breton shore, and drifting in, in a Northwest-
rse.
m the direction in which the Cutter came, veiling her approach,
h the Nova Scotia vessels intervening, none of the persons on
aw the fish actually taken and hauled up, and the further evi-
f the three men on board the *Dusky Lake* becomes very material.
Nickerson says there were about 100 yards from the *A. H.*
, lying between her and the shore. He did not see any fish
r caught by her, he could not see the men hauling any lines or
g bait from the way the sails hid them, but in answer to the 11th
n, he says that he saw the Cutter approaching—she approached
H. Wanson from the south-west, and the witness observed her
anding at the rail, and saw them take their strike-barrels to
l, and throw round mackerel overboard, and when the *Sweep-*
as rounding to, they hauled in their main sheet, and after the
akes fired a gun, they hoisted their colors to the main peak.
xt witness, Joseph H. Grant, says the *A. H. Wanson* was lying
r mainsail and foresail; they appeared to be fishing; he did not
m catch any; as the *Sweepstakes* approached, he observed them

take their strike barrels to leeward, and throw the macker
he could not see any one throwing bait; but saw the tole c
water, as is usual when bait is throwing, in order to raise r
"By the ninth cross interrogatory he was asked 'would
sel drifting along use the same sails and appear in the sam
the *A. H. Wanson?* Is there anything particular in the
sails by vessels employed in mackerel fishing more than
vessels?' To which his answer is: 'I cannot say—never
sel in that position unless she was fishing. There is quite
He had previously said that he had been two years engaged
and line mackerel fishing in the Gulf of St. Lawrence, a
familiar with the way in which the fish are caught.
"The remaining witness, Thomas Roberts, who was desc
hearing as the master, says the *A. H. Wanson* was lying
and about 200 yards from the *Dusky Lake*, they (that is the
A. H. Wanson) catching mackerel, lying head to the south
her mainsail. They were fishing, and the witness saw them
mackerel. She was inside of three miles. He further s
served lines on the starboard side. I saw the men handling,
sixteen or seventeen men. They hauled them in with fish
slatted them off, and threw them out again. . . . I saw
ing bait in the manner usual for attracting mackerel." In h
answer, he says: 'I can positively swear they were catchii
and were within three marine miles of the shores of C
When the *Sweepstakes* ran down upon them from the sou
gave up fishing, and carried their strike-barrels to leewar
the fish overboard." In answer to the eleventh and thirt
interrogatories, he says: 'I saw them heaving bait, casting
ing mackerel, and dumping them overboard, and coiling u
They were slatting fish off of their lines after hauling them
"Let us consider the effect of this mass of evidence,
gone into with a particularity very unusual with me, and on
fied by the nature of the charge, and the necessity of vinc
judgment that is pronounced. Here is a fleet of vessels,
and American, on a fine clear morning, busily engaged i
mackerel rising all around, and no hostile cutter supposec
The Americans think little of the prohibition which the n
vigorous policy of the Dominion has imposed. They are
the exclusive right claimed by the Canadian people on t
of international law, and the faith of treaties; and viola
scruples whenever the opportunity occurs. Hence the e
the openness too, with which these American fishermen ar
task on this particular morning. What should we say, if
that one vessel only was virtuous or strong enough to resis
tions, and to hold their hands from touching their neighl
The captain of the *Wampatuck*, when caught in the act,
self, on the ground, that his crew were so crazy to catch fi
would not stop. But, here on the decks of the *A. H. W*
model crew, who would not catch mackerel within the
though swarming around them. That is the sole defenc
They admit that they were within three miles of the sho
were lying guyed off under mainsail, and with their ancho
south-south east towards the shore in the very position
they were not aware of the arrival of the cutter—and ye
have this Court believe that they were not fishing. It wo
stretch of credulity to believe this in the absence of evidei

But with the mass of testimony just recited—the 8 or 10 men
 ɘ rail—the casting and hauling in of the mackerel lines—the
 ɣ of bait—the emptying of the strike barrels on the approach
 utter, and the clear and positive evidence of three disinterested
 ɪs from the *Dusky Lake*—what is to said of such a defence? In
 of it all, the master and four of the crew of the *A. H. Wanson*—
 of the 16 or 17 men, said to be on board, have sworn that said
 r, or the captain or crew thereof, did not fish, or prepare to fish,
 hree marine miles of the coasts, bays, harbors, or creeks of Canada,
 ιt part of the coasts and bays thereof known as Broadcove and as
  Island on the north-west coast of Cape Breton, on the 3rd day
 ɪmber last, or at any other time during said season. This might
 osed to be a mere formal denial, repeated, however wrongfully
 ɪautiously, by all five, in the very words of the responsive al-
 ., but in the body of their evidence they assert that none of the
 re fishing, or had been fishing that morning, or at any time after
 ιto Broadcove, or were preparing to fish. By what strange cas-
 hese men reconcile such an assertion to their consciences, and
 ɪ right, it is difficult to tell. The human mind practices singular
 ιs upon itself, and the spectacle of conflicting evidence is only
 ιmon in courts of justice. It is enough, in the present case,
 hat the evidence for the prosecution is overwhelming and irre-
 . The allegation that the men were only clearing out their tan-
 .es, besides being inconsistent with the usage and habits of ex-
 hermen, is wholly insufficient to account for the actions of these
 ιile on the rail, as seen and testified to by so many of the wit-

ronounce therefore, for the condemnation of the *A. H. Wanson*,
 kle, apparel, furniture, stores, and cargo, as forfeited under the
 on Acts, and the same having been bailed at the appraised value
 00, I direct that the amount shall be paid into court, to be dis-
 d as directed by the Act of 1868. I pronounce also for the costs
 ι by the first bond, on the defence being put in."

No. 4.

xtract from the Halifax Daily Reporter and Times, February 13th, 1871.]

THE VICE ADMIRALTY COURT, 10TH FEB'Y, 1871.

"*A. J. Franklin.*"—*Sir William Young, Judge Vice Admiralty.*

is is a schooner of 53 tons burthen, owned at Gloucester, in the
 ɔf Massachusetts, under an enrolment of 4th February, 1868, and
 under a fishing license of 28th January, 1870. Attached to her
 are also printed copies of the Treasury Circulars issued at Wash-
 on 16th May and 9th June last, apprising the owners and mas-
 ' fishing vessels of the first article of the Treaty of 1818, of the
 ιion acts of 1868 and 1870, and of the equipment of Canadian sail-
 ssels for the enforcement thereof. This vessel—the *A. J. Frank-
 aving been warned by Captain Tory, of the cutter *Ida E.*, against
 ɪ within the prescribed limits, and having been found on the 11th
 ɪr in the midst of a mackerel fleet at Broad Cove, was overhauled
 sited by the cutter, and was then let go; but, on further informa-

tion that she had been fishing on that day, she was seized on
October, in the Strait of Canso, and libelled in the usual form or
November, and a responsive allegation put in. The vessel aı
were afterward liberated on bail at the appraised value of $2,
depositions were taken both sides, and cross-interrogatories filec
irregularities appear on the face of them, which were waived by
as endorsed, and the case came before me on the 6th instan
pleadings, and eighteen depositions, those of the master, seco
and six of the crew of the *Ida E.*, and of six of the crew of tw
burg vessels, produced on the part of the prosecution, and tho
first mate of the *Ida E.*, and of the master and two of the cre
A. J. Franklin, produced on the defence.

"Captain Tory states that on the morning of the 11th Octobeı
the mackerel fleet close to the shore in Broad Cove, engaged iı
and having run outside until he got about midway, he fired
shot, for the purpose of ascertaining, by their returning the sigı
vessels were British and what not. The *A. J. Franklin* then ı
from the centre of the fleet, and immediately set all sail and rı
from the land, as if trying to avoid detection. To prevent he
the captain ordered a shot to be fired across her bow, when shı
down her jib, and hove to. The two vessels were then about
from Marsh Point in Broad Cove, and less than 2 miles from ₤
Island. The captain at once boarded the *A. J. Franklin*, aı
some mackerel lines coiled up on the rail that were wet, the l
tached thereto being newly or fresh baited, and fresh fish-bl
mackerel gills on deck ; he saw also other lines coiled up under
which were dry. Captain Tory charged Captain Nass with fisb
morning inside the limits, and he admitted that he was lyinɡ
his jib down and sheets off when the first gun was fired, but deı
he had caught any mackerel. He said, however, that he ha
two or three codfish. He accounted for his lines being so recε
by the washing of the deck. His attention was then called to
blood, and bait on deck, but no fresh mackerel being found, a
solemnly denying having caught any, and appealing to two
which he named, for confirmation of his statement, Capt. Tory
him, warning him, however, that if he ascertained that he lı
fishing, or trying to fish, within the limits that morning, that
seize him wherever he caught him, within three miles of the cɔ

"This statement is confirmed by the other men who boarded
sel with Capt. Tory. Matson thinks the *A. J. Franklin* was
than one and a-half miles from the shore when they first saw hε
at first denied that he had his jib down, but afterwards admittε
said he was waiting to see if the other vessels caught any ı
Although this circumstance, and his being so near the shore
picious, it is obvious that on the facts as they then appeared, tł
of the vessel could not have been justified, especially if it bε
stated in the defendants' evidence, that she was then outside of
miles.

"The evidence of the Lunenburg men is, therefore, very mat
we must see what it amounts to. There were two vessels, tł
and the *Nimble*, and the *A. J. Franklin* lay within 60 to 100
them. The crews spoke together while trying to fish. Arn
three of the crew of the *A. J. Franklin* fishing,—saw them ε
fish—three he is sure of ; she was in the position to catch macl
was then about a mile from the shore. The witness saw no
caught, and no fish thrown overboard. Rodenizer states that

lin and his vessel lay 100 yards apart. The skipper of the *A. J. lin* said "mackerel were scarce; he did not do much yet." He , the bait box. The crew were preparing for fishing on the starside, which is the invariable usage. David Heckman says " we in the starboard bow of the *A. J. Franklin* She had her mackues out, and they were heaving bait. She continued trying for rel till after the *Ida E.* fired the second time, when the crew hauled ir mackerel lines, hoisted jib, trimmed their sails, and stood off om the fleet, and set staysail. Thomas Herman says, four of the of the *A. J. Franklin* were fishing for cod-fish—the skipper was ing bait for mackerel, and threw his mackerel lines—others were rail on the starboard side, looking over. She was hove to, jib foresail and mainsail up, and sheets off on port side. Peter nan states that he saw some of the crew of the *A. J. Franklin* to catch mackerel—they threw their lines over the starboard side threw bait over to raise mackerel—they were throwing bait with ver, trying for mackerel, as the *Ida E.* approached—the crew after ed, hauled in the lines, hoisted jib, and stood off the shore. The sheered and shouted as they got out of the fleet, and set their il. George W. Nass says that he saw some of the crew of the *A. inklin* heaving bait, and they had mackerel lines out on the starside. She was hove to, jib down, mainsail and foresail to port, usual in fishing for mackerel—she was then within two miles of l Cove shore, and about three miles to the westward of Seawolf l. When the *Ida E.* came from the westward, the witness heard er Nass call out something to one of the other vessels—the reply m was that it was one of the cutters. The *A. J. Franklin* then d in her mackerel lines, and hoisted her jib, and stood to the north , and then set her staysail.

Teither this witness nor any of the others ever saw any mackerel ht, nor any fish thrown over from the *A. J. Franklin.*

the case for the prosecution is strengthened by certain declarations e crew, which were not objected to at the hearing, and being against interest as sharesmen, are receivable, I think, in evidence.

laptain Tory testifies that he heard several of the crew of the *A. J. klin* say on the day of the seizure at the Strait of Canso, that after ft their vessel at Broad Cove, they advised Captain Nass to clear f the Bay, and go immediately home—that Capt. Tory would find hey had been fishing, and seize them, and that they would lose their to which Capt. Nass replied, that he would like to try a few days r—that Capt. Tory had been aboard, and was not likely to trouble again, or such like words.

ullivan heard one of the crew make a like declaration; and McMas eard one of the crew say, that after the *A. J. Franklin* was seized, they had caught mackerel the morning Capt. Tory boarded them road Cove.

If the depositions for the defence, that of Regis Raimond, who was mate of the *Ida E*, merely repeats what has been already stated— Capt. Tory, after he boarded the *A. J. Franklin*, assigned as his n for not seizing her, that he had found no fish taken that morning, lid not think they had been fishing. The seizure, obviously, re d from information subsequently received.

he depositions of Capt. Nass and two of his crew, go much further, leny a fishing or preparing to fish altogether. They allege that the as let down to prevent their running into another vessel that was l. On no day, say they, between the 1st and 15th October, had

213 F

the *A. J. Franklin*, or any of her crew been fishing or prepari
or had fished, within three marine miles of the North West coa
Breton. On the morning of the 11th they sailed from P
towards Broadcove. After hoisting their jib to go to East
having got outside of the fleet, a gun was fired from the *Ida*
continued on their course, and after running about half-a-mile
gun was fired, when the *A. J. Franklin* hove to, and was boa
after enquiry, was let go. This is the substance of Captain
davit, who states also that Captain Tory was doubtful or re
serve him, and in his statement of what occurred on the 11th
firmed by Morash and Mitchell.

"These three deponents, in fact, are in direct conflict with th
who have given evidence from Lunenburg. All the minute ci
ces they have detailed—the first, that the *A. J. Franklin* v
centre of the fleet,—that, within 100 yards of the Nova Scot
she was in the position for fishing, throwing bait to attract
erel, and with her lines down,—her hasty retreat on the ap
the cutter—all are to be rejected as fabrications, and the six
from Lunenburg, who have no interest in the matter, to be di
I need not say that no Court could come to such a conclusio
all the purposes of this suit, the evidence of these Lunenburg
be taken as substantially true.

"To what result, then, does it tend. On the charge of pr
fish—a phrase to be found in all the British and Colonial Acts,
the treaty—I shall say little in this judgment, because it w
main enquiry in the judgment I am to pronounce in a few d
far more important case of the *J. H. Nickerson*. Had I cons
facts in this case to amount to nothing more than a preparing
would have postponed my decision until the other was pre
delivered. But I look upon the throwing of bait—the beavi
sheets off, and the jib down, and the vessel thus lying in the
catch mackerel, with the mackerel lines out, and hauled in
proach of the cutter—these circumstances, coupled with the d
and actions of Captain Nass, bring the case clearly, as I thi
the meaning of the Dominion Acts of 1868 and 1870, as a fi
subject the vessel and her cargo to forfeiture, although no ma
proved, except by the declarations of the crew, to have been
I am wrong in this conclusion, an appeal to the High Cour
ralty, under the Imperial Act of 1863, will afford the Defendan
and I shall not be sorry to see such appeal prosecuted. Or t
ion Government may see fit to relieve from the penalty in w
part, as they have a right to do, under the Act of 1868, Sec.
sonally, I may say—if a Judge has a right to express any per
ing—as the vessel was appraised at $800, and the cargo, in
crew were largely interested, at a much larger sum, I wo
pleased to see the penalty in this case largely mitigated.

"It is not the policy, as I take it, of the Dominion Gover
is it the disposition of this Court, to press with undue severit
American fishermen, even when they trench upon our undoub
The Court has been accused, I am told, of condemning the
because the steward, in the absence of the master, had ca
codfish within the limits, for the purposes of cooking. Such
was the defence that was set up, and, had it been establi
would certainly have been no condemnation. But the evide
that there was a fishing by three or four men, having lines
as was admitted by the master, and several codfish caught

: curing, and not of procuring food only, as was averred. So, in
se, three or four codfish are admitted to have been taken within
iits; but I have not taken that circumstance at all into account,
ering it too trifling to be a ground of condemnation.
the case of the *Reward*,—2 Dodson Adm. Repts., 269, 270—Sir
m Scott, observed:

e Court is not bound to a strictness at once harsh and pedantic in
plication'of Statutes. The Court permits the qualification implied
ancient maxim, '*De minimus non curat lex.*' When there are
larities of very slight consequence, it does not intend that the
on of penalties should be inflexibly severe. If the deviation were
> trifle, (and the catching of a few codfish for a meal is such),
ing little or nothing in the public interest, it might properly be
oked."

pon the other grounds, however, on which I have enlarged, I con-
t my duty to declare the *A. J. Franklin*, her apparel and cargo, for-
with costs, and her value, when collected from the Bail, distrib-
inder the Act of 1868."

No. 5.

[Extract from the Halifax Daily Reporter and Times, Novr. 15, 1871.]

In the Vice Admiralty Court, 1871.

The "*J. H. Nickerson.*"

ir William Young, Judge Vice Admiralty, pronounced the follow-
idgment in the above cause:—

his is an American Fishing vessel of seventy tons burthen, owned
lem, Massachusetts, and sailing under a Fishing License issued by
ollector of that Port, and dated March 25th, A. D , 1869. In the
h of June 1870, she was seized by Captain Tory of the Dominion
oner *Ida E.*, while in the North Bay of Ingonish, Cape Breton,
; three or four cable lengths from the shore; and it appeared the
ie charged against her was that she had run into that Bay for the
ose of procuring bait, had persisted in remaining there for that
ose after warning to depart therefrom, and not to return, and had
ired or purchased bait while there. This case, therefore, differs
tially from the cases I have already decided. It comes within the
ie of preparing to fish—a phrase to be found in all the British and
iial Acts, but not in the Treaty of 1818. In giving judgment 10th
iary last, in the case of the *A. J. Franklin*, I referred to the case
nd, and stated that I would pronounce judgment in this also in a
lays, which I was prepared to do. But it was intimated to the
t that some compromise or settlement might possibly take place in
ince to the instructions that had been issued from time to time to
ruisers, and to the negociations pending between the two Govern-
s, and I have accordingly suspended judgment until now, when it
ieen formally moved for.

'he same asguments were urged at the hearing of this cause as in
iase of the *Wampatuck* on the wisdom of the Treaty of 1818, and
severe strictures were passed on the spirit and tendency of the
Dominion Acts of 1868 and 1870. To all such arguments and stric-
i the same answer must be given in this as in my former judgments.

The libel sets out in separate articles these two acts'with the trea
the Imperial Acts of 1819 and 1867, all of which are admitted with
questions raised thereon in the responsive allegation. I must tak
therefore, both on general principles and on the pleading, as bin
this court; and it is of no consequence whether the judge appr
disapproves of them. A judge may sometimes intimate a desire t
enactments he is called upon to enforce should be modified or cl
but until they are repealed in whole or in part, they constitute t
which it is his business and his duty to administer.

" Our present enquiry is, what was the law as it stood on the
Book on the 30th of June, 1870, when the seizure was made
court, as I take it, has nothing to do with the instructions of t
ernment to its officers, and which, if in their possession on tl
might have induced them to abstain from the seizure of this ve
may induce the government now to exercise the power confe
them by the 19th section of the Acts of 1868.

" But before pursuing this inquiry, let us first of all ascertain t
as they appear in evidence. For the prosecution, there were ex
the examinations duly taken under the rules of 1859, of Cap
and thirteen of his crew, all of whom were examined on cross-i
atories.

" Capt. Tory testifies that he boarded the vessel at Ingonish.
25th of June, and the master being on shore, that he asked t
then on board, what they were doing there, and they said th
after bait, and had procured some while they were there after
in, and wanted more. About an hour after he saw the master, a
him he had violated the law, that he had no power to allow th
to remain, and that he had better leave. On the 26th the vei
still there in the harbor, and Capt. Tory boarded her and saw fr
ring bait in the ice house; and Capt. McDonald, the master, admi
he had procured said bait since his arrival; and he afterwards a
that he had violated the law, and hoped that Captain Tory w
be too severe with him; and as he promised to leave with hi
Capt. Tory did not then seize her. She went to sea the same nigh
the 30th was found again at anchor in the same place where Ca
boarded her; and judging from the appearance of her deck,
had very recently procured more bait, which he saw the next mo
seized her. In his cross-examination, he says that the herring
on the first occasion in the ice-house on board were fresh, but
a night or two in the nets, which caused them to be a little d
and were large, fat herring, and similar to those caught in the
of Ingonish at that season of the year. The herrings he saw or
ond occasion were also fresh, newly caught, with blood on the
same description, except that they were sound.

" This evidence, in its main features, is confirmed by sever
crew. Grant went into the ice-house by order of his captain, a
saw about five or six barrels of fresh herring bait and a few fre
erel. There were scales of fresh fish on the rails, from whic
judged that they had taken fish that morning. Capt. Tory th
the " Nickerson" and placed witness on board as one of the
take her to North Sydney, the captain of the " Nickerson" rem
board. Witness, on the passage, heard said captain say (and
eral of the other men confirm in words to the like effect) tha
purchased 700 or 800 herrings that morning. He also said
wanted more bait,—that it was of no use going out with th
McMaster says that on the passage to Sydney, he heard son

crew of the "Nickerson" say that they had bought seven barrels of fresh herring bait that morning and that they wanted more. Four of the seamen testify to another conversation with Captain McDonald, in which he said he would not have come in a second time had he known the cutter was at hand, that all the bait he had would not bait his trawls once, and that it was not worth while for him to go off to the Banks with that much. These depositions were taken on the 1st of September, 1870, and the only reply is the examination of John Wills, the steward of the "Nickerson," taken in October under a commission at Boston, which undertakes to deny altogether the purchasing or procuring bait,—nullifying the numerous admissions in proof and supporting the responsive allegation as a whole. Neither the master nor any of the crew of the "J. H. Nickerson" were examined, and I need scarcely say that the evidence of the steward alone, as opposed to the mass of testimony I have cited, is unworthy of credit.

"It being, then, clearly established that the "J. H. Nickerson" entered a British port and was anchored within three marine miles of the coast off Cape Breton, for the purpose of purchasing or procuring bait, and did there purchase or procure it in June, 1870, the single question arises on the Treaty of 1818 and the Acts of the Imperial and Dominion Parliaments. - Is this a sufficient ground for seizure and condemnation? This was said at the hearing to be a test case,—the most important that had come before the Court since the termination of the Reciprocity Treaty of 1854. But it has lost much of its importance since the hearing in February, and the present aspect of the question would scarcely justify the elaborate review which might otherwise have been reasonably expected. If the law should remain as it is, and the instructions issued from Downing street on the 30th of April and by the Dominion Government on the 27th June, 1870, as communicated to Parliament, were to continue, no future seizure like the present could occur; and if the Treaty of 1818 and the 'Acts consequent thereon are superseded, this judgment ceases to have any value beyond its operation on the case in hand.

"The first Article of the Convention of 1818 must be construed, as all other instruments are, with a view to the surrounding circumstances and according to the plain meaning of the words employed. The subtleties and refinements that have been applied to it will find little favor with a Court governed by the rules of sound reason, nor will it attach too much value to the protocols and drafts or the history of the negociations that preceded it. We must assume that it was drawn by able men and ratified by the governments of two great powers, who knew perfectly well what they were respectively gaining or conceding, and took care to express what they meant. After a formal renunciation by the United States of the liberty of fishing, theretofore enjoyed or claimed, wi hin the prescribed limits of three marine miles of any of our bays or harbors, they guard themselves by this proviso: 'Provided, however, that the American fishermen shall be admitted to enter such bays or harbors for the purpose of shelter and repairing damage therein, of purchasing wood and of obtaining water, and for no other purpose whatever. But they shall be under such restrictions as may be necessary to prevent them taking, drying or curing fish therein, or in any other manner whatever abusing the privileges hereby reserved to them.'

"These privileges are explicitly and clearly defined, and to make assurance doubly sure, they are accompanied by a negative declaration excluding any other purpose beyond the purpose expressed. I confine myself to the single point that is before me. There is no charge here

of taking fish for bait or otherwise, nor of drying or curing
obtaining supplies or trading. The defendants allege that th
son" entered the Bay of Ingonish and anchored within th
miles of the shore for the purpose of obtaining water and
two of her men who had friends on shore. Neither the mas
crew on board thereof, in the words of the responsive allega
ing, preparing to fish, nor procuring bait wherewith to fish,
been fishing in British waters, within three marine miles of
Had this been proved, it would have been a complete defense
the Court have been disposed to narrow it as respects either
visions or wood. But the evidence conclusively shows that
tion put in is untrue. The defendants have not claimed in
what their counsel claimed at the hearing, and their evide
terly failed them. The vessel went in, not to obtain water
the allegation says, nor to obtain water and provisions, as th
says; but to purchase or procure bait (which, as I take it, i
ing to fish), and it was contended that they had a right to
that no forfeiture accrued on such entering. The answer i
privilege to enter our harbors for bait was to be conceded to
fishermen, it ought to have been in the Treaty, and it is too
a matter to have been accidentally overlooked. We kn
from the State Papers that it was not overlooked,—that it wa
and declined. But the court, as I have already intimated, c
sist upon that as a reason for its judgment. What may be
fairly insisted on is that beyond the four purposes speci
Treaty—shelter, repairs, water and wood,—here is another
claim not specified; while the treaty itself declares that no
purpose or claim shall be received to justify an entry. It ap
an inevitable conclusion that the "J. H. Nickerson," in e
Bay of Ingonish for the purpose of procuring bait, and ev
purpose by purchasing or procuring bait while there, beca
forfeiture, and upon the true construction of the Treaty
Parliament, was legally seized.

"I direct, therefore, the usual decree to be filed for cond
vessel and cargo, and for distribution of the proceeds acco
Dominion Act of 1871."

APPENDIX Q.

No. 1.

THURSDAY, *October 25.*

The Conference met.

Prof. HENRY YOULE HIND was called on behalf of the Government of Her Britannic Majesty, sworn and examined.

By Mr. Thomson :

Question. Have you made a specialty of examining into marine matters, the effect of tides and winds, the habits of fish, and such things ?—Answer. Yes.

Q. For a number of years back ?—A. Yes; for a number of years, more particularly from the year 1861.

Q. You devoted your attention specially to that subject ?—A. Yes; especially to the subject of marine physics or ocean physics.

Q. Do you belong to any learned society ?—A. No; not any specially learned society.

Q. Now, Mr. Hind, you have made a special study of the action of the Arctic current on the American coast and in the Gulf of St. Lawrence ?—A. Yes.

Q. Also the effect of the Gulf Stream ?—A. Yes; I have.

Q. Well, now, you have also, I believe, paid attention to the habits of the mackerel and cod ?—A. Yes.

Q. Now, take the mackerel. Will you state, if you please, in your judgment, what is the habit of the fish in reference to hibernating ?—A. I think there can be little, if any doubt, that the mackerel, in all our seas, and in some European seas, hibernates, or passes a certain period of the winter in a condition of torpidity in sand banks or mud holes, either close inshore, or far off the coast. For instance, on various parts of the Nova Scotia coast, they have been taken from the mud through the ice, in the act of spearing for eels, as, for instance, on our immediate shore at St. Margaret's Bay, and the Bay of Inhabitants in Cape Breton. They have also been found on the coast of Newfoundland at Christmas, driven ashore there by the ice, or the wind, with what the fishermen call a scale over the eyes. I need scarcely say there is no such thing as a scale, in the ordinary sense of the term, but this is a film that forms over the eyes, and can always be seen in the spring of the year. The object of this film is evidently to protect the eye of the animal during their winter torpidity from parasitic crustaceans. There is an order of parasitic animals in the Northern Seas, specially belonging to the class of Lernæida, which attack the eyes of fishes, particularly the eyes of the shark. You very rarely, for instance, get a shark, without finding one of these parasitical creatures attached to the eye. They feed on the eye as others do upon the gills, and it appears to me that the object of this film is specially to protect the eye when the head is partially immersed in the mud or sand.

Q. From that you infer that the mackerel is not what is ordinarily termed a migratory fish ?—A. No; it is a local fish, frequenting the waters in which it is brought forth. They may have a local run of 40, or 50 miles, their general run being in the form of a circle or eclipse, like most other fish.

Q. Then take the Gulf of St. Lawrence; all the mackerel born there remain ?—A. I believe all the mackerel which are found in the gulf are exclusively a home fish.

Q. And the same is true on the American coast ?—A. Yes; and all other coasts, France, Labrador, Newfoundland, and wherever they are found hibernating. I may mention that on the coast of France they are not unfrequently taken from the sand by means of a trawl-net during the winter. Blanchiere describes them being taken out of the mud or sand by means of ordinary trawls. I speak now of the beam-trawl, which drags over the surface of the sand, very similar to the one on the Speedwell, but not suspended on the two iron heads which you observe in the Speedwell's trawl. By means of this trawl dragging over the surface, shell-fish and others, mackerel for instance, are taken up.

Q. Does the mackerel require a particular temperature of water to live? From what points of temperature does it range ?—A. From observations made in regard to its spawning you will find that it always spawns, as far as can be known, in waters of nearly the same temperature, a temperature characterized by its lowness. Whenever it spawns, there is either an Arctic current, or some current which gives a temperature between 37° and 43°.

Q. Then it is only between 5° and 11° above the freezing point ?—A. Yes; about that temperature.

Q. What about the cod; is it a fish that requires a low temperature ?—A. With regard to the spawning of cod, it always seeks the coldest water wherever ice is not present. In all the spawning-grounds from the Strait of Belle Isle down to Massachusetts Bay, and they are very numerous indeed, they spawn during almost all seasons of the year, and always in those localities where the water is coldest, verging on the freezing point. That is, the freezing point of fresh water, not of salt, because there is a vast difference between the two.

Q. Now state, if you please, how the tides run in the Bay of St. Lawrence, and the effect which they have upon the fish that require cold water ?—A. In order to describe the effect of the tides upon the cold water I must first describe the remarkable condition which exists in all seas, and particularly in the Gulf of St. Lawrence, namely, the temperature zones in the ocean. Very frequently you will find a warm stratum underlying the cold. This has been known for a period of about 30 years in the gulf. It was discovered first by Admiral Bayfield, and the discovery carried to a further degree by Dr. Kelly. Their reports were published, but unfortunately did not attract the attention they merited. But recently, since the Challenger expedition and the investigations of Dr. Carpenter and Sir Wyville Thomson, and more particularly since the Norwegian discoveries and the Swedish discoveries in the Baltic Sea, extraordinary attention has been devoted to the subject of zones of temperature in the sea. They are considered to afford a key to the movements of fishes. Very recently it has been announced with triumph that zones of temperature had been discovered in the Baltic Sea. This fact was discovered 30 years ago, and was then known to exist in the Gulf of St. Lawrence.

Q. Now explain if you please the effect of the Arctic current.—A. The effect of every current in the ocean is to bring the cold stratum of water, which lies at a depth of ten or fifteen or twenty fathoms, near to the surface; and one reason why on Orphan and Bradley Banks the

ter is invariably cold is, that the temperature is thus affected by the
rrents which bring the cold water to the surface. That is the reason
1y the water is always 14° or 16° colder on the Grand Banks than in
e surrounding deep sea, simply because the cold Arctic current is
'ced up and is brought to the surface. On the Georges shoals the
1rine life is that of 40°. So also in the spawning grounds of the mack-
'l in Massachusetts Bay, a tongue of the Arctic current produces a
ld temperature there of about 40°.

With reference to the tidal wave I will refer to a diagram. The great
lal wave at the full and change of the moon strikes the entrance of
e gulf about half past eight in the morning. As this tidal wave en-
rs the gulf it is split into two parts by the Magdalen Islands. One
1rt pursues its course between Cape Breton and the Magdalen group,
1d reaches the southern part of Prince Edward Island at ten o'clock.
e other portion passes around to the north of the Magdalen Islands,
1d over the 60-fathom line of soundings, becoming slower and slower
motion until it reaches this point (referring to Escumenac on map),
four o'clock, and the next point (Richibucto), at six o'clock, and the
'xt point at eight, and finally it meets the wave which came in be-
;een the Magdalen Islands and Cape Breton twelve hours before. It
eets it at a point in the Straits of Northumberland. In precisely the
me way the two tidal waves, one twelve hours later than the other,
eet at a point marked on this chart on the north side of Prince Ed-
ard Island. You will find the words "tides meet." That is to say, the
dal wave twelve hours old meets the incoming tidal wave at this point
nd produces constant high water. There is only one other place where
e phenomenon is well known to any great extent, that is, in the Ger-
an Ocean, where the tidal wave rushing up the English Channel meets
he wave twelve, eighteen, or twenty-four hours old in the German
)cean and produces a permanent high tide. According to Admiral
3ayfield, the tides here (pointing to Northumberland on map) are two
r three times higher than they would be if there was not this meeting
f the tidal wave. Bayfield says it is twice the normal height and in
ome instances three times. The effect of it is that any vessel entering
he Strait of Northumberland with the flood tide goes with the tide to
he point where the tides meet, and goes on in the same course on the
bb tide all the way through. It comes in with the flood and goes on
rith the ebb. The numbers on the map indicate the time at which the
ide passes, and refer only to the full and change of the moon. The
iours would differ between those periods, but at the full and change of
he moon it is high water as indicated by these figures.

Now with regard to the tidal wave that runs up the gulf and produces
'ery remarkable phenomena, I must here draw attention to the fact
hat the channel of the gulf has an average depth of 300 to 250 feet.
All of those depths are not marked on the chart, because owing to the
1bservations which have been made under the instructions of the Min-
;ters of Marine and Fisheries by Mr. Whiteaves and others, much
;reater depths than are here marked have been discovered. For ex-
.mple, there is a depth of 313 fathoms discovered by Mr. Whiteaves, and
ither depths of 250 and 200 fathoms. Under all circumstances the
lepth of the channel varies from 250 to 300 fathoms up as far north as
'oint Des Monts. The fact is, the tidal wave rushes with great rapidity
1p this channel, and also with great volume; but when it reaches the
ontracted channel between Point Des Monts and Cape Chatte, the
itrait is too narrow for the whole body of water to pass through, and
rhile one portion passes through the other returns by an eddy flood

tide all the way down the coast to Gaspé. So that a vessel
the full or change of the moon up the center of this deep wat
and reach Point Des Monts at precisely 12 o'clock, and she
around then and go with the eddy flood and down to Gaspé b
flood tide, which reaches Gaspé at 1.30 p. m.

Q. Now, the effect of that tide is to throw every floating o
inshore ?—A. Yes.

Q. And in some way it has the effect of washing the foc
inshore ?—A. Yes.

Q. Is the peculiar shape of Prince Edward Island due to
Yes; that is the geological cause of the peculiar bend in the
is the result of the ages of action of the tide upon the soft
rock, which it has cut and carried out to sea.

Q. Now, the other portion of the tidal wave which flows
this part of the gulf is split into two parts by the island of A
A. One portion runs inshore with great velocity, but is only
leagues outside. There is no sign of a tide three leagues outs.
ing to Admiral Bayfield, owing to the circumstances of the
wave coming up here. The result is that this tidal wave beit
by friction along the coast, it arrives at Point Des Monts a
entered upon the map as two hours and ten minutes, meeti
tide coming down the Gulf of St. Lawrence, which fills up
The consequence is that the food of fish and floating objects
are all thrown inshore around that portion of the estuary. It
is especially marked with regard to the launce, of which we l
a good deal recently.

Q. Have you been along that shore yourself ?—A. I ha
along a considerable portion of that shore, from the Moisi
Seven Islands, along a magnificent beach, and have watche
erel wait, as it were, until the flood tide came in for the lau
out of the sand, just as the cod are known to watch on tl
Sweden until the flood tide drives the crabs out of the rocks
when they feed upon them.

Q. Then, if I understand you, the effect of this tide is to
food inshore and all other floating objects ?—A. Yes.

Q. Then, along the northern coast of the St. Lawrence, ind
coast of Labrador ?—A. I don't say anything about this por
coast of Labrador.

Q. Then, from the Seven Islands at all events ?—A. Fro
which lies considerably to the east of Point Des Monts, it i
inshore.

Q. What is the food of the mackerel ?—A. It consists chi
all, of launce and small crustaceans.

Q. Well, there is a little fish spoken of by witnesses, call
A. That is a popular name given to what is called the "ey
appears to be the young of the common herring. Although
years ago, it was considered to be of a different species from

Q. They say it is red in color ?—A. I don't know of any
red colored. Perhaps you speak of the so-called cayenne; th
crustacean. It occurs sometimes, in fact frequently, in suc
titudes as to give a distinct color to the sea.

Q. They say the mackerel eat it ?—A. Yes; certainly; the
are sometimes distended with it.

Q. At all events they eat the launce fish and bait. Wha
of the mackerel is brought inshore ?—A. A great many of
marine animals called pteropods, similar to the crustaceans

Q. Are the squid brought inshore also?—A. Not necessarily. The squid is a free swimming animal, but the mackerel food, which consists very largely of these crustaceans, is brought in around the north and south shores of the river Saint Lawrence and the north shore of Prince Edward Island.

Q. It brings in the floating seaweed as well?—A. Yes; in fact everything floating is brought in around this coast.

Q. Knowing the habits of the mackerel, would you say that necessarily all along that shore must be peculiar haunts for them?—A. Yes.

Q. And within three miles?—A. Generally within three miles the food is brought. Then there is another point which has of course to be taken into consideration, namely, the temperature zones. That is a special reason why off the coast in the gulf the mackerel finds its food so near inshore.

Q. Explain that.—A. If you will allow me to exhibit a diagram I can explain it, because it shows what is meant by temperature zones in the gulf. I have here a diagramatic section of the gulf between the two points—Anticosti across Bradley Bank to Prince Edward Island. It is a vertical section, showing the temperature zones according to observations made very many years ago in the Gulf of Saint Lawrence, for example in the years 1832 and 1836, by Admiral Bayfield and Dr. Kelly. They found a series of temperature zones. At 10 fathoms it would be 37°, at 30 fathoms 39°, at 50 fathoms 33°, at 110 fathoms 36°. They were so much surprised at this that they made repeated trials by bringing up the water from the bottom. The mode in which the Swedes and Norwegians effect the same purpose is by the using of a new thermometer. The second temperature table gives the temperature at the surface 51°, at 10 fathoms 38°, at 30 fathoms 32.5, at 50 fathoms 33°, at 80 fathoms 34°, at 110 fathoms 35 degrees.

I am indebted to Professor Baird for the last Swedish observations which give temperature in the Baltic Sea.

The effect of all this is to show where the fish go. They go into the warm or cold zones. It shows also where the food goes during the summer season. The mackerel may for particular years seem to have disappeared, but there is no doubt they are there, but they are in a different zone of water. They are in the zones suited to their different habits or to the food they follow. You have a positive proof of that in the toll-bait used by the American fishermen. They throw toll out. Now, the mackerel are not lying on the bottom, but are in the zone that is suited to their habits. They come to the surface when the bait is thrown, and stay there as long as they can bear the surface temperature, and then go down again.

Q. When the Americans throw their pogie bait they toll them up; then if they cannot stand the temperature they afterwards disappear?—A. Yes.

Q. Now along the shore is the water uniform, or as a rule does it vary between the degrees of 45 and 37?—A. I could not state precisely the temperature, but the effect of the tidal wave on all the coasts of the gulf is to mix the warm surface water with the cold substratum and produce a temperature suitable to the mackerel, whereas on the coast of Massachusetts, where the water is so warm, they are driven off into the cold zone off shore. Whenever the water becomes warm on the coast you will find the mackerel out to sea in the summer, and whenever it is made cold by the mixing of the tides you will find the mackerel inshore.

Q. Now take the American coast; show the Commission where the

cold water strikes.—A. According to Professor Baird's reports there are
three notable points where the Arctic current impinges upon the Banks
and shoals within the limits of the United States waters and where
the cod and mackerel spawning-grounds are found. If you will bear in
mind the large map we had a short time ago, there were four spots
marked upon that map as indicating spawning grounds for mackerel.
If you will lay down upon the chart those points, which Professor Verrill has established as localities where the Arctic current is brought up,
you will find that they exactly coincide. One spot is the George's
Shoals.

Q. For the same reason you have spoken of, that the cold Arctic current is forced to the surface ?—A. Yes ; and the marine life found there
is that of about 40 degrees temperature. There are three localities
where the mackerel spawn, near Block Island, George's Bank, and near
Stellwagen's Bank.

Q. Are those three fishing localities on the American coast, Block
Island, George's Bank, and Stellwagen's Bank, in Massachusetts Bay,
affected every year, and if so, in what way, by the action of the Gulf
Stream ?—A. The whole of the coast of the United States, south of
Cape Cod, is affected by the Gulf Stream during the summer season.
At Stonington the temperature is so warm even in June that cod and
haddock cannot remain there. They are all driven off by this warm
influx of the summer flow of the Gulf Stream. The same observation
applies to certain portions of the New England coast.

Q. Is that the reason, in your judgment, why mackerel are not found
there inshore at all except in spring ?—A. That is chiefly the reason
why they are found on the coast of the United States close inshore
mostly in the spring and fall. They come again in the fall as soon as
the water is cool enough. It is quite possible that owing to the preva-
lence of certain winds the temperature of the water may be sufficiently
cool to permit them, even during the summer months, occasionally to
come quite close inshore. The Arctic current, coming down from the
Spitzbergen seas, passing the southern extremity of Greenland, turning
round and coming down to Labrador, and so on, reaches Newfoundland,
Nova Scotia, and part of the coast of the United States, and passes
underneath the Gulf Stream. Occasionally it comes out in the form of
strips in the Gulf Stream, forming what are termed the different cold
currents of the gulf. The difference in temperature between the Arctic
current on the George's Shoals, for example, and 10 or 20 miles southwest, is from 20 to 25°. The difference between the temperature on the
Grand Banks and the Gulf Stream, even that distance from the coast
of America, is 23°, according to Humboldt. The temperature of the
Gulf Stream, as given on the large map, is marked in several places at
$78\frac{1}{2}°$ in June; the temperature just south of Long Island is marked
$72\frac{1}{2}°$ in July.

Q. Does the Gulf Stream swing in at Block Island ?—A. The summer
flow of the Gulf Stream swings in with every southern wind, as far as
Halifax Harbor, and brings with it southern fishes.

Q. Have you noticed any and what difference between the marine
life on the coast of the United States and that on the cost of the Dominion ?—A. Yes; the marine life on the coast of the United States, in
some parts, is very similar to certain portions on the coast of the Dominion. For instance, north of Cape Cod, in all those parts of the sea where
the depth is over 50, 60, or 70 fathoms, the character of the marine life
is identical with the marine life on the sixty-fathom line of soundings
in the Gulf of St. Lawrence; but it is only where the cold Arctic cur-

ds its way. On George's Shoals the marine life is almost of an
character, according to Verrill, and it resembles an oasis of cold-
l animals surrounded by the Gulf Stream.

ave you ever turned your attention to see whether the present
f fishing on the American coast is capable of, or likely to, de-
hat coast of its codfish and mackerel ? State your views.—A.
egard to that subject, if you will allow me, I will exhibit a map
t, showing the distribution of the cod in Europe and America.
exhibited.) You will find by an examination of this map that it
where extreme cold water exists that cod is found throughout
ir ; and upon the American coast it is only where the Arctic cur-
rikes, that cod is found through the year.

wish to know from you whether the mode of fishing in the United
will deplete those waters of the cod and mackerel, or not ?—A.
ering the mode in which the cod and mackerel spawn, I think
an be no doubt whatever that it is quite possible through human
: to destroy, as has been destroyed on the coast of New England,
l fishery, and also, to a considerable extent, the mackerel fisher-
uply because the area of cold water, which is absolutely necessary
: sustenance of those fish, is so comparatively small, and is being
ntly reduced during the summer season. The proportion of the
f cold water opposite the coast of the United States, compared
he area of cold water opposite the coast of the Dominion, is as 45
; in other words, if the United States has 45,000 square miles swept
Arctic current the Dominion has 200,000 square miles; and every
n of the food supply which comes to the United States has to pass
rh Dominion waters, or by the waters of Newfoundland, simply be-
the Arctic current is constantly bringing the original supply of
rom the north. Although our seas appear to be very abundant in
et, nevertheless, they are almost deserts compared with the won-
l abundance of life in the northern seas, particularly on the Lab-
and Greenland coasts during the summer months. The sea, at
, appears to be perfectly thick with life, and to such an extraordi-
extent does life exist in the northern seas, that the thermometer is
materially influenced during a single night by animal life. In a
ours the animal life disappears utterly, and the thermometer sinks
.hree, or four degrees, and the water becomes colder. On another
he zone of life rises again, but it is always being driven to and fro
eans of the Arctic current, and it follows the course of the great
n of ice which produces the cold in Labrador and the cold gener-
hroughout the Western World.

I understand that where the Arctic current strikes, there are the
to be found which require about 37 degrees of cold ?—A. We are
ted to the Arctic current exclusively for all the cold-water fish, cod,
erel, haddock, pollock, hake, ling, and beside all the minor fish on
ı they feed, such as caplin, smelt, launce, and added to these a vast
ıer of *medusæ*, various kinds of shell-fish and star-fish, all of which
.ost abundant in the northern seas. The Banks on the shores of
ıland are richer than any cod-banks in any other part of the world,
have been so described by various naturalists who have visited

Take the George cod-banks or any other cod banks opposite the
ːd States coast, has the supply of fish on those Banks materially
ıished of late years ? I wish you to contrast the fishing there with
shing on the Grand Banks of Newfoundland or that on the Banks
ıe south of Newfoundland.—A. Personally I know nothing about

the quantities of fish taken on any portion of the coast of th
States, but I have derived the information I have obtained fro
ports of Commissioner Baird and his assistants, and also from
sations with fishermen. Now we know, for instance, that George
are not more than 35 years old as a fishing ground. At first it
quented exclusively for halibut. The halibut seemed to re
supreme. They were finally caught out, as fishermen say.

Q. Halibut is a powerful fish?—A. It is a much more pow
than cod, and drives the cod from all favorite places of resor
after the halibut had been driven away cod began to increase.
here say that cod and halibut were taken together in the first
but much more halibut than cod. The cod taken were of larg
is always the case when a fishing-ground is first established on ar
then they gradually diminish in size and in number except i
localities. Now, although I know nothing of my own knowledg
theless from conversations I have had with fishermen, there is
it is more difficult now to get a cargo of large cod, for exam
withstanding the extensive use of bultows, on Georges and in
cality on the coast of the United States, than it was when th
was first commenced; and in the same way on our own coast.

Q. You mean the trawl?—A. Yes. The reason why I mal
the term " bultow" is because the term "trawling" is applied to
different mode of fishing in Europe.

Q. You mean the long line and minor lines from it?—A. Ye

Q. Take our own fisheries; as far as you are aware are the
cally inexhaustible?—A. As far as all experience goes, judg
history and what we see at the present time, there are certa
ties practically inexhaustible. There is no portion of the worl
there is such a constant and unvarying supply of codfish
Straits of Belle Isle. It has been so for the past 300 years,
may even go farther back, to the time of the old French forts a
including the town of Brest, the ruins of which still exist on
of the Straits of Belle Isle. From the year 1590 down to th
time, the whole of the Straits of Belle Isle, a distance of 60 m
been famed for the uniform quantity of cod. The same holds
regard to the Grand Banks and Newfoundland. The same al.
to that amazing fishing-ground at the south coast of Newf
where the codfish winter at a depth of from 150 to 200 fath
where they can be taken constantly during the winter. Comp
European fisheries, the Newfoundland fisheries and Labrador
are far superior in every particular. The character of the N
fisheries, for instance, is very remarkable. The summer N
fisheries are prosecuted on the northern coast, and are id
regard to character of fish with the Labrador fisheries. The
fish caught are taken at Loffoden, Romsdal, and another local
the quantity of fish there taken, compared with what is take
Newfoundland coast, is on an average as the proportion to 3 to
5 fish or 5 quintals are taken on the coast of Newfoundland,
quintals only are taken on the whole coast of Norway.

By Mr. Whiteway:

Q. That is including Loffoden Islands?—A. Yes; the expor
way very rarely exceed 500,000 or 600,000 quintals.

By Mr. Thomson:

Q. Among the fish for which we are indebted to the Arcti
I do not recollect that you named herring; that is one?—A.
I did not name herring, but it was an inadvertence.

u have spoken of the effect of the tide at Prince Edward Island,
o there being not only water at the temperature the mackerel
, but also the tide. Suppose a body of witnesses swore that
ds of the catch of mackerel, for instance, in Bay St. Lawrence,
n within three marine miles of the coast, and another body of
·s swore that the larger body of the fish is taken outside, and
ller body inside, which would be the party whose evidence would
ith your scientific knowledge of what ought to be the result?—
uld say, as far as the Gulf of St. Lawrence is concerned, that
c evidence all tends toward throwing the food near the shore,
· the food which attracts the fish.

u would, therefore, be inclined to think that the large quantity
erel would be taken inshore?—A. Certainly.   ·. ·by·.·

re you aware that the Dominion Government of late years have
reat pains to restock the rivers?—A. Yes.

ave you any idea whether they would have any appreciable effect
e maintenance of the sea fisheries?—A. I think there can be no
hat in the course of two or three years the effect will be most
, but it takes some time to restock a river. The principal opera-
wever, is no doubt perfect. It is the manner of restoring again
tural condition the food supply of the fish which formerly existed
oast, and that is being done in various localities with all possible
. You allude, I suppose, more particularly to the fish ascending
·awning rivers by means of fish-ways over mill-dams, and restock-
rs in that way and also restocking by means of the ova of different
s of fish, salmon, white fish, bass and others.

hose measures have an important effect on the sea fishery?—A.
important effect on the sea fishery, simply because they bring
·-fish inshore. The cause of the sea-fish gradually ceasing to come
· in various localities is the destruction of the former lure which
t them in, namely, the bait, the fry, young fish.

las the fact of the coasts of Nova Scotia and Prince Edward Isl-
ing studded with small islands any effect on the value of the
·s, and, if so, what?—A. The orographic features of every coast
ert an amazing influence on the fisheries. A sandy shore, sup-
the marine climate is fitted for it, is characterized by an extra-
ry development of shell-fish; whereas a shore which contains
·ays and promontories is distinguished by the ordinary sea-fish
· other classes of animal life—crustaceans for instance. Thus, for
le, when you get on the coast of the United States as far south as
Island, New Jersey, and Delaware, the coast line changes alto-
and with it the character of the marine life. There is there an
ance of all forms of shell-fish, and also many forms of warmer
fish which come in from the Gulf Stream. The shell-fish on our
although the marine climate is well suited to certain varieties,
s the whelk and various kinds of clams, still the quantity which
d on our shores is comparatively small, except in certain localities
there are banks of particular description. Wide expanses of
beach are especially adapted to be the home of the shell-fish;
·s, on the contrary, jutting shores, headlands, and rocky promon·
are especially adapted to the crustacean food for ordinary sea-fish.

By Mr. Dana:
You are testifying to a large extent from the report?—A. I am.

By Mr. Thomson:
The scientific knowledge you have is not to be altered when given

verbally, simply because you have written the same things in a report?—
A. No.

Q. You have spoken of islands along the coast. Some of our witnesses spoke of catching fish in eddies. Is not the effect of the islands
to mackerel eddies ?—A. The food is carried backwards and forwards in
the eddies.

Q. Do the eddies preserve the food for the fish ?—A. Yes; in a very
remarkable way. I had special opportunities last summer of sailing
among eddies for hundreds of miles on the coast of Labrador and of
observing many of the remarkable phenomena connected with this
food.

Q. What is the effect of the eddies?—A. To concentrate food.

Q. And they will consequently be frequented by the fish ?—A. Yes;
it is with that view I have described on these charts the movements of
the mackerel.

Q. How do the eddies preserve the food ?—A. They move in circles
and ellipses and prevent the food from being carried away. The swing
of the tides depends altogether on the locality where they may happen
to be. The swing of the tide in the Bay of Fundy—I mention the Bay
of Fundy because the tides are developed to a greater extent there
than on any other locality on this continent—is about 35 miles. Fish
food is carried up the bay about thirty-five miles and brought back to
the same place with the turn of the tide, thus continually swinging
backward and forward for 35 miles for months together. It frequently
happens that during the winter season vessels caught in the ice will for
three or four weeks swing backward and forward in the middle of the
bay. The swing depends on the heighth of the tide, because that governs its velocity, and it varies from 15 to 35 miles in linear extent.

Q. When practical fishermen state they get fish in the eddies, that
would agree with your scientific information ?—A. Quite so.

Q. In the same way, you say that the statement that more fish is
caught inshore than out in the gulf would square with your scientific
knowledge?—A. More mackerel.

Q. On the American coast, is there a great number of large manufactories on the rivers entering the sea? Are you aware of that; and
state what influence the American manufactories have on the fisheries?—
A. I could not say that the American manufactories have any effect.
I think the quantity of material brought down in the rivers has no
effect on the sea fish, only on the river fish. Damage would be produced by mill-dams obstructing the passage up, but the sea is a reser-
voir so vast, and constantly moving, that a small quantity of foreign
material introduced into a river has no effect on the sea.

Q. What is the effect of throwing overboard gurry on fishing-
grounds ?—A. That depends entirely on the locality. Where there is a
strong current there is little or no effect at all. When fishermen throw
overboard, as they frequently do, the back-bone of the codfish when fish
are cleaned on deck, it has a very prejudicial effect on those fish which
feed on the offal. That is explained in this way : The cod, as fish do as
a general rule, take the food head foremost. The reason is that the fins
would present an obstruction to their passage down the gullet of the
cod, but when they take the fish head foremost they are easily passed
down. When the back-bone of the fish is swallowed, in the endeavors
which the cod constantly makes to throw up, it sticks in the stomach
and remains there, and the cod are very frequently taken in what fishermen call a logy condition, with a portion of the vertebra penetrating
the entrails. That frequently happens when gurry is thrown overboard.

'ith regard to the action of gurry and fish offal in the harbors of New-undland, that will depend entirely on the season of the year, and also on the locality where it happens to be thrown. I consider it has a 'ry prejudicial effect inshore, and I have described this in a paper hich I published some time since.

By Mr. Whiteway:

Q. Will you now state what you know about the distribution of food d the habits of the cod, and your reasons for the great abundance of e fish on the Newfoundland shores?—A. In the first place, with re-ird to the spawning habits of the cod. The cod is known to spawn iring every month of the year on the coast of America. In Trinity ay—I select Trinity Bay as one large place, where the water is not ss than 300 fathoms—cod spawn during six months of the year. We iow this, from the fact that the spawn dealers get the spawn from the 'hermen during that period; moreover, the fishermen catch the cod ith the spawn running from it. In the second place, the Straits of elle Isle is the great spawning place. Cod chiefly spawn there in ugust, at that period of the year when the water has been cooled wn to a great extent by salt-water ice. You will observe an immense ifference between ordinary fresh-water ice and salt-water ice produced y the sea-water itself.

Q. Point out the spawning localities of the cod on the Newfoundland ast.—A. First, there is the Straits of Belle Isle, particularly round out Belle Isle Island. In the second place, along the Newfoundland ast there are Notre Dame Bay, Bonavista Bay, Trinity Bay. I have special knowledge about Conception Bay. The cod spawn from May August all along the south coast of the island, and on the north part f the Grand Banks.

Q. That may be considered as the great spawning ground for the cod nd the great codfishery in the world?—A. Certainly it is, all around hat coast; I also include part of the Great Banks. I know in regard nly to a small portion of the Grand Banks as a place where they spawn. have no doubt they spawn all over the Banks, but I have only received iformation about a certain portion. There is a remarkable fact with espect to the spawning of cod, that while they spawn in May on one ide of the entrance to the gulf, they spawn in September on the other ide, and that arises from the simple fact that the water is not cold nough till September. With regard to the mode of spawning of cod nd all these fish, it is important to bear in mind that they spawn in mid-rater, with the male underneath the female. That is also the way with iackerel. Almost all sea-fish, except those enumerated by Commis-ioner Baird the other day, and two or three I will add immediately, pawn in mid water. You can always distinguish between the egg of he fish whose spawn floats at the surface and the egg of the fish whose pawn adheres to the bottom. The eggs of all those fish whose spawn oats has the orifice through which the fructifying principle of the male nters always downward. The eggs of all those fish whose spawn is at he bottom has the orifice always upwards. The milt of the male is lways poured over the eggs of those adhering to the bottom and un-er those floating

Q. Will you state your views with regard to the bait generally on the hores of Newfoundland and the Dominion; also the habits of the bait self, the places where found, general distribution, and its effect upon he cod-fishery?—A. With regard to herring. which is perhaps gener-lly known to be the best, both in Europe and America, you can always atch fish with herring.

214 F

Q. When upon herring, I will ask you with regard to the sou
of Newfoundland as a herring spawning ground. What are yo
with regard to it?—A. I only know of three or four localitie
herring has been observed to spawn, although I have not a sl
doubt it does spawn to an enormous extent upon the southern

Q. Professor Baird stated that the southern coast of Newfo
is the great spawning ground for herring. Do you concur witl
that statement?—A. Certainly. It is one of the great spawning
There is not a shadow of doubt that the herring spawns from C
to the Straits of Belle Isle.

Q. Professor Baird designates the southern coast of Newfoun
the great spawning ground for herring of America. Do you ag
him?—A. Yes, altogether. There are very erroneous views ent
by fishermen with respect to the spawning grounds of herring,
with regard to the spawning grounds of all fish whose spawn ad
the bottom. The herring spawns in water from 5 to 130 fa
depth. Caplin, instead of spawning only in great number on
as is generally supposed, spawn also in 30 fathoms. The lau
spawn on the Grand Banks, where they have been caught ful
spawn, and they spawn also to some extent on the Newfoundla

Q. Professor Baird pointed out Grand Manan as one of tl
spawning grounds for herring. Do you concur with him?—
tainly.

Q. Having stated your views with regard to herring, would
kind enough to continue to answer the question I put to you wit
to bait?—A. The season of the year, excluding herring, deter
a very considerable extent the bait which is used, especially on t
of Newfoundland. The first kind of bait you have there is ca
caplin is found only as far as the southern portion of the Gu
Lawrence. It is essentially a cold-water fish. It is found in
quantities off Greenland, to an enormous extent upon the nort
tion of Norway, where the cod-fishing in the summer season is
summer cod-fishing, but the caplin fishery, simply from the cod
the caplin inshore. The next bait, as a general rule—but it v.
much each year—is squid. Sometimes launce comes in befo
I have heard of one or two cases of squid coming in as early a

Q. Have you any reason to give why the bait-fish appr
shores—the herring, squid, caplin, and launce?—A. I think
reason, but I think the reason that is generally stated, viz,
approach the shore for the purpose of spawning, is begging
tion. I think it is doubtful whether they approach the shor
that purpose. They approach the shore because they are c
predaceous fishes which feed on them. The cod follows t
and drives it inshore, owing to the circumstance that during tl
ing season, as far as known, all fish have peculiar odors develoj
caplin has the cucumber odor, and so strongly is it developed c
spawning season, that Newfoundland fishermen will tell you
smell caplin for miles. I have smelt it 50, 60, or 80 yards and
any, but there have been men before me with a bag of fres
The smelt has also the odor of the cucumber, which appear.
veloped during the spawning season, and lures the cod insb
herring has also a peculiar odor, but it is totally different fro
the cucumber. And we have a particular reason why it is
only during the spawning season, viz, that afforded by the r
phenomenon which exists in Newfoundland in the winter.
the southern coast, and I have no doubt on the coast of t

'tates, herring are lying under the land during winter at depths of rom 15 to 30 fathoms. There are lying a little farther out seaward, specially on the coast of Newfoundland, from one to two miles out, out in a different zone, millions of cod. You have the herring and its prey lying close together, but they never come in conflict with each other during that season of the year.

Q. Why do they not?—A. The cod is found in from 150, 180, and '00 fathoms. The large herring is, comparatively speaking, near the surface—at a depth of 30 fathoms or so, according to the zone of temperature. The cod is feeding on the young herring, which are found deeper down. When you catch winter cod you will almost invariably find herring or caplin in their stomachs. If it were not so, the species would very soon be destroyed; it seems to be a providential arrangement by which the species is preserved. It is the same with regard to many other fish. Their young separate from them and go into the different zones of water during different periods of the year. The quesion you asked me some time ago with respect to the island is another Illustration. It is the young or fry of the herring which go to the edge of he great deeps off our coast. You have only to go 100 miles to the south of Halifax and you plunge down to a depth of 3 miles. From a depth of 90 fathoms you plunge down a mountain range, only 30 miles south of Cape Sable, with a depth of three miles, or 20,000 feet. So it is at the edge of the Grand Bank, and all along the coast of Newfoundland. Even in Trinity Bay you have a depth of 1,800 feet. In these deep marine valleys and on the mountain ridges you have fish distributed in zones of temperature during the winter. All along the steep banks you have zones of vegetation and of animal life. At a depth of 1,600 feet you discern enormous quantities of sponges, and as you rise to the crest at Sable Island or Grand Bank you come upon an enormous multitude of star-fish of all ages and sizes, and the star-fish always approach the land or shoals in the spring to feed upon the shell fish there. They feed on the enormous multitudes of whelks found all over the Labrador and Newfoundland coasts, and you can see them in very calm weather encircling the whelks and sucking the contents into their protruded stomachs.

Q. The conformation of the coast of Newfoundland, the depth of water, the deep bays and inlets, and numerous islands—do you think these conditions peculiarly adapted to constitute the home of the codfish?— A. Yes. I think there is no part of the world where, owing to the orographic features of the coast-line, all the conditions of life for the cod are developed to such an extent as on the northeast coast of Newfoundland, the northern portion of the Grand Banks, and the southern part of the island. The proof is afforded by the amazing multitude of seals which come every winter, to the extent of three or $_{fou}$r millions, and they feed largely upon codfish. They are found bringing the codfish on the ice. Where the ice drifts into deep bays you will very frequently find the seals, especially the old seals, bringing codfish and placing them on the surface of the ice.

Q. In what month of the year does that occur?—A. From February to the middle of April.

Q. Will you state generally your views as to the progress and development of the Newfoundland fisheries since they have been known, so far as your information goes?—A. I speak now of the Newfoundland fisheries as distinct from the Bank fisheries.

Q. I am speaking now of the Newfoundland inshore fisheries. You are aware that from the coast of Newfoundland the Bank fishery is not

carried on, except to the extent of three, four, or five vessels ?-
About 40 years ago the Bank fishery, so far as regards Newf(
entirely ceased, and the fishery has since been carried on a
within shore, and is extending year by year farther and farth
Labrador. As far as my observation goes, and as far as stat
I am able to show that the increase during the last 60 or 70 yea
for instance, 1804—has been almost perfectly uniform, when
into consideration the increase in the population of the cou
course, it is to a certain extent dependent upon that, and subje
those fluctuations which continually take place in our fisherie:
mackerel and cod fisheries—and in the marine climate on the .
coast, also in the herring fishery.

Q. I think you have prepared a diagram showing the progr
fisheries ?—A. Yes. (Diagram produced.) This shows the an
tuations in the exports of codfish from Newfoundland from 180
and a continuous increase since 1850, since when there has alv
a mean of one million quintals. It reached one million in 1842,
that it either approached to or rose above it continuously.

Q. Those diagrams you prepared from authentic records, I b
A. They are so prepared.

Q. Then from 1804 to 1876 there has been a uniform increase i
ductions of the Newfoundland fisheries ?—A. I would scarcel
word " uniform," otherwise one would suppose the increase w:
uous from year to year; but take a group of years, say five y
the increase is continuous.

Q. You are aware of the different modes of prosecuting the
the island of Newfoundland both by British and French, I b
A. Yes.

Q. Is the cod seine used there to any extent ?—A. It is lar
in the deep bays of Newfoundland, and also by the French
called the French shore; that is to say, on the northern coas
foundland and in the northern portion of the gulf.

Q. Between Cape Ray and Quirpon ?—A. I mean more p
between Cape St. John and Quirpon. The seine is largely u
this coast. I saw it myself largely used there last year; and
seine used by Newfoundlanders in Trinity Bay.

Q. You know as a fact that it is used ?—A. Yes; and larg

Q. At what season of the year is the cod seine used ?—A.
case during what is called the caplin season.

Q. That is when the caplin are on the coast in great abund
Yes; when they first come in.

Q. And when the cod are also there in great abundance ?

Q. Have you any knowledge regarding the quantity of
in these large seines ?—A. Personally, I have no such kno
have never counted them, but I have seen a very large 1
taken. Admiral Cloue states, in his report, that frequently
taken in a cod seine.

Q. In one haul ?—A. Yes. The statement that from 10,00(
and 30,000 cod are so taken at a haul also frequently occurs
ports of Newfoundland fishery officials.

Q. From 50 to 250 quintals are thus taken in one haul of t
A. Yes, fully; and, in many instances, more, because sometim
is composed of large fish.

Q. That is 250 quintals of what are called green fish ?—A
fore they are dried and prepared for market.

this occurs frequently?—A. I believe so; as I have said, I
it myself.

der to use these seines to great advantage,. is it not very de.
t the fish should not be at all disturbed on their grounds in
?—A. Yes; otherwise the schools would be broken up.

, if the bait be disturbed to any considerable extent, and it
ie cod would also be disturbed and follow?—A. Yes; that
· follows.

with regard to the French, how do they carry on the fishe.
ou aware? I do not now refer to St. Pierre and Miquelon,
er portions of the coast.—A. I have seen the French fisher.
reral harbors on the northeast coast of Newfoundland.

you mention the time when the fishing-vessels arrive from
id the tonnage of their vessels, and describe the means and
mode in which they carry on the fishery from their vessels in
se harbors on the northeast coast of Newfoundland where
the privilege of fishing?—A. I will describe what I saw in
r of Fleur de Lis, which is situated on the northeast coast of
land. It has always been a rather celebrated fishing station.
at three large vessels were there last year, and one of them
7 large brig.

it was her size?—A. I could not say exactly, but I think that
f 220 or 240 tons burden. I have a list of the tonnage of all
vhich I obtained from Admiral Cloue's report.

iout going into the particulars, I will simply ask you with re-
ie tonnage of these vessels—between what figures does their
innage vary?—A. Between 200 and 300 tons; some of the
the northeast shore are of larger build.

vhat season of the year do they arrive?—A. They arrive as
ie ice leaves the coast—in other words, as soon as they can get
frequently they first go to St. Pierre and Miquelon, and if
that the ice is off shore, they leave there about the middle of
ie first thing they do is to prepare their stages, and their fish-
s and bakery. They are always well provided with fresh
hey generally when they observe the cod come in after the
vote themselves in the first instance to seining them; as soon
leaves the shore, which they do after the caplin has spawned,
first devote themselves to the taking of bait by means of bait
'hey require a constant supply of fresh bait; they then devote
s to what is called the process of line-fishing, and they con-
from day to day; in the meanwhile they always have their
out, watching for the schools of cod; and the moment that
iool is noticed they immediately take their seines and seine
and this they continue until September, bringing the fruits of
s work inshore, letting the splitting and cleaning and drying
a shore by a regular corps of persons whom they bring out
rpose, completing their operations in the same way as New-
ers are accustomed to do.

i they remove from the coast of Newfoundland with their car-
id in September or October?—A. Yes.

hey leave their stages in charge of some one?—A. Yes; these
illy left in charge of some resident.

7 many men are usually employed in these vessels?—A. I could
ecisely. I do not know, but the number is very large.

Id you give it approximately?—A. The number is 60 or 70.

Q. How many dories or boats have they ?—A. I could not sa
never entered into those particulars.

Q. When do the mackerel appear on the Magdalen Islands ?—A.
mackerel come in there from the 60-fathom line of the sounding
wherever they may winter, about the last of May, from the last of
to the 12th of June. In some instances a good many mackere
caught there before the 1st of June; that is to say, the so-c
spring mackerel or lean mackerel. I have prepared a table sho
the period of their arrival during perhaps 14 or 15 years.

Q. Have you that table with you ?—A. Yes. This always
place about one month after the arrival of the herring. In 185
mackerel arrived there on June 1; in 1860, on June 1; in 1862, on
4; in 1863, on June 12; in 1864, on June 6; in 1865, on May 3
1866, on May 29; in 1867, on June 2. I can get no record for 186
1869, but in 1871 they arrived on May 31. For 1872 I have no re
In 1873, on June 5; in 1874, on June 7; in 1875, on June 8, and in
on June 6.

Q. How do these periods of time correspond with the appeara
the mackerel on the coast of the United States ?—A. There are g
ally from 6 to 8 days' difference between the appearances. I have
a record of their appearance on the coast of the United States,
find that the dates vary in a remarkable manner each year. F
stance, at the Waquoit Weir, in Massachusetts Bay, in 1875 the
erel appeared on the 25th of April, and in 1872 on the 10th of
showing a difference in time of 15 days, whereas at the Magdale
ands they appeared in 1871 on the 31st of May, and in 1872 on the
of June, showing a difference in time of 21 days, though this mus
mistake.

By Sir Alexander Galt :

Q. Would you turn back to your table concerning their arrival
Magdalen Islands ?—A. It must be a mistake. I find that he
1872 no date is given.

By Mr. Whiteway :

Q. Could you, by reference, correct that ?—A. O, yes.

Q. Could you do it to-morrow ?—A. Perhaps I had better do i
viously.

Q. Will you describe the different forms and descriptions of ic
how these operate upon or affect the fishery ?— A. There are three
of ice which exercise an influence over the fisheries in our waters ;
three forms are, first of all, fresh-water ice as it occurs in the fo
icebergs; secondly, the ice which occurs in the form of salt-wat
and thirdly, the ice which occurs in the form of ground ice, or ice
is formed at the bottom of the sea. The most important form of
the floe ice, or salt-water ice ; but icebergs have little or no effect
on the movements of the fish, simply because the cold which the
duce is always brought to the surface, owing to the small specific g
of the water resulting from the melting of icebergs; but the floe
composed of salt-water ice, and always has a temperature of abou
degrees below the ordinary freezing point of water. That is due
circumstance of a very considerable quantity of brine being ent
in the process of freezing, and the result of this is that whereve
water ice is drifted into a sea area it cools the sea area down to i
temperature, which is never less at the bottom of the ice floe t
degrees, and sometimes even 28 degrees. Then, again, when t
water ice melts, the coldest portions always necessarily melt fir

the result is that the brine of the ice being of a specific gravity much greater than the surrounding sea water, this very cold, heavy water sinks down to the bottom of the sea, or to a zone which is of the same specific gravity. Hence the result is those different zones in the Gulf of St. Lawrence which are described in these papers.

By Mr. Doutre:

Q. Are you correct in stating that the coldest parts of the ice melt first?—A. Yes. This does look strange at the first blush; but when you think of it, you will see that the coldest parts must melt first. Now the effect of that is that wherever you have salt-water ice, which is raining down a stream of cold, the moment it gets to the fish, they will not cross this line of cold. The effect of this is most marvelous in the distribution of various kinds of fish in the spring of the year; and, besides, the effect is more marvelous still in the distribution of these zones of cold throughout the gulf, or zones of cold as recently found throughout the Baltic Sea, producing those zones of temperature in which the fish roam during the summer months and find their food.

By the President:

Q. What is the third kind of ice?—A. The third kind of ice is ice that only forms in the coldest waters. It is formed at the bottom of the sea. In a letter which I recently received from Dr. Carpenter, he describes the formation of this ice in the Baltic Sea. It is known in America, especially in relation to fresh-water ice, as anchor-ice: in our rivers it very frequently is found, especially in rapid rivers. There is one condition required for its formation in the sea. You must have a rapid current, or otherwise it cannot form. This arises from the circumstance that the water is reduced down to the temperature of freezing salt water, which is 27 degrees; the sea freezes at 27 degrees only, or at 25 degrees in perfectly still water; and when it is brought down to that temperature, the moment that the cold water impinges on any surface ice crystals start out from it, and these ice crystals accumulate one on the top of the other until they become so light that they break loose and rise to the surface; hence it is that it is always necessary with regard to seal nets—which, during the winter season, are sunk from 18 to 20 and 22 fathoms, by the Newfoundland sealers, on their coast, or on the coast of Labrador—to watch these nets, for fear that the corks, during a perfectly clear night, in a rapid current, should become incrusted with icy particles; and if this happens the whole net will suddenly become incrusted with the icy particles, rise to the surface, and be carried away, causing the loss of the net. They always find that fish, or anything that may be caught in the nets—seals, for example, if they remain for an hour or so in the nets when the anchor-ice is forming—are frozen. One important point of practical importance with regard to the action of ice, to which I would direct attention, is that which the Swedes and Norwegians have now, under the supervision of the Norwegian Government, introduced, namely, the finding out before fishing operations commence the zone or depth at which the fish are to be found. This is the first thing that is done. On the great fishing-grounds on the coast of Norway, for instance, their first step is to find the depth at which the fish are to be found, and whether it be 10, 50, or 90 fathoms, they will sink their nets to that zone. The way in which they find the zone in which the herring are floating is by means of a very narrow net, which they will set, for example, at night. Such a net will be, for instance, 100 fathoms deep—a common seining net inverted. This they sink, and when they take it up they find fish entrapped in it at the zone

or depth in which the fish are to be found. They then set their ¡
according to the depth at which the fish are found.

Q. Do you mean to say that the zone where the fish are to be
is ascertained by the government?—A. Yes; this is done under th
pervision of the government.

Q. For the information of the fishermen?—A. Yes; and the ¡
men are also provided with thermometers to ascertain the zone or
at which the fish are to be found. I ought to say that they di‹
provide the fishermen with thermometers for that particular purpos
ior the testing of the temperature of the sea-water, with the view of
taining the days and hours when the herring fishery is most likely
productive; and in Scotland the fishermen now are provided with
mometers; that is to say, those who are capable of using thermom
So it also is with respect to the Dutch Government, which has pro
most of their fishermen with thermometers to ascertain the temper
of the sea, with a view to instructing them as to the period and ‹
hour when they should sink their nets, how deep they shall sink t
and I have no doubt that these thermometers will, in the course ‹
or three years, become an agent of very great value with regard '
fisheries, enabling us to ascertain the depth at which they are
to find herring in the fall, or, if we can, in the spring, in the dif
zones of water.

By Mr. Whiteway:

Q. Have you any other information to impart regarding the eff
these descriptions of ice upon the fisheries?—A. I have prepared
diagrams, but I did not think them worthy of remark, and consequ
I did not bring them with me. These are merely to show fishing ¡
in the bays, but they lead to results which, if viewed in a proper ma
can be properly interpreted. Very frequently you find, for examp
coming in without caplin and caplin coming in without cod; some
too, you find tons of dead caplin lying upon the surface of the
Now, I think that the explanation of this fact is exceedingly simp
arises from this circumstance: I observed myself last year, whil
dering for weeks, at least for a fortnight, among a field of ice com
of frozen detached pieces, extending over a surface of fifty square
that no cod and no caplin came underneath that ice; they wou
pass through the cold current which was perpetually falling and
ing beneath it. The fishermen prophesied where these fish were
found, and I ascertained that they were found, as they intimated
be the case.   The explanation of this is exceedingly simple.
caplin and cod come in, and meeting the ice, will not strike th
the cold current which is falling the while from the melting ic
is being carried along the coast; but instead of striking across t
customary haunts, they in such event proceed along the edge
field until they reach the grounds at its extremity. They would n‹
through this cold current, and having practical knowledge of thi
the fishermen are enabled to go to the right spot where the fish
be found.

Q. You were on the coast of Labrador last summer, I believe
Yes.

Q. How far did you go up it?—A. I went up 350 miles beyon‹
Isle.

Q. Did you make there any discoveries as regards the existe
banks in the neighborhood of the coast of Labrador?—A. I shou
call them discoveries, for I simply described what the fisherme

known for a long time before. Enormous banks are located there, and I noted down their position and mapped them.

Q. Do these banks extend all along the coast of Labrador, or are they situated off that portion of the coast which you have visited?— A. They do not extend all along the coast. There is very deep water indeed from Belle Isle to a place called Spotted Island, a distance up of ninety miles, where there are no banks; then you go up to Hamilton Inlet, a distance of about sixty miles, where also there are no banks, but when you get to Aillik Head, some forty miles beyond Hamilton Inlet, then the banks commence and continue as far as Mugford, 170 miles up, and I was informed indefinitely along the coast.

Q. As regards the floes of ice and icebergs which are brought down by the Arctic current, have you any information to impart as respects the diatoms, or animalculæ, attached to them,-which form the food of codfish?—A. Yes; in this way: We always find the lowest forms of vegetable life in the Arctic regions associated with the ice in vast profusion. They are described by those naturalists who have been in these northern waters as completely covering the sea for hundreds of thousands of square miles in the northern waters of Greenland seas and Baffin's Bay; tens of thousands of square miles of these peculiar vegetable forms were described by the officers of the Valorous, who went to take provisions to the late Polar Expedition, under Captain Nares. I have with me various descriptions of these animalculæ, and of the enormous extent to which they are developed; I have also appended to this paper here a note, by Dr. Robert Brown, describing the chain of connection which exists between these minute diatoms, found in the Arctic seas, and the food of all fish there up to the whale, and showing the most minute connection between them, and also how it is that in the northern seas many varieties of fish, particularly such as the gigantic basking shark, feed exclusively upon shrimps—a variety of shrimps which form the food of our mackerel—and are specially provided with suitable apparatus for it; so it also is with the seal.

Now, I have succeeded in getting a portion of the mouth-fringe of a shark about 35 feet long with a special apparatus which, in a single moment as you can see, is wonderfully formed for the purpose of sifting out these shrimps. The shark passes through the shrimps with his mouth open, and his mouth is furnished with this peculiar kind of apparatus. These teeth are designed to prevent its food from escaping. The shrimp feed on the animalculæ which feed on the diatoms. It is also a circumstance worthy of mention, in order to show the enormous range of the common squid, that in the northern waters the stomach of the nar-wal is found filled with the beaks of the common squid.

By Mr. Trescot:

Q. How many of these appliances for the taking of food are found in the mouth of the shark?—A. A succession of them are laid along in it.

Q. Are they placed transversely or parallel in the jaws?—A. They move like gills.

By Mr. Whiteway:

Q. As regards the codfishery of Newfoundland, I believe you have stated it is entirely inshore fishery?—A. As far as my experience goes it is exclusively an inshore fishery as now pursued by the Newfoundlanders. Perhaps on the south coast here and there during the winter they may go beyond what is technically termed the three-mile limit. This is quite probable, but taking it altogether this fishery is pursued.

in small boats, and is essentially an inshore fishery. I was in
many of these boats, and I went with the fishermen, especially
great Bay of Notre Dame, where the mackerel frequently appear
-siderable abundance, and where many years ago they made th
pearance in such numbers that it is still a common saying among
men there that they were then "cursed off the coast" because they
the herring nets and were a great nuisance to them, as they cou
no market for these fish, and so they used them for manure.

By Sir Alexander Galt:

Q. At what distance from the shore do the French prosecute t
fishery ?—A. They fish inshore, sometimes to five miles out, but
ally close inshore. The water is deep there quite close inshore.
are fishing all along the shore.

Q. Are the seines which you have described dragged from the
—A. Not necessarily; very frequently they inclose the fish an
them out.

Q. They do not draw them to the shore ?—A. No ; in many ins
they cannot draw these seines to land; the water is so deep a
coast so sheer.

Q. I want to understand how these seines are managed ?—A.
saw one handled once, and I would not like, under the circumst
to give a general description of the way in which they are use
they are managed in the ordinary way in which seines are mana
sea.   They drag the seine together where the bottom of the
will reach the bottom of the sea, for otherwise, of course, the 1
closed would escape.

Q. How do they get the fish to the surface ?—A. In a large
there is always what is called the bag, and they get the fish int
bag.   These seines are not drawn together with strings like purs
but knowing little or nothing about them, I will not venture to
description of them.

FRIDAY, *October 26,*

The Conference met.

The examination of Prof. HENRY YOULE HIND was resumed.

By Mr. Whiteway :

Question. Have you a general knowledge as regards the Fren
ery as carried on, on the coast of Newfoundland and on the
Bank ?—Answer. I have no personal knowledge in this respect
as to what I have seen between Cape St. John and Quirpon.   I w
in one of the harbors there twice, but in the course of conversati
different fishermen, I accumulated as much information as I coul
I have informed myself as far as possible concerning the history
French fisheries, particularly as derived from French works on t
ject and also from official statements relating to the last 40 yea
tained in the records of the various Parliamentary works to be
Newfoundland.

Q. From your information and general knowledge as rega
French Bank fishery and the French coast fishery, what in your
would be the effect, if the French were prevented from getting
any way from the coast of Newfoundland ?—A. With reference
French Bank fishery of course any information which I can giv
subject is necessarily that which I have derived from official docu
because I have no personal knowledge in relation to the French
fishery; but from the information which I have gathered, embr
records that go back over perhaps a period of 40 years, the unifo

ems to be that if they were cut off from the means of obtaining
ring and caplin for use on the Grand Banks, it would be impos-
them to continue that fishery to one-half the extent they now
y have long since exhausted, or nearly exhausted, the caplin
pon the Islands of St. Pierre and Miquelon, where they used to
hemselves, some 40 or 50 years ago, with this bait, and as far
 gather from conversation and also from the statistics I have
, the annual quantity of herring which they require varies from
 100,000 barrels; while the annual quantity of caplin that they
ies from 40,000 to 60,000 hogsheads, and so on.
ive you any knowledge as regards the value which the French
n their fishery rights on the coast of Newfoundland?—A. I
ly the knowledge which history affords in this relation, which is
y have always been most tenacious of those rights, from the
en the Islands of St. Pierre and Miquelon were conceded to
gether with certain supposed rights on the western coast and on
theast coast of Newfoundland. They have not only been, but
 at the present time most tenacious of those rights; and it has
source of constant difficulty between the British fishermen and
nch fishermen, with reference to the supposed encroachments of
fishermen on the fishing grounds they claim.
re you aware as regards the number of men and nets employed
French in these fisheries?—A. I have gathered here the statistics
ire published by Admiral Cloué, who for many years was on
ist, and who is the author of the French work entitled Pilote de
euve, which is the only great authority not only for the French,
en translated also for the British, for a very great deal of our
tion respecting the coast of Newfoundland. Now, these tables
en from his official work, and if necessary I can produce the
self, which I obtained for that purpose from the Library of Par-
 at Ottawa. It comprises two volumes in French, and is entitled
le Terre-Neuve par Le Contre-Admiral G. C. Cloué. These tables
to the different fishing stations, and describe the character, as
ressels and men are concerned, of the French fishing grounds,
nk fishing-grounds, the Gulf fishing grounds, and the northeast
shing grounds, and what they call the dory fishery. Tables Nos.
4, and 5 give the statistics of each kind of fishery, the number of
nployed in them and the kind of vessels engaged in them. I have
 number of boats so engaged.
hose named as coast-fishing vessels are those which fish upon
st between Cape Ray and Cape St. John, I believe?—A. There
 to be two classes of vessels which fish between Cape Ray and
n, forming the western coast, and part of the coast of the Straits
e Isle; and another, and totally different class of vessels which
m Quirpon to Cape St. John. The vessels that fish between
n and Cape St. John are very large, but the fishery is almost
vely carried on in open boats, close inshore, simply because the
s profound and deep close inshore along the northeastern Atlan-
it, whereas upon the gulf coast of Newfoundland in many places
al; and there is a class of fishermen there called the Desfileurs,
e supposed to follow the cod from the Islands of St. Pierre and
on up to the extreme northern point of the Island of Newfound-
here they join the French fishermen at the port of Quirpon.
he *desfileurs* fish sometimes within three miles of the shore and
nes outside of this limit?—A. They fish more frequently, I be-
utside; and then we have a class of men who fish in dories alto-

gether, and who fish altogether inshore. Now, I have here a state
showing the number of men who fish in dories close inshore o
western coast and the number of so-called *desfileurs*, those tha
alleged to follow the cod. I need scarcely say that this term arises
a misinterpretation of the habits of the fish. They merely interce
different schools of cod and caplin as they come in from the gulf t
coast to spawn, according to the gradual rise of the temperature
the seasons, as they progress farther to the north.

Q. And the large vessels that fish between Cape St. John and
pou anchor in the harbors and fish in dories close inshore?—A
dories fish close inshore, but the seiners may coast along for some
siderable distance. You are aware of the fact that the vessels ar
mantled, so to speak, and laid up, for the large vessels have nothi
do with the cod-fishing during the season, on the northeastern Atl
coast. This is altogether a boat-fishery; they require, of course, l
boats than dories to manage large seines.

Q. The vessels anchor in the harbors there during the whole o
fishing season?—A. Yes.

Q. And the fishery is carried on in boats?—A. Yes; that is to
on the northeastern Atlantic coast.

Q. And the fish which are caught in boats are taken within the
mile limit, close inshore, and along the shore?—A. As far as I saw
was the case along the coast between Cape St. John and Part
Point; but, of course, there were certain portions of the coast wh
did not see.

By Mr. Dana:

Q. Professor Hind, I find here a book, purporting to be issu
you, entitled "Fishery Commission, Halifax, 1877. The effect o
Fishery Clauses of the Treaty of Washington on the Fisheries and
ermen of British North America, by Henry Youle Hind, M. A.;
fax, 1877." Is that your product?—A. Yes.

Q. You wrote it?—A. Yes.

Q. And had it printed?—A. Yes.

Q. It is marked "confidential"; will you kindly explain wha
means in this connection?—A. My instructions were to have the
"confidential" printed upon it; and it was not permitted to go
the hands of the printer until special instructions were received fo
purpose.

Q. Then this was not your own private undertaking under you
responsibility?—A. No.

Q. You could not control it?—A. Certainly not.

Q. You furnished it?—A. Yes.

Q. To others?—A. Yes.

Q. Who could control it?—A. Yes.

Q. For whom it was written?—A. I received instructions to pl
when it was written, in the hands of the printer, from the commis
of fisheries of the Dominion of Canada.

Q. The commissioner of fisheries?—A. Yes.

Q. Who holds that office?—A. Mr. Whitcher.

Q. You received such instructions from him?—A. Yes—in relat
the printing of it.

Q. And you placed it in his hands?—A. Yes.

Q. By whom were you requested to prepare it?—A. Original
Mr. Whitcher.

Q. You make a distinction; you say "originally"; was ther

ಣe subsequently ?—A. No ; I say originally, because the history of ṇatter commenced some time back.　Do you wish me to describe it ?

If you please ?—A. It is simply this: When I came from Newfound-in May last, I was requested to put together the various facts with

I was familiar in relation to fisheries, and especially in connection ocean physics, and such like ; so I commenced to do so immediately wards, and this was the result.

Were you requested to do so by any officer of the Dominion Govent ?—A. Yes ; by Mr. Whitcher.

He asked you to put these facts together ?—A. Yes.

You did not confine yourself to Newfoundland ?—A. O, no.

This is a great book, comprising 150 very large pages, relating to ṇackerel, herring, and other fisheries, with chapters on the effect of Vashington Treaty upon the United States, and the general condi-of the United States fisheries, and the total extinction and disap-ınce of cod in certain places, &c.; it purports to be an argument ⁀ding the effect of the fishery clauses of the Treaty of Washington e fisheries and fishermen of British North America ; were your in-tions to prepare such a book ?—A. The matter was left to myself.

To prepare what you like ?—A. Not what I liked ; but to prepare ⁀er on the general subject of fisheries connected with the Washing-reaty.　No definite instructions were given me at all.

Does this title describe fairly the work which you undertook to A. I think it does, at least as far as a title can do so ; but you t describe it in a different way.

At all events your name was put to it and you approved it ?—A. ainly.

. Then of course you understood that you were to write upon the ⁀t of the fishery clauses of the treaty upon the British fisheries and ǐsh fishermen ?—A. No ; I did not understand anything of the kind ; ، was left entirely to me ; no instructions were given me at all with ⁀rd to what I should write ; I was merely to describe what I knew ı respect to the fisheries of British North America, and particularly ı their relation to the Treaty of Washington.

. You were to describe the effect of those clauses upon these fisher-—A. Yes.

. And the fishermen ?—A. Yes.

. And that is what you undertook to do ?—A. Yes.

. And that you put into the hands and left to the discretion of an ⁀er of the Dominion Government ?—A. I beg your pardon.

. When you had finished the manuscript you put it under the con-and discretion of an official of the Dominion Government ?—A. Cer-ly̆ not.

ː. Perhaps I have misunderstood you ?—A. That was not the case. the time when I received the instructions, in the first instance, of rse, I was told to place it in the hands of the printer.

ː. When it was completed ?—A. Yes.

ː. You were not to print it of your own option ?—A. No.

ː. You were to print it or not, according as you received instruc-ıs ?—A. Yes.

ː. Then, having received instructions to print it, you did put it into hands of the printer ?—A. Yes ; I placed my manuscript in the ds of the printer.

ː. And you superintended the printing of it ?—A. I corrected the ofs.

Q. When it was completed, did you take out any copyright?—A. No.

Q. When it was completed, what was done with it?—A. The edition remained at the printer's office; some few copies were, however, taken out of his hands; I, for example, took six copies out, under instructions to send them up to the Waverly Hotel; and that is all I know about it.

Q. You sent them to the Waverly Hotel?—A. Yes.

Q. You took out six copies?—A. Yes.

Q. And the rest, you say, are in the printer's hands?—A. No; I think that nearly the whole of them are there, but some are in my possession.

Q. Was "confidential" suggested by you, or directly by the officer of the government who had charge of it?—A. It was directed to be placed there by the officer of the government.

Q. So that you then had no right to let any one see it without his consent?—A. I had no right to do so.

Q. You were asked by Mr. Thomson, I think, how long you had made a specialty of sea-fish?—A. Pardon me, not of sea-fish, but of ocean physics.

Q. Then you have never made of sea-fish a specialty?—A. Certainly not.

Q. But you have of ocean physics?—A. Yes.

Q. That relates to the animal life of the ocean?—A. No; but it relates to the ocean and its temperature, and, for instance, to winds and ice.

Q. And the formation of the bottom of the sea?—A. O, that would come in, certainly. Every material thing that affects the sea is included under that head.

Q. You have not made a special subject of the fisheries?—A. No.

Q. Then as you are not particularly acquainted with the fisheries, perhaps your attention has been given for many years past to chemistry and geology and mining?—A. Yes; by profession, I am a geologist.

Q. We are familiar with your name in connection with the gold mines of Nova Scotia.—A. Yes.

Q. I believe that when gold-mine stock was put on the market at Boston you presented a certificate touching it?—A. No; never.

Q. Did you never give such a certificate?—A. No.

Q. You are confident of that?—A. Quite.

Q. You issued two or three books about this matter?—A. No; I did not.

Q. They appeared in your name?—A. I have nothing to do with that; they are documents belonging to the government.

Q. We have records of the different gold districts published as late as 1869, 1870, and 1872, by Henry Youle Hind, M. A.—A. If you will kindly turn over a page you will see that these are official documents addressed to the government of Nova Scotia.

Q. This is a record of the Sherbrooke gold district together with a paper on the gneisses of Nova Scotia?—A. Yes.

Q. And a paper on the gold-mining district of Nova Scotia, read before the Geological Society of London and the Society of Arts in London?—A. Yes.

Q. Were they first read there, and then incorporated into reports?—A. They only form part of a report. They were first read before the Geological Society of London, and discussed, and also before the Society of Arts, and discussed there; and then they were introduced in a report.

Q. These were material out of which you form a part of your report?

—A. I should rather say not; the report is given independently of this; they are adjuncts to a report.

Q. And not part of the report at all ?—A. Certainly not.

Q. The report is given with that paper ?—A. Yes.

Q. The paper was read as mentioned, and not the report ?—A. Yes; the paper was read.

Q. The last one is dated 1872; I merely put the question, in order to ascertain the exact field of inquiry to which you have given your attention; then, in addition to mining, &c., your principal occupation during some years past has been the examination of the physics of the sea ?—A. That has been largely the case; but I would not call it my principal occupation. My profession is that of a geologist.

Q. And a mining engineer ?—A. No.

Q. You are a geologist ?—A. Yes; a geologist merely.

Q. And even the geography of the sea—if we may use that expression, though it is a rather contradictory term—is not your primary and principal occupation ?—A. No; it is not my principal occupation.

Q. I will not trouble you with many questions about the habits of fish, as you do not profess to be an expert on that subject; your belief about codfish is, that it is not migratory ?—A. Certainly.

Q. And where do you think it goes; does it disappear during the season, or do you always find it in about the same waters ?—A. It is always in about the same waters; but I imagine that it has a certain very limited migratory movement, following its food a distance perhaps of from 15 to 20, or 50, or 100 miles.

Q. Do you think that it disappears out of the Gulf of St. Lawrence ?—A. Certainly not; the cod is there all the winter through.

Q. It does not go out at any particular time through the Straits of Belle Isle or between Newfoundland and Cape Breton ?—A. No; the cod can be caught in the Straits of Belle Isle up to Christmas.

Q. And how soon afterwards ?—A. As early in the spring as the ice moves, and even under the ice.

Q. The difficulty in catching it in winter is not caused by the absence of the fish but by the presence of the ice ?—A. Yes; the practical difficulty then is to get at the fish.

Q. The fish are then there ?—A. Yes.

Q. Then the cod do not move from place to place in the gulf in pursuit of any particular food ?—A. Certainly not; outside schools may occasionally go in, but this is not generally the case. I believe that all the schools of cod are, comparatively speaking, local in their habits.

Q. And the cod spawn in cold water ?—A. Yes, and in the coldest water.

Q. In the coldest water short of ice ?—A. Yes; short of fresh-water ice—that is to say, a temperature of 32°.

Q. Up to what figure ? You say that is the lowest.—A. That depends entirely upon the marine climate in which the cod are born, so to speak; you are aware that the habits of the fish on the coast of North America differ materially, in connection with the difference in marine climates, from the habits of the same species of fish found on the European coast. All along the coasts of England, Ireland, and Scotland, and of Norway, the diminished effects of the Gulf Stream are experienced.

Q. I would like to have you state if you will undertake to do so, and if this comes within your knowledge, what is the other and highest degree at which cod will spawn; you say that they will spawn when the water is little short of 32 degrees, and is the other limit 34 degrees ?—A. I would put the spawning temperature between 32 and 40 degrees.

Q. I think you have stated in your testimony that the therm
on the New England coast, the Grand Bank and George's Ban
is at 40 degrees at a certain period, owing to the action of the
current ?—A. That is the case at the bottom but not at the surfa

Q. Do you mean to say that ?—A. I certainly say so; and I esp
quoted Professor Verrill on the marine life of the George's Baul
ing that the temperature there is 40 degrees or below it.

Q. I will read a portion of your testimony to see whether I unde
you; it is as follows:

The effect of every current in the ocean is to bring the cold stratum of wat‹
lies at a depth of ten or fifteen or twenty fathoms near to the surface, and on‹
why on Orphan and Bradley Banks the water is invariably cold is, that the t
ture is thus affected by the currents which bring the cold water to the surface
is the reason why the water is always 14° or 16° colder on the Grand Banks
the surrounding deep sea, simply because the cold Arctic current is forced up
brought to the surface. Over the George's shoals the marine life is that of 1
perature of about 40 degrees. So also is the spawning-grounds of the mac
Massachusetts Bay.

Q. Then what do you mean by saying that the temperature of
always about 40 degrees ?—A. That is the temperature indicat
marine life that is found on the rocks on the George's shoals;
stance, the species of shell-fish, the different varieties of shrimj
the different species of star-fish.

Q. Or any other fish ?—A. Well, those are not true fish, but di
marine animals.

Q. You named some fish ?—A. The cod is found there.

Q. Then there is a temperature sufficient for the spawning of ‹
George's Bank ?—A. Most certainly, in the month of Februar;
the temperature rises materially in May. The temperature on G‹
Bank is sometimes that of the Gulf Stream, which in summer flo
it and drives at such times the cod away.

Q. How far must you go down in May to get a current of w
zone of water of the temperature of 40 degrees ?—A. Where ?

Q. On George's Bank ?—A. The water on the George's shoals
eight fathoms deep in some parts.

Q. Just take the lower part of the shoals, or the region just
it ?—A. I should say that in February you would find a portion
water on the George's shoals considerably lower than 40 degr
should imagine that the temperature on these shoals would the
degrees, or lower than that. The mean temperature on the Grand
in February is 31 degrees.

Q. As to the spawning-grounds of mackerel in Massachusett
you say that is the same; you say as to these spawning-grot
mackerel, that the Arctic current there produces a cold tempera
about 40 degrees; is that correctly reported ?—A. Yes; but the
to be understood that for this you take the proper months of th
The temperature of the water varies with every month of the ye

Q. To and fro ?—A. Yes.

Q. Steadily ?—A. It varies to and fro with great regularity.

Q. During what months of the year is the temperature the lo
Massachusetts Bay ?—A. February. In some parts of this ba
water ice forms.

Q. Then we may assume that it is cold enough there for the sp‹
of fish that so spawn ?—A. Certainly.

Q. Will you state what you mean by speaking, as I underst
the mackerel coming into the Bay of St. Lawrence, and striking

[agdalen Islands; do you find that to be the case?—A. I think
must be mistaken.

Which come in the first, mackerel or herring?—A. The herring.

You say that the Grand Banks, the southern coast of Newfound-
and that neighborhood, is the great home of the cod. Perhaps
will also add in this enumeration the Labrador coast, all the way
s far as you are acquainted with it?—A. No; I would not.

What is the great home of the cod?—A. On the American coast
the Grand Banks, and the southern shore and the northeastern
· of Newfoundland.

That is their great home to day?—A. I apprehend that that is
great home.

Their great home, of course, is where there are banks?—A. Yes;
rally where there are banks, but it is not necessarily so.

I do not want theory but facts?—A. As to the southern coast of
foundland, this is not a matter of theory at all, for they are to be
d there in 200 fathoms of water; they are constantly taken there;
00 quintals are caught in that part in from 100 to 200 fathoms of
r.

. They are taken there?—A. Yes.

. Do you mean to say that their home is not necessarily on the
ls?—A. Yes.

. I do not believe that the absolute necessities of the cod are known
cience.—A. It is, perhaps, a misapplication of the word "neces-
y," for which I must apologize. What I meant was this, that the
on why the cod is found on the Grand Banks, and the reason why
found at the depth of 200 fathoms, near to the Grand Banks, is
use the Arctic current is exceedingly broad there, and on the
thern coast of Newfoundland there is a deep passage for it; hence,
asses also between the Grand Bank and the coast of Newfoundland,
the waters are consequently cold enough for and consonant to the
its of the codfish.

. Do you think that the cod is not found where there is no Arctic
rent?—A. I think it is always to be found where there is an Arctic
rent.

. The depth at which the cod must swim in each locality at each pe-
I of the year would depend mainly on the depth of the Arctic cur-
t?—A. I should not put it in that way.

. I dare say that you can state it much more clearly?—A. I would
that the depth at which they swim is entirely dependent on where
r food is to be found. They are not bottom feeders, in the ordinary
se of the term according to the old popular meaning, but at certain
sons of the year they are bottom feeders, and at other seasons of the
r they follow their food elsewhere.

. Will they follow their food irrespective of the coldness of the tem-
ature?—A. I think not.

. Taking their desire for food and their desire for cold baths—taking
ltogether—how do you think it is generally true that they are to be
ad wherever there is an Arctic current flowing?—A. I think there is
doubt that, within certain geographical limits, the cod is always
ad within the Arctic current; and I do not think you can name any
ith during which the cod is not thus found within certain geograph-
limits. I do not say, for example, that on our coast of America,
y are found north of 70 degrees, but in Europe they are found far
th of 70 degrees.

. Taking the coast of America, where do you put these geographical

limits ?—A. At Disco Island, for commercial purposes, but the
maux take cod far north of that.

Q. What is the southern limit ?—A. For commercial purposes,
say Cape Cod.

Q. Not George's Bank ?—A. That is not farther south tha
Cod.

Q. When you speak of cod being found off the coast of Ne
land, to how many fathoms do you refer ?—A. It is caught ther
fathoms.

Q. What distance would that ordinarily be from the shore ?—
varies very much; some deep inlets there vary in depth from 15
fathoms. Of course, I can produce a map or chart, if you like, a
you those localities.

Q. Taking the western shore of Newfoundland—you know th
of course; you have written this book on the subject of the effe
Washington Treaty on the British fisheries and fishermen, and yo
of course—what is the American limit under the Treaty of 18
Yes; I do.

Q. Within those limits, what would ordinarily be the distanc
fathoms from the shore ?—A. Well, I could not say; but it is ve
to the shore—2, 3, or 4 miles from it.

Q. It is not necessarily at a distance of 3 miles from the s
course ?—A. Not necessarily; certainly not; that distance has
at all to do with it.

Q. When you come inside of the Gulf of St. Lawrence, th
places for cod wherever they are to be found are usually in cons
depth of water ?—A. Not necessarily, but usually. For exam
first place, so far as is known, where the cod appears in the Gul
Lawrence is Natashquan, a peninsula on the Labrador coast,
far from the eastern extremity of Auticosti.

Q. Are they found on Banks there ?—A. Yes; outside Nata
and there is a reason why they are found there.

Q. Do you regard the mackerel fishery as a precarious and u
kind of fishing ?—A. Yes.

Q. The habits of fish cannot be understood; we will never
be able to make this fishery anything like a certainty; it is a l
a great extent ?—A. I think not. I think that the Gulf of St.
mackerel fishery can be made much more certain than it now i
you wish, I will describe how this can be done.

Q. If you can do so, and reconcile it with your statement th
precarious and uncertain fishery, yes.—A. It is a precarious and t
fishery in this way: unfortunately, throughout the gulf, the i
fishery is chiefly carried on by means of open boats.

Q. You mean to say that this fishery is thus carried on by
habitants of this country ?—A. Yes; and hence, in the first place,
to a very great extent, the great benefits of the spring macker
in certain localities. For example, they lose the spring macker
on the Bradelle (or Bradley) Bank. They have not decked boa
would enable them to take advantage of the spring macker
there. Secondly, they labor under the great disadvantage of i
able to follow the mackerel when they move under the influen
wind from one side to the other side of the Bay of Chaleurs; a
third place, they cannot follow the mackerel when, under the
of the wind, these fish pass from the north shore of the G
Lawrence, via Point Des Monts and Cape Chatte, to the sou
fishing, as they do, in open boats, they cannot take advantage

ınities. There are three points in this regard. Then, again, on
ıst of Prince Edward Island, owing to the uncertain winds which
there, the mackerel move from one point in the great bight to
r point; and if they possessed sailing-boats or decked boats,
would enable them to remain out one night or two or three nights,
ould then be able to follow these fish to a much greater extent
ıey now do. These are four points in respect of which the use
ked boats or vessels of from 15 to 20 tons would enable them to
aterially to their present profits. At the present time these fish-
make a mere living, but if they were to carry on this fishery in
ıy I have mentioned, it would become to them excedingly profit-

Tou mean that this would be the case if they had large vessels ?—
s ; vessels of larger size, of from 18 to 20 tons, for example.
The Americans have very large fishing-vessels ?—A. Yes.
Is it a precarious and uncertain business to them ?—A. It is, in
ay : The great difficulty with them is to reach the gulf in time to
dvantage of the spring fishery. You very rarely find the Ameri-
ınter the Gulf of Saint Lawrence and reach Orphan or Bradell (or
ɛy) Bank or the Bay of Chaleurs save for what is called the summer
ɣ. This fishery takes place after the fish have spawned ; and in
ıuence of this fact they lose in the gulf the advantages of the
ɣ fishery which they gain on their own shores.
Then there is a spring fishery on the American shore ?—A. Cer-

Which they gain ?—A. Yes.
Is it still true, as you remark somewhere, that the mackerel are
in great numbers on the New England coast in the summer and
ın ?—A. I do not think that is the case there in summer; but I
that in autumn the mackerel come in there; I am not aware of
coming in there in large numbers in summer; I think that the
ɛrature of the water there is too warm for them.
You say :

ın the mackerel has appeared on the coast of the United States and the southern
' New England, they are so poor that they cannot be sold for food; but after
ave spawned, in May, they rapidly increase in fat, and are taken in great num-
, the summer and fall ?

A. Yes.
That is what I read from your book ?—A. Will you refer to the
ɛ
This is on page 79, sixty-sixth article ?—A. You will observe that
ȿ a quotation.
I do not see that—no quotation-marks are here ?—A. It refers to
, and is a quotation from the Report of the United States Commis-
ɛ of Fish and Fisheries.
Indeed, the quotation ends on page 79, with the 1st, 2d, and 3d
ɣraph.—A. True, it is not strictly a quotation, but a reference to
ɩtation.
A reference ?—A. Yes ; to a quotation from the Report of the United
s Commissioner of Fisheries.
You stated that it was a quotation ?—A. It amounts to the same
ɩ; it is a reference.
I cannot agree with you in this; to refer to a book is not to
ɩ?—A. You are quite right; I refer to the book as an authority.
For your own language ?—A. Strictly speaking, it is not a quota-

Q. I was misled by your using the word "quotation"; I
meant a verbal quotation.—A. I did not mean that.

Q. You refer to the United States Commission of Fishe
when you say:

After they spawn in May they rapidly increase in fat, and are taken
bers in the summer and fall.

Did you mean to put that in, thinking that it was incorrect
A. Certainly not. If you refer to the paragraph you will se
"Vide United States Fishery Report, page 64."

Q. That is the place from which you cite as an authority

Q. And did you not suppose it to be true?—A. O, I su]
be true to a certain extent; in fact, I believed it to be true.
that the statements made in Professor Baird's report are tr
his knowledge goes.

Q. Have you changed your mind at all as to the fact 1
"rapidly increase in fat and are taken in great numbers in
and fall?—A. I never formed an opinion touching the fis
New England coast. I state here "on the southern part,"
you will find that this limits the area amazingly.

Q. You allude to the southern part of New England?—A
that limits the area amazingly. I believe that is a spo
Arctic current comes up.

Q. What do you think of the autumn fishery on the N
coast? You have spoken of it in several places in this
think that the mackerel come in there again in the fall.

Q. You think that they disappear during the summer
disappear and go into colder zones of water.

Q. They sink or go out.—A. They sink simply because th
sink; that is to say, the cold zones retire farther and fart
warm coastal waters, and the mackerel follow them, and
approaches the fish come nearer and nearer the coast.

Q. They make another incursion on the New England
autumn?—A. Yes.

Q. Then perhaps you would say that on the southern c
England they increase rapidly in fat and are there caught i
tities in the summer and autumn, and that on the rest of the 1
coast they are caught in the spring, and again as the weat
colder in the autumn?—A. I should think that very proba

Q. And you do not think that the mackerel appear o
as elsewhere described, very fat and in excellent condit
ber and November, coming down there from the Gulf
rence?—A. Certainly not.

Q. You do not adopt what we call the fishermen's theo
spect, in which they still believe?—A. No; in the paper w
request I placed in your hands yesterday, I especially ente
cussion on that subject and point out how it is improba
mackerel pass through so many isothermal lines in ascen
scending order; this is physically improbable, and in th
point it out.

Q. I suppose that you once held the opinion to which I h
and that you did until you examined into the subject, as di
science?—A. I did so until I read a paper written by M
when I had read that very excellent paper, I was perfectly
it was not the case.

Q. And you think that this is the present scientific
Yes.

ne tables appear on page 81 of your book, and you say :

Atwood enumerates in his "Remarks on the Fisheries of the Coast of
etts," published in the Report of the United States Fishery Commissioners for
1.1 the following years as noted for extreme variation in catch.
reat catch, 385,559 barrels inspected.
9—Gradual falling off.
4—Fell to 75,000 barrels in a year.
nly 50,992 barrels.
1—Gradual increase.
'1—200,000 barrels.
—234,000 barrels.

your mind, does that table show a steady falling off and decrease
uackerel fisheries of the United States ?—A. A steady falling

s; and decrease throughout all the period from 1831 to 1871.—
It shows a series of fluctuations.
en you do not consider that the fisheries of New England are in
of ruin ?—A. To what fisheries do you allude in particular ?
illude in the first place to the mackerel fishery; do you consider
mackerel fishery of New England is ruined ?—A. Certainly not.
some respects it is rather increasing, is it not?—A. I think that
le to increase and decrease; it is subject to great fluctuations.
ike halibut, haddock, and that kind of fish; is this fishery in a
ruin, or anywhere near it ?—A. I think that the halibut fishery
in a state of rapid deterioration.
ou think that there are none caught on George's Bank?—A. I
lat there are a great many caught at George's Bank, but not so
r nearly so many, as was formerly the case.
o you not know that there has been a very great catch of them
years, and that there have been found, not on George's, but near
s, at a depth of 200 fathoms of water, a very large quantity of
?—A. I have no doubt that they will find them all round the
Maine at that depth—in what is described as St. George's Gulf,
he same way as I think they will find them throughout the Gulf
awrence, in deep water.
suppose that the necessities of the great market of New York
ewhere has caused more attention to be given to the pursuit of
than was formerly the case ?—A. That is a commercial question
cannot answer.
aving out the reason, has there not, for some reason or other,
re attention paid to the pursuit and discovery of halibut, and a
rease in the product? I do not mean in the number of halibut
sea, but in the number of them taken to market ?—A. I cannot
it I can draw your attention to a very remarkable statement with
to halibut, of which, perhaps, you are aware, namely, the repre-
ns that have been made by American fishermen to the French
n Boston, for permission to fish for halibut on the Newfoundland
t present in the supposed occupation of the French; this shows
g desire to seek halibut in every direction.
ow does that matter bear upon the question whether halibut is
e found on the southern coast of New England, near the George's
r about there, in very great abundance, and that there has been
itional stimulus, for some reason or other, given to the halibut
?—A. I did not understand that you put that question.
lat is my question. Now you say that the Boston fishermen
pplied to the French consul for such permission ?—A. Certain

Boston fishermen have applied to him for that purpose. This wa
years ago.

Q. How many ?—A. It must now be eight or nine years ago.

Q. For liberty to fish on what is called the French coast ?—A.
Newfoundland; that fact is mentioned in the Report of the Unitec
Commissioner of Fish and Fisheries.

Q. Did it go no further? Was the French minister addressec
subject ?—A. I am not aware of that having been the case; bu
as I could and can judge, the extreme jealousy of the French—t
ous manner in which they regard all their fisheries—made it a h
case.

Q. Has the French Government, through its diplomatic a
Washington, or in France, or has the American Government, 1
the Secretary of State or any one else, ever taken up that subje
The subject was brought up through the instrumentality of the
Government; it was also done through the instrumentality (
agent in the United States.

Q. Do you mean the consul at Boston ?—A. No; but thro
agent of the French Government, who was sent to the United
for the purpose of inquiring into their fisheries; and his represe
was made to the French minister; but the applications had bee
to the French consul in Boston.

Q. Then the French minister was told that certain persons in
had so applied to the French consul there ?—A. Yes.

Q. And nothing more came of it ?—A. I am not aware of that
been the case.

Q. On page 91 of your book, under the head of certain con
which you reach on this subject in connection with the Was
Treaty, you say:

The mackerel catch is a special industry, and requires sea-going vessels.

That you are prepared to say ?—A. Yes.

Q. You continue :

The boat equipment so common throughout our British American waters
unsuited to the pursuit of mackerel, which has been so largely carried on
States fishermen.

A. Yes.

Q. That you still consider to be true ?—A. Yes.

Q. That is, that the pursuit of mackerel should be carried on
vessels such as the United States fishermen use ?—A. Pardoi
did not state it at all in that way. I explained a short time ag
was that larger vessels should be used by the inhabitants of th
Chaleurs, of Prince Edward Island, and elsewhere, in order to
them to take advantage of the spring mackerel fishery; and if
done, these fishermen would become wealthy instead of remaini

Q. I did not like to call attention to the poverty or want o
edge or of education of the people of the country.—A. Will you
point out where I have described these conditions ?

Q. There are things which you have more right to say tha
But I did not say them, I think.

Q. You say that—

The boat equipment so common throughout our British waters is wholly u
the pursuit of mackerel, which has been so largely carried on by United Sta
men; and immense schools of mackerel are frequently left unmolested in the
on the coast of Newfoundland, in consequence of the fishermen being unpre
suitable vessels and gear.

Is that so ?—A. Yes; this relates to the spring fishery, on Bradley Bank, for instance.

Q. Is this statement true ?—A. It is; as I interpret it.

Q. As you now interpret it ?—A. Yes; and as I always have interpreted it. It was written with that express view.

Q. It does not contain any limitation. It is said that—

Immense schools of mackerel are left unmolested in the gulf and on the coast of Newfoundland.

A. Yes.

Q. Are there immense schools there ?—A. Yes.

Q. Which are beyond the reach of the boats ?—A. Yes; especially during the spring.

Q. And, therefore, they are left unmolested in the gulf in consequence of the fishermen being unprovided with suitable vessels and gear. You continue:

It is, however, a reserve for the future, which, at no distant day, will be utilized.

Q. It is your hope and expectation that the people of the Dominion may take the fish in larger boats or vessels, which will enable them to put an end to this kind of disability and disadvantage under which they now labor ? You also think that the fish telegraph system might be adopted and used as it is managed in Norway; that is, by telegraphing along the coast the presence of mackerel, I suppose ?—A. Yes; and of fish generally.

Q. You think that eddies contain and hold together a great amount of fish food ?—A. Certainly; of the free-swimming kind of fish food.

Q. And these eddies are formed by the action of currents and tides ?—A. They are formed by the motion of the tide wave being impeded by the shelving coast, while dragging along or moving over any feeding ground.

Q. The tides meet one another ?—A. Yes; but that is a different thing altogether.

Q. Do those eddies contain fish food ?—A. Certainly. I imagine that every eddy will aggregate and draw into itself all the floating substances which it has the power to draw in.

Q. Therefore the eddies as well as the Banks and shoal parts of the gulf would be places where the fish would naturally go to find their food ?—A. Free-swimming food—yes.

Q. To what depth do the tides affect the movement of the water ?—A. That is a very difficult question to answer. It is supposed that they begin to affect, or rather that the bottom begins to affect the tide, which is the proper way of putting it, at a depth of about 500 feet; that is to say, as a tidal wave approaches the coast it begins to be affected when the bottom has a depth of a little less than 100 fathoms, and 100 fathoms is 600 feet; so you may put such depth at about 500 feet; but that effect would be unappreciable to ordinary observation.

Q. At what depth is it appreciable to ordinary observation ?—A. I could not say; I know, for instance, that in the Bay of Fundy, at a depth of 50 fathoms, it is very appreciable, but that is an exceptional case. The geographical features of the province of Nova Scotia and of the coast of Maine have a wonderful effect upon the tides and in determining the depth at which they mix up the waters. But in the open sea the effect begins to be felt at a depth of about 500 feet. Outside of that it is merely an up and down movement of the particles of water, moving at the rate of about 1,000 miles an hour, following a wave like motion. It is only observable when it is multiplied by the tide breaking upon the coast, but

it begins, as I said, at a depth of 500 feet. But in the middle o
ocean it is unappreciable.

Q. You say it is an up and down movement ?—A. It is a ve
movement altogether in the open ocean.

Q. That is, the advance movement is a very small proportion ?—A
motion is especially an undulatory movement at the rate of about
miles an hour. It is very similar to the undulation of sound.]
vertical movement of the particles, and this movement is propagat
other particles.

Q. What do you mean when you speak of the particles moving a
rate ?—A. No; that does not refer to the particles, but to the ur
tion—the wave. The undulation advances at the rate of one thou
miles an hour.

Q. I thought you meant the motion of the particles ?—A. No.

Q. Then you say the mackerel are higher or lower, mainly acco
to the temperature zones ?—A. Yes.

Q. These are affected by the winds ?—A. Yes. They are g
affected by the winds.

Q By other causes ? For instance, by the swing of the curren
A. Yes; by the swing of the tide.

Q. In the shallow coast the appearance of mackerel close in is r
accidental, is it not ?—A. No.

Q. What is it owing to ?—A. The winds.

Q. They are driven in by the winds ?—A. No, not at all. I have
trated that point in the paper which I handed to you last nigl
should like to refer to that. I especially illustrated that point
regard to the movements of the mackerel in the Bay Chaleurs an
effect of the winds on the various portions of the gulf. That
mines the movements of the mackerel to an extraordinary extent.
instance, take the Bay Chaleurs. As a general thing the ma
always go against the wind. An off-shore north wind in the Ba
leurs will cause the mackerel to go from the south coast to the
and a south wind will cause the mackerel to move from the nort
take an exactly contrary direction.

Q. You said something of this sort, that all the food for fish was br
from the northern regions; did I understand you correctly ?—
not exactly in that form. The word which I thought I used, and
in fact I did use, I believe, was that the "source" of all food is
northern regions. I refer to the food of the cold-water fishes.

Q. Then the current does not create the food; it only brings it
Yes.

Q. And you think it is born in the northern regions ?—A. It i
wherever there is ice.

Q. Then does not another generation grow up in this neighbo
or do you have a constant supply from the north? I want
whether I understand one part of your testimony correctly. Yo
"Although our seas appear to be very abundant in life, yet, nev
less, they are almost deserts compared with the wonderful abur
of life in the northern seas, particularly on the Labrador and Gre
coasts during the summer months. The sea, at times, appear
perfectly thick with life, and to such an extraordinary extent do
exist in the northern seas, that the thermometer is very materia
fluenced during a single night by animal and vegetable life. In
hours the animal and vegetable life disappears utterly, and th
mometer sinks two, three, or four degrees, and the water becomes c
On another day the zone of life rises again, but it is always being

by means of the Arctic current, and it follows the course of
stream of ice which produces the cold in Labrador and the
rally throughout the western world." That we are to under-
e so ?—A. No; instead of the word "deserted," read "deserts."
o sense in the word "deserted" in that place. You are com-
imaginary thing with the actual.

y are always deserts ?—A. Comparatively.

pared with the northern abundance, &c.; is that true of cod
s other fish ?—A. No; the reference is more particularly to
æ and diatoms, which form the original source of food.

speak of food then, and not of fish ?—A. Of food.

pears to be perfectly thick." Now, do you mean the ther-
in the water or in the air ?—A. In the water.

you think that the temperature becoming cold affects the fish, or
ish disappearing affects the temperature of the sea ? Do you
nk the life is so great as to affect the general temperature of the

Yes; no doubt of it. That, you observe, is on the authority
rown. I mentioned at the time I was giving that evidence
d the extract here.

s not quoted by you ?—A. No. I mentioned it at the time.

they warm-blooded or cold-blooded animals ?—A. Cold blooded
and the vegetable diatoms.

es it cause the thermometer to rise or fall ?—A. To rise. They
t the surface, and when they disappear the temperature of the
ires its normal condition.

you account in any way for cold-blooded animals causing the
eter which is sunk in the sea to rise ?—A. Certainly. In the
e will you allow me to ask you a question ? What do you mean
l-blooded animal ?

at did you mean when you answered my question ?—A. I
eak of cold-blooded animals. There is no such thing as a cold-
animal.

ere are such things as warm-blooded animals ?—A. Yes.

u said these animals were cold-blooded ?—A. I said so merely
you said it. It is a popular expression. I will describe what
rly meant by a cold-blooded animal, if you like.

t you must have had something in your mind. It must have
ery fine distinction to answer my question as you did and then
a thing does not exist ?—A. A cold-blooded animal is——

ould rather have you state if you please what is the nature of
al that enables it to raise the thermometer ?—A. I can tell you in
ates if you will let me tell you what a cold-blooded animal is.
perature of the blood of most fishes varies from two to four de-
ove that of the medium in which they live. But there is a vari-
nimals whose temperature is much higher than that, and they
d warm-blooded animals. The whale, for instance, is warm-

All those fish breathe in the very same way we do, only they
ess oxygen and somewhat less fuel, so to speak. These minute
s that I have described, or rather which Dr. Brown described,
g the temperature of the sea, generate an amount of heat by
mposition of the carbonic acid gas. They are chiefly diatoms—a
e form.

m not a bit of a chemist, but pray tell me where does the car-
id gas come from ?—A. From the sea water. All sea water
carbonic acid.

Q. Now, the result of this is that they are warm-blooded ?—
They are not. You are a warm-blooded animal.

Q. Then you cannot answer without referring personally to m
Well, I am a warm-blooded animal.

Q. That does not help me, because you do not appear in that ca
but as a witness of certain facts. A man is a warm-blooded :
and so is a seal ?—A. Yes.

Q. Now, are these animals, or creatures, that cause this change
thermometer—are they of the warm-blooded sort ?—A. Certainly

Q. They are not cold-blooded ?—A. There is no such thing as
blooded animal.

Q. Then what can you predicate of them if they are not warm-b
and there is no such thing as a cold-blooded animal ?—A. Fish a1
tures whose temperature is from 2° to 4° above that of the mec
which they live. Diatoms are vegetables.

Q. They have blood ?—A. Fish and animalculæ have.

Q. You did not attribute the fact to the blood ?—A. The bloo(
agent by which the heat is produced in animals.

Q. Then it is the existence of the blood in them that causes tl
to be produced and given out ?—A. It is the existence of the
which is the means of producing the heat.

Q. And that they communicate to the surrounding water ?—A

Q. And that causes the temperature to do which, to rise or fa
To rise.

Q. Now, then, can you tell me hadn't you that in mind wh
answered my question ? I don't mean in the least'to call your sta
in question, but hadn't you all that in your mind when you an
my question that they were cold-blooded ? You answered the
were cold-blooded.—A. I made use of it as a popular phrase.

Q. Would that as a popular phrase apply to a warm-blooded
—A. No, certainly not.

Q. You really think that these animals raise the temperature
degree ?—A. Yes, the mass of minute life raises the temperatur
or 3°, unquestionably so.

By Mr. Foster:

Q. Are they visible to the eye ?—A. Yes. They were also dis
to a considerable extent by Sir Wyville Thomson in the subar
gions. You will find a full description of them published.

By Mr. Dana:

Q. The place where I found the reference in your testimony c
refer to Dr. Brown.—A. Yes, I referred, if you recollect, to th
ments made in this manuscript.

Q. I mean in your testimony yesterday ?—A. I referred to thi
script.

(Witness states at this stage that the remark occurring in h
mony of yesterday, in reference to mackerel coming into the ba,
20th of June, is correct. It appears that he had previously s
was a mistake.)

Q. The mackerel spawn in deep sea, do they not ?—A. Yes, s
have, however, no evidence here in America; but in Europe th
been caught far out in the sea.

Q. Have you any doubt that is true of the American coast ?
I think they will spawn anywhere where the water is cold enou

Q. You think they will spawn in the deep sea ?—A. Yes.

Q. You were asked by Mr. Thomson to compare the two sp

y that he said had been before this tribunal—one class of testi-
ing that the large proportion, say two-thirds, of the mackerel
ght within three miles of the shores all through the gulf; the
iss of witnesses stating that two thirds or three-fourths were
utside and the remainder inside. You were asked which you
insider the true testimony, or, perhaps, the question would be
ch would be the most in accordance with your theory which
e stated here. You answered, as I understood, that the testi-
those who said two thirds were caught inside would be more in
ice ?—A. Yes, for the Gulf of St. Lawrence.
cluding all parts of the gulf; is that taking the gulf as a whole?—
ig the chief mackerel grounds, Prince Edward Island, Bay Cha-
id the north and south shores of the estuary of the St. Law-

ot including the Banks ?—A. No.
ien you didn't mean your answer to apply to the whole gulf,
eddy, and everything ?—A. No.
think it would have been misunderstood otherwise. The question
he greater part are caught depends somewhat, does it not, upon
r the people use boats or vessels, which depends upon conditions
enience and economical considerations. There are various con-
ons which may induce people to fish, inside or outside. People
me in from a distance must come in large vessels, and would nat-
fish outside, whereas people that live along the shores would
with boats; so that, taking the question whether the fishing
e in the bay as a whole, it depends, does it not, upon a variety
imstances ?—A. I understood the question to be more particu-
ith regard to the manner in which the mackerel are caught in-
n the Gulf of St. Lawrence, in contradistinction to the manner in
they are caught upon the American shore, and I think I stated
the Gulf of St. Lawrence the tendency of scientific observation
be to show that the greatest portion of the mackerel are caught
e, whereas on the American shore, owing to the temperature of
ter, the greater portion would be caught outside.
Vould be found, rather ?—A. Yes; would be found.
'he question as to where they would be caught would depend upon
ty of circumstances such as I have referred to. Those you don't
t. You spoke of what was discharged from the mouths of rivers
e dams and factories, which prevented the passage up the rivers
he American coast of the fish from the sea, which you thought
ave the effect of diminishing the number of the commercial fish
followed them. In this connection you spoke of what had been
ere to remedy such evils; are you aware that in New England
reat pains have been taken to secure the passage of the fish up be-
he dam ?—A. Yes.
ind did you know that statutes had been passed, and decisions of
irts given, compelling even the oldest dams to allow a place for
issage of the fish ?—A. Yes.

By Mr. Foster :
u speaking of codfish I wanted to know if you were aware that
the last two or three years, off Block Island, at the mouth of Long
Sound, large quantities of cod have been taken in new places,
they were not known to be before, and where they have not been
for before, through the spring and autumn months?—A. Up to
hey are caught, and then in the autumn.

Q. How do you account for that?—A. I do not. Professor ⌐
accounts for it by a spur of the Arctic current coming in from the
tucket shoals and passing around Block Island.

Q. There is a cold wave of water at that particular point?—A
In the month of June they are driven out by the Gulf Stream.

Q. But the mackerel are taken in substantially the same local
through the season from early spring to late in the autumn, are the⌐
—A. I understand that all around the neighborhood of Block]
they are taken in early spring, and that is their great spawning gr

Q. Undoubtedly they are taken in the early spring. Are they
midsummer?—A. I was not aware of it. I never heard of any
taken then.

Q. Do you think it can be laid down as a rule that the macke
the United States coast are caught nearer inshore in the spring ar
than in the summer months?—A. Certainly.

Q. You are satisfied of that as a fact. I don't mean that it wo
in accordance with your theory, but are you satisfied, from the ob
tions of facts that you have made, that the actual facts will bear or
view?—A. Quite irrespective of theory, I judge solely from the v
descriptions that I have heard that the fish in the spring and f
largely inshore. In the summer it is not so. That is expressly s⌐
Professor Verrill, not in regard to mackerel particularly, but as
fish, in his elaborate report for 1872 as well as in the American Ji
of Science for 1873.

Q. Well, I have seen Professor Verrill's report, but didn't you ⌐
stand that the American skippers have been getting very large h⌐
mackerel in the summer months as well as in the spring and autur
A. You mean away out a good many miles; certainly.

Q. And close in?—A. I don't know about close in; but I know
sail 30 or 40 miles out and get them in abundance.

Q. There is no question about that. Don't they also get them
near inshore?—A. I think they do in Massachusetts Bay and near
wanger Bank.

Q. Would they not get them on the Banks wherever they are,
near shore or far out?—A. Always on the Banks in the locality
Arctic current.

Q. Well, now, one or two more questions about the cod fishery
to ask you. You spoke of the French fishing at St. Peter's; is nc
an uncertain fishery, lasting only a short time?—A. There is .
remarkable circumstance connected with the French fishery.

Q. What is it?—A. It has been pointed out in a very elaborate
ner by Admiral Cloué. It is this: that for the period of three or ⌐
five years the French fishery on the Grand Banks is good, an⌐
declines, but as soon as it begins to decline the French fishery
northeast coast of Newfoundland begins to be good, and many o
vessels go there. That in turn will continue good for a period of
or four years, and then declines. Meanwhile the Bank fishery i⌐
perated.

Q. To what do you attribute that, or what do you infer from it
I should be sorry to draw any special inference from a general
ment like that. All the fisheries fluctuate. It depends very mucl
the seasons of the year, and especially upon the temperature
month of April. I have called especial attention to that in this ⌐

Q. Now, the Gulf of St. Lawrence is a succession of Banks, s⌐
which are laid down on charts and some of which are not big e
to get on the charts.—A. Well, I should not describe it in that w

Well, how many Banks do you know between the south coast of
)sti, and from there down to Prince Edward Island?—A. In the
)lace there is the sixty-fathom line of soundings, and upon that
are several Banks.

Here is a map attached to the British Case (handing map to wit-
can you tell me by whom it was made?—A. No.

Now, there are the Magdalen Islands and there are Bradley,
in, and Miscou Banks, and you know where Fisherman's Bank is.
iot down here. Taking the Magdalens as a center, it appears by
iap that there is excellent fishing all around that region. We
heard of the fisheries on Bradley, Orphan, and Miscou Banks, and
ave stated that Bradley Bank particularly was a great spawning-
d for mackerel. Now, was I not pretty near right in saying that
you get down a little way beyond Anticosti the body of the gulf is
es of Banks?—A. It is nearly all flat. So it is shown on Admiral
eld's chart. The soundings vary from 60 fathoms upward.

I must have got it out of your books, that statement that there
, number of banks so small that they did not get down on the
?—A. I have no doubt that statement is perfectly true, that there
great many Banks that are not on the maps; but there are vast
tudes on the coast of Nova Scotia. It was in reference to that, I
, that I spoke.

Whenever you find these Banks you expect to find mackerel?—A.
bould think so.

Whether these Banks are situated, as some of them are, 25 or 30
from the shore, or whether they are pretty near in?—A. I should
: that made no difference at all.

You don't think there are particular spawning-grounds for mack-
—A. It depends upon the temperature.

Wherever the fish happens to be when it is under the necessity
awning, then it spawns just as an animal delivers its young?—A.

Now, the mackerel do spawn away down south as far as Cape
eras on the American coast?—A. I am not aware of it.

How far south do you think is the most southern point where they
n on the American coast?—A. I don't know; I never heard of any
i of Block Island. I can easily conceive that it is not impossible
e the Arctic current surges up under the Gulf Stream that they
d spawn, but I have never heard of any locality south of Block
d.

I was under the impression that we had some evidence of it a good
further south, but perhaps not. Now, you spoke of a spring fishery
iackerel in the gulf which is not made use of. I would like to know
early you think mackerel could be taken in the gulf that would be
than number three commercially?—A. I could not say.

Well, that would not be until some twenty days after spawning?—
think not. Probably they would be hardly fit to catch. There is
id of food on which they feed immediately after spawning which
us them up with wonderful rapidity.

What is that?—A. The launce. That is the reason why they dis-
ar immediately after spawning on Bradley or on any of these Banks.
disappear in pursuit of the launce.

How early do you think they disappear from these Banks?—A. I
i it is not at all difficult to ascertain if you take a mean of the times
ieir appearance during 12 or 14 years. They didn't appear this

year before the 1st of June. Some years it is considerably befor
some years not until the 7th of June.

Q. When is the spring fishery over, and when does the summ
ery commence ?—A. About a month afterwards.

Q. You think they disappear early in June and reappear abo
1st of July ?—A. They reappear about the 1st of July.

Q. So that the United States fishermen who make their appe
on the Banks about the 1st of July, go there in time for the seco
pearance of the mackerel ?—A. For the summer, yes.

Q. But there is an abundance of earlier and poorer mackere
anybody might get ?—A. A great abundance.

Q. Do you know whether, at that time, they take the hook rea
A. I don't know about that.

Q. That may be one reason why they have not heretofore be
sued ?—A. They have caught them in seines.

Q. I know, but there are no Americans here to catch them, a
provincial fishermen don't use seines ?—A. I think there is a re
an American vessel catching them with seines.

Q. You regard the mackerel fishing of the provincial fisher
undeveloped ?—A. Yes.

Q. The fish are there to be caught, and what the people need
sels and enterprise, skill, and industry to pursue them ?—A.
would not go quite as far as that.

Q. What do they need ?—A. In the first place, I think they
little guidance and instruction. They need also co-operative co
tion, and also capital.

Q. Now, would not those pass under the terms " capital and s
my question ? However, if they know how to do it, and co
money to build vessels, you think they could catch large quant
mackerel early in the season ?—A. If they could get money t
vessels.

Q. Is there any present prospect of that industry developing
think there is.

Q. Has there been anything done in that direction ?—A. I
aware of it on the coast of Prince Edward Island ; I am aware
the coast of Newfoundland ; I am personally aware of a good de
ing been done on the coast of Newfoundland.

Q. Not for mackerel ?—A. Not necessarily.

Q. You refer to the bounties they have offered ?—A. No ; to
operative system being beneficial.

Q. But is there in the provinces any tendency to engage at t
ent time in vessel-fishing for mackerel ?—A. I am not aware ; I
know.

Q. There were vessels fishing a number of years ago here, bu
out ?—A. The mackerel fishery of Nova Scotia is enormous.

Q. Vessels ?—A. I can't say so much for vessels.

Q. It is vessel-fishing I am asking about, because you have
of the necessity of pursuing it in sea-going boats. You are no
that there was a fleet of vessels here that has disappeared ?—A.

Q. Do you know the history of a company formed in Halifax
purpose which has since disappeared ?—A. No ; I never heard

Q. I notice here in your memorandum a report which is from
partment of Agriculture, by J. C. Tache, in which he undertakes
the proportion of the catch from each province ?—A. Yes.

Q. He gives the catch of cod, haddock, herring, and macke
you know whether the figures are according to your views ?

n Quebec as taking seven per cent. of the mackerel, Nova Scotia
er cent., New Brunswick 3 per cent., and Prince Edward Island
per cent. Now, where off the coast of Nova Scotia would there be
quantity taken; 80 per cent. is the estimate on an average catch
50,000 barrels a year. In 1875, it was 126,000; and in 1874, 164,000.
ink a fair average would be 150,000 barrels. Now, 80 per cent. or
is taken off Nova Scotia. Whereabouts is it taken?—A. It is all
and the coast of Nova Scotia and Cape Breton. The mackerel fre-
ntly strike the coast of Nova Scotia for 100 miles in one night.
. These blue marks on the chart are intended to show the general
rse of the mackerel in pursuit of food. They are not always partic-
· to stay out more than three miles or to come in within three miles?
y vary?—A. Yes.
. Well, I was very much surprised to find 80 per cent. given as the
portion taken in Nova Scotia, because from the evidence we should
ik far the greater proportion came from Prince Edward Island.
Ion. Mr. KELLOGG. Is that the percentage for the provinces?
Ir. FOSTER. Yes; it is an estimate of the grand total catch of each
vince, and it follows a total giving the total catch from 1869 to 1875
lusive. It seemed to me a most extraordinary thing, because the
dence of American vessels fishing on the coast of Nova Scotia is very
le indeed.
Q. Can it be. You think it is right?—A. There is a simple explana-
1. They strike the headlands, and are all taken close inshore. They
taken by boats.
. There are no provincial vessels fishing for them, and this particu-
coast is not resorted to very much for mackerel?—A. No, but enor-
us catches are made by the provincial fishermen in boats.
Q. You understand that the Gulf of St. Lawrence is the place where
e United States vessels go for fish?—A. Chiefly.
Q. I observe you spoke of Bay Chaleurs as if there were a good many
ickerel there. Now, the evidence we have had of the amount of
ickerel-fishing in the Bay Chaleurs is that it is quite small. Do you
ow about the quantity caught there?—A. I have been around there
rself in 1863 or 1864, I think two or three years. I have seen a very
rge number of vessels there.
Q. There is no doubt that at that time there were a good many that
nt to Bay Chaleurs, but of late years do you understand there has
en many—for the last four or five years?—A. I don't know.
Q. You omitted one thing that would be necessary to develop the fish-
g industry of the province here, I think. What other things are there
at occur to you as likely to promote the fishing interests of the fisher-
n in the provinces?—A. There are several, I think; that is rather
> wide a field.
Q. They ought to have a market, certainly?—A. I think they ought
have a market, certainly.
Mr. DANA. I wish to explain my ignorance of that book (Professor
nd's book on the fishery clauses of the Washington Treaty.) You
te that half a dozen copies were sent to the Waverly House. They
re not sent to the American counsel?
WITNESS. No.
Mr. DOUTRE That book is not filed here as part of your evidence.
erefore I do not see that this is a matter for investigation.
Mr. DANA. Do you object to my putting the question?—A. If you ob-
t I will not put it.

Mr. DOUTRE proposes to ask witness at whose request he pı
the book.

Mr. DANA. If the subject is to be dropped, that is one thing, b
not think you should ask me to drop it and take it up yourself.

Mr. DOUTRE. O, go on.

Mr. DANA. Do you wish the subject dropped?

Mr. DOUTRE. No, we have nothing to conceal.

Mr. DANA. The unprinted one, the manuscript, I never saw uı
night.

WITNESS. That is a continuation of the present one.

Mr. WEATHERBE observes that if the counsel for the United
had the manuscript book they were better off than the counsel
Britannic Majesty. He had not seen it at all.

Hon. Mr. KELLOGG. What is to be the use of this book? I dı
derstand.

Mr. DOUTRE. It was for our own use in examining the witnes

Hon. Mr. KELLOGG. I only want to know whether it is to be
the board or not.

Mr. DOUTRE. No, not as part of the evidence.

Mr. DANA. I hope we have not been guilty of any mistake. 1
part came here only yesterday, and Mr. Foster got it from the
Agent.

Mr. DOUTRE. Several copies were given to Professor Baird.

Mr. DANA. Not until after he had given his evidence.

By Mr. Trescot:

Q. With regard to the theory of this report, a great portion of wi
have read with a great deal of interest, as I understand, the purpor
the advance in the study of ocean physics has been such that cetra
have been discovered, the application of which, like other scienti
will develop a large fishing industry if properly applied?—A. C

Q. You think that promise of increase in the extension of the
ought to be taken into account in estimating their value?—A.

Q. Has the discovery of these laws advanced far enough to
tically applied within the next two or three years?—A. Certainly
are already practically applied in Norway and by——

Q. Taking the habits of the fish into consideration, the orogra
line of the coast, the operation of the Arctic current and the Gulf
the variation of the zone temperature, together with one or tw
things, the winds and tides; all those considerations govern the ɑ
where the mackerel will be found. Now, is your knowledge of th
sufficiently certain to enable you to say, at any given moment,
mackerel will be there at such and such a time, on such and su
of coast?—A. Certainly not. But there is now being instituteɑ
the auspices of the United States Government, a series of marin
vations, especially under the direction of the Coast Survey, aı
those will pass through the hands of Professor Baird. Those ar
purpose of taking the temperature, not only at the surface but a
depths below. But nothing has been done yet.

Q. That being the case, and you having admitted the America
men under the treaty of 1871, so as to make this practically one
ous line of fisheries dependent on each other, don't you think ɑ
that would end by putting the whole thing under one joint con
would be a great deal better than any award of any kind?—
not capable of answering the question so far as the award is coı
but so far as the development of the fisheries is concerned it
an immense advantage, there is no doubt.

⟨ Mr. Doutre:

mply wish to ask you a question to bring out a full explanation
l of this book —A. 1 have given every explanation.
ℓ government wanted to use your practical knowledge for its
lance and requested you to prepare this information?—A. 1
so, but this manuscript book which I have prepared was pre-
pecially for my own evidence.
ien were you requested by the government to devote yourself
iusiness?—A. Well, I was requested in the first week in May.
d a telegram at St. John's, Newfoundland.
u were requested by the Minister of Marine and Fisheries to go
'a?—A. Yes, and provided that the Newfoundland Government
gree that I should put off the expedition to the Labrador until
r I consented to go. I submitted the request to the Govern-
Newfoundland, made through the Minister of Marine and Fish-
d they agreed in the most cordial manner, and I at once went
'a.
u were put in communication with Mr. Whitcher?—A. Yes.
u were to devote all your time and give the result to the gov-
?—A. Since that I have devoted the whole of my time to the
ion of this report on the subject generally; since that time to
ent moment.

y Hon. Mr. Kellogg:

ere is one point in your evidence with regard to layers of waters
temperature of the water, and I understand you to say that the
ayer would come to the surface. Why would the colder layer
the top, although it is of greater density?—A. In rushing over
ks the cold water, which is at the bottom, forces the warm water
it flows out on either side.
iu don't approve very much of the theory of the mackerel mi-
Probably you don't believe in it? You think they go into the
l hibernate?—A. In the mud and sand.
ell, to what extent do you believe they do so? Is that the way
it part of the mackerel dispose of themselves in the winter?—
nk that is so, not only with the mackerel but with a number of
ih.
ell, does that account for the disappearance of the mackerel dur-
winter to any considerable extent?—A. Yes.
iey go to the bottom or into the sand?—A. Yes.
ell, to what extent do you think they do it?—A. I think they all
te just the same as the sturgeon in fresh water; and on the
States coast, the tautog, the scup, and other fish hibernate.
iw far do you think they go out? What number of fathoms to
⟩ the mud?—A. It depends entirely on the ice. They always
:o select those spots where the salt-water ice shall not be drifted
iat they will not be exposed to the cold current dropping down
ℓ salt ice as it melts in the spring.
here does the American coast mackerel go? They don't have
tic waters there very much?—A. O, yes; the Arctic current is
'inter nearly as far as Cape Hatteras.
iu spoke of the cod schooling. I had not understood that the
ooled in the way that the mackerel schooled. How does the
ig show itself, in the same way as the mackerel?—A. Cod school
:kerel before spawning; they also appear to school at the begin-
each bait season. It is the schooling habit which enables them
ined.

16 F

The following tables are the tables referred to in the evide
fessor Hind :

No. 1.

*Statistics of the French fishery on the Grand Banks, and the northeast coast
land during successive periods from 1826 to 1856.*

From 1826 to 1841.................................374 ships, 10,445 fish
From 1842 to 1847.................................389 ships, 11,378 fish
From 1848 to 1850.................................346 ships, 11,011 fish
From 1851 to 1856.................................383 ships, 11,348 fish

" *Le Pilot de Terre Neuve*," *Vol. I, p. 26.*

No. II.

*Statistics of the French fishery on the Great Banks of Newfoundland and on
Coast.*

Years.	Number ships
1860.	
1861.	
1862.	
1863.	
1864.	
1865.	
1866.	
1867.	

(" *Le Pilote de Terre Neuve*," Vol. 1, page 26)

No. III.

*Statistics of the French fisheries on the northeast coast of Newfoundland, from
to Cape St. John.*

Years.	Number of ships.	Number of men.	
1860	105	6,180	
1861	105	6,058	
1862	112	9,593	
1863	116	5,493	
1864	58	3,264	
1865	55	3,118	
1866	57	2,758	
1867	35	2,068	

(" *Le Pilote de Terre Neuve*," Vol II, page 399.)

No. IV.

Statistics of the French bank-fishery on the Great Banks of Newfoundland. fro

Years.	Bank fishery, with drying at St. Pierre and Miquelon.		Bank fishery, with drying on northeast coast of Newfoundland.		Bank fishery, without drying.	
	Ships.	Men.	Ships.	Men.	Ships.	Men.
1860	68	2,735	4	122	51	1,016
1861	61	2,558	3	93	58	1,172
1862	48	1,591	3	93	41	834
1863	40	1,480	3	90	44	866
1864	38	1,252	7	274	46	986
1865	42	1,515	6	151	55	1,048
1866	47	1,640	17	369	64	1,260
1867	51	1,761	17	384	69	1,466

(" *Le Pilote de Terre Neuve*," Vol. 1, page 25.)

No. V.

Statistics of the French fisheries in the Gulf of St. Lawrence.

Years	Number of French ships.	Number of fishermen sailors.	
....	28	1,080	The Islands of St. Pierre and Miquelon send to the West Coast about 15 schooners manned by 12 men. They dispatch also into the gulf about 120 to 160 men to man from 60 to 80 dol'ys to fish about Cod Roy and Red Island.
....	28	1,088	
....	34	1,354	
....	36	1,519	
....	31	1,399	
....	27	1,209	
....	22	1,043	
....	20	822	

("*Le Pilote de Terre Neuve*," Vol. 1, page 246.)

Affidavits read in rebuttal by Mr. Whiteway.

No. 1.

OUNDLAND.
Saint John's, to wit:

mas Rumsey, aged thirty years, fisherman, residing at Saint
t, aforesaid, maketh oath and saith: Deponent is well acquainted
he fisheries of Newfoundland, and is intimately acquainted with
erring fishery. Deponent, last spring, saw three United States
g seines used by American fishermen in "barring herrings" at
Harbor in Fortune Bay, and knows that large quantities of her-
were "barred" by these seines and taken out afterwards by using
small seines, which these United States fishermen came down pre-
with.
ouent knows that United States fishermen are in the habit of
their own seines to inclose herrings on our coasts, and of employ-
itish fishermen to assist in hauling these seines. Deponent knows
instance in which United States fishermen brought down a large
g seine completely fitted out with seine boat and all necessary
which they sold to a person named Fiander, at English Harbor,
tune Bay. Deponent further has heard and believes that another
seine was sold by United States fishermen to one Burke, at St.
es, in Fortune Bay, and in both cases the value of such seines was
paid for by supplying these United States fishermen with herrings
ninal prices, hauled by these seines, the crews working the same
composed almost wholly of American fishermen. Deponent fur-
ays that he knows of one instance that happened last spring, in
a cargo of fresh herrings was hauled by a United States crew
essel in Fortune Bay, aforesaid, and sold at St. Pierre as bait for
h fishermen; and that it has been stated—and as deponent believes
stated—other United States fishermen did the same thing. De-
t has been informed that United States fishermen intend provid-
emselves with larger seines than those now used by them, (which
uch larger than those by Newfoundland fishermen) and with
seines to engage largely in catching bait on Newfoundland s hores
ply French fishermen at St. Pierre.

THOMAS RUMSEY.

Sworn before me at St. John's, aforesaid, this 9th day
A. D. 1877.

D. W. PRC
Stipendiary Magistrate, St. John's, New

NEWFOUNDLAND,
    Central District, St. John's, to wit:

John Rumsey, of Fortune Harbour, in Fortune Bay, N
maketh oath and saith: I have heard the foregoing dep
brother, Thomas Rumsey, read over. It is correct and t
particular.

The name of one of the American captains is Jacobs.
lived in Green Bay, Newfoundland. I cannot remember
the United States schooner that he commanded.

I have been engaged fourteen years in the herring fisher
Bay. I have been fishing for thirty years in Newfoundlan

his

JOHN +

mark

Sworn before me at St. John's, Newfoundland, this 9th
ber, A. D. 1877.

D. W. PRC
Stipendiary Magistrate, St. John's, Net

No. 2.

Robert Inkpen, aged 33 years, of Burin, Newfoundlan
maketh oath and saith: Deponent has been connected w
eries of Newfoundland since he was fourteen years of age,
ecuted the same almost continuously since that time. De
quainted with the bait-fishery in Newfoundland, and with
of United States vessels in British waters on our coasts.
well aware that no advantages result to British fisherme
operations compared to the injuries to British interests, an
informed that the localities chiefly frequented by United
are marked peculiarly as localities where the inhabitants
the most straitened circumstances. Deponent knows that
fishermen did use their own seines in Fortune Bay last spri
bait, and that they did so in the early part of the spring
tion of a local law that prevented local fishermen hauling h
the 25th day of April, and loaded their vessels with about
barrels herrings, which they carried to St. Pierre, and
French bankers. Captain Kirby was in charge of one of
States vessels. Deponent says, further, that no money p
cans for bait is adequate to the injury they do to local fish
ermen, and that all classes in this country agree in prou
operations a great evil.

ROBER

Sworn before me at St. John's, Newfoundland, this 26tl
ber, A. D. 1877.

D. W. PR
Stipendiary Magistrate, St. John's, Ne

John Mitchell, aged 52 years, residing at Burin,
maketh oath and saith:

I was present when Robert Inkpen made the above sta
I know to be true in all particulars.

JOHN M

Sworn before me, at St. John's, Newfoundland, this 26th day of October, A. D. 1877.

D. W. PROWSE,
Stipendiary Magistrate, St. John's, Newfoundland.

I, Frederic B. T. Carter, a notary public, duly admitted and sworn, practicing at St. John's, Newfoundland, do hereby testify that D. W. Prowse, who has subscribed his name to the jurat of the affidavit of Robert Inkpen and of John Mitchell, on the third page of this sheet of paper, is one of Her Majesty's justices of the peace for the island of Newfoundland; that the signature "D. W. Prowse, stipendiary magistrate, St. John's, Newfoundland," is the true handwriting of the said justice, and that full faith and credit ought to be given thereto in court and thereout.

In testimony whereof I have affixed my notarial seal and subscribed my name this 24th day of October, A. D. 1877.

(L. S.)   FREDERIC B. T. CARTER,

Notary Public.

No. 3.

Stephen Power, aged 38 years, trader and fisherman, residing at Placentia, Newfoundland, maketh oath and saith:

I am practically acquainted with the fisheries of this country, having followed the same since I was 14 years of age. I have been engaged by American fishermen in procuring bait in Placentia Bay. I found the seine and the Americans supplied the crew, and for my services as pilot, hire of seine, and my own aid in working the seine with the American crew I was paid twenty-seven dollars in May last by Captain Hickman, of the American schooner I. S. Glover. I am well aware that American fishermen do haul bait for themselves, and I am well informed that they brought down four large seines this year to Fortune Bay, which were worked exclusively for their purposes and advantages. Such seines were very much larger than those used by our own people, and

curing large quantities of herrings earlier than the local seines, owing to their great length and depth; one of them I heard barreled upwards of (4,000) four thousand barrels of herring at one time. The operations of such large seines are highly injurious to the fisheries.

STEPHEN POWER.

Sworn before me, at St. John's, Newfoundland, the 12th day of October, A. D. 1877.

W. J. S. DONNELLY,
Justice of the Peace for the Island of Newfoundland.

I, Frederic B. T. Carter, a notary public, duly admitted and sworn, practicing at John's, Newfoundland, do hereby certify that W. J. S. Donnelly, who has subscribed his name to the jurat of the affidavit of Stephen Power, on the second page of this sheet of paper, is one of Her Majesty's justices of the peace for the island of Newfoundland; that the signature, "W. J. S. Donnelly, justice of the peace for the island of Newfoundland," is the true handwriting of the said justice, and that full faith and credit ought to be given thereto in court and thereout.

In testimony whereof I have affixed my notarial seal and subscribed my name, this 24th day of October, A. D. 1877.

(L. S.)   F. B. T. CARTER,

Notary Public.

No. 4.

By Stephen Fiander, of Coombs Cove. I reside at Coombs ⟨
Fortune Bay. I was engaged catching or trying to catch herrir
United States vessels at Long Harbor last winter. I was concern
the seine brought by Captain Deagle, of Edwin or Eben Parsons, i
cember last. I was one of the crew who hauled herring with it.
of the crews of United States vessels were concerned or employed i
use of said seine; we had it from Captain Deagle on condition ⟨
selling to him all the herring which should be hauled with it.
hauled about 800 barrels, which we sold to him. We hauled th⟨
Table Beach. Samuel Fiander bought it from him afterwards.
the crew of United States vessel Wildfire engaged hauling herri
Table Beach about first of January last. The captain of said ⟨
was with them; the seine and skiff they used belonged to the vesse
was managed entirely by crews of United States vessels with the e
tion of one man, Bond, whom I saw with them. He, Bond, was
ceive one share only (i. e., one man's share). They inclosed tha
about 300 barrels herring; they were not, however, all saved, as ⟨
of wind came on and the seine burst; I believe over half of the he
were thus lost. Captain Cunningham, master of said vessel, bro⟨
the purse-lines of the seine with him. The crews of United States v
use those purse-lines when they haul herring; we British fishe
never use them. I heard Captain Deagle, of United States sch
Edwin or Eben Parsons; Captain Charles Lee, of United States sch
————, of Gloucester; and Captain Cunningham, of United ⟨
schooner Wildfire, say, that they would have whatever herrings
wanted with their own crews and seines if their crews were quite w
to do so.

his
STEPHEN + FIAND
mark.

Taken and sworn before me at Coombs Cove, the 16th day of Oc
1877.

PHILIP HOBERT,

No. 5.

By Philip Thornhill, of Anderson Cove. I reside at Anderson
Long Harbor. I was at Anderson Cove when Captain Allen,
Bonanza, United States vessel, arrived from head of Fortune B
June, 1876, where, I understood from crew of said vessel and othei
had hauled a large quantity of herring. I believe the hauling
herring was done entirely by the crew of said vessel; there was
two British fishermen on board, but I understood they had no sh
the seine. The seine and skiff they used belonged to the ves
saw the crew of said vessel engaged hauling or trying to haul h
at Anderson Cove in June, 1876. The men employed at it were
of the vessel. I think they hauled some at Anderson Cove and
them on board. I believe the seine and skiff was taken back b
vessel.

his
PHILIP + THORNHI
mark.

Taken and sworn before me at Harbor Breton the 16th October
PHILIP HOBERT,

No. 6.

George Rose, of Jersey Harbor. I now reside at Jersey Harbor, ine Bay. In June, 1876, Captain Allen, of United States schooner nza, arrived at Little Bay (Bay de Lean), where I then resided, old me he wanted to haul about 1,400 barrels herring in Fortune that he had a herring seine and skiff on board of his vessel, and rthing else necessary for hauling, and asked me to go with him as er of his seine, and that he would give me twenty cents per barrel very barrel of herring that was hauled. I agreed, and my son John [went on board at once. We left and sailed for Long Harbor, but iot haul any herring there; from thence we sailed for head of For- Bay, where we hauled about 400 barrels, which were salted on i the vessel. The seine, skiff, and crew belonged to the vessel, as I have said, I was simply engaged as master of the seine. men employed hauling the herring all belonged to the said vessel. r the 400 barrels herring were salted on board we returned to Long ior in her. We (*i. e.*, the crew of vessel and myself helping them) i to haul herring there, but did not succeed. I left the vessel there returned home. Captain Allen, the master of said vessel, paid me uy services the sum of eighty dollars; my son received nothing. I d afterwards that he got at Long Harbor after I left about 1,000 els, but cannot tell if he hauled them all or if he hauled any. He me he intended putting up the herring at Gloucester and reship- ; them for Sweden.

his
GEORGE + ROSE.
mark.

akeu and sworn before me at Jersey Harbor the 17th October, 1877.

PHILIP HOBERT, *J. P.*

No. 7.

VFOUNDLAND,
Saint John's, to wit:

aurice Bonia, of Placentia, aged 58 years, fisherman, maketh oath saith: I have been connected with the fisheries of Newfoundland orty years. I know that United States vessels are accustomed to aited at Fortune Bay with seines they bring themselves, and which r work with the aid of local fishermen. Last June I went pilot with t. Lauchlin McLeod, of the schooner P. L. Whitman, hailing from acester, United States of America, from Placentia to Piper's Hole, 'lacentia Bay, to haul herrings for bait, for which purpose I used my seine, and, with the aid of his crew and myself and my seine, he iured his bait. For my services as pilot and for hire of seine and stance in working it, Captain McLeod paid me twelve dollars. am fully sensible that the American fishermen in our waters, using privileges conferred by the Washington Treaty, are greatly injur our people by their operations, and that absolutely no benefits re from their visits.

his
MAURICE + BONIA.
mark.

worn before me, at St. John's aforesaid, this 19th day of October, A. 877.

H. RENOUF,
J. P. for Newfoundland.

I, Frederic B. T. Carter, a notary public duly admitted and practising at St. John's, Newfoundland, do hereby certify that ' Renouf," who has subscribed his name " H. Renouf, J. P., for Nev land," to the jurat of the affidavit of Maurice Bonia, written on t page of this sheet of paper, is the proper handwriting of said Hei nouf, one of Her Majesty's justices of the peace for Newfoundlanc said, and that full faith and credit should be given to his acts capacity as well in court as thereon.

In testimony whereof I have affixed my hand and seal of off subscribed my name, this 20th day of October, A. D. 1877.

[L. S.]   FRED. B. T. CARTER
                                               Notary P

No. 8.

SOUTHERN DISTRICT, NEWFOUNDLAND,
                    Placentia, to wit :

Humphry Sullivan, of Placentia aforesaid, fisherman, person: peared before me, Thomas O'Reilly, esq., one of Her Majesty's jus the peace for the southern district of the island of Newfoundlai maketh oath and saith that during the last half of the month last, deponent piloted from Placentia to Piper's Hole the Ai schooners Webster Lauburn, Hodgson, master ; the Governor win, McGrath, master ; and the Laura Nelson, Prout, master ; t ponent hauled a sufficiency of herring for bait for the Webster L and Governor Goodwin, and that the master of the Laura Nelso deponent's seine, hauled bait enough for himself on the Sunday.
                                                    his
                            HUMPHRY + SULLI'
                                                  mark.

Sworn to before me at Great Placentia, this 11th day of Octo D., 1877.

                                               T. O'REILLY
                                Commissioner of Affidavits at

I, Frederic B. T. Carter, a notary public duly admitted and practising at St. John's, Newfoundland, do hereby certify that O'Reilly, who has subscribed his name " T. O'Reilly, commissi affidavits," to the jurat of the affidavit of Humphrey Sullivan, on the first page of this sheet of paper, is the proper handwr said Thomas O'Reilly, one of Her Majesty's justices of the peac commissioner of affidavits in Newfoundland aforesaid, and t faith and credit should be given to his acts in said capacity as court as thereout.

In testimony whereof I have affixed my seal of office and su my name, this 23d day of October, A. D., 1877.

[L. S.]   F. B. T. CARTEI
                                               Notary I

APPENDIX R.

No. 1.

Gloucester Mutual Fishing Insurance Company.

No. This Policy of Insurance Witnesseth, That the Gloucester Mutual Fishing Insurance Company, in Gloucester, do by these Presents, cause ——— for whom it may concern, To be Insured, lost or not lost, ——— Hundred ——— Dollars, on seven-eighths ——— of the Schooner ——— and —— Hundred ——— Dollars on the Outfits or Catch, ——— Commencing this day and terminating the thirtieth day of November next, at 12 o'clock, noon ; **Vessel valued at** And to be insured in the manner prescribed by the By-Laws, and to be subject to all the restraints and liabilities therein set forth.

And especially does this Company agree to insure only **$..............** seven-eighths of any one vessel, nor over eight thousand dollars on any one risk.

The owner or owners, in all cases who are insured by this Company, **Vessel Insured,** shall always have one-eighth of said vessel, as valued by the Directors, on his or their own risk, and shall not be allowed to insure said one-eighth, or any portion thereof elsewhere.

$.............. This Company does not insure against Barratry of the Master or mariners.

No claim for loss on, or damage to, Fresh or Frozen Fish, Salt Herring in bulk, Dories, Trawl Gear, Nets, Seine, or Seine Boat, shall be allowed by this Company, unless in case of total loss of vessel.

Cargo Insured, The insurers shall not be liable for any partial loss on Salt, Coal, Grain, Cured Fish, or Fruit, either preserved or otherwise, or other goods that are esteemed perishable in their own nature, when carried on freight, or on the freight thereon, unless it amounts **$.. .** to 10 per cent. on the whole aggregate value of such articles, and happen by stranding.

Outfits Insured, No claims shall be had for Outfits or Catch, insured, unless the loss amounts to or exceeds 10 per cent. on the value of outfits or catch on board at the time of loss, and that loss shall be **$..............** caused by fire or the dangers of the sea.

It is also agreed that this Company shall not be liable in any case for loss on or damage to Outfits or Cargo carried on deck, nor for loss or damage to the cargo of any vessel employed in freighting, unless the loss amounts to 20 per cent. of the value of said cargo, and then for the excess above 15 per cent. only.

Amount of Premium Note. No vessel shall be insured by this Company except those hailing from Gloucester.

No vessel shall be insured by the Company while engaged **$..............** in the business of carrying Sand or Stone.

If there be any Lime on board, one hundred per cent. to be added to the premium for the passage.

Policy, $1 00 No claim for loss on the hull of a vessel shall be allowed by this Company, unless said loss or damage shall amount to the following percentage on the whole value of said vessel as valued in the

Policy, after deductiug one-third for new, viz :— A vess
ued at $7,500 and upwards, 5½ per cent.; $7,000 to $7,
per cent.; $6,500 to $7,000, 6½ per cent.; $6,000 to $6,500, 7 per
$5,500 to $6,·000, 7½ per cent.; $5,000 to $5,500, 8 per cent.; $4,
$5,000, 9 per cent.; $4,000 to $4,500, 9½ per cent.; $3,500 to $4,0(
per cent.; $3,000 to $3,500, 11 per ceut.; $2,500 to $3,000, 12 per
$2,500 to $2,500, 14 per cent.; $1,500 to $2,000, 18 per cent.; $1,
$1,500, 25 per cent.; all under $1,000, 30 per cent.

Cables, Anchors, and Boats to be at the risk of the owners iu all
except a total loss of vessel. Sails, Rigging, Masts, and all other ɛ
tenances belonging to the vessel, to be at the risk of the owners,
cases, except the loss on them at one time amounts to the followin
centage on the whole value of the vessel as valued in the Policy, ·
A vessel valued at $8,000 and upwards, 10 per ceut.; $7,000 to $
12 per cent.; $6,000 to 7,000, 14 per ceut.; $5,000 to $6,000,
cent.; $4,000 to $5,000, 18 per ceut.; $3,000 to $4,000, 20 per
$2,000 to $3,000, 24 per cent.; $1,500 to $2,000, 30 per cent.; all
$1,500, 35 per cent.; and under such adjustmeut one-third shall
ducted for new.

Notice of any claim on the Compaȯy for damages shall be given
Company within ten days of the arrival of the vessel, or no loss ɤ
allowed. No vessel receiving damage, whereby the Company be
liable, shall in any event be sold until directions to ʰhat effect shal
been communicated to the Master or Agent from the Company.

Cables and Anchors lost or sacrificed on the fishing grounds shɛ
be paid for by the Company, in any case, except total loss of vesʂ

Gilt work or carving shall not, when lost or damaged, be paid f
cept in cases of total loss of vessel.

In adjusting partial losses the bowsprit of a vessel shall be consʰ
a spar.

In cases of disaster to any Vessel insured, it shall be lawful
insurers to take possession of aud repair the damage, and to dem
the owners their proportion of the expense thereof, and the acts
insured or insurers in taking possession thereof to save, pres
repair the same, shall not be deemed to be a waiver or accepta
admission of an abaudonment,—provided such Vessel shall be re
and returned to the owners within four months from the date
disaster. No claim for Total Loss shall be allowed by this Co
unless the cost of repairs (according to the Laws of the Compaɪ
one time, after deducting one-third for new, amouuts to fifty peɪ
of the value of the Vessel as in the Policy. Aud the insurers are
any case to be held to pay for any loss or damage by restraint, ʂ
or detention, by auy legal or illegal power whatsoever, or for auɤ
age, accident or loss, which may happen or occur to any Vesseʰ
she may be under such restraint, detentiou or seizure. Nor wɪ
Company, under any circumstances, pay for copper, or any other
lic material, used as a covering for the bottom of vessels except iɪ
of total loss, in which case the copper shall belong to the insurerʂ
copper or other metallic material used as aforesaid, shall not be ɖ
ered at all in the adjustment of a partial loss. Vessels and Ɽ
liable for deposit aud premium notes.   ·

The rates of premium for the current year, to commence on th
of application shall be as follows: From November 16th to Noɤ
30th of next year, 9 per cent.; from December 10th to Novembɛ
of next year, 8 per cent.; from January 1st to November 30th
same year, 7 per cent.; from January 15th to November 30th

ar, 6½ per cent.; from February 1st to November 30th of the
ar, 6 per cent.; from March 1st to November 30th of the same
per cent.; from April 1st to November 30th of the same year,
nt.; from May 15th to November 30th of the same year, 4½ per
rom July 1st to November 30th of the same year, 4 per cent.
1 one-half per cent. extra on the amount insured to be added to
nium of any vessel employed in the Greenland fisheries, or any
s east of Flemish Cap or the forty-fifth degree of longitude; one
.. for any vessel sailing on a voyage to Newfoundland, between
t of November, 1876, and the 1st of March, 1877; one-half of one
.. to be added if employed in the Bay of Island fisheries on or
:tober 1st next, at 12 o'clock, noon; one-half of one per cent. to
d for any vessel engaged in the Georges fishery or any fisheries
nd east of Georges which has not arrived in Gloucester harbor
∌fore October 15th, at 12 o'clock, noon; or for any vessel sailing
yage to Georges or any fishing grounds north or east of Georges,
1 October 15th and November 15th; and one-half of one per cent.
,remium on any vessel sailing on a voyage or employed in any
s easterly from Cape Sable, between October 31st and November
; 12 o'clock, noon. And upon all risks not above provided for,
′ectors shall have power to fix equitable rates for extra premiums
1arged and paid by the insured.
essel shall sail from the harbor of Gloucester on or after the fif-
day of November next, at noon, at the risk of this Company. A
30 sailing is not insured under this Policy. The Policy of any
not having arrived from the voyage she then is on, November
t 12 o'clock, noon, shall be continued until her arrival, a premium
rate of one and one-half per cent per month, to be paid by the
l for such extension.
never the Directors shall require it, a survey shall be called upon
ssel receiving damages supposed sufficient to entitle them to re-
,y the Company, and such repairs, when ordered by said survey,
e made as such survey shall direct, and be done in a faithful and
an-like manner, one-third to be ·deducted for new in the adjust-
,f the loss.
so the President and Directors aforesaid are contented, and do
bind the property of the said Insurance Company, to be insured,
    executors, administrators, and assigns, for the true per-
ice of the premises, confessing themselves paid the consideration
to them for this insurance by the insured, at and after the rate
per cent. for the term, with any extra premium above provided
d in case a further amount shall be required to pay losses, in
of said premium and extras, all such sums as may be levied on
∍miums earned to pay such excess of losses.
/ITNESS WHEREOF, the President hath signed, and the Secretary
ountersigned, at Gloucester, this —— day of —— one thou-
ight hundred and seventy- ——.

GEORGE STEELE, *President.*

— *Secretary.*

No. 2.

BY-LAWS of the Gloucester Mutual Fishing Insurance Company for
years 1876–77.—Adopted November, 1876.—George Steele, Presid
N. D. Cunningham, Vice-President; Cyrus Story, Secretary and Ti
urer.

Article 1. This Company shall be governed by a board of ten Dii
ors, who shall be chosen from the Stockholders at the annual mee
of the Company by a stock vote; one of whom shall be chosen by
Directors to act as President, and another to act as Vice-Presid
The duties of the President (and in his absence the Vice-Presid
shall be to preside at all meetings of the Board, or of the Stockholc
and to perform such other duties as may be required of them.

The Directors shall have power in case there is a vacancy on
Board caused either by non-acceptance, resignation or death, to ch
from among the Stockholders some person or persons to fill the vacai
they shall also have the power to appoint a Secretary and Treas:
and to fix upon salaries to be paid to the officers of the Company.

Article 2. The President and Directors shall superintend the conc
of the Company, and have the management and direction of all th
not otherwise herein provided for. They shall provide a suitable (
for the transaction of business, and furnish it in such a manner as '
shall think proper; they shall cause to be kept by the Secretary a
record of all their transactions, and shall report at the annual mee
in each year, a detailed account of the concerns of the Company, w
report, when accepted, shall be entered upon the records of the (
pany.

Article 3. The Secretary shall keep the books and accounts, shai
lect and receive all monies, and pay the same over to the Treasur
soon as received; shall fill up and record all policies and orders, n
meetings, and perform such other duties of the office as the Presi
and Directors may require.

Article 4. The Treasurer shall take charge of all the funds o
Company, and deposit the same in some Bank in Gloucester, i
name of the company. He shall pay out money by order of the Di
ors, and all checks must be countersigned by the President. He
give such bonds for the performance of his duties as the Directors
require.

Article 5. The President, in addition to his duties of presiding at
ings, shall sign all policies, and shall order the payment of all moni
the Treasurer, with the consent and approval of the Directors,
countersign all checks drawn for the payment of monies aforesaid;
in his absence, the Vice-President shall perform such duties.

Article 6. All applications for insurance shall be made in writing
signed by the person or agent making such application, and shall sp
the amount on the vessel and outfits (catch to be considered as ou
or cargo separately, insurance to commence on the date of the ap]
tion, and shall be binding on both parties until action is taken
said application by the Directors at their next meeting, and unt
expiration of the Policy, unless disapproved by the Directors at
meeting; notice of such disapproval to be given to the applicant ii
diately after such action.

Article 7. No vessel shall be insured by this Company except
hailing from Gloucester.

Article 8. The stock of this Company shall be held in shares v

thousand dollars each; and for each of such shares held by the
olders a promissory note of two hundred dollars, payable on
d, with satisfactory security, shall be given to the Company, and
each amount of said two hundred dollars, assessment may be
by the Directors for such sums as may from time to time be re-
for the use of the Company.

`cle 9. All stock notes shall be signed and endorsed before any
ation for insurance can be received.

`cle 10. Any responsible person who has property to the amount
⸱ hundred dollars to be insured, may take one-half a share of the
of the Company, and one share for each additional thousand dol-
e may wish to have insured.

icle 11. After the closing of the stock-book, no person shall retire
he Company, or cease to be a member thereof, but shall be firmly
intil the business of the Company for the year shall be settled.

icle 12. All matters relating to the government of the Company
be decided by the Directors in all cases where they are not
cted by the stockholders at a regularly notified meeting.

icle 13. The Directors shall call meetings of the stockholders at
imes as they may think proper. And upon notice in writing signed
⸱e or more stockholders, it shall be the duty of the Secretary to call
ting as requested by them.

icle 14. Special meetings of stockholders shall be notified either
lly or by leaving a written or printed notice at each stockholder's
of business two days before the time of holding such meeting.

⸱icle 15. Each stockholder shall be entitled to one vote for each
of stock held by him, and in case a person is the holder of a single
hare, he shall be entitled to one vote.

ticle 16. No alteration shall be made in the laws for the government
iis Company, except at a regularly notified meeting of the stock-
⸱rs, two-thirds of the number of stockholders to constitute a quo-
for the transaction of business, and two-thirds present acting in
ffirmative to decide.

ticle 17. No loss will be allowed by this Company on the hull of a
⸱l, unless said loss or damage shall amount to the following percent-
⸱n the whole value of the vessel as valued in the policy, after de-
ng one-third for new, viz.:—

A vessel valued at $7,500 and upwards,				5½ per cent.
"	" from 7,000	to $7,500,		6 per cent.
"	" " 6,500	to 7,000,		6¼ per cent.
	" " 6,000	to 6,500,		7 per cent.
	" " 5,500	to 6,000,		7½ per cent.
	" " 5,000	to 5,500,		8 per cent.
"	" " 4,500	to 5,000,		9 per cent.
"	" " 4,000	to 4,500,		9½ per cent.
"	" " 3,500	to 4,000,		10½ per cent.
	" " 3,000	to 3,500,		11 per cent.
	" " 2,500	to 3,000,		12 per cent.
	" " 2,000	to 2,500,		14 per cent.
"	" " 1,500	to 2,000,		18 per cent.
	" " 1,000	to 1,500,		25 per cent.
All under 1,000				30 per cent.

bles, anchors and boat to be at the risk of the owners in all cases,
⸱t a total loss of vessel.

ils, rigging, masts, and all other appurtenances belonging to the
⸱l to be at the risk of the owners in all cases, except the loss on

them at one time amounts to the following percentage on the '
value of the vessel as valued in the policy, viz. :—

A vessel valued at		$8,000, and upwards,	10	per cent.
"	" from	7,000 to $8,000,	12	per cent.
"	" "	6,000 to 7,000,	14	per cent.
"	" "	5,000 to 6,000,	16	per cent.
"	" "	4,000 to 5,000,	18	per cent.
"	" "	3,000 to 4,000,	20	per cent.
"	" "	2,000 to 3,000,	24	per cent.
"	" "	1,500 to 2,000,	30	per cent.
All under 1,500			35	per cent.

And under such adjustment one-third shall be deducted for new
the Directors are authorized and empowered, in case of partial
under this article, to compromise with the assured when in their
ment it would be for the interest of the Company so to do.

Article 18. Whenever the Directors shall require it, a survey sh;
called upon any vessel receiving damages supposed sufficient to e
them to repairs by the Company, and such repairs when ordered by
survey, shall be made as they shall direct and be done in a faithfu
workmanlike manner, and with good materials, one-third to be ded
for new in the adjustment of the loss; said repairs to be made i
the direction of the Directors when practicable; notice of such da
to be given within ten days of the arrival of the vessel, or no los
be allowed.

Article 19. In case any vessel insured by this Company sh;
stranded, and the master or owner shall think it for the interest o
Company to get such vessel off and save the property, the Compai
hereby pledge themselves to pay their proportion of all reaso
charges which may arise in consequence of such condition, w
successful or not.

Article 20. No claim for a total loss shall be allowed by this
pany, unless the cost of repairs (according to the laws of the Com
at one time, after deducting one-third for new, amounts to fift
cent. of the value of the vessel as in the Policy.

Article 21. This Company will insure the outfits or cargo o
Gloucester vessel. The amount to be insured on such outfits or
shall be designated in the Policy separately from the vessel, b
claim shall be allowed for the sum so insured, unless the loss am
to or exceeds 10 per cent. of the value of said outfits or cargo on
at the time of loss, and that loss shall be caused by fire or by the d
of the seas. No claim for loss on, or damage to outfits or cargo c
on deck shall be allowed by the Company. In adjusting losses o
fits, the whole catch shall be considered as outfits.

Article 22. Each and every stockholder shall furnish vessels,
or cargo to be insured, the amount of insurance of which shall
least seven-eighths of the amount of stock subscribed by him; sho:
fail to comply with the above requirement, he shall be held to p;
lowest rate of premium on such sum as shall make the required an

Article 23. This Company will not be held for any loss or dama
restraint or seizure by any legal or illegal power whatsoever, or 1
cident or damage which may happen to any vessel while she may
der such restraint or seizure.

Article 24. Sixty days from the supposed or known loss of any
the insured may make the same known to the Company, and furi
written statement of the destination of the vessel, and such othe
as the Directors may deem of importance; and if on mature del

ey should think that sufficient reason has been assigned to cause
lief that the vessel has been lost, they shall cause the Secretary
an assessment upon all the stock notes sufficient to cover the loss
vessel, and such assessment shall be levied and collected within
days, and the loss adjusted with the parties forthwith.

cle 25. In case of disagreement regarding any loss which may
lace in this Company, the parties agrieved shall make a written
tent of the facts in the case, and the Directors shall also make a
r statement, and if the loss cannot be adjusted by the parties, a
ice shall be chosen in the manner pointed out by the laws of the
onwealth, and their decision shall be final. And losses shall be
up by some person not interested in the Company when the in-
so request.

icle 26. This Company will not insure over eight thousand dollars
y one vessel and her outfits or cargo.

icle 27. No vessel insured by this Company receiving damage
by the Company becomes liable, shall in any event be sold until
ions to that effect shall have been communicated to the master or
from the Company.

icle 28. No vessel shall be insured by this Company for more than
eighths of her value as decided upon by the Directors, the owners
e vessel in all cases risking one-eighth of said value.

ticle 29. Gilt work or carving shall not, when lost or damaged, be
for by the Company except in case of total loss of vessel.

ticle 30. Cables or anchors lost or sacrificed on the fishing grounds,
not be paid for by the Company in any case, except total loss of
l.

ticle 31. In adjusting partial losses, the bow-sprit of a vessel shall
nsidered a spar.

ticle 32. No vessel shall sail from the harbor of Gloucester upon
royage whatever after the fifteenth day of November next, at noon,
e risk of this Company. Any vessel not having arrived from the
ge, she then is on November 15th, at 12 o'clock, noon, shall pay a
ium at the rate of one and one-half per cent. per month until her
al. The Policy on such vessel to be continued until her arrival as
said.

ticle 33. This Company will not, under any circumstances, pay for
er or any other metallic material used as a covering for the bottom
essels, except in case of total loss, in which case the copper or other
rial shall belong to the insurers and copper or other metallic mate-
ised as aforesaid, shall not be considered at all in the adjustment
partial loss.

ticle 34. The rates of premium for the current year shall be as
ws:

| om Nov. 16 to Nov. 30 of next year, | 9 per cent. |
| " Dec. 10 " " " " " " 8 " |
| " Jan. 1 " " " " same " 7 " |
| " " 15 " " " " " " $6\frac{1}{2}$ " |
| " Feb. 1 " " " " " " 6 " |
| " Mar. 1 " " " " " " $5\frac{1}{2}$ " |
| " Apr. 1 " " " " " " 5 " |
| " May 15 " " " " " " $4\frac{1}{2}$ " |
| " July 1 " " " " " " 4 " |

it when either of said dates shall fall on Sunday, then the premium
applications made on the next day preceding shall be computed
r the rate of the date so occurring on said Sunday. One per cent.
mount insured to be added to the premium of any vessel employed

in the Newfoundland fisheries between the 15th of November 1st of March next ensuing.

Article 35. A return premium may be allowed whenever an, issued by this company shall be canceled.

Article 36. At the close of the business of the year, if it should that a profit had been made in the business of the company, tl shall be divided among the premiums earned by insurance on tł held by each stockholder; and should there be a loss in the bus the company, the same shall be assessed according to the above conditions as regards profit.

No. 3.

FISHING SHIPPING PAPER.

UNITED STATES OF AMERICA.—DISTRICT OF GLOUCESTE

IT IS AGREED between —— ——, agent or owner of the S —— ——, qualified by law for carrying on the BANK an FISHERIES of the United States, and —— —— Master or : of the said Schooner, and the Fishermen whose names are to thi ment subscribed, that the said —— —— will at —— own e equip the said Schooner —— —— with all the necessary tac apparel for a fishing voyage or voyages; the provision, salt, ar shall be provided and paid for by.—— —— and that said — —— Master or Skipper, with the said Fishermen will pursue the other Fisheries, in the Schooner —— —— —— during the prese ing season, and will use their best endeavors to procure all t Oil, &c., they can, and for the success of the voyage or voya may go; and will be ready at all times, and will never leave Schooner —— —— —— without permission from the Owner o thereof. And it is agreed that the owner or Agent may dispos sell all the Fish, Oil, &c., that may be landed from the said S whenever he may think proper, and after deducting from th Stock all charges for Ice, Bait, Straw for Bait, and Nippers, proceeds to be divided, one-half to the Owner or Owners, the re half among the Fishermen, in proportion to the quantity or nu fish which they shall have respectively caught, each man pa proportion of the expense of Packing Mackerel, Freight and in shipping Fish, &c., home, in accordance with the number or caught, and each one of the Crew with the Skipper to pay an eq of the following charges, viz: Cooking, Sawing, Wood, Water, Medicine, scraping masts, and tarring rigging. And the sai doth hereby stipulate and agree with said fishermen, that he wil a just and true account of the delivery and sales of said Fish,

And it is further Agreed between the parties, that the Master per, together with the fishermen, are entitled to all the benefits ar leges, and subject to all the duties and penalties, provided by the United States, entitled "An Act concerning certain Fisheri United States, and for the Regulation and Government of Fi employed therein."

Time of Entry.	Men's Names.	Quality.	Witness to their Signing.	Time for w Eng:

Countersigned, ——————, Owner or ∠

ALPHABETICAL INDEX.

A.

Affidavits in rebuttal, in support of British case:
1. Rumsey, Thomas: St. John's, Newroundland ....
2. Inkpen, Robert: Burin, Newfoundland.....................
3. Power, Stephen: Placentia, Newfoundland.....................
4. Fiander, Stephen: Coombs Cove, Newfoundland.....................
5. Thornbill, Philip: Anderson Cove, Newfoundland ....
6. Rose, George: Jersey Harbor, Newfoundland.....................
7. Bonia, Maurice: Placentia, Newfoundland ... .
8. Sullivan, Humphry: Placentia, Newfoundland.....................
Affidavits produced on behalf of the United States :
1. Hodgdon, Freeman: Boothbay, Me ....
2. Berry, Thomas: Boothbay, Me ....
3. Eaton, William: Castine, Me.....................
4. Crane, L. G.: Gouldsborough, Me ....
5. Willard, Henry E.: Cape Elizabeth, Me ....
6. Trufant, Albert T.: Harpswell, Me ....
7. Willard, Enoch G.: Portland, Me.....................
8. Trefethen, George: Portland, Me ....
9. Conley, John: Portland, Me ....
10. Whitten, O. B.: Portland, Me ....
11. Chase, Stephen B.: Portland, Me.....................
12. Rich, Marshall N.: Portland, Me.:.....................
13. Swett, Noah: Wellfleet, Mass.....................
14. Pettingill, Charles C.: Salem, Mass.....................
15. Nelson, William H.: Plymouth, Mass ....
16. Small, Asa W.: Nantucket, Mass ....
17. Smalley, Charles E.: Kenny, Reuben C., Nantucket, Mass ....
18. Crowell, Elisha: Brooklyn, N.Y ....
19. Nickerson, Caleb: Brooklyn, N.Y....'.....................
20. Babson, Horatio: Gloucester, Mass ....
21. Friend, Sydney, & Brother: Gloucester, Mass.....................
22. Plumer, George W.: Gloucester, Mass ....
23. Knowlton, Harvey: Horton, Edward A., Gloucester, Mass ....
24. Pierce, Albion K.; Bearse, George; Hamilton, James R.; McDonald, John: Gloucester, Mass.....................
25. Norwood, George; Ayer, James S.: Gloucester, Mass.....................
26. Leighton, Andrew; Falt, Walter M.: Gloucester, Mass ....
27. Wonson, William C.: Gloucester, Mass.....................
28. Friend, George, & Co.: Gloucester, Mass.....................
29. Gerring, Frederick: Gloucester, Mass.....................
30. Wonson, Frederick G.: Gloucester, Mass.....................
31. Pew, Charles H.: Gloucester, Mass ....
32. Mansfield, Alfred: Gloucester, Mass ....
33. Steele, George: Gloucester, Mass.....................
34. Smith, Sylvanus: Gloucester, Mass ....
35. Whelen, Morris: Gloucester, Mass.....................
36. Grady, Thomas: Gloucester, Mass ....
37. Tarr, James G.: Gloucester, Mass.....................
38. Gorman, John E.: Gloucester, Mass.....................
39. Warren, Nicholas: Gloucester, Mass ....
40. Hardy, Henry: Gloucester, Mass ....
41. Saunders, John E.: Gloucester, Mass ....
42. Hannan, Richard: Gloucester, Mass.....................
43. Morey, Stephen B.: Deer Island, Me.....................
44. Webb, Seth; Webb, C. H. S.: Deer Island, Me.....................
45. Staples, John: Swan's Island, Me.....................
46. Perkins Brothers: Gloucester, Mass.....................
47. Pew, John J., & Son: Gloucester, Mass ....
48. Smith & Oakes: Gloucester, Mass ....
49. Walen, Michael: Gloucester, Mass.....................
50. Pettingell, Charles D.: Gloucester, Mass ....
51. Maddox, B., & Co.: Gloucester, Mass.....................
52. Dennis, George, & Co.: Gloucester, Mass ....
53. Proctor, Joseph O.: Gloucester, Mass ....
54. Haskell, Samuel: Gloucester, Mass ....
55. Friend, Joseph: Gloucester, Mass ....
56. Lane, Samuel, & Brother: Gloucester, Mass.....................
57. Steele, George: Gloucester, Mass ....
58. Cunningham & Thompson: Gloucester, Mass.....................

C.

218 F

D.

E.

H.

R.

W.

Witnesses examined on behalf of the United States; their testimony:
1. Bradley, James: Newburyport, Mass.......................
2. Stapleton, Edward: Gloucester, Mass......................
3. Cheney, S. F.: Grand Manan, N. B.......................
4. Ingersoll, David: Gloucester, Mass......................
5. Atwood, Nathaniel E.: Provincetown, Mass................
6. Kemp, Barzilla: Wellfleet, Mass.........................
7. Freeman, Francis M.: Provincetown, Mass.................
8. Cook, Henry: Provincetown, Mass........................
9. Paine, Joshua: Provincetown, Mass......................
10. Freeman, Nathan D.: Provincetown, Mass.................
11. Lewis, Bangs A.: Provincetown, Mass....................
12. Graham, James W.: Wellfleet, Mass......................
13. Newcomb, Daniel C.: Wellfleet, Mass....................
14. Pettingill, Moses: Newburyport, Mass...................
15. Young, Isaiah C.: Wellfleet, Mass......................
16. Daniels, Timothy A.: Wellfleet, Mass...................
17. Oliver, D. W.: Wellfleet, Mass.........................
18. Friend, George: Gloucester, Mass.......................
19. Orne, Charles H.: Gloucester, Mass.....................
20. Maddocks, Benjamin: Gloucester, Mass...................
21. Leighton, Andrew: Gloucester, Mass.....................
22. Riggs, Aaron: Gloucester, Mass.........................
23. Rowe, John J.: Gloucester, Mass........................
24. Gale, John H.: Gloucester, Mass........................
25. Evitt, John S.: Gloucester, Mass.......................
26. Cook, Benjamin F.: Gloucester, Mass....................
27. Smith, Edwin: Gloucester, Mass.........................
28. McInnis, John: Gloucester, Mass........................
29. Procter, Joseph O.: Gloucester, Mass...................
30. Gardner, Sidney: Gloucester, Mass......................
31. Martin, Stephen J.: Gloucester, Mass...................
32. Macaulay, Michael: Gloucester, Mass....................
33. Turner, Ezra: Deer Island, Me..........................
34. Rowe, Samuel T.: Gloucester, Mass......................
35. Tarr, Moses: Gloucester, Mass..........................
36. Ashby, Benjamin: Noank, Conn...........................
37. Brown, Joseph F.: Gloucester, Mass.....................
38. Mills, Peter H.: Deer Island, Me.......................
39. McDonald, William H.: Gloucester, Mass.................
40. Dickey, William A.: Belfast, Me........................
41. Gray, Elvarado: Brooksville, Me........................
42. Hulbert, Robert H.: Gloucester, Mass...................
43. Smalley, Castanus W.: Belfast, Me......................
44. Googins, Edward A.: Portland, Me.......................
45. Burgess, Isaac: Belfast, Me............................
46. Brier, Charles H.: Belfast, Me.........................
47. Walsh, Dexter F.: Belfast, Me..........................
48. Loudrigan, Lawrence: St. Mary's Bay, N. F..............
49. Hopkins, Richard: Belfast, Me..........................
50. Clark, George O.: Belfast, Me..........................
51. Gurrie, James: Picton, N. S............................
52. Perry, William: Sheet Harbour, N. S....................
53. Warren, Thomas: Deer Island, Me........................
54. Fisher, Wilford J.: Eastport, Me.......................
55. Lakeman, Joseph: Grand Manan, N. B.....................
56. Smith, Sylvanus: Gloucester, Mass......................
57. Williams, Gilman S.: Gloucester, Mass..................
58. Low, David W.: Gloucester, Mass........................
59. French, Eliphalet W.: Eastport, Me.....................
60. Davis, William: Gloucester, Mass.......................
61. Cook, William O.: Gloucester, Mass.....................
62. Hill, Edward: Gloucester, Mass.........................
63. Conley, John, jr.: Rockport, Mass......................
64. Knowlton, John C.: Rockport, Mass......................
65. Myrick, James H.: Boston, Mass.........................
66. Nelson, Chresten: Gloucester, Mass.....................
67. Patillo, James W.: North Stoughton, Mass...............
68. Baird, Spencer F.: Washington D. C.....................

Lightning Source UK Ltd.
Milton Keynes UK
UKHW012032121218
333853UK00008B/570/P